~~Terms~~

*Jerry Stephenson

Future:

- Businessman
- Minister
- Politician

Even - odd
Chapter 3

HBJ Federal Tax Course 1986

Ray M. Sommerfeld
University of Texas

Hershel M. Anderson
North Texas State University

Horace R. Brock
North Texas State University

John O. Everett
Virginia Commonwealth University

Harcourt Brace Jovanovich, Publishers

San Diego New York Chicago Atlanta Washington, D.C.

London Sydney Toronto

ISBN: 0-15-535306-3
Printed in the United States of America

Copyrights and Acknowledgments
The authors are grateful to the following publishers for permission to use material reprinted in this book:

Tables 1-1 and 1-2 From *Facts and Figures on Government Finance*, 22nd Biennial Edition, 1983, by courtesy of the publisher, the Tax Foundation, Inc., Washington, D.C.

Table 1-7 Adapted from *Revenue Statistics of OECD Member Countries, 1965–83—A Standardized Classification*, by courtesy of the publisher, the Organization for Economic Co-operation and Development, Paris.

Figures 10-1, 11-3, 11-4, 11-7, 12-1, 12-2, and 13-1 Reprinted and adapted from *An Introduction to Taxation*, 1983 Edition, by Ray M. Sommerfeld, Hershel M. Anderson, and Horace R. Brock, copyright © 1982 by Harcourt Brace Jovanovich, Inc. Reprinted by permission of the publisher.

Self-Study Questions Material from Uniform CPA Examination Questions and Unofficial Answers, copyright © 1969, 1971–84 by the American Institute of Certified Public Accountants, Inc., is adapted with permission.

Preface

This text is for students who are taking their first course in federal income taxation. The book's objective is to make it as easy as possible for them to comprehend both a general overview of our income tax laws and the detailed provisions that most persons will encounter in their personal or professional lives.

The emphasis here is on current tax law provisions, as opposed to the more theoretical approach of *An Introduction to Taxation*, also published by Harcourt Brace Jovanovich. In the *HBJ Federal Tax Course*, the historical and conceptual background material is clearly separated from other portions of the text. Tax planning "workshops" are scattered through the book to make potentially dull tax rules more interesting. The reproduction of tax forms throughout will also help students learn to deal with realistic problems in taxpayer compliance.

Four features of the text that we hope will be especially helpful are the following:

1. At the beginning of each chapter, a clear and concise statement of its primary objectives identifies the subject matter on which students should concentrate.
2. A marginal glossary defines—at the precise point where the definition is most useful—those words and phrases that may be new to students but that students must understand to gain an overall comprehension of the subject matter.
3. At the end of each chapter, a brief summary statement of the most important points should be particularly helpful in reviewing for examinations.
4. At the end of each chapter are 10 to 15 self-study questions (with answers in the back of the book) on material covered in the chapter. To the extent possible, these questions are adapted from uniform CPA examinations to reflect the current law.

In addition, every chapter of the text includes many examples that will help students understand the more difficult provisions of our federal income tax law. There are also many tables, figures, and charts summarizing important data. At the end of each chapter is an expanded selection of questions and several types of problems, to be used as homework assignments or for classroom discussion. At the end of the book is a comprehensive tax return problem and the necessary forms, which can be removed from the book.

The text is organized so that the information required to do basic tax research is introduced early (in Chapter 2), permitting instructors who so desire to assign problems or cases that require work beyond the text. The first 15 chapters emphasize the tax provisions that apply to individual taxpayers; the special rules applicable to corporations and other entities are discussed in the sixteenth and last chapter.

Several chapters have been reorganized from the previous edition. This reorganization (1) separates the material on general requirements for business deductions from that on personal deductions for individual taxpayers (the first half of Chapter 6 in the last edition is incorporated in Chapter 7 in this edition); and (2) brings together the chapters on income (old Chapters 4, 5, and 9; new Chapters 4–6), the chapters on deductions (old Chapters 6, 7, and 10; new Chapters 6–8), and the chapters on property transactions (old Chapters 8, 12, and 15; new Chapters 10–12).

An accompanying Instructor's Manual contains assignment schedules and solutions to end-of-chapter material. It also includes a test bank of multiple choice questions and answers.

A Student Supplement on tax reporting procedures is also available. This supplement, updated each January with the latest tax forms, reproduces more than sixty forms. Case studies of seven hypothetical taxpayers illustrate the most common types of returns, and the supplement also includes ten tax return problems, along with the forms necessary to complete each exercise. Every form included in the supplement is referenced in the margin of the text.

Many persons have made important contributions to the development of this edition, but special recognition must be given to the following: Norma D. Brink, San Jose State University; Alan D. Campbell, University of Texas–Arlington; Edsel Grams, University of Wisconsin–Eau Claire; Dennis R. Lassila, Texas A&M University; Debra A. McGilsky, Northern Illinois University; Robert H. Michaelsen, University of Nebraska–Lincoln; Bruce Mogayzel, St. Anselms College; and John H. Wilguess, Oklahoma State University, who reviewed the text in detail and made numerous suggestions for its improvement.

We also want to give our special thanks to: Arthur Baum, State University of New York–New Paltz; William Caskey, Cerritos College; Eugene C. Elser, Evangel College; M. Ray Gregg, Oral Roberts University; G. L. Kantin, Madison Area Technical College; Frank A. Mayne, University of Texas–El Paso; John P. McLean, University of Scranton; Tony Merlonghi, Napa Valley College; Emily Miklis, Cuyahoga Community College; Judith Odell, Junior College of Albany; Travis A. Pittman, Texas Southern University; John D. Rice, Trinity University; David E. Ritter, Texas Wesleyan College; Uwe Rudolf, Luther College; Jerome R. Scheve, Wilmington Colleg; Francine Simmons, Griffin Business College; and Theodore N. Wood, Gordon College, who completed a detailed questionnaire on the previous edition. Finally,, we owe a special debt of gratitude to Johanna Schmid, of HBJ, who directed the revision, and to Anne Harvey, who served as the production editor of this edition.

Ray M. Sommerfeld
Hershel M. Anderson
Horace R. Brock
John O. Everett

Contents

Chapter Objectives

1. Review briefly the most important tax developments in the history of the United States for the past 80 years.
2. Identify the tax bases most commonly used by the federal, state, and local levels of government.
3. Note how many tax dollars are collected—in both absolute and relative terms—in the United States each year.
4. Identify the diverse objectives common to our tax laws.
5. Identify the three taxable entities for federal income tax purposes.
6. Describe the most important details of the income tax, social security tax, retail sales tax, property tax, and the donative-transfers tax.
7. Explain the difference between proportional, progressive, and regressive tax rates in both a technical and a popular sense.
8. Distinguish between average and marginal tax rates.
9. Compare the tax structure of the United States with that found in other countries of the world.

1 An Introduction

Over 50 years ago Justice Oliver Wendell Holmes described ***taxes*** as the price that we pay for civilized society.[1] Many present day commentators suggest that high taxes are destroying our otherwise healthy society. Who is correct? Do taxes help or hinder the United States in the achievement of its multiple goals? In this introductory chapter we will examine the broad outlines of the tax structure which currently exists at the federal, state, and local levels of government. Our examination will begin with a historical review of the major changes in our tax system during the first 80 years of this twentieth century. Following that discussion we will examine in a general way the taxes that are most heavily relied upon for the production of revenue. We will then review the tax rate structure that applies to those various taxes. Finally, we will make a brief comparison between our own tax system and those found in some of the other nations of the world, to better assess the major current issues in U.S. taxation.

TAX (noun) Any nonpenal yet compulsory transfer of resources from the private to the public sector, levied on the basis of predetermined criteria, and without receipt of a specific benefit of equal value, in order to accomplish some of a government's economic and social objectives.

HISTORICAL PERSPECTIVE

Prior to World War I local taxes accounted for over one-half of all tax revenues collected in the United States. Following that war and throughout the period of the Great Depression, both state and federal taxes increased slowly until, by 1934, no single level of government accounted

[1] *Compañia de Tabacos v. Collector*, 279 U.S. 306 (1927).

for more than half of the total tax revenues collected. With the advent of World War II, however, the federal government became the dominant force in U.S. taxation. Nothing has happened in the years since 1942 to change that picture even though total tax revenues continue to increase almost yearly at all levels of government. This changing picture is implicit in Table 1-1.

The dominance of the federal level of government in our tax system for the past 40 years has had a profound impact on the kinds of taxes that we have come to rely upon most heavily. More specifically, our present heavy reliance upon the income tax could not have occurred without this shift from the local to the federal level of government. Although a significant number of cities, and most states, do impose an income tax, the problems of overlapping jurisdictions create major administrative difficulties for income taxation at all but the highest levels of government. These problems are especially significant for large businesses operating in multiple jurisdictions. The basic problem is, of course, allocating the total income among the various jurisdictions.

AMOUNTS COLLECTED

Although the taxes of state and local levels of government have since 1934 accounted for less than half of all tax revenues collected, the total amounts collected generally continue to increase at all levels of government every year. The increases exist both in terms of the absolute number of dollars collected and in per capita collections. This conclusion is supported by the data of Table 1-2. The dramatic increase in the number of dollars collected in tax revenues from $1.4 billion in 1902 to nearly $730 billion in 1980 reflects the impact of inflation, a growing economy, and a larger population.

Instead of looking at the absolute number of tax dollars collected in various years, we might better compare the number of tax dollars collected to any of several measures of national income. In general terms,

TABLE 1-1
Percentage Distribution of Tax Receipts for Selected Years

YEAR	LOCAL	STATE	FEDERAL
1902	51%	11%	37%
1913	58	13	29
1934	44	22	33
1942	20	22	58
1960	14	16	70
1980	12	20	67
1982	15	19	66

Note: Totals may not add to 100% because of rounding.

SOURCE: Tax Foundation, Inc. *Facts and Figures on Government Finance*, 22nd Biennial Edition, 1983, Table 10, p. 22.

TABLE 1-2
Total Tax Receipts for Selected Years (in billions)

YEAR	LOCAL	STATE	FEDERAL	TOTAL
1902	$ .7	$ .2	$ .5	$ 1.4
1913	1.3	.3	.7	2.3
1934	3.9	2.0	2.9	8.9
1942	4.6	5.0	13.4	23.0
1960	18.1	20.0	88.4	126.7
1980	85.2	151.5	490.4	727.0
1983	113.1	171.4	568.4	852.9

Note: Totals may not add up because of rounding.

SOURCE: Data for 1902–1980 adapted from Tax Foundation, Inc., *Facts and Figures on Government Finance*, 22nd Biennial Edition, 1983, Table 14, p. 26; data for 1983 estimated by author.

both gross national product (GNP) and net national product (NNP) are numerical estimates of the value of all goods and services produced by a nation during a year. GNP measures the value of that output without concern for the capital consumed in the production process; NNP reduces the gross value by the amount of capital consumed. If tax revenues are expressed as a percentage of NNP, it appears that tax collections have really not grown very much in the past 50 years. In 1934 total tax receipts amounted to approximately 31% of the United States' NNP; today that same figure is approximately 34%. This relative stability in the ratio of tax revenues to NNP may explain why politicians of both parties have found it difficult to make major changes in our system of taxation and government expenditure. That is, as a nation, we may have become accustomed to a certain level of taxes and—on balance—prefer to keep it that way.

Ronald Reagan apparently struck a sympathetic chord in the 1980 presidential elections when he promised massive cuts in both the personal and business income taxes. On the other hand, the reluctance of Congress to go along with some of President Reagan's further budget cuts in 1983 and 1984 suggests that there will be substantial resistance to reducing public expenditures much below their present level. The hope for 1985 is to maintain prior year levels which, for many, is tantamount to a budget reduction. Many commentators believe that the present large budget deficit accumulated by the federal government already has or soon will impact negatively on the economy. If the deficits are to be decreased, however, we must either reduce spending or increase taxes (or do some of both). When faced with similar problems in prior years, almost instinctively both Congress and the administration turned to the income tax. It seemed that Congress usually decided that whatever needed to be done could best be handled by changes in the income tax laws. Unfortunately those laws have become so complex—as you will discover in this book—the average citizen can no longer understand what is expected of him or her. The frequency of change in the income tax rules

TABLE 1-3
Revenue Sources by Level of Government in 1983 (in billions)

TAX BASE	LOCAL	STATE	FEDERAL	TOTAL
Income	$ 6	$ 63	$326	$395
Social Security	—	—	187	187
Sales	16	84	44	144
Property	86	3	—	89
Other	4	21	11	36
Total	$112	$171	$568	$851

SOURCE: Bureau of the Census, Washington, D.C., 1984.

during the past decade has done little to increase the nation's trust in its basic fairness. In any case, the events of the past few years may signal the beginning of some major changes in our tax system. The recent willingness of both Congress and President Reagan to consider income tax simplification seriously is encouraging. Unfortunately, however, those efforts do little or nothing to reduce the budget deficits. What Congress and the administration will actually do by way of tax reform and budget reductions in 1985 remains to be seen as we go to press.

REVENUE SOURCES

Historically the federal government has relied most heavily on the income tax, while state governments have used the sales tax, and local governments the property tax. In the recent past, however, the federal Social Security tax has been the most rapidly growing of all taxes. As demonstrated in Table 1-3, the income tax still produces significantly more tax revenue than any other tax. Observe also that a total of about $850 billion in taxes is collected every year, or more than $2.3 *billion* every day of the year, including Saturdays and Sundays! To put these awesome numbers in perspective, reflect upon the fact that the Korean War ended approximately one billion seconds ago; that Christ was on earth slightly more than one billion minutes ago; and that man still lived in caves only one billion hours ago.

> ***BACKGROUND***
>
> Except for recurring disputes over the income tax, few citizens question the legal right of a government to impose and collect taxes. The early litigation over the income tax centered upon an interpretation of Article 1, Section 9, Clause 4, of the Constitution of the United States. It states that "No Capitation, or other direct, Tax shall be laid, unless in Proportion to the Census or Enumeration herein before directed to be taken." Thus, if the income tax is a *direct* tax, this clause
>
> *Continued*

BACKGROUND

in the Constitution seems to say that any federal income tax is unconstitutional because there is no way to make an income tax proportional based upon population.

The first time the Supreme Court considered whether or not the income tax was a direct tax it decided in a unanimous decision that it was not a "direct tax," but an "indirect tax." Accordingly, the Court held in *Springer* v. *United States** that an income tax was entirely constitutional and that the federal government had acted within its authority in imposing and collecting an income tax from 1862 to 1872. Following the Civil War the issue of income taxation became a major social issue. Surprising as it may seem today, the income tax was generally favored by the states of the South and West and opposed by those in the North and East. When another income tax act passed Congress in 1894 (without the signature of President Cleveland!), the same direct tax issue was reintroduced into the judicial system. This time the Supreme Court held by a scant 5 to 4 vote that the income tax *was* a direct tax and, therefore, unconstitutional. See *Pollock* v. *Farmer's Loan and Trust Co.*†

After the *Pollock* decision the citizens who favored the income tax decided that the best way to proceed was to seek a constitutional amendment. The joint resolution to amend passed Congress in 1909 and was ratified by the appropriate number of states. It thus became the Sixteenth Amendment on February 25, 1913. Even before ratification of this amendment, Congress passed, with President Taft's signature, a revenue act that imposed a flat (1%) tax on all corporate income in excess of $5,000. This corporate income tax was tested on constitutional grounds in *Flint* v. *Stone Tracy Co.*‡ and found to be legitimate on the grounds that it was not a direct tax but rather a special form of excise tax on the privilege of doing business in the corporate form.

* 102 U.S. 602 (1880).

† 158 U.S. 601 (1895).

‡ 220 U.S. 107 (1911).

TAX OBJECTIVES

Prior to the years of the Great Depression and the New Deal of the Roosevelt Administration, taxes were generally viewed as nothing more than a way for the government to get the money needed to pay for whatever resources it elected to consume. A number of economists pointed out, however, that taxes do have economic side effects that may be more important than their immediate impact on government budgets. They observed, for example, that an increase in taxes necessarily reduces the private sector's ability either to consume or invest. Because there were large quantities of unemployed resources in the 1930s, some economists advocated an expansion of government programs, even if that necessitated deficit spending, to "get the country going again." These individuals argued that any increase in taxes would serve only to diminish the chance of an early economic recovery; in short, they suggested that the federal government at least could spend its way to prosperity. That possibility, however, is not available to state and local governments. The major single difference between the federal government and the state and local governments was (and is) the exclusive right of the federal government to create money. To this day, if a state or local government desires to spend more than it collects in taxes, it must borrow the difference. And before a state or local government can borrow, it must convince the voters to approve its right to issue additional bonds—a task which is becoming increasingly difficult every year. The federal government, on the other hand, can spend whatever it wishes—without regard for what it collects and without direct regard for how the voters feel about government debt—since only Congress need approve any increase in the federal debt. This right of the federal government to control the monetary system has now been recognized as an additional force of great importance in the way our economy performs. However, recognition of the importance of monetary policy has not eliminated the need to give careful consideration to the secondary effects of every tax law change.

Many of the income tax law changes enacted since World War II were based upon the notion that, if enacted, they would serve to stimulate economic growth. Among the most important of these provisions are those that introduced rapid depreciation deductions and the investment tax credit. Of even more recent vintage are the 1981–1983 tax rate reductions, which were especially large for individuals in the highest income brackets. These rate reductions were enacted in the belief that the incentives to work, save, and invest would be favorably affected by the lower tax liabilities that would attach to marginal amounts of effort and income. Similar economic incentives explain such diverse income tax provisions as the research and experimentation credit, the targeted-jobs credit, percentage depletion, the long-term capital-gain deduction, and ACRS (the Accelerated Cost Recovery System).

Other tax provisions are primarily explained on the basis of social, rather than economic, objectives. The fundamental explanation of the personal exemption is, for example, social in origin. The idea is that no income tax should be paid by persons earning only very small amounts of income. An extension of that same basic idea lies behind our progressive tax rate structure; it implies that those who earn more should pay *relatively* more than those who earn less. Acceptance of that general notion, however, says nothing about either the desired rate of progression in the tax rate structure or the maximum rate to be applied to any amount of income earned. The extra personal exemption deductions allowed for those 65 years of age or older, and for blind taxpayers, are two additional examples of social objectives being addressed through a system of income taxation; so are the medical expense deduction, the right to deduct both interest expense and property taxes on private homes, the child-care credit, and the charitable contribution deduction.

Although economic and social objectives tend to dominate the reasons which explain some of our income tax provisions, other objectives may account for particular legislation. For example, simplification of the tax law and greater equity among taxpayers are frequently cited as the reasons a particular politician or political party supports a proposed change.

BACKGROUND

Although many politicians talk about tax equity, few of them take the time or make an effort to define what they mean by the term. Most U.S. tax scholars agree that there are at least two fundamentally different tax equity concepts. One is called horizontal equity; the other, vertical equity. Horizontal tax equity refers to the equal treatment of two similarly situated taxpayers. For example, if Taxpayer A, an accountant, earns an annual income of $100,000 and pays an income tax of $20,000, and Taxpayer B, a business executive, also earns an annual income of $100,000, but pays an income tax of $35,000, the tax system would be said to be inequitable because two persons earning the same income pay significantly different taxes. Vertical tax equity, on the other hand, refers to the deliberately *different* tax treatment of two *unequally* situated taxpayers. In general, vertical tax equity is deemed to exist when those who earn more pay *relatively more* in taxes. For example, if Taxpayer C, a carpenter, earns an annual income of $20,000 and pays an income tax of $4,000, and Taxpayer D, a dentist, earns an annual income of $200,000 and pays an income tax of $40,000, many persons would contend that the tax system was inequitable because both individuals pay 20% of their income in taxes even though one taxpayer (D) earns 10 times as much as the other taxpayer (C). Vertical tax equity is generally deemed to demand that D pay something more than 20%; unfortunately, however, there is no simple way to determine how much more than 20% D should pay.

The idea behind the standard deduction—which has evolved through the years into a zero-bracket amount—is best explained as a simplification; it allows a majority of all taxpayers to forget record keeping, at least as far as deductions are concerned. The tax tables and the withholding system are two other examples of attempts to simplify our tax laws. Income averaging, on the other hand, is an attempt to achieve greater tax equity between those taxpayers whose incomes are relatively constant over time and those who earn widely fluctuating amounts of income from year to year. Finally, political objectives may explain some otherwise unexplainable tax laws. After all, in the first instance our tax law is designed by the individual members of Congress who must regularly seek reelection.

In summary, since 1930 the objectives of the federal income tax have changed dramatically. The objectives now are:

1. To raise government revenues;
2. To stimulate economic growth;
3. To decrease unemployment;
4. To retard inflation;
5. To stimulate the production of energy;
6. To conserve the consumption of energy;
7. To provide assistance to the needy;
8. To improve our national defense;
9. To simplify the tax law; and
10. To increase tax equity.

The only objective of nearly all taxes *other than* the federal income tax, however, remains that of providing needed government revenues. The diversity of the other tax bases is testimony to the substantial need for tax revenues generally.

OUR MOST IMPORTANT TAX BASES

We have already observed that the most important taxes in the United States are the income tax, the Social Security tax, the sales tax, and the property tax, in that order. To state that we rely heavily upon the income tax (or any other tax) says little or nothing about many details concerning that tax. Because the income tax has come to play such a dominant role in our tax structure, and because there are so many things that you can do to change an income tax liability, the remaining chapters of this text are devoted solely to a discussion of the many details common to our federal income tax. Before we begin a detailed examination of our federal income tax law, however, it seems desirable that we note a few generalities about some of our important tax bases.

THE INCOME TAX

The biggest single problem in income taxation is the definition of income. Anyone who has completed even one semester in financial accounting should automatically understand the problem. Economists, accountants, and lawyers have disagreed for years over the meaning of that simple, six-letter word, "income." Given this disparity of expert opinion over the meaning of the word income, the fact that the United States has come to rely more heavily on an *income tax* than on any other tax, is something of a miracle. How can a government tax so heavily something no one can define?

INCOME: A NET CONCEPT Virtually all authorities agree that income is not the same thing as gross revenues. The income concept clearly suggests that some items, even though poorly defined, must be deducted from gross revenues in the measurement of income. Accountants, generally speaking, argue that income measurement should proceed as follows:

- First: Determine the amount of gross revenue *earned* during a given time period;
- Next: Determine the amount of expense incurred (or still to be incurred) in the production of the revenue measured in step one;
- Then: Deduct the quantity determined in step two from the quantity measured in step one and label this difference "income."

In other words, accountants generally start with a measurement of revenues earned; then, based on a matching concept, they deduct all of the expenses incurred in the production of those revenues to obtain their measure of income. This brief explanation of the accountant's income-measurement technique, however, begs many important questions. For example, exactly what events must transpire before a revenue is deemed to have been earned, or "realized"? Exactly how should expenses be measured: in units of historical cost, current cost, or future cost? If anything other than historical cost measures are to be used, how is one to estimate either current or future costs?

Although accountants can (and do) argue over these and many other important income-measurement questions, tax advisors and taxpayers have no choice but to proceed with their income measurements at least once each year. The government demands that every taxpayer report ***taxable income*** earned and pay a tax liability based on this measure of income. Under these circumstances you should not be surprised to discover that there are literally thousands of pages of official tax law devoted largely to the definition of taxable income. Chapter 2 will explain what is authoritative in tax law and how you can assess authoritative pronouncements. In the meantime, the general idea implicit in our concept of taxable income can be described as follows:

TAXABLE INCOME The arithmetic difference between gross income and deductions.

- First: Determine the amount of ***gross income*** earned by a taxpayer during the year. In making this determination, interpret the word income broadly. *The Code states that income means all income from whatever source derived.* However, every taxpayer may exclude from the measurement of gross income those items specifically designated as *exclusions* in the tax Code.
- Next: Determine the total amount of ***deductions*** that a taxpayer may claim for the year. In making this determination, interpret the word deductions narrowly. In other words, in measuring taxable income you can generally forget the matching concept of financial accounting. Every taxpayer should generally presume that nothing is deductible un-

GROSS INCOME Income (broadly conceived) less exclusions.

DEDUCTIONS Items that by law may be deducted from gross income in the calculation of taxable income.

less he or she can find good authority to support such a deduction.

- Then: Deduct the quantity measured in step two from the quantity measured in step one and label this difference "taxable income."

Example 1: The income of a service business is generally computed for both financial accounting and tax purposes as follows:

Gross Receipts	$100,000
Less Operating Expenses	60,000
Equals "Net Income"	$ 40,000

Example 2: The income of a merchandising business is slightly more complicated; for federal income tax purposes that computation would be made as follows:

Gross Receipts ($220,000) *less* Cost of Goods Sold ($120,000) *equals* "Gross Income"	$100,000
Less Operating Expenses	60,000
Equals "Net Income"	$ 40,000

For financial accounting purposes that same computation would be detailed in a slightly different way, namely:

Sales (i.e., gross receipts)	$220,000
Less Cost of Goods Sold (an expense)	120,000
Equals "Gross Income"	$100,000
Less Operating Expenses	60,000
Equals "Net Income"	$ 40,000

For federal income tax purposes the cost of any property sold is automatically deducted *before* determining any measure of "gross income."

Although taxable income has many similarities to the net income of financial accounting, you will discover that there are numerous differences between the two measures. However, both clearly accept the idea that income is a net concept. The correct determination of taxable income is often a frustrating experience because of the complexity (and ambiguity) of the Code and because of the large number of authoritative pronouncements that must be consulted in making this measurement. With time and experience you may discover that this same complexity and ambiguity makes tax work a lot of fun as well as a big challenge. If so, a career as a tax advisor could prove to be a very rewarding experience.

TAXABLE ENTITIES In addition to measuring taxable income, we must also determine *who* must pay the income tax. In other words, who are the taxpayers or taxable entities for income tax purposes? Generally speaking, that answer is every individual,[2] every corporation,[3] and every estate or trust.[4] Several things are notable about our income tax law. First, it makes every individual a taxpayer without regard for age, marital status, or intelligence. Second, it does not treat partnerships or sole proprietorships as taxpayers. Third, at least initially, the law does not distinguish between citizens and aliens, or between domestic and foreign corporations. *Every* individual, corporation, trust, and estate in the entire world is a viable taxpayer for U.S. income tax purposes! The all-encompassing nature of our income tax law is generally described by the adjective "global," that is, the U.S. income tax is a ***global tax***. On first blush it appears to make no difference who earns the income or where it is earned—all income is subject to the U.S. income tax. Many other countries are less grandiose in their tax laws; those countries impose a ***territorial income tax***, as opposed to a global tax. In other words, they attempt to tax only the income that is earned in their own country.

GLOBAL INCOME TAX An income tax law that applies to all income earned in any country of the world.

TERRITORIAL INCOME TAX An income tax law that applies only to the income earned within a specific governmental jurisdiction.

As you may suspect, the differences between a global and a territorial income tax are often more imaginary than real. As a practical matter, the U.S. government would find it very difficult to get legal jurisdiction over the citizens and corporations of the Soviet Union, Poland, China, France, or any other country. Therefore our Code goes on to provide, in Subchapter N,[5] a host of special rules for foreign-source income. In general, only the U.S. citizen and the domestic corporation are subject to the full panoply of U.S. tax rules on worldwide income; and numerous special provisions apply even to the income of those taxpayers from non-U.S. sources. Aliens, at least nonresident aliens, and most foreign corporations pay a U.S. income tax only on that portion of their income that derives from U.S. sources.

We must also observe that even though partnerships escape designation as taxable entities, the income earned by a partnership does not escape the income tax. Rather, our tax law immediately taxes each partner on his or her share of the partnership's taxable income, whether or not that income is distributed by the partnership to the partners.

Example 3: Suppose that individuals A and B and corporation C are three equal partners in the ABC Partnership which earned a $900,000 taxable income during the year. Further assume that the ABC Partnership distributed only $600,000 to its partners during the year.

In spite of the fact that each partner received only $200,000 from ABC during the year, each must report additional taxable income in the amount of $300,000 because of their partnership interest in ABC.

In short, generally we treat the partnership as a conduit for tax purposes. That same conduit treatment also extends to every sole proprietorship;

[2] Sec. 1.

[3] Sec. 11(a).

[4] Sec. 1(e).

[5] Secs. 861–999.

i.e., any proprietorship income must be reported immediately by (and taxed to) the "proprietor," or owner. The amount distributed from the business venture to the owner does not matter.

UNITARY INCOME TAX An income tax that purports to apply the same tax rate(s) to all kinds of income.

SCHEDULAR INCOME TAX An income tax that deliberately applies a different tax rate(s) to income from different sources.

TAX RATES The final step in any tax calculation involves the multiplication of a tax base by the tax rate; i.e., the tax liability equals the product of some tax base (taxable income) and a tax rate. In general, the United States imposes a ***unitary tax*** on all of the income earned by each taxable entity during the year. This means that the same tax rates will apply to all income, without regard for where or how the income is earned. Many other countries impose a ***schedular income tax***, rather than a unitary tax. In those countries each taxable entity must divide its taxable income for the year into various schedules, such as income from interest on government bonds, income from commercial interest or dividends, income from manufacturing, income from farming, income from trading, etc. There is little uniformity in the number or kind of schedules provided by the several countries following this alternative tax system. What they do have in common is their explicit provisions for different tax rates for different "kinds" of income.

Although the United States purports to apply a unitary tax rate, the differences between our unitary and their schedular systems are once again more imaginary than real. For example, any interest income earned from state and local government bonds is generally exempt from the U.S. federal income tax. In effect, therefore, this exclusion creates a separate tax schedule for interest from state and local bonds (with a zero tax rate). The United States has also given very special treatment to certain capital gains ever since 1922. Although the details of the special treatment have changed frequently, the net effect of our capital-gain provisions is tantamount to a special schedule (with a preferential tax rate) for those items of income that can be classified as long-term capital gains. Congress has also created a special 10-year forward-averaging option that may be used to determine the tax liability payable on the distribution of a lump sum from a qualified pension or profit-sharing plan. This option is also equivalent to a special schedule for income derived from that one source. As noted earlier, therefore, the apparent distinction between the unitary and schedular systems of income taxation is truly more apparent than it is real.

In addition to the different tax treatments provided for different types or kinds of income, the U.S. tax law also provides different tax rate schedules for different taxable entities. To be more precise, our law provides one tax rate schedule for all corporations;[6] another schedule for all trusts and estates;[7] and four different schedules for individual taxpayers. The tax rate schedules for individual taxpayers include those applicable to (*a*) married persons filing joint returns and surviving spouses;[8] (*b*) heads

---

[6] Sec. 11(a).

[7] Sec. 1(e).

[8] Sec. 1(a).

of households,[9] (*c*) unmarried individuals (other than surviving spouses and heads of households),[10] and (*d*) married individuals filing separate returns.[11] These different tax rate schedules are explained in greater detail in Chapter 3.

Although much more could be said about the income tax, let us now turn our attention to some generalities of the other taxes which are an important part of our total tax system. Specifically, let us consider a few important facts about the federal Social Security tax.

THE SOCIAL SECURITY TAX

The Social Security system was originally seen as a form of old-age and survivor insurance. That is, people expected to pay the government the equivalent of an insurance premium—that they might otherwise have paid to a private insurance company—to provide them with a limited amount of life insurance or a retirement annuity. During the past 30 years, however, this Social Security system has been greatly expanded to include many welfare programs (such as medical insurance) not originally deemed to be part of that system. Because the Social Security system is not a funded system—that is, because the amounts currently received are *not* accumulated to pay for later benefits—most people have come to look upon Social Security payments as simply another tax having little or no relationship to the principles of retirement insurance.

The ***Social Security*** tax—or FICA (Federal Insurance Contribution Act) tax—is, in essence, a tax on the value of human labor. Technically this tax can be divided into two parts: that based on the amount of wages and salaries paid to employees and that imposed on self-employed persons. The funds collected from this tax are ***earmarked*** for (or deposited in) one of three funds which can be used only to pay for (*a*) retirement and/or survivorship benefits, (*b*) disability benefits, and (*c*) Medicare benefits. In this brief introduction to the Social Security tax we will consider first the tax on employees and employers, next the tax on self-employed individuals, and finally a few of the major problems currently faced by the Social Security system.

SOCIAL SECURITY The tax authorized by the Federal Insurance Contribution Act, formally known as the FICA tax.

EARMARKING A bookkeeping procedure whereby tax revenues derived from a specific tax are put into a separate governmental fund which, by law, can be used only to pay for government expenditures of a stated variety.

TAX ON EMPLOYEES AND EMPLOYERS The tax on employees consists of two separate parts, namely, (*a*) the part paid by the employee and (*b*) the part paid by the employer. The tax rate paid by both the employer and the employee is the same but it, in turn, is also composed of two separate parts, namely, (*a*) the old-age, survivor, and disability insurance part, and (*b*) the hospital insurance part. Finally, there is an annual maximum wage base, the exact amount of which changes frequently. The current and scheduled future tax rates are shown in Table 1-4. The maximum

---

[9] Sec. 1(b).

[10] Sec. 1(c).

[11] Sec. 1(d).

TABLE 1-4
Social Security Tax Rate for Employees and Employers

YEARS	RATE FOR OLD-AGE, SURVIVORS, AND DISABILITY INSURANCE	RATE FOR HOSPITAL INSURANCE	TOTAL SOCIAL SECURITY TAX RATE
1985	5.70%	1.35%	7.05%
1986	5.70	1.45	7.15
1987	5.70	1.45	7.15
1988	6.06	1.45	7.51
1989	6.06	1.45	7.51
1990	6.20	1.45	7.65

SOURCE: Sec. 3111.

wage base for 1985 is $39,600. This amount automatically changes each year with increases in the Consumer Price Index.

Example 4: In 1985 Dale Davis was paid a total of $24,000 in wages. The Social Security tax payable by both Dale and his employer amounts to $1,692 (i.e., $24,000 × .0705) each.

Example 5: In 1985 Harriet Moore was paid a salary of $50,000. The Social Security tax payable by both Harriet and her employer amounts to $2,792 (i.e., $39,600 × .0705) each. Because Harriet's salary exceeded the maximum, both she and her employer paid Social Security taxes on only the first $39,600 that she earned.

Although the vast majority of all employees in the United States are subject to the Social Security tax, there are a number of exceptions, including federal government employees employed before 1984, railroad workers, newspaper carriers (under 18 years of age), employees of Communist organizations, and a few others. In addition some individual employees will be covered only if they meet certain minimum conditions. The latter group includes agricultural employees, casual and domestic employees, and maritime and aircraft personnel.

If an individual works for more than one employer during a year, each employer must calculate the Social Security tax payable as if the employee worked for only that one firm. Because such an employee could be paid less than the maximum wage base by any single employer, but still earn a total salary that exceeded the maximum for the year, an excess Social Security tax can be paid. The portion of any such excess attributable to the *employee's* share of the tax (but *not* to the employer's share) can be claimed by the employee as a tax credit on his or her individual income tax return. The portion of any excess attributable to the amounts paid by multiple employers is not recoverable by anyone.

TAX ON SELF-EMPLOYED PERSONS The Social Security tax on self-employed persons is similar to the tax on employees except for the fact that self-employed persons must pay the entire amount of the tax themselves. The current and scheduled future tax rates for the self-employed are shown in Table 1-5. The maximum tax base is the same for both employees and the self-employed.

Example 6: Mary Madsen is self-employed. During 1985 Mary earned a total of $24,000 in self-employment income. The Social Security tax payable by Mary amounts to $2,832 (i.e., $24,000 × .118).

If one individual works both as an employee and as a self-employed person, the Social Security tax is first determined by that individual's status as an employee; if the total wages and salary received do not exceed the maximum tax base for the year, any remainder is subject to the self-employed person's tax.

Example 7: Ted Fisher works for Acme Corporation. In addition Ted is self-employed as a fishing guide on weekends. In 1985 Ted earned $32,000 as an employee for Acme and another $10,000 as a fishing guide. Ted's Social Security tax for 1985 would amount to $3,152.80 (i.e., $32,000 × .0705 plus $7,600 × .118).

SOME MAJOR PROBLEMS The biggest problem with the Social Security system is simply the fact that it is short on money. As explained earlier, the Social Security system is not a funded system. In other words, the dollars currently collected by the government in Social Security taxes are *not* put aside to pay for the benefits that will be payable in future years to those presently working; they are, instead, used to pay those presently receiving benefits from the system. Because of the large increase in benefits provided, the increasing life span of retired persons, a declining birth rate and therefore a declining percentage of currently employed persons,

TABLE 1-5
Social Security Tax Rate on Self-Employed Persons

YEAR(S)	RATE FOR OLD-AGE, SURVIVORS, AND DISABILITY INSURANCE	RATE FOR HOSPITAL INSURANCE	TOTAL SOCIAL SECURITY TAX
1985	11.40%	2.70%	14.10%*
1986–87	11.40	2.90	14.30
1988–89	12.12	2.90	15.02
1990	12.40	2.90	15.30

*For 1985 the law allows a 2.3% credit against this rate; hence the real or effective total rate is really 11.8% (or 14.1% less 2.3%).

SOURCE: Sec. 1401.

as well as a number of other factors, the Social Security system will not be able to continue to pay its present and promised future benefits without making changes. This problem has been apparent for a number of years but the politicians in Washington found it very difficult to reach a satisfactory settlement. Finally, in April, 1983, Congress did act on a bipartisan commission's recommendation and shored up the system for the next few years.

Each year it becomes increasingly difficult simply to raise the Social Security tax rate because it already represents the largest single tax paid by a majority of all individuals. To increase it even more creates numerous social and economic problems. Among those problems is the fact that the Social Security tax can not itself be treated as a deduction for federal income tax purposes by the employee or by the self-employed person. Employers, on the other hand, can generally deduct their contribution to Social Security, the tax they pay on behalf of business employees. This difference in tax treatment results in a significantly different after-tax burden for employees and employers. In other words, even though both the employee and the employer appear in the first instance to make an equal contribution to the Social Security tax, their real after-tax burdens are substantially different. In general, the real burden is greater on the employee than it is on the employer.

The difference between treatment of persons who are employed and those who are self-employed creates another difficulty. Many employers would prefer to have those persons who work for them classified as independent contractors. Since independent contractors are treated as self-employed individuals, the "potential employer" is freed from making any contribution to the Social Security system to the extent that any "would-be employee" can be reclassified as an independent contractor. For years this distinction has caused many disputes between the Internal Revenue Service (IRS) and taxpayers. A few of the troublesome classifications—such as that of real estate agents and brokers—have been resolved by specific provisions in the Code. Other disputes will continue to be resolved through administrative and judicial procedures.

In spite of the numerous and serious problems faced by our Social Security system, this tax continues to be among the most rapidly escalating taxes in the United States. In the past 20 years, for example, this one tax has increased from approximately 20% of total federal government receipts to about 31%. During the same period the corporate income tax has declined significantly in its relative importance to total federal tax revenues.

THE SALES TAX

The general sales tax is exactly what its name implies, a tax on the sales transaction. Even though the sales tax could be applied at any or every level of the production process it is most commonly imposed at only the retail sale level. If a sales-type tax is imposed at the manufacturer, wholesaler, *and* retailer level it is commonly known as a value-added tax, rather than as a sales tax, and the taxpayer is allowed to deduct (in the computation of this tax base) the cost of goods purchased from another. By contrast, the sales tax is imposed on the total value of each taxable sale transaction.

Example 8: Jaw Corporation's total retail sales for the year amounted to $2,510,300. Jaw's sales were made in a state which imposes a 5% retail sales tax. Accordingly, Jaw would be expected to remit a total of $125,515 (i.e., $2,510,300 × .05) to the state government as the sales tax paid during the year by those who purchased items from Jaw Corporation.

Example 9: Bone Corporation's total sales for the year also amounted to $2,510,300. Bone purchased raw materials from other suppliers in the amount of $510,300. Bone's sales were made in a country which imposes a value-added tax of 5%. Accordingly, Bone should remit a total of $100,000 (i.e., $2,510,300 less $510,300 times .05) to the government as a value-added tax.

In most instances the retail sales tax is technically imposed on the ultimate purchaser of goods or services. The seller, however, serves as the collecting and remitting agent for the government. In some jurisdictions the seller is allowed to retain the difference between the actual sales tax collected and the amount calculated on total sales, to compensate the seller for the administrative costs associated with this tax. The reason that actual tax collections exceed the amount as computed on total sales is, of course, attributed to the rounding of the tax on individual sales. That is, individual sales are taxed based on tables constructed with rounded amounts as an administrative convenience. When all sales are aggregated, the rounded amounts disappear and an excess sales tax collection remains. A value-added tax, on the other hand, is ordinarily imposed on the seller who must pay the tax without any compensation for the additional cost incurred.

THE EXCISE TAXES

EXCISE TAX A special tax on specific goods or services.

Excise taxes are typically administered in a manner very similar to the sales tax but they apply only to the sale of very specific goods and/or services. For example, a 5¢ excise tax may be imposed on the sale of 1 gallon of gasoline. Because this tax applies only to sales of gasoline, it is not considered to be a sales tax. On the other hand the method of collection and remittance for most excise taxes parallels closely that used in the administration of the sales tax. In other words, most excise taxes are technically paid by the purchaser but they are collected from the buyer and remitted to the government by the seller.

The distinction between sales and excise taxes is sometimes blurred by the practice of excluding various sales from the sales tax base. In numerous states, for example, there is no retail sales tax on sales of food purchased for off-premise consumption, on work clothing, and/or sales of medicines or drugs prescribed by a medical doctor. The broader the list of exceptions from the sales tax, and the more numerous the items subject to an excise tax, the more blurred the distinction between these two taxes becomes. In recognition of this blurred distinction, and to facilitate your comprehension of the big picture in the United States tax system, the dollar amounts collected for all sales, excise, and customs taxes were combined into a single figure (called "sales taxes") in Table 1-3. This loose combination of what really are diverse taxes should not, however, be allowed to hide either the long list of items commonly subject to excise taxation or the administrative problems introduced by the statutory exclusions from sales taxes.

Among the list of commodities and services commonly subject to one or more excise taxes in the United States are:

- Beer and wine
- Bows and arrows
- Coal
- Crude oil
- Diesel fuels
- Distilled spirits
- Fishing equipment
- Gasoline
- Lubricating oils
- Machine guns
- Pistols and revolvers
- Shells and cartridges
- Telephone and teletypewriter services
- Tires
- Tobacco
- Trucks and trailers
- Wagers and accepting wagers

These same commodities and services may also be subject to tax by more than one level of government; for example, gasoline is typically subject to both a federal and a state excise tax. In addition to the excise tax, the sale of many commodities is also subject to the sales tax. In other words, a single sale may actually involve both the sales and one or more excise taxes at the same time.

One important distinction between sales and excise taxes is that only the former are routinely deductible in the computation of the federal income tax. However, in most circumstances this difference is more important for the individual taxpayer than for the business taxpayer because the business taxpayer can usually deduct the total cost of the items purchased, including any excise tax, when calculating taxable income.

Example 10: Ethel Simms purchased a new set of automobile tires for her personal car that were subject to excise taxes totaling $25 and sales taxes totaling $20. In the computation of her personal federal income tax, Ethel may deduct the $20 in sales tax but not the $25 in excise tax, assuming that she itemizes her tax deductions.

Example 11: The Green Company purchased a new set of automobile tires for its delivery truck that were subject to excise taxes totaling $25 and sales taxes totaling $20. In the computation of its federal income tax the Green Company may deduct the total cost of these tires, including the full $45 attributable to the sales and excise taxes.

Since sales and excise taxes are typically most important at the state level of government, people living near a state line sometimes find it advantageous to cross a state border to do their shopping and thereby reduce their sales tax liability. To minimize that kind of tax avoidance, most states impose a ***use tax,*** which is nothing more than a substitute sales tax imposed on goods purchased in one jurisdiction but used in another.

USE TAX A substitute retail sales tax imposed on goods purchased in one governmental jurisdiction but used in another.

Example 12: Mary Maverick purchased a new car in Delaware for $12,000. Because Delaware imposes no retail sales tax, Mary paid no sales tax when she acquired the car. When Mary went to register her new automobile in her home state of Pennsylvania, however, she had to pay a use tax of 6%, or $720, just as if she had purchased the automobile in Pennsylvania in the first place.

Although it is difficult to avoid the sales and excise tax on automobiles and other properties that must be registered, that is not true for other major purchases such as diamonds, home appliances, and clothing.

In addition to the taxes commonly imposed at the time a person purchases various properties, the mere ownership of some properties may also give rise to another tax, commonly called the property tax. The most common forms of property taxation are those typically imposed by local governments on real estate and automobiles.

THE PROPERTY TAXES

Real property may be defined loosely as land and anything permanently attached to land. ***Personal property*** is a residual class; that is, any property that is not real property may be described as personal property. Because real property is immobile and impossible to conceal, it has long been a favorite tax base for local governments, including cities, counties, and school districts. In this brief review we will consider a few of the most important problems commonly associated with the various forms of property taxation.

REAL PROPERTY Land and other properties that are permanently attached to land.

PERSONAL PROPERTY Any property that is not real property (also known as "personalty").

VALUATION Property taxes are referred to as *ad valorem* taxes because they are based on value. Many persons go on to suggest that property taxes are a form of wealth taxation, or a tax on capital, but that generalization is frequently not true for many of the taxpayers who must pay a property tax. The two primary reasons property taxes are not really a form of wealth taxation are (*a*) the tendency to impose property taxes on the gross value of the property, and (*b*) the highly selective nature of most property taxes. The difference between a property tax based on gross value and another based on net value is, perhaps, best understood through an example.

Example 13: Farmer Smith owns 350 acres of rich farmland that is valued at $1.4 million, or $4,000 per acre. Smith purchased this land five years ago by paying $400,000 cash and taking out a 30-year mortgage with the Farmers' Bank and Trust Company for the remaining $1 million. Today Smith still owes $950,000 on that mortgage. In spite of the fact that Smith's equity interest in this farmland is only $450,000, Smith's real property tax liability will be based on the full fair market value, presumably $1.4 million.

Example 14: Farmer Jones, a neighbor of Smith, also owns 350 acres of rich farmland valued at $1.4 million. Jones inherited this land from his parents who paid $60,000 for the land many years ago. Like Smith, Jones' real property tax bill will be based on its current fair market value of $1.4 million. If this property accounts for nearly all of the property owned by Farmer Jones, the property tax will approximate a net wealth tax for Jones. That same conclusion is not, however, equally applicable to Smith (even though both farmers technically own an equivalent property), because Smith's net wealth amounts to only $450,000.

Unlike the taxes on real property, ad valorem taxes on personal property have generally fallen into disuse because of (*a*) the ease of concealment, (*b*) the mobility of the taxed property, and (*c*) the administrative difficulty of valuation. The numerous governments that tried to impose property taxes on such items as radios and television sets, jewelry, stocks and bonds, and household appliances, were quick to discover that most taxpayers were reluctant to admit their ownership of such properties if to do so meant paying a tax. Furthermore, if the government actually engaged tax collectors to go out and locate those properties and collect the tax, they frequently were hidden from view or even moved to other locations. Intangible assets—such as stocks, bonds, and bank-account balances—are especially subject to relocation and very few (if any) governments want to be guilty of driving those kinds of property into another city, county, or state.

The problem of determining a correct value is not unique to personal property. Owners of real estate frequently disagree with the assessments made by the tax authorities. In those instances, however, a board of tax appraisers can usually point to reasonably good evidence to justify any value assigned. For example, recent sales of similar properties often provide a good basis for determining comparable value. An actual purchase price is even better evidence, if the purchase was made at arm's length (that is, between unrelated parties) in the recent past. In other instances the appraisers may have to estimate the cost of reproducing a property or even determine its value by "discounting" the income stream produced by a rental property. In addition, because real estate values are relatively large, small errors in judgment are not critical. Many jurisdictions deliberately value all real estate at only a fraction of true fair market value—such as 50 or 75%—solely to reduce the frequency of arguments with irate taxpayers. As long as all properties are evaluated on the same fractional basis, no harm is done. Unfortunately, however, these same administrative expediencies are not equally pertinent to numerous items of personal property of small value. Therefore, as noted above, ad valorem taxes on many personal properties are rapidly disappearing even though most local governments are desperately looking for additional sources of tax revenues.

SELECTIVITY Many local governments continue to impose significant taxes on automobiles and boats which require registration. The valuation of automobiles is facilitated by a monthly publication prepared by the national automobile dealers' association. This publication reports the average price paid during the prior month for literally hundreds of different cars and trucks. Since owners must register their cars, and since those same cars are relatively easy to value, an ad valorem tax on car ownership is commonplace. One difficulty encountered by those governments that place an especially heavy tax on car ownership is the tendency of local residents to register their cars elsewhere. The only way to detect this kind of tax evasion is to impose periodic checks on major highways at unannounced times and in various locations. Anyone who has been delayed in such a check learns quickly why such extreme measures to enforce a relatively small tax become unpopular in a hurry. And taxes that are unpopular are seldom supported by officials who must seek reelection in a short time.

The only other form of personal property taxation that is still widely used is that imposed on business equipment and/or inventory. A large number of local governments continue to impose and collect an ad valorem tax on selected business assets. In most instances these taxes are relatively small and many businesses consider their payment to be a reasonable contribution to the cost of the services provided by the local government. Obviously business benefits greatly from public education, highways, and police and fire protection. As long as the personal property tax on business assets is deemed to be used for these services, and as long as those taxes remain relatively small, compliance is not a major issue. In a few cases, however, local governments have tried to increase those tax rates significantly in the past few years. When and where that has happened, major disputes have arisen and—in some cases—businesses have even relocated their assets to the detriment of the local government. The relocation of warehouse facilities for inventory assets is perhaps the most common form of tax avoidance in this regard.

Interpersonal inequity is an inevitable cost of selective property taxation. Those individuals who own the few properties that are made the basis for taxation bear a disproportionate share of the cost of local government.

Example 15: Helen owns a $30,000 diamond ring; Bill owns a $30,000 automobile; Barbara owns a $30,000 business inventory; Harry owns a $30,000 stock investment; and Sheila owns a $30,000 vacant lot as an investment. In all probability, Bill, Barbara, and

Sheila will pay some form of property tax while Helen and Harry will escape tax-free even though each individual owns $30,000 worth of property.

The apparent answer to the problem of interpersonal inequity common to property taxation is to convert that tax to a form of net wealth taxation. In other words, if everyone had to pay an annual tax on his or her net wealth at the end of each year, equity would be improved. The cost of greater equity, however, could be achieved only with a major increase in the cost of administering the tax system. Most people apparently are willing to pay the price of inequity to achieve administrative convenience. The only major exception to this conclusion, so far as property-related taxes are concerned, is the estate and gift tax.

THE FEDERAL ESTATE AND GIFT TAX

DONATIVE-TRANSFERS TAX The federal tax imposed on the transfer of property by gift or death.

DONOR A person who makes a gift.

DONEE A person who receives a gift.

Even though the federal estate and gift tax—more correctly known as the ***donative-transfers*** tax—is not a major source of revenue, we will examine its major provisions very briefly just to satisfy a natural curiosity that most people have about this unusual tax.[12] Before we review the rules applicable to the federal estate and gift tax, note that this tax is technically not a property tax. Rather, it is a tax on the right to *transfer* property, either by gift or through inheritance. (By contrast, state inheritance taxes are taxes on the right to *receive* property.) On the other hand, estate, gift, and inheritance taxes are all somewhat like property taxes, in that they are based on the *value* of any property transferred. Gift taxes are generally paid by the ***donor***, that is, by the person who makes the gift. (The lucky person who receives the gift—called the ***donee***—pays neither a gift tax nor an income tax on the value received.) The federal estate tax is paid by the administrator of the deceased taxpayer's estate from assets left by the decedent. Obviously, if the administrator pays an estate tax there is less of an estate left for the heirs. Nevertheless, the estate tax is *not* deemed to be paid by the heirs.

ADMINISTRATIVE CONSIDERATIONS All of the problems of property valuation described above for property taxes are equally applicable to the estate, gift, and inheritance taxes. Because these taxes are imposed relatively infrequently—in most cases, only once at the death of an individual—and because of rather generous exclusion provisions, most governments continue to impose an estate and gift tax to redistribute the assets of those few individuals who accumulate very large amounts of property. The only apparent justification for this tax is vertical equity: that is, the belief that those with large amounts of property should contribute relatively more to the government.

[12] In 1984 death and gift taxes are estimated to have provided approximately $8 billion in taxes, $6 billion for the federal government and $2 billion for all state governments.

The donative-transfer tax is made inapplicable to most gifts because of two provisions. First, anyone can give any number of people up to $10,000 worth of gifts every year and not be subject to the federal gift tax.[13] This generous annual exclusion is more than adequate to excuse most birthday, wedding, and holiday gifts from tax. Second, in addition to the annual $10,000 per donee exclusion, everyone is entitled to a lifetime donative-transfers tax credit. This credit may be claimed against either the tax payable on large gifts or the tax payable at death. The amount of this credit is scheduled to increase from $121,800 in 1985 to $192,800 in 1987 and thereafter.[14] A tax credit of $192,800 is equivalent to an additional exclusion of $600,000. This means, of course, that after 1986 there will be no federal estate or gift tax payable on any gifts or estates of $600,000 or less, even if property valued at that amount (or less) is passed to one person in one year. Finally, there is also an unlimited marital deduction which allows one to give his or her spouse any amount of property tax-free, either while living or at death. Because of the generosity of these exclusions and exemptions the federal estate and gift tax is expected to produce even less government revenue in the next few years than it has in the immediate past.

CALCULATING THE TAX If an individual makes one or more taxable gifts after 1976, the gift tax is computed by the following formula:

Gross gifts for the calendar year measured by the fair market value of the property on the date given

Less: (*a*) An exclusion of $10,000 per donee per year;
(*b*) An unlimited marital deduction (if the gift is to the donor's spouse); and
(*c*) Charitable gifts;

Equals: Taxable gifts.

The rates in Appendix E are used to determine the gross tax. Because of the progressive tax rates, however, taxable gifts during the current period must be added to all prior taxable gifts (made after 1976) to obtain the total base on which the tentative tax is computed. Taxes already paid on prior gifts are then subtracted from the tentative tax, and the remainder is the current tax liability. The unified donative-transfers tax credit can be applied against the gift tax until it has been exhausted. The credit is used to offset the first transfer taxes levied to avoid or reduce current pay-

[13] In addition to the $10,000 annual exclusion per donee, an individual can also exclude *any amounts paid directly* to (1) an educational institution, as tuition for a student enrolled there, or (2) a medical-care facility, for the unreimbursed medical expenses of a patient. Note, however, that these extra exclusions are lost if paid directly to the student or the patient, even if they are actually used by the recipient to pay tuition or medical expenses. (Sec. 2503(e).)

[14] The amount of the annual credit is as follows: 1985—$121,800; 1986—$155,800; 1987—$192,800.

ments to the government. The beginning point for determination of the unified transfer tax imposed at death is calculation of the decedent's taxable estate according to the following formula:[7]

Gross estate—The fair market value of all property, wherever located, in which the decedent had an interest at death

Less: (*a*) Funeral, administrative, and certain other expenses;
(*b*) Debts owed by the decedent;
(*c*) A marital deduction (equal to the fair market value of property passing to the decedent's surviving spouse); and
(*d*) Amounts bequeathed to charities.

Equals: Taxable estate.

If a decedent made no *taxable* gifts after 1976, the rates in Appendix E are then applied to this taxable estate to determine his or her gross estate tax liability. The gross tax may be reduced by credits allowed (*a*) for death taxes paid to states and (*b*) for a portion of all of the estate taxes paid on any property included in the decedent's gross estate if that same property had also been subject to the estate tax of a prior decedent within the last 10 years. Finally, the gross tax is reduced by the unified credit.

Upon the death of any donor who has made lifetime gifts (after 1976) the following calculation must be made to determine the correct estate tax:

Compute the value of the taxable estate as before	$XXX
Add aggregate value of all taxable gifts made during life	XXX
The sum equals the donative-transfers tax base at death	$XXX
Compute the gross tax on the above value using the tax rate schedule printed in Appendix E	$XXX
Subtract the aggregate gift tax paid on all gifts made during life	XXX
The remainder is the federal estate tax payable at death	$XXX

The resulting total tax is approximately the same as that which would have been levied were the decedent's entire wealth transferred at death.

Example 16: To illustrate how the federal donative-transfers tax is computed, assume that Sue Durham died in 1985 leaving a taxable estate of $2,500,000 to her only nephew, Bull. Also assume that before her death Sue made taxable gifts in 1979 totaling $500,000 in value. Finally, assume that Sue paid a gift tax of $117,800 in 1979 ($155,800 gross tax less a $38,000 maximum unified credit available in 1979). Given these assumed facts, the Estate of Sue Durham would pay a federal estate tax of $1,076,700, determined as follows:

Taxable Estate (at death)	$2,500,000
Plus Taxable Gifts (during life)	500,000
Equals Donative-Transfer Tax Base	$3,000,000
Gross Tax Liability (Appendix E)	$1,290,800
Less Gift Tax (already paid)	117,800
Gross Estate Tax	$1,173,000
Less Unified Credit	96,300
Net Tax Payable (at death)	$1,076,700

BACKGROUND

Federal tax policy relative to the wealth transfer taxes has been ambivalent in recent years. The 1976 changes that unified the estate and gift taxes indicated that Congress meant to make the taxes more equitable and close existing loopholes. In 1981 Congress considered seriously the complete repeal of all transfer taxes. While not going that far, the changes made in the Economic Recovery Tax Act of 1981—for example, the reduced rates, the increased unified credit, and the unlimited marital deductions—mean that only a very few wealthy citizens need worry about them. Here, as elsewhere in the tax law, careful planning can reduce the impact of the tax for those fortunate enough to have a problem. However, the details of those plans are best left for a more advanced course in taxation.

IMPORTANT FACTS ABOUT TAX RATES

After a government has decided what items or events it will use as a tax base, it must decide what tax rate(s) it will apply to each tax base. Any one of three fundamentally different tax rate structures may be utilized, namely: proportional, progressive, or regressive. In the next few pages of this chapter we will define each of these terms. Then we will distinguish between marginal, average, and effective tax rates.

DEFINITION OF TERMS

In the simplest way, a tax can be defined as the product of the tax base times the tax rate. In equation form, then,

$$T = B \times R$$

where T stands for tax, B for tax base, and R for tax rate. By elementary algebraic manipulation, this equation can, of course, be rearranged to read:

$$R = \frac{T}{B}$$

PROPORTIONAL TAX RATE A "flat" tax rate. In other words, a single tax rate that is applied to any and all amounts of a tax base.

PROGRESSIVE TAX RATE A tax rate schedule that calls for a continuously higher tax rate with periodic increases in the tax base.

REGRESSIVE TAX RATE A tax rate schedule that calls for a continuously lower tax rate with periodic increases in the tax base.

PROCEDURAL DEFINITIONS Proportional, progressive, and regressive tax rates can be defined readily in terms of the preceding equation. If the ratio T/B remains constant for all possible values of B, then the tax rate R is ***proportional***. If the ratio T/B increases as B increases and decreases as B decreases, then the tax rate R is ***progressive***. Finally, if the ratio T/B increases as B decreases and decreases as B increases, then the tax rate R is ***regressive***.

In other words, when defined in this manner, a tax is proportional if one flat rate is equally applicable to every measure of the tax base. The largest number of our common taxes are in this category. For example, sales, real property, personal property, and excise taxes are generally imposed with a proportional tax rate. If, on the other hand, a higher tax rate is applied to increasingly larger values of the tax base, then the tax is progressive. Typically, income, estate, and gift taxes are imposed with a progressive tax rate structure.

LIMITATIONS OF THESE DEFINITIONS The preceding definitions are based on the premise that the appropriate comparison is between the tax paid and the tax base itself. Thus, for sales taxation, only the amount involved in a *taxable sale* is deemed to be included in the denominator of the ratio T/B; for income taxation, only taxable income is included. As the terms proportional, progressive, and regressive have been used in the popular press and in political propaganda, however, they are not defined in this manner. Rather, they are defined, albeit loosely, by the following ratio:

$$\frac{\text{Aggregate tax liability over some time period}}{\text{Some measure of ability to pay, frequently personal income}}$$

If the ratio above is constant, even roughly so, for most values of personal income, common usage of the terms would classify the tax as a proportional tax. If the ratio tends to decrease with increasing values of personal income, then the tax is alleged to be regressive. Although this alternative definition lacks the precision of the earlier one, it may be the more meaningful of the two. Without doubt, it is the one definition implicit in virtually all nonacademic discussions of tax matters. Unfortunately, it is a very crude measure for several reasons.

INCIDENCE PROBLEMS. The first major problem encountered in any precise application of the popular definition of tax rate structures is our inability to determine who *finally* pays most taxes. The assumption typically postulated by the general public is that the tax is assignable to (borne by) the person who pays it. For example, the retail sales tax is assumed to be borne by the purchaser of the taxed goods or service; the personal income tax is assumed to be borne by the immediate taxpayer.

Several questions can be raised about the validity of this common assumption. Suppose, for example, that a man decides to purchase a new automobile. Because of the competitive nature of the market, he is able to arrange a deal whereby the seller of the car agrees to pay the sales tax via a reduction in the price of the car. Thus the buyer, instead of paying $10,000 plus sales tax, effectively pays $9,500 plus a $500 sales tax. If we could establish that the market price of the car in question actually was $10,000, exclusive of the tax (a very difficult question to establish in fact), the *initial* effect of the transaction would be to shift the retail sales tax from the car buyer to the car seller, even though the tax was legally and technically imposed on the purchaser. Even then we cannot safely conclude that the sales tax has simply been shifted from the purchaser to the seller of the car. To reach an accurate conclusion, we would have to determine if it was possible for the car dealer to shift the tax to: labor, via substandard wages; suppliers of capital, via reduced interest payments; other less-informed purchasers, via higher prices; or some other party, in some other manner. Obviously an accurate answer to these questions remains largely out of reach because of our necessarily limited knowledge of the real world. The complexities of measuring all the pertinent variables make such measurements practically impossible.

Given the state of relative ignorance in which we live, it is not surprising that tax experts are in less than complete accord in their assumptions about ***tax incidence***. And, unfortunately, far too many persons make decisions about taxation based on totally erroneous premises about the incidence of many, if not most, taxes. If, then, we accept the "popular" definition of proportional, progressive, and regressive as applied to taxation, we must understand that our conclusions can be no more valid than our data are accurate. One of the most complicated and unresolved issues in all of taxation is the determination of the final incidence of any tax. Observe that it is necessary to determine who finally must "bear" each tax before we can determine accurately the denominator of the ratio:

TAX INCIDENCE The ultimate occurrence of any tax liability; i.e., who *really* pays a tax.

$$\frac{\text{Aggregate tax liability over some time period}}{\text{Some measure of ability to pay, frequently personal income}}$$

ABILITY TO PAY. The second major problem encountered in any precise application of this popular definition of tax-rate structures lies in our failure to find a truly adequate measure of ability to pay taxes. Progressive-regressive notions have achieved their greatest application in statements related to welfare economics. For example, it is frequently argued that the value-added tax, and the retail sales and (most) excise taxes are regressive because they require a greater relative contribution by the poor than by the rich. They do so, it is explained, because poorer persons are forced to spend a greater percentage of their income for consumer items (which typically are subject to VAT, sales, and/or excise taxes) than persons with larger incomes.

If the assumptions about spending patterns are valid, then the conclusion of regressivity is also valid. Many persons unwittingly go one step further, however, and presume that regressivity necessarily fails to conform to generally accepted notions of ability to pay. This last conclusion

requires a further assumption—that personal income is a meaningful measure of the ability to pay taxes. Without a doubt, annual income is one of the major ingredients of a person's ability to do anything of a financial nature, including the payment of taxes. However, it is certainly not the only ingredient. The amount of a person's accumulated wealth and his or her prospect of earning equal or greater sums in the future are two other items of major significance. Finally, the taxpayer's age, marital status, health, and number of dependents are usually of real importance.

In short, before it is possible to determine whether a tax *is* regressive relative to the taxpayer's ability to pay, we must find some comprehensive measure of tax-paying ability. Although personal income is frequently used in this manner, it is, as we have said, a less than comprehensive measure.

Several of the considerations deemed pertinent to the ability-to-pay concept have been incorporated into our Internal Revenue Code in its definition of taxable income, and will be examined in greater detail in later chapters. Unfortunately, these modifications add one final complication to the definition of the terms proportional, progressive, and regressive as applied to taxation.

This complication can be readily understood in an illustration common to much of the literature that has grown up around the progressive tax controversy. Many writers take care to point out that inclusion of a provision for a personal exemption makes a progressive tax of an otherwise proportional income tax. The arithmetic of their conclusion is simple. Suppose, for example, that country A imposes a (flat) tax of 10% on all income in excess of $500 per year earned by each of its citizens. The progressive nature of this otherwise proportional tax is shown in Table 1-6. In other words, this tax is a proportional (constant 10%) tax on taxable income (defined as all income over $500) but a progressive (increasing percentage) tax on total income.

Whether this tax is judged to be proportional or progressive depends on which income measure is used as the denominator of the ratio to

TABLE 1-6
Example of the Progressive Effect of a Personal Exemption Deduction

	TAXPAYER 1	TAXPAYER 2	TAXPAYER 3
Income earned	$600	$1,000	$1,500
Less $500 exemption	500	500	500
Taxable income (tax base)	$100	$ 500	$1,000
Times tax rate	.10	.10	.10
Equals tax liability	$ 10	$ 50	$ 100
Effective tax rate (tax/income)	10/500 = .02%	50/1,000 = 5%	100/1,500 = 6⅔%

determine the effective tax rate. The only important point of the illustration is very simple: The meanings of the terms proportional, progressive, and regressive, as applied to tax-rate structures, are often elusive, and persons who use the terms to advocate a particular position frequently fail to articulate the assumptions implicit in their analysis. This failure, in turn, often results in misapplication, misstatement, and general misunderstanding.

In conclusion, the student should be aware that in most discussions about progressive and regressive taxation, the writer often assumes both (*a*) that the tax is not shifted—that is, the tax is presumed to be borne by the party it is legally imposed on—and (*b*) that the appropriate measure for determining progressivity (or regressivity) is some vaguely defined but apparently "generally accepted" notion of personal income. From this frame of reference, it is commonly believed that the U.S. personal income tax and the estate and gift tax are progressive, whereas most other taxes (those typically imposed at a uniform rate) are regressive.

MARGINAL, AVERAGE, AND EFFECTIVE RATES

Other distinctions in tax rate structures are the differences among marginal, average, and effective tax rates. First we shall distinguish between marginal and average rates; next we shall consider the differences between the nominal average and the real or effective average rate.

MARGINAL-AVERAGE DISTINCTIONS The ***marginal tax rate*** is the rate that would be applicable to the next unit of any tax base. For any tax that is proportional, in a technical sense of that term, the marginal tax rate is (obviously) the basic tax rate. For any tax that is either progressive or regressive, in a technical sense, the marginal tax rate can be determined only if one knows both (*a*) the rate structure and (*b*) the aggregate measure of the tax base prior to considering any incremental amount. The ***average tax rate*** is simply an arithmetic expression of an aggregate tax liability divided by the given amount of a tax base.

MARGINAL TAX RATE The tax rate that will be applicable to any incremental unit of a tax base; e.g., the tax rate applicable to the next dollar of taxable income.

AVERAGE TAX RATE A tax rate determined by dividing the total tax paid by the total tax base for a given time period.

To demonstrate the difference between the marginal and average tax rates, let us consider the present U.S. income tax on single individuals. The current tax-rate structure applicable to individual taxpayers is reprinted in Appendix A. A single (unmarried) individual who reports a $14,000 taxable income in 1985 will have a marginal tax rate of 20%; this means that an increase in taxable income of $100 would result in the taxpayer's paying $20 of that additional $100 to the government in personal income tax. A $100 increase in the taxable income of a single taxpayer reporting $86,000 taxable income in 1985 would result in the taxpayer's paying $50 of that additional $100 in personal income tax because he or she is in the 50% marginal tax bracket. The average tax rate of the first individual would be approximately 12% (that is, $1,760 tax liability divided by $14,000 taxable income), whereas the average tax rate of the second individual would be approximately 35% ($30,444 divided by $86,000). Obviously, the marginal tax rate is always greater than the average tax rate for any progressive tax after the first step in that progression.

One common misunderstanding about the federal taxation of personal incomes can be clarified by this difference between marginal and average tax rates. Otherwise knowledgeable people frequently tell of someone who experienced a cut in income because of a pay raise that "threw him into the next tax bracket." The marginal tax rates always apply only to the *additional* dollars of income in each new and higher bracket, not to the aggregate income earned. Therefore, as long as the marginal tax rates do not exceed 100%, it is impossible to reap a cut in income from a pay raise. At present, the highest federal income tax rate applicable to income earned by individuals is 50%. Therefore, even if a taxpayer is in the highest possible tax bracket, a $1 pay increase will always yield no less than $.50 after taxes.

It is important for the student, early in the study of taxation, to grasp the significance of the marginal tax rate, because it is the marginal rate that determines how intelligent taxpayers act in many circumstances. In an important sense, the marginal tax rate is to business what the law of gravity is to physics—tax bases tend to seek their lowest level just as water does! In other words, taxpayers tend to arrange their financial affairs so that any tax base will be subject to tax at the lowest possible marginal tax rate. It is this fundamental rule that causes many individuals to (*a*) create short-term trusts for the benefit of their children or parents (and thereby substitute the lower marginal income tax rate of their children or their parents for their own marginal rate), (*b*) to incorporate their sole proprietorships and partnerships (and thereby substitute the lower marginal income tax rate of the corporation for the higher marginal income tax rate of the proprietor and/or partner), and (*c*) to convert what would otherwise be ordinary income into capital gains (and thereby substitute the lower marginal income tax rate applicable to capital gains for the higher marginal income tax rate that would otherwise apply to their ordinary taxable income). Although the multitude of important details pertinent to each of the managerial actions suggested in the preceding sentence is far beyond the comprehension of the student at this juncture, it is not too early to grasp the significance of the marginal tax rate and its bearing on numerous business decisions. Relative to the income tax, financial affairs should nearly always be arranged to report incremental units of taxable income at such times and/or in such ways as to allow the application of the lowest possible marginal tax rates, other things being equal, whereas incremental units of deductions and losses should be reported at such times and/or in such ways as to allow the application of the highest possible marginal tax rates, other things being equal.

NOMINAL-AVERAGE AND REAL-AVERAGE DISTINCTIONS The preceding discussion of average tax rates is based on the premise that the pertinent comparison is that existing between the aggregate tax liability and the tax base determined in a technical way, that is, using a technical rather than a popular definition of the tax base. As explained earlier in this chapter, the popular descriptions of various tax rates are often significantly different from the technical definitions. In the same manner, average tax rates are frequently computed using a popular surrogate for a more technical tax base. The average rate determined in a technical sense might better be labeled the *nominal*-average rate.

For certain purposes, such as making a social value judgment about our existing tax provisions, an average tax rate might be determined better by dividing the aggregate tax liability by an adjusted tax base. The appropriateness of the adjustments depends on the purpose of the calculation. Thus, for example, if one wanted to know an individual's income tax based on a real or economic measure of income, rather than on a technical tax base called taxable income, it would be appropriate to divide the individual's aggregate income tax liability by his or her economic or real income.

To illustrate the notion of a ***real-average tax rate***—(some tax scholars prefer to call this an effective-average or an actual-average tax rate)—consider the calculation pertinent to a single individual who receives each year a $55,000 salary and $100,000 interest in tax-exempt state bonds. Ignoring many additional details, and simply assuming that this individual's salary after all deductions is a $50,000 taxable income on which a $15,000 tax must be paid, we could readily determine that the nominal average tax rate is 30% (that is, $15,000 aggregate tax liability divided by $50,000 taxable income). On the other hand, this same individual's real or effective-average tax rate would be closer to 10% (that is, $15,000 aggregate tax liability divided by $155,000 "real" or "economic" income). As a practical matter, there are many differences between income as commonly perceived by the average person and taxable income as defined in the Internal Revenue Code. We shall examine most of the important differences in a technical way in the remainder of this book.

REAL-AVERAGE TAX RATE
A tax rate determined by dividing the total tax paid by an adjusted tax base for a given period. The adjustments made to the tax base in this calculation are those deemed to make a technically defined tax base more closely resemble its everyday-world counterpart. Often called effective-average tax rate.

Total tax paid / adjusted tax base

PROGRESSIVE INCOME TAXATION AND INFLATION

Before leaving the topic of tax rates, we should examine briefly the impact of inflation on a progressive income tax with a fixed rate structure. The general impact of a fixed rate structure during a period of substantial inflation is, of course, to force taxpayers into higher and higher tax brackets and thus to cause them to transfer to the government a larger and larger portion of their real income. To illustrate this important conclusion, consider the plight of a single taxpayer who reports a $15,000 taxable income in the base year and who receives salary increases exactly equal to the rate of inflation as reflected in the Consumer Price Index. If we assume that the rate schedule applicable to the base year imposes a tax of 10% on a $15,000 taxable income, this person would pay a tax of $1,500 in the base year. If the rate of inflation would cause the taxpayer's monetary salary to double every 10 years, and if the same tax rate structure were still applicable, that taxpayer might pay $6,000 in income taxes just 10 years later. Obviously, this amounts to 20% of his or her income, or a 10% reduction in the real income the taxpayer commands. If salary increases and inflation were to continue at that same pace for another 10 years, the same taxpayer then pays 30% of his or her income in tax. You will observe that even with an annual rate of inflation of substantially less than 10%, a taxpayer might lose control over a good part of his or her real income in just 20 years, solely because of a progressive tax rate structure. The impact is felt often largely because most of the progression in our income tax rates occurs generally at the lower end of the rate scale. In other words, the rate of progression is usually greater on the first $50,000 in taxable income than it is on the next $50,000, and on further increases.

Inflation has additional distorting effects when deductions are either fixed in amount or are subject to maximum limitations that are not increased to compensate for price-level changes. Thus, for example, a personal exemption deduction of any fixed amount that is appropriate at a time when the Consumer Price Index is at 100 would, in all probability, be inadequate when the price index had increased to 150 or 200. For the same reason, a fixed zero-bracket amount would no longer be reasonable if there were a substantial change in the general price level.

The conceptual problems created by a progressive income tax during a period of rapid inflation (or deflation) can readily be corrected in one of two ways. First, it would be possible to require each taxpayer to adjust his or her monetary measure of taxable income to a price-deflated (or price-inflated) equivalent before applying the fixed tax rate at the end of each taxable year. Although the arithmetic involved in such a calculation would not be unduly complicated, it would be beyond the comprehension of many taxpayers and it would complicate taxpayer compliance with what is already deemed to be an intolerably complex tax. Second, it would be possible for the government to adjust the rate schedules, as well as all fixed deductions or deduction limits, automatically and annually in order to accommodate any change in the price level experienced during the prior year. Although this would still create complications for fiscal-year taxpayers, it would provide a relatively straightforward adjustment mechanism for the vast majority of taxpayers.

The invidious effect of inflation on corporate (really, business) income taxes is largely reflected through understated deductions based on historical cost measures, not through the tax rate structure. For example, the determination of a depreciation deduction based on historical costs generally has a greater impact on the determination of a corporation's taxable income than does the fixed rate schedule because the corporate income tax rate schedule has never been highly progressive. Historically, corporations have paid a proportional tax on all corporate taxable income in excess of a relatively low but fixed amount. Consequently, the corrective mechanism appropriate in the case of the corporate income tax should focus on a better measure of historical costs consumed during the year, not on an automatic adjustment of the tax rate.

Although the problems that inflation creates for income taxation were well understood for many years, nothing was done about them prior to the Economic Recovery Tax Act of 1981 (ERTA). In that law both the individual taxpayer's problem and the corporate (business) taxpayer's problem were addressed, but in very different ways. The solution for the individual's problem is found in a provision of the new law which requires that (a) the individual tax rate schedules, (b) the amount of the personal exemption deduction, and (c) the amount of the zero-bracket amount are to be adjusted annually, beginning in 1985, for changes in the consumer price index. This change is an important step forward in U.S. income taxation. Unfortunately there is some reason to believe that the provision could be deferred or even repealed by Congress before 1985. Politicians of both parties have opposed the automatic indexation of taxes for years. They generally do so because "bracket creep" (the name given to this phenomenon by the news media) is a very subtle way of increasing taxes: It allows the government to collect a larger and larger share of the nation's real income without requiring Congress to pass a law calling for increased taxes. In fact, it provides so much additional government revenue that it actually allows Congress frequent opportunity to pass tax reduction bills—always a favorite with voters prior to an election. Because of our large federal deficits, some politicians want to defer or repeal the new rule before it can go into effect.

The 1981 solution to inflation for the business taxpayer came in the form of ACRS, an accelerated cost recovery system. This provision, made retroactive to January 1, 1981, gave business taxpayers the right to deduct the cost of their fixed assets in very short time periods. For example, buildings which will last for 50 years or longer can now be written off over 18 years. Although quick write-offs are a poor substitute for price-adjusted, historical-cost, capital-consumption measures, most business taxpayers are happy to take a bird in hand rather than hope for a theoretically better bird in the bush. The most serious consequence of this patchwork solution to a fundamental problem is the major distortion it provides for income measurements. What now passes for "taxable income" has little or no resemblance to any realistic measure of real income. Indeed, the days of any true *income* tax may have passed already. What remains is a tax on wages and salaries, not a tax on income. However, this perception has not yet filtered down to the average person on the street. If the authors' interpretation of the current situation is at all correct, the average taxpayer and voter is clearly unhappy with the status quo but uncertain about what is really wrong or how to correct it.

THE CURRENT TAX DILEMMA

The presidential election of 1980 unleashed a fair amount of popular sentiment for major reductions in income taxation. Unfortunately, no comparable consensus was reached concerning what other taxes could be increased or what government expenditures (if any) could be reduced. Because of this disparity between tax policy and expenditure policy, the U.S. federal government in 1985 will experience the largest federal deficit ever. Furthermore, the 1984 elections appear to endorse the idea that taxes should not be increased unless absolutely necessary. This dilemma between tax policy and expenditure policy raises several interesting questions. Three of those questions are: Are we really overtaxed? Should income taxes be reduced? And, what other taxes might be increased?

ARE WE OVERTAXED?

Although there can never be a final authoritative answer to this important question, most evidence suggests that we in the United States of America are *not* subject to unduly heavy taxes, considering all taxes at the federal, state, and local levels of government. Evidence supporting this conclusion is derived from two primary sources: one, the majority response to periodic public opinion surveys conducted by the Opinion Research Corporation for the Advisory Commission on Intergovernmental Relations (or ACIR); the other, comparative tax revenue data for the USA and other countries.

In 1975, 1976, 1977, 1979, 1980, and 1982 the ACIR asked a representative sample of U.S. citizens the following question: "Considering all government services on the one hand and taxes on the other, which of the following statements comes closest to your view?

- Keep taxes and services about where they are;
- Decrease services and taxes;
- Increase services and raise taxes; or
- No opinion."

Approximately 42% of the respondents in the most recent survey elected the first alternative; another 8% chose the third response. In summary, therefore, just 50% of our population would either hold the status quo or increase taxes and services. Only 36% favored a reduction in taxes and government services. (Another 14% had no opinion.)[15]

Another measure of the reasonableness of the overall tax burden is the ratio of total tax revenues (for all levels of government) to the gross domestic product of a country. Using this measuring stick, the U.S. ranks 13th in the nations of the world. As is evident in column 1 of Table 1-7, we divert approximately 30% of everything we produce in a year from the private to the public sector, via taxation. This percentage is below that of every country except Japan and the tax revenue data for Japan is not wholly comparable with that for the rest of the world because the peace treaty signed at the end of World War II forbids Japan from having a true national defense force. Consequently, Japan has significantly less need for government revenues than some other countries, such as the United States.

WHY THE INTEREST IN INCOME TAX REDUCTION?

If the majority of our citizens are honestly satisfied with the present level of government expenditures, why did President Reagan's call for a reduction in income taxes in 1980, and for no further tax increases in 1984, receive such a warm reception? The data contained in column 2 of Table 1-7 may give us at least part of the answer. In reliance on income taxes, the U.S. is third behind Denmark and second to Finland. We derive nearly

[15]Annual reports of findings are published by the ACIR, Washington, D.C., 20575.

TABLE 1-7
Comparative Tax Ratios for Selected Countries in 1982

COUNTRY	TOTAL TAX REVENUES / GROSS DOMESTIC PRODUCT	INCOME TAXES / ALL TAXES	TAXES ON GOODS/SERVICES / ALL TAXES
Sweden	50%	44%	24%
Norway	48	42	35
Belgium	47	42	26
Netherlands	45	31	24
Denmark	44	56	37
France	44	18	30
Austria	41	27	31
Italy	40	32	16
United Kingdom	40	38	29
Finland	37	49	40
Germany	37	34	27
Canada	35	44	35
United States	30	45	17
Japan	27	45	15

SOURCE: Adapted from *Revenue Statistics of OECD Member Countries. 1965–83—A Standardized Classification*, Tables 1 and 7, pp. 85 and 87.

half of our total tax revenues from the income tax alone. By comparison, Germany collects only 34% of her revenues from the income tax; the United Kingdom, 38%; and France, only 18%. Our heavy dependence on income taxes could very well explain the recent interest in income tax relief. Incidentally, this conclusion is also supported by responses to the ACIR questions concerning potential sources for additional revenues. At least when couched in terms of state revenue needs, the largest block of respondents consistently favors an increase in sales taxes over additional income taxes, if taxes simply must be increased.

WHAT TAXES MIGHT BE INCREASED?

Finally, if government expenditures are not going to be reduced, and if income tax increases are highly unpopular, where will we get the revenues needed to reduce the very large deficits presently anticipated? The comparative data in column 3 of Table 1-7 support the conclusion that we generally *should* look to additional taxes on goods and services for our revenue needs in the immediate future. In this instance the United States is well below all other economically advanced nations in its dependence on such taxes as the sales, excise, and value-added taxes. We derive only 17% of our revenues from those sources. Nearly all other countries depend on those taxes for at least another 10% or more of their revenues.

In summary, although we might like to believe that we are a nation of heavily taxed individuals, worldwide comparative figures do not support that conclusion. On the other hand there is evidence that we do depend too heavily on income taxation and too lightly on taxes based on goods and services. A value-added tax of just 5% would go a long way in reducing our currently large federal deficit with minimal taxpayer resistance. Unfortunately most politicians do not think the present situation is that dangerous; but some of your authors do.

KEY POINTS TO REMEMBER

1. The federal level of government collects nearly $570 billion in tax revenues each year. This accounts for approximately ⅔ of all tax collections in the U.S.
2. The federal government relies most heavily on the income tax; state governments, on sales and excise taxes; and local governments, on the property tax.
3. The most rapidly growing tax in recent years is the Social Security tax. It is also the largest single tax paid by a majority of the U.S. citizens.
4. Unlike the state and local levels of government, our federal government can (and does) spend significantly more than it receives in tax revenues in most years because it alone controls the monetary system.
5. Many of the federal income tax law provisions that were enacted during the past 25 years were approved because of their intended economic and/or social objective, with minimal regard for their immediate revenue impact.
6. The largest single difficulty in income taxation is finding a satisfactory definition of income. Most of the difficult definitional problems involve the correct timing and measurement of deductions, not items of gross income.
7. For purposes of income taxation there are only three taxable entities: individuals, corporations, and fiduciaries (i.e., estates and trusts).
8. A majority of all provisions in the U.S. federal income tax code apply equally to individuals and corporations. Accordingly, there is neither a separate individual income tax nor a corporate income tax. Different tax rate schedules for different classes of taxpayers, however, do exist.
9. The Social Security tax consists of (*a*) a tax on employees (paid in part by the employee and in part by the employer) and (*b*) a tax on self-employed persons. Although the Social Security tax rates differ for each class of persons, the maximum annual tax base is the same for both.
10. Sales and excise taxes provide over $84 billion in revenue for state governments each year. This represents over 50% of all tax revenues collected by state governments.
11. Property taxes provide $86 billion in revenue for local governments each year. This represents over 75% of all tax revenues collected by local governments.
12. Compared to other countries in the world, the citizens of the U.S. are not overtaxed. We do, however, pay more than most others in income taxes and less than others in taxes on goods and services.

13. In a technical sense, the U.S. income, estate, and gift taxes are imposed with a progressive tax rate schedule; all of our other taxes with a proportional tax rate schedule.

SELF-STUDY QUESTIONS

1. Mr. and Mrs. John Hance gave jointly a $100,000 outright gift in 1985 to an unrelated friend, Fred Green, who needed the money to pay medical expenses. In filing their gift tax returns for 1985, Mr. and Mrs. Hance were entitled to exclusions aggregating

   a) $0
   b) $6,000
   c) $10,000
   d) $20,000

   (AICPA adapted)

2. Which one of the following taxes provides the greatest amount of tax revenue for the U.S. (federal) government?

   a) corporate income tax
   b) donative transfers tax
   c) individual income tax
   d) social security tax

3. Which one of the following federal taxes has been growing most rapidly (in terms of the tax revenues it provides) during the past 10 years?

   a) corporate income tax
   b) donative transfers tax
   c) individual income tax
   d) social security tax

4. Which one of the following taxes has declined most in relative importance, as a source of federal tax revenues, during the past 20 years?

   a) corporate income tax
   b) donative transfers tax
   c) individual income tax
   d) social security tax

5. Approximately how many dollars in taxes were collected, in the aggregate, by our federal, state, and local government units in 1983?

   a) $200,000,000,000
   b) $500,000,000,000
   c) $800,000,000,000
   d) $1,100,000,000,000

6. Approximately what percentage of the United States gross domestic product was diverted to governmental units via taxes in 1982?
   a) 20%
   b) 30%
   c) 40%
   d) 50%
7. Which one of the following entities is *not* a taxable entity for federal income tax purposes?
   a) a corporation
   b) a fiduciary (i.e., an estate or trust)
   c) an individual person
   d) a partnership
8. In a *technical* sense, the state and local retail sales tax rates are generally:
   a) progressive
   b) proportional
   c) regressive
   d) schedular
9. The value-added tax is, in a general sense, a special form of the
   a) excise tax
   b) gift tax
   c) income tax
   d) sales tax
10. After January 1, 1985, which one of the following items will *not* be adjusted each year to reflect changes in the general price level?
   a) depreciation deductions
   b) personal exemption deduction
   c) tax rate schedules
   d) zero bracket amount

Solutions to the self-study questions for each chapter are located after the Appendixes at the back of the book.

QUESTIONS

1. Which of the following payments would you classify as a tax? How would you classify the other payments?
   a) payment for automobile registration (that is, license plates)
   b) payment for a hunting or fishing license
   c) payment for a "safety sticker" on an automobile
   d) payment for parking on a "metered" street

e) payment for federal stamps required on transfer of a real estate deed

f) payment for riding a city-owned and -operated bus

g) payment for a bottle of liquor purchased in a state owned store

2. In what significant way are the "fiscal resources" of a national government different from those of a state or local government?

3. List the objectives, other than raising revenue, for which taxes may be levied.

4. Assume that a city requires that every dog be licensed and that the fee for this annual service is $5. Assume further that the money collected in this way is put into a special fund used to pay the cost of the city dog patrol operation. Is this $5 fee more accurately classified as a "price" or a "tax"? Explain your answer.

5. "The purposes of federal taxes may be significantly different from the purposes of state or local taxes." Discuss.

6. Must taxes involve the transfer of money? Under what circumstances might you expect a government to impose a nonpecuniary tax?

7. Section 164(a) of our Internal Revenue Code (the basic statutory authority for the U.S. federal income tax) authorizes a taxpayer to deduct certain taxes in the determination of taxable income. That subsection reads, in part, as follows:

> Except as otherwise provided in this section, the following taxes shall be allowed as a deduction for the taxable year within which paid or accrued:
> (1) State and local, and foreign, real property taxes.
> (2) State and local personal property taxes.

Based on the authority of Sec. 164(a)(2), taxpayers in some states can deduct the cost of their automobile license plates, whereas taxpayers in other states cannot claim that same deduction. How might you explain the apparent inequity?

8. What good reasons might a free-world government have for imposing a tax of $5 on a pack of cigarettes? If that were done, would it be correct to refer to the $5 charge to the customer as a "tax"? Explain briefly.

9. The federal estate tax allows a tax credit for a limited amount of inheritance tax paid to a state government. Most states impose an inheritance tax equal to the maximum credit allowed against the federal tax, but only a few states are willing to impose additional state inheritance or estate taxes. Why should this be true?

10. In the recent past, personal property taxes—that is, taxes on the value of bank accounts, stocks, bonds, furniture, television sets, refrigerators, and similar personal assets—have been disappearing from

the list of tax bases used by state and local governments. Why are these particular taxes disappearing despite the fact that almost every state and local government is currently looking for new sources of revenue?

11. Forty-six states now impose an income tax. What practical problem does this present for businesses engaged in interstate commerce? What comparable problem exists with the federal government?

12. In revenue yield, which tax base is generally most important at the federal level of government? At the state level? At the local level?

13. Which tax base is growing most rapidly both in absolute dollars collected and in relative significance at the federal level of government? Is this trend likely to continue? Why or why not?

14. If it is true that the income tax was unconstitutional prior to the ratification of the Sixteenth Amendment in 1913, how is it possible that the United States actually imposed and collected an income tax for approximately 10 years in the 1870s and 1880s?

15. What has been done to reduce the effect of inflation on the income tax paid by individual taxpayers in the U.S.?

PROBLEMS

1. Lin Yeh purchased a 20-year City of Los Angeles bond for its $1,000 face value in 1980; this year she sold that same bond for $1,200. Just before she sold this bond, she received a $120 interest check from it. What amount of gross income (if any) must Lin report on her federal income tax return because she first owned and later sold this LA City bond?

2. Sheila Plodzi owns only the four properties described below:

PROPERTY	CURRENT FAIR MARKET VALUE	DEBT OWED ON PROPERTY	SHEILA'S "NET EQUITY" IN PROPERTY
Land	$100,000	$60,000	$ 40,000
Car	20,000	12,000	8,000
Diamond	10,000	-0-	10,000
CD in Bank	70,000	-0-	70,000
Total	$200,000	$72,000	$128,000

a) Which of the four properties (if any) are most likely to be subject to a state and/or local property tax?

b) If Sheila lived in a state that taxed all four of these specific properties using a "flat" 10% tax, how much would she probably owe in property taxes?

c) If Sheila lived in a state that imposed a 10% death (or "inheritance") tax on all properties transferred at death, how much would her estate probably owe in death taxes?

d) What one major difference between most property taxes and most estate (or inheritance) taxes is illustrated in this problem?

3. Two individual taxpayers, A and B, this year earned incomes and paid income taxes in the amounts indicated below:

TAXPAYER	"REAL" OR "ECONOMIC" INCOME	TAXABLE INCOME	TAX PAID
A	$300,000	$100,000	$20,000
B	100,000	100,000	20,000

a) What is A's nominal-average tax rate? Real-average tax rate?

b) What is B's nominal-average tax rate? Real-average tax rate?

c) Does "horizontal equity" exist between taxpayers A and B? Explain briefly.

4. Joe Nation earns *taxable* income from the three different sources indicated below:

SOURCE OF INCOME	AMOUNT OF TAXABLE INCOME
Salary	$ 50,000
Interest and dividends	40,000
Farming	10,000
Total	$100,000

a) If Joe lives in a country that imposes a unitary income tax with the following tax rate schedule, what amount of income tax will he owe?

Tax Rate Schedule:

1st $20,000 — 20%
2nd $20,000 — 30%
Above $40,000 — 40%

b) If Joe lives in a country that imposes a schedular income tax, with the following three rate schedules, what amount of income tax will he owe?

Schedule 1: Income from Wages or Salaries

1st $20,000 — 20%
2nd $20,000 — 30%
Above $40,000 — 40%

Schedule 2: Income from Non-Farm Investments

A "flat" 25%

Schedule 3: Income from Farming

1st \$10,000 — 10%
2nd \$10,000 — 15%
Above \$20,000 — 40%

5. Bill Country earns taxable income in two different countries as indicated below:

SOURCE OF INCOME	AMOUNT OF TAXABLE INCOME
Country A	\$100,000
Country B	\$ 50,000
Total	\$150,000

Assume that Bill is a citizen and resident of Country A which imposes an income tax with the following tax rate schedule:

1st \$20,000 — 20%
2nd \$20,000 — 30%
Above \$40,000 — 40%

a) If Country A's income tax is a global tax, what gross amount of income tax will Bill owe to A at the end of the year?

b) If Country A's income tax is a territorial income tax, what gross amount of income tax will Bill owe to A at the end of the year?

6. Prepare three graphs representing tax *payments* under proportional, progressive, and regressive tax systems. Record the amount of taxes paid on the vertical scale and the tax base on the horizontal scale.

7. Prepare three graphs representing tax *rates* under proportional, progressive, and regressive tax systems. Record the tax rates on the vertical scale and the tax base on the horizontal scale.

8. *a*) Taxpayer Kane earned a total income of \$10,000 in 19X1. Only \$6,000 of his income, however, was included in the tax base for the income tax. Kane paid a tax of \$1,200 during 19X1. What nominal average tax rate is paid by Kane? What is the real or effective average rate paid by Kane?

b) In 19X2, Kane had taxable income (tax base) of \$8,000. That year he paid a tax of \$1,700. Assuming that the tax rate structure was not changed by the government unit imposing the tax, what was the marginal rate of tax paid by Kane on the additional income of \$2,000 in 19X2? What was the nominal average rate paid by Kane in 19X2?

9. In a technical sense, is the present FICA (Social Security) tax progressive, proportional, or regressive in relation to income? Explain with a simple diagram.

10. Examine the 1985 tax rate schedules (see Appendix A) and explain how the amount entered in the "basic amount" column is computed. For example, how is the $1,646.60 figure determined for the taxpayer who is single and earns more than $13,430 but less than $15,610?

11. Assume that Tom earns an annual income of $10,000 per year; Dick earns $100,000; and Harriet earns $500,000. Also assume that Tom pays taxes of $1,000.

    a) How much tax do you think Dick and Harriet should pay in a year?

    b) Compare your answer with those suggested by other members of your class.

    c) Does this problem deal with horizontal or vertical tax equity?

12. Assume that your state legislature were to enact, and your governor were to sign, a new tax law that imposed a tax on the sale of all new and used gasoline engines at the following rates:

0 to 50 horsepower	— $5 per horsepower
50 to 100 horsepower	$250 plus $4 per horsepower over 50
100 to 150 horsepower	$450 plus $3 per horsepower over 100
150 to 200 horsepower	$600 plus $2 per horsepower over 150
over 200 horsepower	$700 plus $1 per horsepower over 200

    a) If A were to purchase a Buick with a 175 horsepower engine and B were to purchase a Ford with a 90 horsepower engine, who would pay the greater tax, A or B?

    b) Who would be in the higher marginal tax bracket, A or B?

    c) What would A's nominal average tax rate per horsepower be?

    d) In a technical sense, would this new tax be progressive, proportional, or regressive?

    e) If the new tax applied only to gasoline engines, what should happen to the price of diesel-powered automobiles? Explain briefly.

13. The government of Neverneverland, a small, strange, island republic in the middle of the Ancient Ocean, imposes two taxes on its citizens and resident aliens. One monthly tax is based on the size (measured in cubic feet) of the taxpayer's residence, an igloo, according to the following rates:

First 3,000 cubic feet	¢ 10 per cu ft
Next 3,000 cubic feet	¢ 18 per cu ft
Next 6,000 cubic feet	¢ 34 per cu ft
Next 12,000 cubic feet	¢ 62 per cu ft
Remainder	¢100 per cu ft

(Note: the basic monetary unit in this imaginary country is the cube, or ¢.)

The second tax is a tax of ¢5 on each ounce of wonderdrug, which is made and distributed only by a secret agency of the government. Neverneverland, you see, is a very strange country indeed: Humans can live there only if they take exactly one ounce of wonderdrug on the first day of each full moon. If they fail to take this drug at the prescribed time or in the prescribed amount, they will die within 20 hours.

a) In a technical sense, is the tax imposed on igloos progressive, proportional, or regressive?
b) In a technical sense, is the tax imposed on wonderdrug progressive, proportional, or regressive?
c) In a popular sense, is the tax imposed on wonderdrug progressive, proportional, or regressive?
d) Fred Jidair's home in Neverneverland contains 9,000 cubic feet of space. Is the nominal average tax paid by Fred on his home less than, equal to, or more than ¢34 per cubic foot?
e) If Fred decided, after the birth of his seventh child, to expand the size of his igloo from 9,000 to 12,000 cubic feet, would his marginal tax rate be less than, equal to, or more than ¢34 per cubic foot?

14. Sam Sharp lives in the Empire of Konform, which is ruled by King Kon. Sam, an employee of King Kon, earns an annual salary of $20,000 (his only source of income). The income tax in Konform is determined according to the following rate schedule:

$ 0–$1,000	—	5% of income
$1,001–$5,000	$ 50 plus 7% of income in excess of $1,000	
$5,001–$100,000	$330 plus 10% of income in excess of $5,000	

In addition, however, any relative of King Kon is entitled to deduct 50% of his salary in the calculation of his income tax base; any employee of King Kon can deduct 10%.

a) Technically, should the income tax in Konform be classified as proportional, progressive, or regressive?
b) Determine Sam's nominal average tax rate.
c) Determine Sam's real or effective average tax rate.
d) Determine Sam's marginal tax rate.

15. Amy Benson spent $100 today on the following purchases:

$60—for food from the grocery store;
$30—for a dress from the department store; and
$10—for wine from the liquor store.

a) Which of Amy's purchases were, in all probability, subject to—
(1) A retail sales tax?
(2) An excise tax?
b) Explain why some of Amy's purchases were, quite possibly, not subject to a retail sales tax even if she lives in a state that does impose a retail sales tax.

16. Ted Carmack earns $20,000 per year as a self-employed businessman.

a) How much Social Security tax must Ted pay in 1985?

b) If Ted were to incorporate his business, and his corporation were to hire Ted as an employee at a salary of $20,000 per year, would Ted's Social Security tax increase or decrease? Explain briefly.

17. Joan Jefferson made gifts of $100,000 this year, as follows:

    $30,000 to her daughter, Eva;
    $ 8,000 to her friend, Harold; and
    $62,000 to her alma mater (The University of Exes)

    a) What is the amount of Joan's *taxable gifts* for the year?

    b) If this is the first year in which Joan has made a taxable gift, must she pay a gift tax? Explain briefly.

18. City X imposes a real property tax at the rate of $.024 per dollar of assessed value. City Y imposes a real property tax at the rate of $.012 per dollar of assessed value. City X assesses property for tax purposes at only 50% of its fair market value; City Y, at its full fair market value. Confound Corporation owns a property in City X that has a market value of $1 million. Confound Corporation owns another property in City Y that is also worth $1 million. Confound Corporation has no debt against its property in City X; it owes a mortgage of $900,000 against the property in City Y. What amount of real property tax must Confound Corporation pay to City X? To City Y?

19. Jenny Jantzen (age 83) died and left her entire estate (valued at $16 million) to her husband, Don (age 26). Assuming that Jenny's funeral and administrative expenses total $100,000, and her predeath debts total $600,000, what is the amount of Jenny's *taxable estate*?

20. During this year Ira Reece earned a salary of $200,000; collected $100,000 interest on State of Florida bonds; and sold a property for $300,000. Ira's tax basis in the property sold was $190,000. What is the amount of Ira Reece's gross income from this year?

TAX PLANNING PROBLEM

Red Whitenblew, a citizen of the United States, has lived and worked for 20 years in a country which imposes no income tax. In all probability Red will never move from his present home. His only income is from a salary. What, if anything, might Red do to be relieved of the U.S. income tax that he pays each year? Locate a copy of the Internal Revenue Code in your library and read Sec. 877. What, in general, does that section provide so far as Red's tax plan is concerned?

Chapter Objectives

1. Introduce the basic sources of all U.S. federal income tax law.
2. Explain how to find answers to tax questions (that are not answered in this text) in other secondary tax-reference services.
3. Describe how the Code is organized and how to reference various parts of the Code in the standard format.
4. Explain the procedure followed by Congress in the enactment of a new tax law.
5. Describe how the Treasury regulations are organized and how to cite a regulation correctly.
6. Explain how revenue rulings originate and how they may be located and cited correctly.
7. Differentiate the various judicial authorities that interpret the Code.
8. Describe how to locate and cite each of the many different judicial authorities.

2 Sources and Uses of Tax Law

Before we begin a detailed study of the most frequently encountered provisions in the federal income tax law, let us examine in a general way the basic sources common to all federal tax laws. A good understanding of these basic sources is important for at least two reasons. First, it may help you locate and assess answers to tax questions that are beyond the information included in this (or any other) tax textbook. Second, it will give you a better appreciation of both the complexity and the uncertainty commonly found in tax problems. At a very minimum, this study of the basic sources of tax law should make you feel a little more at ease when you make your first trip to a tax library in search of an answer either to a real tax problem of your own or one assigned to you by your teacher.

The statutory authority for all current federal tax law is the Internal Revenue Code of 1954, as amended to date. Unfortunately, that document has grown through the years until it now consists of approximately 2,000 pages of technical text. Although a few of the provisions in the Code can be read and understood immediately by anyone who reads English, many other provisions are almost impossible to interpret without a lot of help from other authorities. The "authorities" range all the way from (*a*) governmental institutions created, in large measure, just to issue official interpretations of the Code to (*b*) fly-by-night authors and publishers trying to make a quick buck by selling tax ideas and interpretations to an unsuspecting public. By studying the material in this chapter you will be in a better position to distinguish between those interpretive authorities whose interpretations are dependable and those who generally should be disregarded.

This chapter is subdivided into four major parts. The first part consists of an explanation of how the Code is organized and how new provisions become part of the law. The second part is an explanation of both the primary and secondary interpretations of the provisions included in the statute. The third part is an introduction to some of the commercial tax services which you might use to help find and interpret the tax law. The final part describes the taxpayer compliance process.

THE CODE

All of the current U.S. federal tax laws have been brought together in a single document correctly referred to as the Internal Revenue Code of 1954, as amended. As a practical matter, however, nearly all tax authorities and tax publications simply refer to this document as "***the Code***."

CODE The statutory tax law provisions that are the final authority on all federal income tax issues; technically, The Internal Revenue Code of 1954 as amended.

BACKGROUND

The 1954 Code is only the second tax Code in U.S. history; the other one is technically known as the Internal Revenue Code of 1939. Both the 1954 and the 1939 Codes were, of course, subject to frequent modification. For example, major recent changes were made to the 1954 Code by the Economic Recovery Tax Act of 1981 (commonly known as ERTA), the Tax Equity and Fiscal Responsibility Act of 1982 (frequently cited as TEFRA), and the Tax Reform Act of 1984 (also known as the Deficit Reduction Act of 1984). All of the tax provisions of these recent Acts have been integrated into (and thus become part of) the 1954 Code.

Prior to 1939 there was no tax Code. In those days a taxpayer had to look to the many provisions of numerous individual acts of Congress to determine what the tax law provided in any particular situation. In other words, a single event that took place in 1928 could have been subject to various rules contained in the Revenue Acts of 1921, 1926, and 1928. Although our present-day Code may be unduly complex, at least it brings all of the federal income tax law together in a single document.

You may assume, therefore, that any reference in this text to *the Code* is in fact a reference to the Internal Revenue Code of 1954, as amended.

ORGANIZATION OF THE CODE

The Code has an elaborate organizational scheme that includes subtitles, chapters, subchapters, parts, subparts, sections, subsections, paragraphs, and subparagraphs. The interrelationships of the various divisions, and their method of designation, is outlined in Table 2-1.

TABLE 2-1
Subdivisions of the Code

SUBDIVISION	HOW DESIGNATED
Subtitle	Upper-case English letters, A through G. Subtitle A, for example, is "Income Taxes"; Subtitle B, "Estate and Gift Taxes"; Subtitle C, "Employment Taxes"; etc.
Chapter	Arabic numerals 1 through 98. Although Subtitle A has six chapters, most of the commonly encountered laws are found in Chapter 1, "Normal Taxes and Surtaxes." Chapter 6 includes the consolidation rules for affiliated groups of corporate taxpayers.
Subchapter	Upper-case English letters, A through V. For example, Subchapter A of Chapter 1 is entitled "Determination of Tax Liability"; Subchapter B, "Computation of Taxable Income," etc.
Part	Roman numerals, as required. Some Subchapters are divided into many "Parts"; others have no such subdivision. Subchapter A of Chapter 1 includes six Parts. Part I is entitled "Tax on Individuals"; Part II, "Tax on Corporations"; Part IV, "Credits Against Tax."
Subpart	Upper-case, English letters, as required. Once again, some parts have numerous Subparts; others have none. Part IV of Subchapter A of Chapter 1, for example, has four Subparts. Subpart A is entitled "Nonrefundable Personal Credits."
Section	Arabic numerals, as required. Part 1 of Subchapter A (which has no Subparts) includes Sections 1 through 5. Section 1 is entitled "Tax imposed"; Section 2, "Definitions and special rules."
Subsection	Lower-case, English letters, *in parentheses*, as required. (See text below for important details.)
Paragraph	Arabic numerals, *in parentheses*, as required. (See text below.)
Subparagraph	Upper-case, English letters, *in parentheses*, as required. (See text below.)

This complex organization *could* make reference to any particular part of the Code very cumbersome. For example, one might correctly refer to paragraph 2, of subsection a, of section 1, of part 1, of subchapter A, of chapter 1, of subtitle A, of the 1954 Code, just to find the 1984 tax rate schedule imposed on married persons who file joint income tax returns with their spouse. Fortunately, this entirely correct but unduly complex procedure is *not* necessary.

SECTIONS When the Code was put together the organizers were clever enough to number each Code section with a unique number. In addition, to allow for later expansion, they deliberately skipped some numbers. To illustrate, there has never been a 1954 Code section numbered 6, 7, 8, 9, or 10. These numbers are, therefore, available for future use by Congress. Other sections—like Section 4—have been used but were subsequently repealed. Hence that section, although not in current use, could be used again in the future. In a few areas, however, Congress has already amended or expanded the law more times than the original organizers of the Code anticipated. As a consequence there are now a few sections that contain an English capital letter *as well as* an Arabic numeral.

Example 1: Section 453 is entitled "Installment Method." Another entirely separate section, Section 453A, is entitled "Installment Method for Dealers in Personal Property," and yet another distinct section, Section 453B, is entitled "Gain or Loss on Disposition of Installment Obligations."

Because each section number is unique—that is, because any section number can refer to one and only one part of the tax law—in most cases there is no need to refer to any higher-level subdivision within the Code. Consequently, instead of describing the 1984 tax rates for married persons filing a joint return by the cumbersome method suggested above, it is entirely correct to refer to this same part of the law simply as Sec. 1(a)(2), which is read as "section 1, a, 2."

SUBSECTIONS AND PARAGRAPHS The use of specific subdesignations that exist within a section is often helpful.

Example 2: The subsections of Sec. 1 provide five different income tax rates, as follows:

Sec. 1(a)—those for married persons (and surviving spouses) filing joint returns;

Sec. 1(b)—those for heads of households;

Sec. 1(c)—those for unmarried individuals (other than surviving spouses and heads of households);

Sec. 1(d)—those for married individuals filing separate returns; and

Sec. 1(e)—those for estates and trusts.

This breakdown is useful because it allows one to use a kind of shorthand language when referring to various tax law provisions. Any reference to Sec. 1(e) can only refer to the tax rates on income earned by an estate or trust, whereas a reference to Sec. 1(c) can refer only to the tax rates on income realized by a single (i.e., unmarried) individual.

The use of paragraph references yields still further precision.

Example 3: In 1981 Congress reduced the tax rates on individuals over the next three years (i.e., 1982 through 1984 and beyond). Accordingly, the different income tax rates for single persons in each year can be cited as follows:

Sec. 1(c)(1)—for the 1982 rates;
Sec. 1(c)(2)—for the 1983 rates; and
Sec. 1(c)(3)—for the 1984 rates.

Sec. 1(f) further provides that the 1984 tax rates will be adjusted each year, beginning in 1985, to reflect changes in the CPI (consumer price index) and thus minimize or eliminate future tax increases due solely to inflation.

SUMMARY Because nearly all tax literature explicitly refers only to a section number, or an even lower subdivision of the Code, you must understand clearly what is represented in a common citation. To summarize, suppose that you discover a reference to "the limitation of Sec. 74(b)(2)." What would that reference mean?

Example 4: Regardless of exactly where or how you found it, any reference to Sec. 74(b)(2) should lead you to the following words from the Code:

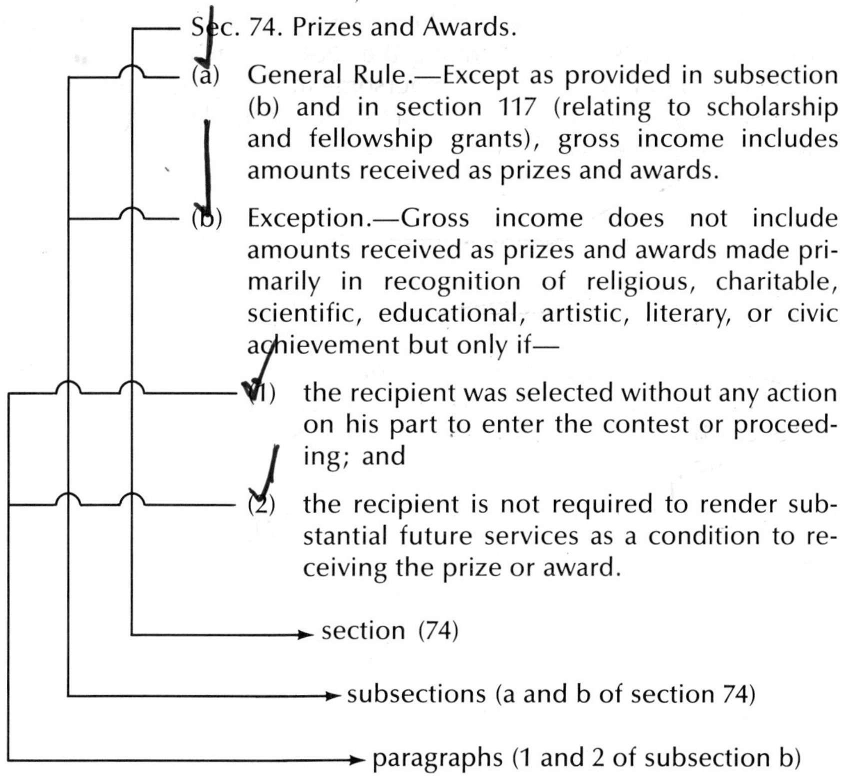

Sec. 74. Prizes and Awards.

(a) General Rule.—Except as provided in subsection (b) and in section 117 (relating to scholarship and fellowship grants), gross income includes amounts received as prizes and awards.

(b) Exception.—Gross income does not include amounts received as prizes and awards made primarily in recognition of religious, charitable, scientific, educational, artistic, literary, or civic achievement but only if—

(1) the recipient was selected without any action on his part to enter the contest or proceeding; and

(2) the recipient is not required to render substantial future services as a condition to receiving the prize or award.

Finding the correct section or subsection of the Code may be just the first step in reaching a correct answer to a tax question. It is, however, a very important first step. Anyone who attempts to do serious tax research will necessarily locate and read the pertinent Code section before giving a tax answer. Reading only someone's interpretation of the Code is often too risky—those who interpret the law may or may not be correct.

SUBCHAPTERS AND OTHER PORTIONS OF THE CODE Since nearly all "popular" references to the Code refer only to a section (or some even lower-level subdivision), you may wonder whether or not the larger subdivisions of the Code have any usefulness at all. Indeed they do. Just as subsection references have become a handy form of shorthand for tax people, so also have parts, subparts, subchapters and chapters.

Example 5: The legislative assistants who draft the language which eventually becomes part of the law, frequently limit the application of a particular provision to only some subdivision of the Code. To illustrate, the definition of the word *property* that is found in Sec. 317(a) is carefully limited by the following words:

Sec. 317. Other Definitions.

(a) Property.—For purposes of this part, the term "property" means money, securities, and any other property; except that such term does not include stock in the corporation making the distribution (or rights to acquire such stock).

The limitation is contained in the words, "for purposes of *this part*." By using these words the individuals who wrote Sec. 317 intended that this definition of property should apply only to *Part 1 of Subchapter C*. Sec. 317(a) could *not* be cited as an authoritative definition of the word property in Sec. 1001 because the latter section is found in Part 1 of Subchapter O, *not* in Part 1 of Subchapter C!

In addition to such critical technical differences, many of the more general subdivisions of the Code also provide a handy shorthand reference for those seriously interested in matters of income taxation. Graduate tax students, for example, frequently refer to a specific college course as "sub C" or "sub K." What they mean by that shorthand reference is implicit in the organization of the Code. Subchapter C deals with those sections (numbered from 301 to 385) that prescribe the tax rules for transactions between a corporation and its own shareholders (in their role as shareholders). Thus a college course "in sub C" really refers to a course in corporate/corporate-shareholder transactions. Subchapter K is entitled "Partners and partnerships." The content of a course "in sub K" is obviously, therefore, a course concerned with the income taxation of transactions between partners and their partnership. Because shorthand references to various subchapters of the Code have become so commonplace, Table 2-2 may on occasion be handy in interpreting an otherwise confusing reference.

Anyone interested in reading a complete list of all the major subdivisions of the Code should visit the tax reference collection in a local library. The Code's Table of Contents typically provides one with an easy reference to each major subdivision. If anyone desires to purchase a personal copy, paperback editions of the Code are updated and printed semiannually by both Commerce Clearing House (CCH) and Prentice-Hall, Inc. (PH).

TABLE 2-2
Titles to Some of the More Common Subchapters of Chapter 1 of Subtitle A of the 1954 Code

SUBCHAPTER	TITLE
C	Corporate distributions and adjustments.
F	Exempt organizations.
H	Banking institutions.
I	Natural resources.
J	Estates, trusts, beneficiaries and decedents.
K	Partners and partnerships.
L	Insurance companies.
O	Gain or loss on disposition of property.
P	Capital gains and losses.
S	Election of certain small business corporations as to taxable status.

AMENDING THE CODE

Changes to the Code ordinarily originate with the Committee on Ways and Means in the House of Representatives.[1] Individual representatives may introduce bills to amend the Code, but these bills are referred to the Committee on Ways and Means before being discussed on the floor of the House. The chairman of the committee exercises a great deal of authority by controlling the fate of the bills referred to Ways and Means. Only after a bill has been favorably voted upon in committee does it ordinarily proceed to the floor of the House. Major bills sent to the floor are accompanied by a Report of the Committee on Ways and Means. The report may become an important source document if the "intent of Congress" becomes a critical factor in the later interpretation of any new law contained in the bill. Upon passage by the House, the bill goes to the Senate for further action.

The idea that most amendments to the Code originate with our elected representatives when they place a new bill in the legislative hopper is a gross oversimplification of the political process. Historically, most major proposals for change are presented to Congress by the secretary of the treasury. New proposals are often a major component of an administration's fiscal policy and reflect the economic philosophy of the president and his most trusted economic advisors. Other amendments originate in the bureaucracy which remains in Washington to administer the laws, regardless of who happens to occupy the oval office.

[1]TEFRA, the 1982 tax act, is an exception to this general rule; for all practical purposes, it originated in the Senate. Because the Constitution requires that all tax bills originate in the House, some members of Congress who opposed TEFRA attempted to contest its legality in the courts. The original trial court held, however, that—because they had suffered no harm—these Congressmen had no standing before the court and thus dismissed their action.

The tax simplification proposal submitted by Treasury Secretary Regan to President Reagan in November 1984 is a good example of the multiplicity of forces that go into the making of a new law. Although that proposal purports to be the joint product of only the staff of the Treasury Department—including top-level Reagan appointees as well as career government employees—it was heavily influenced by the opinions of the President and other high-level Administration advisors. It also appears to reflect the work previously done by, particularly, Senators Kasten (R-Wisconsin) and Bradley (D-New Jersey) and Congressmen Kemp (R-New York) and Gephardt (D-Missouri) as well as the members of their respective staffs. In brief, the latest Treasury Department proposals are really not that different from either the earlier Kemp–Kasten "FAST" tax proposal or the Bradley–Gephardt "FAIR" tax proposal. Hence, if any of the current Treasury proposals ever become law, the true role of numerous congressional advisors, staff members, and government bureaucrats will be difficult to discern but will be very real nonetheless.

Each tax bill sent to the Senate is referred to the Committee on Finance. Once again the chairman of that committee exercises substantial authority in deciding what to do with each bill referred to it. Only bills favorably voted upon in committee can be acted upon by the remainder of the Senate. As in the House, major bills referred favorably to the Senate floor are ordinarily accompanied by a Report of the Senate Finance Committee. These reports may also provide some indication of the intent of Congress implicit in any eventual amendment to the Code. Although bills referred by the Ways and Means Committee to the floor of the House are ordinarily subject to a "closed rule"—i.e., the members of the House are generally not free to amend the Committee version of the bill; they must "take" or "leave" whatever is presented to them—no similar rule ordinarily controls on the floor of the Senate. Accordingly, most tax bills reported by the Senate Finance Committee are freely debated and amended on the floor of the Senate. Because these amendments differ from the Committee version, any intent of Congress on a floor-amended provision must be found in the daily editions of the *Congressional Record*. Because of the deliberations, a bill finally passed by the Senate normally will be different from the one originally passed by the House.

To reconcile the House and Senate bills, a conference committee is appointed to compromise any differences. The compromise reached by this committee is then reported back to both bodies for final ratification. If both houses of Congress adopt the conference bill (which must be accepted or rejected without change), it goes to the president for signature. Once again, most major bills reported by any conference committee will be accompanied by a Report of the Conference Committee. Like the House and Senate reports that preceded it, this Report of the Conference Committee may also become a primary source document for determining the intent of Congress.

The conference procedure increases the power of the two tax committee chairpersons because they appoint the conferees. On rare occasions members of the conference committee may disagree with the chairperson, but the majority will ordinarily favor his or her position. The conference committee can also dispose quickly of any amendments added on the Senate floor against the wishes of the Senate Finance Committee chairperson. Prior to 1976 most conference committees acted only in executive session. The more recent bills, however, have been debated in open sessions which, to some extent, may limit the power of the chair. The president, of course, has the final power of the veto, but this veto is exercised sparingly in tax matters.

Although the reports of the House Ways and Means Committee, the Senate Finance Committee, and the Conference Committee, as well as excerpts from the *Congressional Record*, may be consulted to determine the intent of Congress on any amendment to the Code, those primary source documents should not be confused with the numerous interpretations issued *after* a bill has become part of the Code. Subsequent interpretations of statutory law may be influenced by the intent of Congress, but they are not dependent upon it. In order to provide a satisfactory administration of the tax law, interpretative opinions must be issued even in the absence of any apparent intent of Congress on the issue.

INTERPRETATIONS OF THE CODE

Necessarily, the Code is written in general terms. It is intended to apply to literally millions of taxpayers in widely different factual situations. Given the broad language of the Code, someone must interpret exactly how the general rules apply in specific circumstances. These interpretations can be divided into two major categories: (*a*) primary sources and (*b*) secondary sources. Primary interpretations are those issued by some branch of the government in an official capacity. The two most important primary sources of tax law interpretations can be divided into *administrative* authority and *judicial* authority. Administrative interpretations come largely from the Department of the Treasury, including the Internal Revenue Service (IRS). Judicial interpretations come from the many courts of law which settle disputes between the IRS and taxpayers. Secondary authority can come from anywhere; it carries no "official" sanction and must be handled with care. This text, for example, is secondary authority. Like all other tax texts, it can be no better than the competence of the author(s). This important conclusion is equally true of administrative and judicial interpretations. Nevertheless, interpretations issued by (official) government authorities must be given greater weight than those of secondary authorities, at least until they have been repealed or overruled by a higher level of government authority, such as the Supreme Court.

ADMINISTRATIVE AUTHORITY

The most frequently encountered administrative interpretations of the Code come either from the Department of the Treasury or from the IRS, which is a part of Treasury. Although the Treasury Department issues several different kinds of interpretations, each with different names, the

TREASURY REGULATION An official interpretation of the Code issued by the U.S. Treasury Department that serves as a general guideline to be used by all taxpayers.

REVENUE RULING A specific interpretation of the Code issued by the Internal Revenue Service with respect to the facts submitted by a particular taxpayer.

most common one is called a ***Treasury regulation***. Regulations are general interpretations of the statutory law issued to serve as broad guides for taxpayers in different circumstances. The IRS also issues several different forms of interpretations; its most common one is called a revenue ruling. ***Revenue rulings*** are very specific interpretations of the Code frequently issued in response to a real taxpayer's question about a particular problem. On other occasions the IRS will issue a revenue ruling on its own initiative in an attempt to clarify its own interpretation of the law using assumed facts. The rulings that are issued in response to a taxpayer's actual inquiry may or may not be published by the IRS. Those not published by the IRS are called private letter rulings. Although the IRS does not publish private letter rulings, they are published by commercial publishing companies after the IRS has deleted any references that might identify the taxpayer who initiated the inquiry. These private rulings are not intended to serve as a general interpretation for any taxpayer other than the one requesting it. Even the rulings published by the IRS have limited authority; they disclose the IRS' current position on certain questions, but they can be readily revoked or amended at the IRS' will.

REGULATIONS Treasury regulations, which contain the secretary's interpretation of the Code, have the force and effect of the Code, unless they can be shown to be in conflict with congressional intent.[2] Tax return forms, and the instructions which accompany those forms, constitute part of the regulations. Most regulations contain many helpful examples. Before regulations are officially released on a new or an amended Code provision, *proposed* regulations are published and circulated among interested parties. This process invites comments and suggestions before final regulations are adopted; sometimes the Treasury Department modifies proposed regulations two or three times before final regulations are issued. Final regulations are first issued as Treasury Decisions (TDs). All TDs must have the approval of the Treasury Department. Therefore, after their final release, all regulations may be relied upon as legal precedent; that is, they are binding on the government. They may, however, be challenged by taxpayers.

Once adopted, regulations for all federal taxes are part of Title 26 of the Code of Federal Regulations. Title 26 is subdivided into parts that correspond with the subtitles in the Code. Thus Part 1 of the regulations deals with Subtitle A of the Code; that is, with the income tax. In addition, each part of the regulations is further subdivided into sections that also correspond with sections of the Code. Thus, Part 1, Section 162, of the regulations, deals with the ordinary and necessary expenses of carrying on a trade or business. A complete and correct citation for that section is 26 CFR 1.162, which means Title 26, Code of Federal Regulations, Part 1, Section 162. Fortunately this cumbersome citation—like its counterpart in the Code itself—has been grossly simplified and is typically written as Treas. Reg. Sec. 1.162-x, or just Reg. 1.162-x.

[2] *Maryland Casualty Co.* v. *U.S.*, 251 U.S. 342 (1920).

Every complete citation to a Treasury regulation has four distinct parts, as follows:

1. A number, to the left of the decimal point, that indicates that the regulation deals with a specific tax or a procedural rule, according to the following key:
   - 1. Income tax
   - 20. Estate tax
   - 25. Gift tax
   - 31. Employment tax
   - 48 or 49. Excise tax
   - 301. Administrative and procedural rules
   - 601. Statement of procedural rules
2. A number, between the decimal point and a dash (–), that indicates which Code section the regulation is interpreting.
3. Another number, just to the right of the dash, that indicates the sequential number of the regulation interpreting the Code section that has already been identified (above).
4. And, possibly, one or more letters and/or numbers, immediately following the first number to the right of the dash, to indicate a subreference within a regulation.

Example 6: Treas. Reg. Sec. 1.162-3(b)(2) refers to an income tax regulation (as indicated by the number 1, to the left of the decimal); interprets Code section 162 (as indicated by the numbers between the decimal point and the dash); signifies that this regulation is the third one issued in the interpretation of Sec. 162 (as indicated by the number 3, immediately to the right of the dash); and, finally, refers to part (b)(2) of that third regulation (as indicated by the final letter and number).

Example 7: Reg. Sec. 20.2042-1 refers to the first Treasury regulation issued in interpretation of Code section 2042, a part of our estate tax law.

Although most regulations have the force and effect of the Code, newly issued regulations may not reflect the intent of Congress. If a regulation is challenged by a taxpayer, it is up to the courts to decide whether or not a regulation is a valid interpretation of the Code. Regulations that have been around for a long time are rarely overruled. "Legislative" regulations are also very difficult to overturn, even when they are first issued. The term *legislative* regulation is meant to distinguish between those regulations that are written in response to specific direction by Congress and those issued by the Treasury Department under the more routine authority granted in Sec. 7805. The latter are sometimes referred to as "interpretive" regulations. The regulations issued under Sec. 1502 (dealing with consolidated corporate tax returns) are an example of legislative regulations; those under Sec. 162 (dealing with ordinary and necessary business experiences) are interpretive regulations.

The *Internal Revenue Bulletin* (IRB), a weekly publication of the IRS, contains much of the information referred to in the preceding pages. The *Bulletin*, for example, includes copies of new revenue acts, committee reports accompanying these acts, treasury decisions (that is, new regulations), and all revenue rulings. The weekly IRBs are eventually compiled twice each year in bound volumes called *Cumulative Bulletins*, abbreviated as CB. Thus new rulings can be located in an IRB; older rulings in a CB.

REVENUE RULINGS The IRS Commissioner's interpretation of the statute, as it applies to a specific taxpayer's problem, does *not* carry the same weight of authority as does a regulation. In fact, a commissioner may retroactively revoke an earlier ruling or may elect not to follow his own interpretation (issued in a prior revenue ruling) when confronted with a similar problem by another taxpayer.[3] Incidentally, the IRS is not required to issue a ruling in response to every inquiry made. If one is issued, however, the conclusion is generally binding upon the government as far as that particular taxpayer is concerned, assuming that the taxpayer gave complete and accurate information in making the ruling request.

Each year the IRS issues approximately 12,000 revenue rulings. Since 1976, all revenue rulings must be made available to the public.[4] Although all rulings are a matter of public record, the IRS prints and distributes only 200 to 300 rulings per year. The latter rulings—which are considered to be of general importance for many taxpayers—are technically known as published rulings. The published rulings are consecutively numbered each calendar year and are cited Rev. Rul. 1983-1; 1983-2; etc. The remaining rulings—which the IRS deems to be of sole interest to the taxpayer(s) involved—are referred to as private letter rulings. Letter rulings are numbered in a seven digit series: the first two numbers indicate the year; the remaining five digits involve a chronological (by week) classification and a sequential numbering process. Before they are made public, the IRS deletes the taxpayer's name and any other information that could be used to identify the party making the ruling request. Published rulings may be relied upon and cited as authority by taxpayers having a transaction with facts and circumstances substantially the same as those stated in the ruling. Private or letter rulings, on the other hand, are not deemed to be authority for anyone other than the taxpayer requesting the ruling.

In addition to Treasury regulations and IRS rulings, numerous other official interpretations of the tax law are made every year by various government agencies. They include revenue procedures (cited as Rev. Proc.), technical information releases (TIRs), news releases, technical advice memoranda, and other pronouncements.

Published revenue rulings, like regulations, are cited by reference to the IRB or CB in which they appear. For example, Rev. Rul. 85-122, 1985-23 IRB 10, refers to a *fictitious* ruling that could be described as the 122nd

---

[3] *Dixon* v. *U.S.*, 381 U.S. 68 (1965).

[4] Sec. 6110.

ruling issued in 1985 that was first printed on page 10 of the 23rd *Internal Revenue Bulletin* published in 1985. After the semiannual *Cumulative Bulletin* is published, this same fictitious ruling might then be cited as follows: Rev. Rul. 85-122, 1985-1 C.B. 329. (That is a citation to the same ruling found in volume 1 of the 1985 *Cumulative Bulletin*, beginning at page 329.) Private letter rulings are published by CCH (Commerce Clearing House) in full text as part of their *IRS Letter Rulings Reports*. Digests of those same letter rulings are published by several other publishers as well as CCH.

JUDICIAL AUTHORITY

Any taxpayer who does not agree with the government's interpretation of a tax law is free to litigate that disagreement in court. A judicial review is possible in any one of three courts, namely: the Tax Court of the United States; a U.S. district court; or the U.S. Claims Court. In addition, appeals may be heard from each of these three courts until, possibly, the U.S. Supreme Court finally renders its opinion.

TAX COURT If the IRS interprets the law in such a way as to find that the taxpayer owes more to the government than the taxpayer believes is owed, the taxpayer can refuse to pay the additional assessment and petition the Tax Court for a review of the dispute. This court exists solely to resolve disputes over the Code and its judges are tax specialists. Although the Tax Court is headquartered in Washington, D.C., its judges travel to major cities throughout the United States to hear cases.

> ***BACKGROUND***
>
> Prior to 1943 the Tax court was called the Board of Tax Appeals. As a consequence there are no citations to Tax Court decisions before that date; instead references for the years 1924 to 1942 are to (volume) B.T.A. (page number). A total of 47 volumes were needed to record the opinions of the *United States Board of Tax Appeals* during that 18 year period. Prior to 1924 there was neither a Tax Court nor a Board of Tax Appeals. In those years, therefore, judicial review was possible only in either a district court or the Claims Court, which was then called the Court of Claims.

The Chief Justice of the Tax Court classifies each decision as either a ***regular decision*** or a ***memorandum decision***. The latter classification implies only that, at least in the mind of the Chief Justice, a case adds little or nothing new to the tax law. In addition, regular decisions may or may not be reviewed by the entire court. In other words, after reading a trial judge's opinion, the Chief Justice must decide both (*a*) the status of the opinion as regular or memo, and (*b*) whether or not a regular decision is of sufficient importance to have it "reviewed" by every member of the Tax Court before issuing a final decision. All "regular" decisions (whether or not reviewed by the entire court) are published by the U.S. Government

REGULAR DECISION A decision of the Tax Court deemed by the Chief Justice to include some new and important point in tax law and therefore a decision that will be published by the Government Printing Office in the Tax Court reports.

MEMORANDUM DECISION A decision of the Tax Court deemed by the Chief Justice to include no new or significant point in tax law, hence a decision that will not be printed in the Tax Court reports. (These decisions are nevertheless printed by commercial publishing companies.)

Printing Office in the *Tax Court Reports*, commonly cited (Vol. No.) T.C. (Page No.). The memorandum decisions are not published by the government; they are, however, reproduced and sold in bound volumes by two commercial publishing houses (Prentice-Hall, Inc. and Commerce Clearing House).

The details described in the preceding paragraph do *not* apply to decisions rendered by the small claims division of the Tax Court. That division was created in 1969 to expedite the handling of relatively minor disputes between taxpayers and the IRS. Currently a taxpayer can elect to utilize the small claims division if the amount in dispute involves $10,000 or less. By making that election a taxpayer avoids some of the more formal legal rules of evidence and procedure, but loses any right of appeal to a higher court, should the IRS win the dispute. Furthermore, no formal written opinion of the decision need be rendered by the commissioner hearing the case in the small claims division.

Excluding small-claims division cases, either party that loses a dispute in the Tax Court has the right to appeal the decision to the appropriate circuit court of appeal. In addition, the IRS may publicly announce whether or not it agrees with a decision of the Tax Court. If it does agree with a conclusion of the Tax Court, the IRS will announce its approval in the form of an *acquiescence*; if it disagrees, the IRS may announce its *non-acquiescence* whether or not it decides to appeal the decision. If an appeal is filed by either party both oral and written arguments are made to the circuit court before a decision is reached and an opinion is rendered.

DISTRICT COURT A second line of judicial redress is available to taxpayers in the U.S. district courts. When disagreements arise, taxpayers can either refuse to pay the additional tax demanded by the IRS and take their claim to the Tax Court, or pay the claim and then turn around and sue for a refund in either a district court or the Claims Court.[5] The judges in the district courts hear all kinds of cases, not just those related to tax laws. They are not, therefore, specialists in tax law. They must, however, decide all questions of law in any tax case brought before them. Questions of fact may be decided by either the district court judge or by a jury. The only court in which a taxpayer can be guaranteed a trial by jury—on questions of fact—is a district court.

Official decisions of a district court are published in the *Federal Supplement*, commonly cited (Vol. No.) F. Suppl. (Page No.). Appeals from a district court's decision are also made to the appropriate circuit court of appeal and then, if ***certiorari*** is granted, to the Supreme Court. Incidentally, if at the end of this judicial process the taxpayer's claim for refund is allowed, the government must pay interest on the amount of any overpayment.

CERTIORARI The appellate proceeding that calls for a reexamination by the Supreme Court of a decision by a lower court.

[5] If a taxpayer does not wish to risk having to pay interest on overdue taxes, should his or her interpretation finally be found to be incorrect, it is possible to make a deposit with the Tax Court in advance of the litigation. This deposit procedure will not, however, remove the case from the jurisdiction of the Tax Court.

CLAIMS COURT Taxpayers may also sue for a refund of taxes paid in the Claims Court. All proceedings of this court are held in Washington, D.C. It specializes in suits against the government. Official decisions of the Claims Court are published in the *Court of Claims Reporter,* cited as (Vol. No.) Ct. Cl. (Page No.). Appeals from this court are made to the United States Court of Appeals for the Federal Circuit and, if certiorari is granted, to the Supreme Court. Because of the geographical location of this court, and the expense of litigating in Washington, D.C., in most years relatively few tax cases are brought before it.

CIRCUIT COURTS OF APPEAL As explained in the preceding paragraphs, appeals from both the Tax Court and the district courts first go to one of 12 geographically bounded circuit courts of appeal; appeals from the Claims Court go to the Court of Appeals for the Federal Circuit. The residence of the taxpayer normally determines which circuit court will hear any case appealed from the Tax Court or a district court. The assignment of the 50 states, plus the District of Columbia and four U.S. possessions, to the various circuit courts are as follows:

Alabama:	CCA-11	Oklahoma:	CCA-10
Alaska:	CCA-9	Oregon:	CCA-9
Arizona:	CCA-9	Pennsylvania:	CCA-3
Arkansas:	CCA-8	Puerto Rico:	CCA-1
Canal Zone:	CCA-5	Rhode Island:	CCA-1
California:	CCA-9	South Carolina:	CCA-4
Colorado:	CCA-10	Kansas:	CCA-10
Connecticut:	CCA-2	Kentucky:	CCA-6
Delaware:	CCA-3	Louisiana:	CCA-5
District of Columbia:	CCA-DC	Maine:	CCA-1
Florida:	CCA-11	Maryland:	CCA-4
Georgia:	CCA-11	Massachusetts:	CCA-1
Guam:	CCA-9	Michigan:	CCA-6
Hawaii:	CCA-9	Minnesota:	CCA-8
Idaho:	CCA-9	Mississippi:	CCA-5
Illinois:	CCA-7	Missouri:	CCA-8
Indiana:	CCA-7	South Dakota:	CCA-8
Iowa:	CCA-8	Tennessee:	CCA-6
Montana:	CCA-9	Texas:	CCA-5
Nebraska:	CCA-8	Utah:	CCA-10
Nevada:	CCA-9	Vermont:	CCA-2
New Hampshire:	CCA-1	Virginia:	CCA-4
New Jersey:	CCA-3	Virgin Islands:	CCA-3
New Mexico:	CCA-10	Washington:	CCA-9
New York:	CCA-2	West Virginia:	CCA-4
North Carolina:	CCA-4	Wisconsin:	CCA-7
North Dakota:	CCA-8	Wyoming:	CCA-10
Ohio:	CCA-6		

As implied above, there are eleven "numbered" and two "named" circuit courts of appeal. The named courts are (1) the Circuit Court of Appeals for the District of Columbia, for appeals from any district court located in Washington, D.C., and (2) the Court of Appeals for the Federal Circuit, for all appeals from the Claims Court. The other circuit courts are correctly identified as the First Circuit Court of Appeals; the Second Circuit Court of Appeals; etc. Their current opinions are officially reported in the *Federal Reporter,* Second Series. These decisions would be commonly cited as (Vol. No.) F.2d (Page No).

Once a decision has been rendered by any one of the circuit courts of appeal, the Tax Court is generally bound by that decision when dealing with taxpayers presenting essentially identical facts who reside in that same jurisdiction. The Tax Court is not, however, bound by any circuit court's opinion when it is dealing with a taxpayer who resides in a different circuit. This legal rule is known commonly as the *Golsen Rule* because it was first articulated in *J. E. Golsen,* 54 T.C. 742 (1970). To illustrate, suppose (1) that a dispute between you and the IRS has progressed to the point that you are engaged in litigation before the Tax Court, and (2) that you live in New York, a state assigned to the Second Circuit Court of Appeals. If facts essentially identical to your dispute with the IRS have previously been decided by only the Second Circuit Court, the Tax Court will have no choice but to follow that decision in deciding your case. On the other hand, if you lived in California, a state assigned to the Ninth Circuit Court, then the Tax Court would be free to decide your case without reference to the opinion previously rendered by the Second Circuit Court of Appeals even though the facts in that case were essentially identical to the facts in your case. Obviously the Tax Court may elect to follow the earlier decision of the Second Circuit even if you live in the Ninth Circuit. The important point is simply that the Tax Court is not obligated to follow the decision of an appellate court in every circumstance.

THE SUPREME COURT Neither the IRS nor any taxpayer has an absolute right to have his or her tax case heard by the United States Supreme Court. The party that loses the dispute at the circuit court level may file a *writ of certiorari* and request that the Supreme Court hear the case, but the Court may not grant that request. Generally the Supreme Court will agree to hear no more than 6 to 10 tax cases in any year. The cases which it does agree to hear frequently involve disputes in which the circuit courts of appeal are in disagreement with each other. The official decisions of the Supreme Court are published in the *United States Reporter,* cited (Vol. No.) U.S. (Page No.). Obviously, once the Supreme Court has decided a matter all lower courts must follow that decision in subsequent litigation presenting essentially identical facts.

LOCATING JUDICIAL AUTHORITY

Most judicial interpretations of the statutory tax law (i.e., the Code) are published and made available to the general public. The common form of any judicial citation, as suggested previously, typically consists of two sets of numbers and one set of letters, as follows:

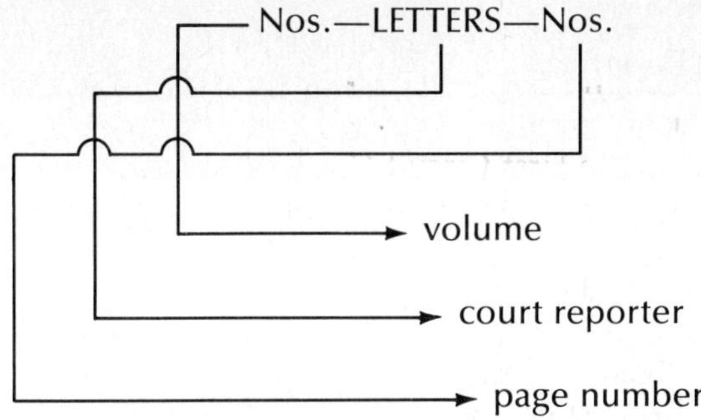

This part of a judicial citation is ordinarily preceded by the name of the plaintiff and defendant, respectively.

Example 8: An earlier footnote in this chapter referred to *Dixon* v. *U.S.*, 381 U.S. 68 (1965). This footnote can be explained, as follows: the reference is to a case in which a taxpayer (Dixon) was suing the United States government and the decision of the United States Supreme Court can be found in volume 381 of the *United States Reports* beginning at page 68. This decision was rendered in the year 1965.

Unfortunately not every judicial citation is as easy to explain as the one in Example 8. Each one, however, contains those same essential features. One reason for additional complexity is the numerous places in which a single court decision may be printed. These publications include both "official" print and "secondary" references. The primary reason for the growth of numerous secondary references is attributable to the substantial cost of a complete law library. Since many courts hear literally thousands of cases that have nothing to do with matters of taxation, their court reporters are full of information that is of little or no value to tax experts. Accordingly, commercial publishing houses have made available to those willing to pay for the service, tax reporters which include only those cases that are concerned with tax matters. As a consequence of this multiplicity of possible sources, many citations to judicial decisions include three or more references to alternative locations for the same decision.

Example 9: *Harris* v. *Commissioner*, 340 U.S. 106, 71 S.Ct. 181, 39 AFTR 1002, 1950-2 U.S. Tax Cas. PP 10,789 (1950), is a citation to but one case—that is, the case in which the taxpayer (Harris) was suing the IRS Commissioner. The same decision of the Supreme Court in this one case can be found in at least four different places, as follows:

1. On page 106 of the 340th volume of the *United States Reporter* series (published by the Government Printing Office); or
2. On page 181 of the 71st volume of the *Supreme Court Reporter* (published by West Publishing Company); or

TABLE 2-3
Tax Court Reporters

CITATION	COURT REPORTER REFERENCED	PUBLISHER
AFTR	American Federal Tax Reporter	Prentice-Hall, Inc.
AFTR 2d	American Federal Tax Reporter, 2nd series	Prentice-Hall, Inc.
USTC	United States Tax Cases	Commerce Clearing House
TC	United States Tax Court Reports	Government Printing Office
BTA	Board of Tax Appeals	Government Printing Office
U.S.	United States Supreme Court	Government Printing Office
S.Ct.	Supreme Court Reporter	West Publishing Co.
Ct.Cl.	Court of Claims Reporter	West Publishing Co.
Fed.	Federal Reporter	West Publishing Co.
F.2d	Federal Reporter, 2nd series	West Publishing Co.
F. Supp.	Federal Supplement	West Publishing Co.
P-H T.C.M.	(Tax Court) Memorandum Decisions	Prentice-Hall, Inc.
T.C.M.	Tax Court Memorandum Decisions	Commerce Clearing House

3. On page 1002 of the 39th volume of the *American Federal Tax Reporter* (published by Prentice-Hall, Inc.); or
4. At paragraph 10,786 of the second volume of the 1950 *United States Tax Cases* (published by Commerce Clearing House).

Both the first and second references are considered "official"; the latter two references are "secondary" sources. Except for the additional headnotes and other "extra" materials, all four citations should lead to exactly the same words of the Supreme Court.

The reason for giving more than one reference in a single citation is intended as a convenience to the reader. That is, the reader can locate (without going through a cross-reference table) the case cited in Example No. 9 if he or she has any one of the four court reporter series available. Table 2-3 lists the abbreviations used for the most common tax reporter series.

Your ability to recognize these abbreviations quickly and their association with the many bound volumes typically found in any tax library, can only be achieved with practice. If you are interested in doing tax research work beyond your text, you should take the time to look over as many of the judicial reporters as are available in your local library. There is, of course, no need to locate each of the reporter series since (as previously explained) many of them are duplicative of materials available in other sources.

Not every tax case will be found in each court reporter series. The following tabulation may help explain where most of the current overlap exists:

DECISIONS OF:	GENERALLY MAY BE FOUND IN:
U.S. Supreme Court	U.S., S.Ct., AFTR 2d, or USTC
Circuit Courts of Appeal	F.2d, AFTR 2d, or USTC
Claims Court	Ct. Cl., F.2d, AFTR 2d, or USTC
District Courts	F. Supp., AFTR 2d, or USTC
Tax Court	
Regular decisions	TC (only)
Memo decisions	P-H T.C.M. or T.C.M.

This means, of course, that a library which contains *both* the TC (i.e., the United States Tax Court Reports) and either (1) the AFTR 2d series (i.e., the American Federal Tax Reporter, Second Series, by Prentice-Hall, Inc.), *or* (2) the USTC series (i.e., the United States Tax Cases series by Commerce Clearing House) will contain virtually all of the cases of current interest, other than the Tax Court memorandum decisions.

LOCATING PERTINENT REFERENCES

As a practical matter the biggest problem in tax research very often is *not* the problem of locating a particular Code section, regulation, revenue ruling, or judicial decision, in a large library. Rather, the biggest problem is figuring out which Code section, regulation, revenue ruling, or judicial decision is even pertinent to your problem. In other words, exactly which of the many authorities really have anything to say about a particular problem? If someone will just tell you *what* to read, finding and reading that authority is not too terribly difficult a task.

Fortunately for the student and the tax advisor alike, numerous publishing companies have found it profitable to print and distribute various tax reference services that will help you locate pertinent authorities for many tax questions. These tax reference works vary from small paperbacks (that sell for $10 or less) to multi-volumed services (that sell for over $2,000 per year). Each of these services is prepared and updated in a unique way, which you can discover through trial and error, through reading descriptive materials distributed by the publisher, or through independent evaluations published in other works.[6] Two very popular and inexpensive tax reference works are the *Master Tax Guide*, published annually by Commerce Clearing House, and the *Federal Tax Handbook*, published annually by Prentice-Hall, Inc. Many instructors use these handy reference services as supplements to regularly published textbooks, both because they provide additional details not available and because they provide an easy cross-reference to additional materials available in the larger tax reference services prepared and sold by their respective publishers. Table 2-4 is a list of larger tax services that are widely

[6]For those interested in additional details about tax research and the related tax services, see Chapter 4, Ray M. Sommerfeld and G. Fred Streuling, *Tax Research Techniques*, 2d ed. AICPA Tax Study No. 5, (New York: American Institute of Certified Public Accountants, 1981).

TABLE 2-4
Major Tax Services

COMMON REFERENCE	FULL TITLE OF TAX SERVICE	PUBLISHER
BNA	Tax Management Portfolios	Bureau of National Affairs
CCH	Standard Federal Tax Reports	Commerce Clearing House
Mertens	Merten's Law of Federal Taxation	Callaghan & Co.
PH	Federal Taxes	Prentice-Hall, Inc.
RIA	Federal Tax Coordinator, 2d	Research Institute of America

used. In addition to these traditional printed tax services, at least three companies now make equivalent materials available through on-line computerized data bases. They are known as: (1) Westlaw, provided by West Publishing Co.; (2) Phinet, provided by Prentice-Hall; and (3) Lexus, provided by Meade Data Corporation.

Each of the printed tax services is a multivolumed service that costs several hundreds of dollars per year; the computerized services include sign-on fees plus time charges that also run to several hundred dollars per year. Each is prepared and arranged in a slightly different way. Nevertheless, regardless of which tax service you may use, and regardless of how you learn to use it, elementary tax research usually begins with a key-word index. It is up to you to figure out what that magic key word might be.

> **Example 10:** Suppose, for example, that you were trying to determine whether or not a $500 award that you had just won in a contest at your school had to be included in your taxable income for the year. You might go to the library, locate the key-word index for any of the tax services listed above, and look up words like—
>
> —Prizes
> —Awards
> —Scholarships
> —Gifts
>
> Each of those words should lead you to a part of tax service which discusses the statutory, administrative, and judicial authority which might be pertinent to your particular tax problem.

A key-word index will ordinarily lead a person to additional references to:

1. The Code (specific sections, subsections, or paragraphs);
2. Treasury regulations;
3. Revenue rulings; and/or
4. Court decisions.

Learning how to use a key-word index successfully takes a bit of practice, but with experience you can quickly learn how to do some elementary forms of tax research. Like any skill, learning how to complete more complex tax research assignments will require long hours of practice, but it can pay handsome dividends for those who find it to be a challenge.

In actual practice, tax research really consists of four separately identifiable skills or tasks. They are:

1. Correctly identifying all of the tax problems (or "issues") implicit in any given set of facts;
2. Locating all of the potential authority that may be needed to resolve the issues identified in step one;
3. Assessing the authorities located in step two and reaching a defensible solution; and
4. Communicating that solution to all interested parties.

This chapter is intended to introduce you to the information needed to carry out the second and third of these four tasks. Learning how to identify issues will become somewhat easier as you progress through the details found in each of the remaining chapters of this text. Improving communication skills is a lifelong process that is achieved with practice and hard work.

TAXPAYER COMPLIANCE AND ADMINISTRATIVE REVIEW

The federal income tax is a self-assessed tax. Every taxpayer has the responsibility for calculation of his or her tax liability, completion and submission of a return form, and payment of the tax. Once a return is filed, the IRS has the responsibility of reviewing and auditing returns. The purpose of this administrative review is to make sure that the tax is computed properly and that the correct tax is paid.

RESPONSIBILITIES OF TAXPAYERS

As stated above, the basic responsibilities of taxpayers are computation of their tax liability, completion and submission of the proper return form, and payment of the tax. The first of these duties is the complicated part. Completion of returns, filing, and payment are more simple procedures. Nevertheless, these duties are important and failure to comply with procedural requirements can result in financial penalties.

All individuals must make their tax computations on Form 1040EZ, Form 1040A, or Form 1040. (These forms are discussed in Chapter 3.) In many situations, one or more schedules accompanying Form 1040 must be filed, depending on the sources of the taxpayer's income and the nature of his or her deductions. Individual taxpayers are on a pay-as-you-go system through (*a*) withholding from wages and (*b*) payments of estimated taxes. A final payment (or refund) is made when the annual return is filed.

Annual returns of individuals are due on the fifteenth day of the fourth month following the end of the tax year. For calendar-year taxpayers, this means April 15. When the due date of any return (or other prescribed act) falls on a Saturday, Sunday, or legal holiday, the due date is the following work day.[7] Also, a return is filed on time by mail if it is postmarked on the due date. The taxpayer may obtain an automatic extension of four months

FORM 4868 by filing Form 4868 on or before the due date of the return and paying at least 90% of the tax due with the extension. Further extensions for rea-

FORM 2688 sonable cause may be obtained by filing Form 2688; however, these extensions should be filed in time for approval by the IRS.

PENALTIES AND INTEREST

The Internal Revenue Code includes a number of penalties intended to encourage taxpayers to file a timely and accurate return and to pay their tax. The more important penalties are:

1. *Failure to file annual returns*. If the taxpayer fails to file a timely return, 5% of the net tax liability is added for each month or part of a month the return is delayed, up to a maximum of 25%. This penalty is not imposed if the taxpayer's failure to file is for a reasonable cause.
2. *Failure to pay tax*. If the taxpayer fails to pay his or her tax on time, interest is added to the tax. The interest runs from the due date of the return without considering extension of time for filing. The interest rate utilized by the IRS is adjusted twice annually on each January 1 and July 1 based on the average prime rate for a prior 6-month period. Interest calculations are made on a daily compounding method.

   In addition to interest, the statute provides a penalty of one-half of 1% per month (or part thereof) for any underpayment. Note that the additional one-half of 1% is a *penalty, not interest*; therefore it is not deductible on subsequent returns. The penalty is not imposed if the taxpayer can show that the underpayment was for a reasonable cause and was not willful neglect.
3. *Deficiencies in tax paid*. If the tax computation is incorrect and the tax payment is less than the tax owed, a penalty of 5% of the understatement is added to the tax where the deficiency is due to negligence. If the deficiency is due to willful negligence or fraud, a penalty of 50% of the deficiency is added to the tax. When the fraud penalty is imposed, the penalty for failure to file and the 5% penalty for negligence are not imposed.

   There is also a 10% penalty for any "substantial underpayment" of tax liability. For individual taxpayers, a substantial underpayment is deemed to exist if the understatement of the tax liability is *the greater of* (*a*) 10% of the correct tax or (*b*) $5,000. In determining

[7] Sec. 7503 and Reg. 301.7503-1(a).

whether or not a substantial underpayment exists, the taxpayer may exclude any item for which either (*a*) there was "substantial authority" (for the position taken by the taxpayer) *or* (*b*) the taxpayer adequately disclosed his or her questionable position.[8] Substantial authority includes the Code, Treasury regulations, judicial decisions, published revenue rulings, and revenue procedures, as well as Congressional intent revealed in committee reports. It does not include private letter rulings. Adequate disclosure ordinarily takes the form of a statement attached to the tax return in which the taxpayer—

a) identifies the statement as one of disclosure under Sec. 6661;
b) identifies the item with respect to which the disclosure is being made;
c) states the amount of the item; and
d) reveals the facts with sufficient detail to allow the IRS (if it reviews the disclosure) to determine the nature of controversy over the questionable tax treatment.[9]

4) *Criminal penalties*. The *willful* failure to pay tax, make a return, or keep adequate records; the willful attempt to evade or defeat the tax; and the willful attempt to make and subscribe to a false return, are criminal acts, misdemeanors or felonies. Fines of up to $10,000, and imprisonment of up to five years, are the punishment for these criminal acts.

The criminal penalties are imposed only after the taxpayer is found guilty in criminal proceedings. The other penalties, however, are imposed by the IRS. The assessment of penalties by the IRS is subject to administrative and judicial review.

This list of penalties is by no means complete. Penalties for underpayment of estimated taxes, for failure to file information returns, and for numerous other acts or failures to act are all aimed at improving the equitable administration of our tax laws. For example, "protesters" who file false statements with respect to withholdings can be penalized $500 for each false statement. They may be punished even more severely by being sentenced to a year of imprisonment. Another penalty is based on the overevaluation of property, for example, a contribution deduction based on a grossly inflated fair market value. The penalty can be as high as 30% of the resulting understatement of the tax.

ROLE OF THE TAX EXPERT

The preceding list of taxpayers' responsibilities leads to an obvious conclusion—many taxpayers are unable to fulfill their duties personally. Rules governing unusual or complex transactions are often beyond the

[8]Adequate disclosure is *not* an adequate defense in the case of "tax-shelter items." A tax shelter is defined as any entity, plan or arrangement which has tax avoidance or evasion as its principal purpose.

[9]Rev. Proc. 83-21 and Prop. Reg. Sec. 1.661-4.

scope of the average citizen's knowledge. Many taxpayers are unable to comprehend the instructions on the return forms. And certainly a taxpayer with a high income will do everything possible to reduce tax liability. For all these reasons, there exists, predictably, a group of specialists or experts willing to assist a taxpayer for a fee.

The number of tax experts offering their services to the public probably exceeds 200,000. Unfortunately, no comprehensive system of regulation exists to assure that persons engaged in tax practice meet reasonable standards of competence. In the past, the only regulation of tax practice has come from the Treasury Department. The department issues Treasury cards to practitioners, which entitle them to represent taxpayers before the IRS. Licensed lawyers and Certified Public Accountants can practice before the IRS without a Treasury card; other individuals must pass an IRS exam in order to obtain a Treasury card. In general, the groups in our society best qualified to give taxpayers advice on tax matters are licensed attorneys and accountants. Yet they are in the minority when it comes to the number of "tax experts" advising taxpayers. This fact raises a serious question. What training and qualifications do the unlicensed "experts" have?

Beyond a doubt, many people who present themselves to the public as tax practitioners have little or no expertise in tax matters. For the most part, state laws are silent on who may engage in tax practice. And, while practitioners holding Treasury cards must observe the provisions of Treasury Circular 230, those practitioners without Treasury cards have no similar restrictions on their activities. They are free to advertise, to represent themselves as "experts," and to make any sort of arrangement regarding fees. It is all too common for a practitioner to rent a vacant building during tax season, engage in extensive advertising, charge a fee based on the "refund" obtained, and then close shop before the IRS has an opportunity to review the returns filed. As an advertising gimmick, some practitioners "guarantee" their returns, promising to pay deficiencies assessed on the returns they prepare. Normally such a guarantee is worthless. A few regulated practitioners are not above doubt either: they look on tax practice as just another business, paying maximum attention to efficient return preparation and minimum attention to equitable administration of the law. In general, CPAs engaged in tax practice will attempt to administer the law fairly and at the same time, take a position of client advocacy when the interpretation of a tax law is not completely clear. In summary, the degree of independence expected of a CPA on an audit engagement is significantly greater than it is on a tax engagement. Furthermore, no one expects the audited financial statements to simply duplicate tax return figures.

The Treasury Department does have some power to ensure that all individuals involved in the preparation of tax returns for remuneration observe nominal rules of conduct. These rules are not necessarily directed at attorneys and licensed accountants, because most of the actions proscribed by the law are also condemned by the standard rules of professional conduct that knowledgeable practitioners routinely observe. For example, the rules make it a misdemeanor, subject to a $1,000 fine and/or imprisonment up to one year, for the unauthorized disclosure of information obtained during the preparation of a return. However, the practitioner can—(and often must)—disclose information to IRS agents and to related taxpayers under certain conditions. The rules also assess civil penalties ranging from $5 up to $500 for each wrongful act related to the preparation of returns. Acts that result in a penalty are (*a*) failure to sign a return as preparer or failure to provide the preparer's identification number, (*b*) failure to retain copies of returns filed for a three-year-period, (*c*) failure to provide the IRS with certain information about employees who prepare returns, (*d*) failure of the preparer to provide the taxpayer with a copy of his or her return, (*e*) understatement of the tax liability due to negligent or intentional disregard for the tax laws, (*f*) endorsement or negotiation of any check issued to the taxpayer. Observe that these penalties do not give the Treasury powers to improve the technical qualifications of return preparers. The criminal and civil penalties only increase the risks for the unscrupulous or uninformed preparer.

The tax law is indeed complex. Many taxpayers will need professional assistance in fulfilling their responsibilities and, incidentally, in minimizing their tax liability. However, in view of the preceding facts, the taxpayer should be cautious when seeking "expert" assistance. Those who advertise their status as experts may be the least qualified, because those with minimal professional qualifications may be forbidden by their professions from claiming such status. Recently, some state bar associations have allowed lawyers specializing in tax matters to identify themselves in advertisements. In addition, the American Institute of Certified Public Accountants made a change in 1978 in its code of ethics that permits limited advertising by CPAs. Under the new rules, members can advertise the firm name and members, services offered, fees charged, and general information about qualifications. The new rule prohibits self-laudatory statements, invidious comparisons with other professionals, and testimonials or endorsements. While CPAs cannot list the "24 reasons" why they should file your return, they can get their names before the public. Despite limited advertising by lawyers and accountants, it remains true that those experts who make public pronouncements about their expertise are generally the least qualified to give taxpayers assistance.

REVIEW BY THE INTERNAL REVENUE SERVICE

Taxpayers file their returns at an IRS regional service center. The United States is divided into ten "regions" and there is a service center in each one. These centers utilize data-processing equipment in handling returns. The United States is also divided into 63 "districts." In recent years the mechanical processing of returns has been shifted from district offices to service centers. Personnel in the district offices, however, still perform most of the important review work.

AUDITING PROCEDURES All returns received by the IRS are checked for mechanical accuracy, which includes the following:

1. Arithmetic, including computation of tax.
2. Transfer of amounts from supporting schedules to return.
3. Matching information returns filed with the income reported on the return. For example, the employer submits a copy of each employee's Form W-2 (withholding) to the IRS. The IRS also receives a veritable mountain of Forms 1099 showing the amounts of interest paid to taxpayers by financial institutions, the dividends paid to shareholders by corporations, and certain other payments. Because of budgetary constraints, the IRS has never matched all information returns to the relevant tax returns. Congress has exerted constant pressure on the IRS to make use of the information returns. As a result, the IRS expects to match up all returns within the next few years.

FORM 1099

The service centers, using automated equipment, do most of this mechanical work. If a mechanical error that results in an understatement of tax is discovered, a bill for the deficiency is sent to the taxpayer. If an error has resulted in an overpayment, the excess payment is credited to the taxpayer or refunded.

In addition to the mechanical processing just described, the computers are programmed to select certain returns for futher examination. Using multiple linear discriminant analysis, the program selects those returns that, upon audit, are most likely to yield additional taxes. In addition, certain returns are automatically tagged for examination based on arbitrary criteria such as large refunds and reported income in excess of a certain amount. Finally, the computer makes a random selection of returns for examination. These returns are used in a "compliance program," where the error rate on the sample selected is used to infer statistically the error rate on all returns. The number of returns selected for examination varies from year to year based mainly on the personnel available to conduct audits.

The returns selected for audit by the service centers are forwarded to the appropriate district office. There, the returns eventually are assigned to revenue agents for audit. This examination may be an "office audit" or a "field audit." For the office audit, the taxpayer is notified of the items under examination and is requested to bring to the district office the necessary records and supporting documents. For taxpayers with extensive records, the agents go to the taxpayer's place of business to perform a field audit.

Upon completion of an examination, normally the agent confers with the taxpayer about his or her findings. In some cases the agent communicates the findings to the taxpayer by letter. The smart taxpayer will have expert help during conversations with an agent if material amounts are involved. Technically, only practitioners with Treasury cards, lawyers, and Certified Public Accountants can represent taxpayers; most agents, however, are willing to work with the preparer—(or advisor to the taxpayer)—

even if that person does not have a Treasury card or is not a lawyer or a certified public accountant.

This contact between taxpayers and the examining agents can have any one of three results:

1. The agent may find that the return, as filed, is correct. In this event, the findings of the agent are reviewed by an audit division supervisor and, if the reviewer agrees with the findings, the audit is finished.
2. The agent may propose adjustments, which normally increase the tax, and the taxpayer may agree. The agent then makes an assessment of the deficiency on Form 870. After review of the findings by the supervisory staff, the taxpayer signs Form 870 and pays the deficiency. The payment normally closes the return, which means that no subsequent adjustments are made to the tax for that year. In a few cases the adjustments may result in a refund to the taxpayer.
3. The agent may propose adjustments resulting in a deficiency and the taxpayer may disagree. When no agreement is reached between the agent and the taxpayer, the taxpayer may either demand a second-level conference in the regional IRS office, or move directly to obtain judicial review. These alternatives are explained later. The auditing process in the IRS is depicted in Figure 2-1.

FORM 870

Taxpayers experiencing their first tax return examination often become apprehensive when they are notified of the impending audit. Undoubtedly some have visions of a merciless inquisition that finally wrings out the last possible tax dollar. Taxpayers with this mistaken notion are sometimes surprised to find that the agents are reasonable persons who are trying to administer a complex law fairly. Only taxpayers guilty of fraud or gross negligence have anything to fear. This does not necessarily mean that the taxpayer will win his or her case. One serious criticism of the tax process at the audit level is the lack of training and expertise of many agents. This criticism is more frequently valid for IRS personnel who conduct office audits. Because of lower pay and a somewhat limited opportunity for advancement within the IRS, the better graduates from strong accounting and law programs in colleges and universities very often opt for careers in public practice or industry.

When the taxpayer refuses to agree to the agent's proposed adjustments, the agent prepares a complete report of the findings, which is submitted to the review staff in the district office. After review (and changes, if required), the report on the examination is mailed to the taxpayer. The cover letter, called the "30-day letter," notifies the taxpayer of the proposed deficiency and normally gives the taxpayer a 30-day period in which to decide on a course of action. Three avenues are open to the taxpayer at this point:

30-DAY LETTER

1. Taxpayer may accept the examiner's findings, sign Form 870, and close the case.

FIGURE 2-1
Income-Tax Audit Procedure of the Internal Revenue Service

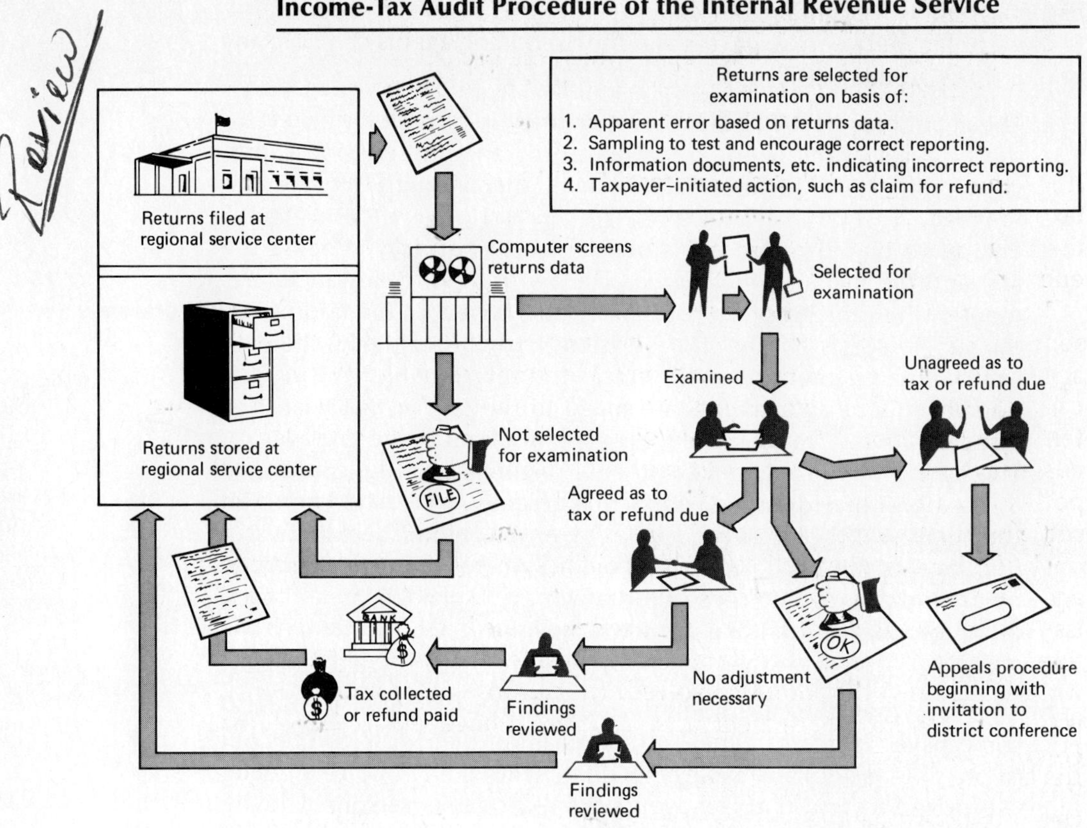

2. Taxpayer may request a conference with the appeals office. The conferees in this office are organized under the chief counsel's office, and have broad powers to settle disputes with taxpayers as explained below.
3. Taxpayer may ignore the 30-day letter and wait for the formal deficiency notice, called the "90-day letter." On receipt of the 90-day letter, the taxpayer either must pay the deficiency or take the case to the courts.

90-DAY LETTER

THE APPEALS CONFERENCE The right of appeal to the appeals office is automatic upon receipt of the 30-day letter. Where the amount of the deficiency is more than $2,500, the taxpayer must file a written protest before the conference. No specific form for the protest is dictated; however, it must include certain elements:

1. A statement that the taxpayer wishes to appeal the assessment.
2. The taxpayer's name and address.
3. The date and symbols of the 30-day letter and the finding that is being protested.
4. The tax year or years involved.

5. An itemized schedule of disputed adjustments.
6. A statement supporting facts in contested factual issues.
7. Arguments and authorities upon which the protest is based.
8. A declaration, signed by the taxpayer, that he or she believes, under penalty of perjury, that facts stated are "true, correct, and complete."

It is generally agreed that the protest should include all issues that the taxpayer intends to raise during the conference. While no rule prohibits the taxpayer from raising new issues, surprise moves during the conference are rarely effective.

The appeals conference is informal. If the taxpayer is being represented by a CPA or lawyer, which is the common practice, the taxpayer's agent must present a power of attorney. The points of departure are typically detailed in the revenue agent's report (RAR) and the taxpayer's protest, if one is filed. The factual and/or legal points at issue are then discussed. The conferees have broad powers of settlement, including the power to compromise an issue based on the hazards of litigation. The settlement authority, however, depends upon whether the case is "non-docketed" or "docketed." Non-docketed cases are those that reach the appeals office before the statutory notice of deficiency (90-day letter) is issued. For non-docketed cases, the appeals office has exclusive jurisdiction. The conferees are required to consider the hazards of litigation without regard to the amount involved. The purpose of the appeals office is to keep disputes out of the courts. If the law is uncertain, the appellate conferees welcome offers to compromise the issues and will themselves make such offers. However, offers of 20% or less of the proposed deficiency generally will be ignored because the conferees are instructed not to accept offers that have only nuisance value. After the conference, agreements reached—if any—are reviewed by the head of the appeals office in the regional office. If, upon review, the settlement is not acceptable, the taxpayer generally is given an opportunity to hold another conference with the reviewer. If agreement is reached, Form 870-AD is completed and the case, for all practical purposes, is closed. If no agreement is reached, the 90-day letter is then issued. **RAR**

Docketed cases are those where the 90-day letter has already been issued and the taxpayer has filed a petition in the Tax Court. Each petition filed is given a docket number and the case formally becomes the responsibility of the regional counsel and is assigned to an attorney who represents the Justice Department but works at the regional office of the IRS. In the period after a case is docketed but before a date for trial is set, settlement authority is effectively shared by the appeals office and the regional counsel, although the latter formally has the final jurisdiction. Thus, the docketed case is referred to the appeals office and an effort is made to reach a compromise. This is generally true even though the same dispute may have already been handled in an appeals conference. At this point, maximum pressure is on both the government and the taxpayer to reach a settlement, since typically, neither wants to incur the bother and costs of court proceedings.

Taxpayers who permit their disputes to reach the docketed status are very often gambling that the regional counsel will take a more cautious stance relative to the hazards of litigation than that taken by the appeals office. After all, some attorney in the regional counsel office must consider the actual trial. On the other hand, any offer previously made by the appeals office before the case is docketed is no longer in effect. The taxpayer may find the regional counsel has a more optimistic outlook. In that case, the taxpayer will be forced to accept a reduced offer, to capitulate entirely, or to go to trial.

After a case is set for trial, settlement authority rests solely with the regional counsel. From this point on, most CPAs can play only an advisory role. Direct negotiations with government counsel by an accountant would generally be construed as the practice of law.[10]

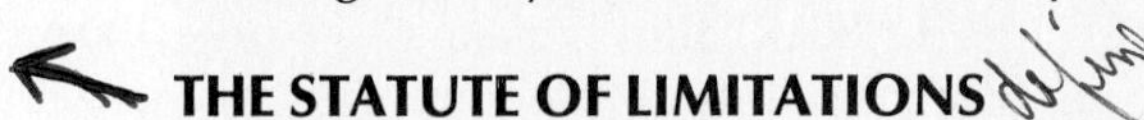

THE STATUTE OF LIMITATIONS

If the IRS wants to assess a tax deficiency, or if a taxpayer wants to file a claim for a refund, that action must be undertaken before the statute of limitations has expired. Old claims can not be prosecuted beyond an arbitrary time period established by the statute of limitations. For most IRS assessments, the general statute of limitations is three years after the due date for an income tax return.[11] The general rule is extended from three to six years, however, if a taxpayer omits one or more items of gross income which in the aggregate exceeds 25% of the gross income reported on the return.[12]

Example 11: Mary Baker filed her 1984 income tax return on April 4, 1985. On this return Mary reported gross income of $20,000. Due to simple oversight, Mary failed to report a bonus of $500 paid to her by her employer. Assuming there were no additional errors on Mary's return, the IRS must assess any deficiency for her underpayment of taxes before April 15, 1988.

Example 12: Tom Shield filed his 1984 income tax return on April 10, 1985. On his return Tom reported gross income of $10,000. Due to an inadvertent error, Tom failed to report interest income of $3,000. The IRS may assess a deficiency against Tom any time prior to April 15, 1991.

If a taxpayer files a fradulent return, or files no return, there is no statute of limitations.[13] This means, of course, that the IRS is free to file a deficiency assessment at any time.

---

[10] A few CPAs, who are not also licensed attorneys, have passed a special examination which specifically authorizes them to practice before the Tax Court.

[11] Sec. 6501(a).

[12] Sec. 6501(e).

[13] Sec. 6501(c).

Taxpayers who overpay their federal income tax generally must file any claim for refund "within three years from the time the return was filed or two years from the time the tax was paid, whichever of such periods expires the later, or if no return was filed by the taxpayer, within two years from the time the tax was paid."[14] Longer periods for refunds exist if the claim relates to bad debts or worthless securities;[15] net operating losses or capital-loss carrybacks;[16] foreign tax credits;[17] and certain other items.

Example 13: Rosa Delgado filed her 1984 income tax return and paid her net tax liability for 1984 on April 15, 1985. Due to an oversight, Rosa failed to claim a $500 travel expense deduction on her return. Rosa must file any claim for a refund by April 15, 1988.

CALCULATING THE ODDS

While the preceding discussion refers to the taxpayer as the active participant, wise taxpayers usually seek professional help in resolving disagreements with the IRS. Indeed, most practitioners will advise their clients not to attend appeals proceedings or to file large refund claims unless they are knowledgeable in tax matters. Representation at conferences by skilled professionals, and filing lengthy documents, costs money. As a result, the betting odds favor the taxpayer with a relatively large amount in dispute because of three factors. First, the *absolute* amount that can be gained from the settlement is greater. Second, the cost of professional representation will increase as the amount in dispute increases, but less than proportionally. Third, the fees paid for professional help are income tax deductions, and the after-tax cost of these services declines relatively as the taxpayer's marginal tax rate increases.

Some simple arithmetic will illustrate the point. Take the situation of two taxpayers, A and B, who are considering the wisdom of hiring a professional to represent them at an appellate conference. Relevant factors are:

	A	B
Amount of tax in dispute	$6,000	$100,000
Accountant's fee for preparing protest and handling conference	$2,000	$ 8,000
Marginal tax rate	25%	50%
After-tax cost of professional service	$1,500	$ 4,000
Estimated probability of winning	50%	50%

Taxpayer A is faced with a $1,500 net cost to gain $6,000, odds of 3 to 1. B, on the other hand, is betting $4,000 to gain $100,000, odds of 24 to 1.

[14] Sec. 6511(a).

[15] Sec. 6511(d)(1).

[16] Sec. 6511(d)(2).

[17] Sec. 6511(e)(3).

Before turning to judicial consideration of tax conflicts, we should note that the tax process has many procedures to protect the rights of taxpayers. First, the law is enacted by elected officials. Before enactment, individual taxpayers and special interest groups are given an opportunity to express their opinions of the proposals at the congressional committee hearings. After enactment, the Administration must set out its interpretation of the law in regulations. Proposed regulations are circulated to interested parties before final adoption. The IRS makes numerous rulings that help taxpayers assess the impact of the income tax on their financial affairs. After the taxpayer files a return, proposed adjustments to the tax calculation are considered carefully in conferences with agents and conferees. Finally, the conflict is considered by the appeals office, whose primary function is settlement of conflicts.

This lengthy process can hardly be termed arbitrary. The government cannot be said to "run roughshod" over the taxpayer. Indeed, a fairer criticism of the process might be that it is too cumbersome, that too much time and effort are spent on safeguarding property rights. In any event, taxpayers who cannot reach an agreement with the IRS may take their cases to the courts. Through appeals, each taxpayer may insist on the protection of his or her rights until a decision has been rendered by a circuit court of appeals or, possibly, the Supreme Court.

JUDICIAL REVIEW

As explained earlier in this chapter, three avenues for judicial review are open to taxpayers. The taxpayer may have his or her case heard first by the Tax Court, a U.S. district court, or the Claims Court. Since the popular alternative is the Tax Court, we will consider it first.

THE TAX COURT ROUTE

Taxpayers who do not reach an agreement with the appeals office receive a 90-day letter, which is their formal deficiency notice. The letter gives the taxpayer a 90-day period within which to file a petition with the Tax Court. If a petition is not filed, the IRS will assess the additional tax and, if the taxpayer fails to pay, will take legal steps to force payment.

If a petition is filed, the conflict will be heard by the Tax Court. This court is specially organized to hear tax cases and is completely independent of the IRS. The 19 judges are appointed to the Tax Court for a 15-year term by the President. Although the Tax Court has its headquarters in Washington, D.C., sessions are held at various times in all major cities, and the taxpayer may request a hearing in his or her general area.

In the Tax Court taxpayers may represent themselves or be represented by counsel. Generally, only attorneys are admitted to practice before the Tax Court, although some CPAs have been granted this right by examination. At the hearing, depositions of witnesses and oral and written arguments of the parties are presented to the Court. There is no jury. The Court arrives at its decision and writes up its findings in an opinion.

The Tax Court also has a small claims division to handle disputes when the amount in contest does not exceed $10,000. Hearings are not before judges but before commissioners appointed by the chief judge of the Tax Court. In the small claims division, formal rules of evidence need not be followed; the Tax Court can prescribe rules of evidence it deems appropriate. The findings of the commissioner are not reported in formal written opinions and the opinions cannot be cited as precedent in other cases. Finally, the decisions in small claims cases cannot be appealed to a higher court—the decision is final for both parties.

Throughout this review process, the taxpayer must take the initiative. He or she must ask for the conferences with the IRS and for the hearing before the Tax Court. In all conferences and hearings the determination of the IRS is presumed to be correct. The taxpayer must carry the burden of proving that any proposed adjustments are incorrect. The decision of the Tax Court, however, may be disputed by either party. If the decision goes against the government, the Justice Department may appeal. Taxpayers also have the right to appeal. (Decisions in the small claims division cannot be appealed by either party.)

Appeals from decisions of the Tax Court are made to one of the Circuit Courts of Appeals. There are 13 Courts of Appeals in the country. Here, again, oral and written arguments are presented by the parties, and a decision is reached by the court. The final appeal is, of course, to the U.S. Supreme Court. Either party to the dispute may ask the court to consider the case by asking for a writ of certiorari. The Supreme Court normally will hear cases only when two or more Courts of Appeals have reached different conclusions on the same issue or where, in the Court's opinion, the constitutionality of tax law is questionable.

If the Tax Court route is selected, throughout the lengthy process of administrative and judicial review, the taxpayer is *not* assessed for the deficiency until the review process is complete. The taxpayer pays the tax according to *his* or *her* computation; additional assessments are made only at the end of the review process. The taxpayer is required, however, to pay interest on any eventual deficiencies. Interest runs from the due date of the return.[18] In addition, other penalties may also be assessed.

THE DISTRICT COURT ROUTE

To avoid a hearing before the Tax Court, the taxpayer merely pays the proposed deficiency at any point in the process before the petition to the Tax Court. He or she may then file a claim for refund of the deficiency paid.

The claim for refund sets in motion the administrative review procedures previously discussed. Thus, the claim is reconsidered by the district

[18]These interest charges can be avoided as explained in footnote 5, p. 1/11.

office. If the claim is denied, as it normally will be, a 30-day letter is sent, which may lead to an Appeals office conference. If no agreement is reached in this conference, the refund claim is denied by the IRS. When a claim for refund is denied, the taxpayer has a statutory right to sue the government for the tax illegally (in the eyes of the taxpayer) assessed and collected.

Most suits to force a refund are brought in U.S. district courts. In this court, the taxpayer must be represented by an attorney. A jury of peers may be used to determine the facts. The judge of a district court, however, decides the law. Once a decision is reached in this court, either party may ask for an appeal to the appropriate Circuit Court of Appeals. The decision of the Appeals Court may, in turn, be appealed to the Supreme Court.

THE CLAIMS COURT ROUTE

The taxpayer may also take a refund suit to the Claims Court in Washington. As noted earlier, this court specializes in claims against the government. The court is composed of a chief judge and four associate judges appointed by the President. Most of the hearings, however, are heard by fifteen commissioners who report their findings to the judges, who then agree or disagree with their findings. Decisions of this court are appealed to the Court of Appeals for the Federal Circuit and, finally, to the Supreme Court.

The procedures for administrative and judicial review of conflicts are briefly summarized in Figure 2-2. Note that agreement may be reached at any step in the process. Even after the petition is filed with the Tax Court, or a suit is filed in a district court or the Claims Court, conferences between the government and the taxpayer are frequent and agreement may be reached at any time.

HOW THE IRS PLAYS THE JUDICIAL GAME

The person not initiated into the subtleties of the tax process would logically assume that if a court reaches a decision and the loser does not appeal that decision, then that decision can be relied on safely by other taxpayers. For example, if a taxpayer wins a fight with the IRS in the Tax Court, and the IRS does not appeal the Tax Court decision, then other taxpayers with the same facts might logically conclude that they could rely on the court's opinion. Unfortunately, while logical, the game is played using more complicated rules.

When the IRS loses in the Tax Court, it may follow any one of four alternative procedures. First, it can appeal the decision as discussed earlier. This appeal is a clear signal that the IRS does not agree with the Tax Court's conclusions. Second, the General Counsel for the IRS may announce an "acquiescence," which lets everyone know that the IRS will follow the decision in other situations with the same facts. Third, the IRS may announce a "non-acquiescence," a clear signal that it will not follow the decision, even though it may not choose to appeal it. Finally, it may

FIGURE 2-2
Income-Tax Appeal Procedure of the Internal Revenue Service

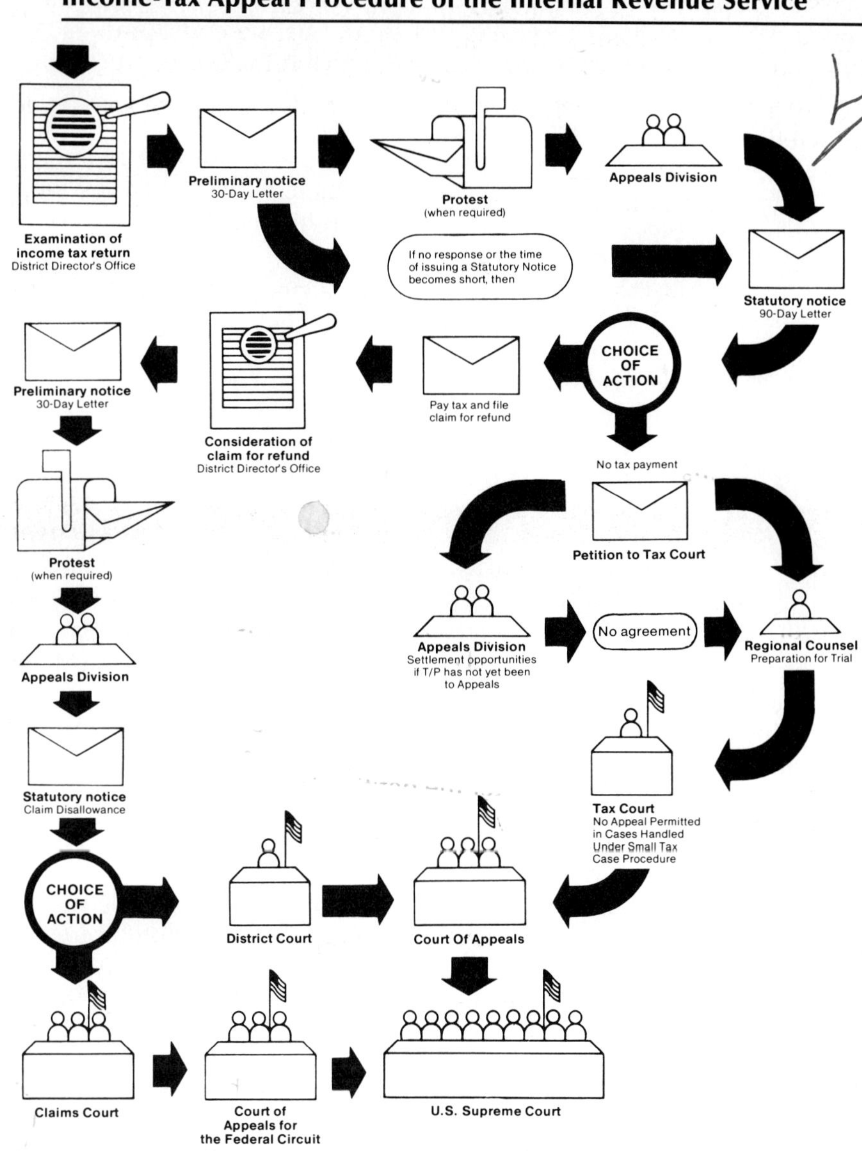

remain silent, in which case we do not know what it will do in similar situations.

For decisions reached by district courts and by the Claims Court, the IRS has two courses of action: either an appeal to the appropriate court or silence. Silence, however, cannot be interpreted as acquiescence. As with Tax Court decisions, silence may signify either agreement or disagreement. Taxpayers and their advisors may rely on a decision of a district court or the Claims Court, but this does not mean that the IRS will not attempt to enforce a rule of law contrary to an earlier decision that was adverse to the IRS position.

What happens if the IRS has appealed a Tax Court or district court decision and has lost again? Logically, this should be the end of the matter. But, again, logic goes for naught. The IRS, like the Tax Court, must follow decisions of the Circuit Courts of Appeals, but *only* in that particular circuit. Often the government will apply a contrary rule in the jurisdiction of other circuit courts. The government's intention is to obtain a conflicting ruling in another circuit. Given a conflict of opinion between two or more Circuit Courts of Appeals, the case *may* then be heard by the Supreme Court and the question finally resolved.

The process just described seems at first glance unfair and wasteful. However, we must remember the extraordinary measures taxpayers take to reduce their taxes and the enormous stakes involved in the annual contest. Remember also that the IRS is charged with the role of protecting the revenues by enforcing the laws passed by Congress. That the government occasionally persists beyond reason to enforce the law, based solely upon *its* interpretation, is a natural result of the process.

Despite the criticisms of the compliance process noted in this chapter, the overall process is a relatively fair one, in which citizens are safeguarded against arbitrary administration and confiscation. Maintenance of a fair, equitable process is essential if the income tax law is to play the vital role assigned to it in our political and economic system. Nevertheless, we must note in passing that it is a complicated process involving many people, including many with a sizable vested interest in the process as it now exists. As a result, tax reforms—changes in the process—are not easily made.

SOME STATISTICS ON THE TAX PROCESS

The process described above is a complicated one. To place the various steps in proper perspective for the student, it might be helpful to review some statistics on how well the taxpayer does relative to the government in the taxpaying process. The statistics are restricted to the administrative and judicial review.[19] How the taxpayer fares in the legislative process cannot be reduced to neat numbers.

In 1983 approximately 100 million income tax returns were filed, including about 95 million individual returns. Of the 100 million returns filed in 1983, the IRS examined about 1.7 million, mostly in the district offices. Usually, about 2% of the individual returns are examined (compared with about 7% of the corporate returns). In recent years the number of returns examined has been decreasing slightly. However, because of inflation and improved techniques for selecting returns, the total addi-

[19]*Annual Report of the Commissioner of the Internal Revenue Service* (Washington, D.C.: U.S. Government Printing Office, 1983), and *Annual Report of Chief Counsel for the Internal Revenue Service* (Washington, D.C.: U.S. Government Printing Office, 1983).

tional assessments resulting from the audits have increased. For 1983, recommended additional taxes and penalties totaled $13.7 billion, an increase of $2.0 billion over 1982.

The vast majority of all disputes are settled at the audit level. In 1983, of the 1.7 million returns audited, which resulted in additional assessments and penalties of $13.7 billion, over 1.5 million disputes were settled at the audit level. In a typical year taxpayers eventually pay about 50% of original assessments for additional taxes and penalties. This percent varies significantly, however, at different levels of income. Unfortunately, the settlement ratio is disproportionately high at the low end of the income scale. This could be due to poor representation on behalf of the low-income taxpayer; a realization that it does not "pay" to dispute small amounts of tax; an unreasonable attitude of agents in small cases; or any of several other factors.

During 1983 the IRS completed 5,785 investigations of criminal violations of the tax laws and recommended prosecution in 2,610 of those cases. Of the 1,646 taxpayers sentenced during the year, 64% received prison sentences.

The number of litigated decisions is very small relative to disputes settled in the administrative review procedures. On the other hand, the backlog of cases related to the federal tax laws in the Tax Court alone increased from 53,440 to 57,869 during the year. That amounts to a sizable body of "new" law still to be revealed and underscores the point that taxation is a human process, never static, but always in a state of flux.

In Chapter 2 we have touched the surface of some rather complex subjects. It is hoped that many students will be sufficiently stimulated by this brief introduction to make a more exhaustive examination of tax research and practice at some future time.

KEY POINTS TO REMEMBER

1. The statutory law in federal income taxation today is the Internal Revenue Code of 1954, as amended.
2. For most purposes, when referring to statutory tax law, it is adequate to refer only to sections and lower subdivisions of the Code; e.g., Sec. 453 or Sec. 453B(a)(1).
3. The "intent of Congress" concerning income tax legislation may be found in the various committee reports that accompany a bill on its way through Congress. The most important of these are the Report of the Committee on Ways and Means, the Report of the Senate Finance Committee, and the Report of the Conference Committee. Occasionally the *Congressional Record* may also contain important references to Congressional intent.
4. The words of the Code are constantly subject to both administrative and judicial interpretation.

5. The most authoritative administrative interpretations of the Code are known as Treasury regulations.
6. The most authoritative judicial interpretations of the Code are those rendered by the Supreme Court.
7. The only court that may involve a jury trial in an income tax dispute is the federal district court.
8. Although a citation to a single judicial authority may include multiple references, it is unnecessary to locate and read more than one of the multiple citations because they duplicate one another as far as the primary judicial authority is concerned.

SELF-STUDY QUESTIONS

1. Fred Wright filed his 1984 income tax return on March 15, 1985, showing gross income of $20,000. He had mistakenly omitted $6,000 of income which, in good faith, he considered nontaxable. By what date must the Internal Revenue Service assert a notice of deficiency?
   a) March 15, 1988
   b) April 15, 1988
   c) March 15, 1991
   d) April 15, 1991

   (AICPA adapted)
2. Ronald Raff filed his 1984 individual income tax return on January 15, 1985. There was no understatement of income on the return, and the return was properly signed and filed. The statute of limitations for Raff's 1984 return expires on
   a) January 15, 1988
   b) April 15, 1988
   c) January 15, 1991
   d) April 15, 1991

   (AICPA adapted)
3. When a CPA prepares a federal income tax return for an audit client, one would expect
   a) the CPA to take a position of client advocacy;
   b) the CPA to take a position of independent neutrality;
   c) the taxable net income in the audited financial statements to agree with taxable net income in the federal income tax return;
   d) the expenses in the audited financial statements to agree with the deductions in the federal income tax return.

   (AICPA adapted)

4. Which one of the following citations refers directly to part of the Internal Revenue Code of 1954, as amended?
   a) Reg. Sec. 1.482-3(a)
   b) Sec. 302(b)(2)
   c) Rev. Rul. 85-19, 1985-1 C.B. 34
   d) 31 U.S. 610
5. Which one of the following citations refers directly to a decision of the Supreme Court?
   a) Reg. Sec. 1.482-3(a)
   b) Sec. 302(b)(2)
   c) Rev. Rul. 85-19, 1985-1 C.B. 34
   d) 31 U.S. 610
6. Which one of the following citations could *not* refer to a decision of the Fourth Circuit Court of Appeals?
   a) 29 F.2d 401
   b) 17 T.C. 882
   c) 50 USTC 349
   d) 11 AFTR 2d 290
7. Which one of the following four courts is solely a court of appellate jurisdiction?
   a) Circuit Court
   b) Claims Court
   c) District Court
   d) Tax Court
8. Assume that you located the following four authorities in a tax service that each support a position you desired to take on your own tax return. Which of these four authorities would carry the *least* weight in any dispute that you might later have with an IRS agent?
   a) a part of the Code
   b) a Treasury regulation
   c) a Circuit Court decision
   d) a private letter ruling
9. Most genuine audits of taxpayers' returns are performed by personnel assigned to the
   a) Chief Counsel's Office
   b) District Director's Office
   c) IRS Service Center
   d) Tax Court

10. Approximately what percentage of all income tax returns filed are actually audited by the IRS?
    a) 2%
    b) 20%
    c) 60%
    d) 98%

QUESTIONS

1. How many Internal Revenue Codes have been enacted by the Congress? Which Code is in effect today?
2. In reading a tax article you note the two following references. Explain briefly what each means.
    a) Reg. Sec. 1.101-2(b)(2).
    b) Rev. Rul. 68-10, 1968-1 C.B. 18.
3. Outline the channels through which federal tax legislation normally passes before enactment.
4. What is the difference between a Treasury regulation and an IRS ruling?
5. In reading an article dealing with the federal income tax you encounter the following citations to court decisions. Identify the "source" of each decision by the court rendering it, and generally discuss the strength of each decision as a precedent relative to the other decisions (Claims Court not included):
    a) *Estate of Brockway*, 18 T.C. 488 (1952)
    b) *Heasty*, 370 F. 2d 525 (10 Cir., 1966)
    c) *Crane*, 331 U.S. 1 (1947)
    d) *Snyder*, 203 F. Supp. 195 (W.D. Ky., 1962)
    e) *Estate of Willis*, 28 B.T.A. 152 (1933)
6. The following nine statements refer to or describe a source of tax law discussed in this chapter. For each, give the appropriate source. For example, Internal Revenue Code of 1954; House, Senate, or Conference Committee Reports; Treasury Regulations; Revenue Rulings; U.S. Tax Court decisions; U.S. District Court decisions; Circuit Court decisions; or Supreme Court decisions.
    a) The basic statutory authority for the income tax.
    b) Normally arise only because of conflicting rules from other sources.
    c) Once tested, they have the same force as the Code.
    d) Generally the best source for an explanation of the intent behind statutory provisions.

e) Statement of IRS position but not generally binding on taxpayers.

f) Put into effect only after taxpayers are given an opportunity to study the rules and make comments.

g) Produced by judges whose jurisdiction is restricted to tax matters.

h) Court decisions that the IRS must follow in all subsequent disputes.

i) Court decisions with generally the least value as precedents.

7. What actions must a taxpayer take before he or she is able to obtain a hearing before the U.S. District Court? How does this procedure differ from the Tax Court route?

8. a) What are the three courts in which legal action may be begun in income tax matters?

   b) Which of these courts may include a jury trial?

   c) What is the appeal route from each court?

9. What is the difference between a *primary* and a *secondary* authority in tax matters?

10. Explain each part of the following (fictitious) judicial citation: *Tax Students United* v. *Commissioner*, 80 T.C. 417 (1983).

11. What is the difference between a *regular* and a *memorandum* decision of the Tax Court?

12. Does every taxpayer have the legal right to force the Supreme Court to settle a tax dispute that he or she may be having with the IRS?

13. Under what circumstances will a reference to a Code *section* include a capital letter as well as an arabic numeral?

14. What is meant by the "closed rule" which usually applies to tax bills considered in the House of Representatives?

15. What is the difference between the *Internal Revenue Bulletin* and the *Cumulative Bulletin*?

PROBLEMS

1. Suppose that a friend came to you and explained the following facts: Fred and Maurine Gardner and their family are members of the Mormon Church. Last year they expended $1,500 to support their son who is undertaking a two-year foreign mission assignment for their church. Of the $1,500 spent, $700 was paid directly to a travel agent for their son's transportation to his new mission assignment; the other $800 was paid directly to him for daily living expenses. The Gardners would like to know whether or not they can deduct this $1,500 on their federal income tax return.

   Without doing any actual research in a tax library, simply list the five "key words" that you would want to investigate in the index of a tax service were you actually going to try to locate primary authority to answer this inquiry. Compare your five key words with those selected by other members of your own class.

2. Suppose that a friend came to you and explained the following facts: Home Show Video Corporation (hereafter, HSV) had engaged in the business of renting video cassettes in Crystal City for five years. Last year the owner of HSV decided to expand by opening a new branch office in Nearby City, just 17 miles from its business' original location. In investigating and opening the new branch, HSV expended $25,000 last year. The owner-manager of HSV would like to know whether or not the $25,000 can be deducted as ordinary business expenses or whether they must be capitalized and amortized as start-up costs of a new business venture.

   Without doing any actual research in a tax library, simply list the five "key words" that you would want to investigate in the index of a tax service were you actually going to try to locate primary authority to answer this inquiry. Compare your five key words with those selected by other members of your class.

3. Suppose that a friend came to you and explained the following facts: Jester Construction Company (hereafter, JCC), is a new corporation preparing to file its first tax return. Before it can complete its tax return, JCC must make numerous decisions about accounting methods. Charles Jester, Jr., the controller of JCC, wonders if it can elect to use both a LIFO inventory method and a completed contract method at the same time. Charley thinks he remembers reading somewhere that such a combination is authorized.

   Without doing any actual research in a tax library, simply list the five "key words" that you would want to investigate in the index of a tax service were you actually going to try to locate primary authority to answer this inquiry. Compare your five key words with those selected by other members of your class.

4. Because of a prolonged illness, Robert McFee filed his income tax return, due April 15, 19X1 on May 12, 19X1. An analysis of his return shows that he made quarterly estimated payments of $8,400, whereas the actual tax liability for the year is $9,200. Describe the penalties and other action that McFee faces.

5. Because of a misunderstanding with her accountant, Gloria Washington filed her income tax return, due April 15, 19X1, on May 12, 19X1. An analysis of her return shows that she made quarterly estimated payments of $9,200, whereas the actual tax liability for the year is only $8,400. Describe the penalties and other action that Washington faces.

6. Harry Breach filed a timely tax return for last year, reporting gross income of $6,000. On this return Harry paid a tax of $320. In reviewing his records during the current year he discovered a "remittance ad-

vice" for $120 that he had received in the prior tax year. Further investigation revealed that he had failed to report this $120 of taxable income on his tax return for last year. What is your advice to him? What types of liabilities will he have if he follows your advice?

7. On his tax return for 19X1, Omar claimed a dependency exemption for his mother. His return was audited, and an agent disallowed the dependency exemption. Omar received a "30-day letter" notifying him of a proposed additional tax liability of $182. Omar is very perturbed over this assessment and comes to you, a tax expert, saying, "I'll take it to court. I'm just not going to pay this $182."
   a) What procedure do you suggest that Omar follow?
   b) What procedure would be necessary to literally "take it to court"?

8. In researching a tax case, you find a decision of the Fifth Circuit Court of Appeals that supports a favorable outcome of your problem. Is it probable that the IRS will follow this decision if—
   a) You reside in Texas? (Texas is in the Fifth Circuit).
   b) You reside in California? (California is in the Ninth Circuit.)

9. a) Explain the difference between a "non-docketed" and a "docketed" case.
   b) Why might a taxpayer refuse an offer of compromise from the appellate conferee and file a petition with the Tax Court, even when he or she does not anticipate actual litigation?
   c) Who has settlement jurisdiction for non-docketed cases? For docketed cases? For cases scheduled for trial?

10. a) Under what circumstances can a taxpayer unquestionably rely on a Tax Court decision, given the same facts?
    b) What signal or signals does the IRS give taxpayers to alert them to the fact that they will not follow a particular Tax Court decision?

11. John Price recently received a letter from the IRS stating that his return for two years ago is being examined. John, an engineer, prepared the return himself. The letter asks John to bring his records for the year under examination when he appears for the office audit. John is convinced that he has made some terrible mistake in the computation of his tax. He is worried. What can you tell him to ease his mind?

12. Loretta Black, a single individual with a large income, is in the 50% marginal tax bracket. In calculating her federal income tax liability, Loretta is uncertain how to treat a $12,000 expenditure. She thinks the entire $12,000 might be deductible in the current year, but she also realizes that the IRS might believe that the $12,000 should be capitalized and written off over 12 years. If she claims the entire $12,000 as a current deduction, Loretta's gross tax liability for the year will amount to $65,000. If she capitalizes the $12,000, and claims only a $1,000 de-

duction in the current year, her gross tax liability will be $70,500. If Loretta takes an aggressive tax position, and claims the entire $12,000 as a current deduction, what can she do to make certain that she will not be subject to the penalty for a "substantial underpayment" for her tax liability?

13. Mike Smith discovered in July 1985 that he had failed to claim a casualty loss deduction of $1,283 on his 1982 federal income tax return. Mike had filed his 1982 return on June 10, 1983, when he returned from a trip to China. Prior to leaving for China Mike had obtained an automatic extension of the normal due date for his return (April 15, 1983). Is it too late for Mike to correct this error or can he still file a claim for refund? Explain briefly.

14. Helen Cass realized in June 1986, that she should have included the value of a new car ($15,000), which she won in a sweepstake contest in November 1981, on her 1981 federal income tax return. She had not included the value of the car on her original 1981 return because she erroneously believed that prizes did not constitute taxable income. She filed her 1981 tax return on February 3, 1982. On that return Helen reported gross income of $14,310. Although her gross tax liability for 1981 amounted to $598, Helen actually received a refund of $110 because of overwithholding. Can the IRS still assess Helen for her underpayment of taxes in 1981, or has the statute of limitations expired on this item? Explain briefly.

RESEARCH PROBLEMS

1. Read problem #1 on pp. 2/41–42. After reading the facts of this problem, go to a tax library and locate as much actual primary authority as you can to answer the inquiry posed there. Write down the citation to each authority you locate and state briefly what that authority seems to suggest as the "correct" answer to the question raised.

2. Read problem #2 on p. 2/42. After reading the facts of this problem, go to a tax library and locate as much actual primary authority as you can to answer the inquiry posed there. Write down the citation to each authority you locate and state briefly what that authority seems to suggest as the "correct" answer to the question raised.

3. Read problem #3 on p. 2/42. After reading the facts of this problem, go to a tax library and locate as much actual primary authority as you can to answer the inquiry posed there. Write down the citation to each authority you locate and state briefly what that authority seems to suggest as the "correct" answer to the question raised.

4. Locate a current copy of the Code. Then, by examining the Table of Contents, determine which subchapter of Chapter 1 deals with the

taxation of cooperatives and their patrons. Finally, identify the section numbers included in that subchapter.

5. Locate a current copy of the Code and copy the words of Sec. 38(b). Explain exactly what is meant by the phrase included there that reads as follows: "*For purposes of this subpart* . . . ."

Chapter Objectives

1. Explain, in a general way, how to compute the federal income tax payable by an individual taxpayer.
2. Define the technical meaning of many tax terms including: gross income, adjusted gross income (AGI), taxable income, exclusion, deduction, tax credit, prepayment, etc.
3. Clarify the amount that any individual taxpayer may deduct as a personal exemption deduction.
4. Explain the five tests that must be satisfied before a taxpayer can claim an exemption deduction for a dependent.
5. Identify which parent of a divorced couple may claim the dependent's exemption for their child.
6. Define the term "unused zero-bracket amount" and explain when it must be added back in the calculation of taxable income.
7. Distinguish between the tax tables and the tax rate schedules and explain when each must be used.
8. Explain who qualifies for both the joint-return and head-of-household tax rates.
9. Explain when an individual must make a quarterly payment in order to avoid paying a tax penalty.
10. Distinguish between a tax deduction and a tax credit.

3 Calculating an Individual's Income Tax

Section 1 of the Code imposes a tax, with specified tax rates, "on the taxable income of every individual." At least two aspects of this very brief quotation from the Code are noteworthy. First, observe that this tax is imposed on *taxable income*; second, note that it applies to *every individual*. The first observation is important because it should alert you to the fact that the base for the income tax is not simply "income"—whatever that may mean—but *taxable income*, a term of the art that can only be defined by the tax law itself. The second observation is important for two reasons: first, it clarifies the fact that the taxpaying unit is *every person*—not a husband-wife team, the family unit, or any other group of individuals—and, second, because it applies to *every* individual, not just to U.S. citizens or adults.

As a practical matter, both of the last two observations noted in the prior paragraph are somewhat misleading. The Code does go on, in other places, to provide for what is commonly known as a "joint return" for married persons. On such a return, technically the husband and the wife are "taxpayers," jointly and severally liable for the entire tax once they elect to file a joint return. Furthermore, although Sec. 1 does indeed impose a tax on the taxable income of every individual, other sections of the Code provide special rules for both nonresident aliens (i.e., individuals who live elsewhere and who are not U.S. citizens) and nonresident citizens (i.e., U.S. citizens who reside in another country). Although these special tax provisions are interesting, they have little or no impact on the tax liability of the vast majority of all U.S. taxpayers. Accordingly, we will dismiss these special rules from further consideration in this introductory text and suggest that those few students who are interested in the additional details examine other tax publications.

Our purpose in this chapter is to develop a general tax formula that can be used to determine the federal income tax liability of the average citizen who lives and works in the United States. *Many of the general concepts used in the development of this formula will be explained further in later chapters of this text. It is important, therefore, that neither the student nor the instructor get too bogged down in details at this early juncture in the course. If we can get a clear perspective of the tax determination process now, other details will fall into place later.*

THE GENERAL FORMULA

In its most generalized form the calculation of an individual's federal income tax can be reduced to the following formula:

Start:	Income (broadly conceived)
Less	Exclusions
Equals	Gross Income
Less	Deductions for adjusted gross income*
Equals	Adjusted Gross Income (or AGI)
Less	Deductions from AGI†
Equals	Taxable Income
Times	Applicable tax rate(s)
Equals	Gross Tax Liability
Less	Tax credits and prepayments
Equals	Net Tax Payable (or Refundable)

*Some authors refer to these deductions as "above-the-line" deductions or as "deductions to reach AGI."
†Some authors refer to these deductions as "below-the-line" deductions or as "personal deductions."

Although this formula looks reasonably simple at the outset, you will soon discover that defining the terms used here is a surprisingly difficult task. In fact, the rules have become so complex that a few taxpayers are convinced that Congress should get rid of our present income tax and replace it with some other tax which (they hope) will be easier to administer; many others hope that Congress will soon simplify the present income tax rules for everyone.

INCOME BROADLY CONCEIVED

The starting point in implementing the income tax formula is the correct identification of all income items. As will be demonstrated in the following examples, even this task can sometimes be difficult.

Example 1: Last month Bill Belt received (*a*) a $1,200 paycheck, (*b*) a $75 wrist watch for fixing a friend's car, and (*c*) a $500 check in full payment for a bike that Bill bought for $400 six months ago. Bill's income for the month, broadly conceived, would total $1,375. That total includes his $1,200 paycheck, the $75 watch, and a $100 gain on the sale of the bike.

As illustrated in Example 1, income does not have to be received in cash. The ***fair market value*** of any goods or services received in exchange for rendering any service is also included in income. As a practical matter it is often difficult for a taxpayer and an IRS agent to agree on the fair market value of any noncash properties. Typically a taxpayer wants to place a low value on such properties; an IRS agent, a high value. Example 1 also illustrates the fact that income can not be equated with gross receipts. Although Bill sold his bike for $500, that sale produced income of only $100. In other words, at least for tax purposes, income derived from the sale of property means only the excess of the sales price ($500) over the cost of goods sold ($400).[1]

FAIR MARKET VALUE The price a willing buyer would pay a willing seller in a transaction in which both parties acted with no compulsion and full knowledge.

Example 2: Last month Barbara Banks received a $1,000 dividend check from AT&T. She also found a $100 bill on the sidewalk and collected a $50 bet from a friend. Barbara's income for the month is $1,150.

As illustrated in Example 2, income may include "windfall gains," such as finding a $100 bill.[2] Example 2 also illustrates the fact that income includes profits from activities that may be considered illegal under state law; that is, Barbara's income will include the $50 bet she collected from a friend, whether or not the state in which she lives considers gambling a legal activity.[3]

Although there are many more interesting things to be learned about the income concept, we will postpone those ideas for further discussion in the next chapter and proceed to develop the general formula for calculating an individual's income tax. After a taxpayer has identified and measured all items of income correctly, he or she must then subtract from that total income the amount of any exclusions.

---

[1] Treas. Reg. Sec. 1.61-3(a).

[2] Rev. Rul. 53-61, 1953-1 C.B. 17; see also *Cesarini* v. *U.S.*, 428 7.2d 812 (CA-6, 1970) *aff'g.* 296 F. Supp. 3 (N.D. Ohio, 1969).

[3] Treas. Reg. Sec. 1.61-14(a).

EXCLUSIONS

EXCLUSIONS Items of income exempted by law from the income tax.

The word ***exclusion*** refers to any item of income that is not subject to the income tax simply because the tax law says that it is not taxable. Many of the exclusions are neatly summarized in Part III of Subchapter B of the Code. That Part includes the sections numbered 101 through 130. Some of these and other Code provisions will be examined in greater detail in Chapter 5. For the moment, we must be satisfied with understanding the general concept of exclusions. That can be easily accomplished with a few examples.

> **Example 3:** Last month Carl Craft received (*a*) an $800 interest check on some State of Ohio bonds; (*b*) a $500 gift from a friend; and (*c*) a $100 door prize from a local restaurant. Although Carl's monthly income, broadly conceived, is $1,400, his gross income for federal income tax purposes would be only $100. Sec. 103(a) authorizes a taxpayer to exclude interest earned on the obligations of any state or political subdivision thereof. Sec. 102(a) authorizes a taxpayer to exclude from gross income "the value of property acquired by gift, bequest, devise, or inheritance."

As suggested by the first three examples in this chapter, a taxpayer must first add together all items of income and then deduct the value of any exclusions. In other words, our income tax law is worded in a manner that has caused both the courts and the administrative authorities to give the word *income* an expansive meaning. You must take the words of Sec. 61(a) literally, where it states "Except as otherwise provided in this subtitle, gross income means all income from whatever source derived." Applying this idea to the facts of Example 3, Carl Craft must include the $100 door prize in his gross income unless he can find good authority to substantiate its exclusion. Secs. 102 and 103 are clearly good authority to exclude the $500 gift and the $800 interest on the Ohio State bonds, respectively; but if Carl can find no authority to exclude the $100 door prize, he must include it in gross income. If Carl looks long and hard enough, he just might find Sec. 74(a), which should clarify any doubt that he has on the need to include the $100 door prize in gross income. Sec. 74(a) states that "Except as provided in subsection (b) gross income includes amounts received as prizes and awards." And, unfortunately for Carl, the exceptions found in subsection (b) do not include door prizes. Therefore, Carl would know that he must include this $100 in his gross income. In many cases a taxpayer will not be able to find such an explicit statement concerning the need to include an item within the gross income concept. As explained above, however, the absence of an explicit statement concerning inclusion does *not* authorize its exclusion from gross income. To the contrary, silence implies inclusion rather than exclusion.

> **Example 4:** Last month Cynthia Cade received a $20,000 distribution of assets from the executrix of the estate of her recently deceased mother. She also received $500 interest on a regular bank

savings account that she established with cash received from her father's estate two years ago. Cynthia may exclude the $20,000 inheritance from her prior month's gross income by operation of Sec. 102(a); she may not, however, exclude the $500 by that (or any other) authority.

As illustrated in Example 4, a taxpayer must read each statutory provision very carefully. Sec. 102(a) does authorize the exclusion of property acquired by inheritance; it does *not* authorize the exclusion of income derived as a result of owning property that was itself acquired by inheritance. In other words, Cynthia must distinguish carefully between the $20,000 direct inheritance and the $500 income that she (personally) earned on a prior inheritance.

After a taxpayer has correctly identified and quantified all items of income and subtracted the correct value of any exclusions, the arithmetic difference between these two amounts is his or her ***gross income***. This is an important technical term. The amount of one's gross income determines whether or not a tax return must be filed. Current law provides that for 1985 any single individual (who is under age 65 and not blind) must file a tax return if his or her gross income exceeds $3,400. Thus if Dave receives $300 each month from state bond interest, while Diane receives a $300 gross monthly salary, Dave need not file a tax return even though Diane must. Dave's gross income for the year is zero; Diane's is $3,600.

GROSS INCOME Income (broadly conceived) less exclusions.

A more complete and accurate statement of the rules which determine who must file a tax return in 1984 and 1985 is as follows:

DESCRIPTION OF TAXPAYER	MUST FILE IF GROSS INCOME EXCEEDS	
	1984	1985
Single, and under 65 years of age	$3,300	$3,430
Single, and 65 years or older	4,300	4,470
Single, and claimed as a dependent on parent's return, and having taxable dividends, interest, or other *unearned* income	1,000	1,040
Qualified surviving spouse under 65	4,400	4,580
Qualified surviving spouse over 64	5,400	5,620
Married couple, filing jointly, both under 65	5,400	5,620
Married couple, filing jointly, one spouse over 64	6,400	6,660
Married couple, filing jointly, both over 64	7,400	7,700

Observe carefully that the correct interpretation of this apparently simple table requires a good understanding of such technical tax terms as "unearned income," "surviving spouse," and "filing jointly." Note also that an individual's gross income is not dependent in any way upon the presence or absence of any income tax deductions. It depends solely on items of income and exclusions.

DEDUCTIONS

DEDUCTIONS Items that by law may be deducted from gross income in the calculation of taxable income.

For purposes of federal income taxation, the word ***deduction*** means any item which can be subtracted from gross income in the calculation of taxable income. It is just as true in the case of deductions, as it is in the case of exclusions, that *nothing is deductible unless a taxpayer can find good authority to authorize the deduction*. In other words, if the Code is silent, this generally means that any particular expenditure or loss is *not* deductible. Unfortunately for both the student and the taxpayer, that general rule—although entirely correct—is of very little practical value. Its limited value stems from the fact that the Code includes both (*a*) some very broadly worded deduction sections and (*b*) some equally broad restrictive sections, and an individual taxpayer discovers frequently that his or her situation arguably falls within either one of these diametrically opposed provisions.

For example, Sec. 162(a) authorizes the deduction of "all the ordinary and necessary expenses paid or incurred during the taxable year in carrying on any trade or business." Sec. 262, on the other hand, states that "no deduction shall be allowed for personal, living, or family expenses." Given only these two Code provisions, can an individual taxpayer deduct the cost of special clothing purchased only because one's employer seems to require that all employees dress in a certain manner? The answer to that question is not at all obvious, even after a thorough investigation of all pertinent authority. The answer seems to depend on just how "special" the special clothing is. If it is unique, and not the kind of thing that can be worn in general usage, it is deductible; otherwise it is not.[4] Obviously trying to decide exactly which clothing is appropriate for general wear leaves room for a great deal of disagreement between a taxpayer and an IRS agent. Further discussion of these and other interesting rules concerning deductions is left for later chapters. For now we must be satisfied with the general conclusion that nothing is deductible unless authorized by the Code or other competent authority.

ADJUSTED GROSS INCOME Gross income less any deductions specified in Sec. 62.

"ABOVE-THE-LINE" DEDUCTIONS Only those deductions, specified in Sec. 62, that may be deducted in the computation of adjusted gross income. (Also known as deductions for AGI.)

"BELOW-THE-LINE" DEDUCTIONS Authorized deductions other than those specified in Sec. 62. (Also known as deductions from AGI.)

To discover that any particular item is deductible is only half the problem for individual taxpayers. They must also correctly classify every deduction as either: (*a*) a deduction *for* adjusted gross income or (*b*) a deduction *from* adjusted gross income. The tax Code defines an intermediary measure of income—somewhere between gross income and taxable income—and calls that measure ***adjusted gross income***, or AGI. Thus, what the person on the street might know as an ***"above-the-line" deduction***, is technically any deduction that can be subtracted from gross income to determine adjusted gross income. Any other deductible item is a ***"below-the-line" deduction***, or a "deduction *from* AGI." In other words, the deductions from AGI are a residual class; that is, they are any authorized deductions not specifically included in the definition of AGI.

---

[4]See, for example, Rev. Rul. 70-474, 1970-2 C.B. 34 or see *Louis M. Roth*, 17 T.C. 1450 (1952); see also *Wilson J. Fisher*, 230 F.2d 79 (CA-7, 1956) *aff'g*. 23 T.C. 218 (1954), and *Barry D. Pevsner*, 636 F2d 1106 (CA-5, 1981) *rev'g*. 38 TCM 1210 (1979).

DEDUCTIONS FOR ADJUSTED GROSS INCOME The deductions which may be subtracted from gross income to determine adjusted gross income are explicitly identified in Sec. 62, which is entitled "Adjusted Gross Income Defined." Observe that Sec. 62 is *not* a section which authorizes any deductions; rather, it simply determines how deductions that are authorized in other Code sections will be treated in the "for AGI"/"from AGI" classification. Because of its importance to many taxpayers, Section 62 is reproduced in its entirety below:

Sec. 62 Adjusted Gross Income Defined.

For purposes of this subtitle, the term "adjusted gross income" means, in the case of an individual, gross income minus the following deductions:

(1) Trade and business deductions.—The deductions allowed by this chapter (other than by part VII of this subchapter) which are attributable to a trade or business carried on by the taxpayer, if such trade or business does not consist of the performance of services by the taxpayer as an employee.

(2) Trade and business deductions of employees:—

(A) Reimbursed expenses.—The deductions allowed by part VI (sec. 161 and following) which consist of expenses paid or incurred by the taxpayer, in connection with the performance by him of services as an employee, under a reimbursement or other expense allowance arrangement with his employer.

(B) Expenses for travel away from home.—The deductions allowed by part VI (sec. 161 and following) which consist of expenses of travel, meals, and lodging while away from home, paid or incurred by the taxpayer in connection with the performance by him of services as an employee.

(C) Transportation expenses.—The deductions allowed by part VI (sec. 161 and following) which consist of expenses of transportation paid or incurred by the taxpayer in connection with the performance by him of services as an employee.

(D) Outside salesmen.—The deductions allowed by part VI (sec. 161 and following) which are attributable to a trade or business carried on by the taxpayer, if such trade or business consists of the performance of services by the taxpayer as an employee and if such trade or business is to solicit, away from the employer's place of business, business for the employer.

(3) Long-term capital gains.—The deduction allowed by section 1202.

(4) Losses from sale or exchange of property.—The deductions allowed by part VI (sec. 161 and following) as losses from the sale or exchange of property.

(5) Deductions attributable to rents and royalties.—The deductions allowed by part VI (sec. 161 and following), by section 212 (relating to expenses for production of income), and by section 611 (relating to depletion) which are attributable to property held for the production of rents or royalties.

(6) Certain deductions of life tenants and income beneficiaries of property.—In the case of a life tenant of property, or an income beneficiary of property held in trust, or an heir, legatee, or devisee of an estate, the deduction for depreciation allowed by section 167 and the deduction allowed by section 611.

(7) Pension, profit-sharing, annuity, and bond purchase plans of self-employed individuals.—In the case of an individual who is an employee within the meaning of section 401(c)(1), the deductions allowed by section 404 and section 405(c) to the extent attributable to contributions made on behalf of such individual.
(8) Moving expense deduction.—The deduction allowed by section 217.
(9) [Repealed]
(10) Retirement savings.—The deduction allowed by section 219 (relating to deduction for certain retirement savings).
(11) Certain portion of lump-sum distributions from pension plans taxed under section 402(e).—The deduction allowed by section 402(e)(3).
(12) Penalties forfeited because of premature withdrawal of funds from time savings accounts or deposits.—The deductions allowed by section 165 for losses incurred in any transaction entered into for profit, though not connected with a trade or business, to the extent that such losses include amounts forfeited to a bank, mutual savings bank, savings and loan association, building and loan association, cooperative bank or homestead association as a penalty for premature withdrawal of funds from a time savings account, certificate of deposit, or similar class of deposit.
(13) Alimony.—The deduction allowed by section 215.
(14) Reforestation expenses.—The deduction allowed by section 194.
(15) Certain required repayments of supplemental unemployment compensation benefits.—The deduction allowed by section 165 for the repayment to a trust described in paragraph (9) or (17) of section 501(c) of supplemental unemployment compensation benefits received from such trust if such repayment is required because of the receipt of trade readjustment allowances under section 231 or 232 of the Trade Act of 1974 (19 U.S.C. 2291 or 2292).
(16) Deduction for two-earner married couples.—The deduction allowed by section 221.

Nothing in this section shall permit the same item to be deducted more than once.

By omission, Sec. 62 also defines deductions *FROM* AGI; i.e., any deduction not specifically listed in Sec. 62 is a deduction from adjusted gross income. The general content of Sec. 62 may be paraphrased as follows:

1. All expenses that can be classified as
   a) Nonemployee trade or business expenses (for example, all routine business expenses associated with the operation of a sole proprietorship or a partnership).
   b) Expenses associated with the production of rents and royalties, whether or not the income-producing activity is a "trade or business."
2. Only the following expenses incurred as an employee:
   a) All expenses of travel away from home.
   b) All transportation expenses (which differs from both (1) the deductible cost of travel away from home and (2) nondeductible commuting from home to work and back).
   c) All reimbursed business expenses but only to the extent of reimbursement.

d) Any expenses associated with activities conducted as an outside salesman.
3. The long-term capital-gain deduction (explained in Chapter 10).
4. Certain losses from the sale or exchange of certain properties (explained in Chapters 10 and 11).
5. Moving expenses.
6. Alimony.
7. The special deduction allowed two-earner married couples.
8. A few miscellaneous deductions.

Although this paraphrased version of Sec. 62 appears to be relatively explicit and straightforward, it hides many problems.

Example 5: Eva Ervine is a self-employed CPA. She paid a $100 registration fee to attend a local seminar on the new tax law. Eva may deduct the entire $100 as a deduction for AGI. Sec. 62(1).

Example 6: Earl Evert, also a CPA, is an employee of Dander & Co., CPAs. Earl pays the same $100 registration fee to attend the same seminar as Eva, but Earl's firm will reimburse him for only $75 of this cost. Earl must deduct $75 for AGI and $25 from AGI. Sec. 62(2)(A).

Example 7: Faye Fox is an artist who occasionally sells one of her oil paintings. Although Faye uses one room in her home as an art studio, she is not deemed to be in the art business. Last year she sold only two paintings for $100 cash. She paid $3,000 to heat and cool her home during the past year. Faye cannot deduct any of the $3,000 on her federal income tax return.

Example 8: Frank Falk is a self-employed artist. Last year Frank was able to sell 68 of his 100 paintings for a total of $6,375. Frank uses one of 10 rooms in his home solely as a studio. He paid $3,000 to heat and cool the studio during the year. Frank may deduct $300 on his federal income tax return. Sec. 162(1).

As implied by Example 8, it is often very important for a taxpayer to be engaged in a trade or business when it comes to determining which expenses are deductible. As you may already suspect, the definition of a trade or business is often uncertain. It seems to include (1) an intent to make a profit; (2) some entrepreneurial effort; (3) a "holding out" of oneself to others; and (4) a degree of "regularity." Mere passive collection of income is not enough. An actual profit, however, is not required. The distinction between a trade or business and certain pleasurable, but sometimes profitable, hobbies is particularly difficult to draw.[5]

[5] See, for example, Treas. Regs. Sec. 1.183-1. See also *Higgins*, 312 U.S. 212, 25 AFTR 1160, 41-1 USTC 9233 (S.Ct., 1941); *Whipple*, 373 U.S. 193, 11 AFTR 2d 1454, 63-1 USTC 9466 (S.Ct., 1963); *Highland*, 124 F.2d 556, 28 AFTR 816, 42-1 USTC 9199 (CA-4, 1942); *Steffens*, 707 F.2d 478, 52 AFTR 2d 83-5227, 83-2 USTC 9425 (CA-11, 1983) and *Moller*, 721 F.2d 810, 52 AFTR 2d 83-6333, 83-2 USTC 9698 (CA-FC, 1983).

DEDUCTIONS FROM ADJUSTED GROSS INCOME As noted earlier, any item that an individual taxpayer may legally deduct, but which is not specified in Sec. 62, is a deduction from AGI. This broad class of deductions can generally be further subdivided into two major categories: (*a*) the itemized deductions (if any) in excess of the zero-bracket amount and (*b*) the personal and dependent exemption deductions. Note that the first category—which includes (among other things) the deductions for home-mortgage interest, state and local income and property taxes, and most charitable contributions—can be claimed only to the extent that they exceed the taxpayer's zero-bracket amount.

ITEMIZED DEDUCTIONS AND THE ZERO-BRACKET AMOUNT. Even though the Code specifically disallows (in Sec. 262) any deductions for personal, living, or family expenses, it goes on in other sections to permit the deduction of a few of those same items. Sec. 262 resolves what would otherwise be a conflict in Code sections with the following words: "Except as otherwise expressly provided in this chapter, no deduction shall be allowed for personal, living, or family expenses" (emphasis added). Therefore, before anyone can be certain of exactly which personal expenses are deductible, and which ones are not deductible, he or she must know and understand all of the deduction sections contained in Chapter 1 of the Code. Such an exhaustive examination of the Code is, quite obviously, beyond reason at this early juncture in your study of income taxation. We can, however, note two important examples of the itemized deduction provisions.

Section 163 authorizes a deduction for "all interest paid or accrued within the taxable year on indebtedness." Although this broad general rule is subject to many exceptions—stated both in later subsections of Sec. 163 and in other provisions of the Code and regulations—there is no exception which prohibits the deduction of interest on purely personal purchases. Accordingly, the interest paid on a debt, the proceeds of which were used to acquire a personal residence, a private automobile, or for personal travel, are deductible. Since this kind of interest expense deduction is *not* specifically mentioned in Sec. 62, it has to be an "other itemized deduction," or a deduction from AGI.

Section 164 authorizes a deduction for all real property taxes, all personal property taxes, all state income taxes, and all general sales taxes, as well as other specified taxes. Once again this broad general rule is subject to a number of explicit exceptions, but none of those exceptions disallows the deduction of any real property taxes imposed on an individual's personal residence, the personal property taxes imposed on a pleasure boat, or the general sales tax imposed on everyday purchases. Accordingly, each of these tax payments can be deducted. Since this kind of tax expense deduction is not specifically mentioned in Sec. 62, it too must be a deduction from AGI.

The net result of these complex deduction rules would make the income tax even more complicated than it already is for the average taxpayer were it not for the zero-bracket amount. What is now called the

zero-bracket amount was for many years known as the standard deduction. The idea behind both the standard deduction and the zero-bracket amount was to simplify the tax calculation for most individuals. As originally worded, individuals could claim the larger of (*a*) their itemized deductions or (*b*) the standard deduction. The dollar amount of the standard deduction was periodically adjusted so that somewhere between 60% and 80% of the entire U.S. population would find that their personal itemized deductions amounted to less than the standard deduction. Accordingly, they had no need to keep any special records of their routine personal expenses for federal income tax purposes. These individuals would automatically elect the standard deduction for which no documentation was required.

ZERO-BRACKET AMOUNT (ZBA) The first of several steps, in the four different individual income tax rate brackets, to which a zero tax rate applies.

A few years ago Congress incorporated the concept of the standard deduction directly into the tax rate schedules. In other words, instead of taxing the first dollar of taxable income earned in any year at some stated percent, the tax rate schedules were rewritten to allow a specified amount of taxable income to be subject to a "zero tax rate." This dollar amount is described as the zero-bracket amount. The zero-bracket amounts for 1984 and 1985 are:

	1984	1985
Single individuals (including heads of households)	$2,300	$2,390
Married persons (including a surviving spouse) filing a joint return	$3,400	$3,540
Married persons filing separate returns	$1,700	$1,770

The net result of a zero-bracket amount is exactly the same as a standard deduction of that same amount because, under the current rules, an individual taxpayer can deduct his or her itemized deductions only if, and to the extent that, they exceed the zero-bracket amount. The excess of a taxpayer's itemized deductions over his or her zero-bracket amount is commonly known as their "excess itemized deductions." For most individuals, itemized deductions will be greater than the zero-bracket amount as soon as they purchase a home because the total of the home mortgage interest expense plus the real property taxes on a residence generally are more than the zero-bracket amount.

Example 9: Gerry Grant, a single taxpayer, is entitled to only two deductions: (*a*) $1,200 in interest expense on a car loan, and (*b*) $1,000 in state income taxes. Because both of Gerry's deductions are deductions from AGI, and because they do not exceed his zero-bracket amount, Gerry has no "excess itemized deductions" and, therefore, is not entitled to any deductions other than a personal exemption deduction.

Example 10: Gene and Hedi Hart file a joint return and claim itemized deductions as follows:

Home mortgage interest	$2,000
Property taxes	1,500
State income tax	800
Charitable contributions	700
Total itemized deductions	$5,000

On their tax return the Harts' deductions from AGI will be $1,600 in 1984 (i.e., their $5,000 total less the $3,400 zero-bracket amount), or $1,460 in 1985, plus any personal and dependent exemptions.

BACKGROUND

Prior to 1982 charitable contributions made by individuals were deductible only as itemized deductions *from* AGI. The Economic Recovery Tax Act of 1981 contained a limited and temporary provision that now makes some amount of charitable contributions a rough equivalent of a deduction *for* AGI. The purpose of this provision was to encourage charitable gifts by low-income individuals.

Beginning in 1982 and extending through 1986, limited amounts of charitable contributions made by persons who do not itemize their personal deductions are treated as a "direct charitable deduction" per Sec. 63(i). As explained in Sec. 170(i), this means that individuals who do not claim any itemized deductions can still claim some amount of deduction for any charitable contributions they make, subject to the following limits:

YEAR(S)	PERCENTAGE OF CHARITABLE CONTRIBUTION ALLOWED	EFFECTIVE MAXIMUM ("DIRECT") DEDUCTION
1982–83	25% of amount given to a maximum of $100	$25
1984	25% of amount given to a maximum of $300	$75
1985	50% of all charitable contributions given	N/A
1986	100% of all charitable contributions given	N/A
1987	No amount allowed	$-0-

Note that Congress did *not* modify Sec. 62 to include charitable contributions in the list of deductions that may be made "for AGI." Instead, it created an entirely new thing—called a "direct deduction"—which has essentially the same effect as a deduction for adjusted gross income, but is subject to stated maximum amounts. Note also that this special provision applies only to individual taxpayers who do *not* itemize deductions and that, unless further modified before then, it will expire on January 1, 1987.

EXEMPTION DEDUCTIONS. Exemption deductions are $1,000 each. They include both personal exemption deductions and dependent exemption deductions. In general, every individual is entitled to claim one ***personal exemption deduction*** for himself or herself on his or her own return. If, on the last day of the taxable year, a taxpayer is blind, he or she may claim another deduction; and if 65 years of age or older, still another. Thus, on his or her own return, any individual taxpayer may claim as little as $1,000 in 1984, $1,040 in 1985, or as much as $3,000 in 1984, $3,120 in 1985, in personal exemption deductions. Because there are two taxpayers on a joint return of a married couple, these minimum and maximum amounts are doubled. Incidentally, according to Treas. Reg. Sec. 1.151-1(c)(2), a person whose birthday falls on January 1 is deemed to be 65 years of age on the day before his 65th birthday!

PERSONAL EXEMPTION DEDUCTION A special deduction of anywhere from $1,000 to $3,000 allowed every individual taxpayer on his or her own tax return. (On the joint return of a married couple this deduction can vary from $2,000 to $6,000.)

Example 11: Juan Hernandez is single, age 22, and not blind. In 1984 Juan may claim a personal exemption deduction of $1,000 on his own return; in 1985 he may claim $1,040.

Example 12: Joe and Helen Haven are 66 and 62, respectively. Joe has normal vision; Helen is legally blind. On a 1984 joint return, Joe and Helen may claim a total of $4,000 in personal exemption deductions; on their 1985 return they may claim $4,160 in personal exemption deductions.

In addition to claiming one or more personal exemption deductions, an individual taxpayer may be able to claim an additional $1,000 in 1984 or $1,040 in 1985 for another individual who is "***dependent***" on him or her. No "special" or "extra" deductions are allowed for dependents who are blind or over age 64. In order to claim another individual as a dependent, that person must satisfy *each* of the following five tests:

DEPENDENT An individual for whom a taxpayer may claim a dependent-exemption deduction. (To be a dependent, a person must satisfy each of five technical tests.)

1. Be either a U.S. citizen or a resident alien;
2. File either no return or a separate return (even if married);[6]
3. Be dependent on the taxpayer for over one-half of his or her support;
4. Have gross income of less than $1,000 for 1984 or $1,040 for 1985; and
5. Either be a relative of the taxpayer or live with the taxpayer throughout the entire year.

Dependents who die during the year may be claimed if the general conditions were satisfied to the day of their death. No dependency deduction is allowed, however, for a stillborn child. In general, the first two requirements need no interpretation. The last three, however, require further explanation and elaboration.

THE SUPPORT TEST. The taxpayer must provide over one-half of the amount *spent* on the ***support*** of the dependent during the calendar year

SUPPORT The total amount spent for necessities during a year.

[6]A married spouse may file a joint return (and still be claimed as a dependent) if (*a*) the couple has *no* gross tax liability and (*b*) they file only to claim a refund of taxes withheld or prepaid.

(or that part of the year that the dependent was alive). Support includes all expenditures for such items as food, clothing, shelter, medical care, education, and child care. A scholarship received by a student who is the taxpayer's *child* is not counted as part of the total support in determining whether the taxpayer provided more than half the student's support.

Example 13: Ida Lopez is a student at State University. This year Ida spent a total of $3,000 for her own support. Her parents contributed $1,200 toward her rent; she earned $1,400 (but spent only $1,000 of this amount); and she received and spent an $800 scholarship to attend college. Ida's parents can claim Ida as a dependent because they provided more than one-half of her "support" determined as follows:

Total spent	$3,000
Less scholarship	800
Total "support"	$2,200

Obviously, $1,200 is more than one-half of $2,200 (even though it is not more than one-half of $3,000). Note, however, that if Ida's brother had provided her with the same $1,200 toward her rent, he could *not* have claimed Ida as a dependent because he would not have satisfied the support test. The right to exclude the $800 scholarship from the total spent in determining "support" extends only to the case where the dependent is the taxpayer's *child*.[7]

A major exception to the general support-test requirements may occur when two or more persons furnish a dependent's support but no one taxpayer provides over half the support. In this event, any one of the taxpayers who provided over 10% of the dependent's support during the year, and who satisfies the relationship test, may claim the dependent's exemption if each of the other eligible claimants will sign a multiple support agreement (Form 2120) agreeing *not* to claim an exemption for the dependent.

FORM 2120

Example 14: Each of four brothers provides 25% of their father's support. Any one of the four brothers may claim the father as a dependent for the year provided the other three brothers sign a multiple support agreement. On the other hand, if two of the brothers each provided 40% of their father's support, and the two others provided only 10% each, the two who gave exactly 10% would *not* be eligible claimants and need not sign the Form 2120 since that requires *over* 10%. In the latter case either one of the two who contributed 40% could claim the father as a dependent if the other 40% contributor would sign the Form 2120.

---

[7]Treas. Reg. Sec. 1.152-1(c).

If both of the divorced or separated parents (of a child) contribute support for their child (or children), the parent who has custody for the major part of the calendar year is generally presumed to have provided more than 50% of the support. There are several exceptions to this general presumption: For example, for persons divorced or separated before 1985, if the divorce decree provides, or if the parents entered into a separate written agreement not included in the divorce decree, that the parent not having custody was to be entitled to the exemption, the noncustodial parent will be entitled to the exemption of the child named in the decree or agreement if he or she actually contributed at least $600 toward support of the child during the year. Note that $600 or more must be paid for each child under this exemption. For parents divorced or separated after 1984, the custodial parent may sign a written statement agreeing not to claim a child as a dependent and thus allow the noncustodial parent to do so if he or she will attach a copy of this agreement to the tax return for the year.

Example 15: Tom and Nancy are the divorced parents of Paul. Paul lives with his mother. The divorce decree makes no mention of any exemption deduction for Paul, and Tom and Nancy have no separate written agreement on that matter. Tom contributes $1,000 per year toward Paul's support. Under these circumstances Nancy will be entitled to claim the exemption deduction for Paul.

Example 16: Assume all facts as in Example 15 except that their divorce took place in 1985 and Nancy signed a written agreement stating that she will not claim Paul as a dependent. Tom attaches a copy of this statement to his 1985 tax return. With this revision, Tom is entitled to claim the dependent exemption deduction for Paul.

Example 17: David and Sharon are the divorced parents of Ken. Ken lives with his father. The 1980 divorce decree provides that Sharon will be entitled to the exemption deduction for Ken. Sharon provides $700 per year toward Ken's support. Under these circumstances, Sharon will be entitled to claim the dependent exemption deduction for Ken.

THE GROSS INCOME TEST. The gross-income test provision of Section 151(e) limits the potential dependent's gross income to less than the amount of an exemption allowance for that year ($1,000 for 1984 or $1,040 for 1985), in order for the taxpayer to claim an exemption for him or her. This test does not apply, however, to a taxpayer's child, or qualified foster child, who is either a full-time student *or* under age 19 at the close of the year. Generally, a "student" is defined as one who during each of any five months of the calendar year was in "full-time" attendance at an educational institution or took a full-time, on-farm training course during any five months of the year. If a taxpayer's child who is either a student or under 19 has sufficient gross income, he or she must, of course, file his or her own tax return. On this return the child may claim an exemption for himself or herself even though he or she is also claimed as a dependent by his or her parents.

> ***BACKGROUND***
>
> These exceptions to the gross-income test are designed to encourage students to earn an income, to foster education or farm training, and to aid those with the greatest financial need (where children must work to aid the family). These special provisions, however, like many others, may be criticized as rather inefficient devices to obtain worthy objectives. The basic criticism is that students who are the children of poor parents may have to earn more than half of their expenses; if so, this deprives their parents of exemptions for them because they will then fail the support test. Wealthier parents, on the other hand, whose children need earn far less, may still be eligible for the dual exemptions.*
>
> *An excellent criticism of these provisions may be found in C. Lowell Harriss, "Parent and Child and Taxes: Some Problems in Dependency," *1959 Compendium*, pp. 531–35. A similar presentation may be found in Groves, *op. cit.*, pp. 39–43.

THE RELATIONSHIP TEST. The Internal Revenue Code also provides that a dependent must be a *relative* of the taxpayer and specifies the necessary definition of relatives as follows:

1. A son or daughter of the taxpayer, or a descendant of either,
2. A stepson or stepdaughter of the taxpayer,
3. A brother, sister, stepbrother, or stepsister of the taxpayer,
4. The father or mother of the taxpayer, or an ancestor of either,
5. A stepfather or stepmother of the taxpayer,
6. A son or daughter of a brother or sister of the taxpayer,
7. A brother or sister of the father or mother of the taxpayer,
8. A son-in-law, daughter-in-law, father-in-law, mother-in-law, brother-in-law, or sister-in-law of the taxpayer.[8]

When a joint return is filed, the relationship test is met if the person claimed as a dependent is a qualified relative of either spouse. Even after termination of a marriage, a relationship established by a prior marriage is continued for tax purposes. In addition, brothers and sisters include those "by the halfblood." Finally, an adopted child is treated as a natural child for dependency purposes. The law goes even further: it provides for the taxpayer to claim an exemption for an individual who *resides in* the taxpayer's home throughout a tax year even though that person is not a relative as specified above. An exemption is allowed for:

[8]Code Sec. 152(a)(1)-(8).

9. An individual (other than an individual who at any time during the taxable year was the spouse, determined without regard to section 143, of the taxpayer) who, for the taxable year of the taxpayer, has as his principal place of abode the home of the taxpayer and is a member of the taxpayer's household.[9]

This provision of the law permits dependency exemptions for persons, such as foster children not legally adopted, or foster parents, who do not meet any of the relationship tests in 1 through 8 above. Foster children who meet the residence test are treated in all respects as though they were blood relatives of the taxpayer. This special provision will not apply, however, if the relationship between the dependent and the taxpayer is contrary to local law. For example, if state law prohibits common-law marriage, no exemption can be claimed for the taxpayer's consort. Children born into such an arrangement, however, can still be dependents.

THE UNUSED ZERO-BRACKET AMOUNT As noted previously, the amount of the zero-bracket varies, depending on the filing status of the taxpayer and the year. The effect of the zero-bracket amount and the personal exemption deduction combined is to exempt wholly from the federal income tax those individuals who earn relatively small amounts of taxable income each year. In most instances this result is entirely justified because it makes little or no common sense to tax away from the poorest members of society any part of the little income that they can earn.

However, in a very few instances the same two tax provisions may be used to create an unintended tax benefit. To illustrate, assume that a wealthy taxpayer who earns a large income each year decided to give his infant child an income-producing asset, such as a $33,000 certificate of deposit paying 10% interest. If this parent had not made this gift, the same interest income of $3,300 (i.e., $33,000 × 10%) would have been subject to an income tax of up to $1,650 (or 50% of $3,300) when received by the parent. If the taxpayer's child can report that same interest income on his or her own tax return, and also claim both a zero-bracket amount and a personal exemption deduction, then the income tax on the $3,300 interest could be reduced to zero. In order to partially plug this unintended tax loophole, the Code requires an individual to add back, in the calculation of taxable income, an amount described as the "***unused zero-bracket amount***" in four specific situations.[10] This unused zero-bracket amount is equal to the excess of (*a*) the stipulated zero-bracket amount over (*b*) the taxpayer's itemized (or "below-the-line") deductions in the three following situations:

UNUSED ZERO-BRACKET AMOUNT An amount that must be added to gross income, in the determination of taxable income, in four specific and somewhat unusual situations.

1. Where married individuals file separate returns *and* either one of them claims itemized deductions;
2. Where the taxpayer is a nonresident alien; or
3. Where the taxpayer claims some very special tax benefits, under

[9] Code Sec. 152(a)(9).

[10] Sec. 63(e).

Sec. 931, that are available only to U.S. citizens who earn income from within a U.S. possession, such as Puerto Rico.

In a fourth situation—that is, in the case where a dependency exemption can be claimed for an individual by another taxpayer *and* the individual so claimed also has some amount of *unearned* income (such as interest income) to report—the unused zero-bracket amount can be defined as the excess of (*a*) the individual's stipulated zero-bracket amount over (*b*) the individual's *earned income*, if earned income exceeds itemized deductions. This fourth situation is, of course, the one described earlier for the parent who transferred a $33,000 certificate of deposit to his infant child.

Example 18: Harry Hopkins transferred a $33,000-10% "CD" to his infant daughter, Lisa. Assume that Lisa's only gross income for 1985 is the $3,300 interest earned in this savings account. Since Lisa has no *earned* income, her unused zero-bracket amount is equal to $2,390 (i.e., a $2,390 zero-bracket amount less nothing). Therefore, Lisa's *taxable income* must be computed as follows:

Gross income	$ 3,300
Less one personal exemption deduction	(1,040)
Plus the "unused zero-bracket amount"	2,390
Taxable Income	$ 4,650

Example 19: Assume that during 1985 Jim, age 16 and a dependent of his parents, earns $1,900 from a part-time job plus $2,500 from interest on a savings account. If Jim is not entitled to any itemized deductions, his taxable income must be computed as follows:

Gross income:		
Wages		$ 1,900
Interest income		2,500
Total		$ 4,400
Add-back "unused zero-bracket amount" determined as follows:		
ZBA	$2,390	
Less earned income	1,900	
Unused ZBA		490
Total		$ 4,890
Less personal exemption deduction		1,040
Taxable income		$ 3,850

Observe that in Example 18 Lisa Hopkins will actually pay a tax on only $2,390 of income, and in Example 19 Jim will pay a tax on only $1,460 of income, because (in both instances) each taxpayer will still utilize a tax rate schedule that incorporates a $2,390 zero-bracket amount.

Example 20: Assume that Joe and Terri Block, a husband and wife, file separate returns for 1985. Joe reports his salary of $11,000 and Terri reports her salary of $14,000. Terri also claims all of this couple's itemized deductions of $4,000; Joe claims no deductions. On *separate* returns, these two married individuals would compute their 1985 taxable incomes as follows:

	JOE	TERRI
Gross income (salary)	$11,000	$14,000
Unused zero bracket amount ($1,770 − $0) (must be added back)	1,770	-0-
Total	$12,770	$14,000
Less itemized deductions in excess of ZBA	-0-	(2,230)
Less personal exemptions	(1,040)	(1,040)
Taxable income	$11,730	$10,730

Note that the $22,460 sum of their two separate taxable incomes is exactly equal to what their combined taxable income would have been on a joint return, computed as follows:

Salaries		$25,000
Less:		
Deductions	$4,000	
Less ZBA	3,540	(460)
Personal exemptions		(2,080)
Taxable income		$22,460

Once a taxpayer has determined the amount of his or her deductions, both for and from AGI, the amount of his or her *taxable income* is easy to figure. It is simply the remainder left after subtracting all deductions from gross income. The amount of taxable income is very important because it is the technical tax base on which our federal income tax is calculated.

APPLICABLE TAX RATES

The general formula on page 3-2 suggests that once an individual knows the amount of his or her taxable income, the next step in determining the income tax liability involves multiplying that taxable income by the applicable tax rate(s). As a practical matter, the actual need to multiply may or may not be required. The administrators of our tax law have prepared tax tables which can be used by many people to determine their gross tax liability without the need for any multiplication. These tables have been designed to simplify the law and minimize the chance for errors. The 1984 tax tables generally had to be used by all individual taxpayers with a taxable income of $50,000 or less. A copy of these 1984 tax tables is included as Appendix B at the end of this text. The tax tables for 1985 will not be available until December of 1985. Individuals reporting a taxable income in excess of $50,000 in 1985 will use one of the four tax rate schedules reprinted in Appendix A.

Example 21: Raul Rios realized a taxable income of $60,000 in 1985. Raul is single. Using the tax rate schedules located in Appendix A, Raul will determine his 1985 gross tax liability as follows:

Tax on first $57,550 (per Schedule X)	$16,770.70
Tax on remaining $2,450 (at 48%)	1,176.00
Gross tax liability for 1985	$17,946.00

Example 22: Paul and Sue Johnson realized a taxable income of $22,418 in 1984. They file a joint return. Using the tax tables located in Appendix B, Paul and Sue will determine their 1984 gross tax liability as follows:

Tax on taxable income of any amount from $22,400 to $22,450 (per column 2)	$ 2,987

Regardless of whether one uses the tax tables or the tax rate schedules, the correct determination of an individual's federal income tax depends upon a correct classification of the taxpayer into one of four categories, namely:

1. Married, filing a joint return;
2. Married, filing separately;
3. Head of household; or
4. Single.

The general intent of the first two categories is, obviously, to allow married persons an option: that is, a married couple may elect to file one joint return or the husband and wife may each file separately. The general intent of the fourth category—that of single persons—is equally apparent: it is intended to apply to individuals who are not married. Both common sense and a brief study of history would support the idea that the third category, labeled "Head of household," must be intended for unmarried individuals with some family-type responsibilities. While these general observations are indeed correct, and most taxpayers know intuitively into which of the four categories they belong, there are enough problem cases to justify a more detailed examination of each category.

JOINT RETURN RATES The Code provides criteria that must be met before a taxpayer may elect to file a joint return.[11] Two taxpayers may generally file a joint return if—

[11] Secs. 1(a) and 143. Sec. 143(b) provides that certain legally married persons who live apart from their spouse for more than one-half of the year may be considered to be "not married." Generally this requires them to maintain their own home, for themself and for a dependent, for at least six months of the year.

1. They are married (not divorced or legally separated) on the last day of their taxable year; and
2. Neither spouse is a nonresident alien.[12]

A single person who qualifies as a ***surviving spouse*** is also eligible to file a joint return.[13] The surviving-spouse status extends only to the first two years following the tax year in which a taxpayer's spouse dies. Furthermore, to be classified as a surviving spouse, a taxpayer must maintain a home in which a dependent child or stepchild lives. The special status as a surviving spouse is automatically terminated (*a*) after the two-year period, (*b*) by remarriage during the period, or (*c*) by the loss of the dependency status of the child or stepchild.

SURVIVING SPOUSE A widow or widower who qualifies for the joint return rate schedule.

Example 23: Ann's husband, Bill, died on May 3, 19X1, leaving in their home a 14-year-old child, Zane, who qualifies as Ann's dependent. For 19X1 Ann may file a joint return and claim three exemption deductions (one each for Ann, Bill, and Zane). If Zane continues to live with Ann, and to qualify as her dependent, Ann may continue to file a joint return for 19X2 and 19X3. In the latter two years, however, Ann may claim only two exemption deductions (one each for herself and Zane).

In most instances the lowest possible tax rates are available by filing a joint return. Consequently, most married persons elect this status. Because both the husband and the wife are jointly and severally liable for the total amount of the correct tax liability on a joint return, however, a few individuals may desire to file separate returns.[14] A few other individuals may elect to file separate returns because one spouse has a large medical deduction or casualty loss subject to the 5% or 10% (of AGI) limitation (discussed in Chapter 6). Otherwise, in most cases married persons will elect to file a joint return if they are eligible to do so.

HEAD OF HOUSEHOLD RATES The major requirements for using the tax rates for heads of households are found in Sec. 2(b). In general, to qualify as a ***head of household***:

1. The taxpayer cannot be classified as married (or as a surviving spouse) *unless* he or she qualifies as an ***abandoned spouse***;
2. The taxpayer maintains a home in which a dependent relative lives for the entire year;
3. The taxpayer pays more than 50% of the cost of maintaining the home; *and*
4. The taxpayer is either a U.S. citizen or a resident alien.

HEAD OF HOUSEHOLD In general, a taxpayer who is not married, but who maintains a home in which a dependent relative lives.

ABANDONED SPOUSE In general, a married taxpayer who does not live with his or her spouse during the last six months of the year, and who furnishes over one-half the cost of maintaining a home in which a dependent child lives for at least 6 months of the year.

[12] Note, however, that a joint return may be filed even if one spouse is a nonresident alien if both agree to include their worldwide income on the return. Sec. 6013(g) and (h).

[13] Sec. 1(a) and 2(a).

[14] An "innocent" spouse may, under very special conditions, be excused from this joint and several liability. Sec. 6013(e) and Treas. Reg. Sec. 1.6013-5.

The apparent intent of this tax rate schedule is to prescribe for persons who are not married, but who have certain family responsibilities, a tax rate schedule that is (in general) slightly higher than that prescribed for married persons filing a joint return, but slightly lower than that prescribed for single individuals.

Example 24: The 1984 tax on a $15,000 taxable income is $1,585 for a married couple filing a joint return; $1,899 for a head of household; and $2,007 for a single person. (See tax rate tables in Appendix B.)

The biggest problem with the head of household rate schedule is found in the definitional requirements. Although the four basic requirements stated above appear to be relatively easy to read and interpret, the Code goes on to make several exceptions to the general requirements in specific situations. Three of these exceptions are worth noting.

Exception 1: If the dependent relative who qualifies a taxpayer for head of household status is the taxpayer's parent, then the parent need not live in the taxpayer's home. This exception allows a taxpayer to qualify as a head of household if he or she supports a dependent parent in a retirement home or similar facility.[15]

Exception 2: If the relative who lives with and qualifies a taxpayer for head of household status is the taxpayer's (*a*) child or child's descendant, (*b*) stepchild, or (*c*) foster child, then that relative need *not* qualify as the taxpayer's dependent as long as that relative remains unmarried.[16]

Exception 3: An "abandoned spouse," who otherwise qualifies, may qualify as a head of household even though he or she is still legally married. To be an abandoned spouse a taxpayer must—

a) Live apart from his or her spouse for the last six months of the entire year;

b) Maintain a household (furnishing over one-half of the cost of that home) during the year;

c) Have a dependent child or stepchild live with him or her for at least six months of the year; *and*

d) Not file a joint return with their legal spouse.[17]

Note that a taxpayer may qualify as an abandoned spouse without qualifying for the head of household tax rates. Before an individual can use the head of household rates, a dependent relative must (subject to exceptions 1 and 2 above) live with him or her for the entire year; to be

[15] Sec. 2(b)(1)(B).

[16] Sec. 2(b)(1)(A)(i).

[17] Secs. 2(c) and 143(b).

an abandoned spouse requires only six months of living together.

These complex rules with their exceptions, and even exceptions-to-exceptions, make it difficult for more than a few taxpayers to determine whether or not they qualify for the head of household tax rates.

SINGLE RETURN RATES The tax rate schedule prescribed for single persons is, in reality, the residual schedule. In other words, this is the rate schedule that must be used if a person does not qualify for any one of the other three schedules. Note that married persons never qualify for the tax rates prescribed for single individuals *unless* (*a*) they are legally separated under a decree of divorce or of separate maintenance or (*b*) they qualify as an abandoned spouse (but not as a head of household).[18] This is an important conclusion because, in some circumstances, two married persons—each of whom earns a sizable income—would pay less tax in total if they could file as two single individuals. In an attempt to alleviate this "***marriage penalty***," the Congress provided a special (above-the-line) deduction for working couples.

MARRIAGE PENALTY The additional income tax that may be payable when two individuals, each of whom earns a substantial income, marry.

This special deduction is equal to 10% of the lesser of (*a*) $30,000 or (*b*) the qualified *earned* income of the spouse who earns the least.[19] Thus, the maximum deduction is $3,000 per year. As illustrated in Example 25 a partial marriage penalty remains for some two-earner families.

FORM SCHEDULE W

Example 25: Both Kristin Klark and Christopher Counts earn a $35,040 annual salary. Assuming they are not entitled to claim any deductions, other than their personal exemption deductions, they would each pay an income tax of $7,306.90 in 1985 as long as they are single, determined as follows:

Salary	$35,040
Less personal exemption deduction	(1,040)
Taxable income	$34,000
Tax (using 1984 rates)	$ 7,306.90
Total tax (for two)	$14,613.80

If these two individuals were to marry and continue to earn their same salaries, their income tax would jump to $16,859, computed as follows:

Combined salaries	$70,080
Less:	
Special deduction	(3,000)
Personal exemptions	(2,080)
Taxable income	$65,000
Tax (using 1985 rates)	$16,859

[18] Secs. 2(c) and 143.

[19] Sec. 221.

Thus this couple still pays a marriage penalty of $2,245.20 for 1985. In general, the larger their earned incomes, the greater the marriage penalty, especially if both incomes are of approximately the same size.

The marriage-penalty deduction is simply the latest of numerous attempts over many years to achieve greater tax equity among diverse groups of individual taxpayers. The problems all started when, in 1948, Congress created the first "joint tax return" rate schedule. Prior to that time there was only one tax rate schedule that applied equally to all individuals, regardless of their marital status. The 1948 problem arose because married taxpayers who lived in "community-property states" often paid significantly less federal income tax than married taxpayers living in "common-law states" because, in the community-property states, each spouse was deemed to have earned one-half of most income earned by his or her spouse. Because the U.S. tax rates on individual incomes were progressive—and, in those days only one spouse typically worked—two times the tax on one-half the couple's total income was generally less than the tax determined on the total income earned by only one of the two parties to the marriage. Hence the width of the initial joint-return tax-rate brackets were set exactly equal to twice the width of the brackets for single persons. As a result of this modification, after 1948 married couples with only one working spouse were treated the same way regardless of the property law of the state in which they lived.

Although the creation of the first joint-return tax-rate schedule did resolve the conflict between some persons living in different states, it created very large differences between the tax liability on single persons and married couples who earned the same total income. To make matters worse, there were some individuals who were not married—because of death or divorce—but who had "family-type" financial obligations. Widows having to support young dependents were treated most unfairly. These persons argued that their tax liabilities should be reduced to reflect their "nearly-married" status. Again, in an attempt to achieve greater equity, Congress in 1951 created what we know now as the head-of-household tax-rate schedule. Being a political solution, it is not surprising to discover that the first head-of-household brackets were exactly half again as wide as those applied to single persons. In other words, if the first (say, 10%) bracket for single taxpayers went from $0 to $2,000 in taxable income (and, therefore, the first (10%) bracket for married persons went from $0 to $4,000), the first (10%) bracket for heads of households went from $0 to $3,000 (etc.) in 1951.

While this modification helped achieve greater equity between some married couples and certain widowed and divorced singles, the big difference between the tax liability of single persons and married couples earning the same total income still remained. Hence, the singles complained to Congress and their views were heeded in 1969 when all prior rate schedules were adjusted in such a way that a single person's tax would never exceed 120% of the tax payable by a married couple earning the same total income. (Head-of-household tax brackets were adjusted at the same time to remain approximately half-way between the other two.)

At the same time, however, this last change necessitated the creation of new brackets for married persons filing separate returns to avoid recreating exactly the same community-property problems that were "resolved" back in 1948! Unintentionally this change also created what we know now as the marriage penalty.

The latest social inequity (due to the differences between the width of the various marginal tax-rate brackets for singles and marrieds) was made even greater by the fact that the zero-bracket amounts for married persons were less than twice the amounts allowed for single individuals. Hence, in 1981, Congress created the very special deduction, discussed above, solely for married couples with two working spouses. As demonstrated in the above example, the degree of equity currently achieved is much less than perfect. Nevertheless, this last change seems, for the moment at least, to have brought the newest inequity to within politically tolerable limits.

After a taxpayer knows his or her gross tax liability—either by reference to one of four columns in a tax table or by using one of the tax rate schedules—he or she must determine his or her tax prepayments and credits.

TAX PREPAYMENTS AND CREDITS

Tax prepayments and credits stem from two very different sources. ***Tax credits*** are, generally speaking, special incentives, in the form of limited tax reductions, put into the law in an attempt to induce taxpayers to take specified actions that they might not otherwise be inclined to take. Tax prepayments, on the other hand, are merely a way of getting people to "pay their tax as they earn their income." In other words, tax credits may be viewed as a special "gift" from Congress while prepayments are nothing but a down payment on taxes.

TAX CREDIT Any of several direct tax reductions in a taxpayer's gross tax liability authorized by the Code for reasons other than a prepayment of a tax liability.

TAX PREPAYMENTS—WITHHOLDING Individuals who work as employees quickly learn that their paychecks are significantly less than their gross wages or salaries. The two biggest differences between an employee's gross wage and his or her take-home pay are generally due to the amounts withheld by the employer for (*a*) social security taxes and (*b*) income taxes. Every employer is required by law to withhold from each paycheck an estimated amount of income tax based on the employee's (*a*) marital status, (*b*) number of exemptions claimed (on Form W-4), and (*c*) earnings for the period, and to remit the amount thus withheld to a depository of the federal government within a prescribed time period.[20] Essentially, the withholding provision is designed to put the payment of income taxes on wages on a "pay-as-you-go" basis. "Wages" include all remuneration for services performed by an employee for an employer, including the cash value of all remuneration paid in any medium other

FORM W-4

[20] Sec. 3402.

than cash. Each January the employer must give the employee a Form W-2, showing the total amount of remuneration subject to income tax paid the employee during the year, the amount of income tax withheld, the amount of earnings subject to social security taxes, and the amount of social security tax withheld. The employee attaches one copy of this form to his or her federal income tax return when it is sent in to the Internal Revenue Service. The amount withheld for income taxes is a prepayment that is subtracted from the gross tax payable, after tax credits, to arrive at the net tax payable or refundable.

FORM W-2

TAX PREPAYMENTS—ESTIMATED PAYMENTS As explained above, every employee is placed on a pay-as-you-go basis when the employer withholds income taxes from the employee's earnings. Individuals who are self-employed are generally required to make "quarterly" payments of their estimated income tax on each April 15, June 15, September 15, and January 15. Technically, every individual is required to make timely payments of estimated tax every year if he or she will owe an income tax at the end of the year. However, there is no penalty for failure to make timely ***estimated payments*** if either of two tests described in Chapter 13 is met. If neither of those tests is met, a penalty for underpayment of the estimated tax will be assessed.

ESTIMATED PAYMENTS The annual prepayments of the federal income tax required of certain individual taxpayers each year, to put them on a pay-as-you-go basis.

Simply stated, the penalty is an annual charge on the difference between the amount paid in each quarter and 80% of the tax due each quarter, computed from the date due until the date paid. The penalty is treated as an addition to the tax. Additional details concerning estimated taxes are discussed later in the text.

TAX PREPAYMENTS—EXCESS SOCIAL SECURITY TAXES Each employer is required to withhold (and match) Social Security taxes from every employee's earnings each pay period up to a specified amount every year. For 1985 the Social Security tax withheld is 7.05% of the first $39,600 paid an employee during the year. Thus, if an employee works for two employers during 1985, earning $30,000 from the first and $15,000 from the second, the first employer would withhold $2,115 and the second would withhold $1,057.50, for a total of $3,172.50. However, an employee is subject to a maximum Social Security tax of only $2,791.80 on a total of $39,600 of wages paid during 1985. This means that the employee has overpaid Social Security taxes by $380.70 through excess withholding by employers. On his or her income tax return for the year, the taxpayer treats the "excess Social Security tax withheld" as a prepayment in computing net tax payable (or refundable).

TAX PREPAYMENTS—EXCISE TAX PAID ON NONHIGHWAY USE OF PETROLEUM PRODUCTS When a consumer purchases gasoline or lubricating oil, the purchase price includes a federal excise tax imposed on users of highways, to provide funds for construction and maintenance of roads. When the gasoline or oil is purchased for nonhighway uses, such as farming or operating a motorboat, the taxpayer must pay the tax on purchase but may file a refund claim for the amounts paid. Section 34 allows the taxpayer to take a credit against his or her federal income tax for the amount of excise taxes paid on gasoline and oil bought for nonhighway use, thus providing a simple refund procedure. In essence, these amounts are treated as prepayments of income taxes.

Tax credits, like prepayments, reduce a taxpayer's gross tax liability on a dollar-for-dollar basis. The most important tax credits are intended as a special incentive to stimulate desired taxpayer behavior. A few other tax credits are intended to improve tax equity. Although the important details of the various tax credits must be deferred to Chapter 14, a few of the most important general rules will be very briefly described here.

THE INVESTMENT CREDIT The investment credit is by far the most important tax credit.[21] The purpose of this credit is to encourage investment by business. Congress tried to encourage investments in only those assets that would have a positive effect on economic activity by limiting the credit to investments in *qualified property*. In general, qualified property means tangible personal property subject to depreciation. The tax credit allowed is generally equal to 10% of the qualified investment. In effect, this works out to 6% for investments in three-year properties[22] and 10% for most other qualified investments. There are various limitations, provisions for recapture, carrybacks and carryovers of unused credits, and other technical provisions that make the investment credit very complex. These details are discussed further in Chapter 14.

TARGETED JOBS CREDIT In an attempt to induce employers to employ various individuals who are chronically underemployed, Congress created a targeted jobs credit (Sec. 51). This allows taxpayers to claim a tax credit equal to 50% of the wages paid to qualified employees (to a maximum of $6,000) in their first year plus 25% of qualified wages in the second year. The targeted persons eligible for this credit include economically disadvantaged youths, persons receiving welfare payments, ex-convicts, etc. Once again the important details of this credit must be left for discussion later in the text.

THE EARNED INCOME CREDIT In order to qualify for the earned income credit (Sec. 32), a taxpayer is required to maintain in the United States a household that is the principal place of abode of the taxpayer and the taxpayer's dependent child. The credit is available only to married taxpayers and to taxpayers qualified to file either as a "surviving spouse" or a "head of household." If the taxpayer is a head of household, an unmarried child living with the taxpayer does not have to qualify as the taxpayer's dependent, although a married child *does*. The credit is based on "earned income," defined as salaries, wages, other employee compensation, and earnings from self-employment.

The gross credit is 10% of a taxpayer's first $5,000 of earned income, so that the maximum credit is $500. However, the gross credit is reduced by 12.5% of that amount of the taxpayer's adjusted gross income or earned

---

[21] Sec. 38.

[22] A 3-year property is one whose cost can be recovered, for tax purposes, in just three years. See Chapter 10 for more details.

income, whichever is larger, that is in excess of $6,000. Thus, if the taxpayer has $10,000 or more of earned income or adjusted gross income, no credit would be allowed. To illustrate the computation, assume that a married taxpayer and spouse live in a home with their 2 dependent children. The taxpayer's adjusted gross income, solely from wages, totals $7,150, so there is no gross tax liability. Nevertheless, the taxpayer will file a tax return and receive a "refund" equal to the earned income credit. Theoretically, the earned income credit is $356.25, computed as follows:

Tentative credit, 10% of earned income of $7,150 limited to $500 maximum	$500.00
Less 12.5% of adjusted gross income in excess of $6,000 ($1,150 × 12.5%)	143.75
Credit (theoretically)	$356.25

The actual amount of credit, however, must be determined from a table developed by the IRS. This table shows that if the amount subject to the credit is at least $7,100 but not over $7,105, the earned income credit is $359. (See Appendix D).

An employee who is eligible for the earned income credit may, by filling out a certificate, have his employer make "advance payment" of the credit to the employee. The amount to be advanced is determined under tables prescribed by the Internal Revenue Service. The employer offsets the advance against the employer's liability for the following taxes, in order: (*a*) income taxes withheld, (*b*) FICA taxes withheld, and (*c*) the employer's share of FICA taxes.

Obviously, the earned income credit is designed to benefit low-income taxpayers. It was passed with the specific intent of offsetting partially the rapidly growing impact of social security taxes.

CREDIT FOR THE ELDERLY Another tax credit is the "credit for the elderly" (Code Sec. 22), which permits taxpayers who are 65 years of age or older to reduce their tax bill by an amount up to $750. The credit is equal to 15% of the taxpayer's adjusted gross income up to $5,000. The credit begins to be phased out when the taxpayer's adjusted gross income reaches $7,500. The provision contains special rules for married couples and for those who receive social security benefits. The original retirement income credit was an effort to equalize, at least partially, the tax effect on (*a*) "retirement income" subject to the income tax and (*b*) tax-free income from social security and railroad retirement benefits.

THE CREDIT FOR POLITICAL CONTRIBUTIONS Sec. 24 authorizes an individual taxpayer to take a credit equal to one-half of "contributions" made to political parties, a candidate for nomination or election to public office, or a candidate's organization. The maximum credit is $50 for a single individual, $50 for a married person filing a separate return, and $100 for a married couple filing jointly.

CREDIT FOR CHILD-CARE AND DEPENDENT-CARE EXPENSES Sec. 21 authorizes a tax credit, subject to several limits, ranging from 20% to 30% of the amount expended for the care of a qualified individual (generally the taxpayer's dependents under 15 years of age, the taxpayer's disabled spouse, or certain other disabled dependents). The base for the credit is limited to $2,400 per year if there is one qualified individual or $4,800 per year for two or more qualified individuals. Additional details of these and several other credits are discussed in Chapter 14. Even without full knowledge of all the details, we are now ready to review the individual tax formula in its entirety.

THE INDIVIDUAL'S FORMULA ILLUSTRATED

To illustrate the general tax formula applicable to the individual taxpayer, let us consider the following income tax-related items assumed for the year 1984:

Marital status: married (files jointly)	
Number of exemptions: 4 (husband, wife, and two young children)	
Income:	
Salary	$10,000
Raffle prize	300
Employee travel allowance	1,800
Dividends (from domestic corporations)	250
Interest (from local bank)	450
Deductions:	
Employee travel expenses	2,000
Interest paid	700
Real property taxes (on residence)	200
Prepayment:	
Tax withheld from salary	390

Plugging the above data into the tax formula for individual taxpayers, we find that the net tax payable for this imaginary taxpayer is a negative $24; that is, the taxpayer is entitled to a refund of this amount. The solution is presented in Table 3-1. Note once again that the arithmetic in this formula is straightforward; the definitions and classifications prerequisite to the arithmetic are the complicating factors.

TAX RETURN ILLUSTRATION

The simplest tax return form available to an individual taxpayer is Form 1040EZ (Figure 3-1). To use this form in 1985 the taxpayer must— **FORM 1040EZ**

1. Be single and claim no "extra" personal exemption deductions for age or blindness;
2. Claim no dependent's exemption deduction;
3. Realize a taxable income of less than $50,000; and
4. Receive all income from wages, salaries, tips, and/or interest. (Furthermore, interest income can not exceed $400.)

TABLE 3-1
Using the Individual Formula

Income broadly conceived	$12,800	($10,000 + 300 + 1,800 + 250 + 450)
less ↓		
Exclusions	(200)	(Dividends—up to $100/taxpayer)
equals ↓		
Gross income	$12,600	
less ↓		
Deductions for AGI	(2,000)	(Employee travel "away from home")
equals ↓		
AGI	$10,600	
less ↓		
Deductions from AGI	-0-	(Excess over zero bracket amount) *
less ↓		
Personal and Dependent Exemptions	(4,000)	($1,000 × 4)
equals ↓		
Taxable income	$ 6,600	
times		
Tax Rate	—	(Tax tables for 1984)†
equals ↓		
Gross Tax	$ 366	
less ↓		
Tax Credits and Prepayments	(390)	(Tax withheld from salary)
equals ↓		
Net Tax Payable/Refundable	$ (24)	(Refund due taxpayer)

*The zero-bracket amount of $3,400 for 1984 exceeds the actual itemized deductions.

†The tax tables must be used because the taxable income is less than $50,000. (See Appendix B for the 1984 tax tables.)

FIGURE 3-1

Department of the Treasury - Internal Revenue Service

1984 **Form 1040EZ Income Tax Return for Single filers with no dependents** OMB No. 1545-0675

Name & address

Use the IRS mailing label. If you don't have one, please print:

▶ Tom X. Jones
Print your name above (first, initial, last)

112 Slippery Road
Present home address (number and street)

Central City, KS 66031
City, town, or post office, State, and ZIP code

Please print your numbers like this.

1 2 3 4 5 6 7 8 9 0

Social security number

284 23 5291

Presidential Election Campaign Fund
Check box if you want $1 of your tax to go to this fund. ▶ ☐

			Dollars	Cents
Figure your tax	1	Total wages, salaries, and tips. This should be shown in Box 10 of your W-2 form(s). (Attach your W-2 form(s).) 1	15,000	.
	2	Interest income of $400 or less. If the total is more than $400, you cannot use Form 1040EZ. 2	300	.
Attach Copy B of Form(s) W-2 here	3	Add line 1 and line 2. This is your **adjusted gross income.** 3	15,300	.
	4	Allowable part of your charitable contributions. Complete the worksheet on page 21 of the instruction booklet. Do not enter more than $75. 4	0	.
	5	Subtract line 4 from line 3. 5	15,300	.
	6	Amount of your personal exemption. 6	1,000	.00
	7	Subtract line 6 from line 5. This is your **taxable income.** 7	14,300	.
	8	Enter your Federal income tax withheld. This should be shown in Box 9 of your W-2 form(s). 8	1,900	.
	9	Use the **single** column in the tax table on pages 31-36 of the instruction booklet to find the **tax** on your taxable income on line 7. Enter the amount of tax. 9	1,866	.
Refund or amount you owe	10	If line 8 is larger than line 9, subtract line 9 from line 8. Enter the **amount of your refund.** 10	34	.
Attach tax payment here	11	If line 9 is larger than line 8, subtract line 8 from line 9. Enter the **amount you owe.** Attach check or money order for the full amount, payable to "Internal Revenue Service." 11	,	.

Sign your return

I have read this return. Under penalties of perjury, I declare that to the best of my knowledge and belief, the return is true, correct, and complete.

Your signature: Tom X. Jones Date: 2/14/85

For IRS Use Only—Please do not write in boxes below.

1 2 3 4 5

For Privacy Act and Paperwork Reduction Act Notice, see page 41.

FORM 1040A **FORM 1040** Individuals who can not use Form 1040EZ must use either Form 1040A (commonly known as the "short form") (Figures 3-2 and 3-3) or Form 1040 (the "long form") (Figures 3-4 and 3-5).

To illustrate the use of Form 1040EZ, we assume the following facts:

> Tom Jones, unmarried, age 30, and with good vision has the following income:
>
> | | |
> |---|---|
> | Wages (subject to withholding) | $15,000 |
> | Interest (from City Bank account) | 300 |
>
> Tom's itemized deductions are less than the zero-bracket amount; he made no charitable contributions. Tom's Form W-2 shows that his employer withheld $1,900 for federal income taxes.

As the form indicates, Tom is entitled to a $34 refund for 1984.

KEY POINTS TO REMEMBER

1. The income concept must be broadly interpreted for federal income tax purposes. In other words, unless you can cite good authority for excluding it, every item of income must be included in income for federal income tax purposes.
2. Whether or not an individual is required to file a federal income tax return is determined by the amount of his or her *gross income*.
3. Nothing is deductible for federal income tax purposes unless the taxpayer can cite good authority authorizing the deduction.
4. Any legally authorized deduction that is not specifically included within Sec. 62 is automatically a "below-the-line" deduction (or a deduction from AGI).
5. Itemized deductions—i.e., below-the-line deductions other than the personal and dependent exemption deductions—can be deducted only if and to the extent that they exceed the taxpayer's zero-bracket amount.
6. Before an individual may claim a dependency deduction for another individual, each of five specific tests must be satisfied.
7. The maximum gross-income limit does not apply in determining the dependency status of a taxpayer's child (or foster child) if either (*a*) that child is 18 years of age or younger, or (*b*) that child is a "full-time" student.
8. An "unused zero-bracket amount" must be added to gross income, in the determination of taxable income, in four specific situations.
9. Any one of four different tax rate schedules may be applicable to the taxable income earned by an individual taxpayer.
10. The gross tax liability may be reduced by tax credits and prepayments of tax to determine the net tax payable (or the net refund).

FIGURE 3-2

Department of the Treasury—Internal Revenue Service

1984 **Form 1040A US Individual Income Tax Return** OMB No. 1545-0085

Step 1
Name and address

Use the IRS mailing label. If you don't have one, print or type:

Your first name and initial (if joint return, also give spouse's name and initial) | Last name | Your social security no.

Present home address (number and street) | Spouse's social security no.

City, town or post office, State, and ZIP code

Presidential Election Campaign Fund

Do you want $1 to go to this fund? . . . . ☐ Yes ☐ No

If joint return, does your spouse want $1 to go to this fund? ☐ Yes ☐ No

Step 2
Check your filing status
(Check only one)

1 ☐ Single (See if you can use Form 1040EZ.)

2 ☐ Married filing joint return (even if only one had income)

3 ☐ Married filing separate return. Enter spouse's social security number above and spouse's full name here. ______

4 ☐ Head of household (with qualifying person). If the qualifying person is your unmarried child but not your dependent, write this child's name here. ______

Step 3
Figure your exemptions

Always check the exemption box labeled Yourself. Check other boxes if they apply.

5a ☐ Yourself ☐ 65 or over ☐ Blind

b ☐ Spouse ☐ 65 or over ☐ Blind

Write number of boxes checked on 5a and b ______

c First names of your dependent children who lived with you ______

Write number of children listed on 5c + ______

d Other dependents:

1. Name	2. Relationship	3. Number of months lived in your home.	4. Did dependent have income of $1,000 or more?	5. Did you provide more than one-half of dependent's support?

Attach Copy B of Form(s) W-2 here

Write number of other dependents listed on 5d + ______

Add numbers entered on lines above = ______

e Total number of exemptions claimed. (Also complete line 18.)

Step 4
Figure your total income

6 Total wages, salaries, tips, etc. This should be shown in Box 10 of your W-2 form(s). (Attach Form(s) W-2.) 6 .

7 Interest income. (If the total is over $400, also complete and attach Schedule 1 (Form 1040A), Part I.) 7 .

8a Dividends. (If the total is over $400, also complete and attach Schedule 1 (Form 1040A), Part II.) 8a .

Attach check or money order here

b Exclusion. See the instructions on page 16. 8b .

c Subtract line 8b from line 8a. Write the result. 8c .

9a Unemployment compensation (insurance), from Form(s) 1099-G. Total received. 9a .

b Taxable amount, if any, from the worksheet on page 17 of the instructions. 9b .

10 Add lines 6, 7, 8c, and 9b. Write the total. This is your **total income.** 10 .

Step 5
Figure your adjusted gross income

11a Individual retirement arrangement (IRA) deduction, from the worksheet on page 19. 11a .

b Write IRA payments made in 1985 that you included on line 11a: ($.)

12 Deduction for a married couple when both work. Complete and attach Schedule 1 (Form 1040A), Part III. 12 .

13 Add lines 11a and 12. Write the total. These are your **total adjustments.** 13 .

14 Subtract line 13 from line 10. Write the result. This is your **adjusted gross income.** 14 .

3

FIGURE 3-3

1984 Form 1040A Page 2

Step 6
Figure your taxable income

15 Write the amount from line 14. 15 .

16 Allowable part of your charitable contributions, from the worksheet on page 21 of the instructions. 16 .

17 Subtract line 16 from line 15. Write the result. 17 .

18 Multiply $1,000 by the total number of exemptions claimed on line 5e. 18 .

19 Subtract line 18 from line 17. Write the result. This is your **taxable income.** 19 .

Step 7
Figure your tax, credits, and payments

If You Want IRS to Figure Your Tax, See Page 21 of the Instructions.

20 Find the tax on the amount on line 19. Use the tax table, pages 31–36. 20 .

21a Credit for child and dependent care expenses. Complete and attach Schedule 1 (Form 1040A), Part IV. 21a .

b Partial credit for political contributions for which you have receipts. See page 24 of the instructions. 21b .

22 Add lines 21a and 21b. Write the total. 22 .

23 Subtract line 22 from line 20. Write the result (but not less than zero). This is your **total tax.** 23 .

24a Total Federal income tax withheld. This should be shown in Box 9 of your W-2 form(s). (If line 6 is more than $37,800, see page 24 of the instructions.) 24a .

b Earned income credit, from the worksheet on page 26 of the instructions. See page 25 of the instructions. 24b .

25 Add lines 24a and 24b. Write the total. These are your **total payments.** 25 .

Step 8
Figure your refund or amount you owe

26 If line 25 is larger than line 23, subtract line 23 from line 25. Write the result. This is the **amount of your refund.** 26 .

27 If line 23 is larger than line 25, subtract line 25 from line 23. Write the result. This is the **amount you owe.** Attach check or money order for full amount payable to "Internal Revenue Service." Write your social security number and "1984 Form 1040A" on it. 27 .

Step 9
Sign your return

Under penalties of perjury, I declare that I have examined this return and accompanying schedules and statements, and to the best of my knowledge and belief, they are true, correct, and complete. Declaration of preparer (other than the taxpayer) is based on all information of which the preparer has any knowledge.

Your signature | Date | Your occupation

X

Spouse's signature (if joint return, both must sign) | Date | Spouse's occupation

X

Paid preparer's signature | Date | Preparer's social security no.

X

Firm's name (or yours, if self-employed) | Employer identification no.

Address and ZIP code | Check if self-employed ☐

For **Privacy Act and Paperwork Reduction Act Notice,** see page 41.

FIGURE 3-4

Form **1040** Department of the Treasury—Internal Revenue Service
U.S. Individual Income Tax Return 1984 (0)

For the year January 1-December 31, 1984, or other tax year beginning , 1984, ending , 19 | OMB No. 1545-0074

Use IRS label. Otherwise, please print or type.

Your first name and initial (if joint return, also give spouse's name and initial)	Last name	**Your social security number**
Present home address (Number and street, including apartment number, or rural route)		**Spouse's social security number**
City, town or post office, State, and ZIP code	Your occupation Spouse's occupation	

Presidential Election Campaign ▶ Do you want $1 to go to this fund? . . . . Yes | No
If joint return, does your spouse want $1 to go to this fund?. . Yes | No
Note: *Checking "Yes" will not change your tax or reduce your refund.*

For Privacy Act and Paperwork Reduction Act Notice, see Instructions.

Filing Status

Check only one box.

1 ☐ Single
2 ☐ Married filing joint return (even if only one had income)
3 ☐ Married filing separate return. Enter spouse's social security no. above and full name here.
4 ☐ Head of household (with qualifying person). (See page 5 of Instructions.) If the qualifying person is your unmarried child but not your dependent, write child's name here.
5 ☐ Qualifying widow(er) with dependent child (Year spouse died ▶ 19). (See page 6 of Instructions.)

Exemptions

Always check the box labeled Yourself. Check other boxes if they apply.

6a ☐ Yourself ☐ 65 or over ☐ Blind
b ☐ Spouse ☐ 65 or over ☐ Blind
Enter number of boxes checked on 6a and b ▶ ☐
c First names of your dependent children who lived with you
Enter number of children listed on 6c ▶ ☐

d Other dependents: (1) Name	(2) Relationship	(3) Number of months lived in your home	(4) Did dependent have income of $1,000 or more?	(5) Did you provide more than one-half of dependent's support?

Enter number of other dependents ▶ ☐
Add numbers entered in boxes above ▶ ☐

e Total number of exemptions claimed (also complete line 36). . . . .

Income

Please attach Copy B of your Forms W-2, W-2G, and W-2P here.

If you do not have a W-2, see page 4 of Instructions.

Please attach check or money order here.

7	Wages, salaries, tips, etc.	7
8	Interest income *(also attach Schedule B if over $400)*	8
9a	Dividends *(also attach Schedule B if over $400)* ____ , **9b** Exclusion ____	
c	Subtract line 9b from line 9a and enter the result	9c
10	Refunds of State and local income taxes, from the worksheet on page 9 of Instructions *(do not enter an amount unless you itemized deductions for those taxes in an earlier year—see page 9)* . . .	10
11	Alimony received	11
12	Business income or (loss) *(attach Schedule C)*	12
13	Capital gain or (loss) *(attach Schedule D)*	13
14	40% of capital gain distributions not reported on line 13 (see page 9 of Instructions) . . .	14
15	Supplemental gains or (losses) *(attach Form 4797)*	15
16	Fully taxable pensions, IRA distributions, and annuities not reported on line 17 . . .	16
17a	Other pensions and annuities, including rollovers. Total received **17a**	
b	Taxable amount, if any, from the worksheet on page 10 of Instructions	17b
18	Rents, royalties, partnerships, estates, trusts, etc. *(attach Schedule E)*	18
19	Farm income or (loss) *(attach Schedule F)*	19
20a	Unemployment compensation (insurance). Total received . . **20a**	
b	Taxable amount, if any, from the worksheet on page 10 of Instructions . . .	20b
21a	Social security benefits. (see page 10 of Instructions) . . . **21a**	
b	Taxable amount, if any, from the worksheet on page 11 of Instructions	21b
22	Other income (state nature and source—see page 11 of Instructions)	22
23	Add lines 7 through 22. This is your **total income** . . . . ▶	23

Adjustments to Income

(See Instructions on page 11.)

24	Moving expense *(attach Form 3903 or 3903F)*	24	
25	Employee business expenses *(attach Form 2106)*	25	
26a	IRA deduction, from the worksheet on page 12	26a	
b	Enter here IRA payments you made in 1985 that are included in line 26a above ▶		
27	Payments to a Keogh *(H.R. 10)* retirement plan	27	
28	Penalty on early withdrawal of savings	28	
29	Alimony paid	29	
30	Deduction for a married couple when both work *(attach Schedule W)*	30	
31	Add lines 24 through 30. These are your **total adjustments** . . . . . . ▶		31

Adjusted Gross Income

32	Subtract line 31 from line 23. *This is your* **adjusted gross income.** *If this line is less than $10,000, see "Earned Income Credit" (line 59) on page 16 of Instructions. If you want IRS to figure your tax, see page 12 of Instructions.* . . . . . . ▶	32

FIGURE 3-5

Form 1040 (1984) Page **2**

Tax Computation (See Instructions on page 13.)

33	Amount from line 32 (adjusted gross income)	33	
34a	If you itemize, attach Schedule A (Form 1040) and enter the amount from Schedule A, line 26. **Caution:** If you have unearned income and can be claimed as a dependent on your parent's return, check here ▶ ☐ and see page 13 of the Instructions. Also see page 13 if: • You are married filing a separate return and your spouse itemizes deductions, OR • You file Form 4563, OR • You are a dual-status alien.	34a	
34b	If you do not itemize deductions, and you have charitable contributions, complete the worksheet on page 14. Then enter the allowable part of your contributions here	34b	
35	Subtract line 34a or 34b, whichever applies, from line 33	35	
36	Multiply $1,000 by the total number of exemptions claimed on Form 1040, line 6e	36	
37	Taxable Income. Subtract line 36 from line 35.	37	
38	Tax. Enter tax here and check if from ☐ Tax Table, ☐ Tax Rate Schedule X, Y, or Z, or ☐ Schedule G	38	
39	Additional Taxes. (See page 14 of Instructions.) Enter here and check if from ☐ Form 4970, ☐ Form 4972, or ☐ Form 5544	39	
40	Add lines 38 and 39. Enter the total ▶	40	

Credits (See Instructions on page 14.)

41	Credit for child and dependent care expenses *(attach Form 2441)*	41			
42	Credit for the elderly and the permanently and totally disabled *(attach Schedule R)*	42			
43	Residential energy credit *(attach Form 5695)*	43			
44	Partial credit for political contributions for which you have receipts	44			
45	Add lines 41 through 44. These are your total personal credits			45	
46	Subtract line 45 from 40. Enter the result (but not less than zero)			46	
47	Foreign tax credit *(attach Form 1116)*	47			
48	General business credit. Check if from ☐ Form 3800, ☐ Form 3468, ☐ Form 5884, ☐ Form 6478	48			
49	Add lines 47 and 48. These are your total business and other credits			49	
50	Subtract line 49 from 46. Enter the result (but not less than zero). ▶			50	

Other Taxes (Including Advance EIC Payments)

51	Self-employment tax *(attach Schedule SE)*	51	
52	Alternative minimum tax *(attach Form 6251)*	52	
53	Tax from recapture of investment credit *(attach Form 4255)*	53	
54	Social security tax on tip income not reported to employer *(attach Form 4137)*	54	
55	Tax on an IRA *(attach Form 5329)*	55	
56	Add lines 50 through 55. This is your **total tax** ▶	56	

Payments (Attach Forms W-2, W-2G, and W-2P to front.)

57	Federal income tax withheld	57			
58	1984 estimated tax payments and amount applied from 1983 return	58			
59	Earned income credit. If line 33 is under $10,000, see page 16	59			
60	Amount paid with Form 4868	60			
61	Excess social security tax and RRTA tax withheld (two or more employers)	61			
62	Credit for Federal tax on gasoline and special fuels *(attach Form 4136)*	62			
63	Regulated Investment Company credit *(attach Form 2439)*	63			
64	Add lines 57 through 63. These are your **total payments** ▶			64	

Refund or Amount You Owe

65	If line 64 is larger than line 56, enter amount **OVERPAID** ▶			65	
66	Amount of line 65 to be **REFUNDED TO YOU** ▶			66	
67	Amount of line 65 to be applied to your 1985 estimated tax ▶	67			
68	If line 56 is larger than line 64, enter **AMOUNT YOU OWE.** Attach check or money order for full amount payable to "Internal Revenue Service." Write your social security number and "1984 Form 1040" on it ▶ (Check ▶ ☐ if Form 2210 (2210F) is attached. See page 17 of Instructions.) $			68	

Please Sign Here

Under penalties of perjury, I declare that I have examined this return and accompanying schedules and statements, and to the best of my knowledge and belief, they are true, correct, and complete. Declaration of preparer (other than taxpayer) is based on all information of which preparer has any knowledge.

▶ Your signature | Date | ▶ Spouse's signature (if filing jointly, BOTH must sign)

Paid Preparer's Use Only

Preparer's signature ▶	Date	Check if self-employed ☐	Preparer's social security no.
Firm's name (or yours, if self-employed) and address ▶		E.I. No.	
		ZIP code	

U.S.GPO:1984-0-423-073 E.I.#430814328

SELF-STUDY QUESTIONS

1. For the year ended December 31, 1984, Elmer Shaw earned $3,000 interest at Prestige Savings Bank, on a time savings account scheduled to mature in 1986. In January 1985, before filing his 1984 income tax return, Shaw incurred a forfeiture penalty of $1,500 for premature withdrawal of the funds from his account. Shaw should treat this $1,500 forfeiture penalty as a

   a) penalty not deductible for tax purposes;

   b) deduction from gross income in arriving at 1985 adjusted gross income;

   c) deduction from 1985 adjusted gross income, deductible only if Shaw itemizes his deductions for 1985;

   d) reduction of interest earned in 1984, so that only $1,500 of such interest is taxable on Shaw's 1984 return.

   (AICPA adapted)

2. John Budd was 58 years old at the time of his death on July 1, 1985. John's wife Emma, age 57, did not remarry in 1985. Emma is executrix of John's estate. With regard to John and Emma's filing status for 1985, Emma should file

   a) as a single individual, and a separate return should be filed for John as unmarried head of household;

   b) as a qualifying widow, and a separate return should be filed for John as married head of household;

   c) as a qualifying widow, and a separate return should be filed for John as a single deceased individual;

   d) a joint return including John, as married taxpayers.

   (AICPA adapted)

3. Jill Norman's filing status for 1984 was that of a single individual. Jill claimed itemized deductions of $5,000 on her 1984 income tax return. How much was Jill's zero bracket amount for 1984?

   a) $1,700

   b) $2,300

   c) $2,700

   d) $3,400

   (AICPA adapted)

4. During 1984 Howard Thompson maintained his home in which he and his sixteen-year old son resided. The son qualifies as his dependent. Thompson's wife died in 1983, for which year a joint return was appropriately filed. Thompson remarried on March 15, 1985. What is Thompson's filing status for 1984?

a) single

b) head of household

c) surviving spouse

d) married, filing jointly.

(AICPA adapted)

5. During 1985, Lucas Andrews, a widower, was the sole support for his aged mother who was a resident of an old age home for the entire year. Mr. Andrews' wife died in 1983. What is Mr. Andrews' filing status for 1985?

a) surviving spouse

b) single with one dependent

c) single with no dependents

d) head of household

(AICPA adapted)

6. Mrs. Irma Felton, by herself, maintains her home in which she and her unmarried son reside. Her son, however, does not qualify as her dependent. Mrs. Felton's husband died in 1984. What is Mrs. Felton's filing status for 1985?

a) single

b) surviving spouse

c) head of household

d) married filing jointly

(AICPA adapted)

7. During 1985, Anita Simms was entirely supported by her three sons Dudley, Carlton, and Isidore, who provided support for her in the following percentages:

Dudley	8%
Carlton	45%
Isidore	47%

Which of the brothers is entitled to claim his mother as a dependent, assuming a multiple support agreement exists?

a) Dudley

b) Dudley or Carlton

c) Carlton or Isidore

d) Dudley, Carlton, or Isidore

(AICPA adapted)

8. Mr. and Mrs. Vonce, both age 62, filed a joint return for 1984. They provided all the support for their daughter who is 19, legally blind, and who has no income. Their son, age 21 and a full-time student at a university, had $4,200 of income and provided 70% of his own support during 1984. How many exemptions should Mr. and Mrs. Vonce have claimed on their 1984 joint income tax return?

a) 2

b) 3

c) 4

d) 5

(AICPA adapted)

9. Alex Kerr was 65 years old on January 21, 1985, and has been legally blind for the past three years. Alex's wife, Rose, lived with him until her death on January 5, 1984, at the age of 50. Rose has no income of her own. Alex did not remarry in 1984. How many personal exemptions was Alex entitled to on his 1984 income tax return?

   a) 1

   b) 2

   c) 3

   d) 4

   (AICPA adapted)

10. During 1985 Robert Moore, who is 50 years old and unmarried, maintained his home in which he and his widower father, age 75, resided. His father had $1,600 interest income from a savings account and also received $2,400 from social security during 1985. Robert provided 60% of his father's total support in 1985. What is Robert's filing status for 1985, and how many exemptions should he claim on his tax return?

    a) head of household and 2 exemptions

    b) single and 2 exemptions

    c) head of household and 1 exemption

    d) single and one exemption

    (AICPA adapted)

QUESTIONS

1. Jim and Mary Barlow are married and have one daughter, Kristin, who is one year old. During the current year, Jim worked for Ace Corporation and earned $18,000; Mary sold cosmetics part-time and earned $4,000. Kris, an unusually beautiful one-year old, modeled infants' clothing for the Best Department Store and earned $5,000. How many taxpayers are there in the Barlow family? As a minimum, how many tax returns must the Barlow family file? How do you account for the discrepancy between the number of taxpayers and the number of returns that must be filed? Would you advise Jim and Mary to file separate returns? Explain each answer.

2. Several years ago, David Nipon became disenchanted with U.S. politics and moved to France. He lives on the Mediterranean Coast, tak-

ing his ease. Although he has not returned to the United States, he continues to draw income from extensive real estate holdings in Illinois and from various American corporate securities. Nipon also has substantial wealth invested in companies located throughout Europe. As a resident of France, he is subject to the French income tax (although he continues to hold a U.S. passport). Is Nipon subject to the U.S. income tax? If so, does the U.S. tax cover his foreign-source income?

3. For each of the following independent situations, can John and Marsha file a joint return for 19X1? Explain your answers.
   a) John and Marsha married on December 20, 19X1, after a whirlwind courtship. On December 28, 19X1, following a violent argument, Marsha packed off home to mother, vowing never to return. No legal action was taken during 19X1.
   b) John and Marsha, after years of marriage, were legally separated on December 30, 19X1.
   c) John, while on temporary assignment in England for a large corporation, married Marsha, a citizen of Great Britain. They were still in London at the end of 19X1, but they returned to the United States in January 19X2. They made no election for 19X1 to include Marsha's worldwide income on a U.S. return.
   d) John died on January 2, 19X1, after years of happy marriage to Marsha. Marsha did not remarry.

4. Indicate in each of the following cases whether taxpayers may file a joint return. If they are not allowed to do so, indicate the reason.
   a) Jones, a widower, and his mother live in the same house. Jones has gross income of $8,000; mother has income of $6,000.
   b) Kuehn, an American citizen, married Greta while he was stationed in Germany. Kuehn and his wife now live in New York. Greta is not yet an American citizen, but at the end of the tax year she was taking steps to become one.
   c) Smith's wife died in the preceding tax year. Smith has not remarried. Smith's 3-year-old daughter lives with him.
   d) Bellmon's wife died on January 2 of the current year. He has not remarried.
   e) Ratliff and his wife's divorce became final on December 18 of the current tax year.
   f) Whitlaw and his wife are both United States citizens. Whitlaw's wife's parents live in England, and both parents are seriously ill. Whitlaw's wife spent the entire tax year in England with her parents.

5. The correct classification of the various subtractions in the individual tax formula is very important.

a) Why is the accurate calculation of gross income important?

b) Why is the accurate calculation of adjusted gross income important?

6. In May of 19X1 a 17-year-old cousin of Mrs. Jones came to live with the Jones family and stayed in the household until she was graduated from high school in May 19X3. At that time the cousin went away to college, but she still calls the Jones household "home." The Joneses provide full support of the cousin, who has had no income. May Mr. and Mrs. Jones claim a dependency exemption for the cousin in 19X1? 19X2? 19X3? Explain.

7. Explain which taxpayers must use the tax tables.

8. Mary and John are married residents of New York and have two small children. They depend on John's salary of $50,000 per annum for their livelihood. In January 19X2, Mary learned that John was in hock to his bookie to the tune of $200,000 and that the bookie was getting impatient. New York is not a community-property state. While Mary has no current income, her family is quite wealthy and she expects to inherit substantial amounts in the near future. What would you advise Mary about filing status for 19X1?

9. Robert and Mary were divorced on January 18, 1985. The divorce decree awarded Mary custody of the couple's child but directed Robert to provide $100 per month of child support. No mention was made about which parent would be entitled to take the exemption. Robert actually made child-support payments totaling $680 during the year. Who is entitled to take the exemption for the child?

10. June and Tom were divorced in 1982. In the current year, Tom contributed $1,800 to June for the support of the couple's three children who were in June's custody. June provided the balance of their support. How many, if any, of the children may Tom claim as dependents?

11. Indicate in each of the following independent cases whether the taxpayer may file as a "surviving spouse."

    a) Taxpayer's husband died in the preceding tax year. Taxpayer maintains a home in which resides her unmarried 20-year-old daughter, a college student, who qualifies as taxpayer's dependent.

    b) Taxpayer's husband died in the preceding tax year. Taxpayer maintains a home in which resides her unmarried 20-year-old sister, a college student, who qualifies as taxpayer's dependent.

    c) Taxpayer's wife died during this tax year. Taxpayer maintains a home in which resides his unmarried 18-year-old daughter, who qualifies as taxpayer's dependent.

    d) Taxpayer's husband died during the preceding year. Taxpayer maintains a home in which reside her married 17-year-old daughter and the daughter's 18-year-old husband. Taxpayer supports both her daughter and son-in-law and properly claims both of them as her dependents.

e) Taxpayer's wife died four years ago. Taxpayer has not remarried and maintains a home in which reside his two stepchildren, ages 7 and 8. Taxpayer properly claims both stepchildren as dependents.

12. In the following situations, can Mac use the head-of-household tax-rate schedule?
    a) Mac maintains a home and his unmarried grandson lives with him. The grandson is 23 years old and has a good job and therefore does not qualify as a dependent for Mac. (Mac is a widower.)
    b) Mac maintains a home for his two dependent children. Mac's wife died last year.
    c) Mac's dependent parents live in an apartment at a resort center in Florida. They have no income, so Mac, who is a bachelor and lives and works in New York, supports them.
    d) Mac is a widower living in New York. His wife died five years ago. Mac pays all the living costs of his 18-year-old unmarried daughter, who has no income and lives in Miami Beach, Florida.

13. Boyd, who is unmarried, maintains a home in which resides his 17-year-old first cousin. Boyd provides over one-half the support of the cousin. Because he is a high school student, the cousin works only during the summer and on the weekends and earns a total of $1,200. May Boyd claim a dependency exemption for the cousin? What rate schedule can Boyd use?

14. During one year, Mrs. Eve Elderly lived in a small apartment, where she was supported by her three adult sons, Shem, Ham, and Japheth. Each son contributed one-third of his mother's financial support. Mrs. Elderly's only income was $1,201 in dividends, which she received on stocks she inherited from her late husband. Could any or all of the sons claim their mother as a dependent?

15. Jane, Mary, and Paul contribute to the support of their mother, age 71. The mother's total living costs for the year were $3,100, received from the following sources:

Jane	$ 800
Mary	1,400
Paul	300
Social Security	600

Who is entitled to claim the mother as a dependent? Explain.

PROBLEMS

1. Jose Castro and Li Chen both earned a gross income of $20,000 and both incurred $4,000 in deductions in 1985. The classification of their deductions differed, however, as follows:

TAXPAYER	*FOR* AGI	*FROM* AGI	TOTAL
Jose	$1,000	$3,000	$4,000
Li	$3,000	$1,000	$4,000

If both Jose and Li are single taxpayers, who are entitled to claim only their own personal exemption deduction in addition to the deductions above, what is the amount of each taxpayer's taxable income?

2. Anne Drue earned a salary of $18,000 in 1985. Her only deductions for the year were: (1) $2,000 in interest expense that she paid on a debt incurred when she purchased a new personal automobile; and (2) $320 in charitable contributions. What is the amount of Anne's taxable income for 1985?

3. Joe Romano just won a new automobile in a magazine sweepstakes contest. The "sticker price" of this car is $22,000; the wholesale price to local dealers is $19,000. According to reports from local dealers, the average retail sale price of this car, during the past month, was $20,500. What amount, if any, must Joe include in his gross income because he won the sweepstakes contest? Explain briefly.

4. Both Carl and Edward each earn a $30,000 salary. Carl pays his ex-wife $1,200 in alimony plus $4,800 in child support each year; Edward pays his ex-wife $6,000 in alimony but no child support each year. Neither Carl nor Edward can claim any deductions from AGI other than their own personal exemption deduction. What will each man's federal income tax liability be for 1985 if there are no other items to complicate their tax computation and each man is single?

5. From January 1 until October 31 Margaret Roosevelt worked as an account executive for Baker Company. During these 10 months Baker withheld $2,750 in social security tax and $7,250 in federal income tax from Margaret's salary. During November and December Margaret worked for Charley Corporation which withheld $500 in social security tax and $1,400 in federal income tax from Margaret's salary. Margaret also made $125 estimated tax payments on April 15, 1985; June 15, 1985; September 15, 1985; and January 15, 1986. Her gross federal income tax liability for 1985 is $9,800. What is Margaret's net tax payable (or her net refund) for 1985?

6. In 1985 James Cochran had adjusted gross income from his employment of $46,000. His allowable itemized deductions totaled $3,500. (This does not include personal exemptions.) His wife, Mary, also was employed and had adjusted gross income of $6,500. Her allowable itemized deductions were $1,800. (This does not include exemptions.) Compute the amount that the family unit saves in income taxes by filing a joint return rather than filing separately. (There are no dependents.)

7. Max and Mary, recent college graduates and employees of an accounting firm, are thinking about marriage. Estimates of their income and deductions for 1985 are:

	MARY	MAX
Gross income from salaries	$32,000	$28,000
Allowable deductions for AGI (job related)	1,500	2,000
Allowable itemized deductions (before the ZBA)	2,200	1,800

They have no dependents. The above deductions will remain unchanged, married or not. What is the tax penalty resulting if they should marry in 1985?

8. Answer the following questions. Use the italicized words in their precise meaning:
   a) Mrs. Jones, a 70-year-old widow, lives with her son and his family in Austin, Texas. During this year she received $5,000 in interest on State of Texas bonds she owns. What is her *gross income*?
   b) Mrs. Smith is also a 70-year-old widow who resides with her son and his family in Austin, Texas. She received $5,000 from the rental of her former residence. Deductions related to the rental property were $4,000 for the year. What is her *gross income*?
   c) Must either Mrs. Jones or Mrs. Smith file a federal income tax return?

9. Mary Burnes, unmarried and age 20, is a full-time student at State University. As a part-time employee, she earned $1,500 during the current year. She also received a $4,200 distribution from a simple trust created by her grandmother. All of the trust's income was from interest on corporate bonds. Mary's parents properly claimed a dependency exemption for Mary. Assume she had no deductions for adjusted gross income and that her itemized deductions were less than $1,500.
   a) Compute Mary's taxable income for the year. (She has no dependents.)
   b) What is Mary's gross tax? What credits may Mary claim, assuming she consumed her entire income for personal use?

10. A review of Taxpayer C's financial records revealed the following data for 1985:

INCOME ITEMS		EXPENDITURES	
Salary	$20,000	Personal living costs (rent, food, etc.)	$8,000
Gross income from a partnership (C's share only)	4,000	Expenses of partnership (C's share only)	3,000
Dividend income*	400	Personal taxes, interest and contributions	3,550
Interest income (from local bank account)	200	Federal income tax withheld from salary	2,200

*For reasons not explained in this chapter, $200 of dividend income can be excluded from gross income.

Compute C's taxable income and net tax liability (or refund due) for 1985, assuming that a joint return is filed. (C and spouse D have no dependents.)

11. Individual Eve does a lot of baby-sitting while attending college. During the current year, Eve received the following for baby-sitting services rendered:

Cash	$2,108
Clothing	500*
Room	1,200*

(*estimated fair market value)

What amount of income has taxpayer Eve realized for federal income tax purposes?

12. One provision that has often been considered by Congress during deliberation of proposed tax legislation would allow taxpayers to take either a deduction of a specified amount or a credit of some other specified amount for each exemption. Assume that the choice was to be a credit of $250 or a deduction of $1,000 for each exemption. What option would be taken by a taxpayer with one exemption whose marginal tax rate is

    a) 20%?

    b) 50%?

13. For each of the independent cases below, calculate the number of exemptions for the taxpayer for the current tax year.

    a) Lopez is 75, blind, and has AGI of $7,200. His wife is 71. They file a joint return.

    b) Mayfield is 54, unmarried. She supports her father, who is age 75 and blind, and her mother, who is 75 and has good vision.

    c) Smith is 34. His wife is 31. They have a 5-year-old son and a 3-year-old daughter. On January 18 of this year, Mrs. Smith gave birth to a son, who died on January 21.

    d) Assume the same facts as in part (*c*) except that the son born on January 18 was stillborn.

    e) Porter is 53. He provides his father, who does not live with him, with $2,500 of living costs. During the year, the father had no income except from rental property. Gross rents totaled $1,200; rent-related expenses totaled $700. The father lived off the support of Porter and the net rentals.

14. In each of the independent cases below, calculate the number of exemptions for the taxpayer for the current tax year.

    a) Taxpayer, age 67, and wife, age 63, file a joint return.

    b) Taxpayer, age 68, and wife, who became 65 on January 1 of the following year after the tax year, are both blind and file a joint return.

c) Taxpayer and husband, both 48, spent $1,600 toward living expenses of their son, who is 25 and in college. The son earned $1,110 during the summer, received a scholarship of $400 and $450 under the GI Bill. The son used all of these funds for his living costs.

d) Taxpayer, a woman, received a decree of divorce on January 8 (this year) and has not remarried. The divorce required the husband to pay $1,000 a year for the support of their child, who is 5 years old and lives with the mother. They have not discussed who is to claim an exemption for the child.

e) Assume the same facts as in (*d*) except that the taxpayer has signed a statement saying she will not claim the child as a dependent. Taxpayer is the mother.

15. For each of the following independent situations, determine the proper number of exemptions to be taken for the current tax year.

a) Taxpayer, age 66, and spouse, age 62, file a joint return. Both have good vision. They have one son, age 22, who is a student at State University. The son earned $1,100 in a summer job and received a scholarship from State University for $1,000. During the year the son's total support cost $3,300, of which $1,200 was paid by the father.

b) Taxpayer and spouse, both under 65 and with good vision, file a joint return. They provided more than 50% of the support for two unmarried children, both under 19. However, one child earned $1,200 from part-time work. Taxpayer also provided most of the support for his blind mother, who is over 65. The mother received $750 in social security payments.

c) Taxpayer, unmarried, under 65 and with good vision, provides more than 50% of the support for his brother's son and the son's wife, who live with the taxpayer while they attend State University. The nephew's wife had no income. The nephew earned $1,200 on a summer job. The nephew filed a separate return, claiming one exemption.

16. Determine the correct number of exemptions for each situation described below.

a) John Smith, a 66-year-old bachelor, maintains a home in which the 24-year-old son of a deceased friend has lived for the past 14 years. The young man is a full-time college student who earned $1,800 during the year. John can prove that he furnishes 65% of the support of the young man.

b) Jacques, a widower for four years, age 63, maintains a home that is the principal abode for himself, his married daughter Joan, and his grandchild Zed. Jacques's son-in-law is a wandering "bum." Jacques provides more than 50% of the support of all those who live with him. Joan and her husband file a joint return, but they do not claim Zed as their dependent because their joint earnings are only $4,800.

c) Alan Standard contributes more than half the support of both his mother and father, who live with him. Alan is 38 and single; his father is 66, his mother, 64. Alan's father earned $1,100 during the year and filed a separate return claiming himself as an exemption.

d) Jack and Jill (30 and 28, respectively) have two children. Andrea, their 5-year-old daughter, models clothes for a local department store and earned $1,200 during the year. Their son Don, who is 2 years old, was born blind. For the past three years Jack and Jill have also been raising (without adopting) a 6-year-old boy, Ted, who was orphaned by an automobile accident. The total support expenditures for Ted amounted to $1,000 during the year. Of the $1,000, Jack and Jill paid $700 from their personal funds; the remainder was provided by a county welfare program.

17. Which rate schedule (X, Y-Joint, Y-Separate, or Z) should each of the following taxpayers use?

   a) Sue's husband died last year. She maintains a home in which live her married son and his wife. Both of them qualify as Sue's dependents.

   b) Mary's husband died last year. She maintains a home in which live her married son and his wife. Mary supports both of them, but the son and daughter-in-law file a joint return to reduce their own taxes.

   c) Herman and Victoria were married on December 31 of the current tax year. Herman earned $18,000 during the year and Victoria earned $7,200. Victoria is a resident alien. Victoria has income from several countries.

   d) Wilma's husband died four years ago. Wilma maintains a home in which her 6-year-old daughter, her 21-year-old son, and her 20-year-old daughter-in-law reside. The son and daughter-in-law file a joint return. Wilma provides all the support for everyone in the household.

   e) Jones, whose wife died earlier in the current tax year, has not remarried. He has no children or other dependents.

   f) Joe, a bachelor, maintains a home in which his nephew resides. The nephew is not a dependent.

   g) Thomas was divorced from his wife in November of the current tax year. Thomas's unmarried dependent daughter lives with him.

18. In each of the following independent cases, indicate whether the amount involved is (*a*) deductible for AGI, (*b*) deductible from AGI, or (*c*) not deductible at all.

   a) Taxpayer paid $2,000 interest on her home mortgage.

b) Taxpayer paid expenses of $1,200 applicable to rental property that he owned.

c) Taxpayer replaced roof on a home at a cost of $1,000.

d) Taxpayer, a nurse, is employed at the local hospital. She spent $105 for uniforms during the year.

e) Millsaps, a public school teacher, spent $40 for magazine subscriptions. The magazines were used in his classroom activities.

f) Herman, a department store buyer, attended an out-of-town "market" at which he examined new merchandise. His total costs including meals, lodging, and transportation were $308. He was not reimbursed by his employer.

g) Taxpayer, an employee working for a public accounting firm, lives in a suburban community and commutes to the city to work. During the year commuting costs were $360.

h) Taxpayer operates an antique shop on the first floor of a house and lives on the second floor. Fire insurance for the entire house was $600 for the year (which does not include insurance on the antique inventory or personal furnishings). Floor space on each floor is approximately equal.

19. Indicate which of the following expenditures by an individual would constitute (*a*) a deduction for AGI; (*b*) a deduction from AGI; or (*c*) a nondeductible personal expense.

    a) Expenses associated with rental property.

    b) Travel expenses (away from home) incurred as an employee.

    c) Travel expenses incurred as a self-employed business person.

    d) Entertainment expenses incurred as an employee:
        1. If no reimbursement is made by the employer.
        2. If the reimbursement is less than the expense incurred.

TAX PLANNING PROBLEMS

1. Ted and Barbara are married and have three children. They recently inherited a substantial sum from Barbara's deceased aunt. Last year, they were distressed by the amount of income tax paid on this inherited wealth and are considering gifts of the property to their children. As they understand the law, each child can realize an annual income of $3,300 without paying any federal tax.

    a) Is their understanding correct? Explain.

    b) Assuming an interest rate of 15%, how much could they give to each child without the child owing federal income taxes? The children have no other income.

    c) Under what circumstances may gifts to the children be a wise plan from a tax standpoint, even if the children do owe some federal taxes on the income from the gifts?

2. Jack Sprat will graduate from State University in December 1985 with

a BBA in accounting. He has accepted a job with Arthur Marwick, a national CPA firm, beginning in January 1986. While in school Jack has lived on help from his parents, earnings from part-time employment, and savings he accumulated during summer employment. He usually invested his summer savings in common stocks in an attempt to increase his pool of financial resources. Generally this strategy has been successful. In one instance, however, it was not: Jack still owns 500 shares of Fat Corporation's common stock that he purchased in August 1985 for $1,500; those 500 shares are currently worth only $500.

Assume that it is December 1985 and that Jack has reluctantly accepted the fact that the value of his Fat stock will not increase in the foreseeable future and that he really needs the $500 as a down payment on a new car he intends to acquire in the very near future. The only question in Jack's mind is: should he (1) sell this Fat stock in time to report the $1,000 short-term capital loss on his 1985 federal income tax return, or should he (2) wait and sell it early in 1986?

Jack's *taxable income without the capital loss* will be (about) $6,000 in 1985 and (about) $24,000 in 1986. Thus, Jack can either (1) decrease his 1985 taxable income from $6,000 to $5000, or (2) decrease his 1986 taxable income from $24,000 to $23,000. Using the 1985 tax-rate schedule for single persons for both 1985 and 1986, determine which action Jack should take. Quantify the approximate amount he will "save" if he follows your advice as a canny tax planner.

RESEARCH PROBLEMS

Mr. and Mrs. Brideparent are trying to determine whether or not they can claim their recently married daughter as a dependent for 1985. The answer to their question turns solely upon the issue of whether or not they can include the cost of their daughter's wedding apparel and reception as part of her "support" for the year. Their daughter, Lydia, expended a total of $10,000 for support-type items during the year, exclusive of her wedding apparel/reception. Her parents provided $4,000 for routine support items plus an additional $5,000 for her wedding apparel/reception. Thus, if the wedding-related items are *not* included within the meaning of support, Mr. and Mrs. Brideparent provided only 40% (or $4,000 ÷ $10,000) of Lydia's support and, therefore, they fail to satisfy the support test. On the other hand, if the wedding apparel and reception are deemed to be part of her support, they provided 60% (or $9,000 ÷ $15,000) of Lydia's support and, therefore, they can claim Lydia as their dependent for 1985.

Using whatever tax services are available in your school's library, and using the tax research technique explained in Chapter 2, determine whether or not Mr. and Mrs. Brideparent can claim Lydia as their dependent for 1985. (Simply assume that the other four tests for dependency can be easily satisfied.) Cite whatever authority you can for your answer. Remember *primary* authority is always better than *secondary* authority.

3

Chapter Objectives

1. Identify the major conceptual differences between "economic" income and income for accounting purposes.
2. Explain the major reasons why the concept of income for tax purposes differs from that of both economic income and accounting income, and describe the importance of the realization concept, the wherewithal-to-pay concept, the need for ease and consistency of administration, and the role of social and economic objectives.
3. Identify the tax accounting period.
4. Describe the primary accounting methods used for tax purposes: the cash basis, the accrual basis, and the mixed basis.
5. Identify concepts that have developed in tax accounting which have caused deviations from a true cash or accrual basis, including the cash-equivalent concept, the constructive-receipt doctrine, and the claim-of-right doctrine.
6. Identify the taxpayer to whom income is taxable, especially in family situations involving income of minor children, the assignment of income (including Clifford Trusts), and income from "community property."
7. Review the Sections of the Internal Revenue Code dealing specifically with inclusions and exclusions of gross income.

4 Gross Income

GENERAL CONCEPTS OF GROSS INCOME

The determination of an *income tax* liability quite obviously must begin with an operative definition of the income concept. Unfortunately for everyone concerned, there are few concepts in the history of economic thought that have been more widely debated than the income concept. To make matters even more difficult, as one moves from a conceptual plane to the pragmatic and often political world of taxation, no logical explanation of the many distortions in the basic concept can be offered as guidance either to the serious student or the confused taxpayer.

In this chapter we will examine some of the fundamental issues underlying the problem of income definition and measurement. We will begin with major distinctions in the concepts of income found in economics, accounting, and taxation, especially with the conflicts between the accounting and tax concepts of income.

ECONOMIC AND ACCOUNTING CONCEPTS OF INCOME

Most economists define income as the algebraic sum of consumption plus the change in the individual's net worth in the year or other accounting period—it asks simply: how much could this individual have spent for consumption during the year while remaining as well off in terms of net worth at the end of the year as he or she was at the beginning of the year?[1]

---

[1]See, for example: Robert M. Haig, "The Concept of Income—Economic and Legal Aspects," *The Federal Income Tax* (New York: Columbia University Press, 1921); Henry C. Simons, *Personal Income Taxation*

Under this concept both consumption and the net change in the individual's store of wealth are evaluated at market price.

Example 1: On January 1, 19X1 Thomas owned assets with a fair market value of $116,000 and had liabilities of $16,000. During 19X1 Thomas consumed food, clothing, shelter, medical care, entertainment, and other goods and services with a total value of $24,000. At the end of that year, Thomas' assets had a market value of $141,000 and his liabilities were $20,000. From the economist's viewpoint Thomas' income, ignoring the effects of change in value of the monetary unit (inflation), would be

Value of net assets, end of year ($141,000 – $20,000)	$121,000
Value of net assets, beginning of year ($116,000 – $16,000)	100,000
Increase in store of wealth during year	$ 21,000
Consumption during year	24,000
"Income" for year	$ 45,000

The major difficulty in using this definition for such practical purposes as taxation is in obtaining reliable measures of net worth and consumption. Basically, the problem is one of valuation. Unfortunately, only a relatively insignificant portion of total assets have easily ascertainable and accurate market values. The "value" of most assets is a subjective characteristic that depends on someone's estimate of the satisfaction to be derived from the object in question compared with the expected satisfaction that could be obtained from other objects that might be purchased as an alternative.

ECONOMIC CONCEPT OF INCOME Income as conceived by economists. "Income equals sum of value of current consumption plus the increase in the value of store of wealth during the period."

Another problem arising from this ***economic concept of income*** is in distinguishing between "monetary" income and "real" income. This difference refers to the familiar problem caused by changes in the value of the monetary unit—in accounting the problem is commonly called the price-level problem. Most economists stress *real* capital accumulation measured by the increase in command over scarce resources. Presumably, fictitious gains that result merely from an increase in price level can be eliminated approximately by deflating them by an index of consumer prices.

There are clearly major discrepancies between the broad definition of income discussed above and the computation of income under generally accepted accounting principles. The primary difference is the absence of any ***realization*** criterion in the economic view of income.

REALIZATION The conversion of assets or services into new assets or into the liquidation of liabilities.

Generally accepted accounting principles suggest that income should be measured on the basis of completed transactions. Note the impor-

(Chicago: University of Chicago Press, 1921); and Melvin I. White, "Consistent Treatment of Items Excluded and Omitted from the Individual Income Tax Base," *1959 Compendium*, p. 318 (The complete reference is *Tax Revision Compendium: Compendium of Papers on Broadening the Tax Base*, submitted to the Committee on Ways and Means, beginning November 16, 1959. This three-volume collection of papers on income taxation is one of the modern classics.)

tance of this distinction: Economists define income in terms of *value*, depending essentially on expectations about the *future*. Accountants define income basically in terms of the *past*, expressed in money measurement; they are concerned with completed transactions—presumably at arm's length—because transactions provide independent judgments of "value" on which accountants can rely. The economists' concept is, in general, deemed by accountants to be too impractical and difficult to apply and lacking the objectivity and accuracy needed as a basis for measuring periodic income in the accounts.

> **Example 2:** Marcus owned land that had a fair market value of $90,000 on January 1, 19X1. During the year the land's value increased and on December 31, 19X1, its fair market price was $160,000. Even though the economist might argue that Marcus has income of $70,000, for accounting purposes no income results from the mere increase in value because it has not been realized through a sale or exchange transaction involving another party.

DIFFERENCES BETWEEN ACCOUNTING INCOME AND TAXABLE INCOME

The economic concept of income is also too subjective to be used generally as a basis for determining income taxes. The measurement of income as computed under generally accepted accounting principles comes much closer to yielding a basis on which income taxes can be computed. Nevertheless, there are still many differences between income determined under generally accepted accounting principles and income computed for tax purposes. These differences are created by the many factors that enter into and influence the federal tax structure. Primary among these factors are the underlying body of economic, social, and legal philosophies of the people and the Congress; the (proper and improper) exercise of power by groups and lobbies with vested interests; the variation in interpretations of laws and regulations by the courts (which often conflict because of opposing values and ideologies of those handing down the decisions and because of changing "public policy"); and the increasing use of tax policy as an instrument of social and economic planning and control.

For our purposes we can attribute differences between income as measured for tax purposes and income as measured for financial accounting purposes to four concepts in taxation that often outweigh the correctness or logic, or both, of financial accounting. These are:

1. Wherewithal-to-pay
2. Realization and objectivity
3. Ease and consistency of administration
4. Social and economic objectives

WHEREWITHAL-TO-PAY
The notion that the tax should be levied when the taxpayer has the cash to make the payment.

WHEREWITHAL-TO-PAY The phrase "***wherewithal-to-pay***" suggests that the levying of the tax should occur at a time when the taxpayer can most readily pay the tax and the IRS can most readily collect it. The concept may be expressed simply as "get the tax when the taxpayer has the money to pay it."

The requirement that unearned revenues be reported in most cases as taxable income in the year received, regardless of the year(s) in which they will actually be earned, is a classic example of application of this concept. This requirement is designed to provide maximum possible assurance that the tax will be collected while the taxpayer has the cash available for paying the tax.

PREPAID INCOME Cash received in advance for services or goods to be delivered in the future.

Although the ***prepaid-income*** rule is frequently cited as a deviation from generally accepted accounting principles that is unfair to the taxpayer, the concept of wherewithal-to-pay more often works to the advantage of the taxpayer. For example, generally a taxpayer may defer the tax recognition of gain on an installment sale until he or she receives the cash, even if financial accounting would report the entire gain in the year of the sale. A taxpayer may similarly defer the recognition of taxable gain in many transactions involving the exchange of assets: in the event of an involuntary conversion of property, in the sale of a personal residence, and in many transactions between the taxpayer and a related business entity. By contrast, prepaid rents must be included in taxable income even though unearned at the end of the year. These and other illustrations of tax provisions that are related to the wherewithal-to-pay concept will be discussed in later chapters.

REALIZATION We have already seen the importance of applying the realization criterion to the measurement of accounting income. Fundamentally, the realization criterion states that income is recognized when, and only when, it is realized through a conversion into new assets or a liquidation of existing liabilities.

The importance of the realization concept to the taxpayer can be readily seen. A mere increase in the value of an asset—even if easily measurable and readily convertible into cash—is not taxed. For example, the taxpayer who purchases shares of stock for $1,000 and finds at the end of the year that the stock has a quoted market value of $1,500, has no income to report because none has been realized; that is, there has been no change in the assets held. Only when the shares are sold or exchanged for other assets will the gain be recognized.

Similarly, the taxpayer who, to his or her good fortune and surprise, discovers oil and gas reserves worth millions of dollars under his or her land, recognizes no income until this increase in value is realized by conversion into other assets through sale or exchange.

On the other hand, the concept may also work to the disadvantage of a taxpayer. Declines in asset values generally are not recognized until they are realized through disposition of the asset, no matter how real the decline seems to be. (There are some minor exceptions to this rule—notably in the case of accounts receivable and merchandise inventory.) Thus, the taxpayer who purchases shares of stock for $1,000 and finds that the stock is worth only $300 at the end of the year has no deductible loss until realization takes place through conversion of the shares by sale or exchange.

A major reason for the rather strict adherence to the realization concept (in addition to the notion of wherewithal-to-pay already discussed) is the need for a high degree of objectivity and certainty in the tax computation. Generally, tax authorities are even more wed to the concept of objectivity than are accountants. This is not surprising, since there must be at least one specific point at which the amount of tax can be computed and levied with reasonable certainty and accuracy. As previously observed, abandonment of the realization criterion would result in considerable subjectivity, making the tax dependent on the whims of personal judgments. This would mean constant litigation and dispute and would become an administrative nightmare.

The realization concept does not dictate that assets must be converted into monetary gains in order for gain to be recognized, even though this requirement would result in greater objectivity and easier tax administration. For example, if the taxpayer exchanges shares of stock for land, generally a gain or loss must be recognized. The amount of the gain or loss depends on the basis of the stock given up and the fair market value of the land (or other asset) received. It is obvious that subjectivity is immediately introduced into this situation; that is, the determination of the fair market value of the land or other asset is often not a simple or objective process. It is also apparent that unless realization is deemed to have taken place at the time of the exchange, a rather simple device for tax avoidance—the barter transaction—could be introduced. Thus, even though the IRS would prefer to use only objective data, it is nevertheless forced to establish market values in many cases even when it retains the basic realization criterion.

EASE AND CONSISTENCY OF ADMINISTRATION Closely tied to the realization concept is the administrative need for a taxable event to be fixed with adequate certainty in order for the IRS to avoid disputes as to the occurrence of the event or the amount involved.

This goal often creates a distinct conflict between what is generally accepted in financial accounting and what is required for tax purposes. The conflict occurs more often in relation to expense items than in relation to income items, because expenses frequently are estimated for financial accounting purposes even though they may not be deductible on the tax return. To quote former Commissioner Cohen:

> It is often proper or even necessary to reflect future events of a contingent nature, such as potential losses or pending lawsuits, in a financial statement. However, an attempt to reflect this type of transaction in the computation of a tax liability could result in protracted controversy between the government and the taxpayer over the likelihood of the occurrence of the event and the amount potentially involved. The tax accounting rule is easier to administer because it involves fewer subjective judgments and estimates.[2]

[2]Sheldon S. Cohen, "Accounting for Taxes, Finance and Regulatory Purposes—Are Variances Necessary?"; speech before the 19th Annual Tax Conference, The University of Chicago Law School, October 1966. Reprinted in *Taxes*, 44, No. 12 (December 1966), p. 784.

Similarly, tax requirements stricter than generally accepted accounting rules are often justified because they are easier to administer and produce more uniform results among different taxpayers. In short, administrative convenience frequently becomes important in explaining differences between taxable income and the net income of accounting.

SOCIAL AND ECONOMIC OBJECTIVES Tax laws often result from a desire to achieve stipulated social or economic goals. More and more frequently, tax laws are changed to secure full employment, to combat inflation, to relieve social pressures, or to attain other goals of the national Administration or the Congress. As a matter of fact, many critics today complain violently that tax laws have become little more than economic tools, whereas others think that's just what they should be.

As a result, many items that would be viewed as income for both economic and financial accounting purposes are excluded from taxation, or items that would not be considered in computing economic income or financial accounting income are allowed as tax deductions. For example, in 1982 and 1983 taxpayers were permitted to exclude from taxable income a limited amount of interest on "all-savers" certificates of deposit issued by financial institutions in order to stimulate savings that could be used largely in making loans for home purchases. Clearly this interest represents both financial and economic income to the recipient even though it was not taxable. Similarly, the deduction allowed under the Accelerated Cost Recovery System (ACRS) enacted in 1981 authorizes a taxpayer to deduct the cost of plant and equipment used in business significantly faster than is allowed for any other income measurement purpose. The purpose was to stimulate investment in productive assets.

THE ACCOUNTING PERIOD

ACCOUNTING PERIOD The period of time covered by the taxpayer's return. The basic period may be either a calendar or fiscal year.

The concept of income is meaningful only if we know the ***accounting period***, or the period of time to which the income applies. The basic period for measuring income is a year. Any taxpayer may use the *calendar* year to report income. Most individuals—almost all individuals whose income is from salary, wages, interest, and dividends—do use the calendar year. However, any taxpayer who maintains adequate records and books may use a *fiscal* year.[3] A fiscal year may be any 12-month period ending on the last day of any month except December (e.g., the period beginning March 1 and ending February 28th or 29th). Alternatively, the taxpayer can adopt a fiscal year ending on the same weekday that last occurs in a calendar month (for example, the last Tuesday in December) or on the same day of the week occurring nearest the last day of the same calendar month each year (for example, a fiscal period that ends on the Saturday occurring nearest to June 30 each year).[4] In both of the last two cases, some accounting periods will contain 52 weeks while others will contain 53 weeks.

[3] Reg. Sec. 1.441-1(b).
[4] Reg. Sec. 1.441-2(a).

With the approval of the IRS, the taxpayer may change the taxable year.[5] Special rules are provided for filing a return for the "short period" resulting from a change in taxable years.[6] Application for a change must be made on Form 1128, "Application for Change in Accounting Period."

FORM 1128

THE METHOD OF ACCOUNTING

The taxable year in which an item is to be included in gross income or is to be deducted in arriving at taxable income may depend on the ***accounting method*** adopted.

ACCOUNTING METHOD The method under which the taxpayer accounts for income and expenses. The primary methods provided are the cash basis and the accrual method. In addition the taxpayer may use a "mixed basis" and in specific cases may use the "installment method" or the "percentage-of-completion" method.

Subchapter E of the Internal Revenue Code contains the ground rules for accounting periods and methods. Sec. 446 provides the specific rules for tax accounting methods:

> (a) General Rule. Taxable income shall be computed under the method of accounting on the basis of which the taxpayer regularly computes his income in keeping his books.
>
> (b) Exceptions. If no method of accounting has been regularly used by the taxpayer, or if the method used does not clearly reflect income, the computation of taxable income shall be made under such method as, in the opinion of the Secretary [of the Treasury], does clearly reflect income.
>
> (c) Permissible Methods. Subject to the provisions of subsections (a) and (b), a taxpayer may compute taxable income under any of the following methods of accounting—
>
> (1) the cash receipts and disbursements method;
>
> (2) an accrual method;
>
> (3) any other method permitted by this chapter; or
>
> (4) any combination of the foregoing methods permitted under regulations prescribed by the Secretary.
>
> (d) Taxpayer Engaged in More Than One Business. A taxpayer engaged in more than one trade or business may, in computing taxable income, use a different method of accounting for each trade or business.
>
> (e) Requirement Respecting Change of Accounting Method. Except as otherwise expressly provided in this chapter, a taxpayer who changes the method of accounting on the basis of which he regularly computes his income in keeping his books shall, before computing his taxable income under the new method, secure the consent of the Secretary.

Additional and more specific procedural requirements on detailed accounting provisions are spread throughout the Code.

THE CASH BASIS

Most individual taxpayers, especially wage earners and individuals in the professions, use the ***cash basis*** of accounting. The cash basis is not only

CASH BASIS An accounting method under which generally income is reported when cash is received and generally expenses are deducted when paid.

[5] Reg. Sec. 1.441-1(b).

[6] Sec. 443.

simpler, in that it requires less record keeping than other methods, but it also gives the taxpayer limited control over the timing of expenses by accelerating or deferring cash receipts and cash payments. A taxpayer on the cash basis *generally* reports income when it is received in cash and deducts expenses when they are paid; however, there are many modifications and exceptions to these two basic rules.

CASH EQUIVALENT The notion that whenever a taxpayer receives a noncash asset in a transaction the fair market value of the asset received serves as a measure of the cash equivalent realized from the transaction.

THE "CASH-EQUIVALENT" CONCEPT Most individuals are prudent, and if taxed only on *cash* receipts they could easily avoid the tax by arranging to receive noncash property for services rendered. To eliminate this tax-avoidance ruse, the concept of "***cash equivalent***" has been developed. Essentially, the cash-equivalent concept suggests that whenever a taxpayer receives a noncash asset in a transaction, the fair market value of the asset received serves as a measure of the cash equivalent realized from the transaction. Thus, income is realized on the exchange of services for a noncash asset even in the case of a cash-basis taxpayer, as made clear in the Regulations which state that gross income

> . . . includes income realized in any form, whether in money, property, or services. Income may be realized, therefore, in the form of services, meals, accommodations, stock, or other property, as well as in cash.[7]

Example 3: Kay's employer sold her 100 shares of stock in Blue Corporation for $6,000. The market value of this stock at date of purchase was $9,500. Kay has $3,500 of gross income.

Example 4: Pelzel, a barber, agreed to shampoo and cut Lawrence's hair every two weeks of the year in return for which Lawrence agreed to mow the grass on the lawn of Pelzel's residence during the summer months. The value of the exchanged services during the current year was $260. Each party has income of $260 from the exchange.

CONSTRUCTIVE RECEIPT If a taxpayer has the right to take receipt of cash (or other assets) at will, the taxpayer is deemed to have received the item even though he or she elects not to take actual receipt.

"CONSTRUCTIVE-RECEIPT" DOCTRINE Another doctrine intended to reduce the opportunity for the cash-basis taxpayer to defer income by not taking cash, even though he or she could do so at will, is the concept of "***constructive receipt***." This doctrine finds clear and explicit expression in Regulation 1.451-2(a):

> Income although not actually reduced to a taxpayer's possession is constructively received by him in the taxable year during which it is credited to his account, set apart for him, or otherwise made available so that he may draw upon it at any time, or so that he could have drawn upon it during the taxable year if notice of intention to withdraw had been given. However, income is not constructively received if the taxpayer's control of its receipt is subject to substantial limitations or restrictions.

Obviously this rule is designed to prevent cash-basis taxpayers from deferring *receipt* of cash, and thus deferring the income tax in order to

[7] Reg. Sec. 1.61-1(a).

take advantage of the "present value" of money or to avail themselves of lower tax rates in later periods of lower income. Nevertheless, it is possible for cash-basis taxpayers to make limited deferrals of income simply by deferring billings for services in some circumstances. The doctrine has little application to accrual-basis taxpayers, since they ordinarily report income when it is earned in any event.

As noted in the quotation from the Regulations, the doctrine of constructive receipt is applied whenever a taxpayer has control, without substantial limitations or restrictions, over the amount involved. In addition, it is often held that for an amount to be constructively received, (*a*) the payer must have credited or set aside that amount for the payee and (*b*) the payer must have been able to make payment. Some of the common applications of the rule will suffice to show its scope and importance:

> **Example 5:** Grey has a savings account at the First National Bank. During 19X1 the bank credited Grey's account with interest of $260. Grey withdrew the interest in 19X2. Since Grey had constructive receipt in 19X1, he must report the entire $260 in 19X1.[8]

> **Example 6:** Black owns stock in National Company. In December 19X1, the corporation declared a dividend. The checks were mailed by the company on December 31, 19X1. Black's check was delivered in the mail on January 2, 19X2. Black includes the dividend in 19X2's income.[9]

> **Example 7:** Zipper, an accountant, performed services for a client in 19X1 and billed the client $200. The client tendered payment on December 31, 19X1, but Zipper asked the client to defer payment, which the client did. The $200 is taxable to Zipper in 19X1.

> **Example 8:** Manor Company issued a check in payment of a bonus to Mattson, an employee, on December 30 of last year. However, because Manor was overdrawn at the bank, the Company's manager asked Mattson not to cash the check until January 5 of the current year. There would be no constructive receipt in last year because the issuer had insufficient funds to pay the debt.[10]

CLAIM-OF-RIGHT DOCTRINE One additional concept needs to be mentioned at this point even though it is applicable to both cash-basis and accrual-basis taxpayers. The "***claim-of-right***" ***doctrine***—a judicial concept—holds that an amount is includable in income when actually or constructively received (or, in the case of an accrual basis taxpayer, is accrued) even though the taxpayer might be required to repay the amount at some future time. Money received by a taxpayer and treated as his

CLAIM-OF-RIGHT DOCTRINE The concept that an amount is includable in income when actually or constructively received.

[8] Reg. Sec. 1.451-2(b).

[9] *Ibid.*

[10] See *L. M. Fischer*, 14 T.C. 792 (1950).

own, under a claim that it is his, will be taxable to him even though the claim is disputed.[11] Following are examples of funds held to be taxable income to the taxpayer.

Example 9: Last year Smith won $10,000 gambling, an illegal activity in the state in which Smith resides. The gains are included in income because Smith exercised a claim of right to the funds.

Example 10: Last year Noel received a bonus of $22,000 from his employer. In the current year it was discovered that the bonus had been improperly computed and Noel was required to return the bonus. Because Noel "at all times controlled and used the full . . . amount unconditionally as his own, in the good faith though mistaken belief that he was entitled to the whole bonus," the entire amount would be includable in last year's income.[12]

Example 11: In the current year Berry, an attorney, received a contingent fee of $50,000 from a client in connection with a district court decision. Berry's agreement with the client is that if the district court decision is reversed on appeal to a higher court Berry will return the $50,000. Berry must report the $50,000 in income this year even though it may have to be returned later.

Taxpayers are offered some relief from potential adverse effects of the claim-of-right doctrine. When amounts required to be reported as income in one year under this doctrine must be repaid in later years, a deduction is allowed in the year of repayment if the amount exceeds $3,000.[13] A special rule is available to the taxpayer in most cases to ensure that the tax benefit in the year of deduction is as great as the increased tax liability in the prior year.

Example 12: If Berry, who received compensation of $50,000 in the current year (Example 11) is required to repay the $50,000 next year because of reversal of the district court decision, Berry will be entitled to a deduction next year. In addition, he will recompute the tax liability that would have resulted in the prior year if the item had not been incorrectly included. This difference in prior year's taxes is then compared with the reduction in tax in the later year resulting from the deduction in that year. The larger of these two amounts is the tax benefit allowed the taxpayer.

The claim-of-right doctrine does not generally apply if the taxpayer knows at the time of receipt that income that might otherwise be subject

---

[11] See *North American Oil Consolidated* v. *Burnet*, 73 S. Ct. 671 (1953), for the basic doctrine of claim of right.

[12] *U.S.* v. *Lewis*, 71 S. Ct. 522 (1951).

[13] Sec. 1341.

to the claim-of-right doctrine is subject to an absolute obligation for repayment by the taxpayer.

> **Example 13:** Mayfair Properties requires all tenants in its apartment houses to make a "damage" deposit of $250. Any amount not necessary to repair damages is refunded when a tenant vacates an apartment. Because of the absolute refund obligation, no income results under the claim-of-right doctrine.[14]

THE ACCRUAL BASIS

ACCRUAL BASIS An accounting method in which income generally is reported when it is earned, even though not received, and expenses generally are deducted when they are incurred even though not yet paid.

A taxpayer on the ***accrual basis*** generally reports income when it is earned, even though not yet received, and deducts expenses when they are incurred, even though not yet paid. Income is deemed earned "when all the events have occurred which fix the right to receive such income and the amount thereof can be determined with reasonable accuracy."[15] In general, the rules of measuring gross income for an accrual-basis taxpayer are the same as those that would be used in financial accounting. The accrual basis *must* be used to account for sales, purchases, and inventories by a taxpayer with inventories of stock in trade.[16] In addition, a few other taxpayers—for example, some corporations engaged in farming, and some partnerships engaged in farming and having a corporate partner—must use the accrual basis.[17] Most controversies between taxpayers and the Internal Revenue Service related to the accrual basis center around the period in which expenses should be deducted rather than when income should be included. Nevertheless there are some disputes over the timing of income inclusion.

One rule of special importance to accrual-basis taxpayers (although it applies to cash-basis taxpayers as well) is the one governing tax treatment of prepaid income. As a general rule, income received in advance is wholly taxable when received rather than over future years when earned. However, an accrual-basis taxpayer, but *not* a cash-basis taxpayer, may defer recognizing income from *services* (but not interest, rents, warranties or guaranties) applicable to services to be rendered in the first tax year *after* the year of receipt *if* all the services will be performed not later than that next tax year. If *any* services are to be performed *after* the next year, *all* of the advance receipts are taxable when received.[18]

> **Example 14:** On June 1 of the current year Jones received $24,000 representing 18 months' rent on property he owned. The entire $24,000 will be taxed to Jones in the current year under either the cash basis or accrual basis of accounting.

---

[14] See *John Mantell*, 17 T.C. 1143 (1952).

[15] Reg. Sec. 1.451-1(a).

[16] Reg. Sec. 1.446-1(c)(2).

[17] Sec. 447.

[18] Rev. Proc. 70-21, 1976-2 C. B. 549.

Example 15: Regina is an appliance dealer. When customers purchase appliances, they are given an opportunity to purchase either one-year or two-year warranty contracts that entitle them to free repair services (both parts and labor) on the appliances. During the current year Regina had the following receipts from sales of contracts:

One-year contracts	$ 4,000
Two-year contracts	10,000
Total	$14,000

Because the warranty or guaranty is related to products manufactured or sold by the taxpayer, no deferral of income is permitted. The entire $14,000 must be included in income in the current year.[19]

Example 16: If, in Example 15, Regina had been in the appliance repair business and not in the appliance sales business, the service contract would not relate to merchandise *manufactured or sold by* the taxpayer. Thus the portion of the one-year contracts that apply to services in the year *after* the payments were received could be deferred until the following year. However, because a portion of the two-year contracts would not be earned within the current tax year or the following tax year, the entire $10,000 applicable to such contracts must be reported in the current year.[20]

In addition to the deferral of prepaid income in limited cases provided in Rev. Proc. 70-21, the Code provides for deferral by accrual-basis taxpayers in a few other specific instances. Code Sec. 455 permits publishers to prorate certain subscription income over the period of the subscription. Code Sec. 456 likewise permits certain "membership organizations" to prorate dues over the membership period. Finally, Reg. Sec. 1.451-5 contains complex rules that permit the seller of goods to defer prepaid income until the year in which the payments are properly accruable under the method of accounting used for tax purposes (but not later than the year in which the payments are recognized as income for financial accounting purposes) if certain tests are met.

THE MIXED BASIS

Although Reg. Sec. 1.446-1(c)(2) generally requires that an accrual basis be used to account for inventories and sales and purchases of inventory items (gross profit), a taxpayer may nevertheless use the cash basis in computing all other items of income and deduction. This procedure is quite commonly followed by owners of small businesses and is called the "***mixed*** ***basis*** of accounting. If a taxpayer uses the cash basis in comput-

MIXED BASIS Gross profit may be based on the accrual basis, but expenses are reported on the cash basis.

[19] Rev. Proc. 70-21, Sec. 3.10(5).

[20] Rev. Proc. 70-21-3.10(4).

ing gross income, however, he or she must also use the cash basis in computing deductions.

Example 17: Saenz operates the Saenz Cash and Carry Retail Grocery Store. Saenz must use the accrual basis in accounting for sales and purchases and must properly account for inventories. Nevertheless, Saenz may use the cash basis in accounting for operating expenses.

OTHER BASES

In addition to the cash, accrual, and "mixed" methods of accounting, a taxpayer may sometimes use either the ***installment method*** or the long-term construction contract method. The former accounting method effectively spreads the gain (or gross income) realized on the sale of goods or property over the years during which the seller receives payment for the asset sold. The latter accounting method allows a contractor to spread the gain realized on the construction of a property over the years during which the construction takes place. Both of these methods are discussed in Chapter 6.

INSTALLMENT METHOD
An accounting method that recognizes gross income in proportion to the cash received each year.

CHANGING METHODS

A taxpayer who desires a change in tax-accounting methods must generally obtain the prior approval of the Commissioner.[21] Form 3115, an application for change in accounting method, is used to seek approval. Such a change often necessitates an adjustment to avoid the duplication or omission of certain items of gross income or deduction. Under some circumstances these "adjustments" may be reported by a taxpayer over a period of up to 10 years, as opposed to total recognition in a single tax year. In still other circumstances the Commissioner may not approve a request for a change in accounting method unless the taxpayer agrees to use the new method for financial accounting as well as tax purposes. And in yet other circumstances, the Commissioner may insist that a taxpayer change his or her accounting method to reflect income more clearly. Obviously, the details of each of these "special circumstances" cannot be investigated at this point in our study of income taxation. It will suffice to observe that, in general, a taxpayer is relatively free in the initial selection of an accounting method, but may be more restricted in electing to change that method at a later date.

FORM 3115

IDENTIFYING THE TAXPAYER

There frequently is a question about which taxpayer should include items in gross income. Sometimes this results from a deliberate attempt of the taxpayer to "***assign income***"—that is, to have the income taxed to some-

ASSIGNMENT OF INCOME
A device for attempting to have income earned by one person paid to another person and taxed to the latter.

[21] Sec. 446(e).

one else, usually a family member with a lower income and consequently a lower tax rate than that of the taxpayer. In other cases the confusion over the taxpayer who should report income arises from the effects of state laws or uncertainty as to who owns the property which generates the income.

INCOME OF MINOR CHILDREN

The Regulations provide:

> Compensation for personal services of a child shall, regardless of the provisions of State law relating to who is entitled to the earnings of the child, and regardless of whether the income is in fact received by the child, be deemed to be the gross income of the child and not the gross income of the parent of the child. . . . The income of a minor child is not required to be included in the gross income of the parent for income tax purposes.[22]

The opportunity immediately obvious in this rule to shift income through transfers of income-earning property to the taxpayer's child, or to pay a child reasonable wages for services rendered in the parent's trade or business, will be discussed subsequently.

INCOME ASSIGNMENT

In general, income derived from a service must be taxed to the person who rendered the service and income from property must be taxed to the person who owns the property. Income earned by one entity cannot be assigned to another entity.

> **Example 18:** Morris holds notes receivable from another person. Morris directs the debtor to pay this year's interest of $6,000 to Morris' son. The interest is taxed to Morris even though the cash is paid to Morris' son.

In spite of the general rule that income of one taxpayer cannot be assigned to another taxpayer, it is possible for one taxpayer to transfer to another *property* that generates the income, with the income earned after date of assignment being taxed to the transferee.

> **Example 19:** Morris owns interest-bearing notes. He gives those notes to his son on March 1, 19X1. If the transfer is a bona fide ***gift***, interest earned after the date of transfer will be taxed to Morris' son.

GIFT A transfer of property that is made for consideration less than the property's value.

The Uniform Gift to Minors Act permits an adult to give a minor child gifts of intangible property such as cash, savings accounts, certificates of

---

[22] Reg. Sec. 1.73-1.

deposit, bonds, and stocks. The Act permits the adult to be the custodian of the fund even though the income belongs, and is taxed, to the child.

Further, a taxpayer may effectively assign income by making a "temporary" gift of the property. This can be achieved if the property owner places the property in a ***Clifford***[23] or "short-term" ***trust*** for the benefit of another person, if the period of the trust is more than 10 years, and if the grantor of the trust (the transferor of property rights) divests himself or herself of control. After the 10-year period, the property can revert to the grantor without affecting the tax status of income distributed during the existence of the trust.[24]

CLIFFORD TRUST A trust to which assets are transferred for more than 10 years, in which income benefits a person other than the transferor.

Example 20: Morris owns notes receivable. He transfers these notes to a trustee to hold the property in trust for a period of 12 years. All income is to be paid to Morris' son during the 12-year period. On termination of the trust, the notes are to revert to Morris. During the period of the trust, the income will be includable in the son's, rather than in Morris' tax return.

INCOME FROM COMMUNITY PROPERTY

Eight states (Arizona, California, Idaho, Louisiana, Nevada, New Mexico, Texas and Washington) have "***community-property***" laws affecting the property rights of married persons. The other 42 states are referred to as "separate-property" or common-law states. In community-property states, property that was acquired by a person before marriage may be deemed to be owned solely by that spouse as "separate property." Similarly, property received by a person through inheritance or gift after that person's marriage may be held as property owned solely by that spouse. All other property acquired by either of the spouses after marriage is deemed to be community property, owned one-half by each spouse, unless that property can be shown to have been acquired using identifiably separate property of one spouse.

COMMUNITY PROPERTY Property deemed to be owned jointly by a husband and wife in the eight community property states.

The federal income tax law follows state laws in determining to whom income earned by spouses is taxable. One-half of income from personal services such as salaries and wages is deemed to belong to each spouse in community property states. Similarly, each spouse is deemed to be taxable on one-half of the income earned from community property. In some states (Idaho, Louisiana, and Texas) income earned on separately-owned property is treated as ***community income***, with one-half being allocable to each spouse. In the other five community property states, income from separate property is deemed to be the income of the spouse owning the property.

COMMUNITY INCOME Income received during marriage which, in the eight "community-property" states, is deemed to belong one-half to the husband and one-half to the wife.

Since 1948, married couples in all states have been permitted to file joint returns, effectively permitting them to treat all gross income of the

[23]The name is derived from *Helvering* v. *Clifford*, 309 U.S. 331 (1940), which dealt with a short-term trust.

[24]The requirements and rules for taxing Clifford trusts are found in Secs. 671-679.

couple as belonging one-half to each spouse. Joint returns are discussed in detail in Chapter 3.

Example 21: John and Mary were married throughout the year and lived in Arizona. During the current year they received the following income: John's salary, $20,000; Mary's salary, $40,000; interest on bonds held as community property, $1,500; interest on bonds held by Mary as separate property, $900. The $900 interest on bonds held as separate property belongs solely to Mary. All the remaining income ($61,500) is deemed to belong equally ($30,750) to each spouse. Thus, if the taxpayers file separate tax returns, Mary should report income of $31,650 and John should report $30,750. (The taxpayers may file a joint return, in which they combine their income, and will probably do so because it will generally result in a lower total tax burden.)

SUMMARY OF THE INCOME CONCEPT FOR TAX PURPOSES

The preceding discussion of the income concept for federal tax purposes can be summarized briefly. Before any taxpayer must report the receipt of income for federal income tax purposes, he or she must answer three fundamental questions—*all* in the affirmative. Those three questions are:

1. Did the taxpayer have any income?
2. Was that income realized?
3. If income was realized, must it be recognized immediately?

Perhaps the best possible test for the presence (or absence) of income is the one suggested by economists: Did the event under consideration for the potential taxpayer cause *either* an increase in net worth *or* in consumption? If the answer to this first question is yes, we ordinarily should presume that income is present. The conclusion that income is present, however, is not sufficient to trigger the income tax. To be taxable, income must also be both realized and recognized.

Realization usually requires *both* (*a*) a change in the form or the substance of the taxpayer's property (or property rights) and (*b*) the involvement of a second party. Income is most commonly realized when a service has been rendered; a property has been sold or exchanged; or a property belonging to the taxpayer has been used by someone else. Thus the receipt of any form of payment for a service rendered—whether it is received in cash or in noncash property—is generally sufficient to cause the realization of income; so is the exchange of one property for another. Not every item of realized income is, however, subject to an immediate income tax. Realized income must also be recognized for federal income tax purposes.

In general, income must be recognized for tax purposes in the same accounting period that it is realized. There are, however, many exceptions to this general rule. Tax nonrecognition, when it occurs, may be either permanent or temporary. Permanent nonrecognition is typically due to an exclusion provision inserted into the Code by Congress. Temporary nonrecognition may be attributed either to (*a*) specific accounting methods (or conventions) or (*b*) special nonrecognition provisions put into the Code by Congress, usually to provide for income taxation at the time that the taxpayer has the wherewithal to pay a tax.

STATUTORY PROVISIONS GOVERNING INCOME

The general concepts of gross income for tax purposes that have been discussed in this chapter stem in part from the Internal Revenue Code, in part from administrative interpretations of the Code, and in part from decisions of various courts. A cursory examination of the statutes reveals that they contain relatively few sections devoted to defining gross income.

Section 61 of the Code purports to define gross income. Although the definition it provides—gross income means all income—does not tell us much, it clearly suggests that any doubtful items are included within the definition. This conclusion is supported by three other phrases in Sec. 61(a) which, in its entirety, reads as follows:

> (a) General Definition. Except as otherwise provided in this subtitle, gross income means all income from whatever sources derived, including (but not limited to) the following items:
> (1) Compensation for services, including fees, commissions, fringe benefits, and similar items;
> (2) Gross income derived from business;
> (3) Gains derived from dealings in property;
> (4) Interest;
> (5) Rents;
> (6) Royalties;
> (7) Dividends;
> (8) Alimony and separate maintenance payments;
> (9) Annuities;
> (10) Income from life insurance and endowment contracts;
> (11) Pensions;
> (12) Income from discharge of indebtedness;
> (13) Distributive share of partnership gross income;
> (14) Income in respect of a decedent; and
> (15) Income from an interest in an estate or trust.

The four statutory phrases that support an expansive interpretation of "gross income" for tax purposes are:

1. *Except* as otherwise provided . . .
2. Gross income means *all* income . . .
3. From *whatever* source derived . . .
4. Including (but *not limited to*) . . .

In view of the all-inclusive nature of Code Sec. 61(a), the taxpayer must look to the phrase "except as otherwise provided" as a basis for omitting an item from gross income. The statutory exceptions are collectively identified as exclusions. In other words, *any item of income that is not included in gross income is known as an exclusion*. The words of Sec. 61 clearly suggest that all exclusions must have a statutory base and that these provisions must be found within Subtitle A of the Internal Revenue Code. In fact, a few exclusions do not have statutory bases, but they are so widely accepted that no one seriously challenges their validity today. Perhaps the best known exclusion based solely on administrative authority is that formerly extended to social security benefits. These benefits were excluded from taxation by a Treasury Department ruling in 1941. Although various proposals were made from time to time to revise the statutes to include social security benefits within the income tax base, none of those proposals was enacted by the Congress until 1983, when a portion of social security benefits was made taxable in certain cases.

A careful examination of a detailed table of contents of the Code might suggest that all of the exclusions are neatly contained within Part III of Subchapter B of Chapter 1. The title for that part of the Code reads "Items Specifically Excluded from Gross Income." Part III includes Sections 101 through 133, the titles of which read as follows:

Sec. 101. Certain death payments.
Sec. 102. Gifts and inheritances.
Sec. 103. Interest on certain governmental obligations.
Sec. 103A. Mortgage subsidy bonds.
Sec. 104. Compensation for injuries or sickness.
Sec. 105. Amounts received under accident and health plans.
Sec. 106. Contributions by employer to accident and health plans.
Sec. 107. Rental value of parsonages.
Sec. 108. Income from discharge of indebtedness.
Sec. 109. Improvements by lessee on lessor's property.
Sec. 110. Income taxes paid by lessee corporation.
Sec. 111. Recovery of tax benefit items.
Sec. 112. Certain combat pay of members of the Armed Forces.
Sec. 113. Mustering-out payments for members of the Armed Forces.
Sec. 114. Sports programs conducted for the American National Red Cross.
Sec. 115. Income of States, municipalities, etc.
Sec. 116. Partial exclusion of dividends received by individuals.
Sec. 117. Scholarships and fellowship grants.
Sec. 118. Contributions to the capital of a corporation.
Sec. 119. Meals or lodging furnished for the convenience of employer.
Sec. 120. Amounts received under qualified group legal services plans.
Sec. 121. One-time exclusion of gain from sale of principal residence by individual who has attained age 55.
Sec. 122. Certain reduced uniformed services retirement pay.

Sec. 123. Amounts received under insurance contracts for certain living expenses.
Sec. 124. Qualified transportation provided by employer.
Sec. 125. Cafeteria plans.
Sec. 126. Certain cost-sharing payments.
Sec. 127. Educational assistance programs.
Sec. 128. Interest on certain savings certificates.
Sec. 129. Dependent care assistance programs.
Sec. 130. Certain personal injury liability assignments.
Sec. 131. Certain foster care payments.
Sec. 132. Certain fringe benefits.
Sec. 133. Interest on certain loans used to acquire employer securities.

The seemingly clear list of 15 inclusions provided in Sec. 61(a), coupled with the 34 specific exclusions located in Part III of Subchapter B, may give the student who is unfamiliar with the myriad controversies surrounding the nature and measure of income a false and unwarranted sense of security about his or her understanding of income. As you will discover throughout the remainder of this text, these few specific items of inclusion and exclusion are but the tip of a very interesting iceberg.

In the next chapter we will analyze the tax rules governing the inclusion or exclusion of a number of specific items that are frequently encountered by taxpayers and by preparers of tax returns. In many instances our discussion must of necessity be oversimplified and superficial. It would be impossible in a book of this type to examine all the exceptions (and exceptions to the exceptions) to the general rule. Only an intensive reading of the Revenue Code Section involved, the related Regulations and other administrative interpretations, and in some instances key court decisions, can result in satisfactory answers to many questions that are raised.

INCOME REALIZED AS NET CAPITAL GAINS

The unique, preferential tax treatment of income realized in the form of capital gains deserves some mention at this point. Income realized and recognized is included in gross income under the rules explained in this chapter. Gains realized on the disposition of property is income and is generally included in gross income. However, a taxpayer who realized a net capital gain in a given year is allowed a deduction equal to 60 percent of such gain. Thus, only 40 percent of the income realized in the form of a net capital gain is recognized. This extraordinarily beneficial rule is a powerful motivation for taxpayers. A major goal of much tax planning is to ensure that the maximum amount of income is realized in this form.

While the detailed rules governing net capital gains are deferred to Chapters 10 and 11, generally a net capital gain arises from the sale or exchange of a capital asset that has been held for more than six months (one year before 1984). The usual capital assets are those assets held for investment, such as corporate securities and undeveloped land, as opposed to ordinary assets that are held for use in a trade or business. Just as net capital gains receive beneficial treatment, taxpayers get only limited deductions from net capital losses. For these limits and other numerous details, see Chapters 10 and 11.

PLANNING WORKSHOP

The general concepts that have been discussed in this chapter are not topics that lend themselves to providing a basis for tax planning. Nevertheless, it is obvious that some of the topics discussed can be helpful to the taxpayer trying to minimize taxes.

ACCOUNTING METHODS

Where a taxpayer is entitled to do so, tax deferral (and thus interest savings because of the time value of money) can be achieved through selecting the cash basis of accounting. Under the cash basis, income is included only when the cash is received, thus deferring some income to a subsequent period for services rendered late in the preceding period. Additionally, expenses are generally deducted when paid under the cash method, permitting the taxpayer to accelerate some payments where doing so would improve the current tax situation without undue additional interest costs.

A few taxpayers are able to benefit from other accounting provisions. For example, a taxpayer who sells merchandise on the installment basis, or a taxpayer who makes casual sales of real estate or personal property, may use the installment method of accounting, reporting the gross profit as the cash in payment for the property sold is received. In general, the taxpayer would prefer to defer tax payment because of the time value of money. On the other hand, if the taxpayer is in a relatively low income tax rate bracket at the time of the sale and expects to have increasing income levels, with resulting higher tax rates, during the period of collections, a careful analysis of the interest applicable to the taxes deferred, and the increase in taxes resulting from deferring the income to the period of higher taxes, would be appropriate.

As we will see in subsequent chapters, where a taxpayer controls a closely-held corporation and is an officer or employee of the corporation, an advantage may often be gained by having the corporation adopt an accrual basis of accounting while the taxpayer adopts the cash basis, or by having the corporation adopt a fiscal year different from the taxable year used by the shareholder-employee. For example, the corporation may adopt a year ending on January 31, while the shareholder-employee adopts the calendar year. By paying

Continued

a bonus to the owner in January, the corporation could utilize the tax advantage of the deduction almost immediately, while the owner-employee could defer at least part of the resulting tax liability until the second-following April 15, i.e., some 14½ months later. These opportunities, and the safeguards against them in the Internal Revenue Code, will be discussed in later chapters.

ASSIGNMENT OF INCOME

As we have seen, a taxpayer cannot simply assign his or her income, and transfer the tax burden related thereto, to another person in a lower rate bracket. Nevertheless, some assignment of income may be possible through the gift of income-producing properties to minor children or other relatives or, even more importantly, through the use of short-term Clifford Trusts.

Example 22: Mr. and Mrs. Isadore Safe, a highly successful locksmith and his wife, report an annual taxable income of $109,400. If Mrs. Safe were suddenly to inherit $100,000 cash from her recently deceased uncle, Willis More, she might be tempted to put the inheritance into a bank savings account or high grade corporate bonds and save the interest to help finance the education of her three small children. If Mrs. Safe were to receive 15% interest on her savings account, she would discover that the additional $15,000 in interest each year would cause an increase of $7,500 in the couple's annual income tax liability. In other words, only $7,500 would be left after taxes to apply toward the children's education fund. With a little tax planning, Mrs. Safe might put the $100,000 that she inherited "in trust" for a period of at least 10 years and 1 day, and instruct the trustee to distribute the $15,000 annual interest equally to her three minor children. Each of the Safe children would now receive $5,000 per year in interest (for 10 years). If we assume that the children receive no other income, they would each pay a 1983 income tax of $536. In this way the aggregate tax liability on the $15,000 of interest each year would have been reduced from $7,500 to $1,608, and the amount left to accumulate in the children's education fund would have increased from $7,500 to $13,392 per year, using 1983 tax rates.

Parents with minor children are afforded another means of shift ing income—namely, by using the Uniform Gift to Minors Act (UGMA) adopted in some form by all the states. Under this Act the parent can make a gift of intangible assets such as bank accounts, certificates of deposit, bonds, etc. to a minor, but with control remaining in the

Continued

PLANNING WORKSHOP

hands of the parent or other adult who serves as custodian. As long as the child's income and assets are not commingled with those of the adult, the custodian has a great deal of freedom in selling the assets, reinvesting sales proceeds and income, and accumulating or distributing the income. The income from the investments, including any gains from sales, are taxed to the child, not to the custodian.

Example 23: By periodic savings, parents accumulate a fund for their child's education. The UGMA permits taxes on the savings to be eliminated completely or greatly reduced because the income is shifted to the child, who is in a lower tax rate bracket.

EMPLOYMENT OF CHILDREN OF THE TAXPAYER

If the taxpayer is in a trade or business, consideration may be given to employing his or her children to perform reasonable jobs at reasonable rates of pay in that trade or business. For example, the child might be hired to perform custodial services, to make deliveries, or perform other suitable jobs. If the pay is reasonable for the work performed, the parent will be able to deduct the payment as a business expense. A part of the income may be taxable to the child, while some of it will not be (an amount equal to the child's personal exemption and "zero-bracket income"). However, even the taxable portion will be taxed at a rate that is probably considerably lower than the rate of the parent. Thus, the family unit saves taxes on income retained within the family.

KEY POINTS TO REMEMBER

1. In general, changes in value of a taxpayer's assets have no effect on the taxpayer's taxable income. Only when income is "realized" through a transaction with another party does income result.
2. The taxpayer usually has a choice of the taxable year. It may be either a calendar year or a fiscal year. The fiscal year can end on the last day of the same month each year. Alternatively, it can end on the same weekday (e.g., Tuesday) that last occurs in the same calendar month (e.g., March) each year, or it can end on the same weekday occurring nearest the last day of the same calendar month.
3. In order to change taxable years, the taxpayer must receive approval of the IRS.
4. The taxpayer may use the cash basis of accounting, the accrual method, or a mixed method. However, if the taxpayer has inventories, the accrual method *must* be used in computing gross profit.
5. Consent of the IRS must be received in order to change accounting methods.

6. Even under the cash basis of accounting, it is not necessary that the taxpayer receive cash to realize income. Under the cash-equivalent concept, the fair value of noncash assets received serves as a measure of cash equivalent.
7. Under the doctrine of constructive receipt, a taxpayer is taxed on amounts that he could have received during the year by drawing on amounts that have been made available to him.
8. Under the claim-of-right doctrine, a taxpayer who has received funds and uses them as his own or her own must include the funds in income even though they may have to be returned.
9. Prepaid income is taxed in the year received, with minor exceptions, even by a taxpayer using the accrual basis.
10. Income of a minor child is taxed to the child—not to the parent.
11. Taxpayers cannot avoid paying taxes by assigning their income to others. However, assignment of income may be effected by transferring income-producing properties to the other party or by using a Clifford Trust.
12. The federal income tax law follows state laws in determining to whom income is taxable in the case of married couples. In the eight community-property states, laws differ on the treatment of income from separately owned property.
13. In general, all income is taxable unless the statutes (or court decisions) provide otherwise.

SELF-STUDY QUESTIONS

1. Carl Tice, an employee of Canova Corp., received a salary of $50,000 from Canova in 1983. Also in 1983, Carl bought 100 shares of Nolan Corp. common stock from Canova for $30 a share, when the market value of the Nolan Stock was $50 a share. Canova had paid $20 a share for the Nolan stock in 1975.

   In addition, Carl owned a building which he leased to Boss Co. on January 1, 1983, for a five-year term at $500 a month. Boss paid Carl $8,000 in 1982 to cover the following:

Rent for January to December 1983	$6,000
Advance rent for January 1984	500
Security deposit, to be applied against the final three months' rent in the fifth year of the lease	1,500

   How much should Carl report on his 1983 income tax return as compensation income received from Canova?

   a) $50,000

   b) $51,000

   c) $52,000

   d) $53,000

   (AICPA adapted)

2. Refer to Question 1. How much rent income should Carl report in his 1983 income tax return for the amounts paid to him by Boss?

   a) $6,000

   b) $6,500

   c) $7,500

   d) $8,000

   (AICPA adapted)

3. Dr. Berger, a physician, reports on the cash basis. The following items pertain to Dr. Berger's medical practice in 1982:

Cash received from patients in 1982	$200,000
Cash received in 1982 from third-party reimbursers for services provided by Dr. Berger in 1981	30,000
Salaries paid to employees in 1982	20,000
Year-end 1982 bonuses paid to employees in 1983	1,000
Other expenses paid in 1982	24,000

   What is Dr. Berger's net income for 1982 from his medical practice?

   a) $155,000

   b) $156,000

   c) $185,000

   d) $186,000

   (AICPA adapted)

4. Dr. Chester is a cash-basis taxpayer. His office visit charges are usually paid on the date of the visit or within one month. However, services rendered outside the office are billed weekly, and are usually paid within two months as patients collect from insurance companies. Information relating to 1982 is as follows:

Cash received at the time of office visits	$ 35,000
Collections on accounts receivable	130,000
Accounts receivable, January 1	16,000
Accounts receivable, December 31	20,000

   Dr. Chester's gross income from his medical practice for 1982 is

   a) $165,000

   b) $169,000

   c) $181,000

   d) $185,000

   (AICPA adapted)

5. Alex Burg, a cash-basis taxpayer, earned an annual salary of $80,000 at Ace Corp. in 1983, but elected to take only $50,000. Ace, which was financially able to pay Burg's full salary, credited the unpaid balance of $30,000 to Burg's account on the corporate books in 1983 and actually paid this $30,000 to Burg on April 30, 1984. How much of the salary is taxable to Burg in 1983?

a) $50,000
b) $60,000
c) $65,000
d) $80,000
(AICPA adapted)

6. Mr. and Mrs. Alvin Charak took a foster child, Robert, into their home in 1981. A state welfare agency paid the Charaks $3,900 during the year for related expenses. Actual expenses incurred by the Charaks during 1981 in caring for Robert amounted to $3,000. The remaining $900 was spent by the Charaks in 1981 toward their own personal expenses. How much of the foster child payments is taxable income to the Charaks in 1981?
   a) $0
   b) $900
   c) $2,900
   d) $3,900
   (AICPA adapted)

7. Bennet Hanover purchased a tract of land for $20,000 in 1974 when he heard that a new highway was going to be constructed through the property and that the land would soon be worth $200,000. Highway engineers surveyed the property and indicated that he would probably get $175,000. The highway project was abandoned in 1976 and the value of the land fell to $15,000. Hanover can claim a loss in 1976 of
   a) $0
   b) $5,000
   c) $160,000
   d) $180,000
   (AICPA adapted)

8. On March 12, 1973, Ivan Turner was injured in a truck accident in the course of his employment. As a result of injuries sustained, he received the following payments in 1973:

Damages for personal injuries	$5,000
Workmen's compensation	500
Reimbursement from his employer's accident and health plan for medical expenses paid by Turner in 1973 (The employer's contribution to the plan was $75 in 1973.)	750

   The amount to be included in Turner's 1973 gross income should be
   a) $6,250
   b) $5,000
   c) $750
   d) $75

e) none of the above

(AICPA adapted)

9. Paul Charles, a cash-basis taxpayer, owns an apartment house. In computing net rental income for 1972, the following information is ascertained:

   - An analysis of the 19X1 bank deposit slips shows rents received in the amount of $15,000.
   - In December 1972, Mr. Charles received a $600 negotiable non-interest-bearing promissory note dated December 1, 1972 as rent for the months of December 1972 and January 1973 (fair market value $550).
   - Pursuant to instructions from Mr. Charles, a past-due rent check of $175 was given to the building superintendent on December 29, 1972. He mailed it to the rental office on the 30th, it was received on January 2, and deposited on January 3, 1973.
   - The lease of the tenant in Apt. 4A expired on December 31, 1972, and the tenant left improvements valued at $500. The improvements were not in lieu of any rent required to have been paid.

   In computing his 1972 taxable income, Mr. Charles will report gross rents of

   a) $16,275

   b) $16,225

   c) $15,725

   d) $15,500

   e) none of the above

   (AICPA adapted)

10. Malakoff reports his taxable income on the accrual basis of accounting. In 19X1, he had the following receipts:

Collections on accounts receivable from customers	$290,000
Sales on account to customers	314,000
Cash received on September 1, 19X1, for sublease of part of his office space covering period Sept. 1, 19X1 through Feb. 28, 19X2	6,000
Cash received in February 19X1 representing sublease of part of office space for December 19X0 and January 19X1	2,000

   The amount Malakoff should include in gross income in 19X1 on account of the above is:

   a) $322,000

   b) $321,000

   c) $320,000

   d) $319,000

   e) none of the above

   (AICPA adapted)

QUESTIONS

1. What is the principal difference between the concepts of income held by accountants and by economists?
2. What is meant by the term "completed transaction"?
3. Explain how the need for ease and consistency of administration affects tax laws.
4. How does the "wherewithal-to-pay" concept affect the tax treatment of prepaid income?
5. Explain the "realization" concept.
6. Give examples of how the income tax law is used to achieve certain social and economic objectives.
7. Explain the taxpayer's choices of "tax year."
8. What is the "cash-equivalent" concept?
9. Define constructive receipt.
10. What is the claim-of-right doctrine?
11. Under what circumstances can a cash-basis taxpayer defer recognition of prepaid income beyond the year of receipt?
12. Under what circumstances can an accrual-basis taxpayer defer recognition of prepaid income beyond the year of receipt?
13. What is meant by the "mixed basis" of accounting?
14. Under what circumstances, if any, must a taxpayer use the accrual basis of accounting?
15. In general, what is the "installment basis" of accounting?
16. A taxpayer is filing a tax return for the first time. Must the taxpayer obtain permission from the Internal Revenue Service to use the cash basis of accounting?
17. What is meant by "assignment of income"?
18. Is a minor child's income taxable to the parent?
19. What is a Clifford Trust?
20. How can the Clifford Trust be used to reduce taxes?
21. Does the federal law dictate to which spouse income is taxed in a community-property state? Explain.

PROBLEMS

1. On June 1, 19X1, Lawrence, a cash-basis taxpayer, purchased the following assets:

100 shares of Zeno Corporation stock for	$ 2,800
A 6-months "certificate of deposit" for	1,000
20 acres of land for	20,000

Lawrence held all of these assets through the remainder of the year. On October 15, Lawrence received $32 as dividends on the Zeno stock. On December 1, the certificate of deposit matured. The principal, along with the earned interest of $50, was automatically reinvested in a new 6-months CD. On December 31, 19X1, the 100 shares of Zeno Corporation stock had a market value of $2,100, the CD had a cash surrender value of $1,054, and the land had a fair market value of $26,000. How much income, if any, must Lawrence report for tax purposes in 19X1?

2. Jane, an accounting student at State University, has worked out a deal with the hairdresser at a local beauty salon. Jane agrees to prepare the hairdresser's federal income tax return in exchange for a shampoo and set each week. The two parties agree that this transaction has a value of $416 per year. The cost of materials used in the hair treatment is $104 per year.

   a) How much income, in the economic sense, does each party have?

   b) How much taxable income, if any, must each party recognize?

   c) What is the difficulty faced by the IRS in making certain that each party recognizes the income that should be reported?

3. Individual Alan works as a salesman at a clothing store while attending college. During the current year, Alan received the following from his employer:

Cash salary	$4,200
Clothing	900*
Cash bonus	300
New television (for being selected as salesperson of the month)	125*

(*estimated fair market value)

What amount of gross income has taxpayer Alan realized for federal income tax purposes?

4. *a*) Taxpayer, an accountant, performed work for his client, a closely held corporation. Based on his normal rate, the services performed in the latter part of 19X1 would have been billed to the client at $2,500. Because of the client's poor cash position, however, the taxpayer, who is on the cash basis of accounting, agreed to present the bill in March 19X2 and was immediately paid on

presentation of the bill. In which year should the taxpayer report the income?

b) Suppose, instead of the facts above, that the accountant, because he was sympathetic with his client's cash position and because he expected the client to be very successful in the future, agreed to accept instead of $2,500 cash a 5-year convertible note bearing interest at 8%. Under the terms of the note, it could be converted into the client's stock at any time in the 5-year period at the rate of 1 share of stock for each $10 face amount of the note. When the note was issued in December 19X1, the stock had a value of $7 per share. In 19X6, the taxpayer converted the note into 250 shares of stock, which at that time had a value of $14 per share.
(1) How much, if any, income does the taxpayer report in 19X1?
(2) How much, if any, income does the taxpayer report in 19X6?

5. The following events affecting Mary Muffet occurred at the end of 19X5:

   a) On December 31, National Corporation mailed Mary a dividend check of $600 from New York. The dividend was received by Mary, who lives in California, on January 6, 19X6.

   b) California Savings Company credited Mary's savings account with "dividends" of $120 on December 31.

   How do these transactions affect Mary's gross income for 19X5?

6. Snuffel opens a "cash-and-carry" retail grocery store in 19X4. In addition, Snuffel works as an employee for an accounting firm and operates a part-time tax service. Snuffel wishes to use the cash basis of accounting for the retail store because he uses the cash basis for his other activities. Will this be possible? Assume, instead, that Snuffel wishes to use the accrual basis of accounting for his retail store. Will this be possible?

7. In November 19X3, Yuri received a check from a well-known medical insurance company for $325. The accompanying stub stated: "In payment of your claim No. 123456." Yuri had made no claim, but he nevertheless cashed the check. In June 19X4, Yuri received a letter from the insurance company telling him that the check sent him in the preceding year resulted from a computer error and asking him to repay the $325. Yuri repaid the amount in July 19X4.

   How do these facts affect Yuri's taxable income in 19X3 and 19X4?

8. Surrey owns an apartment building. In addition to the rents applicable to the current year, Surrey receives the following:

   a) Damage deposits from new tenants. These are refundable when tenants move if no damage is done.

   b) Payments for the last month's rent on rental contracts. These are prepayments for the final month on each contract.

   How do these amounts affect Surrey's income for the year if Surrey uses the cash basis of accounting? If Surrey uses the accrual basis?

9. Jason operates a retail appliance store. He uses the cash basis of accounting except for items related to gross profit from sale of merchandise. Jason offers purchasers of appliances from his store a warranty contract under which Jason agrees to repair free of charge any appliance purchased from him (including parts and labor) for 36 months from date of sale. During 19X4 Jason received $24,000 from the sale of such contracts. He estimates that approximately $20,000 of this amount relates to work to be performed in 19X5, 19X6, and 19X7.

   a) How much of the $24,000 must Jason include in gross income in 19X4?

   b) Assume the same facts as above, except that Jason uses the accrual basis of accounting. How much of the $24,000 must Jason include in gross income in 19X4?

10. Louise, a divorcee, was married to Henry in 19X4. Louise's 6-year-old daughter is a child model. During 19X4 the child's total income from modeling was $60,000. Of this amount, $20,000 was earned before Louise and Henry married, and $40,000 after that date. Louise had the modeling agency put the entire $60,000 into a trust fund for the child, and no part of it was withdrawn during 19X4. Louise and Henry live in a community-property state.

    How does the $60,000 affect the gross income of the various parties during 19X4?

11. Chris made a $10,000 loan, bearing interest at 12%, to a friend. Chris directed the friend to pay the interest to Chris's 15-year-old daughter. During the current year the daughter received $1,200 interest.

    How much income is reported, and by whom, during the current year?

12. In 19X4, Elvis purchased securities for $100,000 and immediately transferred them to a "Clifford Trust." The terms of the trust require all income from the trust's assets to be accumulated and to be distributed to Elvis's son after 12 years. At that time the assets in the trust, except for the income, are to revert to Elvis. A local bank's trust officer is named trustee.

    During the current year, the trust earned income of $10,000. Is the $10,000 taxable to Elvis? Explain.

13. Mary and John both lived in Texas throughout 19X4. They were married on April 1, 19X4. Prior to their marriage, Mary had interest income of $600 and a salary of $3,000 in 19X4. During that period John earned a salary of $4,500 and received dividend income of $300. After marriage, Mary's salary was $9,000 for the remainder of 19X4, while John's salary was $14,000. Mary also received interest of $1,800 on interest-bearing securities owned at the time of marriage. John's dividends after marriage, on stocks owned before marriage, were $1,000. If Mary and John file separate returns for 19X4, how much income will each report?

14. Assume the same facts as in Problem 13 except that Mary and John live in California. How much gross income will they each report in 19X4?

15. Periodically Mrs. Sand makes deposits to a savings account at the Federal Savings and Loan Association. The account was opened by Mrs. Sand in the following name: Mrs. R. T. Sand, Trustee for William Sand. William Sand is her 6-year-old son. The trust was created under the "Uniform Gift to Minors" Act. It is Mrs. Sand's intent to continue such deposits until William becomes an adult, at which time he will have full control of the account. During the current year, Federal Savings and Loan Association credited the account with $430 of "dividends."
   To whom are the dividends taxable?

16. Brian Allen purchased a new automobile for $8,500 during the current year. Two weeks after purchasing the automobile, Allen received a $500 rebate check from the automobile manufacturer. This rebate check was offered to any retail customer who purchased an automobile during the month of October. Should the rebate check be included in Allen's gross income for the current year? Explain.

17. The GAS Corporation is engaged in the sale of gasoline. Because of its simplicity, the corporation keeps its regular financial accounting books on the cash basis of accounting. Can the corporation also report its taxable income on the cash basis? Explain briefly.

18. Taxpayer K found a $100 bill on the streets of San Francisco. Is the $100 taxable to K? Explain.

19. Taxpayer Lawrence owned land with an "adjusted basis" of $100,000. The land was encumbered by a mortgage of $61,000. In 19X1, Lawrence sold the land to Oliver. Oliver assumed the mortgage on the land, paid Lawrence $40,000 in cash and transferred to Lawrence an automobile which cost Oliver $14,000 and had a fair market value of $8,000. What is the amount of income, if any, earned by Lawrence on sale of the land?

TAX PLANNING PROBLEMS

1. Henry and Irma Goode operate a successful retail business and own substantial interests in real estate. They also have large investments in stocks, bonds, and certificates of deposit with present values of $500,000 and yielding cash income of $50,000. Their taxable income has averaged over $200,000 per year for several years, so that their marginal tax rate is 50 percent. It is quite likely that their income will continue to increase.

   The Goodes have three children, ranging in ages from two years to eight years. The Goodes anticipate that all of these children will be sent to private universities for four years when they graduate from high school. The current average cost per year for tuition, fees, lodging, and meals at those universities is $8,000. The Goodes speculate that these costs will probably double by the time their children reach college age. Mr. and Mrs. Goode have decided that they should begin to systematically accumulate funds to pay for this education. Presently the children own no assets and have no income.

From a tax viewpoint (ignoring other factors), what are the most advantageous approaches the Goodes could use to accumulate the funds? Explain.

2. Marole owns a retail furniture store, employing 14 full-time employees and six part-time employees. The part-time employees are involved in sales activities, repair services, and janitorial services. Marole has two teenage children in high school, both of whom wish to work at the furniture store. The primary reason Marole has not hired the two children in the store is his understanding that the amounts paid them would not be deductible for tax purposes. What advice would you give Marole?

3. Ahrens, an accounting professor at State University, conducted an audit of a local business during the first 20 days of December, 19X1, and on December 22 prepared a bill for $1,000 to send the client. The client always pays immediately on receipt of the statement. The professor has stable income from year to year. What is your advice to the professor?

4. Margaret has recently received $1,000,000 life insurance resulting from the death of her husband. Her income from other investments is estimated to be $200,000 per year. Margaret is contemplating investing $100,000 of this amount in bonds. She can purchase at par value top-rated corporate bonds maturing in 20 years and bearing interest at 13 percent. A friend has suggested that Margaret consider investing instead in top-rated and guaranteed municipal securities or in U.S. government bonds. What points should you consider in counseling Margaret? What is the minimum interest rate that Margaret must earn on municipal securities to be as well off as she would be if she invests in corporate bonds?

RESEARCH PROBLEMS

1. Rachel Amaros, a dentist, has maintained her tax records on the accrual basis of accounting. Because of slow pay of some patients and nonpayment by others, and in order to defer taxes, Rachel has decided to switch to the cash basis of accounting.

   a) Will she be required to get the approval of the IRS to make the change?

   b) If your answer to question *a* is *yes*, when must approval be received?

c) How will any adjustments or changes in income resulting from the change in method be handled in the tax return?

2. Ms. Marquis has opened a savings account at the local bank for her four-year-old son, Robert. The account is listed in Robert's name, but Ms. Marquis is named as the person who has authority to make withdrawals. Ms. Marquis expects to make periodic deposits in the account and to make no withdrawals. When Robert enters college, the account balance is expected to be applied toward Robert's expenses. During the current year, interest of $108 was earned on the account and added to the account balance. To whom is the $108 taxable? What advice should you give Ms. Marquis about this account?

3. Grafa, an accrual-basis taxpayer, operates an advertising agency. In 19X1, Grafa received payment of $120,000 from a retail store covering three advertising mailings to be made in December, 19X1, and January and February, 19X2. Each mailing is expected to have costs of $30,000. May Grafa defer until 19X2 the $80,000 applicable to January and February?

4. Janet Penn had her 1982 income tax return prepared by Payless Tax, Inc. A subsequent audit by the IRS disclosed that Payless had improperly reported a deduction of $2,000 and Penn was assessed $820 of additional taxes. Payless offers to reimburse taxpayers for any tax deficiencies due to the preparer's negligence. Payless agreed to pay this tax deficiency for Penn. Is the $820 payment by Payless includable in Penn's gross income? Explain.

Chapter Objectives

1. Explain the limited exclusion from gross income for dividends received by individuals and identify which dividends qualify for the exclusion.
2. Describe the tax treatment of various types of interest income, especially tax-exempt interest.
3. Explain the treatment of rents received from annuities purchased by the taxpayer as well as those purchased by the taxpayer's employer under qualified pension and profit-sharing plans.
4. Demonstrate the proper tax treatment of life insurance proceeds received because of death of the insured, including interest paid on reinvested proceeds.
5. Explain the correct treatment to be given payments made by an employer to beneficiaries of a deceased employee.
6. Identify receipts that qualify as tax-free "gifts" and "inheritances."
7. Describe scholarship or fellowship awards received by the taxpayer which qualify as tax-free.
8. Identify other prizes and awards that are excludable from gross income.
9. Describe the most common "fringe benefits" provided to employees, including premiums paid on life insurance and health insurance, meals and lodging, group legal services, transportation, dependent care, "cafeteria plans," stock options, courtesy discounts, and others, that are excludable from gross income.
10. Demonstrate the exclusion for income earned in foreign countries.
11. Explain the treatment of amounts related to the taxpayer's illness, injury, and absence from work that are paid under insurance policies or other plans.
12. Illustrate the calculation of the portion of unemployment benefits that is tax-free.
13. Identify alimony, separate-maintenance, and child-support payments that are not taxable to the recipient.
14. Explain the rules for determining what part, if any, of Social Security benefits are taxable.
15. Review the basic rules of exclusion for such items as discharge of indebtedness, improvements by lessee on lessor's property, recovery of amounts previously deducted, and rental value of parsonages.

5 Inclusions and Exclusions

Sec. 61 was quoted at the end of Chapter 4. That Section states that all income is includable in gross income unless otherwise provided. Subsequently, the titles of Sections that relate specifically to exclusions were listed. The fact that a Section relates to exclusion of a specific type of income does not mean that *all* income of that type is to be excluded. In some instances, the Section may provide that only limited amounts of a given type of income may be tax-free. In this chapter, most of the types of income that are commonly encountered will be discussed.

Neither the items listed in Sec. 61, nor the items contained in the group of sections dealing with exclusion are found in a sequence that has particular relevance or that provides continuity. For that reason, the topics discussed in this chapter are not organized in the same sequence as listed in the Code. Instead, they have been placed in an order that facilitates their discussion because of the interrelationship of many of the items.

DIVIDENDS

GENERAL RULE

Profits earned by a corporation are subject to a corporate income tax. When these profits are distributed to shareholders as dividends, they represent income to the shareholders. In order to alleviate, to a limited degree, the "double taxation" that results, Code Section 116 permits an unmarried shareholder, or a married shareholder filing a separate return, to exclude from income a total of $100 of qualified dividends received each year from qualified domestic corporations (most companies are

DIVIDEND EXCLUSION Annual exclusion from gross income of up to $100 ($200 on a joint return) of dividends from qualified domestic corporations received by the taxpayer (other than a corporation).

"qualified"). On a joint return, a ***dividend exclusion*** of $200 is permitted, regardless of which spouse owns the shares.[1] (Special rules, discussed in Chapter 16, apply to dividends received by a *corporate* shareholder on stock owned in another corporation.) Obviously the exclusion does not eliminate double taxation because many stockholders receive more than the excludable amount each year.

Example 1: Edna and Manuel, married, living in a non-community-property state, and filing a joint return, received dividends as follows during the year.

PAYING CORPORATION	AMOUNT RECEIVED ON STOCK OWNED BY: EDNA	MANUEL	JOINTLY	TOTAL
Canada Corp. (foreign corp.)		$ 30		$ 30
City Corporation	$600			600
Towne Corporation	140	20		160
Country Corporation			$ 50	50
Total	$740	$ 50	$ 50	$840
Less Exclusion				200
Amount included				$640

Since Edna and Manuel file a joint return, they will exclude $200 from income and must include $640. The amount of dividends received exceeds $400, so they must list each payor and the amount received from each on Form 1040, Schedule B (see Figure 5-1 on page 5/10). On that schedule they will show the entire amount received. On the face of Form 1040, they will subtract the $200 excludable amount to arrive at the amount includable.

FORM 1040—SCHEDULE B

Example 2: Assume that Edna and Manuel, whose dividends were listed in Example 1, file separate returns. Edna would include $665 on her return. Manuel must include $30 since dividends paid by a foreign corporation are not excludable. The computation of the amount includable by each is shown as follows:

PAYING COMPANY	DIVIDENDS REPORTED BY: EDNA	MANUEL
Canada Corporation	$	$ 30
City Corporation	600	
Towne Corporation	140	20
Country Corp. (jointly owned)	25	25
Total	$765	$ 75
Less exclusion	100	45
Amount included	$665	$ 30

[1] Code Sec. 116.

In some community-property states (Texas, Louisiana, and Idaho) dividends on stock that is held as separate property by one of the spouses are treated as community income, with each spouse entitled to one-half, but in the other community-property states (Arizona, California, Nevada, New Mexico, and Washington) dividends on separately-owned shares are deemed to be the income of the separate owner rather than of both spouses.

DIVIDENDS NOT OUT OF EARNINGS AND PROFITS

Dividends distributed by a corporation are taxable to stockholders only to the extent that a corporation has current or accumulated earnings and profits.[2] Current earnings and profits are related closely to taxable income of the current year (although, as discussed in Chapter 16, there are many important differences) and accumulated earnings and profits are related to retained earnings as shown in the financial accounts (although again there are significant differences). If a corporation distributes amounts in excess of its current and accumulated earnings and profits, the shareholders treat their proportionate shares of such excess as a tax-free recovery of basis until all the basis has been recovered. If the distribution received by a shareholder in excess of the stockholder's proportionate share of earnings and profits is greater than the taxpayer's basis in the stock, the distribution in excess of the basis is treated as a capital gain.[3] The corporation notifies the shareholder of the percentage or amount that is nontaxable on Form 1099—DIV, which summarizes dividends paid the shareholder during the year.

FORM 1099—DIV

Example 3: Marty owns 10% of Glo-Company's stock purchased several years ago for $2,000. At the end of the current year, when the company's total earnings and profits were $12,000, the company distributed cash of $40,000. Marty received $4,000. Of that amount, $1,200 will be treated as dividend income, $2,000 as tax-free return of basis, and $800 as capital gain.

STOCK DIVIDENDS AND DIVIDEND-REINVESTMENT PLANS

Most "***stock dividends***" do not represent gross income to the shareholders. After a stock dividend each shareholder merely has more shares to show for his or her investment and each shareholder's proportionate ownership is unchanged by the stock dividend.[4] Stock dividends are discussed further in Chapter 16.

STOCK DIVIDEND
Distribution by a corporation of its own stock.

Example 4: Rosita owned 4,000 shares of Little Corporation common stock for which she paid $8,800. During the current year the corporation declared a 10% stock dividend, issuing each common shareholder one share of common stock for each 10 shares the

[2] Sec. 316(a).

[3] Sec. 301(c).

[4] *Eisner v. Macomber*, 40 S.Ct. 189 (1920). Sec. 305(a).

shareholder owned. Rosita received 400 new shares as a stock dividend. She realized no income from the dividend. Rosita merely allocated the $8,800 cost among the 4,400 shares owned after the dividend, so that each share is deemed to have a basis of $2.

If, however, a shareholder is given the right to choose between receiving cash or stock at the shareholder's election, even though he or she elects to receive the stock it is generally deemed to be a cash dividend equal to the value of the stock received.[5]

DIVIDEND-REINVESTMENT PLAN Plan under which cash dividends payable to a shareholder are reinvested in additional shares of stock.

Many corporations have adopted formal "***dividend-reinvestment plans***" under which the shareholder may elect to receive cash dividends regularly or, instead, to receive additional shares of stock in lieu of the cash. Dividend-reinvestment plans have been especially popular with public utility companies as a means of generating funds for capital investments. Under the general rule of Sec. 305(1), the value of such stock is treated as a dividend and that amount is deemed to be the cost of the shares acquired. However, for the years 1982 through 1985 Congress provided a device to help public utilities retain internally generated funds while remaining competitive in the financial markets. For those years, dividend-reinvestment plans of public utility corporations are subject to a special election[6] by individual shareholders if the plan meets a host of complex qualifying restrictions. If an individual chooses under such a qualified plan to receive stock in lieu of cash, he or she may exclude up to $750 per year ($1,500 on a joint return).[7] This exclusion is in addition to the regular dividend exclusion of $100 or $200. Election is made by the shareholder by indicating that fact on the tax return. Stock acquired under this exclusion has a basis of zero, so that if the stock is subsequently sold the entire sales price will be treated as a gain. If the stock is held for more than one year after receipt, the gain on sale will be a capital long-term gain.[8]

Example 5: Karen owns shares of stock in East Central Utility Company. In 1985 dividends on these shares totaled $2,000. Under a qualified dividend-reinvestment plan, Karen chose to receive the entire amount in the form of 40 shares of stock, with a value of $50 per share. Karen may exclude $750. Of the remaining $1,250, $100 is subject to the regular dividend exclusion. The basis of the 15 shares received under the exclusion election is zero; the basis of the other 25 shares is $50 per share.

"DIVIDENDS" THAT ARE NOT DIVIDENDS

Taxpayers sometimes erroneously think that payments from savings associations, credit unions, insurance companies, and cooperatives qualify

[5] Sec. 305(1).
[6] Sec. 305(e).
[7] *Ibid.*
[8] *Ibid.*

for the dividend exclusion because the savings in these institutions are often referred to as "shares" and the institutions frequently call the interest payments "dividends."

Example 6: Coe maintains a savings account in an employee's credit union. During the current year, Coe's account was credited with "dividends" of $210 on Coe's shares. Coe must report *interest* income of $210.

Example 7: James Martin, a farmer, belongs to an agriculture cooperative (a "co-op"). Martin purchases feed, seed, fertilizer, and chemicals from the co-op. At the end of the year, the co-op computed the excess of its revenues over its expenses and distributed the excess in the form of a patronage dividend to its members, basing the distribution to each on the net purchases made by that member during the year. Martin's dividend was $604. This rebate is not a dividend for tax purposes, but is ordinary income (although many taxpayers erroneously treat it as a reduction of purchases).

Example 8: Arnold Arnoff acquires from the World Mutual Insurance Company a life insurance policy covering his life. During the current year Arnold paid the insurance company premiums of $2,600 on the policy. He received a dividend check from the company for $800. The company pointed out that this dividend was based on the company's claims record for the preceding year. This rebate is not dividend income to Arnold; it is merely a refund of premiums paid.

Example 9: Sharon owns shares in a mutual investment fund. In the current year she receives dividends totaling $120. The Form 1099 received by Sharon from the fund indicates that $80 of the $120 represents ordinary income, while $40 represents long-term capital gain. The $80 of ordinary income is dividend income subject to the exclusion rules; the remaining $40 is treated as long-term capital gain and is not eligible for the $100 dividend exclusion.

INTEREST INCOME

Under Sec. 61(a) interest income is (with a few exceptions provided in other Code Sections) fully taxed to the recipient. Thus, interest received on notes receivable, loans receivable, corporate bonds, refunds of federal income taxes, and U.S. treasury bonds are all taxable. The major exception to the taxability of interest income is interest received on obligations (bonds and notes) "of a State, or Territory, or a possession of the United States, or any political subdivision."[9] The exclusion does not apply

[9]Sec. 115(a).

to interest received on open accounts of such governments nor on such debts as an overpayment of state income tax.[10]

Example 10: During the current year Madden received the following interest: on bonds of U.S. Steel Corporation, $500; on his savings account at the bank, $200; on his investment in a liquid asset money market fund, $900; on City of New York bonds, $100; on Port of New York Authority bonds, $600; on a refund of state income taxes, $20; and on bonds of the United States, $60. All of these amounts are taxable except the $100 interest received on the City of New York bonds and the Port of New York Authority bonds, so Madden must report interest income of $1,680.

TAX-EXEMPT INTEREST

BACKGROUND

The exclusion of interest on obligations of states and political subdivisions (Sec. 103 and Sec. 103A) has historically been supported on a constitutional basis on the grounds that taxing of income from such bonds was essentially taxing the bonds themselves and was therefore an encroachment on a sovereign power of the state. However, the major reason for this continued exclusion is probably political—stemming from the fact that removing the exclusion would substantially increase the costs of operating state and local governments. The traditionally low interest rates on bonds issued by these governments have existed because high-income purchasers have been willing to accept a low tax-free income on bonds that have in the past had a high degree of security, in preference to substantially higher interest income subject to the federal income tax. The exclusion has been controversial over the years. The controversy has been heightened by the fact that many municipalities and other governmental units have issued bonds to secure funds which were then loaned either to nonprofit or profit-seeking groups for various purposes. In other cases, governmental units have borrowed money and then used it to acquire assets for lease or resale to those groups.

Frequently, special governmental subdivisions are created to carry on certain types of activities or to construct assets with funds provided by issuance of tax-free bonds. Most of these activities are designed to attract new industry to the municipality, but frequently have been used to finance residential buildings, recreational facilities, or other nonbusiness property. In other situations, state and lo-

Continued

[10] *Kieselbach v. Comm.*, 63 S.Ct. 303 (1943).

BACKGROUND

cal governmental units have engaged in so-called "arbitrage transactions" in which they have issued tax-exempt securities and then reinvested the proceeds in federal and corporate obligations bearing interest at higher rates than those paid by the government units.

Example 11: During the current year Mark received $1,500 interest on bonds issued by the South State Utility District. Those tax-free bonds were issued by the District to obtain funds to build a sewage system. The $1,500 interest received by Mark is excluded.

In recent years many amendments to Code Sec. 103, along with new Code Sec. 103A, have been enacted to limit the use of industrial development bonds and arbitrage bonds by state and local governments. For example, Sec. 103(b) provides that no tax exemption will be allowed for interest on bonds if the proceeds are to be used directly or indirectly by a business, unless (*a*) the issue is for $1,000,000 or less (although the uses that may be made of such bonds are now limited), (*b*) the proceeds are used to finance an industrial park, or (*c*) the proceeds are used to finance public services such as communications facilities, transportation facilities, sewage or waste disposal systems, electric energy facilities, pollution control facilities, and a host of others. The statutes similarly restrict the use of arbitrage bonds.*

In late 1984 and early 1985 many officials in the U.S. Government, including then-Secretary of the Treasury Regan called for additional restrictions on state and local bonds in order for the interest thereon to be classified as tax-exempt.

---

* Sec. 103(c).

Fortunately, the investor or tax preparer generally does not have to know the dozens of detailed rules necessary to determine whether interest on state or local bonds qualifies as being tax-exempt. Attorneys examine the bonds for the issuing governmental unit and issue an opinion on whether the interest qualifies for exclusion. The taxpayer relies on this opinion.

In addition to the direct purchase of tax-free bonds, investors may also invest in tax-free bond *funds*. Distributions representing interest on tax-free securities made by these funds to investors are exempt to the investors. The fund managers notify the taxpayer each year of the tax status of distributions made during the year.

Although the interest on state and local bonds is generally tax-free, gains and losses on the sale or redemption of such securities are recognized for tax purposes. Discounts and premiums on tax-exempt securities do not affect the tax-free status of interest on the securities. However, there are special rules (discussed in Chapter 10) for computing the basis to be used in measuring gain or loss when such securities were purchased at a premium or discount.

SAVINGS BONDS AND OTHER OBLIGATIONS OF THE U.S. GOVERNMENT

Interest on obligations of the U.S. government and its agencies is taxable. Sometimes taxpayers are confused as to the *time* that interest on some types of U.S. bonds is to be reported. For example, Series E "savings bonds" (issued prior to 1980) and their successor, Series EE bonds, have been popular investments for many individuals. Both of these series are issued at a discount and are subsequently redeemable at their face value. *Cash*-basis taxpayers have a choice on when to report interest on these bonds. They may report no interest income until the bond is redeemed for cash and at that time report the entire excess of proceeds over the original cost as interest.[11] Alternatively, the investor may report the increase in redemption value each year as interest income during that year. The election to accrue interest is thereafter binding for all bonds owned or subsequently owned by the taxpayer. Most bond holders choose the first alternative. *Accrual*-basis taxpayers must generally report the increase in redemption value each year as interest income for that year.

The Series E and EE bonds need not be redeemed at their maturity dates. They can be retained by the taxpayer and continue to accrue interest. However, after 30 years from the date of issue (40 years for Series E bonds issued before May 1, 1942), all accrued interest not previously reported as income *must* be reported, even if the bonds are not redeemed. However, cash-basis taxpayers are allowed to convert Series E bonds into Series HH bonds within one year of that final maturity date without reporting the accrued interest. Interest on Series HH bonds is paid semiannually and that payment will be taxable. However, only when the Series HH bonds are redeemed will the interest accrued on the original converted Series E bonds be taxable.[12]

Example 12: Marilyn purchased Series EE bonds during the current year, paying $375 for them. No interest is paid on the bonds, but when they mature at the end of ten years the face value of $500 will be paid. At the end of the current year, the redemption value is $386. Since Marilyn is on the cash basis, she may elect to report no interest this year and instead to report the entire $125 excess of redemp-

---

[11] Sec. 454(a).

[12] Treas. Dept. Circulars No. 1-80, No. 2.80, 1980-1, C.B. 714, 715.

tion value over purchase price as income in the year of redemption. Alternatively, she may report the increase in value as income each year. If she chooses the latter option, the income this year will be $11.

If noninterest bearing governmental obligations issued at a discount mature within one year of the date of issue, no accrual of increase in value is recognized, even by an accrual-basis taxpayer.[13] Instead, when the obligations are redeemed or otherwise disposed of, the excess of proceeds over cost is treated as interest income at that time. When U.S. savings bonds are redeemed, the government issues to the owner a Form 1099-INT, showing interest income equal to the difference between the issue price and the redemption price. The taxpayer should report as interest income on Schedule B the entire amount reported by the government on the Form 1099 and should show as an offset against the total such interest received any amount which the taxpayer has already reported as income. Interest received on interest-bearing U.S. obligations will be treated as ordinary income in the year received by a cash-basis taxpayer or as accrued by an accrual-basis taxpayer.

BONDS PURCHASED AND SOLD BETWEEN INTEREST DATES

When bonds are sold between interest dates, the amount of interest accrued through the date of sale is added to the selling price. The seller reports as income the interest accrued to the date of sale. The purchaser reports as income the interest earned after the date of sale.

Example 13: Raynard owned $10,000 par value, 12 percent, bonds of Washington Corporation. Interest is payable on September 1 and March 1. On March 21, 19X2, Raynard sold the bonds to Laney for $10,600, plus accrued interest of $66.67 for 20 days—a total of $10,666.67. Laney received semiannual interest of $600 on September 1, 19X2. The $600 of interest received by Laney on September 1 represents a nontaxable return of the $66.67 paid to Raynard and taxable income of $533.33. Raynard should include in income in 19X2 the $66.67 accrued to date of sale of the bonds.

PREMIUM AND DISCOUNT ON CORPORATE BONDS

A taxpayer who purchases corporate bonds for more than their par value (at a premium) has an election to amortize the premium as a deduction against the bond interest.[14] If the premium is not amortized, the tax "basis" of the bonds remains at their original cost. When the bonds are

[13] Reg. Sec. 1.1232A(b).
[14] Sec. 171(a)(1).

later redeemed or sold, the difference between proceeds and cost will be recognized as a capital gain or loss. If the premium is amortized, the amortization reduces the basis for measuring gain or loss. Premium amortization is discussed in Chapter 10.

If the taxpayer purchases corporate bonds for less than the maturity value, the discount represents an adjustment of the face interest rate to the market interest rate at the date of purchase. In general, if the bonds were originally issued for par value or a greater amount, a secondary purchaser who acquired them at a discount is *not* required to recognize any of the discount as income until the bonds are sold or mature. If the bonds were originally issued at a discount, the taxpayer may be required to include in income each year a portion (depending on several factors) of the original issue discount.[15] These rules, examined in somewhat greater detail in Chapter 10, are extremely complex. Fortunately, original discount bonds are seldom encountered.

REPORTING INTEREST AND DIVIDEND INCOME

The Schedule B shown on page 5/12 (Fig. 5-1) reflects the following data for Sidney K. and Maggie Bloom.

Interest received on:		
Great Northern Corp. bonds		$ 200
Second mortgage resulting from sale of their home to Leon Lewis		1,800
Savings at Big Star Credit Union		300
National Money Market Funds		800
Total		$3,100
Dividends:		
From 100 shares of Windsor Window Corp., a Canadian Corporation ($80 − $12 Canadian tax withheld)		68
From American Net Company paid to ABC Brokerage Company, as nominee. ABC issued check to Mr. Bloom.		80
From Consolidated Mutual Fund, reported as:		
Dividends	$30	
Long-term Capital Gain	70	100
From Northern Power & Light Co., $280, reinvested under a qualified reinvestment plan		280
Eastern Mining Company ($12 of this amount is deemed to be a tax-free return of capital)		30

The information from Schedule B is transferred to the front page of Form 1040 as shown in Figure 5-2.

[15] Secs. 1232 and 1232A.

EXCLUSION OF INTEREST AND DIVIDENDS

BACKGROUND

Through the years the tax laws controlling treatment of both dividends and interest have changed frequently. Most of the changes in taxation of dividends have been related to the problem of double taxation. However, some of the dividend rule changes, like most of the changes involving taxation of interest income, have been caused by the perceived need to stimulate investment.

Prior to taxable year 1981 each taxpayer could exclude up to $100 of dividends. If a married couple in a non-community-property state received dividends, each could exclude $100 only if that person owned the stock. This was true, even on a joint return. In community-property states dividends that were community income would, of course, be deemed to belong one-half to each taxpayer.

In 1980 the Congress, primarily to encourage taxpayers to save and invest their money, passed a temporary provision that increased the annual exclusion for calendar years 1981 and 1982 to $200 per taxpayer ($400 on joint return) *and* extended the exclusion to interest as well as to dividends if the interest was received from certain domestic sources. The Administration and Congress concluded after only one year that the provision was not effective and in 1981 (effective for 1982) reinstated the original pre-1981 rules permitting married persons filing joint returns to exclude $200, no matter which spouse received the dividends.

Another exclusion introduced in 1981 was intended to increase the amount of funds available for the purchase of residential property. Code Sec. 128 gave individuals (and, within certain limits, estates) a once-in-a-lifetime exclusion of up to $1,000 ($2,000 on a joint return) of interest earned on special qualified tax-exempt savings certificates. The exclusion was for interest received on qualified certificates in tax years ending after September 30, 1981, and before 1984, where the certificate was issued after September 30, 1981 and before January 1, 1983 by a bank, a qualified savings institution, a qualified credit union, or qualified industrial loan association.

One provision in the 1981 act designed to encourage savings has become effective for tax years beginning after 1984. Sec. 128 provided that for any such tax year an individual could exclude from income 15% of the smaller of:

1. $3,000 ($6,000 on a joint return), or
2. the taxpayer's net interest for the year.

This relatively cumbersome rule effectively would have provided a maximum interest exclusion of $450 for single taxpayers and $900 for married taxpayers filing a joint return. This Section was, not surprisingly, repealed by the Tax Reform Act of 1984.

FIGURE 5-1

Schedules A&B (Form 1040) 1984 **Schedule B—Interest and Dividend Income** 08 OMB No. 1545-0074 Page 2

Name(s) as shown on Form 1040 (Do not enter name and social security number if shown on other side.) Sidney K. and Maggie Bloom — Your social security number 111 11 1111

Part I Interest Income

(See Instructions on pages 8 and 22)

Also complete Part III.

If you received more than $400 in interest income, you must complete Part I and list ALL interest received. If you received interest as a nominee for another, or you received or paid accrued interest on securities transferred between interest payment dates, or you received any interest from an All-Savers Certificate, see page 22.

Interest income		Amount
1 Interest income from seller-financed mortgages. (See Instructions and show name of payer.) ▶ Leon Lewis	1	1,800
2 Other interest income (list name of payer) ▶		
Great Northern Corporation	2	200
Big Star Credit Union		300
The National Money Market Fund		800
3 Add the amounts on lines 1 and 2. Write the total here and on Form 1040, line 8 ▶	3	3,100

Part II Dividend Income

(See Instructions on pages 8 and 22)

Also complete Part III.

If you received more than $400 in gross dividends (including capital gain distributions) and other distributions on stock, or you are electing to exclude qualified reinvested dividends from a public utility, complete Part II. If you received dividends as a nominee for another, see page 22.

Name of payer				Amount
4 Windsor Window Corporation (Canadian)			4	80 *
ABC Brokerage Co.				80
Consolidated Mutual Fund				100
Northern Power & Light Co. (DR)				280
Eastern Mining Co.				30
5 Add the amounts on line 4. Write the total here			5	
6 Capital gain distributions. Enter here and on line 15, Schedule D.*	6	70		
7 Nontaxable distributions. (See Schedule D Instructions for adjustment to basis.)	7	12		
8 Exclusion of qualified reinvested dividends from a public utility. (See page 23 of Instructions.)	8	280		
9 Add the amounts on lines 6, 7, and 8. Write the total here			9	362
10 Subtract line 9 from line 5. Write the result here and on Form 1040, line 9a ▶			10	208

**If you received capital gain distributions for the year and you do not need Schedule D to report any other gains or losses, do not file that schedule. Instead, enter 40% of your capital gain distributions on Form 1040, line 14.*

Part III Foreign Accounts and Foreign Trusts

(See Instructions on page 23)

If you received more than $400 of interest or dividends, OR if you had a foreign account or were a grantor of, or a transferor to, a foreign trust, you must answer both questions in Part III.	Yes	No
11 At any time during the tax year, did you have an interest in or a signature or other authority over a bank account, securities account, or other financial account in a foreign country? (See page 23 of the Instructions for exceptions and filing requirements for Form TD F 90-22.1.)		X
If "Yes," write the name of the foreign country ▶		
12 Were you the grantor of, or transferor to, a foreign trust which existed during the current tax year, whether or not you have any beneficial interest in it? If "Yes," you may have to file Forms 3520, 3520-A, or 926		X

For Paperwork Reduction Act Notice, see Form 1040 Instructions. **Schedule B (Form 1040) 1984**

*NOTE: The $12 of Canadian taxes withheld may be treated by the Blooms as either a credit against their income tax liability or as a deduction, as discussed in Chapter 14.

FIGURE 5-2

Form 1040 Department of the Treasury—Internal Revenue Service
U.S. Individual Income Tax Return 1984 (0)

For the year January 1-December 31, 1984, or other tax year beginning , 1984, ending , 19 . OMB No. 1545-0074

Use IRS label. Otherwise, please print or type.	Your first name and initial (if joint return, also give spouse's name and initial) Last name *Sidney and Maggie Bloom*	Your social security number
	Present home address (Number and street, including apartment number, or rural route)	Spouse's social security number
	City, town or post office, State, and ZIP code	Your occupation Spouse's occupation

Presidential Election Campaign ▶ Do you want $1 to go to this fund? . . . Yes / No
If joint return, does your spouse want $1 to go to this fund? . . . Yes / No
Note: *Checking "Yes" will not change your tax or reduce your refund.*

For Privacy Act and Paperwork Reduction Act Notice, see Instructions.

Filing Status

Check only one box.

1 ☐ Single
2 ☐ Married filing joint return (even if only one had income)
3 ☐ Married filing separate return. Enter spouse's social security no. above and full name here. ______
4 ☐ Head of household (with qualifying person). (See page 5 of Instructions.) If the qualifying person is your unmarried child but not your dependent, write child's name here. ______
5 ☐ Qualifying widow(er) with dependent child (Year spouse died ▶ 19). (See page 6 of Instructions.)

Exemptions

Always check the box labeled Yourself. Check other boxes if they apply.

6a ☐ Yourself ☐ 65 or over ☐ Blind
b ☐ Spouse ☐ 65 or over ☐ Blind
} Enter number of boxes checked on 6a and b ▶ ☐

c First names of your dependent children who lived with you ______ } Enter number of children listed on 6c ▶ ☐

d Other dependents: (1) Name	(2) Relationship	(3) Number of months lived in your home	(4) Did dependent have income of $1,000 or more?	(5) Did you provide more than one-half of dependent's support?

Enter number of other dependents ▶ ☐

Add numbers entered in boxes above ▶ ☐

e Total number of exemptions claimed (also complete line 36) . . .

Income

Please attach Copy B of your Forms W-2, W-2G, and W-2P here.

If you do not have a W-2, see page 4 of Instructions.

Please attach check or money order here.

7	Wages, salaries, tips, etc.	7	
8	Interest income *(also attach Schedule B if over $400)*	8	*3100 00*
9a	Dividends *(also attach Schedule B if over $400)* *208 00*, **9b** Exclusion *128 00*		
c	Subtract line 9b from line 9a and enter the result	9c	*80 00*
10	Refunds of State and local income taxes, from the worksheet on page 9 of Instructions *(do not enter an amount unless you itemized deductions for those taxes in an earlier year—see page 9)*	10	
11	Alimony received	11	
12	Business income or (loss) *(attach Schedule C)*	12	
13	Capital gain or (loss) *(attach Schedule D)*	13	
14	40% of capital gain distributions not reported on line 13 (see page 9 of Instructions)	14	
15	Supplemental gains or (losses) *(attach Form 4797)*	15	
16	Fully taxable pensions, IRA distributions, and annuities not reported on line 17	16	
17a	Other pensions and annuities, including rollovers. Total received 17a		
b	Taxable amount, if any, from the worksheet on page 10 of Instructions	17b	
18	Rents, royalties, partnerships, estates, trusts, etc. *(attach Schedule E)*	18	
19	Farm income or (loss) *(attach Schedule F)*	19	
20a	Unemployment compensation (insurance). Total received 20a		
b	Taxable amount, if any, from the worksheet on page 10 of Instructions	20b	
21a	Social security benefits. (see page 10 of Instructions) 21a		
b	Taxable amount, if any, from the worksheet on page 11 of Instructions	21b	
22	Other income (state nature and source—see page 11 of Instructions)	22	
23	Add lines 7 through 22. This is your **total income** ▶	23	

Adjustments to Income

(See Instructions on page 11.)

24	Moving expense *(attach Form 3903 or 3903F)*	24	
25	Employee business expenses *(attach Form 2106)*	25	
26a	IRA deduction, from the worksheet on page 12	26a	
b	Enter here IRA payments you made in 1985 that are included in line 26a above ▶		
27	Payments to a Keogh *(H.R. 10)* retirement plan	27	
28	Penalty on early withdrawal of savings	28	
29	Alimony paid	29	
30	Deduction for a married couple when both work *(attach Schedule W)*	30	
31	Add lines 24 through 30. These are your **total adjustments** ▶	31	

Adjusted Gross Income

32	Subtract line 31 from line 23. *This is your* **adjusted gross income.** *If this line is less than $10,000, see "Earned Income Credit" (line 59) on page 16 of Instructions. If you want IRS to figure your tax, see page 12 of Instructions.* ▶	32	

ANNUITY INCOME

ANNUITY A contract under which one or more persons will be paid a specified amount for a specified period or for life. A *simple* annuity or *term* annuity is paid for a specified time. A *life* annuity is paid for life. A *joint or survivor* annuity is paid for as long as either of two people lives. A *refund* annuity is one in which the annuitant or beneficiary is guaranteed that rents will at least equal cost.

RENTS The amount paid an annuitant each period under an annuity contract.

ANNUITANT The person receiving rents under an annuity.

An ***annuity*** is a contract calling for an insurance company or other payor to make a series of monetary payments (***rents***) at stated intervals for either a fixed or a contingent time-period to the ***annuitant*** (the person receiving payment). A *simple* or *term* annuity is payable for a fixed time-period. A *life* annuity is one that is payable for as long as the annuitant shall live. A *joint and survivor* annuity is one that provides for a series of payments for as long as either the annuitant or another person, usually the annuitant's spouse, shall live.

Obviously, if an insurance company is to make payments to the annuitant, the insurance company must have first been provided with funds from some source with which to make payment. The annuitant may have "purchased" the annuity contract with a single payment. However, most private annuities are accumulated from a series of deposits or payments made during an individual's working years. In some cases only the annuitant's employer makes contributions to the fund that eventually pays the retirement annuity; this type of annuity is described as a *noncontributory* plan. If the employee-annuitant makes some or all of the contributions to the fund, the plan is described as a *contributory* one. In all types of annuities the insurance company or fund manager invests the contributed funds in income-earning assets.

Because of the risk of a short life by the annuitant, some plans, called *refund* annuities, guarantee the annuitant and the annuitant's heirs that they will receive back at least an amount equal to the annuity's cost. Other annuities simply terminate on death of the annuitant.

Annuity contracts typically permit the annuitant to withdraw a lump sum of cash in lieu of receiving rents. The withdrawal may be made prior to the maturity date, based on the "cash-surrender value" of the contract, or it may be made at the maturity date.

ANNUITIES PURCHASED BY THE ANNUITANT

EXCLUSION RATIO The percentage of annuity rents that may be excluded from income as return of cost.

AMOUNTS RECEIVED AS RENTS Where the annuitant purchased the contract, amounts received by the annuitant as rents are treated in part as income and in part as recovery of cost. In most cases the return of capital element and the income element are prorated proportionately over all rents received. The approach is to first determine the ***exclusion ratio***—the proportionate part of each rent that is to be treated as recovery of cost. This exclusion ratio is computed as follows:[16]

$$\frac{\text{Investment in Contract}}{\text{Known or Expected Return}} = \text{Exclusion ratio}$$

If the annuity is a simple annuity to be paid for a fixed number of periods and was purchased for a lump sum by the annuitant, calculation of the amount to be excluded is simple.

[16] Sec. 72.

Example 14: Thompson purchased a simple annuity by making a lump sum payment of $20,000. Under the contract Thompson began receiving rents two years ago on his 60th birthday and is to receive $300 per month for 120 months. Of the $3,600 received during the current year, Thompson will exclude $2,000.

$$\text{Exclusion ratio} = \frac{\text{Investment, \$20,000}}{\text{Known return, \$36,000}} = 55.555\%$$

$$\text{Exclusion this year} = \$3{,}600 \times .55555 = \$2{,}000$$

The remaining $1,600 ($3,600 minus $2,000) received during the current year will be included in gross income.

If the contract is a life annuity, the expected return is the annual amount to be received under the contract multiplied by a multiple representing the annuitant's life expectancy at the time payments begin. The multiple is contained in an annuity table (Table 5-1) in the Regulations.[17]

Example 15: Lohman purchased a life annuity from an insurance company for $99,000. When Lohman reached age 65, he began drawing monthly payments of $1,000, which will continue until Lohman's death. The multiple for a male age 65, as shown in Table 5-1, is 15.0. Thus, Lohman's exclusion ratio is 55%, computed as follows:

$$\frac{\text{Investment, \$99,000}}{\text{Expected Return (\$12,000} \times \text{15.0)}} = .55$$

Of the $12,000 received each year Lohman will exclude $6,600 (.55 × $12,000) and will include the remaining $5,400 in gross income.

Once the exclusion ratio is computed, it will be applied to all future rents even though the annuitant lives for a period longer than the life expectancy determined at the starting date.

Example 16: Using the data for Lohman in Example 15, if Lohman should live to be 92 years old he would continue to receive $1,000 each month and would continue to exclude 55% of the amount received each year.

Special tables are provided for finding the multiple to be used in computing expected returns for refund annuities and for joint and survivor annuities. These tables and a discussion of their use may be found in Reg. Sec. 1.72-9.

SURRENDER FOR CASH AT MATURITY If the taxpayer surrenders the annuity contract before, on, or after the starting date for a lump sum

---

[17] Reg. Sec. 1.72-9.

TABLE 5-1
Ordinary life annuities—one life—expected return multiples (for monthly rents)*

AGES		MULTIPLES	AGES		MULTIPLES	AGES		MULTIPLES
MALE	FEMALE		MALE	FEMALE		MALE	FEMALE	
6	11	65.0	41	46	33.0	76	81	9.1
7	12	64.1	42	47	32.1	77	82	8.7
8	13	63.2	43	48	31.2	78	83	8.3
9	14	62.3	44	49	30.4	79	84	7.8
10	15	61.4	45	50	29.6	80	85	7.5
11	16	60.4	46	51	28.7	81	86	7.1
12	17	59.5	47	52	27.9	82	87	6.7
13	18	58.6	48	53	27.1	83	88	6.3
14	19	57.7	49	54	26.3	84	89	6.0
15	20	56.7	50	55	25.5	85	90	5.7
16	21	55.8	51	56	24.7	86	91	5.4
17	22	54.9	52	57	24.0	87	92	5.1
18	23	53.9	53	58	23.2	88	93	4.8
19	24	53.0	54	59	22.4	89	94	4.5
20	25	52.1	55	60	21.7	90	95	4.2
21	26	51.1	56	61	21.0	91	96	4.0
22	27	50.2	57	62	20.3	92	97	3.7
23	28	49.3	58	63	19.6	93	98	3.5
24	29	48.3	59	64	18.9	94	99	3.3
25	30	47.4	60	65	18.2	95	100	3.1
26	31	46.5	61	66	17.5	96	101	2.9
27	32	45.6	62	67	16.9	97	102	2.7
28	33	44.6	63	68	16.2	98	103	2.5
29	34	43.7	64	69	15.6	99	104	2.3
30	35	42.8	65	70	15.0	100	105	2.1
31	36	41.9	66	71	14.4	101	106	1.9
32	37	41.0	67	72	13.8	102	107	1.7
33	38	40.0	68	73	13.2	103	108	1.5
34	39	39.1	69	74	12.6	104	109	1.3
35	40	38.2	70	75	12.1	105	110	1.2
36	41	37.3	71	76	11.6	106	111	1.0
37	42	36.5	72	77	11.0	107	112	.8
38	43	35.6	73	78	10.5	108	113	.7
39	44	34.7	74	79	10.1	109	114	.6
40	45	33.8	75	80	9.6	110	115	.5
						111	116	0

*NOTE: Adjustments in multiples must be made if rents are payable at intervals other than monthly (*see* Reg. Sec. 1.72-5).

instead of receiving periodic rents, any excess amount received over the investment in the contract is treated as gross income.[18]

Example 17: Richards purchased an annuity at a total cost of $60,000. In the current year the annuity matured and Richards elected to take the cash value of $100,000. Richards has gross income of $40,000 as a result of surrender of the policy.

PARTIAL SURRENDER OR CASH WITHDRAWALS PRIOR TO STARTING DATE Historically, amounts received from an annuity before the annuity starting date have been treated as return of investment in the contract. If the total of such withdrawals exceeded the investment in the contract, the excess was treated as income. However, since August 13, 1982 partial surrenders are treated first as income, to the extent that the cash value of the contract exceeds the investment in the contract, with the remainder being treated as a return of capital.[19] The rule does not apply to income amounts allocable to investments made prior to August 14, 1982.[20] In addition, early withdrawals made after December 31, 1982 may be assessed a 5% penalty.[21] Even more severe is the rule that loans against the contract, or loans acquired by pledging the contract, will be treated as withdrawals.[22]

EMPLOYEE ANNUITIES

When an employer has established a "qualified" pension or profit-sharing plan, amounts contributed by the employer to the trust fund on behalf of an employee are not taxed to the employee at the time of contribution by the employer. (A "***qualified***" ***plan*** is one that meets a host of requirements, the primary one being that the plan is not discriminatory.) Only when the employee receives benefits from a plan does the employee recognize income. Commonly, the fund is used to acquire retirement annuities for employees. Since the employer's contributions used to purchase the annuity have not been taxed to the employee, the employee has no investment in the contract unless the employee has also contributed from his or her own funds to the purchase of the annuity. If the employee has, in fact, paid part of the cost of the annuity under a contributory plan, those contributions become the annuitant's investment in the contract.

QUALIFIED PLAN A retirement plan that qualifies for special favorable tax treatment under Sec. 401.

Annuity rents received from a qualified employee annuity may be taxed in one of three ways.

1. If the employee contributed nothing towards the annuity's cost, or if the employee's contribution was itself tax deductible, all rents are taxable as ordinary income.

[18] Reg. Sec. 1.72-11(d).
[19] Sec. 72(e)(1), (2) and (3).
[20] Sec. 72(e)(5)(B).
[21] Sec. 72(q).
[22] Sec. 72(e)(h).

Example 18: Louise retired during the current year. She received $3,600 retirement pay from a qualified pension plan that was financed entirely by the employer. The $3,600 is includable in Louise's income.

2. If the employee has contributed part of the cost of the annuity, and if the rents to be received during the 3-year period beginning on the date on which the first rent is received are equal to or greater than the employee's investment, all amounts received are excluded until the taxpayer has recovered his or her investment. After that point, the entire amount received is income.[23]

Example 19: Ronson, a public school teacher, retired in 19X1. Ronson was covered by the state teacher retirement system. During his working years, Ronson contributed $18,000 to the retirement fund. Ronson received $6,800 in retirement benefits in 19X1; $9,400 in 19X2, and $9,400 in 19X3. Since in a period of 3 years Ronson is to receive an amount greater than his investment of $18,000, Ronson has no includable income in 19X1 and no includable income in 19X2. In 19X3 he will exclude $1,800 ($18,000 − $6,800 − $9,400) and will include $7,600 ($9,400 − $1,800).

3. If the annuitant will not receive proceeds within a three-year period equal to or greater than his or her investment, the proceeds under an employee annuity are treated in the same manner as an annuity purchased by the taxpayer.

Example 20: Harrison retired in 19X1 at age 65 and began receiving benefits under a qualified employee annuity. During his working years Harrison contributed $45,000 to the cost of the annuity and his employer contributed $50,000. Harrison is to receive $833.33 per month during the remainder of his lifetime (estimated to be 15 years). During 19X1 Harrison received four monthly payments, totaling $3,333.32. Since Harrison will not recover his $45,000 cost within three years, he will compute an exclusion ratio in the usual manner:

$$\frac{\text{Investment, \$45,000}}{\text{Expected return, (15 yrs. @ \$10,000)}} = .30$$

Thus of the $3,333.32 received in 19X1, Harrison will exclude $1,000 (.30 × $3,333.32) and include $2,333.32.

Amounts received in lump-sum distributions from qualified plans receive special treatment as discussed in Chapter 13.

[23] Sec. 72(d).

LIFE INSURANCE PROCEEDS

GENERAL RULE

With limited exceptions insurance proceeds paid to the beneficiary because of the death of the insured under a policy issued prior to 1985 are exempt from the federal income tax,[24] although they are usually included in the decedent's estate that may be subject to the federal estate tax.

Example 21: In March of the current year Brown died. His daughter was paid $50,000 as beneficiary of a life insurance policy which Brown had acquired several years prior to death. The $50,000 is not included in the daughter's income.

For contracts issued before January 1, 1985 "flexible-premium" life insurance policies must meet very complex requirements in order to be excluded under Code Sec. 101(a). Flexible-premium policies, also called "universal life" or "adjustable-life" policies, allow the policy holder an option of paying substantial sums into the policy's cash value fund without increasing the amount of the policy's death benefit.[25] Because of the complexity of these rules and the relative infrequency with which such policies are found, the special qualifying rules are not explained here.

In the case of policies issued after 1984, Code Sec. 7702 provides that the contract must qualify as a life insurance contract under the applicable state or federal law. In addition the contract must meet either (1) a cash accumulation test, or (2) a "guideline premium/cash value corridor" test. If these complex requirements are not met, the policy will be treated as a combination of term insurance or a deposit fund on which the income is currently taxable to the policyholder. Most life insurance policies will qualify.

POLICIES OBTAINED FOR CONSIDERATION

The principal exception to the exclusion of life insurance proceeds relates to proceeds on a policy whose rights have been assigned to the beneficiary for a consideration.[26] In that event, the excess of the proceeds over the sum of the consideration plus any further premiums paid by the assignee will be included in income.

Example 22: Cherry loaned Candy $12,000 several years ago. Candy was unable to repay the loan and in settlement of same transferred to Cherry a life insurance policy with a face amount of $50,000 and a cash surrender value of $5,000 that Candy had obtained on her own

[24] Sec. 101(a).
[25] Sec. 101(f).
[26] Sec. 101(a)(2).

life. Subsequent to assignment of the policy, Cherry paid premiums of $800 on the policy. In the current year, Candy died and Cherry received $50,000, representing the face amount of the policy. Cherry must report $37,200 as income ($50,000 − $12,000 − $800).

In order to accommodate certain types of business transactions, exceptions are made to the general rule of taxability of proceeds from a policy obtained for a consideration. For example, in order to facilitate the funding of "buy-out" agreements between businesses and their owners, three exceptions are provided.[27] No income results from the receipt of insurance proceeds paid because of death of the insured if:

1. a partner of the decedent is the beneficiary,
2. a partnership in which the decedent was a partner is the beneficiary, or
3. a corporation in which the decedent was a shareholder or officer is the beneficiary.

Example 23: Miles, Lane, and Kelley are partners in the MLK partnership. They agree that on the death of any partner the partnership can purchase the decedent's equity for the book value of that partner's interest as of date of death. As part of the plan, to provide funds for the partnership to purchase his interest, Miles transfers to the partnership a life insurance policy on his life with $100,000 face value. The partnership is named as the new beneficiary. The partnership pays Miles $18,000, the cash surrender value of the policy at date of transfer. After the transfer and before Miles' death, the partnership pays premiums of $7,000 on the policy. In the current year Miles dies and the partnership receives the $100,000 face amount. The partnership has no income as a result of receiving the insurance proceeds of $100,000.

INTEREST ON LIFE INSURANCE PROCEEDS

In general, interest received on life insurance proceeds left with the insurer or on the reinvestment of proceeds will be taxable income. However, a surviving wife or husband is entitled to exclude up to $1,000 of interest each year on life insurance proceeds from the death of a deceased husband or wife if the beneficiary has elected to receive installment payments under an option provided in the insurance contract.[28] This exclusion is not affected by remarriage.

Example 24: Larry died during the current year. Life insurance proceeds of $100,000 were payable to Larry's wife. Under an option permitted in the contract, she elected to receive $24,000 per year for five years beginning in the year after death. Of each $24,000 annual

[27] Sec. 101(a)(2)(A).

[28] Sec. 101(d).

payment, $20,000 represents a tax-free distribution of proceeds and $4,000 represents interest income. She may exclude $1,000 of the interest, but must include the other $3,000 in interest income.

Example 25: Assume the same facts as in Example 24, except that the beneficiary is Larry's mother. The mother may exclude the $20,000 distribution of face amount each year, but must include the full $4,000 of interest received each year.

EMPLOYEE DEATH BENEFITS

Frequently employers make a cash payment to the surviving spouse or children of an employee who dies. If payments are made by, or on behalf of, an employer and are paid solely because of the employee's death, the beneficiary(ies) may exclude from income a portion of the amount paid, not to exceed an exclusion of $5,000 per decedent.[29] Where the decedent has more than one beneficiary who receives payments, the exclusion is prorated among the beneficiaries in proportion to the amount that each receives.[30]

Example 26: Solely because of the death of Smith, his employer makes payments of $8,000 to Smith's widow and $4,000 to each of his two children. Of the $16,000 paid to the beneficiaries, they may exclude a total of $5,000, divided as follows:

Wife = $8,000/$16,000 × $5,000 = $2,500
Each child = $4,000/$16,000 × $5,000 = $1,250

If the payment represents payment for nonforfeitable rights accrued to the decedent prior to death, such as accrued salary, the entire amount is taxable.[31] There are, however, rather complex rules that extend the $5,000 ***employee death benefit*** exclusion to amounts received from stock-bonus plans, pension plans, profit-sharing plans, and employee annuities. The $5,000 exclusion is available for lump-sum distributions from qualified pension, profit-sharing, or stock-bonus plans even though the employee's rights may have been nonforfeitable.[32]

EMPLOYEE DEATH BENEFITS Amounts paid by the employer to beneficiaries of a deceased employee because of the employee's death.

Generally a self-employed person is not an employee.[33] Nevertheless, in the case of a lump-sum distribution, the term "employee" includes a self-employed individual if the person dies after December 31, 1983 and if the benefits are paid under a qualified pension, profit-sharing, or stock bonus plan.[34]

---

[29] Sec. 101(b)(2)(A).
[30] Reg. Sec. 1.101–2(c)(1).
[31] Sec. 101(b)(3)(A).
[32] Sec. 101(b).
[33] Sec. 101(b)(2)(B).
[34] Sec. 101(b)(3)(B).

Distributions from stock-bonus plans, pension plans, profit-sharing plans and annuities other than lump-sum payments are eligible for the $5,000 exclusion only if the employee's rights were forfeitable at the time of death.

Example 27: Roger is covered by a "qualified" profit-sharing plan established by his employer. Roger's rights are nonforfeitable. During the current year Roger died and his widow was paid $36,000, the amount of Roger's accumulated benefits, in a lump sum. Since the plan was "qualified" and payment was made in a lump sum, the widow is entitled to exclude $5,000.

GIFTS

GIFT A transfer made without valuable consideration and not related to performance of services.

A bona fide ***gift*** is not taxable to the recipient.[35] To be excluded from income, a gift must clearly be a transfer made without valuable consideration and not related to the performance of services. The Supreme Court has stated that a gift must have been made because of "affection, respect, admiration, charity or like impulses."[36]

Example 28: During the current year, Clarence made gifts of $20,000 to each of his two children and $30,000 to his girl friend. None of the recipients has taxable income as a result of the gifts.

Obviously the donor's intent is of paramount importance in determining whether a payment is a gift. In situations involving transfers of property between two persons who have a business relationship, the IRS will look carefully to see if a taxable transfer is involved.

Example 29: Markham voluntarily supplies Whitson with the names of potential customers. Subsequently Whitson makes a gift of a new automobile to Markham. Markham will probably be deemed to have received income equal to the fair market value of the automobile.[37]

As discussed later in this chapter, the general rule is that any payment of *cash* made by an employer to an employee will probably be treated as taxable income even though it is called a gift and even though it is made at Christmas or at other holidays or times of celebration. On the other hand, traditional gifts of property with small value, for example, a turkey at Thanksgiving, will be tax-free gifts to the recipient and the employer will be allowed to deduct the gifts as a business expense.

Even though a gift is excluded from income taxation by the recipient,

---

[35] Sec. 102(a).

[36] *Robertson v. U.S.*, 72 S.Ct. 994 (1952).

[37] See, for example, *Comm. v. Duberstein*, 80 S.Ct. 1190 (1960).

the giver may be required to pay a federal gift tax on all or part of the amount given. (The gift tax does not apply to contributions made to "charitable organizations.")

INHERITANCES

Amounts received as ***inheritances*** on the death of a decedent are almost always exempt from income taxes.[38] This is true whether or not the decedent is related to the beneficiary. If, however, the bequest represents payments to the beneficiary for services rendered by the beneficiary to the decedent during the latter's lifetime, the inheritance may be taxable.[39]

INHERITANCE An amount received because of death of decedent.

Example 30: Katie died in 19X1, bequeathing her estate to her best friend, Charles. The value of the estate inherited by Charles was $220,000. No income results from Charles' inheritance.

Example 31: Prior to the death of Klausen, Carpenter, a certified public accountant, assisted Klausen in his estate planning. In return, Klausen agreed to make a bequest of $10,000 to Carpenter in his will. Carpenter will be deemed to have received income of $10,000 on receipt of the inheritance.

SCHOLARSHIPS AND FELLOWSHIPS

Scholarships represent amounts "paid or allowed to, or for the benefit of, a student, whether an undergraduate or a graduate, to aid such individual in pursuing his studies."[40] ***Fellowships*** are amounts "paid or allowed to, or for the benefit of, an individual in the pursuit of study or research."[41] Code Sec. 117 provides that any amount received (*a*) as a scholarship at a qualified educational organization or as a fellowship grant, including the value of contributed services and accommodations and (*b*) to cover travel, research, clerical help, or equipment—which are incidental to such a scholarship or fellowship grant and that is so expended by the recipient—shall not be included in gross income.[42]

SCHOLARSHIP Amount paid or allowed to a student to aid the student in pursuing his or her studies.

FELLOWSHIP Amount paid to an individual in the pursuit of study or research.

Regulations dealing with scholarships and fellowships are quite voluminous and there have been many court cases covering the subject. The key test is whether the grant is intended primarily to benefit the recipient or is intended primarily to benefit the grantor;

[38] Sec. 102.

[39] See, for example, *Walder v. Comm.*, 493 F. 2d 608 (CA-2, 1974).

[40] Reg. Sec. 1.117-3(a).

[41] Reg. Sec. 1.117-3(b).

[42] Sec. 117(a).

. . . whether a payment qualifies as a scholarship or fellowship grant excludable from gross income under Section 117 of the 1954 Code depends upon whether the primary purpose of the payment is to further the education and training of the recipient or whether the primary purpose is to serve the interest of the grantor. The problem is usually somewhat difficult of solution because of the fact that in most of the situations there is a dual or mutual benefit involved. The question of necessity must be resolved on a factual basis and depends upon the facts and circumstances in each particular case.[43]

In general, a grant received by a college student who is working toward a degree is tax exempt unless the recipient is obligated to perform duties before, during, or after the period of the grant.[44]

Example 32: Susan is an undergraduate accounting student at State University. During the current year she was the recipient of two scholarships. One was awarded by Big Electric Company based on Susan's grades. The other was awarded by the university based on financial need. Neither scholarship requires Susan to render a service. All amounts received under both of these scholarships will be excludable.

Although most payments to students for teaching, grading papers, or assisting in research are merely taxable compensation, if all students in the same degree program are required to perform the same duties, such as teaching or research, payment for the services may be treated as a scholarship and excluded.[45] (Obviously a university or college cannot abuse this provision by requiring *all* degree students to perform services.) There have been many court cases involving payments to medical students for work as interns and residents in hospitals. If the principal purpose of the medical facility is to train medical specialists rather than to provide care for patients *and* if the "student" is not replacing personnel who would otherwise have been employed for patient care, the payments may be excludable.[46] On balance, however, most interns and residents have lost their battle for an exclusion when litigating this dispute with the IRS. Amounts of tuition reduction granted to employees for education below the graduate level by academic institutions are excludable from the employee's income for education furnished after June 30, 1985.[47]

Interest subsidy payments made to lenders on student loans are treated as scholarships and are not taxable to the student.

A scholarship or fellowship received by an individual who is not a candidate for a degree must meet the same tests as those for degree-seeking

---

[43] C. P. Bhalla, 35 T.C. 13 (1960).

[44] Reg. Sec. 1.117-4(c).

[45] Sec. 117(b)(1).

[46] *Wrobleski v. Bingler*, 161 F. Supp. 901 (D. Ct., Pa., 1958).

[47] Sec. 117(d).

students. In addition, other rules are imposed. The scholarship or fellowship must have been awarded by a tax-exempt nonprofit organization, a governmental unit or agency, or one of a limited number of other organizations. Only $300 per month for each month of the scholarship or fellowship period may be excluded.[48] Furthermore, an exclusion is available for a maximum of 36 months. Amounts that the recipient receives for expenses incidental to the scholarship or fellowship are not excludable under the $300 per month rule. However, they are excludable to the extent that they are offset by actual expenses incurred.[49]

Example 33: Larry is a post-doctoral fellow in biology at State University. He was awarded a fellowship from a tax-exempt medical foundation and is to receive a stipend of $700 per month for a maximum of 48 months, receiving the first such payment in June of the current year. In addition, he is to be given $200 per month to cover supplies and other research costs. He receives a total of $6,300 for the stipend and expenses during the current year ($900 per month for seven months). His actual research costs were $900. Larry may exclude $2,100 of the stipend (seven months @ $300 per month) and must include the remaining $2,800 of stipend. He may exclude $900 of the amount received for expenses, but must include the remaining $500. Thus, he will include a total of $3,300 in gross income.

Example 34: Caruth received a post-doctoral research fellowship from Great Ways Foundation, a qualified tax-exempt organization. The grant for $6,300 was for a nine-month period beginning September 1 of the current year. The entire amount was received by Caruth in September. Since the grant covers a nine-month period, Caruth may exclude $2,700 (nine months at $300 per month) and must include the remaining $3,600 in the current year.

EDUCATIONAL ASSISTANCE PROGRAMS

Another exclusion related to education benefits is an amount received by an employee under certain "***educational-assistance plans***." In recent years many employers have encouraged employees to undertake additional education by providing assistance through such acts as paying tuition, purchasing books and supplies, and paying other costs. Before 1979, such benefits were generally includable in an employee's income, and the employee may or may not have been able to deduct the related expenses (see Chapter 7). In order to reduce the administrative difficulties in determining whether such costs were deductible in these circumstances, Sec. 127 was introduced by the Revenue Act of 1978. For years beginning after December 31, 1983 and before January 1, 1986, payments made by the employer on behalf of the employee for costs such as tuition and books

EDUCATIONAL-ASSISTANCE PLAN Plan by employer to pay part of education costs of employees.

[48] Sec. 117(b).

[49] Rev. Rul. 59-81, 1959-1 C.B. 37.

(but not for supplies other than textbooks that the employee retains after the course, transportation, lodging, or meals) are tax-free to the employee if made through a written nondiscriminatory educational-assistance program.[50] The limit on the exclusion is $5,000 per year for the student. At the same time, no deduction is allowed the employee for expenses for which he or she has been reimbursed under such tax-free plans.[51]

Example 35: Bethard's employer, National Corporation, maintains a nondiscriminatory educational-assistance plan for its employees. During 1984 Bethard received the following amounts as reimbursement for costs he incurred in attending classes at the university: tuition, $500; books, $180; supplies consumed in the classes, $50; transportation, $400. Bethard may exclude the $730 reimbursement for tuition, books, and supplies, but must include in income the $400 received as reimbursement for transportation. No deduction will be allowed for expenses represented by the $730 excluded. Whether the $400 spent for transportation is deductible depends on whether the tests discussed in Chapter 7 are met. That determination is not affected by Code Sec. 127.

PRIZES AND AWARDS

Section 74(a) contains a very terse statement concerning the taxability of prizes and awards, stating simply that with two exceptions prizes and awards are includable in gross income.[52] The two exceptions are scholarships and fellowships, discussed above, and "amounts received as prizes and awards made primarily in recognition of religious, charitable, scientific, educational, artistic, literary, or civic achievement," if the recipient was selected without any action on his or her part *and* if the recipient is not required to render substantial future services as a condition of receiving the prize or award.[53]

Obviously, there may be different interpretations of such terms as "artistic" and "civic" achievements. The Regulations state that amounts received from radio and television shows, door prizes, contest awards and prizes and similar items are taxable, but that awards such as a Nobel prize or Pulitzer prize are excludable.[54] The courts have rather consistently supported this strict interpretation of Sec. 74.

Example 36: Edna purchases groceries at Big Supermarket. With each purchase Edna receives a card with a number. The stubs are detached and cards placed in a basket. Each week a "lucky number" is drawn. The holder of the stub corresponding to the number of the

---

[50] Sec. 127.

[51] *Ibid.*

[52] Sec. 74(a).

[53] Sec. 74(b).

[54] Reg. Sec. 1.74-1(b).

card drawn wins free groceries with a value of $100. During the year Edna was a lucky winner. She must include in income the $100 value of the groceries she received.

Example 37: Margaret won first prize in a state-wide beauty pageant. The prize was a $1,000 check. The $1,000 is includable in Margaret's gross income.

Example 38: Yeoman, a college professor, was chosen by the students of his university as the winner of an award for being an "outstanding professor." The award included a $500 prize. This amount is tax-free to Yeoman.

Where prizes or awards are in the form of non-cash assets or services, the amount of income is the "fair market value" of the assets or services. Obviously, fair market value may be difficult to measure.

COMPENSATION FOR INJURIES, SICKNESS, OR DAMAGES

Sec. 104 permits the taxpayer to exclude from gross income certain amounts received relating to injury or sickness. The most important exclusions are those received:

1. under workmen's compensation acts as compensation for personal injuries or sickness;[55]
2. as damages (whether by suit or agreement) on account of personal injuries or sickness;[56]
3. through accident or health insurance for personal injuries or sickness (except for certain amounts received as an employee).[57]

AWARDS UNDER WORKMEN'S COMPENSATION

The exclusion of workmen's compensation benefits is made clear in Sec. 104(a)(1).

Example 39: Hendricks was injured in an accident while working at his job. He received $1,500 in workmen's compensation benefits for 5 weeks loss of work. The $1,500 is excludable from Hendricks's income.

AWARDS FROM LAWSUITS OR AGREEMENTS

The treatment of amounts received as damages and other awards through lawsuits or compromise settlements resulting from injuries, or from such

[55] Sec. 104(a)(1).

[56] Sec. 104(a)(2) and Reg. Sec. 1.104-1(c).

[57] Sec. 104(a)(3).

actions as libel and slander, has given rise to many disputes between taxpayers and the IRS. Payments received as compensation for personal injury are tax-free. Personal injury has been interpreted to be broader than physical injury. For example, damages awarded to a taxpayer for libel, slander, battery, and invasion of privacy are excluded from gross income. Payments received for these "damages" are excludable on the theory that they compensate the taxpayer for the loss of a right or attribute that was previously enjoyed tax-free; thus the payments to compensate for loss of that right are also deemed to be tax-free.[58]

However, awards received as a substitute for lost wages[59] and damage payments that are intended to punish the defendant for gross negligence or willfulness[60] (including "treble damages") are includable by the recipient.

Example 40: While staying at the Big Lodge Hotel, Isaacs fell over a toolbox left on the floor of the room in which he was lodged, suffering severe internal injuries. As part of the settlement, Isaacs received the following amounts:

For pain and suffering	$105,000
Reimbursement for loss of wages	16,200
Reimbursement of medical costs	12,610
Total	$133,810

Isaacs may exclude the payment of $105,000 for pain and suffering. The reimbursement for loss of wages is taxable. The reimbursement of medical costs is taxable to the extent that the actual costs were deducted and resulted in a tax benefit in a prior year. To the extent the actual costs were incurred in the present year, the reimbursement will be offset against them in computing the current year's net medical costs.

BENEFITS FROM HEALTH OR ACCIDENT INSURANCE NOT PROVIDED BY EMPLOYER

When the taxpayer collects benefits related to personal injury or sickness under an accident or health insurance policy the benefits are generally excluded if the premiums on the policy were not paid by the taxpayer's employer. The recipient has taxable income only to the extent that the reimbursement is attributable to a "deduction" allowed for "medical expenses" on the taxpayer's tax return in a prior year.[61] Even if the amount received exceeds actual costs incurred, no income results if the taxpayer paid the premiums on the policy.

---

[58] *C. A. Hawkins v. Comm.*, 6 B.T.A. 1023 (1927).

[59] *Glenshaw Glass Co. v. Comm.*, 75 S.Ct. 473 (1955).

[60] *Ibid.*

[61] Sec. 105(b).

Example 41: Stephanie pays premiums on a medical and disability insurance policy that pays her $250 per week as disability benefits while she is unable to work because of illness or injuries. During the current year, she received $800 of benefits under the policy. Since Stephanie paid the premiums, the benefits are exempt from federal income tax.

Example 42: In the current year Alfonse received $900 reimbursement for medical expenses incurred for care of his wife. The payment was received under a health insurance policy on which Alfonse paid all the premiums. The $900 represents $400 reimbursement for medical expenses paid during the current year and $500 paid during last year. Of the $500 reimbursement for last year's expenses, $200 represents an amount that was deducted in arriving at Alfonse's taxable income for that year. Of the $900 received, only the $200 representing the amount giving a tax benefit last year is included in the current year's income.

BENEFITS ATTRIBUTABLE TO EMPLOYER CONTRIBUTIONS

When payments received through accident or health insurance for personal injuries or sickness (*a*) are attributable to contributions by the *employer* that were not included in gross income of the employee or (*b*) are paid directly by the employer, special rules apply.

REIMBURSEMENT OF AMOUNTS EXPENDED FOR MEDICAL CARE Amounts received as reimbursement of medical expenses of the taxpayer, the taxpayer's spouse, and the taxpayer's dependents under an accident or health policy provided by the employer may be treated in the same way as reimbursement under a policy on which premiums were paid by the taxpayer. Similarly, amounts paid directly to doctors, hospitals, and others under such policies may also be excludable by the employee. However, if amounts received under policies paid for by the employer exceed actual costs incurred, the excess is taxable to the employee.

MEDICAL EXPENSE REIMBURSEMENT PLAN Sec. 105(e) makes it clear that amounts received from the employer under an accident or health plan for employees are generally treated as having been received through accident or health insurance.[62] Many corporations, especially closely-held corporations, have used this provision to provide tax-free reimbursement of medical expenses incurred by selected employees and their families. Section 105(h), added in 1978, curtailed this practice to some extent by stipulating that payments made under a *direct* health and accident reimbursement plan (that is, one not provided under an insurance policy) will be tax-free to the recipient only if the plan does not discriminate in favor of stockholders or highly compensated individuals.[63]

MEDICAL EXPENSE REIMBURSEMENT PLAN Plan under which the employer directly reimburses or pays medical costs for employees without utilizing an insurance policy.

[62] Sec. 105(e).

[63] Sec. 105(h).

However, if payments are made through a plan using an insurance policy, the exclusion is permitted even though the insurance plan discriminates in favor of stockholders or selected employees.

Example 43: T Corporation has a plan which reimburses all employees for 80% of the medical expenses paid by employees for themselves, their spouses, and their dependents. In addition, the company pays the remaining 20% of such expenses for all officers of the corporation. In the current year Sterling, the corporation's controller, was reimbursed $2,000 for medical expenses ($1,600 under the general reimbursement plan and $400 under the special plan for officers). The $1,600 general reimbursement is tax-free, but Sterling must include the $400 supplemental payment in gross income.

PAYMENTS UNRELATED TO ABSENCE FROM WORK Receipts of amounts that constitute payments for permanent loss of, or loss of use of, a body member or function, or the permanent disfigurement of the taxpayer, his spouse, or a dependent, are also excluded from gross income if they are computed with reference to the nature of the injury, without regard to the period the employee is absent from work.[64]

Example 44: Clarence was injured on the job and, as a result, lost sight in his right eye. Under an insurance policy carried by his employer, Clarence received $10,000 solely because of loss of the eye. The entire amount is tax-free.

There are special rules for retired military personnel and certain public servants.[65]

Disability payments received from the taxpayer's employer (or under an insurance plan paid for by the employer) in lieu of wages are taxable. A permanently and totally disabled individual may be able to qualify for a special credit (discussed in Chapter 14).

COMPENSATION FOR SERVICES

For most taxpayers, compensation for services is the most important source of income. Sec. 61(a) provides that compensation for services includes fees, commissions, and similar items.[66] Reg. Sec. 1.61-2(a), a portion of which is quoted below, elaborates on the nature of items included.

> (a) *In general*. (1) Wages, salaries, commissions paid salesmen, compensation for services on the basis of a percentage of profits, commissions on insurance premiums, tips, bonuses (including Christmas bonuses), termi-

[64] Sec. 105(c).
[65] Sec. 104.
[66] Sec. 61(a).

nation or severance pay, rewards, jury fees, marriage fees and other contributions received by a clergyman for services, pay of persons in the military or naval forces of the United States, retired pay of employees, pensions, and retirement allowances are income to the recipients unless excluded by law.[67]

Example 46: Roger works as a waiter in a restaurant. During the year he received the following amounts related to his work.

Hourly wages	$10,200
Tips	3,860
Commission, based on the total purchases by his customers	610
Cash bonus based on restaurant's profit	92
Christmas bonus (cash)	100

All of these items are included in Roger's income.

As discussed in Chapter 4, compensation from services may involve more than mere cash payments received. Unless otherwise provided, it includes all payments to or on behalf of an employee, substantial discounts on the price of property sold to the employee by the employer, and the fair value of all noncash compensation. The taxation of "fringe benefits"—those goods and services which are made available to the employee as part of the employer-employee relationship—has been controversial and in some cases unclear.

EMPLOYEE FRINGE BENEFITS

BACKGROUND

The tax treatment of ***fringe benefits*** has been both controversial and paradoxical. On the one hand, Congress continues to enact statutes that tend to curtail the tax-free status of fringe benefits. At the same time, Congress has added new benefits to the list of tax-free items and has taken specific action to prevent the Internal Revenue Service from requiring taxpayers to include a number of items that have been excluded in practice but for which no specific exclusion is provided in the law.

For example, in recent years Sec. 120 (permitting the exclusion of amounts received under qualified group legal services plans), Sec. 124 (permitting the exclusion of qualified transportation provided by the employer), Sec. 125 (relating to cafeteria plans), Sec. 127 (allowing the exclusion under educational-assistance programs), Sec. 129 (excluding benefits under dependent-care assistance programs),

Continued

FRINGE BENEFITS Benefits provided to employees which are not paid in cash.

[67] Reg. Sec. 1.61-2(a).

BACKGROUND

and Sec. 122A (reinstating a tax-favored employee stock-option plan) have all been enacted, dramatically enlarging the range of tax-free benefits. All of these Code Sections have been the result of efforts to achieve specific economic or social goals. Even more noteworthy, and perhaps surprising, has been the Congressional action to block the Service's announced intention to issue regulations specifying that certain fringes must be included in gross income. In 1978 the Congress enacted a statutory barrier prohibiting the issue of such Regulations before June 1, 1981, and again in 1981 enacted a ban on the issuance of any fringe benefit Regulations before 1984.

Almost simultaneously, several Code Sections have been amended to "tighten" the conditions under which certain fringe items may be excluded. For example, Code Sec. 79(d) was enacted, specifying additional nondiscrimination requirements for group term-life insurance, and Code Sec. 105(h) restricted the use of medical expense reimbursement plans. The overall result of these statutes has been to increase the variety of tax-free fringe benefits, while at the same time moving toward greater assurance that fringe-benefit plans do not discriminate in favor of officers and highly-paid employees.

In 1984, Congress partially faced up to the problem of taxing fringe benefits. Several Sections of the Code were revised (or added) reflecting a concern for the problem. The three major revisions and additions are as follows:

1. In Section 61, defining gross income, the words "fringe benefits" were included in the examples of inclusions relating to compensation for services.
2. Section 280F (discussed in Chapter 7) limited the deductions related to certain types of business property (autos and other vehicles, entertainment or recreation property, and computers) that are used in part for personal activities (in effect fringe benefits) by either employees or self-employed persons.
3. Section 132 specified four types of fringe benefits (no-additional-cost services, qualified employee discounts, working condition fringes, and *de minimis* fringes) that are to be excluded from income if certain tests are met.

The Internal Revenue Service wasted little time in taking steps to interpret the Code changes. Temporary Regs. issued in October 1984 contain rules relating to the reduction in costs and credits allowable as "listed property" where such property is not used at least 50 percent of the time in business or where the business use of such property declines in relation to personal use in subsequent tax years.* (These rules are discussed in Chapter 7.)

Then in early 1985, the IRS announced plans to issue new regulations concerning the documentation and record-keeping necessary

Continued

BACKGROUND

for "listed property." Also in early 1985, a regulation[†] was issued establishing guidelines for the inclusion in income of the value "of an employee's personal use of employer-owned cars and airplanes (including free or discounted flights by airline personnel)."

The Commissioner of Internal Revenue has stated that the regulations issued have not covered the waterfront and that additional ones will be forthcoming. The tax treatments of some of the most important fringe benefits are reviewed on the following pages.

*Temporary Regs. 1.280F-1T—6T.

[†]Temporary Reg. 1.61-2T.

INSURANCE PREMIUMS PAID BY EMPLOYER

Many employers pay all or part of the premiums on insurance policies covering the lives of employees, with the proceeds benefitting the employees' beneficiaries. In addition, employers often pay all or part of the premiums on insurance policies providing reimbursement for medical expenses for employees and the employees' families, or for payments relating to absence from work because of illness or injury of employees. The taxability of the premiums paid ("contributions") by the employer on behalf of employees depends on the type of insurance coverage, the amount of coverage, and the degree to which the insurance plan does not discriminate in favor of higher paid and key employees. Several Sections of the Code provide for specific limited exclusions of premiums paid by the employer on insurance policies.

LIFE INSURANCE PAID FOR BY EMPLOYER

Premiums paid by the employer on life insurance policies covering the lives of employees and payable to the employees' beneficiaries are generally taxable to the employee when the premiums are paid.[68] There is, however, one very important major exception to this general rule. Premiums paid by an employer for an employee for ***group term-life insurance***, up to a $50,000 face amount, may be excluded by the employee under Code Section 79. (The term employee does not include either a sole proprietor or a partner in a partnership.) The Regulations under Section 79 are lengthy and rather complex. For example, Reg. Sec. 1.79-1(a)(4) defines the word "group" as including *all* employees of the employer, or *less than all* if membership in the group is based on factors such as age, marital status, etc. Reg. Sec. 1.79-1 defines the meaning of "term" insurance. A group term-insurance policy must meet specified nondiscrimina-

GROUP TERM-LIFE INSURANCE Life insurance plan covering a group of people. Insurance builds no permanent (cash surrender) value.

[68]Reg. Sec. 1.61-2(d)(2)(ii)(a).

TABLE 5-2
Uniform Premiums for $1,000 of Group Term-Life Insurance Protection

5-YEAR AGE BRACKET	COST PER $1,000 OF PROTECTION FOR 1-MONTH PERIOD
Under 30	$ .08
30 to 34	.09
35 to 39	.11
40 to 44	.17
45 to 49	.29
50 to 54	.48
55 to 59	.75
60 to 64	1.17

tion rules in order for key employees to obtain the exclusion.[69] Sec. 79(d) contains detailed rules defining "nondiscrimination."

The Regulations contain explicit instructions for computing the excludable amount of premiums where more than $50,000 of protection is provided. For each $1,000 of coverage *above* $50,000, the employee must *include* the amount shown in Table 5-2 for each month of such coverage.[70] However, if the employee pays any part of the cost of the insurance, the entire amount paid reduces dollar for dollar the amount the taxpayer would otherwise include in income.

Example 46: Klaren, age 38, is covered by a nondiscriminatory $80,000 group term-life insurance policy on which all premiums are paid by Klaren's employer. During the current year the premiums paid by the employer for Klaren's coverage totaled $1,536. The amount that must be included by Klaren is $39.60:

$$\frac{\$80{,}000 - \$50{,}000}{\$1{,}000} \times \$.11 \times 12 \text{ months} = \$39.60$$

Premiums paid by the employer on group term-life insurance covering the lives of the taxpayer's spouse or dependents are not excludable under Sec. 106. If, however, such life insurance is "incidental" (coverage of $2,000 or less for the spouse and each child) the premiums may be excluded; otherwise such amounts are taxable to the employee.[71]

The Regulations contain complex provisions for determining the taxable portion and excludable portion of group life insurance contracts that provide both "permanent" and "term benefits."[72] The portion of pre-

[69] Sec. 79(d).
[70] Reg. Sec. 1.79-3(d)(2).
[71] Reg. Sec. 1.61-2(d)(2)(ii)(b).
[72] Reg. Sec. 1.79-1(d).

miums allocated to permanent benefits cannot be excluded. This allocation process is beyond the scope of this book.

If the employer is named as the beneficiary of a life insurance policy purchased by the employer on the life of an employee, no benefit accrues to the employee, so the premiums paid are not taxable to the employee. (Incidentally, the premiums are also not deductible by the employer.)

Example 47: Ace Corporation purchases a life insurance policy on the life of its president. The corporation is named as beneficiary. During the current year, premiums of $2,500 were paid by Ace. The premiums are not taxed to the president, nor are they deductible by the corporation.

ACCIDENT AND HEALTH PLANS PAID FOR BY EMPLOYER

Contributions by the employer to accident or health plans that compensate employees for personal injuries or sickness of the employee, the employee's spouse, or the employee's dependents, are not includable in gross income of the employee.[73] (The taxability of benefits received under such policies is discussed on pages 5/28–5/29.) If such insurance plans provide other benefits in addition to accident or health plans, only the portion of the contribution which is allocable to accident or health benefits is excludable.[74] (Incidentally, Sec. 106 does not require that accident and health plans be nondiscriminatory in order for the employee to exclude the employer's contributions.)

Example 48: Wheaton Company pays 80% of the premiums on a medical-care policy covering its employees and their dependents. During the current year, Wheaton paid premiums of $1,920 to provide coverage for an employee, James Dunn, and his wife and children. The $1,920 is not included in gross income by Dunn.

The same exclusion is available for payments made by a former employer for medical insurance coverage for the retired employee and his or her spouse and dependents. Similarly, premiums paid for the benefit of a surviving spouse and dependents are tax free.

MEALS AND LODGING PROVIDED FOR THE EMPLOYER'S CONVENIENCE

Certain forms of compensation have been made tax-free on the basis that they are paid for the convenience of the employer. The two most commonly encountered items that may be excludable under this concept are meals and lodging provided to the employee.

---

[73] Code Sec. 106.

[74] Reg. Sec. 1.106-1.

MEALS

In order for the value of meals provided by the employer to the employee, the employee's spouse, and the employee's dependents to be tax-free, the meals must be furnished *for the convenience of the employer* and must be provided *on the employer's business premises.*[75] If meals are furnished without charge to the employee for a substantial noncompensatory business reason of the employer, they will be deemed to have been provided for the convenience of the employer.[76] Generally meals furnished before or after working hours will not be regarded as being for the employer's convenience and are not excludable, and meals on nonworking days do not qualify for exclusion.[77] However, in the case of a food-service employee, meals are considered to be for a substantial noncompensatory reason regardless of whether the meal is furnished during, immediately after, or immediately before the employee's working hours.[78] Regulation 1.119-1 contains examples of other situations in which meals for which no charge is made and meals for which a charge is made are to be considered excludable.

> **Example 49:** Saleh is a waiter at the Big Time Restaurant. He eats two meals each day at the restaurant at no charge. One is eaten just before he begins work; the other is eaten during working hours. Value of the meals consumed by Saleh during the year was $2,800. That value is not included in Saleh's gross income if they were offered to benefit the business and not as a means of additional compensation.

The Supreme Court has held that a cash allowance for meals does not qualify for exclusion when the employer does not *provide* the meals.[79] Nevertheless, "supper money," or cash allowance for a meal when the employee works overtime, has been held to be tax-free.[80] Although this ruling is very old, there appear to have been no subsequent rulings or decisions directly challenging it.

LODGING

In order for the value of lodging provided by the employer to an employee to be excluded, the employee must have been required to accept the lodging on the business premises of his or her employer as a condition of employment for substantially noncompensatory reasons.[81]

---

[75] Sec. 119(a)(1).
[76] Reg. Sec. 1.119-1(a)(2).
[77] Reg. Sec. 1.119-1(d).
[78] Reg. Sec. 1.119-1(a)(2)(d).
[79] *Comm. v. Kowalski*, 98 S.Ct. 315 (1977).
[80] O.D. 514, 2 C.B. 90 (1920).
[81] Sec. 119(a)(2).

Example 50: Zant is manager of City Apartments. As a condition of employment, Zant is required to live in one of the apartments in order to be accessible to tenants. The fair rental value of the apartment occupied by Zant during the current year was $5,200. Zant does not have any income to report as a result of occupying the apartment.

Example 51: Assume the same facts as in Example 50 except that Zant was given an option either to occupy the apartment or to receive instead, a cash allowance of $4,500. The fair rental value, $5,200, of the apartment that Zant occupied must be reported as gross income by Zant.[82]

OTHER FRINGE BENEFITS OF EMPLOYEES

The Code, Regulations, and various court decisions give tax-free status to a variety of other specific fringe benefits provided to employees by employers. Some of the most commonly found benefits are summarized in the following paragraphs.

QUALIFIED GROUP LEGAL-SERVICES PLANS

An employee may exclude from income amounts contributed by an employer on behalf of the employee, the employee's spouse, and the employee's dependents to a qualified ***group legal-services plan*** and may also exclude the value of legal services received under the plan.[83] In order to be qualified, a legal services plan must be in writing, must be for the exclusive benefit of employees and their families, and must provide personal legal service through prepayment of, or provision in advance for, legal fees. The plan must not discriminate in favor of officers, shareholders, or highly compensated employees.

GROUP LEGAL-SERVICES PLAN A plan by the employer to provide or pay for specified legal services for a group of employees.

Example 52: Patsy's employer has established a qualified group legal-service plan under which attorneys are available to perform specified services free of charge to employees. During the current year Patsy used the attorneys to prepare her will, to examine several contracts, and to give her tax advice. These services had a fair value of $600. Patsy has no gross income from these free services.

QUALIFIED TRANSPORTATION PROVIDED BY EMPLOYER

Under Sec. 124, an employee is entitled to exclude the value of qualified transportation provided by the employer between the employee's residence and place of employment. Several restrictions are placed on this exclusion in order to prevent abuses. For example, the vehicle transport-

[82] Reg. Sec. 1.119-1(d), Ex. (6).

[83] Sec. 120(a).

ing the employee must have a seating capacity of at least 8 adults, not including the driver. The transportation plan must be in writing and must not be discriminatory. Also, the transportation must be in addition to, not in lieu of, compensation otherwise payable.

Example 53: Arcon works for a large oil company. The company provides commuter buses to transport employees, free of charge, from "pickup" points throughout the city and suburban areas to the company's offices. During the current year, Arcon rode the company bus almost every day. The $420 value of his transportation on the bus is excludable by Arcon.

DEPENDENT-CARE ASSISTANCE PROGRAMS

DEPENDENT-CARE ASSISTANCE PROGRAM A plan under which the employer provides or pays for care of employees' dependents during hours of employment.

The gross income of an employee does not include amounts paid or incurred by the employer for ***dependent-care assistance*** under a written, nondiscriminatory plan. The amount excluded cannot exceed the "earned income" of an unmarried taxpayer. In the case of a married employee, the exclusion is limited to the earned income of the employee or the earned income of the spouse, whichever is less.[84] The expenses must have been incurred in order for the taxpayer and spouse to be gainfully employed.[85]

Example 54: Clarice's employer has established a qualified dependent-care assistance program. In order for both spouses to be employed, Clarice and her husband leave their 4- and 6-year-old children at a child-care center. Clarice's employer paid the child-care center $4,200 for care of the two children during the year. Clarice's earned income for the year was $16,000; her husband's earned income was $4,000. They may exclude $4,000 of the $4,200 paid by the employer.

"CAFETERIA" PLANS

CAFETERIA PLAN A fringe benefit plan under which employees are permitted to choose from a variety of fringe benefits.

Historically, where employers have offered employees a choice to take either cash or an otherwise nontaxable fringe benefit, the option to take cash was deemed to have created taxable income even if the employee chose the fringe benefit that would otherwise have been tax-free. (Plans with optional benefits are referred to as "***cafeteria***" ***plans***.) Section 125 now provides that, with minor exceptions, no amount shall be included in the gross income of a participant in a nondiscriminatory cafeteria plan solely because the participant may choose between receiving (1) cash and (2) otherwise nontaxable benefits.[86] Proposed regulations require that a taxable benefit (cash) "should at no time become currently available to

---

[84] Sec. 129.

[85] The dependent-care assistance program exclusion is based on the same type of expenses that would be subject to a credit for child and dependent care if the expenses were not reimbursed, as discussed in detail in Chapter 14.

[86] Sec. 125.

the participants."[87] Thus, the plan should require participants to elect the specific benefits that they will receive *before* the period in which the taxable benefits become currently available.

Example 55: Tinkle's employer has established a nondiscriminatory cafeteria plan. The employees may choose to take either cash, premium payments on health and hospital insurance, or a qualified dependent care assistance program. Tinkle chose to accept the health and hospital insurance policy. Premiums paid by the employer on behalf of Tinkle will not be taxed to him.

OTHER BENEFITS SPECIFICALLY EXCLUDED OR INCLUDED

Employers frequently provide a variety of other benefits that generally escape taxation. For example, free parking, payment of dues in professional organizations and routine (minimal) courtesy discounts on merchandise purchased by the employee from the employer have usually been treated as excludable if the same benefits are offered to other employees on a nondiscriminatory basis, although there was no statutory basis for such exclusions prior to the Tax Reform Act of 1984. As a matter of fact, Reg. Sec. 1.61-2(d) made it clear that if property or services are transferred to an employee for less than their fair value, income results. However, a strict enforcement of this rule would lead to continuous controversy between taxpayers and the Internal Revenue Service and would probably result in very expensive enforcement. Thus there has been lax (but inconsistent) enforcement of these rules. The Tax Reform Act of 1984 identified certain types of fringe benefits that will not be included in income beginning in 1985.[88] There are four broad categories of tax-free fringes:

a) "No additional cost" services,
b) Qualified employee discounts,
c) Working condition fringes, and
d) *De minimis* fringes.

Study

NO "ADDITIONAL COST" SERVICES

In situations where the employer provides to the employee, the employee's spouse or surviving spouse, or the employee's dependent child, free of charge a service that is offered for sale to customers in the ordinary course of the employer's line of business no includable income results. The employer should not incur substantial additional cost in providing the service to the employee.[89]

Example 56: Akron is a retired pilot of Big Sky Airline. His dependent son, James, flew without cost from New York to Los Angeles on

[87] Proposed Reg. 1.125-1(Q15).
[88] Sec. 132(a).
[89] Sec. 132(b) and Temporary Reg. 1.61-2T.

a regularly scheduled flight on Big Sky. The flight was made on a "standby" basis (space available) pursuant to the airline's policy which permits all employees and retired employees, their spouses, and dependent children to do so. The normal fare is $275. Neither Akron nor James has taxable income.

A similar exclusion is allowed if the service is provided by an unrelated employer on a basis provided: (1) the two employers are engaged in the same line of business, (2) they have entered into a written reciprocal agreement, (3) both provide the services to their employees, and (4) neither employer incurs any substantial additional cost because of the service.[90]

Example 57: Akron is a pilot for Wide Blue Airline. Akron's wife flies without cost on a "standby" basis from New York to Los Angeles via Stormy Airline. The two airlines have a written reciprocal agreement under which they offer this service to the employees of both airlines. Neither Akron nor his wife has includable income because of the flight.

QUALIFIED EMPLOYEE DISCOUNTS

No income results when an employee purchases qualified property or services at a price less than the price at which the property is regularly sold to customers, provided the discount does not exceed the limits established in the Code. The term "qualified property and services" means all property (other than personal property of a kind held for investment) and services offered for sale to customers by the employer in the normal course of the line of business in which the employee works.[91]

The limits on excludable discounts are:

a) for personal property, the normal gross profit percentage multiplied by the price at which the property is being offered for sale to customers,
b) for services, 20 percent of the price at which the services are being offered by the employer to customers.[92]

Example 58: Apple works for a retail department store. The employer has a stated policy of giving all full-time employees a "courtesy" discount of 30% on purchases of merchandise made from the employer during the year. The employer's gross profit rate is 48%. Apple took courtesy discounts totaling $160. This will probably be excludable from Apple's income.

---

[90] Sec. 132(g)(2).
[91] Sec. 132(c)(4).
[92] Sec. 132(c)(1).

Example 59: Stella is employed as an accountant in a shoe factory. She purchases from the employer a tract of land for $20,000. Its fair market value at date of purchase was $22,000. Stella has includable income of $2,000.

WORKING CONDITION FRINGE BENEFITS

Property or services provided to the employee by the employer are excludable to the extent that, if the employee paid for such services they would be allowable as a business expense or allowable through depreciation.[93] In addition, parking provided to the employee on or near the employer's premises[94] and "on-premises" athletic facilities[95] are specifically listed as "working condition fringes."

Example 60: Sinclair is a staff accountant for a public accounting firm. During this year the firm paid $120 for Sinclair's subscription to two professional accounting periodicals. Since these costs would be deductible by Sinclair as an employee business expense if she had paid for the subscriptions, the payments by Sinclair's employer are excludable by her.

DE MINIMIS FRINGE BENEFITS

A *de minimis fringe* benefit is property or service of which the value is so small that accounting for it is unreasonable or administratively impractical.[96] An employer-operated eating facility for employees is to be treated as a nontaxable fringe benefit if the facility is located on or near the employer's business premises and if revenue from the facility normally equals or exceeds the operating costs of the facility.[97]

THE SPECIAL PROBLEMS OF BUSINESS AUTOMOBILES AVAILABLE FOR PERSONAL USE

Temporary Reg. 1.61-2T, issued in October 1984, provides guidelines for determining the amount that an employee should include in income from personal use of employer-provided automobiles. The Temporary Regulation established an "annual lease value" based on the fair market value of the auto as of the first date of its availability to the employee. The percentage of the time the automobile is utilized for personal use is multiplied by the fair value to obtain the taxable fringe benefit. There is a daily allocation of the lease value if the automobile is not available throughout the year.[98] A portion of the annual lease value is shown in Table 5-3.

---

[93] Sec. 132(a) and (d).
[94] Sec. 132(h)(4).
[95] Sec. 132(h)(5).
[96] Sec. 132(e)(1).
[97] Sec. 132(e)(2).
[98] Temporary Reg. 1.61-2T.

TABLE 5-3
Annual Lease Value Table

AUTOMOBILE FAIR MARKET VALUE	ANNUAL LEASE VALUE	AUTOMOBILE FAIR MARKET VALUE	ANNUAL LEASE VALUE
$ 0–999	$ 600	$22,000–22,999	$ 6,100
1,000–1,999	850	23,000–23,999	6,350
2,000–2,999	1,100	24,000–24,999	6,600
3,000–3,999	1,350	25,000–25,999	6,850
4,000–4,999	1,600	26,000–27,999	7,250
5,000–5,999	1,850	28,000–29,999	7,750
6,000–6,999	2,100	30,000–31,999	8,250
7,000–7,999	2,350	32,000–33,999	8,750
8,000–8,999	2,600	34,000–35,999	9,250
9,000–9,999	2,850	36,000–37,999	9,750
10,000–10,999	3,100	38,000–39,999	10,250
11,000–11,999	3,350	40,000–41,999	10,750
12,000–12,999	3,600	42,000–43,999	11,250
13,000–13,999	3,850	44,000–45,999	11,750
14,000–14,999	4,100	46,000–47,999	12,250
15,000–15,999	4,350	48,000–49,999	12,750
16,000–16,999	4,600	50,000–51,999	13,250
17,000–17,999	4,850	52,000–53,999	13,750
18,000–18,999	5,100	54,000–55,999	14,250
19,000–19,999	5,350	56,000–57,999	14,750
20,000–20,999	5,600	58,000–60,000	15,250
21,000–21,999	5,850	over $60,000	(Car's fair market value × 0.25) + $500

Example 61: Beginning November 15, 19X1, Coe's employer made available to her an automobile for business purposes, which she may also use for personal activities. Her daily log showed that during the remainder of the year she drove 1,600 miles for business purposes and 400 miles for personal activities. At the date the auto was made available to her, it had a fair market value of $11,500. She must include in income $111.97 for the year, computed as follows:

$$\frac{61 \text{ days}}{365 \text{ days}} \times \frac{400 \text{ miles}}{2{,}000 \text{ miles}} \times \$3{,}350 = \$111.97$$

INTEREST-FREE LOANS

One interesting exclusion that has been permitted by court action is the benefit accruing to an employee or employee-shareholder who is extended a loan by his or her employer at an interest rate less than the market rate. The Tax Court has held that the benefit is not taxable. The ground used by the Court to arrive at this decision was that the imputed income from the lower rate is offset by an imputed allowable deduction for interest deemed to have been paid.[99] This conclusion has not, however, been generally accepted by the IRS. The Tax Reform Act of 1984 provides that effective June 6, 1984, the imputed interest on interest-free loans or on below-market loans shall be treated as income to an employee and a deduction by the employer.[100] The amount taxable is the difference between the amount loaned and the present value (based on specified federal rates) of all payments to be made. There is no taxable amount on loans less than $10,000.

FOREIGN-EARNED INCOME

Income earned by a U.S. citizen is generally taxable, without regard to the country in which the income was earned. In addition, income earned by a U.S. citizen in a foreign country may be taxed by that country. Because of this potential double taxation and the fact that, presumably, Americans living abroad incur extra living costs and do not receive the same benefits from services and facilities provided by the U.S. government within the United States, Congress, in Sec. 911, has provided some tax relief to those taxpayers by allowing the exclusion of a limited amount of income earned abroad.

"***Foreign-earned income***" is defined as the amount received from sources within a foreign country constituting earned income for services performed abroad (except as an employee of the U.S. Government).[101] The exclusion is available to an individual who is a bona fide resident of a foreign country, or who is present in a foreign country or countries for 330 days out of any 12 consecutive month period.[102] The ceiling on the amount of earnings excludable is $80,000 in 1984 through 1987. If the taxpayer is abroad only part of a taxable year, the exclusion is computed on a daily basis. The maximum daily exclusion for 1984 was $218.58 ($80,000/366) and for 1985 it is $219.18 ($80,000/365).

FOREIGN-EARNED INCOME Income earned from personal services by a U.S. citizen in a foreign country.

Example 62: Sanchez, a U.S. citizen, arrived in London, England, on June 1, 1984, where he remained until July 31, 1985, when he returned to the U.S. During that period Sanchez was paid $9,000 per month. Sanchez can exclude $46,557.54 (213 full days @ $218.58 per day) in 1984 and $46,246.98 (211 full days @ $219.18 per day) in 1985.

In addition to the exclusion for earned income, the reasonable expenses of housing for the taxpayer and the taxpayer's family in a foreign country are excludable to the extent that they exceed a statutory "base amount."[103] The base amount is 16% of the salary of an employee of the

---

[99] Nax Zager, 72 T.C. 1009 (1979).

[100] Sec. 7872.

[101] Sec. 911(d) and Reg. 1.911-1.

[102] Sec. 911 and Reg. 1.911-7.

[103] Sec. 911(c)(1).

FORM 2555 U.S. Government who has a rank of GS-14, Step 1.[104] (This salary level for 1984 was $42,928.)

In lieu of excluding foreign earned income, the taxpayer may include all amounts earned and may take a credit for foreign taxes paid. In most instances the taxpayers will elect to take the exclusion.

UNEMPLOYMENT BENEFITS

Payments made to individuals as unemployment compensation under federal and state government programs may be totally or partially excluded from gross income of the recipient.

UNEMPLOYMENT BENEFITS Payments to a taxpayer under federal and state-funded programs, payable because of unemployment.

Such ***unemployment benefits*** are included in gross income, but only to the extent of one-half the excess of (*a*) the sum of the taxpayer's adjusted gross income (before the special deduction that is allowed to a "two-earner" married couple) other than unemployment compensation benefits, all unemployment compensation received, and all excludable disability income over (*b*) the taxpayer's "base amount."[105] The base amount is $18,000 in the case of a married individual filing a joint return, zero in the case of a married individual filing a separate return (unless the taxpayer lived apart from his or her spouse for the entire year), and $12,000 for all other individuals.[106]

Example 63: For the current year, Kevin and Gerri file a joint return. During the year Kevin earned $9,000 and Gerri earned $8,000. They had no other income except $1,600 state unemployment compensation received by Kevin while he was unemployed for part of the year. Of the $1,600 unemployment compensation, $300 is includable and $1,300 is excludable, computed as follows:

Adjusted gross income (before "two wage-earner" deduction)	$17,000
Unemployment compensation	1,600
Total	$18,600
Less "base amount"	18,000
Excess	$ 600
Amount includable (½ of excess)	$ 300

Unemployment benefits received from employer-financed or other privately-financed unemployment compensation plans are fully taxable.[107]

Example 64: Bugg Corporation has contributed to a private supplementary unemployment-benefit plan as part of a contract with its

[104] Sec. 911(c)(2).

[105] Sec. 85(a).

[106] Sec. 85(b).

[107] Reg. Sec. 1.85-1(b)(1).

employees' unions. In the current year, Agnes, an employee of Bugg, was temporarily laid off from her job. During the period of unemployment, she received $300 as supplementary benefits. The $300 is taxable.

ALIMONY, SEPARATE MAINTENANCE, AND CHILD-SUPPORT PAYMENTS

The treatment of amounts received by a former spouse under a divorce decree or by a nondivorced spouse under a written separate maintenance or a decree of support depends on whether the divorce or agreement was entered into prior to 1985 or after 1984.[108]

PRE-1985 SETTLEMENTS

Periodic alimony payments are deductible by the payor[109] and are taxable to the recipient if they are made pursuant to either[110] (*a*) a decree of divorce or separate maintenance entered into prior to 1985 or (*b*) a written agreement or a decree of support entered into before 1985, if they are in "discharge of a legal obligation arising from the marital or family relationship."[111] Thus, purely voluntary payments to a former spouse would not be taxable to the recipient, nor would they be deductible by the payor, because they are not in discharge of a legal obligation.

PERIODIC ALIMONY Payments under a divorce decree or settlement where the payments are to be made periodically for an indefinite period or for a period in excess of 120 months.

"PERIODIC" DEFINED

Much of the controversy over treatment of alimony and separate maintenance payments has resulted from the requirement that payments must be "periodic" before they are to be includable in the income of the recipient and deductible by the payor. Numerous court cases and regulations have dealt with this requirement.

PAYMENTS OVER AN INDEFINITE PERIOD If a pre-1985 divorce settlement provides for payment for an indefinite period—for example, until the death of either spouse or until the marriage of the recipient—these payments are considered periodic payments.[112]

Example 65: Mindy and Lee, who live in a state where there is no law providing for alimony payments, were divorced in June of 1984. In the divorce settlement they agreed that "in lieu of alimony" Lee would pay Mindy $500 per month beginning on July 10, 1984, and continuing until Mindy's death or such time as she would remarry.

---

[108] Pre-1985 settlements can be modified to expressly elect the post-1974 tax provisions.

[109] Sec. 215.

[110] Sec. 71 (prior to 1985).

[111] Sec. 71(a) (prior to 1985).

[112] Reg. Sec. 1.71-1(d)(3).

The $6,000 paid in the current year (12 payments at $500 each) is taxable to Mindy and is deductible by Lee.

INSTALLMENT PAYMENTS OF A PRINCIPAL-SUM AMOUNT Settlements often are stated as a single monetary amount ("principal sum"), with payments of the principal-sum amount to be made over a period of years. If the principal-sum amount under a pre-1985 settlement is to be paid over a period of 10 years or less from the date of the agreement, the payments are not deemed to be periodic and thus are neither deductible by the payor nor taxable to the recipient.[113]

Example 66: Zelda and Victor were divorced in 1984. The divorce decree provided that Victor will pay Zelda alimony of $20,000 per year for six years, beginning in 1984. Since the payments are to be completed within 10 years, the payments received by Zelda are not includable in income and Victor will not be entitled to any deduction for alimony paid.

On the other hand, if the principal sum is to be paid over a period ending more than 10 years from the date of a pre-1985 agreement, all or part of each payment may be considered periodic. Code Sec. 71 provides that in those circumstances payments in any one year of up to 10% of the principal sum will be treated as periodic, while amounts paid in any year in excess of 10% of the principal sum will not be considered periodic.

Example 67: Will and Clara were separated in 1984. The written separation agreement requires Will to pay Clara $10,000 per year for a period of 13 years. All of the current year's payment of $10,000 will be considered periodic and thus taxable to Clara and deductible by Will.

Example 68: Richmond and Edna were divorced in 1984. The divorce decree requires Edna to pay Richmond a total of $150,000 over a period of 12 years, with $10,000 to be paid in 1984 and each of the following nine years and $25,000 to be paid in each of the final two years. Since the payments in each of the first 10 years are less than 10% of the principal sum, the entire amount received in each of those years is deemed to be periodic. In each of the last two years, however, only $15,000 (10% of $150,000) will be considered periodic and thus taxable to Richmond and deductible by Edna. The remaining $10,000 in each of the final two years will not be taxable to Richmond nor deductible by Edna.

DIVISION OF PROPERTY Frequently a divorce decree or a separation settlement includes a division of property that has been accumulated during the couple's marriage. The receipt of property by a spouse in this

[113] Sec. 71(c) (prior to January 1, 1985).

situation under a pre-1985 settlement does not give rise to income, nor is the transferor entitled to a deduction resulting from the transfer. (However, if the value of property owned by one spouse is tranferred to the other spouse in the settlement and if the value of the property at the date of transfer exceeds its tax basis, the transferor must recognize the excess as gain in the year of transfer[114] if the transfer is made on or before July 18, 1984.) For post-July 18, 1984, no gain or loss is recognized on such transfers.

Example 69: Hector and Martha live in a non-community-property state. As part of a divorce settlement in 1983, Hector transferred to Martha 10,000 shares of Big Sky Corporation stock with a fair market value of $200,000 and a basis of $20,000. As a result of the transfer, Martha recognizes no income and Hector has no deduction for alimony paid. Hector, however, was required to recognize gain of $180,000 as a result of the transfer. If the transfer had been made after July 18, 1984, no gain would have been recognized.

CHILD-SUPPORT PAYMENTS The treatment of child-support payments is clearly distinguished in the law from the treatment given periodic alimony. Payments made by one party to the other for support of a dependent child are nondeductible personal expenses to the payor[115] and are not taxable to the recipient. The decree or the agreement between the divorced or separated parties must clearly specify what part of payments are for child support. If this is not done, no part of the payments will be treated as being for child support.[116]

Example 70: Pender and Nelda were divorced last year. The divorce settlement required Pender to pay Nelda $600 per month, adjusted each year for inflation, for the support of their child until the child reaches the age of 21. In addition, Pender is to pay Nelda $800 per month as alimony during her lifetime or until such time as she remarries. The payments designated as child support are neither taxable to Nelda nor deductible by Pender, whereas the periodic alimony is taxable to Nelda and deductible by Pender.

POST-1984 SETTLEMENTS

Payments under divorce or separation settlements executed after 1984 will no longer have to be periodic in order to be considered as alimony. Cash payments that do not extend beyond the death of the payee spouse and that are not made between spouses who occupy the same household, are treated as alimony if they are not designated as child support payments.[117]

---

[114] *U.S. v. Davis*, 82 S.Ct. 1190 (1962).

[115] Sec. 71(b).

[116] *Comm. v. Lester*, 81 S.Ct. 1343 (1961).

[117] Sec. 71(b).

Example 71: Susan and Peter were separated under a decree of separate maintenance on February 15, 1985. Under the decree, Peter is to have custody of their child. Susan is to pay Peter $12,000 per year for five years. Of this amount, $4,000 per year is designated as child support payments. Peter will include $8,000 per year in income and Susan will be able to deduct that amount.

No gain or loss is recognized on property transfers to a spouse or to a former spouse (if incident to a settlement) made after July 18, 1984.[118]

If the payment in any calendar year exceeds $10,000, the amount paid in excess of $10,000 is not to be considered as alimony unless payments are to be made by the payor in each of the six post-separation years, except for terminations resulting from the death of either spouse or remarriage of the payee spouse.[119] (There are complex recapture provisions where payments decrease by more than $10,000 in a year.)

OTHER EXCLUSIONS

A number of miscellaneous exclusions affecting many taxpayers have been provided in the Code, have arisen from court decisions, or have simply developed as a result of administrative action or inaction.

SOCIAL SECURITY AND WELFARE PROGRAM BENEFITS

The recipient must include in gross income the lesser of (*a*) one-half of Social Security benefits (including "Tier 1" Railroad Retirement benefits) received during the year, or (*b*) one-half of the amount by which the sum of Social Security benefits received during the year plus the "modified adjusted gross income" exceeds the "base amount."[120]

"Modified gross income" is (*a*) adjusted gross income before considering Social Security benefits, before the deduction for two-earner married couples, and before the exclusion for U.S. citizens living abroad, plus (*b*) tax-exempt interest.[121]

The "base amount" is generally $25,000, except that it is $32,000 for a married couple filing jointly and zero for a married person filing a separate return if the married person did not live apart from his or her spouse for the entire year.[122]

Example 72: Roger and Thelma are married and file a joint return. Roger is retired. Thelma is employed and earned $25,000 during the

---

[118] Sec. 1041.

[119] Sec. 71(f).

[120] Sec. 86(a).

[121] Sec. 86(b)(2).

[122] Sec. 86(c).

year. They received taxable interest of $3,200 and tax-exempt interest of $2,000. Roger received Social Security benefits of $4,800. The taxable portion of their Social Security benefits is $300, the lower of:

1. one-half of Social Security benefits (½ × $4,800) = $2,400, or
2. one-half of the excess of (1) the sum of modified adjusted gross income and one-half of Social Security benefits over (2) the base amount.

One-half of Social Security benefits	$ 2,400
Taxable interest	3,200
Tax-exempt interest	2,000
Salary	25,000
Total	$32,600
Less base amount	32,000
Excess	600
One-half of excess	$ 300

Public welfare benefits such as food stamps, amounts received under the Aid-to-Dependent-Children program and state "old age" pensions are excludable.

BACKGROUND

As previously pointed out, the former exclusion of Social Security benefits did not result from Congressional action, but from an administrative decision made in 1941 and reiterated in 1970. Many attempts were made in Congress to tax Social Security benefits in the same way as similar benefits under other annuity plans. This would, however, be difficult to implement because measurement of the expected benefits under Social Security is virtually impossible since Congress frequently changes benefit formulas, and benefits may change as amounts earned by the taxpayer from other sources change. However, the greatest impediment to taxing Social Security benefits has been the sheer political unpopularity of such a move.

In the late 1970s and early 1980s the solvency of the Social Security system was threatened by the spiraling increase in the excess of benefit payments made from the fund over the inflow of Social Security taxes coming into the fund. As part of a comprehensive program to "save the Social Security program" a special commission recommended that some Social Security benefits to higher-income recipients be included in gross income. Finally, Congress passed the Social Security Amendments act of 1983, discussed above, which levies a tax on a portion of Social Security benefits and "Tier 1" Railroad Retirement benefits received by taxpayers with relatively high incomes.

DISCHARGE OF INDEBTEDNESS

In general if a taxpayer transfers property with a value in excess of its basis to settle a debt, the transaction is treated as a sale of the property and a subsequent payment of the debt with the proceeds.[123] As a result, gain is recognized. However, there are many exceptions to this rule.

If a debt owed by an individual to a party who is related by blood or marriage is canceled, the forgiveness is generally treated as a gift to the debtor.

Example 73: James borrowed $10,000 from his mother three years ago. In the present year, James' mother canceled the debt owed to her by James. James has no income from the forgiveness.

If a shareholder forgives a debt owed to him or her by a corporation, the shareholder is generally deemed to have made a contribution to the corporation's capital.[124] No income results to the corporation as a result of a capital contribution.[125] On the other hand, if the corporation forgives a debt owed to it by a shareholder, the corporation is deemed to have made a distribution to the shareholder that will be taxed as a dividend if the corporation has adequate earnings and profits.

Example 74: Peak loaned $10,000 to a corporation in which he is a majority shareholder. During the current year, Peak canceled the debt. The corporation has no income from the debt. Both Peak and the corporation treat the $10,000 as a contribution to capital.

Section 108 and the related Regulations contain very complicated rules for the forgiveness of debt in other circumstances. In general, a taxpayer's gross income does not include the discharge of the taxpayer's debt if the forgiveness occurs in a Title 11 (bankruptcy) case, if the discharge occurs when the taxpayer is insolvent, or if the indebtedness discharged is "qualified business indebtedness."[126] In the case of insolvency, the exclusion is limited to the amount by which the taxpayer is insolvent after the forgiveness.[127]

Example 75: Cohen borrowed money from several creditors for personal uses. At a time when Cohen's assets were worth $120,000 and he had debts of $140,000, the creditors agreed on a compromise settlement in which they forgave $26,000 of the debt. Cohen must report as income $6,000 of the amount forgiven—the amount by which he is solvent after the forgiveness ($120,000 − $114,000).

---

[123] *Crane v. Comm.*, 67 S.Ct. 1047 (1947).

[124] Reg. Sec. 1.61-12(a).

[125] Sec. 118.

[126] Sec. 108(a)(1).

[127] Sec. 108(a)(3).

A more complex set of rules about how forgiven debt excluded from income affects the taxpayer's "tax attributes" comes into play when the forgiveness arises because the debtor is insolvent or because the debt is discharged in bankruptcy proceedings. As an alternative to reducing such favorable tax attributes as net operating losses, credit-carryovers, and capital loss carryovers, the debtor may elect to reduce the basis of depreciable property owned by the amount of the excluded income.[128] In the case of *forgiveness* of business indebtedness, the amount excluded from gross income may be applied to reduce the basis of the depreciable property of the taxpayer.[129]

FORM 982

RECOVERY OF AMOUNTS PREVIOUSLY DEDUCTED

In general if a taxpayer receives a payment or reimbursement or otherwise recovers all or part of an item for which a deduction was taken on a tax return in a prior year, the subsequent recovery produces taxable income. However, to the extent that the recovery represents an amount which did not result in a reduction of the taxpayer's tax in the prior year, the recovery does not result in includable income.[130] This is generally called the "***tax-benefit" rule***. Several provisions contain similar rules for specific items. For example, Reg. Sec. 1.213-1(g) requires this treatment for reimbursement of expenses paid in prior years. The Regulations under Section 111 extend this concept to "all other losses, expenditures, and accruals made the basis of deductions from gross income for prior taxable years."[131] Earlier in this chapter the application of this concept, when an amount received under health and hospitalization insurance represented recovery of an amount deducted in the preceding year, was illustrated.

TAX-BENEFIT RULE The concept that amounts received in one period representing a recovery of an amount deducted in a prior period are to be included in income to the extent that the prior deduction resulted in a decrease in taxable income in that year.

Example 76: Last year Snelson deducted property taxes of $900 on his residence as an itemized personal deduction. In the current year he received a rebate of $300 of that amount because of detection of an error by the taxing authority. An analysis of last year's tax return indicated that only $180 of the taxes deducted actually resulted in a reduction of taxable income (because of the interaction of the "zero-bracket" amount, discussed in Chapter 3). In the current year, Snelson must include in gross income $180 under the "tax benefit" rule.

RENTAL VALUE OF A PARSONAGE

Sec. 107 provides a valuable exclusion to "ministers of the gospel." Under that Section the rental value of a home furnished the minister as part of his or her compensation, or the rental allowance paid him or her (to the extent that it is used to rent or provide a home), will be excluded.

---

[128] Sec. 108(b) and Reg. Sec. 7a.1.

[129] Sec. 108(c).

[130] Sec. 111(a).

[131] Reg. Sec. 1.111-1(a)(1).

The Regulations define "minister of the gospel" rather broadly.[132] The Regulations also define rental value to include expenses "directly related to providing a home."[133] Thus, an allowance for utilities would be included in the exclusion. However, Reg. Sec. 1.107-1 provides specifically that expenses for food and servants are not considered to be related to "providing a home."

Example 77: Uhrich is pastor of the First Church. His remuneration for the year consisted of salary, $18,000; contribution to qualified pension plan, $2,400; rental allowance, $6,000; utility allowance, $2,400; and value of housecleaning services, $1,500. Uhrich may exclude the rental allowance, the utility allowance, and the pension contribution. All other items must be included in income.

IMPROVEMENTS BY LESSEE ON LESSOR'S PROPERTY

A lessor (property owner) has no includable income either at the time a tenant constructs improvements on the lessor's property or at the time the property, including improvements, reverts to the lessor on termination of the lease.[134] However, the improvements have a zero tax basis to the lessor. If the improvements are constructed *in lieu of rents*, however, the lessor must report as income the fair value of the improvements when the property reverts to the lessor.[135]

Example 78: Apex Corporation owned unimproved land. In 19X1 it leased the property to Hamilton Property Management Corporation under a 20-year lease at an annual rental rate of $10,000 per year. In 19X2 Hamilton constructed a building on the property at a cost of $400,000. On August 1 of the current year the lease expired and all property rights reverted to Apex. On that date the building had a fair market value of $100,000. Apex has no income either when the building is built or when the lease terminates. Apex Corporation's tax basis in the improvements is zero.

PAYMENTS TO MEMBERS OF ARMED FORCES AND VETERANS

Although regular pay for members of the armed forces is taxable, certain benefits and allowances to service personnel and their dependents may be excluded. For example, the value of quarters provided a serviceman (or the cash payment made to him in lieu of quarters) is tax-free, as is the basic allowance for quarters for the serviceman's dependents. Similarly, the value of subsistence (or cash payment in lieu of subsistence) is not taxable. Uniform and equipment allowances are likewise excluded.[136]

---

[132] Reg. Sec. 1.107-1(a).

[133] Reg. Sec. 1.107-1(b).

[134] Sec. 109.

[135] Reg. Sec. 1.109-1.

[136] Reg. Sec. 1.61-2(b).

Former servicemen also receive certain tax breaks. The mustering-out pay on termination of service is tax exempt.[137] Although pensions paid to military retirees who have retired because of length of service are taxable, pensions or other allowances based on personal injury or sickness resulting from active duty are exempt. Under Sec. 104, personnel entering service after September 24, 1975 may exclude disability pensions only if the benefits are based on a combat-related injury. Payments made for education and training allowances (the "GI Bill") are excluded, as are bonus payments received by veterans from state governments.

PLANNING WORKSHOP

Obviously the fact that some income items may be wholly or partially tax-free offers many opportunities for saving taxes, especially for individuals who own incorporated businesses and those who have funds to invest.

For example, taxpayers in higher income brackets, especially those approaching the 50% ceiling, may consider investing in tax-free state and local bonds. The rates on these securities have in recent years far exceeded half the rate on corporate bonds, and often on short-term investments. For example, a taxpayer in the 50% bracket, who is considering a $100,000 bond investment, may have the opportunity to invest in a corporate bond bearing interest at 13% or a high-grade municipal bond bearing interest at 10%. If the risks are equal, the investor would be well advised to acquire the municipal bonds, whose total after-tax yield will be $10,000 compared to an after-tax yield of $6,500 ($13,000 minus 50% of $13,000) on the corporate bonds.

There are also opportunities for deferring taxes on income. For example, an investment in an annuity contract earns income which is tax-free and is automatically reinvested. Only when proceeds are withdrawn is there a tax to be paid. Purchase of Series EE bonds, especially when coupled with the Uniform Gift to Minors Act, may provide tax-savings opportunities. The parents who are saving for their child's education may purchase bonds periodically for the child, then have the child elect to report the increase in value as income each year. Since the child would have little income, no tax need be paid on the income. When the bonds are redeemed, no income will be reported because it will have been reported in prior years.

For the taxpayer who owns and controls his or her own corporation, the opportunities for tax-favored fringe benefits abound. The establishment of group term-life insurance plans and the purchase of health and hospital insurance policies are only two of the po-

Continued

[137] Sec. 113.

PLANNING WORKSHOP

tential tax-free benefits. Similary, establishment of employee pension and profit-sharing plans provides means for deferring income for the owner. One consideration is the requirement that most such plans not discriminate in favor of highly-paid employees or owner-employees. Other obvious planning devices include provision for lump-sum payments to the owner-employee's beneficiaries in case of the employee's death, education-allowance plans, meals, lodging, qualified transportation plans, etc.

Planning, however, is not restricted to income from investments or business. Two people getting divorced have opportunities for minimizing their total tax burden by arranging the terms of their financial settlement properly.

KEY POINTS TO REMEMBER

1. All income is taxable unless otherwise provided.
2. Individuals may usually exclude up to $100 ($200 on a joint return) of dividends from domestic corporations.
3. Interest income, except for amounts received on obligations of states or other political subdivisions is taxable.
4. When annuities mature and periodic rents are received, a portion of each rent is excluded (based on the ratio of investment to expected return) if the annuitant paid for the contract. If an annuity was paid for entirely, or in part, by the employer of the taxpayer, the exclusion ratio applies *unless* the rents in the first 36 months exceed the taxpayer's investment. In that case, the taxpayer excludes all rents until the investment is recovered. All further rents are fully taxable.
5. Life insurance proceeds paid because of death of the decedent are tax-free unless the policy was obtained by the beneficiary for a consideration. In addition, a spouse of the decedent may exclude $1,000 of interest on proceeds to be paid in installments.
6. Up to a total of $5,000 paid by an employer to beneficiaries of a deceased employee, paid solely because of death, may be excluded.
7. Gifts received solely because of affection, etc., are excluded from gross income by the recipient.
8. Amounts received as a scholarship or fellowship that do not require the rendering of services are generally excluded if the individual is working toward a degree. For persons not working toward a degree such awards are exempt only if given by a tax-exempt organization and only to the extent of $300 per month for a maximum of 36 months.
9. Prizes and awards given for artistic, literary, or other achievement without active effort by the recipient are tax-free. All others are taxable.
10. Certain fringe benefits are tax-free. These include payments of premiums on health and hospital insurance policies, premiums on up to $50,000 face amount of nondiscriminatory group term-life insurance,

meals and lodging provided on the employer's premises for the benefit of the employer, nondiscriminatory group legal services, certain transportation plans, qualified incentive stock option plans, qualified employee discounts, "no additional cost" services, "working condition" fringes, "*de minimis*" fringes, and a few others.

11. U.S. citizens who are bona fide residents of a foreign country or reside there for at least 330 days out of a 12-month period may exclude the amounts (with limitations) earned abroad during the period.
12. Generally amounts received by the taxpayer as reimbursement for medical costs and amounts received for injury are tax-free. Amounts received as wage continuation from the employer, even under an insurance policy, are generally taxable.
13. A portion (depending on the taxpayer's income) of unemployment benefits may be taxable.
14. Alimony is taxable. Child-support payments are tax-free.
15. Welfare benefits are tax-free.
16. A portion of Social Security benefits are taxable if the taxpayer's adjusted gross income is above a specified amount.
17. Discharge of indebtedness is taxable except in the case of bankruptcy. Where creditors compromise and forgive part of the debt, the forgiveness is taxable only to the extent of the taxpayer's solvency.

SELF-STUDY QUESTIONS

1. Laura Lewis has been legally separated from her husband, Herman, since 1982. Their three-year-old son, Ronald, lived with Laura for the entire year 1983. Under the written separation agreement between Laura and Herman, Herman was obligated to pay Laura $300 per month for alimony and $200 per month for child support, or a total of $6,000 annually. However, Laura received a total of only $300 from Herman during 1983. Laura's other income in 1983 was from the following sources:

Salary	$20,000
Interest on insurance dividents left on deposit with a life insurance company	100
Interest on federal income tax refund	60

In addition, Laura's father, Albert, gave Laura a gift of 500 shares of Liba Corporation common stock in 1983. Albert's basis for the Liba stock was $4,000. At the date of this gift, the fair market value of the Liba stock was $3,000.

How much alimony was includable in Laura's 1983 taxable income?

a) $0

b) $300

c) $3,600

d) $6,000

(AICPA adapted)

2. Refer to Question 1. How much interest was includable in Laura's 1983 taxable income?

   a) $0

   b) $60

   c) $100

   d) $160

   (AICPA adapted)

3. Refer to Question 1. How much was includable in Laura's 1983 taxable income for the 500 shares of Liba stock?

   a) $0

   b) $3,000

   c) $3,500

   d) $4,000

   (AICPA adapted)

4. During the current year Alfred Allen sustained a serious injury in the course of his employment. As a result of this injury, Allen received the following amounts during the same year:

Workers' compensation	$2,400
Reimbursement from employer's accident and health plan for medical expenses paid by Allen	1,800
Damages for personal injuries	8,000

   How much of the above amounts should Allen include in his gross income for the current year?

   a) $12,200

   b) $8,000

   c) $1,800

   d) $0

   (AICPA adapted)

5. John Budd was 58 at the date of his death on July 1, 1983. Upon John's death, Emma received life insurance proceeds of $60,000 under a group policy paid for by John's employer. In addition, an employee death benefit of $7,500 was paid to Emma by John's employer. How much of the group life insurance proceeds should be excluded for 1983 taxable income?

   a) $0

   b) $5,000

   c) $50,000

   d) $60,000

   (AICPA adapted)

6. Refer to Question 5. How much of the employee death benefit should be excluded from 1983 taxable income?

   a) $0

   b) $4,500

   c) $5,000

   d) $7,500

   (AICPA adapted)

7. On November 1, 1958, Sam Lerner leased a building to Kenneth Tate for a period of fifteen years at a monthly rental of $400 with no option to renew. At that date the building had a remaining useful life of twenty years.

   Prior to taking possession of the premises, Tate made improvements at a cost of $20,000. These improvements had an estimated useful life of twenty years at the commencement of the lease period. The lease expired on October 31, 1973, at which point the improvements had a fair market value of $3,000. The amount Lerner should include in his 1973 gross income resulting from the leased buildings is

   a) $12,000

   b) $9,000

   c) $7,000

   d) $4,000

8. Mr. and Mrs. Carl Nido own 5,000 shares of common stock of Niagara Power Corporation, a qualified domestic public utility. Instead of receiving their dividends in cash on the Niagara stock, the Nidos have elected to receive common stock under Niagara's qualified dividend reinvestment plan. The Nidos earned $2,000 in dividends on their Niagara stock in 1982. What portion of these dividends could the Nidos exclude from gross dividend income (before other allowable dividend exclusions) on their 1982 joint return?

   a) $2,000

   b) $1,800

   c) $1,500

   d) $0

   (AICPA adapted)

9. Henry Adams, an unmarried taxpayer, received the following amounts during 1980:

Interest on savings accounts	$1,000
Interest on municipal bonds	500
Dividends on General Steel common stock	750
Dividends on life insurance policies	200

   Adams should report taxable income, after exclusions, if any, from dividends and interest for 1980 in the total amount of

a) $1,650
b) $1,750
c) $1,850
d) $2,150

(AICPA adapted)

10. Sam Mitchell, a calendar-year taxpayer, purchased an annuity contract for $3,600 that would pay him $120 a month beginning on January 1, 1976. His expected return under the contract is $10,800. How much of this annuity is excludable from gross income for the 1976 calendar year?

    a) $0
    b) $480
    c) $960
    d) $1,440

    (AICPA adapted)

11. Lila Lux retired on December 31, 1980, with a monthly pension of $300. Her contributions to the pension plan totaled $6,000, while her employer's contributions to the plan totaled $12,000. How much of the pension is taxable in 1981?

    a) $0
    b) $1,800
    c) $2,400
    d) $3,600

    (AICPA adapted)

12. Roger Burrows, age 19, is a full-time student at Marshall College and a candidate for a bachelor's degree. During 1980 he received the following payments:

State scholarship for ten months	$3,600
Loan from college financial aid office	1,500
Cash support from parents	3,000
Cash dividends on qualified investments	700
Cash prize awarded in a contest	500
	$9,300

    What is Burrows' adjusted gross income for 1980?

    a) $1,100
    b) $1,200
    c) $4,800
    d) $9,300

    (AICPA adapted)

13. On January 1, 1979, James Davis was awarded a post-doctorate fellowship grant of $4,500 by a tax-exempt educational organization. Davis is not a candidate for a degree and was awarded the grant to continue his research. The grant was awarded for the period March 1, 1979, through July 31, 1980.

    On March 1, 1979, Davis elected to receive the full amount of the grant. What amount should be included in his gross income for 1979?

    a) $0

    b) $1,500

    c) $3,000

    d) $4,500

    (AICPA adapted)

14. Mrs. Grant, a widow, elected to receive the proceeds of a $50,000 face value life insurance policy on the life of her deceased husband in ten annual installments of $6,800 each beginning in 1978. Of the $6,800 received in 1978, the amount subject to income tax is

    a) $800

    b) $1,800

    c) $5,000

    d) $6,800

    (AICPA adapted)

15. Edward Ryan, who is single, had adjusted gross income, other than unemployment compensation, of $25,000 in 1981. Ryan had no disability income exclusion, but received $3,000 in unemployment compensation benefits during the year. How much of the unemployment compensation is taxable in 1981?

    a) $0

    b) $1,500

    c) $2,500

    d) $3,000

    (AICPA adapted)

QUESTIONS

1. What is the reasoning underlying the "dividends-received" exclusion?
2. What types of dividends are subject to the exclusion?
3. What is the tax treatment given to most stock dividends?
4. Under what circumstances are shares of stock received under "dividend-reinvestment plans" excludable?

5. For what reason is interest on state and local bonds tax-exempt?
6. What is an annuity?
7. In what ways may proceeds received under an annuity contract be taxed if the taxpayer paid the entire cost of the annuity?
8. A taxpayer is covered by a "qualified annuity." Both the employer and employee contribute to the annuity's cost. If, on retirement, the taxpayer receives proceeds in the form of periodic "rents," how will the rents be taxed?
9. In general, how are proceeds from life insurance policies taxed if they are paid because of death of the insured? What is the major exception to this rule?
10. A client tells you that she has heard that amounts paid by an employer to the spouse of a deceased employee are tax-exempt. Explain the rules to her.
11. Under what circumstances, if any, is interest on life insurance proceeds left with the insurance company tax-free?
12. Are gifts and inheritances taxable to the recipients?
13. Under what circumstances are scholarships tax-exempt?
14. What is an "educational-assistance plan"? Under what conditions are benefits under such plans tax-free?
15. Are awards and prizes such as those given to winners of beauty pageants taxable? Explain.
16. Are amounts received related to sickness under a health insurance policy purchased by the taxpayer ever taxable? Explain.
17. What is a medical expense reimbursement plan? Explain the tax treatment given payments received under such plans.
18. Explain the tax treatment of benefits received under disability income payments.
19. Under what conditions are premiums on life insurance policies paid by an employer on an employee's life tax-free to the employee if the employee names the beneficiary?
20. Are meals provided to an employee by the employer taxable? Explain.
21. Under what conditions is the value of lodging provided by the employer taxable to the employee?
22. What is a cafeteria plan?
23. How should an employee treat "discounts" on purchases from the employer?
24. What are "working condition" fringe benefits?

25. Under what circumstances, and to what extent, can an individual exclude income earned abroad?

26. Explain the tax treatment of unemployment benefits.

27. How does the recipient treat amounts received as alimony?

28. How is forgiveness of debt treated for tax purposes?

29. Why are "*de minimis*" fringe benefits excluded from income?

30. How are interest-free loans treated by the borrower?

PROBLEMS

1. During the current year, Thomas, who is single, received the following items:

   a) Cash dividends on US Steel stock, $75.

   b) Interest on corporate bonds, $125.

   c) Interest on City of Denver bonds, $300.

   d) Dividends from a Canadian corporation, $90.

   e) "Dividends" on his savings account at the credit union, $220.

   f) "Dividends" on his life insurance policy, $300. (The insurer was a "mutual" company, and the dividend represented a return of part of the premiums paid.)

   How much gross income does Thomas recognize because of these items?

2. State the amount to be included in gross income in each of the following cases.

   a) Saul Maro and his wife Sue live in a community-property state where 50% of the income belongs to the husband and 50% to the wife. During the current year they received dividends of $800 on common stock. All the stock is held in the name of Sue, as owner. They plan to file a joint return.

   b) Fairchild had savings accounts at a bank and at a credit union. On December 31 of the current year, the two institutions credited Fairchild's account for a total of $385, but Fairchild did not withdraw the money during the year.

3. In January 1983 Raman purchased 1,000 shares of City Electric Company (a public utility) stock. In August 1985 the company declared a cash dividend of $3 per share. The dividend notice permitted shareholders to receive either cash or stock under a qualified reinvestment plan for any part or all of the dividend at the rate of $50 per share. Raman elected to receive 20 new shares of the company's stock and to apply the nonrecognition provisions. How much income must Raman report in 1985?

4. In January 19X1 Ms. Skekel purchased a Series EE U.S. Savings bond for $750. On December 31, 19X1, the bond's redemption value was $779.

   a) If Ms. Skekel is on the cash basis, how much income will she report for the year?

   b) If she is on the accrual basis, how much income will Ms. Skekel report for the year?

5. *a*) A taxpayer and his employer each contributed $25,000 to a retirement annuity, which pays the taxpayer $5,000 during each of his retirement years. The employer's contributions were *not* treated as taxable income of the employee at the time they were deposited in a tax-free employee trust fund. At retirement, the appropriate "multiple" to be used in computing expected return was 18.0. How much of his annual $5,000 retirement income must the employee report as taxable income?

   b) B. D. Evers retired from employment on December 31, 19X0. Beginning on January, 10, 19X1 Evers received monthly payments of $320 from his employer's qualified profit-sharing and pension plan. In recent years, the employer had made all contributions to the fund. Several years ago, however, the plan provided for optional contributions by the employee, and during that time Evers contributed $8,000 to the plan. At the date of retirement, Evers was 65 years old. Compute the amount Evers will include in income in 19X1.

   c) Chang worked for her employer for 30 years. During that time she contributed $5,400 to a qualified retirement annuity program. She retired in June of 19X1 and began drawing monthly retirement checks of $200 per month, starting in August 19X2. During 19X2 she received checks totaling $1,000; in 19X3 she received $2,400; in 19X4 she received $2,400; and in 19X5 she received $2,400. How will Chang treat these receipts on her tax return each year?

   d) Roger invested $20,000 in an annuity. Beginning in 19X1 and continuing through 19Y0, a total of 10 years, he is to be paid $3,000 each year. How much, if any, of the $3,000 received in 19X1 must be included in gross income?

6. In each of the following independent cases, indicate the amount that the taxpayer should report as "gross income" for the year.

   a) Regina's husband died during the current year, leaving a life insurance policy with a face value of $50,000 payable to Regina. She received the $50,000 from the insurance company, but after consultation with friends she returned the money to the insurance company and they agreed to pay her $13,000 per year for five years. During the year she received one of the $13,000 checks.

   b) Assume the same facts as in part (*a*), except that the $50,000 was not withdrawn from the insurance company at time of death of the insured, but was left with the company under an option provided in the policy, with five installments of $13,000 each to be paid her. During the year she received her first installment of $13,000.

c) Faro's mother died during the current year, leaving an insurance policy with face value of $50,000 payable to Faro. Under an option provided in the policy, he left the proceeds with the insurance company to be paid in five equal annual installments of $13,000 each. During the current year he received the first installment of $13,000.

7. In each of the following independent cases, indicate the amount that the taxpayer should report as "gross income" for the year.

   a) McAdams surrendered his life insurance policy and received a lump sum of $8,000. He paid total premiums of $7,200 on the policy in previous years.

   b) Mr. Nelson lent $5,000 to his neighbor, Jones. Jones ran into financial difficulty, so he agreed to assign a life insurance policy to Nelson naming Nelson beneficiary. Face amount of the policy was $7,000. After receiving the policy, Nelson paid premiums of $420. At that point, Jones died and Nelson received a check for $7,000 from the insurance company.

   c) In 19X3 Raymond transferred a life insurance policy on his life, face value $100,000, cash value $22,000, to a partnership in which he was a partner. The partnership paid him $22,000 for the policy and paid premiums of $4,000 on the policy before Raymond died during the current year. The partnership (the taxpayer) received the face amount of $100,000.

8. In each of the following independent cases, indicate the amount that the taxpayer should report as "gross income" for the year.

   a) Kline, who had been holding two jobs, died during the current year. Because of Kline's death, the first employer paid Mrs. Kline $8,000 and the second employer paid her $6,000.

   b) Mrs. Easley died during the current year. Her employer paid Mr. Easley $8,000 and each of their two children $3,500. Payments were made solely on account of death. (Both Mr. Easley and the children are taxpayers.)

   c) Toro died during the current year. His wife was paid $10,000 under a group term-life insurance policy that had been paid for by Toro's employer. In addition, the employer paid Toro's wife $4,000 on account of Toro's death.

9. In each of the following independent cases, indicate how much, if any, of the amounts involved must be reported as income by the recipient.

   a) Mal inherited several bonds of the State of Illinois upon the death of her uncle during the current year. The bonds had a fair value of $60,000 at date of the uncle's death. After receiving the bonds, Mal was paid an additional $1,800, representing interest earned on the bonds after the uncle's death.

b) Parker inherited land from a deceased aunt. The land had a fair market value of $60,000 when inherited.

10. State the amount to be included in gross income in each of the following cases.

a) Candy, a university student working on her B.B.A. degree, received a scholarship of $2,000 from the university. The scholarship was based on grades, and she had no service to render.

b) Assume the same facts as in part (a), except that the scholarship was awarded by an industrial firm.

c) Assume the same facts as in part (a), except that Candy is working on a Ph.D. degree.

d) Vanecek received his Ph.D. degree in 19X1. Beginning in September 19X1, and continuing to December 19X4, he received a postdoctoral fellowship from a tax-free foundation to continue study and research. The fellowship paid him $1,000 per month. How much of this, if anything, must be included in 19X1, 19X2, 19X3, and 19X4, assuming he received $4,000 in 19X1, $12,000 in 19X2, $12,000 in 19X3, and $12,000 in 19X4?

e) Nancy is working toward a Ph.D. in chemistry. She receives a $5,000 scholarship from the school. In order to get the scholarship she is required to work 10 hours each week in the laboratory. This laboratory work is required of all students working toward the Ph.D. in chemistry at that university.

f) A graduate student at State University received a $1,000 fellowship grant, $350 for grading accounting papers, and $2,000 from her father. She used the $3,350 to finance her year at school.

11. Northern Corporation adopted a plan under which the corporation would pay the costs of tuition, books, and supplies for any officer of the corporation or for any operating department head who enrolled in not more than two courses at an accredited university. Pat Hicks, the corporation's controller, enrolled in a tax course. The corporation reimbursed Hicks $270 for tuition, $22 for books, and $6 for other consumable supplies. What part, if any, of the reimbursement is taxable to Hicks?

12. In each of the following independent cases, determine the amount to be included in gross income.

a) Professor Mason was selected by the business students at State University as their outstanding teacher and was given a cash award of $1,000 by the student association.

b) Sue was chosen "Miss City." She won both the bathing suit contest and the talent contest. Many speculate that she will ultimately become Miss America. As an award for being chosen Miss City she was given cash and merchandise totaling $2,000.

c) Mohat, an avid baseball fan, attended every home game of the city team. He was surprised one evening when his ticket stub contained the "lucky number" and he won an automobile with a fair value of $10,000 in the ticket drawing.

d) Professor Buzman was awarded a Pulitzer Prize of $50,000 for writing a book on the history of the American antelope.

13. In each of the following independent cases, determine the amount to be included in gross income.

a) During all 12 months of the year, taxpayer, a city policeman, was provided a free apartment in an apartment complex in exchange for "keeping an eye on the place" when he was off duty. He also was "on call" for emergencies. The apartment had a rental value of $500 per month.

b) Robinson, a CPA employed by a national accounting firm, regularly audits the accounts of the local professional baseball team in the National League. The client gave the taxpayer a season pass to all home games. The pass had a value of $500 if used for all home games. Robinson attended approximately 50% of the games.

c) Anderson, a college professor, was invited to deliver a one-hour lecture as part of a "great tax issues" series at another university. Anderson expected an honorarium of $300 at the close of his presentation, but was presented a check for $750.

14. In each of the following independent cases, determine the amount to be included in gross income.

a) Lum was involved in an accident and as a result received a $5,000 personal damage judgment plus $800 reimbursement for medical costs incurred during the year of the accident.

b) Abner was injured on the job. As a result of his injury, he was paid $400 under workmen's compensation insurance and also received $800 under health and accident insurance policies to reimburse him for medical costs. Additionally, he received $500 under a disability income policy that he purchased and paid for himself.

c) Sid and his wife were injured in an automobile accident during the year. Because of the accident, Sid and his wife were paid $1,300 to reimburse them for medical costs and $8,900 for personal injury and suffering.

d) Mr. Aldo's car was struck in the rear by a speeder in September of last year. Mr. Aldo suffered from whiplash and had severe pains in the neck and upper back. He filed a claim for damages against the speeder and his insurance company. Aldo went to the doctor with the problem but was never hospitalized because the doctor could not diagnose the ailment. To avoid a costly court fight, the speeder's insurance company settled with Aldo in February of the current year for $1,000 and agreed to pay the medical costs incurred by Aldo.

15. In each of the following independent cases, determine the amount to be included in gross income.
    a) Mr. Carr has two health and accident policies on which he pays all the premiums. During 19X2, when he was hospitalized for hepatitis, his hospital and doctor bills amounted to $2,500. Carr paid these bills and, before the end of 19X2, collected $1,300 on one policy and $1,800 on the other.
    b) In 19X5 Smith has a job where the employer pays premiums for a health and accident policy for each employee. During the year the employer paid $1,250 on behalf of Smith and $800 on behalf of Smith's child.

16. In each of the following independent cases, determine the amount to be included in gross income.
    a) Tony's employer carries a substantial insurance program for his employees. During the current tax year the employer paid premiums of $1,960 on health and hospital insurance policies for Tony. In addition, the employer paid life insurance premiums of $400 under a group term insurance program. This life insurance provides for a death benefit of $40,000 payable to Mrs. Tony in the event of Tony's death.
    b) Maxley's employer purchased an ordinary whole-life insurance policy for each employee. During the current year the employer paid premiums of $400 on Maxley's policy.

17. In each of the following independent cases, determine the amount to be included in gross income.
    a) Darrell works as an airline steward for Great Fly Airlines. One of his fringe benefits is the right to fly free of charge on the airline. On his days off and during vacation, Darrell takes advantage of this right. He estimates that during 19X1 the flights taken on short vacations would have cost him $1,200 if he had been required to pay for them.
    b) Sonja is a real estate salesperson. During the year she purchased a residential lot from her employer for $4,500. Similar lots were sold to purchasers at an advertised price of $5,500.
    c) A college student worked for Grady Corporation during the summer months. In return for her services, the student received $500 cash and 50 shares of Grady stock. The 50 shares had a par value of $500 and a fair market value of $2,000. Their book value was $1,500.

18. In each of the following independent cases, determine the amount to be included in gross income.
    a) Barry is a university student. He works in the university cafeteria

and receives as payment three meals each day. Total value of the meals consumed during the current year was $1,450.

b) Steve manages an apartment house throughout the year. He is required by his employer to live in one of the apartments, which is given to Steve rent free. Similar apartments were rented to tenants for $6,000 per year. Steve's salary as manager is $12,000 per year.

c) Alan manages an apartment house throughout the year. He is making a cash salary of $4,000 for the year. In addition, his employer offered to give him another $200 per month in cash or to let him live rent free in an apartment. Choosing the latter, Alan received an apartment that has a fair rental value of $4,000 per year.

d) Debra is a waitress in a local cafe. Her income for the year consists of wages of $6,500 and tips of $3,200. In addition, she eats her noon meal while on duty at the cafe, free of charge. She estimates that the value of meals consumed during the year was $650.

e) Watchman lived rent free during the year in a house owned by his employer on the employer's premises. The rental value of the house was $1,800 for the year. Although Watchman lived in the house for the convenience of the employer, he was not required to live there and could have lived somewhere else.

19. *a*) In the current year, Anthony, single, was employed during the first nine months of the year, earning $20,600. He lost his job in early October, and then drew unemployment benefits under the state unemployment compensation plan during the remainder of the year. The unemployment benefits totaled $800. What amount, if any, of the unemployment compensation benefits will be included in gross income?

b) Assume the same facts as in part (a), except that Anthony's salary during the first nine months of the year had been $19,600. What amount, if any, of the unemployment benefits will be included in gross income?

c) Michael was ill during most of the current year. He received $500 per month for nine months under a wage-continuation insurance policy. Michael paid all premiums on the policy. What part of the $4,500 is excludable?

20. *a*) Wayne and Deirdre Willis were divorced during the current year. The divorce decree provided that Wayne should pay Deirdre a lump sum of $42,000, which he paid this year. What part, if any, of this is taxable to Deirdre?

b) Thomas and Sheila Patterson were divorced in 1984. The divorce decree provided that Thomas should pay alimony of $500 per month for 15 years and also should pay child support to her of $300 per month. During the current year Thomas made payments of $3,000 for alimony and $1,800 for child support. How much, if any, of this is taxable to Sheila? How much, if any, is taxable to the children covered by the child-support agreement?

c) Karen and Wesley Boyd were divorced during the current year. In the divorce decree, Wesley was directed to pay Karen a total of $19,000, with $8,000 to be paid in the year of the divorce and $1,000 per year to be paid in each of the succeeding 11 years. What part of the $8,000 received in the year of the divorce is taxable?

d) Janet and Jacob were divorced in the current year. Under the terms of the settlement Jacob is to pay Janet alimony of $500 per month until her remarriage or death ($4,500 paid this year) and $300 per month as child support for the two children ($2,700 paid during this year). In addition, Janet received title to their home, which had a fair market value of $40,000. Jacob is to make mortgage payments on the home ($2,400 this year) and to pay all utilities ($920 during the current year). How much must Janet include in her income during the current year on account of the divorce settlement?

21. What amount must be included in gross income in each of the following independent cases?

a) Johnny is single and employed by King Brick Company. Under a written nondiscriminatory plan, the employer provides a nursery to care for employees' children under five years of age. Johnny's 3-year-old daughter was kept in the nursery during 1982. Johnny's salary was $21,000 for the year. The value of the dependent's care provided the daughter was $3,600.

b) Several years ago Alex leased a piece of land that he owned to a local businessman. During the current year, the lease expired and the land use reverted to Alex. He discovered that the tenant had constructed a building on the property, and on the date the lease expired the building had a fair market value of $22,000.

22. Glen owned a small plot of land in Midcity. In 1960 he leased the land to ABC Company. ABC Company built a small building on the property. When the lease expired in the current year, the building became the property of Glen. At that time the building had a fair market value of $6,000. When the building was built in 1960 it had cost ABC $24,000 to construct. This amount was also considered to be the building's fair market value at that time.

a) How much income did Glen have in 1960 as a result of the building's being constructed?

b) How much income did he have in the current year when the lease expired?

23. Moore was a candidate for mayor during the current year. She received contributions from friends totaling $13,200. Her expenses in the campaign were $11,800. The additional $1,400 was retained by

Moore for use in subsequent campaigns. How much, if any, income must Moore include in gross income?

24. Robert had been in business for many years. Because of his illness in the current year, Robert's corporation suffered severe losses. As a result, on September 1 the corporation's assets totaled only $180,000 while its liabilities were $231,000. Because Robert had been a valuable customer for many years, and because he had recovered from his illness and the outlook for future profits was good if Robert could solve the immediate insolvency, the creditors agreed to reduce the corporation's debt. Indicate the amount of taxable income that would result to Robert's corporation under each of the following circumstances:

    a) The debts were reduced to $200,000.
    b) The debts were reduced to $171,000.

25. Helen Preachmore retired as minister of the Crosstown Church on December 31, 19X1. For 19X1 her remuneration was:

Salary	$30,000
Housing allowance	7,200
Home utilities allowance	4,800
Auto allowance	3,600

    On December 31 the congregation of the church held a special meeting at which Preachmore received the following letter. "To show our appreciation for your devotion to this church, the trustees and congregation have voted to present you a gift, the sum of $1,000 per month for as long as you may live, beginning January 15, 19X2." At that time her life expectancy was 15 years.

    a) What part of the $45,600 paid in 19X1 is taxable to Preachmore?
    b) What is the proper tax treatment of the $1,000 per month beginning January 19X2?

26. Mitchum Corporation made an interest-free loan of $6,000 to an employee on February 1 of the current year. The loan was repaid on August 1—six months later. Based on the appropriate "federal rate," the loan had a present value of $5,700 at the date the loan was made. This is the only debt owed to Mitchum during the year. Does Mitchum have gross income to report as a result of the interest-free loan? If so, how much?

27. Susan Feldhouser has lived in the U.S. throughout her life. In February 1984 Susan accepted her employer's offer to transfer to London, England for a period of three years. Susan left New York on February 29 and arrived in London at noon on March 1. She continued to live there through 1984 and all of 1985. Her salary in 1984 was $6,500 per month. On January 1, 1985, her salary was increased to $7,500 per month.

    What amount may Susan exclude in 1984? in 1985?

TAX PLANNING PROBLEMS

1. Abel Smithers died recently, leaving an insurance policy of $50,000 payable to his wife. Ms. Smithers expects to have taxable income from real estate and stock investments of approximately $61,000 (ignoring any income that she may earn on the life insurance proceeds) for the next three years so that she is expected to be in a marginal tax rate bracket of 45%. Ms. Smithers is considering the alternatives of (1) withdrawing the policy proceeds and investing them in high-grade five-year corporate notes yielding interest at 13%, and (2) leaving all or part of the proceeds in the insurance company to be paid in installments over a five-year period. The effective interest rate paid by the insurance company is 11%.

   What is your advice to Ms. Smithers?

2. US Bank was formed 15 years ago. It has been profitable, but has never paid a cash dividend. Instead, each year the bank has issued a stock dividend ranging from 12% to 15% and market price of the stock per share has increased at an average of 2% each year.

   One of the shareholders is your tax client. She has expressed to you her disappointment that the bank has not paid cash dividends and informs you that she plans to sell all her shares. She plans to invest in interest-bearing securities paying interest of 12%. The client's marginal tax rate is 50%.

   Considering only the income tax factors, what advice would you give your client?

3. Thulman Corporation has twelve shareholders, all of whom are officers or employees of the corporation. In addition, there are thirteen other employees. The corporation's board of directors is considering various fringe benefits to be made available to all employees. Among those being discussed are:

   a) A cash bonus equal to 20% of the corporation's pre-tax profits to be allocated on the basis of earnings. (Estimated cost: $2,000 per year per employee.)

   b) A vacation trip to Hawaii for each employee and the employee's spouse or a friend. (Estimated cost: $2,000 per employee per year.)

   c) Term life insurance in a face amount equal to twice the employee's annual salary limited to $100,000 face value. (Estimated average cost: $600 per employee per year.)

   d) A discount of 33⅓% on all merchandise purchased by the employee from the company. (Estimated cost: $300 per employee per year.)

   e) A liberal health and hospitalization insurance policy providing almost complete medical care coverage of the employee and the employee's dependents. (Estimated average cost: $2,000 per employee per year.)

f) An additional one-week vacation per year for each employee. (Estimated average cost: $700 per employee per year.)

g) Payment of employee parking at nearby parking lot. (Estimated cost: $600 per employee per year.)

The corporation's controller has asked you to analyze the proposals and to suggest which proposals would be of the greatest tax benefit *to the employees*. What is your response?

RESEARCH PROBLEMS

1. Daphne, an accounting major at your college, won the "Miss State" contest in May of the current year. Her award included a four-year tuition scholarship to your college beginning in the current fall semester. The tuition this semester is $1,000. The present value of future tuition payments at the date of the award, assuming no change is made in rates, is $6,500.

   How much income, if any, should Daphne report this year?

2. On January 2 of the current year Dumont retired from his job as managing partner of an accounting firm. As part of his termination agreement, he is to be paid $200,000 per year for five years, with the first payment to be made this year. On January 2 of the current year, he took a three-year appointment as advisor to a company having financial problems. Since Dumont does not need the cash from employment, he has worked out an agreement with the company to pay him $25,000 per year during the three-year period and then $100,000 per year for five years.

   How will Dumont treat these items on the current year's tax return?

3. During the current year Professor Zamonski and his wife organized a tour group to visit China. Because they were able to get 30 participants for the group, the Zamonskis received their tours free of charge. Each other person paid $1,650 for the tour. The cost to the operator of the tour was approximately $1,200 per person.

   What amount of income, if any, should the Zamonskis report this year because of the tour?

4. Taliaferro completed college and was married in May of last year. He and his bride wished to purchase a new home, but did not have the funds for the down payment. On April 1 of the current year Taliaferro's father made an interest-free loan of $30,000 to Taliaferro, to be used as the down payment. Under the agreement (in writing) Taliaferro agreed to begin repayment five years from the date of the loan and is to repay his father $5,000 per year for six years.

   Discuss the tax implications, if any, of this loan.

Chapter Objectives

1. Identify the three permissible accounting periods and understand how annualization of income is performed when accounting periods are changed.
2. Explain the differences between the cash and accrual methods for tax purposes, with special emphasis on tax concepts overriding the cash or accrual distinctions.
3. Recognize the special income deferral opportunities for deposits for merchandise inventory and long-term construction contracts.
4. Differentiate between the cumulative adjustment procedures required by changes of accounting methods (a) initiated by a taxpayer and (b) initiated by the IRS.
5. Explain the determination of inventory value with cost and lower-of-cost or -market procedures.
6. Explain the general purpose of dollar value LIFO inventory methods and the advantages of inventory pooling procedures.
7. Describe the tax requirements for writing down the value of obsolete or excess inventories, with particular emphasis on the Thor Power Tool Case.
8. Explain the gross profit calculation for installment reporting procedures of both dealers and nondealers.

6 Business Income

The choice of accounting periods and accounting methods has a significant effect on the reported tax liability of all business taxpayers. A judicious choice of accounting periods may provide an opportunity to postpone income recognition temporarily and/or reduce the costs of meeting several tax reporting requirements. More importantly, the choice of accounting method may provide more long-run opportunities to postpone income recognition and/or mitigate the incidence of the income tax liability.

The first part of this chapter contains a discussion of the alternative accounting periods available to a taxpayer. This is followed by a discussion of permissible accounting methods, with special emphasis on changes of accounting method and the choice of inventory method. Finally, one of the more important exceptions to the annual reporting requirement for business income, the installment sales method, is discussed. This section also includes a discussion of installment sales of noninventory properties, since the reporting procedures for these sales are similar to those required for inventories.

ACCOUNTING PERIODS

PERMISSIBLE ACCOUNTING PERIODS

Sec. 441 states that "Taxable income shall be computed on the basis of the taxpayer's taxable year." This annual reporting requirement is a firmly established principle of tax law. The term "taxable year" is defined in Sec. 441(b) to include a calendar or fiscal year, as well as periods of less than 12 months, when permissible by law. If a taxpayer fails to keep books and records, a calendar year must be used as the taxable year. A fiscal year must end on the last day of a month other than December. However, realizing that this requirement created an undue hardship for some industries (such as retail sales) that preferred to end their taxable years on the same day of the week each year, Congress in 1954 enacted Sec. 441(f) to include a "***52–53 week*" *taxable year*** within the definition of a fiscal year. This is simply a tax year which ends on the same day of the week falling closest to the end of the calendar month. Thus, in some years the taxpayer's reporting period will encompass 52 weeks, and in other years (approximately every sixth year) the reporting period will cover 53 weeks.

52–53 WEEK TAXABLE YEAR A tax year that ends on the same day of the week each year, with the final week of the tax year ending on that day of the week closest to December 31.

Example 1: A taxpayer begins business on May 15, 19X1 and adopts a taxable year ending May 15 of each year. This does not qualify as a fiscal year, since the period does not end on the last day of a month other than December. The year also does not qualify as a 52–53 week year. Therefore, the taxpayer will be required to use a calendar year, with a short taxable year for 19X1.

CHANGES OF ACCOUNTING PERIODS

The election of a taxable year is determined by a timely filing of the initial tax return. Thus, an individual electing a calendar year must file the first return by April 15 of the second taxable year. A reporting period can never be longer than a year. It is important, therefore, for corporate taxpayers to determine exactly when the company's first year begins (under state law) so that a timely return can be filed.

The initial accounting period selected must be followed in all subsequent years unless prior approval is obtained from the IRS. Generally the IRS will not grant permission unless a valid business reason exists for the requested change. For example, a new retail business organizing in midyear may choose to extend the initial year of doing business beyond the end of the first calendar year so that more expenses will be available to offset the year-end peak seasonal sales. This may also save time and money by taking year-end inventories during a slack period when quantities are low. This conformity of the natural tax year with the business tax year is accepted by the IRS as a valid business reason for changing tax years.[1]

---

[1]Rev. Proc. 74-33, 1974-2 C.B. 489.

A change of accounting periods always creates an interim tax year of less than 12 months. For example, a calendar-year taxpayer who decides to switch to a fiscal year ending March 31 after 19X1 must file a short-period return for January 1 through March 31, 19X2. Subsequent returns will be for fiscal years ending March 31.

SHORT-PERIOD RETURN PROCEDURES

The tax liability for a short period caused by a change in accounting period must be computed with an ***annualization*** procedure specified in Sec. 443.[2] Basically this procedure calculates an annual tax based on the assumption that the same rate of short-period income and expenses is incurred throughout a 12-month period. This annual tax is then apportioned to the short period, based on the fraction of a year covered by the short period. The annualization procedure is designed to eliminate any incentive for taxpayers to change accounting periods in order to split income over two periods to take advantage of the lower marginal tax rates (i.e., start at "$0 income" twice within a 12-month period).

ANNUALIZATION A procedure for computing the tax liability of a short tax period, which extrapolates the short-period income for a 12-month period, calculates a tax liability, and allocates a portion of the annual tax to the short period.

Sec. 443 specifies several requirements to be followed in computing the short-period income to be annualized. First, a taxpayer must apportion the personal-exemption deductions based on the ratio of the number of months in the short period to 12 months. Secondly, a taxpayer *must* itemize deductions for the short period. This is accomplished by deducting total itemized deductions and then adding back the zero-bracket amount *after* the total income has been annualized. This annualization is accomplished by multiplying the short-period income by a fraction, the numerator being 12 and the denominator being the number of months in the short period.

Example 2: G (single, age 40), a calendar-year taxpayer, has received permission to switch to a fiscal year ending March 31. This creates a need to file a short-period return for the period 1/1/X2 to 3/31/X2. For the three months, G had $6,820 of gross income and $1,340 of itemized deductions. G's annualized taxable income is determined as follows:

Gross income	$ 6,820
Less: Prorated exemption (3/12 × $1,040)	(260)
Total itemized deductions	(1,340)
Short-period modified income	$ 5,220
Annualization factor	× 12/3
Subtotal	$20,880
Add zero-bracket amount	2,390
Annualized taxable income	$23,270

[2] Such procedures are not necessary for short-period returns caused by other reasons (e.g., a taxpayer's first or last tax return). For example, a corporation may choose to end its first taxable year before the end of 12 months in order to keep its income in the lower tax brackets. One possibility would be to end the

Note in Example 2 that the zero-bracket amount must be added back because the total of itemized deductions (on an annualized basis) has been subtracted in determining the $20,880 subtotal. If a taxpayer's annualized itemized deductions are less than the zero-bracket amount, the required add-back will compensate for the automatic deduction built into the tax rate schedules and, in effect, force the taxpayer to itemize.

The final step in the annualization procedure is to calculate the tax on the annualized income and apportion this tax to the short period based on the ratio of short-period months to 12 months. The resulting tax is the tentative tax liability for the short period. In certain instances this annualization procedure will unfairly penalize a taxpayer. In such cases a taxpayer may be able to elect a special relief provision.

Example 3: Continuing with the facts in Example 2, the tax due on the annualized taxable income of $23,270 would be $3,974 (1985 rates). The tax for the short period is presumed to be 3/12 of $4,042, or $994. Note that the marginal tax rate on the $23,270 annualized income was 26%. If the taxpayer were not required to annualize, the marginal tax rate on $5,780 of taxable income ($6,820 − $1,040 exemption) would be only 14%.

BACKGROUND

The short-period annualization procedure may penalize a taxpayer if the short-period income is higher (or expenses lower) than at other times during the taxable year. For example, the short period may occur during the peak sales period of a seasonal business. Reg. Sec. 1.443-1(b)(2) provides an alternative calculation of short-period tax liability, and if the *larger* of two special calculations results in a smaller tax liability, then a credit (or claim for refund) may be obtained for the difference. (The alternative calculations can be made only after 12 months have elapsed from the beginning of the short period.)

The alternative calculations can be demonstrated by continuing the facts of Examples 2 and 3. Assume that G's actual gross income and itemized deductions for the 12 months ended 12/31/X2 were $21,850 and $5,440 respectively. The two alternative calculations are:

1. Calculate a tax on the actual income for the 12-month period which begins with the short period and prorate this tax to the short period based on the ratio of short-period taxable income to the 12-month taxable income:

Continued

---

year at $50,000 of taxable income, when tax rates of only 15% (on the first $25,000) and 18% (on the second $25,000) would apply. The rates applying to corporate taxable income in excess of $50,000 are 30% (on the third $25,000), 40% (on the fourth $25,000) and 46% (on any taxable income exceeding $100,000).

BACKGROUND

Gross income (12 months)	$21,850
Less: Personal exemption	(1,040)
Excess itemized deductions (5,440 − 2,390)	(3,050)
12-Month taxable income	$17,760
Tax on 12-month income (1985 rates)	2,577
Tax on short period (5,220/15,370* × 2,577)	891

2. Calculate a tax on the sum of short-period taxable income and the zero-bracket amount (which, in effect, requires the taxpayer to itemize):

Short-period taxable income Example 2	$5,220
Add zero-bracket amount	2,390
Taxable income	$7,610
Tax liability (Schedule X)	$ 684

Since the larger of these two amounts ($875) is less than the original short-period tax of $994 paid per Example 3, G may now file a claim for credit or refund with the IRS for the $119 difference. Note that the $875 liability under method (1) demonstrates that the taxpayer did not earn income at the same rate for the actual 12-month period. Furthermore, the method (2) calculation is required so that the taxpayer will not pay *less* tax than would have been due without annualization (e.g., if the other nine months resulted in a net loss).

*Since the short-period income of $5,220 did not reflect the zero-bracket amount, the 12-month income figure must also be based on a subtraction of total itemized deductions, or $2,390 less income than the actual 12-month figure.

ACCOUNTING METHODS FOR BUSINESS INCOME

Sec. 446(a) requires taxable income to be computed "under the method of accounting on the basis of which the taxpayer regularly computes his income in keeping his books." This method must be used consistently and clearly reflect income; otherwise, the Commissioner has the authority—Sec. 446(b)—to impose an accounting method which does reflect income clearly.

For a salaried employee, the tax return and supporting documentation will usually be sufficient as "accounting records." A more demanding standard is established for business taxpayers. Reg. Sec. 1.446-1(a)(4) requires that such records include at a minimum detailed inventory information (if applicable), proper classification of expenditures as capital or expense, and any information necessary to reconcile differences between book and taxable income.

The expression "method of accounting" includes an overall method (such as cash or accrual), a hybrid (combination) method, and a method applied to a specific item, such as inventory. Sec. 446(c) specifically allows the use of the cash receipts and disbursements method, the accrual method, and any specific method permitted elsewhere in the Code; e.g., installment method, long-term construction, etc. Combinations of acceptable methods are also permitted. Additionally, a taxpayer having more than one trade or business may adopt different methods, as long as separate records are maintained for each activity.

An introduction to the basic accounting methods was given in Chapter 4. The following discussion highlights the special accounting method considerations applicable to business taxpayers.

PERMISSIBLE ACCOUNTING METHODS

CASH METHOD The cash receipts and disbursements method is the simplest and most widely used method of accounting. Income is taxed in the year in which it is actually or constructively received, regardless of when it is earned. However, a mere right to receive income is not taxable until actual or constructive receipt occurs.

> **Example 4:** A sells services on account for $800. The accounts receivable, though representing a right to receive income, is not an actual or constructive receipt of income. However, if the customer gives A a negotiable note for the balance, the fair market value of the note will be taxable to A immediately. The negotiable feature is the equivalent of constructive receipt of the income by A.

Expenses are generally deductible under the cash method when they are paid. There are, however, two significant exceptions to this general rule. First, Reg. Sec. 1.461-1(a)(1) requires the deferment of a portion of any expenditure creating an asset having a useful life which extends "substantially beyond" the end of the tax year. However, if the useful life of the expenditure overlaps only into the next tax year, a taxpayer may deduct the item in the year paid if such a practice is used consistently and does not result in a material distortion of income.[3]

> **Example 5:** B, a cash-basis calendar-year taxpayer, prepays $7,200 for three years of insurance coverage for her business on October 1, 19X2. B's deduction on her 19X2 tax return would be $600 ($\frac{3}{36} \times$ $7,200); the remaining $6,600 would be deferred until actually used. However, if B prepaid only six months coverage, she could deduct the entire payment, if such a practice is followed consistently in the future.

[3] Reg. Sec. 1.461-1(a)(3)(i).

A second limitation on the use of the cash method applies when inventories are a significant component of income. In this case a taxpayer is required to use the accrual method for gross profit computations (e.g., sales and purchases).[4] This can be done by adjusting cash sales and purchases by the annual changes in the receivable and payable balances, respectively. Furthermore, the cost of goods sold computation must disclose the change in the beginning and ending value of the inventory, as reflected by year-end physical counts.

Example 6: C, a cash-basis taxpayer, collected $105,000 from 19X2 cash sales and collections on account and paid $64,000 for cash purchases and payments on account. C's ledger records disclose the following information.

	1-1-X2 BALANCE	12-31-X2 BALANCE
Accounts receivable	$ 3,200	$3,800
Accounts payable	$ 4,000	$2,800
Inventory (per count)	$10,300	$9,600

Gross profit on the accrual basis would be $42,100 computed as follows:

Sales ($105,000 + $3,800 − $3,200)		$105,600
Cost of goods sold:		
Beginning inventory	$10,300	
Purchases ($64,000 + $2,800 − $4,000)	62,800	
Available for sale	73,100	
Ending inventory	(9,600)	
Cost of goods sold		(63,500)
Gross profit		$ 42,100

Note that the cash sales are adjusted to reflect the sales on account not received in cash (the $600 receivables increase), and the cash purchases are adjusted to reflect payments made on prior year purchases (the $1,200 payables decrease).

ACCRUAL METHOD Income is recognized under the accrual method when all events which determine a contractual right to receive the income have occurred. Generally the amount of such income must be determinable with reasonable accuracy.[5] Significant contingencies or lack of a reasonable estimate may justify a deferral of recognition. For example, an income item subject to litigation may be deferred until a settlement or judgment is made. Furthermore, if property is sold or exchanged and the selling price is based on a contingency, such as a share of future profits,

[4] Reg. Sec. 1.461-1(c)(2)(i).
[5] Reg. Sec. 1.446-1(c)(1)(ii).

the seller may use a cost recovery approach of recognizing income, since the value of these payments cannot be reasonably estimated at the time of sale. Such an open transaction approach treats payments as nontaxable until the taxpayer recovers his or her cost basis. However, it is important to note that Reg. Sec. 1.1001-1(a) states that the right to receive these payments cannot be valued only in ". . . rare and extraordinary cases."

Example 7: T sells her retail business (adjusted basis $82,000) for $30,000 cash and a 20% share of the profits for the next 10 years. Since these payments are not subject to reasonable estimation, T may use a cost-recovery method. None of the future payments is taxable until T recovers her $82,000 cost basis.

A major exception to the accrual method of income recognition is the claim-of-right doctrine. As discussed in Chapter 4, this concept requires a taxpayer to include an amount in income not later than when it is actually or constructively received, provided that there are no restrictions on the disposition of such amount by the taxpayer. This concept, equally applicable to both cash- and accrual-basis taxpayers, is based on both the wherewithal-to-pay concept and the annual accounting period concept. Several modifications to this concept have been enacted over the years, but the fact remains that the practicality of insuring adequate tax collections is an overriding consideration in the development of tax laws.

Example 8: D Corporation, an accrual-basis taxpayer, leases a warehouse to E Corporation, a cash-basis taxpayer. If E pays 3 years of rent in advance, D Corporation must recognize the entire payment as income in the year received. Furthermore, E must prorate the payment over the 3 years, even though the cash basis is used.

BACKGROUND

Generally, financial accounting principles are acceptable for tax purposes only when the financial reporting and tax collection objectives are congruent. For example, the realization principle is fundamental to both financial and tax accounting because of the uniformity and certainty of measurement. On the other hand, the claim-of-right doctrine is unique to tax accounting because of the tax objective of insuring an orderly tax administration.

In a landmark tax case, the Supreme Court disallowed the proration of dues of a membership organization over the life of the membership. In supporting the Commissioner's criteria for an annual reporting of income, the Court noted that:

> . . . in performing the function of business accounting the method employed by the Association "is in accord with generally accepted

Continued

BACKGROUND

commercial accounting principles and practices. It is not to hold that for income tax purposes it so clearly reflects income as to be binding on the Treasury."*

It is interesting to note that occasionally the IRS has used "generally accepted accounting principles" (GAAP) to support their position; for example, GAAP was cited as justification for the allocation of a portion of fixed overhead to inventories.† Despite these aberrations, the Supreme Court recently reaffirmed the dichotomy of tax and financial reporting objectives:

> The primary goal of financial accounting is to provide useful information to management, shareholders, creditors and others properly interested . . . the primary goal of the income tax system . . . is the equitable collection of revenue. . .‡

**American Automobile Association*, 367 U.S. 687 (1961).

†*All-Steel Equipment Company*, 54 T.C. 1749 (1978).

‡*Thor Power Tool Company*, 99 S. Ct. 773 (1979).

Generally an expense is deductible under the accrual basis when all events have occurred to determine the contractual liability. In addition, the Tax Reform Act of 1984 requires the deferral of year-end expense accruals until "substantial economic performance" occurs. (These requirements are discussed in Chapter 7.) An expenditure based on a contingency or not subject to a reasonable estimation may not be deducted currently. However, Sec. 461(f) permits the deduction of a liability paid under protest, and any amount refunded to the taxpayer in a subsequent year must be recognized as income under the tax-benefit rule.

The requirement that an expense can be reasonably estimated effectively eliminates for tax purposes the use of reserves for estimated expenses. Although such practices are common in financial accounting, the Code specifically provides for the use of a reserve only in the case of bad debts (Sec. 166). This prohibition against the use of reserves is justified primarily as a means of administrative convenience, since the use of subjective estimates would create practical audit difficulties for the IRS. Thus, deductions have been denied for additions to reserves for warranty service, self-insurance, and estimated repairs.[6]

Example 9: F operates an appliance dealership and knows from past experience that approximately 4% of annual sales prices of appliances will be spent on warranty guarantees. This amount is ac-

[6]It is interesting to note that in 1954 Congress enacted Code Sec. 462, which allowed a company to deduct additions to reserves for future maintenance costs on products. However, the provision was repealed retroactively when projections of large revenue declines were developed.

crued each year for financial accounting purposes in order to match revenues and expenses properly. However, for tax purposes, F can deduct warranty expenses only when they actually occur. The same would be true if F deposited the accrued amount in a special account each year.

HYBRID METHODS Sec. 446(c)(4) specifically permits the use of a combination of cash, accrual, and other acceptable methods of accounting, provided that the hybrid method is consistently applied and properly reflects income. Some restrictions are present; for example, a taxpayer using the cash method for income must also use the cash method for expenses.

Perhaps the most common hybrid procedure is the use of the accrual method for gross profit calculations and the cash method for other expenses. You will recall that a taxpayer must use the accrual method for sales and purchases when inventories are a significant component of income. This hybrid method, specifically allowed by the Regulations,[7] has the advantage of simplifying accounting records.

SPECIAL INCOME DEFERRAL ELECTIONS

As discussed previously, most income prepayments are taxed immediately to the recipient under the claim-of-right doctrine. For various reasons, Congress and the IRS have permitted several exceptions to this basic rule for certain types of prepaid business income. Two important exceptions applicable to taxpayers are discussed in the following text.

PREPAYMENTS FOR INVENTORY Reg. Sec. 1.451-5 permits an accrual-basis taxpayer to defer advance payments on sales of inventory until the income is recognizable under the accrual basis, i.e., usually at the time of delivery. Generally this regulation permits a taxpayer to achieve a proper matching of income and expenses for both financial and tax purposes. However, certain occurrences may require the taxpayer to accelerate income recognition.

If the advance payments are for goods which are either included in the taxpayer's ending inventory or are available through normal supply channels, the advance payments must be included in income no later than the end of the second year following the year in which "substantial advance payments" are received. Substantial advance payments are defined as those exceeding reasonable estimated costs and expenses associated with the inventory item. In these circumstances the IRS view is that a wherewithal to pay exists, the sale could be closed with available inventory, and these factors taken together justify a two-year limit on the deferral period.

---

[7]Reg. Sec. 1.446-1(c)(1)(iv).

Example 10: H, a calendar-year accrual-basis taxpayer enters into a contract in March 19X1 for delivery of an inventory item (currently available) in March of 19X6. The inventory item has a total estimated cost of $6,500 to H, and during 19X1 H received a $5,000 advance payment under the contract for the goods. Under these circumstances H may defer recognition of the $5,000 prepayment until the date of delivery, March 19X6.

Example 11: Assume that H in Example 10 received another advance of $2,000 in 19X2 under the contract. In this case, the total advances received ($7,000) exceed the estimated cost of the goods ($6,500), and H must recognize the advances as income no later than the end of 19X4.

An interesting question arises when a taxpayer is required to recognize an advance payment as income in a tax year before actual delivery. Specifically, can the taxpayer also take an advanced deduction for the estimated cost of goods sold and related expenses? Reg. Sec. 1.451-5(c)(2) permits a taxpayer to deduct the estimated cost of goods sold in the year of income inclusion. Obviously, such costs would not also be deductible in the year of delivery if previously deducted, although adjustments for incorrect estimates of earlier years would be made in that year.

Example 12: Assume the same facts as in Examples 10 and 11. Since H is taxed on the $7,000 advances in 19X4, H may also deduct the estimated costs of $6,500 associated with the goods on the 19X4 return. Any other payments received by H are fully taxable when received. Additionally, if the cost of the goods is determined in 19X6 to be $6,650, H may deduct an additional $150 in 19X6, the year of delivery.

LONG-TERM CONSTRUCTION CONTRACTS Because of the potential distortions of income inherent in comparing advance payments with actual expenses in long-term construction contracts, Reg. Sec. 1.451-3 provides two special elective methods of reporting income for building, installation, or construction contracts that are not completed during the tax year in which the contract is initiated.[8] A basic requirement for such an election by a manufacturer of products is that the item must require more than 12 calendar months to complete and is not normally available in the taxpayer's finished goods inventory.

Generally the allowable methods are similar to the two methods considered to be acceptable for financial reporting purposes. A change to or from one of these methods requires the permission of the Commissioner

[8]Reg. Sec. 1.451-5, which provides for the deferral of advances received on inventory discussed above, also permits the deferral of advances received on long-term construction contracts.

of the IRS, although the method is not necessarily required for all long-term construction contracts.

PERCENTAGE-OF-COMPLETION METHOD A long-term construction contract procedure where gross income is recognized on an annual basis according to some measure of the incremental work effort performed during the period.

The ***percentage-of-completion method*** requires recognition of a portion of the total gross profit each year based on the estimated percentage of the contract work completed that year. This percentage estimate can be based on either the ratio of work performed in the tax year compared to the total work to be performed or the ratio of costs incurred during the tax year compared to total estimated costs of the contract. (The latter basis is commonly used for financial accounting purposes.) Any costs incurred during the tax year (other than ending materials and supplies inventories) are deducted from the computed gross income. This method offers the advantage of spreading the income over several tax periods.

Example 13: J, a calendar-year taxpayer, enters into a contract to construct a bridge for the city of Allentown for $2,000,000. J begins work on the contract on March 1, 19X1 and completes the contract on November 20, 19X4. At the end of each year J obtained a certificate from the construction engineer estimating the percentage of work completed. Assuming the following estimated completion percentages (on a cumulative basis) and actual costs, J would report the following profit each year:

YEAR	PERCENTAGE COMPLETED	GROSS PROFIT REPORTED	ACTUAL COSTS	TAXABLE PROFIT
19X1	35%	$ 700,000	$ 640,000	$ 60,000
19X2	55%	400,000	330,000	70,000
19X3	80%	500,000	410,000	90,000
19X4	100%	400,000	280,000	120,000
		$2,000,000	$1,660,000	$340,000

COMPLETED-CONTRACT METHOD A long-term construction contract procedure in which all income and expenses associated with the contract are deferred until the project is finished and accepted by the purchaser.

The ***completed-contract method*** defers recognition of the entire profit (or loss) from the contract until the year that the contract is completed and accepted by the purchaser. All progress payments and costs directly allocable to the contract are accumulated until the contract is completed, although indirect expenses such as officer salaries which are not directly attributable to the contract are deductible in the year paid or incurred. This method provides an opportunity for the taxpayer to defer income recognition possibly for several tax years; however, Reg. Sec. 1.451-3(b)(2) specifically prohibits unnecessary delays in the completion of the contract when the primary purpose of such delays is to defer the federal income tax. A taxpayer is permitted to defer recognition after the completion date when disputes with buyers involve amounts so substantial that it is impossible to determine if a profit or a loss on the contract will ultimately be realized.[9]

[9] Reg. Sec. 1.451-3(d)(2)(ii).

Example 14: Assume the same facts as in Example 13. If J uses the completed-contract method of reporting income from the construction contract, no profit will be reported until 19X4, the year of completion. At that time, J will report $2,000,000 of gross income and $1,660,000 of costs and expenses, or a net profit of $340,000. Any progress payments J receives during these four years will not change the final result.

As part of the search for additional revenue sources, in the *Tax Equity and Fiscal Responsibility Act of 1982*, Congress instructed the Treasury Department to amend its regulations related to the completed-contract method of accounting.[10] These new regulations will be designed to accomplish several objectives. For example, taxpayers will no longer be able to defer income artificially by treating several contracts as a single contract. Additionally, the new regulations are to reclassify as deferrable contract costs certain expenditures which under the old rules were treated as currently deductible period costs. These costs included bidding expenses, shipping costs, general and administrative expenses, and scrap and spoilage costs. The new rules will not apply to construction contracts for real property improvements if the contract is expected to be completed within three years or if the taxpayer has average annual gross receipts of $25 million or less for the prior three years.

CHANGES IN ACCOUNTING METHODS

On his or her first tax return, a taxpayer may adopt any permissible accounting method. However, consent of the Commissioner is normally required for taxpayers who wish to change their method of accounting. Form 3115 is used to obtain such permission and should be filed within 180 days after the beginning of the tax year of the proposed change, although a showing of "good cause" can extend the deadline until nine months from the beginning of that tax year.[11] For certain changes, such as depreciation or bad-debts methods, a taxpayer may assume the Commissioner's consent if the Form 3115 is filed on time.

FORM 3115

Reg. Sec. 1.446-1(e)(ii) defines a change in the method of accounting as including both a change in the overall plan of accounting (e.g., cash to accrual) or a change in the treatment of a material item used under the overall plan (e.g., inventory). A change of accounting method does not include corrections of mathematical, posting, or classification errors, which can be corrected simply by filing amended returns (if the filing deadline has passed). Similarly, changes in accounting estimates such as reserve for bad debts or useful lives for depreciation are not considered to be changes in accounting methods—such changes should be made by adjustments in the current and future years.

[10] *Tax Equity and Fiscal Responsibility Act of 1982*, Sec. 229. It should be noted that this provision represents a compromise with the Reagan administration, which had proposed to abolish the completed-contract method altogether.

[11] Rev. Proc. 80-51, 1980-2 C.B. 818.

Example 15: J, a calendar-year taxpayer, purchased a portable copier on January 1, 1979 and began depreciating the $5,000 cost on a 10-year useful life straight-line basis. On January 1, 1984 circumstances indicated that the machine had a remaining useful life of only three years. As of January 1, 1984 the undepreciated basis of the asset is $2,500. J's revised depreciation deduction for 1984, 1985, and 1986 will be $833 per year ($2,500 ÷ 3).

DETERMINING THE SEC. 481 CUMULATIVE ADJUSTMENT When an accounting method change occurs, income of the year preceding the year of change is determined under the old method of accounting and income for the year of change and succeeding years is determined under the new method. Such a procedure generally requires a ***Sec. 481 cumulative adjustment*** to avoid duplication or omission of income or deductions.[12] Otherwise, such items would escape taxation altogether.

SEC. 481 CUMULATIVE ADJUSTMENT An adjustment for additional income and/or expenses caused by a change of accounting method. The adjustment is generally for items not recognized under the old method and not properly reportable under the new method.

Example 16: Assume that C changes from the cash to the accrual method. C had used the cash basis prior to 19X2 and relevant information from C's records included the following:

	1-1-X2 BALANCE	12-31-X2 BALANCE
Accounts receivable	$ 3,200	$3,800
Accounts payable	4,000	2,800
Inventory (per count)	10,300	9,600

In converting from the cash to the accrual basis in 19X2, C will be required to make a positive cumulative adjustment (addition) to income of $9,500, determined as follows:

1-1-X2	Accounts receivable balance (never reflected as income on the cash basis, and not accruable in a year (19X2) after the sale)	$ 3,200
1-1-X2	Accounts payable balance (never deducted on the cash basis, and not deductible in a year (19X2) after incurrence)	(4,000)
1-1-X2	Inventory balance (previously deducted on the cash basis or reflected in the above payables adjustment)	10,300
	Total Sec. 481 cumulative adjustment	$ 9,500

Note that a cash basis taxpayer would have deducted cash purchases and payments on account as cost of goods sold; therefore, the $10,300 adjustment is necessary.

Once the cumulative adjustment is determined, a question arises as to how the additional income or deductions should be reported. As a gen-

[12] Sec. 481(a)(2).

eral rule, Rev. Proc. 80-51 requires the adjustment to be recognized over a period considered appropriate by the Commissioner. This may be in the year of change; in Example 16, for instance, C would add the $9,500 to the 19X2 taxable income computed under the new (accrual) method. (See Example 6 (page 6/7) for the necessary calculations to convert income from the cash to the accrual basis.) As a practical matter, the adjustment period depends on whether the adjustment is positive or negative and also whether the change of method is initiated by the taxpayer (a voluntary change) or the IRS (an involuntary change).

VOLUNTARY CHANGES Sec. 481 and Rev. Proc. 80-51 offer some guide lines for the appropriate period for taking the cumulative adjustment into account. For a voluntary change initiated by the taxpayer (through Form 3115 procedures), Rev. Proc. 80-51 establishes three possible periods for recognizing a cumulative adjustment. First, if the entire adjustment relates to the tax year preceding the year of change, the entire adjustment is taken into account in the year of change. Secondly, if the former method has been used for more than one year, the adjustment is reported ratably over the number of years that the former method was used (not to exceed 10 years). Finally, if the former method has been used for more than three taxable years and at least 67% of the cumulative adjustment is attributable to either the 1-year, 2-year, or 3-year period preceding the year of change, a special rule applies. Basically, the highest percentage (of the cumulative adjustment) attributable to either of these periods must be taken into account over the 3-year period beginning with the year of change.[13] Any balance is allocated over the remaining number of years the taxpayer had used the former method (not to exceed 10 years).

In general, these rules reflect an IRS belief that a cumulative adjustment should be recognized prospectively over basically the same number of years that caused the adjustment, unless a significant portion of the adjustment occurred in recent years. In the latter case, either the taxpayer or the government would benefit from an unreasonable deferral of recognition.

Example 17: In 19X7 L voluntarily changes accounting methods for inventory and is required to recognize $42,000 as a Sec. 481 cumulative adjustment. The former inventory method was used for six prior years and resulted in understatements (overstatements) of income of those years as follows:

19X1—$ 8,000	19X3—($6,000)	19X5—$ 6,000
19X2—$14,000	19X4— $1,000	19X6—$19,000

L will be required to spread the $42,000 adjustment over the current year and the next five years, recognizing $7,000 of additional income each year. The adjustment is recognized over the same number of years that the former method of accounting was used.

[13] If the old method was used less than four years, a 75% test replaces the 67% test.

Example 18: Assume that the $42,000 cumulative adjustment (Example 17) was distributed as follows:

19X1—$8,000	19X3—($6,000)	19X5—$ 6,000
19X2—$1,000	19X4— $1,000	19X6—$32,000

Since at least 67% of the $42,000 cumulative adjustment is now attributable to the 1-, 2-, or 3-year period preceding the change, a portion of the $42,000 will be recognized on an accelerated basis during the next three tax years (including the current year). The highest percentage of the total adjustment for the three possible time periods is 92.8% for the 19X4–19X6 period (since all three years involved positive adjustments). This percentage represents the $39,000 total adjustments for the 3-year period divided by the $42,000 total adjustment. Thus 92.8% of the total adjustment, or $39,000, must be recognized in 19X7, 19X8, and 19X9 at the rate of $13,000 per year. The remaining adjustment of $3,000 will be recognized in 19Y0, 19Y1, and 19Y2 at the rate of $1,000 per year.

INVOLUNTARY CHANGES One of the purposes of Rev. Proc. 80-51 was to encourage voluntary compliance in changing from improper accounting methods to acceptable accounting methods. This is accomplished by eliminating any benefits of a spread-forward period when a taxpayer is using an "erroneous" method of accounting at the time of being contacted by the Internal Revenue Service for the purpose of examining the tax return. An "erroneous method of accounting" is defined as a method not specifically permitted by the Code, Regulations, or Supreme Court decisions. The denial of spread-forward benefits would seem to offer an incentive for taxpayers to change from an erroneous accounting method before being contacted by the IRS. However, this is not necessarily the case for taxpayers who have used an erroneous method of accounting for tax years prior to 1954.

BACKGROUND

Court decisions prior to the adoption of the 1954 Internal Revenue Code generally allowed a taxpayer to avoid cumulative adjustments due to involuntary changes of accounting method.* However, for tax years beginning in 1954 or later, the Code requires a taxpayer to make the necessary cumulative adjustments, regardless of whether the change is voluntary or involuntary. This provision was not made retroactive to years prior to 1954; anytime a taxpayer undergoes an *involuntary* change of accounting method, the government can not make cumulative adjustments for tax years beginning prior to 1954. However, if the taxpayer *voluntarily* initiates the change of method, the IRS has a free hand to adjust for *all* prior taxable years (including pre-1954 years).

This anomaly in the tax law has in some cases created an interest-

Continued

BACKGROUND

ing stalemate between certain taxpayers and the IRS. Although the IRS may encounter a taxpayer using a clearly erroneous method of accounting, the government may choose not to force the taxpayer to change accounting methods, because such an involuntary change closes off adjustment possibilities for pre-1954 tax years. Thus, the government may play a "wait and see" game in case the taxpayer may voluntarily choose to change accounting methods, possibly because of changing economic conditions or related effects on financial statements. Obviously, it becomes critical in such cases to determine which party initiates a change in accounting method.†

---

*For example, see C. J. Dwyer, 203 F.2d 522 (CA-2, 1953).

†See *Brookshire v. Commissioner*, 273 F.2d 638 (CA-4, 1960). In this case a taxpayer was deemed to initiate the change when the IRS agent suggested that it would be a "good idea to change" and the taxpayer subsequently did so.

Example 19: M Company has used the direct-costing method for its manufacturing inventories for the past 12 years. Such a method of inventory costing is specifically prohibited by Reg. Sec. 1.471-11. If M voluntarily elects to change to an absorption (full cost) inventory method, the company may be able to spread any positive adjustment over a period as long as 10 years (Rev. Proc. 80-51). However, if the IRS audits the return before a request for change of accounting method is made, M must recognize the entire positive adjustment at that time. Of course, if the total cumulative adjustment was *negative*, i.e., in M's favor, Sec. 481 and Rev. Proc. 80-51 allow the Commissioner to determine an appropriate adjustment period.

Sec. 481(b) provides some tax relief for a taxpayer undergoing an involuntary change which results in a positive adjustment of more than $3,000. The general rule of total recognition in the year of change is relaxed by allowing the taxpayer to add one-third of the total adjustment to each of the two prior tax years, determine the marginal tax on such additions, and add the two marginal tax figures to the tax liability of the year of change (which includes the tax on the other one-third of the adjustment). This averaging procedure may help the taxpayer avoid a bunching of income in the year of change.

Example 20: N is required to make a $30,000 cumulative adjustment because of a change in accounting method in 19X6. Including the $30,000 in 19X6 taxable income will increase N's tax liability by $13,800. However, if N included $10,000 additional income on her 19X4, 19X5, and 19X6 tax returns, the additional tax liabilities would be $3,000, $4,800, and $4,600 respectively. In this case, N would elect the 3-year averaging and pay a total of $12,400 ($3,000 + $4,800 + $4,600) tax on the adjustment in 19X6.

A related provision[14] provides a further opportunity for the taxpayer to possibly reduce the incidence of tax in the year of change. This provision allows a taxpayer to recompute taxable income using the new accounting method for one or more consecutive years prior to the year of change, and add the resulting marginal tax liabilities to the tax liability for the year of change. (The tax liability for the year of change includes any portion of the cumulative adjustment not allocated to the prior years under the new method.) This option provides the taxpayer the flexibility of allocating a portion of the adjustment to tax years with low marginal income tax rates.

Example 21: Assume the same facts as in Example 20, and assume that N's marginal income tax rates for the past five years when the old method was used and the current year (19X6) are:

19X1—50%	19X3—31%	19X5—48%
19X2—48%	19X4—30%	19X6—46%

Depending on the dollar effect of recomputing income under the new accounting method, N may elect to recompute income back to 19X3 to take advantage of the lower marginal tax rates in 19X3 and 19X4. Note that the years must be consecutive, so N must also recompute income for 19X5 (where a 48% rate applies). Any portion of the cumulative adjustment not carried back through this procedure will be added to the 19X6 taxable income.

INVENTORY METHODS

The choice of inventory method is a significant factor in the determination of both financial accounting income and taxable income. Reg. Sec. 1.471-1 requires adjustments for inventories at the beginning and end of each tax year so that taxable income will be correctly reflected. And as discussed previously, the accrual basis must be used for gross profit computations when inventories are a factor in computing taxable income.

Sec. 471 states that inventories should be taken ". . . as conforming as nearly as may be to the best accounting practice in the trade or business and as most clearly reflecting the income." As a result, there is a great deal of similarity between tax and financial accounting rules for inventories. For example, Sec. 1.471-2(f) prohibits the use of reserves for price declines or base-stock methods and excludes from inventory the cost of inventory in transit where title has not passed to the taxpayer. However, it should be noted that Sec. 471 reserves for the Commissioner of the IRS the right to determine what may be the "best accounting practice." This power will invariably lead to conflicts (see the discussion on the Thor Power Tool Case).

Questions invariably arise as to what goods should be inventoried. In-

[14] Sec. 481(b)(2).

ventories should include not only all finished goods inventories held for resale, but also all work-in-process, materials, and supplies which eventually will be embodied in the final product offered for resale. The latter category includes containers (e.g., kegs, bottles, and cases) when title has passed to the buyer. However, containers furnished under a deposit arrangement are not includable in inventory.[15] Materials and supplies which are not embodied in the final physical product may be expensed in the year of purchase, unless separate inventories are necessary to avoid a distortion of income.

VALUATION OF INVENTORIES

Sec. 471 requires that an inventory method clearly reflect income and conform to the best accounting practice in the business. For the latter requirement, the Regulations indicate that consistency of treatment should be given greater weight than any particular inventory method, provided that an acceptable inventory method is used.[16] In general, the two bases of inventory valuation permitted by the Regulations are (*a*) cost and (*b*) the lower of cost or market.

COST METHOD The valuation of inventories at cost depends on whether the inventory is purchased or produced. In the case of a retailer who purchases inventory during the year, cost is defined as the invoice price less trade discounts plus transportation and other necessary acquisition charges. Cash discounts which represent a fair rate of interest may be deducted either from the inventory cost or added to gross income.

In the case of a manufactured product, the cost of an inventory item includes the costs of (*a*) raw materials, (*b*) direct labor, and (*c*) all indirect production costs necessary for the production of the article, other than costs of selling or return on capital.[17] It is important to distinguish items includable in the latter category, because this question of classification has led to many taxpayer-IRS disputes.

Reg. Sec. 1.471-11(a) specifically requires that the computation of inventoriable costs be in accordance with the "full-absorption" method of inventory costing. The ***full-absorption costing*** method requires that a portion of all indirect production costs be included in inventory, including such nonvariable (fixed) costs as factory rent and supervisory salaries. The "direct-costing" method, which inventories only the variable direct and indirect factory costs, is specifically prohibited by Reg. Sec. 1.471-11(a). This regulation provides a general guide line for applying the absorption costing method by classifying indirect factory costs into one of three categories: (1) those includable in ending inventory; (2) those excludable from ending inventory; and (3) those costs which are to re-

FULL-ABSORPTION COSTING An inventory cost procedure required for manufacturers. A portion of all factory costs must be allocated to ending inventory, including fixed overhead.

[15] Reg. Sec. 1.471-1. If customers fail to return the containers, any forfeited deposit is treated as capital gain or loss (Rev. Rul. 75-34, 1975-1 C.B. 271).

[16] Reg. Sec. 1.471-2(b).

[17] Reg. Sec. 1.471-3(c).

TABLE 6-1
Examples—Classification of Indirect Manufacturing Costs—Reg. Sec. 1.471

CATEGORY 1 COSTS (REQUIRED INCLUSION IN INVENTORY COST)	CATEGORY 2 COSTS (OPTIONAL EXCLUSION FROM INVENTORY COST)	CATEGORY 3 COSTS (EXCLUSION ONLY IF TREATED SIMILARLY ON FINANCIAL STATEMENTS *)
Repairs and Maintenance	Marketing and Distributing Costs	Taxes (Inventory and Factory Assets)
Utilities and Rent	Selling and Advertising	Depreciation (Incident to Manufacturing)
Indirect Labor and Materials	Interest	Employee Benefits (Direct and Indirect Labor)
Tools and Equipment	Research and Experiment	Scrap, Rework, Strike, and Spoilage Costs
Quality Control	Losses	Factory Administrative Expenses

* Financial treatment must be under generally accepted accounting principles.

ceive the same treatment as reporting in the financial statements provided to shareholders and creditors. Table 6-1 summarizes the major cost classifications of the three categories. Any item not included in (or similar to) one of the three categories will be treated the same as for financial reporting purposes. It is important to note that Category 3 classifications are acceptable only if the financial accounting treatment is in conformity with "generally accepted accounting principles."

Example 22: O Corporation manufactures canned beverages, and has consistently omitted normal expected spoilage costs from inventory valuations (i.e., the amount is expensed each year). This violates an accepted industry accounting practice of inventorying normal spoilage costs and expensing only abnormal spoilage costs. Therefore, O Corporation must inventory the normal expected spoilage costs, since the financial reporting treatment of this category (3) must be under generally accepted accounting principles.

Because indirect costs cannot be traced directly to the products being produced, an estimation procedure must be used to apply such costs to the products. Reg. Sec. 1.471-11(2) specifically allows two methods of applying these costs to the ending inventory. The *manufacturing-burden-rate* method applies the costs on a basis of a predetermined rate based on some appropriate level of factory activity (e.g., direct labor hours, machine hours, etc.). The *standard-cost* method is similar, in that a predetermined cost per unit (based on expected costs) is assigned to each inventory item. Regardless of the method chosen, material variances between applied and actual overhead incurred must be allocated to both the ending inventory and cost of goods sold.

LOWER OF COST OR MARKET Reg. Sec. 1.471-2 specifically allows a taxpayer to use a lower-of-cost or -market procedure in determining an inventory value. "Market" for purchased inventory is the applicable bid price for the inventory item on the inventory date in the volume in which it is normally purchased. Market for manufactured inventory items, including work-in-process inventories, is the total reproduction cost at current prices for inventory items in a similar state of completion. Inventory items subject to a firm sales contract with fixed sales prices are always valued at cost.[18]

In applying lower-of-cost or -market procedures, comparisons of cost and market must be made for each inventory item. A taxpayer is not permitted to derive an inventory figure by comparing total costs with total market value for the entire inventory of nonsimilar items.[19] Instead, comparisons are made for each product.

Example 23: P uses lower-of-cost or -market procedures in valuing his inventory of three types of paint products. Relevant data at the end of 19X2 include the following:

	COST	MARKET	LOWER-OF-COST OR -MARKET
Paint A	$2,000	$2,700	$2,000
Paint B	$3,000	$2,800	$2,800
Paint C	$4,200	$4,000	$4,000
	$9,200	$9,500	$8,800

P will value his ending inventory at $8,800. The $9,200 and $9,500 totals are irrelevant for these purposes.

INVENTORY COST FLOW ASSUMPTIONS, PARTICULARLY LIFO

Generally a taxpayer must use actual costs when he or she is able to identify the particular goods in inventory through accounting or production records. For example, a wholesaler of heavy construction equipment may be able to trace original cost by referring to serial and invoice numbers. On the other hand, such procedures would not be economically feasible for a parts dealer who handles literally hundreds of similar items. In these cases, a taxpayer must assume an order of cost flow. Three possible assumptions are average cost, FIFO (first-in, first-out), and LIFO (last-in, first-out).

[18] Reg. Sec. 1.471-4.

[19] Ibid.

Example 24: A's inventory records for 19X4 disclose the following:

DATE	UNITS PURCHASED	COST PER UNIT	TOTAL COST
Beginning inventory	100	$ 4	$ 400
1-18-X4	300	$ 6	1,800
5-14-X4	200	$ 8	1,600
12-1-X4	200	$11	2,200
	800		$6,000

If A uses the average cost method, each unit in ending inventory will be valued at $7.50 ($6,000 ÷ 800). Thus, if 300 units are in ending inventory, they will be valued at $2,250. If A elects the FIFO procedure, the ending inventory will be valued at $3,000 (200 units @ $11 and 100 units @ $8) under the assumption that the first units purchased were the first units sold, and therefore the ending inventory of 300 units represents the most recent purchases. If A elects the LIFO procedure, the ending inventory will be valued at $1,600 (100 units @ $4 and 200 units @ $6) under the assumption that the ending inventory represents the earliest purchases (with the most recent purchases being sold).

Although a FIFO assumption may more realistically represent the actual physical flow of goods, a taxpayer is nevertheless permitted to elect the LIFO method.[20] This inventory method was incorporated into the tax law in order to cushion the impact of price increases in an inflationary economy. This may be seen by referring to Example 24. A's cost of goods sold under the FIFO method would be $3,000 ($6,000 goods available − $3,000 ending inventory), and under the LIFO method would be $4,400 ($6,000 goods available − $1,600 ending inventory). The LIFO method matches the current inventory costs more realistically against current revenues. Because of this economic incentive for electing LIFO, Congress has established specific requirements for its usage.

BACKGROUND

One of the first attempts to eliminate paper inventory profits was the "base-stock" method, where a permanent layer of inventory prices were frozen as a base stock in future years. However, this method was later rejected and is still prohibited by Reg. Sec. 1.471-2(f).

Congress first approved the use of a LIFO method in Sec. 22(d) of the Revenue Act of 1938; however, its applicability was limited to the leather tanning and nonferrous metal industries. One year later, Sec. 22(d) was amended to allow all taxpayers to use the LIFO method.

Continued

[20] Reg. Sec. 1.472-1(a)(2).

> ***BACKGROUND***
> However, the method did not immediately receive widespread usage, primarily because of the computational difficulties with item inventory methods and the possible adverse tax effects of liquidating old low-cost layers of inventory.
>
> In 1947 and 1948, two important court decisions paved the way to a more widespread acceptance of LIFO. In these decisions the Tax Court approved the use of "dollar-value" inventory methods, which used price indexes developed across several inventory items to value inventories.* These methods simplified LIFO calculations for changing inventory compositions and lessened the adverse tax effects of a liquidation of one particular inventory item by pooling similar inventory items. These methods were eventually incorporated into the Regulations.
>
> *Hutzler Bros. Co., 8 T.C. 14 (1947), and Edgar A. Basse, 10 T.C. 328 (1948).

ELECTING LIFO A taxpayer must elect LIFO by filing a request on Form 970 for the tax year in which the change is made. Note that prior approval of the Commissioner is not necessary, although the election cannot be revoked unless prior approval is obtained from the Commissioner. If the election is revoked, any cumulative adjustment must be recognized under the general rules of Rev. Proc. 80-51 previously discussed, and the taxpayer must also agree not to elect LIFO again for a 10-year period, unless consent is granted by the IRS.[21]

FORM 970

LIFO is considered to be a cost method of inventory valuation; therefore, lower-of-cost or -market procedures may not be used in conjunction with this method. If a taxpayer has used lower-of-cost or -market procedures before electing LIFO, any previous write-downs related to the beginning inventory in the year when LIFO is elected must be restored to income.[22] For tax years prior to 1982, the IRS required that the full adjustment be included in income in the year of change. As part of the Economic Recovery Tax Act of 1981, Congress added Sec. 472(d) which permits taxpayers to spread such an adjustment over three years (beginning with the year of change) for tax years beginning after 1981.

Example 25: P elects to use the LIFO inventory method beginning in 19X3. P's ending inventory for 19X2 was valued at $30,600, using lower-of-cost or -market procedures. The cost of this ending inventory was $37,700. P must therefore restore the $7,100 of markdowns to income by recognizing $2,367 ($7,100 ÷ 3) of additional income in 19X3, 19X4, and 19X5.

[21] Rev. Proc. 80-51, supra note 17.

[22] Reg. Sec. 1.472-2(c).

DOLLAR-VALUE LIFO METHODS Applying LIFO inventory procedures to each different item of inventory is a difficult, if not impossible, task for many businesses. Such an "item" method may be sufficient for a taxpayer with one type of inventory (such as in Example 24) but this procedure would be quite cumbersome for a manufacturer of hundreds of household products. To overcome this deficiency, Congress amended the tax regulations to allow the use of "dollar-value" methods of inventory.[23]

Dollar-value methods simplify inventory calculations by determining inventory cost on the basis of total dollars (for a base year) rather than the quantity and price of each inventory item. The primary advantage of these methods is that the inventory is viewed as a pool, not as a series of individual items. In addition to minimizing the laborious calculations associated with LIFO, the use of pools can lessen the possible tax impact of liquidation of the oldest and lowest cost layers of one particular inventory item.

DOLLAR-VALUE LIFO An inventory procedure in which ending and beginning inventories are valued at a base-period price to determine if inventories increased or decreased during the year (in terms of total dollar values). Increases are valued as new LIFO layers according to a current price index, and decreases are taken from the most recently added layers.

Perhaps the most commonly used method of ***dollar-value LIFO*** valuation is the double-extension method, a procedure sanctioned by the Regulations. Table 6-2 displays a comprehensive example of the double-extension technique. Although students may be inclined to dismiss such an illustration as being too complicated or confusing, we urge them not to do so. A close examination of Table 6-2 reveals the tax advantages of pooling inventory items and helps explain the popularity of dollar-value methods, from both a computational and a tax-saving standpoint.

The starting point for the double-extension method is the establishment of a base price for each unit of inventory at the time that LIFO is adopted. In the example of Table 6-2, the base prices of the four inventory items A, B, C, and D at December 31, 19X0, are $7, $12, $4, and $8, respectively. These base prices are used in the double-extension procedure to value ending inventories. The following sections describe this procedure in terms of three basic steps by referring to the 19X1 results of Table 6-2.

1. *Determining the Net Increment or Decrement at Base-Year Prices.* The first step in applying the double-extension procedure is to value the quantity of each ending inventory item at base-year prices. The current price of each inventory item is irrelevant at this point. Table 6-2 discloses that the 12/31/X1 inventory consists of 3,000 units of A, 2,000 units of B, 7,000 units of C, and 3,000 units of D. Valuing these quantities at the base-year (19X0) prices of $7, $12, $4, and $8 (respectively) results in a total inventory value of $97,000.

   This ending inventory value at base prices is then compared to the prior year's ending inventory value at base prices to determine if an overall increment (increase) or decrement (decrease) in inventory has occurred. A comparison of the 12/31/X0 and 12/31/X1 valuations at base prices discloses a net increment in 19X1 of $8,000 ($97,000 −

[23] T.D. 5756, 1949-2 C.B. 21.

$89,000). This increment indicates that a new "layer" of inventory must be added to the ending inventory. This layer must be valued at 19X1 prices.

2. *Determining a Price Index to Value an Incremental Layer of Inventory*. A net increment for the current year, stated in terms of base-period prices, must now be valued at current-year prices. This is accomplished by developing an aggregate price index for the current year, based on the following formula:

$$\text{Current-Year Price Index} = \frac{\text{Ending Inventory Value (Current Prices)}}{\text{Ending Inventory Value (Base-Period Prices)}}$$

Referring again to Table 6-2, the 12/31/X1 ending inventory value at the current 12/31/X1 prices ($10 for A, $7 for B, $5 for C, and $10 for D) totals $109,000. Therefore, the 19X1 price index is 112.4%, determined as follows:

$$\text{19X1 Price Index} = \frac{\$109{,}000\ \text{(Current Prices)}}{\$97{,}000\ \text{(Base-Year Prices)}} = 1.124$$

3. *Applying the Increment or Decrement to the Prior Year's Ending Inventory*. The last step in the double-extension procedure is to adjust the inventory layers for any current increment or decrement. In the example of Table 6-2, a net increment of $8,000 (base-year prices) resulted in 19X1. Therefore, a new "layer" of inventory must be added to the 19X0 layer of $89,000. This new layer is valued at 19X1 prices by multiplying the $8,000 base price increment by the 19X1 price index of 112.4% (computed in step 2). The resulting value of $8,992 is added to the beginning inventory value of $89,000 which results in a final ending inventory value of $97,992. The 19X1 ending inventory can now be viewed as consisting of the following two layers:

19X0 (Base Layer)	$89,000
19X1 ($8,000 × 1.124)	8,992

It is important to identify each layer of this inventory, because future decrements in inventory must be subtracted in LIFO order.

Similar calculations are made in 19X2 to convert a $34,000 inventory increase in terms of 19X0 base prices ($131,000 minus $97,000) to 19X2 average prices of $39,202 ($34,000 times the 19X2 price index of 115.3%). The 19X2 ending inventory of $137,194 consists of the following three layers:

19X0 (Base Year)	$89,000
19X1 ($8,000 × 1.124)	8,992
19X2 ($34,000 × 1.153)	39,202

In 19X3 a $31,000 decrement occurs; again, the increment or decrement is initially valued at base-period prices. This decrement is first subtracted from the 19X2 layer, since this was the last layer added to the ending inventory. Note that the decrement of $31,000 is subtracted from the $34,000 base-period value of the 19X2 layer,

TABLE 6-2
Dollar Value LIFO—Double Extension Method

R Corporation adopts the dollar value method of LIFO inventory valuation on December 31, 19X0, when the inventory consisted of the following:

ITEM	QUANTITY	COST PER UNIT	TOTAL COST
A	3,000	$ 7.00	$21,000
B	1,000	$12.00	12,000
C	6,000	$ 4.00	24,000
D	4,000	$ 8.00	32,000
			$89,000

Inventory quantities and costs at the end of 19X1, 19X2, and 19X3 were as follows:

	DECEMBER 31, 19X1	
ITEM	BASE PRICES	CURRENT PRICES
A	(3,000 @ $ 7) = $21,000	(3,000 @ $10) = $30,000
B	(2,000 @ $12) = 24,000	(2,000 @ $ 7) = 14,000
C	(7,000 @ $ 4) = 28,000	(7,000 @ $ 5) = 35,000
D	(3,000 @ $ 8) = 24,000	(3,000 @ $10) = 30,000
	$97,000	$109,000

Increment (Decrement) at Base Prices	$97,000 − $89,000 = $8,000
Price Index	$109,000 ÷ $97,000 = 112.4%
Ending Inventory (By Layer)	19X0 − Base Year = $89,000
	19X1 − $8,000 × 1.124 = 8,992
	$97,992

DECEMBER 31, 19X2

BASE PRICES	CURRENT PRICES
(5,000 @ $ 7) = $ 35,000	(5,000 @ $ 8) = $40,000
(2,000 @ $12) = 24,000	(2,000 @ $15) = 30,000
(4,000 @ $ 4) = 16,000	(4,000 @ $ 8) = 32,000
(7,000 @ $ 8) = 56,000	(7,000 @ $ 7) = 49,000
$131,000	$151,000

Increment (Decrement) at Base Prices	$131,000 − $97,000 = $34,000
Price Index	$151,000 ÷ $131,000 = 115.3%
Ending Inventory (By Layer)	19X0 − Base year = $ 89,000 19X1 − $8,000 × 1.124 = 8,992 19X2 − $34,000 × 1.153 = 39,202 $137,194

DECEMBER 31, 19X3

BASE PRICES	CURRENT PRICES
(4,000 @ $ 7) = $ 28,000	(4,000 @ $ 8) = $ 32,000
(1,000 @ $12) = 12,000	(1,000 @ $13) = 13,000
(5,000 @ $ 4) = 20,000	(5,000 @ $ 4) = 20,000
(5,000 @ $ 8) = 40,000	(5,000 @ $10) = 50,000
$100,000	$115,000

Increment (Decrement) at Base Prices	$100,000 − $131,000 = ($31,000)
Price Index	$115,000 ÷ $100,000 = 115.0%
Ending Inventory (By Layer)	19X0 − Base Year = $ 89,000 19X1 − $8,000 × 1.124 = 8,992 19X2 − $3,000 × 1.153 = 3,459 $101,451

since both values are stated in terms of base prices. The 19X3 ending inventory of $101,451 consists of the following three layers:

19X0 (Base Year)	$89,000
19X1 ($8,000 × 1.124)	8,992
19X3 ($3,000 × 1.153)	3,459

If the 19X3 decrement was larger than $34,000 (in terms of base prices), the 19X1 layer would be reduced next. (This process of first "peeling off" the most recently added layers retains the LIFO cost flow. Sometimes it is easy to forget that the purpose of this detailed procedure is simply to reflect a LIFO cost of goods sold.)

Example 26: Assume the same facts as in Table 6-2, except that the 19X3 inventory decrease in terms of base-year prices was $40,000. This results in a complete liquidation of the 19X2 inventory layer (base price of $34,000) and a $6,000 base-price reduction in the 19X1 layer. The 19X3 ending inventory would be valued at $91,248, consisting of a 19X0 layer of $89,000 (base year) and a 19X1 layer of $2,248 ($2,000 × 1.124).

As mentioned earlier, one of the advantages of pooling inventory items under a dollar-value method is that it neutralizes the possibly adverse tax effects of significantly depleting the stock of one particular inventory item. Note in Table 6-2 that all increments, decrements, and price indexes are based on aggregate numbers which reflect all four inventory items. As a general rule, it is to the taxpayer's advantage to group as many inventory items as possible into one pool. Reg. Sec. 1.472-8(e) requires that inventory be grouped into "homogeneous" pools. For manufacturers, a pool is usually defined as a "natural business unit," which consists of the raw materials, work-in-process, and finished goods of one or more related product lines. For wholesalers and retailers, a pool is a major line, type, or class of goods.

Example 27: Refer to product C in Table 6-2. Note that the number of units of product C decreased from 7,000 units in 19X1 to 4,000 units in 19X2. If product C was accounted for separately, the 3,000 unit decrease would have liquidated the 1,000 additional units acquired in 19X1 (at $5 cost) and also 2,000 units of the original 19X0 base layer (at $4 cost). One of the dangers of a unit method of LIFO is that an inventory decrease will cause significantly higher tax liabilities because low-cost inventory layers of earlier years will be liquidated. However, by pooling product C with products A, B, and D under the dollar-value method, the reduction in quantity of C is offset by increases in the other items in the pool.[24]

[24]As an additional incentive for small businesses to elect the LIFO method, Congress included a special pooling rule in the *Economic Recovery Tax Act of 1981*. Sec. 474 allows a business with less than $2 million of average gross receipts for three years to elect one inventory pool for dollar value LIFO purposes.

For some taxpayers, the use of the double-extension method may be impractical. For example, the items in inventory at any one time may change so rapidly that the development of base-year prices for new items may be almost impossible. In such cases the IRS may accept other dollar-value methods. Two such methods, the "index method" and the "link chain" method, are described in Reg. Sec. 1.427-8(e).

SIMPLIFIED DOLLAR-VALUE PROCEDURES Congress established a simplified alternative dollar-value method in the *Economic Recovery Tax Act of 1981*. Sec. 472(f) authorizes the IRS to draft regulations which permit taxpayers to elect a LIFO procedure using indexes published by the government. Specifically, taxpayers will calculate inventories at year-end prices and convert this value to base-year prices with the government index figures. This base price inventory is then compared to the beginning inventory (at base prices) to determine the net increment or decrement. If an increment occurs, the government index is used to value this new inventory layer.

Example 28: On January 1, 19X5 Q Company decides to elect LIFO procedures under the government index method. Q's ending 19X4 inventory was $100,000, and the 19X5 inventory was $120,000. Assume that the government indexes for Q's particular inventory were 110% for 19X4 and 115% for 19X5. Q's 19X5 inventory would be valued at $115,455, and consists of the following two layers:

19X4 (base period)	$100,000
19X5 incremental layer	15,455*
	$115,455

*$120,000 × 1.10/1.15 = $114,783 at 19X4 base prices
$114,783 − 100,000 = $14,783 increment at 19X4 base prices
$14,783 × 1.15/1.10 = $15,455 increment at 19X5 base prices

Note that the calculations did not require base-period prices for any of the inventory items. Note also that the LIFO cost flow is retained because none of the base-period inventory of $100,000 was depleted.

In March 1982 the IRS issued the necessary regulations for Sec. 472(f). These regulations authorize all taxpayers to use appropriate indexes from either the Consumer Price Index or the Producer Price Index. These indexes are prepared monthly and may be obtained from the U.S. Government Printing Office for $20 each. A controversial provision in these regulations requires taxpayers with average annual sales of greater than $2 million in the prior three years to compute LIFO inventories using only 80% of the percentage change in the applicable index. All other taxpayers will be allowed to use 100% of the applicable changes in the index.

It remains to be seen how many taxpayers will select this simplified LIFO procedure. Much depends on how well the government indexes approximate actual price fluctuations in a taxpayer's inventory pool (See Planning Workshop, p. 6/43–44). Many taxpayers may find the index methods attractive simply because base-period costs will not be required for each inventory item.

FINANCIAL STATEMENT CONFORMITY WITH LIFO One of the controversial requirements of a LIFO election is that financial reports to owners and creditors must also be prepared on the basis of LIFO.[25] In other words, a company electing LIFO because it results in a lower taxable income will also have to report a lower income to the company shareholders and creditors. Many taxpayers have complained about this requirement, but nevertheless this conformity rule has been strictly enforced by the IRS.

It is questionable if the conformity rule is justification by itself for not electing LIFO procedures. If owners and creditors are sophisticated enough to "see through" the low financial accounting income number and recognize that significant tax savings are accruing, then the conformity rule is of little importance. This is especially true in the light of regulations proposed in 1979, which would permit a taxpayer to make a footnote disclosure of what net income would have been realized under alternative inventory procedures such as FIFO.[26]

BACKGROUND

The LIFO conformity rule has caused much anguish over the years for some corporate taxpayers who would like to present a high income figure to shareholders (using FIFO), and at the same time present a low income figure to the government (using LIFO). One way that corporations could possibly achieve this objective was suggested in a 1979 Tax Court case.* In this decision, the LIFO conformity rule was ruled inapplicable to certain consolidated financial statements of affiliated (related) corporations.

Some taxpayers interpreted this rule as implying that taxpayers could avoid the conformity rule by simply creating subsidiary corporations and filing consolidated returns. To prevent this possibility, Congress enacted Sec. 472(g)(1) as part of the Tax Reform Act of 1984. This provision treats all members of a "group of financially related corporations" as a single taxpayer for purposes of the LIFO conformity rule. Thus, if either a parent or a subsidiary uses LIFO for tax purposes, a consolidated financial statement issued to shareholders must be based on the LIFO method.

---

*Insilco Corporation, 73 T.C. 589 (1979).

---

[25] Sec. 472(c).

[26] Prop. Reg. Sec. 1.472-2(e).

GOODS UNSALABLE AT NORMAL PRICES

Inventory items which cannot be sold at normal prices (e.g., imperfections, odd lots, style changes) should be valued at bona fide selling prices less the direct cost of disposition. For these purposes, a bona fide selling price is the actual offering price of the goods during a period not later than 30 days after the inventory date. This rule applies regardless of whether the inventory is taken under cost or lower-of-cost or -market procedures.[27]

In a landmark court case, the Supreme Court determined that this rule applies to excess inventory.[28] The taxpayer valued its inventory of spare parts according to an aging schedule, and parts in excess of anticipated future sales were written down in value or written off completely. Although such a procedure is considered to be a generally accepted accounting principle, the IRS disallowed the procedure because the inventories were not offered for sale at the write-down prices or scrapped (as in the case of complete write-offs). The Supreme Court concluded that the Treasury should not be limited by such concepts as "generally accepted accounting principles." This is somewhat ironic, in that Sec. 471 states that an inventory method should be ". . . conforming as nearly as may be to the best accounting practice in the trade or business."

Example 29: V owns a retail store specializing in limited editions of collectors' plates. V has 3,000 unsold plates from the 19X0 edition. These plates cost $18 apiece and normally sold for $30 each. Although V estimates their current value to be no more than $6, she refuses to offer the plates for sale at this amount. Obviously, it would not help her business if a customer who paid $30 a plate now finds the same plate on sale for $6. Nevertheless, V cannot write down the cost of the plates unless she first offers them for sale at the reduced price within 30 days of the inventory date.

FARM INVENTORY METHODS

Over the years Congress and the IRS have attempted to simplify the tax accounting for farmers and ranchers. For example, these taxpayers are allowed to use the cash method for expenses of raising crops and livestock, thus negating the need for inventories. In this situation the cost basis for raised crops and livestock is zero (since all costs are expensed), and the cost basis for purchased livestock is simply the purchase price with no future increases for expensed items. As part of the Tax Reform Act of 1976 Congress added Sec. 447, which requires the accrual basis for certain farm corporations. This requirement was aimed at tax-shelter ventures such as cattle-feeding operations which otherwise obtained immediate deductions for large prepayments for feed and other farm supplies.

---

[27] Reg. Sec. 1.471-2(c).

[28] *Thor Power Tool Company v. Commissioner*, 99 S.Ct. 773 (1979).

A farmer may elect to use the accrual method, which will require inventory procedures. A farmer may also elect cost or lower-of-cost or -market procedures. Generally the cost includes the purchase price and the costs of raising the crops or livestock to maturity. Because of the difficulties inherent in determining these actual costs, the Regulations permit several special reporting procedures for such inventories. For example, Reg. Sec. 1.471-6(d) allows a farmer to use a "farm-price" method, which values inventories of livestock and crops at market price less direct costs of disposition.

A farmer who disposes of crops (other than timber) in a tax year later than the year of planting may elect a special crop-basis method of reporting income.[29] Under this procedure, all costs of producing the crop are deferred until the tax year in which the gross income is realized. This provides a better matching of revenues and expenses for farmers by eliminating the problem of incurring expense deductions in one year and revenues in the next year.

INSTALLMENT METHOD OF REPORTING INCOME

As a general rule the claim-of-right doctrine requires that each annual accounting period stands on its own. In some cases this imposes hardships for taxpayers and special reporting procedures have been developed to mitigate these problems. Two important exceptions to the annual reporting concept are the installment methods available for (*a*) sales by dealers and (*b*) sales by nondealers.

INSTALLMENT METHOD A method of recognizing income from deferred-payment contracts on a wherewithal-to-pay basis by recognizing a portion of each payment as gross income and the remainder as a tax-free recovery of cost.

The ***installment-method*** procedures were enacted by Congress to allow a taxpayer to report gain from the sale of property as deferred contract payments are received. The tax incidence parallels the taxpayer's wherewithal-to-pay, and the installment method eliminates the question of whether or not all of the profit should be taxed in the year of sale.

Generally the installment method can be applied to most sales arranged on a deferred payment basis. However, in some cases the fair market values of an obligation cannot be determined (e.g., when sales price is based on future profits). In such rare cases, the taxpayer will use a cost-recovery method of reporting income. None of the payments is taxable until the taxpayer recovers his or her adjusted basis in the property.

It is interesting to note that the installment method is not considered to be generally acceptable for financial accounting statement purposes. *Opinion No. 10 (Omnibus Opinion)* of the Accounting Principles Board (1966) limits the use of the installment method to those exceptional cases where ultimate collectibility is not reasonably assured. As a result, taxpayers electing the installment method for tax purposes are often required to use regular accrual accounting methods for financial statement purposes.

---

[29] Reg. Sec. 1.61-4.

INSTALLMENT SALES BY DEALERS IN PERSONALTY Sec. 453 specifies special reporting procedures for dealers in personal property who regularly sell on the installment plan. The dealer does not have to sell a specified percentage of inventory on the installment basis; it is merely required that the dealer regularly offer inventory for sale on such a plan. The installment method may be adopted by a new business without the prior approval of the Commissioner, although a change *from* the installment method cannot be made without the prior approval of the IRS. Under the installment method, a dealer in personalty reports a percentage of each payment received as income; this percentage is based on the ratio of the gross profit to the total sales price. This gross profit ratio may be computed on the basis of each sale or, as is more commonly the case, the total sales made during the tax year.[30] If the annual sales approach is used, it is necessary for cash collections in a tax year to be segregated by the year of original sale so that the appropriate gross profit percentage may be applied to the collection.

Example 30: V Corporation regularly offers its inventory of appliances for sale on the installment basis. Results for the first three years of operation were:

YEAR	GROSS SALES	COST OF GOODS	GROSS PROFIT	GROSS PROFIT PERCENTAGE
19X6	$300,000	$210,000	$90,000	30%
19X7	$360,000	$270,000	$90,000	25%
19X8	$400,000	$312,000	$88,000	22%

V Corporation collects $250,000 on account in 19X8, of which $180,000 is from 19X8 sales, $50,000 from 19X7 sales, and $20,000 from 19X6 sales. V must recognize a total of $58,100 gross profit in 19X8, composed of $39,600 from 19X8 sales ($180,000 × .22), $12,500 from 19X7 sales ($50,000 × .25), and $6,000 from 19X6 sales ($20,000 × .30).

OTHER INSTALLMENT SALES The Installment Sales Revision Act of 1980 significantly liberalized the rules for casual (nondealer) sales of personalty and all sales of realty. Prior to 1980, the installment method had to be affirmatively elected by a taxpayer, and such an election was subject to several restrictions on sales price and initial year payments. Effective October 20, 1980, any sale of noninventory property (but *not* services) must be reported on an installment basis, unless the taxpayer makes a special election to report the entire gain in the year of sale, even though payments may be received over several tax years.[31] In some cases such an election may be advisable (see Planning Workshop, p. 6/44).

[30] Reg. 1.453-2(c). "Gross profit" is total sales price less cost of goods sold. Note that selling and administrative expenses do not affect gross profit (these are expense deductions).

[31] Reg. Sec. 1.453-1(d).

The only requirement for a nondealer installment sale is that at least one payment be received after the tax year in which the sale took place. It is not necessary to receive a payment in the year of sale.[32] The taxable portion of each payment is computed in a manner similar to that for dealers, although important definitional differences exist. Specifically, the portion of each payment reported as income is the ratio of the gross profit to the total contract price. Gross profit is determined by comparing the selling price with the adjusted basis of the property. The definition of each of these items is important in applying the installment rules, and each may be described as follows:

- *Selling price*—Selling price represents the total amount received (actually and constructively) by the seller. This includes cash, the fair market value of property received, and any liabilities and expenses paid, assumed, or taken by the buyer subject to the property.
- *Adjusted basis*—This represents the taxpayer's tax basis for gain purposes as normally computed under the Code (e.g., Code Sec. 1011-1019). Commissions and selling expenses are *added* to this basis for nondealers, although dealers in real estate may deduct such items as business expenses.
- *Total contract price*—Total contract price represents the total amount to be received by the seller. This does not include mortgages assumed by the buyer unless the amount of the mortgage exceeds the basis of the property sold.[33] In this case, the excess must be included as part of the total contract price and treated as a payment received in the year of sale.

Example 31: W sells realty having an adjusted basis of $21,000 (tax basis of $20,000 plus $1,000 of selling expenses added to basis). The property is not subject to a mortgage. The buyer will pay $30,000, with $9,000 in the year of sale and $7,000 a year for the next three years. W's gross profit percentage is determined as follows:

$$\text{Gross Profit Percentage} = \frac{\text{Gross Profit}}{\text{Total Contract Price}} = \frac{(\$30{,}000 - \$21{,}000)}{\$30{,}000}$$

$$= \frac{\$9{,}000}{\$30{,}000} = 30\%$$

W must recognize $2,700 of gain ($9,000 × 30%) in the year of sale and $2,100 of gain ($7,000 × 30%) in each of the next three years. The gain is taxed as the taxpayer has a wherewithal-to-pay.

Example 32: Assume the same facts as in Example 31 except that the buyer's down payment consists of $4,000 cash and a $5,000 purchase money mortgage (payable on demand). In this case, the result

[32] Sec. 453(a).

[33] Reg. Sec. 1-453(1)(b)(2).

is the same as Example 31, since a mortgage note payable on demand is considered the equivalent of cash.[34]

Particular consideration should be given to the treatment of mortgages assumed by the purchaser. As long as the mortgage assumed is less than the basis of the property, then the amount is not considered to be a "payment" received by the seller. Clearly the taxpayer's wherewithal-to-pay should be related to the actual payments received. However, any portion of the assumed mortgage exceeding the basis of the property is automatically treated as part of the total contract price and is considered to be a payment received in the year of sale. In effect, the excess is considered to be a constructive distribution of cash in the year of sale. This is consistent with other provisions of the Code[35] and limits the gross profit percentage to 100%. In fact in these situations the gross profit will always equal the total contract price, which results in a 100% gross profit ratio.[36] The effects of mortgages are illustrated in the following examples.

Example 33: Assume the same facts as in Example 31 except that the property was subject to a $6,000 mortgage which is assumed by the buyer. The buyer will pay $3,000 down in the year of sale and $7,000 a year for the next 3 years for a total selling price of $30,000. W's gross profit percentage is now determined as follows:

$$\text{Gross Profit Percentage} = \frac{\text{Gross Profit}}{\text{Total Contract Price}} = \frac{(\$30{,}000 - \$21{,}000)}{\$24{,}000}$$

$$= \frac{\$9{,}000}{\$24{,}000} = 37.5\%$$

W must recognize $1,125 ($3,000 × 37.5%) of gain in the year of sale and $2,625 ($7,000 × 37.5%) of gain in the next three taxable years. Note that the mortgage assumed is considered to be part of the selling price but is *not* considered in determining the total contract price, since the mortgage did not exceed the basis of the property. Over the 4-year period, the entire $9,000 gain is recognized ($1,125 + $2,625 + $2,625 + $2,625 = $9,000).

Example 34: Assume the same facts as in Example 33 except that W's basis in the property is only $4,000 (i.e., less than the mortgage assumed of $6,000). W's gross profit percentage is now determined as follows:

$$\text{Gross Profit Percentage} = \frac{\text{Gross Profit}}{\text{Total Contract Price}} = \frac{(\$30{,}000 - \$4{,}000)}{(\$24{,}000 + \$2{,}000)}$$

$$= \frac{\$26{,}000}{\$26{,}000} = 100\%$$

---

[34] Such payments are treated as being received in the year of sale; otherwise the seller could completely control the timing of the gain by demanding payment or selling the obligations. See Sec. 453(f)(4).

[35] For example, see Sec. 357(c), relating to excess liabilities in certain nontaxable exchanges.

[36] Recall that the mortgage exceeding basis is in both the gross profit and the total contract price.

W must recognize $5,000 ($3,000 + $2,000 × 100%) gain in the year of sale and $7,000 of gain in the next three taxable years. Note that the excess of mortgage over basis of $2,000 is treated as a constructive receipt of cash in the year of sale and is reflected as a part of total contract price.

FORM 6252

Form 6252 is used to report nondealer sales of property on an installment basis. Figure 6-1 illustrates this form, using the information contained in Example 33.

INSTALLMENT REPORTING—SPECIAL PROBLEMS The preceding discussion focused on the basic gross profit computations for the installment methods. Some of the practical problems encountered in applying the installment method are discussed in the following sections.

CHARACTER OF THE INSTALLMENT GAIN. The use of the installment method does not change the ordinary income or capital gain status of the gain. The character of the recognized gain is determined by the character of the property being sold. Thus, a taxpayer who sells a capital asset held longer than a year (at the date of sale) on an installment basis will report the taxable portion of each gain as long-term capital gain on Schedule D.

FORM 1040—SCHEDULE D

In some instances, a portion or all of the gain recognized on sales of depreciable property may be "recaptured" as ordinary income. In such a case, all ordinary income must be recognized before any other type of gain is reported. In addition, Sec. 453(i), added by the Tax Reform Act of 1984, requires the recognition of *all* depreciation recapture income in the year of sale, regardless of the amount of principal payment(s) received in the year of sale. These provisions, which drastically alter tax planning for installment sales of depreciable property, are discussed in detail in Chapter 11.

IMPUTED INTEREST RULES. In an arm's length transaction it is expected that an installment sales contract provides for a reasonable rate of interest on the deferred payments. Since such interest payments are taxed as ordinary income, a taxpayer entitled to long-term capital gains treatment on an installment sale may be tempted to increase the selling price of the assets in lieu of charging a fair rate of interest. The interest income would then be converted to capital gain. Of course, such a designation in the sales contract may cause the buyer to lose interest deductions, and the adverse tax interests of the seller and buyer may adjust the interest in the contract to a rate acceptable to both parties. Nevertheless, Congress has chosen to establish some minimum interest rate guide lines for selling prices exceeding $3,000 through the ***imputed interest*** rules of Sec. 483.

IMPUTED INTEREST A procedure used by the IRS to impose a minimum interest return on deferred-payment contracts which provide for little or no interest.

The imputed interest rules of Sec. 483 were signficantly altered by the Tax Reform Act of 1984. Prior to this act, Reg. Sec. 1.483-1(d)(1) required that an installment contract provide for at least a simple interest rate of 9%. In order to determine whether this requirement was met, all payments (including any *stated* interest) deferred more than six months must

FIGURE 6-1

Form **6252** Department of the Treasury Internal Revenue Service	**Computation of Installment Sale Income** ▶ See instructions on back. ▶ Attach to your tax return. Use a separate form for each sale or other disposition of property on the installment method.	OMB No 1545-0228 **1984** 79

Name(s) as shown on tax return: *Taxpayer W* — Identifying number: *111-22-3333*

A Description of property ▶ *10 Acres of Real Estate*

B Date acquired (month, day, and year) ▶ *6/2/76* C Date sold (month, day, and year) ▶ *8/13/84*

D Was property sold to a related party after May 14, 1980? (See instruction C) ☐ Yes ☒ No

E If the answer to D is "Yes," was the property a marketable security? ☐ Yes ☐ No

If you checked "Yes" to question E, complete Part III.
If you checked "No" to question E, complete Part III for the year of sale and for 2 years after the year of sale.

Part I Computation of Gross Profit and Contract Price *(Complete this part for year of sale only.)*

1 Selling price including mortgages and other indebtedness (Do not include interest whether stated or unstated)			1	30,000
2 Mortgages and other indebtedness buyer assumes or takes property subject to (Do not include new mortgages from a bank or other source.)	2	6,000		
3 Subtract line 2 from line 1	3	24,000		
4 Cost or other basis of property sold	4	20,000		
5 Depreciation allowed or allowable	5	0		
6 Adjusted basis (subtract line 5 from line 4)	6	20,000		
7 Commissions and other expenses of sale	7	1,000		
8 Income recapture from Form 4797, Part III (see instructions)	8	0		
9 Add lines 6, 7, and 8			9	21,000
10 Subtract line 9 from line 1. If result is zero or less, do not complete rest of form			10	9,000
11 If question A is a principal residence, enter the sum of Form 2119, lines 12,15, and 19			11	—
12 Gross profit (subtract line 11 from line 10)			12	9,000
13 Subtract line 9 from line 2. If line 9 is more than line 2, enter zero			13	0
14 Contract price (add line 3 and line 13)			14	24,000

Part II Computation of Taxable Part of Installment Sale
(Complete this part for year of sale and any year you receive a payment.)

15 Gross profit ratio (divide line 12 by line 14) (for years after the year of sale, see instructions)			15	37.5%
16 For year of sale only—enter amount from line 13 above; otherwise enter zero			16	0
17 Payments received during year (Do not include interest whether stated or unstated)			17	3,000
18 Add lines 16 and 17			18	3,000
19 Payments received in prior years (Do not include interest whether stated or unstated)	19	0		
20 Taxable part of installment sale (multiply line 18 by line 15)			20	1,125
21 Part of line 20 that is ordinary income under recapture rules (applies only to sales before 6/7/84)			21	0
22 Subtract line 21 from line 20. Enter on Schedule D or Form 4797			22	1,125

Part III Information and Computation for Related Party Installment Sale
(Do not complete this part if you received the final installment payment this tax year.)

F Name, address, and taxpayer identifying number of related party

G Did the related party, during this tax year, resell or dispose of the property? ☐ Yes ☐ No

H If the answer to question G is "Yes," complete lines 23 through 30 below unless one of the following conditions is met (check only the box that applies).

☐ The first disposition was a sale or exchange of stock to the issuing corporation.
☐ The second disposition was an involuntary conversion where the threat of conversion occurred after the first disposition.
☐ The second disposition occurred after the death of the original seller or purchaser.
☐ It can be established to the satisfaction of the Internal Revenue Service that tax avoidance was not a principal purpose for either of the dispositions. If this box is checked, attach an explanation. (See instruction C.)

23 Selling price of property sold by related party	23	
24 Enter contract price from line 14 for year of first sale	24	
25 Enter the smaller of line 23 or line 24	25	
26 Total payments received by the end of your 1984 tax year. Add lines 18 and 19	26	
27 Subtract line 26 from line 25. If line 26 is more than line 25, enter zero	27	
28 Multiply line 27 by the gross profit ratio on line 15 for year of first sale	28	
29 Part of line 28 that is ordinary income under recapture rules (applies only to sales before 6/7/84)	29	
30 Subtract line 29 from line 28. Enter on Schedule D or Form 4797	30	

For Paperwork Reduction Act Notice, see back of form. Form **6252** (1984)

be discounted back to the date of sale at 9% using the tables provided in the Regulations at Sec. 1.483-1(g)(2). If the net present value was less than the portion of the stated sales price (excluding any stated interest), then unstated interest existed in the contract.

Example 35: J sells property in 1982 with an adjusted basis of $60,000 for $100,000 with $10,000 received at the time of sale and six annual payments of $18,000 beginning one year later ($3,000 of each payment is designated in the contract as interest). Using the tables provided in the Regulations, the present value of the six annual payments at a 9% discount rate is $83,278. Since this amount is less than the portion of the principal sales price deferred more than six months ($100,000 − $10,000 = $90,000), unstated interest exists in the contract.

Interestingly, once it was determined that unstated interest existed in the contract, another calculation had to be made to determine the *amount* of the unstated interest. This is the same computation as described above, except that the discount rate used is 10%.[37] In effect, a 1% "penalty" was charged for failure to specify an adequate rate of interest in the installment contract.

Example 36: Refer to Example 35. Using the tables provided in the Regulations, the present value of the six annual payments at a 10% discount rate is $77,824. The difference of $12,176 between the $90,000 of principal payments and the present value of $77,824 is treated as unstated interest, to be recognized as ordinary income ratably over the period of the deferred payments. This creates a new actual selling price of $87,824 ($100,000 − $12,176) for purposes of computing the long-term capital gain. Rather than reporting a $40,000 gain ($100,000 − $60,000 basis), J will report a $27,824 long-term capital gain ($87,824 − $60,000 basis).

BACKGROUND

As part of the changes instituted by the Tax Reform Act of 1984, Congress expanded the applicability of the original issue discount rules. These rules require the use of effective interest methods in determining actual interest income and expense amounts on certain corporate obligations. The 1984 changes were designed to ensure that obligations bear market rates of interest for tax purposes. Specifically, when corporate obligations were issued for property, it was sometimes difficult to determine an allocation between the issue

Continued

[37] Reg. Sec. 1.483-1(c)(2)(ii).

BACKGROUND

price of an obligation and the related interest. Congress addressed this problem by establishing test rates for imputed interest on such obligations. Unlike the 9% rate used in Sec. 483, these test rates were tied to current market rates of interest. These test rates were then incorporated into Sec. 483 to ensure that virtually all obligations (corporate and noncorporate) provide for market rates of interest for tax purposes.

Sec. 483(c)(1) was amended to provide imputed interest rules which were more in line with current market rates of interest. Specifically, the new test rate to determine if unstated interest exists in a deferred payment contract was set at 110% of the "applicable federal rate," which represents an average of various federal interest rates (e.g., treasury notes and treasury bills). The test rate so determined will be compounded semiannually. Three separate rates would be determined and published every six months by the Treasury for three categories of obligations: (1) short-term (maturities of three years or less), (2) mid-term (maturities of over three but not more than nine years), and (3) long-term (maturities of more than nine years). The applicable test rate would be determined on the first day on which there is a binding installment contract.

As was true under prior law, the existence of unstated interest in a contract required another calculation to determine the *amount* of the unstated interest. Once again, a "penalty" for unstated interest is involved; the discount calculations are made using a rate of *120%* of the applicable federal rate, compounded semiannually (Sec. 483(b)).

The imputed interest rules as originally drafted in the 1984 Act caused much consternation among taxpayers and tax preparers, who believed that the test rates were set at very high levels and that the complex original issue discount rules would apply to a variety of commonplace transactions. Sensing that perhaps they had engaged in overkill, Congress delayed the effective date of the imputed interest rules until July 1, 1985 as part of H.R. 5361, enacted in October of 1984. For the interim period, a 9% test rate will apply to a seller-financed sale of property for $2 million or less. Taxpayers failing to meet this hurdle will have interest imputed at a 10% rate. Sales in excess of $2 million will be subject to a test rate based on a weighted average of 9% and 110% of the "applicable federal rate." Some members of Congress have called for a return to the old 9% test rate for all transactions, and the status of the 1984 provisions relating to imputed interest is at best uncertain as this text goes to press.

The imputed interest rules also apply to both sales of property at a loss and sales where future payments are based on a contingency. In the latter case, the imputed interest rules are applied to each payment on an ex post facto basis. Finally, it is interesting to note that Sec. 483(g) provides for a 7% maximum imputation rate for sales or exchanges of land for $500,000 or less between family members (as defined in the related party rules of Sec. 267(c)(4)). This change was justified because ". . . the use of a single test rate in times of unusually high interest rates places an undue burden on sales of land between related individuals."[38] Unfortunately, no explanation was given as to why a similar burden apparently doesn't exist on a sale between unrelated parties.

DEFAULTS AND REPOSSESSIONS. The tax treatment for defaults and repossessions on personalty are basically the same for both dealers and nondealers. If a buyer defaults on the remaining payments of an installment contract and the personal property is not repossessed, the seller is entitled to a bad debt deduction for the unrecovered cost of the contract.[39] The portion of the remaining payments which represent deferred gross profit are not deductible, since these amounts have not been included in income and therefore have a zero basis. If the property is repossessed, the bad debt deduction is reduced by the fair market value of the property at repossession and the fair market value is the tax basis. Any gain recognized on repossession is reported as ordinary income or capital gain, depending on the character of the original sale.

Example 37: After paying $300 of the $500 sales price of a 19X1 installment sale, the buyer defaulted on the remaining payments. The seller's 19X1 gross profit percentage was 20%. The seller is entitled to a bad debt deduction of $160 ($200 remaining balance × 80% cost percentage). If the seller repossesses the property at a time when it has a value of $100 and incurs $30 of repossession costs, the bad debt deduction is $90 ($160 − $100 + $30). The inventory has a tax basis of $100, the fair market value at repossession.

Special rules apply for repossessions of real property. In general, Sec. 1038 provides for no loss recognition on the repossessed realty; the loss is deferred by assigning the adjusted basis of the debt (net of the profit portion) as the basis of the realty. Because of the appreciation potential of realty, Sec. 1038 limits the potential gain recognized on the repossession of realty. Such gain recognized is limited to the gain recognized on the original sale less any amounts previously reported as income and less any repossession costs.[40] Thus a taxpayer avoids paying tax on any appreciation in value of property since the original sale. Since the basis of the repossessed property is increased only by repossession costs and the gain

---

[38] *Joint Committee on Taxation, General Explanation of the Economic Recovery Tax Act of 1981* (H.R. 4242, 97th Congress, Public Law 97-34), p. 60.

[39] Reg. Sec. 1.453-1(d).

[40] As an alternative, the taxpayer may recognize the total collections on the installment contract less any gain previously taxed as income from such payments. Generally this method produces a gain larger than the method described above.

actually reported for tax purposes, this appreciation in value will be taxed on a later sale.

Example 38: N repossesses realty at a time when the buyer defaulted on $40,000 of remaining installment payments. The original sale was for $100,000 three years ago, and the gross profit on the sale was $30,000. Repossession costs were $2,000, and the land had a fair market value of $140,000 at the time of repossession. N's gain on repossession is limited to $10,000 ($30,000 original gross profit less $2,000 repossession costs and less $18,000 [$60,000 × 30%] of gross profit included in income from the $60,000 amounts collected before default). N's tax basis in the land is $40,000, the sum of the $28,000 unrecovered cost basis of the defaulted payments ($40,000 × 70%), the $10,000 gain recognized on repossession, and the $2,000 repossession costs.

DISPOSITION OF INSTALLMENT OBLIGATIONS. Sec. 453B was specifically enacted to prevent a taxpayer from avoiding income recognition by selling an installment obligation or by assigning the obligation to other taxpayers. If the installment obligation is sold, the difference between the amount realized and the adjusted basis of the obligation (net of any deferred profit) must be recognized as taxable gain or loss. Additionally, a gift of the installment obligation usually requires the donor to immediately recognize the unreported deferred profit. Such treatment is justified under the theory that without the installment provisions the income properly accrues to the seller at the time of entering the installment contract and such income cannot be assigned away to another person. Sec. 453B(f) specifically requires immediate recognition by the holder if an obligation is canceled, with a further stipulation that the face value of the note is always used to measure gain or loss on a cancellation between related parties. (Exceptions to the immediate recognition rule are provided for certain nontaxable exchanges covered elsewhere in the Code.)

Example 39: G sells property (adjusted basis, $20,000) for $25,000 on a 5-year installment basis. After collecting $13,000 of payments, G sells the remaining notes for their fair market value of $10,500. G must recognize a gain of $900. This represents the difference between the amount realized ($10,500) and the unrecovered cost basis of $9,600 for the remaining payments ($12,000 × 80% cost percentage).

Example 40: Assume the same facts as in Example 39 except that G cancels the note with $12,000 of payments remaining. G must still recognize the $900 of gain (presuming the fair market value of the notes is $10,500). However, if G is related to the buyer, the $12,000 face value of the notes must be used to compute gain, resulting in a gain of $2,400 ($12,000 − $9,600).

RELATED PARTY SALES. Sec. 453(e) was enacted by Congress in 1980 to accelerate income recognition in certain related party installment sales. Usually such schemes were structured in the following manner: Taxpayer A would sell property on an installment basis to a related party B who in turn would immediately resell the property for cash (at approximately the same value) to a third party C (not necessarily a related party). Since B's basis in the property is the value of the installment obligations issued to A, no gain is recognized on the sale to C for cash. The net result of this series of transactions is that the family unit (A and B) has the immediate enjoyment of the cash, although taxes on the gain realized by A are reported only as payments are received over the life of the installment note issued by B. Taxpayers were surprisingly successful with similar schemes in a number of court cases prior to 1980.[41]

Sec. 453 addresses this problem by accelerating the recognition of gain by the initial seller when the related purchaser resells the property. The net effect is to tax the original seller as though he or she had disposed of the original installment obligation for the amount realized on the second sale (limited to the original contract price). For purposes of applying these provisions Sec. 453(f)(1) defines a related party as including the initial seller's spouse, children, grandchildren, and parents, as well as corporations, partnerships, estates, and trusts in which the taxpayer has an interest (directly or indirectly, through Code Sec. 318 stock attribution rules).

Example 41: On November 1, 19X2 B sold property to his mother M for $800,000, payable with $100,000 down payment and seven equal $100,000 annual installments beginning one year from the date of sale. B's adjusted basis in the property was $480,000. The gross profit to be recognized on the sale is $320,000 or 40% of the total contract price. On January 3, 19X3, M sells the property to an unrelated third party for $800,000. B, a calendar-year taxpayer, reports $40,000 of gross profit on his 19X2 return ($100,000 down payment × 40% gross profit ratio). The sale by M in 19X3 forces B to recognize the remaining $280,000 of deferred gain ($700,000 × 40%). The same result would occur if M sold the property for $820,000; however, M would also have to recognize her $20,000 realized gain. Future payments received by B on the installment note will not be taxable.

Special rules limiting the acceleration of gain apply in cases where the second sale is for less than the amount of outstanding installment obligations.[42] The acceleration rule applies only when the related party resells the property within two years of the initial sale. However, there is no time limit for sales of marketable securities. Various other exceptions not discussed here are specified in Sec. 453(e)(6).

---

[41] The leading case in this area was *Rushing v. Commissioner*, 441 F. 2d 593 (CA-5, 1971), which involved the use of a family trust in the related party transaction.

[42] Sec. 453(e)(3).

Finally, Sec. 453(g) provides a special rule for sales of depreciable property to an 80%-owned (controlled) partnership or corporation. Such a sale triggers total income recognition in the year of sale, so that the buyer's depreciation deductions (or total sales price) will not be taken immediately while the seller's income recognition is deferred. Without such a provision, related taxpayers could take advantage of an unwarranted timing difference.

PLANNING WORKSHOP

ACCOUNTING METHOD SELECTION

The choice of accounting method should be tailored to the particular business. A publicly-held corporation may be required to use the accrual basis for financial accounting purposes, although specific methods can be chosen for such important items as inventories and depreciation. On the other hand, a sole proprietor may find the cash method to be the simplest method for his or her business. Records may be as simple as a checking account, and accrual-basis calculations for sales and purchases can be easily made with beginning and ending inventory balances.

Additionally, the cash basis offers some opportunity (within reason) for tax planning by delaying or accelerating year-end billings of revenues or payment of expenses. This income deferral opportunity makes the cash method particularly attractive to service-oriented taxpayers such as physicians, attorneys, and accountants. These businesses dealing in services will generally elect the cash basis of reporting for tax purposes.

CHANGING ACCOUNTING METHODS

Businesses change accounting methods for a variety of reasons. It is important for taxpayers to realize the cumulative adjustment implications of such changes. Revenue Procedure 80-51 may require acceleration of an unfavorable cumulative adjustment in some cases, and such an acceleration may create cash-flow problems for the taxpayer. On the other hand, the new accounting method may produce immediate tax benefits which will offset the cumulative adjustment. For example, a taxpayer switching from a lower-of-cost or -market procedure to LIFO will have to restore previous write-downs to income over a 3-year period. However, if the taxpayer's inventory cost is increasing, the tax savings from LIFO procedures may offset the income restoration.

LIFO INVENTORIES

LIFO inventory procedures offer taxpayers an opportunity to postpone the payment of taxes on "paper profits" in inventory during

Continued

PLANNING WORKSHOP

inflationary periods. Even if a taxpayer must liquidate the oldest low-cost layers of inventory, at a minimum he or she has received an interest-free loan from the government on the cumulative tax savings generated during the LIFO years. The index methods of the proposed Regulations will make LIFO procedures easier to apply for many taxpayers. However, it remains to be seen if the pooling procedures permissible with such indexes will generate the same tax savings available under the double-extension method. This is especially true for businesses subject to the 80% limit on the use of such indexes.

The decision in the Thor Power Tool Company case on obsolete or excess inventories may actually be an incentive to switch to LIFO. A taxpayer who has made improper write-downs to inventory will be required to restore these adjustments to income. Since the restoration of previous write-downs is a necessary prerequisite to adopting LIFO, one of the major barriers to electing LIFO for taxpayers making such write-downs will be removed.

INSTALLMENT SALES

The installment method offers a dealer in personalty the opportunity to defer a portion of income each year until collections occur. This may lead to a smoothing of income and avoids possible lags between the recognition of sales and bad debts on the accrual basis.

The installment method for nondealers offers several advantages. The tax liability is postponed on a wherewithal-to-pay basis, and the spreading of the income may keep the taxpayer in a lower marginal tax bracket. Additionally, spreading the gain over several years may help avoid a minimum tax problem (see Chapter 13).

One major disadvantage of an installment election is that the taxpayer does not have the immediate use of the funds representing the full contract price. A taxpayer may decide that the cost of recognizing the gain in the year of sale is not that significant, particularly if losses are available to offset the gain and/or the taxpayer can benefit from income averaging. An installment election will necessarily involve interest income, either stated in the contract or imputed by the IRS.

One potential problem with an installment election is the definition of contract price and initial-year payments. Recall that any excess of a mortgage assumed over the adjusted basis of the property sold will be considered an initial-year payment (a constructive distribution of cash). This often happens when a taxpayer sells low-basis realty which has been remortgaged. In some cases, taxpayers are surprised to discover that this is a payment received, even though no wherewithal-to-pay exists.

KEY POINTS TO REMEMBER

1. Taxpayers may elect to file returns on a calendar-year basis, a fiscal-year basis, or a 52–53 week year. Changes from one period to another usually require annualization of income procedures to tax the resulting short-period income at an annual marginal tax rate.
2. Taxpayers electing the cash method must still report sales and purchases of inventory on the accrual basis, and expenses may not be deducted until incurred.
3. The claim-of-right doctrine usually taxes an amount as income at the time constructive receipt occurs. Special deferrals are available for advances received on future inventory deliveries.
4. Taxpayers entering into long-term construction contracts may elect either of two special reporting procedures for tax purposes. The percentage-of-completion method recognizes income each year by stages of work performed, and the completed-contract method defers recognition until the contract is satisfied.
5. Changes of accounting methods may require cumulative adjustments for income or expense items reported under the prior method. If the change is initiated by the taxpayer, an adjustment period of up to 10 years is possible. If the change is initiated by the IRS, the total adjustment is recognized immediately, subject to a special averaging procedure for positive adjustments exceeding $3,000.
6. Taxpayers may value inventories at cost or the lower-of-cost or -market. In cases where taxpayers are unable to identify the specific goods in inventory, a cost flow assumption such as LIFO, FIFO, or average cost may be used.
7. Dollar value LIFO inventory procedures enable a taxpayer to apply LIFO inventory procedures on a basis of total dollars, rather than identifying the price and quantity of each item. The double-extension method requires base-period costs for each item; simplified procedures under new Regulations are designed to overcome this potential problem.
8. Damaged, obsolete, or excess inventories can be written down only if the items are offered for sale at the write-down prices within 30 days of the inventory date.
9. Installment reporting procedures recognize the gross profit on sales or exchanges as the deferred payments are received. Such procedures are elective for dealers of personalty and are mandatory for other sales unless the taxpayer elects to report the entire gain in the year of sale.
10. Bad debt deductions may be taken for defaults on installment sales. The deduction is limited to the unrecovered cost portion of the deferred payments, reduced by the value of the property (if repossessed), and increased by any repossession costs.

SELF-STUDY QUESTIONS

1. Jill Abram, a single taxpayer, elects to change her tax year from a calendar year to a fiscal year ending each September 30. Abram's adjusted gross income for the January 1–September 30 short tax year was $36,200, and her itemized deductions for this period were $8,800. Abram's annualized taxable income for the short period is
   a) $26,620
   b) $35,420
   c) $35,493
   d) $37,883

2. Katherine Norton is required by the IRS to switch from the cash to the accrual basis of accounting in January, 19X4. Relevant information from Norton's accounting records for 19X4 includes the following:

	12-31-X3 BALANCE	12-31-X4 BALANCE
Accounts receivable	$62,000	$58,000
Accounts payable	46,000	50,000
Merchandise inventory	38,000	46,000

   Norton's sales on the cash basis for 19X4 were $320,000, and her purchases on the cash basis were $230,000. The total Sec. 481 cumulative adjustment required for Norton as a result of the change of accounting method is
   a) $54,000
   b) $70,000
   c) $82,000
   d) $146,000

3. In 19X8, Myra Thomas voluntarily changed accounting methods. The change requires a $60,000 cumulative adjustment, caused by the following understatements of income in the four prior years:

   19X4—$24,000 19X6—$10,000
   19X5—$14,000 19X7—$12,000

   Assuming that Thomas elects the maximum spread-forward period available under Rev. Proc. 80-51, she will increase her 19X8 income on account of the adjustment by
   a) $6,000
   b) $12,000
   c) $15,000
   d) $60,000

4. Charles Carson owns and operates Carson Grocery as a self-employed individual. For the calendar year 19X0 the opening inventory was

$15,000—purchases $40,000, and closing inventory $12,000. The following information for 19X0 is also available:

- Stock in trade which was included in the opening inventory and had a basis of $3,500 (fair market value $4,300) was donated to qualified charitable organizations.
- Included in purchases is merchandise having a basis of $2,200 (fair market value $2,900) used personally by Mr. Carson and his family.
- Excluded from both ending inventory and purchases was $1,600 of merchandise on hand that was consigned from a new manufacturer of diet foods and $5,400 for purchased goods which were in transit on December 31; title to the latter had passed to the Carson Grocery at year's end. It is estimated that the value of the closing inventory will decline 20% early in 19X1.

The cost of goods sold to be used in computing 19X0 taxable income would be

a) $42,700

b) $37,300

c) $35,800

d) $32,640

(AICPA adapted)

5. On December 31, 19X1, Kern Company adopted the dollar value LIFO inventory method. All of Kern's inventories constitute a single pool. The inventory on December 31, 19X1, using the dollar value LIFO inventory method was $600,000. Inventory data for 19X2 are as follows:

12/31/X2 inventory at year end prices	$780,000
Relevant price index at year end (base year 19X1)	120

Under the dollar value LIFO inventory method, Kern's inventory at December 31, 19X2 would be

a) $650,000

b) $655,000

c) $660,000

d) $720,000

(AICPA adapted)

6. Roger Morse is a self-employed home appliance dealer who derives most of his gross income from sales of merchandise on the installment basis. During 19X3, Morse recorded installment sales of $120,000. The cost of these sales was $80,000, excluding selling and administrative expenses of $10,000, which were incurred and paid in 19X3. Collections of the 19X3 sales were made as follows:

19X3	$20,000
19X4	$64,000
19X5	$36,000

What is the amount of income that Morse should report for 19X5 with respect to the 19X3 installment sales?

a) $7,800

b) $10,000

c) $10,800

d) $12,000

(AICPA adapted)

7. George Singleton, owner of Singleton Appliance Company, uses the installment method for reporting gross profit on retail sales. His gross profit percentage was 30% in 19X7 and 35% in 19X8. An appliance sold in 19X7 for $500 had a cost of $375. It was repossessed on January 15, 19X8 as the buyer had not paid an installment since November of 19X7. Its fair market value on January 15, 19X8 was $75 and the balance owed on the contract was $150. The gain or loss on the repossession was

a) $52.50 gain

b) $45.00 gain

c) $30.00 loss

d) $17.50 loss

(AICPA adapted)

8. On January 15, 19X1, Gene Bolin bought a vacant lot for $75,000 as a parking lot for his customers. The parking lot had been in use five months when the town began providing free parking facilities nearby. Mr. Bolin sold the lot on June 20, 19X1 for $100,000 ($20,000 cash and four $20,000 12% notes due on June 20 of each of the next four years). If Mr. Bolin elects to report the gain on this sale on the installment basis, the gain to be reported in the year of sale would be

a) $25,000

b) $20,000

c) $6,250

d) $5,000

(AICPA adapted)

9. Bob Cratchett sold six acres of land in 19X6 for a total of $25,000, which was allocated as follows: $3,000 cash down payment, $1,000 purchase money mortgage payable on demand, and a $16,000 note in which the purchaser agrees to pay $4,000 a year (plus 14% interest) for the next four years beginning in 19X7. In addition, the purchasers agrees to assume a $5,000 outstanding mortgage on the property. Cratchett had purchased the property in 19X1 for $9,000, and he incurred $1,000 selling expenses in closing the sale. Under the installment method, Cratchett must recognize a gross profit in 19X6 (before considering any 60% long-term capital gains deduction) of

a) $2,250
b) $3,000
c) $4,000
d) $10,000

10. Max Adams sold 20 acres of land to his father on June 15, 19X5. His father subsequently resold the property. Max would not have to accelerate the recognition of any deferred gain on the installment note if
    a) his father sells the property at a gain,
    b) his father sells the property to an unrelated party,
    c) the installment contract provided for at least 9% interest,
    d) his father sold the property after more than two years had elapsed.

QUESTIONS

1. What restrictions are imposed on the selection of a tax year?
2. Explain the purpose of the annualization requirement for short-period tax returns. Can these calculations unfairly penalize a taxpayer? Explain.
3. Len Redgrave, a tax attorney using a calendar tax year, completed three consulting engagements in December 19X4. Client A paid $500 cash for the service, Client B gave Len a 12%, 90-day note (fair market value of $475), and Client C was billed for $500 through Redgrave's normal accounts receivable procedures (unpaid at year-end). When will these fees be taxed to Redgrave, assuming that he uses (*a*) the cash basis, and (*b*) the accrual basis?
4. "The reporting of expense deductions by a cash-basis taxpayer closely resembles the reporting of such deductions by an accrual-basis taxpayer." Do you agree? Explain.
5. On October 1, 19X4 Apple Company prepays two years rent of $48,000 to Banana Company. How will this payment be reported by each party for tax purposes, assuming that (a) Apple is a cash-basis taxpayer and Banana is an accrual-basis taxpayer, and (b) Apple is an accrual-basis taxpayer and Banana is a cash-basis taxpayer?
6. Give an example of a change in accounting estimate and a change in accounting method. Are the two changes treated the same for tax purposes? Explain.
7. Barbara Johnson voluntarily makes a change of accounting method in 19X4 which results in a Sec. 481 cumulative adjustment of $80,000. How will Barbara report this adjustment, assuming that the incorrect method of accounting had been used for (a) one year, (b) six years, and (c) 13 years? (In each case, assume that the misstatements of income in each of the prior years were approximately equal.)

8. Markov Corporation uses lower-of-cost or -market procedures in valuing its inventory of 15 consumer products. Explain how the lower-of-cost or -market technique would be applied to this inventory.

9. Hightech Company is a retail dealer in personal computers. During recent months a large consumer demand has resulted in a decreased wholesale cost of the computers. What factors should Hightech consider in choosing an inventory cost flow assumption?

10. Prior to 19X4, Candle Corporation has used lower-of-cost or -market (LCM) procedures for valuing its ending inventory. The December 31, 19X3 inventory had an original cost of $98,000 and was valued at $83,000 using LCM procedures. Assuming that Candle changes to the LIFO method on January 1, 19X4, what tax adjustments must be made to reflect the change?

11. One of the advantages of electing a dollar-value LIFO method of inventory valuation is the acceptability of pooling various inventory items. Explain how pooling procedures can offer tax advantages over unit (item) LIFO procedures.

12. Minton Company uses a computer aging schedule for its inventory of replacement equipment parts. In accordance with generally accepted accounting procedures, Minton writes down the value of the inventory to an expected net realizable value. Is this inventory method acceptable for tax reporting purposes? Explain.

13. Is the term "total contract price" defined in a manner to reflect a wherewithal-to-pay principal when computing the gross profit ratio for installment sales? Explain.

14. Why are the imputed interest rules of Code Sec. 483 a necessary component of the installment sales provisions? Explain by means of an example.

15. Code Sec. 453(e) was enacted in 1980 to prevent a taxpayer from using the installment method for nondealer sales of property when his or her family currently enjoys immediate possession of the total sales price of the property. Give an example of such a transaction, and explain how the new rules eliminate this problem.

16. A taxpayer must itemize his or her deductions in computing short-period taxable income for annualization purposes. Explain how this is accomplished in the short-period computation.

17. What information is necessary to convert cash sales and collections on account to the accrual basis?

18. The recognition of income from advance payments for inventory is governed by the year in which "substantial advance payments" are received. Explain.

19. A taxpayer who has been using a particular accounting method for eight years voluntarily changes to another accounting method in

19X4. Under what conditions will the taxpayer have to recognize more than one-eighth of the Sec. 481 cumulative adjustment in 19X4?

20. Will the new simplified dollar-value LIFO procedures be attractive to all businesses? Explain.

21. Is it possible for a business taxpayer to recognize a gain on the repossession of an inventory item (personalty) that was sold on the installment basis? Explain.

22. Explain the concept of "applicable federal rate," as used in the imputed interest rules of Sec. 483, for installment sales occurring after 1984.

PROBLEMS

1. Rita Penn (single, age 31) has been filing her sole proprietorship tax returns on a calendar-year basis. She has received permission from the IRS to switch to a fiscal year ending May 31. For the period January 1 to May 31, 19X4 (the year of the change), Penn had $14,300 of gross income and $1,500 of itemized deductions.
   a) Compute Penn's correct tax liability for the short taxable year ended May 31, 19X4, using annualization procedures.
   b) Would the annualization calculation potentially penalize Penn if the 5-month period is during peak seasonal business? Explain.

2. Bill Ackle owns and operates a hardware store. Bill keeps his accounting records on the cash basis. Cash receipts and payments for 19X4 were as follows:

Cash sales	$320,000
Cash collections on account	225,000
Cash purchases of inventory	103,000
Cash payments on account	120,000
Utility expenses (paid in cash)*	4,200
Store rental payments†	24,000
Fire insurance payments‡	9,600
Salaries of employees	62,500
Miscellaneous expenses	13,500

*The December 19X4 bill for $480 has not been paid and is not included in the total.
†Includes a prepayment of $2,000 for the January 19X5 rent.
‡The amount represents a prepayment for 4 years of insurance coverage, beginning on September 1, 19X4.

An analysis of Ackle's business records discloses the following balances:

	1/1/X4 BALANCE	12/31/X4 BALANCE
Accounts receivable	$35,000	$43,000
Accounts payable	28,000	31,000
Merchandise inventory	18,000	16,000

Assuming that Ackle elects to file his 19X4 tax return on the cash basis, determine the correct 19X4 income reportable from the hardware business.

3. Concrete Construction Company agreed to construct a new athletic stadium and dormitory complex for Wheeling University. The contract for a total of $20 million dollars was signed on January 1, 19X4 and work began shortly thereafter. A record of completion percentages, payments, and expenses under the contract is charted below:

YEAR	CUMULATIVE PERCENTAGE OF TOTAL JOB COMPLETED (PER ARCHITECT)	TOTAL PAYMENTS RECEIVED FROM UNIVERSITY	TOTAL EXPENSES ALLOCABLE TO CONTRACT
19X4	28%	$5,000,000	3,800,000
19X5	64%	$8,000,000	6,000,000
19X6	100%	$7,000,000	5,300,000

a) Compute Concrete Company's taxable income from the contract for 19X4, 19X5, and 19X6 using the percentage-of-completion method.

b) Same as (a) except that Concrete Company uses the completed-contract method.

c) Are the advance payments received from the university in 19X4 and 19X5 treated differently under the two methods of reporting long-term construction income? Explain.

4. Identify the correct tax reporting procedure for the following accounting changes as either prospective in nature, retroactive with an amended tax return, or retroactive with a Sec. 481 cumulative adjustment:

a) Due to technological changes, a personal computer (purchased in 1979) with eight years of remaining depreciable life is expected to be used for only three more years.

b) Taxpayer changes from the lower-of-cost or -market procedure to the LIFO method of valuing inventories.

c) Taxpayer determines that last year's cost of goods sold was understated by $10,000 due to a posting error.

d) Taxpayer changes from the cash to the accrual method of accounting.

e) Taxpayer revises downward the reserve for bad debts.

5. Beverly Hunt has been incorrectly using the cash method of reporting sales and cost of goods sold for her retail equipment sales business. Her tax records for 19X7 disclosed the following information:

	CASH INFLOW (OUTFLOW)	1/1/X7 BALANCE	12/31/X7 BALANCE
Cash sales and collections on account	$420,000	—	—
Cash merchandise purchases and payments on account	(310,000)	—	—
Accounts receivable ledger balances	—	$82,000	$89,000
Accounts payable ledger balances	—	24,000	21,000
Merchandise inventory per physical count	—	18,000	14,000

a) Assuming that Hunt changes to the accrual method in 19X7, determine the cumulative Sec. 481 adjustment due to the change in accounting method.

b) How will this cumulative adjustment be reported by Hunt in the following situations:

(1) Hunt voluntarily makes the change, and the incorrect method has been used only in 19X5 and 19X6 (her first two years of business);

(2) Hunt voluntarily makes the change, and the incorrect method has been used for the preceding six years (with each year misstated by approximately the same amount);

(3) Same as (2), except that the total misstatement of income over the 6-year period was as follows:

19X1—$ 3,000	19X4—$16,000
19X2—$ 6,000	19X5—$18,000
19X3—$10,000	19X6—$23,000

6. As of the end of 19X3, Blanton Corporation has been using an inventory method not specifically sanctioned by the Code, Regulations, or Supreme Court decisions. This method has been used since 1948; however, Blanton has never been audited by the Internal Revenue Service. What factors should Blanton Corporation take into account when considering the feasibility of voluntarily changing to an acceptable accounting method?

7. Wayne Combest is (involuntarily) required by the IRS to change his method of valuing his appliance inventory. The net effect of the Sec. 481 cumulative adjustment is an $18,000 increase in income. Combest's marginal income tax rate for the year of change (19X5) is 40%. His marginal income tax rates for 19X3 and 19X4 were 35% and 32%, respectively.

a) How would you suggest that Combest report this Sec. 481 adjustment?

b) Assume that Combest had used the erroneous method for the years 19X0 through 19X4, resulting in the following understatements of income:

TAX YEAR	MARGINAL TAX RATE	INCOME UNDERSTATEMENT
19X0	48%	$ 8,000
19X1	20%	3,000
19X2	32%	2,000
19X3	35%	4,000
19X4	32%	1,000
		$18,000

Given these facts, how would you suggest that Combest report the $18,000 adjustment?

8. Paula Graham uses lower-of-cost or -market (LCM) procedures for valuing her liquor store inventory. Relevant data at the end of 19X4 include the following:

	COST	MARKET
Domestic beers	$3,600	$4,200
Imported beers	4,100	3,400
Domestic wines	6,250	7,980
Imported wines	9,400	9,850
Liquors	2,650	1,900

a) What will be Graham's ending inventory using LCM procedures?

b) Will any adjustments be required if Graham decides to adopt the LIFO inventory method? Explain.

9. Microtech Corporation adopts dollar-value LIFO procedures on 12/31/X3. Their 12/31/X3 inventory consisted of the following:

PRODUCT	QUANTITY	COST PER UNIT	TOTAL COST
Microcomputers	6,000	$150	$ 900,000
Software packages	10,000	80	800,000
Video games	4,000	30	120,000
Printers	8,000	90	720,000
			2,540,000

Ending inventories for 19X4 and 19X5 at end-of-year prices were as follows:

	19X4		19X5	
	QUANTITY	COST	QUANTITY	COST
Microcomputers	4,000	$160	5,000	$155
Software packages	12,000	90	8,000	85
Video games	5,000	28	3,000	25
Printers	11,000	100	7,000	110

a) Determine the correct 19X4 and 19X5 ending inventory values for Microtech Corporation using the double-extension dollar value LIFO procedure.

b) Would there be any possible tax advantages for Microtech to elect the new Index LIFO procedures prescribed in the Regulations? Explain.

10. Books, Incorporated, a textbook publisher, values its ending inventory at an estimated net realizable value. Costs of publishing a particular edition of a book are such that the marginal cost of running about 10,000 extra copies of an edition is minimal. In the event that these volumes are not ordered by distributors within 18 months, the company will write off the entire cost of the excess copies. This appears to comply with generally accepted accounting principles. Will these write-offs be allowed for tax purposes? Explain.

11. Giant Retail Corporation regularly offers an installment sales plan for its inventory sales. The results of the past four years were as follows:

YEAR	GROSS SALES	COST OF GOODS	RECEIVABLES WRITTEN OFF	VALUE OF REPOSSESSIONS
19X1	$ 600,000	$450,000	$30,000	$18,500
19X2	750,000	600,000	36,000	17,000
19X3	800,000	624,000	40,000	28,000
19X4	1,000,000	760,000	50,000	34,000

a) Assuming that Retail collected $300,000 from 19X2 sales in 19X4, how much gross income would be reported from these collections in 19X4?

b) What would be Retail's bad debt deduction for the $50,000 of receivable balances written off for 19X4 sales? For 19X3 sales?

12. Bill Summit sold 12 acres of unimproved land in 19X4 for a total consideration of $100,000 payable as follows: $20,000 cash in 19X4, a $10,000 note payable on demand received in 19X4, a $40,000 mortgage on the property assumed by the purchaser, and an installment note for six annual payments of $5,000, bearing interest of 12% on the unpaid balance. Summit had purchased the land in 19X1 for $65,000. Summit does not elect to be taxed on the entire gain in 19X4.

a) Determine Summit's recognized taxable gain in the year of the sale (19X4) and the following year (19X5).

b) How would your answers to (a) change if Summit's basis in the land was $35,000?

c) Would your answer to (a) change if the installment note provided for 6% interest on the unpaid balance? Explain.

13. Rebecca Mason sold her vacation home on August 1, 19X4 for $50,000, payable as follows: $20,000 down at sale date and four annual payments of $7,500 plus 10% interest on the unpaid balance beginning on August 1, 19X5. Mason had purchased the vacation home in 19X0 for

$34,000. What are the tax consequences to Mason of the following dispositions of the installment note:

a) On August 2, 19X5, after receiving the first installment payment, Mason sells the note for $21,000 cash.

b) On August 2, 19X5, Mason gives the note to her daughter.

c) Assume that the original sale by Mason was to her brother, and after receiving the August 2, 19X5 payment, Mason canceled the debt obligation.

14. Bryan Jenkins sold his personal coin collection on April 1, 19X6 to a trust set up to benefit his children. The collection was purchased by Jenkins on May 5, 19X3 for $80,000. The terms of the sale to the trust were as follows: $40,000 down payment at the sale date and 4 annual payments of $40,000, plus 12% interest on the unpaid balance, beginning on April 1, 19X7. The trust sold the coin collection on December 10, 19X6 for $205,000. What are the 19X6 tax consequences of these transactions to (a) Bryan Jenkins and (b) the trust?

15. Mary Scott uses the cash method of reporting for her supermarket business (except for accruals required by law). Her 19X5 results of operations included the following:

	1/1/X5 BALANCE	12/31/X5 BALANCE	19X5 TOTAL
Accounts receivable	$17,000	$13,500	—
Accounts payable	12,000	10,800	—
Merchandise inventory	10,000	13,400	—
Cash sales	—	—	$ 56,000
Cash collections on account	—	—	138,000
Cash purchases of inventory	—	—	41,000
Cash payments on account	—	—	106,000

Determine Scott's reportable gross profit for 19X5.

16. James Hardy is an accrual-basis, calendar-year taxpayer. In June 19X3, he entered into a contract to deliver an inventory item (currently available through normal channels) by June 19X8. The item had a total estimated cost of $11,500, and Hardy received a $12,250 advance payment in June, 19X3. When is the latest that Hardy can recognize these advance payments as income?

17. Bello Manufacturing Company produces gidgets. During 19X3, its first year of operations, Bello incurred the following costs in producing 10,000 units:

Direct materials	$120,000
Direct Labor	420,000
Variable factory overhead	200,000
Fixed factory overhead	110,000

If Bello sold 9,000 gidgets in 19X3, what value would be assigned to the inventory of 1,000 gidgets?

18. M, Inc., uses the simplified government index method of valuing inventories. The base period index is 1.08, and 19X3 results were:

	12/31/X2	12/31/X3
Ending inventory (19X3 at year-end prices)	$200,000	$240,000
Government price index	1.20	1.25

What will be the value of M's 19X3 ending inventory?

19. On June 12, 19X8, Helen Dresden sold ten acres of land for a total consideration of $60,000. The land was originally acquired in 19X1 for $35,000. The sales contract provided for a down payment of $10,000, eight semi-annual payments of $5,000 plus 12% interest on the unpaid balance beginning on December 12, 19X8, and the assumption of a $10,000 outstanding mortgage on the land by the purchaser. Assuming that unstated interest does not exist in the contract, how will Dresden report the total 19X8 collections of $17,400 on her return?

20. Explain how the imputed interest rules of Sec. 483 would be applied to the following installment sales of property, assuming that all sales occur after 1984:

   a) a sale of a used automobile for $2,500 on a 4-year installment note;

   b) a sale of investment land for $300,000 on a 20-year installment note;

   c) a sale of personal residence for $400,000 on a 10-year installment note.

TAX PLANNING PROBLEMS

1. Ryan Co. has been using an improper accounting method in its sole proprietorship business since 1948. If Ryan voluntarily changes its accounting method, it will have to report a cumulative Sec. 481 adjustment of $100,000 over a 10-year period, as provided in Rev. Proc. 80-51. On the other hand, if the IRS forces Ryan to make the change, it will have to report cumulative adjustment of $81,000 in the year of change (no adjustment is made for pre-1954 years with involuntary changes of accounting method). Ryan's marginal income tax rate has been a relatively constant 46% and is not expected to change in the foreseeable future. Ryan can earn a 10% after-tax rate of return on any idle funds.

   Ryan has just discovered this year that the accounting method used was an incorrect one, and it is concerned about an IRS audit in the future. Ryan asked you if it should voluntarily change accounting methods so that it can preserve the 10-year deferral period for reporting the effects of the change. What would you suggest? (Hint—compare the net present values of the two methods of reporting the change by discounting the marginal tax liabilities at 10% to the point of the first tax payment under both methods.)

2. Susan Gruber, a 50%-bracket taxpayer, has been using the lower-of-cost or -market (LCM) in valuing her inventories. Her 19X6 ending inventory has a value of $82,000 using this method. The actual cost of these items in ending inventory is $100,000. Gruber is considering a switch to the LIFO method, but she is concerned about the additional income to be recognized by the required restoration to income of the $18,000 write-downs to market in previous years.

   She estimates that the quantity of ending inventory will remain about the same in future years, but the prices will increase about 10% a year. If Gruber switches to the LIFO method, approximately how many years will it take for the tax savings generated by the use of the LIFO method to exceed the tax costs of restoring the previous LCM write-downs to income? (Compare the present value of the marginal tax costs of the 3-year restoration adjustment with the present value of the LIFO tax savings on a year-by-year basis. The LIFO savings are measured by the incremental ending inventory values times the marginal tax rate.) Gruber can earn a 10% after-tax return on idle funds.

CASE PROBLEM

John and Nancy Wilson, both age 38, are married taxpayers who will file a joint return in 1985. John is a college professor who received a salary of $36,000 in 1985, of which $9,500 was withheld in federal income taxes. He also received a post-doctorate, 3-month summer research grant for $1,500 from the National Science Foundation.

Nancy owns and operates her own automobile repair business. In 1985 she voluntarily changed her accounting method from the cash to the accrual basis. She had used the cash method for the past eight years, with misstatements in income of approximately the same amount each year. She will report any cumulative adjustment over the maximum period permitted by Rev. Proc. 80-51. Her business records indicate the following summary totals for 1985:

	CASH PAYMENTS AND EXPENSES	BALANCE 12/31/84	BALANCE 12/31/85
Cash sales and collections	$262,000	—	—
Cash purchases and payments	153,000	—	—
Business expenses (cash)	24,000	—	—
Allowable depreciation deduction	16,400	—	—
Accounts receivable	—	$46,000	$32,500
Accounts payable	—	30,000	24,000
Merchandise inventory	—	38,000	24,000
Estimated federal income taxes paid	19,000	—	—

The Wilsons' only other sources of income in 1985 were $850 interest on certificates of deposit, $620 dividends on General Motors common stock, and a total of $10,000 collected on a 1985 installment sale of 10 acres of land. The land was originally acquired as an investment in 1981 for $20,000, and was sold on 6/1/85 for a total consideration of $50,000, payable as follows: $4,000 down payment, followed by ten semiannual payments of $4,000 beginning on 12/1/85. Each installment payment will include 10% interest on the unpaid balance. (The unstated interest rules do not apply in this case.) In addition, the purchaser agreed to assume a $6,000 outstanding mortgage on the property. John and Nancy provide 85% of the support of John's mother, whose only sources of income in 1985 consisted of $800 interest and $2,000 of social security. John and Nancy's legitimate itemized deductions in 1985 total $16,400.

Required: Determine the net tax liability (or refund due) for John and Nancy Wilson in 1985. Assume that the income tax liability must be increased by a self-employment tax of $4,673 on Nancy's self-employment income. (As explained in Chapter 13, self-employed individuals report and pay their social security taxes on their annual federal income tax returns. The estimated self-employment tax is also reflected in the $19,000 of estimated tax payments.)

RESEARCH PROBLEMS

1. Ronco, Inc., a mail-order accrual-basis corporation, ships many of its products C.O.D. (cash on delivery), guaranteeing the arrival of goods and advancing posting and collection charges which are repaid by the purchaser. At the end of 19X3 Ronco had $38,000 cost of inventory items shipped to customers for which repayments had not been received. The retail sales value of these items is $60,000. How should these items be reflected on Ronco's 19X3 tax return? Explain.

2. Brandon Corporation is an accrual-basis taxpayer which uses a 52–53 week taxable year ending on the Friday closest to December 31. In one tax year having 53 weeks, *two* years of real property taxes accrued in the same year (the accrual date was January 1). Can Brandon Corporation deduct two years of property taxes in this one year? Discuss.

Chapter Objectives

1. Define the phrase "trade or business."
2. Apply the tests of "positive criteria" to determine whether an expense is deductible.
3. Apply the tests of "negative criteria" to determine whether an expense is deductible.
4. Identify the types of expenses that are deductible.
5. Demonstrate the general rules for the time for deducting expenses of cash-basis and accrual-basis taxpayers.
6. Determine whether an individual is an employee or self-employed.
7. Identify the activities that are necessary for an employee to be classified as an "outside salesman."
8. Distinguish between employee expenses that are deductible *for* AGI, deductible *from* AGI, and not deductible.
9. Identify employee transportation costs that are deductible and those that are not deductible.
10. Calculate the deductible amount of automobile expenses and other transportation costs of employees.
11. Identify the entertainment expenses that are deductible.
12. Determine the deductible portion of business gifts.
13. Recognize deductible miscellaneous expenses of employees.
14. Demonstrate how to report properly an employee's expense reimbursement.
15. Specify the types of records that must be maintained to support deductions for travel, transportation, entertainment, etc.
16. Demonstrate how to report properly expenditures for education activities.
17. Identify and compute deductible "moving costs."
18. Determine whether expenses of an "office in the home" are deductible.

7 General Requirements for a Deduction and Employment-Related Deductions

As explained in Chapter 3, the income tax is levied against taxable income, a statutory and legalistic quantity determined by subtracting authorized deductions from gross income.

The term "deductions," as used in federal income taxation, can be defined only procedurally—for example, as those items that collectively constitute the difference between the quantity called "gross income" and the quantity called "taxable income." A few considerations implicit in this purely procedural definition are, however, important. Note that the two quantifications, gross income and taxable income, describe purely legalistic quantities; outside the realm of federal income taxation, neither quantity has particular meaning. It is a widely accepted notion in federal income taxation that *nothing is deductible unless authorized by the Code or the Regulations*.

In accounting, income is itself a net concept, generally defined as the difference between properly matched revenues and expenses for some arbitrary time period. Thus, it seems implicit that all "properly matched expenses" must be "deductions" for purposes of determining income. Ignoring possible differences in timing—that is, ignoring the accounting refinements common to the "matching concept"—the accounting notion of income is only partially appropriate for matters of federal income taxation. As a general proposition, most of the items that would fall into the accountant's classification called "expenses" are also "deductions" for tax purposes; in addition, however, the Code provides for many other deductions in the calculation of taxable income. Thus, the term "deduction" is a much broader, more generic and legalistic term than the term "expense." This is especially true for the individual taxpayer, although the comment also has limited relevance for the corporate taxpayer.

The deductions allowed for trade or business activities are roughly comparable to the expenses that appear on the annual income statement of a business, prepared in accordance with generally accepted accounting principles. This generalization applies equally to the computation of taxable income for a corporation, a sole proprietorship, or a partnership. There are, however, numerous and major exceptions to the general rule. Some of these exceptions relate only to differences in the timing of deductions; others involve the aggregate amount to be deducted in the long run.

It is for individual taxpayers that the accounting concept of "expenses" fails to approximate the tax concept of "deductions." For individuals, deductions may be grouped into three broad categories:

1. Deductions applicable to a trade or business, including business-related expenses of an employee.
2. "Nonbusiness" deductions related to production of "nonbusiness" income.
3. Purely personal deductions specifically provided for individual taxpayers.

These deductions for individuals are discussed in this and the following two chapters. First, we will examine some general concepts governing allowable deductions. Then we will concentrate on certain business-related expenses of an employee. (Many of these expenses are incurred also by individual taxpayers who conduct a trade or business as self-employed persons.) Deductions that are available primarily to taxpayers (including entities other than sole proprietorships) engaged in operating a trade or business are discussed in Chapter 8. Deductions related to the production of "nonbusiness" income and purely personal deductions specifically provided for individual taxpayers will be covered in Chapter 9.

GENERAL REQUIREMENTS FOR A DEDUCTION

In order to deduct any item, the taxpayer must be able to point to some provision of the Internal Revenue Code that authorizes the deduction.[1] It is not necessary that the statute list the specific item by name, but the item must clearly fall under one of the provisions of the law. In this regard, a mere reading of the Code may not reveal whether or not an item is deductible, since Treasury Regulations, Revenue Rulings, and court decisions constantly interpret the meaning of the statute. It is knowledge of these *interpretations* that constitutes the real stock in trade of the tax practitioner.

---

[1] See, for example, *New Colonial Ice Co. v. Helvering*, 54 S.Ct. 788 (1934).

In addition to being able to prove that he or she is entitled to the deduction, the taxpayer must maintain adequate records to support any deduction claimed. Although in most situations neither the Code nor the Regulations dictate the form or content of the necessary records, taxpayers should retain reasonable records to protect their right to all tax deductions.

The Code provides for a multitude of deductions for very dissimilar items, including losses, expenses, and "special" items not necessarily involving monetary outlays. These provisions can be divided into two major categories: the general (or universal) provisions and the specific deduction authorizations.

GENERAL PROVISIONS

Two code sections that serve as the most general basis for deductions are Sec. 162, Expenses of Carrying on a Trade or Business, and Sec. 212, Expenses for Production of Income. In addition, Sec. 165 permits a deduction for certain losses (i.e., Sec. 165(c)(3) covers losses incurred in a transaction entered into for a profit, though not connected with a trade or business). The importance of these sections warrants a closer examination of the three provisions.

EXPENSES OF TRADE OR BUSINESS The broadest provision pertaining to deductions—and, incidentally, the provision that comes closest to approximating the expense concept in accounting—is located in Sec. 162(a), which reads in part as follows:

> (a) In General—There shall be allowed as a deduction all the ordinary and necessary expenses paid or incurred during the taxable year in carrying on any trade or business, including—
> (1) a reasonable allowance for salaries or other compensations for personal services actually rendered;
> (2) traveling expenses (including amounts expended for meals and lodging other than amounts which are lavish or extravagant under the circumstances) while away from home in the pursuit of a trade or business; and
> (3) rentals or other payments required to be made as a condition to the continued use or possession, for purposes of the trade or business, of property to which the taxpayer has not taken or is not taking title or in which he has no equity.

Although these general words may suggest to the unsuspecting taxpayer (or student) that virtually every "business expense" is deductible, an investigation of the interpretations given these words by tax administrators and courts would not support such a conclusion. In the following paragraphs a few of the factors affecting these interpretations are reviewed.

INTENT TO MAKE A PROFIT The definitional boundaries of a *trade or business*, although they are of particular importance to the individual taxpayer, are as elusive as the definitions of "ordinary" and "necessary." The intention to make a profit is necessary; the actuality of a profit is not. On the other hand, the intention to make a profit is not a sufficient condition. Many transactions and business ventures are profit-oriented, but they are not deemed to constitute a trade or business for tax purposes. Rather, there must be some personal effort of an entrepreneurial nature before any income-producing activity can be said to constitute a trade or business. This distinction becomes particularly difficult to draw with relatively passive investment ventures.

Example 1: Marco owns a duplex. He lives in one unit and rents the other unit to a tenant. Marco's ownership of a single rental unit probably does not constitute a trade or business.

HOBBY An activity entered into for purely personal enjoyment.

HOBBY LOSSES A second major problem arises in determining whether a particular venture constitutes a trade or business or whether it is a ***hobby***. Many taxpayers, particularly those of financial means, enjoy such expensive endeavors as building race cars, breeding race horses, and feeding beef cattle. Obviously, such endeavors may be very sound and profitable business ventures. In those cases in which a taxpayer consistently reports losses, however, the tax administrators suspect that the real motivation is purely personal enjoyment rather than a desire to conduct a profitable business. Whenever the IRS can prove these suspicions, expenses related to the hobby activity are deductible only to the extent of hobby income.[2] Further, Sec. 183 provides that, unless the IRS establishes to the contrary, an activity is presumed to be engaged in for profit if the gross income for two or more out of five consecutive tax years (two out of seven consecutive years if the activity involves the breeding, training, showing, or racing of horses) exceeds the deductions attributable to the activity.[3] If the gross income from the activity does not exceed expenses for at least two out of five consecutive years, there is no automatic presumption that the activity is not engaged in for profit. However, the burden of proof is on the *taxpayer*, and not the IRS, if the two out of five year test is not met. Expenses otherwise deductible, such as interest and taxes, are not disallowable merely because they are related to a hobby. If the gross income from the hobby exceeds the expenses that are deductible in any event, such as taxes and interest, other expenses can be deducted to the extent of the excess.[4]

Example 2: Giese, a college professor, owns a ranch on which he raises cattle. During 19X6 Giese's farm activities resulted in a loss. The farm activity also showed a loss for 19X5 and 19X4. The farm was profitable in 19X3 and 19X2. Since the farm activity was profitable in

---

[2] Sec. 183(a) and Reg. Sec. 1.183-1—4.
[3] Sec. 183(d).
[4] Sec. 183(b).

2 of the 5 years including 19X6, the presumption (which the IRS may refute) is that Giese's farm activity is a business, not a hobby, in 19X6.

Example 3: Assume that Henson carried on an activity that is deemed to be a hobby. Gross receipts for the year were $26,000. Expenses were:

Interest	$ 9,200
Property taxes	8,400
Utilities	5,000
Supplies	5,000
Misc.	4,000
Total	$31,600

Since the activity is a hobby, the loss of $5,600 is not deductible. However, the interest of $9,200 and the taxes of $8,400 are deductible in any event. In addition $8,400 of the other expenses can be deducted to absorb the remainder of the revenues ($26,000 minus $9,200 minus $8,400 equals $8,400). Note that the interest and taxes which are deductible under other sections are the first expenses to be offset against the hobby income.

COSTS OF INVESTIGATION OF A BUSINESS The IRS generally maintains that many anticipatory expenditures cannot be deducted as losses unless a taxpayer has already established himself or herself as being "in business." Thus, expenditures for travel incurred by a taxpayer to investigate the possibility of opening a business similar to that in which the taxpayer is already engaged may be deducted when paid or incurred, regardless of whether the new business is or is not acquired.[5] (However, Sec. 195 permits the taxpayer to capitalize such costs if the new business is acquired and to amortize the costs over a period of 60 months.)

If the taxpayer is not already engaged in a business similar to that being investigated, the expenses of investigation are generally nondeductible if the business is not acquired.[6] If a *new* business (whether or not similar to one in which the taxpayer is already engaged) is acquired, the investigation costs may be capitalized and amortized over a period of 60 months.[7] In those cases where a taxpayer has decided to acquire a *specific* business and, for reasons beyond the taxpayer's control, is subsequently prevented from doing so, the expenses related to the attempt may be capitalized and deducted as losses,[8] although the IRS contends that this option applies only to those expenses that are incurred *after* the decision to acquire the business and does not apply to expenses related to the investigation leading to the decision.[9]

---

[5] *York v. Commissioner*, 261 F.2d 421 (CA-4, 1958).

[6] Rev. Rul. 57-418, 1957-2 C.B. 143. See also *Morton Frank*, 20 T.C. 511 (1953).

[7] Sec. 195.

[8] *Harris W. Sneed*, 52 T.C. 880 (1969).

[9] Rev. Rul. 77-254, 1977-2 C.B. 63.

Example 4: Mack operates a hamburger shop in Cheyenne, Wyoming. He learns of a bookstore for sale in Seattle and travels there to investigate a possible purchase. He concludes that he does not have adequate experience to operate a bookstore and decides not to purchase it. Mack's travel costs to investigate the new business were $810. The costs are not deductible.

Example 5: Assume the same facts as in Example 4, except that Mack did acquire the bookstore. Mack may capitalize the $810 investigation costs and amortize them over a 60-month period (at the rate of $13.50 per month) beginning in the month that business is begun.

Example 6: Thomas operates a launderette in New Orleans. He learns of a chain of launderettes in Jackson, Miss. and goes there to investigate possible purchase. He spends $350 for travel costs and $500 for fees to an attorney to investigate the lease contracts of the chain. Thomas decides that he will not acquire the launderettes. The $850 expenses of investigation are deductible.

EMPLOYEE BUSINESS EXPENSES Expenses incurred by a taxpayer in connection with his or her business activities as an employee.

BUSINESS ACTIVITIES OF AN EMPLOYEE A few ***employee business expenses*** also are allowable under Sec. 162 as deductions related to trade or business. Generally, the employee must be able to demonstrate that any "business expenses" deducted are directly related to the performance of duties or are required by an employment agreement. Travel, transportation, and entertainment are deductible employee business expenses frequently encountered. The Code and the Regulations are rather precise in describing the purpose and nature of costs that may be deducted as travel, transportation, and entertainment, and the Regulations specify the nature of records that must be maintained when such expenses are claimed. Entertainment expenses in particular are often held to be personal expenditures and therefore not deductible. Although the IRS requirements are frequently criticized, it is obvious that when it comes to travel and entertainment there is a fine line between bona fide business costs and personal expenditures by either an employee or a self-employed individual. Here, again, the importance of the tests of reasonableness, necessity, appropriateness, and "direct business connection" become crucial in deciding whether an item is or is not deductible.

Obviously, the difficulty created by allowing deductions of this type lies in the rather arbitrary distinctions used in deciding what constitutes a personal business expense. It might be argued, for example, that every person employed outside the home incurs extra costs because of his or her job. The cost of commuting to work, the extra expense incurred in eating restaurant meals, the additional costs of wearing appropriate clothing and of personal grooming all result from the taxpayer's employment, but they are all considered to be personal expenses. Cost of special clothing not suitable for off-duty wear, union dues, tools of trade, and membership dues of professional employees in professional organizations are typical examples of employee business expenses that are properly deductible.

Deductions for employee business expenses are examined in detail later in this chapter.

EXPENSES FOR PRODUCTION OF INCOME As already explained, many business-oriented activities do not qualify as a trade or business for tax purposes because no personal effort of an "entrepreneurial nature" is involved. Until the Revenue Act of 1942 deductions for expenses related to these income-producing activities were frequently denied because they did not qualify as a "trade or business." For example, in 1941 the United States Supreme Court found that expenses incurred by a wealthy taxpayer to maintain an office for the purpose of managing his securities and real estate were not those of a trade or business and were therefore nondeductible personal expenses. [*Higgins v. Commissioner*, 61 S.Ct. 475 (1941)] Following this decision, Congress enacted the first two paragraphs of the present Sec. 212. (The third paragraph, relating to deduction of expenses incurred in connection with the determination of taxes, was incorporated later by the Revenue Act of 1954.) The present section reads as follows:

> Sec. 212. Expenses for Production of Income. In the case of an individual, there shall be allowed as a deduction all the ordinary and necessary expenses paid or incurred during the taxable year—
> (1) for the production or collection of income;
> (2) for the management, conservation, or maintenance of property held for the production of income; or
> (3) in connection with the determination, collection, or refund of any tax.

The result of this section is to make many income-related expenses deductible even though they are not incurred in a trade or business. For example, an expense attributable to the renting of a single property is not deductible under Sec. 162 because such limited rental activity does not constitute a trade or business. Nevertheless, Sec. 212 authorizes such a deduction. The Regulations help delineate what is meant by "production of income." Regulation 1.212-1(b) states in part:

> The term "income" for the purpose of section 212 includes not merely income of the taxable year but also income which the taxpayer has realized in a prior taxable year or may realize in subsequent taxable years; and is not confined to recurring income but applies as well to gains from the disposition of property. For example, if defaulted bonds, the interest from which if received would be includable in income, are purchased with the expectation of realizing capital gain on their resale, even though no current yield thereon is anticipated, ordinary and necessary expenses thereafter paid or incurred in connection with such bonds are deductible. Similarly, ordinary and necessary expenses paid or incurred in the management, conservation, or maintenance of a building devoted to rental purposes are deductible notwithstanding that there is actually no income therefrom in the taxable year, and regardless of the manner in which or the purpose for which the prop-

> erty in question was acquired. Expenses paid or incurred in managing, conserving, or maintaining property held for investment may be deductible under section 212 even though the property is not currently productive and there is no likelihood that the property will be sold at a profit or will otherwise be productive of income and even though the property is held merely to minimize a loss with respect thereto. . . .

Section 212 is the primary authority for the deduction of such expenses as safety deposit box rental and investment counsel fees that relate to investments in securities that produce taxable income. Many other expenses associated with property or an activity intended to produce income also become deductible under Sec. 212. In determining whether any expense is deductible, the major consideration is whether it is related to an activity entered into with the hope of making a profit or is merely engaged in for pleasure or personal reasons. In a few cases, expenses associated with the production of income may be subject to special, restrictive rules. For example, there is a limit on the deduction permitted taxpayers (other than corporations) for interest paid on indebtedness incurred to purchase or carry property held for investment. This limitation is discussed later in this chapter.

DEDUCTIONS FOR LOSSES The general authorization for the deduction of losses is found in Sec. 165(a), which reads as follows:

> There shall be allowed as a deduction any loss sustained during the taxable year and not compensated for by insurance or otherwise.

Subsection 165(c), however, restricts the general provision for individual taxpayers as follows:

> In the case of an individual, the deduction under subsection (a) shall be limited to—(1) losses incurred in a trade or business; (2) losses incurred in any transaction entered into for profit, though not connected with a trade or business; and (3) except as provided in subsection h, losses of property not connected with a trade or business or a transaction entered into for profit, if such losses arise from fire, storm, shipwreck, or other casualty, or from theft. . . .

Here again we observe the same three-way classification of losses incurred by an individual taxpayer: that is, a loss may be (*a*) incurred in a full-fledged trade or business, (*b*) incurred in a "nonbusiness" but profit-oriented transaction, or (*c*) incurred in a purely personal connection. In the event of losses to purely personal properties, no deduction is allowed unless the loss is attributable to a casualty or theft.

Unfortunately, each set of facts is to some extent unique, and in order to determine whether or not any particular loss is deductible it may be necessary to determine the intent and motive of the taxpayer for entering into a particular transaction. This is a difficult, if not impossible, task in many cases. Losses of anticipated gains are denied; only actual losses sustained (as measured by the adjusted basis of the property) can be deducted. And losses must be those of the taxpayer before a deduction can be granted. The other subsections of Sec. 165 are of less general interest, although they, too, deal with deductible losses.

THE NET OPERATING LOSS DEDUCTION One other Code Section of interest at this point is Sec. 172, dealing with a "Net Operating Loss Deduction." Under Sec. 172, a ***net operating loss*** (essentially the net loss from the taxpayer's trade or business) can be allowed as a deduction against income of other tax years. The "NOL" is carried back and offset against income of the third year preceding the year in which the loss occurred. Any amount not used in the third prior year is then offset against income of the second year preceding the loss year, and then against income of the first year preceding the loss year. Any amount unused in the three years preceding the loss year is then carried forward and offset against income of the year following the loss year, and any amount of loss still unused is then carried forward for 14 more years in sequence. Thus, the net operating loss can be carried back three years and forward for a total of 15 years. The taxpayer, however, may elect (irrevocably) to relinquish the carryback right and carry the loss forward for only 15 years. This special deduction is discussed in more detail in Chapter 8.

NET OPERATING LOSS Essentially the net loss from the operation of a taxpayer's trade or business.

GENERAL PROVISIONS: POSITIVE CRITERIA

In both Secs. 162 and 212 (but not in Sec. 165), the terms "ordinary" and "necessary" are used. In addition, Sec. 162 contains a "reasonableness" test. The meaning of each of these words in income taxation differs somewhat from customary usage. An expense need not be incurred frequently by the taxpayer in order to be ***ordinary***. The essence of the ordinary criterion seems to be that the expense would be acceptable or commonplace among other taxpayers who find themselves in comparable circumstances.[10] In the usual meaning of the term, the "comparable circumstances" may indeed be extraordinary. In the case of *Welch v. Helvering*, the Court, struggling with the meaning of the word "ordinary," said that

ORDINARY EXPENSE An expense resulting from an activity acceptable or commonplace among taxpayers in comparable circumstances.

> the decisive distinctions are those of degree and not of kind. One struggles in vain for any verbal formula that will supply a ready touchstone. The standard set up by the statute is not a rule of law; it is rather a way of life. Life in all its fullness must supply the answer to the riddle.[11]

To be ***necessary*** an expense must be capable of making a contribution to a trade or business. Fortunately for the taxpayer, the courts and tax administrators do not insist that necessity be determined on an ex post facto basis; it is sufficient if the expense appeared to be appropriate and helpful at the time it was incurred. The "prudent person" test is applied; if, in the same circumstances, a prudent person would have incurred the expense in the expectation that it would be helpful in the taxpayer's busi-

NECESSARY EXPENSE A test of whether an expense is capable of making a contribution to a trade or business.

[10] See *Deputy v. DuPont*, 60 S.Ct. 363 (1940).

[11] *Welch v. Helvering*, 54 S.Ct. 8 (1933).

ness, it will likely be deemed "necessary."[12] The courts generally do not second-guess business people on the necessity of making expenditures. As a practical matter, therefore, this positive criterion is probably the least significant of those considered. When invoked, it frequently relates to illegal activities.

REASONABLE EXPENSE A test of whether, in the circumstances, the *amount* of an expense is reasonable.

Finally, even an ordinary and necessary expense incurred in a trade or business or in connection with the production of income must be ***reasonable*** *in amount* before it can be deducted for tax purposes. Technically, this requirement is stated in Sec. 162(a)(1) only in relation to compensation, but the courts have found that the element of reasonableness was inherent in the phrase "ordinary and necessary."[13] As a practical matter, the reasonableness criterion is important most frequently in the case of related taxpayers. For example, a corporation may attempt to pay its sole stockholder-executive (or his or her children) an unreasonably large salary, interest, or rental payment. If allowed, these expenses could be used to disguise payments that in reality are dividends—a result of particular importance, since dividends, unlike business expenses, are not deductible by the corporation paying them. Therefore, the IRS is constantly screening transactions between related parties to determine their reasonableness.[14]

Example 7: Ewing owns 90% of the stock of Town Corporation; his son owns the other 10% of the stock. The corporation pays Ewing $380,000 per year as salary for his services as president. The normal salary for a president in similar companies would be $100,000. The $380,000 salary will very likely be deemed to be unreasonable, and it is likely that only $100,000 will be deductible by Town Corporation. The remaining $280,000 will probably be treated as a dividend.

GENERAL PROVISIONS: NEGATIVE CRITERIA

In addition to the positive criteria, there exist four negative criteria that must also be satisfied before any unspecified expense may be tax deductible. Any expenditure not specifically authorized as a deduction will be disallowed if it is found to be *purely personal*, a *capital expenditure*, *related to tax-exempt income*, or *contrary to public policy*. The most important Code sections pertaining to nondeductible expenses in general include:

- Sec. 262.—Personal, Living, and Family Expenses.
- Sec. 263.—Capital Expenditures.
- Sec. 265.—Expenses and Interest Relating to Tax-Exempt Income.
- Sec. 162.—(Expenses contrary to public policy.)

---

[12] *Ibid.*

[13] *Dunn and McCarthy, Inc. v. Comm.*, 139 F.2d 242 (CA-2, 1943).

[14] See, for example, *James D. Kennedy*, 72 T.C. 793 (1979).

There are, in addition, many other Code provisions that prohibit such specific expenses as certain entertainment expenses, etc. (Sec. 274), and selected taxes (Sec. 275). As explained earlier, our concern at this point is limited to the provisions of more general application.

PERSONAL, LIVING, AND FAMILY EXPENSES Section 262 states in its entirety, that "Except as otherwise expressly provided in this chapter, no deduction shall be allowed for personal, living, or family expenses." In light of the earlier discussion, we can suggest that all expenses can be categorized as either (*a*) directly related to a trade or business, (*b*) related to a profit-making venture that is not a trade or business, or (*c*) incurred without any intention of profit. Only the last category, the purely personal expenses, are categorically disallowed unless some section of the law specifically provides for their deduction. The difficulty in everyday tax practice, of course, comes in fitting actual expenses into the proper category. In Chapter 9 we will examine some of those personal expenses that are specifically allowed.

CAPITAL OUTLAYS Section 263(a) states that

> (a) General Rule—
> No deduction shall be allowed for—
> (1) any amount paid out for new buildings or for permanent improvements or betterments made to increase the value of any property or estate. . . . [or]
> (2) any amount expended in restoring property or in making good the exhaustion thereof for which an allowance is or has been made.[15]

(The omitted portion of Code Sec. 263 recognizes that other Code provisions specifically authorize the immediate deduction of a number of expenditures that could be classified as capital expenditures.) Any student acquainted with intermediate accounting is well aware of the practical difficulties in determining whether or not a particular expenditure is a "capital expenditure" or a "revenue expenditure." In general, the tax solutions to such riddles parallel the accounting solutions; therefore, no detailed consideration of them is presented here.

However, the mere fact that a ***capital outlay*** is not deductible at the time of the outlay does not prevent its recovery (deduction against income) at a later date through depreciation, depletion, or amortization deductions or through an offset against the amount realized on the sale or other disposition of the asset.

CAPITAL OUTLAYS
Expenditures that benefit more than one year.

EXPENSES RELATED TO TAX-EXEMPT INCOME Sec. 265 disallows a deduction for any interest or other expense that is paid or incurred in order to realize tax-exempt income. This provision closes a loophole that would otherwise exist for persons in the higher tax brackets. That is, if it were not for this provision, a person in a top tax bracket might, because

[15] Sec. 263(a).

of income taxation, actually obtain a positive cash flow by borrowing high-interest money and investing it in low-interest state or local obligations. To illustrate, let us assume that a taxpayer in the 50% marginal tax bracket borrowed $1 million at 12% and invested the proceeds in a 10% state bond issue. The annual interest expense would amount to $120,000, which, if it were not for Sec. 265, would reduce the borrower's tax liability by $60,000 (50% of $120,000). The tax-exempt interest earned on the state bonds would amount to $100,000, thus producing a net positive cash flow of $40,000 per year to the taxpayer. As stated above, Sec. 265 prevents this kind of tax legerdemain.

EXPENSES CONTRARY TO PUBLIC POLICY Prior to the 1969 Tax Reform Act, no statutory authority specifically disallowed such "expenses" as bribes, kickbacks, and fines. Nevertheless, the courts frequently disallowed such expenses on the grounds that allowing the deduction would frustrate public policy, and taxpayers were frequently required to go to court to determine whether various items were contrary to public policy. Now, Sec. 162(c) specifies several types of expenditures that controvert public policy and are disallowed:

1. Fines or penalties for violation of law.
2. Illegal bribes or kickbacks paid to public officials.
3. A portion (usually two-thirds) of treble damages paid under antitrust laws in criminal proceedings.
4. Payments such as kickbacks and bribes other than to government officials and employees if such payments are illegal under any generally enforced United States or state law providing for a criminal penalty or loss of license or privilege to engage in trade or business.
5. Any kickback, rebate, or bribe under medicare or medicaid.

Kickbacks, bribes, and so on, other than those specified above, would still be deductible if ordinary and necessary. Payments to officials of foreign governments are not deductible if such payments would be a violation of U.S. laws.

Example 8: Jones, a public accountant, pays a bank loan officer $200 for referring clients to Jones. This type of payment is prohibited under the state regulatory body's code of ethics and would, under state law, lead to the suspension of Jones' license if it were known. The $200 is not deductible by Jones.

Example 9: State Aircraft Manufacturing Company pays the Minister of Defense of a foreign country $2,000,000 as a fee to get a $200,000,000 contract for aircraft sales to that country. The $2,000,000 fee is illegal under U.S. law and is, therefore, not deductible.

However, the addition of these provisions does not solve all the questions involving public policy. The boundaries of this prohibition are especially difficult to specify because the courts have consistently held that expenses are deductible even if the income that the expense produces is illegal. For example, the expenses incurred by a gambler are deductible for tax purposes even if the gambler operates his business in a state that prohibits gambling. In a way, this is only equitable, because the illegal income has been held to be fully taxable. On the other hand, the granting of the deduction does eliminate another potential penalty which might be added to the penalties prescribed by the state.

Another gray area related to public policy, the deductibility of lobbying expense, is covered by Sec. 162(e)(2).

> (e) Appearances, etc., with Respect to Legislation.—
>
> (1) In general.—The deduction allowed by subsection (a) shall include all of the ordinary and necessary expenses (including, but not limited to, traveling expenses described in subsection (a)(2) and the cost of preparing testimony) paid or incurred during the taxable year in carrying on any trade or business—
>
> (A) in direct connection with appearances before, submission of statements to, or sending communications to, the committees, or individual members, of Congress or of any legislative body of a State, a possession of the United States, or a political subdivision of any of the foregoing with respect to legislation or proposed legislation of direct interest to the taxpayer.
>
> (B) in direct connection with communication of information between the taxpayer and an organization of which he is a member with respect to legislation or proposed legislation of direct interest to the taxpayer and to such organization,
>
> and that portion of the dues so paid or incurred with respect to any organization of which the taxpayer is a member which is attributable to the expenses of the activities described in subparagraphs (A) and (B) carried on by such organization.
>
> (2) Limitation.—The provisions of paragraph (1) shall not be construed as allowing the deduction of any amount paid or incurred (whether by way of contribution, gift, or otherwise)—
>
> (A) for participation in, or intervention in, any political campaign on behalf of any candidate for public office, or
>
> (B) in connection with any attempt to influence the general public, or segments thereof, with respect to legislative matters, elections, or referendums.[16]

The Congress, through this Section, recognizes that business people may have a direct economic interest in legislative and administrative matters, justifying the expenditure of funds. At the same time, the law attempts to prohibit a tax deduction for costs incurred in attempting to influence voters, or to influence legislators *through* voters.

Example 10: In the current year, Goodson, an importer of steel products, spent $1,500 on a trip to Washington to visit Congressmen to urge them to roll back import restrictions on steel. He also contributed $10,000 to a trade association to help finance a television

[16] Sec. 162(e)(2).

campaign urging voters to write their Congressmen to vote for the rollback. The $1,500 of travel costs is deductible, but the $10,000 contribution will probably not be allowed.

SUMMARY OF CRITERIA FOR A DEDUCTION

In sum, then, an expense is ordinarily deductible in the computation of taxable income if it either is authorized by a specific Code section or satisfies eight general criteria. An unspecified expense may be deducted if it is

1. ordinary,
2. necessary,
3. reasonable in amount, and
4. incurred in connection with a trade or business or in the production of income

and if it is *not*

5. a capital expenditure,
6. a personal expenditure,
7. related to tax-exempt income, or
8. contrary to public policy.

TIME FOR TAKING DEDUCTIONS

CASH-BASIS METHOD Accounting procedure under which, essentially, income is reported when cash is received and expenses are deducted when payment is made.

ACCRUAL-BASIS METHOD Accounting method under which, essentially, income is reported when earned and expenses are deducted when services or goods are used. (However, income received in advance is generally taxable when received.)

The quoted portions of Secs. 162 and 212, earlier in this chapter, include the words "paid or incurred during the taxable year" in specifying which deductions are allowable. A ***cash-basis*** taxpayer ordinarily deducts expenses only when paid, whereas the ***accrual-basis*** taxpayer is entitled to take a deduction as soon as there is a fixed and determinable liability incurred by the taxpayer.

Regulation 1.461-1(a) further explains how to determine the year in which a deduction is to be taken by a cash-basis taxpayer.

> Under the cash receipts and disbursements method of accounting, amounts representing allowable deductions shall, as a general rule, be taken into account for the taxable year in which paid. Further, a taxpayer using this method may also be entitled to certain deductions in the computation of taxable income which do not involve cash disbursements during the taxable year, such as the deductions for depreciation, depletion, and losses under sections 167, 611, and 165, respectively. If an expenditure results in the creation of an asset having a useful life which extends substantially beyond the close of the taxable year, such an expenditure may not be deductible, or may be deductible only in part, for the taxable year in which made. . . .[17]

Note that the payment must actually be made; there is no doctrine of constructive payment equivalent to the doctrine of "constructive re-

[17] Reg. Sec. 1.461-1(a).

ceipt," which was explained in Chapter 4. (However, a deduction may be allowed for a payment made with a noncash asset.) When payments are made by mail, the usual rule is that mailing constitutes payment because the postal system is deemed to be the agent of the addressee as well as the mailer, but there are conflicting court decisions on this point.

Questions are frequently raised about prepayment of expenses. Ordinarily a prepayment, such as a purchase of supplies, can be deducted in the year of payment even if the supplies are not used until the following year. If the payment creates an asset extending substantially beyond the end of the year, however, only that part used up in the current year is deductible. There are conflicting decisions over the proper period for deduction of prepaid rent and insurance by cash-basis taxpayers. As a generalization, however, it can be said that such prepayments must be allocated over the period for which payment was made if to do otherwise would result in a material distortion of income. The IRS has argued frequently that prepaid insurance and prepaid rent must be allocated in almost every case. In a 1980 decision, the Ninth Circuit Court of Appeals held that rent prepaid for 11 months beyond the close of the tax year was deductible in the year paid. In that case, the court specified a 12-month period beyond the end of the tax year as being a period for which prepaid rent is deductible.[18] However, the amount involved in that case probably would not be considered material. Code Sec. 461(g) requires cash-basis taxpayers to deduct prepaid interest over the period of the loan, except for points on home (personal residence) mortgages, which, as discussed later in this chapter, generally can still be deducted on a current basis.[19] "Tax shelters" using the cash basis of reporting generally are allowed to deduct prepaid amounts only if the related economic performance (providing of the services or property involved) occurs within 90 days after the close of the taxable year.[20]

Deposits made in advance on goods or services are deductible in years when the goods or services are received.[21] Obviously, expenditures for capital assets such as equipment must be capitalized and depreciated, even by the cash-basis taxpayer. Deposits on inventory goods also become a part of the cost of the goods acquired.

Normally, an accrual-basis taxpayer is entitled to a deduction whenever all the events have occurred that determine that a liability exists and the amount can be determined with reasonable accuracy. Thus, if there are substantial contingencies, or no reasonable estimate of the amount of expense can be made, there is no deduction. There are many "timing differences" between deductions on the tax return and those that are generally accepted in financial accounting. Many of these exist because there is no "fixed" liability even though an expense may be estimated with reasonable accuracy for financial accounting purposes. A good example is the

---

[18] *Zaninovich*, 616 F.2d 429 (CA-9, 1980).

[19] Sec. 461(g).

[20] Sec. 461(i).

[21] *G. R. Shippy*, 308 F.2d 743 (CA-8, 1962).

timing difference resulting from a deduction in the financial reports for estimated costs of guarantees and warranties at the time the related product or service is sold; these costs cannot be deducted on the tax return until the service under the warranty is actually rendered because the event which "fixes" the liability (e.g., the equipment failure) has not yet occurred.

Section 461(h), added in 1984, stipulates that, in general, no accrual can be made until economic performance occurs. In other words, the related service must be provided, the related property must be provided, or use must be made of the property involved before an accrual can be made. An exception is made in the case of immaterial amounts where economic performance will take place within 8½ months after the end of the taxable year.[22]

Individuals cannot deduct charitable contributions until the year in which payment is made or in which the amount is charged on a bank credit card even though the taxpayer is on an accrual basis.[23] Similarly, medical expenses are deductible only in the year paid.

EMPLOYMENT-RELATED EXPENSES

With this basic understanding of the *general requirement* for a deduction and of the rules governing the *time* for claiming deductions, we may now proceed to examine the deductibility of specific costs, beginning with employment-related expenses. First, it is necessary to examine the factors used to determine whether an individual is deemed to be self-employed or an employee.

EMPLOYEE ACTIVITIES DEFINED

On first thought one would surmise that the determination of whether an individual is an employee could be made easily. However, frequently this is not the case. The Regulations define an employee in very simplistic terms as:

> . . . every individual performing services if the relationship between him and the person for whom he performs such services is the legal relationship of employer and employee.[24]

Obviously this is of little help if it is the legal relationship that is in question initially. The Regulations do, however, go on to offer limited clarification by stating:

> (b) Generally the relationship of employer and employee exists when the person for whom services are performed has the right to control and direct

[22] Sec. 461(h)(1), (2), and (3).

[23] Reg. 1.170A-1(a)(i) and Rev. Rul. 78-38, 1978-1, C.B. 68.

[24] Reg. Sec. 31.3401(c)-1(a).

the individual who performs the services, not only as to the result to be accomplished by the work but also as to the details and means by which that result is accomplished. That is, an employee is subject to the will and control of the employer not only as to what shall be done but how it shall be done. In this connection, it is not necessary that the employer actually direct or control the manner in which the services are performed; it is sufficient if he has the right to do so. The right to discharge is also an important factor indicating that the person possessing the right is an employer. Other factors characteristic of an employer, but not necessarily present in every case, are the furnishing of tools and the furnishing of a place to work to the individual who performs the services. In general, if an individual is subject to the control or direction of another merely as to the result to be accomplished by the work and not as to the means and methods for accomplishing the result, he is not an employee.[25]

Example 11: Mary works full-time typing dissertations, term papers, and theses. She charges on a per-hour basis for her work. Mary is not classified as an employee, but is deemed to be self-employed because she determines how and when her work will be performed.

Example 12: Mary, from Example 1, hires Josh, a student, as a part-time typist to assist her. Josh is paid an hourly rate, works under Mary's direct supervision and follows her instructions. Josh is an employee.

Example 13: Martin is a court reporter. He takes depositions and records other hearings and interviews. He is one of several reporters provided an office and services by a "court reporting firm." The firm receives telephone calls from attorneys and in turn contacts the reporters. The reporters are free to accept or reject any jobs. Martin bills the legal firms directly for his services and in turn pays the court reporting firm 35% of his fees as a payment for facilities, services, and arranging jobs. Martin is probably a self-employed person rather than an employee.

There are still many conflicts between the IRS and individual taxpayers over whether, in light of specific circumstances, the individual is an employee or is self-employed.

THE BASIS FOR DEDUCTING EMPLOYEE EXPENSES

The basic authorization for deduction of business-related expenses is found in Sec. 162 of the Revenue Code, which merely provides that expenses of carrying on a trade or business shall be deductible. That Section of the Code does not refer to employees except to the extent that it defines the place of residence of a member of Congress.[26] The most con-

[25]Reg. Sec. 31.3401(c)-1(b)

[26]Sec. 162(a).

crete reference to deduction of employees' business-related expenses is found in Section 62, the purpose of which is to specify the deductible employee expenses that are deductible *for AGI*. Section 62 states in part:

> For purposes of this subtitle, the term "adjusted gross income" means, in the case of an individual, gross income minus the following deductions:
>
> (1) Trade and Business Deductions—The deductions allowed by this chapter (other than by part VII of this subchapter) which are attributable to a trade or business carried on by the taxpayer, if such trade or business does not consist of the performance of services by the taxpayer as an employee.
>
> (2) Trade and Business Deductions of Employees—
>
> (A) Reimbursed Expenses—The deductions allowed by part VI (sec. 161 and following) which consist of expenses paid or incurred by the taxpayer, in connection with the performance by him of services as an employee, under a reimbursement or other expense allowance arrangement with his employer.
>
> (B) Expenses for Travel Away from Home—The deductions allowed by part VI (sec. 161 and following) which consist of expenses of travel, meals, and lodging while away from home, paid or incurred by the taxpayer in connection with the performance by him of services as an employee.
>
> (C) Transportation Expenses—The deductions allowed by part VI (sec. 161 and following) which consist of expenses of transportation paid or incurred by the taxpayer in connection with the performance by him of services as an employee.
>
> (D) Outside Salesmen—The deductions allowed by part VI (sec. 161 and following) which are attributable to a trade or business carried on by the taxpayer, if such trade or business consists of the performance of services by the taxpayer as an employee and if such trade or business is to solicit, away from the employer's place of business, business for the employer.[27]

Thus most of the guidelines for deductibility of employee expenses are found in the Regulations, in Revenue Rulings, and in court decisions. The Regulations under Section 62 contain additional references to the expenses of employees. For example, in determining whether expenses incurred in attending a convention or other meeting are deductible, "no distinction will be made between self-employed persons and employees."[28] The Regulations under Section 162 provide that certain education expenses are deductible if the education "maintains or improves skills required by the individual in his employment or other trade or business."[29] Section 274 and the related Regulations govern the disallowance of entertainment and certain other expenses incurred by both self-employed individuals and employees.

---

[27] Sec. 62.

[28] Reg. Sec. 1.162-2(b)(2)(d).

[29] Reg. Sec. 1.162-5(a)(1).

EMPLOYEE DEDUCTIONS *FOR* AGI AND *FROM* AGI

As previously pointed out, the purpose of Sec. 62 is to specify which expenses incurred by employees in connection with their employment are deductible *for* AGI. (In addition, the deduction allowed for "moving costs" and that allowed for certain "retirement savings," both deductions *for* AGI, may be viewed as related to employment.) All other allowable employment-related expenses are deductible *from* AGI. As discussed in Chapter 3, the significance of having expenses classified as deductible *for* AGI is that they are deductible no matter whether the taxpayer does or does not itemize "personal" deductions. Any deductible employee expenses other than those listed above are deductible *from* AGI as part of the total of the personal deductions, but only if the total of all such items exceeds the "zero-bracket" amount will a deduction be allowed for such items. The key difference between business expenses deductible by a self-employed person engaged in a trade or business and expenses related to trade or business activities as an employee is that the former are *always* deductible *for* AGI while many employee expenses are deductible only *from* AGI.

Example 14: Clarence, an employee, has deductible travel costs of $600. In addition he paid professional association membership fees of $200, which are deductible employee expenses. Clarence, single, has other itemized personal deductions of $1,020. The $600 travel costs are deductible *for* AGI. However, Clarence will not be able to deduct the professional association fees, because, when they are added to the personal deductions of $1,020, the total of $1,220 does not exceed the zero-bracket amount.

The importance of properly classifying deductible expenses is obvious from Example 14.

THE SPECIAL CASE OF OUTSIDE SALESMEN

Sec. 62(2)(D) stipulates that all deductible expenses attributable to an employee's trade or business as an ***outside salesman*** are deductible *for* AGI. Thus, for this purpose, the outside salesperson is treated essentially as a self-employed individual. One can quickly (and correctly) surmise that the determination of whether an individual is or is not an outside salesman has frequently been a subject of contention between taxpayers and the Internal Revenue Service. Perhaps the best definition of an outside salesperson is found in the Regulations:

OUTSIDE SALESMAN One who solicits business as a full-time salesman for his employer away from his employer's place of business.

> An outside salesman is an individual who solicits business as a full-time salesman for his employer away from his employer's place of business. The term "outside salesman" does not include a taxpayer whose principal activities consist of service and delivery. For example, a bread driver-salesman or a milk driver-salesman would not be included within the definition. However, an outside salesman may perform incidental inside activities at his

employer's place of business, such as writing up and transmitting orders and spending short periods at the employer's place of business to make and receive telephone calls, without losing his classification as an outside salesman.[30]

In spite of this definition provided by the Regulations, there have been many court cases and many Revenue Rulings about whether a taxpayer in a specific situation should be considered to be an outside salesman or merely an employee.

Example 15: An industrial insurance agent employed by an insurance company to collect, service, and sell weekly and monthly insurance policies is not an outside salesman because the agent's primary job is not selling.[31]

Example 16: An employee of a brokerage firm is required to be at the employer's place of work from 9:30 to 2:30 p.m. During other hours, the employee is engaged in outside selling. The employee is not an outside salesman.[32]

Example 17: Jones sells chemical products to wholesale customers in a 14-county area. He travels for nine days in each 2-week period and spends one day in the office preparing reports, analyzing sales, calling customers, etc. Jones is an outside salesman because the work done in the office is merely incidental to his sales activities.

Example 18: Assume that Jones in Example 17 had the following business-related expenses—none of which was reimbursed: travel, \$16,200; transportation, \$2,900; telephone calls, \$120; membership in trade organization, \$200. Since Jones is classified as an outside salesman, all of the expenses would be deductible *for* AGI. If Jones had not been classified as an outside salesman only the travel and transportation would be deductible *for* AGI under Sec. 62. The expenses of telephone calls and membership dues would be deductible *from* AGI, and would thus be fully deductible only if the total of other deductions *from* AGI equaled or exceeded the zero-bracket income.

TRANSPORTATION EXPENSES

TRANSPORTATION COST Cost of transporting the employee from one place to another.

Transportation costs incurred by a taxpayer in connection with services performed as an employee are deductible *for* AGI, as we have seen in Sec. 62. The Regulations point out that "transportation" is a narrow concept, which includes:

---

30 Reg. Sec. 1.62-1(h).

31 Rev. Rul. 58-175, 1958-1 CB 28.

32 *S. Novak*, 51 T.C. 7 (1968).

> . . . only the cost of transporting the employee from one place to another in the course of his employment, while he is not away from home in a travel status. Thus, transportation costs may include cab fares, bus fares, and the like, and also a pro rata share of the employee's expenses of operating his automobile, including gas, oil, and depreciation. All transportation expenses must be allowable expenses under part VI (section 161 and following), subchapter B, chapter 1 of the Code, as ordinary and necessary expenses incurred during the taxable year in carrying on a trade or business as an employee. Transportation expenses do not include the cost of commuting to and from work; this cost constitutes a personal, living, or family expense and is not deductible.[33]

TRANSPORTATION TO "SECOND JOB"

Although routine commuting costs from the taxpayer's residence to his normal place of work are not deductible, if the taxpayer has more than one job the additional costs of going from the first job to the second one are deductible.[34]

Example 19: Louis is employed on a full-time job from 8 a.m. to 5 p.m. In addition he "moonlights," working at a second job from 6 p.m. to 8:30 p.m. He drives 20 miles from his home to the first job, 6 miles from the first job to the second, and 26 miles home from the second job. He may deduct only the cost of driving 6 miles from the first job to the second.

Example 20: Assume the same facts as in Example 19 except that Louis travels 20 miles from his home to the first job, 6 miles from the first job to the second job, and then 18 miles home from the second job. Since the additional mileage resulting from performing a second job is four miles a day (44 miles compared to 40 miles), only the cost of that four miles is deductible.

Similarly, a taxpayer whose sole employment requires movement from one location to another during a single day may be entitled to a transportation deduction, excluding the cost of getting from home to the first location and from the last assignment to home.

In recent years there have been several court cases involving the transportation costs of commuting employees who at the same time transported tools or equipment required on the taxpayer's job. The IRS maintains that the taxpayer is entitled to deduct only the difference between the cost of transportation actually used and the cost of the same mode of transportation without carrying the tools.[35] In many cases, therefore, the deductible cost amounts to very little, or nothing, under the IRS interpretation. This may appear to be grossly unfair to the worker who would

---

[33] Reg. Sec. 1.62-1(g).

[34] Internal Revenue Service Publication No. 463, "Travel, Entertainment, and Gift Expenses."

[35] Rev. Rul. 75-380, 1975-2 C.B. 59.

ordinarily ride a bus to work but because he or she is carrying tools must take an automobile—thus increasing his or her transportation cost because of the need for tools. In *Fausner v. Comm.*, the Supreme Court held that a taxpayer can deduct costs of the different transportation mode (an automobile) only if the taxpayer can show that the different mode would not have been used if it had not been necessary because of the transportation of the tools.[36]

Example 21: Scott normally rides a bus to work at a cost of $1.80 for the round trip from his home. On one day, Scott takes a large mower to be used on his job. In order to transport the mower he drives his automobile and rents a trailer. The automobile expenses were $5.20. Rental of the trailer was $16. Scott is clearly entitled to deduct the cost of the trailer rental. In addition, it should be possible for Scott to show that he would not have taken the automobile had it not been necessary to do so in order to transport the mower. Thus, he may be able to deduct the automobile expenses, although the IRS would probably challenge this deduction.

USE OF PERSONAL AUTOMOBILE

The taxpayer (either an employer or a self-employed person) who uses his or her personal automobile in business-related activities may generally choose between two methods in computing the allowable automobile expenses. First, the actual operating costs of the automobile for the business miles driven may be deducted. Second, the taxpayer may use the "standard mileage" rate. Taxpayers who use their personal automobiles only *occasionally* generally elect the standard mileage allowance because it is a simple computation, although the deduction for actual operating costs would often be greater.

If actual costs are to be used, the taxpayer must keep a record of costs incurred for gasoline, oil, repairs, taxes, insurance, tags and licenses, depreciation (cost recovery), and other operating expenses. The operating costs during the months the automobile is actually used in business are then allocated on a mileage basis between the business use and personal use during those months.

If the standard rate is used in lieu of actual expenses, the taxpayer may deduct 20½¢ per mile for the first 15,000 miles each year.[37] The standard allowance for each mile of use in excess of 15,000 miles each year is 11¢ per mile. After a car has been used for 60,000 business miles at the 20½¢ rate, it is considered to have been fully depreciated and the allowable rate for additional mileage after that point is only 11¢ per mile, even for the first 15,000 miles each year.

[36] *Fausner v. Comm.*, 93, S. Ct. 820 (1973).

[37] Form 2106, 1984.

Example 22: Clarence uses his automobile for business purposes as an employee. Prior to the current year he had driven the car for 59,000 miles, for which the maximum rate (20½¢ for 1984) had been deducted. During the current year, he drove 2,600 miles for business-related purposes. His total standard mileage allowance is $381:

1,000 miles @ $.205	$205
1,600 miles @ $.11	176
Total	$381

The standard mileage rate method cannot be used if more than one car at a time is being used for business purposes.

In addition to a deduction for the proportionate share of operating costs or for the standard mileage allowance, the taxpayer is entitled to deduct parking fees, bridge and road tolls, etc.[38] Also, the "business portion" of interest and state taxes on the automobile will be deductible as transportation expenses.[39] The business portion of such costs is the total of those items for the months during which the auto was used in business multiplied by the ratio of business miles to the total miles driven during those months. (These taxes and interest would normally be deductible as itemized deductions *for* AGI and would thus be deductible even if they were not allocated to business-related transportation.) However, if total itemized deductions are less than the zero-bracket amount, no deduction could be taken *from* AGI.

Example 23: Shirley uses her personal automobile infrequently in her business-related activities as an employee. During the current year she used the automobile 800 miles in March and 1,200 miles in September for business purposes. Total mileage driven in each of those months was 1,500 miles. Property taxes on the automobile were $48 and interest paid on the automobile was $1,200 for the year. Thus $4 of taxes and $100 of interest are allocable to each month. Shirley's total deduction for business-related automobile expenses is thus $548.66:

Mileage (2,000 miles @ $.205)	$410.00
Taxes (2,000/3,000 × $8.00)	5.33
Interest (2,000/3,000 × $200)	133.33
Total	$548.66

The remaining property taxes and interest may be included in itemized deductions *from* AGI.

[38] IRS Form 2106.

[39] *Ibid.*

TRAVEL EXPENSES

TRAVEL COSTS Costs of lodging, meals, etc., incurred by taxpayer while "away from home."

Sec. 62 of the Internal Revenue Code provides that *deductible* ***travel costs*** of employees will be deductible *for* AGI. However, the basic authority for deducting travel costs rests in Sec. 162(a)(2), which provides for the deduction by self-employed persons and employees of all ordinary and necessary expenses paid or incurred during the year in carrying on a trade or business, including:

> traveling expenses (including amounts expended for meals and lodging other than amounts which are lavish or extravagant under the circumstances) while away from home in the pursuit of a trade or business. . .[40]

The Regulations expand on this general statement about the deductibility of travel costs:

> (a) Traveling expenses include travel fares, meals and lodging, and expenses incident to travel such as expenses for sample rooms, telephone and telegraph, public stenographers, etc. Only such traveling expenses as are reasonable and necessary in the conduct of the taxpayer's business and directly attributable to it may be deducted. If the trip is undertaken for other than business purposes, the travel fares and expenses incident to travel are personal expenses and the meals and lodging are living expenses. If the trip is solely on business, the reasonable and necessary traveling expenses, including travel fares, meals, and lodging, and expenses incident to travel, are business expenses.[41]

Several phrases in the paragraph quoted above from the Regulations have proved to be far from clear and have resulted in countless disputes between taxpayers and the Internal Revenue Service. Most of these controversies have involved either (*a*) what types of costs qualify as deductible travel costs, (*b*) what is meant by the term "away from home", and (*c*) what is necessary for costs to be ordinary and necessary and related to the taxpayer's trade or business.

TYPES OF DEDUCTIBLE TRAVEL EXPENSES

Perhaps the most comprehensive listing of travel expenses is to be found in Internal Revenue Publication 463:

> (1) Air, rail, and bus fares;
> (2) Operation and maintenance of your automobile;
> (3) Taxi fares or other costs of transportation between the airport or station and your hotel, from one customer to another, or from one place of business to another;

[40] Sec. 162(a)(2).

[41] Reg. Sec. 1.162-2(a).

(4) Transportation from the place where you obtain your meals and lodging to your temporary work assignment;
(5) Baggage charges and transportation costs for sample and display material;
(6) Meals and lodging when you are away from home on business;
(7) Cleaning and laundry expenses;
(8) Telephone and telegraph expenses;
(9) Public stenographers' fees;
(10) Operation and maintenance of house trailers;
(11) Tips that are incidental to any of these expenses; and
(12) Other similar expenses incident to qualifying travel.[42]

"AWAY FROM HOME"

The question of whether a taxpayer was ***away from home*** when expenses were incurred has frequently been controversial. Both the words "away" and "home" have proved difficult to define.

AWAY FROM HOME The taxpayer's absence from the general locale of his principal place of duty for a period long enough to require sleep and rest.

Traditionally the IRS has emphasized that the taxpayer must be away from home *overnight*. In recent years, however, the word "overnight" has been abandoned. Instead, the IRS stresses that the taxpayer needs to be away from the general area of home for a period substantially longer than an ordinary day's work, and, during released time while away, it is reasonable for the individual to need and to get sleep or rest to meet the demands of employment or business. However, this does not mean napping in the taxpayer's car. The employee need not be away from his or her tax home for an entire 24-hour period or from dusk to dawn, so long as relief from duty during the absence is a sufficient period of time in which to get necessary sleep or rest.[43]

Example 24: You are a railroad conductor. You leave your home terminal on a regularly scheduled round-trip run between two cities and return home 16 hours later. During the run you are released for six hours at your turnaround point, where you eat two meals and rent a hotel room to get necessary sleep before starting the return trip. You are considered to be away from home.[44]

Another aspect of the "away-from-home test" is defining "home." Home has been identified by the IRS as (*a*) the taxpayer's regular place of business (***principal place of business*** if the taxpayer has more than one place of business)[45] or (*b*) the principal place of abode if, because of the nature of the taxpayer's work, the taxpayer has no regular or principal place of business.[46]

PRINCIPAL PLACE OF BUSINESS Place where taxpayer conducts the greatest portion of business, based on income, profits, time spent, and other factors.

---

[42] IRS Publication 463, "Travel, Entertainment, and Gift Expenses."

[43] IRS Publication 463. See also, *U.S. v. Correll*, 88 S. Ct. 445 (1967).

[44] IRS Publication 463.

[45] *Markey v. Comm.*, 490 F. 2d 1249 (6th Cir., 1960).

[46] IRS Publication 463.

In identifying the "principal place of business" when the taxpayer has more than one place, several factors are considered, such as: (*a*) the amount of time spent in each location, (*b*) the amount of business in each, and (*c*) the amount of financial return in each location.

Example 25: You live in Cincinnati where you have a seasonal job for 8 months and earn $15,000. You work the remaining 4 months in Miami, also at a seasonal job, and earn $4,000. Cincinnati is your principal place of employment since you spend most of your time there and earn most of your income there.[47]

Where the taxpayer has no regular or principal place of business, practical tests are applied for determining whether the taxpayer's abode can be treated as a "tax home." The taxpayer must:

1. have part of his or her business in the area of the taxpayer's principal home and use that home for lodging while doing business there,
2. have living expenses at home that are duplicated because business requires the taxpayer to be away from that home, and
3. have not left the area in which both his or her traditional place of lodging and principal home are located; have a member or members of the taxpayer's family living at the principal home; or often use that home for lodging.

If the taxpayer satisfies all three requirements, the taxpayer will be considered to have a tax home and may have deductible travel expenses. If only two of the factors are satisfied, the taxpayer may have a home, depending on all the facts and circumstances. If at least two of the requirements are not satisfied, the taxpayer will be considered an itinerant and "home" will be wherever the taxpayer happens to work.[48]

Example 26: You are an outside salesperson and have a sales territory covering several states. Your employer has its main office in City X, and you return there for approximately one month each year for business and nonbusiness reasons. Your business work assignments are temporary and you have no way of knowing where future assignments will be located. You have lived in City X for 14 years, first with your spouse in your own house until your divorce, and presently with your married sister in her house. You pay her $50 a month for a room in her house where you also keep your furniture and any clothing which you do not take on your out-of-town business trips.

You have satisfied all three objective factors listed previously, including the traditional lodging aspects of factor (*c*). Therefore, you

---

[47] *Ibid.*

[48] *Ibid.*

are considered to have a home in City X for travel costs deduction purposes.[49]

Another aspect of the "away-from-home" test is that the absence from home must be *temporary*, rather than for an *indefinite* period. In order to be temporary, termination of duty away from the taxpayer's regular post must be foreseen within a fixed and reasonably short period. This determination must be made at the time work is begun in the new location. Usually an assignment expected to last for a year or more is not deemed temporary.[50] Nevertheless, the Courts have often held that construction workers who accept employment for an indefinite period in locations where it is not desirable or feasible to establish long-term homes for their families may deduct the costs of living at such locations.[51]

COMBINED BUSINESS AND PLEASURE TRIPS

Two sentences in Reg. Sec. 1.162-2(a) relate to the requirement that expenses must be reasonable and necessary and must relate to the taxpayer's business in order to be deductible. "Only such traveling expenses as are reasonable and necessary in the conduct of the taxpayer's business and directly attributable to it may be deducted." "If the trip is solely on business the reasonable and necessary traveling expenses . . . are business expenses."

The basic test as to whether travel expenses are reasonable is that they not be lavish in the circumstances. Controversies over reasonableness have been relatively limited. However, there have been almost endless controversies over whether specific expenses are ordinary and necessary. Many of these disputes have dealt with whether the costs involved were for trips "solely for business" or for trips that were for both business and pleasure.

If, while away from home, the taxpayer engages in both business and personal activities, a determination must be made of whether the trip was made primarily for personal reasons or was primarily business related. If the trip is within the United States and is primarily personal in nature, the costs of traveling to and from the destination are not deductible, even though the taxpayer engages in business activities while there. Nevertheless, expenses at the destination which are properly allocable to business are deductible.[52] On the other hand, if the trip is primarily for business purposes and is within the United States, the cost of transportation and other costs incurred in connection with business activities are deductible even though the incremental costs related to personal activities are not deductible. The facts and circumstances in each situation determine

---

[49] *Ibid.*

[50] Rev. Rul. 60-189, 1960-1 C.B. 60.

[51] See, for example, *R.A. Sanders*, 439 F2d 296 (C.A. 9, 1971) and *W. R. McKinley*, 37 TCM 1769 (1978).

[52] Reg. Sec. 1.162-2(b)(1).

whether a trip is primarily related to the taxpayer's trade or business. Such factors as the amount of time during the trip which is spent on personal activities compared to that spent directly on business activities is an important factor.[53]

Example 27: Morgan, a salesperson of industrial supplies, lives in New York. In February of the current year, she went to San Diego on business. She spent four days conducting business and two days vacationing. Her air fare was $460, taxi fares related to business in San Diego, $45, her meal costs during the four days of business, $131, her hotel room (including taxes) for the four business days, $372, her meal costs during the two days of vacation, $31, and her hotel room during the two days of vacation, $186. Morgan's trip was primarily business related, so all of the costs are deductible except the $186 for the hotel and $31 for meals during the two days of vacation.

Example 28: While at a destination, a taxpayer spends one week on activities which are directly related to business and subsequently spends an additional three weeks there on personal activities. The trip will be considered primarily personal in nature in the absence of a clear showing to the contrary. Thus the costs of transportation between home and the destination will not be deductible. Costs directly related to business activities at the destination will be deductible.

Example 29: Sharon works in Atlanta and is required to make a business trip to New Orleans. On her way home, she stops in Mobile to visit her parents. She spends $450 during the nine days she is away from home for transportation, meals, lodging, and other travel expenses. Had she not stopped in Mobile, she would have been gone only six days and her total cost would have been $400. Sharon may deduct only $400 for her trip to and from New Orleans.[54]

FOREIGN TRAVEL

In recent years many taxpayers have found it "necessary" to make "business" trips to foreign countries and have taken the opportunity to combine personal vacations with the business trips. If the taxpayer travels on business, or attends a convention, seminar, etc., in a foreign country, special rules apply. If the travel does not exceed one week, or if the portion of the taxpayer's time outside the U.S. that is not attributable to trade or business activity is less than 25% of the total time on such travel, all the transportation costs may be deductible. If more than one week is spent abroad and 25% or more of the time is spent on nonbusiness activities, the transportation costs must be allocated on the basis of time spent, and

---

[53] Reg. Sec. 1.162-2(b)(2).

[54] *Ibid.*

the nonbusiness portion is not deductible.[55] All expenses attributable to such activities are nondeductible. Costs of attending a foreign convention or seminar are not deductible unless it is as reasonable for that meeting to be held outside the North American area as within it. (The North American area includes the U.S., its possessions, the Trust Territory of the Pacific Islands, Canada, and Mexico. There are special rules involving Caribbean countries.)

Factors considered in determining whether it is reasonable for a convention to have been held outside the North American area are:

1. The purpose of the meeting and activities taking place.
2. The purposes and activities of the sponsoring group or organization.
3. The places of residence of active members of the organization and places of other meetings of the group.
4. Other relevant information.[56]

Expenses of attending conventions, seminars, or other meetings aboard cruise ships are not deductible unless the cruise ship is a vessel registered in the United States and all ports of call are in the United States or its possessions. In addition, the taxpayer, as well as the sponsoring group, must submit certain written information about the program or seminar. The maximum amount deductible for programs on cruise ships in a calendar year is $2,000.[57]

TRAVEL COSTS OF ACCOMPANYING SPOUSE

Questions frequently arise in connection with the deductibility of travel costs of a spouse or other family member who accompanies the taxpayer on business trips. The spouse's travel costs are not deductible unless the spouse's presence had a bona fide business purpose. The spouse's performance of incidental service does not cause the expenses to qualify as deductible business travel.[58]

> **Example 30:** A taxpayer travels to Chicago on business in her automobile and takes her spouse with her. No business purpose is served by the spouse's presence. The taxpayer pays $75 a day for a double room. A single room would cost $67 a day. The taxpayer may deduct the total cost of operating her automobile to and from Chicago, but only $67 a day for her hotel room. If she had used public transportation, her fare but not that of her spouse would be deductible.[59]

Although travel costs are deductible *for* AGI, such costs as convention registration fees and payments for materials used in attending a conven-

[55] Reg. Sec. 1.274-4 contains detailed rules governing deduction of expenses of foreign travel.
[56] Sec. 274(h)(1).
[57] Sec. 274(h)(2) and (4).
[58] Reg. Sec. 1.162-2(c).
[59] IRS Publication 463. See also Rev. Rul. 56-168, 1956-1 C.B. 93.

tion or seminar are not considered to be travel costs and therefore are not deductible *for* AGI unless they are reimbursed. Nevertheless, they are business-related expenses and will be deductible *from* AGI if the total of such deductions exceeds the zero-bracket amount.

Even though the various rules followed in determining if travel costs are deductible may be "logical," the application of the rules is often difficult, and the facts of each case must be studied carefully. Even then, skillful and rational people may disagree in their conclusions in a specific case.

ENTERTAINMENT COSTS

Most of the criticisms of "expense account" spending as a means of tax avoidance have dealt with entertainment costs. The reasons are obvious, as a single example will illustrate. Suppose the taxpayer enjoys the theater (or the night club, or any other particular form of entertainment). An individual with whom he has some business connection is coming to town, so the taxpayer purchases theater tickets for himself, his wife, and the visiting businessman. Is this expenditure really for business? What are the motives in making the expenditure? Was the attendance of the taxpayer's wife reasonable and necessary? As a result of this entertainment and the goodwill generated, the taxpayer may very well achieve important business objectives even though the two do not directly discuss business during the evening. The inherent problems are obvious.

MEALS, AMUSEMENT AND RECREATION

With few exceptions, Sec. 274(a) denies the taxpayer a deduction for meals and entertainment unless the activity is "directly related to" or is "associated with" the active conduct of trade or business.

> (1) In General—No deduction otherwise allowable under this chapter shall be allowed for any item—
>
> (A) Activity—With respect to an activity which is of a type generally considered to constitute entertainment, amusement, or recreation, unless the taxpayer establishes that the item was directly related to, or, in the case of an item directly preceding or following a substantial and bona fide business discussion (including business meetings at a convention or otherwise), that such item was associated with, the active conduct of the taxpayer's trade or business. . . .[60]

DIRECTLY-RELATED ENTERTAINMENT

The regulations under Sec. 274 lay down four requirements, all of which must be met, in order for entertainment to be considered as "directly related."

---

[60] Sec. 274(a)(1)(A).

1. The taxpayer must have more than a general expectation of deriving some specific benefit (other than simple "goodwill") from the meeting.
2. An actual business discussion took place during the meeting.
3. In light of all the facts and circumstances, the principal character of the business entertainment was active conduct of the taxpayer's trade or business, and
4. The persons involved were the taxpayer and a person with whom the taxpayer engaged in the active conduct of trade or business during the entertainment.[61]

Meetings or discussions at night clubs, theaters, and sporting events, or during essentially social gatherings like cocktail parties, are not conducive to such business discussions, and it will be difficult to classify these costs as ***directly-related business discussions***.[62]

DIRECTLY-RELATED BUSINESS DISCUSSION Discussion between taxpayer and second individual about specific business activities, conducted in an atmosphere conducive to serious business conversations.

"ASSOCIATED" ENTERTAINMENT

Expenses that are not directly related to, but are associated with, the active conduct of the taxpayer's trade or business are deductible only if the entertainment directly preceded or followed a substantial or bona fide business discussion.[63] This is commonly referred to as the "***associated entertainment***" rule.

ASSOCIATED ENTERTAINMENT Entertainment just before or just after a substantial "directly-related" business discussion.

Example 31: Rolando, a salesman, takes a customer to see a play at a New York theater. After the play, the two discuss a new product that Rolando is seeking to sell the customer. The cost of the theater tickets represents costs of entertainment "associated with" conduct of Rolando's business. However, because it is not possible for the two to discuss business during the time at the theater, it is not "directly related" entertainment.

Example 32: Morrison, a banker, took several businessmen to a discotheque. Although no business was discussed, the banker felt that he was building goodwill that might subsequently lead to new accounts. The cost is not deductible as entertainment.

THE "QUIET-MEAL" RULE

The major exception to the requirement that entertainment meet the provision of being directly related to or associated with the taxpayer's trade or business is found in the "quiet-meal" rule. In general, expenses for food or beverages are deductible when "furnished to any individual under circumstances which (taking into account the surroundings in which furnished, the taxpayer's trade, business, or income-producing ac-

[61] Reg. Sec. 1.274-2(c)(3).
[62] Reg. Sec. 1.174-2(c)(7).
[63] Reg. Sec. 1.274-2(d)(1).

tivity and persons to whom the food and beverage are furnished) are of a type generally considered to be conducive to a business discussion."[64] There is no requirement that business actually be discussed in order for costs of such meals to be deductible.[65] However, if the meals or beverages are furnished in circumstances where there are distractions such as at night clubs, sporting events, large cocktail parties, or other major distracting influences, the taxpayer must show that business was actually discussed at the entertainment just before or after the event.[66]

Example 33: Ronson, a banker, invited several local businessmen to lunch at a local restaurant. Although no business was discussed, Ronson feels that the goodwill generated might subsequently lead to new accounts. Under the "quiet-meal" test, the cost will probably be deductible.

ENTERTAINMENT FACILITIES

ENTERTAINMENT FACILITIES Physical facilities provided for entertainment. Includes country clubs and other clubs in which taxpayer holds membership.

Taxpayers have frequently abused the tax laws that made entertainment costs deductible. One frequent abuse by self-employed persons in the past was the acquisition of ***entertainment facilities*** such as yachts, hunting lodges, and fishing camps that could be used for entertaining business associates, but could also be available for personal use. The Code prohibits the deduction of costs "with respect to a facility used in connections with" entertainment activities.[67] Although "dues or fees to any social, athletic, or sporting club or organization shall be treated as items with respect to facilities,"[68] the dues or fees may be deductible if the taxpayer can establish "that the facility for which the dues or fees were paid was used primarily for the furtherance of the taxpayer's trade or business and that the item was directly related to the active conduct of such business."[69]

In order to deduct dues and fees to a club, the taxpayer must show that the facility was used "primarily for the furtherance of his trade or business . . . more than 50% of the total calendar days of use of the facility by . . . the taxpayer during the taxable year."[70] Any use of a facility during one calendar day is considered a day of business use if the facility was used for *directly related* purposes, including quiet business meals, even though the facility may be used on the same day by the taxpayer or the taxpayer's family for personal use.[71] *Associated* use does not qualify as business use for this purpose.

---

[64] Sec. 274(e)(1).

[65] Reg. Sec. 1.274-2(f).

[66] Reg. Sec. 1.274-2(f)(2)(i)(b).

[67] Sec. 274(a)(1)(B).

[68] Sec. 274(a)(2)(A).

[69] Sec. 274(a)(2)(C).

[70] Reg. Sec. 1.274-2(e)(4)(iii).

[71] *Ibid.*

Example 34: During the current year, Smith paid $600 in dues to the local country club. During the year, Smith took customers to the club for business lunches on 32 days. On six of those same 32 days Smith's wife used the club for personal use. In addition, Smith and his wife used the club solely for personal use on 30 other days. A total of $310 of the dues is deductible ($^{32}/_{62}$ × $600) because of the 62 days of use, 32 days were directly related to business purposes. The costs of business meals will be deductible, while meals and other costs incurred during personal use will not be deductible.

Although the costs of "facilities" (except dues and fees) are not generally deductible, costs incurred in *using* these facilities for business entertainment will be deductible. For example, depreciation, rent, utility charges, repairs, salaries of caretakers, and other operating expenses of a hunting lodge are not deductible. However, the costs of meals and beverages served, the costs of a hunting guide, and the cost of ammunition used in hunting trips at the lodge while entertaining business customers would be deductible. In addition, all costs of operating recreational facilities for employees are deductible.[72]

Entertainment costs are deductible *for* AGI in the case of self-employed persons. Such costs are deductible *from* AGI by employees unless they are reimbursed. To the extent that they are reimbursed, they are deductible *for* AGI.

BUSINESS GIFTS

The Revenue Code severely restricts the deductions allowable for business gifts. In general, the total amount deductible is limited to $25 per donee each year.[73] For this purpose a gift is defined as any amount excludable as a bona fide gift under Code Sec. 102. However, items that cost the taxpayer not in excess of $4, on which the name of the taxpayer is clearly and permanently imprinted, and which is one of a number of identical items distributed generally by the taxpayer, are not included in "gifts" for this purpose.[74]

Example 35: During the year the taxpayer made the following gifts to business customers:

- to Thurgood, two gifts, one valued at $16, one at $12
- to Iris, one gift valued at $100
- to six other customers, one gift each, valued at $15 each.

Of the amounts given, $3 of the gifts to Thurgood and $75 of the gift to Iris will not be deductible.

---

[72] Sec. 274(e)(5).

[73] Sec. 274(b)(1).

[74] Sec. 274(b)(1)(A).

In addition, tangible personal property which is awarded to an employee because of length of service, productivity, or safety achievement is deductible if the cost of the item does not exceed $400 or if the item is a "qualified-plan award."[75] Qualified-plan awards must be granted under written nondiscriminatory plans, the average cost of all items under all the employers' plans must be $400 or less, and the individual item awarded under the plan must not cost more than $1,600.[76]

The general $25 limit applies to gifts made directly and indirectly to the donee. In general, a gift made to the spouse of the person who has a business relationship with the donor is deemed to have been made indirectly to the person with the business relationship.[77] Similarly, a gift to a corporation or other business entity where the gift is intended for the individual use or benefit of a person is deemed to be an indirect gift to that person.[78]

Example 36: Burbank, a salesman, gave a radio valued at $40 to Claiborn, a customer, and a camera valued at $70 to Claiborn's wife. Both gifts are deemed to have been given to Claiborn. Thus only $25 of the total of $110 will be deductible.

Like entertainment costs, deductible gifts are deductible *for* AGI by self-employed persons. Deductible gifts made by employees are deductible *from* AGI, except that they are deductible *for* AGI to the extent they are reimbursed.

RECORD-KEEPING AND REPORTING REQUIREMENTS: TRAVEL, ENTERTAINMENT, AND GIFTS

The Code and related Regulations are rather precise in specifying the reporting and accounting requirements for traveling, entertainment, and gift expenses.

> (d) Substantiation Required—No deduction shall be allowed—
> (1) under section 162 or 212 for any traveling expense (including meals and lodging while away from home),
> (2) for any item with respect to an activity which is of a type generally considered to constitute entertainment, amusement, or recreation, or with respect to a facility used in connection with such an activity, or
> (3) for any expense for gifts,
> unless the taxpayer substantiates by adequate records or by sufficient evidence corroborating his own statement (a) the amount of such expense or other item, (b) the time and place of the travel, entertainment, amusement, recreation, or use of the facility, or the

[75] Sec. 274(b)(1)(C).
[76] Sec. 274(b)(3).
[77] Reg. Sec. 1.274-3(d)(1).
[78] Reg. Sec. 1.274-3(d)(2).

date and description of the gift, (c) the business purpose of the expense or other item, and (d) the business relationship to the taxpayer of persons entertained, using the facility, or receiving the gift. The Secretary may by regulations provide that some or all of the requirements of the preceding sentence shall not apply in the case of an expense which does not exceed an amount prescribed pursuant to such regulations.[79]

Regulation 1.274-5 contains a detailed description of the information required about each "element" (amount, time, place, business purpose, business relationship, amount, description, etc.) for each expenditure for travel, for entertainment, and for gifts.[80]

Prior to 1985, taxpayers were required to keep "adequate" records of travel expenses, entertainment costs, and business gifts, prepared at or near the time of each expenditure,[81] supported by appropriate documentary evidence. After 1984, however, taxpayers are required to keep "adequate contemporaneous" records to substantiate:[82]

(1) traveling expenses,
(2) entertainment expenses,
(3) business gifts, and
(4) the business use of "listed property." (Listed property includes automobile and other transportation vehicles susceptible of personal use, computers or peripheral equipment, and property of a type generally used for entertainment, recreation, or amusement.)[83]

In the case of vehicles, the records must include a log showing the date of the trip, the business purpose, the number of miles driven, and the user.[84] Similarly, records showing the use of computers must be maintained unless the computer is used exclusively at a regular business establishment. The person preparing the tax return and the person signing the return are both saddled with unusual responsibilities for verifying the substantiations required.[85]

Documentary evidence, such as receipts or paid bills, is required for (a) any expenditure for lodging and (b) for any other expenditure of $25 or more, except for transportation charges if such documentation is not readily available.[86]

However, special rules apply to the reporting and substantiation of employee's expenses in certain cases. If the employee is required to make an "adequate accounting" to his or her employer, the employee is not required to report business expenses or reimbursements on his or her own

---

[79] Sec. 274(d).
[80] Reg. Sec. 1.274-5(b).
[81] Reg. Sec. 1.274-5(c).
[82] Sec. 1.274(d).
[83] Listed property is defined in Sec. 280F(d)(4).
[84] Temp. Reg. 1.280F-2T and Temp. Reg. 1.274-5T.
[85] Sec. 6695(b).
[86] Reg. Sec. 1.274-5(c)(2)(iii).

FIGURE 7-1

Form **2106** | **Employee Business Expenses** | OMB No. 1545-0139
Department of the Treasury
Internal Revenue Service

(Please use Form 3903 to figure moving expense deduction.)
▶ **Attach to Form 1040.**

1984
54

Your name	Social security number	Occupation in which expenses were incurred
Helen G. Wills	333 33 3333	Sales Representative

Part I Employee Business Expenses Deductible in Figuring Adjusted Gross Income on Form 1040, Line 32

1	Reimbursed and unreimbursed fares for airplane, bus, boat, taxicab, train, etc	1	3,890
2	Reimbursed and unreimbursed meal, lodging, and other expenses while away from your tax home	2	4,385
3	Reimbursed and unreimbursed car expenses from Part II. (Mileage is larger)	3	3,970
4	Reimbursed and unreimbursed outside salesperson's expenses other than those shown on lines 1 through 3. **Caution:** *Do not use this line unless you are an outside salesperson (see instructions).* Entertaining Clients	4	2,620
5	Reimbursed expenses other than those shown on lines 1 through 3 (see instructions)	5	
6	Add lines 1 through 5	6	14,865
7	Employer's payments for these expenses only if not included on Form W-2	7	12,200
8	If line 6 is more than line 7, subtract line 7 from line 6. Enter here and on Form 1040, line 25	8	2,665
9	If line 7 is more than line 6, subtract line 6 from line 7. Enter here and on Form 1040, line 7	9	

Part II Car Expenses (Use either your actual expenses or the mileage rate.)

	Car 1	Car 2	Car 3
A Number of months you used car for business during 1984	12 months	months	months
B Total mileage for months on line A	25,000 miles	miles	miles
C Business part of line B mileage	20,000 miles	miles	miles
D Date placed in service	11/15/83	/ /	/ /

Actual Expenses (Include expenses on lines 1 and 2 only for the months shown on line A, above.)

		Car 1	Car 2	Car 3
1 Gasoline, oil, lubrication, etc.	1	3,560		
2 Other	2	120		
3 Total (add lines 1 and 2)	3	3,680		
4 Divide line C by line B, above	4	80 %	%	%
5 Multiply line 3 by line 4	5	2,944		
6 Depreciation (see instructions)	6	820		
7 Business parking fees and tolls	7	110		
8 Add lines 5 through 7. Also enter in Part I, line 3.	8	3,874		

Mileage Rate

9	Enter the smaller of (a) 15,000 miles or (b) the total mileage (Car 1+ Car 2+ Car 3) from line C, above	9	15,000 miles
10	Multiply line 9 by 20½¢ (.205) (11¢ (.11) if applicable, see instructions)	10	$3,075
11	Enter the total mileage, if any (Car 1 + Car 2 + Car 3) from line C that is over 15,000 miles	11	5,000 miles
12	Multiply line 11 by 11¢ (.11) and enter here	12	$550
13	Business part of car interest, parking fees, tolls, and State and local taxes (except gasoline tax)	13	345
14	Total (add lines 10, 12, and 13). Enter here and in Part I, line 3.	14	$3,970

Part III Information About Educational Expenses Shown in Part I or on Schedule A (Form 1040)

1 Did you need this education to meet the minimum educational requirements for your business or profession? ☐ Yes ☐ No

2 Will this study program qualify you for a new business or profession? ☐ Yes ☐ No

Note: *If your answer to question 1 or 2 is "Yes," stop here. You cannot deduct these expenses, even if you do not intend to change your business or profession.*

3 If "No," list the courses you took and their relationship to your business or profession ▶

Changes You Should Note

New rules apply that may limit the amount of your recovery deduction for depreciation and investment credit for certain property used in your trade or business and placed in service after June 18, 1984.

- For calendar year 1984, the recovery deduction for a "passenger automobile" may not exceed $4,000, and the investment credit may not exceed $1,000. In figuring your recovery deduction, for purposes of this limitation, the section 179 expense deduction is treated as a recovery deduction. These amounts are reduced if your business use is less than 100%.
- The section 179 expense deduction and investment credit are not allowed for certain property such as "passenger automobiles" and other transportation property used 50% or less in your trade or business. Additionally, if you use the property 50% or less in a trade or business, you must use the straight-line method of depreciation.
- No deduction for recovery depreciation or investment credit will be allowed for an employee's "passenger automobile" or other transportation property unless such use is for the convenience of the employer and required as a condition of employment.
- New recordkeeping rules for trade or business expenses will apply beginning in 1985. See **Important Tax Law Changes** on page 2 of your 1984 Form 1040 Instructions.

See **Publications 572**, Investment Credit and **534**, Depreciation, for more detail on the kinds of property to which the above limitations apply. Also, see **Forms 3468**, Computation of Investment Credit, and **4562**, Depreciation and Amortization, for additional information.

For Paperwork Reduction Act Notice, see instructions on back. Form **2106** (1984)

return if reimbursements equal expenditures.[87] Instead, the employee simply affirms on his or her tax return that reimbursements did not exceed expenses. If, however, the reimbursements exceed the deductible expenses, the employee must include the excess in income.[88] Similarly, an employee who makes an adequate accounting to his or her employer but wishes to deduct expenses incurred in excess of the amount of reimbursement, must submit the same information as an employee who is not required to account to his employer and must maintain adequate records to substantiate the deduction.[89]

In cases where an employee is not required to make an adequate accounting to his or her employer, the employee is required to submit with the tax return a statement showing the total reimbursement from the employer, the nature of occupation, the number of days away from home on business, and the total amount of business expenses paid or incurred, broken down into such categories as transportation, meals and lodging while away from home overnight, entertainment, gifts, and other business expenses. In addition, the employee must maintain adequate records to substantiate the deductions.[90] In almost all cases, employees will use Form 2106 to report expenses and reimbursements. This form is illustrated in Figure 7-1.

FORM 2106

OTHER EMPLOYEE EXPENSES

Other expenses of employees related to their business activities have been specifically allowed by court decisions, Revenue Rulings, and Regulations. Those expenses are deductible *for* AGI to the extent that they are for travel or transportation or reimbursed. Other nonreimbursed costs are deductible *from* AGI.

For example, fees paid to an employment agency for aid in securing employment are deductible.[91] In addition, all expenses that a taxpayer incurs in seeking employment in the same trade or business are deductible, even if the search is unsuccessful.[92] However, if a taxpayer is seeking employment in a *new* trade or business (including seeking the taxpayer's *first* job) no deduction is allowable for such expenses.[93]

Example 37: Regina is employed as a secretary. During the current year she changed jobs. She paid an employment agency $1,000 in connection with finding the new job. In addition she paid $10 to have resumés printed and she incurred travel costs of $300 to be in-

---

[87] Reg. Sec. 1.274-5(e)(2)(i).
[88] Reg. Sec. 1.274-5(e)(2)(ii).
[89] Reg. Sec. 1.274-5(e)(2)(iii).
[90] Reg. Sec. 1.274-5(e)(3).
[91] Rev. Rul. 77-16, 1977-1 C.B. 37.
[92] *Ibid.*
[93] *Ibid.*

terviewed for the job. The travel costs are deductible *for* AGI. All of the other items are itemized deductions *from* AGI.

A deduction is allowed for dues, initiation fees, and out-of-work assessments paid to labor unions or professional associations or societies.[94] Assessments made by a union for such purposes as sickness or death benefits are not deductible as trade or business-related expenses.

Example 38: Sue is employed as an accountant by a public accounting firm. During the year she paid $60 for subscriptions to professional publications and $200 for membership dues in professional organizations. Her employer reimbursed Sue for the membership dues. Thus, that cost is deductible *for* AGI (and the reimbursement is included in gross income) while the subscription costs will be deductible *from* AGI.

An employee may deduct the cost of special items of clothing required in the employee's work if the items are not generally suitable for off-duty wear and if the items are required as a condition of employment.[95] In addition the costs incurred in the upkeep of deductible items of clothing, (such as laundry, cleaning, and repair) are also deductible.

Example 39: Ronald is employed as a CPA. He is required to wear a suit and tie each day. This requirement causes Ronald to spend $600 for clothing this year that he would not have spent otherwise. Since these clothing items are suitable for off-duty wear, Ronald is not entitled to deduct their cost.

Example 40: Laura is a registered nurse. She is required to wear uniforms on the job. These uniforms, which cost her $600 this year, are not suitable for off-duty wear. She may deduct their cost. If she is an employee, Laura would deduct the costs *from* AGI. If she is self-employed they are deductible *for* AGI.

EDUCATION EXPENSES

Most expenses related to education are nondeductible personal expenses. The costs are deductible only if the education

(1) maintains or improves skills required by the individual in his employment or other trade or business, or
(2) meets the express requirements of the individual's employer, or the requirement of applicable law or regulations, imposed as a condition to the retention by the individual of an established employment relationship, status, or rate of compensation.[96]

---

[94] Rev. Rul. 72-463, 1972-2, C.B. 93.

[95] Rev. Rul. 70-474, 1970-2 C.B. 34.

[96] Reg. Sec. 1.162-5(b).

The intention of this regulation is to permit deductions only for education expense incurred purely for business purposes. This has been interpreted to mean that the costs of acquiring the basic education necessary for the taxpayer's *entrance* into his or her trade, business or profession are *not* deductible, because they represent personal expenditures.[97] However, after the taxpayer has attained the minimum education requirements and is active in a job, he or she may deduct expenditures made to maintain or improve the skills of the job. Also, expenses of education *required* by the taxpayer's employer or by law as a condition of continued employment will be deductible. Costs of education undertaken *primarily* to obtain a promotion, an increase in pay, or a new job are not deductible. It is extremely difficult in many cases to determine why education costs are incurred by the taxpayer.

Example 41: Lawrence is a high school teacher of business subjects. The state legislature passed a law this year requiring all business teachers to have taken, or to take, at least one semester of computer familiarization. Lawrence enrolls at the local university in a computer course. Lawrence can deduct the expenses of the course.

Frequent changes in the Revenue Service's rules and sometimes conflicting court cases have caused further confusion over the deductibility of education expenses. Although a taxpayer cannot deduct the costs of preparing for a *new* trade or business, a change of duties is not considered to be a new trade or business if the new job involves many of the same duties as the present job. For example, a teacher who meets minimum educational requirements to teach in one state may deduct the costs for required educational courses necessary to qualify to teach in another state.[98] The U.S. Tax Court has allowed a teacher already certified to teach in Canada to deduct the costs of three courses required for certification to teach in New Jersey.[99]

Additionally, the Tax Court has permitted an unemployed high school principal (who had resigned his position) to deduct the expense of getting his Ph.D. in educational administration.[100]

Many educational activities clearly relate to the taxpayer's trade or business and are clearly undertaken to improve the taxpayer's skills. For example, the costs incurred by a practicing CPA to attend a 3-day seminar on computer auditing, or those incurred by a teacher in attending a seminar on motivating students, would be deductible. However, the costs incurred by a noncertified employee of a public accounting firm in attending a "CPA review" seminar would be deemed to be a cost of preparing to enter the profession rather than for improving skills and knowledge.[101]

---

[97] Reg. Sec. 1.161-5(b)(2).

[98] Rev. Rul. 71-58, 1971-1, C.B. 55.

[99] *R. Lawrence*, 69 T.C. 723. (1978).

[100] *R. J. Picknally*. 36 TCM 1292 (1977).

[101] Rev. Rul. 69-292, 1969-1 C.B. 84.

(Similarly, the fee paid the State Board of Accountancy for taking the CPA exam would be a nondeductible personal expense.)

If educational expenses incurred by an employee are reimbursed by his or her employer under a qualified educational-assistance plan, the amounts received as reimbursement by the employer are not included in gross income, as discussed in Chapter 5, and the employee is not entitled to deduct the expenses for which reimbursement is received. Amounts received as reimbursement that are not made by the employer under an educational-assistance plan must be included in gross income whether or not the related expenses are deductible.

REIMBURSEMENT OF EMPLOYEE BUSINESS-RELATED EXPENSES

Generally, amounts received as reimbursement for costs incurred by a taxpayer are includable in gross income.[102] The actual procedure for handling reimbursement on the tax return is to offset the reimbursement and the expenses against one another and report the difference as adjusted gross income or as a deduction.[103] As discussed earlier in this chapter, however, if the employee is required to account to the employer for expenditures, and if the expenses are equal to the reimbursement, the taxpayer is not required to report the reimbursement and will not deduct the expenses. Instead the employee merely states that the amounts received as reimbursement did not exceed expenses.[104] If reimbursement exceeds expenditures, the excess must be included in AGI. If expenses exceed reimbursement, the excess is deductible either *for* AGI or *from* AGI, depending on the nature of the expense.

Since Sec. 62 provides that deductions for adjusted gross income for employee-related expenses are limited *only* to: (*a*) transportation costs, (*b*) travel costs, (*c*) all expenses of outside salesmen, and (*d*) other deductible *reimbursed* expenses, the taxpayer must carefully match reimbursements with expenditures.

Example 42: In the current year, the taxpayer spent the following amounts for deductible employee expenses: $800 for travel, $400 for transportation, $20 for business gifts, $200 for entertainment, $100 for professional memberships, and $80 for subscriptions to trade periodicals. The employer reimbursed the employee $1,200 for travel and transportation. None of the other costs was reimbursed.

The taxpayer will have no net deduction for travel and transportation, since those amounts are exactly reimbursed. Entertainment, business gifts, subscriptions, and dues are all not deductible *for* AGI if they are *not* reimbursed. Thus, the $400 spent for these items will be included in deductions *from* AGI along with allowed personal ex-

---

[102] Reg. Sec. 1.62(f)(2).

[103] IRS Form 2106 and Reg. Sec. 1.162(b).

[104] Reg. Sec. 1.162-17(b).

penditures. The excess of *all* the deductions *from* AGI over the zero-bracket amount will be deductible. However, if there is no excess over the zero-bracket amount, the taxpayer will have received no tax deduction for these business expenses.

Example 43: Assume the same expenditures ($1,600 total) as in Example 42 and the same reimbursement ($1,200). However, the reimbursement is specifically $800 for travel, $20 for gifts, $200 for entertainment, $100 for professional memberships, and $80 for subscriptions. The transportation costs are not reimbursed. In this case all of the costs are deductible *for* AGI. The travel and transportation are always deductible *for* AGI, whether or not reimbursed. Since the amounts spent for gifts, entertainment, dues and subscriptions were fully reimbursed, they, too, are deductible *for* AGI.

If the employee is reimbursed in an amount less than the total deductible expenses incurred and the reimbursement is not designated to cover specific expenses, an allocation of the reimbursement must be made between the different expenses incurred.[105] The procedure for making this allocation is shown in the following example taken from the Regulations.[106]

Example 44: S, who is not a full-time outside salesman, received a salary of $20,000 and an expense allowance of $1,200 for the calendar year. He expended $800 for travel, meals, and lodging while away from home, $500 for local transportation expenses, and $300 for the entertainment of customers. His adjusted gross income is computed as follows:

Salary	$20,000		
Expense allowance	1,200		
Gross income		$21,200	
Less: Travel, meals, and lodging while away from home	$ 800		
Transportation expense	500		
Reimbursed expenses*	225	1,525	
Adjusted gross income			$19,675

*The amount of the reimbursement allocable to entertainment expenses is determined as follows:

Travel, meals and lodging away from home	$ 800	
Transportation expense	500	
Expenses deductible in arriving at adjusted gross income (whether or not reimbursed)	$1,300	
Entertainment expense	300	
Total expenses	$1,600	
Deductible for adjusted gross income: $300/$1600 × $1,200 (expense allowance)		$225

[105] Reg. Sec. 1.62-1(f)(1).

[106] Reg. Sec. 1.62-1(f)(2).

The remaining $75 ($300 minus $225) of entertainment costs in Example 44 is deemed to be unreimbursed and will be included in itemized deductions *from* AGI. If the taxpayer in the example were single and had other itemized deductions of only $1,600, he would get no tax benefit from the $75 of unreimbursed entertainment expenses because the total of all items deductible *from* AGI would be less than the amount of zero-bracket income.

MOVING EXPENSES

MOVING COSTS Costs related to taxpayer's move to a new job location.

An individual, either an employee or a self-employed person, is allowed to deduct, within limits, ***moving costs*** paid or incurred "in connection with the commencement of work by the taxpayer as an employee or as a self-employed individual at a new principal place of work."[107] Allowable moving expenses are deductible *for* AGI.[108] There are two major requirements which must be satisfied in order for a deduction of moving expenses to be allowed. The first is a minimum distance requirement and the second is a minimum period of employment requirement.[109]

For a taxpayer who has a former principal place of work, no deduction is allowable unless the distance between the former residence and the *new principal job site* is at least 35 miles farther from the old residence than was the old job site. If the taxpayer had no former principal job site, the new principal job site must be at least 35 miles from the former residence. Individuals who are obtaining full-time employment for the first time—for example, a recent college graduate—would be included in the latter category.[110]

An *employee* must be a full-time employee at the new job location for at least 39 weeks during the 12-month period immediately following his or her arrival at the new job location. A self-employed person must perform services on a full-time basis in the new location for at least 39 weeks out of the next 12 months and also for at least 78 weeks in the 24-month period following the move.[111] The minimum work period does not apply in the case of a taxpayer who dies, is disabled, is involuntarily separated (other than for willful misconduct), or is transferred for benefit of the taxpayer's employer.[112] Generally the taxpayer may elect to claim the expenses in the year paid or incurred, or instead to wait until all requirements, including the 39 or 78 weeks of employment condition, have been met. In the latter event, the taxpayer will file an amended return or a refund claim for the year the costs were incurred.

Example 45: A is transferred by his employer from Boston, Massachusetts to Cleveland, Ohio. He begins working there on November

---

107 Sec. 217(a).
108 Sec. 62(8).
109 Reg. Sec. 1.217-2(c)(1).
110 Reg. Sec. 1.217-2(c)(2).
111 Reg. Sec. 1.217-2(c)(4).
112 Reg. Sec. 1.217-2(d)(1).

1, 19X0. Moving expenses are paid by A in 19X0 in connection with this move. On April 15, 19X1, when he files his income tax return for the year 19X0, A has been a full-time employee in Cleveland for approximately 24 weeks. Although he has not satisfied the 39-week employment condition at this time, A may elect to claim his 19X0 moving expenses on his 19X0 income tax return as there is still sufficient time remaining before November 1, 19X1, to satisfy the residence requirements.[113]

Example 46: Assume the same facts as in Example 45 except that on April 15, 19X1 A has voluntarily left his employer and is looking for other employment in Cleveland. A may not be sure he will be able to meet the 39-week employment condition by November 1, 19X1. Thus he may, if he wishes, wait until such condition is met and file an amended return claiming as a deduction the expenses paid in 19X0. Instead of filing an amended return, A may file a claim for refund based on a deduction for the expenses. If A fails to meet the 39-week employment condition on or before November 1, 19X1, no deduction is allowable for such expenses.[114]

Deductible moving costs may be classified into two broad groups.[115]

1. Direct costs that are deductible without limit and
2. Indirect costs that are deductible within specified limits.

Direct costs include:

a) expenses of moving household goods and personal effects and
b) travel costs of the taxpayer and family en route from the former residence to the new place of residence.

If the family uses a personal automobile in the move, the actual out-of-pocket costs incurred for gasoline and oil may be deducted, or a standard allowance of 9 cents per mile may be used.

Indirect costs are limited to a total deduction of $3,000.[116] There are three main elements of indirect costs:

a) ***Premove househunting*** costs at the new location *after* new employment has been obtained.[117]
b) Temporary living costs for the taxpayer and taxpayer's family at the new principal job location (up to 30 days).[118]
c) Costs related to disposing of the taxpayer's old residence and obtaining a new one. Allowable costs related to disposing of an old residence include real estate commission, attorney's fees, title fees,

PREMOVE HOUSEHUNTING COSTS Costs incurred by taxpayer and family for travel in seeking living quarters at new job location.

[113] Reg. Sec. 1.217-2(d)(2)(iii), Ex. (1).
[114] Reg. Sec. 1.217-2(d)(2)(iii), Ex. (2).
[115] Reg. Sec. 1.217-2(b)(9)(i).
[116] Reg. Sec. 1.217-2(b)(9)(ii).
[117] Reg. Sec. 1.217-2(b)(5).
[118] Reg. Sec. 1.217-2(b)(6).

escrow fees, state transfer taxes, etc.[119] Allowable expenses incident to acquiring a new residence include, for example, attorney's fees, appraisal fees, title costs, and similar expenses.[120] In addition, expenses incident to settling an unexpired lease on the taxpayer's former dwelling quarters and expenses incident to acquisition of a lease on new quarters are allowable.[121]

FORM 3903 Although the overall limitation on all indirect costs is $3,000, a further limit of $1,500 is placed on the total of house-hunting expenses and temporary living costs.

Example 47: McDougal moved to a new job from Atlanta, Georgia to Los Angeles, California on June 1, 19X1. His related costs were:

Shipping household goods	$5,200
Costs of travel of McDougal and his family en route to new job	700
Costs of broker's fees, title policy, legal fees, etc. on selling home in Atlanta	6,800
Temporary living costs in Los Angeles for four days	600
Cost of house-hunting trip to Los Angeles for McDougal and his wife	1,300

The costs of shipping household goods ($5,200) and the travel costs en route ($700) are direct costs and are deductible in full. The deductions for house-hunting expenses ($1,300) and temporary living costs ($600) are limited to a total of $1,500. Since the total deduction for all indirect costs is $3,000, McDougal can deduct $1,500 spent on costs of disposing of the old residence. Thus the total deduction allowed McDougal for living costs is $8,900.

Direct Costs	$5,900
Indirect Costs	3,000
Total	$8,900

Special rules apply to U.S. military personnel and to individuals whose new place of employment is outside the United States. For example, the former are not required to meet the 39-week test.[122] For a taxpayer whose new place of employment is outside the United States, the period during which temporary living costs may be deducted is 90 days rather than 30 days. Similarly, the limit on overall costs that may be deducted is $6,000 rather than $3,000, and the limit on the amount deductible for house-hunting costs and temporary living costs is $4,500 instead of $1,500.[123]

---

[119] Reg. Sec. 1.217-2(b)(7)(i).
[120] Reg. Sec. 1.217-2(b)(7)(ii).
[121] Reg. Sec. 1.217-2(b)(7)(iii) and (iv).
[122] Sec. 217(g).
[123] Sec. 217(h).

OFFICE IN THE HOME

Prior to 1976 many taxpayers, including employees, deducted all or part of the expenses of maintaining an office in the taxpayer's home. Frequently the "office" was used only incidentally and sometimes consisted of nothing more than a desk or table in the taxpayer's bedroom or den, resulting in frequent conflicts between taxpayers and the IRS. As a consequence, the Congress in the Tax Reform Act of 1976 severely curtailed the deduction for costs of a home used as an office. No costs related to a portion of a home may be deducted as a business-related expense unless that portion of a home is *exclusively* used on a *regular basis* as a principal place of business, or as a place for meeting with clients or customers in the normal course of the taxpayer's business.[124] In addition to meeting the exclusive-use test, an employee seeking to deduct costs of an office in his or her home must show that the office is maintained for the convenience of the employer.[125] This provision has gone far toward eliminating such deductions by employees.

Example 48: Webb is a college professor. In his home he has set aside one room which is used exclusively as an office. Webb uses this office for grading papers, preparing exams, writing articles, etc., because he finds his office at the university too noisy. Webb will not be able to deduct the costs of an office in his home.

Nevertheless, in a recent case[126] an appeals court held that a professor, who maintained an office in his home where he did the bulk of his research and writing (activities which consumed 80 percent of his working hours and which were required to retain his teaching position), should be allowed to deduct home office expenses. The court found that the office was the focal point of the professor's business activities. Because of an inadequate employer-provided office, it was held to be a practical necessity for the home office to be used and thus the deduction was allowed.

P L A N N I N G   W O R K S H O P

TRAVEL AND ENTERTAINMENT

Travel and entertainment deductions have been the source of many tax controversies, since it is often difficult to separate business and personal expenses. The importance of keeping adequate records which document these expenditures can not be overemphasized. Recall that the burden of proof is always on the taxpayer to substan-

Continued

[124] Sec. 280A(c)(1).

[125] *Ibid*.

[126] *D. J. Weissman*, CA-2, 85-1 USTC, par. 9106.

PLANNING WORKSHOP

tiate travel and entertainment deductions; the IRS is not required to provide a "reasonable allowance" for undocumented expenditures.

The deduction for the business use of an automobile is a recurring source of taxpayer/IRS disputes. An estimate of the percentage of time that an automobile is used for business purposes is necessary for actual expense calculations, but this estimate by itself will not suffice as documentation for a standard mileage allowance. The actual business miles driven should be documented by a detailed mileage diary. Since the taxpayer can deduct the larger of actual costs or the standard mileage allowance, it is in the taxpayer's best interest to keep detailed records for both calculations. In this case, one set of records can serve as documentation for the other.

Example 49: Griffin used her automobile throughout 19X3 for business purposes. She maintains a detailed mileage diary, and records all actual costs. Her mileage diary indicates that the car was used 75% of the time for business purposes in 19X3. A comparison of the standard mileage allowance with 75% of actual operating costs indicates that Griffin should use the mileage allowance on her 19X3 return. However, her actual expense receipts will help document the time and place of her business trips, should the mileage allowance be questioned by the IRS.

Travel and entertainment deductions sometimes create a dilemma for a tax return preparer. Specifically, is a preparer required to "audit" or "verify" a client's deduction for travel and entertainment? Generally the Code and Regulations do not require a preparer to verify the deductions. However, Reg. Sec. 1.6694-1(b)(2)(ii) states that:

> The preparer shall make appropriate inquiries of the taxpayer to determine the existence of facts and circumstances required by a Code section or regulations incident to claiming a deduction.

In addition, after 1984, the preparer is required to advise the taxpayer of the substantiation requirements of Section 274 and obtain written confirmation that such requirements were met with respect to any deduction claimed. In essence, this provision requires preparers to satisfy themselves that the client has records which comply with the substantiation requirements.

MOVING EXPENSES

A taxpayer who incurs selling expenses in disposing of his or her personal residence has a choice when reporting these selling expenses on his or her tax return. These expenses may be either (*a*) deducted as an indirect moving expense (subject to the limits dis-

Continued

PLANNING WORKSHOP

cussed in this chapter), or (*b*) deducted as selling expenses in computing the gain on the sale of the residence.

Generally it is to the taxpayer's advantage to deduct these items as moving expenses. If the taxpayer purchases a new residence within two years of selling the old one, the special nonrecognition rules of Sec. 1034 and/or Sec. 121 (Chapter 12) may indefinitely postpone any gain realized on the house sale. Furthermore, any recognized gain on the residence sale is usually reported as long-term capital gain, which qualifies for a special deduction equal to 60% of the net long-term capital gain. Since only 40% of the resulting gain is taxable, the value of the selling expense deduction (in terms of tax savings) is correspondingly reduced.

Example 50: Blestoe sold his personal residence in 19X4 for a total realized gain of $10,000 before considering $1,000 of selling expenses. Assuming that Blestoe's only other income in 19X4 was a $40,000 salary, a comparison of the two options discloses $600 of additional tax deductions by reporting the expenditure as a moving expense deduction:

	REPORT AS A SELLING EXPENSE	REPORT AS A MOVING EXPENSE
(1) Salary	$40,000	$40,000
Gain on sale of the residence:		
Selling price	$50,000	$50,000
Less selling expenses	(1,000)	—
Less cost basis of residence	(40,000)	(40,000)
Total realized gain	$ 9,000	$10,000
Less 60% long-term capital gains deduction	(5,400)	(6,000)
(2) Net taxable gain	$ 3,600	$ 4,000
(3) Moving expense deduction	—	(1,000)
Adjusted gross income (1 + 2 − 3)	$43,600	$43,000

OFFICE IN THE HOME

In enacting Sec. 280A in 1976, Congress attempted to curtail abuses in the reporting of home office expense deductions. However, events subsequent to 1976 indicate that these provisions are being

Continued

PLANNING WORKSHOP

interpreted quite liberally by the courts, and taxpayers should be advised to keep abreast of judicial findings in this area. For example, the Tax Court allowed a deduction for a specific portion of a room, as opposed to requiring a separate room for the home office.* In addition, as previously noted, an appeals court has allowed a professor a deduction even though the office in his home was not primarily for his employer's convenience.†

It is important to note that Sec. 280A as presently drafted permits a deduction for the portion of a residence used exclusively on a regular basis for *any* trade or business of the taxpayer. Thus, it is possible for a taxpayer to have a principal place of business for *each* trade or business in which he or she engages. A taxpayer's home office does not necessarily have to be associated with his or her "primary" business activity.

**D. J. Weightman*, 45 TCM 167 (1982).

†D. J. Weissman, CA-2, 85.1 USTC Par. 9106.

KEY POINTS TO REMEMBER

1. To be deductible an expense must fall under some provision of the Code that permits its deduction.
2. Expenses incurred in a trade or business (except as an employee) are generally deductible *for* AGI.
3. Costs of investigating a business similar to that in which the taxpayer is engaged are deductible. Expense of investigating a new business in a field in which the taxpayer is not engaged are nondeductible if the business is not acquired; if the business is acquired, the costs are capitalized and amortized.
4. Expenses relating to production of income other than in a trade or business are deductible *from* AGI.
5. To be deductible, an expense must be ordinary, necessary, and reasonable.
6. Expenses of a hobby are deductible only to the extent that there is gross income from the hobby activity.
7. Expenses related to tax-exempt income are nondeductible.
8. Prepaid expenses are generally not deductible, even by a cash-basis taxpayer.
9. Business-related expenses of an employee are deductible. The only employee expenses deductible *for* AGI are those for travel, transportation, and reimbursed amounts of other deductible expenses. All expenses of an outside salesman are deductible *for* AGI.

10. Transportation costs (incurred either out of town or in town) related to business activities are deductible. However, costs of commuting between the taxpayer's home and office are not deductible.
11. If the taxpayer uses an automobile partly for business, the actual costs related to business miles driven or a standard mileage rate may be deducted.
12. Travel costs including lodging, food, laundry, etc., are deductible only if the taxpayer is "out of town." This requires that the taxpayer be gone overnight or reasonably long enough to require sleep and rest.
13. Entertainment expenses are deductible if specific business discussions took place during, just before, or just after the entertainment. Costs of a "quiet business meal" may be deducted even if no specific business was discussed.
14. The taxpayer can deduct the costs of "business gifts" up to a total of $25 of such gifts made to each donee during the year. Special rules apply for "advertising" gifts and for employee-incentive awards.
15. Miscellaneous employee expenses such as union and professional association dues, costs of uniforms not suitable for off-duty wear, subscriptions to business-related publications, and supplies used on the job are deductible.
16. If the employee adequately reports expenses to the employer and if reimbursement exactly equals expenses, the employee is not required to report details of expenses on the tax return. If actual expenses do not equal reimbursement, certain details must be shown. Also, if the employee does not adequately report to the employer, details of expenses and reimbursements must be shown.
17. Costs of an office in the taxpayer's home can be deducted only if the office is used exclusively as the taxpayer's principal place of business for meeting customers, etc. An employee must also show that the home office is maintained for the benefit of the employer.
18. Costs of acquiring an education to prepare for a job are not deductible. Costs incurred to maintain skills or improve performance are deductible. In most cases if the taxpayer is working towards his or her first degree, the costs are not deductible.
19. An employee or self-employed person can deduct certain expenses of moving to a "new job." Generally the taxpayer must remain at the new home for at least 39 weeks out of the 12-month period after the move (78 weeks out of 24 months for a self-employed person). There is no limit on the amount deductible for direct moving expenses. "Indirect expenses" (costs of disposing of an old residence, travel costs to look for a new home and temporary living costs at the new location, and costs related to acquiring a new residence) are limited to $3,000, of which not more than $1,500 can be for costs relating to house-hunting expenses and temporary living costs combined.

SELF-STUDY QUESTIONS

1. Charles Gilbert, a corporate executive, incurred business-related, unreimbursed expenses in 1982 as follows:

Entertainment	$900
Travel	700
Education	400

Assuming that Gilbert does not itemize deductions, how much of these expenses should he deduct on his 1982 tax return?

a) $700

b) $1,100

c) $1,300

d) $1,600

(AICPA adapted)

2. Martin Hart, who is not an outside salesman, earned a salary of $30,000 during the current year. During the year he was required by his employer to take several overnight business trips, and he received an expense allowance of $1,500 for travel and lodging. In the course of these trips he incurred the following expenses which were either adjustments to income or deductions from adjusted gross income:

Travel	$1,100
Lodging	500
Entertainment of customers	400

What is Hart's adjusted gross income?

a) $28,000

b) $29,500

c) $29,600

d) $29,900

(AICPA adapted)

3. Herbert Mann is an engineer employed by a major chemical company. During 1981 he paid the following business-related expenses:

Travel expenses incurred while away from home overnight	$2,500
Executive search consultant fees paid in securing a new job in same profession	1,500
Professional society dues	600
Transportation expenses	350

Mann received travel expense reimbursements totaling $2,300 from his employer during 1981. How much should Mann deduct as employee business expenses in arriving at his adjusted gross income for 1981?

a) $550

b) $2,050

c) $2,650

d) $2,850

(AICPA adapted)

4. Richard Putney, who lived in Idaho for five years, moved to Texas in 1980 to accept a new position. His employer reimbursed him in full for all direct moving costs, but did not pay for any part of the following indirect moving expenses incurred by Putney:

House-hunting trips to Texas	$800
Temporary housing in Texas	900

How much of the indirect expenses can be deducted by Putney as moving expenses?

a) $0

b) $900

c) $1,500

d) $1,700

(AICPA adapted)

5. In January 1976, Ray Hodges, a New York resident, accepted a position in Arizona with a new employer by whom he is still employed. His new employer paid him a $2,000 moving expense allowance which Hodges applied to the following expenses incurred in moving to Arizona:

Plane fare for Mr. Hodges	$ 300
Bus fare for Mrs. Hodges and children	500
Cost of moving household effects	1,500
Meals and lodging of Mrs. Hodges and children during trip	200
New lightweight clothes for family	400
	$2,900

For 1976, Hodges included the $2,000 payment in his income. In computing his adjusted gross income, he can deduct

a) $1,800

b) $2,300

c) $2,500

d) $2,900

(AICPA adapted)

6. Martin Dawson, who resided in Detroit, was unemployed for the last six months of 1981. In January 1982, he moved to Houston to seek employment, and obtained a full-time job there in February. He kept this job for the balance of the year. Martin paid the following expenses in 1982 in connection with his move:

Rental of truck to move his personal belongings to Houston	$ 800
Penalty for breaking the lease on his Detroit apartment	300
	$1,100

How much can Martin deduct in 1982 for moving expenses?

a) $0

b) $300

c) $800

d) $1,100

(AICPA adapted)

7. Sam Peterson is a plumber employed by a major contracting firm. During 1978 he paid the following miscellaneous personal expenses:

Specialized work clothes (required by employer)	$410
Union dues	600
Preparation of will	150
Cost of income tax preparation	100
Safe deposit box rental (used only for personal effects)	20

If Peterson were to itemize his personal deductions, what amount could he claim as miscellaneous deductible expenses?

a) $680

b) $770

c) $1,110

d) $1,130

(AICPA adapted)

8. In gathering information for her income tax return for 1978, Mabel Herzog listed the following miscellaneous expenses incurred and paid for in 1978:

Hobby expenses (not engaged in for profit)	$500
Union dues	400
Employment agency fees paid in securing a new job in same profession	200
Legal fees paid in connection with a libel suit	700

What can Herzog report as allowable deductions from adjusted gross income?

a) $600

b) $1,100

c) $1,300

d) $1,800

(AICPA adapted)

9. Harold Brodsky is an electrician employed by a contracting firm. During the current year he incurred and paid the following expenses:

Use of personal auto for company business (reimbursed by employer for $200)	$300
Specialized work clothes	550
Union dues	600
Cost of income tax preparation	150
Preparation of will	100

If Brodsky were to itemize his personal deductions, what amount should he claim as miscellaneous deductible expenses?

a) $1,300

b) $1,400

c) $1,500

d) $1,700

(AICPA adapted)

10. Which of the following is deductible to arrive at adjusted gross income?

a) Unreimbursed dues to AICPA by an employee of an accounting firm.

b) Unreimbursed union dues by an employee of a company.

c) Medical expenses of a self-employed individual.

d) None of the above

11. During 1981 Culbert, Inc. made the following expenditures:

Promotional materials for use on customers' premises (1,000 @ $40)	$40,000
Business gifts to customers (60 @ $100)	6,000
Contribution to a candidate for public office	1,000

How much of the above expenditures should Culbert deduct in determining its taxable income for 1981?

a) $26,500

b) $41,500

c) $42,500

d) $47,000

12. During 1979 Ashley Corporation charged the following payments to miscellaneous expense:

Travel expense of $300 for the company president to offer voluntary testimony at the state capital against proposed legislation regarded as unfavorable to its business
Christmas gifts to 20 customers at $75 each
Contribution of $600 to local political candidate

The maximum deduction that Ashley can claim for these payments is

a) $800
b) $1,400
c) $1,800
d) $2,400

13. During the 1976 holiday season, Barmin Corporation gave business gifts to 16 customers. The value of the gifts, which were not of an advertising nature, was as follows:

4 @ $10
4 @ $25
4 @ $50
4 @ $100

For 1976, Barmin can deduct as a business expense

a) $0
b) $140
c) $340
d) $740

QUESTIONS

1. Distinguish between a "trade or business expense" and a "nonbusiness expense related to income production."
2. What is meant by the terms "reasonable," "ordinary," and "necessary"?
3. Section 262 of the Internal Revenue Code of 1954 specifically disallows the deduction of "personal, living, and family" expenses. Yet many persons may deduct a purely personal contribution to a local charity. Explain the apparent contradiction.
4. In what fundamental way do the deductions allowed individual taxpayers differ generally from the deductions allowed corporate taxpayers? What forces explain this difference?
5. Distinguish between a tax-deductible "nonbusiness expense" and a nondeductible "personal expense."
6. A taxpayer who owns a textile manufacturing plant in New York is visited by an important customer. The taxpayer "wines and dines" this customer and his wife during their stay in New York. Total cost of his entertainment is $350. Is this a reasonable, ordinary, and necessary business expense? Explain.
7. List and explain the "negative" criteria that may be applied to determine whether an expenditure is deductible.
8. a) What tax treatment is given expenses of a "hobby"?
   b) How does one distinguish between a hobby and a business venture?

9. No interest deduction is allowed on loans made to carry an investment if the income from the investment is tax-exempt, or on loans made to obtain a single-premium policy. Assume that this rule did not exist. Devise two schemes, one related to state municipal bonds and one related to life-insurance contracts that would result in financial windfall from the loophole.
10. Which employment-related expenses are deductible *for* AGI?
11. How does the meaning of the term "travel expenses" differ from the term "transportation expenses"?
12. In what ways are the deductions allowed outside salesmen different from those allowed other employees?
13. What are the distinguishing characteristics of an "outside salesperson" for tax purposes?
14. In your opinion, if it is true that many employees would be entitled to a larger deduction for transportation expenses if they would compute actual costs rather than taking the standard mileage deduction, why do employees almost always elect the standard deduction?
15. Explain how the amount of transportation expenses related to a "second job" is determined?
16. What is meant by the term "away from home?"
17. Is it necessary that an employee be away from home overnight in order to deduct travel expenses? Explain.
18. If a trip is primarily for personal vacation purposes, can any part of the travel costs be deducted as business-related? Explain.
19. What is the basic test for determining whether travel expenses are "reasonable"?
20. How do the rules for determining the deductible portion of foreign travel expenses differ from the rules for determining the deductible portion of expenses within the North American area?
21. Under what circumstances, if any, could a taxpayer deduct the expenses of a spouse accompanying him or her on a business trip?
22. Distinguish between expenses that are "directly related to" and those that are "associated with" business activities.
23. Explain the "quiet meal" rule.
24. What is meant by the term "entertainment facilities"?
25. Are dues to a country club ever deductible? If so, under what circumstances?
26. For an employee, are entertainment expenses deductible *for* AGI or *from* AGI?

27. Explain the limits on business "gifts."

28. Explain briefly what type of record keeping is required for travel expenses if the taxpayer seeks to deduct the expenses.

29. May the employee ever omit from his or her tax return the amount of reimbursement received from the employee's employer?

30. Which expenses related to seeking a job are deductible?

31. Under what conditions may an employee deduct the cost of clothes worn to work?

32. What types of education-related expenses are deductible by an employee? In other words, for what purposes must the education be undertaken?

33. Are education expenses deductible *for* AGI or *from* AGI for an employee? Explain.

34. An employee incurs some expenses that are deductible *for* AGI and some that are deductible *from* AGI. The taxpayer's employer makes a lump-sum reimbursement for exactly half of the total expenses. How would this situation be handled on the taxpayer's tax return?

35. What are the requirements for an employee to deduct "moving costs"?

36. Explain the limits on the deduction for employee moving costs.

37. Under what circumstances can an employee deduct the costs of an office in his or her home?

PROBLEMS

1. Indicate whether each of the following items is deductible. In those cases where only part is deductible, indicate the amount to be deducted.
   a) Taxpayer operates a truck on a contract basis. While hauling gravel under a contract, he was stopped for speeding. He paid a fine of $25 for speeding and a fine of $30 for carrying an overweight load.
   b) Assume the same facts as in part (a) except that the taxpayer is an employee instead of an independent contractor. He was not reimbursed by his employer for either fine.

2. Indicate whether each of the following items is deductible. In those cases where only part is deductible, indicate the amount to be deducted.
   a) Contribution to purchase gift for employee's supervisor, $100
   b) Penalty for late payment of federal income taxes, $82
   c) Costs incurred in divorce trial, $2400

3. Indicate whether each of the following items is deductible. In those cases where only part is deductible, indicate the amount to be deducted.

   a) Warner, who is an attorney, also operates a farm. During each of the past five years he has had expenses on the farm of $9,000 and income of only $4,000. During the current year he has income of $4,800 and expenses of $9,200.

   b) A gambler won $45,000 during the year. In order to earn this income, however, he incurred expenses for travel and other items totaling $10,200.

4. *a*) The president of Unlimited Aviation Corporation traveled to a foreign country to talk to a group of military officers in that country about purchasing military aircraft manufactured by Unlimited. The officers hinted that a "gift" to them might increase the likelihood that Unlimited would receive the contract sought. The president thus authorized payment, and the company paid $500,000 to each of the six officers (a total of $3,000,000). Are these payments deductible by Unlimited?

   b) During a severe cold wave in 19X1, Rayford Company paid $50,000 to officers of a natural gas pipeline company to "ensure" that gas supplies to the company were not curtailed. Although supplies to Rayford's competitors were greatly reduced, Rayford had no curtailment. Can Rayford deduct the $50,000 payment?

5. Indicate whether each of the following items is deductible. In those cases where only part is deductible, indicate the amount to be deducted.

   a) Leo owns 60% of King Corporation's outstanding stock. During the current year, King Corporation paid Leo a salary of $82,000. Executives in similar situations earn about $40,000 per year.

   b) Kickbacks to purchasing agents of companies who buy substantial amounts of Corona's products, $4,000.

   c) Kickbacks to purchasing agents of four cities buying Corona's products, $2,000.

   d) Trip to Washington, D.C., to testify before Congressional committee holding hearings on proposed legislation to restrict foreign imports of electronics equipment. Corona is very interested in curtailing imports and asked to be heard. Transportation, $280; lodging, $92; meals, $43.

6. Indicate whether each of the following items is deductible. In those cases where only part is deductible, indicate the amount to be deducted.

   a) Cost of keeping watch in good repair. (Taxpayer is a registered nurse.)

   b) Ramon purchased a piece of land for $45,000 in order to get a location for his new office building. However, he has to tear down an old building on the property, paying $3,200 to a demolition company for clearing the building.

7. Reginald operates a retail store. He follows the cash basis of accounting for expenses. At the end of 19X1, he had the following prepaid items:

Property insurance through February 19X2	$ 160
Store supplies on hand	64
Rent paid through June 19X2	6,000
Office supplies	100

Which, if any, of these amounts are deductible in 19X1?

8. Richard Rice, an auto mechanic, lost his job in April 19X1, when his employer decided to close shop. After futilely seeking employment, Richard arranged for potential financing to open his own shop. He concluded that his best opportunity would be in another city, so Richard spent four days in a town located 200 miles from his home, investigating possible locations, studying competition, and engaging in other activities to determine the likelihood of success of a new shop. Richard spent $208 on this trip, but decided against opening the new business.

   a) What are the effects of the $208 spent?

   b) Would your answer be different if Richard had decided to open the new business? Explain.

9. In 1983 Mr. Lee, an outside salesperson, drove his car 36,000 miles, of which 24,000 miles pertained to business. The total operating costs and other costs were as follows:

Gas and oil	$3,250
Auto license tag	50
Insurance	380
Repairs	320
Tires	200
Parking (incurred during business use)	175
Depreciation for business use of car	2,000

What is Mr. L's allowable auto expense deduction?

10. Day is sales manager of Ace Product Company. During this year he went to the national convention of sales managers held in Hawaii for three days. He took his wife, since the convention offered a good reason for taking his vacation at the same time. Although the convention ended on July 13, Day and his wife stayed in Honolulu for an additional four days. The following costs, none of which was reimbursed by Day's employer, were incurred on the trip:

   a) Taxi fare from Day's home to airport for him and wife, $15.

   b) Airline tickets for Day and wife, $900. Normal fare for one person is $600; because of a special family travel plan, Day's wife's ticket was only $300.

c) Limousine fare from airport to hotel for Day and wife, $8.00 each.

d) Hotel room (double rate) for seven days, $700. The room rates are $90 for a single room and $100 for two people.

e) Registration for Day at conference, $60. No registration fee for Mrs. Day.

f) Cost of official meals (at meetings) for Day, $70. Mrs. Day did not attend these.

g) Cost of registration for women's activities for Mrs. Day, $75.

h) Cost of seven breakfasts for seven days, $70. This was for both persons at rate of $5.00 per meal each.

i) Cost of meals, other than breakfast, taken together during convention for Mr. and Mrs. Day, at $15 per meal, $30.

j) Cost of meals during 4 days of vacation, $212.

Determine the total amount deductible by Day, and categorize the deductions as either *for* AGI or *from* AGI.

11. Determine the amount deductible by the taxpayer in the following cases and whether they are *for* AGI or *from* AGI.

    a) Taxpayer, an employee, spent $1,000 for transportation during the year. Of this amount, $600 was allocated to the cost of going from home to work sites and back, while $400 was spent on transportation between work sites during the workday.

    b) Taxpayer, a self-employed plumber, incurred costs of $1,500 for transportation, which represented depreciation, gas, and oil, for the truck used in his business. One-third of the mileage driven was for trips from his home to his shop and returning, while two-thirds was for trips connected with on-the-job activities.

12. Taxpayer, a physician, attended two professional conventions on the West Coast connected with his practice. The first convention was held on Monday, Tuesday, and Wednesday in Los Angeles. The second convention was held on Monday and Tuesday of the following week in San Francisco. Between the two conventions, the taxpayer stayed at Carmel for a short vacation. The costs were: air travel from his home to Los Angeles and from San Francisco to his home, $425; hotel and meals for three days in Los Angeles, $390; auto rental for trip from Los Angeles to Carmel and from Carmel to San Francisco, $280 (one-third of this cost represents the cost of pleasure trips while in Carmel); hotel and meals for two days in San Francisco, $205. What amount may the taxpayer deduct?

13. Roane lives and is employed in Stamford, Connecticut. Roane went to New York for one day in connection with his employment, driving 120 miles. Roane also spent $15 for parking fees and $8.50 for his lunch.

Roane returned to Stamford at 6 p.m. The employer reimbursed Roane 18¢ per mile for automobile use and all $15 of the parking fee. However, no part of Roane's lunch cost was reimbursed. How are these facts reported on Roane's tax return?

14. Thomas, a construction worker, maintains a home in Cleveland, where his wife and children live. Thomas takes a job in Illinois on a road construction project that may last as long as four years. In the current year, Thomas's expenses in Illinois included, among others: apartment rent, $4,300; meals, $2,100; and laundry, $320. In addition, Thomas made six trips to Cleveland to visit his family at a cost of $740. What amount may Thomas deduct this year for the above expenses?

15. In the current year, Razor, a sales manager for a manufacturing company, paid $1,600 for membership dues in a hunting lodge in Canada for the purpose of entertaining clients and prospective clients. In November Razor took three clients to the lodge for hunting. He paid their transportation costs, totaling $620; their meals for the 3-day period at the lodge ($543 for guests and $181 for Razor); their room costs ($900 for the guests and $300 for himself); $220 for a hunting guide; $210 for use of guns and ammunition; and $120 for miscellaneous items such as phone calls and drinks. What part of the expenditures named above will be deductible by Razor, assuming none of these costs is reimbursed?

16. In each of the following independent cases, indicate the amount, if any, that would be deductible by the taxpayer. If an appropriate answer depends on the circumstances, explain.

    a) Ruiz is an importer of Spanish boots. In July of this year a group of Spanish boot manufacturers and commerce officials visited this country. Ruiz invited them to be his guests for one evening. Cost of attending a Broadway show, cocktails, dinner, and after-dinner entertainment for the taxpayer and the seven guests totaled $1,120.

    b) Morgan is a sales representative for a national machine manufacturer. In September of this year a convention of machine manufacturers was held in Morgan's hometown. Morgan entertained six visiting manufacturers at a "western dance hall" at a cost of $360.

17. Evelyn is a salesperson for a book company. In the current year, two book dealers from St. Louis came to New York, where Evelyn lived. Because they have been customers for several years, Evelyn took them to a nightclub (cost $200) and to dinner (cost $248). No business was discussed at either place. How much, if any, of these expenses can Evelyn deduct?

18. During the current year, Mark, an employee, made the following unreimbursed gifts to his customers.

    To Jane Avery, a video game, cost $102.
    To Peter Compton, a color television, cost $360.
    To Larry Lawrence, a record album, cost $18.

What amount, if any, is deductible by Mark because of these three gifts?

19. In April of the current year, Phyllis, an airline employee, lost her job. She incurred the following costs in seeking and acquiring a similar job with another airline.

Cost of telephone calls to airline personnel managers	$ 4
Travel and transportation costs to another city to seek job (no job acquired)	96
Fee paid an employment agency to acquire a job for Phyllis	900
Transportation costs to interview for job secured	6

What amount, if any, of the above may Phyllis deduct?

20. Don, an auto mechanic, is an employee. During the year he spent $200 (unreimbursed) for clothing not suitable for off-duty wear. Would this cost be deductible?

21. Indicate how much, if any, is deductible as educational expenses in each of the following independent cases. Briefly explain your answer, and indicate in each case whether the amount deductible is *for* AGI or *from* AGI.

a) Haskins is a senior in college, majoring in accounting. His college expenses for the current year were: tuition, $1,200; books and supplies, $340; room, $540; and meals, $1,680.

b) Bernard was a practicing Certified Public Accountant in the tax department of a national accounting firm. During July of this year Bernard decided that he should secure a law degree in order to further his career, so he resigned from the accounting firm and entered law school. His expenses related to law school this year were: tuition, $1,200; supplies, $120; books, $180; auto expenses communting to classes, $110.

c) Raymond works for an accounting firm. During this year he attended several professional development programs sponsored by the American Institute of Certified Public Accountants. These programs were 2- or 3-day seminars or workshops held in other cities (requiring overnight travel), dealing with areas of accounting in which Raymond is involved. His expenses in attending these programs totaled $800, and they were not reimbursed by his employer. The costs were: registration fees, $200; transportation, $400; lodging, $110; meals, $90.

d) Assume the same facts as in part (c) above except that Raymond is a self-employed accountant with his own public accounting practice.

22. Determine the amount deductible by the taxpayer in the following cases. (Is the amount deductible, if any, a deduction *for* AGI or a deduction *from* AGI?)

a) Clifton is employed as a public school teacher. He possesses a B.A. degree, but the school board has stipulated that each teacher in the school system must return to college for additional course work at least each third summer. During this year Clifton returned to the state university. His costs were: tuition, $360; meals, $540; lodging, $285; transportation from his home town to the university and return, $23; and books, $40. Clifton is unmarried.

b) Myrtle is an elementary-school art teacher. She has found that in recent years there has been a great increase in interest in ceramics, so this summer Myrtle returned to college to take some courses in ceramics. Her expenses were: tuition, $185; lodging, $200; food, $320; transportation, $18; and supplies, $65.

c) Professor Williams holds an M.A. degree. She is a nontenured assistant professor at a local college. The college administration has ruled that no one could be promoted to a rank higher than assistant professor unless she or he possesses the Ph.D. degree, so Williams returned to the university this fall to work on a doctorate. Her expenses for the four months were: tuition, $680; meals, $1,200; room, $800; supplies, $180; and transportation to the university and return (one round trip), $32.

23. During the current year, Jill, an employee, incurred the following deductible expenses related to her job:

Transportation	$1,210
Travel	990
Entertainment	1,000
	$3,200

Jill's employer does not reimburse employees for all expenses incurred, but instead gives each employee $2,000 each year as an "expense allowance." Explain how Jill will handle these facts on her tax return.

24. In July of this year Arthur quit his job in Spokane and accepted a job with an oil company in Singapore. The following costs were incurred by Arthur.

Commission and closing costs incurred in selling his home in Spokane	$3,600
Transportation for Arthur and his wife to Singapore	1,800
Cost of transporting personal effects from Spokane to Singapore	1,900
Temporary living costs for 45 days while seeking permanent living accommodations	4,000

The employer paid Arthur $3,900 representing reimbursement of $900 for his transportation costs and $3,000 for temporary living costs.

Determine the effects of all the items named above on Arthur's taxable income.

25. Taxpayer changed jobs in January of the taxable year. The new place of employment was 300 miles from the old one. Expenses of moving to a new home near the new job amounted to $500 and were not reimbursed. At year end, taxpayer was still employed on the new job. How may the taxpayer handle these facts on the tax return?

26. Allen Brown received his degree in accounting in June of this year. He took a job with a public accounting firm in a city 90 miles away from the university. He spent $850 to have his furniture moved to the new home. He and his wife drove their automobile to the new home. How much, if any, may they deduct as moving expense?

27. In each of the following independent cases, indicate whether the taxpayer will be entitled to deduct expenses (depreciation, utilities, insurance, etc.) applicable to an "office in the home."

    a) Pete is an accounting professor at a state university. In his home, one room has been converted into an "office" used by Pete solely for such tasks as grading papers, preparing exams, and reading journals.

    b) Joe is a law professor in a state university. In his home one room has been converted into an "office" used solely by Joe for grading papers and other class-related activities, and also for writing and revising textbooks from which Joe receives substantial royalties. His office at the university is shared with two other professors and he finds it difficult to work.

    c) Marilyn, married, operates a part-time typing service in her home. In her bedroom, she has an "office" with a desk, typewriter, file cabinet, etc. She uses the office approximately 15 hours per week in her typing service.

    d) Jane is a sales representative for several companies. She uses a room in her home solely as an office in which she takes orders, makes telephone calls, prepares reports, and so on.

28. Al Acorn is employed as a high school principal. He also owns and manages six rental properties. He lives in a 2-bedroom condominium and uses one bedroom exclusively as an office for bookkeeping and other tasks associated with the property management activities.

    a) Is the property management activity a "business"? Is the office a "principal place of business activity"?

    b) Can the costs (depreciation, utilities, taxes, interest) related to the office be deducted by Al?

    c) Can the transportation expenses incurred in driving from the office to the rental properties be deducted by Al as business expenses?

TAX PLANNING PROBLEMS

1. Steele, who lived in Capital City for several years, was transferred by his employer to a city 900 miles away. Steele sold his home (which cost $100,000) in Capital City for $160,000. In selling the home, he paid a sales commission of $9,600 to a realtor. Other "closing" costs were $200. Steele paid $2,000 for transporting his household goods and $240 for costs of transporting himself and his family to the new job location. On arriving there, Steele and his family lived in a hotel for four days while they purchased a new residence. Costs of the four days included lodging of $520 and meals of $310. The new home cost $180,000; as a result, Steele has no taxable gain to report on the sale of the old home. How should Steele handle the costs incurred in order to get the maximum tax benefit? (Steele's marginal tax rate is 50 percent.)

2. Noel Howard and his wife, Betty, both graduated from State University in August, 19X1. He took a job with a Big Eight accounting firm in Dallas, beginning on September 15, 19X1. The Howards' moving costs included $2,500 for transportation of household possessions and $300 for their own transportation. In 19X1, the Howards' income was as follows:

Howards' part-time earnings while in school	$ 1,400
Salary in new place of employment (September–December, 19X1)	8,500
Wife's earnings from part-time job	1,000
Total	$10,900

The Howards have no children.

For 19X2 the Howards' expected earnings are:

Noel's salary	$32,000
Wife's salary	16,000
Total	$48,000

What can you advise the Howards about deducting their moving costs?

RESEARCH PROBLEMS

1. Merino is a partner in a public accounting firm. He occasionally conducts seminars on international taxation for International Seminars, Inc. In July of the current year he went to Stockholm, Sweden, to conduct a three-day seminar. He left the U.S. on July 12, arriving in Stockholm on the morning of the 13th. He conducted the seminar on the 14th, 15th, and 16th. On the morning of the 17th, he left Stockholm

for a four-day vacation tour of Sweden. He left Stockholm on July 21. Merino was paid $1,000 per day for each of the three days of seminars.

Expenses reimbursed by International Seminars, Inc. were as follows:

Airfare to Stockholm and return	$1,080
Taxi (airport to hotel and hotel to airport)	28
Lodging on July 13 through July 17	400
Meals: Lunch July 13 through breakfast July 17	126
Transportation from home to airport and airport to home	36

Expenses not reimbursed

Lodging: July 17 through July 20	400
Meals: Lunch July 17 through lunch July 20	192
Transportation during tour of Sweden	201

How should Merino treat these expenses in his tax return?

2. Kuehn, a wealthy taxpayer, owns 82 percent of the stock of Newtime Corporation. Kuehn serves as Chairman of the Board and President of the company. The corporate offices are located in Jackson, Mississippi. Last year Kuehn moved to Gulfport, Miss., where he bought an expensive shore-front home. Because the corporation is functioning well, Kuehn spends every second week in Jackson. While there he usually works ten hours each day on corporate business. During the alternate weeks, Kuehn stays in Gulfport dealing with his stock and bond investments and frequently making phone calls to the corporation's offices and to customers of the corporation. He estimates that he spends one-fourth of each work week dealing with corporate matters. Kuehn has asked you as his tax return preparer to deduct the transportation cost of all his trips betweeen Gulfport and Jackson, the cost of his meals and lodging while in Jackson, and the cost of telephone calls from his home in Gulfport to the corporate offices and of telephone calls to customers. (He is reimbursed by the corporation for both types of telephone calls.)

   What is the proper tax treatment of all these costs?

Chapter Objectives

1. Identify the type of property qualifying for a cost-recovery deduction and determine the appropriate cost-recovery basis for tax purposes.
2. Determine the depreciation deduction for an asset acquired before 1981 by permissible tax methods which reflect tax considerations such as salvage value, useful life, and additional first year depreciation.
3. Categorize assets acquired after 1980 under the ACRS procedure and determine appropriate ACRS deductions and/or optional straight-line recovery deductions.
4. Identify the intangible assets subject to cost-recovery deductions, with special emphasis on the recovery options for R&E expenditures.
5. Determine if a debt qualifies as a bad-debt deduction under Sec. 166 and the amount allowable as a deduction for both business and nonbusiness bad debts.
6. Describe three basic steps in determining and applying net operating loss deductions.
7. Compare the requirements for deductibility for contributions to qualified corporate retirement plans, self-employed (HR-10/Keogh) retirement plans, and individual retirement account (IRA) plans.
8. Identify the special tax considerations inherent in the deductions for construction period interest and taxes, start-up expenses, and certain farm expenditures.

8 Business Deductions

The general requirements for an expense deduction were discussed previously in Chapters 6 and 7. The focus of this chapter is a discussion of deductible business expenses and losses allowed within the general framework of Sec. 162 and Sec. 165, respectively. For discussion purposes, these deductions are grouped into three classes: cost-recovery deductions, net operating loss deductions, and miscellaneous business deductions.

A taxpayer is permitted to recover the cost of goods or services consumed in a trade or business or an income-producing activity. In many cases the incurrence and consumption of the goods or services occur at the same time (e.g., a repair expense). In other cases, an expenditure must be capitalized and recovered through other procedures permitted in the Code. The first part of this chapter discusses the most common extended-cost recoveries applicable to business taxpayers: depreciation and Accelerated Cost Recovery, amortization, and bad debt deductions.

The second part of this chapter describes the determination and utilization of net operating loss deductions. This topic was introduced briefly in Chapter 7 with the general discussion of loss deductions under Sec. 165. Because of the unique tax-saving opportunities offered by these procedures, a detailed discussion of these provisions is given in this chapter.

The final part of this chapter is devoted to a variety of business expenses which involve special tax considerations. Special emphasis is given to the deductibility of retirement plan payments, since the tremendous growth in formal retirement plans in recent years may be explained in part by special tax incentives.

In studying these business deductions, it may prove beneficial to refer to the discussion on the requirements of an expense (Chapter 7). You will recall that the basic rules for expense deductions apply to all taxpayers, although trade or business expenses are classified further as deductions *for determining* adjusted gross income for individual taxpayers.

COST-RECOVERY METHODS

DEPRECIATION AND ACRS DEDUCTIONS

DEPRECIATION A systematic procedure for providing a reasonable allowance for the exhaustion, wear and tear, and obsolescence of trade or business or income-producing property.

The deduction for ***depreciation*** has become one of the most visible and important components of tax policy in recent years. The advent of the Accelerated Cost Recovery System (ACRS) in 1981 marks a radical change in the nature of tax depreciation. A system which was once closely allied to the financial accounting concept of depreciation has been changed to a mechanical computation which ignores such time-honored accounting concepts as useful life and salvage value. Because the old depreciation rules continue to apply to assets acquired before 1981, the provisions of both Sec. 167 (depreciation) and Sec. 168 (ACRS) are covered in the following discussion.

BACKGROUND

The myriad of depreciation rule changes over the years reflects a conscious attempt by Congress to stimulate private investment. Such a national goal reflects an acceptance of the basic relationship between aggregate investment and national income first espoused by John Maynard Keynes in 1935. In general, an increased level of investment spending will set off a recurring cycle of income and consumption throughout the economy which results in an increase in national income several times the size of the original investment.

Such an increase in investment expenditures must come from either public or private sources. One way to increase the private demand for investment is to increase the marginal efficiency of such investments. Accelerated depreciation methods represent an attempt to increase the returns on investment by accelerating the timing of tax savings from depreciation deductions. The ACRS procedure represents a bold attempt by Congress to increase capital investment dramatically by offering accelerated deductions over artificially short lives.

Cost-recovery deductions under both sets of laws are allowed only on property used in a trade or business or held for the production of income (note the parallel to Sections 162 and 212). The use of the property determines its deductibility: in some cases a property may have both business and personal uses. In such instances, only the business portion would be subject to cost recovery.

A cost-recovery deduction is allowed only on property with a limited useful life. Land is generally not depreciable, but improvements such as paving and fences, which normally have limited useful lives, are subject to cost-recovery methods. In addition, certain intangible assets such as goodwill are not subject to cost recovery.

Generally the cost of a property eligible for recovery deductions is the tax basis used in determining gain on a sale or exchange. For purchased property, this includes such acquisition costs as commissions and fees, as well as any installation costs. (Taxpayers may also elect to capitalize certain sales taxes.) For constructed property, all necessary building costs are capitalized, including such overhead expenditures as depreciation on machinery and equipment used in the construction. Furthermore, necessary costs of excavating and grading associated with a new building are added to the building cost.

For personal assets converted to a business use, the tax basis for cost recovery is the lesser of the adjusted basis of the property or fair market at the conversion date.[1] This requirement prevents the indirect deduction (through cost-recovery procedures) of a loss in value which occurred when the property was held for personal reasons. This would violate Sec. 262, which disallows deductions for purely personal expenses.

Example 1: D purchased a personal automobile in 19X3 for $7,500. In 19X5 D started his own business and began using the car 70% of the time in the business. The value of the car at that time was $6,000. D's basis for cost recovery deductions is $6,000; furthermore, D can only deduct 70% of the appropriate cost recovery deduction each year, since the automobile is still used 30% of the time for personal reasons.

DEPRECIATION FOR ASSETS ACQUIRED PRIOR TO 1981 Sec. 167(a) allows ". . . as a depreciation deduction a reasonable allowance for the exhaustion, wear and tear (including a reasonable allowance for obsolescence)—(1) of property used in a trade or business; or (2) of property held for the production of income." In order to qualify for such deductions, a taxpayer must use a reasonably consistent method of allocating the depreciable basis over the useful life of the asset. In accomplishing this objective for assets acquired prior to 1981, a taxpayer was subjected to a variety of elections and restrictions. The following sections describe the more important rules and options for such property.

USEFUL LIFE. The determination of an asset's useful life has been a constant source of controversy between taxpayers and the IRS. On several occasions the IRS has published guideline lives to aid taxpayers in

---

[1] Reg. Sec. 1.167(g)-1.

this determination. Nevertheless, many taxpayers choose to use their previous experience or the experience of others in assigning useful lives. Such an informal guide is known as a "fact-and-circumstances" system, a phrase coined in 1962 when Revenue Procedure 62-21 established a new set of asset guideline lives:

> The depreciation deduction claimed by the taxpayer will not be disturbed if the class life used by the taxpayer is justified for the taxable year under examination on the basis of all facts and circumstances.[2]

Although the adoption of useful lives equal to or exceeding the IRS guideline lives could reduce disputes with the IRS, many taxpayers attempt to justify shorter lives because of their unique "facts and circumstances." Many times the taxpayer's arguments have merit; for example, rapid advances in technology may cause abnormal obsolescence for many assets.

Example 2: K Company purchased desk-top microcomputers for its sales personnel in 19X2, and began depreciating them over an 8-year guide-line useful life. In 19X4 the same computing capacity was made available in smaller models, and K Company plans to change to the new model within two years. K Company would be justified in changing to a shorter useful life of four years.

Normally, depreciation calculations are made for each month that an asset is used in service. Fractional computations may be necessary in the year that an asset is purchased or sold. Additionally, it may sometimes be necessary to change the estimated life of an asset. As discussed in Chapter 6, the undepreciated basis of the asset will be spread over the remaining useful life of the property (a prospective change).

SALVAGE VALUE. Reg. Sec. 1.167(a) states that an asset should never be depreciated below a reasonable salvage value. Salvage value represents the estimated realizable sales price of the asset at the end of its useful life. Obviously, assigning a salvage value to an asset involves a degree of subjectivity and invariably disputes between taxpayers and the IRS occur on this issue. Sec. 167(f) was added to the Code in 1962 in an attempt to minimize these disputes. This provision allows a taxpayer to ignore up to 10% of the basis of the property when assigning a salvage value to tangible personalty (other than livestock) with a useful life of at least three years.

Example 3: F purchased a new business machine in 19X4 for $8,000. The machine has an estimated useful life of ten years and salvage value of $1,000. For depreciation purposes, F can assign a salvage value of $200 ($1,000 − [$8,000 × .10]) and depreciate $7,800. If the

---

[2] Rev. Proc. 62-21, 1962-2 C.B. 418.

estimated salvage value were $800 or less, the entire $8,000 cost could be depreciated over the useful life.

DEPRECIATION METHODS. Code Sec. 167(b) allows the following methods of depreciation: (*a*) straight-line, (*b*) declining balance (not to exceed twice the straight-line rate, i.e., "double-declining balance"), (*c*) sums-of-the-years' digits, and (*d*) any other consistent method, as long as the deductions during the first two-thirds of the property's useful life do not exceed the deductions allowed under the double-declining balance method. The various depreciation methods can be demonstrated by means of a simple example.

Example 4: G purchased a new metal plating machine on 1/1/19X1 for $3,000. The machine has an expected useful life of five years (or approximately 15,000 machine hours) and an expected salvage value of $200. Table 8-1 displays the appropriate depreciation amounts under four different methods of depreciation. For the machine-hours method, it is assumed that the plating machine was used the following hours: 19X1—4,000; 19X2—4,000; 19X3—3,000; 19X4—2,000; 19X5—2,000. Following is a brief description of each method.

The *straight-line method* is the easiest procedure to apply, with the depreciable cost spread evenly over the useful life. This constant charge method has been in use since the first U.S. income tax laws. Note in the above example that salvage value was ignored, since it is less than 10% of the $3,000 cost.

The *declining-balance method* applies a constant percentage (expressed as a percentage of the straight-line rate) to a declining book value (the undepreciated cost). In the example the straight-line rate is 20%, so the double-declining-balance rate, the maximum allowed under Sec. 167(b), is 40%. In 19X1 this rate is applied to the total cost of the asset, unreduced by any salvage value, regardless of the 10% reduction rule. (However, the asset cannot be depreciated below a reasonable salvage value after reflecting the 10% reduction, if applicable.) Thus, the depreciation deduc-

TABLE 8-1
Sample Depreciation Calculations

	DEPRECIATION METHOD			
Year	Straight-line	200% Declining Balance	Sum-of-the-years' Digits	Machine Hours
19X1	$600	$1,200	$1,000	$800
19X2	600	720	800	800
19X3	600	432	600	600
19X4	600	324	400	400
19X5	600	324	200	400

tion for 19X1 is $1,200 ($3,000 × .40). The deduction for 19X2 is the undepreciated book value at the beginning of the year of $1,800 ($3,000 − $1,200) times the 40% rate, or $720. The deduction for 19X3 is computed in a similar manner.

If the same procedure were used in 19X4 and 19X5, the total depreciable cost of $3,000 would not be recovered. This can be overcome by switching to the straight-line method in 19X4, which is allowed without the consent of the Commissioner of the IRS.[3] (Most other changes require prior approval by the Commissioner.) Generally, the switch to straight-line should be made when such a deduction exceeds the declining-balance deduction, either at the middle year of the useful life or one year later. In the example, the 19X4 deduction under the declining-balance method would have been only $259.

The *sum-of-the-years'-digits method* applies a decreasing percentage to a constant depreciable cost (after reduction for salvage value). The fractional percentage for each year is a function of the useful life of the asset. The numerator of the fraction is the remaining useful life as of the beginning of the tax year, and the denominator is the sum of the numbers representing each year of the asset's useful life, which can be calculated with the formula $n(n + 1)/2$. The numerator will decrease by one each year while the denominator remains constant; this allows the acceleration of deductions for the early years of asset life. In the example, the percentage recovery for 19X1 is $5/15$, the remaining useful life at the start of the year divided by the sum of the years' digits $(1 + 2 + 3 + 4 + 5$, or $5(5 + 1)/2 = 15)$. The recovery percentage for 19X2 would be $4/15$, for 19X3, $3/15$, and so on.

A machine hours method will also qualify as an acceptable recovery method as long as it is consistently applied. This method provides equal charges per work unit; for example, the uniform charge for the machine in Example 4 would be $.20 per machine hour ($3,000/15,000 estimated machine hours). The deduction each year is simply the number of machine hours used for the year times the cost per machine hour.

RESTRICTIONS ON DEPRECIATION RECOVERY. In 1969 Congress established maximum depreciation rates for properties, with the higher rates (expressed as a percentage of straight-line) going to new properties and residential (rental) properties. At this time Congress wanted to channel available investment funds into the construction of ***residential*** (rental) buildings, as opposed to ***commercial*** (business) buildings. To qualify as residential property, at least 80% of a building's gross rents must come from dwelling units (i.e., rented to nontransients).[4]

RESIDENTIAL REALTY
For tax purposes, residential realty includes buildings where dwelling unit rentals (nontransient rentals) account for more than 80% of the gross rental income.

COMMERCIAL REALTY
For tax purposes, commercial realty includes all buildings where dwelling unit rentals (nontransient rentals) account for less than 80% of the gross rental income.

Table 8-2 summarizes these restrictions on maximum depreciation rates. Note that the sum-of-the-years'-digits method is available only when the property otherwise qualifies for the double-declining-balance method. These are restrictions only as to maximum recovery rates; a tax-

[3] Sec. 167(e)(1).
[4] Sec. 167(j)(2)(B).

TABLE 8-2
Maximum Allowable Depreciation Rates—Tangible Property, Code Sec. 167(j) Expressed As a Percentage of Straight-line

	NEW	USED
Personal property (physical property other than land or buildings)	200% of S/L*	150% of S/L
Residential real property (rental property)	200% of S/L*	125% of S/L†
Commercial real property (business property)	150% of S/L	S/L

*Sum-of-the-years' digits allowed *only* where 200% of S/L is allowed.
†Useful life must exceed 20 years.

payer may always elect a smaller recovery rate or simply use the straight-line method.

ADDITIONAL FIRST-YEAR DEPRECIATION. Congress enacted this special provision in 1958 to provide additional recovery incentives for small business. This provision, which applies only to assets purchased before 1981, allows a taxpayer to deduct 20% of the first $10,000 cost of qualifying property ($20,000 on a joint return) as depreciation in addition to the normal depreciation recovery in the first year. Qualifying property is defined as tangible personalty (new or used) with a useful life of at least six years. Any amount deducted as additional first-year depreciation reduces the cost basis subject to regular depreciation.

> **Example 5:** K Corporation purchased a new copy machine on 1/1/X6 for $14,000. The machine has an estimated useful life of ten years and no salvage. If K elects to use a straight-line recovery, the additional first-year depreciation will be $2,000 (20% of the first $10,000 of qualifying cost), and the regular 19X6 depreciation will be $1,200 ($12,000 remaining cost ÷ 10 years).

MULTIPLE-ASSET ACCOUNTS. Thus far the discussion has been limited to depreciation calculations on a property-by-property basis, commonly referred to as "item accounts." Reg. Sec. 1.167(a)-7 allows a taxpayer to combine a number of assets into a single account and take a single depreciation deduction for the entire account. There are three types of multiple-asset accounts: group (similar assets with similar useful lives), classified (similar uses without regard to useful life), and composite (any asset, without regard to character or useful life). An average depreciation rate must be determined for each multiple-asset account. A detailed discussion of these procedures is beyond the scope of this text.

ASSET DEPRECIATION RANGE SYSTEM. In 1971 the Nixon administration introduced a special multiple-asset depreciation procedure known as the Asset Depreciation Range (ADR) system. Such a system would group similar assets by each year of purchase into "vintage accounts."

TABLE 8-3
Overview of Accelerated Cost Recovery System

TYPE OF ASSET	CLASS LIFE (YEARS)	QUALIFYING PROPERTY	REDUCTION IN BASIS	RECOVERY TABLE METHOD	ACQUISITION YEAR ASSUMPTION	STRAIGHT-LINE OPTIONS
PERSONALTY	3	Auto, light trucks, R&D equipment, other ADR of 4 years or less, and certain racehorses	One-half of allowable investment or energy credit (unless reduced rate is elected)	150% declining balance (see Table 8-4)	Half-year convention	3, 5, or 12 years (half-year convention, all properties in class must use S/L)
	5	Most tangible personal property (i.e., machinery, furniture, etc.) greenhouses, chicken coops	Same as above	Same as above (Table 8-4)	Half-year convention	5, 12, or 25 years (half-year convention, all properties in class must use S/L)
	10	Most public utility personalty (ADR to 25), realty of 12.5 ADR or less (such as theme park structures), and railroad tank cars	Same as above	Same as above (Table 8-4)	Half-year convention	10, 25, or 35 years (half-year convention, all properties in class must use S/L)
	15	Public utility with an ADR greater than 25	Same as above	Same as above (Table 8-4)	Half-year convention	15, 35, or 45 years (half-year convention, all properties in class must use S/L)
REALTY	15	Realty placed into service before 3/16/84 (and all low-income housing)	100% of rehabilitation expenditure credit, if applicable (50% for certified historic structures)	175% declining balance (200% for low-income housing) (Table 8-5)	Full-month convention	15, 35, or 45 years (full-month convention, separate elections for each property)
	18	Realty placed into service after 3/15/84	Same as above	175% declining balance (Table 8-5)	Mid-month convention (full-month for acquisitions after 3/15/84 and before 6/23/84)	18, 35, or 45 years (mid-month convention, separate elections for each property)

The asset(s) could then be depreciated over a useful life falling within a "range" of acceptable years. This range simply included useful lives up to 20% less or 20% greater than the guideline lives for assets published by the IRS in 1962. Thus the principal benefit of electing ADR was the ability to select a shorter useful life than the former IRS guidelines without having to offer "facts and circumstances" proof. The ADR system is replaced by the Accelerated Cost Recovery System (ACRS) for properties placed into service after 1980.

COST RECOVERY FOR ASSETS ACQUIRED AFTER 1980 The ***Accelerated Cost Recovery System (ACRS)*** established by the Economic Recovery Tax Act of 1981 provides a radical departure from previously acceptable tax depreciation methods. The new rules of Sec. 168 eliminate several sources of disagreement between taxpayers and the IRS, including estimated salvage value, estimated useful life, "facts-and-circumstances" justifications, and component depreciation.

ACRS The accelerated cost recovery system (ACRS) is the statutory procedure used to compute cost recovery deductions for all tangible assets acquired after 1980.

The ACRS rules apply to all depreciable assets purchased on or after January 1, 1981 other than intangible assets and assets depreciated on nontime-based methods (e.g., units of production, income forecast, etc.). The preexisting rules continue to apply only to assets purchased prior to 1981.

The following discussion highlights the major characteristics of the ACRS procedure. Table 8-3 summarizes these characteristics. The reader is encouraged to refer frequently to this table throughout the ACRS discussion.

CLASS LIFE. In general, the ACRS procedure classifies property into the two broad categories of ***personalty*** and ***realty***. These terms are defined in substantially the same manner as before, except that a few special-purpose buildings are considered to be personalty under the new provisions. Under the ACRS procedure, all depreciable personalty is grouped into either a 3, 5, 10, or 15-year category, and depreciable realty (other than a few special-purpose buildings in the 10-year class) is classified in either a 15-year or an 18-year category, depending on the date of acquisition (except for residential realty, which is always in the 15-year class). These categories represent the fixed recovery periods for ACRS property; the useful life of the asset is no longer relevant.

PERSONALTY Tangible property other than land, buildings, and permanent building components.

REALTY Tangible property which is either land, buildings, or permanent additions (or components) of buildings.

QUALIFYING PROPERTIES. Table 8-3 discloses the major classes of qualifying property for each class life under ACRS. The notation "ADR" refers to the midpoint life under the old ADR system; for example, personalty having an ADR midpoint life of four years or less is in the 3-year classification. Note that most personalty of nonutility companies will be in either the 3 or 5-year class. The 10-year class life for personalty includes some items formerly classified as realty under the old law, such as theme (amusement) park structures and manufactured mobile homes.[5]

[5] Sec. 168(h)(3).

BASIS REDUCTION. Sec. 48(q), added by the *Tax Equity and Fiscal Responsibility Act of 1982*, requires a reduction in the depreciable cost basis of certain assets which otherwise qualify for the investment tax credit, energy tax credit, or rehabilitation tax credit. The basis of such assets must be reduced by 50% of the allowable credit. Optionally, a taxpayer may elect to reduce the allowable credit percentage by two percentage points and recover the full cost of the asset. A detailed discussion of these basis adjustments is reserved for Chapter 14. However, the following examples demonstrate the application of the general-basis reduction rule and the optional-credit reduction rule.

Example 6: Baker purchased a new business machine on 1/1/85 for $10,000. This machine would be classified as 5-year ACRS property, which normally qualifies for a 10% investment tax credit. Accordingly, Baker's two tax options for this machine are as follows:

- *Basis Reduction*—Baker would take an investment tax credit of $1,000 (10% of $10,000) and assign a depreciable basis to the machine of $9,500 (the $10,000 cost less one-half of the investment tax credit).
- *Credit Reduction*—Baker would take an investment tax credit of $800 (8% of $10,000) and assign a depreciable basis to the machine of $10,000 (the original cost).

Example 7: Carter purchased a new business automobile on 1/1/85 for $5,000. This automobile would be classified as 3-year ACRS property, which normally qualifies for a 6% investment tax credit. Accordingly, Carter's two tax options for this automobile are as follows:

- *Basis Reduction*—Carter would take an investment tax credit of $300 (6% of $5,000) and assign a depreciable basis to the automobile of $4,850 (the $5,000 cost less one-half of the investment tax credit).
- *Credit Reduction*—Carter would take an investment tax credit of $200 (4% of $5,000) and assign a depreciable basis to the automobile of $5,000 (the original cost).

This special basis adjustment was enacted to eliminate what Congress perceived as an incentive to make tax-motivated investments which distort economic efficiency:

> Cost recovery deductions for most personal property allowed currently under ACRS in combination with the regular investment tax credit generate tax benefits which have a present value that is more generous than the tax benefits that would be available if the full cost of the investment could be deducted in the year when the investment was made, i.e., more generous than the tax benefits of immediate expensing.[6]

---

[6] *Report of the Committee on Finance*, United States Senate, H.R. 4961 (July 12, 1982), p. 122.

TABLE 8-4
Rates for ACRS Personal Property and 10-Year Real Property

	PERCENTAGE BY PROPERTY CLASS			
Recovery Year	3-Year	5-Year	10-Year	15-Year Public Utility
1	25	15	8	5
2	38	22	14	10
3	37	21	12	9
4		21	10	8
5		21	10	7
6			10	7
7			9	6
8			9	6
9			9	6
10			9	6
11				6
12				6
13				6
14				6
15				6

RECOVERY-TABLE METHOD. The ACRS procedure greatly simplifies the depreciation calculation by requiring that the original cost of the asset (subject to the basis adjustment rule discussed above) must be multiplied by a statutory percentage for each year of its class life. The recovery tables are based on accelerated depreciation methods (declining-balance) with a switch to straight-line at the optimum point.

The personalty recovery percentages are based on the 150% declining-balance method.[7] These statutory recovery percentages are detailed in Table 8-4. Note that the sum of each column of percentage recoveries totals 100%. This effectively eliminates any salvage-value considerations. The original provisions of the 1981 Act provided for a gradual increase in the personalty recovery methods to a 200% (double) declining-balance method. However, this scheduled increase was repealed as part of the budget-cutting measures of the *Tax Equity and Fiscal Responsibility Act of 1982*.[8]

The realty recovery percentages are based on the 175% declining-balance method. Realty acquired on or before March 15, 1984 is subject to a 15-year ACRS recovery period, as are all acquisitions of low-income housing. These statutory percentages are detailed in the first two categories of Table 8-5.

---

[7] Sec. 168(b)1.

[8] *Tax Equity and Fiscal Responsibility Act of 1982*, Sec. 206, amending Code Sec. 168(b)(1).

TABLE 8-5
Rates for ACRS Real Property

1. ALL REAL ESTATE (EXCEPT LOW-INCOME HOUSING) ACQUIRED BEFORE MARCH 16, 1984

IF THE RECOVERY YEAR IS:	THE APPLICABLE PERCENTAGE IS: *(USE THE COLUMN FOR THE MONTH IN THE FIRST YEAR THE PROPERTY IS PLACED IN SERVICE)*											
	1	2	3	4	5	6	7	8	9	10	11	12
1	12	11	10	9	8	7	6	5	4	3	2	1
2	10	10	11	11	11	11	11	11	11	11	11	12
3	9	9	9	9	10	10	10	10	10	10	10	10
4	8	8	8	8	8	8	9	9	9	9	9	9
5	7	7	7	7	7	7	8	8	8	8	8	8
6	6	6	6	6	7	7	7	7	7	7	7	7
7	6	6	6	6	6	6	6	6	6	6	6	6
8	6	6	6	6	6	6	5	6	6	6	6	6
9	6	6	6	6	5	6	5	5	5	6	6	6
10	5	6	5	6	5	5	5	5	5	5	6	5
11	5	5	5	5	5	5	5	5	5	5	5	5
12	5	5	5	5	5	5	5	5	5	5	5	5
13	5	5	5	5	5	5	5	5	5	5	5	5
14	5	5	5	5	5	5	5	5	5	5	5	5
15	5	5	5	5	5	5	5	5	5	5	5	5
16	-	-	1	1	2	2	3	3	4	4	4	5

2. LOW-INCOME HOUSING

IF THE RECOVERY YEAR IS:	THE APPLICABLE PERCENTAGE IS: *(USE THE COLUMN FOR THE MONTH IN THE FIRST YEAR THE PROPERTY IS PLACED IN SERVICE)*											
	1	2	3	4	5	6	7	8	9	10	11	12
1	13	12	11	10	9	8	7	6	4	3	2	1
2	12	12	12	12	12	12	12	13	13	13	13	13
3	10	10	10	10	11	11	11	11	11	11	11	11
4	9	9	9	9	9	9	9	9	10	10	10	10
5	8	8	8	8	8	8	8	8	8	8	8	9
6	7	7	7	7	7	7	7	7	7	7	7	7
7	6	6	6	6	6	6	6	6	6	6	6	6
8	5	5	5	5	5	5	5	5	5	5	6	6
9	5	5	5	5	5	5	5	5	5	5	5	5
10	5	5	5	5	5	5	5	5	5	5	5	5
11	4	5	5	5	5	5	5	5	5	5	5	5
12	4	4	4	5	4	5	5	5	5	5	5	5
13	4	4	4	4	4	4	5	4	5	5	5	5
14	4	4	4	4	4	4	4	4	4	5	4	4
15	4	4	4	4	4	4	4	4	4	4	4	4
16	-	-	1	1	2	2	2	3	3	3	4	4

TABLE 8-5 *Continued*

3. ALL REAL ESTATE (EXCEPT LOW-INCOME HOUSING) ACQUIRED AFTER JUNE 22, 1984

IF THE RECOVERY YEAR IS:	THE APPLICABLE PERCENTAGE IS: *(USE THE COLUMN FOR THE MONTH IN THE FIRST YEAR THE PROPERTY IS PLACED IN SERVICE)*											
	1	2	3	4	5	6	7	8	9	10	11	12
1	9	9	8	7	6	5	4	4	3	2	1	0.4
2	9	9	9	9	9	9	9	9	9	10	10	10.0
3	8	8	8	8	8	8	8	8	9	9	9	9.0
4	7	7	7	7	7	8	8	8	8	8	8	8.0
5	7	7	7	7	7	7	7	7	7	7	7	7.0
6	6	6	6	6	6	6	6	6	6	6	6	6.0
7	5	5	5	5	6	6	6	6	6	6	6	6.0
8	5	5	5	5	5	5	5	5	5	5	5	5.0
9	5	5	5	5	5	5	5	5	5	5	5	5.0
10	5	5	5	5	5	5	5	5	5	5	5	5.0
11	5	5	5	5	5	5	5	5	5	5	5	5.0
12	5	5	5	5	5	5	5	5	5	5	5	5.0
13	4	4	4	4	4	4	5	4	4	4	5	5.0
14	4	4	4	4	4	4	4	4	4	4	4	4.0
15	4	4	4	4	4	4	4	4	4	4	4	4.0
16	4	4	4	4	4	4	4	4	4	4	4	4.0
17	4	4	4	4	4	4	4	4	4	4	4	4.0
18	4	3	4	4	4	4	4	4	4	4	4	4.0
19	-	1	1	1	2	2	2	3	3	3	3	3.6

4. OPTIONAL 18-YEAR STRAIGHT-LINE RECOVERY METHOD

IF THE RECOVERY YEAR IS:	THE APPLICABLE PERCENTAGE IS: *(USE THE COLUMN FOR THE MONTH IN THE FIRST YEAR THE PROPERTY IS PLACED IN SERVICE)*					
	1–2	3–4	5–7	8–9	10–11	12
1	5	4	3	2	1	0.2
2	6	6	6	6	6	6.0
3	6	6	6	6	6	6.0
4	6	6	6	6	6	6.0
5	6	6	6	6	6	6.0
6	6	6	6	6	6	6.0
7	6	6	6	6	6	6.0
8	6	6	6	6	6	6.0
9	6	6	6	6	6	6.0
10	6	6	6	6	6	6.0
11	5	5	5	5	5	5.8
12	5	5	5	5	5	5.0
13	5	5	5	5	5	5.0
14	5	5	5	5	5	5.0
15	5	5	5	5	5	5.0
16	5	5	5	5	5	5.0
17	5	5	5	5	5	5.0
18	5	5	5	5	5	5.0
19	1	2	3	4	5	5.0

As a means of cutting back on the use of realty for tax shelter purposes, Congress decided to extend the ACRS writeoff period for buildings, other than low-income housing, to 18 years. These recovery percentages are also based on the 175% declining-balance method and are detailed in the third category of properties in Table 8-5. Generally, the 18-year recovery period applies to all realty (other than low-income housing) acquired after March 15, 1984.

HALF-YEAR CONVENTION. The ACRS procedure specifies that one-half year's depreciation is allowed on all personalty purchased during the year, regardless of when the property was actually acquired during the year. However, the ACRS tables do not extend an extra half-year to fully recover the cost of the asset; rather, the remaining recovery years "catch up" this difference, and at the end of the last whole year the asset cost is fully recovered.

Example 8: L purchased a new word processor on November 14, 19X1. The cost basis for recovery deductions after credit adjustment is $10,000. This asset would be classified as 5-year recovery property under ACRS procedures. L's recovery deductions for the asset would be:

19X1—$1,500 ($10,000 × .15)
19X2—$2,200 ($10,000 × .22)
19X3, 19X4, and 19X5—$2,100 ($10,000 × .21)

Note that the first year ACRS recovery percentage is one-half the normal 150 percent declining-balance factor of 30% (20% straight-line rate times 1.50) for the first year of a 5-year asset. Additionally, no recovery deduction is taken in the sixth year, 19X6; the recovery table adjusts for this within the five years.

A half-year convention is not used for realty; rather, the recovery deduction is calculated on a per-months service use for the first and last year of recovery. As a result of this requirement, the ACRS tables for realty (Table 8-5) are divided into 12 columns, one for each of the possible months that the asset could have been placed into service. Additionally, the ACRS tables extend into the 16th year (or 19th year, for 18-year realty) if the asset is placed into service after the first month of the tax year (as opposed to the "catch-up" adjustment for personalty).

Example 9: M purchased a new office building on 10/1/81 for $100,000. This asset is classified as 15-year recovery property under ACRS procedures. M's recovery deductions for the asset would be:

1981—$ 3,000
1982—$11,000
1983—$10,000
1984—$ 9,000
1985—$8,000
1986—$7,000
1987, 1988, and 1989—$6,000
1990 to 1995—$5,000
1996—$4,000

Note that the first year recovery percentage is 3/12 (rounded) of the normal 175% declining-balance factor of 12% (6.7% straight-line rate times 1.75). Likewise, the 4% recovery in the year 1996 reflects a deduction for nine months.

Example 10: Assume the same facts as in Example 9, except that the asset was acquired on 10/1/84. In this case, the asset is classified as 18-year realty (i.e., acquired after 3/15/84), and M's recovery deductions would be:

1984—$ 2,000	1991 to 1995—$5,000
1985—$10,000	1996 to 2001—$4,000
1986—$ 9,000	2002—$3,000
1987—$ 8,000	
1988—$ 7,000	
1989 and 1990—$ 6,000	

There is a slight difference in the calculation of the recovery percentages for 15-year and 18-year realty. The 15-year tables are based on a *full-month convention*, an assumption that the asset is placed into service on the first day of the month of acquisition. On the other hand, the 18-year tables are based on a *mid-month convention*, an assumption that the asset is placed into service in the middle of the month (Sec. 168(b)(2)(A)). This mid-month convention applies to realty (other than low-income housing) acquired after June 22, 1984.

BACKGROUND

At this point in the discussion, the reader is probably confused about the effective dates for the required 18-year recovery (property acquired after *March 15, 1984*) and the effective date for the required mid-month convention (property acquired after *June 22, 1984*). There is a simple answer to this dilemma: It *is* confusing!

The original Senate version of the Tax Reform Act of 1984 provided for an extended recovery period for realty of 20 years, which would be gradually reduced to 18 years by 1986. This provision was to be effective for realty acquired after March 15, 1984. Why March 15? The answer to this question is probably based on political realities: The effective date of an unpopular provision is often chosen to roughly correspond with the date the proposed legislation was first discussed in Congress. Any date before this time would retroactively penalize some taxpayers, and any date after this time would provide a "window" for taxpayers to take immediate action to avoid the effects of the proposed law.

The final version of the 1984 Act drafted by the Conference Committee reduced the recovery period for realty to 18 years for all realty other than low-income housing which was acquired after March 15, 1985. In addition, the Conference Committee instructed

Continued

BACKGROUND
the Treasury Department to prescribe recovery tables based on a mid-month convention. The conferees agreed on a final tax bill on June 23, 1984, and as a result, the mid-month convention rules were made effective for acquisitions on or after that date. For acquisitions of realty in the "twilight zone" interim period of March 16–June 22, taxpayers will use special recovery tables (not displayed in this text) based on an 18-year recovery period and a full-month convention. In fact, Treasury Release R-2890, which contains the 18-year recovery rates, included a total of 9 possible recovery tables for 18-year realty!

STRAIGHT-LINE RECOVERY OPTIONS. In proposing the ACRS procedure, Congress recognized that some businesses may prefer to use straight-line depreciation and/or longer recovery periods. To provide some flexibility in the ACRS procedure, Congress provided three optional straight-line periods for each recovery class.[9] These optional lives are disclosed in Table 8-3; note that the first optional straight-line period in each class is the actual ACRS recovery period for that class.

If the straight-line option is elected for one item of personalty during a year, then it must be elected for all personalty purchased in that class life during the year (but *not* necessarily other class lives).[10] Electing straight-line recovery on personalty requires the use of the half-year convention for the first *and last* years of the recovery period (which requires an extension of one-half year to the normal recovery period).

Example 11: Assume the same facts as in Example 8, except that L elects a straight-line recovery over a 5-year period (although a 12- or 25-year period could be selected). L's recovery deductions for the asset would be:

19X1—$1,000 ($10,000 × ⅕ × ½)
19X2–19X5—$2,000 ($10,000 × ⅕)
19X6—$1,000 ($10,000 × ⅕ × ½)

Note that a straight-line election necessitates a recovery deduction in 19X6, unlike normal ACRS procedures (see Example 6). The election will also require the taxpayer to use straight-line recovery on any other 5-year personalty purchased during the year.

A straight-line option for realty is elected on a property-by-property basis; there is no requirement that straight-line recovery apply to all 15- or 18-year real properties purchased during the year. Additionally, straight-line calculations for realty are not based on a half-year convention; deductions for the first and last recovery years are calculated on a months-in-service basis (similar to regular depreciation deductions).

---

[9] Sec. 168(b)(3)(A).

[10] Sec. 168(b)(3)(B).

Example 12: Assume the same facts as in Example 9 except that M elects a straight-line recovery over a 15-year period (35- or 45-year recoveries are also possible). M's recovery deductions for the building would be:

1981—$1,667 ($100,000 × 1/15 × 3/12)
1982 to 1995—$6,667 ($100,000 × 1/15)
1996—$5,000 ($100,000 × 1/15 × 9/12)

Note that the straight-line option requires a recovery deduction in the 16th year, unless the asset is purchased in the first or second month of the taxable year.

As illustrated in Example 12, the straight-line calculations for 15-year realty are relatively simple, since a whole-month convention is used for such acquisitions. The straight-line computations become more complex for 18-year real properties acquired after June 22, 1984, because of the necessity of incorporating the mid-month convention. For this reason, Treasury Release R-2890 (the source for all 18-year recovery tables) includes recovery tables for the three optional straight-line recovery periods. The 18-year straight-line recovery table is shown as the fourth table in Table 8-5. (And to think that, as accountants, we always thought that we knew how to compute straight-line depreciation!)

Example 13: Assume the same facts as in Example 10, except that M elects a straight-line recovery procedure over an 18-year period (35- and 45-year recovery periods are also available). M's recovery deductions for the building, based on Table 8-5, would be:

1984—$1,000
1985 to 1993—$6,000
1994 to 2002—$5,000

IMMEDIATE EXPENSING ELECTION. The 1981 Act eliminated the additional first-year depreciation rules and substituted Sec. 179 as another form of tax relief for small businesses. This provision allows a taxpayer to expense in the year of acquisition limited amounts of purchased personalty which otherwise qualifies for the investment tax credit (referred to as "Sec. 38 property," discussed in Chapter 14). The maximum annual write-off is $5,000 in 1982 through 1987, $7,500 in 1988 and 1989, and $10,000 in 1990 and thereafter. The maximum deduction may be taken on one asset or allocated to several assets. There is a significant cost to such an election, however; the 6% or 10% investment credit is not allowed on that portion of the cost of the ***Code Sec. 179*** property.

CODE SEC. 179 PROPERTY Tangible depreciable property which otherwise qualifies for the investment credit and may be expensed at the option of the taxpayer (up to a limited amount each year).

Example 14: N Company purchased a new drill press (5-year personalty) on 1/1/X6 for $5,000. N can elect to expense this amount immediately on its 19X6 return; however, no investment credit will be allowed on the property. Alternately, N could elect to use a 5-year ACRS recovery on the asset and claim a $500 ($5,000 × .10) investment credit against its 19X6 tax liability. (However, you will recall that one-half of this credit reduces the recovery basis.)

Although Congress originally justified this provision as an aid to small business, such an election may actually be less beneficial than the combination of normal ACRS procedures and the investment tax credit. This is especially true for taxpayers with low marginal tax rates (see "Planning Workshop," on page 8/46).

BUILDING COMPONENTS AND ADDITIONS. A common practice under the old depreciation rules was to allocate the total cost of realty to as many component parts as possible (i.e., plumbing, wiring, etc.). This was done because many components had useful lives shorter than the building shell. Code Sec. 168(f)(1) prohibits this practice under the ACRS procedures; composite recovery is now required for the entire structure. Apparently, Congress felt that a 15-year recovery for buildings, as opposed to 30- or 40-year guideline lives under the old law, should eliminate the need for component methods.

The tax treatment of building improvements was also modified by the 1981 Act. Any improvements made to buildings acquired after 1980 which exceed 25% of the adjusted basis (computed without recovery deductions) may be treated as a separate building for purposes of ACRS procedures.[11] If the improvement does not meet the 25% test, the expenditure must be recovered under the option elected on the original building. As a transitional rule, the first component placed in service after 1980 on a building owned before 1981 will be treated as a separate building, regardless of the 25% rule.[12] However, the recovery method elected on this addition (e.g., ACRS or straight-line) must also be used on subsequent additions. Furthermore, any improvements made after March 15, 1984 will be subject to 18-year recovery procedures.

> **Example 15:** In 1982 O invested $20,000 in an addition to a building (purchased in 1978) which had an adjusted basis of $150,000 (ignoring depreciation recoveries). Although this improvement does not meet the 25% test, the taxpayer may elect any available recovery option under ACRS. This recovery option will continue to apply to future additions.

ASSET DISPOSITIONS. ACRS deductions reduce the adjusted basis of an asset (for purposes of determining gain or loss) similar to depreciation deductions. However, the tax treatment of personalty and realty differ in the tax year of disposition. Sec. 168(d)(2)(B) specifies that no recovery deduction is allowed on personalty in the year of disposition. On the other hand, Sec. 168(b)(2)(B) states that the deduction for realty in the tax year of disposition should ". . . reflect only the [full] months during such year the property was in service." Additionally, the adjusted basis of

---

[11] Code Sec. 168(f)(1)(C).

[12] Code Sec. 168(f)(1)(D).

property subject to a Sec. 179 expensing election is automatically reduced by the allowed immediate deduction. ACRS properties are also potentially subject to the depreciation recapture rules, discussed in Chapter 11.

ANTI-CHURNING RULES. An elaborate set of special rules was included in the ACRS provisions, Sec. 168(e)(4), to prevent sham transactions (through related parties) which attempt to qualify property purchased before 1981 under the new ACRS rules. These provisions, referred to as the "anti-churning rules," have the same basic intent as the related-party rules for loss deductions of Sec. 267, in that control (through family members or controlled entities) may be equated with ownership.

> **Example 16:** P and her spouse together own 85% of the outstanding stock of X Corporation. In 1983 P sells a plating machine to X Corporation. P had purchased the machine in 1979 for her business. X Corporation cannot use the ACRS procedures for cost recovery on the machine, since the asset is not considered as being "acquired" after 1980.

SPECIAL LIMITATIONS FOR "LISTED PROPERTY". Two special limitations on ACRS deductions and investment tax credits were included in the Tax Reform Act of 1984. These reform provisions, which have far-reaching implications, were enacted by Congress to prevent what they perceived as the use of ACRS and the investment tax credit to subsidize the personal use of business assets. These two provisions deal with "mixed use property" (property used for both business and personal uses) and "luxury automobiles."

Sec. 280F establishes special cost recovery and investment tax credit limitations on certain "listed property" acquired after June 18, 1984 that is not used predominantly in a trade or business. Listed property includes passenger automobiles, computers, amusement properties, and other properties to be specified by the regulations. Any listed property which is not used more than 50% of the time in a qualified trade or business will not qualify for the investment tax credit or accelerated recovery. Depreciation must be claimed using a straight-line method over extended recovery periods of either five years (3-year property), 12 years (5-year property), or 35 years (other properties). For purposes of the 50% threshold test, only use of the property in a trade or business is considered; any usage in the production of income is ignored. However, if business usage alone exceeds 50%, any usage in the production of income may also be used to determine the total qualifying cost for the investment tax credit and ACRS deductions.

> **Example 17:** Mark Asman purchased a personal computer for $6,000 on 8/1/84 that will be used 40% of the time for business purposes, 20% of the time for income-producing purposes (rental properties), and 40% of the time for personal reasons. Since the business usage alone does not exceed 50%, Asman cannot take an investment

tax credit on the computer, and he must compute cost recovery deductions on a straight-line basis over a 12-year period.

Example 18: Assume the same facts as in Example 17, except that usage of the computer will be as follows: 60% for business purposes, 15% for income-producing purposes, and 25% for personal purposes. In this case, Asman is allowed an investment tax credit and ACRS recovery on 75% of the cost, or $4,500.

Sec. 280F also establishes two additional tax limitations on "luxury automobiles," which are defined as four-wheeled passenger vehicles rated at 6,000 pounds or less and manufactured primarily for use on public roads. First, the investment tax credit on such a vehicle is limited to $1,000 ($667 if 4% rate is elected). Secondly, the maximum recovery deduction (ACRS or straight-line) is limited to $4,000 in the first year of service and $6,000 for each year thereafter. If the total cost is not recovered over the prescribed ACRS period, deductions of up to $6,000 may be taken in the following years. The $1,000 (or $667), $4,000, and $6,000 limits are reduced proportionately for any nonqualified business uses (automobiles are also "listed properties"). Beginning in October 1985, these three values will be adjusted annually for inflation by changes in the automobile component of the Consumer Price Index (using October 1983 as the base figure).

Example 19: Francis Bourne purchased a new automobile for $20,000 on October 1, 1984. She will use the automobile as follows: 60% of the time in her business, 30% of the time in managing her rental properties, and 10% of the time for personal transportation. She elects to use the maximum 6% investment tax credit rate. Since 90% of the cost of the automobile qualifies for the credit, her allowable investment tax credit is the lesser of:

a) Regular computation ($20,000 × .90 × .06)	$1,080
b) Sec. 280F limit ($1,000 × .90)	$ 900

Therefore, her investment credit is limited to $900, and one-half of this amount, or $450, will reduce her cost recovery basis from $18,000 ($20,000 cost × .90 qualifying usage) to $17,550. Her allowable cost recovery deductions are computed as follows:

1984 ($17,550 × .25 = $4,388, limited to $4,000 × .90)	$ 3,600
1985 ($17,550 × .38 = $6,669, limited to $6,000 × .90)	5,400
1986 ($17,550 × .37 = $6,494, limited to $6,000 × .90)	5,400
1987 ($17,550 − $14,400 allowed in earlier years)	3,150
Total ACRS Deductions	$17,550

In addition to the limitations imposed on owners of luxury automobiles, Congress also enacted special income inclusion rules applicable to lessees. These rules essentially have the same effect as the limitations applicable to owners. For example, temporary Reg. Sec. 1.280f-5T(d) requires an annual income inclusion of 7.5% of the excess of the fair market value of the automobile over $16,500 for the first three lease years. The income inclusion for the fourth and later years is 6% of the excess of the fair market value over the sum of $16,500 plus $6,000 × the number of lease years in excess of three.

Sec. 280F(e) instructs the Secretary of the Treasury to prescribe regulations as may be necessary to carry out the purposes of these special rules. The first two drafts of these regulations issued by the IRS were highly controversial and almost universally criticized, because they would require taxpayers to keep detailed diaries of business and personal usage of listed properties. As we go to press, President Reagan signed into law, P.L. 99-44 on May 24, 1985. This measure repeals the contemporaneous record-keeping rule. However, the "price" of this repeal, for purposes of revenue neutrality, was to reduce the $1,000, $4,000, and $6,000 limits to $675, $3,200, and $4,800 respectively, for autos acquired after April 2, 1985.

REPORTING PROCEDURES. Form 4562 is used to report cost recovery deductions and is illustrated in Figure 8-1. Note that lines 1 and 2 of the form are used to report ACRS deductions for assets acquired in 1984.

AMORTIZATION

The term ***amortization*** generally refers to cost recovery procedures for intangible assets. Intangible property must have a definite and limited useful life to qualify for cost recovery deductions. Sec. 167(c) limits recovery deductions for intangible assets to the straight-line method (recall that ACRS does not apply to intangible assets). In addition, Congress has established special rapid amortization elections for certain tangible properties.

AMORTIZATION
Systematic straight-line cost-recovery procedures for intangible assets.

INTANGIBLE ASSETS In general, the cost of an intangible asset should be recovered over the period of the estimated useful economic life it will have for the taxpayer. For some intangibles, this life may be established by law (e.g., 17 years for patents). For other intangible assets, contractual agreements may specify an economic useful life (trademarks, tradenames, franchises, designs, drawings, and patterns). Thus, most leasehold costs are amortized over the life of the lease. Depreciable improvements made to leased property are amortized over the remaining lease life unless the asset life (actual, ADR, or ACRS) is less than the lease term, in which case the improvement cost can be recovered through depreciation of ACRS procedures (i.e., as a "tangible" asset).

Reg. Sec. 1.167(a)-3 specifically prohibits an amortization deduction for goodwill on the theory that such an intangible asset has an unlimited life. However, a taxpayer may amortize payments for such related items as covenants not to compete, customer lists, and location contracts, if the value of these assets is distinct from goodwill and a useful life can be estimated with reasonable accuracy.[13]

---

[13] Rev. Rul. 74-456, 1974-2 C.B. 65.

FIGURE 8-1

Form **4562**

Department of the Treasury
Internal Revenue Service

Depreciation and Amortization

▶ See separate instructions.
▶ Attach this form to your return.

OMB No. 1545-0172
1984
67

Name(s) as shown on return: Gloria S. Gretna
Identifying number: 583-66-4410

Business or activity to which this form relates: Gretna Garment Company

Part I Depreciation For transportation equipment (e.g. autos), amusement/recreation property, and computer/peripheral equipment placed in service after June 18, 1984, and used 50% or less in a trade or business, the section 179 deduction is not allowed and depreciation must be taken only on line 2(h).

Section A.—Election to expense recovery property (Section 179)

A. Class of property	B. Cost	C. Expense deduction
Automatic Shirt Press	4,930	4,930
1 Total (not more than $5,000). (Partnerships or S corporations—see the Schedule K and Schedule K-1 Instructions of Form 1065 or 1120S)		4,930

Section B.—Depreciation of recovery property

A. Class of property	B. Date placed in service	C. Cost or other basis	D. Recovery period	E. Method of figuring depreciation	F. Deduction
2 Accelerated Cost Recovery System (ACRS) (see instructions): *For assets placed in service* **ONLY** *during taxable year beginning in 1984*					
(a) 3-year property Vans		$14,550*	3	Pre	3,638
(b) 5-year property Presses		$57,000*	5	Pre	8,550
(c) 10-year property					
(d) 15-year public utility property					
(e) 15-year real property—low-income housing		*Adjusted for ITC			
(f) 15-year real property other than low-income housing					
(g) 18-year real property Warehouse	9/1/84	$100,000	18	Pre	3,000
(h) Other recovery property				S/L	
				S/L	
3 ACRS deduction for assets placed in service prior to 1984 (see instructions)					34,300

Section C.—Depreciation of nonrecovery property

4 Property subject to section 168(e)(2) election (see instructions)	
5 Class Life Asset Depreciation Range (CLADR) System Depreciation (see instructions)	
6 Other depreciation (see instructions)	16,400

Section D.—Summary

7 Total (Add deductions on lines 1 through 6). Enter here and on the Depreciation line of your return (Partnerships and S corporations—DO NOT include any amounts entered on line 1.)	70,818

Part II Amortization

A. Description of property	B. Date acquired	C. Cost or other basis	D. Code section	E. Amortization period or percentage	F. Amortization for this year
Total. Enter here and on Other Deductions or Other Expenses line of your return					

See Paperwork Reduction Act Notice on page 1 of the separate instructions.

Form **4562** (1984)

SPECIAL 5-YEAR AMORTIZATIONS For various social and economic reasons, Congress has enacted special 60-month elective amortization procedures for certain tangible and intangible costs. This practice began during World War II, when the costs of certain property necessary for the war effort could be amortized over five years. Today elections are available for such diverse expenditures as rehabilitation of low-income housing [Sec. 167(K)], pollution-control facilities (Sec. 169), and child-care facilities (Sec. 188). Additionally, longer elective amortization periods are available for reforestation expenditures (Sec. 194) and railroad grading and tunnel bores (Sec. 185). Each of these elections is subject to various qualifications.

Congress has also enacted special 60-month elective amortizations for various intangible costs which otherwise have a longer (or unlimited) useful life. These qualifying expenditures include the costs of starting up and organizing a business (discussed later in this chapter).

RESEARCH AND EXPERIMENTATION EXPENDITURES A systematic program of research and experimentation (R&E) has long been a key ingredient in the technological progress of American industry. Realizing the importance of providing tax incentives for such activities, Congress has consistently provided preferential tax treatment for such expenditures. Sec. 174 provides three possible tax treatments to existing trades or businesses for ***R&E expenditures*** which meet the definitional qualifications of Sec. 174 and related regulations.

RESEARCH AND EXPERIMENTATION EXPENDITURES All costs incident to the development (or improvement) of a model, process, formula, or invention.

Reg. Sec. 1.174-2(a) defines research and experimentation expenditures as including ". . . generally all such costs incident to the development of an experimental or pilot model, a plant process, a product, a formula, an invention, or similar property, and the improvement of already existing property of the type mentioned." The use of the term "experimentation," as opposed to "development," was intentional; ordinary testing, inspection, promotions, management surveys, or promotional expenditures do not qualify (these are not "laboratory" expenses). Additionally, any capital expenditures related to land or depreciable property must be recovered under the ordinary cost recovery rules, i.e., depreciation or ACRS. Qualifying expenditures may be incurred by either the taxpayer or by another organization on behalf of the taxpayer.

Under Sec. 174, a taxpayer may elect to deduct R&E expenditures in the year of occurrence, amortize the expenditures over a period of not less than 60 months (beginning with the first month of benefit), or simply capitalize the expenditures (no amortization). The first two of these options (immediate expensing or amortization) reflect a Congressional recognition of the problems of trying to allocate R&E expenditures to individual projects over uncertain useful lives. If the 60-month (or more) amortization method is elected, the amortizable costs include the annual depreciation (ACRS) deduction on tangible R&E properties.

Example 20: P Company, a calendar-year corporation, spent $75,000 in January 19X3 to construct a new research laboratory (15-year ACRS property). P also incurred $30,000 of operating expenses (materials, salaries, utilities, etc.) in connection with research activities at the lab during 19X3. In 19X4 P company first realizes the benefits of the 19X3 research and elects a 60-month recovery for the qualifying expenditures. The maximum amount subject to the 60-month amortization will be $39,000. All $30,000 of lab operating expenditures qualify, but only $9,000 of the lab construction costs qualify. The $9,000 represents the normal first-year ACRS recovery for commercial realty placed in service in the first month of the taxable year (12% ACRS factor). If the lab is not used for R&E activities after 19X3, the remaining unrecovered cost will be subject to the normal ACRS procedures.

Congress provided an additional incentive for R&E activities by adding Sec. 44F in the Economic Recovery Tax Act of 1981. In certain cases, taxpayers can take a 25% credit for qualified R&E expenditures incurred after June 30, 1981 which exceed a base-period amount (based on prior levels of R&E activity). This credit is a bonus for incremental R&E expenditures, since it does not affect the Sec. 174 deduction. Requirements for this credit are discussed in Chapter 14.

BAD DEBT DEDUCTIONS

Sec. 166 allows a deduction for any debt obligation which during the tax year becomes worthless (or in some cases, partially worthless). The deduction allowed is the adjusted basis of the debt. This requirement effectively eliminates the possibility of a bad debt deduction for a cash-basis trade or business. In this case, the taxpayer has a zero basis in such a receivable, since no revenue from the sale has been recognized and any costs associated with the sale were deducted immediately when paid.

The burden of proof concerning worthlessness is on the taxpayer. Bankruptcy of the debtor is considered an indication of at least partial worthlessness of a bad debt. Evidence of legal action against the debtor may also be an indication of worthlessness, although the absence of such action is not necessarily determinative of a final result. For example, statements from legal counsel indicating that legal action would in all probability be a fruitless endeavor may be sufficient evidence of worthlessness.[14]

An additional burden is placed on taxpayers who incur bad debts on loans to related parties. Unless the loan has all of the characteristics of a loan to an independent third party (e.g., reasonable interest, definite repayment schedule, etc.) the IRS may contend that the loan was a gift, with no repayment expected.

BUSINESS VS. NONBUSINESS BAD DEBTS The distinction between business and nonbusiness bad debts is an important one for several reasons. First, a business bad debt can be taken as an ordinary loss deduction (and be part of a net operating loss), while a nonbusiness bad debt can be taken only as a short-term capital loss (possibly subject to the

[14] Reg. Sec. 1.166-2(b).

$3,000 annual limitation).[15] Secondly, no deduction for partial worthlessness is allowed on nonbusiness bad debts; the debtor must wait until a final determination as to the status of the debt is made.

Example 21: R, who owes S $15,000, went through bankruptcy proceedings in 19X6. At that time it was estimated that creditors could expect to receive only 20¢ on the dollar. In 19X7 a final settlement of 15¢ on the dollar was made to each creditor. If the debt is a business bad debt to S, she may deduct $12,000 ($15,000 × .80) in 19X6 and $750 ($15,000 × .05) in 19X7 as ordinary expense deductions. However, if the debt is a nonbusiness bad debt to S, she must wait until the final settlement in 19X7 to deduct the $12,750. Furthermore, if S has no capital gains in 19X7, the deduction for that year will be limited to a maximum $3,000 offset against noncapital-gains income with a carryover of the unused loss to the following year.

The business or nonbusiness determination is made at the time the debt was created. Thus, a taxpayer who sells his or her business and retains the receivables may obtain an ordinary deduction for future bad debts even though he or she is no longer in the trade or business. Obviously, a taxpayer in the trade or business of lending money is normally entitled to ordinary deductions. Additionally, loans made by a corporation are always assumed to be related to a trade or business purpose. However, a loan from a shareholder to a corporation is generally considered to be a nonbusiness bad debt, unless the taxpayer can show a primary business motive (e.g., protecting a shareholder-employee's salary).[16] Thus being an investor in and of itself does not constitute a trade or business. Sec. 166(f) specifies that losses of endorsers or guarantors of loans are deductible as ordinary losses only if related to the guarantor's trade or business (i.e., endorsements and guarantees are treated as direct loans).

TAX ACCOUNTING FOR BAD DEBTS Sec. 166 permits a taxpayer to deduct a debt in the year it becomes worthless (the "direct write-off" method) or to deduct a reasonable addition to a reserve for bad debts (the "reserve" method). The use of the direct write-off method permits a taxpayer to deduct the adjusted basis of a debt at the time that the debt is judged to be worthless. Deductions for partial worthlessness are also available under the direct write-off method; however, the taxpayer has the burden of substantiating the amount of worthlessness to the IRS.

Under the reserve method, a taxpayer does not reduce taxable income directly for specifically identified bad debts; rather, these accounts are charged against a reserve allowance. The annual deduction for bad debts is determined by computing a "reasonable addition" to the reserve. This method is one of the few instances in the Code where a taxpayer is permitted to use estimates of expenses in calculating tax liability.

---

[15] Sec. 167(d)(1)(B).

[16] *U.S. v. Generes*, 92 S.Ct. 827 (1972).

The subjective nature of the "reasonable addition" to a reserve account causes practical administrative problems for the IRS. The Regulations offer only general guidelines in making this determination:

> What constitutes a reasonable addition to a reserve for bad debts shall be determined in the light of facts existing at the close of the taxable year of the proposed addition. The reasonableness of the addition will vary as between classes of business and with conditions of business prosperity. It will depend primarily upon the total amount of debts outstanding as of the close of the taxable year, including those arising currently as well as those arising in prior taxable years, and the total amount of the existing reserve.[17]

Normally the addition to the reserve is based on the prior collection history of the business. Since the Regulations specify a relationship with the "total amount of debts outstanding," a common procedure used by taxpayers and the IRS is the development of an "experience ratio" representing the relationship between net bad debts written off (write-offs less recoveries) and average accounts receivable. Once determined, this percentage is multiplied by the ending accounts receivable balance to determine an estimate of the appropriate year-end reserve balance (which indirectly determines the amount of the permitted addition to the reserve, e.g., the tax deduction). The IRS currently uses a court-approved formula for determining a reasonable experience ratio, based on the ratio of the average bad debts and accounts receivable for the current year and the past five years. (See *Black Motor Co., Inc. v. Commissioner*, 125 F2d 977 (CA-6, 1942).)

Example 22: R uses the reserve method in determining a tax deduction for bad debts. R's accounting records disclose the following:

YEAR	NET BAD DEBT WRITEOFFS*	YEAR-END ACCOUNTS RECEIVABLE
19X1	$ 18,600	$ 440,000
19X2	20,200	460,000
19X3	21,500	520,000
19X4	24,800	430,000
19X5	27,500	360,000
19X6	26,000	310,000
Total	$138,600	$2,520,000
Average	$ 23,100	$ 420,000

*Total Bad Debts Written Off Less Recoveries

At the end of 19X6, R's reserve account was as follows:

RESERVE FOR BAD DEBTS

19X6 Write-offs	$28,340	1/1/X6 Balance	$28,800
		19X6 Recoveries	2,340

[17] Reg. Sec. 1.166-4(b)(1).

Thus, the year-end reserve balance before adjustment is a credit of $2,800 ($28,800 + 2,340 − 28,340). R's average bad debt experience ratio for the past five years and the current year is 5.5% ($23,100 ÷ 420,000); therefore, the required ending 19X6 balance in the reserve account to reflect this past experience would be $17,050 ($310,000 × .055). Since the reserve balance before adjustment is a $2,800 credit, R will increase the reserve account by $14,250 ($17,050 − 2,800), which represents the 19X6 bad debts deduction. Future write-offs of realized bad debts will be against the reserve, rather than income.

BACKGROUND

The reserve method for accounting for bad debts was first approved by Congress in the Revenue Act of 1921, Sec. 214(a)(7). Interestingly, the procedure was justified as ". . . a method of providing for bad debts much less subject to abuse than the method of deducting bad debts required by the present law."* Obviously, this statement did not anticipate the subsequent taxpayer-IRS disputes over what constitutes a "reasonable addition" to the reserve.

The endorsement of such a subjective reporting procedure did little to enhance an easy and consistent administration of the tax laws by the IRS. The IRS would obviously prefer a mechanical computation of a reasonable addition, since such a method would be more objective and thus easier to audit. In the Black Motor Co.† case of 1942, the Sixth Circuit Court of Appeals approved the 6-year experience ratio calculation described in Example 22. This calculation, referred to as the "Black Motor Company formula," has generally been applied by the IRS to test the "reasonableness" of bad debt deductions. Although occasionally taxpayers have been able to deduct more than the formula allows (and in some cases, the IRS has allowed *less* than the formula‡), the formula approach has generally been approved by the Courts, including the Supreme Court:

> Common sense suggests that a firm's recent credit experience offers a reasonable index of the credit problems it may suffer currently. And the formula possesses the not inconsiderable advantage of enhancing certainty and predictability in an area peculiarly susceptible of taxpayer abuse. In any event, after its 40 years of universal acceptance, we are not inclined to disturb the Black Motor Company formula now.§

Some critics of the formula maintain that in some cases the 6-year computation of an experience ratio does not truly reflect a company's most recent bad-debt history. Reference is frequently made to the statement in Reg. Sec. 1.166-4(b) that ". . . reasonableness will vary as between classes of business and with conditions of busi-

Continued

BACKGROUND

ness prosperity." For example, the computed experience ratio in Example 22 was 5.5%; however, if only the last 3 years were used, the ratio would be 7.1% ($78,300 ÷ $1,100,000). Thus, the formula may not reflect rapidly deteriorating business conditions, especially when early years have larger receivable balances. It remains to be seen how taxpayers, the IRS, and the courts will interpret the above reference by the Supreme Court to a firm's "recent credit experience."

* *Report of the Ways and Means Committee*, 67th Congress, 1st Session, H Report 350, p. 11.

† *Black Motor Co., Inc. v. Commissioner*, 125 F 2d 977 (CA-6, 1942).

‡ Rev. Rul. 76-362, 1976-2, C.B. 45 stated that ". . . whatever formula may have been applied, the taxpayer bears the burden of showing that the proposed adjustment constitutes an abuse of discretion." Thus, the IRS maintained the flexibility of allowing more or less than the formula addition.

§ *Thor Power Tool v. Commissioner*, 99 S. Ct. 773 (1979).

A taxpayer may elect either the reserve method or the direct write-off method on the first tax return filed. Of course, such a choice is subject to later IRS scrutiny. An election to use the reserve method is binding in future years unless the taxpayer receives permission from the Commissioner to change methods. In addition, Rev. Proc. 70-27[18] requires specific computations for taxpayers switching from the direct write-off method to the reserve method. In general, the initial reserve balance is determined in a manner similar to Example 22, except that the experience ratio is based on the five prior years. Additionally, this reserve balance must be deducted ratably over ten years (although specific bad debts identified in the year of change are deductible in that initial year of electing the reserve method).

The treatment of bad debt recoveries depends on the taxpayer's method of reporting bad debts. Under the specific charge-off method, recoveries are included in income in the year received, but only to the extent that the original deduction reduced tax liability in the earlier years (after considering any net operating loss or capital loss carryback or carryover effects caused by the original deduction). This is an application of the tax-benefit rule discussed earlier. Under the reserve method, recoveries are credits against the reserve and not included in income. Indirectly, this is similar to an increase in income, in that future "reasonable additions" to the reserve are correspondingly decreased.

NET OPERATING LOSS DEDUCTIONS

Sec. 165(a) authorizes a deduction for any loss not compensated by insurance or other means. This provision assumes that all losses incurred by a corporation are trade or business losses. However, Code Sec. 165(c) lim-

[18] Rev. Proc. 70-27, 1970-2 C.B. 509.

its the deduction for individuals to those losses (*a*) incurred in a trade or business, (*b*) incurred in a transaction entered into for profit, or (*c*) resulting from a casualty or theft. Note that this provision follows the consistent pattern delineated by Code Sections 162 (trade or business expenses), 212 (income-producing activity expenses), and 262 (personal expenses). The only purely personal loss deductions available to individuals are casualty and theft losses. The rules for deducting both business and personal casualty and theft losses are discussed in Chapter 9.

Sec. 165 is the general authority for deducting all losses. In this respect, a taxpayer is permitted to offset a net business loss from one activity against income from other activities, as long as the loss activity was carried on for a profit. In effect, the loss is justified by qualifying the expenses under either Sec. 162 or Code Sec. 212. Sec. 172 provides additional relief to the taxpayer by allowing a deduction in other years for any portion of the net business loss not used to reduce tax liability in the year of occurrence.

The ***net operating loss*** provisions of Sec. 172 were enacted by Congress to mitigate the effect of the annual reporting requirement on businesses which have negative incomes. If businesses were not permitted to deduct these excess expenses, the income tax could turn into a tax on capital. Thus the net operating loss provisions provide an averaging procedure to equate the effective tax liabilities of highly cyclical businesses with those of stable businesses. This is accomplished by allowing carryovers of the excess losses as deductions in other tax years. For an individual taxpayer, the net operating loss deduction is a deduction for determining adjusted gross income (AGI) in the carryover year.

NET OPERATING LOSS
The taxable loss reported per the return as adjusted to an economic business loss by adding back certain personal and artificial deductions.

The net operating loss computations can be somewhat complex for an individual, since the individual tax computation includes a mixture of both business and personal incomes and expenses. There are three distinct steps in the net operating loss procedure: (*a*) determining the economic net operating loss; (*b*) applying the net operating loss as a deduction in the appropriate tax year; and (*c*) determining if any net operating loss deduction remains available for carryforward to the next tax year. Each step is discussed in detail in the following sections. To illustrate each of these steps, the hypothetical tax return data of taxpayers Harold and Maude Anderson displayed in Table 8-6 will be used. This illustration includes data for the loss year and the first carryback year. For simplicity, 1984 zero-bracket and exemption amounts are used.

DETERMINING THE NET OPERATING LOSS

The purpose of Sec. 172 is to provide tax relief when a taxpayer's *business* expenses and losses exceed *business* incomes and gains. (An exception for casualty losses is described below.) Therefore, the net operating loss of a taxpayer is usually not the net loss figure shown on the tax return. Sec. 172(d) specifies several modifications necessary to convert a negative taxable income figure into a net operating loss. These modifications are designed to convert the taxable loss into a more realistic measure of economic loss. The following items are not deductible in determining a net operating loss and should be *added back* to the taxable loss shown on the return:[19]

1. Any net operating loss deduction from another year.
2. Any net long-term capital-gains deduction.
3. Any net capital-loss deduction. In applying this adjustment, nonbusiness capital losses in excess of nonbusiness capital gains are not deductible.
4. Any personal-exemption deductions.
5. An excess of nonbusiness expenses (other than casualties) over nonbusiness income. For these purposes, a salary is business income.
6. Any deduction for contributions to a self-employed (H-R 10/Keogh) retirement plan.

A logical reason exists for each of these adjustments. For example, adjustments (2) and (3) represent artificial (noncash-flow) deductions which do not necessarily affect a taxpayer's economic income. Also, adjustments (4), (5), and (6) are personal deductions which should not be part of a business loss. Finally, adjustment (1) is made so that the net operating loss of each year stands alone (not making this adjustment would duplicate the loss and would also start a fresh carryforward period for the old loss).

Applying these adjustment rules to the data for the Andersons in Table 8-6 converts a $10,650 tax loss to a $7,725 net operating loss, based on the following computations:

Taxable income (loss) per return		$(10,650)
Add-back adjustments:		
1. Any NOL deduction from another year	0	
2. Any L/T capital-gain deduction (875 × .60)	525	
3. Any capital loss reducing income	0	
4. Any personal exemption deductions	2,000	
5. Any excess non-business deductions	400*	
6. Any contributions to HR-10 (Keogh) Plan	0	
Total add-back adjustments		2,925
		$ (7,725)

*$900 − ($300 + $200) = $400

Note particularly the adjustment for the excess of excess itemized deductions ($900) over nonbusiness income ($300 dividends and $200 interest). Only excess itemized deductions are used in this adjustment, since only that amount was deducted in determining the original $10,650 taxable loss. In this respect the zero-bracket amount can be a complicating factor. For example, if the Andersons' excess itemized deductions were only $100, a *negative* adjustment of $400 ($100 − $500) must be made to *increase* the net operating loss! The purpose of this adjustment is to allow personal deductions only to the extent of personal income. However,

[19]Sec. 172(d).

TABLE 8-6
Sample Problem Net Operating Loss—Individuals

Harold and Maude Anderson (married, no children) owned and operated an appliance store in the years 19X0 through 19X3. Their original tax returns for 19X0 and 19X3 disclose the following:

		19X0		19X3
Net profit (loss) from business		$6,000		$(8,600)
Dividend income (after exclusion)		400		300
Interest income		700		200
Net LT capital gain (after 60% ded.)*		400		350
Adjusted gross income		$7,500		$(7,750)
Less excess itemized deductions:				
Taxes	$1,100		$3,070	
Interest	1,050		1,000	
Contributions	1,350		0	
Medical expenses	800		230	
Less 3% of AGI	(225)		(0)	
Total itemized deductions	4,075		4,300	
Less zero-bracket amount	(3,400)		(3,400)	
Excess itemized deductions		(675)		(900)
Less personal exemptions		(2,000)		(2,000)
Taxable income		$4,825		$(10,650)
Net tax liability due (Schedule Y for 1981)		$ 200		$ 0

*All capital gains and losses were business gains and losses.

the Andersons' *total* personal deductions were $3,500, although only $100 is subtracted in determining taxable income (because of the $3,400 zero-bracket amount incorporated in the Tax Rate Schedules). The $400 negative adjustment would be made because total nonbusiness deductions do not actually exceed total nonbusiness income.

Finally, it is important to note that a casualty or theft loss can be part of a net operating loss. This is accomplished by omitting casualties and thefts from the total nonbusiness expenses used in making adjustment (5). This provision was incorporated into the tax law in 1951[20] to provide additional tax relief (through loss carryovers) for taxpayers who suffer large uninsured losses in a tax year. Without this provision, the only relief available would be to reduce the loss year's tax liability to zero. Note that a taxpayer whose only income is a salary may still be able to benefit from the net operating loss provisions if he or she has a large uninsured casualty loss during the year.

[20] *Revenue Act of 1951*, Sec. 344(a), amending Sec. 122(d)(5).

APPLYING THE NET OPERATING LOSS DEDUCTION

Once the net operating loss is determined, the next step is to apply the deduction (*for* AGI) against the gross income of the appropriate carryback or carryforward tax year. For net operating losses incurred after 1975 the loss is first carried back to the third prior taxable year and can be taken as a deduction (in chronological order) for the three years preceding the loss year and up to 15 years following the loss year.[21] Any loss not deducted after the 15 years carryforward is permanently lost. However, a special provision [Sec. 172(b)(3)(C)] allows a taxpayer to forgo the 3-year carryback and simply carry the loss forward for 15 years. This may be beneficial in cases where the taxpayer expects his or her marginal tax rate to be significantly higher in the carryforward years than the carryback years, or the carryback adversely affects credits of the earlier years. (Of course, a taxpayer will have to wait until the tax returns of the future years are filed before the benefits are received. See Planning Workshop, page 8/47.)

FORM 1040X

FORM 1045

If the taxpayer elects to carry the loss back to the third year, an amended return (Form 1040X) or a special refund claim form (Form 1045) must be filed, requesting a refund of taxes previously paid. If the loss is carried back, it is mandatory that the loss be applied against the third prior year first.

Continuing the example of Table 8-6, the tax liability for 19X0 would be recomputed with one additional deduction *for* AGI—the net operating loss deduction. This computation completely eliminates the 19X0 tax liability:

Net profit (business)		$ 6,000
Dividend income (after exclusion)		400
Interest income		700
Net LT capital gain (after 60% deduction)		400
Net operating loss deduction		(7,725)
Recomputed adjusted gross income		$ (225)
Less excess itemized deductions:		
Taxes	1,100	
Interest	1,050	
Contributions	1,350	
Medical expenses	800	
Less 3% of recomputed AGI	(0)	
Total itemized deductions	4,300	
Less zero-bracket amount	(3,400)	
Excess itemized deductions		(900)
Less personal exemptions		(2,000)
"Recomputed" taxable income		(3,125)
Tax originally paid in 19X0		200
Tax due on recomputed income		0
Refund due		$ 200

[21] Sec. 172(b)(1).

Note that a negative AGI results, which eliminates the 3% floor (assumed applicable in 19X0) on the medical expense deduction (the entire $800 of medical expenses is deducted). Similar adjustments may be necessary for casualty losses exceeding 10% of AGI for carryover years after 1982. However, the charitable deduction, normally limited to a percentage of adjusted gross income, is *not* retroactively reduced.[22] In this respect, a taxpayer is not retroactively penalized for a charitable deduction, although net operating loss deductions will affect the charitable limits in the 15 carryforward years.

The loss carryback to 19X0 results in a revised taxable income figure, a $3,125 loss. Therefore, no tax is due on the 19X0 return, and a claim for refund will be filed for the $200 tax originally paid.

DETERMINING THE REMAINING LOSS CARRYOVER

The final step in the net operating loss procedure is to determine if any of the net operating loss is available to carry forward to future years (after eliminating the tax liability of the first carryover year). To determine any available carryover, the taxable income of the first carryback year must be modified in a manner similar to those adjustments made in determining the net operating loss of the loss year. It should be noted, however, that these modifications have nothing to do with the revised tax liability for the first carryback year; the adjustments are made solely for purposes of determining how much (if any) of the net operating loss deduction carried back to the first carryover year is available for deduction in the second carryover year.

The modifications required in the taxable income of the carryover year are not as demanding as those required in the loss year. Specifically, adjustments are made only for (*a*) any net long-term capital-gains deduction, (*b*) any net capital-loss deduction, and (*c*) any personal-exemption deduction.[23] Since no adjustment is made for any excess of nonbusiness income over nonbusiness expenses, it is not necessary to adjust for any excess of nonbusiness capital losses over nonbusiness capital gains. However, since either the adjustment for the long-term capital-gains deduction or the adjustment for net capital losses would have increased the "modified" AGI for the carryover year, any medical-expense deduction (or casualty-loss deduction for years after 1982) must be correspondingly reduced to reflect the modified AGI.

Referring once again to the facts of Table 8-6, the Andersons' net operating loss carryover to 19X1 is computed as follows:

[22] Reg. Sec. 1.172-5(a)(3)(ii).

[23] Sec. 172(b)(2).

Taxable income as originally reported (19X0)		$ 4,825
Add-back adjustments:		
1. Any LT capital-gain deduction (1,000 × .60)	600	
2. Any capital loss reducing income	0	
3. Any personal exemption deductions	2,000	
Medical-expense adjustment (600 × .03)	18	
Total add-back adjustments		2,618
"Modified" (original) taxable income		7,443
NOL available to use in 19X0		(7,725)
Subtotal		(282)
Add zero-bracket amount		(3,400)
NOL carryover to 19X1		$(3,682)

Note particularly the adjustment for the zero-bracket amount. Once again this seemingly simple concept complicates other tax calculations. Since no adjustment is required in the carryover year for the excess of nonbusiness deductions over nonbusiness income, the taxpayer should be given credit for the *total* itemized deductions of 19X0, rather than just those that exceeded the zero-bracket amount (as originally reported). Stated differently, the $3,400 zero-bracket amount is incorporated into the tax tables and rate schedules, and the taxpayer should not be required to reduce a net operating loss carryover for an amount included in reported income which is never subject to tax.

In summary, of the total net operating loss of $7,725 carried back to 19X0, $3,682 remains available to be taken as a deduction in 19X1. The taxpayer will repeat this procedure in 19X1, and any unused loss can be applied in 19X2, and then possibly to the years 19X4–19Y8 (15 carryforward years) until any remaining carryovers are utilized. Sec. 6511(d) permits a refund claim to be filed up to three years after the due date (including extensions) for filing the return following the end of the year in which the loss was incurred.

MISCELLANEOUS BUSINESS EXPENSES

The discussion thus far has centered on several major business expense and loss deductions permitted under specific Code sections other than Sec. 162. Obviously, a variety of other expenditures qualify under the general requirements of Sec. 162. Several expenses which involve special consideration are discussed in the following sections.

RETIREMENT PLAN PAYMENTS

In defining trade or business expenses, Sec. 162(a) allows a deduction for ". . . a reasonable allowance for salaries or other compensation for personal services actually rendered." This includes current or deferred compensation, although Sec. 404 places additional restrictions on the deductibility of deferred compensation.

Over the years Congress has offered tax incentives to encourage employers, employees, and self-employed individuals to participate in private retirement plans. Although these plans may take many different forms, they all have three major tax advantages: (*a*) immediate deductions for contributions to a plan, (*b*) tax-free income on contributions through working years, and (*c*) deferral of income tax until the recipient receives payments from the retirement fund. These tax advantages are reserved for the so-called "qualified plans." Plans failing to meet stipulated requirements receive no special tax treatment.

QUALIFIED CORPORATE PLANS In order to receive the special qualified tax treatment, a corporation's retirement plan must meet the various requirements specified in Code Sec. 401(a). These rules are based on the Employee Retirement Income Security Act (ERISA), passed in 1974 to regulate private pension systems. Among the most important of these requirements are the following:

1. The plan must be for the exclusive benefit of the employees (or their beneficiaries).
2. The plan must not discriminate in favor of certain classes of employees (such as officers or shareholders). This requirement can be met if 70% or more of the employees participate in the plan (or 70% of the employees are eligible, and 80% of these employees participate).
3. The plan must provide a reasonable vesting schedule under Sec. 416. This requirement can be met by one of three schedules providing nonforfeitable rights to (*a*) 100% of the benefits for employees with at least ten years service; or (*b*) 25% of the benefits for five years of service, with gradual increases to 100% after 15 years of service; or (*c*) 50% of the benefits for employees with a minimum of five years service whose sum of age and years service equals 45, with gradual increases to 100% for ten years of service and a sum of 55. (This is commonly referred to as the ***Rule of 45***.)
4. Employees must be allowed to participate at age 25 with one year of service; however, a 3-year service period can be required when 100% immediate vesting is possible.

RULE OF 45 A reasonable vesting schedule based on the sum of an employee's age and years of service; an employee's benefits must be at least 50% vested when this sum is 45 (and the employee has at least 5 years of service).

Assuming that these and other requirements are met, a corporate employer may deduct limited amounts of contributions to such plans on behalf of the employees. The employee may or may not contribute to the plan. These contributions are generally made to a trust organization which manages the funds, although the corporation may choose to purchase the annuity coverage from outside agencies such as insurance companies. Regardless of the method chosen, the corporate deduction depends on the type of retirement plan.

In discussing these retirement plans it is important to note the distinction between the maximum tax *deduction* and maximum allowable *con-*

tribution; these two amounts are not necessarily the same (in fact, in some cases they are quite different). The maximum deduction is either expressed actuarially (pension plans) or as a percentage of compensation (other plans). On the other hand, the maximum contribution is a stated amount which cannot be exceeded in any one year on behalf of any employee. This amount may be larger than the deduction, which in turn involves carryover amounts for possible later deduction. Table 8-7 summarizes these differences for the various types of qualified retirement plans discussed in the following sections.

PENSION PLANS. A pension plan is usually referred to as a defined benefit plan in that the plan provides for specific dollar payments to employees after retirement. In general, Sec. 404(a)(1) permits a corporation to deduct the amount necessary to fund the ultimate employee benefits. These amounts must be determined actuarially, since estimates of life expectancies and rates of return for invested funds must be used. Since benefits are normally based on the employee's length of service, it may also be necessary for the corporation to fund credits for past service. Sec. 404(a)(1)(A) allows a deduction to amortize these past service costs over a period of not less than ten years. Thus, the total deduction permitted in any tax year is the amount necessary to fund normal future costs plus up

TABLE 8-7
Maximum Contribution and Deduction Amounts for Contributions to Qualified Retirement Plans

FOR THIS TYPE OF QUALIFIED RETIREMENT PLAN	THE MAXIMUM AMOUNT THAT CAN BE CONTRIBUTED ON THE BEHALF OF ANY ONE EMPLOYEE IS:	BUT THE MAXIMUM AMOUNT DEDUCTIBLE BY THE EMPLOYER IS LIMITED TO:
Pension plans	The lesser of 100% of the employee's compensation or the present amount necessary to fund an annual retirement benefit of $90,000	An actuarial calculation of the amount necessary to fund the stated contract benefit (plus up to 10% of past service costs)
Profit-sharing, stock-bonus, and money-purchase plans	The lesser of $30,000 or 25% of the employee's compensation	15% of total annual aggregate compensation of employees
More than one plan existing at one time	Individual limits (above)	25% of total employee compensation

to 10% of past service costs. Amounts contributed in excess of this amount may be carried forward and deducted in future years (if contributions for that year are less than the maximum).

> **Example 23:** U Corporation's normal cost for funding retirement benefits in the current year is $13,300, and the amount necessary to fund service costs before the adoption of the plan is estimated to be $146,000. U's maximum deduction for the current year is $27,900 ($13,300 + ($146,000 × .10)).

Sec. 415(b) limits the maximum annual *contribution* benefit per employee (regardless of deduction limit) which may be used in the actuarial calculations to determine the maximum deduction. This annual maximum is currently the lesser of $90,000 or 100% of the employee's annual compensation for defined benefit plans. This limitation is to remain constant until 1988, when certain cost of living adjustments may be permitted.[24]

PROFIT-SHARING, STOCK-BONUS, AND MONEY-PURCHASE PLANS. Profit-sharing and money-purchase pension plans are referred to as "defined-contribution plans," in that the employer agrees to a predetermined contribution, such as a percentage of company income or a percentage of an employee's compensation. Similarly, in a stock-bonus plan, the contributions are invested in the company's stock, and this is used later to pay accrued benefits. For all three plans, the maximum *contribution* to an employee's account (regardless of deduction limit) cannot exceed the lesser or $30,000[25] or 25% of total compensation.

An employer is permitted to deduct up to 15% of the aggregate earned compensation of employees covered under a profit-sharing, money-purchase, or stock-bonus plan—Sec. 404(a)(3). Contributions in excess of the 15% limit may be carried over to future years. Additionally, if the contributions in any year are *less* than the 15% limit, a "credit carryover" for the deficiency is allowed, which increases the next year's 15% limit dollar for dollar. However, any "credit carryover" used in a particular year cannot exceed 10% of that year's total compensation. In other words, the total deduction in any one year cannot exceed 25% of total compensation.

> **Example 24:** For the years 19X0–19X4, X Corporation had an annual payroll of $400,000. Contributions to a qualified profit-sharing plan during those years were: $69,000 (19X1), $50,000 (19X2), $40,000 (19X3), and $86,000 (19X4). X's deduction, contribution carryover, and credit carryover for each year would be as follows:

---

[24] Prior to 1983, annual cost-of-living adjustments were made to the dollar maximum. This had resulted in a $136,475 maximum limit for 1982. As part of the budget-cutting measures of the *Tax Equity and Fiscal Responsibility Act of 1982*, Congress reduced this maximum to $90,000 and froze cost-of-living adjustments until 1986. This freeze was extended to 1988 by the Tax Reform Act of 1984.

[25] This amount will also be subject to cost-of-living adjustments beginning in 1988. Under prior law, the adjusted maximum had reached $45,475 for 1982.

YEAR	ACTUAL CONTRI-BUTIONS	DEDUCTION	CONTRI-BUTION CARRYOVER	CREDIT CARRY-OVER
a) 19X1	$69,000	$60,000	$9,000	—
b) 19X2	50,000	59,000	—	$ 1,000
c) 19X3	40,000	40,000	—	$21,000
d) 19X4	86,000	81,000	$5,000	—

(a) Limited to 15% of total compensation ($400,000).
(b) $50,000 current contribution plus a $9,000 contribution carryover from 19X2. (Total deduction is less than the $60,000 maximum, so a $1,000 *credit* carryover of $1,000 is allowed.)
(c) Limited to actual contribution, which is $20,000 less than the $60,000 maximum. Thus, the total credit carryover to 19X4 is $21,000.
(d) Limited to $60,000 plus the $21,000 credit carryover.

COMBINATION PLANS. Frequently a company will offer a combination of pension, profit-sharing, or stock-bonus plans to its employees. When two or more retirement plans exist, Sec. 404(a)(7) limits the employer *deduction* to 25% of total compensation paid.

TOP-HEAVY PLANS. As part of the Tax Equity and Fiscal Responsibility Act of 1982, Congress added Sec. 416, which establishes certain restrictions for "top-heavy plans." A top-heavy retirement plan (or group of plans) is one that provides more than 60% of its aggregate accumulated benefits (or account balances) to key employees. Sec. 416(i)(1) defines a key employee as any employee (including beneficiaries and self-employed individuals) who at any time during the four preceding plan years is (or was) an officer, an employee who owns directly or indirectly one of the ten largest interests in the employer, a more-than-5% owner, or a more-than-1% owner who earns more than $150,000 a year. This definition was amended by Congress in 1984 to exclude any officer whose annual compensation is no more than 150% of the defined contribution limits for plans, i.e., $45,000 for 1984.

In general, Sec. 416 requires a top-heavy plan to use accelerated vesting schedules, imposes a compensation ceiling of $200,000 (adjustable by cost of living allowances after 1987) per employee for purposes of computing contributions or benefits, and provides for a minimum level of contributions and benefits for non-key employees. Obviously, the top-heavy requirements will have their largest impact on small and/or closely-held businesses. For small employers caught by the top-heavy net, the costs of complying with such restrictions could be significant.

SEC. 401(K) PLANS. A company that provides a qualified profit-sharing or stock bonus plan may also offer a qualified cash or deferred compensation arrangement to its employees. Sec. 401(k) provides that employer contributions to such a plan will not be taxable to the employee, even though he or she has the option of receiving cash (which, of course, would be taxable). Earnings on the contributions to the plan, including any employer contributions, are also deferred. The plan may also be cast in the form of a salary reduction plan, where employees elect either to reduce present compensation or forgo an increase in compensation. Finally, a 401(k) plan is the only type of deferred compensation that may be offered as part of a Sec. 125 "cafeteria plan" (discussed in Chapter 5), where an employee can choose from a variety of taxable and nontaxable fringe benefits.

SELF-EMPLOYED RETIREMENT PLANS In 1962 Congress amended Sec. 404(e) to permit self-employed individuals to establish retirement plans for their own benefit and obtain some of the advantages of qualified retirement plans. These plans are referred to as "Keogh" or "HR-10" plans. Such plans are available only to individuals who participate in active trades or businesses.

Prior to 1983 self-employed plans were subject to rules which were generally more restrictive than the corporate rules for qualified retirement plans. For example, the plan had to provide full vesting for all employees with at least three years of service, and annual deductions on behalf of the owner-employee were deductions *for* adjusted gross income and were limited to the lesser of 15% of earned income or $15,000.

In the *Tax Equity and Fiscal Responsibility Act of 1982*, Congress responded to criticism of the preferential corporate treatment by making self-employed plans subject to the same Sec. 415 limits as corporate retirement plans. Thus the rules for defined benefit and defined contribution plans now apply equally to incorporated and unincorporated businesses. For these purposes, employees will now include the self-employed person(s).

Example 25: Q owns a sole proprietorship service business and covers herself and her 20 employees with a money-purchase (defined contribution) pension plan. Her maximum deduction for contributions in any one year is limited to 15% of total compensation (including her own). Additionally, the annual addition on behalf of any employee (including Q) cannot exceed the lesser of $30,000 or 25% of total compensation. Thus the limits on tax deductions and dollar contributions are the same as corporate plans.

INDIVIDUAL RETIREMENT ACCOUNTS Sec. 404(e) permits any individual to establish his or her own individual retirement account (IRA), with deductible contributions of 100% of compensation up to a maximum of $2,000 annually. The three advantages of a qualified retirement plan apply to IRAs: current deductions for contributions, tax-free accumulation of income on trusteed contributions until retirement, and deferral of tax liability until withdrawal at retirement. Any one who receives earned compensation during the year may contribute to an IRA, even though he or she is covered by another retirement plan. Earned compensation includes wages, tips, commissions, services income, and income from active trades or businesses. For tax years beginning after 1984, taxable alimony received by a divorced spouse will also qualify as compensation

(Sec. 219(f)(1)). Additionally, self-employed individuals may choose to contribute up to the maximum IRA limits as an addition to an existing self-employed (HR-10) plan (as opposed to using a separate IRA). An IRA may also be combined with a "simplified employee pension plan" (See BACKGROUND, below).

The maximum contribution deduction (100% of compensation up to $2,000 annually) is taken as a deduction *for* adjusted gross income on the individual's tax return. Sec. 219(a) permits a married couple to establish a special "spousal IRA" when only one spouse has earned income. (Of course, if both spouses have earned income, each can establish a separate IRA). The maximum deduction for contributions to such an account is limited to 100% of the working spouse's compensation, up to a maximum of $2,250. The contribution can be divided in any manner between the two spouses, subject to the constraint that no more than $2,000 can be allocated to the working spouse's account.

Example 26: S received $26,000 salary during 1982, and S's spouse T received $4,200 of dividend income and $6,300 of interest income in 1982. T may not establish an IRA by himself, since he had no earned income. S may establish a separate IRA and contribute up to $2,000 (deductible *for* adjusted gross income). Optionally, S may establish a spousal IRA and contribute up to $2,250, although only $2,000 may be allocated to her accumulation.

FORM 5329

Any contributions to an IRA which exceed the maximum annual limitation are subject to a special 6% annual (nondeductible) excise tax until this excess is either withdrawn from the account or is qualified under the maximum limit of a future year. Additionally, any withdrawals by a taxpayer before he or she reaches age 59½ are subject to a nondeductible 10% penalty tax (as well as being includable in income in the year withdrawn).

BACKGROUND

In the middle 1970s, some small businesses that initially established qualified corporate plans later abandoned them because of the complexities inherent in meeting the requirements. In 1978 Congress responded somewhat to this problem by establishing a new "simplified employee pension plan" (SEP).

The SEP was designed to incorporate some of the advantages of qualified corporate plans, HR-10 plans, and IRAs. For years prior to 1983, Sec. 408(j) permitted employers to contribute and deduct up to 15% of each qualifying employee's compensation, limited to $15,000 (the maximum permitted for HR-10 plans). Although such employer payments must be included in the employee's gross in-

Continued

BACKGROUND

come, the employee was permitted a deduction *for* adjusted gross income to offset this inclusion (up to the 15%, $15,000 limit). Additionally, an employee could make contributions to the plan if the employer failed to contribute the maximum (up to the IRA limits). The plan had to cover all employees age 25 or older with three years of service.

As mentioned earlier, the *Tax Equity and Fiscal Responsibility Act of 1982* extended the basic corporate qualified plan rules to HR-10 plans. This act extends the same qualified requirements of Sec. 415 to SEP plans. Although this increases the contribution limit to the lesser of $30,000 or 25% of compensation (the corporate limit on defined contribution plans), the new provisions also revive some of the complexities that the original SEP provisions were designed to overcome in the first place.

MISCELLANEOUS CONSIDERATIONS The preceding discussion highlights the basic deduction rules for contributions to qualified corporate plans, HR-10 plans, and IRA plans. Obviously, each set of provisions is subject to extensive sets of requirements and limitations, most of which are beyond the scope of an introductory text. However, two provisions are worthy of special consideration.

First, it should be noted that for each type of retirement plan, the taxpayer may deduct contributions up until the due date of the tax return. This special grace period provides the advantage of "hindsight" to the taxpayer, since the exact amount of compensation or earned income is known at that time. Secondly, the advantages of the special 10-year averaging for lump-sum distributions (discussed in Chapter 13) are available only for qualified corporate or HR-10 distributions; IRA distributions do not qualify (although regular income averaging may be a possibility).

COMPENSATION

Sec. 162(a) provides a deduction for ". . . a reasonable allowance for salaries or other compensation . . .". As a practical matter, the reasonableness of compensation issue arises most frequently when a relationship exists between the employer and the employee. The most common example is the case of an officer-shareholder in a closely-held corporation. This relationship receives particular IRS scrutiny because of the possibility of disguising nondeductible dividend payments as deductible salary expenses. This issue has been a constant source of friction between taxpayers and the IRS. Factors to be considered in judging the reasonableness of compensation include amounts paid by other employers in similar circumstances, the complexity of the job, the entrepreneurial skills of the employee, and the relationship of the employee's salary to previous years and to other employees.

BACKGROUND

Sec. 280G, enacted by Congress as part of the Tax Reform Act of 1984, represents an interesting variation of the "reasonableness" concept for compensation. This new provision limits the deduction for any excess compensation paid or incurred pursuant to a "golden parachute contract." A golden parachute contract is basically an employment contract which provides for unusually high payments to an employee in the event of a change of corporate ownership. Such a contract provision would soften the landing for those corporate executives who are squeezed out in an unfriendly corporate takeover. Congress has been increasingly concerned about hostile takeovers of corporations, and sees no reason for taxpayers to subsidize such activities through deductions for the entire amount of such inflated payments by the new ownerships.

Congress attacked the golden parachute problem in two ways. First, Sec. 280G disallows a deduction for any payments in excess of 300% of a base amount (annualized compensation in the last five years) that are due to a change in ownership. This provision applies to any contracts entered into or renewed after June 14, 1984. Secondly, Sec. 4999 provides for a nondeductible excise tax of 20% of the excess payment, payable by the recipient in addition to normal income taxes.

The timing of the compensation deduction is another potential problem area. Generally an employer deducts compensation expenditures when paid (cash basis) or incurred (accrual basis). Special rules apply to vacation pay and bonuses. Sec. 463 permits a taxpayer to accrue and deduct specific liabilities for vacation pay earned by employees during the tax year, even though payment may actually be made up to 12 months later. A special suspense account is used by the taxpayer to ensure that amounts are not deducted twice (i.e., as accrued and as paid). Additionally, Revenue Ruling 55-446 (1955-2 C.B. 531) permits an accrual-basis taxpayer to deduct reasonable estimates of bonuses to be paid in the following tax year, if such payments are calculated with an existing formula and the employer is obligated to make the payment as soon as feasible within the next tax year.

Sometimes the deductibility of employer payments depends on the character of the payment to the employee. For example, an employer receives no deduction in connection with issued stock options unless the employee is required to recognize ordinary income because the special qualification requirements for capital-gains treatment is not met. This would be the case, for example, when an employee does not meet the 1 or 2-year holding period requirements for an incentive stock option. (These requirements are discussed in Chapter 10.)

Example 27: X Corporation granted an option to Y on 2/1/X1 to purchase 100 shares of company stock at $80 a share. Y exercised the option on 1/3/X2 when the stock was selling at $87 a share, and subsequently sold the stock on 1/13/X3 for $90 a share. Although Y held the stock for more than 1 year after exercise, he did not hold the stock for at least two years after the date the option was granted (2/1/X1). Therefore, Y must recognize $700 of ordinary income on the 1/13/X3 sale ([$87 − 80] × 100 shares), and X Corporation can deduct the $700 as compensation. The remaining $300 of gain is recognized as capital gain by Y and is not deductible by X Corporation.

CONSTRUCTION-PERIOD INTEREST AND TAXES

In general, any interest and real estate taxes incurred during the period of construction of real property must be capitalized by most taxpayers. Such capitalized costs are then to be amortized over a 10-year period. This provision does not apply to low-income housing and real estate that cannot reasonably be expected to be put to use in a trade or business or income-producing activity.

Example 28: During the 9-month construction period for a new apartment complex, Taxpayer Z incurred $1,700 of interest expense and $1,900 of property taxes. This total of $3,600 must be capitalized and amortized over a 10-year period (on a straight-line basis).

START-UP EXPENSES

Normally the costs of organizing a business enterprise are considered to be nondeductible capital expenditures, to be recovered only when the business is liquidated. These expenses, frequently referred to as "start-up" or "preopening" expenses, are usually considered to be nondeductible capital expenditures. However, Sec. 195 permits a taxpayer to elect to amortize such expenditures over a period of not less than 60 months. These preopening expenses include such expenditures as advertising, training of employees, expenses of lining up suppliers, and the costs of investigating the new business.

Two special provisions permit corporations and partnerships an election to amortize most start-up costs over a period of 60 months or more. These elections for "organization expenses" are discussed in Chapter 16.

SPECIAL FARM DEDUCTIONS

Over the years Congress has enacted special tax provisions for farmers. Some of these provisions were designed to simplify farm accounting procedures, and others were designed to promote the national interest by encouraging efficient land use by farmers. The special farm inventory methods discussed briefly in Chapter 6 are examples of simplified farm accounting. Several other special expense provisions are described briefly in the following sections.

FORM 1040—SCHEDULE F

FIGURE 8-2

SCHEDULE C (Form 1040)
Department of the Treasury
Internal Revenue Service

Profit or (Loss) From Business or Profession
(Sole Proprietorship)

Partnerships, Joint Ventures, etc., Must File Form 1065.
▶ Attach to Form 1040 or Form 1041. ▶ See Instructions for Schedule C (Form 1040).

OMB No. 1545-0074
1984
09

Name of proprietor: *Gloria S. Gretna* | Social security number: *583 66 4410*

A Main business activity (see Instructions) ▶ *Garment Manufacturing* | Product or Service ▶ *Work Clothing*

B Business name and address ▶ *Gretna Garment Company* | C Employer ID number: *22 6045131*

D Method(s) used to value closing inventory:
(1) ☒ Cost (2) ☐ Lower of cost or market (3) ☐ Other (attach explanation)

E Accounting method: (1) ☐ Cash (2) ☒ Accrual (3) ☐ Other (specify) ▶

	Yes	No
F Was there any change in determining quantities, costs, or valuations between opening and closing inventory? If "Yes," attach explanation.		X
G Did you deduct expenses for an office in your home?		X

Part I Income

1 a	Gross receipts or sales	1a	864,520
b	Less: Returns and allowances	1b	1,220
c	Subtract line 1b from line 1a and enter the balance here	1c	863,300
2	Cost of goods sold and/or operations (from Part III, line 8)	2	522,600
3	Subtract line 2 from line 1c and enter the **gross profit** here	3	340,700
4 a	Windfall Profit Tax Credit or Refund received in 1984 (see Instructions)	4a	
b	Other income	4b	
5	Add lines 3, 4a, and 4b. This is the **gross income** ▶	5	340,700

Part II Deductions

6	Advertising	6,320
7	Bad debts from sales or services (Cash method taxpayers, see Instructions)	4,500
8	Bank service charges	
9	Car and truck expenses	2,340
10	Commissions	43,620
11	Depletion	
12	Depreciation and Section 179 deduction from Form 4562 (not included in Part III below)	70,818
13	Dues and publications	2,050
14	Employee benefit programs	
15	Freight (not included in Part III below)	
16	Insurance	4,820
17	Interest on business indebtedness	6,340
18	Laundry and cleaning	
19	Legal and professional services	3,600
20	Office expense	2,506
21	Pension and profit-sharing plans	
22	Rent on business property	
23	Repairs	6,450
24	Supplies (not included in Part III below)	3,008
25	Taxes (Do not include Windfall Profit Tax here. See line 29.)	3,850
26	Travel and entertainment	920
27	Utilities and telephone	4,750
28 a	Wages 118,400	
b	Jobs credit	
c	Subtract line 28b from 28a	118,400
29	Windfall Profit Tax withheld in 1984	
30	Other expenses (specify):	
a		
b	*Pattern Leases*	16,020
c	*Maintenance*	800
d		
e		
f		
g		
h		
i		

31	Add amounts in columns for lines 6 through 30i. These are the **total deductions** ▶	31	301,112
32	**Net profit or (loss).** Subtract line 31 from line 5 and enter the result. If a profit, enter on Form 1040, line 12, and on Schedule SE, Part I, line 2 (or Form 1041, line 6). If a loss, you **MUST** go on to line 33	32	39,588

33 If you have a loss, you **MUST** answer this question: "Do you have amounts for which you are not at risk in this business (see Instructions)?" ☐ Yes ☐ No
If "Yes," you **MUST** attach **Form 6198.** If "No," enter the loss on Form 1040, line 12, and on Schedule SE, Part I, line 2 (or Form 1041, line 6).

Part III Cost of Goods Sold and/or Operations (See Schedule C Instructions for Part III)

1	Inventory at beginning of year (if different from last year's closing inventory, attach explanation)	1	83,200
2	Purchases less cost of items withdrawn for personal use	2	518,140
3	Cost of labor (do not include salary paid to yourself)	3	94,300
4	Materials and supplies	4	3,020
5	Other costs	5	
6	Add lines 1 through 5	6	698,660
7	Less: Inventory at end of year	7	176,060
8	**Cost of goods sold and/or operations.** Subtract line 7 from line 6. Enter here and in Part I, line 2, above.	8	522,600

For Paperwork Reduction Act Notice, see Form 1040 Instructions. **Schedule C (Form 1040) 1984**

SOIL AND WATER CONSERVATION EXPENDITURES Sec. 175(b) permits a current deduction for expenditures paid or incurred during the year for soil and water conservation, limited to 25% of the gross farm income. Amounts not currently deductible may be carried forward to future years. The 25% limit was imposed as an attempt to limit deductions available to part-time or hobby farmers. Additionally, such expenditures may be subject to recapture (see Chapter 11).

LAND CLEARING EXPENDITURES Costs incurred in land clearing, including the moving of earth, are currently deductible under Sec. 182, limited to the lesser of $5,000 or 25% of taxable income. No carryovers of excess amounts are allowed (though such amounts may be capitalizable). These expenditures may also be subject to special recapture rules discussed in Chapter 11.

FERTILIZER AND LIME EXPENDITURES Sec. 180 permits a farmer to deduct unlimited amounts for fertilizer, lime, and other materials designed to enrich or condition the soil. Although such expenditures are obviously designed to benefit more than one tax year, the special election guarantees current deductibility.

TAX REPORTING PROCEDURES FOR SELF-EMPLOYED INDIVIDUALS

FORM 1040—SCHEDULE C

A self-employed individual reports his or her trade or business income on Form 1040, Schedule C. This tax form is in a format similar to an income statement (see Figure 8-2) with the final net income figure (line 32) carried over to line 12 of Form 1040 as an addition to (or subtraction from) gross income (since Sec. 162 expenses are deductions *for* adjusted gross income). Note also that this figure will be used to compute the self-employment tax on Schedule SE.

P L A N N I N G   W O R K S H O P

CONSIDERING STRAIGHT-LINE OPTIONS

In some situations it may be quite logical for a taxpayer to consider straight-line and possibly extended-recovery periods for depreciation. For example, a newly-formed business may reasonably expect to incur losses in the first years of its operations. Accelerated deductions would not generate tax savings in these years, and deductions in later years when the business generates a profit would be less than a straight-line recovery. Furthermore, a business may elect an extended-recovery period to lessen the possibility that net operating loss deductions (caused to a degree by recovery deductions) will possibly expire before being fully utilized. Finally, a straight-line re-

Continued

PLANNING WORKSHOP

covery for realty may be used as a means of eliminating ordinary income recapture on disposition, especially in the case of commercial realty (see Chapter 11).

EVALUATING THE SEC. 179 ELECTION

Simple present value analysis can be used to compare the tax savings of the immediate expensing election (Sec. 179) with the savings generated by normal ACRS recovery (including an investment credit). For example, if N Company in Example 14 is in a 40% marginal income tax bracket, the tax savings generated under the two options would be as follows:

YEAR	SEC. 179 ELECTION	ACRS AND INVESTMENT CREDIT	
1	($5,000 × 1.00 × .40) = $2,000	($4,750* × .15 × .40) + ($5,000 × .10)	= $ 785
2		($4,750* × .22 × .40)	= $ 418
3		($4,750* × .21 × .40)	= $ 399
4		($4,750* × .21 × .40)	= $ 399
5		($4,750* × .21 × .40)	= $ 399
			$2,400

*Reflects the basis reduction for ½ of the investment credit.

Obviously, the only way to compare the $2,000 and the $2,400 is in a time-value of money context, since the savings occur at different points in time. The key question is this: at what rate of return can the $2,000 of tax savings under the Sec. 179 election be invested to equal the savings of the ACRS/Investment Credit option (also invested at the same rate)? Through a trial and error process, this rate is determined to be 12%. In other words, N Company should make the Sec. 179 election only if they feel that the tax savings can earn an *after-tax* rate of return of 12%. This rate of return is necessary to offset the loss of the 10% investment credit.

The Sec. 179 election is even less attractive when the marginal tax rate decreases. Using the same trial and error procedure, it can be found that a 30% tax bracket requires a 20% after-tax rate of return, and a 19% tax bracket requires an astronomical 51% after-tax rate of return.

CAPITALIZATION OF RESEARCH AND EXPERIMENTATION EXPENDITURES

Although time-value of money considerations cause most taxpayers to elect either an immediate or a 5-year recovery for R&E expenditures, the option of capitalizing the expenditures without amortization may appeal to some taxpayers. For example, a company with

Continued

little or no current revenues may prefer to defer cost recovery until a project or product is sold, so that the matching of revenues and cost recovery results in a lower marginal tax rate in the year of disposition. Additionally, a deferral election guarantees an eventual cost recovery; deducting the expenditures in loss years limits the potential deductibility to the net operating loss carryback and carryforward periods.

JUSTIFYING ADDITIONS TO A BAD-DEBT RESERVE

Occasionally taxpayers believe that they should be permitted to increase their bad-debt reserve by more than the amount calculated by using the Black Motor Company formula. Obviously, these extra charges must stand up to IRS scrutiny. Comparative agings of accounts receivable for several years may disclose a recent deterioration in credit collection procedures. Additionally, evidence of an extraordinary credit reversal of a major customer may justify an unusually large charge. For example, the Tax Court permitted such a deduction for the bankruptcy of a major customer.* Industry averages may also be of some help to firms with an otherwise brief operating history as a base for reserve additions.

NET OPERATING LOSSES

The key tax planning question to be answered with net operating losses is whether or not the taxpayer should forgo the 3-year carryback period. In some cases the question cannot be answered simply by comparing the marginal tax rates of the carryback years with the expected rates of carryforward years. For example, a carryback may eliminate or reduce credits taken in the carryback year which are limited to a portion of the tax liability, e.g., the investment credit. A carryback may also eliminate capital loss deductions or affect income averaging calculations. Finally, the reduction or elimination of tax liability may create or add to a minimum tax problem in the carryback year (see Chapter 13). In summary, numerous factors should be considered in evaluating carryover options.

EVALUATING RETIREMENT PLAN OPTIONS

Many factors enter into the choice of an appropriate retirement plan by a business. Perhaps the most important question to be answered is whether or not the company can financially afford to meet the various requirements for a qualified plan. The nondiscrimination rules of Code Sec. 401 are designed to ensure participation by a broad group of employees. Projections of total expected future funding costs are essential when deciding on a retirement plan. Such projections should also be on an after-tax basis (i.e., a $100,000

Continued

PLANNING WORKSHOP

deductible contribution to a retirement plan by a 40% bracket taxpayer involves an after-tax outlay of $60,000). If cash flow is a critical variable in such a decision, a stock-purchase plan may permit the corporation current deductions simply by transferring unissued shares to the trustee at the end of the year. Similarly, a profit-sharing plan would eliminate outlays in loss years.

Projections of ultimate benefits to employees may also be an important consideration to employers as a means of acquiring or retaining valuable employees. Generally, the younger the age of an employee, the greater the advantage of a defined contribution plan (assuming maximum contributions are made). However, the projected benefits are greater under defined benefit plans if contributions (at the maximum rate) begin when an employee is roughly 50 years of age or older.

---

* *Westchester Development Co.*, 63 T.C. 198 (1974).

KEY POINTS TO REMEMBER

1. Cost-recovery deductions (depreciation, ACRS, and amortization) are allowed only on properties with limited useful lives which are either used in a trade or business or held for the production of income.
2. The tax basis for recovery deductions for an asset is generally its total cost, reduced for any special credit adjustments for certain personalty acquired after 1982. However, the recovery basis for personal property converted to a business use is the lesser of original cost or fair market value at the date of conversion.
3. Assets acquired before 1981 must be depreciated with a consistent method over their expected useful lives. Generally, these expected useful lives must conform to the IRS guide-line lives, unless the taxpayer can justify unique "facts and circumstances." Additionally, an election to use the Asset Depreciation Range System provides an opportunity to select a useful life from a range of lives equal to 20% more or less than the guide-line life.
4. Salvage value must be considered in determining depreciation deductions for assets acquired before 1981; however, up to 10% of the original cost of the property may be ignored when assigning a salvage value to tangible personalty with at least a 3-year life.
5. A taxpayer may use any consistent method of calculating depreciation for assets acquired before 1981. The use of accelerated methods is permissible, subject to the prescribed maximum rates specified in Sec. 167(j). These rates give preferential treatment to new versus used property, and to residential versus commercial realty.

6. The Accelerated Cost Recovery System greatly simplifies the cost recovery deduction for assets acquired after 1980 by categorizing assets into one of five statutory recovery-period classes (3, 5, 10, or 15 years for personalty, and 15 or 18 years for realty). Recovery deductions are then computed by multiplying the recoverable cost (unreduced by salvage value) by a statutory recovery percentage. The statutory percentage for personalty is based on the 150% declining balance method with a half-year convention, and the realty percentage is based on a 175% declining-balance method (200% for low-income housing) with monthly adjustments for service use.
7. A taxpayer may elect straight-line recovery for assets acquired after 1980. Three optional recovery periods are provided for each of the five asset categories.
8. A taxpayer may elect to immediately expense limited amounts ($5,000 through 1987) of purchased personalty which otherwise qualifies for the investment credit. However, no investment credit is allowed on that portion of the cost.
9. The cost of intangible properties with limited and definite useful lives may be amortized under the straight-line method over their expected useful economic lives. In some cases, Congress has established special rapid amortization procedures for certain expenditures.
10. Qualifying research and experimentation (R&E) expenditures may be deducted currently, amortized over a period of not less than 60 months, or capitalized with no amortization. However, the cost of any tangible properties used in the R&E process must be recovered under normal depreciation or ACRS procedures.
11. Sec. 166 permits a deduction for bad debts. Business bad debts are taken as ordinary loss deductions, and nonbusiness bad debts are taken as short-term capital losses.
12. A business taxpayer may use either the direct write-off or the reserve method for calculating bad debt deductions. The IRS requires the use of a court-approved formula for determining additions to a bad-debt reserve. This formula derives an experience ratio based on the net bad debts and average accounts receivable of the current year and five prior years.
13. A net operating loss is determined by modifying the negative taxable income for the loss year. The modifications reduce the reported loss by adding back items which are either artificial deductions or personal in nature.
14. A net operating loss so determined is taken as a deduction for adjusted gross income in the appropriate carryover year. A net operating loss deduction may be used (in chronological order) in the three preceding tax years and 15 future years, or simply in 15 future years.
15. The Internal Revenue Code offers special tax incentives to employers, employees, and individuals to participate in certain "qualified" retirement plans. These provisions permit immediate deductions for plan contributions (subject to certain limits), tax-free income on contribu-

tions through working years, and deferral of income tax until withdrawal at retirement.

16. Corporations and self-employed individuals must meet certain nondiscriminatory requirements of Sec. 401 in order to receive the preferential treatment mentioned in Item 15. Self-employed plans are commonly referred to as HR-10 or Keogh plans.
17. An individual may establish his or her own retirement account (IRA) with the same qualifed plan advantages. Deductions are limited to the lesser of $2,000 or 100% of compensation. Special rules apply to certain spousal IRAs.
18. Special deduction rules have been established as an administrative convenience to simplify the accounting for certain expenditures. These include the provisions for "start-up expenses," construction-period interest and taxes, and farm deductions.

SELF-STUDY QUESTIONS

1. Bill Atley purchased a new machine for use in his business on 8/1/X5 for $8,000. Atley elects to expense immediately as much of the cost of the machine as possible, and take a 10% investment tax credit on any excess. Atley's ACRS deduction for 19X5 will be based on a depreciable basis of

   a) $8,000
   b) $3,000
   c) $2,850
   d) $2,700

2. Earl Cook, who worked as a machinist for Precision Corp., lent Precision $1,000 in 19X0. Cook did not own any of Precision's stock, and the loan was not a condition of Cook's employment by Precision. In 19X4, Precision declared bankruptcy, and Cook's note receivable from Precision became worthless. What loss can Cook claim on his 19X4 income tax return?

   a) $0
   b) $500 long-term capital loss
   c) $1,000 short-term capital loss
   d) $1,000 business bad debt

   (AICPA adapted)

3. Bud Ace, a self-employed carpenter, reports his income on the cash basis. During 19X8, he completed a job for a customer and sent him a bill for $3,000. The customer was not satisfied with the work and indicated that he would pay only $1,500. Ace agreed to reduce the bill to $2,000, but before payment was made the customer died. Ace could not collect from the customer's estate and should treat this loss as

a) an ordinary business deduction of $3,000

b) an ordinary business deduction of $2,000

c) a short-term capital loss of $1,500

d) a nondeductible loss as no income was reported

(AICPA adapted)

4. Paramount Corporation has consistently used the reserve method to compute the bad debt deduction on its tax returns. The year-end reserve for bad debts reported on the 19X9 tax return was $11,200. Additional information is available as follows:

	ACCOUNTS RECEIVABLE AT END OF YEAR	BAD DEBT LOSSES	BAD DEBT RECOVERIES
19X5	$ 255,000	$12,000	$1,150
19X6	265,000	13,500	1,300
19X7	270,000	11,500	1,450
19X8	250,000	12,000	1,500
19X9	280,000	14,000	1,920
19Y0	300,000	18,000	2,400
Totals	$1,620,000	$81,000	$9,720
% of receivables		5.0%	0.6%

In December of 19Y0 one of Paramount's important customers experienced financial difficulties, which could result in a bad debt write-off of $10,000 during 19Y1 in respect of this customer. What is the maximum bad debt deduction that Paramount can claim on its tax return for 19Y0?

a) $13,200

b) $17,600

c) $19,400

d) $27,600

(AICPA adapted)

5. Joe Dailey's house was destroyed by fire during the year. The uninsured loss was greater that his entire income for the year. The net loss (above the $100 and 10% of AGI floors) may be

a) carried forward indefinitely

b) carried forward 15 years only

c) carried back three years and forward 15 years only

d) carried back three years and forward 15 years, or carried forward 15 years

(AICPA adapted)

6. Which of the following items is not an add-back adjustment to taxable income in determining a net operating loss for a taxable year:
   a) a personal exemption deduction
   b) a capital loss deduction
   c) a capital gains deduction (60% of the long-term capital gain)
   d) a deduction for business bad debts

7. Z Company contributed the following amounts to the company's qualified (defined contribution) profit-sharing plan: $18,000 (19X2), $11,000 (19X3), and $17,500 (19X4). Assuming that aggregate employee compensation was $100,000 in each of the three years, Z Company's allowable 19X4 deduction would be
   a) $15,000
   b) $16,000
   c) $17,500
   d) $19,000

8. Under the provisions of ERISA, the maximum contribution to a qualified retirement plan (a defined contribution money-purchase plan) on behalf of a self-employed individual whose earned income is $20,000 is limited to
   a) $3,000
   b) $5,000
   c) $20,000
   d) $30,000

   (AICPA adapted)

9. Roger Efron, who is single and has no dependents, earned a salary of $50,000 in 19X3, and had an adjusted gross income of $60,000. Roger has been an active participant in a qualified noncontributory pension plan since 19W2. Roger itemized his deductions on his 19X3 income tax return. Among Roger's 19X3 cash expenditures was a contribution to an individual retirement account of $2,000 ($200 interest was earned on this IRA in 19X3). How much could Roger deduct for the contribution to his individual retirement account in arriving at his 19X3 adjusted gross income?
   a) $0
   b) $1,500
   c) $1,800
   d) $2,000

   (AICPA adapted)

10. For the year 19X8 Fred and Wilma Todd reported the following items of income:

	FRED	WILMA
Salary	$40,000	—
Interest income	1,000	$ 200
Cash prize won on a T.V. game show	—	8,800
	$41,000	$9,000

Fred is not covered by any qualified retirement plan and he and Wilma established retirement accounts at the end of the year. Assuming a joint return was filed in 19X8, what is the maximum amount that they can be allowed for contribution to their individual retirement accounts?

a) $1,500

b) $2,000

c) $2,250

d) $4,000

(AICPA adapted)

QUESTIONS

1. Which of the following assets are eligible for depreciation/cost recovery deductions?
   a) Factory plant location, which includes land, building, fences, and paved parking areas
   b) Personal automobile (estimated useful life of four years)
   c) $25,000 cost of purchased goodwill as allocated by the original sales contract for purchase of a business
   d) Cost of carpet cleaning machines leased to customers on a daily basis
   e) Furniture and appliances in a rental duplex
2. Explain how the following elections could be used to maximize or accelerate depreciation deductions in the early years of an asset's life for properties placed into service before 1981: additional first-year depreciation, salvage value reduction, and the Asset Depreciation Range System.
3. What was the maximum rate of depreciation allowable, expressed as a percentage of the straight-line method, for the following properties acquired before 1981:
   a) a new business duplicating machine (useful life of eight years)
   b) a used factory warehouse (useful life of 25 years)
   c) a new residential apartment complex (useful life of 40 years)
   d) a used drill press machine (useful life of five years)

e) a new factory building (useful life of 35 years)

f) a used residential rental duplex (useful life of 30 years)

4. What is the correct ACRS classification (3-, 5-, 10-, or 15-year property) for each of the following properties (all acquired before 1984):
   a) residential rental duplex building
   b) used delivery automobiles
   c) greenhouses used for growing vegetables
   d) new metal plating machine
   e) tangible amusement park rides (12-year ADR life as realty under prior law)
5. Even though the Sec. 179 immediate expensing election was enacted to benefit small businesses, many small businesses may actually find it preferable not to make this election. Explain this apparent inconsistency.
6. Explain the basic differences in ACRS tax treatment between personalty and realty for the following factors:
   a) recovery-table method
   b) immediate-expensing election
   c) cost-recovery deduction for first year and last year of service
   d) straight-line election
7. What is the appropriate cost-recovery period for the following items: pollution control expenditures, research and development costs, patents, and goodwill? Can accelerated recovery be used for any of these items?
8. Explain why it is important to distinguish between business and nonbusiness bad debts. When should such a determination be made?
9. Some commentators contend that the Black Motor Company formula is not truly representative of a firm's bad-debt experience during times of a sudden economic downturn. Explain how this could sometimes occur.
10. What adjustments to an individual's taxable income are necessary to convert a tax loss to a net operating loss? What do these adjustments have in common?
11. Why may some taxpayers elect to forgo the 3-year carryback period for net operating deductions? Are there any potential disadvantages in making such an election?
12. What effect (if any) do casualty losses have on net operating loss calculations?
13. Rancor Corporation was recently formed under the State of Delaware statutes. The corporation will have five shareholder-officers and ap-

proximately 40 staff and line employees. The officers of Rancor would like to establish a qualified retirement plan which benefits primarily the officer-employees. Do you foresee any problems with this plan? Discuss.

14. All qualified retirement plans (pension, profit-sharing, stock-bonus, HR-10, and IRAs) offer essentially the same tax advantages. List the basic tax advantages common to all qualified plans, and describe what happens if the qualifications for special tax treatment are not met.

15. Are there instances where a self-employed individual may choose to establish an IRA rather than an HR-10/Keogh plan, even though the latter provides larger annual deductions for owner contributions? Explain.

16. Explain the difference in cost recovery procedures for (a) a business building acquired on January 15, 1984, and (b) a business building acquired on July 15, 1984.

17. How is the adjusted cost recovery basis of personalty acquired after 1982 affected by the investment tax credit? Explain.

18. What restrictions are imposed on cost recovery deductions and investment tax credits for business automobiles acquired after 1984?

19. What limitations are imposed on cost recovery deductions and investment tax credits for "listed personal property" that is acquired after 1984?

20. Able, a 30% shareholder in Waco Corporation, lent the Corporation $16,000 in 19X5. Waco continued to experience financial difficulties and was unable to repay the loan. Under what circumstances would Able be able to deduct the loss as an ordinary business bad debt?

21. Is it possible for a taxpayer to have a net operating loss without operating a trade or business or being a partner in a business venture? Explain.

22. A taxpayer purchased a new business machine in 1985 for $8,000. The machine will be used solely for business purposes. The taxpayer may choose from a total of 16 possible combinations of investment tax credit and cost recovery options. Explain.

PROBLEMS

1. Determine the appropriate tax basis for cost recovery purposes for the following assets. Assume that all properties except (b) do *not* qualify for an investment credit.
   a) Abe Washington receives a typewriter as a gift from his brother in 1984. The typewriter had originally cost $1,500 and was worth $800

at the time of the gift. His brother's adjusted basis in the typewriter at the time of the gift was $600.

b) Brenda Irby purchased a new rotary saw in 1984 to use in her business. The total cost of the saw was $8,200, and Brenda spent $700 having the saw installed. She also paid the dealer a $100 commission for obtaining the saw from another dealer.

c) On 1/6/84 Tamara Wells began a landscaping business and converted her personal automobile to 75% business usage. The car had cost $7,600 in 1983 and was worth $6,000 on 1/6/84.

2. For each of the following assets, determine the corrected adjusted basis at the end of 1981 (note that all assets were acquired before 1981). The taxpayer elects the salvage-value reduction and bonus depreciation where applicable:

a) Helen Anderson purchased a new lathe for her business on 1/2/80. The lathe cost $8,000, has a useful life of five years, and an expected salvage value of $1,000. Helen elects to use the straight-line depreciation method.

b) Bob Welch purchased a new office desk on 1/4/80. The desk cost $2,000, has a useful life of ten years, and an expected salvage value of $200. Bob elects to use the double-declining balance method.

c) Tom Abbey purchased a used business collator on 1/6/80. The collator cost $2,500, has a useful life of six years, and an expected salvage value of $200. Tom elects to use the maximum depreciation rate available under the Code.

d) Mary Woods purchased a new slide projector for her business on 1/7/80. The projector cost $800, has a useful life of four years, and an expected salvage value of $50. She elects to use the sum-of-the-year's-digits method.

3. During January 1980, Bill Robinson acquired the following three assets:

ITEM	USE	COST	USEFUL LIFE	SALVAGE VALUE
Used rental duplex building	Tenant rental	$80,000	40 Years	$10,000
New furniture	Tenant rental	2,000	10 Years	300
New warehouse building	Business use	40,000	25 Years	5,000

Bill elects to depreciate these items using the highest permitted rates of recovery. Compute the maximum 1980 depreciation deductions for these three assets, making any elections which increase the potential deduction.

4. Cindy Curry began a sole proprietorship landscaping business in 1984. She acquired the following business assets during that year:

DATE	ITEM	COST	USEFUL LIFE	SALVAGE VALUE
1-8	Business auto (100%)*	$ 8,000	4 Years	$ 1,000
1-12	Business pickup truck*	7,000	5 Years	2,000
2-15	Heavy-duty trucks†	15,000	8 Years	4,000
7-14	Office furniture†	4,000	10 Years	500
7-30	Business building	60,000	30 Years	15,000

*Qualifies for 6% investment credit.
†Qualifies for 10% investment credit.

Determine Cindy's total ACRS deductions for 1984 and 1985. Assume that she does not elect either the Sec. 179 immediate-expensing option or the optional straight-line recoveries.

5. Refer to Problem 4. Assume that Cindy elects to use straight-line recovery for all of the assets. Recompute the 1984 and 1985 deductions assuming that Cindy elects to use:
   a) the shortest possible straight-line recovery.
   b) the longest possible straight-line recovery.

6. Raymond Evans purchases a new business machine for $12,500 on 6/2/84. The machine qualifies as 5-year ACRS property and also potentially qualifies for a 10% investment tax credit. Determine the appropriate ACRS deduction and investment credit for Evans, assuming that (a) Evans elects the Sec. 179 immediate-expensing option, and (b) Evans does not elect the immediate-expensing option. Would you advise Evans to elect Sec. 179 if he is in a very low marginal tax bracket? Explain.

7. Crane Chemical Company owns and operates its own research facility. During 1984 Crane spent the following amounts on research and experimentation: $56,000 salaries, $12,000 utilities, $18,000 materials, and $50,000 for equipment (appropriate ACRS deduction—$7,500). What are the tax options available to Crane Company in reporting these expenditures, assuming that the economic benefits from these expenditures begin in November 1984?

8. On 2/1/82 Meagan Armstrong lent $9,000 to Ronald Wade. In November of 1984 Wade instituted bankruptcy proceedings. At that time it was estimated that Wade's creditors would be able to collect 75¢ for each dollar of liability. In 1985 the bankruptcy proceedings were completed, with each creditor receiving 70¢ on the dollar. How would Meagan report the bad-debt deduction on her 1984 and 1985 income tax returns, assuming that:
   a) the loan was for a personal boat purchase by Wade, a former friend of Meagan;
   b) the loan was to ensure a steady inventory supply for Meagan, as Wade was her primary wholesale source of supply;
   c) the loan was made to ensure that Wade, a personal friend, could

retain his machinery repair business (a business unrelated to Meagan's enterprise).

d) Assume the same facts as (c), except that Meagan had cosigned a $9,000 note as a guarantor and had to pay that amount when Wade defaulted on the note.

9. Randolph Company uses the reserve method for bad debts and deducted $48,000 as a reasonable addition to the reserve in 1984. Randolph's records disclose the following information:

ALLOWANCE FOR BAD DEBTS

1984 Write-offs	$72,500	1/1/84 Balance	$82,000
		1984 Recoveries	4,400

An examination of current and prior year records disclosed the following:

YEAR	BAD-DEBT WRITE-OFFS	BAD-DEBT RECOVERIES	ENDING ACCOUNTS REC. BALANCE
1979	$ 45,975	$ 5,600	$ 650,000
1980	44,000	4,400	630,000
1981	53,000	3,800	660,000
1982	59,000	4,000	610,000
1983	67,000	3,500	580,000
1984	72,500	4,400	585,000
Totals	$341,475	$25,700	$3,715,000

a) Assuming that the IRS audits Randolph's 1984 tax return, are they likely to accept the $48,000 bad-debt deduction? Discuss.

b) Has Randolph Company's bad-debt experience been stable over the 6-year period? Explain.

10. Blackmore Corporation sold an inventory item on account in 1982 for $10,000. The item had a cost of $6,000. In 1985, at a time when a $4,000 balance existed on this receivable, the debt was judged completely worthless.

a) How would Blackmore report this bad debt, assuming that the company uses the following tax accounting methods: (1) the cash method, (2) the accrual method, and (3) the installment method?

b) Assume that in 1986, the customer unexpectedly repays the $4,000 debt. How would this recovery be reported on (1) the cash method, (2) the accrual method, and (3) the installment method?

11. Dan Rivers incurs a $70,000 net operating loss in 19X4. His tax returns for the previous three years disclose the following:

YEAR	TAXABLE INCOME	MARGINAL TAX RATE
19X3	$26,000	35%
19X2	22,000	31%
19X1	15,000	23%

Business has improved considerably in the first three months of 19X5, and Rivers expects business income to be at least $50,000 a year in the future. What factors should Rivers consider when deciding on the proper treatment of the 19X4 net operating loss?

12. Wanda Fairchild operates her own equipment leasing business. Her tax returns for the years 19X1 and 19X4 disclose the following:

		19X1		19X4
Net business income (loss)		$11,500		($23,000)
Interest income		300		1,000
Net long-term capital gain (net)		—		4,000
Net capital loss		(600)		—
Adjusted gross income		11,200		($18,000)
Less excess itemized deductions:				
Medical expenses	620		600	
Less 5% of AGI	(560)		(0)	
Taxes	1,600		1,800	
Interest	1,800		3,400	
Contributions	1,200		0	
Casualty loss (net)	0		800	
Total itemized deductions	4,660		6,600	
Less zero-bracket amount	(2,300)	(2,360)	(2,300)	(4,300)
Less personal exemptions		(1,000)		(1,000)
Taxable income		$7,840		($23,300)
Net tax liability		$ 947		$ 0

a) Determine Fairchild's 19X4 net operating loss.

b) Determine the net operating loss available to carry forward to 19X2 after applying the net operating loss deduction in 19X1.

c) What happens to the $600 capital loss deduction of 19X1 after applying the net operating loss?

13. During 19X4, Randolph Brown incurred $3,800 of interest expense and $4,250 of property taxes in constructing a new company warehouse. How should these costs be reported for tax purposes?

14. Determine the appropriate tax deduction and carryover amounts (if any) for the following qualified corporate retirement plans:

a) A Company provides a qualified pension plan for its employees. The actuarially determined amount necessary to fund current year pension costs is $61,500, and the total remaining amount necessary to fund past service costs for employees who joined the company before the pension plan was adopted is $192,000.

b) Delco Corporation provides a combination of pension and profit-sharing plans for its employees. During the year Delco paid a total of $1,000,000 compensation to its employees and contributed $180,000 to the pension plan (based on actuarial calculations) and $85,000 to the profit-sharing plan.

c) Zeller Corporation established a qualified profit-sharing plan for its employees in 1983. Zeller made the following contributions during the first three years of the plan's existence:

YEAR	EMPLOYEE COMPENSATION	PROFIT-SHARING CONTRIBUTION
1983	$300,000	$42,000
1984	400,000	65,000
1985	500,000	44,000

Determine the appropriate tax deduction and carryover (if any) for each year.

15. Darryl Norton owns and operates a sole proprietorship dry cleaning service. Darryl has 10 employees and elects to establish a qualified defined-contribution (money) pension plan. Each of his ten employees will be paid $30,000 salary a year, and Darryl's earned income ("compensation") as the owner of the business is expected to average $250,000 a year. Darryl would like to contribute and deduct 15% of each employee's annual compensation (including his own) to the plan. Do you foresee any problems with this plan? Explain.

16. Determine the maximum deduction to an Individual Retirement Account (IRA) in each of the following situations:

a) Melvin Turner received $28,000 salary as a college professor and contributed $2,400 to an IRA.

b) Bob and Melva Armstrong each work for Alloy Aluminum Company. Each received $32,000 of salary, and both are covered under Alloy's qualified corporate retirement plan. Bob and Melva each establish an IRA in 19X5, with Bob contributing $1,700 and Melva contributing $2,150.

c) Harry and Maude Thunderbird establish a spousal IRA. Harry earned $22,000 as a court stenographer in 19X5 and contributed $2,100 to the joint account in his name. Maude did not work in 19X5; however, she contributed $100 to the joint account in her name.

d) Barry Heinbaugh wishes to establish an IRA in 19X5 and contribute the maximum amount. His 19X5 income consists of $26,000 interest and $14,500 of taxable dividends.

17. Joe Bryant purchased a new business computer in February, 1985 for $7,000. He does not elect to immediately expense any of the cost of the computer. Determine the allowable investment tax credit and ACRS deductions for 1985 assuming that (a) the computer is used 20% of the time for personal reasons, and (b) the computer is used 60% of the time for personal reasons.

18. Marsha Mason purchased a new business automobile in March, 1985, for $20,000. Assuming that she uses the automobile 80% of the time for business purposes, determine Mason's maximum investment tax credit and cost recovery deductions for (a) 1985 and (b) 1986.

19. Determine the appropriate cost recovery deductions for the following buildings acquired in 1985:
    a) a business building acquired on September 15, 1985, for $80,000 (ACRS recovery is elected)
    b) a residential apartment building acquired on December 1, 1985 for $100,000 (the building qualifies as low-income housing, and ACRS recovery is elected)
    c) a business building acquired on August 12, 1985 for $150,000 (18-year straight-line recovery is elected)

20. Determine the appropriate ACRS classification (3-, 5-, 10-, 15-, or 18-year property) for the following assets acquired after 1980:
    a) a business typewriter
    b) a business warehouse acquired on 3/1/83
    c) a pickup truck used in a farming business
    d) a rental building acquired on 8/1/84 (does not qualify as low-income housing)
    e) a business dictaphone which had a midpoint life of three years under the ADR system

TAX PLANNING PROBLEMS

1. Jan Beals owns and operates her own business. In 19X5, she purchased a new computer for $8,000. The computer will be used 100% of the time in her business. She asks your advice on the advisability of immediately expensing the first $5,000 of the cost of the asset. Jan's marginal tax rate is expected to be approximately 25% for the next three years, and she can invest tax savings at an after-tax rate of 8%. Assuming that she will use the 10% rate for any applicable investment tax credit, what would be your advice? (Hint: Compare the net present values of the expected tax savings with and without the immediate expensing option by discounting the tax saving of each year

to the end of 19X5, the point at which the 19X5 tax savings are first realized.)

2. Wanda Brown, a 30-year-old, 50%-bracket taxpayer, established an individual retirement account (IRA) in December, 19X1, by contributing $2,000 to a trusteed fund that will pay 12% interest a year (less a $40 annual management fee). Brown was somewhat reluctant to establish the account, since she feels that she may need the funds in a few years to purchase a home, and she does not want to incur the 10% penalty on a premature withdrawal. However, her financial adviser, Bombshell Bushkin, told her that after six or seven years she would accumulate enough cash in the fund that she could afford to pay the penalty and still realize more cash than she would have if she invested $1,200 of her (after-tax) salary in an 8% nontaxable municipal bond fund. Do you agree with this statement? Explain. (Hint: Compare the future value of the municipal bond investment after six years with the future after-tax value of the IRA, assuming that it is withdrawn after six annual investments of $2,000 each. Assume that a 44% marginal tax rate will apply in the year of withdrawal because of the income recognition of the entire amount. Assume that any interest earned in the municipal fund can be reinvested into the fund.)

CASE PROBLEM

Harold Williams is a 28-year-old cash-basis, calendar-year unmarried taxpayer. He owns and operates his own machine shop. His only other income in 1985 consisted of $1,200 interest on State of Arizona bonds, $1,250 dividends on Ford Motor Company stock and $1,125 dividends on Arizona Power and Electric Company stock (of which $900 was reinvested in the company's dividend reinvestment plan).

Harold has summarized his cash receipts and disbursements for the year and balances at year-end of receivables, payables, and inventories as follows (inventories are assumed to be a significant component of income):

	CASH RECEIPT (PAYMENT)	12/31/84 BALANCE	12/31/85 BALANCE
Sales and account collections	$480,000	—	—
Purchases and account payments	(260,000)	—	—
Deductible business expenses	(132,500)	—	—
Accounts payable	—	$38,000	$32,000
Accounts receivable	—	52,000	59,000
Merchandise inventory	—	28,000	34,300

Harold also provides the following summary of assets used during the year in his business operations:

ASSET	DATE ACQUIRED	COST	RECOVERY METHOD	BONUS DEPR. TAKEN
Shop building	1/2/80	$120,000	150% DB (40 years)	—
Drill presses	1/6/80	27,500	SYD (10 years)	—
Office equipment	1/8/80	10,000	200% DB (10 years)	2,000
Delivery trucks	8/2/81	12,000	3-year ACRS	—
Office equipment	10/2/83	6,000	5-year ACRS	—
Lathes	2/6/85	18,000	5-year ACRS	—
Personal computer	9/1/85	7,000	5-year ACRS	—
Warehouse	11/2/85	82,000	18-year ACRS	—

Harold elects to take the maximum investment credit on any qualifying acquisitions (including 1983); however, he also elects to immediately expense as much of the cost of the lathes acquired in 1985 as permitted by the Code. Harold's deductible expenditures for 1985 include a $13,500 net operating loss carryover from 1984, $3,200 of medical expenses (before applying the 5% of adjusted gross income floor), $6,000 of state and local taxes, $5,300 of interest expenses, and $3,200 of charitable contributions. In addition, Harold made $22,000 of estimated tax payments in 1985 and contributed $2,000 to an individual retirement account in February, 1986.

Determine the final 1985 tax liability (or refund due) for Harold Williams. Assume that the lathes and the personal computer qualify for a 10% investment credit. (Note: The final 1985 gross tax liability must be increased by a self-employment tax of $4,673, which is paid with the filing of the income tax return.)

RESEARCH PROBLEMS

1. As a result of an embezzlement by a bank employee, John Austin lost $10,500 of uninsured deposits because of the bank's insolvency. Can Austin deduct the $10,500 loss as a theft loss under Sec. 165, or is the loss a nonbusiness bad debt under Sec. 166? Explain.

2. Barbara Huff is in the trade or business of constructing small regional shopping centers. During 19X3 she paid a loan commitment fee to a potential lender. The fee ($12,000) guarantees that the lender will make funds available for a specific period at a fixed interest rate. Is the fee deductible as an ordinary and necessary business expense, capitalizable as a start-up cost, or capitalizable as an option? Explain.

Chapter Objectives

1. Explain the deductions allowed individuals that are "personal" in nature, as opposed to those related to a trade or business or a transaction for profit.
2. Determine the amount of deductible interest expense.
3. Compute the deductible portion of taxes paid.
4. Calculate the "charitable contributions" deduction.
5. Properly carry forward contributions in excess of the amount deductible.
6. Identify expenditures that qualify as deductible medical expenses.
7. Calculate the deduction for medical expenses.
8. Compute and report casualty and theft losses of business property.
9. Determine the deductible portion of casualty and theft losses of nonbusiness properties.
10. Identify other items that may be deductible by individual taxpayers.

9 Personal Deductions for Individual Taxpayers

In Chapter 7, it was pointed out that the tax laws allow deductions (*a*) related to carrying on a trade or business, (*b*) associated with "nonbusiness" income production, and (*c*) of a purely personal nature that are deductible because of specific provisions of the law. Certain types of expenditures may sometimes be found under all three categories. For example, interest may be paid on loans acquired in trade or business, to purchase income-producing rental properties, or to be used solely for personal purposes. In this chapter we will examine a number of deductions specifically allowed by the Internal Revenue Code. In general, we will discuss these deductions from the viewpoint that they are personal expenditures that are specifically allowed as deductions, or that they are allowed because they are incurred in connection with nonbusiness income, keeping in mind that some of them may also be allowed as trade or business expenses. If these expenses are incurred in connection with a trade or business or in connection with property held for production of rents and royalties, they are deductible *for determining* AGI; otherwise they are deductible *from* AGI.

INTEREST EXPENSE

Since the early days of the modern income tax law, nearly all interest expense has been deductible. Although it is agreed almost unanimously that interest incurred in a trade or business, or in connection with the production of any other taxable income, should be treated in the same manner as other deductible expenses, there is far less agreement over the propriety of a deduction for interest paid on funds to finance the purchase of personal consumer goods and services. Nevertheless Code Sec. 163 authorizes the general deduction of interest. Sec. 163 reads as follows:

> (a) General Rule.—There shall be allowed as a deduction all interest paid or accrued within the taxable year on indebtedness.[1]

Some common deductions allowed as "interest" are:

- Actual interest on home mortgages and/or personal loans of all types
- Interest on bank credit card balances[2]
- Finance charges on revolving charge accounts[3]
- Other financing charges separately stated[4]
- "Points" paid by the buyer of a *principal residence*[5]
- Discount on notes payable[6]
- Interest on delinquent Federal taxes[7]

Similarly, a list of nondeductible "interest" would include:

- Credit investigation fees[8]
- Interest related to tax-exempt income[9]
- "Points" paid by seller of property[10]
- Interest paid on "single-premium" life insurance policies[11]

A number of the most important restrictions and limitations on interest deductions are discussed below.

DEBT MUST BE THAT OF THE TAXPAYER

In order for interest to be deducted, there must be a bona fide debt—that is, there must be an actual expectation shared by both the debtor and creditor that the debt will be repaid by the taxpayer. Additionally, the debt must be that of the taxpayer. A taxpayer cannot deduct interest paid on the debt of another person.[12]

---

[1] Sec. 163(a).
[2] Rev. Rul. 71-98, 1971-1, C.B. 57 as modified by Rev. Rul. 72-315, 1972-1 C.B. 49.
[3] Rev. Rul. 72-215, 1972-1 C.B. 49.
[4] *Ibid.*
[5] Sec. 461(g)(2).
[6] *J. R. Hopkins*, 15 T.C. 160 (1951).
[7] Rev. Rul. 70-284, 1970-1 C.B. 34.
[8] Rev. Rul. 67-297, 1967-2 C.B. 87.
[9] Sec. 265(a).
[10] The debt is not that of the taxpayer.
[11] Sec. 264(a)(2).
[12] *Arcade Realty Co.*, 35 T.C. 256 (1960).

Example 1: Ray and Marsha, married, file separate returns. Ray borrowed $100,000 but was unable to pay the interest due on the loan. Marsha paid the interest of $16,000 on the loan this year. The debt is not Marsha's debt and, since she and Ray file separate returns, she cannot deduct the interest paid.[13]

FINANCING CHARGES

The "Truth in Lending" Act[14] now requires that finance charges on a retail installment contract, bank credit card, and similar credit arrangements be disclosed as an annual percentage rate. All such charges are deductible on the tax return.[15]

Example 2: During the current year Ruth paid $200 in "financing charges" on installment debt incurred to purchase furniture for her home. The $200 is deductible as interest expense.

"POINTS" AND OTHER CHARGES RELATED TO REAL ESTATE LOANS

In recent years, mortgage finance companies have required both buyers and sellers of real estate to pay ***points*** on mortgage loans at the time the sale of property occurs. These points are finance charges for placing and processing the loan, and are sometimes used to "equalize" the allowed interest rate on a loan and the market rate of interest. They are expressed as a percentage of the loan. (One point equals 1% of the loan.) In addition there are often service charges and credit investigation fees assessed in connection with the transaction. Points (as well as loan placement fees) paid by the *seller* are not deductible,[16] but are considered to be a reduction of the sales price. Points that represent service charges, credit investigation fees and payment for other specific services are not deductible as interest[17] by either the seller or buyer. A cash-basis buyer may deduct points if three specific tests are met:

POINTS Fees charged buyers and/or sellers of property at the time of sale by the lender providing funds to finance the purchase.

1. the points are incurred (and currently paid) in obtaining a mortgage loan on the buyer's principal place of residence,
2. the charging of points is a normal business practice in the area, and
3. the points charged do not exceed what is "normally" charged in the area.[18]

Example 3: In the current year Ruiz sold her residence. Terry, the buyer, used a government-guaranteed loan to finance the purchase.

---

[13] See, for example, *Colston v. Burnet*, 59 F. 2d 867 (C.A.-D.C., 1932).

[14] P.L. 90-321, 82 Stat. 146 (1968).

[15] Rev. Rul. 72-215, 1972-1 C.B. 49.

[16] *Robert T. Hunt*, 24 TCM 915 (1965).

[17] Rev. Rul. 69-188, 1969-1, C.B. 54, as amplified in Rev. Rul. 69-189, 1969-1, C.B. 55.

[18] Sec. 461(g)(2).

Because the maximum interest rate allowable under the guarantee program was less than the going market rate, the lender required both the buyer and the seller to pay points. The buyer's points totaled $6,000 and the seller's points were $4,000. Ruiz, the seller, will offset the $4,000 she paid against the selling price of the residence, while Terry will be able to deduct the $6,000 he paid, provided such points are normal business practice in that area and the amount involved is also normal. (If the points are paid out of loan proceeds, however, they will likely be held to be nondeductible.)

If the points paid by a buyer are not deductible when paid, they are treated as prepaid interest and amortized over the life of the loan.[19] However, if the points are not normal in the area, the amount paid may be treated as part of the cost of the property.

INTEREST ON DEBT TO ACQUIRE OR CARRY TAX-EXEMPT SECURITIES

Under Sec. 265 no deduction is allowed for expenses related to tax-exempt income.[20] Sec. 265(2) and the Regulations go on to state specifically that *interest* on debt incurred to acquire or carry securities on which interest received is tax exempt shall not be deductible.[21] In many instances, it may be difficult to determine whether a debt was "incurred or continued to purchase or carry" exempt obligations.

Obviously, if the proceeds of indebtedness are used for, and are directly traceable to, the purchase of tax-exempt obligations, the interest expense will be nondeductible. If, however, "proceeds of a bona fide business indebtedness are temporarily invested in tax-exempt obligations," deductibility of the interest expense is not precluded.[22] If tax-exempt securities are pledged as collateral, indebtedness is deemed to be "direct evidence of a purpose to carry tax-exempt obligations" and interest paid on such indebtedness will be nondeductible.[23] The general rule for deductibility of interest on debt by a taxpayer who owns tax-exempt securities is aptly stated in Rev. Proc. 72-18:

> In the absence of direct evidence linking indebtedness with the purchase or carrying of tax-exempt obligations . . . section 265(2) of the Code will apply only if the totality of facts and circumstances support a reasonable inference that the purpose to purchase or carry tax-exempt obligations exists.[24]

Example 4: In 19X3 Lee borrowed $60,000 to purchase shares of stock. As collateral, he pledged the shares purchased, along with

---

[19] Sec. 461(g)(1).
[20] Sec. 265(1).
[21] Sec. 265(2) and Reg. Sec. 1.265-2.
[22] Rev. Proc. 72-18, 72-1 C.B. 740.
[23] *Ibid.*
[24] *Ibid.*

tax-exempt local bonds with a par value and fair market value of $16,000. Of the $60,000 loan, $16,000 will be deemed to "carry" tax-exempt securities and interest on that amount will not be deductible.

PREPAID INTEREST

Although generally a cash-basis taxpayer deducts interest in the year paid, *prepaid* interest is not deductible, even by a cash-basis taxpayer, to the extent that it applies to a period later than the year of payment. Amounts prepaid beyond the year are capitalized and are deducted over the period to which applicable.[25]

Example 5: In December 19X3 Alex, a cash-basis taxpayer, paid in advance interest of $2,000 applicable to 19X4, hoping to deduct that amount in his 19X3 income tax return. Under Code Sec. 461(g), the $2,000 is not deductible in 19X3.

INSTALLMENT PAYMENTS

When loans are repaid in installments, a portion of each payment is treated as interest and a portion as repayment of principal. Where the amount of interest in each payment is specified, that amount of each payment is deductible (assuming that an amount at least equal to the computed interest is paid on each payment date).

Example 6: On October 4, 19X7 Bailey borrowed $1,000 from the bank. The interest rate was 12%. Bailey was to repay the loan by making 12 monthly installment payments of $88.85 each, beginning on November 4, 19X7. Payments were made when due. A loan amortization table provided by the bank showed that the first two monthly payments were to apply as follows:

PAYMENT	INTEREST	PRINCIPAL	TOTAL
1	$10.00	$78.85	$88.85
2	9.21	79.64	88.85

Bailey may deduct $19.21 ($10.00 + $9.21) as interest expense in 19X7.

If the amount of interest in each payment is not stated, a cash-basis taxpayer may prorate the total interest over the number of payments to be made. No deduction is allowed a cash-basis taxpayer until payment is actually made.[26]

Example 7: In October 19X3 Charles borrowed $1,000 from a friend. They agreed that Charles would repay the loan over a period of one year by making 12 monthly payments of $88.85 each, with the first payment being due on November 18, 19X3. Charles made the two payments due in 19X3 and may deduct $11.04 computed as follows:

[25] Code Sec. 461(g)(1).

[26] Sec. 1275(b).

Total amount to be paid (12 × $88.85)	$1,066.20
Principal	$1,000.00
Interest	$ 66.20

$$\text{Interest in each monthly installment} = \frac{\$66.20}{12} = \$5.52$$

Payments made in 19X3 = 2
Total interest = 2 × $5.52 = $11.04

Another provision related to installment sales is that if an installment contract from the purchase of personal property or educational services states the carrying charge separately, but does not specify the interest, the deduction is limited to an imputed amount equal to one-half of 1% (0.5%) of the unpaid balance on the first day of each month.[27] This situation is seldom encountered.

DISCOUNTED NOTES

Sometimes taxpayers borrow by discounting their own notes payable, which means that the lender advances the face amount of the note less the amount of discount (interest) charged. If the principal and interest are payable in a single payment at maturity, a cash-basis taxpayer can generally deduct interest only when payment is made.[28] However, an accrual-basis taxpayer will amortize the discount over the period of the loan, using either the effective rate of interest or simply amortizing the discount ratably over the period of the loan.[29]

> **Example 8:** Thurgood, an accrual-basis taxpayer, signed a note for $1,200 on October 1, 19X3, with repayment to be made one year later. The bank discounted the note at $200 and advanced Thurgood $1,000. Thurgood may deduct $50.00 (3/12 × $200) in 19X3.

The 1984 Act added extensive rules in Sections 1271–1275 governing the treatment of "original issue discounts" (OID). While Congress was primarily concerned with the holders of obligations (lenders) to avoid the deferral of interest income until maturity of notes, the new rules also apply to the issuer or borrower and permit the deduction of discounts as the holder reports income.[30] The rules given above and the result in Example 8 are still correct because of exceptions to the new rule. Coverage of the rules for OIDs is beyond the scope of this introductory text.

EXCESSIVE INVESTMENT INTEREST

Prior to 1969 taxpayers could deduct all interest expense except that related to tax-free income. This rule permitted taxpayers to incur voluntarily

[27] Sec. 163(b).
[28] *J. R. Hopkins*, 15 T.C. 160 (1951).
[29] *B. Foster*, 32 TCM 243 (1975).
[30] Sec. 1278(b).

substantial interest expense on funds borrowed to acquire or carry investment assets. Often these funds were used to purchase stocks that had growth potential but returned little or no dividends currently. This gave rise to an immediate deduction and permitted the taxpayer to report gain on sale of the appreciated securities as long-term capital gain. Undeveloped real estate offered the same kind of tax parlay. In order to curtail excessive abuse of this tax break, tax laws now limit the amount of interest deductible on funds borrowed by noncorporate taxpayers to purchase investment property. The limitation for interest on such indebtedness is the sum of (*a*) $10,000 ($5,000 if married and filing separately) plus (*b*) net investment income for the year.[31]

Investment income is defined as the gross income from interest, dividends, royalties, rents, net short-term gains from the disposition of investment property, and amounts treated as ordinary income under depreciation recapture rules for real and personal property, where such property is held for investment.[32] Expenses relating to investment properties are deducted from investment income to compute net investment income. These expenses include such items as taxes, amortizable bond premiums, and bad debts.[33]

Example 9: An individual paid interest of $45,000 this year on funds borrowed to purchase investment property. During the year she received investment income consisting of interest and dividends totaling $5,000 and incurred investment expenses of $2,000. Her investment interest deduction is limited to $13,000, computed as follows:

Basic amount deducted without restriction	$10,000
Excess of investment income over investment expenses ($5,000 − $2,000)	3,000
Amount of investment interest deducted this year	$13,000

In the example above, the remaining $32,000 investment interest paid by the taxpayer is not deductible this year. However, any excess amount is carried foward and treated as interest paid or accrued in the succeeding tax year.[34] Thus, there is, in effect, an unlimited carryover. FORM 4952

Increased limits exist when the taxpayer, the taxpayer's spouse, or the taxpayer's children own more than 50% of a partnership or corporation and the investment indebtedness is incurred in connection with the acquisition of the interest in the corporation or partnership.[35]

Where investment interest is paid on indebtedness incurred on or after September 11, 1975 (known as "post-1975 interest"), as well as on indebt-

[31] Sec. 163(d)(1).
[32] Sec. 163(d)(3)(B).
[33] Sec. 163(d)(3)(c).
[34] Sec. 163(d)(2).
[35] Sec. 163(d)(7).

edness incurred before that date (known as "pre-1976 interest"), separate computations must be made for the excess investment interest for the two periods. The rules governing pre-1976 interest are not discussed in this book.

Another deviation from the normal rules for deducting interest arises from a requirement that interest and taxes incurred during the "construction period" of assets must be capitalized. This requirement is discussed in Chapter 8.[36]

REPORTING INTEREST DEDUCTIONS ON INDIVIDUAL RETURNS

The purpose for which related funds are borrowed determines whether interest deducted by an individual is deductible *for determining* AGI or *from* AGI.[37] Thus, interest paid or incurred by an individual on indebtedness related to conduct of the taxpayer's trade or business (other than as an employee) is deductible *for determining* AGI.[38] The same is true of interest on debt incurred in connection with the production of rents or royalties.[39] All other interest, such as on the taxpayer's home mortgage, on personal loans, on income tax liability, and on funds borrowed to purchase stock, bonds, or other investment assets, will be deductible *from* AGI to the extent that the total of all deductions from AGI exceeds the zero-bracket amount.

Example 10: Larry, married, filing jointly, operates a retail store and also owns an apartment building. During the current year he paid interest as follows:

on working capital loans for his business	$ 3,200
on the mortgage on the apartment house	28,000
on funds borrowed to buy shares of stock	700
on his home mortgage	900
on personal bank credit cards, installment accounts, etc.	200

The first two items are deductible *for determining* AGI. The last three are included with other itemized deductions from AGI and all of the deductions from AGI will be deductible to the extent they exceed the zero bracket.

TAXES

Certain taxes paid to state and local governmental units are deductible even though they are not incurred in connection with a trade or business or other income-producing activity. Section 164(a) provides:

[36] Sec. 189(a).

[37] *Wharton v. U.S.*, 207 F.2d 526 (CA-5, 1953).

[38] Sec. 62(1).

[39] Sec. 62(5).

(a) General Rule. Except as otherwise provided in this section, the following taxes shall be allowed as a deduction for the taxable year within which paid or accrued:
(1) State and local, and foreign, real property taxes.
(2) State and local personal property taxes.
(3) State and local, and foreign, income, war profits, and excess profits taxes.
(4) State and local general sales taxes.
(5) The windfall profit tax imposed by section 4986.

In addition, there shall be allowed as a deduction State and local, and foreign, taxes not described in the preceding sentence which are paid or accrued within the taxable year in carrying on a trade or business or an activity described in Section 212 (relating to expenses for production of income).

Thus all taxes paid or incurred in carrying on a trade or business or in the production of income are generally deductible, while only those taxes named specifically in Sec. 164(a) are deductible if they are not incurred in trade or business or in connection with income-producing activities.

The Regulations describe a number of taxes that are not deductible. These include:[40]

(a) Federal income taxes;
(b) Federal war profits and excess profits taxes;
(c) Estate and gift taxes;
(d) Foreign income, war profits and excess profits taxes *if* the taxpayer has elected to take a credit for the foreign taxes;
(e) Real property taxes required to be treated as imposed on another taxpayer;
(f) Federal duties and excise taxes;
(g) Taxes for local benefits; and
(h) Excise tax on real estate investment trusts.

Some of the more commonly encountered problems relating to deductions for taxes are discussed below.

PROPERTY TAXES

A deduction for "personal property taxes" is limited to ***ad valorem taxes*** (taxes based on value) on personal property.[41] Thus, a tax based on some other factor—such as an automobile's "weight, model year, and horsepower"—does not qualify for deduction as a "tax."[42]

AD VALOREM TAXES
Taxes based on value of property.

Example 11: Darnell lives in a state which imposes a tax on motorized vehicles. The tax is based on the vehicle's gross weight. The tax is not deductible.

---

[40] Reg. Sec. 1.164-2.
[41] Sec. 164(b)(1).
[42] Reg. Sec. 1.164-3(c)(1).

Regulation 1.164-4 elaborates on the prohibition of a deduction for so-called taxes assessed for local benefits. Assessments for such local benefits as

> . . . streets, sidewalks, and other like improvements, imposed because of and measured by some benefit inuring directly to the property against which the assessment is levied are not deductible as taxes.[43]

However, insofar as such assessments "are made for the purpose of maintenance or repair or for the purpose of meeting interest charges with respect to such benefits," they are deductible.[44]

Example 12: In the current year Easton made three payments to the city for taxes levied on land owned by Easton:

Ad Valorem taxes	$1,900
Special assessment for construction of streets and gutters adjoining the property	280
Special assessment for repairs to sidewalk adjoining the property	30

The ad valorem taxes and the special assessment for sidewalk repairs are deductible. The "construction taxes" are not.

When real estate is sold "during any real property tax year" (during the fiscal year of the taxing authority) the portion of taxes relating to the period up until the date of sale is properly deductible by the seller, while the portion of taxes beginning with the date of sale is properly deductible by the buyer.[45]

Example 13: The real property tax year in County R is April 1 to March 31. A, the owner of real property located in County R on April 1, 1984 sells the real property to B on June 30, 1984. B owns the real property from June 30, 1984 through March 31, 1985. The real property tax for the real property tax year April 1, 1984 to March 31, 1985 is $365. For purposes of section 164(a), $90, (a portion representing 90 days—April 1, 1984 through June 29, 1984—of the real property tax) is treated as imposed on A, the seller, and $275, (the portion for the balance of the year of 275 days—June 30, 1984 through March 31, 1985—of such real property tax) is treated as imposed on B, the purchaser.[46]

Generally, taxes for the tax year during which the sale occurs will be paid by the purchaser. The buyer treats that portion of cost applicable to

---

[43] Reg. Sec. 1.164-4(a).

[44] Reg. Sec. 1.164-4(b)(1).

[45] Sec. 164(d) and Reg. Sec. 1.164-6(b)(1)(i).

[46] Reg. Sec. 1.164-6(b)(3), Example 1.

the period the property was owned by the seller as additional purchase price, but takes a tax deduction for that portion of taxes beginning with the date of purchase.

> **Example 14:** Assume in Example 13 that B subsequently pays the taxes of $365. Of that amount, B will treat $90 as an additional capitalized cost of the real estate and will take a tax deduction for $275 representing taxes after date of purchase.

SALES TAXES AND EXCISE TAXES

Sec. 164(a) provides that ***general sales taxes*** are deductible. The Regulations explain that to qualify as a general sales tax, a tax must meet two tests:[47]

GENERAL SALES TAX A tax based on retail sales and levied at one rate for a broad range of items.

1. It must be on "retail" sales.
2. The tax must be general—that is, it must be imposed at one rate with respect to retail sales of a broad range of classes of items, including either commodities or services.

Thus, a selective sales tax which applies only to sales of alcoholic beverages, tobacco, admissions, luxury items, and a few other items is not "general," and such taxes would not be deductible (unless incurred in trade or business or for income production).[48]

The sales tax must be separately stated and passed on to the consumer. In general, this test is met where "at the time of sale to the consumer the tax was added to the sale price and collected or charged as a separate item."[49]

Although Reg. Sec. 1.164-3(f) provides that a sales tax must be imposed at one rate, Paragraph (g) of that Regulation states, "The fact that a sales tax applies to food, clothing, medical supplies, and motor vehicles, or any of them, at a rate which is lower than the general rate of tax will not prohibit the tax being considered as a general sales tax."[50]

> **Example 15:** Reynolds purchased a new automobile for $10,000 in the current year. Although a general retail sales tax of 5% is levied in the state, automobiles are taxed at a rate of 4%. Reynolds may deduct the $400 tax paid on the automobile purchase.

To assist the taxpayer in determining a reasonable deduction for state sales taxes in the absence of an accurate record of expenditures, the IRS has provided a series of tables (one for each state) that stipulate an acceptable sales-tax deduction. The tables, reproduced in Appendix C, are based on the amount of the taxpayer's adjusted gross income plus

---

[47] Reg. Sec. 1.164-3(b).

[48] Reg. Sec. 1.164-3(g)(1).

[49] Reg. Sec. 1.164-5.

[50] Reg. Sec. 1.164-3(g)(3).

nontaxable receipts such as social security benefits, the capital-gain deduction, dividend exclusion, etc., and on the number of persons in the taxpayer's family. Most taxpayers use these standard tables rather than keeping detailed records of taxes paid on countless small purchases.

Taxpayers living in a city that imposes an additional sales tax can prorate an appropriate amount, in addition to the amount stipulated in the IRS table for that state, to determine the total amount deductible, if the table does not already contain a provision for local sales taxes. Finally, in addition to the amount shown in the tables, a deduction is allowed for sales taxes paid on automobiles, boats, airplanes, materials to build a new home (under certain conditions), and mobile homes.

Example 16: Mr. and Mrs. Weil, residents of New York, file a joint return. They have three dependents and their adjusted gross income for the year is $49,800. In addition, they received $600 of tax-free interest and excluded $200 of dividends received. The city in which they live also levies a 2% general sales tax. Based on a recomputed income amount of $50,600 ($49,800 + $600 + $200) and the New York table in Appendix C, their standard state sales tax deduction is $747:

State tax related to the first $40,000 of income	$506
State tax related to remaining $10,600 ($17 × 3)	51
Total sales tax	$557
Add: city tax (2 × .26 × $557)	290
Total	$747

EXCISE TAX A tax levied on the sale of a single item or relatively narrow group of items.

Excise taxes are not deductible as "taxes," even though they may be deductible as an expense if related to a profit-seeking activity.

Example 17: Thomason purchases tires for his personal automobile. Included in the purchase price of $256 are state excise taxes of $16. In addition a sales tax of $12.80 is levied on the $256 sales price. The sales tax of $12.80 will be deductible, but the excise taxes of $16 are not deductible.

If the tires had been purchased for business use, the entire cost of $268.80 would have been deductible as a business expense.

INCOME TAXES

Although federal income taxes paid are *never* deductible, generally an *individual* taxpayer can deduct state, local, or foreign income taxes as personal deductions *from* AGI. This is true even though the individual's only source of income is from business, rents or royalties.[51] However, if a state or local tax is levied on gross income attributable to a trade or business,

[51] Rev. Rul. 70-40, 1970-1 C.B. 50.

the tax qualifies as a deduction *for* determining AGI. A corporate taxpayer is entitled to deduct such taxes as business expenses. Taxpayers can (and usually do) elect to take a credit rather than a deduction for foreign income taxes paid.

A common question arising in connection with state income taxes relates to the time that an individual taxpayer should deduct state income taxes withheld by the taxpayer's employer from the employee's pay. A cash-basis taxpayer will deduct the amount *paid* during the year, whether paid through withholding by the employer or by direct payments by the taxpayer. If a taxpayer deducts the amount withheld by an employer in a year and, because the amount withheld exceeds the actual tax liability, receives a refund in the subsequent year, the amount of refund is treated as gross income to the extent that it represents a tax benefit resulting from the deduction in the prior year.

Example 18: Sue is a cash-basis taxpayer. In 19X5 Sue's employer withheld $420 in state income taxes from Sue's earnings. She itemized deductions from AGI in 19X5, deducting the entire $420 withheld.

On May 1, 19X6 Sue filed her state income tax return for 19X5. The state return showed actual taxes of $360 for the year, so Sue received a refund of $60. To the extent that the $60 represents an amount which gave rise to a tax benefit in 19X5, it will be included in gross income in 19X6.

OTHER TAXES

Social Security taxes imposed on the employee, as well as railroad retirement taxes, are not deductible by the employee. The employer can, of course, deduct the employer's portion of such taxes if it is incurred in connection with a trade or business. However, employer taxes related to domestic labor or other activities not related to income production are not deductible by the employer.

Estate taxes, inheritance taxes, legacy taxes, and succession taxes are nondeductible, as are federal and state gift taxes.

Example 19: Graham operates a business that is not incorporated. In 19X4, Graham paid the following taxes related to his employees' earnings:

Social Security taxes (federal)	$8,920
Unemployment taxes (federal)	810
Unemployment taxes (state)	3,200

In addition Graham paid federal self-employment taxes of $1,900 on his own self-employment income.

Graham may deduct all of the $12,930 in taxes related to earnings of his employees. The self-employment taxes of $1,900 are not deductible.

CHARITABLE CONTRIBUTIONS

CHARITABLE CONTRIBUTION Contribution made to or for the use of one of the types of organizations listed in Sec. 170(c).

At the present time, both individual and corporate taxpayers may deduct ***charitable contributions*** made to qualifying recipients. Most questions regarding contribution deductions involve either the determination of a gift's eligibility for deduction or the determination of the amount that may be deducted.

PRESENT PROVISIONS RELATING TO CONTRIBUTIONS BY INDIVIDUALS

Contributions made by individuals are deductible, within limits, if they are made to (or "for the use of") one of the types of organizations listed in Sec. 170(c), which reads as follows:

> (1) A State, a possession of the United States, or any political subdivision of any of the foregoing, or the United States or the District of Columbia, but only if the contribution or gift is made for exclusively public purposes.
>
> (2) A corporation, trust, or community chest, fund, or foundation—
>
> (A) created or organized in the United States or in any possession thereof, or under the law of the United States, any State, the District of Columbia, or any possession of the United States;
>
> (B) organized and operated exclusively for religious, charitable, scientific, literary, or educational purposes or to foster national or international amateur sports competition . . . , or for the prevention of cruelty to children or animals;
>
> (C) no part of the net earnings of which inures to the benefit of any private shareholder or individual; and
>
> (D) which is not disqualified for tax exemption under section 501(c)(3) by reason of attempting to influence legislation, and which does not participate in, or intervene in (including the publishing or distribution of statements), any political campaign on behalf of any candidate for public office.
>
> A contribution or gift by a corporation to a trust, chest, fund, or foundation shall be deductible by reason of this paragraph only if it is to be used within the United States or any of its possessions exclusively for purposes specified in subparagraph (B) . . .
>
> (3) A post or organization of war veterans or any auxiliary unit or society of, or trust or foundation for, any such post or organization—
>
> (A) organized in the United States or any of its possessions, and
>
> (B) no part of the net earnings of which inures to the benefit of any private shareholder or individual.
>
> (4) In the case of a contribution or gift by an individual, a domestic fraternal society, order, or association, operating under the lodge system, but only if such contribution or gift is to be used exclusively for religious, charitable, scientific, literary, or educational purposes, or for the prevention of cruelty to children or animals.
>
> (5) A cemetery company owned and operated exclusively for the benefit of its members, or any corporation chartered solely for burial purposes as a

cemetery corporation and not permitted by its charter to engage in any business not necessarily incident to that purpose, if such company or corporation is not operated for profit and no part of the net earnings of such company or corporation inures to the benefit of any private shareholder or individual.

Note that in order to be deductible, charitable contributions must be made to a qualifying organization that fits into one of the classes listed in Code Sec. 170(c). Contributions to individuals, no matter how needy, are not tax deductible.[52]

A contribution made to a qualifying organization is just what the words imply—a direct gift to the organization. A contribution made "for the use of" an organization involves an indirect gift. For example, an individual might make a gift to a trust and, in turn, direct the trustee to contribute that gift (and, possibly, any income that it produces) to a qualifying charity. Alternatively, an individual might pay a liability originally incurred by a charitable organization. In either of the latter two cases, the gift is deemed to be "for the use of" the recipient organization, and is subject to the special limits applicable to contributions to private foundations (discussed later in this chapter).

MEASURING THE AMOUNT CONTRIBUTED

To be deductible, a charitable contribution must be in money or property; the taxpayer cannot deduct the value of services donated to an organization.[53] Contributions of tangible, personal property must be of "present interest"—that is, a taxpayer cannot get a deduction now for a transfer that will take place at his or her death if the property involved is tangible, personal property. Contributions of "future interests" in real property are, however, possible under certain circumstances.

In some instances it is difficult to determine if a particular contribution consists of a property or a service; for example, the donation of blood has been held to be a service, not a property.[54] Similarly, the law denies a taxpayer the value of "lost rents" as a deduction when the taxpayer permits a charity to occupy rental property free of cost.[55] A taxpayer who uses a personal automobile on behalf of a charitable organization is entitled to deduct only the out-of-pocket costs (gasoline, oil, etc.) or to deduct a flat amount of 12 cents per mile.[56]

When the taxpayer contributes cash, there can be no question about the amount of the contribution. If the taxpayer contributes other property, generally the fair market value of the property at the date of contri-

[52] *S. E. Thomason*, 2 T.C. 441 (1943).

[53] Rev. Rul. 67-236, 1967-2 C.B. 103.

[54] Rev. Rul. 53-153-2 C.B. 127.

[55] Sec. 170(f)(3).

[56] Sec. 170(j).

bution is the measure of the amount given. However, in many instances the amount deemed to have been contributed depends on the nature of the property and, in some cases, the nature of the donee organization.

ORDINARY INCOME PROPERTY If property, the sale of which would have resulted in ordinary income, is contributed, the taxpayer may generally deduct only an amount equal to the fair market value of the property, less the amount that would have been recognized as ordinary income if the property had been sold for its fair market value at the date of the contribution.[57] This means that generally the cost or adjusted basis of the property is the amount of the contribution. Note that the net effect of this provision is equivalent to the taxpayer selling the property at its fair market value, recognizing the taxable gain, and contributing the sales proceeds to the charity.

ORDINARY-INCOME PROPERTY Property, the sale of which would have resulted in ordinary income.

Ordinary-income property includes several types of assets, for example:

- Inventory held for sale in the taxpayer's trade or business.
- Capital assets, such as shares of stock, land, and other investments, if held for one year or less.
- Art objects, literary works, etc., produced by the taxpayer.
- Property used in business or held for investment to the extent that its sale would result in ordinary income (usually through depreciation recapture, as discussed in Chapter 11).
- Inventories of consumable supplies that would be charged to expense when used in the business.
- Letters and memoranda written by or to the taxpayer.

Example 20: A retail furniture dealer contributed furniture from his inventory to a charitable organization. The items cost the taxpayer $2,000 but had a fair retail value of $3,800. The amount of the contribution would be $2,000.

Example 21: Martha purchased 100 shares of stock in November 19X2 for $1,800. In June 19X3, when the shares had a fair market value of $2,800, she contributed them to her church. The amount of her contribution is $1,800.

Example 22: Martha purchased 100 shares of stock in November 19X1 for $1,800. In June 19X3, when the shares had a fair market value of $1,300, she contributed the shares to her church. The amount of the contribution is $1,300. (Obviously Martha would have been wiser to sell the shares for $1,300, recognizing a loss on the sale, and then contributed the $1,300 to the church.)

[57] Sec. 170(e)(1).

BACKGROUND

Prior to 1970, a taxpayer was entitled to deduct the fair market value of *any* noncash property contributed to a charity. As a result, it was possible to achieve a greater positive cash flow from making a contribution than from selling. For example, if a taxpayer in the 70% rate bracket in 1969 contributed to a qualified organization merchandise inventory that cost $1,000 but had a fair market value of $2,000, he or she would deduct $2,000 as a contribution, resulting in an income-tax saving of $1,400. Thus, the tax saving would exceed the cost of the item contributed by $400. Had the taxpayer sold the same inventory, the $1,000 ordinary income would have been subject to a $700 tax, thus leaving only $300 in excess of the cost after taxes.

CAPITAL-GAIN PROPERTY If property, the sale of which would have resulted in *long-term* capital gain, is contributed to a qualified organization, the fair market value of the property is deemed to be the amount contributed with the following two exceptions:

1. Tangible *personal* property unrelated to the donee organization's exempt function (for example, an object of art that will be resold by the donee charity).[58]
2. Any capital-gain property contributed to a nonoperating *private* foundation that does not meet certain technical requirements. (Because this exception is rarely encountered, we will not discuss it further.)

The property involved under this provision is ***capital-gain property*** held for more than one year. The most common capital assets would be shares of stock, land, buildings, and purchased works of art.

CAPITAL-GAIN PROPERTY Property, the sale of which would result in a *long*-term capital gain.

Example 23: Larson purchased 100 shares of stock for $1,800 in November 19X2. In December 19X3, when the shares had a fair market value of $3,100, Larson contributed them to his church. The amount of the contribution is $3,100.

In the case of property that fits into the two exceptions above, the amount deemed to have been contributed is the property's fair market value minus 40% of the amount of the property's appreciation over the taxpayer's basis in the property. Once again, the tax result is equivalent to selling the property at its fair market value, recognizing the taxable gain (40% of the appreciation), and contributing the sales proceeds to the charity.

[58] Sec. 170(e)(1)(B).

Example 24: Mounts paid $1,000 for a painting four years ago and this year, when its fair market value was $4,000, contributed the painting to a university. The amount deductible depends on the intended use of the property made by the university. If it is hung in the university's art gallery, the amount deductible will be the fair market value of $4,000. On the other hand, if it is resold by the university, the amount deductible will be $2,800: $4,000 fair market value minus $1,200 (40% of the $3,000 "gain").

THE MAXIMUM AMOUNT DEDUCTIBLE

The deduction for contributions by an individual can in no case exceed 50% of the taxpayer's adjusted gross income for the year.[59] However, the limit in some cases may be less than 50% of adjusted gross income, depending on the nature of the property given and type of donee to which the contribution is made. As a practical matter, these limits are only rarely applicable.

CONTRIBUTIONS TO 50%-LIMIT ORGANIZATIONS The deduction for contributions made directly to "public charities" generally is limited to 50% of AGI. Public charities include churches, educational institutions, organizations for medical care, governmental units or other organizations that get a substantial portion of their support from the public or from a governmental unit, and a relatively small number of "private foundations" that meet specific requirements.[60]

The deduction for contributions to public charities of appreciated capital-gain properties is, however, subject to a special limit of 30% of AGI.

Example 25: In the current year, Mason, whose AGI is $9,000, contributes a work of art (that cost him $2,000 ten years ago and had a fair market value of $8,000 at the date of gift) to the city art museum to be used as part of its permanent exhibition. The current deduction for this contribution would be limited to 30% of Mason's AGI, or $2,700.

When applying the overall 50% limit, contributions of 30%-limit property are the last to be considered, assuming that there are no contributions to private foundations.[61]

Example 26: Siegfried, who has AGI of $10,000, gives $2,600 cash to public charities and a capital-gain property with a fair market value of $4,000 to a public museum. He can deduct only $5,000, or 50% of his AGI this year. The deduction consists of the $2,600 cash contribution and $2,400 of the value of the capital-gain property.

---

[59] Sec. 170(b).

[60] Sec. 170(b)(1)(A).

[61] Sec. 170(b)(1)(C)(1).

(The $1,600 excess of capital-gain property contributed over the 50% limit can be carried forward to future years, as discussed later in this chapter.)

SPECIAL ELECTION FOR INCREASING CEILING FOR CONTRIBUTION OF CAPITAL-GAINS PROPERTY Under a special election provided in Section 170(b), the taxpayer may elect to disregard the 30% of AGI ceiling on deductions for contributions of capital-gain property and to treat such contributions under the usual 50% ceiling for other contributions. In doing so, however, the taxpayer must reduce the fair market value of the capital-gain property by an amount equal to 40% of the difference between the fair market value of the property and its adjusted basis.[62]

Example 27: During the current year, Dickerson's AGI was $30,000. His sole contribution was a gift made to his church of stock that had cost Dickerson $13,000 several years previously and had a fair market value of $14,000 at the date of the gift. Under the general rules, the amount of Dickerson's contribution is deemed to be $14,000 and the amount deductible is limited to $9,000 (30% of AGI). The amount not deductible in the current year, $5,000, would be carried over to the next year and treated as a contribution of capital-gain property in that year.

Example 28: Under the special election described above, Dickerson can measure the amount of the contribution as $13,600 ($14,000, minus 40% of $1,000) and, in doing so, may increase the ceiling on the deduction to $15,000 (50% of $30,000). Thus, the entire contribution of $13,600 will be deductible in the current year.

It is obvious from Example 28 that many factors must be considered in making this election: the amount of potential gain involved; the relationship between the taxpayer's AGI, the property's fair market value, and the property's adjusted basis; other capital gains and losses; and the taxpayer's present and future income levels.

LIMIT ON DEDUCTIONS TO CERTAIN PRIVATE FOUNDATIONS The deduction for contributions to *private* foundations that do not meet specified requirements is limited to 20% of the taxpayer's AGI. The same limit also applies to contributions made *for the use of*, rather than *directly to*, public charities. If contributions are made to both public charities and private foundations, the contributions to public charities must be deducted first. These rules can be illustrated by two simple examples.

Example 29: Conrad has AGI of $20,000. His only contributions were $5,500 cash to Harvard University and $6,000 cash to a private foundation. His deduction is limited to $9,500, consisting of the

[62] Sec. 170(b)(1)(C)(iii).

$5,500 given Harvard University and $4,000 of the contribution to the private foundation, which is limited to 20% of AGI.

Example 30: Assume the same facts as in Example 29, except that Conrad's contribution to Harvard was $9,000. His deduction would be limited to $10,000 (50% of AGI). The deduction would consist of $9,000 given to Harvard and $1,000 of the gift to the private foundation.

For cases in which the value of capital-gain properties contributed to public charities exceeds 30% of AGI and contributions are also made to private foundations, the computation of the limit on the amount deductible for the private foundation contributions becomes more complex. Since this situation is rarely encountered, it is not discussed in this text.

CONTRIBUTIONS CARRYOVER

Any contributions to public charities in excess of 50% of the individual taxpayer's AGI can be carried over to the following year and treated as having been paid that year. If the sum of the carryover and the actual contributions made to public charities in the second year again exceeds 50% of the taxpayer's AGI, the excess may be carried over to the next following year. This procedure can be repeated for up to five years.[63] If, because of the percentage limitation, a contribution cannot be deducted fully during the 5-year carryover period, any unused amount is simply lost as a deduction. In each year, the contributions actually paid during that year must be deducted before any of the contribution carryover can be applied.[64] If excess contributions are carried over from more than one tax year, the carryovers are used in order of occurrence (on a FIFO basis).

Contributions to private foundations can never be used to determine a contribution carryover; there is a carryover only if contributions to public charities exceed 50% of AGI (with the exception of carryovers of contributions of capital-gain property in excess of the 30% limit). Thus, in both Examples 29 and 30, above, the taxpayer (Conrad) would lose some of the tax benefit associated with his contributions to a private charity.

The calculation of the contribution carryover can be illustrated by the following tabulation, prepared for an individual with an AGI of $10,000.

	AMOUNT CONTRIBUTED TO: PUBLIC CHARITIES	PRIVATE FOUNDATIONS	MAXIMUM DEDUCTION IN CURRENT YEAR	CONTRIBUTION CARRYOVER
Case A	$6,000	$ 0	$5,000	$1,000
Case B	0	6,000	2,000	0
Case C	5,500	800	5,000	500
Case D	3,500	2,500	5,000	0

[63] Sec. 170(d)(1).

[64] Sec. 170(d)(1)(A).

The relationship between the contribution carryover and the contributions actually made during a year can also be illustrated in a simple tabulation. Assume that a taxpayer's only contributions were made in cash to public charities in the amounts shown in the tabulation below. Also, assume that the taxpayer had AGI of $60,000 each year. This taxpayer must exhaust the 19X6 contribution carryover by December 31, 19X9, since it comes from the 19X4 excess contributions.

	AMOUNT CONTRIBUTED (ALL TO PUBLIC CHARITIES)	NOT DEDUCTIBLE IN CURRENT YEAR	CONTRIBUTION CARRYOVER
19X1	$50,000	$30,000	$20,000
19X2	40,000	30,000	30,000
19X3	20,000	30,000	20,000
19X4	32,000	30,000	22,000
19X5	20,000	30,000	12,000
19X6	20,000	30,000	2,000

Contributions of appreciated capital-gain property that are in excess of the 30% limitation may be carried over to future years and added to the capital-gain contributions of the future years, subject to a 5-year carryover.[65]

REPORTING CONTRIBUTIONS OF INDIVIDUALS

Contributions made by individual taxpayers are deductible *from* AGI. Prior to 1982, all charitable contributions were added to other itemized deductions and if the total of all such deductions exceeded the zero-bracket amount, the excess was deductible. Because of the increases in the zero-bracket amount prior to 1982, many taxpayers did not have enough in itemized deductions to secure a benefit from itemizing. Thus, there was less incentive for those taxpayers to make contributions. In order to encourage contributions, Section 170(i) was added in 1981.

Under this Section a ***direct charitable contribution*** is allowed as a deduction from adjusted gross income even though the taxpayer's itemized deductions do not exceed the zero-bracket amount. The "direct charitable contribution" for 1985 is 50% of eligible contributions made during the year, with the regular ceiling placed on "eligible" contributions. Then, in 1986, 100 percent of contributions can be deducted directly from gross income with the regular limits applicable to contributions.

DIRECT CHARITABLE CONTRIBUTION A contribution of property (rather than the mere use of property) to a charitable organization.

For contributions made after 1986 the pre-1982 rules will again become effective and contributions will be added to other itemized deductions, with the excess over the zero-bracket amount being deductible.

Example 31: In 1985 Mr. and Mrs. Alkire had adjusted gross income of $20,000. Their itemized deductions included:

---

[65] Sec. 170(b)(1)(C)(ii).

Interest	$1,700
Taxes	900
Contributions	350
Total	$2,950

Although the Alkires' itemized deductions do not exceed the zero-bracket amount of $3,400, they will be entitled to deduct $175 as a "direct charitable contribution" (50% of charitable contributions).

The "direct charitable contribution" ceiling is the same for single persons and married couples. However, for a married person filing a separate return, the ceiling is half of the amounts shown for other taxpayers.[66] If Congress raises taxes in 1985, the amount of the direct deduction for contributions will probably be reduced with the dollar limit of $75 that was applicable to 1984 extended to 1985 and 1986.

Generally the taxpayer is not required to include in the tax return the names of donees of cash contributions. However, Form 1040, Schedule A, on which contributions are reported, specifies that if cash contributions total $3,000 or more to any one organization, the name of the organization and the amount of contribution must be shown. In addition, if contributions of noncash property exceed $200 in a year, the taxpayer must attach a statement to the return which shows the name and address of the donee, the date of the donation, the kind of property contributed, the fair market value of the property at the time of contribution, and the method of determining the fair market value.[67] The IRS has issued guidelines for appraising contributed property.[68]

Under most circumstances an individual taxpayer is allowed to deduct contributions only in the year in which he or she actually transfers the cash or other property to the qualified recipient. Pledges of contributions are not deductible until paid. This restriction is applicable equally to accrual-basis taxpayers and to cash-basis taxpayers. Payments by credit card, however, are treated as cash payments in the year the credit slip is signed.

The contributions deduction for corporations is discussed in Chapter 16.

MEDICAL EXPENSES

Every individual taxpayer is entitled to a limited deduction for expenses paid during the year for the medical care of the taxpayer, the taxpayer's spouse, and the taxpayer's dependents. (For this purpose, a "dependent" does not have to meet the gross-income test nor the "joint-return test" discussed in Chapter 3.)[69]

---

[66] Sec. 170(i)(3).

[67] Reg. Sec. 1.170A-1(a)(2)(ii).

[68] Rev. Proc. 66-49, 1966-2 C.B. 1257.

[69] Reg. Sec. 1.213-1(a)(3).

GENERAL RULE

The basic authority for deduction of medical expenses is Sec. 213, which reads in part as follows:

> (a) Allowance of Deduction.—There shall be allowed as a deduction the expenses paid during the taxable year, not compensated for by insurance or otherwise, for medical care of the taxpayer, his spouse, or a dependent (as defined in section 152), to the extent that such expenses exceed 5 percent of adjusted gross income.
>
> (b) Limitation with Respect to Medicine and Drugs.—An amount paid during the taxable year for medicine or a drug shall be taken into account under subsection (a) only if such medicine or drug is a prescribed drug or is insulin.

THE PROBLEM OF DEFINING MEDICAL EXPENSES

"Medical care" is further defined in Sec. 213(e)(1) as follows:

> (1) The term "medical care" means amounts paid—
> (A) for the diagnosis, cure, mitigation treatment, or prevention of disease, or for the purpose of affecting any structure or function of the body,
> (B) for transportation primarily for and essential to medical care referred to in subparagraph (A), or
> (C) for insurance . . . covering medical care referred to in subparagraphs (A) and (B).

Thus, medical costs include unreimbursed amounts paid for medical and dental care, such as physician's charges, hospital rooms, nursing care, laboratory charges, dentures, optical care, glasses, and similar costs. In addition, some costs of medicines and drugs, transportation and travel related to medical care, capital outlays for devices and equipment related to infirmity or physical handicaps, nursing care, and ***medical insurance*** premiums may be deductible. The final medical expense deduction is the *excess* of the qualifying medical expenditures over 5% of adjusted gross income. Because of the uncertainty surrounding these items, however, they are examined in greater detail.

MEDICAL INSURANCE Insurance that provides payment for medical care.

MEDICINES AND DRUGS The term "medicines and drugs" includes only drugs and medicines obtained by prescription and the costs of insulin (whether or not prescribed).[70] Prior to 1984, qualifying "medicines and drugs" did not have to be prescribed; however, the total deduction for medicines and drugs was allowed only to the extent that it exceeded 1% of adjusted gross income.

Example 32: Rasould, whose adjusted gross income was $20,000, incurred the following expenditures during the current year.

[70] Sec. 213(b).

A b c c b

Prescription drugs	$194
Aspirin and other items for relief of aches and pains	16
After-shave lotion	3
Toothpaste	9
Vitamins for general health	28
Total	$250

Only the prescription drugs are included in the definition of medicines and drugs. Thus, Rasould can include $194 of these costs in medical expenses.

TRANSPORTATION AND TRAVEL Transportation costs "primarily for and essential to" medical care are considered medical costs. For example, the costs of taxi fares, ambulance hire, airline fares, etc., incurred in acquiring medical care are deductible. The taxpayer who uses his or her personal automobile for transportation to secure medical care may deduct either the actual expenses incurred or use the standard allowance of 9¢ per mile, plus parking fees and toll charges. (This mileage allowance will probably be raised to 12¢ later in 1985.)

The deductible costs of transportation to and from the place of treatment include the costs of meals and lodgings while in transit if the taxpayer is "away from home."[71] Once the taxpayer reaches the place of treatment, the costs of lodgings up to $50 per day are treated as medical expense as long as the care is in a hospital under the direction of a physician.[72] The cost of meals is not included. This rule became effective in 1984; before that date the costs of lodgings were not medical expenses.

Example 33: Hampton traveled by automobile to Mayo Clinic for diagnosis of his health problem. Hampton stayed overnight in a motel during this trip, and took his meals in restaurants along the way. Once at the clinic, Hampton lived in a hotel adjacent to the clinic, paying $75 per night for the room. He also spent $30 per day for meals. Hampton can include as medical expenses 12¢ per mile for the automobile, the meals and lodgings while in transit, and $50 per day for lodgings while at the clinic. The meals while at the clinic are not deductible.

The allowance of the lodging costs while in out-patient status applies only where care is provided by a licensed physician and only if there is no "significant element of personal pleasure" in the travel.

Example 34: Henrietta, a native of Buffalo, eats too much, a fact that causes a potential health problem. Her doctor recommends a dieting and grooming spa in Tucson that panders to wealthy, overweight women. Henrietta visits the spa for a month in February and

[71] *Montgomery v. Comm.*, 428 F. 2d 243 (C.A. 6, 1970).

[72] Sec. 213(d)(2).

looks much better afterward, according to her fifth husband. The cost of the spa is not a medical expense.

The line between legitimate health care and a pleasure trip is not always clear.

CAPITAL EXPENDITURES Capital expenditures related specifically to the illness of an individual may also be deductible. For example, the cost of a wheelchair would be deductible in full in the year purchased. However, capital expenditures that increase the value of property will not be allowed as a deduction to the extent of the increase in value of the property.[73]

Example 35: Laramie suffers a degenerative muscle disease. As part of a treatment of physical therapy, Laramie's physician recommended that Laramie install a swimming pool at his home and that he swim at least two hours each day. Laramie had the pool installed at a cost of $14,000. The pool increased the value of Laramie's home by $10,000. The remaining $4,000, which did not result in an increase in value, will be deductible as medical expense in the year paid.[74]

Costs of such items as crutches and braces are fully deductible.

NURSING CARE Amounts paid nurses during a hospital stay are clearly deductible. Similarly, the cost of nursing care in the taxpayer's home would also be deductible. If, however, an individual is hired to perform both nursing care and household work in the taxpayer's home, only that portion of the cost applicable to nursing care would be considered a medical cost. (If the expense is allowed as the basis for credit for child care, as discussed in Chapter 14, it cannot be treated as a medical expense.)[75]

Example 36: Nero was dismissed from the hospital after surgery but needed medical care for two weeks at home. Because Nero was unmarried, he hired a nurse to provide medical care for him and also to do housework such as cleaning and cooking. The total amount paid the nurse during the two weeks was $750. Of the time spent by the nurse, two-thirds was reasonably allocated to medical care and one-third to housework. Nero could treat $500 of the amount as medical expense.

Another common situation in which it is difficult to distinguish between a bona fide medical expense and simply a personal expenditure arises when a member of the family is placed in a nursing home or home for the aged. If the individual is placed in the institution because of his or

---

[73] Reg. Sec. 1.213-1(e)(1).

[74] See, for example, *Riach v. Frank*, F.2d 374 (CA-9, 1962).

[75] Sec. 213(e).

her physical condition and the availability of medical care in the institution, all the costs incurred (including meals and lodging) would be considered medical costs.[76] If, however, the main reason for placing the individual in the institution is simply personal convenience or desire, only the costs actually spent for medical care would be deductible.[77]

MEDICAL INSURANCE PREMIUMS Premiums paid for medical-care insurance for the taxpayer, the taxpayer's spouse, and the taxpayer's dependents are treated as medical expenses. Deductible premiums include the premium paid for supplemental Medicare medical insurance (referred to as "Part B supplementary") for the aged.[78] However, amounts included in self-employment taxes and employee Social Security taxes for basic medicare coverage are not deductible. When an insurance policy covers loss of life, limb, etc., no part of the premiums is included in medical expenses unless the contract specifically states the coverage for medical care.

Example 37: Sampson's only medical expenses in 1984 were medical insurance premiums of $1,720. Sampson's adjusted gross income for the year was $60,000. Sampson has no "medical expenses" because the costs incurred were less than 5% of AGI:

Medical costs (Insurance premiums)	$1,720
Less 5% of AGI	3,000
Medical expenses included in itemized deductions	0

OTHER EXPENSES The variety of expenditures that taxpayers might seek to classify as medical expenses is almost endless. A few examples will show the breadth of possibilities. The cost of birth-control pills,[79] of a vasectomy,[80] and of a legal abortion[81] have all been held to be deductible. Marriage counseling costs are not deductible[82] although costs incurred by a married couple for psychiatric treatment of sexual inadequacy are deductible.[83]

The cost of special schooling for a physically handicapped[84] or mentally retarded[85] child qualifies as a medical expense if the schooling has a direct relationship to treatment and the school has special facilities for treatment. It has been held that expenses of a hair transplant performed by a dermatologist or plastic surgeon are deductible.[86] Similarly fees paid

---

[76] Reg. Sec. 1.213-1(e)(1)(v).

[77] Reg. Sec. 1.213-1(e)(1)(v)(b).

[78] Reg. Sec. 1.213-1(e)(4)(i)(a)(3).

[79] Rev Rul. 73-200, 1973-1 C.B. 140.

[80] Rev Rul. 73-201, 1973-1 C.B. 140.

[81] *Ibid.*

[82] Rev. Rul. 75-319, 1975-2 C.B. 88.

[83] Rev. Rul. 75-187, 1975-1 C.B. 97.

[84] Rev. Rul. 68-212, 1968-1 C.B. 91.

[85] Rev. Rul. 58-280, 1958-1 C.B. 157.

[86] Rev. Rul. 82-111, I.R.B. 1982-22, 10.

a plastic surgeon to perform cosmetic surgery, at the request of the patient, have been held deductible.[87]

This list could be extended to include hundreds of other items, but those mentioned demonstrate the uncertainty over whether a particular item will pass the tests for being a medical expense.

REIMBURSEMENT OF EXPENSES

The taxpayer may deduct only unreimbursed medical expenses. Thus, reimbursements from insurance policies, employer reimbursement plans, or other sources must be offset against gross expenditures before the medical expense calculation is commenced.

If reimbursement is received in a year after the expenditure was made, treatment of the reimbursement depends on whether the expenditure was deductible in the prior year. As discussed in Chapter 4, to the extent that the reimbursement represents a deduction that resulted in a tax benefit in a prior year, it must be included in gross income in the year of reimbursement.

CASUALTY AND THEFT LOSSES

Sec. 165(c) permits the deduction of losses sustained during the year to the extent of any amount "not compensated for by insurance or otherwise" if the loss is incurred in a trade or business or in a transaction entered into for a profit. In addition, for individual taxpayers, Sec. 165(c)(3) provides for the deduction of unreimbursed losses

> . . . except as provided in subsection (h), losses of property not connected with a trade or business, if such losses arise from fire, storm, shipwreck, or other casualty, or from theft. [Subsection (h) deals with the limitations on the deduction, discussed later in this chapter.]

DEFINING "CASUALTY" AND "THEFT"

Code Sec. 165(c) specifically includes "fire, storm, or shipwreck" in the definition of casualties, and it provides for the general inclusion of "other casualties." However, "other casualties" are not identified, and it is often difficult to determine if loss of property resulting from a particular event constitutes a casualty for tax purposes. In general, a sudden, unexpected, or unusual event, as well as an external force, is required before a given event can be considered a ***casualty***.[88] Thus losses caused by vandalism, car and boat accidents, earth slides, hurricanes, and sonic booms have been held deductible. No deduction is allowed for breakage of china, glassware, furniture and similar items under normal conditions, and tax deductions have been disallowed for damage due to rust, corrosion, ter-

CASUALTY Loss of taxpayer's property due to sudden, unexpected, or unusual event as the result of an external force.

[87] Rev. Rul. 76-332, 1976-2 C.B. 81.

[88] *Matheson v. Comm.*, 54 F.2d 537 (C.A.-2, 1931).

mites[89] (although some courts have allowed deductions for termite damage where the damage has been caused over a short period of up to 15 months),[90] insects, disease, and other slow-acting destructive forces. Although a casualty loss may be deductible even though the taxpayer is at fault, if the damage was caused by the taxpayer's willful act or willful negligence, no deduction will be allowed.[91] Because of the imprecision of the general criteria pertinent to the determination of a deductible casualty loss, litigation of specific facts is commonplace.

The definition of a theft loss is somewhat clearer, but whether a theft has taken place is still a matter of factual determination. The term "theft" is deemed to include, but is not limited to, larceny, embezzlement, and robbery.[92] No deduction is allowed for property the taxpayer simply lost or misplaced.[93] The reasons for the stringent rules are apparent if you consider the multiple opportunities for tax evasion that would arise under more lenient rules.

A deduction is allowed for loss to the taxpayer's own property only; thus no deduction is allowed for damage caused by the taxpayer to the property or body of another. The regulations under Sec. 165 make it clear that a loss is allowed even if the taxpayer is at fault, but not if the loss is due to the willful act or willful negligence of the taxpayer.[94]

DETERMINING THE BASIC AMOUNT OF LOSS

The amount of loss for physical damage to the taxpayer's property is basically the decrease in value of the property resulting from the casualty, not to exceed the adjusted basis of the property.[95]

Example 38: A taxpayer's property had an adjusted basis of $8,000, a fair market value of $6,000 just before a casualty, and a fair market value of $2,000 just after the casualty. The basic measure of loss sustained would be $4,000.

Example 39: A taxpayer's property had an adjusted basis of $3,000 and a market value of $6,000 just before a casualty, and a fair market value of $2,000 just after the casualty. The measure of loss sustained is $3,000.

However, if property used in trade or business or held for income production is *completely* destroyed, the adjusted basis of the property is the basic measure of loss regardless of the fair market value.[96]

---

[89] *Fay v. Helvering*, 120 F.2d 253 (C.A.-2, 1941).
[90] *Rosenberg v. Comm.*, 198 F.2d 46 (1952).
[91] Reg. 1.165-7(a)(3)(i).
[92] Reg. Sec. 1.165-8(d).
[93] *Mary Frances Allen*, 16 T.C. 163 (1951).
[94] Reg. Sec. 1.165-7(a)(3)(i).
[95] Reg. Sec. 1.165-7(b)(1).
[96] Reg. Sec. 1.165-7(b)(1)(ii).

Example 40: A taxpayer's property used in trade or business had an adjusted basis of $4,000 and a fair market value of $2,000. It was completely destroyed by a casualty. The amount of loss is $4,000.

In some cases, the cost of repairs to the property damaged is acceptable as evidence of the loss of value if (*a*) the repairs are necessary to restore the property to its condition immediately before the casualty, (*b*) the amount spent for such repairs is not excessive, (*c*) the repairs do not improve the property beyond the damage suffered, and (*d*) the value of the property after the repairs does not exceed the value immediately before the casualty.[97]

One final complication in measuring the amount of loss should be mentioned. In losses from casualty or theft related to business property, each single identifiable item damaged or destroyed is treated separately in measuring the decrease in value.[98] For example, if a storm damages a building used in trade or business and also damages or destroys ornamental shrubs on the premises, the decrease in value of the building will be computed separately from the decrease in value of the shrubs. However, in the case of property not used in a trade or business, the real property and any improvements must be considered an integral part of one property.[99] Thus, if a storm damaged the building and shrubs on the premises, the decline in value would not be computed for each item, but a single figure for the total decline in overall value of the property would be determined.

DETERMINING THE AMOUNT DEDUCTIBLE

The amount of loss deductible for casualty or theft of the taxpayer's property depends on a number of factors: the decrease in value; whether the property is used in trade or business or for income production, or is held for purely personal purposes; whether the property is completely destroyed or only partially destroyed; and the amount of insurance or other reimbursement.

In every case, the amount of potential loss must be reduced by amounts recovered under insurance or from other sources to arrive at the actual loss.[100] There are additional severe restrictions on losses of property not used in trade or business.

BUSINESS PROPERTY COMPLETELY DESTROYED If property used in trade or business or held for income production is completely destroyed, the adjusted basis of the property, less any amount of reimbursement, is deductible.[101]

---

[97] Reg. Sec. 1.165-7(a)(2)(ii).
[98] Reg. Sec. 1.165-7(a)(6)(b)(2)(i).
[99] Reg. Sec. 1.165-7(a)(6)(b)(2)(ii).
[100] Reg. Sec. 1.165-1(c)(4).
[101] Reg. Sec. 1.165-7(b)(1)(ii).

Example 41: A property with an adjusted basis of $20,000 and a fair market value of $15,000 that is used in the taxpayer's business, is completely destroyed by fire. The taxpayer collects insurance proceeds of $12,000 for the loss. The amount of deductible loss is $8,000.

BUSINESS PROPERTY PARTIALLY DESTROYED Where property is only partially destroyed, the amount of deductible loss is the adjusted basis of the property or its decrease in fair market value, whichever is smaller, reduced by insurance proceeds or other reimbursement.[102]

Example 42: A property used in the taxpayer's trade or business is damaged by fire. The property's fair market value before the fire was $8,000; after the fire it was appraised at $2,500. Insurance proceeds of $3,000 were received under a policy covering the fire. Adjusted basis of the property was $5,000. The amount deductible is $2,000:

Value before fire	$8,000
Value after fire	2,500
Decline in value	$5,500
Basis of property	$5,000
Lesser of value decline or adjusted basis	$5,000
Less insurance proceeds	3,000
Deductible loss	$2,000

Example 43: Assume the same facts as in Example 42, except that the adjusted basis of the property was $9,000. The amount deductible is:

Lower of decline in value ($5,500) or adjusted basis ($9,000)	$5,500
Less insurance proceeds	3,000
Deductible loss	$2,500

If insurance proceeds exceed the adjusted basis of the property, the taxpayer will recognize a gain on the excess.

NONBUSINESS PROPERTY For property not used in a trade or business the initial measure of the loss is always the smaller of the property's adjusted basis or the decline in value resulting from the casualty. This is true whether the property is completely destroyed or only partially destroyed. As in the case of business property, amounts recoverable from insurance or other sources are offset against the loss. In addition, only the excess of *each* nonbusiness loss over $100 can be treated as a casualty

---

[102] Reg. Sec. 1.165-7(b)(1).

loss. This $100 floor applies to each casualty, even when more than one property is damaged. Finally, only to the extent that the total of all such excesses exceeds 10% of the taxpayer's AGI can losses be deducted.[103]

Example 44: In 19X5, Knutsen suffered the following casualties.

1. A fire destroyed his home. The home, which cost $84,000, had a fair market value of $90,000. Insurance proceeds of $60,000 were received.
2. Knutsen was involved in an automobile accident. Damage to his personal car, which cost $12,000, was $1,800. Insurance proceeds of $900 were received.

Knutsen's AGI was $30,000. The amount deductible as a casualty loss is $21,700, determined as follows:

	HOME	AUTO-MOBILE	TOTAL
Lower of decline in value or adjusted basis	$84,000	$1,800	
Less insurance proceeds	60,000	900	
Balance	$24,000	$ 900	
Less $100 floor	100	100	
Loss considered	$23,900	$ 800	$24,700
Less 10% of AGI			3,000
Loss deductible			$21,700

If married spouses file a joint return, they are subject to a single $100 floor for each casualty. Thus, if a thief stole items belonging to both husband and wife, they would have a floor of $100 each for their personal casualty loss if they file separate returns. If they file a joint return, a single floor of $100 is imposed.[104]

REPORTING CASUALTY LOSSES

A number of complications arise regarding the year in which a casualty or theft loss should be deducted. In general, a loss is allowed as a deduction only for the year in which the loss is sustained. A loss arising from theft, however, shall be treated as sustained in the year that the theft is discussed, unless an unsettled insurance claim defers the year of recognition.[105] If there exists a claim for reimbursement and there is a reasonable prospect of recovery, no portion of the loss with respect to which re- **FORM 4684**

---

[103] Sec. 165(h).
[104] Reg. Sec. 1.165(b)(4)(iii).
[105] Reg. Sec. 1.165-8(a).
[106] Reg. Sec. 1.165-8(a)(2).

imbursement may be received is deductible until it can be determined with reasonable certainty whether reimbursement will be received.[106] Any portion of the loss not covered by a claim for reimbursement will be deductible, however, in the year the casualty occurred or the theft was discovered.

Example 45: In December 19X2 burglars entered the home of Sidney and took property with a fair value of $8,000 (which is less than cost). Sidney's property is covered by an insurance policy, but settlement (for $7,200) was not reached until May 19X3. Sidney is not entitled to a deduction in 19X2, but may deduct $800 in 19X3 (subject to the $100 and 10% of adjusted gross income limitations).

In some cases, if a loss results from a disaster in an area that the President of the United States subsequently declares to be a "disaster area" warranting federal assistance, the taxpayer may deduct the loss in the year the loss occurs or may elect to deduct the loss on the tax return for the year preceding the year in which the loss actually occurred. This is accomplished by filing an amended return for the prior tax year.

If a taxpayer deducts a loss in one year and in a subsequent tax year receives reimbursement, he does not recompute the tax for the taxable year in which the deduction was taken, but includes the reimbursement as income in the year it is received, to the extent that the reimbursement represents recovery of an amount that gave rise to a tax benefit when the deduction was taken.

The procedures for reporting casualty or theft losses on the tax return may be quite complex. If the individual taxpayer has a deductible nonbusiness casualty or theft loss only, the loss is included as an itemized deduction *from* AGI. Similarly, if the taxpayer has only a casualty or theft loss on business property, the loss is deductible as a business expense for determining AGI. Where the taxpayer has both business and nonbusiness losses and gains, special rules, discussed in Chapter 11, apply.

OTHER DEDUCTIONS FOR INDIVIDUALS

A number of other deductions are available to individual taxpayers. Some of the more important are reviewed briefly below. Most of these items are discussed in greater detail in other chapters.

PERIODIC ALIMONY

In Chapter 5, the taxability of alimony payments to the recipient was discussed. A simple rule to follow is that if the alimony is taxable to the recipient, it is deductible to the payer.[107] Thus periodic alimony is deduct-

[107] Sec. 215.

ible for AGI.[108] Nonperiodic alimony is not deductible. Child-care payments are never deductible.

RETIREMENT SAVINGS

Individuals are permitted to deduct contributions to several types of formal retirement savings plans. The two most common plans, discussed in some detail in Chapter 8, are Individual Retirement Accounts (IRAs) and "Keogh" plans (for self-employed persons).

Under IRA plans an individual may deduct cash contributions to certain types of retirement accounts. The ceiling is the lower of the taxpayer's earned income or $2,000.[109] Special rules apply to married couples. "Keogh" or "HR 10" plans permit *self-employed* individuals to deduct amounts contributed on his or her own behalf (as an employee) to a company pension plan.

EXPENSES FOR PRODUCTION OF INCOME

It has been pointed out several times in this chapter that Sec. 212 permits several types of deductions related to the production of income.

Thus such costs as rental charges for a safety deposit box in which to keep income-producing securities, travel costs to oversee real estate held as an investment, investment counsel fees, custodian fees, state and local transfer taxes, and other expenses incurred by the taxpayer in connection with investments are deductible. These costs are included in itemized deductions *from* AGI, unless they are for travel and transportation, in which case they are deductible *for* AGI.

Where the taxpayer must forfeit interest to a savings organization for premature withdrawal of funds, the amount of forfeiture is deductible *for* AGI (but the contractual amount of interest must be included in gross income).[110]

One final authorized deduction that merits mention is the deduction for certain adoption expenses. A taxpayer may deduct from AGI up to $1,500 for expenses incurred in connection with the legal adoption of a child "with special needs."[111]

REPORTING ITEMIZED DEDUCTIONS

FORM 1040—SCHEDULE A

Form 1040, Schedule A, is used to report total itemized deductions of an individual taxpayer. This form is illustrated in Figure 9-1. Note that the net deduction carried over to page two of the 1040 is total itemized deductions less the applicable zero-bracket amount.

---

[108] Sec. 62(13).

[109] Sec. 219.

[110] Sec. 62(12).

[111] Sec. 222.

FIGURE 9-1

SCHEDULES A&B (Form 1040)
Department of the Treasury
Internal Revenue Service

Schedule A—Itemized Deductions

(Schedule B is on back)

▶ Attach to Form 1040. ▶ See Instructions for Schedules A and B (Form 1040).

OMB No. 1545-0074
1984
07

Name(s) as shown on Form 1040: *Robert and Martha S. Simka*

Your social security number: *222 22 2222*

Section	Line	Description	Line	Amount	Line	Total
Medical and Dental Expenses (Do not include expenses reimbursed or paid by others.) (See Instructions on page 19)	1	Prescription medicines and drugs; and insulin	1	144		
	2 a	Doctors, dentists, nurses, hospitals, insurance premiums you paid for medical and dental care, etc.	2a	900		
	b	Transportation and lodging	2b	40		
	c	Other (list—include hearing aids, dentures, eyeglasses, etc.) ▶	2c			
	3	Add lines 1 through 2c, and write the total here	3	1,084		
	4	Multiply the amount on Form 1040, line 33, by 5% (.05)	4	1,000		
	5	Subtract line 4 from line 3. If zero or less, write -0-. **Total** medical and dental ▶			5	84
Taxes You Paid (See Instructions on page 20)	6	State and local income taxes	6	820		
	7	Real estate taxes	7	1,250		
	8 a	General sales tax (see sales tax tables in instruction booklet)	8a	380		
	b	General sales tax on motor vehicles	8b			
	9	Other taxes (list—include personal property taxes) ▶	9			
	10	Add the amounts on lines 6 through 9. Write the total here. **Total** taxes ▶			10	2,450
Interest You Paid (See Instructions on page 20)	11 a	Home mortgage interest you paid to financial institutions	11a	2,230		
	b	Home mortgage interest you paid to individuals (show that person's name and address) ▶	11b			
	12	Total credit card and charge account interest you paid	12	85		
	13	Other interest you paid (list) ▶ *First City Bank*	13	240		
	14	Add the amounts on lines 11a through 13. Write the total here. **Total** interest ▶			14	2,555
Contributions You Made (See Instructions on page 20)	15 a	Cash contributions. (If you gave $3,000 or more to any one organization, report those contributions on line 15b.)	15a	960		
	b	Cash contributions totaling $3,000 or more to any one organization. (Show to whom you gave and how much you gave.) ▶	15b			
	16	Other than cash (attach required statement)	16			
	17	Carryover from prior year	17			
	18	Add the amounts on lines 15a through 17. Write the total here. **Total** contributions ▶			18	960
Casualty and Theft Losses	19	Total casualty or theft loss(es). (You must attach Form 4684 or similar statement.) (see page 21 of Instructions) ▶			19	0
Miscellaneous Deductions (See Instructions on page 21)	20	Union and professional dues *Union Local 563*	20	210		
	21	Tax return preparation fee	21	40		
	22	Other (list type and amount) ▶ *Safety Boots*	22	80		
	23	Add the amounts on lines 20 through 22. Write the total here. **Total** miscellaneous ▶			23	330
Summary of Itemized Deductions (See Instructions on page 22)	24	Add the amounts on lines 5, 10, 14, 18, 19, and 23. Write your answer here.			24	6,379
	25	If you checked Form 1040 { Filing Status box 2 or 5, write $3,400; Filing Status box 1 or 4, write $2,300; Filing Status box 3, write $1,700 }			25	3,400
	26	Subtract line 25 from line 24. Write your answer here and on Form 1040, line 34a. (If line 25 is more than line 24, see the Instructions for line 26 on page 22.) ▶			26	2979

For Paperwork Reduction Act Notice, see Form 1040 Instructions.

Schedule A (Form 1040) 1984

P L A N N I N G   W O R K S H O P

The objective of planning for personal deductions is obviously the maximization of the tax benefits. For many taxpayers, this means that the deductions must be properly timed.

TIMING OF ITEMIZED DEDUCTIONS

The itemized deductions of many taxpayers do not exceed the zero bracket amount year in and year out. For these taxpayers, the deductions should be bunched into alternate years. Property taxes, for example, can often be paid every other year without incurring penalties.

Example 46: For the year, T and J, who file jointly, have itemized deductions of $1,800 consisting of sales taxes, contributions, and interest. In December, their property taxes of $1,500 can either be paid now or in January of next year without a penalty. If they pay the taxes this year, their itemized deductions total only $3,300. If they pay these taxes next year (along with other deductions for that year), their itemized deductions will exceed the zero bracket amount.

Contributions and medical costs can also be bunched in alternate years.

UTILIZING THE ZERO BRACKET AMOUNT

Taxpayers with savings that earn interest income can sometimes save taxes by using their savings to pay off mortgages and other indebtedness and save taxes. The interest paid on such indebtedness results in a tax benefit only if itemized deductions exceed the zero bracket amount. Interest income on savings increases the taxable income in every event.

Example 47: T and J file a joint return. They have savings that produce $5,000 of interest income each year. They contribute about $1,000 to the church each year and their taxes amount to $1,200 a year. They have no other itemized deductions in most years. They have a small mortgage on their residence and the interest paid on this mortgage amounts to $1,500. Itemized deductions total $3,700, $300 more than the zero bracket amount. If they pay off the mortgage, they still get the benefit of the $3,400 zero bracket amount.

AVOID THE LIMIT ON INVESTMENT INTEREST

Taxpayers who borrow money to buy growth investments may have their interest deduction limited to $10,000 (plus the net investment

Continued

PLANNING WORKSHOP

interest). Growth investments enjoy a favored tax position because gain realized on their disposition is usually taxed as a long-term capital gain. Deduction of the interest paid on money borrowed to carry these investments substantially reduces the cost of holding such properties and improves the chances of a large, eventual profit.

Money borrowed in a trade or business, or for personal use, is not subject to a limit. Taxpayers can shift debt or property from one category to another to avoid the limit on investment interest.

Example 48: T invested in 500 acres of farmland, borrowing most of the money. He leases the land to a farmer. He pays interest on the $25,000 he borrowed and has no net investment income. T will get a deduction of only $10,000. T can avoid this disastrous result by farming the land himself or by borrowing some of the money needed by mortgaging his personal residence. If a taxpayer cannot shift debt to a trade or business or into the personal category, he or she must balance out the investments between growth and yield properties.

KEY POINTS TO REMEMBER

1. All interest is generally deductible, except that related to acquiring and carrying assets that yield tax-free income.
2. The deduction for "investment interest" is limited.
3. Ad valorem taxes on property, state, and local income taxes, state and local general sales taxes, and the windfall profits tax are deductible. Other taxes are deductible only if incurred in trade or business or in income-producing activities.
4. Contributions to qualified domestic charitable organizations are deductible.
5. For individuals, the limit on deductions for charitable contributions is 50% of AGI.
6. The limit on deductions for contributions of capital-gains property is 30% of AGI, and the limit on deductions of contributions to certain private foundations is 20% of AGI.
7. Contributions in excess of the ceiling on deductions may be carried forward for five years by both individuals and corporations.
8. Medical expenses in excess of 5% of AGI are deductible.
9. Medical expenses include such items as physician's charges, dental care, hospital care, nursing care, premiums on health and hospital insurance, medicines and drugs, and other costs.
10. Losses from theft and casualty of business property are deductible without regard to AGI.
11. Losses from theft and casualty of nonbusiness property are deductible only to the extent that (*a*) they exceed $100 for each casualty, and

(*b*) the total of all such excess over $100 for each casualty exceeds 10% of AGI.

12. The measure of theft and casualty loss for nonbusiness property is the smaller of decline in fair value or the adjusted basis, reduced in either case by insurance or other reimbursement.
13. The measure of theft and casualty loss for a business asset that is only partially destroyed is the same as that for a nonbusiness asset. However, if a business asset is completely destroyed, the measure of the loss is its adjusted basis.
14. All expenses related to the production of income are deductible, as are all costs in connection with the collection or refund of any tax.

SELF-STUDY QUESTIONS

1. Eric Ross, who is single and has no dependents, had an adjusted gross income of $80,000 in 1983, comprised of the following:

Salary	$74,000
Net investment income	6,000

During 1983, uninsured art objects owned by Eric, with a basis of $50,000 and a fair market value of $70,000, sustained casualty fire damage reducing the fair market value to $60,000. Also during 1983, Eric made the following payments:

Interest on margin account at stockbroker	$18,000
Real estate taxes on condominium owned by Eric's mother, in which Eric resides	3,000
State and city gasoline taxes	180
Medical insurance premiums	300
Unreimbursed dental expenses	4,500
Contribution to political committee of elected public official	500

Eric elected to itemize his deductions for 1983. How much can Eric claim in his itemized deductions for interest on his 1983 return?

a) $6,000

b) $12,000

c $16,000

d) $18,000

(AICPA adapted)

2. Refer to Question 1. How much can Eric claim as taxes in itemized deductions on his 1983 return?

a) $0

b) $180

c) $3,000

d) $3,180

(AICPA adapted)

3. Refer to Question 1. How much can Eric claim in his itemized deductions for medical and dental expenses on his 1983 return?

   a) $2,400
   b) $800
   c) $300
   d) $150

   (AICPA adapted)

4. Refer to Question 1. How much can Eric claim in his itemized deductions for the casualty loss on his 1983 return?

   a) $0
   b) $1,900
   c) $2,000
   d) $9,900

   (AICPA adapted)

5. Dan Barlow, who itemizes his deductions, had an adjusted gross income of $70,000 in 1983. The following additional information is available for 1983:

Cash contribution to church	$5,000
Purchase of art object at church bazaar (with a fair market value of $1,000 on the date of purchase)	1,600
Donation of used clothing to Salvation Army (fair value evidenced by receipt received)	800

   What is the maximum amount Barlow can claim as a deduction for charitable contributions in 1983?

   a) $5,600
   b) $6,400
   c) $6,600
   d) $6,800

   (AICPA adapted)

6. During 1979, Mr. and Mrs. Benson provided substantially all the support in their own home for their son, John, age 26, and for Mrs. Benson's cousin Nancy, age 17. John had $1,100 of income for 1979, and Nancy's income was $500. The Bensons paid the following medical expenses during the year:

Medicines and drugs:	
For themselves	$400
For John	500
For Nancy	100
Doctors:	
For themselves	600
For John	900
For Nancy	200

What is the total amount of medical expenses (before application of any limitation rules) that would enter into the calculation of excess itemized deductions on the Bensons' 1979 tax return?

a) $1,000

b) $1,300

c) $2,400

d) $2,700

(AICPA adapted)

7. During 1978, Albert Mason purchased the following long-term investments at par:

   $10,000 in general obligation bonds of Tulip County (wholly tax exempt)
   $10,000 in debentures of Laxity Corporation

   He financed these purchases by obtaining a loan from the Community Bank for $20,000. For the year 1978, he paid the following amounts as interest expense:

Community Bank	$1,600
Interest on mortgage	3,000
Interest on installment purchases	300
	$4,900

   What amount can Mason deduct as interest expense in 1978?

   a) $4,900

   b) $4,100

   c) $3,600

   d) $3,300

   (AICPA adapted)

8. Al Daly's adjusted gross income for the year ending December 31, 1982, was $20,000. He was not covered under any medical insurance plan. During 1982, he paid $500 to a physician for treatment of a heart condition. He also owed the physician a balance of $900 for an operation performed in December, 1982, which he paid in January 1983. In addition, Daly incurred a $1,700 hospital bill in 1982, which he charged to his bank credit card in December 1982 and paid to the bank in January 1983. Daly's total allowable medical deduction in 1982 is

   a) $0

   b) $500

   c) $1,200

   d) $2,500

   (AICPA adapted)

9. The following information is available for Seymour and Ruth Atkinson, who reside in Pennsylvania, for 1981:

Adjusted gross income	$31,500
Tax-exempt interest received	$1,500
Exemptions (including exemption claimed for their son John, a full-time student at State University)	3

An abstract from the Optional Sales Tax Table for Pennsylvania is presented below:

INCOME	SALES TAX FAMILY SIZE 1 & 2	SALES TAX FAMILY SIZE OVER 2
$30,001–$32,000	$219	$248
$32,001–$34,000	$230	$261

Assuming that the Atkinsons elect to use the Optional Sales Tax Table, what is the maximum amount of general sales taxes that they can utilize in calculating excess itemized deductions for 1981?

a) $219

b) $230

c) $248

d) $261

(AICPA adapted)

10. Frank Lanier is a resident of a state that imposes a tax on income. The following information pertaining to Lanier's state income taxes is available:

Taxes withheld in 1981	$3,500
Refund received in 1981 of 1980 tax	400
Deficiency assessed and paid in 1981 for 1979:	
Tax	600
Interest	100

What amount should Lanier utilize as state and local income taxes in calculating excess itemized deductions for his 1981 federal tax return?

a) $3,500

b) $3,700

c) $4,100

d) $4,200

(AICPA adapted)

11. Mr. and Mrs. Donald Curry's real property tax year is on a calendar-year basis, with payment due annually on August 1. The realty taxes on their home amounted to $1,200 in 1981, but the Currys did not pay

any portion of that amount since they sold the house on April 1, 1981, four months before payment was due. However, realty taxes were prorated on the closing statement. Assuming that they owned no other real property during the year, how much can the Currys deduct on Schedule A of Form 1040 for real estate taxes in 1981?

a) $0

b) $296

c) $697

d) $1,200

(AICPA adapted)

12. Eugene and Linda O'Brien had adjusted gross income of $30,000 in 1979. Additional information is available for 1979 as follows:

Cash contribution to church	$1,500
Tuition paid to parochial school	1,200
Contribution to a qualified charity made by a bank credit card charge on December 14, 1979. The credit card obligation was paid on January 11, 1980	250
Cash contribution to needy family	100

What is the maximum amount of the above that they can utilize in calculating excess itemized deductions for 1979?

a) $1,500

b) $1,750

c) $2,700

d) $3,050

(AICPA adapted)

13. Burt Morgan's adjusted gross income for 1975 was $30,000. On December 10, 1975, he made the following contributions to qualified charitable organizations:

Cash, $700

100 shares of common stock of Cal Company (acquired on October 22, 1975, at a cost of $500)

The fair market value of the donated common stock on December 10, 1975, was $900.

What should be Morgan's deduction for charitable contributions for 1975?

a) $1,100

b) $1,200

c) $1,400

d) $1,600

(AICPA adapted)

QUESTIONS

1. Once a taxpayer has purchased a home, he or she will almost always have excess itemized deductions. Explain why generally this statement is accurate.
2. Explain the reasons for the limitation on the deduction for "investment interest."
3. What limits are imposed on the total medical expense deduction?
4. Define the terms "drugs" and "medical care" as used in federal income taxation. List several items in each category that would be included and several that would be excluded.
5. Under what circumstances, if any, would amounts paid by a taxpayer for costs of living in a retirement "nursing" home be deductible?
6. What differences, if any, are found in measuring the deductible amount of a casualty loss on property held for personal use and property used in trade or business?
7. Under what circumstances, if any, may the taxpayer treat the amount of a repair bill as a measure of loss from a casualty?
8. To what extent, if any, does the quality of medical care or its luxuriousness determine the extent to which it is deductible? For example, are different rules applied in determining deductibility of a bed in a hospital ward compared with one in a luxurious private room in an exclusive hospital? Or for contact lenses versus ordinary glasses?
9. Compare the tax treatment of premiums on health and hospitalization insurance and casualty insurance premiums on the taxpayer's home or personal automobile.
10. Under what, if any, circumstances can costs related to adopting a child be deductible?
11. In what year is a theft loss deductible?
12. A taxpayer's home was destroyed by fire in 19X4. At the end of the year, the amount of reimbursement by the insurance company had not been determined. In the following year, the final insurance settlement was reached and partial reimbursement was received. How should these facts be handled in the tax returns?
13. Which of the following taxes are deductible for federal income tax purposes? (Assume all taxes were paid in the current year.)
    a) Gift tax.
    b) FICA tax on business employees.
    c) State gasoline (excise) tax on gasoline used in family auto.

d) Federal gasoline tax on gasoline used in family auto.
e) State income tax.
f) Property tax on family residence.
g) State excise tax on cigarettes for personal consumption.
h) State excise tax on liquor consumed while entertaining business clients.
i) State excise tax on liquor for private consumption.
j) Automobile license (your state) for family auto. (If you are an out-of-state student, solve this problem for the state in which your school is located.)

14. R operates a retail store as a proprietor. During the year he paid $6,000 representing the employer's share of the FICA tax. He also paid $2,000 for his FICA tax on his self-employment income. Are these taxes deductible? If so, under what provision?

15. Basilica, a U.S. resident, owns a home in his native land, Spain. He pays real estate taxes to Spain on this residence which he uses for vacations. Can he "itemize" these foreign taxes?

16. Thelma, who lives in New Mexico, flew to Houston, Texas to undergo therapy for cancer. While in Houston, Thelma spent $60 a night for a room in a hotel and $30 a day for meals. What can Thelma treat as medical expenses?

17. During the year T bought some undeveloped land and gave the seller a note for a large part of the purchase price. To save taxes, T paid the interest on the note for the current year and for the following year. Can this interest be deducted?

18. T's wife divorced him last year. The judge awarded her $6,000 a year for support of their child and $9,000 a year for alimony. T paid these amounts this year. How much can T deduct?

19. T had too much to drink at the office Christmas party, straightened out a curve and lost a contest with a brick wall. His personal car was "totaled" and he had no collision insurance. After his release from jail, he wondered if his loss is deductible. Advise him.

20. In December, T, who files a joint return, calculates that his itemized deductions are only $1,800 for the year. He has not yet paid his property taxes of $1,500. Should he pay the taxes now, or wait until next year?

PROBLEMS

1. Powers, unmarried, paid the following interest:

On loan to finance summer vacation	$ 162
On home mortgage	7,680
On loan to purchase tax-exempt securities (income earned on the tax-free certificate was $800)	920
On loan to obtain money to open an IRA account	100
On loan obtained from bank by Powers's mother	600
Finance charges on purchases made on bank credit cards	124

What amount can Powers deduct for interest?

2. Wheeler Corporation had the following interest payments in the current year:

On loans to provide corporate working capital	$126,200
On mortgage on fixed assets	64,800
On loan to purchase tax-exempt industrial development bonds	12,000
On funds borrowed to make contribution to employee's tax-sheltered pension plan	31,000
On loan from corporation's president (interest rate equal to prime rate)	16,000

What amount may the corporation deduct as interest for the year?

3. In the current year, Brandon and his wife filed a joint return showing adjusted gross income of $80,000. Included in their tax information were the following items:

Interest paid on funds borrowed last year to purchase stocks and bonds	$48,000
Investment income	12,000
Investment-related expenses	800
Interest paid on home mortgage	6,200
Interest on personal loans	3,500

Compute the Brandons' deduction for interest for the year.

4. Jill, a cash-basis taxpayer, borrowed $15,000 from a bank on September 1, 19X1. The loan, plus interest at a rate of 12%, is due on March 1, 19X2. On December 30, 19X1, Jill paid all the interest for the six-month period of the loan, $900, but no part of the principal.

   a) What amount of interest, if any, may Jill deduct in 19X1?

   b) What amount of interest, if any, may Jill deduct in 19X2?

5. During 19X1 Maryanne Boswell paid the following interest:

Interest on home mortgage	$3,600
Installment charge accounts	60
Interest on loan used to purchase tax-exempt bonds	300

In addition, $20,000 was borrowed from a bank on September 1, 19X1 for financing a new business venture. Interest of $2,400 was deducted by the bank in advance, and the loan is being repaid in 12 equal monthly installments. Beginning October 1, 19X1 Maryanne made all payments when due. What amount will she claim as interest expense in her itemized deductions?

6. In each of the following independent cases, indicate the amount that the taxpayer may deduct as interest on his or her federal income tax return.

   a) Miranda paid interest of $2,100 on a loan secured to purchase bonds of the city of Centerville on which he received interest of $2,800.

   b) On October 9, 19X1 Bradley purchased a refrigerator, which had a cash price of $550. He elected to use the installment-payment method and made a down payment of $70, agreeing to pay the balance of $480 plus carrying charges of $60 in 12 equal installments of $45 each. Payments were made promptly on November 9 and December 9. (Answer for 19X1.)

   c) In 19X2 Bradley in part (b) above made all payments when due and the final payment was made on October 9. (Answer for 19X2.)

   d) Palmore made the following interest payments during the year: $60 on a loan obtained to buy his wife some jewelry on their 25th wedding anniversary; $670 on the mortgage on his home; $45 on a loan obtained at the bank by his dependent 23-year-old son (Palmore also paid the loan principal in order to protect the family name even though he had no legal liability for the note or interest); $48 to the life insurance company on the loan value of his life policy withdrawn to pay for his daughter's high school graduation present; and $92 on amounts owed on gambling debts.

   e) Goodwoman had a rather sizable income in 19X1, so she decided to make large contributions to various charities in order to get the tax deduction in 19X1. Unfortunately, her cash position was quite low, so she borrowed $30,000 for the purpose of making these contributions. In 19X2 her interest payments on these loans totaled $2,400. (Answer for 19X2.)

   f) Patsy is a majority stockholder in City Corporation. In 19X1 City suffered a financial reverse. In order to protect the corporation's good name, Patsy paid $6,000 of interest owed by the corporation to a local bank.

7. In each of the following independent cases, indicate the amount that the taxpayer may deduct as "taxes" on his or her federal income tax return. Indicate whether any amount deductible is *for* AGI or *from* AGI.

   a) In July of this year, Geraldo inherited some property from a deceased aunt. He paid a state inheritance tax of $1,200 on the inheritance.

b) During the year, Arnold purchased various bottles of alcoholic beverages for personal use. The amount he paid for these beverages included $118 federal excise tax, $32 state excise tax, and $8 state retail sales tax.

c) Planter had the following expenditures for taxes during the year 19X2: payment of 19X1 state income tax, $84; quarterly estimates of his 19X2 federal income tax, $4,600; final payment of net amount due on 19X1 federal income tax return, $310.

d) Raymond purchased real estate on May 1 of this year for $18,000. The estimated taxes for the year were prorated and the cash payment to the seller was reduced by $80, the estimated taxes through April 30. In December Raymond paid the real estate taxes due for the year, $272.

e) Gomer operates a business. During the year he remitted to the federal government $19,000 of income taxes withheld from employees' earnings. He also remitted $9,000 in FICA taxes, representing $4,500 deducted from employees' paychecks and Gomer's matching contributions. He also paid $170 federal unemployment compensation taxes and $920 state unemployment compensation taxes on his employees' earnings.

f) Tradesman operates a business. During the year he imported jewelry for resale in the business, paying an import tariff of $980. In addition he imported some furs for his wife's personal use, paying an import tariff of $230.

g) Peggy operates a retail gift shop. During 19X1 she paid $720 of "self-employment" taxes on her net earnings for the preceding year, 19X0. (Answer for year 19X1.)

8. In each of the following independent cases, indicate the amount that may be deducted as charitable contributions.

a) Paulson has AGI of $22,000. During the year he made the following cash contributions:

Boy Scouts	$3,000
Local church	6,000
Local university	4,200

b) Agatha had AGI of $16,500. During the year she made the following cash contributions:

Girl Scouts	$5,000
Democratic Party	2,000
Needy family in neighborhood	400
American Legion	200
London School of Economics (England)	800
Local hospital	1,000

c) Concord owned 1,000 shares of X Corporation stock for which he paid $10,000 in 1962. During the current year he contributed 600 shares of this stock to the First Church of Midtown. On the date of the contribution the shares had a market price of $25 per share. Concord's AGI this year was $25,000.

d) Manney operates a retail furniture store. In July of this year he contributed to the local hospital a number of items of furniture (tables, chairs, and sofas) from his merchandise inventory. These items had cost him $3,800 but had a normal retail value of $7,400. Manney's AGI this year was $20,000.

e) Assume the same facts as in part (d) except that Manney contributed the furniture to a private foundation.

f) English is active in the Boy Scouts. During the past year he served as a scoutmaster. At the end of the year he calculated that he had spent $80 for various scout activities such as fund-raising drives. In addition, he had driven his automobile an estimated 300 miles in connection with scout work. He also had lost 38 working hours from his job with a loss in pay of $228.

9. What amount may the taxpayer deduct as "contributions" in each of the following cases?

   a) Paul purchased five tickets from the Boy Scouts. These tickets were to a local benefit performance of the city symphony, with all proceeds going to the Scouts. Normal cost of these tickets would have been $2.50 each, but because they were for a benefit, the cost was $5 each. Paul and his family attended the performance, using all five tickets.

   b) Assume the same facts as in part (a) except that Paul purchased the tickets as a purely charitable gesture with the intent of throwing them away—and he did so.

10. In 19X1 the Thrift family decided to have a "garage sale" to dispose of unused clothing. To their surprise, the Thrifts found they had discarded almost none of their old clothes through the years. They found dresses, pants, shirts, coats, and other items that had been outgrown by the children, relatively unused clothing of Mrs. Thrift that had been made obsolete by style changes, and many usable suits discarded by Mr. Thrift because of the dress requirements of his job as attorney. Proceeds from the two-day sale were $180, but over half the clothes were unsold. As a matter of fact, the "price tags" on the unsold clothes totaled $210, which represented about 15% of the original cost. The Thrifts contributed the unsold items to the Salvation Army. Mr. Thrift is interested in the possibility of a tax deduction for the contribution. Advise him.

11. Charity contributed to two "funds" during the year, giving $100 to the City United Fund drive and $20 to the Remembrance Fund of the office where she is employed. The Remembrance Fund is used to buy flowers for employees who are ill, die, or get married. Also it is used to buy Christmas presents for custodial workers and for similar purposes. What part, if any, of these contributions will Charity be entitled to deduct on her tax return for the year?

12. Richard and Ora reported AGI of $20,000 in 1984, a year in which they incurred the following medical expenses:

Dentist's charges	$ 450
Physician's charges	900
Hospital costs	1,800
Drugs (prescription)	180
Medical insurance premiums	700

The insurance company reimbursed Richard and Ora for $1,700 of their hospital bill and $800 for their physician's charges. What is their medical-expense deduction for the year?

13. Compute the medical deduction in the following cases:
The year is 1985.

	CASE A	CASE B	CASE C
Adjusted gross income	$12,000	$12,000	$12,000
Medicine (prescription)	150	100	200
Medical costs (net of insurance claims)	500	200	200
Premiums on medical insurance	220	220	220

14. Oliver Perce retired from Chicago to Miami, Florida after 50 years of service with Drake Corporation. Each June Oliver flies back to Chicago for an annual physical examination by Dr. Wilkerson, the heart specialist who started treating Oliver ten years ago. The examination is conducted in the doctor's office. This annual physical requires approximately one week to complete. Between trips to the physician's office, Oliver visits family and friends. The trip costs him $500 for transportation, $300 for a hotel, $140 for food, $200 for medical expenses, and $100 for incidentals. Which of these costs, if any, can Oliver deduct? Explain your answer.

15. Marzel Rand, age 65, and wife, Cara, age 39, filed a joint return for the current tax year showing an AGI of $45,000. A son of Mrs. Rand by a former marriage is now a full-time university student and is fully dependent on the Rands. They also provide over 50% of the support of Mr. Rand's mother, who is 85 and bedridden. Grandmother Rand receives a $1,200-a-year payment from a trust fund. Medical expenses in excess of reimbursements were paid by Marzel and Cara in the amounts stated below:

	FOR MARZEL	FOR CARA	FOR SON	FOR MOTHER
Hospital insurance premiums	$240	$ --	$ --	$ --
Drugs (prescription)	150	350	10	400
Medical expenses	200	300	100	300
Nurse				5,200

Show your computation for the medical-expense deduction that can be taken on Mr. and Mrs. Rand's joint tax return.

16. *a*) Patsy, a college student, has for several years been concerned about her "overbite" and its impact on her personal appearance. She visited a local orthodontist, who suggested that she have her teeth realigned and straightened. Total cost of her work is expected to be $3,000. During the current year, Patsy paid $1,400 to the orthodontist. What amount, if any, is treated as medical expense this year? Explain.

    b) Damita had a legal abortion at a cost of $1,020. What part of this cost, if any, is a medical expense? Explain.

    c) Marian, unmarried, had a legal abortion at a cost of $1,500, which was paid directly to the doctor by James, who caused the pregnancy. What amount can James claim as medical costs?

17. In each of the following cases, indicate the amount of "casualty loss" deductible before considering the 10% of AGI floor, and indicate how the loss would be handled on the income tax return. Assume there are no other casualties or thefts.

    a) Pearl was vacationing in Miami. While Pearl was swimming, a thief stole her wristwatch (cost, $220, with a fair market value of $180) and her wallet. The wallet, which was not recovered, contained $120 cash. The wallet itself, with a value of $5, cost $10. There was no insurance.

    b) Barry owned a lake cabin with an adjusted basis of $16,000. On January 18, the cabin had a fair value of $14,000. On the next day, a tornado completely demolished the cabin. It was not insured. The cabin was held solely for personal use.

    c) Clarence owned a frame building with an adjusted basis of $20,000. In July of this year the building caught fire and was partially destroyed. The value just before the fire was $21,000 and just after the fire was $4,000. There was no insurance. The building was Clarence's personal residence.

    d) Assume the same facts as in part (c) above except that insurance proceeds of $12,000 were received.

    e) Gregory backed his car out of his garage into a neighbor's automobile. Gregory's automobile suffered $600 damage. (Its basis was $3,500.) Damage suffered by the neighbor's automobile was $520, which Gregory paid out of his own pocket, since he carried no insurance of any kind.

    f) Jones's home was burglarized. The thief took Mrs. Jones's jewelry, which had a fair market value of $1,800. The jewelry had a basis of $1,200. He also took Jones's watch, which had a fair market value of $150 and a basis of $200. There was no insurance. Jones and his wife filed a joint return.

g) Assume the same facts as in part (f) except that the Joneses filed separate returns.

h) Carlos owns an automobile used 50% for business and 50% for pleasure. The automobile had cost $8,000 and Carlos had taken depreciation of $1,200 on the business portion. In August of this year he had an accident. At that time the fair value of the auto was $4,400. Just after the accident the auto had a value of $3,000. Insurance proceeds of $1,240 were recovered.

i) Harper went hunting with his rifle, which had a basis of $160 and a fair market value of $150. Somehow, Harper laid his rifle down in the woods and never was able to find it again. He had no insurance.

j) In the current year Benson was in an auto accident. As a result, he was sued by another individual in the accident and was required to pay "damages" of $16,000 to the other party.

18. Gerald owned a home. In his front yard he had a number of trees that he had set out some 15 years ago. This year a high wind demolished all the trees. A man from the local tree service estimated the trees were worth $1,200, although Gerald had paid only $120 for them. Just before the wind, his home had an appraised value of $32,000 (cost, including trees, $20,000). Just after the wind, his home had an estimated value of $31,500. Gerald paid $160 to have the debris cleaned up. What is the amount of his casualty loss deduction before considering the 10% of AGI floor?

19. In the current year a single taxpayer's receipts were:

Salary (gross)	$10,000
Reimbursement from insurance company for medical costs incurred and paid by taxpayer in the preceding year. (Taxpayer did not have itemized deductions in excess of zero-bracket income in the preceding year.)	300

The taxpayer's disbursements included the following items in the current year:

Payments to doctors for medical care	700
Premiums on health and hospital insurance policies that would reimburse taxpayer for a part of his medical bills.	960
Premiums on an insurance policy that would pay the taxpayer $50 per day for each day he is hospitalized, without regard to the actual cost incurred by the taxpayer.	180
Premium on "wage continuation plan" policy that contracts to pay the taxpayer 60% of his normal wages for each day he is hospitalized, beginning after a waiting period of 60 days.	240

What is the amount of medical expenses that can be included in itemized deductions in the current year?

20. Tommy provided $600 per month during 19X1 toward the cost of maintaining his mother in the Sunshine Nursing Home for the Aged.

The Sunshine home was chosen in preference to several others because it had a physician and nurse on duty at all times. Tommy's mother had had a series of heart attacks in recent years and, although her situation was not critical and she was not confined to her bed, Tommy felt it necessary to have medical care immediately available for her. In addition to the $7,200 provided by Tommy, his mother also received $3,600 from Social Security benefits and $2,000 from a fully taxable pension during 19X1, all of which was used for the living costs of Tommy's mother.

What part, if any, of the $7,200 will Tommy be allowed to treat as medical expenses on his 19X1 tax return?

21. Buck, a college professor in Indiana, left his home for a 3-week vacation in England on December 18, 19X1 as soon as he finished grading his final exams for the fall semester. When he returned in January 19X2 he discovered that his home had been burglarized. Two items were missing: a set of silver dinner ware that had cost $1,000 and had a fair value of $2,400, and a stereo sound system that had cost $1,000 and had a fair value of $500. In 19X2, he received insurance reimbursement totaling $800. A neighbor's home was burglarized on December 27, 19X1 and police speculate that the two burglaries occurred on the same night. How should Buck treat these facts on his tax returns for 19X1 and 19X2? Ignore the 10% of AGI floor.

TAX PLANNING PROBLEMS

1. Casals is a real estate developer with AGI in the current year of $200,000. He wants to make a substantial gift of $50,000 to the local university this year and is considering the following properties as the subject for the gift:

   1. $50,000 cash
   2. Corporate stock held as an investment with a fair market value of $50,000 and a basis of $10,000, owned for five years.
   3. A small tract of land held for resale with a fair market value of $50,000 and a basis of $35,000.

   a) Advise Casals on this contribution, giving amounts wherever appropriate.

   b) Does your advice change if his AGI is only $100,000?

2. Linda, a young CPA, has an opportunity of a lifetime, a chance to buy a tract of land favorably located on the outskirts of a large city. The tract would cost $250,000, with Linda paying $50,000 down using her savings, and the seller to finance $200,000 at an interest rate of 12%. Linda can lease the land for farming with an annual rental of $3,000. Real estate taxes will cost $2,200 per year.

   Linda's only other investment is in common stock that yields $4,000 in dividends. She practices accounting as a sole proprietor and has no money borrowed for the practice. Her assets in the practice are valued at $175,000, including $125,000 of accounts receivable.

a) What tax problem does acquisition of the land create?

b) How can Linda plan around this problem?

CASE PROBLEM

Emmit and Leah Hartman file jointly and claim exemptions for their two children. For 1985, their income was:

Emmit's salary	$38,000
Leah's salary	18,000
Dividends (U.S. corporation)	5,000
City of Dayton bonds	3,000
Interest—S & L association	1,200
Reimbursement from health insurance	800

The S & L interest was paid on accounts in the name of the children showing the parents as guardians. For the year, they incurred the following costs:

IRA deposits ($2,000 each)	$4,000
Job-related travel expenses (Emmit)	2,500
Dental bills (no insurance)	1,200
Hospital bill	1,000
Doctors and prescribed drugs	600
Property taxes	1,750
Mortgage interest	3,600
Interest—Visa	220
Nurse's uniforms (Leah)	180
Lock box (securities)	12
Cash contributions	850

During 1985, Emmit drove 300 miles while serving on the church budget committee. Also, high winds damaged the roof of their residence. Replacement cost was $6,000 and this amount represented the decrease in value in the property.

Calculate the 1985 gross tax for the Hartmans.

RESEARCH PROBLEMS

1. Two years ago, taxpayer constructed a residence in Encino, California at a cost of $210,000. The residence is located on a mountain side. The cost of the residence included $30,000 for a retaining wall designed to keep the mountain and the house separated. Taxpayer's architect insisted on the wall. In fact, the architect warned the taxpayer that the footings for the wall and the house were marginal.

   During the current year heavy rains fell, causing mud and the totally destroyed house to shift downhill onto the next lot. Is the taxpayer entitled to a casualty deduction?

2. Boris suffers from a heart condition. Because of a bad back, he cannot exercise by walking. His doctors recommended daily swimming. Because of the remote location of his residence, he built his own swimming pool at a cost of $45,000. Real estate experts estimated that the value of Boris's home increased by $15,000 as a result of this addition. Based on these facts, Boris deducted $30,000 as a medical expense.

   The IRS, on the other hand, claimed that a reasonable cost for the pool would be $18,000, and therefore disallowed $12,000, claiming the pool's cost was lavish and unnecessary. Who is right, Boris or the IRS?

Chapter Objectives

1. Explain how to calculate the amount of any capital gain or loss realized.
2. Explain how to determine the adjusted tax basis of purchased property, inherited property, and property acquired by gift.
3. Distinguish between capital gains and losses and ordinary gains and losses for federal income tax purposes.
4. Distinguish between "short-term" and "long-term" capital gains and losses.
5. Describe the different tax treatment that may be given to varying amounts of net short-term and net long-term capital gains and losses realized by individual taxpayers.
6. Define the long-term capital gain deduction.
7. Explain the correct treatment of net capital losses realized by individual taxpayers.
8. Describe how year-end tax planning for capital assets can save an individual tax dollars.
9. Illustrate how capital gains and losses are reported on Schedule D, Form 1040.

10 Sales of Investment Properties

In Chapters 3 and 4 we learned that any gains realized on the sale of property were part of gross income and therefore subject to the income tax. Although that conclusion is indeed correct, it tells only a small part of a very complex story. Ever since 1922 the United States tax law has included a host of special rules that govern the income taxation of capital gains and losses. Investments in some properties create capital gains and losses while investments in other properties produce ordinary income or loss. In this chapter we will learn how the tax law taxes the gains and losses that derive from investments in capital assets.

The proper treatment of a property disposition, either by sale, exchange, or otherwise, involves the solution of three distinct questions. First, what is the amount of gain or loss arising from the disposition? The law provides specific measurement rules that must be used to determine the gain or loss. Second, is the gain or loss recognized in the current year? As explained in Chapter 4, many realized gains are not recognized currently, if ever. Other rules either limit or defer the recognition of losses. Third, how are the recognized gains and losses taxed? Capital gains receive very favorable treatment usually, while ordinary gains are taxed at regular rates. This chapter addresses these three questions in the order just mentioned with most of the coverage on the capital gain and loss rules.

MEASUREMENT OF GAINS AND LOSSES

Stated briefly, the amount of a gain or loss is the difference between the "amount realized" and the "adjusted basis" of the asset that has been sold, exchanged, or otherwise disposed of. The phrases "amount realized" and "adjusted basis" obviously are technical terms that need to be studied with care.

AMOUNT REALIZED

AMOUNT REALIZED The sum of (*a*) any cash received plus (*b*) the fair market value of any property received plus (*c*) the amount of debt transferred to another by the taxpayer who sells or exchanges any property.

Section 1001(b) defines the term ***amount realized*** as follows:

> Amount Realized.—The amount realized from the sale or other disposition of property shall be the sum of any money received plus the fair market value of the property (other than money) received. In determining the amount realized—
>
> (1) there shall not be taken into account any amount received as reimbursement for real property taxes which are treated under section 164(d) as imposed on the purchaser, and
> (2) there shall be taken into account amounts representing real property taxes which are treated under section 164(d) as imposed on the taxpayer if such taxes are to be paid by the purchaser.

For our purposes, subparagraphs (1) and (2) add little to the general definition, but they demonstrate a basic quality of the Code—extensive cross-referencing—that is often frustrating to the tax student. In addition, the student of taxation must be aware that case law—i.e., that law decided by judges—often constitutes an important adjunct to understanding statutory law. In determining the amount realized, the courts have held that the assumption of a seller's mortgage by a buyer constitutes a positive element in the calculation of amount realized just as much as do money and the fair market value of property received.[1]

> **Example 1:** Suppose the buyer of a home gave the seller $10,000 cash and a secondhand car with a fair market value of $1,500, and that the buyer assumed the seller's mortgage on the home in the amount of $48,000. The amount realized by this seller would be $59,500 ($10,000 + $1,500 + $48,000), not just $11,500 ($10,000 + $1,500) as Sec. 1001(b) seems to suggest.

One of the most *administratively* difficult aspects of this definition is establishing the fair market value of any noncash property received. The practical importance and complexity of establishing such valuations in the real world should not be underestimated. The phrase "fair market

---

[1] *Crane* v. *Commissioner*, 331 U.S. 1 (1935). If the face value of the debt is greater than the fair market value of the property, the debt amount must be used in computing the amount realized. (See *Tufts* v. *Commissioner*, 103 S. Ct. 1826 (1983).)

value" assumes a willing buyer and a willing seller acting with full knowledge and without obligation in an arm's-length transaction. Value is, therefore, ultimately a question of fact that frequently must be determined by a court. Fortunately for the student, fair market values are almost always explicitly stated in the textbook and thus a major problem in actual tax administration has been circumvented in the classroom.

ADJUSTED BASIS

Adjusted basis is much more difficult to define than "amount realized." The applicable Code section is deceptively brief:

ADJUSTED BASIS The portion of the amount realized (in a sale or exchange of property) that may, by law, be treated as a tax-free return of capital; in other words, the portion of the amount realized that is *not* considered to be a part of gross income.

> Sec. 1011. Adjusted Basis for Determining Gain or Loss.
> (a) General Rule.—The adjusted basis for determining the gain or loss from the sale or other disposition of property, whenever acquired, shall be the basis [determined under section 1012 or other applicable sections of this subchapter and subchapters C (relating to corporate distributions and adjustments), K (relating to partners and partnerships), and P (relating to capital gains and losses)], adjusted as provided in section 1016.

The necessarily elementary discussion of adjusted basis that follows will proceed by considering, in turn, purchased property, inherited property, and property acquired by gift, because the method of acquisition is usually the critical factor in determining the adjusted basis of a particular property. (The cost basis of property acquired in a nontaxable exchange can be exceedingly difficult to determine. It is not discussed here but is deferred to Chapter 12 for separate consideration.)

PROPERTY ACQUIRED BY PURCHASE The determination of the tax basis of purchased property generally coincides closely with the determination of "book value" in accounting. That is, under most circumstances the adjusted basis of any purchased property is the sum of the historical cost of the original property, plus the cost of any capital improvements made to that property subsequent to acquisition, less the depreciation or ACRS deduction claimed (for tax purposes) on the same property and improvements since acquisition.

> **Example 2:** Suppose that a building was purchased in 1970 for \$100,000 and that an addition costing \$25,000 was constructed in 1975. If the depreciation deductions allowed on the building and the addition total \$50,000 through last year, then the adjusted basis for tax purposes on January 1 of this year would be \$75,000 (\$100,000 + \$25,000 − \$50,000).

Obviously, in implementing this kind of basis definition, the tax accountant shares many of the financial accountant's problems. For example, in determining historical cost at acquisition, the following problems are typical: separating a single purchase price into costs of component assets (for which the financial accountant and the tax accountant both resort to a common solution—allocation of purchase price on the basis of relative fair market values of the component assets); determining fair market values of noncash acquisitions; and allocating overhead and other indirect costs to assets constructed by the taxpayer for his or her own use. Another common problem, although greater for tax than for financial accounting, is the strong pressure to charge to expense (and hence to obtain an immediate tax deduction) what is actually a capital expenditure that should be charged to an asset account. As one might expect, controversy in this area of income taxation is commonplace.

PROPERTY ACQUIRED BY INHERITANCE The basis of property received from a decedent generally is the fair market value of the property on the date of the decedent's death. An exception to this general rule applies if the executor or executrix of the estate elects the alternate valuation date for estate tax purposes; in that event, the basis is generally the fair market value six months after the decedent's death.

Example 3: Assume that Tom Tucket purchased stock A for $10,000 on February 5, 1980 and stock B for $20,000 on September 5, 1980. If Tom died on October 16, 1984, when the fair market values of stock A and stock B were $15,000 each, any beneficiary of Tom's estate who received those shares would take as his or her basis the $15,000 fair market value on Tom's death, assuming that Tom's executor or executrix made no election to value properties on the alternate valuation date. This means, of course, that the $5,000 unrealized or "***paper*** ***gain***" implicit in stock A would go unrecognized forever for income tax purposes, and the $5,000 unrealized or "***paper*** ***loss***" implicit in stock B would also go unrecognized forever for income tax purposes.

"PAPER" GAIN/LOSS An economic gain or loss that has not yet been realized.

Example 4: Assume that Tina Torres purchased stock A for $10,000 on April 16, 1981, and that she died on November 24, 1984, when this stock had a value of $16,000. Suppose also that the value of stock A decreased from $16,000 to $15,000 by May 24, 1985. If the executor or executrix of Tina's estate elects to value Tina's property on the alternate valuation date, the heir's basis in stock A will be $15,000.

If an executor or executrix elects the alternate valuation date *and* also distributes some property prior to that date, then—for the property distributed before the valuation date—the basis shall be the fair market value of the property on the date it was distributed.

Example 5: Assume that Zeek Adams invested in ten ounces of gold bullion on January 3, 1983, when gold was selling for $430/ounce. Zeek died on February 10, 1984, when gold was selling for $560/ounce. The executor of Zeek's estate elected the alternate valuation date, August 10, 1983; however, he distributed this ten ounces of gold to Zeek's widow (the sole heir of all of Zeek's property) on June

23, 1983. If gold were selling for $490/ounce on June 23, 1983, Zeek's widow's basis in this gold would be $4,900.

PROPERTY ACQUIRED BY GIFT A third common method by which an individual taxpayer acquires property is by gift. January 1, 1921 marked a major change in the rules for determining the basis of property received by gift. A taxpayer's basis for property acquired by gift after December 31, 1920 is generally the donor's adjusted basis. A major exception to the general rule just stated controls if the fair market value of the property given is less than the donor's basis on the date of the gift. In that event, the donee's basis for loss (only) becomes the fair market value on the date of the gift. This means, of course, that a donee may have two different tax bases for properties; that is, one basis for gain and another for loss.

Example 6: Mary Ann Bliss gave her grandson, Jeb, 100 shares of AB stock. Mary Ann purchased this stock for $12,000 on September 6, 1980. It had a fair market value of $20,000 on March 29, 1984, the day she gave it to Jeb. Jeb's tax basis in these shares (for both gain and loss) is $12,000, if Mary Ann was not required to pay a gift tax on this transfer.

If the donor's basis on the date of the gift exceeds the fair market value of the property given *and* the donee eventually sells the gift for some amount greater than its value on the date of the gift, but less than the donor's cost, then the donee's basis will automatically equal its sales price. In that event, no gain or loss will be recognized.

Example 7: Jimmie Don gave his daughter, Anna, 100 shares of DEF stock. Jimmie Don purchased this stock for $12,000 on September 6, 1980. It had a fair market value of $10,000 on March 29, 1984, the day he gave it to Anna. If Jimmie Don is not required to pay a gift tax on this transfer, Anna's tax basis in the shares is: (*a*) $12,000 if she eventually sells the stock for more than $12,000; (*b*) $10,000 if she eventually sells the stock for less than $10,000; *or* (*c*) whatever she sells it for, if she eventually sells the stock for any amount between $10,000 and $12,000.

BACKGROUND

To understand the idea behind the basis rules for properties acquired as gifts, we need only observe the possibilities for tax avoidance in the absence of such wording. If the law provided simply that in all cases the donee would take the donor's cost basis (as it did prior to 1921), then a donor in a low tax bracket could give a property with a substantial "paper loss" to a family member, friend, or acquaintance in a higher tax bracket, and the two individuals com-

Continued

BACKGROUND

bined could achieve a significantly greater tax benefit from the one economic or paper loss than the donor alone could have received. On the other hand, suppose the law provided simply that the donee had to take the *lesser* of the fair market value of the property on the date of the gift or the donor's cost basis. In that case, if the donor's cost basis was higher than fair market value at date of gift, and if the donee eventually sold the property for more than that cost basis, an unrealistically large gain (in a consolidated sense) would have to be reported. Hence the law is written as it is—trying concurrently to close a loophole and yet not to create an unduly harsh tax result.

The provisions that relate to gift taxes further complicate the rules used to determine the cost basis of property acquired by gift. For gifts acquired after September 2, 1958 and before January 1, 1977, if the donor paid a federal gift tax on the transfer of the property, the donee can increase the donor's basis by the total amount of the gift tax as long as the sum of the two (donor's cost and gift tax) does not exceed the fair market value on the date of the gift. If the sum of these two amounts does exceed the fair market value, then the donee's basis will be the fair market value on the date of the gift. Note that if the donor's cost exceeds the fair market value on the date of the gift, none of the gift tax paid can be added to the donee's basis, even if the property is eventually sold for more than the donor's cost. To illustrate the basis rules applicable to gifts made before January 1, 1977, consider Examples 8, 9, and 10.

Example 8: Taxpayer A purchased stock for $15,000. On the date of the gift, June 1, 1976, the stock had a fair market value of $20,000. Gift taxes of $1,000 were paid. In this case, the donee's basis for gain and loss will be $16,000 ($15,000 cost plus $1,000 in gift taxes).

Example 9: Taxpayer B purchased stock for $15,000. On the date of the gift, June 1, 1976, the stock had a fair market value of $10,000. Gift taxes of $1,000 were paid. In this case, the donee's basis for gain is $15,000; the donee's basis for loss, $10,000. If the stock is sold by the donee for any amount greater than $10,000 and less than $15,000, he or she will report neither gain nor loss.

Example 10: Taxpayer C purchased stock for $15,000. On the date of the gift, December 28, 1976, the stock had a fair market value of $15,500. Gift taxes of $1,000 were paid. In this case, the donee's basis for gain and for loss is $15,500 (the sum of the donor's basis plus the gift tax paid, but not in excess of the fair market value of the property on the date of the gift).

The Tax Reform Act of 1976 changed the rules for property acquired by gift after December 31, 1976 insofar as the step-up in basis for gift taxes is concerned. The 1976 Act provides that the gift tax to be added to appreciated property shall be calculated as follows:

$$\text{Addition to basis} = \text{Gift tax paid} \times \frac{\text{Net appreciation in gift property}}{\text{Total value of gift property}}$$

The "net appreciation" is equal to the excess of the gift's fair market value on the date of the gift over the donor's basis at that time. To illustrate the step-up in basis for gift taxes paid on gifts made after December 31, 1976, consider Examples 11, 12, and 13.

Example 11: Taxpayer X purchased securities at a cost of $20,000 in 1970. This year he gave these securities to a donee when their fair market value was $50,000. Total gift tax paid on the transfer was $10,000. The donee's basis for gain and loss is $26,000, computed as follows:

Donor's basis	$20,000
Gift tax adjustment:	
$\$10{,}000 \times \frac{\$50{,}000 - \$20{,}000}{\$50{,}000}$	6,000
Total	$26,000

Example 12: Taxpayer Y purchased securities at a cost of $20,000 in 1970. This year he gave these securities to a donee when their fair market value was $15,000. Total gift tax paid on the transfer was $1,000. No portion of the gift tax can ever be added to the donee's basis, since the fair market value on the date of the gift was less than the donor's cost. Thus, the donee's basis for gain is $20,000; the basis for loss is $15,000.

Example 13: Taxpayer Z purchased securities at a cost of $48,000 in 1970. This year she gave these securities to a donee when their fair market value was $50,000. Total gift tax paid on the transfer was $10,000. The donee's basis for gain and loss is $48,400:

Donor's basis	$48,000
Gift tax adjustment:	
$\$10{,}000 \times \frac{\$50{,}000 - \$48{,}000}{\$50{,}000}$	400
Total	$48,400

TRANSFERS SHORTLY BEFORE DEATH What happens if a donor taxpayer dies shortly after giving property to another? Will the recipient determine his or her basis according to the gift rules or according to the inherited property rules? The answers to these questions have been changed several times during the past few years. At the moment, however, gifts made to a person shortly before his or her death will generally be treated as any other gifts. And inherited property, regardless of how the decedent acquired the property, will generally be treated as any other inherited property. However, one major exception to this rule exists for property given to a decedent within one year of his or her death *if* that same property is subsequently inherited back by the donor or the donor's spouse. In that event the "heir" must carry over the donor's basis in spite of the fact that he or she technically inherited the property from the deceased donee. Although the reason for the new rule may not be obvious, suffice it to say that it does away with some tax benefits previously associated with deathbed giving.

SUMMARY In summary, the amount of a capital gain or loss is the difference between the amount realized on the sale or exchange of a capital asset and the adjusted basis of that capital asset on the date it is sold or exchanged.

The amount realized is equal to the sum of—

- Money received, *plus*
- Fair market value of other property received, *plus*
- Amount of debt transferred from the seller to the buyer.

The adjusted basis of property *acquired by purchase* generally is equal to—

- Cost of the property surrendered, *plus*
- Cost of capital improvements to that property, *less*
- Depreciation or ACRS deductions claimed on the property.

The adjusted basis of property acquired by inheritance or by gift is determined according to special rules.

RECOGNITION OF GAINS AND LOSSES

As a general rule, taxpayers who dispose of assets in a sale must recognize any gain realized. For this purpose, a sale is a disposition in which the seller receives cash consideration and must be distinguished from exchanges and other forms of dispositions. While gains from sales must be recognized, losses realized by individual taxpayers are recognized only if the property was used in a trade or business or was held for investment. Losses from sales of property held for personal use are not deductible. (As explained in Chapter 9, taxpayers can deduct losses related to property held for personal use if the loss results from a casualty.)

Example 14: T sells a boat that he held for personal use. If the sale results in a gain, the gain is recognized by including it in gross income. If the sale results in a loss, such loss is not recognized and no deduction is allowed.

Example 15: Assume the same facts as in Example 14, except that the boat is used in a business. Both gains and losses are recognized upon the sale of this property.

In a number of special circumstances, gains and losses that have been fully realized will not be recognized immediately for federal income tax purposes if the disposition is not a sale. The Code provisions which govern the tax consequences in these special circumstances are generally known as the nontaxable exchange sections. To interpret the phrase *nontaxable exchange* literally, however, would be a mistake; several of the transactions which are given nontaxable treatment involve sales and other dispositions, as well as literal exchanges. Furthermore, the nontaxable consequence is generally temporary. In most instances, the gain or loss that is not recognized immediately in a nontaxable exchange is simply deferred until the newly acquired property is disposed of in a later taxable transaction.

One of the more important nontaxable-exchange sections for many individual taxpayers is Sec. 1031. That section requires a taxpayer to defer any amount of gain or loss realized on the direct exchange of one productive-use or investment property for another property of "like kind." As usual, this paraphrased version of Sec. 1031 is exceedingly dangerous because the words and phrases used in the Code do not have the same meaning for those who interpret the Code that they have for the average person on the street. Because the important details are so lengthy, further discussion of this topic is deferred to Chapter 12.

A second nontaxable-exchange section of general interest to individual taxpayers is Sec. 1034. That section provides that any gain realized on the sale of a person's primary residence will not be recognized immediately if the taxpayer acquires a second primary residence within 24 months before or after the sale of the first residence, at a cost that is equal to (or greater than) the adjusted sales price of the residence sold. Sec. 1034, like Sec. 1031, contains a significant amount of additional detail that must be studied at length if a person is to understand its full significance. Consequently it too is deferred to Chapter 12.

A third important nontaxable-exchange section is found in Sec. 1091. That section denies a taxpayer the right to claim a deduction for any *loss* realized on the sale of a stock or other security if, within 30 days before or after the sale, the taxpayer purchases any "substantially identical securities." This section is commonly known as the "wash-sale provision." Any loss disallowed by operation of Sec. 1091 is recognized on the later taxable disposition of the security acquired because the disallowed loss is added to the basis of the security acquired within the forbidden period. Note that Sec. 1091 has no effect on sales where a gain is realized.

Example 16: On December 27, 19X1 Jane Rivers sold 100 shares of ABC Corporation's common stock for $20,000. Jane had purchased these shares 2 years ago at a cost of $25,000. On January 10, 19X2 Jane repurchased another 100 shares of ABC common stock for $22,000. On July 15, 19X3 Jane sold these same shares for $35,000.

By operation of Sec. 1091, the $5,000 loss realized by Jane's sale of 100 ABC shares of common stock on December 27, 19X1 will *not* be recognized on her 19X1 federal income tax return, because she repurchased substantially identical stocks within the 30-day period. Although Jane realized a gain of $13,000 when she sold her second investment in ABC common stock on July 15, 19X3 only $8,000 of that gain need be recognized. In summary, the $5,000 loss that was realized but not recognized in 19X1 will reduce the gain realized in 19X3 so that the final gain recognized ($8,000) will equal the aggregate difference between the amount Jane invested in the 200 shares of stock ($25,000 + $22,000) and the amount she realized on the sale of those same 200 shares ($20,000 + $35,000).

Example 17: Ed Carson sold 100 shares of DEF common stock for $25,000 on December 27, 19X1. Ed had purchased these shares for $20,000 two years earlier. On December 28, 19X1 Ed repurchased another 100 shares of DEF common stock for $25,500. The wash-sale rule of Sec. 1091 will not apply to Ed Carson's sale of December 27, 19X1, because that sale resulted in a gain.

When a taxpayer disposes of property, he or she must first measure the realized gain or loss using the rules for amount realized and adjusted basis just explained. Second, the taxpayer must decide if the realized gain or loss is recognized by applying these rules and the rules explained in Chapter 12. In the remainder of this chapter, we will assume that all dispositions will be sales and that the properties sold will be held for investment. Under these circumstances, both gains and losses are recognized.

CAPITAL GAIN AND LOSS DEFINED

CAPITAL GAIN/LOSS The gain or loss realized on the sale or exchange of any capital asset.

CAPITAL ASSET All assets are capital assets unless specifically excluded from that classification by Code Sec. 1221(1) through (5).

The Internal Revenue Code does not define ***capital gains and losses*** *per se*; rather, it defines a capital asset and then states that a capital gain or loss is the gain or loss realized on the sale or exchange of a ***capital asset***. It should be observed further that the Code defines capital assets negatively as *all property except that specifically exempted by the Code*. The complete statutory definition of a *pure* capital asset reads as follows:

> Sec. 1221. Capital Asset Defined.
> For purposes of this subtitle, the term "capital asset" means property held by the taxpayer (whether or not connected with his trade or business), but does not include—
> (1) stock in trade of the taxpayer or other property of a kind which would properly be included in the inventory of the taxpayer if on hand at the close of the taxable year, or property held by the taxpayer primarily for sale to customers in the ordinary course of his trade or business;
> (2) property, used in his trade or business, of a character which is subject to the allowance for depreciation provided in section 167, or real property used in his trade or business;
> (3) a copyright, a literary, musical, or artistic composition, a letter or memorandum, or similar property, held by—

(A) a taxpayer whose personal efforts created such property.
(B) in the case of a letter, memorandum, or similar property, a taxpayer for whom such property was prepared or produced, or
(C) a taxpayer in whose hands the basis of such property is determined, for the purpose of determining gain from a sale or exchange, in whole or in part by reference to the basis of such property in the hands of a taxpayer described in subparagraph (A) or (B);

(4) accounts or notes receivable acquired in the ordinary course of trade or business for services rendered or from the sale of property described in paragraph (1); or

(5) a publication of the United States Government (including the Congressional Record) which is received from the United States Government or any agency thereof, other than by purchase at the price at which it is offered for sale to the public, and which is held by—
(A) a taxpayer who so received such publication, or
(B) a taxpayer in whose hands the basis of such publication is determined, for purposes of determining gain from a sale or exchange, in whole or in part by reference to the basis of such publication in the hands of a taxpayer described in subparagraph (A).

Even a cursory reading of Sec. 1221 will suggest that not every investment is to be treated as an investment in a capital asset. For example, if an individual business person invests in "inventory" or "stock-in-trade," Sec. 1221(1) clearly excludes that investment from the category treated as a capital asset for income tax purposes. To the surprise of many taxpayers, a business person's investment in a retail store building, a warehouse, a cash register, or a typewriter, will also be excluded from capital asset treatment—by operation of Sec. 1221(2)—*if* that asset is used in a "trade or business." Unfortunately for the student and taxpayer alike, this is not the end of this story. Chapter 11 will explain in detail the correct tax treatment of the gains and losses realized on the sale of these and other typical business assets.

In a vast majority of the cases, an individual intuitively knows whether or not a particular property is part of his or her inventory. Similarly, most taxpayers know whether or not they are engaged in a trade or business. However, you would not have to prepare too many tax returns to discover how uncertain the definitional boundaries of Sec. 1221 really are.

Example 18: Suppose that a taxpayer inherited some jewelry that he or she had no intention of keeping and, in fact, promptly disposed of through another party. Would those jewels be "property held by the taxpayer primarily for sale to customers"? If so, any gain on their sale would be ordinary income; if not, the gain would be capital gain.[2]

[2]For a decision of the First Circuit Court of Appeals on these facts, see *R. Foster Reynolds* v. *Commissioner*, 155 F. 2d 620 (1946).

Example 19: Suppose that a salaried employee owns and rents out a single dwelling unit. Does this rental activity constitute a second and separate trade or business for the taxpayer? If it does, the rented dwelling becomes depreciable property used in a trade or business and therefore is not a capital asset. If the rental activity is not a trade or business, then the property is a capital asset.[3]

Sec. 1221(3) is an interesting example of a conceptual problem inherent in capital-gain taxation. The only way that most persons can earn a living is by "selling" a service that involves a physical or mental process or both. For example, a person might dig a ditch, diagnose an illness and prescribe a medication, or repair an automobile. A few persons, however, create property that, when sold, provides an income. For example, artists create art objects; authors and composers create copyrighted works; and inventors create patentable ideas. If all properties were capital assets, then persons whose efforts produced property would reap the benefits of the capital-gains tax, whereas all other persons would be subject to the less favorable ordinary tax rates. To preclude this result, Sec. 1221(3) was inserted into the Code. Observe, however, that the statute does not exclude patents. Further, observe that the exclusion for created properties in general extends only to the individual whose efforts created the property and to those who assume the creator's tax basis because the property is received as a gift.

BACKGROUND

The exclusion contained in Sec. 1221(3)(B) was added to the Code in 1969 to put an end to the large tax deductions previously available to former presidents of the United States. Under prior law, whenever an ex-president contributed his papers and other memorabilia to a specially created library named in his honor, a major charitable deduction was created. After lengthy debate, Congress decided that Lyndon Johnson was to be the last of the presidents to be so privileged. As explained in Chapter 6, the present law states that the measure of the deduction for a charitable contribution of property depends on the classification of that property. "Ordinary income property" creates a deduction equal only to the taxpayer's basis in the property. Since a president's basis in his papers is generally zero, and since Sec. 1221(3)(B) makes such properties "ordinary income properties," future presidents will no longer be able to get major personal tax benefits from their public service.

One final observation relative to the definition of capital assets ought to demonstrate the care that must be exercised in dealing with this por-

[3] *Hazard*, 7 T.C. 372 (1946).

tion of the Code. Suppose a local accountant sells his entire practice to another accountant for a fixed sum, payable immediately. Is all or any part of the sale's proceeds to be allocated to the sale of a capital asset? More specifically, if the proceeds exceed the fair market value of the tangible assets and uncollected receivables, does the excess represent the sale of goodwill, and if so is this intangible asset a capital asset? As a general rule it is; however, a slight difference in facts may modify this conclusion. If, for example, the sale includes an agreement not to compete, all or part of the excess may be ordinary income. Careful tax planning by an expert is absolutely essential to guarantee the tax rights of both the purchaser and seller in these and other similar arrangements.

For tax purposes, the most numerically important capital assets are stocks and bonds. Except when held for resale by brokers or dealers, these assets generally are capital assets, and therefore the gain or loss on their sale or exchange is a capital gain or loss.

BACKGROUND

Every general rule in taxation is subject to one or more important exceptions, including the rule that stocks and bonds are always capital assets. In a benchmark decision—*Corn Products Refining Co.*, 76 S.Ct. 20 (1955)—the U.S. Supreme Court held that corn futures owned by a corn product manufacturing company were equivalent to inventory and therefore the gain realized on their sale was ordinary income rather than capital gain. In this case the taxpayer (because of limited storage facilities) had purchased the corn futures for protection against a price rise and a corn supply shortage. Because of these unusual facts, the Court held that the corn futures were tantamount to inventory. The Corn Products Doctrine has been extended to the ownership of common stocks where the acquisition of those stocks was made primarily to protect a source of raw materials supply; for example see *Booth Newspapers, Inc.*, 303 F. 2d 916 (Ct. Cl., 1962). Thus, if the dominant reason behind the acquisition of stock is a business purpose (such as ensuring a source of supply) rather than an investment purpose, the gain or loss realized on the sale of that stock may be found to be ordinary income rather than capital gain. If a taxpayer has *both* a substantial investment purpose and a substantial business motive for acquiring a stock, the sale of that stock will still generate capital gain or loss, rather than ordinary income or loss, according to *W. W. Windle Co.*, 65 T.C. 694 (1976). See also Rev. Rul. 78-94, 1978-1 C.B. 58.

Personal assets such as residences, family automobiles, and pleasure boats are other common capital assets. Observe that a single asset may be both capital and noncapital—for example, a car that is used 50% of the time for family driving and 50% for business uses is treated for tax purposes as two assets—one capital, the other not.

SHORT- OR LONG-TERM CAPITAL GAIN AND LOSS

The tax consequences of a capital gain or loss are significantly affected by its categorization as short- or long-term. How, then, is this distinction determined? The answer to that question is contained in Sec. 1222:

> Sec. 1222. Other Terms Relating to Capital Gains and Losses. For purposes of this subtitle—
> (1) Short-term capital gain.—The term "short-term capital gain" means gain from the sale or exchange of a capital asset held for not more than six months, if and to the extent such gain is taken into account in computing gross income.
> (2) Short-term capital loss.—The term "short-term capital loss" means loss from the sale or exchange of a capital asset held for not more than six months, if and to the extent that such loss is taken into account in computing taxable income.
> (3) Long-term capital gain.—The term "long-term capital gain" means gain from the sale or exchange of a capital asset held for more than six months, if and to the extent such gain is taken into account in computing gross income.
> (4) Long-term capital loss.—The term "long-term capital loss" means loss from the sale or exchange of a capital asset held for more than six months, if and to the extent that such loss is taken into account in computing taxable income.

NET SHORT-TERM CAPITAL GAIN/LOSS The net gain or net loss realized during a tax year on the sale or exchange of all capital assets held for six months or less.

NET LONG-TERM CAPITAL GAIN/LOSS The net gain or net loss realized during a tax year on the sale or exchange of all capital assets held for longer than six months.

Obviously, the distinction between the short- and long-term categorization depends simply on the period of time the seller has owned the capital asset. As a general proposition, no tax benefit attaches to a ***net short-term capital gain***, whereas substantial tax benefits attach to a ***net long-term capital gain***. Just why a short holding period should be an appropriate method of separating the tax-gifted from the tax-deprived capital gain has never been clear. An examination of appropriate congressional records yields only the suggestion that this distinction is sufficient to separate an "investment" gain from a purely "speculative" profit.

BACKGROUND

Congress cannot make up its mind about the holding period for long-term gains and losses. For recent years until 1977, the required holding period was "over six months." In 1977, it was changed to "over one year." The 1984 Act changed the holding period back to six months for properties acquired after June 22, 1984. (Note that after June 22, 1985, the six-month period will apply to all dispositions—until that date, properties purchased before June 22, 1984 may not have been held for a full year.)

But wait! The change back to six months in 1984 is only temporary. For properties acquired after December 31, 1989, the one-year period will apply again—unless Congress changes its mind again.

Although the theoretical rationale of the holding period requirement may be elusive, the application of the requirement to specific factual circumstances is not particularly difficult. As usual, there are some administrative rules that ought to be noted, since they can have considerable importance in practical applications.

> **Example 20:** A stock purchased on September 10, 1984 will be assumed to have been owned for exactly six months on March 10, 1985. To be categorized as a long-term capital gain, a capital asset must be held for *more than* six months; hence a stock purchased on September 10, 1984 cannot be sold before March 11, 1985, if the gain (or loss) on its sale is to be categorized as long-term. The gain or loss on a security purchased on the last day of any month must be held until the first day of the seventh subsequent month, regardless of the number of days in any month, before it will be classified as long-term. (See Rev. Rul. 66-7, 1966-1 C.B. 188.)

> **Example 21:** T acquired a block of stock on June 22, 1984. June 23, 1984 is the effective date for the change from the one-year to the six-month holding period. If T sells this property on or before June 22, 1985, the resulting gain or loss will be short-term.

Relative to securities transactions, the purchase and sale dates, which are referred to as the "trade" or "execution" dates in the financial community, are the critical dates in determining how long a security has been held. The trade dates must be carefully distinguished from order dates, settlement dates, and other special dates that may determine the year in which a particular transaction is to be reported for income tax purposes. Generally, the year of reporting follows routine accounting conventions: Cash-basis taxpayers use settlement dates and accrual-basis taxpayers use execution (that is, "trade") dates. An important exception to the usual rule exists in the case of *loss* sales by cash-basis taxpayers.[4] In this instance, a loss must be recognized for tax purposes in the year the sale is executed, even though settlement takes place in the next year. Note, however, that the usual rule generally applies for gains. Hence a cash-basis taxpayer generally must place sell orders several days prior to the year end if he or she wishes to record a gain for tax purposes in a year about to end. The New York Stock Exchange generally follows a five-business-day delivery rule. Therefore, in some years, cash-basis taxpayers desiring to establish *gains* have to execute their orders no later than December 23 if they wish to report the gain on their current year's income tax return. A cash-basis taxpayer can, however, elect under Sec. 453(d) *not* to report this gain in the normal manner but rather to speed up recognition into the year of sale. Such an election must be made on a timely basis when filing the tax return for the year.[5]

---

[4] Rev. Rul. 70-344, 1970-2 C.B. 50.

[5] Rev. Rul. 82-227, 1982-2 C.B. 89.

Example 22: Assume that a cash-basis calendar-year taxpayer ordered his or her broker to purchase 100 shares of ABC common stock at the market price on July 26, 19X1. Further assume that this purchase order was actually executed on the exchange the following day and that the investor paid the brokerage firm the $2,400 purchase price, including a $75 brokerage fee, on August 8, 19X1. If this investor ordered the broker to sell these same shares at the market price on December 28, 19X1 and the broker executed the sale on that date for $2,875 less another $75 brokerage fee, the investor would report a short-term capital gain on the sale of $400 (that is, $2,800 − $2,400), but this gain would not be reported until he or she filed a 19X2 tax return unless the taxpayer carefully elected not to use the normal installment sale rules on the 19X1 tax return. The gain would be short-term because a capital asset purchased on July 27, 19X1 was sold on December 28, 19X1 and was thus held for less than one year. The gain, however, would not be included with 19X1 transactions because (*a*) the taxpayer reported on a cash basis; (*b*) the transaction resulted in a gain; (*c*) the settlement date occurred in 19X2; *and* (*d*) the taxpayer failed to elect out of the normal rules per Sec. 453(d). If any one of these factors had not been true, the transaction would have been reported with the taxpayer's other 19X1 transactions. For example, if the transaction had resulted in a loss, or if the taxpayer had reported on an accrual basis, then the transaction would have been included on the 19X1 tax return.

The date on which a taxpayer can start to count his or her holding period obviously is as important as the date on which it ends. We shall refer to the former date as the "date basis" of property. Like the adjusted ("cost") basis, the date basis is dependent in large measure on the method of acquisition.

The rule for *purchased* property is that the date basis is the day on which the property is actually purchased, that is, the date title passes. A major exception to this rule applies to property acquired in a barter, or trade, transaction. In that event, the date basis of the newly acquired property *may* be the date the property surrendered in the trade was acquired if the transaction is considered a nontaxable exchange. (Since a discussion of the cost basis of property acquired in a nontaxable exchange was deferred to Chapter 12 for separate consideration, so also is any further consideration of its date basis.)

The date basis of a capital asset acquired from a decedent is immaterial. The Code provides in Sec. 1223 (11) that all gains and losses on the sale or exchange of inherited capital assets are *long-term* gains or losses.

In one sense, the date-basis rules applicable to property acquired by *gift* parallel the cost-basis rules for the same property. That is, if in the calculation of gain or loss the donee takes the donor's cost as his or her cost basis, then the donee's date basis is the date the *donor* acquired the property. If the donee takes as the basis the fair market value on the date of the gift (because this value is lower than the donor's cost basis and because the property is eventually sold for less than this amount), then the date basis is the date of the gift. See Sec. 1223(2).

Example 23: Dale Ashburne inherited a boat from his deceased mother's estate. Dale's mother died on May 8, 19X1; Dale received the boat on July 10, 19X1. Dale's basis in this boat was $5,000. Dale sold the boat for $6,500 on September 23, 19X1. His $1,500 capital gain realized on the sale of this boat will be classified as a long-term capital gain.

Example 24: Jean Best gave her daughter, Lisa, a gem on July 2, 19X1. Jean's basis in the gem was $14,000; it had a fair market value of only $4,000 on the day Jean gave it to Lisa. Lisa sold the gem on December 10, 19X1 for $3,500. The $500 capital loss realized by Lisa on the sale of this gem will be classified as a short-term capital loss.

Example 25: Belinda Ruiz purchased 10 ounces of gold for $3,200 on March 28, 19X2. She gave this gold to her son, Manuel, on October 3, 19X2 when it had a fair market value of $2,800. Manuel sold this gold for $3,700 on March 17, 19X3. The $500 gain realized by Manuel on the sale of this gold will be classified as a long-term capital gain.

Although much more could be said about the rules used to determine the holding period of capital assets, these rules do little to expand our appreciation of the basic problem—the tax treatment of capital gains and losses. To appreciate that aspect of the problem we must turn next to the statutory requirements relative to short-term and long-term transactions.

COMBINING SHORT- AND LONG-TERM GAIN AND LOSS

In order to determine the important tax results, it is necessary to consolidate all ***short-term capital gains and losses*** into one group and all ***long-term capital gains and losses*** into another, and thus to determine the *net* short-term capital gain or loss and the *net* long-term capital gain or loss for a given tax period. For example, suppose that in a given year a taxpayer had three transactions that could be categorized correctly as short-term capital transactions: one resulting in a $600 gain, a second resulting in a $100 loss, and a third resulting in a $200 loss. This taxpayer would have a net short-term capital gain of $300 ($600 minus $100 minus $200). Suppose that instead of the $200 loss assumed above, the third transaction had resulted in a loss of $1,000; then the taxpayer would have had a net short-term capital loss of $500 ($600 minus $100 minus $1,000). In the same manner, the taxpayer must combine all long-term capital gains and losses to determine net long-term capital gain or loss.

SHORT-TERM CAPITAL GAIN/LOSS The gain or loss realized on the sale or exchange of a capital asset held for six months or less.

LONG-TERM CAPITAL GAIN/LOSS The gain or loss realized on the sale or exchange of a capital asset held for longer than six months.

FIGURE 10-1

NET LONG-TERM CAPITAL POSITION (columns) / **NET SHORT-TERM CAPITAL POSITION** (rows)

	Gain	Zero	Loss
Loss	Cell (1) − 0 +	−	−
Zero	+	0	−
Gain	+	+	Cell (2) − 0 +

CAPITAL GAIN NET INCOME The excess of any capital gains over capital losses realized during a tax year.

Finally, it is possible for the taxpayer to combine net short-term and net long-term capital gains and losses into a single net capital gain or loss, an amount that the Code refers to as ***capital gain net income***.[6] This final combination, however, is meaningful only in certain select cases. (If it were always meaningful, there would be no reason to distinguish between short- and long-term capital transactions in the first place.) Before trying to understand the tax treatment applicable to each of the potential "cases," you should understand clearly the range of possibilities that can obtain. The 13 possibilities can be presented concisely in the form of the simple matrix shown in Figure 10-1. The necessity of entering all three symbols in cell (1) of the matrix can be better understood if we let quantity a equal the net long-term capital gain and quantity b equal the net short-term capital loss. Then the relationship between the quantities a and b can be any one of three:

a may be greater than b
a may be equal to b
a may be less than b

If $a > b$, the result is a net gain (+); if $a = b$, the result is neither capital gain nor capital loss (0); if $a < b$, the result is a net loss (−).

The reason for entering three symbols in cell (2) of the matrix is exactly the same. The net long-term capital loss in the vertical column can exceed, equal, or be exceeded by the net short-term capital gain in the horizontal row yielding, respectively, a combined minus, zero, or plus.

[6]Unfortunately for everyone, in the name of simplification Congress coined some truly nonsensical phrases. The everyday English interpretation of the phrase "net capital gain" (or NCG) would seem to demand the definition: LTCG plus STCG minus LTCL minus STCL equals NCG. Believe it or not, after the 1976 Reform Act, the Code defines "net capital gain" as NLTCG minus NSTCL! See Sec. 1222(11). Under the present Code, what common sense and good English would describe as "net capital gain" is now technically known as "capital gain net income." See Sec. 1222(9).

Example 26: Tom and Nancy Harris realized five capital gains and losses during 19X2. Details of those five transactions can be described as follows:

DATE OF SALE	GAIN or (LOSS)	CLASSIFICATION AS SHORT- OR LONG-TERM
Feb. 28	$3,100	Long-term
May 5	($500)	Short-term
June 18	$1,600	Short-term
Aug. 11	($2,200)	Long-term
Nov. 30	$5,000	Long-term

On their federal income tax return for 19X2, Tom and Nancy will report a net long-term capital gain of $5,900 ($3,100 − $2,200 + $5,000) and a net short-term capital gain of $1,100 ($1,600 + $500).

Although it has little or no significance for tax purposes, their capital gain net income will amount to $7,000 ($5,900 + $1,100).

Example 27: Martha VanNostrand realized three capital gains and losses during 19X7. Details of those three transactions can be described as follows:

DATE OF SALE	GAIN or (LOSS)	CLASSIFICATION AS SHORT- OR LONG-TERM
March 2	$6,700	Long-term
April 9	($4,000)	Short-term
July 22	($2,200)	Long-term

On her federal income tax return for 19X7, Martha will report a net long-term capital gain of $4,500 ($6,700 − $2,200) and a net short-term capital loss of $4,000.

This process of combining capital gains and losses can be illustrated in another manner, which may be easier to understand. Think of capital gains and losses as small, round cells showing the appropriate plus or minus sign. Further, think of short-term gains and losses as, say, black cells and long-term gains and losses as, say, gray cells. Now imagine that these cells can be combined in the chemical apparatus illustrated in Figure 10-2.

Up to this point, all we have done is net the short-term capital gains and losses on the one side and the long-term ones on the other. When we try to understand how the two net quantities are then treated for tax purposes, however, complications arise because at least three distinct alternatives exist:

1. Some part or all of a net gain (in Code parlance, "capital gain net income") may get special tax treatment in the form of a long-term capital-gain deduction.
2. Some part or all of a net gain (again, in Code parlance, "capital gain

FIGURE 10-2

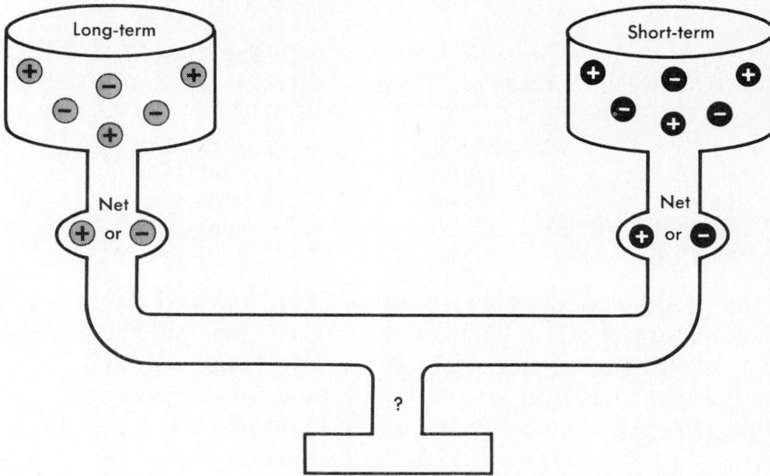

net income") may be treated in the same manner as an equivalent amount of ordinary income.

3. If the result is a net loss, the taxpayer may be entitled to deduct part or all of the loss.

In order to understand the eventual tax treatment given capital gains and losses reported by individual taxpayers, the student must study carefully the rules applicable to the long-term capital-gain deduction and the treatment of net capital losses. Other rules, explained in Chapter 16, apply to any capital gains and losses realized by corporations.

THE LONG-TERM CAPITAL-GAIN DEDUCTION DEFINED

The statutory authority for the long-term capital-gain deduction is found in Sec. 1202, which reads in part as follows:

> Sec. 1202. Deduction for Capital Gains.
> If for any taxable year, a taxpayer other than a corporation has a net capital gain, 60 percent of the amount of the net capital gain shall be a deduction from gross income.

NET CAPITAL GAIN The excess of any net long-term capital gain over any net short-term capital loss realized during a tax year.

And Sec. 1222(11) defines a ***net capital gain*** as "the excess of the net long-term capital gain for the taxable year over the net short-term capital loss for such year." This definition can be stated concisely in a simple formula:

LTCG deduction equals 60% (NLTCG minus NSTCL) where NLTCG equals net long-term capital gain and NSTCL equals net short-term capital loss. The larger the NLTCG and the smaller the NSTCL, the greater the long-term capital-gain deduction.

The outcome of capital asset transactions for a year benefits a taxpayer only when a net capital gain results. When the short-term and long-term capital gains and losses are combined, only four outcomes are significant:

1. The taxpayer's net long-term capital gain exceeds his or her short-term capital loss. The excess is the net capital gain and the taxpayer enjoys the 60% deduction.
2. The taxpayer has a net long-term capital gain *and* a net short-term capital gain. The net capital gain subject to the deduction is the net long-term capital gain. The net short-term capital gain is treated the same as ordinary income.
3. The taxpayer's net short-term capital gain exceeds his or her net long-term capital loss. In this case, there is no net capital gain (and no deduction). The excess is ordinary income.
4. The taxpayer's capital losses, either short-term or long-term, exceed his or her capital gains. A *net capital loss* results for the year. Special rules explained later in this chapter apply to the deductibility of net capital losses.

Table 10-1 illustrates the four possibilities.

Several aspects of the table deserve emphasis. First, notice that the first two columns are *net* quantities; it is immaterial how many individual long- and short-term gains and losses are realized to arrive at these net quantities. Second, note that, in common sense English, the "net capital position" is *not* the base for determining the long-term capital-gain deduction. Unfortunately, however, the Code uses the phrase "net capital gain" to mean "NLTCG minus NSTCL." In Code language, the net capital position is called capital-gain net income. Third, observe that whenever a *net* short-term capital gain is reported (even if that net quantity includes several individual short-term capital losses), a zero is substituted for NSTCL in the formula suggested earlier. Fourth, notice that no long-term

TABLE 10-1
The Long-term Capital-Gain Deduction

NET LONG-TERM GAIN (LOSS)	NET SHORT-TERM GAIN (LOSS)	CAPITAL-GAIN NET INCOME	NET CAPITAL GAIN	AMOUNT OF LTCG DEDUCTION
$ 8,000	$ 0	$ 8,000	$8,000	$4,800
8,000	(2,000)	6,000	6,000	3,600
8,000	(10,000)	(2,000)	0	0
8,000	5,000	13,000	8,000	4,800
0	5,000	5,000	0	0
(5,000)	8,000	3,000	0	0
(5,000)	(8,000)	(13,000)	0	0

capital-gain deduction can be derived from an excess of net short-term gains over net long-term losses, but that net long-term capital losses are offset against net short-term capital gains.

Example 28: Tom and Nancy Harris (of Example 26) reported a net long-term capital gain of \$5,900 and a net short-term capital gain of \$1,100. They would, therefore, be entitled to claim a long-term capital gain deduction of \$3,540 (i.e., 60% × (\$5,900 − \$-0-)).

Example 29: Martha VanNostrand (of Example 27) reported a net long-term capital gain of \$4,500 and a net short-term capital loss of \$4,000. She would, therefore, be entitled to claim a long-term capital-gain deduction of \$300 (i.e., 60% × (\$4,500 − \$4,000)).

The long-term capital-gain deduction provides a potential benefit to every taxpayer who has taxable income sufficiently large to make him or her subject to even the lowest income tax rate. That is, regardless of the marginal bracket at which he or she pays tax, and regardless of the ability to itemize deductions, the taxpayer who is fortunate enough to record net long-term capital gains in excess of net short-term capital losses will be automatically entitled to a tax deduction equal to 60% of that excess.

Example 30: Assume that a single taxpayer had a \$12,000 ordinary taxable income and a \$5,000 long-term capital gain. This taxpayer would compute his or her tax liability as follows:

Ordinary taxable income		\$12,000
Long-term capital gain	\$ 5,000	
Less LTCG deduction	(3,000)	
Taxable portion of capital gain		2,000
Total taxable income		\$14,000

Observe that the highest marginal tax rate applicable to individual taxpayers is 50%. Thus, the effect of the long-term capital-gain deduction is, for all practical purposes, to place a *maximum* 20% tax rate on the excess of net long-term capital gains over net short-term capital losses—50% of (100% minus 60%). In Example 30, the taxpayer's highest marginal rate is only 20% and the net capital gain is taxed at 8% or less.

In the third possible outcome just listed, the net short-term capital gain exceeds the net long-term loss. In this case, no tax benefits accrue to the net gain that is treated as ordinary income.

Example 31: T has a net short-term capital gain of \$10,000 and a net long-term capital loss of \$6,000. The \$4,000 excess of gain over loss is ordinary income.

The fourth possibility is that capital losses exceed capital gains and a *net capital loss* results.

NET CAPITAL LOSSES

Tax detriment, as well as tax benefit, can result from transactions involving capital assets. The detriment can arise from any one of three provisions. First, many capital losses simply are not deductible for tax purposes. As explained earlier, the capital loss sustained on the sale of a personal automobile is *not* deductible, even though the gain on the sale of the identical asset would be taxable. This rather peculiar situation results from two basic Code provisions noted in Chapter 3: (*a*) that all income, regardless of source, is subject to the income tax unless it is specifically excluded by another Code section; and (*b*) that no deduction is allowed unless specifically provided by the Code. And the Code authorizes neither the exclusion of any gain realized on the sale of personal capital assets nor the deduction of any loss realized on the sale or exchange of personal capital assets. Because casualty losses are deductible under Sec. 165(c), however, the destruction (total or partial) by theft, fire, flood, or wind of a personal automobile *could* result in a tax deduction, while the routine loss on the sale or exchange of that asset could not achieve the same tax status. The precise treatment of deductible casualty losses was discussed in Chapter 9. At this juncture, it is necessary only to realize that many capital losses simply are not tax deductible.

A second possible tax detriment in transactions involving capital assets occurs because even those capital losses that are deductible are subject to maximum limitations. As a general proposition, in any given year ***net capital losses*** are deductible (if deductible at all) only to the *lesser* of (*a*) $3,000 or (*b*) taxable income determined without subtracting personal exemptions. (The maximum capital loss deduction for a married taxpayer filing a separate return is $1,500.) Notice that the rule just stated is concerned with *net* capital losses; in other words, capital losses can be offset against capital gains without limit.

NET CAPITAL LOSS The excess of any capital losses over capital gains realized during a tax year.

A third and final tax detriment in transactions involving capital assets occurs when net *long-term* capital losses are offset against ordinary income. For all such losses incurred after December 31, 1969 the losses must be offset on a $2-for-$1 basis. That is, it requires $2,000 of a net long-term capital loss to create a $1,000 deduction from ordinary income. This 50% dilution is applicable only to net long-term losses; short-term losses are applied on a dollar-for-dollar basis.

> ***BACKGROUND***
>
> This provision, instituted in the Tax Reform Act of 1969, was intended to bring the tax treatment of net long-term capital losses in line with the treatment of net long-term capital gains (which then were taxed at only one-half their value). The parity of gain and loss treatment was not continued in the Revenue Act of 1978, however, because that law did *not* change the 2-for-1 loss provision when it increased the LTCG deduction from 50% to 60%.

If the deductible net capital loss in any particular year exceeds the maximum, for all noncorporate taxpayers the excess is carried forward to subsequent tax years until exhausted. In each of the subsequent years the capital loss retains its short- or long-term character, as established in the year it was realized. The taxpayer with both net short-term and net long-term capital losses in any given year must deduct short-term capital losses first.

Example 32: Assume that in 19X1 a taxpayer had a $20,000 ordinary taxable income and that, in addition, he recognized a deductible net long-term capital loss of $5,800 and a net short-term capital loss of $500. This taxpayer would offset the maximum net capital loss of $3,000 against his ordinary income (the $500 short-term loss and $2,500 long-term loss) but he would use up $5,000 of his $5,800 net long-term capital loss to do so. He could carry forward only the remaining $800 net long-term capital loss into 19X2. His net taxable income would be calculated as follows:

Ordinary taxable income	$20,000
Less: $3,000 maximum net capital-loss deduction, determined as follows:	
Net short-term capital loss first (on dollar-for-dollar basis)	(500)
Net long-term capital loss next (on a 2-for-1 basis) $800 carried to 19X2	(2,500)
Net taxable income for 19X1	$17,000

If this taxpayer had no further capital transactions in 19X2, the $800 long-term loss carried forward would yield only a $400 deduction from his ordinary income.

It should be noted that the taxpayer in Example 32 is not given an option in deciding whether or not to offset his net capital losses against ordinary income in a particular year; he or she must do so if possible. If this were not stipulated, a taxpayer, under some circumstances, might be tempted to defer deducting losses until he or she could use them dollar-for-dollar. As a practical matter, of course, this means that a little year-end tax planning can often pay sizable dividends.

Table 10-2 demonstrates the proper handling of net capital losses and the determination of the ***capital-loss carryforward***. This tabulation assumes a taxpayer with taxable income, excluding capital transactions and personal exemptions, of more than $3,000. (In other words, the $3,000 maximum capital loss offset against ordinary income is assumed to be available each year.)

CAPITAL-LOSS CARRYFORWARD The excess of any net capital loss over the maximum capital loss deduction allowed for one tax year which may be carried forward and deducted in later years.

The rules that determine the tax treatment of long- and short-term capital gains and losses for individual taxpayers can now be illustrated, as in Figure 10-3, with an extension of the chemical-beaker apparatus of Figure 10-2. On initial examination, both the student and the instructor may

TABLE 10-2
Individual Net Capital Losses and the Capital-Loss Carryforward

YEAR	ASSUMED CAPITAL GAINS AND LOSSES EXCLUDING CARRYFORWARD		CAPITAL LOSSES TO BE CARRIED FORWARD TO SUBSEQUENT YEAR	EXPLANATION OF LOSS USED AND LOSS CARRYFORWARD
19X1	NLT	$(2,000) *	$(2,000)LT	Carried forward
	NST	(3,000)	0	$3,000 deducted from ordinary income (maximum)
	Net capital	$(5,000)		
19X2	NLT	$(4,000)	$(6,000)LT	19X1 $(2,000) + 19X2 $(4,000)
	NST	$(4,000)	$(1,000)ST	$3,000 deducted from ordinary income (maximum); $1,000 carried forward
	Net capital	$(8,000)		
19X3	NLT	$ 7,000		Offset all LT carryforward + $1,000 short-term loss of current year
	NST	(4,000)	$(1,000)ST	$3,000 (maximum) deducted from ordinary income; $(1,000) carried forward†
	Capital gain net income	$ 3,000		
19X4	NLT	$ 1,000	0	
	NST	$ 1,000	0	Offset by ST carryforward
	Net capital	$ 2,000		

*Parentheses denote capital loss; absence of parentheses indicates capital gain.
†Observe that the $6,000 long-term carryforward is used to offset the current year's $7,000 long-term capital gain before applying any of the current year's short-term capital loss against the current year's long-term capital gain. If the opposite procedure were required, no carryforwards would have been left.

be inclined to dismiss Figure 10-3 as too confusing. Our experience, however, has been that this one illustration is more readily digested than the hundreds of words required to replace it. In working with this illustration, note, for example, that all gray positives and negatives first combine into a single net quantity. Similarly, all black positives and negatives also combine into another single net quantity. These two net quantities, however, will combine into another single net quantity *only if they are of opposite signs*. That is, net long-term gains will always combine with net short-term losses to form a single net gain or loss. Also, net long-term losses will always combine with net short-term gains to form a net loss or gain. If the grays and the blacks are of the same sign, positive or negative, they will never combine. If they are both net positives, the one (the long-term gains) gets special treatment, whereas the other (the short-term

FIGURE 10-3

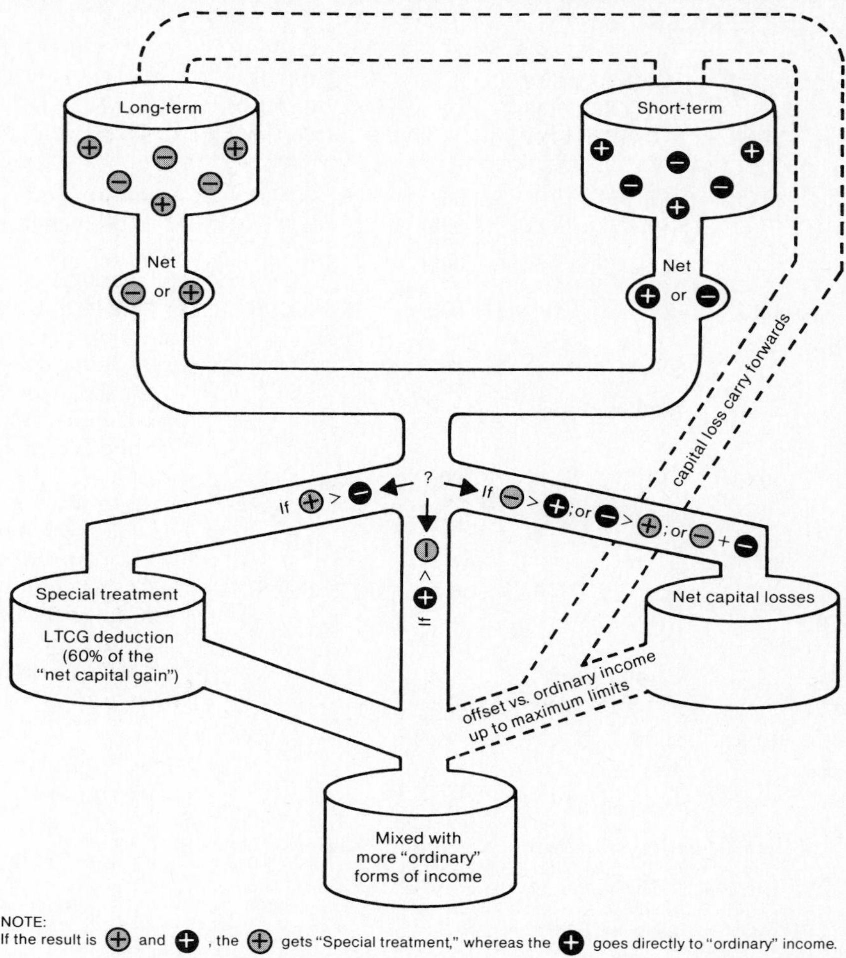

gains) gets the same treatment as ordinary income. If both nets are negative, the short-term negatives go through the system first; additionally, the long-term negatives must be diluted by 50% if and when they are used to offset ordinary income.

MISCELLANEOUS SPECIAL RULES

The rules discussed in the preceding pages of this chapter constitute the more important general rules applicable to the sales of investment properties. Unfortunately all general rules in tax matters are subject to numerous special exceptions. No introductory tax text can cover all of the special rules; nevertheless, a few of those rules must be introduced briefly to give the student a more realistic picture of the income taxation of investments. The special provisions selected for further discussion by the authors of this text include those for worthless securities, related-party losses, short sales, options, Sec. 1244 stock, and bond transactions.

WORTHLESS SECURITIES

Worthless securities present an interesting special problem. A very careful reading of Sec. 1001(c) suggests that the loss incurred if and when a security becomes worthless can not be deducted. That is, Sec. 1001(c) states that "the gain or loss . . . *on the sale or exchange* of property shall be recognized." (Emphasis added.) If a security is truly worthless, how can a taxpayer either sell or exchange it? Clearly no intelligent person would pay anything for a *worthless* security; neither would he or she exchange anything of value for it. If it were not for some special rules, therefore, a taxpayer might be left with a nondeductible loss on a worthless security for want of a sale or exchange.

In this instance, however, Sec. 165(g)(1) comes to the taxpayer's rescue. That provision reads as follows:

> (1) General rule.—If any security which is a capital asset becomes worthless during the taxable year, the loss resulting therefrom shall, for purposes of this subtitle, be treated as a loss from the sale or exchange, on the last day of the taxable year, of a capital asset.

In effect this special rule does two important things: first, it creates an artificial sale or exchange; and second, it provides a date for that event. The artificial sale or exchange solves the sale-or-exchange dilemma created by the wording of Sec. 1001(c) and the determination of an artificial sale date allows the taxpayer to classify any capital loss as a short- or long-term capital loss.

RELATED-PARTY LOSSES

Section 267(a) disallows the recognition of any loss realized on the sale or exchange of property with a "related party." The term related party is defined in Sec. 267(b) to include, among others, members of the taxpayer's family and any corporation controlled directly or indirectly by the taxpayer. (For this purpose, control is defined as stock ownership of 50% or more.)

Example 33: Phil Brown sold 100 shares of XYZ common stock to his sister, Maude Phillips. Phil's basis in these shares was \$20,000. Maude paid Phil \$15,000 for the shares—their fair market value on the day they were sold. The \$5,000 capital loss realized by Phil on the sale of these shares will not be recognized for federal income tax purposes.

Any loss disallowed because of Sec. 267(a) can be used to reduce a gain subsequently recognized by the related purchaser. Sec. 267(d).

Example 34: If Maude Phillips (Example 33) later sold the 100 shares of XYZ common stock for a gain, that gain (to the extent of $5,000) would also go unrecognized.

For example, if Maude sold these shares for $22,000, she would recognize only $2,000 of the $7,000 capital gain that she had realized.

On the other hand, if Maude later sold the XYZ shares for $17,000, she would not have to recognize any of the $2,000 gain that she had realized. The remaining $3,000 of the $5,000 loss sustained by Phil would, however, be "lost" forever.

SHORT SALES

Short sales can be of two general types: namely, ordinary short sales or short sales against-the-box. In an ordinary short sale a taxpayer sells something that he or she does not currently own. In order to complete a short sale, the seller obviously must borrow the property sold short. In the case of securities, brokers typically provide the shares sold short by an investor. The reason an investor would sell short is his or her belief that the value of the security sold short is about to decline. If an investor can sell a security for $1,000 today; borrow that security for a short period of time; and then acquire the same security for a cost of $600 (to repay the broker who loaned the stock to the taxpayer in the interim period), he or she will have made a profit of $400 (less any fee paid to the broker for the interim loan).

A short sale against-the-box is just like an ordinary short sale except that the seller already owns as much or more of the property as he or she has just sold short. Nevertheless, even though he or she already owns that same property, the investor still goes through the motions of borrowing the property to complete the initial short sale. Then, at some later date, the investor delivers to the lending party the property previously sold short. This last transaction is described as closing the short sale.

The primary reason for utilizing a short sale against-the-box is to defer the recognition of a gain or loss for federal income tax purposes. The act of selling short, in this case, simply freezes the economics of the transaction. In other words, because the taxpayer already owns that which he or she has just sold short, the true amount of the economic gain or loss realized is determined at the time of the short sale (except for the service charge paid to the broker for making the temporary loan). However, for tax purposes a short sale is not deemed to be complete until the taxpayer delivers the property sold short; hence, the recognition of that sale transaction can be deferred until a time that is most convenient to the taxpayer.[7] Even though a taxpayer can use a short sale against-the-box to defer the recognition of a capital gain or loss, he or she can not use that technique to convert a short-term capital gain or loss into a long-term

[7]Treas. Reg. Sec. 1.1233-1(a)(1).

capital gain or loss. For federal income tax purposes, the act of making a short sale against-the-box terminates the holding period for the shares already owned.[8] Section 1233(a) guarantees a taxpayer the right to claim a capital gain or loss on a short sale—rather than an ordinary gain or loss—as long as the property sold short is a capital asset in the hands of the taxpayer.

Example 35: Donald Evans sold short 100 shares of RMS common stock on May 8, 19X1. The amount realized by Donald on this sale was $8,000. Donald borrowed the 100 shares of RMS stock from his broker to make delivery. On August 10, 19X1 Donald purchased 100 shares of RMS stock for $6,500 and immediately delivered those shares to his broker to close the previous short sale. Assuming that RMS common stock is a capital asset to Donald Evans, this short sale results in a $1,500 short-term capital gain.

Example 36: Dee Lyman purchased 100 shares of TDY common stock for $3,000 on July 24, 19X1. On October 29, 19X1, Dee sold short 100 shares of TDY common stock for $5,000. On February 1, 19X2 Dee closed her short sale of October 29, 19X1 with the shares purchased on July 24, 19X1. Given these facts, Dee Lyman must report a short-term capital gain of $2,000 on her 19X2 federal income tax return. Although her short sale against-the-box in 19X1 did permit her to defer the recognition of the gain realized in 19X1 into the year 19X2, it did not allow her to convert what was a short-term capital gain into a long-term capital gain.

If a taxpayer does not already own substantially identical property on the date he or she makes a short sale, but acquires such property on or before the date the short sale is closed, any gain or loss realized on closing the sale will be short-term.[9]

OPTIONS IN GENERAL

In lieu of investing directly in a property, a taxpayer might elect to buy and/or sell options in that same property. Generally speaking, the cost of an investment in an option is substantially less than the cost of purchasing an equivalent amount of property directly since the option merely provides the investor with the right to acquire (or to sell) the property at a given price—not with the property itself. Alternatively, an investor who already owns a property may be willing to sell another party a call option which gives the purchaser the right to acquire his or her property, at a given price, for a stipulated period of time.

---

[8] Treas. Reg. Sec. 1.1233-1(a)(3).

[9] Sec. 1233(b) and Treas. Reg. Sec. 1.1233-1(c).

Section 1234 provides the general tax treatment for any gain or loss realized on the sale or exchange of an option to buy or sell. Section 1234(a) provides that any gain or loss realized will be a capital gain or loss if the property subject to option would be a capital asset in the hands of the investor. Thus, if an investor writes a call option on a capital asset that he or she already owns, and the purchaser of the option elects not to exercise that option (because the price of the property did not increase as expected during the option period), the investor who wrote the call option would recognize a short-term capital gain on the date the option lapsed.[10] On the other hand, if the purchaser of the option exercises a call option, the grantor of the option must add the amount received on the sale of the option to his or her sales price to determine the amount of gain or loss realized when the option is called.

Example 37: Shawn Brown purchased 100 shares of GHI stock for $4,000 on April 14, 19X3. On September 5, 19X5 Shawn wrote a call option on her 100 shares of GHI, giving the option holder the right to purchase these shares within the next 90 days at a price of $6,500. Shawn was paid a call premium of $600 for writing this option.

If the purchaser fails to exercise this option, Shawn must recognize a $600 short-term capital gain on the day the option lapses.

On the other hand, if the option holder elects to exercise the option, and pays Shawn $6,500 for the 100 shares of GHI stock on September 29, 19X5, Shawn must recognize a $3,100 long-term capital gain on that date. That is, $7,100 amount realized ($6,500 + $600) less $4,000 adjusted basis (or cost of stock) equals the gain realized.

A put option is similar to a call option except that it authorizes the option holder to force the other contracting party to acquire an optioned property at a stipulated price. In other words, an option holder can exercise a put and force the grantor of the option to purchase a property at a stated price.

Taxpayers sometimes purchase offsetting put and call options to establish a "tax straddle." Frequently the ploy behind such a straddle was to allow the taxpayer to sell the option with the loss just before year-end, and the other option with the gain just after year-end. The result was a tax-deferral but with little or no economic risk. Congress adopted a new rule in 1984 that severely limits the usefulness of a straddle. Under the new rule, the taxpayer must defer the recognition of a loss on a tax straddle until the year when the gain is recognized.[11]

The preceding discussion of options is concerned only with general options in stocks, securities, commodities, commodity futures, and other properties. It is not pertinent to stock options granted by a corporation to

---

[10] Sec. 1234(b)(1).

[11] Sec. 1092(a)(1)(A) & (B).

an employee, officer, or shareholder, as part of a special "compensation" package. The tax provisions governing the latter kind of stock options are found in Secs. 421, 422, and 422A.

INCENTIVE STOCK OPTIONS

The most important employee stock options today are those governed by Sec. 422A, called ***incentive stock options***. The important requirements for an incentive stock option plan are detailed in Sec. 422A(b). Among those requirements are the following:

INCENTIVE STOCK OPTION A plan under which as an incentive the employer gives one or more employees an option to purchase shares of the employer's stock.

1. The option must be granted pursuant to a plan which states the maximum number of shares that can be granted, and identifies the employees (or class of employees) to receive the option. This plan must be approved by the stockholders of the corporation within 12 months before or after the date the plan is adopted.
2. The option must be granted to the employee within ten years from the earlier of (*a*) the date the plan was adopted or (*b*) the date the plan was approved by the stockholders.
3. The option must be exercised within ten years from the date it is granted.
4. The option price must be equal to (or greater than) the fair market value of the stock on the date granted.
5. The option can not be transferable (except upon the death of the option holder).
6. Either the option holder can not own more than 10% of the outstanding stock of the corporation granting the option (using the attribution rules of Sec. 267) *or* (if the stockholder does own directly or indirectly more than 10% of the grantor corporation's stock) the option price must be at least 110% of the fair market value of the stock on the grant date.
7. The aggregate fair market value of the stock granted to any one employee can not exceed $100,000 plus a special carryover, defined in Sec. 422A(c)(4) in any one calendar year.

If an employee stock option satisfies all of the requirements of Sec. 422A(b), there will be no tax consequences to either the grantor or the grantee on the date the option is granted or the date the option is exercised. If the employee holds the stock for more than one year, any gain realized on its disposition will be long-term capital gain (assuming that the disposition takes place at least two years after the date it was granted and assuming that the taxpayer remains an employee of the grantor from the date the option was granted until at least three months prior to its exercise).

Example 38: Mary Friou was granted an option to acquire 1,000 shares of her employer-corporation's stock for $12 per share. This option satisfies all of the requirements of Sec. 422A; hence it is an "incentive stock option" as that term is defined by the Code.

Three years after this option was granted, Mary exercised the option and acquired the 1,000 shares for $12,000. On this date the stock had a fair market value of $20,000.

Two years after exercising the option, Mary sold the 1,000 shares for $30,000. Mary remained an employee of the grantor corporation until the day she sold the shares and retired. Under these circumstances, Mary will report a long-term capital gain of $18,000 (i.e., $30,000 amount realized less $12,000 adjusted basis) on the sale of the shares.

Incidentally, the employer corporation is not given a deduction for any amount associated with an incentive stock option if the employee meets the holding period requirements.[12]

If the holding period requirements are not satisfied (but the option otherwise satisfies all of the conditions of Sec. 422A), a portion of the gain realized on the sale of the stock must be reported as ordinary income by the employee-optionee. The portion reported as ordinary income is equal to the difference between the value of the stock on the date the option was exercised and the option price. Any additional gain will be short- or long-term capital gain or loss, determined by the period of time that has elapsed between the exercise and sale dates. And, if the employee must recognize some amount of ordinary income, because of the holding period requirements, then the employer-corporation may also deduct an equivalent amount as compensation.

Special rules apply to closely related corporations (such as a parent and subsidiary corporations); also to situations modified by the subsequent reorganization or liquidation of the grantor corporation, and to insolvent employees. These rules, however, are better left for study beyond an introductory course in income taxation.

SECTION 1244 STOCK

Under most circumstances the sale of corporate stock at a loss results in a capital loss for the shareholder. Furthermore, for reasons already explained, capital losses are generally not as desirable as ordinary losses. In order to increase the attractiveness of investments in the stock of small business corporations, Congress enacted Sec. 1244. The important consequence of this section is to convert what otherwise would be capital loss into ordinary loss. This special privilege is restricted to sales and exchanges of "small business stock," also known as "Sec. 1244 stock."

Prior to the Revenue Act of 1978 the status of Sec. 1244 stock was restricted to corporations with a capitalization of $500,000 or less and to stock issued under a written plan adopted within two years before or after the stock was issued. Those requirements were retroactively re-

[12] Sec. 421(a)(2).

pealed, however, and Sec. 1244 now authorizes this special treatment on the first $1,000,000 of capital stock issued by any corporation for property regardless of the total capitalization of the corporation and whether or not any special plan for a Sec. 1244 stock issue was ever intended.

The special privilege of claiming an ordinary loss (in lieu of a capital loss) on the sale of Sec. 1244 stock is restricted to individual taxpayers (including stock held by partnerships who are the *original* owners). The maximum amount that may be reported as an ordinary loss under Sec. 1244 is $50,000 per year per taxpayer. Therefore, on the joint return of a married couple, up to $100,000 per year may be so reported.

> **Example 39:** Robert White purchased 1,000 shares of Mite Corporation's common stock for $5,000 on June 16, 19X4. Robert sold these same shares for $1,000 on November 12, 19X5. The shares purchased qualified as Sec. 1244 stock because they were part of the first $1,000,000 in capital stock issued by Mite Corporation. On his 19X5 federal income tax return, Robert should report an ordinary loss of $4,000 from the sale of Mite's common stock.

BOND TRANSACTIONS

Investments in bonds present interesting and unusual tax problems in certain circumstances. The two special cases to be considered here involve the sale of bonds issued by state and local government units and the sale of bonds issued at a premium or a discount.

THE SALE OF TAX EXEMPT BONDS As explained in Chapter 3, Sec. 103 generally excludes from gross income any amount of interest received on state and local government bonds. That section does *not*, however, go on to exclude any gain or loss on the sale or exchange of those same bonds. Some taxpayers are surprised, therefore, to discover that they must report a taxable capital gain when they sell a state or local bond for more than they paid for it. By the same token, those taxpayers may be pleasantly surprised to discover that they can also deduct any capital loss realized on the sale of an otherwise "tax-exempt" bond.

BOND PREMIUM AND BOND DISCOUNT If the rate of interest stipulated on the face of a bond is either more or less than the current rate of interest for an investment subject to an equivalent risk, that bond will sell at a premium or at a discount, respectively. Suppose, for example, that a corporation issues $5,000,000 in bonds paying a 12% rate of interest. If the market deems this rate of interest to be greater than the market rate for an investment of equivalent risk, the bond will sell for more than its face value. A $1,000 face-valued bond might, under these circumstances, sell for $1,200. The extra $200 paid for the bond is called a "premium." On the other hand, if investors deem the stated 12% rate of interest to be less than the market rate for investments of similar risk, a $1,000 face-valued bond will sell for less than $1,000. In that event the difference between the sales price and the face is called a "discount."

Generally speaking, the tax law recognizes the fact that bond premiums and bond discounts are market adjustments to a stated rate of interest and require taxpayers to adjust their reported interest income or interest expense accordingly. The adjustment process is referred to as "amortization" of the bond discount or bond premium. The most important rules are contained in Secs. 1271, 1272, 1273, and 1016(a)(5). Original issue discount on bonds issued prior to July 1, 1982 could generally be amortized on a straight-line basis. For bonds issued after July 1, 1982 with an original issue discount, the amortization rule has been modified so that the additional income that must be reported by the purchaser is calculated at a constant rate of interest using effective interest methods.

Two examples may be helpful. First, assume that a $1,000 face-value bond is sold for $1,200. If this bond is payable 20 years from the date of issue, the $200 premium received by the debtor must be amortized so that, on the maturity date of the bond, no amount of premium will remain. For bonds issued prior to July 1, 1982, this amortization could have been made on a straight-line basis; hence $10 might have been amortized each period. From the point of view of the issuer of the bond, this $10 amortization would have reduced the interest expense otherwise deductible. Under these circumstances the debtor-taxpayer *must* amortize the premium. From the point of view of the taxpayer purchasing the bond, however, the same premium amortization serves to reduce the interest income otherwise reportable. If this is taxable interest, the taxpayer *may* amortize the premium, but he or she is not required to do so. On the other hand, if the interest is tax-exempt interest, the premium amortization must be made so that no loss will remain to be realized when the bond is paid (at face value) on maturity.

Exactly the opposite situation exists with bond discounts. If a taxpayer issues a $1,000 face-valued bond for $800, the $200 discount serves to increase the interest expense otherwise deductible. Under these circumstances the taxpayer may (but is not required) to amortize the discount. The purchaser of that same bond, however, is required to amortize the $200 bond discount because it serves to increase his or her otherwise reportable interest income.

The general rules for bond discounts and bond premiums which have been stated here are just that: general rules! They should not be used in actual applications of the law without further checking of appropriate authorities because each rule is subject to numerous special exceptions. For example, the rules described for discounts are applicable only to "original-issue discounts," a term that only our Tax Code can define. A bond discount that is not an original-issue discount (in the technical sense of that term) need not be amortized. The 1984 Tax Reform Act expanded significantly the scope of the rules for original issue discount and extended the rules to notes issued by natural persons. At the time of this writing (February, 1985), Congress is debating changes in the rules adopted in 1984, and as a result is creating further uncertainty.

REPORTING CAPITAL GAINS AND LOSSES

If an individual taxpayer has any recognizable capital gains or losses for the tax year, he or she must file ***Schedule D***, Form 1040. An example of the 1984 form appears as Figures 10-4 and 10-5. Ignoring the numbers that we have entered on that form for the moment, observe that the 1984 form is divided into five "parts," two parts appearing on the front of the first page. Part I is used to report only short-term capital transactions and, as such, serves much the same purpose as the short-term beaker in our chemical-apparatus simulator. Part II does the same thing for long-term capital transactions. Part III is the "directing" mechanism that, in effect, routes the various components and possible combinations of net capital gains and losses to their proper container (that is, to special treatment, ordinary income, and/or net capital loss, in our apparatus). Observe also that the instructions on line 22 serve to give the taxpayer the benefit of the long-term capital-gain deduction. Line 25 of Part III in effect allows the taxpayer to deduct up to $3,000 of net capital loss from ordinary income. Part IV is a record of capital-loss carryforwards, Part V is an information section concerning the election to opt out of the installment sales method, and Part VI provides a space to reconcile the amounts reported on Schedule D with amounts shown on Form 1099-B.

FORM 1040—SCHEDULE D

SCHEDULE D The tax form on which capital gains and losses are reported.

FORM 1099-B

In order to discover the various rules for tax basis, holding period, and so on, you would have to read the "Instructions for Schedule D" that accompany this form. We have not reproduced those instructions here. Observe, however, that the rules become operative whenever the taxpayer enters the amounts in the various columns of this form. Thus, column e. of Part I should reflect the cost basis (which differs, as we have seen, with the method of acquisition). The time lapse between columns b. and c. determines the correct holding period and, therefore, the correct classification as a short- or long-term component.

The amounts entered on Schedule D in Figure 10-4 are based on the following assumed transactions for a married couple filing a joint return:

1. Sale of ABC stock at a $10,000 short-term capital gain;
2. Sale of XYZ stock at a $5,000 long-term capital gain;
3. Sale of land held as an investment at a $12,000 long-term capital gain; and
4. A $2,000 long-term capital-loss carryforward from last year.

In this example, line 23 (Figure 10-5) instructs the taxpayer to carry $16,000 to line 13 of Form 1040. The effect of that instruction is, of course, to cause the following to be taxed as ordinary income:

1. All the $10,000 net short-term capital gain, but only
2. 40% of the $15,000 net long-term capital gain.

This completes our discussion of the sale of investment properties. To complete your understanding of all the capital gain and loss rules, however, you must also study Chapter 11: Sales of Business Properties.

FIGURE 10-4

SCHEDULE D (Form 1040)

Department of the Treasury Internal Revenue Service (0)

Capital Gains and Losses

(Also reconciliation of sales of stocks, bonds, and bartering income from Forms 1099-B)

► Attach to Form 1040. ► See Instructions for Schedule D (Form 1040).

OMB No. 1545-0074

1984

12

Name(s) as shown on Form 1040: T. H. Taxpayer

Your social security number: 444 44 4444

Part I Short-term Capital Gains and Losses-Assets Held One Year or Less (6 months if acquired after 6/22/84)

a. Description of property (Example, 100 shares 7% preferred of "Z" Co.)	b. Date acquired (Mo., day, yr.)	c. Date sold (Mo., day, yr.)	d. Gross sales price	e. Cost or other basis (see instructions)	f. LOSS If column (e) is more than (d) subtract (d) from (e)	g. GAIN If column (d) is more than (e) subtract (e) from (d)
1 1,000 Shares ABC stock	7/10/84	11/10/84	$40,000	$30,000		$10,000

Line	Description	f	g
2	Short-term gain from sale or exchange of a principal residence from Form 2119, lines 7 or 11		
3	Short-term gain from installment sales from Form 6252, lines 22 or 30		
4	Net short-term gain or (loss) from partnerships, S corporations, and fiduciaries		
5	Add lines 1 through 4 in columns f and g	( )	$10,000
6	Combine columns f and g of line 5 and enter the net gain or (loss)		$10,000
7	Short-term capital loss carryover from years beginning after 1969		( )
8	Net short-term gain or (loss), combine lines 6 and 7		$10,000

Part II Long-term Capital Gains and Losses-Assets Held More Than One Year (6 months if acquired after 6/22/84)

a. Description of property	b. Date acquired	c. Date sold	d. Gross sales price	e. Cost or other basis	f. LOSS	g. GAIN
9 100 Shares XYZ	10/12/75	8/14/84	$14,000	$9,000		$5,000
50 Acres of Land	6/10/75	5/8/84	52,000	40,000		12,000

Line	Description	f	g
10	Long-term gain from sale or exchange of a principal residence from Form 2119, lines 7, 11, 16, or 18		
11	Long-term gain from installment sales from Form 6252, lines 22 or 30		
12	Net long-term gain or (loss) from partnerships, S corporations, and fiduciaries		
13	Add lines 9 through 12 in columns f and g	( )	$17,000
14	Combine columns f and g of line 13 and enter the net gain or (loss)		$17,000
15	Capital gain distributions		
16	Enter gain from Form 4797, line 6(a)(1)		
17	Combine lines 14 through 16		$17,000
18	Long-term capital loss carryover from years beginning after 1969		($2,000)
19	Net long-term gain or (loss), combine lines 17 and 18		$15,000

Note: *Complete the back of this form. However, if you have capital loss carryovers from years beginning before 1970, do not complete Parts III or IV. See Form 4798 instead.*

For Paperwork Reduction Act Notice, see Form 1040 instructions. **Schedule D (Form 1040) 1984**

FIGURE 10-5

Schedule D (Form 1040) 1984 **12** Page **2**

Name(s) as shown on Form 1040 (Do not enter name and social security number if shown on other side)	Your social security number
T. H. Taxpayer	444 44 4444

Part III Summary of Parts I and II

20	Combine lines 8 and 19, and enter the net gain or (loss) here		20	$25,000
	Note: *If line 20 is a loss, skip lines 21 through 23 and complete lines 24 and 25. If line 20 is a gain complete lines 21 through 23 and skip lines 24 and 25.*			
21	If line 20 shows a gain, enter the smaller of line 19 or line 20. Enter zero if there is a loss or no entry on line 19. . . .	21 $15,000		
22	Enter 60% of line 21		22	$9,000
	If line 22 is more than zero, you may be liable for the alternative minimum tax. See Form 6251.			
23	Subtract line 22 from line 20. Enter here and on Form 1040, line 13		23	$16,000
24	If line 20 shows a loss, enter one of the following amounts:			
	a If line 8 is zero or a net gain, enter 50% of line 20;			
	b If line 19 is zero or a net gain, enter line 20; or			
	c If line 8 and line 19 are net losses, enter amount on line 8 added to 50% of the amount on line 19 .		24	
25	Enter here and as a loss on Form 1040, line 13, the smallest of:			
	a The amount on line 24;			
	b $3,000 ($1,500 if married and filing a separate return); or			
	c Taxable income, as adjusted. . . .		25	

Part IV Computation of Post-1969 Capital Loss Carryovers from 1984 to 1985
(Complete this part if the loss on line 24 is more than the loss on line 25)

26	Enter loss shown on line 8; if none, enter zero and skip lines 27 through 30, then go to line 31	26	
27	Enter gain shown on line 19. If that line is blank or shows a loss, enter zero	27	
28	Reduce any loss on line 26 to the extent of any gain on line 27	28	
29	Enter smaller of line 25 or line 28	29	
30	Subtract line 29 from line 28. This is your short-term capital loss carryover from 1984 to 1985 . . .	30	
31	Subtract line 29 from line 25. (Note: If you skipped lines 27 through 30, enter amount from line 25)	31	
32	Enter loss from line 19; if none, enter zero and skip lines 33 through 36	32	
33	Enter gain shown on line 8. If that line is blank or shows a loss, enter zero	33	
34	Reduce any loss on line 32 to the extent of any gain on line 33	34	
35	Multiply amount on line 31 by 2	35	
36	Subtract line 35 from line 34. This is your long-term capital loss carryover from 1984 to 1985	36	

Part V Complete this Part Only If You Elect Out of the Installment Method and Report a Note or Other Obligation at Less Than Full Face Value

☐ Check here if you elect out of the installment method.
Enter the face amount of the note or other obligation. ▶ ....
Enter the percentage of valuation of the note or other obligation. ▶

Part VI Reconciliation of Forms 1099-B With Tax Return (Complete this part if you received one or more Forms 1099-B or equivalent statement reporting sales of stock, bonds, etc. or bartering income.)

SECTION A.—Reconciliation of Sales of Stocks, Bonds, etc.

37	Total sales of stock, bonds, etc. from Forms 1099-B or equivalent statement received from your brokers	37	
38	Proceeds from sale or exchange of capital assets reported on Schedule D, but not included in line 37	38	
39	Add lines 37 and 38. . . .	39	
40	Part of line 37 not reported on Schedule D this year, attach explanation	40	
41	Subtract line 40 from line 39	41	

Note: *The amount on line 41 should be the same as the total of all amounts on page 1, lines 1 and 9 of column d.*

	SECTION B.—Reconciliation of Bartering Income Indicate below the amount of bartering income reported on each form or schedule		Amount of bartering from Form 1099-B or equivalent statement
42	Form 1040, line 22. . . .	42	
43	Schedule C (Form 1040)	43	
44	Schedule D (Form 1040)	44	
45	Schedule E (Form 1040)	45	
46	Schedule F (Form 1040)	46	
47	Other (identify) (if not taxable, indicate reason—attach additional sheets if necessary) ▶	47	
48	Total (add lines 42 through 47)	48	

Note: *The amount on line 48 should be the same as the total bartering on all Forms 1099-B or equivalent statements received.*

☆U.S. GOVERNMENT PRINTING OFFICE: 1984-423-091 23 188 59/9

PLANNING WORKSHOP

YEAR-END PLANNING

In addition to making it easier to learn the basic rules, we have found that the use of Figure 10-3 also helps to identify major tax-planning opportunities. Consider the fact that this system of beakers "dumps" or "flushes" only once each year, at midnight on the last day of the taxpayer's taxable year. Therefore, the taxpayer is often in a position to modify the final result in a most advantageous way shortly before the year ends. To illustrate just a couple of opportunities, consider a year in which a taxpayer has recognized no long-term capital gains or losses but in which she has already realized (and must recognize) a $10,000 net short-term capital gain. In terms of our chemical apparatus, we can picture a system that is about ready to "flush" as follows:

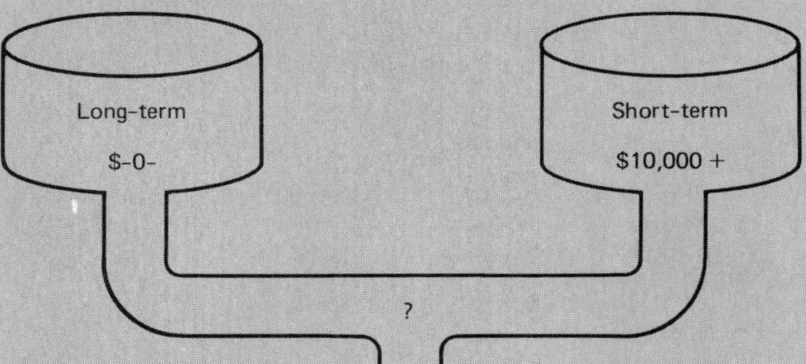

If this taxpayer does nothing further, we know that at the end of the year the $10,000 net short-term capital gain will proceed through the system and end up being taxed as ordinary income. This would be a perfect time, therefore, for this taxpayer to realize and recognize a $10,000 long-term capital loss (assuming that the taxpayer already holds capital assets with such a "paper loss" in her portfolio that would otherwise not be sold at this time). In this manner, a $10,000 long-term capital loss can be used to offset an equivalent of $10,000 in ordinary income on a one-for-one basis! If that same capital loss were deferred and not so effectively used, it might have to offset an otherwise tax-favored long-term capital gain in another year, or it might be parceled out as capital loss deductions against ordinary income over several years on a 2-for-1 basis and thus be of much less monetary value. Of course, the taxpayer making such a disposition could not, for 30 days, repurchase shares identical to those just sold at a loss or she would run afoul of the wash-sale provisions.

As a second illustration of possible year-end tax planning, consider the situation of a taxpayer who has already recognized both a

Continued

$10,000 long-term capital gain and a $10,000 short-term capital loss. The illustrative beakers for this taxpayer would appear as follows:

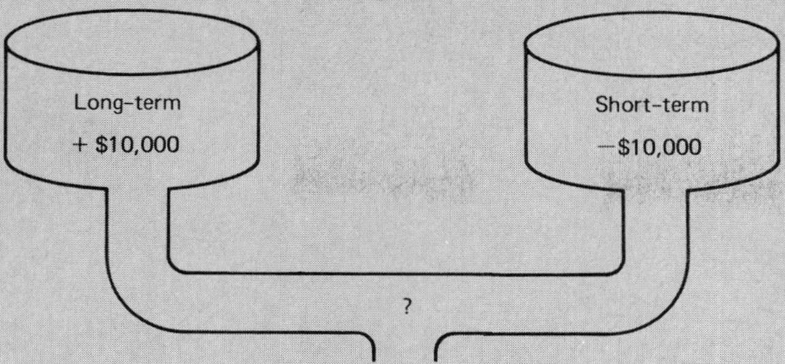

If this taxpayer does nothing further before the end of the year, we know that the short-term capital loss will completely devour the tax-favored long-term capital gain. Therefore, this would be a good time to introduce a $10,000 short-term capital gain into the system, if at all possible. To do so would cause the previously realized short-term capital loss to combine with the newly induced short-term capital gain and thereby allow the long-term capital gain to pass untouched through the system and to be taxed in the most favorable manner. Obviously, the final result does increase the tax payable for the current year, but a taxpayer can seldom, if ever, do better than realize gains in the form of a net long-term capital gain (which exceeds net short-term capital losses). Incidentally, in this instance, the taxpayer could *immediately* repurchase the shares just sold if he or she desired to return to the former portfolio position; the wash-sale rules apply only to losses. The only cost in doing this would be the broker's fee.

AVOIDING "ORDINARY" CLASSIFICATION FOR ASSETS

The distinction between an investor or trader in property and a broker or dealer in property is very important. Dealers hold property for resale to customers and their gains are ordinary income. For securities, this vital distinction is usually clear-cut because security dealers are subject to tight regulation. In real estate, however, the line between the investor and the dealer is often unclear.

The taxpayer who buys and sells real properties from time to time and is not a licensed real estate broker is trading capital assets. At the other extreme, a broker who subdivides and markets real estate on a regular basis is a dealer. Taxpayers with large investments in real estate should keep a safe distance from brokerage activity. In some instances, a corporation or partnership can be used by an investor to undertake the subdivision and development of his or her investment property, provided great care is taken to ensure that the "dealer" status of the entity is not attributed to the investor.

KEY POINTS TO REMEMBER

1. The amount of any capital gain or loss realized is equal to the difference between the amount realized and the adjusted basis of the property sold or exchanged.
2. The adjusted tax basis of any property acquired by purchase is generally equal to—
   a) Its original cost plus
   b) The cost of any capital improvements, less
   c) The tax depreciation deductions claimed by the taxpayer in prior years.
3. The adjusted tax basis for *most* property acquired by inheritance is equal to the fair market value of the property on the date of the decedent's death.
4. The adjusted tax basis of property acquired by gift depends on the date of the gift; the amount of gift tax paid (if any), and the fair market value of the property on the date of the gift. The many possible different basis results are too numerous to summarize here.
5. The loss realized on the sale or exchange of a purely personal capital asset—such as a person's residence or the family automobile—is not deductible for federal income tax purposes; nevertheless, any gain realized on the sale of those same assets is taxable as a capital gain.
6. All assets are capital assets unless specifically excluded from that classification in the Code.
7. The major statutory exclusions from the capital asset category are—
   a) Inventory and other properties held primarily for resale;
   b) Real and depreciable properties used in a trade or business;
   c) Created properties (other than patents) owned by the creator;
   d) Ordinary trade accounts and notes receivable; and
   e) Government publications if they were not purchased.
8. The sale or exchange of any capital asset held for six months or less results in the realization of a short-term capital gain or loss. A capital asset held for more than six months triggers a long-term capital gain or loss when it is sold or exchanged.
9. The long-term capital-gain deduction allowed individual taxpayers is equal (by definition) to 60% of the excess of the net long-term capital gain over the net short-term capital loss for the year.
10. If an individual taxpayer realizes both net long-term and net short-term capital gains in one year, only the net long-term gain will give rise to a long-term capital-gain deduction. The net short-term gain will be treated as an equivalent amount of ordinary income.
11. Individual taxpayers can offset a maximum of $3,000 in capital losses against ordinary income in any one year. Furthermore, long-term capital losses must be reduced by 50% before being offset against ordinary income.
12. Losses realized on sales or exchanges between related parties are not deductible for tax purposes. However, such nonrecognized losses can offset gains on a subsequent sale of the property to an unrelated party.

13. Special recognition rules apply to worthless securities, short sales, options, Sec. 1244 stock, and certain bond transactions.

SELF-STUDY QUESTIONS

1. Mike Karp owns machinery, with an adjusted basis of $50,000, for use in his car-washing business. In addition, Karp owns his personal residence and furniture, which together cost him $100,000. The capital assets amount to

   a) $0

   b) $50,000

   c) $100,000

   d) $150,000

   (AICPA adapted)

2. On March 1, 1984, Harry Beech received a gift of income-producing real estate with a donor's adjusted basis of $50,000 at the date of the gift. Fair market value of the property at the date of the gift was $40,000. Beech sold the property for $46,000 on August 1, 1984. How much gain or loss should Beech report for 1984?

   a) no gain or loss

   b) $6,000 short-term capital gain

   c) $4,000 short-term capital gain

   d) $4,000 ordinary loss

   (AICPA adapted)

3. On March 1, 1983, Lois Rice learned that she was bequeathed 1,000 shares of Elin Corp. common stock under the will of her uncle, Pat Prevor. Pat had paid $5,000 for the Elin stock in 1980. Fair market value of the Elin stock on March 1, 1983, the date of Pat's death, was $8,000 and had increased to $11,000 six months later. The executor of Pat's estate elected the alternate valuation date for estate tax purposes. Lois sold the Elin stock for $9,000 on May 1, 1983, the date that the executor distributed the stock to her.

   Lois' basis for gain or loss on sale of the 1,000 shares of Elin stock is

   a) $5,000

   b) $8,000

   c) $9,000

   d) $11,000

   (AICPA adapted)

4. Refer to Question 3. Lois should treat the 1,000 shares of Elin stock as a

   a) short-term Section 1231 asset

   b) long-term Section 1231 asset

c) short-term capital asset

d) long-term capital asset

(AICPA adapted)

5. Rose Budd owns 55% of the outstanding stock of Kee Corp. During 1983, Kee sold a machine to Rose for $80,000. This machine had an adjusted tax basis of $92,000, and had been owned by Kee for three years. What is the allowable loss that Kee can claim in its 1983 income tax return?

   a) $12,000 Section 1245 loss

   b) $12,000 Section 1231 loss

   c) $12,000 ordinary loss

   d) $0

   (AICPA adapted)

6. Laura Lewis' father, Albert, gave her a gift of 500 shares of Liba Corporation common stock in 1983. Albert's basis for the Liba stock was $4,000. At the date of this gift, the fair market value of the Liba stock was $3,000.

   If Laura sells the 500 shares of Liba stock in 1984 for $5,000 her basis is

   a) $5,000

   b) $4,000

   c) $3,000

   d) $0

   (AICPA adapted)

7. Refer to Question 6. If Laura sells the 500 shares of Liba stock in 1984 for $2,000, her basis is

   a) $4,000

   b) $3,000

   c) $2,000

   d) $0

   (AICPA adapted)

8. On January 1, 1977, Hubert Toast sold stock with a cost of $4,000 to his sister Melba for $3,500, its fair market value. On July 30, 1977, Melba sold the same stock for $4,100 to a friend, in a bona fide transaction. In 1977 as a result of these transactions

   a) neither Hubert nor Melba has a recognized gain or loss

   b) Hubert has a recognized loss of $500

   c) Melba has a recognized gain of $100

   d) Melba has a recognized gain of $600

   (AICPA adapted)

9. In June 1982, Olive Bell bought a house for use partially as a residence and partially for operation of a retail gift shop. In addition, Olive bought the following furniture:

Kitchen set and living room pieces for the residential portion	$ 8,000
Showcases and tables for the business portion	12,000

How much of this furniture comprises capital assets?

a) $0

b) $8,000

c) $12,000

d) $20,000

(AICPA adapted)

10. For the year 1978 Michael King reported salary and taxable interest income of $40,000. His capital asset transactions during the year were as follows:

Long-term capital gains	$2,000
Long-term capital losses	(8,000)
Short-term capital gains	1,000

For 1978 King should report adjusted gross income of

a) $35,000

b) $37,500

c) $38,000

d) $39,000

(AICPA adapted)

11. For the year 1979 Susan Otis had salary income of $19,000. In addition she reported the following capital transactions during the year:

Long-term capital gain	$7,000
Short-term capital gain	3,000
Long-term capital loss	(2,000)
Short-term capital loss	(4,000)

There were no other items includable in her gross income. What is her adjusted gross income for 1979?

a) $19,000

b) $20,600

c) $21,400

d) $23,000

(AICPA adapted)

12. Paul Beyer, who is unmarried, has taxable income of $30,000 exclusive of capital gains and losses and his personal exemption. In 1980 Paul incurred a $1,000 net short-term capital loss and a $5,000 net long-term capital loss. His long-term capital loss carryover to 1981 is

a) $0
b) $1,000
c) $2,500
d) $5,000

(AICPA adapted)

13. On March 10, 1975, James Rogers sold 300 shares of Red Company common stock for $4,200. Rogers acquired the stock in 1972 at a cost of $5,000.

    On April 4, 1975, he repurchased 300 shares of Red Company common stock for $3,600 and held them until July 18, 1975, when he sold them for $6,000. How should Rogers report the above transactions for 1975?

    a) a long-term capital loss of $800
    b) a long-term capital gain of $1,000
    c) a long-term capital gain of $1,600
    d) a long-term capital loss of $800 and a short-term capital gain of $2,400

    (AICPA adapted)

QUESTIONS

1. Courts and tax commentators have for years compared capital to a tree and income to the fruit of that tree. That is, income is viewed as something that can be separated from capital, leaving the productive base "unscathed." Discuss the possible weaknesses of this simile.
2. Assume that ten years ago a high-school teacher earned an annual salary of $12,000 and that today his or her annual salary has risen to $18,000. If we can establish that the general price level increased 50% in the interim, what increase in real income did the teacher have in his (original) "base" salary in the 10-year interval? What portion of the $6,000 increase would be treated as a capital gain for tax purposes?
3. Based on your own intuition, how would you describe a "capital gain"? (In responding to this question, *ignore* this textbook and base your answer on any general notions you may have gathered from your other studies thus far in college.) As a part of your class discussion, be prepared to explain why basic differences in concepts exist.
4. Assume that your grandfather purchased a property in 1900 and that your mother inherited that property from him in 1945. Further assume that your mother died in 1977 and left the property to you and that you sold it today for $1,001,000. How much taxable income (capital gain) do you believe that you should have to report on the sale of this property if:

- Your grandfather paid $1,000 for it in 1900;
- It had a fair market value of $500,000 in 1945 when your mother received title to it; and
- It had a fair market value of $991,000 when you took title in 1977?

Explain your answer briefly. (NOTE: This question does not ask you to answer based on what the law provides; rather, it asks you to determine how you personally feel about one very important issue in capital-gains taxation today.)

5. In 1963 Betty paid $10,000 for property A and Bob earned $10,000 for his services. In 1985 Betty sold property A for $20,000 and Bob was paid $20,000 for his services. If the consumer price index (CPI) increased from 100 in 1963 to 200 in 1985:
   a) How much real income has Betty realized on property A in 1985?
   b) How much of an increase in real wages has Bob realized after working 20 years?
   c) Do you believe that Betty should pay an income tax on the sale of the property in 1985? Explain briefly. (NOTE: This question asks for personal opinion, not the answer per the Code.)
   d) On what amount of income do you believe Bob should pay an income tax in 1985? Explain briefly. (NOTE: State your personal opinion.)
   e) Based on our current tax law (the Internal Revenue Code of 1954, as amended), will either Betty or Bob automatically get a tax break? If so, which one—Betty or Bob? What will this "tax break" be called?

6. Approximately 55% of all outstanding corporate stock in the United States is owned by 1% of the population. That same 1% owns 60% of all outstanding bonds and 90% of all trust assets. Of what significance are these facts to the taxation of capital gains?

7. Harry Fox operates a retail hardware store and owns the following property. Indicate whether each property is, for federal tax purposes, a capital asset or a noncapital asset in Fox's hands.
   a) A sailboat used solely for pleasure.
   b) The building that houses his retail store.
   c) A warehouse in which he stores his hardware.
   d) The hardware items in the store.
   e) The hardware items in the warehouse.
   f) His personal residence.
   g) His automobile, used 25% of the time for business, 75% for pleasure.
   h) One hundred shares of Alpha Corporation stock.
   i) A valuable painting, inherited from a favorite aunt.

j) Land on which the warehouse is located.

k) "Goodwill" purchased by Fox when he acquired the business from its previous owner.

8. The *Washington Dispatch*, a Delaware corporation, sold the following assets during the current year:

   a) A letter it received a year earlier from a well-known politician.

   b) A letter from a former U.S. president to a New York attorney, which the *Washington Dispatch* purchased (from the attorney) in conjunction with a story it published this year.

   c) A set of 25 photographs, taken by a staff photographer, which graphically depict the terror associated with a recent skyjacking.

   d) Above normal sales (say, 100,000 extra copies) of a special edition of the *Dispatch*.

   e) A set of classified government documents given to the *Dispatch* by an anonymous person.

   f) All the common stock of a subsidiary corporation that publishes another newspaper in another city.

   g) A 3-year-old printing press deemed obsolete.

   h) Illinois State bonds, which the *Dispatch* treasurer purchased as a temporary investment for excess corporate cash.

   Which of the sales by the *Washington Dispatch* corporation involved capital assets?

9. Helen and Maria, two University of Hartford students, have almost covered the walls of their apartment with oil paintings. Helen's favorite painting is not a capital asset; Maria's favorite is a capital asset. Explain how this could be true.

10. Taxpayer, a surgeon, realized the following gains and losses during the current year:

    - Personal car sold at $1,600 loss.
    - Business car sold at $200 gain.
    - Personal home sold at $2,000 loss.
    - Rental property sold at $3,000 gain.
    - Purchased oil painting, from personal art collection, sold at $100 gain.
    - Bronze statue, cast by taxpayer in spare-time hobby, sold at $20 loss.
    - Bronze statue, cast by taxpayer in spare-time hobby, stolen from uninsured private collection, cost, $180.

    a) Which of the gains and losses above can be classified as capital gains and losses? Explain any troublesome classifications.

    b) Which of the gains and losses above would not be recognized for tax purposes in the current year?

11. Taxpayer Y, a dealer in appliances, sold the following properties during the year. In every case the property was sold *at a loss*. Which of the losses is recognized for tax purposes? Is the loss a capital loss or an ordinary loss?

    a) Automobile used by wife for personal transportation.

    b) Farm land inherited from father but held for investment.

    c) Vacant lot used in trade or business.

    d) Corporate securities purchased from business funds.

    e) Diamond ring purchased by wife for personal use.

12. Which of the following assets, owned by Mary and Don Persons, is a pure capital asset per Sec. 1221?

    a) Half of the duplex in which taxpayers live.

    b) Other half of duplex, which taxpayers rent to a couple of students. (Assume this is the Persons' only rental property and that they are not, therefore, deemed to be in the trade or business of renting property.)

    c) A valuable oil painting purchased by Mary to hang in their living room. Artist is Mary's great-aunt.

    d) A valuable letter written to Mary and Don on their wedding, signed by their uncle, the president of the United States.

    e) Land on which their duplex is built.

    f) The Persons' car used solely for personal transportation.

    g) An oil painting painted by Mary, an amateur artist.

13. Jack E., a single taxpayer, realized the following capital gains and losses this year:

    LTCG, $10,000; STCL, $9,000

    What effect will these two transactions have on Jack's adjusted gross income for the year?

14. Older, wealthy taxpayers who own capital assets that have appreciated substantially in value often contend that they are "locked-in" to their investments by the high rate of tax on capital gains.

    a) Explain what these taxpayers mean when they say they are "locked-in."

    b) If Congress were to leave the gift provisions as they presently read, but modify the rules applicable to property held at death and to treat death as a realization event (thus triggering all previously unrealized gains and losses for inclusion with the decedent's final tax return), what would you expect wealthy taxpayers to do? Would the change you anticipate be "good" or "bad" for the economy? Explain briefly.

    c) How might other tax provisions relating to gifts be modified to minimize any problems you saw implicit in the suggestion in part (*b*)?

d) If both death transfers and gift transfers were treated as a realization event, what social or economic ill might be exacerbated? Explain briefly, as best you can.

15. Some authorities have proposed the elimination of all taxes on capital gains. They argue that such a change would eliminate many complexities from the law. Do you agree? Why or why not?

16. Explain the tax treatment of an incentive stock option plan.

17. "Related party losses and wash-sale losses are not disallowed entirely: they are merely deferred." Do you agree? Explain.

18. Explain the special tax recognition rules for worthless securities and Sec. 1244 stock.

PROBLEMS

1. In the six cases that follow, a donee has received property as a gift and subsequently disposed of it through sale. For each case, compute the donee's gain on the subsequent sale if:

   a) The gifts were made in 1976.

   b) The gifts were made in 1977 or a later year.

CASE	DONOR'S ADJUSTED BASIS	FAIR MARKET VALUE AT DATE OF GIFT	GIFT TAX PAID	AMOUNT REALIZED
1	$10,000	$20,000	$1,000	$21,000
2	10,000	15,000	1,000	15,000
3	10,000	15,000	1,000	9,000
4	10,000	8,000	500	11,000
5	10,000	8,000	500	7,500
6	10,000	8,000	500	9,000

2. Taxpayer Y sold a building to taxpayer Z. Z paid Y $10,000 cash and assumed the $52,000 mortgage on the property. In addition, Z agreed to pay property taxes of $320 accrued to the date of the sale. What is the amount realized by Y? What is Z's adjusted basis at the time of purchase?

3. In March of the current year, Massad purchased a 300′ by 300′ tract of land for a cash payment of $200,000. He plans to build a small office building on the site next year or the following year. During the remainder of the current year Massad:

   a) Paid $6,000 to have an old building removed from the lot.

   b) Paid $3,000 for local property taxes on the site, $700 of which were allocated to the period before the purchase by Massad.

c) Paid $600 to have the grass and weeds mowed as required by city ordinance.

What is Massad's basis in the lot at year's end?

4. On August 10 Linn Berg, an airline pilot, sold 100 shares of Trimotor Aircraft Corporation stock (a listed security) for $1,000. What gross amount of capital gain or loss should Linn report if:

   a) He purchased the shares on February 15 for $800?

   b) He received the shares as a gift from his Uncle Jim on July 2 when their fair market value was $900? (Assume that Jim purchased the shares for $300 in 1962, and that he paid a gift tax of $60 on this transfer after 1976)

   c) If all facts are as in part (*b*) except that Jim purchased the shares for $1,020 rather than for $300?

   d) He inherited the shares from his father, Charles, who died July 8 last year? Charles had purchased the shares for $300 in 1962. The fair market value of the shares on July 8 was $1,200. The executrix of Charles's estate elected to value all assets in the estate six months after Charles's death. On December 31 the shares had a fair market value of $900. On January 8 (this year) the shares had a fair market value of $880. The shares were distributed by the executrix to Linn on June 21, when they had a fair market value of $1,100.

5. Assume that on February 14, a donee sold, under the alternative conditions detailed below, an investment property she had received as a gift on January 8. Assume further that the donor had purchased the property on October 26, 1974. State the amount and class (short-term/long-term) of capital gain or loss realized.

	DONOR'S ADJUSTED BASIS	GIFT TAX PAID BY DONOR	VALUE ON DATE OF GIFT	AMOUNT REALIZED ON SALE
a)	$11,000	$ 600	$12,000	$13,000
b)	11,000	1,200	12,000	13,000
c)	11,000	500	10,000	9,000
d)	11,000	500	10,000	12,000
e)	11,000	1,500	10,000	10,500

6. Determine the amount and the short- or long-term classification of each of the following capital-asset transactions. The year is 1985.

   a) On December 1 taxpayer sold ABC shares for $1,000. The shares had been purchased for $800 on January 30.

   b) On October 7 taxpayer sold DEF shares for $2,500. The shares were acquired from taxpayer's deceased grandmother's estate. Grandmother died on November 5, 1980. Grandmother had purchased the shares on February 10, 1960 for $500; they had a fair market value of $1,500 on November 5, 1980. The shares were distributed to taxpayer on October 2, when they had a fair market value of $1,800.

c) On July 28 taxpayer sold GHI shares for $10,000. Shares were acquired by gift from Aunt Mary, who purchased them for $5,000 on January 24, 1954. Mary gave GHI shares to taxpayer on February 14, 1977, when their value was $12,000. Mary paid gift tax of $600 on the transfer.

7. Jim inherited four properties from his Aunt Zelda, who died on September 30. The executrix of Zelda's estate valued all properties on the date of death for estate tax purposes. Using the following information, determine Jim's tax basis in each property.

PROPERTY	DATE PURCHASED BY ZELDA	COST TO ZELDA	FMV ON SEPT. 30
Stock A	3/8/62	$10,000	$20,000
Bond B	6/22/68	20,000	10,000
Land	9/1/75	30,000	50,000
Oil painting	11/14/78	2,000	2,500

8. Determine the adjusted basis of the three assets detailed below.

a) A building purchased for $100,000 16 years ago. Taxpayer paid $20,000 down and signed an $80,000 12% note payable. To date only $35,000 in principal has been paid on this $80,000 note. After acquiring the building, taxpayer incurred $10,000 in repairs (which were expensed) and made $25,000 worth of capital improvements. Taxpayer has claimed depreciation of $50,000 on the building since acquisition.

b) Taxpayer received a gift of 100 shares of ABC stock from his girl friend. She purchased the stock in 1975 for $500. On the date of the gift the shares were worth $11,500. A gift tax of $180 was paid.

c) Taxpayer received stock two years ago as a gift from her grandmother. On the date of the gift the stock was valued at $10,000; no gift tax was paid. Grandmother had purchased the stock in 1929 for $500. Grandmother died this year when the stock was valued at $11,000. Taxpayer, who was executrix of her grandmother's estate, did not elect the alternate valuation date. Six months after her grandmother's death, the same shares were valued at $12,000.

9. Arnold Roger sold the following securities: in 1985

DATE ACQUIRED	SECURITY	DATE SOLD	COST	SALES PRICE
9/21/83	ABC	10/4	$2,000	$1,800
10/29/84	DEF	3/10	6,000	6,600
1/15/84	GHI	8/16	1,700	1,400
1/20/84	JKL	3/10	3,000	4,500
5/8/84	MNO	12/31	5,000	4,700
5/8/84	PQR	12/31	5,000	5,300

Assuming that Mr. Roger is a cash-basis taxpayer and that the above transactions constitute all of his "Schedule D" transactions for this year, calculate:

a) His net short-term capital gain or loss.

b) His net long-term capital gain or loss.

c) His long-term capital-gain deduction.

d) His capital-loss carryforward to next year.

10. Bert has $40,000 of taxable income for the year calculated before considering his capital gains and losses. In the following four situations, what is Bert's taxable income?

	CASE A	CASE B	CASE C	CASE D
Net short-term capital gain (loss)	($4,000)	$ 6,000	$6,000	($8,000)
Net long-term capital gain (loss)	$10,000	$10,000	($2,500)	$2,000

11. Assume that Harold Vine, a married taxpayer who files a joint return, had the following components of taxable income this year:

Salary	$53,200
Interest, rents, etc. (after exclusions)	30,000
Net short-term capital gain	10,000
Net long-term capital gain	75,000
Excess deductions from AGI (including exemptions)	(20,000)

a) What is Vine's taxable income for the year?

b) What is his "net capital gain"?

c) Calculate Vine's minimum income tax liability. Use the current tax rates.

12. Adam Smith, who earned a $23,200 taxable income from ordinary sources in each of the years 19X1 through 19X3, also realized the following capital gains and losses:

YEAR	NET SHORT-TERM*	NET LONG-TERM*
19X1	$ 0	$(7,000)
19X2	(3,600)	(3,200)
19X3	4,000	0

*Excluding any losses carried forward

a) Assuming that Smith is married and files a joint return, complete the following table by entering the amount of capital loss that he should carry forward in each case. Assume that Smith had no capital transactions prior to 19X1.

	SHORT-TERM	LONG-TERM
From 19X1 to 19X2	________	________
From 19X2 to 19X3	________	________
From 19X3	________	________

b) By what amount is Smith's ordinary taxable income in 19X3 reduced because of the capital loss?

13. Sandra Beckett, a single individual, had the following components of taxable income this year:

Salary	$38,200
Dividends from domestic corporations (after exclusion)	30,000
Net short-term capital loss	(10,000)
Net long-term capital gain	80,000
Excess itemized deductions (including exemptions)	(10,000)

Determine Ms. Beckett's minimum gross tax liability for this year.

14. The following properties were held by John Price. Which of these properties is a capital asset?
    a) 1,000 shares of a publicly-traded company held as an investment.
    b) Used automobiles that John hopes to resell on his used car lot.
    c) Notes from customers who purchased used cars from the lot.
    d) Copyright to a C & W song written by John's ex-wife. She gave the copyright to John before entering a drug-abuse clinic.
    e) 1,000 shares of the Price Company, representing 100% of the capital stock of a corporation John formed to market DeLorean automobiles.
    f) John's Rolex received as a gift from his daughter last Christmas.
    g) A letter to John from Richard Nixon, thanking John for tips on how to affect illegal entry undetected.

15. Determine Kathy Little's minimum federal income tax liability assuming that she (*a*) is single, (*b*) had a $40,200 ordinary *taxable* income, and (*c*) realized a $70,000 net capital gain.

16. Dan D., a single taxpayer, realized the following capital gains and losses this year: LTCG, $2,000; LTCL, $3,200; STCG, $6,500; STCL, $8,000.

    Dan also had a long-term capital loss carryforward of $2,000 from last year.

    Dan's ordinary taxable income is $30,000.

    a) What is Dan's taxable income for the current year?
    b) What capital loss carryforward (if any) does Dan have for next year?

17. *a*) Jan Burns purchased 1,000 shares of WX Company stock on 1/1/X5 for $9,000. She sold 800 of these shares on 10/6/X5 for $5,600, and purchased 600 additional shares of WX on 10/23/X5 for $4,800. What is Jan's recognized gain or loss on the 10/6/X5 sale?
    b) Assume that Jan sells all of her remaining shares of WX Stock on 11/3/X5 for $8.50 per share. What is her recognized gain or loss on the sale?

18. On 6/1/X3 Martin Williams sold 100 shares of BC stock to his sister Pat for $3,500. Martin had originally purchased the shares in 19X0 for $4,700. On 11/15/X3 Pat sells these shares to an unrelated party for $4,850. What are the 19X3 tax consequences of these transactions to Martin and Pat?

19. In January of 1982 McDonald Corporation issued its president, Ben Smith, qualified stock options to purchase 2,000 shares of the corporation's stock at $20 per share. On the date of issue the stock had a value of $19 per share. Smith exercised the option on 3/15/82 when the stock had a market value of $22 per share. He sold the stock on 4/1/84 for $30 per share. What amount and character of income does Smith have in 1982? 1983? 1984?

20. Determine the tax consequences of the following unrelated securities transactions:

   a) Miller purchased 1,000 shares of DEF Corporation stock on 9/3/X3 for $2,500. DEF Corporation was judged to be bankrupt in July 19X4, and all assets were distributed to creditors.

   b) On 6/1/X8 Graham (a single taxpayer) purchased $65,000 of newly issued stock of Banker Corporation. Banker Corporation was organized on this date and issued a total of $800,000 of capital stock. The Company immediately experienced financial difficulties, and Graham sold his shares on 9/2/X9 for $13,000.

   c) Barlow entered into a contract to deliver 100 shares of BC stock in six months for $5,000. Barlow owned no BC stock at the time of entering into the contract, but she delivered the stock six months later by borrowing 100 shares from her broker. Ten days later, Barlow purchased 100 shares of BC stock for $3,200 and delivered those shares to her broker.

TAX PLANNING PROBLEMS

1. Dan, who will graduate from your university in December of this year with a B.B.A. degree, will earn a total salary of $3,400 during the current year. His new job, which begins January 1 next year, will pay him a salary of $18,500. Throughout his college career Dan has managed to save and invest relatively modest sums of money. At the present time (assume that you are near the end of the current year), Dan owns two stocks, as follows:

STOCK	DATE PURCHASED	COST	CURRENT VALUE
ABC	February 8, last year	$1,200	$2,200
DEF	September 1, this year	3,500	2,500

Dan is most discouraged by his last purchase and therefore is about to sell both of his stocks and invest the $4,700 in a badly needed new car and a few pieces of essential furniture, including a good stereo.

Because you are completing a course in taxation, Dan asked you if there were any tax aspects that he should consider before selling the shares in the next few days. Because you understand the rules of capital gain and loss taxation, you tell Dan that it would be wiser for him to sell only his ABC shares prior to December 31 and the DEF shares early next year. To prove your point, *calculate the total tax saving that Dan will realize if he follows your advice and explain, as best you can, what accounts for the tax savings.*

In making your calculations you may assume that Dan is single and claims only himself as an exemption; that Dan will not itemize deductions in either the current or the next following year; that the market price of DEF will not change materially before early next year; and that Dan had no other capital asset transactions in either year.

2. Near the end of the year Neal Downs reviewed his completed capital transactions and discovered that thus far he had realized a net short-term capital gain of $800 and a net long-term capital gain of $2,100. He further reviewed his portfolio of stocks and discovered that his unrealized or "paper" gains and losses included a total of $1,800 in additional short-term gains, $2,100 in short-term losses, $3,200 in long-term losses, and $10,800 in long-term gains. Neal also is aware that he will have ordinary taxable income of approximately $45,000 this year.
   a) Assuming that Neal's ordinary income is not likely to change drastically in the next few years, what would you recommend that he consider by way of year-end tax planning relative to his capital asset position? Explain your recommendations.
   b) Assuming that Neal is about to retire and therefore anticipates a substantial reduction in his ordinary taxable income in future years, what would you recommend that he consider by way of year-end tax planning relative to his capital asset position? Explain your recommendations.
   c) Assuming that Neal will begin to receive a much larger ordinary income in future years, because of a large inheritance, what would you recommend that he consider by way of year-end tax planning relative to his capital asset position? Explain your recommendations.
   d) How would each of your answers have differed in (a) through (c) if Neal had already realized a $2,100 net long-term capital loss (instead of gain, as originally stated)? Assume all other facts as before.

CASE PROBLEM

Able and Clarise Dodson file a joint return and claim two dependents. For 1985, their records show the following:

Able's salary	$65,000
Clarise's salary	20,000

Dividends (taxable, U.S. corporation)	3,000
Travel expenses (Able)	(2,500)
IRA deposits ($2,000 each)	(4,000)
Mortgage interest	(3,500)
Property taxes	(3,200)
Investment counseling	(1,100)

During 1985, the Dodsons sold the following securities:

SECURITY	ACQUIRED	SOLD	REALIZED	BASIS
XYZ Stock	10/15/84	2/15/85	$10,000	$12,500
ABC Stock	3/20/80	8/24/85	$42,000	$28,000
MNO Stock	7/18/84	5/10/85	$15,000	$19,500

In June 1985, Able's Lincoln caught fire and was totally destroyed. To the Dodsons' astonishment, their insurance had lapsed. The auto cost $21,000 and had a fair market value of $12,500 when destroyed. It was used for pleasure.

Calculate their gross tax for 1985.

RESEARCH PROBLEMS

1. Basto owns and operates a large wheat farm in Kansas. Over the years, he has built on the farm a substantial capacity to store his wheat crop. In June 1984, his own crop was below average due to bad weather. As a result, on June 25, 1984, he bought wheat at a cost of $175,000 from his neighbors and stored it on his farm. At the time, he believed wheat prices would be higher in early 1985. (He also stored his own crop.) Basto's records clearly show the cost of the purchased wheat.

   Basto was right, the price increased, and in March 1985 he sold his own 1984 crop plus the additional wheat purchased. He realized $210,000 on the purchased wheat. How does Basto treat the profit on this purchased grain?

2. Tom Thibs operated as a proprietor for many years (he specialized in the income tax) until a heart attack broke his health in April of this year. In June, a large local firm agreed to buy the practice for a total consideration of $300,000. Of this amount, $160,000 was allocated to the value of tangible properties and the uncollected accounts. The sales-purchase agreement specified that $60,000 of the remainder was compensation for Tom's covenant not to compete for a 5-year period. How should Tom treat this $60,000 and the remaining $80,000 not allocated in the agreement?

Chapter Objectives

1. Identify and group transactions qualifying under Sec. 1231.
2. Compute and characterize the net gain or loss on Sec. 1231 transactions occurring during the tax year.
3. Understand how a series of personal and business property transactions are consolidated into ordinary income through a process of sequentially netting casualty and theft, Sec. 1231, and capital transactions.
4. Identify transactions qualifying under Sec. 1245 and compute the gain subject to ordinary income treatment.
5. Identify transactions qualifying under Sec. 1250 and compute the gain subject to ordinary income treatment for both commercial and residential real properties.
6. Understand how the pervasive nature of the recapture provisions affects installment sales, nontaxable exchanges, and charitable contributions.
7. Identify the basic philosophy underlying the expense recapture provisions for farm losses, soil and water conservation expenditures, and intangible drilling costs.
8. Describe the prerequisites for capital-gains treatment on transfers of patents, franchises, subdivided realty, and securities (by dealers).
9. Explain the tax implications of goodwill and covenants not to compete in a sale of a going-concern business.

11 Sales of Business Properties

This chapter is concerned with the sale, exchange, or involuntary conversion of properties used in a trade or business. The preferential treatment accorded long-term capital gains on the sale of investment properties was discussed in Chapter 10. Likewise, the limitations on the deductibility of capital losses were also explained in conjunction with the capital-gain and -loss netting procedure.

Both considerations are relevant in studying the tax treatment for sales of business properties. In some cases the sale of a business property may be treated the same as the sale of a capital asset, and in other cases the sale may be subject to ordinary gain and loss rules. The first part of this chapter explains Sec. 1231 and the related recapture provisions which create this "chameleon" category of business properties.

The second part of this chapter discusses the tax treatment of several business properties which, because of their somewhat peculiar nature, have caused statutory modifications in the definition of a capital asset. In some cases, these statutory actions have only partially resolved the tax controversies.

CODE SEC. 1231

RATIONALE FOR SEC. 1231

The definition of capital assets in Sec. 1221 expressly excludes depreciable property and real property used in a trade or business. As a consequence, gains and losses on the sale or exchange of such properties would be recognized normally as ordinary gains and losses. Such treatment would be favorable to an individual taxpayer selling such an asset at a loss, since the ($3,000) capital-loss limitations would not apply, and such losses would not offset long-term capital gains which are eligible for the 60% capital-gains deduction. Such ordinary loss deductions would also be preferred by corporate taxpayers, since corporate capital losses can only offset corporate capital gains (which possibly include long-term gains eligible for the alternative tax rate).

A complementary ordinary income treatment accorded to gains on the sales or exchanges of such property, however, would be to the detriment of business taxpayers. Corporations and individuals could pay the government in taxes up to 46% or 50% of the gain. Such a tax penalty could discourage businesses from disposing of old unproductive assets and purchasing newer, more productive properties. ***Sec. 1231*** and its predecessors were enacted partly to encourage the free mobility of capital in the economy by granting long-term capital-gains treatment to a "net Sec. 1231 gain."

SEC. 1231 PROPERTY An asset used in a trade or business for more than a year which is sold or exchanged, and also a business or capital asset held longer than a year which is involuntarily converted. The holding period is more than six months for properties acquired after 6/22/84 and before 1/1/88.

The net effect of Sec. 1231 is to provide the taxpayer with the best of both tax worlds: long-term capital-asset treatment for net Sec. 1231 gains, and ordinary loss deductions for net Sec. 1231 losses. Unfortunately, this desired result is often overshadowed by the complexities of defining Sec. 1231 properties, applying the consolidation rules, and evaluating the potential impact of the depreciation recapture rules.

DEFINITION OF SEC. 1231 PROPERTY

Sec. 1231(a) defines two basic types of property transactions qualifying for the special tax netting:

1. Recognized gains and losses from the sale or exchange of property used in a trade or business and held on a long-term basis; and
2. Recognized gains and losses from the involuntary conversion of such properties and also capital assets used in a trade or business and income-producing activities. Both must be held on a long-term basis.

The long-term holding period conforms to the long-term definition of capital assets in Sec. 1222; therefore, properties acquired after 6/22/84 and before 1/1/88 need only be held longer than six months. Several points should be noted in reference to these transactions.

First, only *recognized* gains and losses are included in the Sec. 1231 definition; any gains or losses deferred through the operation of one of the nontaxable exchange provisions of the Code would not be included. Additionally, the entire recognized gain or loss is initially included in the computations, unreduced by any capital-gains deduction or loss limitation.

INVOLUNTARY CONVERSION The conversion of a property into money or other similar property as a result of destruction, theft, seizure, condemnation, or threat of condemnation.

Second, Sec. 1231 encompasses ***involuntary conversions*** of business properties and income-producing properties. An involuntary conversion refers to the destruction, theft, seizure, condemnation, or the threat of condemnation of these two types of properties. Thus, the term involuntary conversion refers to a broader class of transactions than those covered by the casualty and theft rules. Such a distinction is important because of the special casualty and theft netting procedure and also because of the prohibition against deducting losses on the condemnation of personal properties.

Third, the Sec. 1231 provisions apply only to properties with a long-term holding period. Gains and losses on the sale, exchange, or involuntary conversion of business properties held less than the requirement will always be ordinary gains and losses, since such properties are not covered by the definition of either Sec. 1231 assets or capital assets.

Fourth, Sec. 1231 includes gains and losses from the involuntary conversion of business or income-producing assets but not the gains and losses on the involuntary conversion of personal assets. Personal casualties and thefts are subject to a special nettings process.

Finally, it should be noted that Sec. 1231 does not provide the authority for loss deductions. This authority is granted by Sec. 165, which permits a deduction for trade or business losses, income-producing losses, and casualty or theft losses. Furthermore, Sec. 1231 does not alter the basic requirement that casualty or theft losses on nonincome-producing capital assets must be deducted *from* adjusted gross income by individuals.

SPECIAL SEC. 1231 PROPERTIES

The best of both tax worlds treatment offered by Sec. 1231 is available only for properties used in a trade or business (unless a capital asset is involuntarily converted). Therefore, it is not surprising to find political pressures by various groups to have their business transactions covered by the definition of "property used in a trade or business." The Sec. 1231(b) definition of qualifying trade or business property has been modified over the years to accommodate a variety of transactions.

TIMBER, COAL, AND DOMESTIC IRON ORE ROYALTIES Code Sec. 631(a) grants a taxpayer the right to treat the cutting of timber as a sale or exchange, and if elected, the transaction qualifies as a sale or exchange of property used in a trade or business under Sec. 1231.[1] This provision was intended to encourage selective cutting of timber and to avoid a bunching of ordinary income which actually accrues over many years. To qualify, the taxpayer must own or have a contract right to cut the timber for more than the appropriate long-term holding period. Such an election is binding upon the taxpayer for the election year and all subsequent years, unless permission to revoke the election is received from the Commissioner.

If such an election is made, the gain or loss recognized by the taxpayer is the difference between the fair market value of the timber (as of the first day of the taxable year when cut) and the adjusted basis of the timber for depletion purposes. The fair market value used in this calculation will

[1] Sec. 631(a).

be used as the new cost basis of the timber for future transactions. Gain on a later sale of the timber will be recognized as ordinary income.

Example 1: T, a calendar year tree farmer, cut five acres of timber in May, 19X2. At that time, the timber had a fair market value of $48,000 and an adjusted depletion basis of $16,000. The fair market value of the timber on January 1, 19X2 was $47,000. T sold the cut timber on November 5, 19X2 for $49,500. T's 19X2 tax return will include a Sec. 1231 gain of $31,000 ($47,000 − $16,000) and ordinary income of $2,500 ($49,500 − $47,000).

Congress eventually extended similar Sec. 1231 treatment to sales or exchanges of coal and domestic iron ore held on a long-term basis by a royalty owner who retains an economic interest in the property.[2] Congress justified this special treatment for timber, coal, and domestic iron ore by equating the sale of the natural resource with a sale of capital, as opposed to receiving net income from property which remains intact. Of course, the same arguments could apply to oil and gas royalties, which do not receive Sec. 1231 treatment. These amendments to the definition of Sec. 1231 property have been quite controversial in that they reflect a mixture of economic, social, and political objectives.

LIVESTOCK In 1951 Congress extended the definition of Sec. 1231 property to include cattle, horses, and other livestock (but *not* poultry) held for draft, breeding, dairy, or sporting purposes. In order to qualify, cattle or horses must have been held by the taxpayer for more than 24 months, and other livestock must have been held for more than 12 months.[3] This provision was enacted to resolve the controversy over whether livestock was inventory or trade or business property:

> Our tax collectors, however, have never been able to understand that cattle, sheep, hogs, and horses used by a farmer for breeding, dairy, or draft purposes are just as much the tools and machinery of farming as the lathes, tools, and dies of a manufacturer. So they took it to court and the Tax Court, the Federal district courts, and the circuit courts of appeals decided the obvious fact that breeding, dairy, and draft animals are depreciable property used in the trade or business of the taxpayer-farmer.[4]

LAND WITH UNHARVESTED CROPS Prior to 1951 the IRS ruled that the sales price received for land with unharvested crops or unripe fruit should be allocated, with gain on the crops or fruit being treated as ordinary income (e.g., the sale of inventory). However, several district courts granted capital-gains treatment to the sale of the unharvested crop of fruit on the theory that these items constituted property used in a trade or business. Congress resolved this inconsistency in 1951 by providing

---

[2] Sec. 631(c).

[3] Code Sec. 1231(b)(3). The holding period for these items was not changed by the 1984 act.

[4] *Congressional Record*, Vol. 97, p. 6976, Mr. Granger speaking.

Sec. 1231 treatment to the unharvested crop if the land was used in a trade or business and held on a long-term basis (the holding period of the crop is irrelevant).[5] To qualify, both the land and the crop must be sold at the same time to the same person, and any costs of producing the crop must be capitalized as part of the cost of the crop.

THE SEC. 1231 NETTINGS PROCESS

The effect of Sec. 1231 is to treat some noncapital assets the same as capital assets when the net gains from sales, exchanges, or involuntary conversions of such assets exceed the losses from such assets during the tax year. Since Sec. 1231 applies only to such properties held on a long-term basis, the net gain would be long-term and thus eligible for preferential-tax treatment. On the other hand, if the losses from such transactions exceed the gains, each gain or loss is ordinary. The net effect of this ordinary treatment is to allow a net loss deduction without regard to the limitations on deductibility of capital losses. Thus, the net Sec. 1231 gain or loss always receives the more favorable capital- or ordinary-tax treatment.

The following sections describe the year-end consolidation procedure for all property transactions. This procedure can be described as a sequence of four separate gain and loss consolidations for personal casualty and theft transactions, business casualty and theft transactions, Sec. 1231 transactions, and capital transactions. These consolidations are referred to as netting processes in the following discussion.

BACKGROUND

Before 1938, properties used productively in a trade or business were capital assets largely by default, because this type of property was not included in the list of exclusions from capital-gain-and-loss treatment. In the Revenue Act of 1938, Congress modified Sec. 117(a) so that the term capital assets ". . . does not include property used in the trade or business, of a character which is subject to the allowance of depreciation provided in Sec. 23(l);."* Congress justified this change on the following basis:

> As a result of this change, losses realized on the sale or exchange of such depreciable assets will be deductible in full from ordinary income. Corporations will not, as formerly, be deterred from disposing of partially obsolete property, such as machinery or equipment, because of the limitations imposed by Sec. 117 upon the deduction of capital losses.†

This provision was instituted primarily to confer the benefits of ordinary loss deductions to the sellers of productive business assets

Continued

[5] Sec. 1231(b)(4).

BACKGROUND

during a depression. However, these revisions did not anticipate the increasing prices of machinery and equipment brought about by World War II. The complementary ordinary-gain treatment for non-capital assets potentially impeded the efficient allocation of capital during World War II.

In 1942 Congress modified Sec. 117 (the forerunner of Sec. 1231) in three major respects. First, if the gains on sales or exchanges of Sec. 117 property exceeded the losses on such property, the gains and losses would be treated as long-term capital gains and losses; however, if such losses exceeded gains, the ordinary-gain and loss treatment instituted in 1938 would continue to apply. Secondly, the definition of property qualifying for this special treatment was expanded to include the sale or involuntary conversion of *any* property used in a trade or business (depreciable and nondepreciable) and held on a long-term basis. Finally, gains and losses from the involuntary conversion of long-term capital assets, whether business or personal, were included in the definition of Sec. 117 property.

---

* *Revenue Act of 1938*, Sec. 117(a)(1).

† *Report of the Ways and Means Committee*, 75th Congress, 3d Session, House Report 1860, p. 34.

PERSONAL CASUALTY AND THEFT NETTING PROCEDURE In addition to applying to sales or exchanges or properties used in a trade or business and held on a long-term basis, Sec. 1231 also encompasses involuntary conversions of such properties. Prior to 1969, any gain or loss on the involuntary conversion of a *personal* capital asset was also included in the Sec. 1231 definition. However, in 1969 Congress decided to exempt certain involuntary conversions from Sec. 1231 treatment. Specifically, if the *net losses* from fire, storm, shipwreck, other casualty, or theft of Sec. 1231 properties exceed the net gains from such transactions, each gain and loss was treated as ordinary for a *net* loss from casualties during the tax year. Otherwise, such a loss would potentially offset Sec. 1231 gains eligible for long-term capital-gains treatment, as opposed to the more favorable tax treatment of offsetting income subject to ordinary tax rates.

The effect of this modification to Sec. 1231 was to require a taxpayer to net casualty and theft gains and losses incurred during the year first. If a net gain resulted, the casualty and theft gains and losses were combined with Sec. 1231 gains and losses. If a loss resulted, all gains and losses were treated as ordinary gains and losses. This special netting applied only to casualties and thefts; all other involuntary conversions (condemnations or the threat thereof) were always included in the Sec. 1231 category.

You will recall that personal casualty and theft loss calculations involve application of the $100 floor reduction rule (to *each* loss) and the 10% of adjusted gross income (AGI) rule (to *total* casualty and theft and theft losses of a personal nature which are incurred after 1982). In enacting the latter limitation, Congress unintentionally created a circular computation, because the net Sec. 1231 result is used in the determination of AGI, and AGI is used in the determination of casualty and theft losses. Thus, the Sec. 1231 netting and the casualty and theft netting are interrelated.

Congress removed this circular computation in 1984 by creating a *separate* netting for personal casualty and theft gains and losses on properties held on a long-term basis. Sec. 165(h)(2) was amended by the Tax Reform Act of 1984 so that if gains exceed losses from such casualties and thefts, the net gain will be taxed as a long-term *capital* gain, and the losses will *not* be subject to the 10% of AGI floor. On the other hand, if the losses exceed the gains on such transactions, the net loss is deductible as an ordinary (itemized) deduction, but only to the extent that it exceeds 10% of AGI. Thus, personal casualties and thefts are completely removed from the Sec. 1231 nettings process.

Example 2: During 19X6, TP, a single taxpayer with $34,000 AGI, incurred a $3,000 gain on the insurance settlement for fire damage to his personal automobile. In addition, TP suffered a $2,000 uninsured loss (after the $100 floor reduction) from storm damage to his personal residence. Since the personal casualty and theft gains ($3,000) exceed the personal casualty and theft losses ($2,000), the net gain of $1,000 will be treated as a long-term capital gain, to be combined with other capital gains and losses. Note that the $2,000 casualty loss is not subject to the 10% of AGI floor.

Example 3: Assume the same facts as in Example 2, except that the loss from storm damage to the residence was $8,000 (after the $100 floor reduction). In this case, the personal casualty gains and losses net to a $5,000 loss, of which $1,600 is allowed as an itemized (ordinary) deduction. The $1,600 is the excess of the $5,000 net loss over $3,400, or 10% of the $34,000 AGI.

BUSINESS CASUALTY AND THEFT NETTING PROCEDURE The netting of casualty and theft losses on business and income-producing properties was not changed by the Tax Reform Act of 1984. (For the balance of this discussion, the word "business" will refer to both trade or business properties and income-producing properties, such as rental properties.) The netting procedure for such transactions retains the "best of both tax worlds" feature which was first enacted in 1969 for casualty and theft losses on all properties. If business casualty and theft gains exceed losses, the net gain is taxed as a Sec. 1231 gain, to be combined with other Sec. 1231 gains and losses under procedures described in the following section. If the business casualty and theft losses exceed gains, the net loss is treated as an ordinary loss, deductible in the determination of AGI.

Example 4: During 19X6, XY incurred a $4,000 gain from the insurance settlement on a partially damaged business building. XY also suffered a $2,500 loss in the same year from fire damage to a business lathe. Since the business casualty and theft gains ($4,000) exceed the business casualty and theft losses ($2,500), the net gain of $1,500 will be taxed as a Sec. 1231 gain, to be combined with other Sec. 1231 gains and losses.

Example 5: Assume the same facts as in Example 4, except that the loss on the business lathe was $4,700. In this case, the business casualty and thefts net to a $700 loss, which is allowed in full as a deduction for AGI. Recall that business casualty and theft losses are not subject to either the $100 or the 10% of AGI floors.

SEC. 1231 PROPERTY NETTING PROCEDURE Once the business casualty and theft netting is completed, the next step in the procedure is the netting of all Sec. 1231 transactions. You may recall that these Sec. 1231 transactions automatically include gains and losses on sales or exchanges of properties used in a trade or business and held on a long-term basis and also gains and losses from the condemnation (or threat thereof) of trade or business properties held on a long-term basis. Additionally, the Sec. 1231 transactions include any excess of gains over losses derived from the business casualty and theft nettings procedure. If the Sec. 1231 gains exceed the Sec. 1231 losses, the excess is treated as a long-term capital gain; if the Sec. 1231 losses exceed the Sec. 1231 gains, the net loss is treated as an ordinary loss.

Example 6: C, a sole proprietor, had the following property transactions during the current year:

1. $6,000 gain (excess of insurance reimbursement over adjusted basis) on the complete destruction by fire of her business automobile (owned 6 years);
2. $10,000 loss on the theft of uninsured tools (owned 4 years) used in her business;
3. $8,000 gain on the sale of land (owned 8 years) used in her business; and
4. $9,000 loss on the sale of business machinery (owned 3 years).

On her tax return for the current year, C will report net ordinary-loss deductions of $5,000. The first two transactions are netted separately as business casualties and thefts, and the resulting $4,000 loss is taken as an ordinary deduction (the 10% of AGI and $100 floors do not apply to business casualties). The land sale and the machinery sale are Sec. 1231 transactions, and since the $9,000 loss exceeds the $8,000 gain, the $1,000 net loss is also taken as an ordinary deduction.

Example 7: Assume the same facts as in Example 6, except loss on the theft of the tools was $1,000, instead of $10,000. In this case, the two business casualty and theft transactions net to a $5,000 gain, which is now treated as a Sec. 1231 gain. Combining this gain with the other Sec. 1231 transactions results in a $4,000 excess of Sec. 1231 gains over Sec. 1231 losses. This gain is considered to be a long-term capital gain, to be combined with other capital gains and losses.

CAPITAL ASSET NETTING PROCEDURE The final step in the property transaction netting procedure is to combine all gains and losses from sales or exchanges of capital assets. This procedure was discussed in Chapter 10 and simply involves the determination of a net short-term and a net long-term result. Sec. 1231 affects this netting only when the Sec. 1231 gains exceed the Sec. 1231 losses. In this case, the excess gain is treated as a long-term capital gain. Additionally, a net gain from the personal casualty and theft netting would be treated as a long-term capital gain.

Example 8: Assume the same facts as in Example 7, and also assume that C incurred the following gains and losses:

1. $3,000 short-term gains
2. $4,500 short-term losses
3. $6,000 gain on a personal casualty
4. $8,000 long-term losses

The $4,000 Sec. 1231 gain will be treated as a long-term gain, and the final long-term result is a $2,000 gain ($4,000 + $6,000 − $8,000). Note that the personal casualty gain is taxable as a long-term capital gain. The final short-term result is a $1,500 loss ($3,000 − $4,500). Since the short-term and long-term results are opposite signs, they are combined, and the resulting $500 gain is treated as a long-term gain. This gain is subject to the 60% capital-gain deduction, resulting in $200 of taxable ordinary income.

CONSOLIDATION OF PROPERTY TRANSACTIONS The four nettings procedures (personal casualty and theft, business casualty and theft, Sec. 1231, and capital) may be combined into a 5-column work sheet format for purposes of analyzing the effects of various property transactions on taxable income. Such a work sheet approach is illustrated in Figure 11-1. The first four columns are used to summarize the four netting procedures, and the fifth column is used to summarize the final effect of the transactions on ordinary income.

In using the 5-column procedure, all recognized gains and losses would first be listed in the appropriate column. Then, each of the first four columns will be netted in order and closed to another column to the right, depending on the final gain or loss result. Ultimately, the final effect of all

FIGURE 11-1
5-Column Work Sheet Approach to Analyzing the Tax Consequences of Property Transactions

PERSONAL CASUALTY & THEFT GAINS & LOSSES	BUSINESS CASUALTY & THEFT GAINS & LOSSES	SECTION 1231 GAINS & LOSSES	CAPITAL GAINS & LOSSES	ORDINARY INCOME*
			Short-Term:	
$ XXX	$ XXX	XXX	XXX	
(XXX)	(XXX)	(XXX)	(XXX) } XXX	
		(XXX)		
○	○ — Net Gain →	XXX	Long-Term:	→ ○
			XXX	
			(XXX)	
		○ — Net Gain →	XXX } XXX	
			(XXX)	
Net Gain →		→	XXX	
		Net Loss →		○
	Net Loss →			○
				AGI
Net Loss →	○ Less 10% of AGI →			○
				Taxable

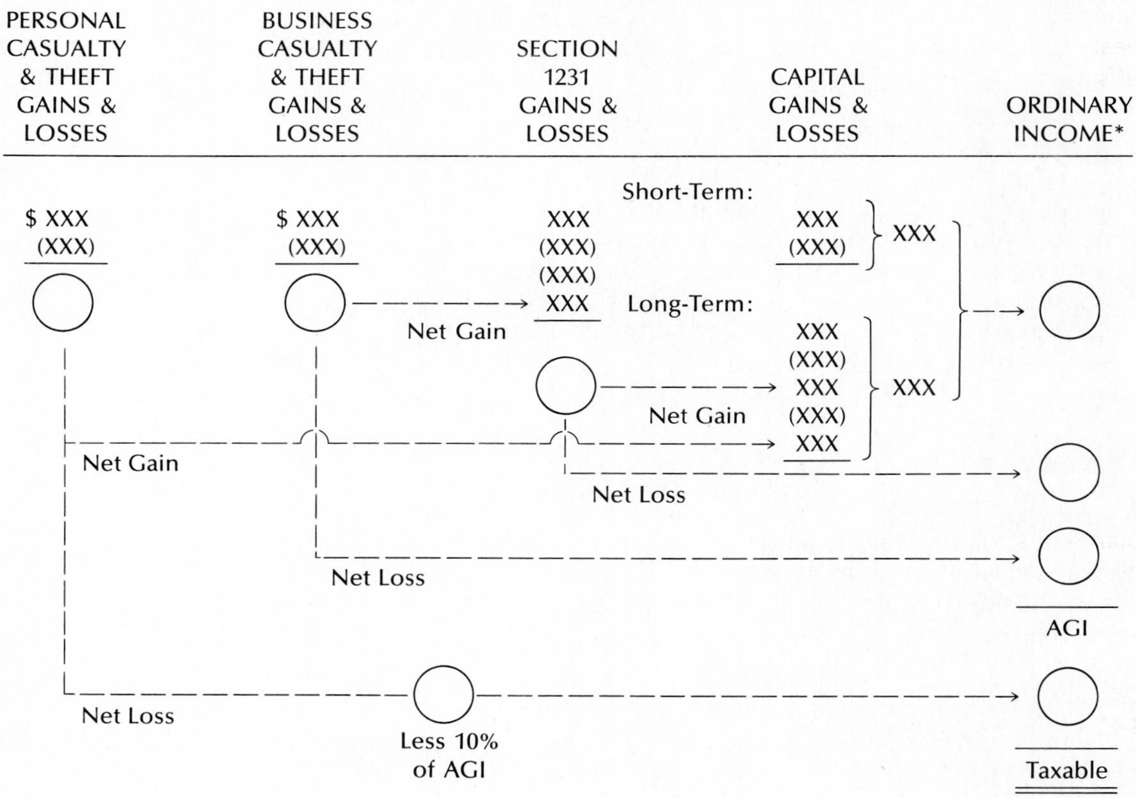

*Includes Any Depreciation Recapture

property transactions will be closed to the ordinary income column. Figure 11-2 illustrates the procedure, using the information provided in Examples 7 and 8. Note that since the capital transactions net to a long-term capital gain, only 40% of the gain is ultimately included in ordinary income.

Any depreciation recapture (discussed later in the chapter) on Sec. 1231 properties would be listed in the ordinary income column of the work sheet. For example, if a business machine owned for more than a year is sold at a $3,000 gain and $2,500 of the gain must be recaptured as ordinary income, $500 will be listed in the Sec. 1231 gain and loss column and $2,500 will be listed in the ordinary income column. The 5-column procedure can also be used for corporate taxpayers, since three separate property nettings are required for all tax-paying entities (the personal casualty and theft netting would not be applicable to corporations). However, the capital gain and loss netting procedure is different for a corporation. This is discussed in Chapter 16.

RECAPTURE OF PRIOR SEC. 1231 NET LOSSES Since the Sec. 1231 nettings process ensures the best of both tax worlds treatment, a common business planning strategy in the past was to attempt to group all Sec. 1231 gains into one tax year and all Sec. 1231 losses into another tax year. After all, if both gains and losses were recognized in the *same* year, the best of both tax worlds treatment of gains and losses would, to an extent, offset one another.

> **Example 9:** In 19X3, G sold a business building at a $40,000 gain and a business machine at a $36,000 loss. If these were the only Sec. 1231 transactions recognized in the year, the $36,000 loss would be used up to offset a $40,000 gain which would otherwise be taxed at the preferential long-term capital gains rate, assuming that this was the only Sec. 1231 transaction incurred during the year. G would be much better off to split the two transactions over two tax years. Then, the $36,000 loss would be deductible as an ordinary loss, and the $40,000 gain in the other tax year would be taxed as a long-term capital gain.

As part of the Tax Reform Act of 1984, Congress severely limited such a planning strategy by adding Code Sec. 1231(c), effective for tax years beginning after 1984. In the future, when a taxpayer's Sec. 1231 transactions net to a gain, the net gain will be taxed as *ordinary* income to the extent

FIGURE 11-2
5-Column Work Sheet Example

PERSONAL CASUALTY & THEFT GAINS & LOSSES	BUSINESS CASUALTY & THEFT GAINS & LOSSES	SECTION 1231 GAINS & LOSSES	CAPITAL GAINS & LOSSES		ORDINARY INCOME
			Short-Term:		
	6,000	8,000	3,000	(1,500)	
	(1,000)	(9,000)	(4,500)		
	5,000 →	5,000	Long-Term:		200*
		4,000 →	4,000		
6,000 →			6,000	2,000	
			(8,000)		
				AGI	200

*$500 Long-Term Capital Gain Less 60% Capital Gains Deduction

that the taxpayer realized a net Sec. 1231 loss in the five most recent prior years occurring after 1981. Once a Sec. 1231 loss is recaptured under this rule, it will not be subject to additional recapture in a succeeding tax year.

Example 10: Assume that taxpayer G in Example 9 elected to recognize the $36,000 loss in 19X5 and the $40,000 gain in 19X6. In this case, $36,000 of the $40,000 Sec. 1231 gain in 19X6 must be recognized as ordinary income. The remaining $4,000 of gain will be reported as Sec. 1231 gain, to be combined with long-term capital gains. If G recognized another Sec. 1231 gain in 19X7, the 19X5 Sec. 1231 loss would not be recaptured again. Note that G could have avoided the recapture if he had recognized the $40,000 gain in 19X5 and the $36,000 loss in 19X6. However, any Sec. 1231 net gains recognized in the five tax years following 19X6 will be ordinary income to the extent of the $36,000 net Sec. 1231 loss recognized in 19X6.

RECAPTURE OF CERTAIN COST RECOVERIES

DEPRECIATION (COST RECOVERY) RECAPTURE

DEPRECIATION RECAPTURE The conversion of Sec. 1231 gain into ordinary income, generally in proportion to some or all previous depreciation deductions.

The ***depreciation recapture*** provisions of Code Secs. 1245 and 1250 were enacted to close an unintended loophole that resulted through the interaction of accelerated depreciation and Sec. 1231. This interaction is sometimes referred to as "converting ordinary income into capital gains" because the depreciation deductions reduce ordinary income dollar for dollar, but the gain caused by the rapid depreciation is taxed at favorable capital-gains rates. Secs. 1245 and 1250 were actually preceded by another depreciation-recapture provision, Sec. 1239, which addressed a more blatant and immediate abuse of Sec. 1231 by related taxpayers.

CODE SEC. 1239 Prior to the enactment of Sec. 1239, some taxpayers were not satisfied with merely achieving ordinary income to capital gain conversion on business properties; they would sometimes use related party sales to repeat the benefits on the same property. For example, a shareholder could sell a business asset to an entity which he or she controlled at capital gains rates under Sec. 1231; the entity would depreciate the higher cost basis with accelerated depreciation, and finally sell the asset once again at capital gains rates.

Sec. 1239, passed in 1939, provides that *any* gain realized on the sale of a depreciable property to a related taxpayer must be reported as ordinary income. For purposes of applying this rule, related taxpayers include (*a*) a husband and wife, (*b*) an individual and an 80% controlled entity (corporation or partnership), (*c*) two entities commonly controlled (80%) by the same individual and (*d*) a related employee association. In determining "control" for purposes of the 80% test, the attribution rules of Sec. 318 apply. For example, a taxpayer is considered to own constructively any shares of corporate stock (or interest in a partnership) owned by his or her spouse, children, grandchildren, parents, as well as a pro rata portion of holdings of any estate, trust, or partnership in which the taxpayer is a beneficiary. The 80% test is made immediately before the sale.

Example 11: M sells a plating machine to O Corporation at a $12,000 gain. Of the outstanding shares of O Corporation stock, M owns 40%, M's spouse owns 30%, M's daughter owns 15%, and M's cousin owns 15%. In applying Sec. 1239, M is considered to own 85% of the O Corporation shares; only the cousin's shares are not covered by the constructive-ownership rules. Therefore, M must report the entire $12,000 gain as ordinary income.

It is important to note that Sec. 1239 applies to the entire recognized gain. Sec. 1245 and 1250 recapture provisions, enacted later to apply to bona fide third party sales, are generally limited to a portion or all of the depreciation deductions taken on the asset.

BACKGROUND

In 1962 the Internal Revenue Service liberalized the accelerated depreciation rules with the issuance of Revenue Procedure 62-21. At the same time, Congress reconsidered the impact of Sec. 1231 in conjunction with a more liberalized depreciation policy;

> Whenever the depreciation deduction reduces the basis of the property faster than the actual decline in its value, then when it is sold there will be a gain. Under present law this gain is taxed as a capital gain, even though the depreciation deductions reduced ordinary income. The taxpayer who has taken excessive depreciation deductions and then sells an asset, therefore, has in effect converted ordinary income into a capital gain.*

This potential conversion of ordinary income into capital gain provided a logical justification for Congress to modify Sec. 1231. To encourage both accelerated ordinary deductions and a favorable potential capital-gains treatment upon disposition of the property was an obvious inconsistency. The Congressional solution to this problem was the enactment of the depreciation-recapture provisions in 1962 (Sec. 1245) and 1964 (Sec. 1250). The term recapture comes from the idea of converting what would otherwise be Sec. 1231 gain into ordinary income. Some or all of the dollar-for-dollar ordinary depreciation deductions are being "recaptured" when the asset is sold, exchanged, or involuntarily converted.

**Report of the Senate Finance Committee*, 87th Congress, Report 1881, p. 94.

CODE SEC. 1245 Sec. 1245 provides that gain on the disposition of certain depreciable personalty will be treated as ordinary income to the extent of any depreciation allowed or allowable after 1961. To the extent

TABLE 11-1
Sec. 1245 Recapture

B purchased a new business machine on 8/1/82 for $50,000. The machine was held until 1/3/84, at which time it had an adjusted basis of $31,500. The character of the gain (loss) for sales prices of $30,000, $42,000, and $52,000 would be as follows:

	A	B	C
Calculation of gain (loss):			
Amount realized	$ 30,000	$ 42,000	$ 52,000
Adjusted basis	(31,500)	(31,500)	(31,500)
Recognized gain (loss)	$ (1,500)	$ 10,500	$ 20,500
Character of gain (loss):			
Sec. 1245 gain	—	$ 10,500*	$ 18,500*
Sec. 1231 gain	—	—	2,000†
Sec. 1231 loss	$ (1,500)†	—	—

*Ordinary Income Recapture Limited to ACRS Deductions Allowed
†To be Combined With Other Sec. 1231 Gains and Losses

that a taxpayer has benefited from ordinary depreciation deductions, the gain on disposition will also be recognized as ordinary income. For an asset acquired after 1981, the maximum recapture is measured by the total ACRS deductions allowed or allowable.

SEC. 1245 PROPERTY A depreciable personal asset which is held on a long-term basis and sold at a gain.

Sec. 1245 property has three basic characteristics; it is (*a*) depreciable personalty, (*b*) held on a long-term basis, and (*c*) sold at a gain. Most tangible depreciable assets other than buildings and permanent building components are included in this category. Sec. 1245 also includes elevators and escalators, livestock (for depreciation after 1969 only), intangible assets subject to amortization, professional athletes' contracts, and properties subject to special elective rapid amortizations (such as pollution-control facilities). Additionally, certain real properties which qualify for the investment credit because of their productive nature are also Sec. 1245 properties.

The operation of Sec. 1245 can be illustrated by reference to the three examples in Table 11-1. These examples disclose the character of the recognized gain or loss for three hypothetical disposal values of a business machine. Several points regarding Sec. 1245 deserve special emphasis.

First, the definition of Sec. 1245 property (primarily depreciable personalty) also falls within the broader definition of Sec. 1231 property (property used in a trade or business). For that reason, the loss in example A is a Sec. 1231 loss (Sec. 1245 applies only to gains), and the gain in excess of depreciation recapture in example C is a Sec. 1231 gain. Note that the $2,000 Sec. 1231 gain in example C represents that portion of the amount realized in excess of the original cost of the property.

Second, the amount of depreciation recapture is limited to the recognized gain. The recapture provision usually determines only the character, and not the amount, of the recognized gain. However, for certain corporate and partnership distributions, the ordinary income recapture may override other nonrecognition provisions in the Code.

Third, if a taxpayer uses the Sec. 179 election to expense immediately a portion or all of the cost of depreciable personalty, Sec. 1245 will be applicable to any realized gain on a subsequent disposition of the property. The amount expensed (subject to the Sec. 179 limits) is treated as a depreciation deduction, and accordingly, will be recaptured upon disposition. Similarly, any basis-reduction amounts due the investment credit on properties acquired after 1982 will be recaptured. (However, any investment credit recapture may increase the adjusted basis, as explained in Chapter 14.)

Finally, it is important to note that commercial realty subject to accelerated recovery was reclassified as Sec. 1245 property by the Economic Recovery Tax Act of 1981. This is a significant change from prior law, which taxed such dispositions of real property under the more liberal Sec. 1250 recapture rules. The tax implications of this change are discussed in the next section.

In summary, Sec. 1245 serves to convert to ordinary income some or all of what normally would be considered as Sec. 1231 gain. The Sec. 1245 rules can be illustrated by a simple graph (Figure 11-3) which illustrates the functional relationship between potential Sec. 1245 recapture and the holding period of the asset. The recapture potential is measured by the total depreciation (or ACRS recovery) taken after 1961 (distance AB). Any depreciation taken before 1962 is not subject to the recapture rules. If the asset is sold for more than its original cost (more than $A), the total gain

FIGURE 11-3
Secs. 1231 and 1245 Rules for Assets Acquired After 1961

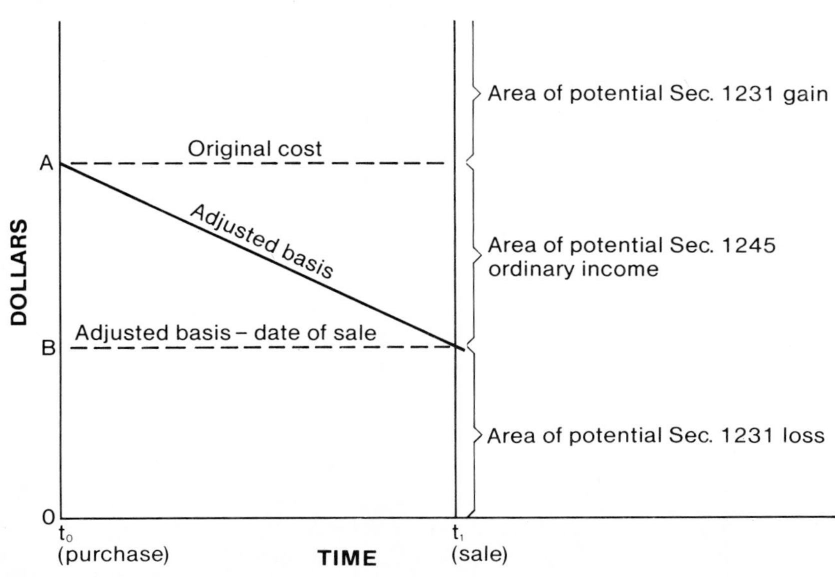

will be larger than the Sec. 1245 recapture, and the excess is taxed as a Sec. 1231 gain.

CODE SEC. 1250 Congress initially did not include real property in the recapture provision of 1962 because of the appreciation potential of real property over a long period of time. Congress believed that such a recapture provision applied to realty would unduly impede sales or exchanges of real estate. However, the same potential for converting ordinary depreciation deductions into capital gains existed for realty. In 1964 Congress adopted a compromise measure by enacting a realty-recapture provision but limiting the recapture to a portion or all of the depreciation deductions taken in excess of a straight-line write-off (hereafter referred to as "excess depreciation").

SEC. 1250 PROPERTY A depreciable real property held on a long-term basis, sold at a gain, and which is subject to accelerated depreciation.

Sec. 1250 property has four basic characteristics; it is (*a*) depreciable realty (*b*) held on a long-term basis, (*c*) sold at a gain, and (*d*) is property on which an accelerated cost recovery method was used. Sec. 1250 also includes intangible real property which meets the four characteristics, such as a leasehold of land used in a trade or business. The Sec. 1250 calculations differ for commercial and residential realty; furthermore, the procedure was modified for assets acquired after 1980 in order to conform to the ACRS calculations. These rules are summarized in the following sections.

REALTY ACQUIRED BEFORE 1981. In 1964 Congress enacted the first recapture provision for depreciable realty. These rules, which applied to both commercial and residential realty, specified a sliding scale based on a holding period for the percentage of "excess depreciation" to be recaptured as ordinary income. These rules were changed by the Tax Reform Act of 1969, and for dispositions occurring after 1979 there is no recapture for excess depreciation taken before 1970.[6]

The 1969 rules differentiated the recapture calculations for commercial and residential realty. Similar to the depreciation changes also instituted that year, the less preferential treatment was given to commercial realty (primarily buildings used by, or rented to, a trade or business, as defined in Chapter 8). For these properties, 100% of the excess depreciation will be recaptured as ordinary income, limited to the total recognized gain. Any gain in excess of this ordinary income recapture will be Sec. 1231 gain, because Sec. 1250 property (depreciable business realty) also fits the broader definition of Sec. 1231 property (property used in a trade or business).

The recapture percentage established in 1969 for residential realty (primarily buildings rented to nontransients, as defined in Chapter 8) was 100% less 1% for each full month the property was held in excess of 100 months. For example, a building held for 10 years would be subject to a maximum recapture potential of 80% (100% − [120 − 100] × 1%) of the

[6]The recapture percentage for excess depreciation taken before 1970 was 100% less 1% for each month the property was held in excess of 20 months. Any property acquired before 1970 would have been held at least 120 months as of 1980; therefore, this recapture is 0% for dispositions after 1979.

excess depreciation. For excess depreciation taken after 1975, the recapture percentage is 100%, regardless of the holding period.[7]

Therefore, it is important to note that residential realty has three possible recapture rules, summarized as follows:

PERIOD	MAXIMUM RECAPTURE (PERCENTAGE OF EXCESS DEPRECIATION)
Pre-1970	0% (Unless Disposed of Before 1980)
1970–1975	100%—(1% × Number of Months Held in Excess of 100)
Post-1975	100% of Excess Depreciation

The pre-1981 rules for Sec. 1250 recapture are illustrated in the examples displayed in Table 11-2. Accelerated and straight-line depreciation calculations are shown for a business building held for nine full years. This is followed by gain and loss calculations for three hypothetical sales prices, assuming that the building is (*a*) commercial realty and (*b*) residential realty. Several observations deserve special emphasis.

The maximum recapture potential on commercial realty is always 100% of the post-1969 excess depreciation; there are no phase-out rules based on the period of ownership. For residential realty, however, the excess depreciation must be partitioned into pre-1976 and post-1975 components, since the former is subject to the 100-month phase-out rule and the latter is always 100% recaptured. For purposes of applying the 100-month rule, the entire holding period of the realty is used, and not just the holding period between 1970 and 1975.

Excess depreciation is computed by comparing the aggregate accelerated and straight-line totals across all years, including those years in which straight-line depreciation exceeds accelerated depreciation. Therefore, the maximum recapture potential begins to decrease once the depreciation calculations reach the crossover point where straight-line deductions exceed accelerated deductions. There is no recapture potential for an asset held for its entire useful life, because excess depreciation at that point is zero.

Transaction A in both examples of Table 11-2 illustrates that a loss on the sale of depreciable realty held on a long-term basis will always be a Sec. 1231 loss; Sec. 1250 applies only to gains. Finally, it should be noted that a taxpayer who elects straight-line depreciation for depreciable realty would not have to worry about depreciation recapture; Sec. 1250 applies only to the "excess depreciation" caused by an accelerated recovery method.

REALTY ACQUIRED AFTER 1980. In the Economic Recovery Tax Act of 1981, Congress modified the depreciation recapture rules for realty placed into service after 1980. The recapture rules for residential realty were not changed by the 1981 Act; such dispositions are still subject to a maximum recapture potential of 100% of the excess depreciation (the post-1975 re-

[7]The 100-month rule was not eliminated for realty which qualified as low-income housing. This procedure continues to apply to excess depreciation taken after 1969 until the date of disposition.

TABLE 11-2
Depreciation Recapture—Realty Acquired before 1981

C purchased a new building on January 1, 1974 for $100,000. The building had a 40-year useful life and no salvage value. C elected to use the 150% declining-balance method of depreciation. The building was sold on January 2, 1983. The allowable depreciation, total gain or loss, and character of gain or loss for sales prices of $70,000, $75,000, and $80,000 would be as follows:

TOTAL DEPRECIATION ALLOWED

YEAR	150% DECLINING-BALANCE DEPRECIATION	STRAIGHT-LINE DEPRECIATION	EXCESS DEPRECIATION	
1974	$ 3,750	$ 2,500	$ 1,250	$2,359
1975	3,609	2,500	1,109	
1976	3,474	2,500	974	
1977	3,344	2,500	844	
1978	3,218	2,500	718	
1979	3,097	2,500	597	$4,246
1980	2,981	2,500	481	
1981	2,870	2,500	370	
1982	2,762	2,500	262	
	$29,105	$22,500	$ 6,605	

CALCULATION OF GAIN (LOSS)	A	B	C
Amount realized	$70,000	$75,000	$80,000
Adjusted basis	(70,895)*	(70,895)*	(70,895)*
Recognized gain (loss)	$(895)	$4,105	$9,105

CHARACTER OF GAIN (LOSS)	A	B	C
Assuming commercial realty:			
Sec. 1250 gain	—	$4,105†	$ 6,605†
Sec. 1231 gain	—	—	2,500
Sec. 1231 loss	$(895)	—	—

CHARACTER OF GAIN (LOSS)	A	B	C
Assuming residential realty:			
Sec. 1250 gain	—	$4,105‡	$ 6,416‡
Sec. 1231 gain	—	—	2,689
Sec. 1231 loss	$(895)	—	—

*$100,000 Cost − $29,105 accumulated depreciation (150% DB)
† Ordinary income recapture limited to 100% of excess depreciation
‡ Ordinary income recapture is 100% for post-1975 excess depreciation ($4,246) and 92% for pre-1976 excess depreciation ($2,170, or $2,359 × .92), a total of $6,416. The 92% is 100% less 1% for each month the property was held in excess of 100 months. The property was held for 108 months; therefore, the maximum reduction in 100% recapture is 8%.

capture rules). Under ACRS, excess depreciation is now the difference between the accelerated percentage recovery (over the statutory 15-year or 18-year period) and a 15-year or 18-year straight-line recovery.[8] As was true under prior law, there is no depreciation recapture if the taxpayer elects an optional straight-line recovery.

One of the major changes enacted in 1981 was the reclassification of commercial realty subject to accelerated recovery as Sec. 1245 property.[9] Thus, the maximum recapture potential for such property is now the *total* ACRS deductions allowed on the property, rather than being limited to the excess depreciation. Interestingly, if a taxpayer elects straight-line recovery for commercial realty, the property is considered to be Sec. 1250 property once again. This means that any gain on disposition will be Sec. 1231 gain, because there will be no excess depreciation. Thus, the same commercial building can be classified as either Sec. 1245 or Sec. 1250 property, depending on the selected method of cost recovery. This anomaly in the tax law is causing some indecision for taxpayers and tax practitioners who must compare the time value of money savings offered by ACRS deductions with the potentially significant ordinary income recapture costs at disposition.

BACKGROUND

The new commercial realty-recapture provisions represent the most significant differentiation in treatment of commercial and residential realty to date. Apparently, this provision was designed to discourage short-term investments in commercial rental property, especially by tax shelter syndicates seeking the advantages of an accelerated 15-year write-off for realty. For commercial realty which retains its value or possibly appreciates in value, the recapture cost at disposition can be substantial.

For example, assume that after 1980 an individual 50%-bracket taxpayer invests $500,000 in a new building to be rented to commercial interests. If the individual elects to use an accelerated recovery method, significant tax savings will result in the first five years of use, since ACRS percentages are significantly higher than straight-line deductions for this period. These savings may be more than offset, however, by a higher tax cost at disposition. If the asset retains its $500,000 value and is sold after the 15-year (or 18-year) recovery period, the tax cost at disposition would be $250,000. Since the asset would have a $0 adjusted basis, the gain on disposition under Sec. 1245 would be ordinary income to the extent of *all* prior ACRS deductions of $500,000. Thus, the $500,000 gain would be taxed at the 50% ordinary income rate.

Continued

[8] Sec. 1250(a)(1)(a).

[9] Sec. 1245(a)(5).

BACKGROUND

On the other hand, the taxpayer has the option of electing a straight-line recovery for the building. Such an election classifies the building as Sec. 1250 property, and consequently there is no recapture on disposition because no excess depreciation was taken. Therefore, the taxpayer's $500,000 gain at disposition would be a Sec. 1231 gain, and if the taxpayer's 1231 gains during the year exceed 1231 losses, only 40% of the gain, or $200,000, would be subject to tax. The resulting $100,000 tax on disposition (at a 50% rate) is $150,000 less than the $250,000 tax due if accelerated recovery had been elected.

This possibility of substantial recapture may cause some owners of commercial realty to elect a straight-line recovery. Of course, such a recapture provision may also persuade taxpayers seeking real estate tax shelters to channel their investments into residential rental properties, where the more lenient Sec. 1250 recapture provisions apply when accelerated recovery is used.

Table 11-3 displays several examples summarizing the depreciation recapture rules for depreciable realty acquired after 1980. Again, three assumed sales prices are used to illustrate the possible tax results for both residential and commercial realty. The key difference in treatment for commercial and residential realty is the potential recapture; for commercial realty, this amount is $58,500 (*total* ACRS deductions), and for residential realty, this amount is $18,500 (*excess* ACRS deductions). Also, note that depreciable realty acquired after 1980 is still classified as Sec. 1231 property for purposes of characterizing losses or gains in excess of the ordinary-income recapture.

As part of the Tax Equity and Fiscal Responsibility Act of 1982, Congress curtailed several special deductions and tax preferences available to corporate taxpayers (the tax treatment of these items for other taxpayers remains unaffected). One of the special-preference cutbacks is the potential Sec. 1231 capital-gains treatment on dispositions of Sec. 1250 property for tax years beginning after 1982. Code Section 291 now requires that 20% (15% for 1982, 1983, and 1984) of any gain that would have been treated as Sec. 1231 gain (after reduction for any Sec. 1250 recapture) be treated as ordinary income to the extent that it would have been recaptured as such under the Sec. 1245 recapture rules for personalty. This conversion of 20% of the Sec. 1231 gain into ordinary income occurs for both commercial and residential realty, regardless of whether straight-line or ACRS recovery is selected.

Example 12: Assume that taxpayer D in the example of Table 11-3 elects to use straight-line recovery for the building and sells the building on 1/4/85 for $130,000. The total gain on the sale is $20,000 ($130,000 less $110,000 adjusted basis). If D is a noncorporate taxpayer, the *entire* gain is Sec. 1231 gain. However, if D is a corporate

TABLE 11-3
Depreciation Recapture—Realty Acquired After 1980

D purchased a new building on 1/1/81 for $150,000. D elected to use a 15-year ACRS percentage recovery. The building was sold on 1/4/85. The allowable ACRS deductions, total gain or loss, and character of gain or loss for sales prices of $90,000, $105,000, and $120,000 would be as follows:

TOTAL COST RECOVERY ALLOWED

YEAR	ACRS RECOVERY	15-YEAR STRAIGHT-LINE RECOVERY	EXCESS RECOVERY DEDUCTIONS
1981	$18,000	$10,000	$ 8,000
1982	15,000	10,000	5,000
1983	13,500	10,000	3,500
1984	12,000	10,000	2,000
	$58,500	$40,000	$18,500

	A	B	C
Calculation of Gain (Loss)			
Amount Realized	$90,000	$105,000	$120,000
Adjusted Basis	(91,500)*	(91,500)*	(91,500)*
Recognized Gain (Loss)	$(1,500)	$ 13,500	$ 28,500
Character of Gain (Loss)			
Assuming Commercial Realty:			
Ordinary Income (Sec. 1245)	—	$ 13,500†	$ 28,500†
Sec. 1231 Gain	—	—	—
Sec. 1231 Loss	$(1,500)	—	—
Character of Gain (Loss)			
Assuming Residential Realty:			
Ordinary Income (Sec. 1250)	—	$ 13,500‡	$ 18,500‡
Sec. 1231 Gain	—	—	10,000‡
Sec. 1231 Loss	$(1,500)	—	—

*$150,000 cost less $58,500 ACRS deductions
†Ordinary income recapture is governed by Sec. 1245 and is limited to the total ACRS deductions allowed ($58,500)
‡Ordinary income recapture is governed by Sec. 1250 and is limited to 100% of the excess recovery deductions ($18,500).
NOTE—If the taxpayer had used straight-line recovery, *all* gain would have been Sec. 1231 gain.

FIGURE 11-4
Sec. 1250 and 1231 Rules for Commercial and Residential Buildings

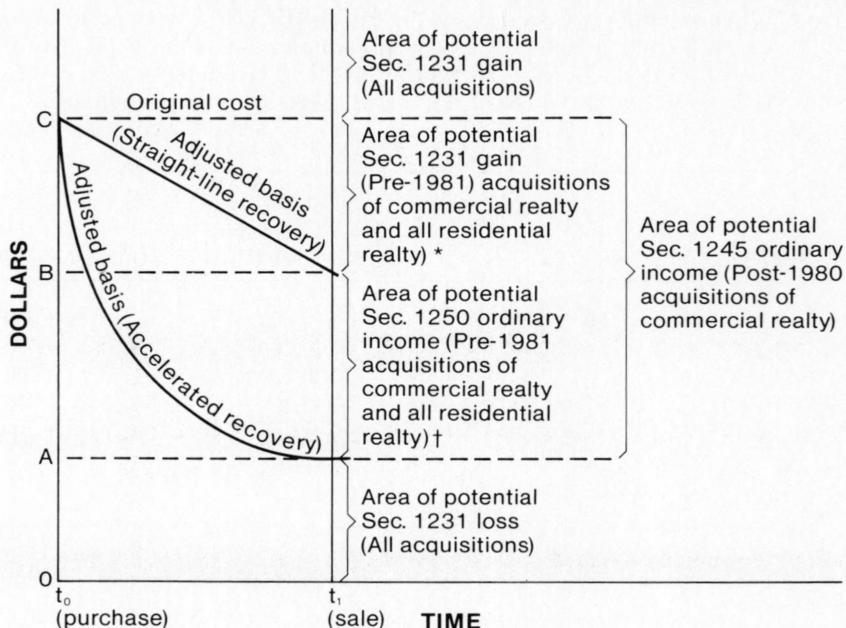

* Corporate taxpayers must report 20% of this Sec. 1231 gain as ordinary income for dispositions in tax years beginning after 1984. This percentage was 15% for 1982, 1983, and 1984.

† Residential realty acquired before 1976 will be subject to less than 100% recapture on 1970–1975 excess depreciation if the property is held for longer than 100 months.

taxpayer, 20% of the gain, or $4,000, is reported as ordinary income and the remaining $16,000 is reported as Sec. 1231 gain.

The recapture rules for commercial and residential realty can be illustrated on a graph (Figure 11-4). Distance OC represents the original cost of the building, and distances OB and OA represent the adjusted bases of the building at the date of sale (ti) using straight-line and accelerated depreciation recoveries, respectively. Therefore, distance AB, the difference in accumulated depreciation under the two recovery methods, represents "excess depreciation." This is the maximum ordinary income recapture under the Sec. 1250 rules, applicable to all pre-1981 acquisitions of commercial realty and all acquisitions of residential realty. Distance AC, the total depreciation taken on the building is the maximum ordinary-income recapture under the Sec. 1245 rules applicable to post-1980 acquisitions of commercial realty using an accelerated cost recovery.

RELATED EFFECTS OF RECAPTURE When Code Secs. 1245 and 1250 were enacted, Congress intended for these provisions to override all other provisions of the Code. Both sections contain the following statement: "Such gain shall be recognized notwithstanding any other provision of this subtitle."[10] This requirement affects several other sections of the Code, including the following:

INSTALLMENT SALES. Property subject to depreciation recapture may be sold on an installment basis. However, for installment sales prior to June 7, 1984, the income portion of each payment was treated as ordinary income until all of the Sec. 1245 or Sec. 1250 gain has been recaptured. The balance of the gain (if any) was Sec. 1231 gain.

Example 13: G sells a business machine for $20,000 on 2/1/83, to be paid for in five annual installments of $4,000 plus 10% interest beginning in 1983. G had purchased the machine for $15,000 five years previously, and had deducted a total of $9,000 depreciation. Therefore, the total gain to be recognized is $14,000 ($20,000 − $6,000 basis), of which $9,000 will be recaptured as ordinary income. G's gross profit percentage on the installment sale is 70% ($14,000/ $20,000), resulting in $2,800 of gross profit each year, to be recognized as follows (ignoring interest):

YEAR	SEC. 1245 (ORDINARY) GAIN	SEC. 1231 GAIN
1	$2,800	$ 0
2	2,800	0
3	2,800	0
4	600	2,200
5	0	2,800

In 1984 Congress enacted a major change in the recognition rules for depreciation recapture on installment sales. Code Sec. 453(i) was modified to provide that *all* depreciation recapture income on an installment sale after June 6, 1984 must be recognized in the year of sale, regardless of the payments (if any) received in the year of sale. Any recapture income so recognized will increase the adjusted basis of the property for purposes of determining the gross profit percentage for the actual payments received.

Example 14: Assume the same facts as in Example 13, except that the installment sale occurs on 2/1/85. In this case, the entire $9,000 of Sec. 1245 recapture must be recognized in 1985, even though only $4,000 of principal payments are received in that year. The $9,000 recapture income increases G's adjusted basis in the property to $15,000, so that the recomputed remaining gross profit on the installment sale is $5,000 ($20,000 − 15,000), and the recomputed gross profit percentage is 25% ($5,000 gross profit divided by $20,000 total

[10] Sec. 1245(a)(1) and Sec. 1250(a)(1).

contract price). Thus, 25% of each $4,000 installment payment, including the 1985 payment, will be taxed as Sec. 1231 gain. G's total gain of $14,000 will be reported as follows:

YEAR	SEC. 1245 (ORDINARY) GAIN	SEC. 1231 GAIN
1	$9,000	$1,000
2	0	1,000
3	0	1,000
4	0	1,000
5	0	1,000

Note that the practical effect of the new provision is to deny installment reporting for any depreciation recapture income. One practical consequence of the new provision may be that sellers will demand more up-front cash in order to fund payment of the taxes due to recapture in the year of sale.

Example 15: Refer to Example 14. If G restructured the transaction to receive $10,000 in the year of sale and $2,500 in each of the following four years, the incremental Sec. 1231 gain recognized in 1985 would be only $1,500 (25% of the $6,000 additional cash received), of which only 40% would be taxable, assuming that Sec. 1231 transactions for 1985 netted to a gain. This may ease any liquidity problems for G in 1985.

NONTAXABLE EXCHANGES. Chapter 12 describes the tax treatment of a number of transactions where the Code permits a deferral of realized gain on qualifying exchanges and involuntary conversions of certain properties. All of the gain is not necessarily deferred in some of these nontaxable transactions; for example, the receipt of nonsimilar property in an otherwise "like-kind" exchange of business properties may cause recognition of a portion of the realized accounting gain. Such a gain will be ordinary income to the extent that a sale of the property at its fair market value would have caused depreciation recapture.[11] Again, the recapture provisions have precedence over other Code provisions.

Example 16: H exchanges an old business machine with an adjusted basis of $3,000 for a new machine worth $4,000 and $500 cash. The old machine had cost $4,800 six years previously. Under Sec. 1031, a gain of $500 must be recognized on the exchange (equal to the nonsimilar property received). All of this gain must be reported as ordinary income under Sec. 1245, since a sale of the old machine at its fair market value of $4,500 (the value received) would have generated Sec. 1245 income of $1,500, which was less than the total depreciation allowed in prior years of $1,800.

---

[11] Sec. 1245(b)(4) and Sec. 1250(d)(4).

CHARITABLE CONTRIBUTIONS. Contributions of Sec. 1245 or Sec. 1250 properties to recognized charities are considered to be contributions of ordinary income property for purposes of applying the Sec. 170 limits on contributions of property. As discussed in Chapter 9, the allowable deduction is determined by reducing the fair market value of the property by the gain that would have been recognized had the property been sold at its fair market value. For depreciable business personalty and realty, this gain is determined by the application of Code Secs. 1245 and 1250, respectively.

> **Example 17:** J Corporation donates a residential building to a recognized charity at a time when the building has an adjusted basis of $60,000 and a fair market value of $72,000. J Corporation had taken depreciation deductions in excess of straight-line of $7,000 during the five years the building was used. J's charitable deduction will be $72,000 less $7,000 of Sec. 1250 recapture potential, or $65,000.

CARRYOVER OF RECAPTURE POTENTIAL. In some cases the Code requires a carryover of the recapture potential to either a new property or a new owner of the same property. These provisions are designed to prevent a later conversion of ordinary income into capital gain through the use of a nontaxable transfer such as a gift, a like-kind exchange, or an involuntary conversion.[12] In the case of gifts, this recapture taint remains even if the donee converts the property to a personal use.

> **Example 18:** Refer to Example 16. In the exchange, H recognized $500 of ordinary income under Sec. 1245. However, the recapture potential on a sale of that machine at its fair market value was $1,500; therefore, H must carry over $1,000 of this recapture potential to the new machine. If the new machine is later sold or exchanged, at a minimum the first $1,000 of recognized gain will be reported as ordinary income.

MISCELLANEOUS RECAPTURE PROVISIONS The concept of "recapturing" some or all of any previous deductions against ordinary income was extended by Congress to other areas of perceived abuse. These situations were primarily cases where tax-shelter investors were reaping tax benefits originally intended for taxpayers engaged in particular trades or businesses. These provisions were enacted to discourage short-run tax-shelter investments in certain activities while at the same time retaining the tax incentives of accelerated deductions for bona fide trade or business taxpayers.

SEC. 1252 LAND EXPENDITURES RECAPTURE. The special deductions for soil and water conservation expenditures (Sec. 175) and land clearing expenditures (Sec. 182) provide an incentive for nonfarmers to make

---

[12] Sec. 1245(b) and Sec. 1250(d).

short-term tax-motivated investments in farm land. Again, current deductions against ordinary income were later exchanged for capital-gains treatment under Sec. 1231. Congress addressed this problem in 1969 by enacting two recapture provisions designed to apply primarily to short-term investments in farm property. (One of these provisions, Sec. 1251, was repealed as deadwood in 1984.)

Sec. 1252 provides for a percentage recapture of the total land-clearing and conservation expenditures occurring after 1969. The percentage recapture is a function of the holding period of the land. The recapture is 100% of the total deductions if the land is held for five years or less and decreases 20% a year, for each year, beginning with dispositions in the sixth year. There is no recapture after the land is held for more than nine years. Note that the holding period is measured from the date of the land acquisition, rather than the date that the expenditures were incurred.

Example 19: K purchased a farm in February 1975 and incurred land-clearing expenditures of $14,000 in January 1976 and soil conservation expenditures of $10,000 in December 1978. K sold 20 acres of the land in April 1982 at a $16,000 gain. Since the land was sold in the eighth year, K's recapture potential under Sec. 1252 is $24,000 × .40, or $9,600. This amount is recognized as ordinary income, with the remaining $6,400 of gain qualifying as Sec. 1231 gain.

SEC. 1254 INTANGIBLE DRILLING-COST RECAPTURE. The Sec. 263(c) election allowing taxpayers to expense various intangible drilling and development costs provides another opportunity for taxpayers to convert ordinary income into capital gains. Once again, Congress responded with a recapture provision in 1976 designed to discourage short-term, tax-motivated investments in oil and gas properties.

Sec. 1254 recapture applies only to intangible drilling and development costs incurred after 1975. Gain on the sale of the property is ordinary income to the extent that the immediate deductions taken exceed the amounts that would have been deducted had the taxpayer originally capitalized the costs and deducted them over the useful life of the property. Additionally, the immediate deduction of such expenses may create a tax-preference item subject to the minimum tax (Chapter 13).

Example 20: P acquired an interest in an oil well in 19X1 for $20,000. In 19X1 P deducted $8,000 of intangible drilling costs. Cost depletion on this amount up to the date of property sale in 19X4 would have been $1,200. If P sells the property in 19X4, a maximum of $6,800 of gain could be recaptured as ordinary income under Sec. 1254. The $6,800 represents the excess of the $8,000 immediate deduction over $1,200, the total allowable cost depletion for three years had the costs been capitalized.

INVESTMENT CREDIT RECAPTURE. A sale or exchange of investment tax credit properties held for less than five years (or seven years for older properties) may require a recapture of a portion or all of an investment credit taken against taxes in the year that the property was acquired. Unlike the recapture provisions discussed thus far, the investment credit recapture increases the current year's tax liability, rather than ordinary income. The detailed rules for the computation of the investment credit and related recapture are discussed in Chapter 14.

SALES OF OTHER BUSINESS-RELATED ASSETS

The statutory definition of a capital asset has been modified in several instances to resolve ambiguities concerning the tax status of several other types of business properties. In the case of patents, trademarks, trade names, and franchises, legislation was enacted to define exactly when a sale or exchange of a capital asset has occurred, as opposed to a mere rental arrangement. In other instances, such as the sale of subdivided realty and the sale of securities by dealers, the focus of the legislation was on distinguishing sales of personal capital assets from sales of business inventory.

COPYRIGHTS AND PATENTS

Sec. 1221(3) expressly excludes a copyright, as well as any literary, musical, or other artistic composition or letter, from the definition of a capital asset. This prohibition against capital asset treatment applies equally to the creator, a taxpayer for whom a letter or memorandum was produced, or a taxpayer who assumes the creator's tax basis (such as a gift recipient). This provision was enacted in order to equate the tax treatment of taxpayers whose mental or physical efforts result in the sale of a product (similar to inventory) with those taxpayers whose efforts result in the sale of services. In both cases, the net increase in wealth is taxed as ordinary income.

Interestingly, the Sec. 1221 definition of a capital asset does not exclude ***patents***. Congress felt that inventive activities should be encouraged and in 1954 enacted Sec. 1235, which automatically grants long-term capital-gains treatment to an amateur or professional inventor on the sale or exchange of a patent which involves a transfer of all substantial rights. The differing tax treatments accorded copyrights and patents has been the subject of much controversy.

PATENT An intangible asset representing an exclusive privilege granted for a term of 17 years by the U.S. Government to exclude others from making, using, or selling an invention.

Sec. 1235 grants long-term capital-gains treatment to the "holder" of a patent, defined as the creator or any other individual who acquires an interest from the creator for a fair consideration prior to the marketing of the invention. However, neither the employer of the creator nor an individual related to the creator (within the meaning of the related party rules of Sec. 267 slightly modified) may be included in this category. In these two cases, the tax treatment would be determined by the character of the asset in the taxpayer's hands (i.e., inventory, capital asset, or Sec. 1231

BACKGROUND

The question of capital-asset status for copyrights and patents was not formally addressed by Congress until 1950. Prior to that time, the tax status of such assets was determined primarily on the basis of whether the taxpayer was considered to be a professional or an amateur. In a celebrated case, the government granted capital-gains status to General Dwight D. Eisenhower for payments for the publishing rights of his book "Crusade in Europe."* This decision in favor of amateur status for a "first time" effort, was highly controversial and was a major impetus for the Congressional action.

In 1950 the House of Representatives passed an amendment to Code Sec. 117, excluding patents and copyrights from the definition of capital assets. The intent of this provision was to tax all such transfers as ordinary income under the theory that a taxpayer engaging in such activities is always engaging in a trade or business, even though it may be the taxpayer's first and only effort. The Senate, however, excluded only copyrights from the capital-asset definition:

> The House bill also would have treated as ordinary income gains from the sale of an invention or patent by the occasional inventor. Your committee believes that the desirability of fostering the work of such inventors outweighs the small amount of additional revenue which might be obtained under the House bill, and, therefore, the words "invention," "patent," and "design" have been eliminated from this section of the bill.†

The Senate version of the bill was passed by Congress, with the result that transfers of copyrights were then considered ordinary income, and transfers of patents were either capital gains or ordinary income, depending on the status of the taxpayer (amateur or professional). In 1954 Congress passed Code Sec. 1235, removing the amateur vs. professional categorization by automatically granting long-term capital gains treatment to a transfer of all substantial rights by qualified holders.

The preferential tax treatment accorded patents has been very controversial. While some writers feel that such a provision fosters technological progress, others feel that the provision represents a form of discrimination against cultural pursuits. Regardless of one's beliefs, it is difficult to argue with a commonly-quoted tax axiom that "it is better to invent than create."

---

*The memoirs were sold for a lump sum in 1950. This led to the Congressional Changes of 1950, which are sometimes referred to as the "Eisenhower Amendment."

†*Report of the Senate Finance Committee*, 81st Congress, 2d Session, Report 2375, p. 44.

property). The capital-gains treatment is unaffected by the method of payment for the patent whether it be lump sum, installment, or contingency payments.

The focus of Sec. 1235 is directed to the question of whether a transaction resulted in the transfer of "all substantial rights" in the patent or an undivided interest in all such rights. Depending on the circumstances, a transfer may be considered to be a sale qualifying for capital-gains treatment or a license to use the patent, the latter taxable as ordinary royalty income. Generally, if the exclusive rights to make, use, and sell the product are transferred, a sale is presumed to have occurred. A transfer of all substantial rights does not occur if the rights to the patent are limited geographically (within the country of issuance), limited in duration (compared to the remaining life of the patent), or restricted to less than all claims or inventions having value at the time of the grant.[13]

Example 21: J transfers to K, an unrelated party, all patent rights to manufacture and sell a product developed by J. K will pay J $50,000 immediately and 5% of all gross revenues from the product for the life of the patent. This transfer qualifies as a sale of a capital asset because all substantial rights are transferred; the contingency payments based on revenues do not affect the final result. Additionally, J would be entitled to a tax-free recovery of any patent costs in the year of sale.

Example 22: Assume the same facts as in Example 21 except that the rights to manufacture and sell the product are limited to a period of five years. If the patent is expected to have a remaining economic useful life of more than five years, then all substantial rights have not been transferred. Therefore, the transfer is treated as a licensing arrangement for tax purposes, with all payments treated as ordinary rental income. Note that J would not be entitled to an immediate tax-free recovery of any patent costs, since a sale has not occurred.

FRANCHISES, TRADEMARKS, AND TRADE NAMES

The transfer of a franchise, trademark, or trade name involves many of the same tax questions raised in the transfer of a patent. A transfer may be either a sale qualifying as the sale of a capital asset or a license to use qualifying as ordinary rental income. The growing popularity of franchise arrangements caused Congress to enact specific legislation in 1969 to govern such transfers.

Sec. 1253 states that a transfer (including renewal) of a franchise, trademark, or trade name will not be treated as the sale or exchange of a capital asset if the transferor retains any significant power, right, or continuing interest. A ***franchise*** is defined as an agreement granting the right to distribute, sell, or provide goods, services, or facilities within a specified

FRANCHISE An intangible asset representing an agreement giving the transferee the right to distribute, sell, or provide goods, services, or facilities within a specified area.

[13]Reg. Sec. 1.1235-2(b)(1).

area. The Senate Finance Committee provided the following examples of significant powers, rights, or continuing interests:

> For example, a transferor may participate in the business by conducting such activities as sales promotion (including advertising), sales and management training, employee training programs, holding of national meetings for transferees, providing the transferees with blueprints or formulae, and other forms of continuing assistance.[14]

In addition to these types of powers, Code Sec. 1253 lists the following as significant rights or continuing interests: a right to disapprove any assignment of interest; a right to terminate the arrangement at will; a right to control product quality, advertising, and sources of supply; and a right to receive substantial contingency payments, based on productivity, use, or disposition of the interest. Interestingly, Sec. 1253 does not apply to the transfer of a professional sports franchise.

Example 23: B grants C the right to sell their special chili mixture in a three-state area. B will control all supplies for preparing the product in order to ensure product quality. This would be considered a significant retained right, and any payments received by B will be taxed as ordinary income.

Sec. 1253 also specifies the tax consequences of such a transfer to the transferee. Basically, the tax ramifications to the transferee are consistent with those of the transferor; for a sale, the purchase price will be amortized, and for a licensing arrangement, the payments are deductible as ordinary expenses.

SUBDIVIDED REALTY

Sec. 1237 was enacted to make it easier for taxpayers who hold real property for investment purposes to subdivide their property (for easier disposition) and still receive capital-asset treatment. Without this provision, such an individual may be classified as a dealer in real estate and subjected to ordinary income tax rates under the theory that the land was held primarily for resale (e.g., inventory).

Three conditions must be met in order to receive the special tax treatment of Sec. 1237; the taxpayer (*a*) must not be a dealer in real estate, (*b*) must not have made a substantial improvement in the property, and (*c*) must have held the property for five years, unless inherited. A substantial improvement is one that increases the value of the lot by more than 10%,[15] although this does not necessarily void Sec. 1237 treatment if the property has been held for at least ten years and certain basis adjustments are waived by the taxpayer.

---

[14] *Report of the Senate Finance Committee*, 91st Congress, Report 91-552, p.213.

[15] Reg. Sec. 1.1237-1(c)(3). Among the improvements listed as "substantial" in Reg. Sec. 1.1237-1(c)(4) are shopping centers, other commercial or residential buildings, and the installation of hard-surface roads or utilities such as sewers, water, gas, or electric lines.

Sec. 1237 does not grant capital-gains treatment automatically to all sales of subdivided realty. Rather, if the three conditions are met, gain on the sale of the lots will be capital gain until the tax year in which the sixth lot is sold. On the sixth and all subsequent lot sales, 5% of the gross sales price will be recognized as ordinary income, with any remaining gain taxable as capital gain. Any selling expenses incurred by the taxpayer can be used to offset the 5% ordinary income portion of the gain first. In counting the lot sales, adjoining lots sold to the same purchaser in the same tax year count as one sale.[16] Furthermore, all gains in the year of the sixth lot sale are subject to the 5% rule, rather than just the sixth and subsequent lot sales.

Example 24: G owns 10 acres of land and subdivides it into ten 1-acre plots, numbered so that consecutive numbers represent adjoining lots. G had originally purchased the 10 acres for $20,000 six years ago. In 19X2 G sells lots 1 and 2 to L, 3 and 10 to M, and 4 to N, all for $4,500 each, less selling expenses of $200 per lot. For purposes of Sec. 1237, G is considered to have sold 4 lots in 19X2 (lots 3 and 10 are not adjoining) and will recognize $2,300 of long-term gain on the sale of each lot ($4,500 less $2,000 less $200), or a total of $11,500 (five separate lots were sold).

Example 25: Assume that in 19X3 G sold lot 5 to P, lot 6 to Q, and lot 7 to R, all for $5,000 each, less selling expenses of $200 per lot. In applying Sec. 1237, G is considered to have sold three more lots. Since this is the year in which the sixth lot was sold, the 5% rule is applied to *all* sales in 19X3. Of the $2,800 gain recognized on each lot, $50 will be recognized as ordinary income and $2,750 will be capital gain. The $50 ordinary income is the difference between 5% of the sales price of $5,000 and the selling expenses of $200. Note that the selling expenses should first be subtracted in determining the total recognized gain and then merely compared to 5% of the sales price to determine how much, if any, of the gain is capital gain. Care should be taken not to deduct the selling expenses twice in the computations.

Example 26: Assume that in 19X4 G added a blacktop road and sewage and water lines to lots 8 and 9. These improvements increased the value of each lot from $5,000 to $6,000. In 19X4 G sells both lots to R for $6,000 each, less $300 selling expenses per lot. Since the improvements are considered substantial within the meaning of Sec. 1237, G does not automatically receive capital-gains treatment. G may still be able to argue that the land is a capital asset, although the IRS may contend that the substantial improvements are the actions of a dealer in real estate. In this case, the gain would all be ordinary income.

[16] Reg. 1.1237-1(e)(2).

The practical effect of Code Sec. 1237 is to tax an individual under one of three different characterizations. In Example 24, G is taxed as a non-dealer investor because all tests of Sec. 1237 are met. In Example 25, G is taxed as a real estate agent with a 5% "commission," since even though he is not a dealer he has sold several properties to several individuals. (In fact, 5% was the normal real estate commission at the time of the enactment of Sec. 1237.) In Example 26 G may be taxed as a dealer in real estate because the substantial improvements are characteristic of a trade or business.

SECURITIES DEALERS

Sec. 1236 solves a potential dilemma for a taxpayer classified as a securities dealer. Because the securities dealer's business inventory consists of stocks and bonds, he or she might find it difficult to convince the IRS that certain sales or exchanges involve only personal capital-asset investments. Obviously, the temptation would be to label the profitable sales as personal transactions, qualifying for capital-gains treatment, and the loss sales as business transactions, qualifying for ordinary-loss treatment.

Congress resolved this problem in 1951 by enacting Sec. 1236, which requires a dealer to clearly identify within 30 days of acquisition purchases made for investment purposes. Failure to do so results in ordinary-gain-or-loss treatment. In the Economic Recovery Tax Act of 1981, Congress amended this provision to require identification of investment shares no later than the close of business on the day of acquisition. This change was enacted because the prior 30-day waiting period for identification was providing some unintended tax incentives:

> Some taxpayers considered security dealers' unique tax-planning opportunities so significant that they established themselves as broker-dealers solely to exploit these opportunities. Large broker-dealer partnerships passed these tax benefits through to hundreds of partners. Many of these broker-dealer partnerships sold shares in their operations for fees which were based on a percentage, usually 10%, of the tax loss sought by the investor.[17]

SALES OF A BUSINESS ENTERPRISE

The sale of a going concern has significant tax consequences for both the seller and the purchaser. The allocation of sales price among the individual assets transferred will have tax ramifications for years to come for both parties. As a rule, the seller and the purchaser have competing tax interests in such an allocation. For example, the seller would prefer as little as possible to be allocated to inventories since any gain there is taxed as ordinary income. On the other hand, the purchaser would prefer a high value allocated to inventory, since this cost can be recovered im-

[17] Joint Committee on Taxation, *General Explanation of the Economic Recovery Tax Act of 1981*, H. R. 4242, p. 311.

mediately upon resale. These adverse interests alone may cause the courts or the IRS to accept the allocations of sales price agreed to by the buyer and the seller. However, the IRS and the courts are not required to accept an agreed-upon allocation if it appears that it does not conform to the realities of the transaction.[18]

Although Rev. Rul. 55-79[19] requires a complete allocation of sales price when a going concern is sold, buyers and sellers sometimes refuse to stipulate any allocation in the contract. Each party may be willing simply to hope for the best in any disputes with the IRS. Obviously, each party to the contract should thoroughly understand the tax implications of any allocation of sales price. Two important considerations in the sale of a going concern are the tax treatments of goodwill and a covenant not to compete. In both cases, the seller and purchaser have adverse tax interests.

GOODWILL ***Goodwill*** is a capital asset, generally presumed to represent the capitalized value of a firm's potential to earn an above-normal return on its investment in capital assets. Goodwill is normally measured as the excess of the purchase price paid for a going concern over the total fair market values of the individual assets transferred. Goodwill is considered to have an indeterminate useful life for tax purposes, and therefore may not be amortized in any way (although goodwill is amortized for financial accounting purposes). In some cases, a purchaser may be able to remove the value of some assets with limited lives, such as customer lists, and depreciate these items over a reasonable useful life.[20]

GOODWILL The excess of the selling price of a business over the sum of the fair market values of the individual assets, with the excess representing intangibles such as reputation and customer goodwill that promise above-normal profits in future years.

COVENANT NOT TO COMPETE A ***covenant not to compete*** is a contractual agreement made by a seller agreeing not to compete with the buyer for a specified term of years. Such a covenant represents a substitute for lost income, and therefore is not considered to be a capital asset, and a payment for same is always taxed to the seller as ordinary income. Since the covenant normally has a fixed life, the payments made by the buyer may be amortized over that period.

COVENANT NOT TO COMPETE As part of the sales contract for a going concern, a seller agrees not to compete actively with the purchaser in a similar business for a fixed period of time.

REPORTING SALES OF BUSINESS PROPERTIES

Reporting sales of properties used in a trade or business is sometimes as difficult as understanding the applicable tax provisions. Form 4797 is used to report sales of real or depreciable property used in a trade or business, and Form 4684 is used to report casualty and theft losses for both business and personal properties. These two forms are illustrated by the following comprehensive example. The problem is first solved using the 5-column property transactions format, and then placed on the appropriate tax forms (including Form 1040 and Schedule D).

---

[18] *Copperhead Coal Co.* v. Commissioner, 272F. 2d 45 (6th Cir. 1959).

[19] Rev. Rul. 55-79, 1955-1-C.B. 370.

[20] Rev. Rul. 74-456. 1974-2 C.B. 65.

COMPREHENSIVE EXAMPLE

Jan Washington is a self-employed taxpayer who owns and operates several parking lots. During 1984 he had a $40,000 net income from his regular business and made the following property transactions:

(a) Sold 100 shares of XYZ Corporation stock for $50 a share on 3/2/84. Jan had purchased the shares for $60 a share on 4/12/83.
(b) Sold one-half acre of land used in the business on 7/12/84 for $8,000. The land originally cost $9,400 on 1/4/76.
(c) Sold a business storage building on 6/2/84 for $50,000. The storage building was originally purchased on 6/18/83 for $52,000, and a total of $1,850 depreciation had been deducted as of the date of sale.
(d) Received $3,200 on 8/2/84 as an insurance settlement on a business machine completely destroyed by fire. The machine originally cost $4,800 on 3/1/79 and had an adjusted basis of $3,550 on the date of the fire (which was less than its fair market value of $3,900).
(e) Sold four auto elevators (personalty) on 9/3/84 for a total of $9,600. The elevators were originally purchased for $9,000 on 6/1/80, and a total of $2,200 of depreciation had been deducted as of the date of sale.
(f) Sold a business warehouse and one acre of land on 11/4/84 for a total of $100,000, with $30,000 allocated to the land and $70,000 to the building. The land and building were originally purchased for $85,000 on 11/1/79, with $25,000 allocated to the land and $60,000 allocated to the building. Accelerated depreciation deducted on the building up to the date of sale was $12,000; straight-line depreciation would have been $8,000.
(g) Received $2,100 on 12/1/84 as insurance recovery on an office painting. The painting had originally cost $1,300 on 5/1/73.
(h) Realized a $6,200 loss on the 6/1/84 theft of an uninsured diamond ring.

WORKSHEET SOLUTION

Figure 11-5 reflects the given transactions within the context of the property transaction netting procedure. Each entry is keyed by letter to the original transaction. The final effect of the property transaction on taxable income is an increase of $54,081. The following points are relevant in analyzing the solution:

- Transactions (d) and (g) are both included in the business casualty and theft netting procedure. The fire loss on the machine is not reduced by the $100 floor, since the machine is business property.[21] Since the casualties and thefts net to a gain, the net gain of $450 is combined with Sec. 1231 gains and losses.
- Sec. 1231 gains and losses include the loss on the sale of business land from transaction (b) and the gain on the sale of the land compo-

[21] For the same reason, the 10% of AGI limit on personal casualties does not apply to the loss.

FIGURE 11-5
Property Transaction Netting Procedure for Comprehensive Example

PERSONAL CASUALTY & THEFT GAINS & LOSSES	BUSINESS CASUALTY & THEFT GAINS & LOSSES	SEC. 1231 GAINS & LOSSES	CAPITAL GAINS & LOSSES	ORDINARY GAINS & LOSSES
			Short-term:	BUS 40,000
(h) (6,100)	(d) (350)	(b) (1,400)	(a) (1,000)	(c) (150)
	(g) 800	(e) 600		(e) 2,200
		(f_1) 5,000		(f_2) 4,000
(6,100)	450 →	(f_2) 18,000	Long-term:	→ 8,660*
		450		
		22,650 →	22,650	AGI $54,710
↳	Less 10% of AGI, or $5,471			→ (629)
				Net Taxable $54,081

*Computed as Follows:
$21,650 Net Long-term Capital Gain
(12,990) 60% Capital Gains Deduction

$8,660 Net Taxable Gain

nent in transaction (f). The Sec. 1231 nettings procedure also includes the gains in excess of depreciation recapture on the sales of the elevators—transaction (e)—and the warehouse—transaction (f). The gain on the elevators was larger than the total depreciation deductions of $2,200 allowed (Sec. 1245 recapture), and the gain on the warehouse was larger than the excess depreciation of $4,000 allowed (Sec. 1250 recapture for commercial realty acquired before 1981). Note that the depreciation recapture amounts of $2,200 and $4,000 are shown in the ordinary income column.

- Since Sec. 1231 gains exceed Sec. 1231 losses, the net difference of $22,650 is treated as a long-term capital gain. Transaction (a) resulted in a $1,000 short-term capital loss, and when netted with the $22,650 long-term gain, results in a $21,650 net long-term capital gain. After subtracting a 60% long-term capital-gains deduction, a final gain of $8,660 is included in ordinary income.
- The $150 loss on the sale of the storage building is treated as an ordinary loss. Since the property was held for less than a year, the loss cannot be a Sec. 1231 loss. Furthermore, the storage building is not a capital asset, because property used in a trade or business is specifically excluded from the capital-asset definition.
- The $6,200 personal theft loss—transaction (h)—is reduced by the $100 floor and 10% of AGI. The net loss of $629 is allowed as a deduction only if the taxpayer itemizes.

TAX RETURN SOLUTION

All of the property transactions ultimately increase Washington's taxable income by a total of $54,081. Deriving this result on the appropriate tax forms is not quite as efficient as the property transaction netting procedure illustrated in Figure 11-5. The following pages illustrate the proper placement of these transactions on Forms 4684 and 4797. The front page of the individual Form 1040 (Figure 11-6), Form 1040—Schedule A (Figure 11-6a), and Form 1040—Schedule D (Figures 11-6b and 11-6c) are also used to illustrate how the final adjusted gross income of $54,710 is determined.

FORM 4684

The preparation of the tax return proceeds in a sequence similar to the property transaction netting procedure. First, Form 4684 (Figures 11-6d and 11-6e) is used to determine the net casualty and theft gain or loss. In the example, the business casualties and thefts net to a gain of $450 (line 21 of Section B), which is transferred to Part I, line 2 of Form 4797. Note that the personal casualties and thefts net to a $629 loss (line 18 of Section A), which is transferred to line 19 of Schedule A, itemized deductions (Figure 11-6a).

FORM 4797

Form 4797 (Figures 11-6f and 11-6g), used by individual and corporate taxpayers, is divided into three main sections. Part I is used to summarize gains and losses under Sec. 1231. This includes the net business casualty and theft gain of $450 from Form 4684 on line 2. This section also includes any gains in excess of depreciation recapture on properties covered by Sec. 1245 and Sec. 1250. These recapture transactions are summarized in Part III of the Form 4797, so that section of the form should be completed before Part I is totaled.

Part II of the Form 4797 is used to summarize any ordinary gains and losses, including those on properties held one year or less. Line 8 of Part II includes the total ordinary income from recapture properties described in Part III; therefore, Part III should also be completed before Part II is totaled.

Part III of the form is used to divide gains on the sale of recapture properties into ordinary income and Sec. 1231 components. Line 26 of Part III summarizes the total gains on all of these properties, and this total is divided into an ordinary income portion (line 27, transferred to Part II) and a Sec. 1231 portion (line 28, transferred to Part I).

Once all transactions are entered on the Form 4797, the next step is to total Part III and transfer the results to Parts I and II. Part I is then totaled, with the final result representing the net Sec. 1231 gain or loss. A net gain is transferred to Schedule D (capital gains and losses), and a net loss is transferred to line 7 of Part II. In the present example, the $22,650 net gain is transferred to line 16 of Schedule D, where it is combined with other capital transactions.

Finally, Form 4797 is completed by totaling Part II. The net ordinary gain or loss of $6,050 (line 14) is transferred to the front page of Form 1040, line 15.

In summary, the tax reporting procedures for dispositions of trade or business properties are both confusing and cumbersome. However, it

FIGURE 11-6

Form **1040** Department of the Treasury—Internal Revenue Service
U.S. Individual Income Tax Return 1984 (0)

For the year January 1-December 31, 1984, or other tax year beginning , 1984, ending , 19 | OMB No. 1545-0074

Use IRS label. Otherwise, please print or type.	Your first name and initial (if joint return, also give spouse's name and initial) Last name: *Jan Washington*	Your social security number: *222 33 4444*
	Present home address (Number and street, including apartment number, or rural route): *1115 Monument Avenue*	Spouse's social security number
	City, town or post office, State, and ZIP code: *Carytown, New York 10061*	Your occupation: *Parking Lot Operator* Spouse's occupation

Presidential Election Campaign ▶ Do you want $1 to go to this fund? Yes ☐ No ☒
If joint return, does your spouse want $1 to go to this fund? Yes ☐ No ☐
Note: *Checking "Yes" will not change your tax or reduce your refund.*

For Privacy Act and Paperwork Reduction Act Notice, see Instructions.

Filing Status

Check only one box.

1 ☒ Single
2 ☐ Married filing joint return (even if only one had income)
3 ☐ Married filing separate return. Enter spouse's social security no. above and full name here.
4 ☐ Head of household (with qualifying person). (See page 5 of Instructions.) If the qualifying person is your unmarried child but not your dependent, write child's name here.
5 ☐ Qualifying widow(er) with dependent child (Year spouse died ▶ 19). (See page 6 of Instructions.)

Exemptions

Always check the box labeled Yourself. Check other boxes if they apply.

6a ☒ Yourself ☐ 65 or over ☐ Blind
b ☐ Spouse ☐ 65 or over ☐ Blind
Enter number of boxes checked on 6a and b ▶ *1*
c First names of your dependent children who lived with you
Enter number of children listed on 6c ▶

d Other dependents: (1) Name	(2) Relationship	(3) Number of months lived in your home	(4) Did dependent have income of $1,000 or more?	(5) Did you provide more than one-half of dependent's support?

Enter number of other dependents ▶
Add numbers entered in boxes above ▶ *1*

e Total number of exemptions claimed (also complete line 36)

Income

Please attach Copy B of your Forms W-2, W-2G, and W-2P here.

If you do not have a W-2, see page 4 of Instructions.

Please attach check or money order here.

7	Wages, salaries, tips, etc.	7	
8	Interest income *(also attach Schedule B if over $400)*	8	
9a	Dividends *(also attach Schedule B if over $400)* , 9b Exclusion		
c	Subtract line 9b from line 9a and enter the result	9c	
10	Refunds of State and local income taxes, from the worksheet on page 9 of Instructions *(do not enter an amount unless you itemized deductions for those taxes in an earlier year—see page 9)*	10	
11	Alimony received	11	
12	Business income or (loss) *(attach Schedule C)*	12	*40,000*
13	Capital gain or (loss) *(attach Schedule D)*	13	*8,660*
14	40% of capital gain distributions not reported on line 13 (see page 9 of Instructions)	14	
15	Supplemental gains or (losses) *(attach Form 4797)*	15	*6,050*
16	Fully taxable pensions, IRA distributions, and annuities not reported on line 17	16	
17a	Other pensions and annuities, including rollovers. Total received 17a		
b	Taxable amount, if any, from the worksheet on page 10 of Instructions	17b	
18	Rents, royalties, partnerships, estates, trusts, etc. *(attach Schedule E)*	18	
19	Farm income or (loss) *(attach Schedule F)*	19	
20a	Unemployment compensation (insurance). Total received 20a		
b	Taxable amount, if any, from the worksheet on page 10 of Instructions	20b	
21a	Social security benefits. (see page 10 of Instructions) 21a		
b	Taxable amount, if any, from the worksheet on page 11 of Instructions	21b	
22	Other income (state nature and source—see page 11 of Instructions)	22	
23	Add lines 7 through 22. This is your **total income** ▶	23	*54,710*

Adjustments to Income

(See Instructions on page 11.)

24	Moving expense *(attach Form 3903 or 3903F)*	24	
25	Employee business expenses *(attach Form 2106)*	25	
26a	IRA deduction, from the worksheet on page 12	26a	
b	Enter here IRA payments you made in 1985 that are included in line 26a above ▶		
27	Payments to a Keogh *(H.R. 10)* retirement plan	27	
28	Penalty on early withdrawal of savings	28	
29	Alimony paid	29	
30	Deduction for a married couple when both work *(attach Schedule W)*	30	
31	Add lines 24 through 30. These are your **total adjustments** ▶	31	

Adjusted Gross Income

32	Subtract line 31 from line 23. *This is your* **adjusted gross income.** *If this line is less than $10,000, see "Earned Income Credit" (line 59) on page 16 of Instructions. If you want IRS to figure your tax, see page 12 of Instructions.* ▶	32	*54,710*

FIGURE 11-6a

SCHEDULES A&B (Form 1040) Department of the Treasury Internal Revenue Service	**Schedule A—Itemized Deductions** (Schedule B is on back) ▶ Attach to Form 1040. ▶ See Instructions for Schedules A and B (Form 1040).	OMB No. 1545-0074 **1984** 07

Name(s) as shown on Form 1040: Jan Washington — Your social security number: 222 33 4444

Medical and Dental Expenses (Do not include expenses reimbursed or paid by others.) (See Instructions on page 19)	1	Prescription medicines and drugs; and insulin	1			
	2 a	Doctors, dentists, nurses, hospitals, insurance premiums you paid for medical and dental care, etc.	2a			
	b	Transportation and lodging	2b			
	c	Other (list—include hearing aids, dentures, eyeglasses, etc.) ▶	2c			
	3	Add lines 1 through 2c, and write the total here	3			
	4	Multiply the amount on Form 1040, line 33, by 5% (.05)	4			
	5	Subtract line 4 from line 3. If zero or less, write -0-. **Total** medical and dental ▶			5	
Taxes You Paid (See Instructions on page 20)	6	State and local income taxes	6			
	7	Real estate taxes	7			
	8 a	General sales tax (see sales tax tables in instruction booklet)	8a			
	b	General sales tax on motor vehicles	8b			
	9	Other taxes (list—include personal property taxes) ▶	9			
	10	Add the amounts on lines 6 through 9. Write the total here. **Total** taxes ▶			10	
Interest You Paid (See Instructions on page 20)	11 a	Home mortgage interest you paid to financial institutions	11a			
	b	Home mortgage interest you paid to individuals (show that person's name and address) ▶	11b			
	12	Total credit card and charge account interest you paid	12			
	13	Other interest you paid (list) ▶	13			
	14	Add the amounts on lines 11a through 13. Write the total here. **Total** interest ▶			14	
Contributions You Made (See Instructions on page 20)	15 a	Cash contributions. (If you gave $3,000 or more to any one organization, report those contributions on line 15b.)	15a			
	b	Cash contributions totaling $3,000 or more to any one organization. (Show to whom you gave and how much you gave.) ▶	15b			
	16	Other than cash (attach required statement)	16			
	17	Carryover from prior year	17			
	18	Add the amounts on lines 15a through 17. Write the total here. **Total** contributions ▶			18	
Casualty and Theft Losses	19	Total casualty or theft loss(es). (You must attach Form 4684 or similar statement.) (see page 21 of Instructions) ▶			19	629
Miscellaneous Deductions (See Instructions on page 21)	20	Union and professional dues	20			
	21	Tax return preparation fee	21			
	22	Other (list type and amount) ▶	22			
	23	Add the amounts on lines 20 through 22. Write the total here. **Total** miscellaneous ▶			23	
Summary of Itemized Deductions (See Instructions on page 22)	24	Add the amounts on lines 5, 10, 14, 18, 19, and 23. Write your answer here.			24	
	25	If you checked Form 1040 { Filing Status box 2 or 5, write $3,400; Filing Status box 1 or 4, write $2,300; Filing Status box 3, write $1,700 }			25	
	26	Subtract line 25 from line 24. Write your answer here and on Form 1040, line 34a. (If line 25 is more than line 24, see the Instructions for line 26 on page 22.) ▶			26	

For Paperwork Reduction Act Notice, see Form 1040 Instructions. — **Schedule A (Form 1040) 1984**

FIGURE 11-6b

SCHEDULE D (Form 1040)

Department of the Treasury
Internal Revenue Service

Capital Gains and Losses

(Also reconciliation of sales of stocks, bonds, and bartering income from Forms 1099-B)

► Attach to Form 1040. ► See Instructions for Schedule D (Form 1040).

OMB No. 1545-0074

1984

12

Name(s) as shown on Form 1040: Jan Washington

Your social security number: 222 33 4444

Part I **Short-term Capital Gains and Losses-Assets Held One Year or Less (6 months if acquired after 6/22/84)**

a. Description of property (Example, 100 shares 7% preferred of "Z" Co.)	b. Date acquired (Mo., day, yr.)	c. Date sold (Mo., day, yr.)	d. Gross sales price	e. Cost or other basis (see instructions)	f. LOSS If column (e) is more than (d) subtract (d) from (e)	g. GAIN If column (d) is more than (e) subtract (e) from (d)
1						
100 Shares of XYZ Corp. Stock	4/12/83	3/2/84	5,000	6,000	1,000	

Line	Description		f. LOSS	g. GAIN
2	Short-term gain from sale or exchange of a principal residence from Form 2119, lines 7 or 11	2		
3	Short-term gain from installment sales from Form 6252, lines 22 or 30	3		
4	Net short-term gain or (loss) from partnerships, S corporations, and fiduciaries	4		
5	Add lines 1 through 4 in columns f and g	5	(1,000)	0
6	Combine columns f and g of line 5 and enter the net gain or (loss)		6	(1,000)
7	Short-term capital loss carryover from years beginning after 1969		7	( )
8	Net short-term gain or (loss), combine lines 6 and 7		8	(1,000)

Part II **Long-term Capital Gains and Losses-Assets Held More Than One Year (6 months if acquired after 6/22/84)**

a.	b.	c.	d.	e.	f.	g.
9						

Line	Description		f. LOSS	g. GAIN
10	Long-term gain from sale or exchange of a principal residence from Form 2119, lines 7, 11, 16, or 18	10		
11	Long-term gain from installment sales from Form 6252, lines 22 or 30	11		
12	Net long-term gain or (loss) from partnerships, S corporations, and fiduciaries	12		
13	Add lines 9 through 12 in columns f and g	13	( )	
14	Combine columns f and g of line 13 and enter the net gain or (loss)		14	
15	Capital gain distributions		15	
16	Enter gain from Form 4797, line 6(a)(1)		16	22,650
17	Combine lines 14 through 16		17	
18	Long-term capital loss carryover from years beginning after 1969		18	( )
19	Net long-term gain or (loss), combine lines 17 and 18		19	22,650

Note: *Complete the back of this form. However, if you have capital loss carryovers from years beginning before 1970, do not complete Parts III or IV. See Form 4798 instead.*

For Paperwork Reduction Act Notice, see Form 1040 instructions. **Schedule D (Form 1040) 1984**

FIGURE 11-6c

Schedule D (Form 1040) 1984 12 Page 2

Name(s) as shown on Form 1040 (Do not enter name and social security number if shown on other side)	Your social security number
Jan Washington	222 33 4444

Part III **Summary of Parts I and II**

20	Combine lines 8 and 19, and enter the net gain or (loss) here	20	21,650
	Note: *If line 20 is a loss, skip lines 21 through 23 and complete lines 24 and 25. If line 20 is a gain complete lines 21 through 23 and skip lines 24 and 25.*		
21	If line 20 shows a gain, enter the smaller of line 19 or line 20. Enter zero if there is a loss or no entry on line 19 — 21: 21,650		
22	Enter 60% of line 21	22	12,990
	If line 22 is more than zero, you may be liable for the alternative minimum tax. See Form 6251.		
23	Subtract line 22 from line 20. Enter here and on Form 1040, line 13	23	8,660
24	If line 20 shows a loss, enter one of the following amounts: a If line 8 is zero or a net gain, enter 50% of line 20; b If line 19 is zero or a net gain, enter line 20; or c If line 8 and line 19 are net losses, enter amount on line 8 added to 50% of the amount on line 19	24	
25	Enter here and as a loss on Form 1040, line 13, the smallest of: a The amount on line 24; b $3,000 ($1,500 if married and filing a separate return); or c Taxable income, as adjusted	25	

Part IV **Computation of Post-1969 Capital Loss Carryovers from 1984 to 1985**
(Complete this part if the loss on line 24 is more than the loss on line 25)

26	Enter loss shown on line 8; if none, enter zero and skip lines 27 through 30, then go to line 31	26	
27	Enter gain shown on line 19. If that line is blank or shows a loss, enter zero	27	
28	Reduce any loss on line 26 to the extent of any gain on line 27	28	
29	Enter smaller of line 25 or line 28	29	
30	Subtract line 29 from line 28. This is your short-term capital loss carryover from 1984 to 1985	30	
31	Subtract line 29 from line 25. (Note: If you skipped lines 27 through 30, enter amount from line 25)	31	
32	Enter loss from line 19; if none, enter zero and skip lines 33 through 36	32	
33	Enter gain shown on line 8. If that line is blank or shows a loss, enter zero	33	
34	Reduce any loss on line 32 to the extent of any gain on line 33	34	
35	Multiply amount on line 31 by 2	35	
36	Subtract line 35 from line 34. This is your long-term capital loss carryover from 1984 to 1985	36	

Part V **Complete this Part Only If You Elect Out of the Installment Method and Report a Note or Other Obligation at Less Than Full Face Value**

☐ Check here if you elect out of the installment method.

Enter the face amount of the note or other obligation. ▶ ....

Enter the percentage of valuation of the note or other obligation. ▶

Part VI **Reconciliation of Forms 1099-B With Tax Return** (Complete this part if you received one or more Forms 1099-B or equivalent statement reporting sales of stock, bonds, etc. or bartering income.)

SECTION A.—Reconciliation of Sales of Stocks, Bonds, etc.

37	Total sales of stock, bonds, etc. from Forms 1099-B or equivalent statement received from your brokers	37	
38	Proceeds from sale or exchange of capital assets reported on Schedule D, but not included in line 37	38	
39	Add lines 37 and 38	39	
40	Part of line 37 not reported on Schedule D this year, attach explanation	40	
41	Subtract line 40 from line 39	41	

Note: *The amount on line 41 should be the same as the total of all amounts on page 1, lines 1 and 9 of column d.*

SECTION B.—Reconciliation of Bartering Income
Indicate below the amount of bartering income reported on each form or schedule

			Amount of bartering from Form 1099-B or equivalent statement
42	Form 1040, line 22	42	
43	Schedule C (Form 1040)	43	
44	Schedule D (Form 1040)	44	
45	Schedule E (Form 1040)	45	
46	Schedule F (Form 1040)	46	
47	Other (identify) (if not taxable, indicate reason—attach additional sheets if necessary) ▶	47	
48	Total (add lines 42 through 47)	48	

Note: *The amount on line 48 should be the same as the total bartering on all Forms 1099-B or equivalent statements received.*

☆ U.S. GOVERNMENT PRINTING OFFICE : 1984-423-091

FIGURE 11-6d

Form **4684** | Department of the Treasury Internal Revenue Service

Casualties and Thefts

▶ See separate instructions.
▶ To be filed with Form 1040, 1041, 1065, 1120, etc.
Use a separate Form 4684 for each different casualty or theft.

OMB No. 1545-0177
1984
26

Name(s) as shown on tax return: Jan Washington | Identifying Number: 222-33-4444

SECTION A.— Personal Use Property
*(Casualties and thefts to property that is **not** used in a trade or business or for income-producing purposes.)*

	Item or article	Item or article	Item or article	Item or article
1 (a) Kind of property and description	Diamond Ring			
(b) Date of purchase or acquisition	1975			
2 Cost or other basis of each item	6,200			
3 Insurance or other reimbursement you received or expect to receive for each item	0			
Note: *If line 2 is more than line 3, skip line 4* 4 Gain from casualty or theft. If line 3 is more than line 2, enter difference here and skip lines 5 through 13				
5 Fair market value before casualty or theft	6,200			
6 Fair market value after casualty or theft	0			
7 Subtract line 6 from line 5	6,200			
8 Enter smaller of line 2 or line 7	6,200			
9 Subtract line 3 from line 8	6,200			

10 Casualty or theft loss. Add amounts on line 9	6,200
11 Enter the amount from line 10 or $100, whichever is smaller	100
12 Subtract line 11 from line 10	6,100
Caution: *Use only one Form 4684 for lines 13 through 18.* 13 Add the line 12 amounts from all Forms 4684, Section A	6,100
14 Add the line 4 amounts from all Forms 4684, Section A	0
15 If line 14 is more than line 13, enter difference here and on Schedule D, and do not complete the rest of form. Otherwise, enter zero and complete lines 16 through 18 (see instructions). If line 14 is equal to line 13, do not complete the rest of form	0
16 If line 13 is more than line 14, enter difference	6,100
17 Enter 10% of adjusted gross income (Form 1040, line 33). Estates and trusts, See instructions	5,471
18 Subtract line 17 from line 16. If zero or less, enter zero. Enter on Schedule A(Form 1040), line 19. Estates and trusts, see instructions	629

For Paperwork Reduction Act Notice, see page 1 of separate instructions. Form **4684** (1984)

FIGURE 11-6e

Form **4684** (1984) 26 Page 2

Name(s) as shown on tax return (Do not enter name and identifying number if shown on other side)	Identifying Number
Jan Washington	222-33-4444

SECTION B.— Business and Income-Producing Property

*(Casualties and thefts to property that **is** used in a trade or business or for income-producing purposes.)*

PART I. Casualty or Theft Gain or Loss (Use a separate Part I for each different casualty or theft.)

	Item or article	Item or article	Item or article	Item or article
1 (a) Kind of property and description	Bus. Machine	Office Painting		
(b) Date of purchase or acquisition	3/1/79	5/1/73		
2 Cost or other basis of each item	$3,550	$1,300		
3 Insurance or other reimbursement you received or expect to receive for each item	3,200	2,100		
Note: *If line 2 is more than line 3, skip line 4*				
4 Gain from casualty or theft. If line 3 is more than line 2, enter difference here and on line 11 or 16, column C. However, see instructions for line 15. Also, skip lines 5 through 10		800		
5 Fair market value before casualty or theft	3,900			
6 Fair market value after casualty or theft	0			
7 Subtract line 6 from line 5	3,900			
8 Enter smaller of line 2 or line 7	3,550			
Note: *If the item was totally destroyed by a casualty, or lost from theft, enter on line 8, in each column, the amount from line 2.*				
9 Subtract line 3 from line 8	350			
10 Casualty or theft loss. Add amounts on line 9. Enter here and on line 11 or 16				350

PART II. Summary of Gains and Losses (From separate Parts I)

	(A) Identify casualty or theft	(B) Losses from casualties or thefts: (i) Trade, business, rental or royalty property	(B) Losses from casualties or thefts: (ii) Income-producing property	(C) Gains from casualties or thefts includible in income
	Casualty or Theft of Property Held One Year or Less (6 months if acquired after 6/22/84)			
11				
12	Totals. Add amounts on line 11 for each column			
13	Combine line 12, columns (B)(i) and (C). Enter the net gain or (loss) here and on Form 4797, Part II, line 9. (If Form 4797 is not otherwise required, see instructions.)			
14	Enter the amount from line 12, column (B)(ii) here and on line 19 of Schedule A (Form 1040). Partnerships, S Corporations, Estates and Trusts, see instructions			
	Casualty or Theft of Property Held More Than One Year (6 months if acquired after 6/22/84)			
15	Casualty or theft gains from Form 4797, Part III, line 28			0
16	From Line 4			800
	From Line 10	(350)		
17	Total losses. Add amounts on line 16, columns (B)(i) and (B)(ii)			
18	Total gains. Add lines 15 and 16, column (C)			800
19	Add amounts on line 17, columns (B)(i) and (B)(ii)			(350)
	Partnerships, enter the amount from line 20 or line 21 on your Schedule K-1, line 6. S Corporations, enter the amount from line 20 on your Schedule K-1, line 5.			
20	If the loss on line 19 is more than the gain on line 18:			
	(a) Combine line 17, column (B)(i) and line 18. Enter the net gain or (loss) here and on Form 4797, Part II, line 9. (If Form 4797 is not otherwise required, see instructions.)			
	(b) Enter the amount from line 17, column (B)(ii) here and on line 19 of Schedule A (Form 1040). Estates and Trusts, see instructions			
21	If the loss on line 19 is equal to or smaller than the gain on line 18, combine these lines and enter here and on Form 4797, Part I, line 2. (If Form 4797 is not otherwise required, see instructions.)			450

☆ U.S.GPO:1984-0-423-241 E.I.#430814328

FIGURE 11-6f

Form **4797**

Department of the Treasury
Internal Revenue Service (O)

Supplemental Schedule of Gains and Losses

(Includes Gains and Losses From Sales or Exchanges of Assets Used in a Trade or Business and Involuntary Conversions)

▶ **To be filed with Forms 1040, 1041, 1065, 1120S, 1120, etc.—See Separate Instructions**

OMB No. 1545-0184

1984

27

Name(s) as shown on return: Jan Washington

Identifying number: 222-33-4444

Part I **Sales or Exchanges of Property Used in a Trade or Business, and Involuntary Conversions From Other Than Casualty and Theft—Property Held More Than 1 Year (6 Months if Acquired After 6/22/84) (Except for Certain Livestock)**

Note: *Use Form 4684 to report involuntary conversions from casualty and theft.*

Caution: *If you sold property on which you claimed the investment credit, you may be liable for recapture of that credit. See Form 4255 for additional information.*

Note: *If you report a loss below and have amounts invested in the activity for which you are not at risk, you will have to file Form 6198. (See instructions under "Special Rules.")*

a. Description of property	**b.** Date acquired (mo., day, yr.)	**c.** Date sold (mo., day, yr.)	**d.** Gross sales price	**e.** Depreciation allowed (or allowable) since acquisition	**f.** Cost or other basis, plus improvements and expense of sale	**g.** LOSS (f minus the sum of d and e)	**h.** GAIN (d plus e minus f)
1							
½ Acre Land	1/4/76	7/12/84	8,000	—	9,400	1,400	
1 Acre Land	11/1/79	11/4/84	30,000	—	25,000		5,000

	g. LOSS	h. GAIN
2 Gain, if any, from Form 4684, Section B, line 21		450
3 Section 1231 gain from installment sales from Form 6252, line 22 or 30		
4 Gain, if any, on line 28 from other than casualty and theft		18,600
5 Add lines 1 through 4 in column g and column h	(1,400)	24,050
6 Combine columns g and h of line 5. Enter gain or (loss) here, and on the appropriate line as follows:		22,650

(a) For all except partnership returns:

(1) If line 6 is a gain, enter the gain as a long-term capital gain on Schedule D. See specific instructions for Part I.

(2) If line 6 is zero or a loss, enter that amount on line 7. (S corporations, enter on Schedule K (Form 1120S), line 6.)

(b) For partnership returns: Enter each partner's share of line 6 above, on Schedule K-1 (Form 1065), line 7.

Part II **Ordinary Gains and Losses**

a. Description of property	**b.** Date acquired (mo., day, yr.)	**c.** Date sold (mo., day, yr.)	**d.** Gross sales price	**e.** Depreciation allowed (or allowable) since acquisition	**f.** Cost or other basis, plus improvements and expense of sale	**g.** LOSS (f minus the sum of d and e)	**h.** GAIN (d plus e minus f)
7 Loss, if any, from line 6(a)(2)							
8 Gain, if any, on line 27							6,200
9 Net gain or (loss) from Form 4684, Section B, lines 13 and 20(a)							
10 Ordinary gain from installment sales from Form 6252, line 21 or 29 (Applies only to sales before 6/7/84)							
11 Recapture of section 179 deduction (see instructions)							
12 Other ordinary gains and losses (include property held 1 year or less, (6 months or less if acquired after 6/22/84)):							
Storage Building	6/18/83	6/2/84	50,000	1,850	52,000	150	
13 Add lines 7 through 12 in column g and column h						(150)	6,200

14 Combine columns g and h of line 13. Enter gain or (loss) here, and on the appropriate line as follows: 6,050

(a) For all except individual returns. Enter the gain or (loss) from line 14, on the return being filed. See instructions for Part II for specific line references.

(b) For individual returns:

(1) If the loss on line 7 includes a loss from Form 4684, Section B, Part II, column B(ii), enter that part of the loss here and on line 19 of Schedule A (Form 1040). Identify as from "Form 4797, line 14(b)(1)" . . . 0

(2) Redetermine the gain or (loss) on line 14, excluding the loss (if any) on line 14(b)(1). Enter here and on Form 1040, line 15 . . . 6,050

For Paperwork Reduction Act Notice, see page 1 of separate instructions. Form **4797** (1984)

FIGURE 11-6g

Form 4797 (1984) Page 2

Part III Gain From Disposition of Property Under Sections 1245, 1250, 1252, 1254, 1255

Skip section 1252 on line 23 and in the instructions, if you did not dispose of farmland, or if a partnership files this form.

15 Description of sections 1245, 1250, 1252, 1254, and 1255 property:	Date acquired (mo., day, yr.)	Date sold (mo., day, yr.)
(A) Auto Elevators	6/1/80	9/3/84
(B) Business Warehouse	11/1/79	11/4/84
(C)		
(D)		

Relate lines 15(A) through 15(D) to these columns ► ► ► ►	Property (A)	Property (B)	Property (C)	Property (D)
16 Gross sales price	9,600	70,000		
17 Cost or other basis plus expense of sale	9,000	60,000		
18 Depreciation (or depletion) allowed (or allowable)	2,200	12,000		
19 Adjusted basis, subtract line 18 from line 17	6,800	48,000		
20 Total gain, subtract line 19 from line 16	2,800	22,000		
21 **If section 1245 property:**				
(a) Depreciation allowed (or allowable) (see instructions)	2,200			
(b) Enter smaller of line 20 or 21(a)	2,200			
22 **If section 1250 property:** (If straight line depreciation used, enter zero on line 22(g) unless you are a corporation subject to section 291.)				
(a) Additional depreciation after 12/31/75		4,000		
(b) Applicable percentage times the smaller of line 20 or line 22(a) (see instructions). (100%)		4,000		
(c) Subtract line 22(a) from line 20. If line 20 is not more than line 22(a), skip lines 22(d) and 22(e)		18,000		
(d) Additional depreciation after 12/31/69 and before 1/1/76		0		
(e) Applicable percentage times the smaller of line 22(c) or 22(d) (see instructions)		0		
(f) Section 291 amount (For Corporations only.)		0		
(g) Add lines 22(b), 22(e), and 22(f)		4,000		
23 **If section 1252 property:**				
(a) Soil, water, and land clearing expenses				
(b) Line 23(a) times applicable percentage (see instructions)				
(c) Enter smaller of line 20 or 23(b)				
24 **If section 1254 property:**				
(a) Intangible drilling and development costs deducted after 12/31/75 (see instructions)				
(b) Enter smaller of line 20 or 24(a)				
25 **If section 1255 property:**				
(a) Applicable percentage of payments excluded from income under section 126 (see instructions)				
(b) Enter the smaller of line 20 or 25(a)				

Summary of Part III Gains (Complete Property columns (A) through (D) through line 25(b) before going to line 26)

26 Total gains for all properties (add columns (A) through (D), line 20)	24,800
27 Add columns (A) through (D), lines 21(b), 22(g), 23(c), 24(b), and 25(b). Enter here and on Part II, line 8	6,200
28 Subtract line 27 from line 26. Enter the portion from casualty and theft on Form 4684, Section B, line 15; enter the portion from other than casualty and theft on Form 4797, Part I, line 4	18,600

Part IV Complete this Part Only if You Elect Out of the Installment Method And Report a Note or Other Obligation at Less Than Full Face Value

☐ Check here if you elect out of the installment method.

Enter the face amount of the note or other obligation ►

Enter the percentage of valuation of the note or other obligation ►

U.S. GOVERNMENT PRINTING OFFICE 1984-423-247 (31-0598032)

should be noted that the tax forms generally follow the property transaction netting sequence (Figure 11-1) of casualties and thefts, Sec. 1231 transactions, capital transactions, and ordinary income. The mastery of the line-by-line details of Forms 4684 and 4797 is certainly secondary in importance to a basic understanding of the tax implications of sales or exchanges of business properties.

PLANNING WORKSHOP

TIMING OF SEC. 1231 TRANSACTIONS

A clear understanding of the Sec. 1231 nettings process provides some useful guides for planning dispositions of trade or business properties. A decision to sell a Sec. 1231 asset should be made only after considering other Sec. 1231 transactions recognized to date. For example, assume that near year-end a taxpayer is considering selling a Sec. 1231 asset at a $100,000 loss. Assume further that the taxpayer's other Sec. 1231 transactions for the year to date net to a $150,000 gain and that the taxpayer expects to be in the 50% tax bracket. Should the taxpayer complete the sale before year-end? The answer under normal circumstances would be no, because the $150,000 gain would be offset by the $100,000 loss. Thus, the $100,000 loss would offset a gain which otherwise would be subject to a maximum effective tax rate of only 20% (50% tax rate times only 40% of the Sec. 1231 gain, since the gain is treated as a long-term capital gain). If the taxpayer defers the loss transaction for a few days until the new tax year, the long-term capital-gains treatment will still be available for the $150,000 gain. Furthermore, the $100,000 loss could then be taken as an ordinary-loss deduction in the later year, since Sec. 1231 losses exceed Sec. 1231 gains. Thus, the loss would offset ordinary income subject to the maximum 50% rate.

The same logic would not necessarily work in the opposite situation, when a large Sec. 1231 loss is incurred in the earlier tax year. Recall that such losses are now subject to a 5-year recapture rule. Thus, the splitting of Sec. 1231 gains and losses into different tax years provides at best a one-year opportunity to sell the gain assets before the loss assets.

Additionally, the regular capital-gain-and-loss netting procedure should not be ignored when contemplating a Sec. 1231 transaction. For example, a taxpayer may not want to create a net Sec. 1231 gain in a year when he or she has large amounts of short-term capital gains and long-term capital losses. Using the long-term losses to offset short-term gains which are otherwise taxable as ordinary income provides the maximum tax benefit from such losses. A net Sec. 1231 gain would create long-term capital gains which would first be offset by the long-term losses.

Continued

PLANNING WORKSHOP

EVALUATING DEPRECIATION RECAPTURE

The initial study of depreciation recapture may give a reader the impression that it is "all bad" and is to be avoided at all costs. This is not necessarily the case; in fact, in most instances the recapture provisions provide an interest-free loan from the government to the taxpayer. After all, the amount being recaptured is at most an amount that was deducted years earlier. In the meantime, the taxpayer could invest the tax savings caused by the deductions. The amount recaptured is the amount that was deducted; there is no interest charge at the time of disposition of the property. Of course, there is some penalty if the taxpayer is in a higher tax bracket in the year of disposition as compared to the deduction years.

The preceding comments no longer apply to post-1980 acquisitions of commercial realty subject to an accelerated recovery. Congress has added a new wrinkle to tax planning for such assets by applying the Sec. 1245 recapture rules to dispositions of such realty. The key point to remember is that the Sec. 1245 rules do not apply if the taxpayer elects a straight-line cost recovery. In this case, the realty is once again considered to be Sec. 1250 property, which results in Sec. 1231 treatment for *any* gain recognized. This anomaly in classification leads to a much larger potential taxable gain at disposition if accelerated recovery methods are used. The dollar amount of gain will be larger because of the lower adjusted basis, but more importantly, the gain will be subject to ordinary tax rates, as opposed to potential long-term capital-gains rates through Sec. 1231 if straight-line recovery is elected.

The basic question to be answered when choosing a recovery method for commercial realty is this: Will the benefits from the time-value-of-money gained by accelerated deductions outweigh the potential additional tax costs of recapture on disposal of the property? Several variables must be considered when attempting to answer this question. These include projections of the marginal tax rate(s), holding period of the property, rate of return earned on the tax savings, potential disposal value, and method of disposition. A taxpayer using the realty in a trade or business may not intend to dispose of the property in the foreseeable future, and this factor alone may justify accelerated recovery. On the other hand, consider a syndicated partnership that owns an office building and leases it primarily to obtain the tax shelter benefits in the early years of ownership. Many of these partnerships sell the properties after short holding periods at relatively high disposal values, and the recapture potential for such a property may be large. One possible solution for the partnership would be to engage in a tax-free exchange (Chapter 12) for another property and begin the process all over again.

Continued

PLANNING WORKSHOP

However, the recapture potential of the old property carries over to the new property, and this "pyramiding" of tax-shelter investments will eventually lead to a final tax reckoning.

Taxpayers should also carefully evaluate the tax consequences of selling depreciation recapture properties on the installment basis. The requirement that all recapture income be recognized in the year of sale may create the wherewithal-to-pay problems that the installment method was designed to eliminate.

TAX ASPECTS OF SELLING A BUSINESS

In the sale of a going concern, the buyer and seller are usually attempting to achieve mutually exclusive tax objectives. A favorable tax treatment for the seller usually leads to an unfavorable tax result for the buyer, and vice versa. When a business is sold, the proceeds must be allocated to the various properties, which can include capital assets, ordinary assets, and Sec. 1231 assets. Once a total price is agreed upon, the tax objective of each party is obviously to maximize the favorable tax treatments.

For a seller, the tax objective is to allocate as much of the price as possible to goodwill, which receives capital-gains treatment. Of course, this amount is generally limited to the excess of the total purchase price over the fair market values of the individual assets. However, the seller should avoid any clause labeling a part of this goodwill as a covenant not to compete and having it taxed as ordinary income. A seller would also like to allocate as much of the price as possible to land or perhaps some buildings where recapture costs are minimal or nonexistent.

Usually for a buyer the tax objective is to allocate as much of the price as possible to assets subject to rapid cost recoveries, such as inventories and 3- and 5-year ACRS properties. If the total selling price exceeds the fair market values of the assets, the buyer may demand that a portion or all of the excess be labeled as an agreement not to compete, since this may be amortized over its useful life. However, the buyer must make sure that such a covenant is realistic and valuable; otherwise, it may be considered merely a part of goodwill.

KEY POINTS TO REMEMBER

1. Sec. 1231 applies to sales of properties used in a trade or business and involuntary conversions of either business or income-producing properties. In both cases, the property must have been held on a long-term basis. The term "properties used in a trade or business" also includes certain livestock, unharvested crops, timber, and coal and iron ore royalties.

2. Sec. 1231 provides a "best of both tax worlds" treatment for the net gain or loss from Sec. 1231 transactions incurred during the tax year. A net gain is treated as a long-term capital gain, and a net loss signifies ordinary loss treatment. Sec. 1231 gains include a net gain on business casualties and thefts.
3. Casualty and theft gains and losses on personal properties held on a long-term basis are netted separately. A net casualty and theft gain for the year is treated as a long-term capital gain, and a net casualty and theft loss for the year provides ordinary-loss treatment for the net loss, after reduction for 10% of AGI.
4. The year-end consolidation procedure for property transactions involves a sequential netting of casualty and theft, Sec. 1231, and capital transactions. A 5-column work sheet approach can be used to consolidate these transactions.
5. Sec. 1245 applies to dispositions of depreciable personalty held on a long-term basis and sold at a gain. Gain on the sale of such properties is ordinary income ("recaptured") to the extent of all depreciation allowed or allowable after 1961. Any excess gain is Sec. 1231 gain, because Sec. 1245 property fits the broader definition of Sec. 1231 property.
6. Sec. 1250 applies to dispositions of depreciable realty held on a long-term basis and sold at a gain. However, the provision only applies when an accelerated depreciation method is used which generates "excess depreciation" (amounts greater than straight-line).
7. Sec. 1250 recapture for properties acquired before 1981 is generally limited to a percentage of "excess depreciation," with residential properties held longer than 100 months possibly subject to less than 100% recapture. The same rules generally apply to post-1980 acquisitions of residential realty; however, post-1980 acquisitions of commercial realty are subject to Sec. 1245 recapture if accelerated recovery methods are used. This recapture can be avoided by electing straight-line recovery.
8. All Sec. 1231 assets are not necessarily either Sec. 1245 or Sec. 1250 properties. For example, land used in the business or any business asset sold at a loss may be Sec. 1231 properties and not depreciation-recapture properties.
9. The depreciation-recapture provisions override all other provisions of the Code. Recapture income must be recognized first in all taxable transactions.
10. To curb potential abuses by tax-shelter investors, the recapture concept was extended to certain expenses and losses of farm and oil and gas operations.
11. Over the years Congress has extended capital-asset treatment to several business-related assets if certain conditions are met. In the case of patents and franchises, capital-gains treatment is available if all substantial rights to the property are relinquished. For subdivided realty and securities owned by securities dealers, rules were established to separate personal and business transactions.

12. The sale of a business enterprise usually creates adversary tax positions between the buyer and the seller. This is especially true in the case of goodwill and covenants not to compete.
13. Form 4797 is used to report sales and exchanges of business properties and involuntary conversions of business and personal properties. A separate schedule, Form 4684, is used to report casualties and thefts.

SELF-STUDY QUESTIONS

1. The following assets were among those owned by Yolanda Corporation at December 31, 19X2:

Delivery truck	$12,000
Land used as a parking lot for customers	20,000

The capital assets amount to

a) $0

b) $12,000

c) $20,000

d) $32,000

(AICPA adapted)

2. Ben Green operates a parking lot that yielded net income of $13,000 during 19X1. The only other transactions that Mr. Green had during the year were a gain of $16,000 on the sale of some Westinghouse Corporation stock that he bought two years ago, a loss of $10,000 on the sale of one acre of the land used in his parking lot business, and a gain of $4,000 on the sale of one-half acre of the land used in his parking business. All of the land used in his parking lot operations was purchased seven years ago. Mr. Green's net gain from sale or exchange of capital assets for 19X1 would be

a) $8,000

b) $6,400

c) $4,800

d) $4,000

(AICPA adapted)

3. During the current year, a corporation retired obsolete equipment having an adjusted basis of $30,000 and sold it as scrap for $1,000. The only other transactions affecting taxable income resulted in $50,000 net income from operations. The taxable income of the corporation was

a) $21,000

b) $35,000

c) $47,000 with a capital loss carryover of $26,000

d) $50,000 with a capital loss carryover of $14,500

(AICPA adapted)

4. Gelinda Shane incurred the following transactions in 19X5:

   $4,000 personal casualty loss on an asset held on a long-term basis
   $5,500 personal casualty gain on an asset held on a long-term basis
   $3,200 business casualty loss on an asset held on a long-term basis

   These transactions will be reported on Shane's 19X5 tax return as

   a) $1,700 ordinary loss deductions

   b) $7,200 ordinary loss deductions and $5,500 long-term capital gain

   c) $3,200 ordinary loss deductions and $1,500 long-term capital gain

   d) $1,700 Sec. 1231 gain

5. Wayne Sharp's only Sec. 1231 transaction in 19X6 resulted in a $15,000 gain. His only other Sec. 1231 transactions in the last eight years were a $5,000 net Sec. 1231 gain in 19X3 and an $8,000 net Sec. 1231 loss in 19X4. Sharp will report the 19X6 gain as

   a) $15,000 ordinary income

   b) $8,000 ordinary income and $7,000 long-term capital gain

   c) $3,000 ordinary income and $12,000 long-term capital gain

   d) $15,000 long-term capital gain

6. Arch Corp. sold machinery for $80,000 on December 31, 19X3. This machinery was purchased on January 2, 19W9, for $68,000, and had an adjusted basis of $40,000 on the date of sale. For 19X3 Arch should report

   a) ordinary income of $12,000 and Section 1231 gain of $28,000

   b ordinary income of $28,000 and Section 1231 gain of $12,000

   c) ordinary income of $40,000

   d) Section 1231 gain of $40,000

   (AICPA adapted)

7. Thayer Corporation purchased an apartment building on January 1, 19X6, for $200,000. The building was depreciated on the straight-line basis. On December 31, 19X9, the building was sold for $220,000, when the asset balance net of accumulated depreciation was $170,000. On its 19X9 tax return, Thayer should report

   a) Section 1231 gain of $20,000 and ordinary income of $30,000

   b) Section 1231 gain of $30,000 and ordinary income of $20,000

   c) ordinary income of $50,000

   d) Section 1231 gain of $50,000

   (AICPA adapted)

8. Soft Cream sells franchises to independent operators. In 19X2 it sold a franchise to Edward Trent, charging an initial fee of $20,000 and a monthly fee of 2% of sales. Soft Cream retains the right to control such matters as employee and management training, quality control and promotion, and the purchase of ingredients. Mr. Trent's 19X2

sales amounted to $200,000. From the transactions with Trent, Soft Cream, an accrual basis taxpayer, would include in its computation of 19X2 taxable income

a) long-term capital gain of $24,000

b) long-term capital gain of $20,000, ordinary income of $4,000

c) long-term capital gain of $4,000, ordinary income of $20,000

d) ordinary income of $24,000

(AICPA adapted)

9. Don Mott was the sole proprietor of a high-volume drug store which he owned for 15 years before he sold it to Dale Drug Stores, Inc., in 19X2. Besides the $900,000 selling price for the store's tangible assets and goodwill, Mott received a lump sum of $30,000 in 19X2 for his agreement not to operate a competing enterprise within ten miles of the store's location, for a period of six years. The $30,000 will be taxed to Mott as

a) $30,000 ordinary income in 19X2

b) $30,000 short-term capital gain in 19X2

c) $30,000 long-term capital gain in 19X2

d) ordinary income of $5,000 a year for six years

(AICPA adapted)

10. Mr. Beth, a sole proprietor on the accrual basis, prepared the following balance sheet for his business on December 15, 19X4:

ASSETS		
Accounts receivable		$ 8,000
Inventory		14,000
Equipment (purchased in 19W4)	$40,000	
Accumulated depreciation	30,000	
		10,000
Goodwill (tax basis)		15,000
		$47,000
CAPITAL		
Beth, capital		$47,000

On December 15, 19X4, Mr. Beth sold this business. The allocation of the selling price of $63,000 was stipulated in the sales agreement as follows:

Accounts receivable	$ 8,000
Inventory	17,000
Equipment	16,000
Goodwill	22,000
Total selling price	$63,000

How should this sale be reported in Mr. Beth's 19X4 individual tax return? The long-term capital gain deduction, if any, should be ignored.

a) zero long-term capital gain and $16,000 ordinary income

b) zero ordinary income and $16,000 long-term capital gain

c) $3,000 ordinary income and $13,000 long-term capital gain

d) $9,000 ordinary income and $7,000 long-term capital gain

(AICPA adapted)

QUESTIONS

1. It is often said that Sec. 1231 confers the "best of both tax worlds" to sales or exchanges of business properties. Explain.

2. Blake Corporation owns three acres of land. On 12/14/X3, this land was sold at a gain of $15,000. How would this gain be taxed, assuming:
   a) the land was purchased in 19X0 and was used as the location for the manufacturing operation;
   b) the land was purchased in 19X1 and was held as an investment for speculative purposes;
   c) the land was purchased in 19X0 and was held for resale to customers in the ordinary course of business (land sales);
   d) the land was purchased on 1/12/X3 and was used as the location of a factory (which was subsequently sold with the land).

3. During 19X3 Sara Tennyson incurred a $14,000 uninsured loss on the theft of an engagement ring and a $2,500 gain on the excess of insurance proceeds over cost from the destruction of her personal residence. How will these transactions be reported on her 19X3 tax return? Assume that Sara's 19X3 AGI is $40,000.

4. "To the extent feasible, a taxpayer should attempt to recognize Sec. 1231 gains in a tax year different from the year used to recognize Sec. 1231 losses." Do you agree? Explain.

5. Explain the purpose of the depreciation recapture provisions. Do the recapture provisions create taxable gain in situations where a gain would otherwise not be recognized? Explain.

6. Marvin Linhart owns 90% of the outstanding stock of M Corporation. During the current year Marvin sold a machine to M Corporation for $35,000. Marvin purchased the machine four years ago for $28,000 and had deducted $6,000 of depreciation as of the date of sale. How will Marvin report this transaction on his current year tax return?

7. "All Sec. 1245 and Sec. 1250 properties are Sec. 1231 properties, but all Sec. 1231 properties are not necessarily either Sec. 1245 or Sec. 1250 properties." Do you agree? Explain.

8. Distinguish the maximum depreciation recapture potential between (a) residential realty acquired before 1981 and residential realty acquired after 1980, and (b) commercial realty acquired before 1981 and commercial realty acquired after 1980.
9. Is depreciation recapture on the sale of commercial realty acquired after 1980 calculated in the same manner as Sec. 1245 recapture when accelerated cost recovery is used? Would your answer be different if straight-line recovery is used? Discuss.
10. For corporate taxpayers, the use of straight-line depreciation on business realty no longer guarantees Sec. 1231 treatment for the total gain on a disposition of the property. Explain.
11. Ellen Goodman contributes a machine used in her business to charity. Is it possible for the machine to be both "ordinary-income property" and "capital-gains property" for purposes of determining the maximum charitable deduction? Explain.
12. When will a purported sale of a patent, franchise, trademark, or trade name not be recognized as a sale or exchange for tax purposes? Give an example.
13. Sec. 1237 provides three possible tax implications for nondealer sales of subdivided realty. Describe the circumstances in which a noncorporate taxpayer may be taxed as (*a*) an investor selling an investment asset, (*b*) a real estate broker selling a "listed property," and (*c*) a real estate dealer selling a property held for resale in the ordinary course of business.
14. Why is it necessary to have a special tax rule for the personal securities holdings of a securities dealer? How was this rule modified by the Economic Recovery Tax Act of 1981?
15. Why is the IRS usually willing to accept the allocation of total sales price specified in a contract for the sale of a business enterprise? What factors may cause the IRS not to accept this allocation?
16. Over the years, Sec. 1231 has been expanded to cover a variety of properties other than simply those used productively in a trade or business. Give some examples of these properties.
17. A taxpayer is considering two year-end sales of land used in her business. One will generate a gain of $60,000, and the other will generate a loss of $50,000. How and when would you suggest that she realize these two transactions for tax purposes? Explain.
18. "The special Sec. 1231 loss recapture rules are similar to the depreciation recapture rules." Do you agree? Explain.
19. Bill Moss purchased a new business typewriter in 1982 for $4,800, and he elected to expense the entire cost under Sec. 179. Assuming that Moss sells the typewriter in 1984 for $2,400, how will he report this transaction on his 1984 tax return?

20. Explain the tax consequences of selling depreciation recapture properties on an installment basis after June 6, 1984.
21. What factors indicate that the transfer of a franchise is a leasing arrangement, rather than a sale or exchange of a capital asset?
22. Explain the tax treatment of payments received for (a) goodwill and (b) a covenant not to compete.

PROBLEMS

1. Which of the following properties would be classified as Sec. 1231 properties (ignore depreciation-recapture possibilities):
   a) a plating machine used in the business (held for three years);
   b) a 15% stock interest in B Corporation (held by C Corporation as a speculative investment);
   c) an office desk used in the business (held for four months);
   d) a personal automobile (owned for 3 years) which is destroyed by fire (the insurance proceeds exceeded the adjusted basis of the automobile);
   e) farm land which is sold together with an unharvested crop during the current year (held for four years);
   f) cattle held for breeding purposes (owned for 18 months);
   g) timber cut but unsold at the end of the tax year (held for 20 years).
2. During 19X3 Max Erman's business truck was destroyed by a fire. The truck had a tax basis of $5,800 in 19X1 and Max received $4,200 of insurance proceeds from the accident. Max's business warehouse was also destroyed by a storm in 19X3. The warehouse, acquired in 19X0, had an adjusted basis of $32,000. Max received $38,000 of insurance proceeds as compensation for the destruction. The warehouse was depreciated using the straight-line method, so there is no recapture.
   a) How will these transactions be reported on Max's 19X3 return?
   b) Would your answer to (a) be different if the $38,000 was a condemnation award from the city under the right of eminent domain, rather than from a storm?
3. Determine the final ordinary-income tax result of the following 19X3 transactions of Wanda Jones, whose only other income was $40,000 from a sole-proprietorship business:
   a) sale of a business copier (held five months) at a $100 gain;
   b) sale of a business plating machine (held four years) at a $3,200 loss;
   c) uninsured theft loss of $8,000 on a diamond watch purchased six years ago;
   d) sale of a rental building (held 11 years) at a $1,000 gain (straight-line depreciation had been used);

e) sale of 40 shares of IBM stock held for three years as an investment for $2,000 gain.

4. Refer to Problem 3. Assume that Wanda had one additional transaction in 19X3, a $12,000 gain from the excess of insurance proceeds over the adjusted basis of a personal boat (acquired in 19X0) which was destroyed by a tornado. Redetermine the final ordinary-income tax result for these transactions.

5. John Cello is in a 45% marginal-income-tax bracket. During 19X3 he sold a business building at a gain of $60,000. The building was acquired in 19X0, and straight-line depreciation was used. This is his only property transaction realized to date. John is considering selling another business building (acquired six years ago) before the end of 19X3. This sale would generate a $90,000 loss. Should Cello make this sale before the end of 19X3 or wait until 19X4? Explain.

6. Ann McCain acquired a personal computer to use in her business for $6,000 on 1/2/X2. She took ACRS deductions of $900, $1,320, and $1,260 during 19X2, 19X3, and 19X4, respectively, and then sold the computer on 1/4/X5. Determine the amount and character of the gain (loss) recognized on the sale of the computer, assuming a sales price of:
   a) $2,400,
   b) $6,350,
   c) $4,600.

7. John Regal invested in a new residential apartment building on 1/3/74. The building cost $200,000, and Regal elected to use double-declining balance depreciation based on a 40-year life. As of 1/4/84, a total of $80,252 depreciation had been deducted (including $19,500 before 1976). On 1/4/84 Regal sold the apartment building for $168,000.
   a) Determine the amount and character of the recognized gain (loss) to Regal from the sale of the apartment building.
   b) How would your answer change if the building was used as Regal's business headquarters (commercial realty)?

8. Determine the final ordinary-income result for the following transactions of Meagan Ferraro, whose only other 19X6 income was a $32,000 salary:
   a) an uninsured theft loss of $8,300 on her personal automobile which was acquired 12 years ago;
   b) a sale of 50 shares of Jeb Co. common stock (held 14 years) at a $10,000 gain;
   c) a receipt of $6,000 on an insured personal boat which was destroyed by fire (the boat was acquired four years ago for $3,000).

9. Assume the same facts as in Problem 8, except that the insurance proceeds on the boat were $14,000. Determine the final 19X6 ordinary-income result.

10. Linda Stosch acquired a business machine on 2/12/X3 for $50,000. The machine was subject to ACRS recovery deductions of $7,500 in 19X3, $11,000 in 19X4, and $10,500 in 19X5. On 1/8/X6, the machine had a fair market value of $35,000. Determine the income tax consequences of the following possible dispositions of the machine:

    a) Linda sells the machine on 1/8/X6 for $35,000;

    b) Linda contributes the machine to a local university;

    c) Linda exchanges the machine for a new machine worth $33,000 and also receives $2,000 cash.

11. *a*) Craig Thomas purchased 200 acres of farm land for $60,000 on March 3, 19W5. During July of 19W5 Craig spent $20,000 for the necessary expenses of clearing the land and $5,200 for soil-conservation purposes. Craig sold the land on November 16, 19X3 for $78,000. Determine the amount and character of the taxable gain (loss) reported by Craig on his 19X3 tax return.

    b) Paul Martinez, an oil and gas operator, acquired Blackacre property in April 19X3 for $30,000. Paul deducted $9,000 of intangible drilling costs in 19X3. Paul sells the property in May 19X7 for $34,000. The adjusted basis in the property at that time was $24,000. How much (if any) of the $10,000 realized gain will be taxed as ordinary income, assuming that the cost depletion allowable on the drilling costs would have been $3,500?

12. Kathryn Taylor has a cost basis of $8,000 in a patent for a new duplicating process which she developed. In 19X4 Kathryn entered into an agreement with Ocra Corporation to transfer an interest in the patent for $100,000 cash. Ocra Corporation had the right to use the patent for the remainder of its useful life of 10 years; however, Ocra's interest in the patent was a nonexclusive one in that Kathryn reserved the right to create additional interests by making additional future assignments after an initial 3-year period. How will the $100,000 payment be taxed to Kathryn in 19X4? Discuss.

13. For each of the following situations determine the character of the realized gain (loss). Treat each item independently, assuming that each is the only property transaction of the taxpayer during the tax year:

    a) Belinda Bell sells rights to use her patent (acquired seven years ago) for a metal plating system to Zeno Corporation. Zeno is granted an exclusive right to use the patent in a 12-state area of the southeastern United States.

    b) Marvin Hamilton sold the copyright on the musical score for a new Broadway play which he had written.

    c) Ralph Morgan's personal residence is condemned by the city and he is forced to sell the residence to the city at a $6,000 loss.

    d) Marian Onansan, a registered securities dealer, sells 80 shares of IBM stock at a $4,000 gain on 3/1/X4. Marian had purchased the shares on 4/2/X2 and identified them as a personal investment on the date of purchase.

e) Christine Sieller developed and registered a trademark for a new diet soft drink. She sold the trademark to Kola Corporation for an $80,000 gain. Kola has an exclusive right to use the trademark in the future.

f) Sam Maxwell developed a special chicken recipe in 19X8 and immediately began selling franchise restaurant agreements. The agreement grants the purchaser an exclusive right to sell the product in a 50-mile radius, as long as the purchaser agees to allow Sam to control advertising, supplies, and product quality.

g) Susan Beale sold her sole proprietorship business in 19X3, with the total sales price allocated as follows:

	BASIS	SALES PRICE
Accounts receivable	$20,000	$ 20,000
Inventory	82,000	122,000
Machinery*	34,000	62,000
Building†	92,000	106,000
Land	80,000	150,000
Goodwill	-0-	40,000
Covenant not to compete	—	25,000

*$90,000 cost less $56,000 accumulated depreciation.
†$140,000 cost less $48,000 accumulated (straight-line) depreciation.

14. Richard Egan purchased 10 acres of land for $82,000 in 19X0 as an investment. In 19X6, Richard divides the land into 10 1-acre plots and offers them for sale. The land is divided and numbered as follows:

1	3	5	7	9
2	4	6	8	10

Determine the tax consequences to Egan of the following sales:

a) Plots 1, 2, and 8 are sold to Galvin in 19X6 for $36,000. No selling expenses were incurred.

b) In 19X7 plots 3 and 4 are sold to Conrad, plot 5 to Deacon, plot 6 to Eagleton, and plot 7 to Eggersman. The selling price of each lot was $14,000 and $800 selling expense was incurred on each lot sale.

c) Plots 9 and 10 were sold in 19X8 to Davis for $15,000 each, less selling expenses of $800 for each lot.

d) Would your answer to (c) change if Conrad had spent $4,500 in 19X7 to install city water, sewage, and street lights in order to make lots 9 and 10 easier to sell?

15. The following is a summary of transactions of four different individual taxpayers:

	ALTON	BENDER	CAUTHEN	DRESDEN
Regular income	$60,000	$50,000	$60,000	$40,000
Sec. 1231 gains	8,000	10,000	12,000	5,000
Sec. 1231 losses	(12,000)	(3,000)	(15,000)	(2,000)
Sec. 1245 gains	6,000	-0-	3,000	-0-
Sec. 1250 gains	5,000	1,000	-0-	4,000
Short-term capital gains	4,000	1,000	2,000	3,000
Short-term capital losses	-0-	(3,000)	(3,000)	-0-
Casualty gains (business)	6,000	-0-	9,000	-0-
Casualty losses (business)	(4,000)	(8,000)	(2,000)	(3,000)
Long-term capital gains	3,000	2,000	4,000	8,000
Long-term capital losses	(1,000)	(7,000)	(5,000)	(14,000)
Casualty gains (personal)	2,000	-0-	4,000	8,000
Casualty losses (personal)	-0-	-0-	(13,000)	(2,000)

For each taxpayer, determine the correct adjusted gross income, after reflecting all property transactions, capital-loss deductions, and/or capital-gain deductions. Also determine the amount and character (short-term or long-term) of any capital-loss carryover, if applicable. Treat each case independently and assume that all casualties are before any floor reductions.

16. Allen Parker (single, age 34) is the sole proprietor-owner of Parker Manufacturing. During 1984 Parker had $65,000 of net income from normal business operations and incurred the following property transactions:

    a) Sold 100 shares of Rayburn Corporation stock on 1/15/84 for $18,000. The stock was originally acquired as a gift from Parker's mother in 1978. His mother had paid $6,000 for the shares, and the stock was worth $9,000 at the time of the gift.

    b) Sold three typewriters used in the business on 2/16/84 for $1,600. The typewriters were originally purchased in 1981 for $3,000 and $2,100 of straight-line depreciation had been taken.

    c) Sold a word processor used in the business on 3/18/84 for $5,400. The word processor had been originally purchased on 2/3/82 for $4,900, and a total of $1,950 of depreciation (ACRS) had been deducted.

    d) Sold the old factory location on 6/15/84 for a total of $180,000, allocated $50,000 to the land and $130,000 to the building. The factory had been acquired in 1974 for $120,000 ($20,000 allocated to the land), and a total of $38,000 depreciation had been taken on the building (straight-line depreciation would have been $25,000).

e) Parker's business warehouse was totally demolished in an accident on 8/4/84. The warehouse was purchased for $62,000 in 1981, and a total of $15,000 straight-line recovery deductions had been taken up to the date of destruction. Parker received $52,000 insurance compensation for the destruction and chooses not to replace the warehouse.

Determine the final effect of these transactions on Parker's 1984 taxable income.

17. June Taylor's 19X8 Sec. 1231 transactions netted to a $13,000 gain. Her only other Sec. 1231 transactions in recent years include a $5,000 net Sec. 1231 loss in 19X4, a $4,000 net Sec. 1231 gain in 19X6, and a $9,000 net Sec. 1231 loss in 19X7. How will Taylor report the $13,000 gain recognized in 19X8?

18. Z Corporation owns a business warehouse which was purchased on 1/1/80 for $90,000. The building was sold for $80,000 on 1/3/85, at a time when its adjusted basis was $68,000 (straight-line recovery). How will Z Corporation report this transaction on its 1985 tax return?

19. George Melton sold a business machine on 6/1/85 for $30,000. He received a $6,000 down payment and an installment note which provided for four additional installments of $6,000 plus 12% interest on the unpaid balance, beginning on 6/1/86. The machine was originally acquired on 3/1/80 for $24,000, and a total of $9,000 depreciation had been allowed on the asset. What is the amount and character of the taxable gain reportable by Melton in (a) 1985? (b) 1986?

20. Gene Stallings purchased a business machine on 9/1/81 for $12,000, and he elected to immediately expense the first $5,000 of the cost, as permitted by Sec. 179. Stallings elected ACRS recovery for the remaining portion of the cost. If Stallings sells the machine on 1/1/85 for $8,200, what is the amount and character of the recognized gain or loss?

TAX PLANNING PROBLEMS

1. Brenda Collier, a self-employed parking lot operator, comes to you for tax advice near the end of 19X6. Her regular business income usually keeps her in a constant 50% tax bracket, and she can earn an after-tax rate of return of 10% on any idle cash funds. She is considering the sale of two parcels of land used in her business. Parcel A was purchased for $40,000 in 19X2, and can now be sold for $70,000. Parcel B was purchased in 19X3 for $55,000, and can now be sold for $35,000. She asks for your advice as to the timing of the two sales. Compare the net present values of the projected tax liabilities of four possible timing sequences: (1) both properties are sold in 19X6; (2) parcel A is sold in 19X6 and parcel B is sold in 19X7; (3) parcel B is sold in 19X6 and parcel A is sold in 19X7; (4) both parcels are sold in 19X7. Assume

that the 19X7 tax payments will be made one year later than the 19X6 payments.

2. John Anson purchased a new office building on 1/2/85 for $200,000. The building will be used to house the administrative functions of his construction business. John asks for your assistance in deciding which cost recovery method to use for the property. Specifically, John asks if the tax dollars he could save and invest by electing ACRS (instead of straight-line recovery) would equal or exceed the additional tax costs from recapture if he sold the building in January 1991 for approximately $190,000. John's marginal-income-tax rate for all tax years is expected to be 50%, and John can invest the ACRS tax savings in a nontaxable municipal fund paying 10% interest (compounded annually).
   - *a*) Determine the total projected tax savings plus interest (from the excess ACRS deductions) accumulated by January 1, 1991. Assume that the tax savings occur at the end of the tax year. For example, the tax savings in 1985 would be $4,000—($18,000 ACRS deduction less $10,000 straight-line recovery) × .50 tax bracket. This $8,000 savings, caused by electing ACRS recovery, will be invested at the end of 1985 and earn a nontaxable 10% interest return compounded annually for the years 1986 through 1990. Similarly, the 1986 tax savings will earn interest for the years 1987 through 1990.
   - *b*) Compute the additional tax liability on disposition in January 1991 caused by the ACRS election by computing (1) the tax due on the total gain if ACRS is elected and (2) the tax due on the total gain if straight-line recovery is elected. (Note—the different recovery methods will create different adjusted bases as of January 1991.)
   - *c*) Would you advise Anson to use ACRS or straight-line recovery? Explain. (NOTE: Refer to Table 8-5 on pp. 8/12–13. for ACRS and straight-line recovery factors.)

CASE PROBLEM

Ralph and Joan Nicholson (both age 38) are married taxpayers who will file a joint return in 1985. Ralph is a salaried outside salesman who earned $42,000 in 1985, of which $18,000 was withheld in federal income taxes and $1,400 in state income taxes. Ralph incurred $400 of entertainment expenses in 1985 which were not reimbursed by his employer.

Joan owns and operates a plumbing repair business. During 1985, her net operating business income was $54,000, before considering the following transactions:

- *a*) On 1/8/85, Joan sold a business machine for $9,000. The machine was originally purchased on 2/3/80 for $12,000, and a total of $4,500 depreciation was taken on the machine.

b) On 3/4/85, Joan sold a business warehouse and one-half acre of land. The warehouse was originally acquired on 6/1/80 for $80,000 ($20,000 allocable to the land), and was sold for $105,000 ($30,000 allocable to the land). Total depreciation allowed on the building was $22,000 using an accelerated method; straight-line depreciation would have been $17,000.

c) On 6/3/85, another acre of business land was sold for $4,000. The land was originally acquired on 1/1/80 for $10,500.

d) On 8/4/85, a storm totally destroyed an uninsured delivery truck used in Joan's business. The truck was originally acquired on 6/1/80 for $9,000, and had an adjusted basis of $1,200 at the time of the accident. The same storm also damaged the Nicholsons' personal residence. Only $4,000 insurance was recovered for a loss calculated to be $18,500.

The Nicholsons' only other source of income in 1985 was $15,000 from the sale of 80 share of ABC stock on 12/1/85 (the stock was originally acquired on 2/1/80 for $27,000). The Nicholsons also have an unused $3,500 short-term capital loss carryover from 1984. Their 1985 legitimate deductions include $2,600 of state and local taxes (other than the withholdings of state income tax), $3,000 of unreimbursed physician charges, $4,000 of personal interest, and $3,200 of contributions to qualified charities.

Compute the Nicholsons' final 1985 tax liability (or refund due). Assume that Joan made $18,000 of estimated income tax payments on her 1985 business income, and that the gross income tax liability must be increased for $4,673 of self-employment taxes on Joan's business income.

RESEARCH PROBLEMS

1. Elizabeth Boynton, an authorized automobile dealer, has four types of automobiles on her lot: new cars for sale, used cars for sale, demonstrators (which are usually sold eventually), and loaners (which are used for errands, loans to customers, and/or courtesy loans to the local college). Will any of the cars qualify as Sec. 1231 assets? Explain.

2. In 19X4 Bill Baxter contributed $10,000 cash to a local university. Two days later, the university purchased a microcomputer from Baxter for $10,000. The computer, originally purchased in 19X1 for use in Baxter's business, had cost $15,000 and had an adjusted basis of $6,000 on the date of sale. The fair market value of the computer on the date of sale was $10,000. Can Baxter deduct the entire $10,000 as a charitable contribution in 19X4? Explain.

Chapter Objectives

1. Describe the basis rules for like-kind exchanges and how these rules defer the gain or loss realized.
2. Identify the properties that qualify as like-kind for purposes of gain and loss deferral.
3. Explain the effects of including cash "boot" in like-kind exchanges and its effects on basis.
4. Explain the recognition of gain or loss when noncash "boot" is used.
5. Describe how gains (but not losses) are deferred when property that is converted involuntarily is replaced by qualified property.
6. Explain the meaning of "qualified replacement property" in involuntary conversions and the time available for replacement.
7. Calculate the gain recognized, if any, upon the sale of a personal residence when the residence is replaced on a timely basis.
8. Explain when a taxpayer's gain from the sale of his or her personal residence is excluded from gross income.
9. Introduce other nontaxable exchanges that are included in the statute.
10. List other nontaxable exchanges commonly encountered.

12 Nontaxable Exchanges

A taxpayer who *sells* property generally recognizes the resulting gain or loss in the year of the sale. Chapter 10 sets out the rules related to sales of investment property; Chapter 11 treats the added complications that arise when business property is sold.

Note carefully that the rules in Chapters 10 and 11 assume that the disposition of the property takes the form of a sale, a transaction in which the seller receives cash or a near-cash asset in exchange for the property. Under these circumstances, resulting gain or loss is currently recognized because the transaction is complete and the taxpayer has the cash (wherewithal) to pay the tax. The same is not true in many instances where the taxpayer *exchanges* one noncash property for another, and thus the law provides for the nonrecognition and/or deferral of gain or loss for numerous exchanges.

> **Example 1:** T owns an unimproved building lot that cost him \$25,000 several years ago. If T sells the lot for \$40,000 cash, the \$15,000 gain is recognized currently (and taxed according to the rules in Chapters 10 and 11). However, if T trades his lot for other real property, the gain may be deferred under the rules explained in this chapter.

Generally the law provides for deferral of gain or loss on exchanges only if: (*a*) the taxpayer has a continuing investment in comparable property; and (*b*) the exchange produces no cash or near-cash asset that can be used to pay the tax. Usually, when these two conditions are met, an exchange is a *nontaxable* exchange.

Nontaxable exchanges covered below are "like-kind" exchanges, involuntary conversions of property through casualties and condemnations, and sale and replacement of a personal residence.

BACKGROUND

Most of the nontaxable exchanges discussed in this chapter have been included in the law since 1921. The conceptual predecessor of these rules is the Supreme Court's decision in *Eisner* v. *Macomber*.* That decision held that the fair market value (FMV) of stock received as a dividend on stock could not be taxable gross income based on the rationale that the taxpayers' continuing investment in the declaring corporation remained unchanged. The income or gain from the stock dividend is not realized or severed from the underlying asset until the stock is sold.

The like-kind rules were added at a time (1921) when barter transactions were much more common than today when elaborate market systems exist for just about everything. In the 1920s, "horse" power was still the common means of locomotion for most of the U.S., and horse and mule trading was a way of life. The fair administration of the income tax law would have been difficult given the volume of barter transactions.†

Some terminology used to describe these nontaxable barter transactions originates from the horse-trading era. The word "boot" which is used later in the text is an example and refers to the other property, usually cash, that one party to an exchange must put up "to boot" to even out the values.

The impetus for the addition of the provisions deferring gains on involuntary conversion, also added in 1921, was World War I.‡ Many taxpayers engaged in the shipping trade lost substantial properties during the war either through requisition by the U.S. government or enemy actions. The tax logic of involuntary conversions was extended to sales of personal residences in 1951 to encourage home ownership.

---

*252 U.S. 189 (1920).

†See Boris I. Bittker, *Federal Taxation of Income, Estates, and Gifts*, Volume II (Boston: Warren, Gorham & Lamont, 1981) pp. 44-8 and 44-9.

‡*Ibid*. p. 44-3.1.

Section 1031 of the IRC provides for the following results when a taxpayer exchanges property *solely* for property of a like kind:

- No gain or loss is recognized.
- The adjusted bases of the property received in the exchange is the same as the old property exchanged.
- The holding period of the new property is the same as that of the old property.[1]

The above result is obtained only if there is a qualified exchange and no ***boot*** is included in the exchange. As will be explained later, the inclusion of nonqualifying property (boot) in the exchange can result in the recognition of gain and necessitate an adjustment to the basis of the new property.

BOOT Property, usually cash, added to the consideration by one party in a barter or exchange transaction. The boot is added to the trade to equalize the values exchanged.

Example 2: T owns an undeveloped lot that cost $75,000 when acquired on July 1, 19X1. On October 1, 19X3 T exchanges the lot for a rental house that has a fair market value of $110,000. The two properties meet the like-kind definition. T's gain of $35,000 is not recognized. The basis of the rental house is $75,000 and its acquisition date is that of the unimproved lot, July 1, 19X1.

Application of the like-kind rules to an exchange only results in a deferral of the gain or loss not recognized. The substitution of the basis of the "old" property as the basis for the "new" property accomplishes this deferral or postponement.

Example 3: In January 19X4 T sells the rental property received in Example 2. T realizes in cash the fair market value (FMV) of $110,000. Since the basis is only $75,000 (that of the old property), the gain of $35,000 is now recognized. This example assumes that no depreciation is deducted on the rental property in the interim.

Nonrecognition applies to both gains and losses. Taxpayers holding property which has depreciated in value significantly will usually avoid like-kind exchanges and opt for a sale. The cash proceeds from the sale can then be used to acquire the desired property.

Example 4: T acquired for investment a lot in Aspen, Colorado for $50,000. She acquired the property in 19X1 at the height of a real estate bubble. In 19X3, when the above lot is worth $40,000, she decides to dispose of the Aspen property and acquire investment

[1]Sec. 1223(1).

property in New Mexico. If T wishes to recognize her loss, she will avoid an exchange, sell the Colorado property, and then purchase the new property.

DEFINITION OF LIKE-KIND PROPERTY

The term "like kind" as used in Section 1031 refers to the nature of property and not to its quality or grade.[2] Liberal court interpretations have held that real property is "like" other real property and personal property is like personal property. The statute further restricts the definition to property that is either held as an investment or used in a trade or business and specifically excludes from this latter category property that is either inventory or securities.[3] Thus, property held for personal use and enjoyment cannot be ***like-kind property***.

LIKE-KIND PROPERTY For purposes of tax-free like-kind exchanges, personal property is like personal property and real property is like real property, provided the property is used in a trade or business, or is held for investment. Property held as inventory and corporate securities can never be like-kind property.

The nontaxable exchange rules apply only if the properties exchanged meet the following two tests:

1. The exchange is of real estate for real estate, or of personal property for personal property; and,
2. The properties exchanged are either held for investment or for use in a business, excepting inventory items and corporate securities.

The exception for inventories prevents nonrecognition when merchants swap items held for resale. The exception for corporate securities prevents nonrecognition from "barter" exchanges which would otherwise replace cash transactions in our securities markets.

Example 5: T owns an apartment house that he wishes to exchange for unimproved farm land. This exchange of real estate for real estate qualifies despite the difference in quality or grade (improved for unimproved). The fact that the apartment rentals constitute an active business while the unimproved land is held as a passive investment is of no consequence.

Example 6: T, engaged in the manufacture of widgets and didgets, wishes to exchange machinery used in his widget business for a fleet of delivery trucks for use in his didget business. This exchange of personal property for personal property qualifies even though the "grades" differ and the properties exchanged are used in different businesses.

Example 7: T owns a sailboat that she races for pleasure. She exchanges the boat for an unimproved lot held for investment. This exchange fails on two counts: Personal property is exchanged for

---

[2]Reg. Sec. 1.1031(a)-1(b).

[3]Sec. 1031(a).

real property and the sailboat was not held for investment or for use in a business.

Example 8: T, a dealer in real estate, exchanges a lot held as inventory for the common stock of a corporation. Both properties, inventory and corporate securities, are excluded by statute from the like-kind definition.

The nonrecognition rules for like-kind exchanges extend only to *direct* exchanges of qualified properties. A series of exchanges involving nonqualified properties such as cash, inventory, or securities as intermediate steps do not enjoy the nonrecognition rules, even if the ultimate position of the taxpayer is unchanged.

Example 9: T holds for investment a building lot which cost $50,000 and has a fair market value of $125,000. He sells the lot for cash and reinvests the $125,000 proceeds immediately in a duplex that he plans to rent. T's $75,000 gain must be recognized. The exchange is *indirect*, and when he received the cash he had the wherewithal to pay the tax on his gain. The tax is levied despite his continuing investment in real estate.

Example 9 illustrates the importance of *form* in this area of the tax law. T's argument that he has *in substance* exchanged real properties and that he has no money left over would carry no weight.

The requirement of a direct exchange, as just explained, does not mean that an exchange must be *simultaneous* in order to qualify. Often the exchange of title is not simultaneous because one party to the exchange has not yet acquired the property to be used in the exchange.

Example 10: In order to expand operations, Giant Corporation needs land owned by T. T does not want to sell because of a large resulting gain. Under a binding contract, T delivers title to his land to Giant. Later, T selects real estate comparable in value. Giant buys this real estate and delivers title to T. This "three cornered" exchange qualifies as a like-kind exchange to T provided the timing rules below are satisfied.

When an exchange is not simultaneous, the property to be exchanged must be identified by the parties within 45 days following the date when the first property is relinquished. Furthermore, the exchange must be completed within a 180-day period, or, if earlier, before the due date of the return of the taxpayer who first relinquishes property.[4]

---

[4]Sec. 1031(a)(3).

BACKGROUND

Congress included the 180-day requirement for completion of like-kind exchanges in the Tax Reform Act of 1984 to curtail the use of abusive three-cornered exchanges. Perhaps a prototype of the scheme Congress had in mind is the one found in *T. J. Starker v U.S.**

In that case, Starker relinquished his titles to several tracts of timberland to a large lumber–paper corporation in 1967. Starker was credited with the fair market value of the tracts. Starker then had the right to select parcels of land to be bought for him by the corporation. Starker's "balance" was also credited with a growth factor of 6% per annum. Between 1967 and 1969, Starker had the corporation buy twelve tracts of land equal in value to the value originally credited, plus the growth factor. While the court held that the 6% growth was interest income, it basically accepted the three-cornered exchange as tax free. The addition to the law of the required 180-day completion period curtails the use of schemes such as this.

The Tax Reform Act of 1984 also resolved another long-standing conflict between taxpayers and the government by providing that an interest in a partnership cannot be like-kind property.

---

*602F, 2d 1342 (9th Cir., 1979)

EXCHANGES INVOLVING CASH BOOT

WHEREWITHAL-TO-PAY A taxpayer who receives cash or near-cash assets in a transaction is said to have the means or wherewithal to pay the tax. In exchanges where the taxpayer receives no boot, he or she may not have the means of paying the tax.

In the usual case where property is exchanged directly for other property, the values are not identical. One party must usually pay something "to boot" in order to even out the values. The most convenient form of boot is cash. (More complex problems involving noncash boot are discussed below.) The party who receives cash in an otherwise like-kind exchange has the ***wherewithal to pay*** the tax on any gain, at least to the extent of the boot received. The party who pays cash boot has increased the basis of his or her continuing investment.

When cash boot is included, the general rules stated earlier become:

- Recognition of gain or loss:

  No losses are recognized.
  To the party who gives (pays) boot, no gain is recognized.
  To the party who receives boot, gain is recognized in the amount of whichever is lesser—the gain realized or the boot received.

- Basis of the new property is:

  Fair market value of the new property—
  Plus any losses deferred or,
  Less any gain deferred.

- Holding period of the new property begins on the acquisition date of the old property.

The recognition rules take account of the ability of the party who receives the boot to pay the tax. According to the basic rules, a hypothetical sale at fair market value that would result in recognition of the deferred gain or loss may be used to determine the basis of the new property.

Example 11: Five general cases illustrate all applications of the rules just listed. In each case, the basic exchange qualifies as a like-kind exchange.

	CASE A	CASE B	CASE C	CASE D	CASE E
Fair market value of the property received	$100	$100	$100	$100	$100
Basis of the property exchanged	110	110	80	105	90
Cash paid or given	15	none	8	none	none
Cash received	none	6	none	15	15
Realized gain (loss)	(25)	(4)	12	10	25
Recognized gain (loss)	-0-	-0-	-0-	10	15
Basis of new property	125	104	88	100	90

Case A: T realizes a loss of $25 (amount realized $100 fair market value of new property less $110 basis of old property plus $15 cash paid). The loss is not recognized. The basis of the new property is:

Fair market value of new property	$100
Plus loss not recognized (deferred)	25
	$125

If T sells the new property for its FMV of $100, this $125 basis then gives a loss of $25, the amount deferred on the nontaxable exchange.

Case B: T receives cash of $6 but still has a realized loss of $4 (amount realized is $100 FMV of new property plus the cash of $6, or $106, less the basis of $110 for the old property). No loss is recognized. The basis of the new property is $104, its FMV of $100 plus the $4 loss deferred on the exchange.

Case C: T realizes a gain of $12 (amount realized of $100 FMV of new property less the $80 basis of the old property plus the $8 cash paid). No gain is recognized because T *gives* boot and has no wherewithal to pay the tax. The basis of the new property is $88, its $100 FMV less the $12 gain deferred.

Case D: T's realized gain is $10 (amount realized of $115, the $100 FMV of the new property plus the $15 cash received, less the $105 basis of the old property). The entire gain of $10 is recognized because the boot of $15 exceeds the gain realized. Since no gain or loss is deferred, the basis of the new property is $100, its fair market value.

Case E: T realizes a gain of $25 (the amount realized of $115, the $100 FMV of the new property plus the cash of $15, less the basis of $90 for the old property). The recognized gain is limited to $15, the amount of the boot received. The basis for the new property is $90, its $100 FMV less the unrecognized or deferred gain of $10 ($25 realized less $15 recognized).

Referring to Example 11, in every instance the holding period of the new property runs from the acquisition date of the old property. In effect, it is assumed that the new investment is merely a continuation of the old investment.

The statutory formula for the determination of the basis of the new property begins with basis of the old property (unlike the method in Example 11 which begins with the FMV of the new property and makes appropriate adjustments for boot given or received and any gain recognized):[5]

Basis of old property exchanged
Plus: Boot given or gain recognized
Less: Boot received (and, in some cases (explained later) loss recognized)
Equals: Basis of the new property.

Reflection on this method reveals it to be a restatement of the accounting journal entry necessary to record the exchange, with the credits having a plus sign and the debits a minus sign.

Example 12: Refer to Case D in Example 11. The journal entry to record the exchange is:

	DR.	CR.
New property	?	
Cash (boot received)	$15	
Old property		$105
Gain recognized		10

The debit needed for the new property is $100, the basis earlier determined.

EXCHANGES INVOLVING NONCASH BOOT

Taxpayers sometimes use property other than cash as boot in a like-kind exchange. Any nonqualified property in an otherwise nontaxable exchange is boot.

[5] Sec. 1013(d).

Example 13: T exchanges real estate for real estate in a like-kind exchange. To even out the exchange, T also receives personal property, e.g., an automobile or corporate securities. The personal property is boot.

When noncash property is used as boot, the measure of the amount of the boot is the property's fair market value. The party that "gives" or transfers the property recognizes gain or loss because the transfer is a taxable disposition of such property.

The party receiving the noncash property treats the fair market value of such property as cash received in the exchange. The basis of the property is its fair market value under the usual cost acquisition rules.[6]

Example 14: T exchanges a tract of real estate held for investment for a new tract. The old tract had a basis of $50,000 and a fair market value (FMV) of $65,000. The new tract received had a FMV of $75,000. To even up the exchange, T also transferred corporate securities with a FMV of $10,000 and a basis of $6,000. T's disposition of the securities is taxable and the $4,000 gain ($10,000 FMV less $6,000 basis) is recognized. However, since T is giving boot in the like-kind exchange, no gain is recognized in that exchange. T's basis in the new property is $60,000, its $75,000 FMV less the $15,000 gain not recognized on the land.

Example 15: Assume the same facts as in Example 14, except that the securities have a basis of $12,000. Now T has a recognized $2,000 loss from disposition of the boot property. All other amounts are unchanged.

Example 16: X is the other party to the exchange in Example 14. X's property, with a FMV of $75,000, had a basis of only $35,000. X has a realized gain of $40,000 (amount realized of $75,000, the FMV of T's land of $65,000 plus the $10,000 FMV of T's securities, less X's $35,000 basis). X recognizes gain of only $10,000, the FMV of the boot. X's basis for the new real estate is $35,000, the $65,000 FMV less the $30,000 gain not recognized. X's basis in the securities received from T is $10,000.

EXCHANGES INVOLVING INDEBTEDNESS

A common form of boot when real estate is exchanged is mortgage indebtedness. Commonly both properties are mortgaged and the new holders resulting from the exchange assume the mortgages on the new properties or take the new properties subject to the mortgages. In these instances, the indebtedness is treated like cash—the party who assumes

[6] Sec. 1012.

the debt is treated as having paid cash and the party relieved of the debt is treated as having received cash.[7]

Example 17: T owns unimproved real estate with a fair market value of $100,000, subject to a mortgage of $35,000 placed on it several years ago. T's basis in the land is $50,000. X owns land valued at $65,000 with a basis of $40,000. T and X agree to an exchange and the properties qualify as like-kind to both parties. Note that the values are equal: X's land is worth $65,000; T's equity is $65,000 ($100,000 FMV less the $35,000 mortgage).

T's realized gain is $50,000 and he must recognize $35,000, the amount of the mortgage assumed by X. T's basis in the new land is $50,000, its $65,000 FMV less the $15,000 gain not recognized.

X has a realized gain of $25,000, T's $65,000 equity in his property ($100,000 FMV less the $35,000 mortgage) less X's $40,000 basis. X recognizes no gain because he is giving boot when he assumes the debt. X's basis in the new property is $75,000, its $100,000 FMV less the gain of $25,000 not recognized.

If both properties in the exchange are subject to debt, only the net difference in the two debts is treated as cash boot.

Example 18: T owns real estate with a fair market value of $150,000 subject to $90,000 mortgage. X owns real estate valued at $165,000 subject to a mortgage of $105,000. T and X exchange properties. The $15,000 difference between the mortgages is treated as cash payment from T to X. The trade is even since both have an equity of $60,000 in their property. X's debt, however, is decreased by $15,000 and T's increased by $15,000, the same effect as a cash payment from T to X.

INVOLUNTARY CONVERSIONS

INVOLUNTARY CONVERSION A disposition of property resulting from a casualty, condemnation, or threat of condemnation.

CONDEMNATION Exercise of the power of "eminent domain" by a governmental unit, whereby the government takes a citizen's property for its own use, but with a fair consideration.

Taxpayers sometimes dispose of property against their will. Such ***involuntary conversions*** occur when property is destroyed in a casualty or when a government unit condemns property under its power of eminent domain. In the former instance, casualty insurance can result in a payment for, or a direct replacement of, the destroyed property. In the latter instance, the governmental unit may purchase the property under a threat of ***condemnation***, pay for the property as a result of condemnation proceedings, or directly replace the property condemned with new property.

When destroyed or condemned property is replaced directly by property that is "similar or related in service or use," a term defined below, any gain resulting therefrom is not recognized and the basis of the new

---

[7]Reg. Sec. 1.1031(d)-2, Example 2.

property (and its holding period) are the same as the old property. Any loss realized on the conversion is recognized. Note here that the law does not penalize the taxpayer by deferring any resulting loss, since the taxpayer's disposition of the old property is involuntary. Where a loss results and is recognized, the basis of the replacement property is its fair market value.[8]

Example 19: Miss Maggie T's personal residence was condemned by the city for a new roadway. Because of her age, the city government bought Miss Maggie a new home and moved her into it. Miss Maggie's old residence cost her $15,000 and had a value of $60,000 when condemned. The city paid $60,000 for Maggie's new residence. Maggie's gain of $45,000 is not recognized. However, her basis in the new property is only $15,000 and the gain is only deferred.

Direct involuntary conversions into "similar" property are rare these days. Usually, the insurance company or the governmental unit pays cash for the property, the rules for which are explained in the following section.

While not technically an involuntary conversion, livestock sold because of a drought and livestock destroyed because of disease are treated as involuntary conversions.[9] As explained below, gain resulting from such dispositions can be deferred if replacement property is acquired on a timely basis.

INVOLUNTARY CONVERSIONS INTO CASH

When property is involuntarily converted into cash, the following rules apply.[10]

- Losses are recognized. In this event, the basis of any replacement property is its cost. You will recall from Chapter 9 that special rules apply to the deduction of casualty losses related to property held for personal use.
- If a gain results, the taxpayer has an election either to: (*a*) Recognize the gain. In this event, the basis of any replacement property is its cost. (*b*) Recognize gain only to the extent the proceeds of the conversion are not used to acquire "similar" property within the prescribed replacement period. When gain is deferred under this election, the basis of the new property is its fair market value less the gain *not* recognized.

Only one of the above alternatives is a "nontaxable exchange"—the election to defer or postpone gain when qualified replacement property

[8]Sec. 1033(a)(1).
[9]Sec. 1033(d) and (e).
[10]Sec. 1033(a)(2).

is acquired. If the taxpayer spends the proceeds of the conversion for new property, he or she has a continuing investment and no wherewithal to pay a tax. The other outcomes, the recognition of losses and the election to recognize gains, are "taxable" transactions. The gain deferral is the important alternative nevertheless, since it permits the postponement of the income tax.

Example 20: Four general cases illustrate the rules of involuntary conversion. Assume that qualified replacement property, if necessary to the case, is acquired within the replacement period by T:

	CASE A	CASE B	CASE C	CASE D
Cash proceeds received upon the conversion	$200	$200	$200	$200
Basis of the "old" property converted	$225	$180	$180	$180
Cost of replacement property, if applicable	N/A	N/A	$205	$192
Gain (loss) realized	($25)	$20	$20	$20
Gain (loss) recognized	($25)	$20*	-0-	$8
Basis of the new property	N/A	N/A	$185	$180

*Taxpayer's election

Case A: T realizes a loss of $25, the excess of the basis of $225 over the proceeds of $200. T's basis in any replacement property is its cost.

Case B: T realizes a gain of $20 ($200 proceeds less basis of $180). This case assumes that T elects to recognize his gain. Thus, replacement of the property is irrelevant and the basis of any new property is its cost.

Case C: T realizes a gain of $20 ($200 proceeds less T's basis of $180). However, upon T's election, no gain is recognized because all of the proceeds are invested in the replacement property. T's basis in the new property is $185, the cost and presumed FMV of the new property less the $20 gain not recognized.

Case D: T realizes a $20 gain. Here, a gain of $8 must be recognized because that amount of proceeds is not reinvested ($200 proceeds less $192 cost of new property). T's basis in the new property is $180, its cost of $192 less the $12 gain not recognized.

In Cases C and D, the holding period of the new property runs from the acquisition date of the property converted. Note that in Cases C and D results comparable to those under like-kind exchanges occur, where the concept of boot is replaced by the notion of proceeds that are not reinvested.

When only a part of a tract of real estate is condemned, the governmental unit sometimes pays "severance damages" as compensation for the decreased value of the remaining tract. Generally, the amount received as severance damages is not included as proceeds from the condemnation but instead reduces the basis of the remaining property.[11]

QUALIFIED REPLACEMENT PROPERTY

Taxpayers may defer gains from involuntary conversions only if ***qualified replacement property*** is acquired during the prescribed time period. The statute uses the term "property similar or related in service or use" but does not define the term.[12] While the interpretation of the meaning of this term by the Internal Revenue Service and by the courts leaves considerable room for doubt, the boundaries of the definition are clear enough:

REPLACEMENT PROPERTY "Qualified" replacement property that permits the deferral of gain in involuntary conversions is property that is similar or related in service or use.

- For *real estate* that is held for investment or used in a business and disposed of in a condemnation, any other real estate acquired for investment or for use in a business is qualified replacement property. "Similar in use" for this property means nothing more than like-kind explained earlier in this chapter.[13] Condemnation of a personal residence would not fit under this liberal rule because it would not be held for investment or business purposes.
- For *personal* property converted in a casualty, the replacement property must have the same functional use as the destroyed property. This test of functional use is restrictive.

The most common involuntary conversion not covered by these clear-cut boundaries is the destruction by ***casualty*** of buildings and other real property. Generally, the test of functional use applies here also. However, if rental real estate, e.g., an apartment building, is destroyed by fire, any new rental real estate is qualified replacement property.

CASUALTY A sudden, unexpected event, often referred to as an "act" of nature or God, that destroys property, e.g., storms, fires, wrecks, explosions.

Example 21: T's farm land is condemned by the federal government because of the construction of a new lake. T acquires an apartment house as a replacement. This replacement is qualified property; the like-kind test applies.

Example 22: In Example 21, T also receives a condemnation award for his personal residence. T can defer gain under the involuntary conversion rules only if he acquires a new residence (functional use). The like-kind test does not apply because the residence is not held for business use or for investment. (The rules related to the sale of residences in the following section could also apply to T's residence.)

---

[11] *Rev. Rul.* 59-173, 1959-1 C.B. 201.

[12] Sec. 1033(a)(1) and (2).

[13] Sec. 1033(g)(1).

Example 23: T operated a discount furniture store. The store fixtures and inventory were destroyed in a fire (the building was leased). T uses the insurance proceeds to enter the retail clothing business, acquiring inventory and fixtures. The functional use of the replacement property is *not* similar to the old property and it is not a qualified replacement. To defer gain, T must remain in the same business, though the precise "mix" of the inventory can vary.

Example 24: In Example 23, the lessor of T's building replaces the building with another store building that he leases to T for T's retail clothing store. This replacement qualifies because both buildings are rental properties.

Special, more complicated rules apply to the replacement of livestock sold because of drought.[14]

Qualified replacement property can be obtained by acquiring the controlling interest in a corporation that owns property that is functionally similar. Control means 80% of the combined voting power of all stock plus 80% of all other shares outstanding.[15] This method of replacement cannot be used for the like-kind replacement of condemned real estate.[16]

REPLACEMENT PERIOD

The qualified replacement property must be acquired within a time period specified by law:[17]

- Beginning date—The date of disposition of the property or the date of the beginning of the threat of condemnation, whichever is earlier.
- Ending date—Generally two years from the end of the taxable year within which the first gain is realized. For condemned real estate used in a business or held for investment, the period is three years.[18]

If a taxpayer can advance cogent reasons, e.g., absence in a foreign country, the Internal Revenue Service will usually extend the ending date.

Example 25: Fire destroyed T's fireworks manufacturing plant on July 4, 19X1. T uses the calendar year for tax purposes. T received the insurance settlement on April 30, 19X2 resulting in a gain. The replacement period begins on July 4, 19X1 and ends on December 31, 19X4.

Example 26: On November 1, 19X1, T learned that a new city park would result in the condemnation of his rental property. Under

---

[14] Sec. 1033(f).
[15] Reg. Sec. 1.1033(e)-1.
[16] Sec. 1033(g)(2).
[17] Reg. Sec. 1.1033(a)-2(c)(3).
[18] Sec. 1033(g)(4).

threat of condemnation, T sold the property to the city on February 2, 19X3, resulting in a gain. T uses the calendar year. The replacement period begins on November 1, 19X1 when the threat arose and ends on December 31, 19X6, three years after the end of the year when the gain arose.

In Examples 25 and 26, the end of the period can be extended if an extension of time is granted by the IRS.

REPORTING INVOLUNTARY CONVERSIONS

Taxpayers recognizing losses on involuntary conversions report them on Form 4797, or on Form 4684 if they are casualties. **FORM 4797** **FORM 4684**

If a gain is realized and no replacement is planned, the gain is reported in the normal manner (see Chapters 10 and 11). If a replacement is anticipated, supporting facts should be reported with the return for the year when the replacement is made. Failure to report the gain when realized is automatically treated as an election to defer the gain by replacing the property.[19] If a property replacement is not made, or the replacement results in only a partial deferral, an amended return is required for the taxable year when the gain was realized.

SALE OF A PERSONAL RESIDENCE

A taxpayer who sells his or her personal residence and realizes a loss receives no tax benefit because losses from the sale of property held for personal use are not recognized.[20] (But see Chapter 9 for the recognition of casualty losses.) On the other hand, the taxpayer who sells his or her personal residence and realizes a gain must generally pay tax on the gain. Two provisions of the Internal Revenue Code mitigate this harsh effect:

- Section 1034—If the taxpayer reinvests the proceeds from the sale of the old residence in a new residence, recognition of the gain on the old residence is deferred or postponed. This deferral of gain works in the same way as an involuntary conversion except that deferral of the gain on a residence is not elective but mandatory.
- Section 121—A taxpayer who is 55 or older on the date of sale of his or her residence may elect to exclude from taxation the resulting gain, but is limited to $125,000 of gain, provided certain conditions are met.

These important relief provisions are discussed in this section.

DEFERRAL OF GAIN UNDER SECTION 1034

For many taxpayers, their personal residence is their principal (only) investment property. Encouragement of homeownership has been a

[19] Reg. Sec. 1.1033(a)-2(c).

[20] Sec. 165(c).

national economic policy for many years. To further this policy and to facilitate the sale of an old residence and the acquisition of a new one because of increased family size or a new job location, the law provides for a deferral of gain if the proceeds from the sale of the old residence are reinvested in a new residence.

OPERATING RULES Specifically, if a taxpayer sells his or her principal residence and acquires a new principal residence within the required time:

- Gain is recognized only to the extent the *adjusted sales price* of the old residence is not reinvested in the new residence.[21] The adjusted sales price is the amount realized on sale of the old residence (sales price less selling costs) less the "fixing up costs." Fixing up costs are noncapital expenditures related to the sale of the old residence for work performed in the 90-day period before the sale of the old residence and paid within 30 days after the sale.[22]
- The basis of the new residence is its cost less any gain not recognized on the sale of the old residence.[23] The cost of the new residence includes all capital expenditures made before the end of the replacement period.

The rules applicable to the sale of a personal residence and its replacement are summarized in Figure 12-1. This figure reads from upper left to lower right, where the recognized gain and the basis of the new residence are determined.

Note that the adjustments to the basis of the new residence result in a *deferral* of the unrecognized gain and not a permanent exclusion of the gain from taxation.

Example 27: The following cases A and B illustrate these rules. Assume that T's old principal residence was used as such for several years, that T's new principal residence is acquired on a timely basis, and that the new residence is not sold within two years of the sale of the old residence.

	CASE A	CASE B
Amount realized on sale of old residence	$100,000	$100,000
Basis of old residence	55,000	55,000
"Fixing-up costs"	1,500	1,500
Capital cost of the new residence	125,000	90,000
Gain realized	45,000	45,000
Gain recognized	-0-	8,500
Basis of the new residence	80,000	53,500

[21] Sec. 1034(a).

[22] Sec. 1034(b).

[23] Sec. 1034.

FIGURE 12-1
Diagram of Section 1034

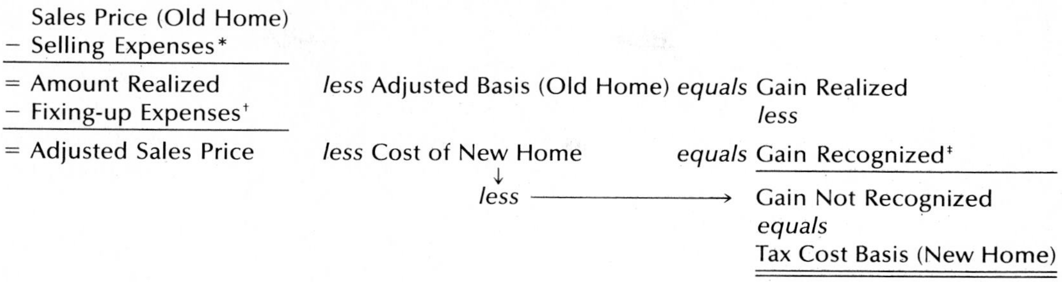

Sales Price (Old Home)		
− Selling Expenses[*]		
= Amount Realized	*less* Adjusted Basis (Old Home) *equals*	Gain Realized
− Fixing-up Expenses[†]		*less*
= Adjusted Sales Price	*less* Cost of New Home *equals*	Gain Recognized[‡]
	↓ *less* →	Gain Not Recognized
		equals
		Tax Cost Basis (New Home)

[*] Perhaps the most important "selling expense" is the broker's commission. See Reg. Sec. 1.1034-1(b)(4).

[†] "Fixing-up expenses" are defined rather narrowly in Reg. Sec. 1.1034-1(b)(6). The phrase refers to expenses incurred to help sell a property and includes such things as painting and papering a home. To qualify, however, these expenses must be incurred and paid within specified time periods.

[‡] Only if > 0; also, "gain recognized" can never be > "gain realized."

From *An Introduction to Taxation*, Tenth Edition, Ray M. Sommerfeld, Hershel M. Anderson, and Horace R. Brock (New York: Harcourt Brace Jovanovich, 1984) p. 567.

Case A: T's realized gain is $45,000 ($100,000 − $55,000) but none of this gain is recognized because the cost of the new residence is $125,000. That amount is greater than the amount realized and the adjusted sales price (amount realized less fixing-up costs) has no relevance. The basis of the new residence is $80,000 (its cost of $125,000 less the $45,000 gain not recognized). T's gain on the old residence is therefore postponed until sale of the new residence.

Case B: T's realized gain is $45,000. The recognized gain is $8,500, the excess of the $98,500 adjusted sales price ($100,000 amount realized less $1,500 fixing-up costs) over the $90,000 paid for the new residence. The law provides here that amounts spent to sell the old residence are not available to pay the tax. The basis of the new residence is $53,500, its cost of $90,000 less $36,500 gain not recognized ($45,000 − $8,500).

Figure 12-2 shows how Figure 12-1 can be used to summarize the calculation, based on the facts in Example 27, Case B. For this purpose assume the sales price was $106,000 and that selling commissions of $6,000 were paid. The figure contrasts the amount realized to adjusted basis to obtain the realized gain of $45,000 and the adjusted sales price to the cost of the new residence to obtain the recognized gain of $8,500. Finally, the unrecognized gain of $36,500 is subtracted from the $90,000 cost of the new residence to obtain the new basis of $53,500.

REPLACEMENT PROPERTY AND TIME The deferral provisions of Section 1034 apply only if the taxpayer's principal residence is sold and re-

FIGURE 12-2
Applying Section 1034

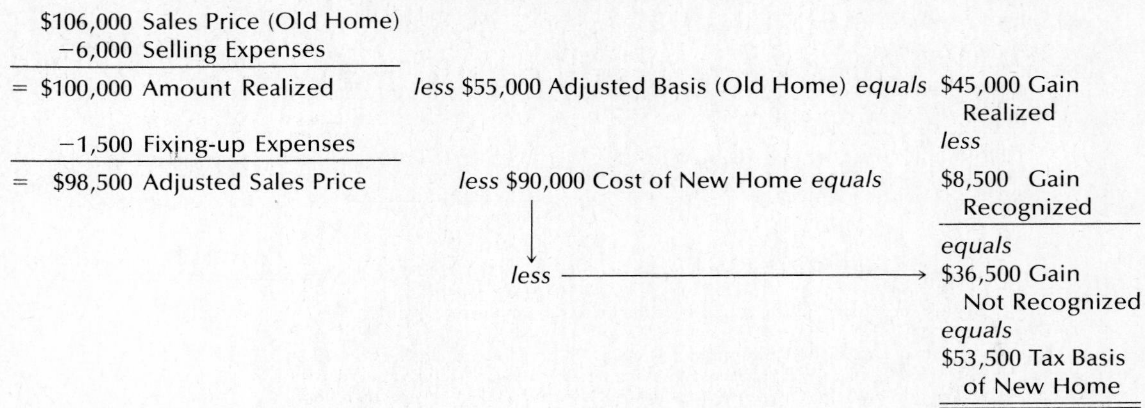

$106,000 Sales Price (Old Home)
−6,000 Selling Expenses
= $100,000 Amount Realized
less $55,000 Adjusted Basis (Old Home) equals
$45,000 Gain Realized
−1,500 Fixing-up Expenses
less
= $98,500 Adjusted Sales Price
less $90,000 Cost of New Home equals
$8,500 Gain Recognized
equals
less
$36,500 Gain Not Recognized
equals
$53,500 Tax Basis of New Home

From *An Introduction to Taxation*, Tenth Edition, Ray M. Sommerfeld, Hershel M. Anderson, and Horace R. Brock (New York: Harcourt Brace Jovanovich, 1984) p. 568.

placed with a new principal residence. The principal residence of a taxpayer who has more than one residence is a question of facts; the rules cannot be extended to second or vacation homes. A houseboat or a house trailer can be the principal residence if so used by the taxpayer.[24] If a residence is converted to business use before the sale, Section 1034 does not apply; however, temporary rental prior to sale does not always mean a conversion to business use.[25] The replacement residence may be constructed by the taxpayer, in which event its cost is the sum of all capital expenditures.[26]

The new principal residence must be acquired during the period beginning two years before the sale of the old residence and ending two years after the sale.[27]

> **Example 28:** T sells her old residence on September 1, 19X3. She has until September 1, 19X5 to acquire a new residence.

A taxpayer who buys more than one principal residence within two years following the sale of an old residence must use the cost of the last residence acquired to calculate the gain deferred.[28]

---

[24] Reg. Sec. 1.1034-1(c)(3)(i).
[25] Rev. Rul. 78-146; 1978-1 C.B. 260.
[26] Sec. 1034(e)(2).
[27] Sec. 1034(a).
[28] Sec. 1034(c)(4).

Example 29: T sold his long-time principal residence on September 1, 19X1. He purchased a new residence on January 15, 19X2. This second residence was sold on June 10, 19X3 and replaced by a third residence acquired on August 15, 19X3. The purchase and sale of the second residence is not covered by Sec. 1034. The cost of the third residence is used to determine the gain not recognized on the sale of the first residence. The preceding rule is waived if the sale and purchase within the 2-year period is made necessary by a change of job locations that meets the test for moving expenses in Section 217.[29]

REPORTING PROCEDURES A taxpayer who sells a residence and does not plan to replace it should report any gain on Schedule D (see Chapter 10). If he or she plans a replacement, but none is made within the prescribed time period, an amended return must be filed for the year when the old residence is sold. If a replacement is planned and is made, the taxpayer files Form 2119 that shows the gain deferred and the basis of the new residence. If replacement is made after the year of sale and something less than the entire gain is postponed, an amended return is required for the year of sale.

FORM 2119

EXCLUSION OF GAIN UNDER SECTION 121

As mentioned earlier, the personal residence represents the principal investment property for many taxpayers. Elderly taxpayers who acquired their residences years ago have enjoyed substantial appreciation, mainly due to the decreased value of the dollar. To afford these citizens some tax relief when they sell their homes and acquire no replacement or a smaller one, and to reduce or eliminate the tax on gains that are partly fictitious, Congress added Section 121 to the law.

Under this section, an electing taxpayer can exclude gain on the sale of a personal residence up to $125,000 ($100,000 for sales before July 20, 1981) provided:

- He or she has not previously made an election under this provision;
- He or she has attained the age of 55 years before the date of sale, and
- He or she has used the property sold as the principal residence for at least three of the five years preceding the disposition (five out of eight in some instances) (Section 121(a)).

Example 30: T, a widower, has owned the same principal residence for many years. In 19X1, when T is 57 years old, he sells the residence for $130,000 (net of selling expenses). His basis in the residence is $42,000. T moves into a rented apartment in a retirement

[29] Sec. 1034(d).

village where many widows live. T's realized gain is $88,000. If T so elects, the entire gain is excluded from taxation.

The election under Section 121 is available only once during the lifetime of a taxpayer. A taxpayer over 55 with a small gain from the sale of residence who expects to reinvest in a new residence should, if possible, defer the gain under Section 1034. However, if a taxpayer is moving into a smaller residence, the election should probably be used for even small gains since future gains on a new residence are speculative and the exclusion saves taxes now.

Example 31: T, aged 56, sells her residence for $125,000, realizing a $40,000 gain. T plans to move into a condominium that costs $80,000. Based on past experience, she expects the condominium to double in value in the next five years. If T elects now to exclude the $40,000, no exclusion is available later if the new property produces a gain of $80,000. The election applies to a single disposition; it is not a $125,000 exclusion applicable to several sales.

For a married couple filing a joint return the election can be made if either spouse is 55 years old and has used the property as a principal residence for three of the five years before the sale.[30] In every case, however, an election by one spouse "spends" the election for both.

Example 32: T was married to A in 19X1, when T was 53 and A was 56. A used the election under Section 121 that year. In 19X2, T divorced A and married B in 19X3. In 19X7, when both T and B are over 55 and have used the same residence for four years, they sell the residence at a gain. No election is available to T and B. A's election tainted T and T in turn taints B.

The exclusion can be combined with the deferral rules discussed earlier (including the rules for involuntary conversions) if the principal residence is replaced. Application of both rules will be necessary only when the gain exceeds $125,000. The gain excluded is treated as an amount spent for a new residence to determine the amount which must be spent to defer the remaining gain.[31]

Example 33: T sells her residence for $200,000 (net of expenses). There were no fixing-up costs. She paid $60,000 for the residence several years ago. Her realized gain is:

Amount realized	$200,000
Basis	60,000
Realized gain	$140,000

[30] Sec. 121(d).

[31] Sec. 121(d)(7).

T meets the requirements of Section 121 and elects to exclude $125,000 of the gain. T's adjusted sales price for purposes of applying the deferral rules of Section 1034 is:

Amount realized	$200,000
Less gain excluded	125,000
Adjusted sales price	$ 75,000

If T acquires a new residence on a timely basis costing $75,000 or more, none of the $140,000 gain is recognized.

The election under Section 121 can be made and revoked at any time before the statute of limitations runs out for the return of the year of sale.[32] The election is made by filing a signed statement (Form 2119 can be used).

OTHER NONTAXABLE EXCHANGES

The statute contains numerous nontaxable exchanges in addition to like-kind exchanges, involuntary conversions, and sales of a residence discussed above. A brief explanation of the more important ones follows:

- Property transferred to a controlled corporation—Shareholders who transfer property to a corporation which they control recognize no gain or loss.[33] This common exchange is covered in Chapter 16.
- Tax-free reorganizations—Shareholders who exchange stock in one corporation for stock in another corporation in a merger or other reorganization recognize no gain or loss.[34] The rules for reorganizations are beyond the scope here.
- Stock splits—Exchanges of common stock for common stock of the same corporation in a stock-split are nontaxable. This rule also applies to exchanges of preferred stock for preferred stock of the same corporation.[35]
- Exchanges of insurance policies—No gain or loss is recognized when taxpayers exchange one insurance contract for another insurance contract of the same type.[36] The exchange is not tax-free if the new policy results in the possible recognition of income at a later date or results in the nonrecognition of income. An endowment contract can be exchanged for another endowment contract if payments under the new contract are not deferred, but the exchange of an endowment contract for a life insurance contract is taxable.
- Exchange of property in a divorce—A spouse who transfers prop-

---

[32] Sec. 121(c).

[33] Sec. 351(a).

[34] Sections 354 and 368.

[35] Sec. 1036.

[36] Sec. 1035.

erty to the other spouse incident to a divorce recognizes no gain or loss.[37] Congress added this tax-free exchange to the law in 1984 to change a court-made rule that treated these exchanges as taxable.

PLANNING WORKSHOP

The nonrecognition rules explained in this chapter are critical to many traditional, successful tax plans. Examples include everything from the many corporate reorganizations completed every year down to the local businessman who trades in his old delivery truck for a new one. For the most part, "plans" based on the tax rules are easy to make. In the following paragraphs some less obvious planning problems are discussed.

ACQUISITION OF PROPERTY WHERE SELLER IS LOCKED IN

The like-kind exchange rules are often a valuable aid in the acquisition of needed real estate by a business. Some taxpayers are reluctant to sell highly appreciated property because of the resulting tax bite. They are said to be "locked in" to their investment. While they may resist an outright sale, a tax-free exchange may free up the property for new use.

To illustrate, Farmer J owns land used in a farming operation which has a value of $1 million but a basis of only $100,000. Company K needs J's land for an expansion of its plant. If J sells the land to K, J's wealth is reduced by approximately $180,000, the 20% capital-gains tax on J's $900,000 gain. However, if K can find another tract of land worth $1 million equally suited to J's farming needs, K can acquire that land by purchase and then exchange it for J's land. K is out $1 million in both events. J still has property valued at $1 million, and the Treasury must wait until a recognition event occurs to collect its $180,000.

On some occasions, a taxpayer with a large gain may wish to avoid the like-kind rules in order to recognize the gain. This can happen, for example, when the taxpayer has a large net operating loss or capital loss carryover. Recognition of gain may merely reduce the carryover at no tax cost. Note, however, that the basis of any new property acquired will equal its purchase price.

EXCHANGE OF LOSS PROPERTIES

Taxpayers with loss properties will generally want to avoid the like-kind rules. The outright sale of the property will result in recogni-

Continued

---

[37] Sec. 1041.

PLANNING WORKSHOP

tion of the loss with tax savings. This result is desirable unless the taxpayer has a net operating or capital loss carryover.

RECOGNITION OF GAINS ON INVOLUNTARY CONVERSIONS

Taxpayers usually gain a tax advantage from the acquisition of replacement property and deferral of gains on involuntary conversions. If a "good" investment is not available, however, the tax tail should not wag the economic dog.

Deferral of gain results in a decrease in basis (compared to the cost of the replacement property) and this means that subsequent deductions for cost of goods sold, depreciation, or amortizations may be less. Thus, the deferral is not an unmixed blessing.

In a few instances, taxpayers are in a better tax position when they elect to recognize gain on an involuntary conversion. For example, gain on land held for investment is taxed at capital-gain rates. If the new replacement property is depreciable property, the present value of the future depreciation deductions can be more than the present cost of capital-gain tax. The result, however, is unlikely during periods of high interest rates.

ELECTION UNDER SECTION 121

Taxpayers over 55 who sell a residence at a gain will usually wish to elect the benefits of Sec. 121 if gain would otherwise be currently recognized, even if the gain is small and they expect to have another sale later. Under "a bird in the hand" notion, avoidance of a tax now is usually the wise choice.

The expectation of a larger gain on a future residence must be weighed against the value of money (a pressing consideration given forecasts of continued high interest rates), against the likelihood of continued inflation in real estate prices, given the "bubble" prices that currently exist in many parts of the country, and against the general economic malaise that afflicts the U.S. and its trading partners.

KEY POINTS TO REMEMBER

1. No gain or loss is recognized when a taxpayer exchanges property solely for property of a like-kind.
2. The term "like-kind" refers to the nature of property—real property or personal property—and not to its quality or grade. Inventory, securities, and property held for personal use are excluded from the tax-free exchange rules.
3. When boot is received in a like-kind exchange, any gain realized is recognized, but limited to the fair market value of the boot.

4. Gain or loss not recognized in a like-kind exchange is deferred or postponed by making the proper adjustments to the basis of the property received in the exchange. The basis of the new property is its fair market value less any gain (or plus any loss) not recognized.
5. A taxpayer who has property that is involuntarily converted may elect to defer any gain realized on the conversion provided he or she spends the proceeds of the conversion to acquire qualified replacement property on a timely basis. Losses arising from involuntary conversions are recognized (subject to general rules). Gain must be recognized if less than the entire proceeds are reinvested.
6. Deferral of gain in an involuntary conversion is accomplished by reducing the basis of the replacement property by the unrecognized gain.
7. Qualified replacement property is property that is "similar in use" to the property converted.
8. The replacement period ends two years from the end of the taxable year in which the gain is first recognized. The period is three years for condemned real property.
9. A taxpayer who sells his or her personal residence at a gain may defer the gain if an amount equal to the adjusted sales price of the old residence is invested in a new personal residence on a timely basis. Losses from the sale of a personal residence are not recognized.
10. Deferral of gain on the sale of a residence is accomplished by reducing the basis of the new residence by the gain not recognized.
11. Other tax-free exchanges in the law include corporate reorganizations, stock splits, transfers to a controlled corporation, and exchanges of property between spouses in a divorce.

SELF-STUDY QUESTIONS

1. On July 1, 1984, Louis Herr exchanged an office building with a fair market value of $400,000, for cash of $80,000 plus an apartment building with a fair market value of $320,000. Herr's adjusted basis for the office building was $250,000. How much gain should Herr recognize in his 1984 income tax return?

   a) $0

   b) $80,000

   c) $150,000

   d) $330,000

   (AICPA adapted)

2. John Budd, who was 58 at the date of his death on July 1, 1983, was married to Emma Budd, age 57. A month before John died, John and Emma sold their house for $225,000. They had lived in the house since 1970 and held the property as tenants by the entirety. Their basis for

this property was $100,000. No replacement property was purchased and Emma did not remarry in 1983. Emma is executrix of John's estate. How much of the gain on sale of the residence should be excluded from 1983 taxable income?

a) $125,000

b) $100,000

c) $ 75,000

d) $0

(AICPA adapted)

3. David Price owned machinery which he had acquired in 1972 at a cost of $100,000. During 1975, the machinery was destroyed by fire. At that time it had an adjusted basis of $86,000. The insurance proceeds awarded to Price amounted to $125,000, and he immediately acquired a similar machine for $110,000.

   What should Price report as ordinary income resulting from the involuntary conversion for 1975?

   a) $14,000

   b) $15,000

   c) $25,000

   d) $39,000

   (AICPA adapted)

4. Robert Efron owned an apartment house that he bought in 1970. Depreciation was taken on a straight-line basis. In 1982, when Efron's adjusted basis for this property was $100,000, he traded it for an office building having a fair market value of $300,000. The apartment house has 100 dwelling units, while the office building has 50 business rental units. The properties are not located in the same city. What is Efron's reportable gain on this exchange?

   a) $0

   b) $200,000 long-term capital gain

   c) $200,000 Section 1231 gain

   d) $200,000 Section 1250 gain

   (AICPA adapted)

5. Stanley Brown, a self-employed individual, owned a truck driven exclusively for business use. The truck had an original cost of $4,000 and had an adjusted basis on December 31, 1976, of $1,800. On January 2, 1977, he traded it in for a new truck costing $5,000 and was given a trade-in allowance of $1,000. The new truck will also be used exclusively for business purposes and will be depreciated with no salvage value. The basis of the new truck is

a) $4,000
b) $4,200
c) $5,000
d) $5,800

(AICPA adapted)

6. On October 1, 1981, Donald Anderson exchanged an apartment building, having an adjusted basis of $375,000 and subject to a mortgage of $100,000, for $25,000 cash and another apartment building with a fair market value of $550,000 and subject to a mortgage of $125,000. The property transfers were made subject to the outstanding mortgages. What amount of gain should Anderson recognize in his tax return for 1981?

   a) $0
   b) $ 25,000
   c) $125,000
   d) $175,000

   (AICPA adapted)

7. During 1973, Mikey Corporation exchanged an old machine used in its business for a similar machine to be used in its business. The following chart summarizes the relevant data on the date of exchange:

	ADJUSTED BASIS	FAIR MARKET VALUE
Old machine (to Mikey)	$4,000	$5,500
New machine (to the seller)	$3,000	$3,500

   As part of the exchange, Mikey Corporation received $2,000 cash. What is the recognized gain on this exchange, and what is the tax basis of the new machine to Mikey, respectively?

   a) $0 and $1,000
   b) $0 and $2,000
   c) $1,500 and $3,500
   d) $2,000 and $4,000

   (AICPA adapted)

8. An office building owned by Elmer Bass was condemned by the state on January 2, 1982. Bass received the condemnation award on March 1, 1983. In order to qualify for nonrecognition of gain on this involuntary conversion, what is the last date for Bass to acquire qualified replacement property?

   a) August 1, 1984
   b) January 2, 1985

c) March 1, 1986

d) December 31, 1986

(AICPA adapted)

9. On February 15, 1973, Barry Waters, age 52, sold his personal residence which was purchased May 8, 1965, at a price of $35,000. The contract price was $50,000, and he received a down payment of $12,500. No other payments were received in 1973, and Mr. Waters elected to report the gain on the installment method. On October 10, 1973, he purchased another principal residence at a price of $45,000. The 1973 tax effect of these transactions, before considering the 60% long-term capital gain deduction and disregarding any selling expense or other adjustments to basis and imputed interest, should be

   a) recognized gain of $3,750 and a basis of the new residence of $45,000

   b) recognized gain of $3,750 and a basis of the new residence of $35,000

   c) recognized gain of $1,250 and a basis of the new residence of $40,000

   d) recognized gain of $1,250 and a basis of the new residence of $35,000

   (AICPA adapted)

10. On January 20, 1972, Tom Ferry, age 55, sold his residence for $30,000. The house had been purchased in 1953 at a cost of $22,000. In order to make it salable it had been painted in December 1971 at a cost of $500 which was paid in December. On March 12, 1972, Mr. Ferry purchased a two-family house for $55,000. The rental portion is 50% and the remainder will be used as a personal residence. For 1972, Mr. Ferry will include a long-term capital gain on the sale of his residence of

   a) $8,000

   b) $2,500

   c) $2,000

   d) $0

   (AICPA adapted)

QUESTIONS

1. What is the definition of properties that qualify for like-kind exchanges? Does property held for personal use qualify?

2. Under what circumstances would a taxpayer try to avoid the like-kind rules?

3. What is meant by the term "boot"? How does boot affect the amount of gain recognized to the party that gives it? Receives it?
4. What is meant by the statement "Like-kind rules only defer gains and losses to later years"?
5. What are the rules used to determine the basis of property received in a like-kind exchange?
6. What is the holding period for property received in a like-kind exchange?
7. Must the transfers of property in a like-kind exchange be simultaneous? If not, what are the time limits?
8. Losses on involuntary conversions are recognized but gains are deferred if the taxpayer replaces the property. Why?
9. Does the same rationale apply to both like-kind exchanges and involuntary conversions? Explain.
10. Define qualified replacement property under the involuntary conversion rules.
11. How long does a taxpayer have to replace property involuntarily converted in a casualty? In a condemnation?
12. How is the basis of replacement property determined when the taxpayer defers gain by acquiring qualified replacement property?
13. Under what circumstances would a taxpayer elect to recognize gain on an involuntary conversion even when replacement property is acquired?
14. If a taxpayer elects to defer gain from an involuntary conversion but fails to acquire replacement property within the time period, how is the deferred gain reported?
15. Contrast the rules for gain deferral from an involuntary conversion to the rules for sale of a personal residence.
16. How are losses realized on the sale of a personal residence treated?
17. How do fixing-up costs affect the amount of gain recognized on the sale of a personal residence?
18. If a taxpayer owns more than one personal residence, do the special-gain deferral rules apply to all of them?
19. Why does the tax law include the special provision for the exclusion of gain on residences for taxpayers 55 or older?
20. How is the basis of a new residence determined where some of the gain on an old residence is deferred?
21. How long does a taxpayer have to acquire a new residence if he or she wishes to defer gain on an old residence?

22. How much gain can an elderly taxpayer exclude under Sec. 121? Can this exclusion be used for all residences sold after the age limit is reached?

PROBLEMS

1. Dusty Rhodes, a road contractor, owned a light airplane used in his business. This plane had an adjusted basis of $8,000 when he exchanged it for a smaller plane with a fair market value of $10,000. Dusty *received* $3,000 cash when he made this trade. Straight-line depreciation claimed on the old plane since acquisition totaled $10,000.
   a) How much gain was *realized* on this exchange?
   b) What minimum gain must be *recognized* on this exchange?
   c) Is the recognized gain a capital gain, ordinary income, or part of Sec. 1231? Explain.
   d) What is Dusty's tax basis in the new plane?
2. The following five cases apply to like-kind exchanges of productive use or investment properties. For each case, determine the recognized gain or loss, and the basis of the new property.

CASE	ADJUSTED BASIS OF PROPERTY SURRENDERED	CASH GIVEN (OR RECEIVED)	FMV OF PROPERTY RECEIVED
a)	$10,000	$2,000	$9,000
b)	10,000	(2,000)	7,000
c)	10,000	3,500	15,000
d)	10,000	(3,500)	15,000
e)	10,000	(5,000)	8,000

3. Assume the following facts apply to a like-kind exchange of productive use or investment property and complete the schedule.

	ADJUSTED BASIS OF PROPERTY SURRENDERED	CASH GIVEN (OR RECEIVED)	FMV OF PROPERTY RECEIVED	RECOGNIZED GAIN (OR LOSS)	BASIS OF NEW PROPERTY
a)	$19,000	$5,000	$30,000	________	________
b)	8,000	(4,000)	20,000	________	________
c)	17,000	0	25,000	________	________
d)	17,000	0	15,000	________	________

4. Assume the following facts apply to an involuntary conversion of business property, and complete the schedule. The taxpayer wants to defer gain where possible.

	ADJUSTED BASIS OF PROPERTY DESTROYED	INSURANCE PROCEEDS	AMOUNT EXPENDED FOR IMMEDIATE REPLACEMENT OF PROPERTY	RECOGNIZED GAIN (OR LOSS)	BASIS OF NEW PROPERTY
a)	$26,000	$16,000	$24,000	________	________
b)	17,000	21,000	20,000	________	________
c)	20,000	25,000	27,000	________	________

5. Investo Corporation purchased several acres of land in 1936 for $400. This year the land was taken by the state government to be used for highway right-of-way, and the taxpayer was awarded $21,000 for the land. Investo first received notification of the prospective conversion on January 4 and received full payment for the land on November 30. In each of the following cases, compute (1) the recognized gain or loss on the conversion under Sec. 1033 and (2) the tax basis of the replacement property in those cases where the property was replaced.
   - *a*) The land was not replaced.
   - *b*) New land was purchased on June 1 for $16,000.
   - *c*) New land was purchased on December 1 for $22,000.
   - *d*) New land was purchased on December 1 for $10,200.
   - *e*) New land was purchased on December 1 of the next following year for $24,000.
   - *f*) New land was purchased on June 10 of the second following year for $30,000.

6. The following four cases relate to an involuntary conversion in which qualified replacement property is acquired within the relevant time period. For each case determine the amount of recognized gain or loss, assuming that the taxpayer wishes to defer gain if possible, and the basis of the new property.

CASE	ADJUSTED BASIS OF PROPERTY CONVERTED	INSURANCE PROCEEDS	COST OF REPLACEMENT PROPERTY
a)	$20,000	$16,000	$25,000
b)	20,000	26,000	30,000
c)	20,000	26,000	25,000
d)	20,000	26,000	18,000

7. Categorize each of the following as (1) a like-kind exchange, (2) a replacement of similar property, or (3) neither.
   - *a*) Inventory of a trade or business is exchanged for an automobile to be used in a trade or business.
   - *b*) Land and a building used in a trade or business are exchanged for unimproved land that will be held for investment.

c) Common stock held by an individual is traded for land that will be held as an investment.

d) Manufacturing machinery used to produce metal tanks is destroyed by fire; proceeds are used to acquire machines used to produce combat boots.

e) An office building held as rental property is condemned by the city for a new park. Proceeds are used to acquire farm land, which is rented immediately following acquisition.

f) A dump truck used by a dirt contractor is exchanged for a family car.

g) Machinery used to produce farm equipment is exchanged for office furniture that will be placed in rental property.

h) Unimproved land is exchanged for machinery to be used in a trade or business.

8. In 1960 Tom Fahr purchased an $18,000 frame house for his family. Eventually this house was too small for Tom and his growing family, so in April of this year he sold the frame house for $62,000. The broker's fee on the sale was $3,700. Tom incurred $600 in fixing-up expenses prior to completing the sale. On June 1 the Fahr family moved into their new brick house. What gross income must the Fahrs report this year because of the sale of their frame house if

   a) The new residence cost them $80,000?

   b) The new residence cost them $60,000?

   c) The new residence cost them $56,000?

   What is the tax basis for the Fahrs' brick house in each of the above situations?

9. The following four cases relate to the sale of a personal residence and the acquisition of a new qualifying residence within the relevant time period. For each case determine the amount of recognized gain or loss and the basis of the new residence. All taxpayers are under 55 years of age.

CASE	BASIS OF OLD RESIDENCE	AMOUNT REALIZED ON SALE OF OLD RESIDENCE	FIXING-UP COSTS	COST OF NEW RESIDENCE
a)	$60,000	$58,000	$1,500	$75,000
b)	60,000	75,000	1,500	82,000
c)	60,000	75,000	1,500	72,000
d)	60,000	75,000	1,500	58,000

10. This year Mr. Elder (age 63) sold his residence for $140,000. He and Mrs. Elder had lived in this home since 1940. They originally paid $18,000 for the home, but they remodeled it immediately at a cost of $3,000. Since then only routine upkeep was required. The Elders paid

a realtor $8,400 commission for selling the house; they also incurred fixing-up expenses of $500 one month prior to the sale. One month after selling their home, the Elders purchased a small cottage on a nearby lake for $48,000. They intend to make this lake cottage their home whenever they are not traveling.

a) What minimum amount of gain must the Elders include on their tax return this year because of the sale of their old home?

b) Would this be a capital gain or ordinary income?

c) If Mr. Elder had been 54, rather than 64, when he sold this home, what minimum amount of gain would he have to report as taxable income?

11. On April 18, Tom's Cleaners, Inc. had one of its delivery vans completely destroyed in an auto accident. The van had an adjusted basis of $3,200 at the time of the accident. Straight-line depreciation of $4,000 had been claimed on the van before the accident. Insurance proceeds of $5,000 were received on May 1. On April 20, Tom's Cleaners, Inc. purchased a new delivery van for $8,000.

a) What amount of gain did Tom's Cleaners, Inc. realize because of the accident?

b) What *minimum* amount of gain must Tom's Cleaners, Inc. recognize because of the accident?

c) If Tom's Cleaners, Inc. recognizes only the minimum amount of gain, what is its tax basis in the van purchased on April 20?

d) What *maximum* amount of gain may Tom's Cleaners, Inc. recognize because of the accident? What kind of gain is this?

e) If Tom's Cleaners, Inc. recognizes the maximum amount of gain, what is its tax basis in the van purchased on April 20?

12. Taxpayer purchased a primary residence in 1965 for $18,000. She sold that same residence for $38,000 this year. In order to sell the home, however, taxpayer incurred and paid fixing-up expenses of $400 and a real estate commission of $2,280. Three months after this sale, but within the current year, taxpayer purchased a new home for $35,500. Taxpayer is 40 years old.

a) What amount of gain did taxpayer realize because of the home sale?

b) What *minimum* amount of gain must taxpayer recognize because of the home sale?

c) If taxpayer recognizes only the minimum amount of gain, what is the tax basis of the new home?

13. For each of the independent situations below, determine (1) the amount of gain or loss realized; (2) the amount of gain or loss recognized; and (3) the tax basis of the new land. Assume that during the current year the taxpayer exchanged one parcel of farm land for an-

other; further assume that the taxpayer had held the original land for six years and that it had an adjusted tax basis of $50,000 at the time of the exchange.

a) Taxpayer received only the "new" land, which had a fair market value of $60,000.

b) Taxpayer received the new land, with a fair market value of $60,000, and $15,000 cash.

c) Taxpayer gave the other party to the exchange $5,000 cash, in addition to the land, and received in return land worth $45,000.

d) Taxpayer received only the "new" land, which had a fair market value of $60,000, and the other party to the exchange assumed taxpayer's mortgage on "old" land in the amount of $20,000.

e) Taxpayer took the "new" land and assumed a mortgage against the land in the amount of $10,000. The other party to the exchange also assumed taxpayer's mortgage on "old" land in the amount of $6,000. "New" land has estimated value of $60,000.

14. On October 10, 1946, Rancher Alpha purchased 500 acres of land on the Colorado River for $40,000. He used this land to graze cattle until this year when, on November 1, he traded the ranch for a small complex of land and buildings that had just been completed in Nearby City. This complex was intended to constitute a neighborhood shopping center. At the time of the trade, the estimated fair market value of the ranch was $250,000; that of the shopping center, $300,000. To equate the exchange, Rancher Alpha gave the builder 1,000 shares of Tractor stock, which had cost him $20,000 in 1965 but was worth $50,000 at the time of the exchange. Builder Beta, the contractor who constructed the shopping center complex, works independently with a small group of men. He makes his living by building homes and office buildings and selling them to interested parties. His construction cost in this particular complex was $270,000; he started construction on February 4 of last year.

a) Relative to Rancher Alpha:

(1) What amount of gain (or loss) did he *realize* on the exchange of the ranch and Tractor shares for the shopping center?

(2) What minimal amount of gain (or loss) must he *recognize* on this same exchange?

(3) What is the tax basis in the shopping center after the exchange has been completed, assuming he elects to pay a minimum tax now?

(4) What is the "date basis" in the shopping center?

(5) Is the shopping center a capital asset in Rancher Alpha's hands after the exchange? Explain.

(6) Can you foresee any reason why Rancher Alpha may prefer to make this a taxable (rather than a nontaxable) event? Explain.

b) Relative to Builder Beta:

(1) What amount of gain (or loss) did he *realize* on the exchange of the shopping center for the ranch and Tractor stock?

(2) What amount of gain (or loss) must he *recognize* on the exchange?

(3) What is his tax basis in the ranch after the exchange has been completed?

(4) What is his tax basis in the Tractor shares after exchange?

(5) What is his "date basis" in the ranch and the shares?

(6) Is the ranch a capital asset to Beta? Explain.

(7) Are the shares of Tractor stock capital assets to Beta? Explain.

15. H and W, both over 65, retired to Brownsville this year. They paid $85,000 for a small oceanside condominium. Earlier this year they sold their residence of 30 years in the snowbelt for $225,000. Their adjusted basis in the old residence was only $55,000.

a) Should they make the election under Sec. 121? Explain.

b) How much gain, if any, must be recognized?

c) What is their basis in the new condominium?

16. T owns farmland with a value of $140,000 and a basis of $65,000. He wants to trade the land for a small apartment house owned by Able. Able's apartment house has a value of $175,000 and a basis of $130,000. T agrees to add boot of $35,000 in the form of corporate stock with a $35,000 value and a basis of $20,000. T holds the stock as an investment. The parties agree to an exchange.

a) With respect to Able:

(1) How much gain or loss must Able recognize? What is the nature of it (capital, ordinary, etc.)?

(2) What is Able's basis in the land? In the corporate stock?

b) With respect to T:

(1) How much gain or loss must T recognize? What is the nature of the gain or loss?

(2) What is T's basis in the apartment house?

17. T owns land with a basis of $80,000, a fair market value of $125,000, and subject to a mortgage of $55,000. Able owns a small building with a fair market value of $140,000 but subject to a mortgage of $70,000, with a basis of $100,000. The parties agree to an exchange with the mortgages assumed.

a) With respect to T:

(1) How much gain or loss must T recognize?

(2) What is T's basis in the building?

b) How much gain must Able recognize? What is Able's basis in the land?

18. Matt T sold his principal residence on January 15, 19X1. The amount realized was $95,000. Matt's basis in the house was $62,000. Matt moved to a new city and bought a new residence in June, 19X1. The purchase price of the new residence was $105,000. Matt became unhappy in that city in February, 19X2. He therefore sold his new house; amount realized, $102,000. In yet another city, the third, Matt bought a new residence in July, 19Z2 at a cost of $87,000.
    a) How do these transactions affect Matt's returns for 19X1 and 19X2?
    b) How is your answer changed, if at all, if Matt is transferred by his employer to the two new locations?

TAX PLANNING PROBLEMS

1. Sam Jones has operated a dairy farm on the outskirts of a large city for a number of years. He owns 200 acres of land for which he originally paid $150 per acre. The land is situated adjacent to a railway track, and a freeway through the area (but not on Sam's place) was recently completed. The Boyce Corporation has approached Sam about buying his place to use as the site for a large manufacturing plant. They offered Sam $1,000 per acre. Sam intends to continue in the dairy business but does not want to sell his land because he will get less than its value after paying the tax. Devise a plan that will allow Boyce to obtain Sam's land and leave Sam without diminution of the value of his investment in land.

2. Nijinski suffered a loss earlier this year from a fire that completely destroyed a small warehouse used in his business. This building originally cost $175,000 but Nijinski had deducted straight-line depreciation on it of $100,000. After the fire, he immediately had a new warehouse built on the same location at a cost of $270,000. Insurance proceeds from the old building were $225,000. Nijinski will use straight-line depreciation for the new building also (to avoid the harsh recapture rules), but with the shortest possible life.

    Nijinski is trying to decide whether he should elect to defer the gain on the old structure. His marginal tax rate is 50% and he faces a 12% interest rate. What choice should he make? Support your answer with all the necessary calculations.

3. Mrs. Fritz divides her year equally between her home in Fort Lauderdale, Florida and her co-op apartment on Fifth Avenue, N.Y. She paid $350,000 for the apartment 10 years ago but it now has a value of $600,000. Mrs. Fritz has decided to sell the apartment and live in a hotel during her six months per year in New York. She is 80 years old but she is in no hurry to make this change. What actions should she take now looking forward to the sale?

CASE PROBLEM

Dave Spenser and his wife have two dependent children. Analysis of their personal checkbooks for 1985 is as follows:

Salary income	$85,000
Dividends (qualified)	5,000
State and local taxes	(3,200)
Mortgage interest on home	(4,500)

During 1985, Dave disposed of several properties:

1. On June 30, 1985, sold 1,000 shares of Chemco Common held as an investment. Acquired January 15, 1982 for $52,000. Net sales price was $46,500.
2. On April 1, 1985, sold the family residence for $130,000 (net of commission). The residence cost $68,000 in 1978. They bought a new residence in May, 1985 for $122,000. No fixing-up costs.
3. Sold 100 acres of farmland used in farming on Sept. 1, 1985. Dave's basis in the land was $70,000. Total sales price was $180,000 to be paid as follows: $45,000 cash down payment, assumption of a $35,000 mortgage, $100,000 in notes due over five years beginning in 1986.
4. On March 15, 1985, the city condemned a lot Dave had bought in 1980 at a cost of $26,000. The lot was held for an investment. Condemnation award was $45,000. He plans to buy farmland to replace this lot but has not yet found a suitable tract.
5. On Jan. 3, 1985, sold a house used as rental property for $90,000 (net of commissions). The house and lot were purchased in December, 1980 for $65,000 and the following amounts of depreciation were deducted (25-year life, DDB):

1981	$5,200
1982	4,784
1983	4,400
1984	4,050

Calculate Dave's gross tax liability for 1985.

RESEARCH PROBLEMS

1. Sheila's employer transferred her from San Francisco to Los Angeles in March of 19X1. Because of high interest rates she could not sell her home in San Francisco. She therefore rented the house in May, 19X1. In the meantime, she purchased a new home in Los Angeles in April, 19X1. The mortgage rates finally decreased in February, 19X3 and Sheila was able to sell the older residence. Can she use the benefits of Sec. 1034?

2. The state condemned 60 acres of a taxpayer's farm for an interchange on a new freeway. The taxpayer used the proceeds from the condemnation to build a new motel on his farm at the interchange. Taxpayer did not operate but only leased the farm. Likewise, the new motel will be leased to an operating company. Does this motel qualify as replacement property under Sec. 1033?

Chapter Objectives

1. Review the general rules related to the various rate schedules and to the computation of the gross tax liability.
2. Identify the individual taxpayers who are eligible for, and will benefit from, the use of income averaging.
3. Explain the mechanics of the income averaging computation and illustrate this computation on Schedule G.
4. Describe the circumstances under which taxpayers may become subject to the alternative minimum tax.
5. Explain the computation of alternative minimum taxable income and how the tax is computed on that base.
6. Describe how the alternative minimum tax can be avoided by shifting income and deductions between years.
7. Distinguish the alternative minimum tax from the add-on minimum tax formerly applicable to individuals (and still applicable to corporations).
8. Explain the rules related to payment of the estimated tax on income not subject to withholdings and the penalty that applies to underpayment of same.
9. Discuss the computation of the self-employment tax, the Social Security tax paid by taxpayers who are not employees.
10. Explain how taxpayers correct errors made on past returns.

13 The Tax Computation

The tax formula for individuals explained in Chapter 3 includes the following steps:

Taxable income	$XX
Times tax rates	X
Equals gross tax liability	$XX

Chapter 3 contains the rules for application of the basic tax rates from Schedules X, Y, and Z to taxable income to obtain the gross tax liability. The present chapter covers several important provisions that are added taxes or that are alternatives to the regular calculation explained in Chapter 3. These provisions are income averaging, the alternative minimum tax, and the tax on self-employment income. This chapter also explains some complications in the tax calculation that were in force in past years and are still referred to in the tax law.

Recall from Chapter 3 that there are four basic rate schedules applicable to individuals:

- Schedule X—Applicable to unmarried individuals who are not entitled to use the Head-of-Household Schedule.
- Schedule Y (Joint)—Applicable to married individuals who do not elect to file separately.
- Schedule Y (Separate)—Applicable to married individuals who do not want the joint liability that accompanies the joint return.

- Schedule Z—Applicable to unmarried individuals who maintain residences for children or dependents and otherwise qualify for head-of-household status.

The lowest tax liability normally results from Schedule Y (Joint), the highest from Schedule Y (Separate). Schedule Z gives to heads-of-households some of the reduction enjoyed by married individuals filing jointly.

As noted in Chapter 3, these schedules do not always give an equitable result. For example, a two-earner household may pay more tax on a joint return than would be paid if the taxpayers remained unmarried and each filed as single individuals. The deduction for two-earner incomes reduces but does not eliminate this inequity.

The provisions in this chapter further complicate the tax calculation. Income averaging replaces the usual tax calculation explained above to reduce inequities where a taxpayer's income fluctuates. Also, a 10-year averaging convention applies to a lump-sum distribution from qualified pension trusts. The alternative minimum tax places a floor on the regular tax. For the social security tax where the taxpayer is self-employed, the tax on self-employment income takes the place of withholdings.

INCOME AVERAGING CONVENTIONS

The law contains two conventions that mitigate the effects of our progressive rates when taxpayers have abnormally high incomes. The 4-year income averaging convention applies to virtually all sources of income. The 10-year convention is used only for lump-sum distributions from qualified pension and profit-sharing trusts.

FOUR-YEAR INCOME AVERAGING

Because of the progressive rates applicable to individuals on the basic rate schedules, a taxpayer who enjoys unusually high income in a year pays a high tax that year. Where income varies, the annual determination, combined with the progressive rates, creates an inequity. Income averaging alleviates this inequity by treating the unusually high income as though received over a 4-year period, for purposes of applying the progressive rates. To qualify for averaging, a taxpayer must generally be self-supporting during the base period as defined below.

BACKGROUND

Congress recognized in 1939 that the "bunching" of income combined with the progressive rate structure resulted in an inequitable tax. The original averaging provision applied only to compensation and "back pay" and could be used only if 80% of the compensation earned over a period greater than 36 months was received in a single year.*

Continued

BACKGROUND

From this beginning, the law gradually developed into a comprehensive 5-year averaging convention that was adopted in 1969. During the 1940's income subject to averaging was extended from compensation to include income from inventions and artistic works. The averaging period was increased from a 3-year to a 5-year period in 1964. The 1964 change also extended the averaging computation to most forms of income.

The Tax Reform Act of 1984 restricted the benefits of income averaging by shortening the averaging period from five years to four years. This 1984 change, which is effective for 1984 and later years, also decreased the amount of income that can be treated as received over the averaging period. These changes were made to increase tax revenues without directly raising the tax rate.

The gradual development of the averaging rules illustrates how our tax laws slowly evolve, usually becoming more equitable as our experience and understanding grow.

---

*Sommerfeld, Anderson, and Brock, *An Introduction to Taxation*, 1983 Edition (San Diego: Harcourt Brace Jovanovich, 1982) p. 28-7.

COMPUTATION OF TAX UNDER INCOME AVERAGING The computation of the tax under income averaging involves the use of several new terms:

- ***Computation year***—This is the year when the taxpayer has unusually high income.
- ***Average base-period income***—The three taxable years preceding the computation year comprise the base period. The average of the taxable income for this 3-year period is the base-period average.[1]

  Example 1: T, a single individual who qualifies for income averaging, had taxable income as follows: 19X1, $10,000; 19X2, $12,000; and 19X3, $14,000. In 19X4, T accepts a much better job and has income of $30,000. 19X4 is the computation year and the base-period average is:

19X1	10,000
19X2	12,000
19X3	14,000
Total for base period	$36,000
Average base-period income	$12,000

- ***Nonaverageable income***—To decrease the number of cases where the averaging rules apply, the base-period average is increased by

COMPUTATION YEAR The taxable year in which the averaging provision is applicable is called the computation year.

AVERAGE BASE-PERIOD INCOME The mean of the taxable incomes for the three years preceding the computation year is the average base-period income. This amount is used to compute the nonaverageable income.

NONAVERAGEABLE INCOME The average base-period income times 140% is nonaverageable income. Averaging applies to a year only if taxable income for the year exceeds nonaverageable income by more than $3,000.

---

[1]Sec. 1302 (b).

40% of the average to determine the nonaverageable income. Only the computation year taxable income in excess of nonaverageable income is subject to the averaging rules.[2]

Example 2: Extending the facts in Example 1, T's nonaverageable income is $16,800, 140% of $12,000, the base-period average.

AVERAGEABLE INCOME The amount taxed as though received over a 4-year period is averageable income, the excess of taxable income for the computation year over nonaverageable income. Taxpayers may use the averaging provisions only in years when their averageable income exceeds $3,000.

- ***Averageable income***—The excess of taxable income in the computation year over the nonaverageable income is the averageable income, subject to the special computation. Only taxpayers whose averageable income is more than $3,000 may use this special tax computation.[3] Application of the special computation where the averageable income is less than $3,000 would not produce a lower tax in most cases.

Example 3: From Example 2, the averageable income is $13,200, the computation year taxable income of $30,000 less the $16,800 nonaverageable income.

Computation of the gross tax under averaging provision is accomplished in the following manner:

1. The averageable income is divided by 4—the 3-year base period and the computation year.
2. The amount obtained in 1 (one-fourth of the averageable income) is added to nonaverageable income and a tax is figured on this amount using the appropriate rate schedule.
3. A tax on the nonaverageable income is computed using the appropriate rate schedule.
4. The difference between the tax in 3 and in 2 is the tax on one-fourth of the averageable income. The reduction in tax under the averaging provision results because this partial tax is computed on this amount at lower marginal rates.
5. The total tax is then the remainder in 4 multiplied by 4, which is the averageable income, *plus* the tax in 3 on the nonaverageable income.

Example 4: To continue Example 3, the tax calculation for T in 19X4 is:

Step 1:	One-fourth of averageable income ($13,200 divided by 4)	$3,300
Step 2:	Nonaverageable income	$16,800
	Plus amount in Step 1	3,300
		$20,100

[2] Sec. 1301.
[3] Sec. 1301.

	Tax on this amount using Schedule X for 1984 (rounded)	$3,231
Step 3:	Nonaverageable income	$16,800
	Tax on this amount from Schedule X for 1984	$2,415
Step 4:	Tax on one-fourth of averageable income:	
	Tax in Step 2	$3,231
	Less tax in Step 3	(2,415)
	Tax on one-fourth of averageable income	$816
Step 5:	Total tax for 19X4 is:	
	Tax on one-fourth of averageable income	$816
		×4
		3,264
	Plus tax on nonaverageable income (computed in Step 3)	2,415
	Gross tax for 19X4	$5,679

The tax on $30,000 for T in 19X4 without the averaging convention is $6,113 (based on 1984 rates), and the savings from use of the averaging rules are $434 ($6,113 − $5,679).

The averaging convention is available in any computation year in which the averageable income exceeds $3,000. A taxpayer whose income increases at a rapid rate over several years can enjoy this benefit until the average base period income catches up with current income.

Figure 13-1 may aid your understanding of the computations made in Examples 3 and 4. The distance ab is the nonaverageable income of $16,800

FIGURE 13-1

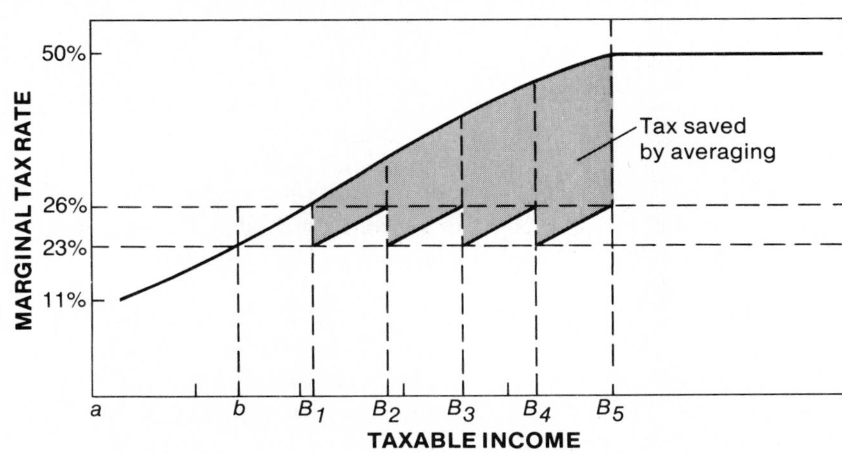

and is taxed at the usual rates for 1984 beginning at 11% and rising to 23%. The tax on this income is $2,415. The distance aB_1 is nonaverageable income *plus* one-fourth of the averageable income. This segment is taxed at rates from 11% up to 26%, for a tax of $3,231. The difference between the tax on ab and the tax on aB_1 is $816, representing the tax on distance bB_1, which is one-fourth of the averageable income. The same rates, and therefore the same tax, apply to distances B_1B_2, B_2B_3, and B_3B_4. That is, the rates from 23% to 26% are used for the other three-fourths of the averageable income. The tax for 19X4 is $2,415 plus 4 × $816, for a total of $5,679.

Example 5: In 19X5, T, the taxpayer in Example 4, has taxable income of $32,000. For 19X5, T's averageable income is:

	TAXABLE INCOME
19X2	12,000
19X3	14,000
19X4	30,000
Total base-period	$56,000
Average base-period	$18,667
Nonaverageable income (140% of $18,667)	$26,134
Averageable income ($32,000 − $26,134)	$ 5,866

T can use the averaging computation in 19X5.

Income averaging is an elective provision. The computation is chosen by claiming the benefits on Schedule G of Form 1040. Averaging should usually be elected when averageable income exceeds $3,000 and the taxpayer meets the following eligibility requirements. When the averageable income is small, however, the averaging computation may produce the same tax as the regular computation. This results when the entire averageable income falls within the same bracket on the rate schedule and is therefore subject to a single marginal rate.

ELIGIBILITY FOR INCOME AVERAGING The averaging convention applies to income from all sources, with two minor exceptions discussed below. While Congress originally included this relief provision to help taxpayers whose incomes were earned in large sums in an irregular pattern, e.g., authors of books, Congress gradually extended the averaging provision to most sources of income, provided the taxpayer is self-supporting throughout the base period.

Example 6: T, a clerk, has had a taxable income of $10,000 a year for several years. T's rich aunt dies and leaves her several million. As a result, T's taxable income for the current year skyrockets to $200,000. The averaging convention applies, if T has been self-supporting for the entire base period.

The only sources of income not eligible for averaging are premature distributions from qualified pension plans[4] and accumulation distributions from trusts subject to the throw-back rules.[5]

To be eligible for averaging, an individual must:

- Be a citizen or resident of the U.S. during the computation year and throughout the base period.[6]
- Furnish more than 50% of his or her own support throughout the base period.[7]

The second requirement is the restrictive one. It means that most students entering the job market or a profession for the first time will not qualify for averaging. Three important exceptions to the support test are included in the law:[8]

1. If the taxpayer is at least 25 years of age during the computation year and has not been a full-time student for at least four tax years after age 21, he or she may average income. This provision extends the benefits of income averaging to taxpayers who have experienced prolonged unemployment.
2. If the taxpayer's income in the computation year is attributable to work performed substantially in two or more of the base-period years, he or she may also average income. This provision is included for artists, inventors, and others who depend on others for support until they produce a valuable property.
3. A married individual who files a joint return with his or her spouse may use the averaging rules if the spouse who provided his or her own support in the base period accounts for 75% or more of the combined adjusted gross income in the computation year.

The objective of the self-support rule is to prohibit taxpayers from enjoying unintended benefits from averaging. Incidentally, income from a scholarship cannot be counted as self-support income by a college student; furthermore, the scholarship is deemed to be support provided by someone else.

FORM 1040—SCHEDULE G

REPORTING THE AVERAGING COMPUTATION Income averaging is reported on Schedule G of Form 1040 (Figure 13-2). The procedures used on Schedule G to compute the tax are somewhat different from those illustrated above and, for that reason, a completed illustration of Schedule G is appropriate.

For this illustration, assume that a qualified married individual has the

[4]Sec. 72(m)(5).

[5]Sec. 667(a).

[6]Sec. 1303(b).

[7]Sec. 1303(c).

[8]Sec. 1303(c)(2).

FIGURE 13-2

Schedule G (Form 1040) Department of the Treasury Internal Revenue Service

Income Averaging

▶ See instructions on back. ▶ Attach to Form 1040.

OMB No. 1545-0074 1984 16

Name(s) as shown on Form 1040: *Married Taxpayer* | Your social security number

Step 1 Add your income from 1981—1983

1981	1	Fill in the amount from your 1981 Form 1040 (line 34) or Form 1040A (line 12). If less than zero, enter zero	1	10,000
1982	2	Fill in the amount from your 1982 Form 1040 (line 37), Form 1040A (line 16), or Form 1040EZ (line 7). If less than zero, enter zero	2	9,000
1983	3	Fill in the amount from your 1983 Form 1040 (line 37), Form 1040A (line 19), or Form 1040EZ (line 7). If less than zero, enter zero	3	17,000
Total	4	Fill in all income less deductions earned outside of the U.S. or within U.S. possessions and excluded for 1981 through 1983 (include housing exclusion in 1982 and 1983)	4	0
	5	Add lines 1 through 4	5	36,000

Step 2 Figure your averageable income

6	Divide the amount on line 5 by three (3)	6	12,000
7	Multiply the amount on line 6 by 140% (1.4)	7	16,800
8	Fill in your taxable income for 1984 from Form 1040, line 37	8	50,000
9	If you received a premature or excessive distribution subject to a penalty under section 72, see instructions	9	
10	Subtract line 9 from line 8	10	50,000
11	If you live in a community property state and are filing a separate return, see instructions	11	
12	Subtract line 11 from line 10. If less than zero, enter zero	12	50,000
13	Write in the amount from line 7 above	13	16,800
14	Subtract line 13 from line 12. This is your averageable income. If this line is $3,000 or less, do not complete the rest of this form	14	33,200

Step 3 Figure your tax

15	Multiply the amount on line 14 by 25% (.25)			15	8,300
16	Write in the amount from line 7 above			16	16,800
17	Add lines 15 and 16			17	25,100
18	Write in the amount from line 11 above			18	
19	Add lines 17 and 18			19	25,100
20	Tax on amount on line 19 (from Tax Rate Schedule X, Y, or Z)			20	3,590
21	Tax on amount on line 17 (from Tax Rate Schedule X, Y, or Z)	21	3,590		
22	Tax on amount on line 16 (from Tax Rate Schedule X, Y, or Z)	22	1,885		
23	Subtract line 22 from line 21	23	1,705		
24	Multiply the amount on line 23 by 3			24	5,115
	If you have no entry on line 9, skip lines 25 through 27 and go to line 28.				
25	Tax on amount on line 8 (from Tax Rate Schedule X, Y, or Z)	25			
26	Tax on amount on line 10 (from Tax Rate Schedule X, Y, or Z)	26			
27	Subtract line 26 from line 25			27	
28	Add lines 20, 24, and 27. Write the result here and on Form 1040, line 38 if less than the tax figured using the tax rate schedules or table. Also, check the Schedule G box			28	8,705

For Paperwork Reduction Act Notice, see Form 1040 instructions. | **Schedule G (Form 1040) 1984**

following amounts of taxable income during the base period and the computation year:

Year 1	= 1981	$10,000
2	= 1982	9,000
3	= 1983	17,000
4	= 1984	50,000

A 1984 Schedule G is shown in Figure 13-2. The computation on Schedule G is the same as that in the text with some exceptions. In Step 1, the taxable incomes for the three base years are shown. At line 7, the base period average is multiplied by 140% to obtain the nonaverageable income. Lines 9 and 11 deal with required adjustments beyond our scope here. At line 24, the tax on one-fourth of the averageable income is multiplied by 3 and then added to the tax at line 20 which is the tax on the nonaverageable income plus one-fourth of the averageable income. The results are the same as those for the computation required by the statute.

TEN-YEAR AVERAGING FOR LUMP-SUM DISTRIBUTIONS

Employees who receive lump-sum distributions from qualified pension and profit-sharing trusts have unusually high taxable incomes for that year. The statute contains a special relief measure, a 10-year averaging rule, that reduces the tax on the lump-sum distribution. A lump-sum distribution is one that liquidates the employee's entire interest in the trust due to death, disability, separation from service, or retirement after the age of 59½.[9]

AMOUNT SUBJECT TO AVERAGING RULE The 10-year averaging conventions apply only to the *taxable distribution* that is treated as *ordinary income*. The *taxable distribution* is the total distribution less: (*a*) the employee's contributions to the plan; and (*b*) any appreciation in the employer's securities included in the plan.[10]

Example 7: T worked for several years for Corporation Y. Y provided a qualified pension plan that permitted contributions by employees. Upon separation from service with Y, T received $80,000 cash in complete liquidation of his interest in the trust. T had contributed $8,000. The taxable distribution is $72,000.

Example 8: T receives a lump-sum distribution that consisted in part of Y Corporation's stock. Y Corporation was T's employer. The Y stock had a fair market value of $15,000 when received but its "cost" to Y when contributed to the trust was only $10,000. T's taxable distribution includes only $10,000.

---

[9] Sec. 402(e)(4)(A).

[10] Sec. 402(e)(4)(D) (called "total taxable amount" in the statute).

A taxable distribution attributable to an employee's service after 1973 is treated as ordinary income subject to the 10-year averaging convention. The portion of the taxable distribution attributable to service before 1974 may be treated as a long-term capital gain.[11] Generally, the entire amount of a lump-sum distribution was a capital gain prior to changes in the law in 1969 and 1974. The allocation between the pre-1974 capital gain portion and the post-1973 ordinary income portion is based on the months of active participation before and after December 31, 1973.

Example 9: Recently T received a $72,000 taxable distribution. He had participated in the plan for 180 months, 60 of which occurred before 1974. The capital-gain portion, then, is:

$$\$72{,}000 \times \frac{\text{60 months pre-1974}}{\text{180 months total}} = \$24{,}000$$

The remaining $48,000 is ordinary income subject to the 10-year averaging rules.

A taxpayer may elect to treat an entire distribution as ordinary income subject to 10-year averaging even though partly attributable to the pre-1974 period. This election will often produce a lower tax than the partial allocation to capital gains.[12] (See Example 10.) Such is usually true except for very large lump-sum distributions or where the taxpayer's taxable income excluding the lump-sum distribution is very low.

The value of assets in qualified pension and profit-sharing trusts are generally excluded from the federal estate tax up to a limit of $100,000. However, this death tax exclusion is lost if the beneficiary who receives a lump-sum distribution uses the 10-year averaging rule.[13]

THE TAX COMPUTATION The 10-year averaging computation specifies a "partial" tax on the ordinary income portion of the taxable distribution. The regular tax computation applies to the other taxable income for the year, including the capital-gain allocation of the lump-sum distribution. The tax due is the sum of the "partial" tax and the regular tax. The partial tax is computed as follows:[14]

FORM 4972

- Taxable distribution (less any portion allocated to capital gain)
- Less: A minimum distribution allowance equal to:
  - a) The *lesser* of $10,000 or one-half of the taxable distribution
  - b) Reduced (but not below zero) by 20% of the taxable distribution in excess of $20,000.
- The net distribution is divided by 10 (thus, 10-year averaging)

[11] Sec. 402(e)(4)(E).
[12] Sec. 402(e)(4)(L).
[13] Sec. 2039(f)(2).
[14] Sec. 402(e)(1).

- Tax on this is one-tenth plus $2,300 using the rates on Tax Rate Schedule X (single individuals)
- Ten times the tax above is the partial tax.

The minimum distribution allowance gives an effect approximately equal to the long-term capital-gain deduction for smaller distributions. Note that the allowance rises to a maximum of $10,000 as the taxable distribution goes from zero to $20,000 and then decreases to zero as the taxable distribution goes from $20,000 to $70,000. The zero-bracket amount of $2,300 on Tax Rate Schedule X must be added to one-tenth of the net amount before the rate schedule can be used. Rate Schedule X is used by all taxpayers without regard to marital status or other circumstances.

Example 10: In 1984 T, a single individual, received a lump-sum distribution of $72,000. T's contributions amounted to $12,000 leaving a taxable distribution of $60,000. T's taxable income before the distribution was $81,800. T elects to treat the entire $60,000 as ordinary income. T's regular tax from Schedule X (1984) on $81,800 is $28,835. The partial tax is:

Taxable distribution		$60,000
Minimum distribution allowance:		
Lesser of $10,000 or $30,000	$10,000	
Less: 20% of $60,000 less $20,000	(8,000)	(2,000)
Net amount		$58,000
Divided by 10		$ 5,800
plus zero-bracket amount on Schedule X		2,300
		$ 8,100
Tax from Schedule X (1984) on $8,100		$ 775
Multiply by 10 for partial tax		$7,750

Total tax for 1984 is $36,585, the regular tax of $28,835 plus the $7,750 partial tax.

In Example 10 the highest marginal rate applicable under 10-year averaging is only 15%. If the entire $60,000 were treated as a capital gain, T's total tax would increase by $12,000, a 20% rate on the $60,000, since T's other income of $81,800 places him in the 50% marginal rate. The top marginal rate applicable under 10-year averaging will usually be lower than the marginal rate applicable to capital gains.

THE ALTERNATIVE MINIMUM TAX

Through careful planning that utilizes the many preferential provisions in the law, individual taxpayers can substantially reduce their income taxes. Often taxpayers and their tax advisors have such success that their tax liability is nominal. The capital-gain provisions, losses from real estate investments and other shelters, and large tax credits are the ***preferences*** that result in nominal liabilities. For taxpayers who enjoy too much success in tax reductions, Congress provides an ***alternative minimum tax (AMT)*** that puts a "floor" on the tax payments for any year. The AMT applies to 1983 and later years.

PREFERENCES A provision of the tax law that confers a benefit through lower taxes is known as a preference. Some preferences are assigned dollar values and included in the bases for the add-on minimum tax and for the AMT.

ALTERNATIVE MINIMUM TAX (AMT) A tax based in part on the taxpayer's preferences that is levied when it exceeds the regular tax. This tax is included in the law to assure a nominal tax payment when preferences such as the capital-gain deduction drastically reduce the regular tax. Corporations are not subject to this tax.

ADD-ON MINIMUM TAX A tax levied in addition to the "regular" tax on taxable income and added to the regular tax. Based on the taxpayer's preferences for the year, the add-on minimum applied to all taxpayers before 1983 but applies only to corporations after 1982.

BACKGROUND

The alternative minimum tax (AMT) for individuals is the product of a tax reform movement that began in 1969. In the late 1960s, the popular press carried numerous stories about taxpayers with incomes of $1 million or more who paid virtually no income taxes because of various preferences such as the deduction for net capital gains, percentage depletion for oil and gas, etc. The Congressional response was the imposition of a minimum tax based on the preferences used.

As originally enacted in 1969, the minimum tax was an add-on tax; that is, a taxpayer calculated his or her tax in the normal manner, then calculated a tax on his or her preferences using a special rate, and *added* the minimum tax to the regular tax to obtain the total tax due for the year. Congress adopted this method of "reform" rather than the repeal or amendment of the various preferential provisions.* But Congress was never happy with this solution and it made numerous changes to the ***add-on minimum tax*** during the 1970s and finally removed the net capital-gain deduction from the preferences subject to the tax.

Then, in 1978, Congress added an AMT applicable only to individuals, designed primarily to exact some income tax from taxpayers with large incomes from capital gains and also large deductions. The add-on minimum tax also applied to individuals. Finally, in 1982, the add-on minimum tax on individuals was repealed and the AMT explained in the text was enacted. The base for the AMT includes the capital-gain deduction as well as other preferences previously used for the add-on minimum.

Corporations are still subject to the add-on minimum tax on preferences, as explained in Chapter 16.

*Sommerfeld, op. cit., p. 28-4.

The base for the AMT is:

Adjusted gross income	$XX
Less: Certain deductions from AGI allowed	X
	X
Plus: Tax preferences	X
Alternative minimum income taxable	$XX

To this alternative minimum taxable income a minimum exemption applies based on the following schedule:

	EXEMPTION
Married couples filing jointly and surviving spouses	$40,000
Single individuals	$30,000
Married individuals filing separately	$20,000

After subtracting the exemption, a rate of 20% applies to determine the AMT. Except for the foreign tax credit, nonrefundable credits cannot be used to reduce the AMT.

Example 11: T, a single taxpayer, has alternative minimum taxable income for a year after 1982 of $80,000. T's AMT is:

Alternative minimum taxable income	$80,000
Exemption	(30,000)
Base for AMT	$50,000
	×20%
AMT	$10,000

If T's regular tax liability is only $7,000, T must pay the $10,000 AMT.

Calculations of alternative minimum taxable income and preferences are discussed in the following sections.

ALTERNATIVE MINIMUM TAXABLE INCOME

The beginning point for the calculation of the AMT is the ***alternative minimum taxable income***. That amount is the taxpayer's adjusted gross income less *some* of the deductions from AGI plus the tax preferences. Several of the usual deductions allowed for AGI must be further adjusted for this purpose. The deductions from AGI allowed for the AMT calculation are:[15]

ALTERNATIVE MINIMUM TAXABLE INCOME The base for the AMT is alternative minimum taxable income. The base is AGI plus tax preferences less some of the deductions from AGI.

- Medical expense deduction—The deduction for medical expenses is allowed but only to the extent such expenses exceed 10% of AGI. The floor on this deduction for the regular tax is only 5%.
- Casualty loss deduction—The losses are allowed in the same amount as in the regular computation, to the extent that they exceed 10% of AGI.
- Charitable contribution deduction—Contributions are allowed in the same amount as for the regular tax.
- Qualified interest deduction—Interest expense is deductible only: (*a*) if it is qualified housing interest; and (*b*) for other interest only to the extent of investment income (interest, dividends, gains, etc.) realized during the year. Qualified housing interest means interest

[15] Sec. 55(e).

paid on mortgages and other pledges related to the taxpayer's principal residence or other dwelling, but only if the pledged indebtedness was incurred before July 1, 1982.

- Estate tax deduction—The deduction allowed for estate taxes paid on income in respect of a decedent.

Taxpayers who have a net operating loss must make several required adjustments to determine the net operating loss allowed for the AMT.[16] These adjustments are beyond the scope of this introduction.

Example 12: For 1984, H's and W's regular taxable income and the tax thereon was computed in the following manner:

Gross income:	
Salary	$100,000
Dividends (net of $200 exclusion)	11,000
Net capital gain	350,000
Gross income	$461,000
Less deductions for AGI:	
Loss from partnership	(25,000)
Capital-gain deduction (60% of $350,000)	(210,000)
Adjusted gross income	$226,000
Less deductions from AGI:	
State taxes	($30,000)
Charitable contributions	(50,000)
Interest expense—residence	(12,000)
Other interest	(26,000)
Miscellaneous deductions	(5,000)
Exemptions	(4,000)
Total	($127,000)
Less zero-bracket amount	(3,400)
Deductions from AGI	($123,600)
Taxable income	$102,400
Regular tax for 1984 from Schedule Y (Joint)	$33,480
Less: Foreign tax credit	(1,000)
Investment tax credit	(2,000)
Net tax due	$30,480

Based on these facts, H's and W's alternative minimum taxable income (before adding preferences) is computed as follows:

Adjusted gross income	$226,000
Less allowed deductions:	
Contributions	($50,000)
Interest on residence	(12,000)
Other interest	(26,000)
Alternative minimum taxable income (before preferences)	$138,000

[16] Sec. 55(d).

The deductions for state taxes, miscellaneous items, and exemptions are not allowed. The other interest of $26,000 is allowed because it is less than the investment income (dividends of $11,200 plus the $350,000 capital gain).

Example 13: T has AGI of $80,000 and incurred medical expenses of $7,500. For the regular tax calculation, T is allowed a medical expense deduction of $3,500, the excess of $7,500 over $4,000, 5% of $80,000. However, no deduction is allowed for medical expense in calculation of the AMT because the limit is $8,000, 10% of AGI.

PREFERENCES FOR THE AMT

Once the taxable income is adjusted in the manner described above, the tax preferences are added to obtain the basis for the AMT. The preferences that will affect most taxpayers are:[17]

- Net capital-gain deduction—The preference that will usually trigger the AMT is the 60% net capital-gain deduction.
- Dividend and interest exclusion—This preference includes the $100 ($200 on joint returns) dividend exclusion under Section 116 and interest on All-Savers certificates excluded under Section 128.
- Excess of accelerated depreciation on real property over straight-line—Taxpayers who invest in real estate shelters usually elect the most rapid capital recovery available and the "excess" depreciation is a preference. For ACRS (Accelerated Cost Recovery System) property, the excess is the depreciation claimed over straight-line based on 18 years.

The law contains several other preferences that affect fewer taxpayers than those listed above:

- Allowable depletion (statutory) of mineral properties over the adjusted basis of the property.
- Intangible drilling costs for oil and gas properties in excess of income from such properties.
- The market value over the option price of stock acquired under an incentive stock option.
- Excess depreciation for leased personal property.
- Excess amortization of pollution control devices recovered over a 5-year period.
- Excess of deductions for mining exploration costs, circulation expenses, and research and development expenses over the amounts allowable if such costs were capitalized and recovered over a 10-year period.

[17] Sec. 57(a).

Detailed explanations and illustrations of these preferences are beyond the scope of this introduction.

Example 14: Refer to the computation of alternative minimum taxable income before preferences for H and W in Example 12. Assume further in that example that the partnership in which H and W own an interest ($25,000 loss reported) has excess depreciation of real estate and that H's and W's share of the excess is $20,000. The base of minimum tax and the tax calculation is:

Alternative minimum taxable income from Example 12	$138,000
Add preferences:	
Dividend exclusion	200
60% capital-gain deduction	210,000
Excess depreciation from partnership	20,000
Alternative minimum taxable income including preferences	$368,200
Less exemption allowed on joint return	(40,000)
Base for AMT	$328,200
Applicable rate	20%
AMT for 1983 before credits	$65,640
Less credit allowed for foreign income taxes	(1,000)
AMT for 1983	$64,640

From Example 12 the 1984 regular tax for H and W is only $30,480. The AMT applies for this year and H and W owe a tax of $64,640.

When the AMT applies to a year and, as a result, tax credits other than the foreign tax credit are disallowed, the credits are available as a carryback and carryover.[18]

Example 15: Refer to Examples 12 and 14. For 1984, H and W were disallowed a $2,000 investment tax credit because the AMT applied to 1984. This $2,000 credit is available for carryback and carryforward as explained in Chapter 14.

The AMT can increase substantially the tax for a year when there are large amounts of preferences. However, important planning opportunities exist in years when the AMT applies. See the Planning Workshop at the end of this chapter.

REPORTING THE AMT

FORM 6251 Taxpayers subject to the AMT must file Form 6251. Since the AMT affects only a relatively few taxpayers, Form 6251 is not illustrated in the text.

---

[18] Sec. 55(c)(3).

SELF-EMPLOYMENT TAX AND DECLARATION OF ESTIMATED TAX

Most individuals in the U.S. derive the bulk of their incomes from wages and salaries. These payments are subject to withholdings and for most taxpayers only a nominal payment of the income tax is due with the return on April 15. Indeed, withholdings may result in an overpayment and an annual return becomes a claim for refund. The typical taxpayer also pays his or her Social Security (FICA) tax through withholdings so that no payment is due on this tax at year end.

Self-employed individuals and other taxpayers with substantial amounts of income not subject to withholdings face a more complicated problem. Their payments for the income and Social Security taxes are not made entirely by their employers through withholdings. Nevertheless, their tax payments must be on a pay-as-you-go basis through quarterly estimated tax payments. Otherwise, they may also owe substantial penalties.

SELF-EMPLOYMENT TAX

FORM 1040—SCHEDULE SE

Individuals who have net earnings from self-employment of $400 or more are subject to the self-employment tax.[19] An individual who is an employee and also self-employed does not pay the self-employment tax if his or her wages or salaries subject to withholdings equal or exceed the ceiling for the FICA taxes. For 1985, the ceiling on Social Security taxes is $39,600. The rate for the self-employment tax for 1985 is 11.8 percent.[20]

Example 16: For 1985, T has ***self-employment income*** of $20,000 from the practice of law. He is also employed by the county as an assistant district attorney and earns $40,000, all subject to withholdings. T has paid his full Social Security taxes through withholdings and no self-employment tax is due.

SELF-EMPLOYMENT INCOME The base for the Social Security tax on self-employed individuals is self-employment income, the net taxable income from the operation of a trade or business.

Example 17: Assume in Example 16 that T's salary from the county is $24,000. T's self-employment income subject to the tax is $15,600 (the $39,600 ceiling, less the wages of $24,000 subject to withholdings). His self-employment Social Security tax for 1985 is $1,840.80 ($15,600 × .118).

The base for the self-employment tax is net earnings from self-employment. This term means the gross income from the trade or business less the deduction *for* AGI related to the business operation.[21] This definition translates into the "net income from the business" except that gains and losses from the sale or exchange of property other than inventory are excluded. The final amounts on Schedule C (trade or business) and on Schedule F (farming) are net earnings from self-employment. Also excluded from the base are all items of passive income such as dividends,

---

[19] Sec. 6017.

[20] Sec. 1401(a) and (b).

[21] Sec. 1402(a).

interests, etc. Where a partnership engages in self-employment activities, the net earnings from self-employment of the partnership are divided up among the partners and each reports and pays the tax on his or her share.

The distinction between self-employment and the employee status is often unclear. Employers prefer the self-employment category for workers because the Social Security tax is thereby shifted to the worker. As a result, a substantial body of law exists on this point and the statute contains numerous exceptions and special rules.[22] To be self-employed, an individual must be in the position of an *independent* contractor. An independent contractor is one who controls the hours and schedules of work, who has a substantial investment in tools or other assets (other than an automobile) used on the job, and who does not use the employer's place of business as a normal work place. Realtors and persons engaged in direct-sales activities are generally treated as independent contractors even when they do not meet the above tests.[23]

PAYMENT OF ESTIMATED TAXES

FORM 1040—ES

ESTIMATED TAX Taxpayers with income that is not subject to withholdings must pay their estimated tax for each year quarterly to avoid a penalty. The estimated tax is the excess of the expected gross tax over available credits and withholdings.

Individuals who have income from sources not subject to withholdings are required to declare and pay their estimated taxes during the tax year. The ***estimated tax*** is the excess of a taxpayer's gross tax over his or her credits and withholdings. For 1984, the minimum is $400; it increases to $500 in 1985 and later years. Prior to 1983, taxpayers were required to file a declaration of estimated tax under certain specified conditions, even when no estimated tax payment was due.[24] There was no penalty for failure to file the declaration; the penalty came from failure to pay the estimated tax on a timely basis.[25] While the declaration is no longer required, the penalty is still in effect for underpayment of the estimated tax.

FORM 2210

For calendar year taxpayers, quarterly payments of the estimated tax are due on April 15, June 15, September 15 of the taxable year, and January 15 of the following year. The penalty is assessed on *underpayments* of the estimated quarterly amount. An underpayment is the excess, if any, of the quarterly installment required by law over the actual amount paid for the quarter.[26] The required quarterly installment is generally 20% of the actual taxes shown on the return for the year.[27] Use of 20% to determine the required installment means that no penalty is due if the estimated tax paid in equal quarterly installments equals 80% of the tax shown on the return. The penalty is computed using the interest rate charged by the government for late payments of the tax (13% at the time this is written) applied from the time of the underpayment until such time as the tax is due, compounded daily. The penalty is treated as an additional tax, not as deductible interest.

---

[22] Sec. 1402(c) and (e).

[23] Sec. 3509.

[24] Sec. 6015.

[25] Sec. 6654(a).

[26] Sec. 6654(b).

[27] Sec. 6654(d).

Example 18: T, a calendar taxpayer, computes an estimated tax of $4,000 for 19X1. He makes no payment of this estimated tax during 19X1 but pays the tax when his return is filed on April 15, 19X2. The estimated quarterly payments are $1,000 and the underpayment on April 15, 19X1 is $800 (80% of $1,000 less the actual payment of zero on that date). The penalty on this $800 is computed by using the current interest rate, compounded daily, for the entire year from April 15, 19X1 to the time of payment on April 15, 19X2. On June 15, 19X1, the underpayment is again $800 but the penalty is for only 10 months, from June 15, 19X1 to April 15, 19X2. Penalties for the other quarters are calculated in a similar way. The interest rate used to calculate the penalty in this example may change on January 1 and July 1 of each year.

The statute contains two exceptions to the application of the underpayment penalty. First, no penalty applies if each of the quarterly installments equals 25% of the tax shown on the return for the preceding year.[28] A zero tax liability for the preceding year can be used only if the preceding year was a 12-month year and if the taxpayer filed a return for such year. Second, no penalty is assessed if the quarterly payment equals 20% of the annualized tax for the year, based on the actual transactions of the taxpayer for the months of the year preceding the due date of the installment.[29] This provision protects taxpayers whose taxable incomes unexpectedly increase after the payments of earlier installments.

Numerous other exceptions and special rules related to the calculation of the estimated tax and the underpayment penalty exist, but are beyond the scope of this introduction.

CORRECTION OF PAST RETURNS

Chapter 2 describes the steps taken by the IRS after a taxpayer has assessed himself or herself for the income tax. If the IRS determines that the self-assessed tax is incorrect, the IRS will refund any excess payment or assess the taxpayer for an underpayment, under the procedures described in Chapter 2.

A taxpayer can also correct his or her mistakes on past returns. While such corrections can result in additional tax payments, the usual case involves a claim for refund of overpayments. Both taxpayers and the government can correct errors within limited time periods specified in the statute and called ***statute of limitations***. Once the statute of limitations has expired, underpayments and overpayments cannot generally be corrected.

STATUTE OF LIMITATIONS
The period during which the IRS and taxpayers may correct errors in tax returns is referred to as the statute of limitations. For income tax returns, the period is generally three years.

[28] Sec. 6654(d)(1)(B). Prior to 1985, four "escape" clauses existed for the underpayment penalty.

[29] Sec. 6654(d)(2).

STATUTE OF LIMITATIONS

Taxpayers and the government generally have three years from the date a return is filed to correct errors on the return.[30] If a return is actually filed *before* the due date, the period runs from the due date, not from the filing date.[31]

Example 19: T, a calendar year taxpayer, files his income tax return for 19X1 on April 1, 19X2. The return is treated as filed on April 15, 19X2, its due date. The statute of limitations expires on April 16, 19X5. Both T and the IRS have until April 15, 19X5 to correct the 19X1 return.

Many exceptions exist to the three-year period just explained. The more important exceptions are:

- Refund Claims—Refund claims can be initiated by taxpayers within three years from the filing date of the return, or two years from the date when the tax is paid, whichever is later.[32]

Example 20: Assume that T in Example 19 does not pay his 19X1 tax until June 1, 19X3. T has until June 1, 19X5 to file a refund claim against his 19X1 tax. (Note that T will be subject to interest and perhaps penalties for failure to pay his tax on a timely basis.)

- Statutory Fraud—The statute of limitations runs for six years when a taxpayer omits gross income in excess of 25% of the gross income reported.[33] Such an omission subjects the taxpayer to the special penalties for statutory fraud.
- Criminal Fraud—The government can bring charges of criminal fraud against a taxpayer at any time. Neither the three-year nor the six-year period affords protection to the taxpayer who willfully defrauds the government.

FORMS USED TO AMEND PAST RETURNS

Taxpayers who wish to correct erroneous past returns, usually to obtain a refund, have several options available. Some options are better than others, depending on the circumstances.

FORM 1040X

The simplest form is one specifically designed for this purpose, Form 1040X, Amended Return. This form requires an explanation of the correction or corrections and a recalculation of the added tax due or the refund. The rates, exemptions, zero-bracket amounts, and other rules of law ap-

---

[30] Sec. 6501(a) and Sec. 6511(a).

[31] Sec. 6501(b)(1).

[32] Sec. 6511(a).

[33] Sec. 6501(e).

plicable to the year corrected must be used to complete Form 1040X. Claims for refunds of the income tax must be made on this form.

If numerous errors were made, the regular return form, e.g., Form 1040, for that year may be used, conspicuously marked "Amended Return" at the top of the front page. This method is used for underpayments of the income tax.

Refund claims that originate from carrybacks of net operating losses or investment tax credits should be reported on Form 1045, Tentative Adjustment for Carryback. Use of this form speeds up the IRS processing of the refund claim.

P L A N N I N G   W O R K S H O P

The provisions in this chapter related to income averaging offer few opportunities for tax planning. Indeed, income averaging is most important when a taxpayer cannot avoid the bunching of income into a single year. On the other hand, careful planning is necessary to minimize the impact of the AMT and the penalty on underpayments of estimated taxes.

PLANNING AROUND THE AMT

The AMT applies only to taxpayers who take advantage of the numerous preferences in the tax law. Except for taxpayers involved in the oil and gas industry, the 60% capital-gain deduction is the preference that will usually give rise to the AMT. Arrangements that spread the realization of a large capital gain over several years can often avoid the imposition of the AMT. Note that if a large capital gain is realized in one year and the 20% AMT rate applies to it, the taxpayer does not get the full benefit from the 60% deduction. Spreading the gain over several years, usually through an installment sale, will solve this problem.

Example 21: T plans to sell some real estate in 19X1 that she has held for several years. The sale will result in a large capital gain. T's ordinary income in 19X1 is unusually low and she has several large deductions in 19X1. As a result, the AMT will apply to 19X1. T should probably sell the property on installments and defer some of the gain to later years.

Taxpayers should make tentative calculations before their taxable years end to determine if the AMT will be imposed for that year. If the AMT is applicable to a given year, taxes can usually be saved by taking the following steps:

Continued

PLANNING WORKSHOP

- Accelerate into the current year the recognition of ordinary income (but not capital gains).
- Defer deductions from the current year into the next year when the regular tax applies. Deductions not allowed in the computation of alternative minimum taxable income, e.g., state and local taxes, should be deferred to a later year. Since most individuals use the cash basis, deferral is easily accomplished by delaying the payment.

The amount of ordinary income recognized early and/or the deductions deferred is the amount necessary to make the regular tax equal the AMT. The planning moves reduce taxes in the later years *without a corresponding increase in the current tax*. Planning opportunities such as this are rare.

Example 22: T owes local property taxes on his residence and on land held for investment. The taxes amount to $5,000 and are due in December 19X1. For 19X1, T's federal income tax liability will be based on the AMT and local taxes are not deductible in computing that tax. If T pays the taxes in 19X1, he gets no benefit. If he pays the taxes in January of 19X2, they will be deductible for the regular tax computation in 19X2 and could reduce T's 19X2 taxes by as much as 50% (the maximum marginal rate).

Foresight is the key to obtaining the advantages just described. Projections of the possible application of the AMT should be made early in the year.

Note that the acceleration of income recognition and the deferral of deductions increase both the regular tax and the AMT. Use of this strategy means that the taxpayer must pay more taxes now to achieve a greater reduction of later taxes, not a wise course of action if the taxpayer's financial future is uncertain. Also, in every case where you pay now to save later, you must consider the time value of money.

PAYMENT OF THE ESTIMATED TAX

The penalty for underpayment of the estimated tax is based on the interest rate used by the government for underpayments and overpayments of the regular tax liability. This interest rate is adjusted twice annually on January 1 and July 1, based on the average prime rate in effect for 6-month periods ending on March 31 and September 30. Given our volatile interest rates of recent years, the interest rate that a taxpayer pays on money borrowed (or forgone on savings) to pay the tax can be quite different from the rate charged by

Continued

PLANNING WORKSHOP

the government. If the government rate is higher, then the estimated tax should be fully paid in every instance.

Note that the penalty for underpayment of the estimate, though calculated using an interest rate, is a *penalty*, and is therefore not deductible. Interest paid on borrowed money is deductible and the effective, after-tax rate is much lower.

Example 23: T underpaid his estimated tax for 19X1 by $1,000 and a $130 penalty was assessed using the current 13% Code rate. The penalty is not deductible. Assume that T's marginal tax rate is 40% and that T could have borrowed the $1,000 needed to avoid penalty by paying interest of 13% to a lending institution. However, the interest is deductible and T's effective interest cost is only $78 (based on a 7.8% after-tax effective interest rate). T should choose to borrow the $1000 and avoid the penalty.

The government rate must be substantially lower than the borrowing rate to offset the fact that penalty is not deductible.

KEY POINTS TO REMEMBER

1. To be eligible for income averaging, an individual must provide his or her own support throughout the base period and the averageable income must exceed $3,000.
2. The averaging computation applies the taxes rates to averageable income, which is the taxable income of the computation year in excess of 140% of average base-period income, as though the averageable income were received over a 4-year period.
3. A 10-year averaging rule applies to lump-sum distributions from pension and profit-sharing trusts. The resulting tax on such distributions is usually lower than that obtainable by allocation of the pre-1974 distributions to capital gains.
4. Alternative minimum taxable income is adjusted gross income plus tax preferences less certain deductions *from* AGI allowed for this calculation.
5. The AMT is 20% of alternative minimum taxable income reduced by the appropriate exemption ($30,000 for single individuals, $40,000 on joint returns). The AMT is the gross tax when it exceeds the "regular" tax.
6. Taxpayers can avoid the AMT by accelerating the recognition of ordinary income and/or by deferring deductions.
7. Generally taxpayers must pay the income taxes in advance through withholdings and quarterly payments of the estimated tax. Failure to "prepay" at least 80% of the actual tax will usually result in the imposition of an underpayment penalty.

8. The underpayment penalty, while computed on the government's interest rate, is not interest and is not deductible. As a result, the after-tax cost of the penalty is usually greater than the cost of borrowing money to pay the estimated tax.
9. Self-employed individuals, who do not pay their Social Security taxes through withholdings on salaries and wages earned, must pay the self-employment tax at a rate of 11.8% in 1985.
10. Form 1040X is the most convenient method of amending incorrect past returns and must be used for an income tax refund claim.

SELF-STUDY QUESTIONS

1. Ronald Raff filed his 1983 individual income tax return on January 15, 1984. There was no understatement of income on the return, and the return was signed and filed. The statute of limitations for Raff's 1983 return expires on

   a) January 15, 1987

   b) April 15, 1987

   c) January 15, 1990

   d) April 15, 1990

   (AICPA adapted)

2. Richard Baker filed his 1982 individual income tax return on April 15, 1983. On December 31, 1983, he learned that 100 shares of stock that he owned had become worthless in 1982. Since he did not deduct this loss on his 1982 return, Baker intends to file a claim for refund. This refund claim must be filed no later than April 15,

   a) 1984

   b) 1986

   c) 1989

   d) 1990

   (AICPA adapted)

3. During 1979 William Clark was assessed a deficiency on his 1978 federal income tax return. As a result of this assessment he was required to pay $1,120 determined as follows:

Additional tax	$900
Late filing penalty	60
Negligence penalty	90
Interest	70

   What portion of the $1,120 would qualify as itemized deductions for 1979?

   a) $0

   b) $ 70

c) $150

d) $220

(AICPA adapted)

4. George Rathman received a salary of $45,000 as an actor in 1968 and had a taxable income of $42,000. Taxable income for the four preceding years was $6,000, $10,000, $14,000, and $18,000, consisting entirely of salary. For income averaging in 1968 Rathman's averageable income is

   a) $14,000

   b) $15,400

   c) $22,400

   d) $45,000

   (AICPA adapted)

5. Edward Grace, a cash-basis taxpayer, is the sole proprietor of a shoe store. In operating his store during 1976, he realized the following:

Net profit from sale of shoes	$8,000
Gain from sale of display cases	2,000
Winning lottery ticket purchased in store's name	3,000
Damage to store fixtures arising from flood	1,000

   What should Grace report as net earnings from self-employment for 1976?

   a) $ 7,000

   b) $ 8,000

   c) $ 9,000

   d) $12,000

   (AICPA adapted)

6. The records of Paul Thorpe, a cash-basis proprietor, for 1979 include the following information:

Gross receipts	$60,000
Dividend income (on personal investment)	400
Cost of sales	30,000
Other operating expenses	6,000
State business taxes paid	600
Federal self-employment tax paid	1,600

   What amount should Thorpe report as net earnings from self-employment for 1979?

   a) $21,800

   b) $23,400

   c) $23,800

   d) $24,000

   (AICPA adapted)

7. Gilda Bach is a cash basis self-employed consultant. For the year 1978 she determined that her net income from self-employment was $80,000. In reviewing her books you determine that the following items were included as business expenses in arriving at the net income of $80,000:

Salary drawn by Gilda Bach	$20,000
Estimated federal self-employment and income taxes paid	6,000
Malpractice insurance premium	4,000
Cost of attending professional seminar	1,000

Based on the information above, what should Gilda Bach report as her net self-employment income for 1978?

a) $ 91,000

b) $105,000

c) $106,000

d) $110,000

(AICPA adapted)

8. Alex Berger, a retired building contractor, earned the following income during 1981:

Director's fee received from Keith Realty Corp.	$ 600
Executor's fee received from the estate of his deceased sister	7,000

Berger's self-employment income for 1981 is

a) $0

b) $ 600

c) $7,000

d) $7,600

(AICPA adapted)

9. Fred Wright filed his 1981 income tax return on March 15, 1982, showing gross income of $20,000. He had mistakenly omitted $6,000 of income which, in good faith, he considered nontaxable. By what date must the Internal Revenue Service assert a notice of deficiency?

a) March 15, 1985

b) April 15, 1985

c) March 15, 1988

d) April 15, 1988

(AICPA adapted)

10. Harold Thompson, a self-employed individual, had income transactions for 1979 (duly reported on his return filed in April 1980) as follows:

Gross receipts	$400,000
Less cost of goods sold and deductions	320,000
Net business income	80,000
Capital gains	36,000
Gross Income	$116,000

In March 1983 Thompson discovers that he had inadvertently omitted some income on his 1979 return and retains Mann, CPA, to determine his position under the statute of limitations. Mann should advise Thompson that the six-year statute of limitations would apply to his 1979 return only if he omitted from gross income an amount in excess of

a) $ 20,000

b) $ 29,000

c) $100,000

d) $109,000

(AICPA adapted)

QUESTIONS

1. Four different rate schedules X, Y (Joint), Y (Separate), and Z (Head of Household) apply to individuals, depending on their marital status, dependents, etc. Which schedule produces the highest tax? The lowest tax?
2. What conditions must exist before an individual is eligible for income averaging?
3. Only taxpayers with averageable income in excess of $3,000 may use the averaging computation. Will a lower tax result from averaging in every case where averageable income is over $3,000? Explain.
4. Why are the averaging rules included in our tax law?
5. If a taxpayer used the averaging rules last year, can he or she enjoy the benefits this year? Explain.
6. What is the difference between the add-on minimum tax (now applicable to corporations only) and the alternative minimum tax applicable to individuals?
7. What inequity does the alternative minimum tax mitigate?
8. Briefly describe the "formula" used to calculate the alternative minimum tax.
9. What is a tax preference? Give examples of the preferences commonly encountered.

10. List the deductions that are *not* allowed in the computation of the alternative minimum taxable income.

11. Because of a large net capital gain, Mr. Rich expects to be subject to the alternative minimum tax for the current year. What would Rich do before year end to minimize the effect of the AMT?

12. Under what conditions is an individual subject to the self-employment tax?

13. What are the current rate and maximum base for the self-employment tax?

14. Why would an employer claim that his employees are independent contractors? Under what conditions would such a claim be successful?

15. Explain generally how the penalty for underpayment for the estimated tax is calculated.

16. Must a taxpayer pay 100% of his or her tax in installments to avoid an underpayment? If not, under what conditions is an underpayment avoided?

17. Mr. Guy usually pays the state and local property taxes on his residence and investment properties in December of each year. This year Guy is subject to the AMT. Should he pay his property taxes as usual? Explain.

18. T receives a lump-sum distribution from a pension trust. Part of the distribution is attributable to the period before 1974. Will 10-year averaging always result in the lowest tax (as opposed to an allocation to capital gains)? Explain.

19. S filed her income tax return for 19X2 on March 10, 19X3 and paid the tax due on that date. She later discovered a $1,000 deduction omitted from the return. How long does S have to file a refund claim? What form should she use?

PROBLEMS

1. Hank, a lawyer, expects to have taxable income of $40,000 for the year. Debbie works for an advertising agency and her taxable income will be $30,000. Neither has dependents, both use the zero bracket amount and have no deductions for AGI. After an extended courtship, the two plan to marry before the year-end.
   a) Calculate their combined tax liability if they decide to forgo marriage.
   b) What amount of additional tax results from the marriage?

2. For five years after being graduated from law school, Melanie Brand worked for the Justice Department and was assigned to the IRS. In

January 19X5, she took a position as an associate with a large local accounting firm. As a result her income increased substantially. Her taxable income for the relevant years was: 19X1, $20,000; 19X2, $22,000; 19X3, $25,000; 19X4, $23,000; and 19X5, $47,500. She remains happily unmarried, having supported herself since graduation.

a) Calculate her gross tax liability for 19X5 using current tax rates.

b) Melanie's taxable income for 19X6 was only $45,000 due to increased deductions when she purchased a residence. Can she use the averaging provisions in 19X6? Explain.

3. John Umber is single. He attended night school for six years to obtain a law degree. His parents are not wealthy and therefore John made his own way, working as a machinist in a local plant. His taxable income for the years 19X1–19X4 was as follows: 19X1, $5,400; 19X2, $5,800; 19X3, $6,200; 19X4, $7,400. He was graduated with honors in January 19X5 and took a position with a prominent local law firm. His taxable income for 19X5 was $14,240.

   a) Compute his gross tax liability for 19X5; use current tax rates.

   b) Compute his gross tax liability for 19X6, assuming his net taxable income for that year was $17,292.

   c) Compute his gross tax liability for 19X7, assuming his taxable income is still $17,292.

4. In the independent situations below, indicate whether T, the taxpayer, is eligible for income averaging. If not, explain why.

   a) T was a student during the base period. She worked in the summers but her parents provided over half of her support.

   b) T is married. He earned $30,000 in the computation year and provided his own support during the base period. W, T's wife, earned $6,000 in the computation year, the first year of their marriage. W was a student, supported by her parents, during the base period.

   c) T is 26 and he dropped out of high school when he was 17. T was a dependent of his mother for two of the three base-period years due to a slack economy.

5. Lotte Luck, unmarried, is a staff accountant for Peat Price. This year, however, Lotte hit a bonanza—a $300,000 long-term capital gain on the shares of a small oil company. Other relevant information is:

Salary from Peat Price	$ 30,000
Net capital gain	300,000
Interest on residence	6,000
State taxes on residence	2,500
Contributions	20,000

   Lotte has no dependents, credits, or other tax items.

   a) Calculate Lotte's gross tax using the regular method (1985 rates).

b) Calculate Lotte's alternative minimum tax.

c) What steps should Lotte have taken during the year, assuming she could not defer the gain from the sale of the stock (because the price was going down).

d) Calculate the effects of your advice in (c) above on Lotte's gross tax.

6. Horace and Thelma are married and file a joint return. For the current year, their records show the following amounts for income and deductions:

Salary	$110,000
Dividends from taxable U.S. corporations	10,200
Net capital gain	300,000
Loss on operation of apartment house	(35,000)
Medical expenses	(12,000)
Contributions	(25,000)
State and local property taxes	(10,000)
Interest paid	(30,000)
Miscellaneous (tax deductible)	(2,000)

Horace and Thelma have two dependent children. The loss of the operation of the apartment house includes $25,000 of excess accelerated depreciation over straight line. The interest expense includes $18,000 paid on the mortgage for their personal residence that was acquired in 1980. They have no credits for the year.

a) Calculate their regular tax liability (using current rates).

b) Calculate their tax liability considering the alternative minimum tax.

7. Tom Tuff is assistant controller for A Corporation and earned a salary of $40,000 in the current year. He also does tax work on the side out of an office in his home. This year, his "net" from this activity was $12,000.

a) Calculate Tom's self-employment tax using 1985 rates.

b) How does your answer in (a) above change if Tom's salary is only $25,000?

8. Consider each of the following independent cases and determine if the taxpayer is an employee subject to FICA or an independent contractor subject to the tax on self-employment income:

a) T, a licensed electrician, installs wiring, fixtures, etc. in homes built by Y, a general contractor. T furnishes his own tools and is compensated on a "per job" basis.

b) T is a salesman for an office supply house. He works for salary plus commission. He reports each morning to his employer's business location and calls on customers as directed by his employer.

c) T is a real estate agent who works on commission. She works out of her employer's place of business.

d) T is a carpenter. He works for Y, a general contractor, on an hourly rate, doing frame work. He provides his own tools.

9. Frank Follet estimates that his income tax (after credits) for the current year will be $8,000. Last year his tax was $5,000. Frank's employer will withhold $5,500 on Frank's pay.

   a) What is Frank's estimated tax for the year?

   b) Will Frank be subject to the penalty for underpayment if he fails to pay the estimated tax in installments? Explain.

10. In 1984 Harris received an $80,000 lump-sum distribution from a noncontributory pension plan. The distribution was in cash. Harris is married and his taxable income, excepting the distribution, was $50,000 for 1984. The distribution attributable to the period before 1974 was $20,000.

    a) Compute Harris's tax for 1984 if he elects to treat the entire distribution as ordinary income.

    b) Did he make the right election? Demonstrate the correctness of your answer.

11. Benny, a citizen of Texas, (a community property state) was married to Beatrice during 19X1 and 19X2. They filed joint returns for those years showing a taxable income of $24,000 for 19X1 and $30,000 for 19X2, all community income. Benny and Beatrice were divorced in 19X3 and Benny filed a "single" return showing taxable income of $20,000. For 19X4, Benny, who is still single, has taxable income of $27,000.

    a) Can Benny use the 4-year averaging rules for 19X4? Explain.

    b) Calculate Benny's 1984 gross tax liability.

12. Herman's tax liability after credits last year was $8,000, the tax due on Herman's income from the operation (as a sole proprietor) of a pool hall. Because of police harassment, Herman's business was slow. Based on his business through March annualized for the year, Herman paid a quarterly estimate of $1,000 on April 15. Using the same procedure, he paid $1,000 on June 15. Due to a new police chief, business began to improve in the summer and continued at unprecedented levels for the remainder of the year, resulting in a tax liability of $15,000. For the last two installments on September 15 and January 15, Herman paid $3,000 per installment.

    a) Calculate Herman's underpayment for each quarter.

    b) Is Herman subject to the underpayment penalty? Explain.

TAX PLANNING PROBLEMS

1. Jacque Belleu expects to realize a very large long-term capital gain in June of 1985 and he has asked you if 1985 affords any planning opportunities. Upon inquiring you develop the following facts relative to 1985:

   a) LT gain is $400,000 from the sale of Jacque's 5% interest in the common stock of X Co. The sale will be made in June 1985 for cash and deferral of the gain is undesirable and impossible.

   b) Jacque is an independent consultant on fashions. He usually nets about $150,000 a year from this activity. For 1985, however, his net will be only $50,000. At year end he will have fees of $40,000 which can be billed and collected in 1985 if desirable (making the income for 1985 $90,000).

   c) For 1985 he expects a loss of $40,000 from a real estate shelter and $25,000 of this loss arises from "excess" depreciation.

   d) He will make the following expenditures for deductible personal items: $50,000 cash contribution to his university; $15,000 interest on indebtedness related to his personal residence; $8,400 state and local taxes on his residence and some land held for investment. Except for interest, these expenses can be deferred.

   Jacque is married but with no dependents.

   a) Calculate Jacque's regular gross tax and his alternative minimum tax, assuming no "planning" changes for the year.

   b) What would you advise Jacque to do in 1985?

   c) Calculate the effects of your advice in (b) above on the regular and alternative taxes.

2. John Jakes estimates that his income tax for 1985 will be $8,000. None of his income is subject to withholdings. He would like to pay the estimated tax and avoid the penalty but he has no cash. If he borrows the money, he will pay interest of 12%. Advise him and make calculations to support your advice.

CASE PROBLEM

Thomas, married with two dependents and on the cash basis, serves as president of a local bank at an annual salary of $80,000. The bank reimburses him fully for all employment-related expenses. During 1984, he sold two properties:

1. Unimproved real estate on July 15, 1984—The land originally cost $125,000. Thomas received cash of $200,000 and three notes of $100,000 each due annually on July 15 beginning July 15, 1985. The notes bear interest at 14%.

2. Small office building on January 2, 1984—The sales price was $400,000 of which $80,000 was allocated to the land. The adjusted basis of the land was $50,000 and the cost of the building was $300,000 when placed in service on January 1, 1980. Depreciation deducted on the building using 150% declining balance and a 20-year life was as follows:

1981	$22,500
1982	20,812
1983	19,252
1984	17,808

During 1984 Thomas paid the following:

Contributions—church, university	$50,000
Interest (including interest on 1975 mortgage)	30,000
State property and sales taxes	12,000

Calculate Thomas's tax liability for 1984.

RESEARCH PROBLEMS

1. Della Hermes owns and operates a 30-acre mobile home park. The park includes spaces for 75 mobile homes. Della grossed $75,000 in rents this year and incurred total costs, including interest, taxes, and operating expenses, of $40,000. Each tenant pays for his or her own electrical power but Della furnishes water from a deep well on the property. Della maintains all common areas (playgrounds, game room, etc.) and also provides a trash garbage service. Della asks you to determine whether her net income from the park is self-employment income subject to the self-employment tax. Naturally, she prefers not to pay the tax.

2. Basil Benoit signed a contract in May 19X4 to play professional football with a NFL team. The contract called for a salary of $75,000 for the 19X4–X5 season with escalation clauses in later years based on Basil's performance. Basil also received a bonus of $25,000 at the time of signing. Basil graduated from Southern University in June 19X4. His support during the preceding years was from the following sources:

	19X0	19X1	19X2	19X3
Parents	$2,000	$2,000	$2,000	$2,000
Athletic scholarship	1,500	1,500	1,500	1,500
Summer employment*	–0–	1,500	1,500	4,000
Total	$3,500	$5,000	$5,000	$7,500

*Provided by Southern's athletic department.

Can Basil use the averaging provisions in 19X4?

Chapter Objectives

1. Identify the properties that qualify for the "regular" investment tax credit (ITC), the rehabilitation tax credit, and the credit for energy properties.
2. Describe how the ITC is calculated, the annual limits that apply, and the rules for carrybacks and carryovers.
3. Explain how the ITC is "recaptured" by an addition to the tax when qualified property is prematurely withdrawn from service.
4. Describe the targeted jobs credit, the credit for expanded research activities, and the credit for the use of alternative fuels.
5. Describe the rules governing the credit for the care of young and incapacitated dependents.
6. Explain how the earned income credit works as a negative income tax for some people in the lower income groups.
7. Describe the computation of other credits that affect the taxes of individuals, including the residential energy credits, the credit for elderly taxpayers, and the credit for political contributions.
8. Explain how the foreign tax credit reduces or eliminates the double tax on income from foreign sources.

14 Tax Credits

The preceding chapter explained how the gross tax liability is computed for individuals. Also covered in Chapter 13 were the rules related to the payment of the tax. The present chapter deals with the computation of the many credits allowed against the gross tax.

A tax credit is an amount subtracted from the gross tax to determine the net tax due. Credits, then, are like prepayments of the tax, and are *not* a part of the computation of taxable income, the tax base.

For discussion purposes, the credits in this chapter are divided into three groups. The first group consists of credits related to business operations, the investment tax credit being the principal one. The second group consists of credits allowed individuals only because of some special need. The child-care credit is an example. The third group consists of credits related to prepayments and includes the credit allowed for income taxes paid to foreign countries.

CREDITS RELATED TO BUSINESS OPERATIONS

Congress often uses the federal income tax laws to control economic activity. During recessions the tax law is often amended to provide the business community with incentives to invest in new plants and to hire new employees. These incentives often take the form of increased tax deductions such as the Accelerated Cost Recovery System added in 1981. Other forms of incentives are the various tax credits discussed in the following

CREDITS While exclusions and deductions are subtracted from income to arrive at the tax base (taxable income), credits are subtracted from the gross tax to determine the net amount due the government. Credits have the same effect as prepayments.

pages. These ***credits***, principally the investment tax credit, are direct subsidies from the government to business.

BACKGROUND

Prior to 1960 tax credits played only a minor role in our income tax laws. The foreign tax credit, which eliminates the double taxation of foreign sources income subjected to taxes by another country, dates from 1918.* In 1954 Congress added a credit to lower the taxes on citizens and residents over 65 years old. This credit, much modified, continues in the law as the "credit for the elderly."

With these two major exceptions, the numerous credits now included in the law were added after the addition of the investment tax credit in the early 1960s. Beginning with the ITC, Congress has added numerous credits in response to various economic and social problems, ranging from the ITC designed to stimulate investment to the credit for political contributions that is designed to broaden the base of financial support for political parties.

The increased use of credits rather than exclusions or deductions is usually explained two ways. First, credits neutralize the effects of progressive tax rates. A relief measure added to the law as a deduction or exclusion gives more benefits to taxpayers in the higher brackets than to those in the lower brackets. For example, a new $100 deduction reduces by $50 the tax of someone in the 50% bracket, but reduces by only $20 the tax of someone in the 20% bracket. Second, compared to deductions and exclusions, credits are more *visible*, and have a more direct effect on the taxes paid. Presumably, taxpayers feel that Congress has done something about a problem when they see their taxes reduced directly by a new credit.

*Boris I. Bittker and Laurence F. Ebb, *United States Taxation of Foreign Income and Foreign Persons*, 2nd Edition (Branford, Conn.: Federal Tax Press, 1960), p. 211.

INVESTMENT TAX CREDIT

ITC Abbreviation for Investment Tax Credit.

TENTATIVE CREDIT The tentative ITC is the base, qualified investment, times the appropriate rate. This amount is "tentative" since it may not be the amount allowed because of limits, carrybacks, and carryforwards.

Originally added to the law in 1963 and changed almost annually since, the investment tax credit (hereinafter ***ITC***) is now a permanent part of our tax law. Taxpayers who acquire "qualified" property can reduce their tax payments to the government by amounts generally equal to 10% of the cost of such property. The specific rules governing the amount of the credit allowed are complex. A step-by-step analysis of the rules follows.

TENTATIVE ITC To determine the credit allowed a taxpayer for any year, we must first determine the tentative ITC for the year.[1]

Qualified investment × Rate = ***Tentative credit***

[1] Sec. 46(a).

Qualified investment is 100% of the cost of qualified property placed in service during the year, except that only 60% of the cost of qualified 3-year property under ACRS is included.[2]

QUALIFIED INVESTMENT
The base for the ITC is qualified investment, the cost of qualified property times the percentages related to the life of the property. For 3-year property, qualified investment is 60% of the cost of the property; for 5-year property, 100% of the cost.

Example 1: During the year, T spent $100,000 for 5-year property, $75,000 for 10-year property, and $50,000 for 3-year property. All properties qualify for the ITC and all were placed in service during the year. T's qualified investment for the year is $205,000:

PROPERTY	COST	PERCENT INCLUDED	QUALIFIED INVESTMENT
3-year	$ 50,000	60%	$ 30,000
5-year	100,000	100%	100,000
10-year	75,000	100%	75,000
Qualified investment			$205,000

Properties placed in service before 1981 when the ACRS was adopted were subject to different percentages based on their estimated useful lives.[3] These percentages must be used for the recapture of the credit in the case of premature dispositions of such properties (see the recapture discussion later in this chapter).

ESTIMATED USEFUL LIFE	PERCENTAGE IN QUALIFIED INVESTMENT
3 years or more but less than 5 years	33⅓%
5 years or more but less than 7 years	66⅔%
7 years or more	100%

The reader will recall from the discussion of ACRS in Chapter 10 that estimated useful life is no longer directly relevant to the depreciation calculation and is therefore not used to determine qualified investment for property placed in service after 1980.

If the ***qualified property*** is *used* property, the cost of such property included in the calculations of qualified investment is limited to $125,000.[4] The maximum dollar limit can be assigned to assets in different classes to obtain the maximum qualified investment.[5]

QUALIFIED PROPERTY
The term qualified property designates those properties that receive the regular ITC. Depreciable, tangible personal property, certain depreciable real properties (other than buildings) used as an integral part of a productive process, and a few other specific properties designated in the statute are qualified properties.

Example 2: During the year (after 1980), T acquired and placed in service the following *used* properties:

PROPERTY	COST
3-year property	$ 50,000
5-year property	100,000

[2] Sec. 46(c)(7).
[3] Sec. 46(c)(2).
[4] Sec. 48(c)(2).
[5] Reg. Sec. 1.48-3(c)(4).

The $125,000 limit on used property should be used first for the 5-year property since 100% of its cost is included in qualified investment. The remaining $25,000 is assigned to 3-year property, but only 60% of this cost, or $15,000, is included in qualified investment.

Generally, the cost of qualified property is not included in qualified investment until the property is placed in service or use. An exception exists for "qualified progress expenditures," payments made on long-term (more than two years) construction contracts.[6]

The rate of the "regular" credit is 10%. (Sometimes 3-year ACRS property is referred to as "6% rate" property, because 10% × 60% of the original investment equals a 6% effective rate.)

Example 3: In Example 1 the qualified investment is $205,000. The tentative credit is 10% of this amount, or $20,500.

For the period between 1975 and ending December 31, 1982, some corporations with ESOP's (Employee Stock Option Plans) could claim an additional 1% (1.5% in some instances). Also, the technical structure of the ITC in the statute includes the percentages allowed for rehabilitation expenditures and for energy properties. For simplicity, these credits are treated separately.

You will recall from Chapter 8 that Section 179 permits taxpayers to expense the cost of certain acquisitions, subject to some rather low limits. The properties that qualify for the expensing election are the same as those that qualify for the ITC. The maximum cost that can be expensed is $5,000 (scheduled to increase to $7,500 in 1988).

If the Section 179 election is made for a property, the cost expensed is not subject to the ITC. The wisdom of such an election is evaluated in the planning workshop for Chapter 8.

REDUCTION IN BASIS OF QUALIFIED PROPERTY If a taxpayer claims the full 10% regular credit on property placed in service after 1982, the adjusted basis of the property must be reduced by 50% of the credit claimed on such property.[7] No reduction is required for property placed in service before 1983.

Example 4: T acquired a $50,000 3-year property and a $100,000 5-year property, both qualified for the regular ITC, both placed in service after 1982. T used a 10% rate for the credit. The basis reductions required are:

PROPERTY	QUALIFIED COST	QUALIFIED INVESTMENT	CREDIT CLAIMED	BASIS REDUCTION
3-year	$ 50,000	$ 30,000	$ 3,000	$1,500
5-year	$100,000	$100,000	$10,000	$5,000

[6] Sec. 46(d).

[7] Sec. 48(q)(1).

For depreciation purposes the 3-year property has a basis of $48,500, the 5-year property a basis of $95,000.

This basis reduction is treated as depreciation for purposes of the depreciation recapture rules under Sections 1245 and 1250 (Chapter 11).

As an alternative to the reduction of basis, a taxpayer may elect to reduce the basic rate of the credit by two percentage points, from 10% to 8%. The rate applicable to 3-year property under this election is 4%.[8] The election to reduce the credit rate permits the taxpayer to use the original cost of the property as its basis.

Example 5: In Example 4, in lieu of the basis reduction, T could elect to claim the following credit:

PROPERTY	QUALIFIED COST	REDUCED RATE	TENTATIVE CREDIT
3-year	$ 50,000	4%	$ 2,000
5-year	100,000	8%	8,000
Total credit			$10,000

This $10,000 compares to a credit of $13,000 allowed using the full 10% rate. However, the taxpayer's adjusted bases n the properties will be the original costs of $50,000 and $100,000.

This election can be made on a property-by-property basis. As explained in the Planning Workshop at the end of this chapter, taxpayers will usually elect the reduced rates when the tentative credit is not allowed in the current year because of the limits described on page 14/24.

DEFINITION OF QUALIFIED PROPERTY The property subject to the ITC is defined in Section 48(a)(1) as recovery property with a life of at least three years under ACRS which falls into one of the following categories:

- Tangible depreciable personal property (other than air conditioning or heating units). Intangible properties do not qualify for the ITC. *Personal* used here refers to the legal characterization of *real* vs. *personal*.

Example 6: During the year, T acquired and placed in service a patent with a remaining life of 10 years, a work of art used as decoration of the company offices, and a new computer that is 5-year recovery property. All properties are personalty. However, the patent (though subject to depreciation) is not ITC property because it is intangible. The work of art, while tangible personalty, is not ITC property because it is not depreciable. (Note that some "decorations" could be depreciable.) Only the computer is qualified ITC property.

- Real property (except for buildings and their structural components), but only if such property is an integral part of some productive pro-

[8] Sec. 48(q)(4)(b).

cess (as opposed to having a service function). Production processes are manufacturing, production, transportation, and extraction. Research facilities and bulk (fungible) storage facilities related to a productive process also qualify. The critical distinction is between a building (and structural components) that do not qualify and productive real property that does.

Example 7: T, engaged in the wholesale production of flowers, built two structures: a greenhouse and a shed used for the storage of tractors and tools. The storage shed does not qualify. The greenhouse, though it *looks* like a building, is an integral part of T's productive process.

Example 8: In conjunction with a new office and plant building, T constructs two asphalt drives and parking areas. One accommodates the administrative and sales office, and the other the loading docks used for receiving and shipping. Only the second lot, which is related to production, qualifies for the ITC.

- Other miscellaneous items including certain elevators and escalators, coin-operated vending machines, and single-purpose agricultural and horticultural structures.

Example 9: T, engaged in the dairy business, constructs a milking barn that is completely automated. While this barn clearly looks like a building, it is ITC property.

The statute contains many exceptions and special rules. Personal property used to furnish lodging, e.g., furniture in an apartment house, does not qualify. But, furniture in a hotel used more than half the time by transients does qualify for the credit. Property used predominantly outside the U.S. does not qualify for the ITC, but numerous exceptions exist for commercial airplanes, railroad rolling stock, ships, etc.

LIMITS AND CARRYOVER OF ITC While most tax credits can be used to offset all the gross tax liability, Congress has placed a limit on the ITC allowed as a reduction of the gross tax. While the limit has been more restrictive in earlier years, the limit for taxable years ending after 1982 is:

- 100% of the gross tax liability up to $25,000,
- Plus 85% of the gross tax liability in excess of $25,000.[9]

Example 10: T has a tentative ITC for 19X3 of $130,000. T's gross tax liability for 19X3 is $100,000. The ITC allowed as a credit in 19X3 (1983 or later) is:

First $25,000	$25,000
85% of $75,000 ($100,000 − $25,000)	63,750
ITC allowed	$88,750

[9]Sec. 38(c).

The remaining tentative credit of $41,250 ($130,000 − $88,750) is carried back or forward as explained below.

For years before 1982 the limit was more restrictive. For 1978 the limit was $25,000 plus 50% of the excess. Beginning in 1979 the percentage increased to 60%, with an additional increase of 10% per year until it reached 90% for 1982. Then, the rate was reduced to 85% for years after 1982.

For years after 1983, the limit just explained applies to most business credits, not just to the ITC. The statute requires that the tentative ITC be combined with the targeted job credit, the alcohol fuel credit, and the employee stock ownership credit for purposes of applying this limit. These other credits, which affect only a few taxpayers, are described briefly later in the chapter. The tax liability used to calculate the limit is the gross tax liability reduced by nonrefundable personal credits, i.e., the child care credit, plus the foreign tax credit, the credit for increasing research activities, and some other minor credits beyond our scope.[10]

A tentative credit not allowed in the current year is carried back for three years and, if not absorbed there, is carried forward for 15 years (the carryforward period was shorter for years before 1974). The unused credit must first be carried to the third preceding year and, if not fully used in that year, to the second preceding year, etc. These carryback and carryforward rules apply to business credits generally, just as the limits as explained above. In every year, the tentative credit for each year plus any carrybacks or carryforwards to that year is allowed subject to the limits explained. Note that for recent past years the limits have been changing each year—90% in 1982, 80% in 1981, etc.

Example 11: In Example 10, only $88,750 of T's 19X3 tentative credit of $130,000 is allowed in 19X3 because of the limit. T treats the excess of $41,250 as a carryback to 19X0, the third preceding year. Assume that T's gross tax for 19X0 was $200,000 and the credit claimed that year was $30,000. By filing an amended return for 19X0, T can now claim an additional credit of $41,250 for 19X0 and obtain a refund of taxes paid.

Example 12: In Example 11, if T's gross tax in 19X0 had been only $60,000 (not $100,000) then the carryback allowed would be subject to the limit:

Limit (if 19X0 is 1982):

First $25,000	$25,000
90% of $35,000 ($60,000 − $25,000)	31,500
Total ITC allowed for 19X0	56,500
Tentative credit for 19X0 acquisitions	30,000
19X3 carryback allowed in 19X0	$26,500

[10] Sec. 38 (b) and (c).

The remainder of the 19X3 carryback, $14,750, which is the $41,250 less the $26,500 allowed in 19X0, is carried back to 19X1 and, if not absorbed there, to 19X2, then, if still not expended, is carried forward to 19X4, etc.

Taxpayers who have credits disallowed because of the expiration of the 15-year carryforward period may add back the basis reduction required for property placed in service after 1982.

RECAPTURE The ITC claimed on properties that are subsequently disposed of prematurely is "recaptured" by adding a prorata of the ITC back to the gross tax. Rules for proration differ for properties placed in service after 1980 from those properties placed in service before that date.

RECAPTURE OF ITC FROM PREMATURE DISPOSITIONS Taxpayers who dispose of qualified property before holding it for a specified period must ***recapture*** all or part of the credit originally allowed. The portion of the credit recaptured is an addition to the tax in the year of disposition. This recapture rule prevents the nonproductive turnover of property merely to obtain the credit.

For property placed in service after 1980, when ACRS became effective, the portion of the allowed credit recapture is specified in the statute:[11]

DISPOSITION OCCURS WITHIN	RECAPTURE 3-YEAR PROPERTY	PERCENTAGE OTHER PROPERTY
First year	100%	100%
Second year	66%	80%
Third year	33%	60%
Fourth year	-0-	40%
Fifth year	-0-	20%

The idea behind the schedule is that the ITC is "earned" as the property is used for its intended minimum life under ACRS. Thus, 3-year property must be used for three years to *earn* the credit and 5-year (and other properties) for five years.

Example 13: T acquired 3-year property at a cost of $100,000 and placed it in service in January 19X1. For the year 19X1 she claimed a credit of $6,000, 10% of $60,000 (since only 60% of the cost of 3-year property is qualified investment). In June 19X3, within the third year of its use, T sold the property. The recapture is $1,980 (33% of $6,000). This amount is added to T's gross tax for 19X3.

A convenient way to remember the recapture rule is that 2% of the cost of an asset is earned as credit for each full year an asset is held. Or, alternatively, the recapture is 2% for each year the asset is *not* held. In Example 13, T held the property two full years and earned 4% credit while 2% of the cost was recaptured. This convenient rule also applies to 5-year property. (However, this rule cannot be applied to cases in which a taxpayer elected

---

[11] Sec. 47(a)(5).

to reduce the credit, rather than the basis of the asset. The recapture percentages shown above must be used in these circumstances.)

For property placed in service prior to 1981, the recapture depends on the percentages allowed as qualified investment, based on estimated useful life. For property acquired before ACRS, the qualified investment was determined by the following schedule:[12]

ESTIMATED USEFUL LIFE	PERCENTAGE OF COST ALLOWED
3 or 4 years	33⅓%
5 or 6 years	66⅔%
7 years	100%

For these older properties, a premature disposition is one occurring before the expiration of the term used to compute the qualified investment.

Example 14: In 1980 T acquired a qualified asset at a cost of $10,000. He used an estimated useful life of five years for the property and claimed a credit of $667 (10% of $10,000 × 66⅔%). T disposed of the property in 1982 after only two years of use. The entire ITC of $667 is recaptured because no credit was allowed under the pre-1981 rules unless the property was held at least three years.

Example 15: In Example 14 assume that T disposes of the property in 1983 after three years of use. One-third (33⅓%) of the cost is earned by actual use but the remaining credit $333 is recaptured.

Recapture of the credit also applies when the property ceases to be "qualified" because of a change in its use.[13] This can occur, for example, when property is devoted to nonqualifying foreign use. If a tentative credit is not allowed because of the limits, premature disposition or cessation of qualified use results in an adjustment of the carryback or carryforward allowances.

The recapture of ITC for properties placed in service after 1982 results in a restoration of any basis reduction required when the 10% rate is used.[14] The amount restored is 50% of the credit recaptured. The restoration is made immediately before the disposition that triggers the recapture. As a result, depreciation calculations for earlier years are not disturbed but the property's basis for gain or loss includes the restored basis.

Example 16: T acquired qualified property (*not* 3-year property) after 1982 at a cost of $100,000. T claimed an ITC of $10,000 and reduced the basis of the property to $95,000. With two years of use the

[12] Sec. 46(c)(2).
[13] Sec. 47(a)(1).
[14] Sec. 48(q)(2).

property was sold within the third year, after claiming depreciation of $35,000. The law requires a recapture of $6,000 of ITC, 60% of the credit claimed. This recapture in turn results in a restoration of $3,000 (50% of $6,000) to the property's basis, which becomes $63,000 for purposes of computing gain or loss on the disposition.

REPORTING THE ITC To claim the ITC, a taxpayer must file Form 3468. Recapture of the credit requires Form 4255. Form 1045 is normally used for carrybacks.

FORM 3468

FORM 4255

An illustration of Form 3468 will prove helpful at this point (Figure 14-1). This form is designed for the regular ITC as well as the credit for energy properties and the credit for rehabilitation expenditures. Our example will deal only with the regular ITC.

Assume that Herman Hesse (SS# 465-80-4600), with a gross tax liability of $26,000, acquired the following properties in 1984:

ITEM	NEW/USED?	COST
Automobile	new	$ 12,000
Heavy truck	used	60,000
Dragline	new	120,000
General purpose warehouse	new	200,000

The cost of the new automobile is entered at line 1(a) and only 60% is extended to column (4) since it is 3-year property. The used heavy truck is reported at line 1(c) because it is used. The entire $60,000 qualifies since it is less than the $125,000 limit on used property and because it is 5-year property. The cost of the new dragline is entered at line 1(b) and the entire cost qualifies because it is 5-year property. The warehouse is not ITC property. (Lines 1[e] through 1[h] are used when the 8% rate is elected.)

Column 4, the qualified investment, is totaled and entered at line 5, $187,200 in this case. Since these properties are "regular" ITC items, a 10% credit is taken at line 7. Line 16 is the total tentative credit for the year.

Lines 17 through 21 are used to compute the limit based on the gross tax. Herman's gross tax is $26,000 and the limit is $25,850 for 1984. Thus, the entire tentative credit of $18,720 is allowed.

Refer to the note following line 14 on Form 3468. A taxpayer who claims business credits other than ITC in 1984 must combine the ITC with these other credits on Form 3800 and calculate the limit for all such credits on that form.

REHABILITATION OF OLDER STRUCTURES

Generally, the ITC does not apply to buildings or their structural components. Congress, however, has provided a special incentive for the continued use and rehabilitation of older structures in an effort to arrest urban decay. This credit was overhauled substantially in 1981 and we will limit our attention to the rules applicable to qualified expenditures incurred after 1981.

FIGURE 14-1

Form **3468**

Department of the Treasury
Internal Revenue Service

Computation of Investment Credit

▶ Attach to your tax return.
▶ Schedule B (Business Energy Investment Credit) on back.

OMB No. 1545-0155

1984
24

Name(s) as shown on return: *Herman Hesse*

Identifying number: *465-80-4600*

Part I Elections (Check the box(es) below that apply to you (See Instruction D).)

A I elect to increase my qualified investment to 100% for certain commuter highway vehicles under section 46(c)(6) . . . . ☐

B I elect to increase my qualified investment by all qualified progress expenditures made this and all later tax years . . . . ☐
Enter total qualified progress expenditures included in column (4), Part II ▶

C I claim full credit on certain ships under section 46(g)(3) (See **Instruction B** for details.) . . . . ☐

Part II Qualified Investment (See instructions for new rules on automobiles and certain property with any personal use)

1 Recovery Property		Line	(1) Class of Property	(2) Unadjusted Basis	(3) Applicable Percentage	(4) Qualified Investment (Column 2 x column 3)
Regular Percentage	New Property	(a)	3-year	*12,000*	60	*7,200*
		(b)	Other	*120,000*	100	*120,000*
	Used Property	(c)	3-year		60	
		(d)	Other	*60,000*	100	*60,000*
Section 48(q) Election to Reduce Credit (instead of adjusting basis)	New Property	(e)	3-year		40	
		(f)	Other		80	
	Used Property	(g)	3-year		40	
		(h)	Other		80	

2	Nonrecovery property—Enter total qualified investment (See instructions for line 2)	2	
3	New commuter highway vehicle—Enter total qualified investment (See **Instruction D(1)**)	3	
4	Used commuter highway vehicle—Enter total qualified investment (See **Instruction D(1)**)	4	
5	**Total qualified investment in 10% property**—Add lines 1(a) through 1(h), 2, 3, and 4 (See instructions for special limits)	5	*187,200*
6	Qualified rehabilitation expenditures—Enter total qualified investment for:		
	a 30-year-old buildings	6a	
	b 40-year-old buildings	6b	
	c Certified historic structures (You must attach NPS certification—see instructions)	6c	

Part III Tentative Regular Investment Credit

7	10% of line 5	7	*18,720*
8	15% of line 6a	8	
9	20% of line 6b	9	
10	25% of line 6c	10	
11	Credit from cooperatives—Enter regular investment credit from cooperatives	11	
12	Regular investment credit—Add lines 7 through 11	12	
13	Business energy investment credit—From line 11 of Schedule B (see back of this form)	13	
14	Current year investment credit—Add lines 12 and 13	14	

Note: If you have a 1984 jobs credit (Form 5884), credit for alcohol used as fuel (Form 6478), or employee stock ownership plan (ESOP) credit (Form 8007), in addition to your 1984 investment credit, you must stop here and go to new ***Form 3800****, General Business Credit, to claim your 1984 investment credit. If you have only the investment credit (which may include business energy investment credit) or an investment credit carryforward from 1983, you may continue with lines 15 through 22 to claim your credit.*

15	Carryforward of unused regular or business energy investment credit from 1983	15	
16	Total—Add lines 14 and 15	16	*18,720*

Part IV Tax Liability Limitations

17	a Individuals—From Form 1040, enter amount from line 46 b Estates and trusts—From Form 1041, enter tax from line 26a, plus any section 644 tax on trusts c Corporations—From Form 1120, Schedule J, enter tax from line 3 (or Form 1120-A, Part I, line 1) d Other filers —Enter tax before credits from return	17	*26,000*
18	a Individuals—From Form 1040, enter credits from line 47, plus any orphan drug, nonconventional source fuel, and research credits b Estates and trusts—From Form 1041, enter any credits from line 27d c Corporations—From Form 1120, Schedule J, enter credits from lines 4(a) through 4(e) (Form 1120-A filers, enter zero) d Other filers—See instructions for line 18d	18	
19	Income tax liability as adjusted (subtract line 18 from line 17)	19	*26,000*
20	a Enter smaller of line 19 or $25,000. (See instructions for line 20)	20a	*25,000*
	b If line 19 is more than $25,000—Enter 85% of the excess	20b	*850*
21	Investment credit limitation—Add lines 20a and 20b	21	*25,850*
22	Total allowed credit—Enter the smaller of line 16 or line 21. This is your **General Business Credit** for 1984. Enter here and on Form 1040, line 48; Form 1120, Schedule J, line 4(f); Form 1120-A, Part I, line 2 ; or the proper line of other returns	22	*18,720*

For Paperwork Reduction Act Notice, see separate instructions.

Form **3468** (1984)

The amount of the credit depends on the age and status of the structure:[15]

AGE AND TYPE OF BUILDING	PERCENTAGE FOR CREDIT
At least 30 years old	15%
At least 40 years old	20%
Certified historical structure	25%

The credit applies only to properties used in a trade or business, or held for investment. Also, "residential" properties qualify only if they are certified historical structures (listed in the National Register or located in a registered historic district and certified by the Interior Department as having historic significance).

Example 17: During 19X1 (after 1980), T spends $100,000 to rehabilitate a 35-year-old building used as his law offices. His tentative credit is $15,000.

Example 18: During 19X1 (after 1980), T spends $100,000 to rehabilitate a 35-year-old apartment house used as rental property. The apartment house is not a certified historical structure. No credit is allowed in this case.

REHABILITATION EXPENDITURES Rehabilitation expenditures are "qualified property" for the rehabilitation credit. The category includes amounts spent to "fix up" buildings at least 30 years old and certified historical structures.

To qualify as a ***rehabilitation expenditure*** the subject building must be substantially rehabilitated after having been placed in service. At least 75% of the old exterior walls must remain in place. The credit does not apply to cost to acquire or enlarge a property. Unlike the regular ITC, the credit allowed for rehabilitation reduces the basis for depreciation by 100% of the credit except for certified historical structures. For certified historical structures rehabilitated after 1982, the basis must be reduced by 50% of the credit allowed.

The credit allowed for rehabilitation is technically a part of the ITC. The rehabilitation credit is added to the tentative ITC for purposes of limits, carryovers, and recapture.

CREDIT FOR ENERGY PROPERTIES

ENERGY PROPERTIES Energy properties subject to the special ITC credit include solar and wind generating properties, alternative-energy properties, and other properties specified by Congress that conserve energy.

Congress provided on a temporary basis an additional credit for the acquisition of properties responsive to the nation's energy crisis. Qualified ***energy properties*** were such things as "alternate energy property," e.g., equipment that uses fuel other than petroleum, or property that conserves petroleum, and "solar and wind energy properties." Numerous other properties too complicated to define here also qualified for the temporary credit.

Most energy properties qualify for a credit only if acquired before January 1, 1983. Other properties (ocean thermal property!) qualify only

[15] Sec. 46(a)(2)(f).

if acquired before January 1,1985. This special investment credit for energy properties was not extended by Congress in 1984. At the time of this writing (February, 1985), the Reagan Administration has still not decided whether it should ask for an extension of the credit. Given our federal budget problems and the continued decline in crude oil prices, one would expect Congress to take no action.

The rate of the credit for most energy properties is 10%, but some properties carry a rate up to 15%. Solar, wind, and geothermal energy properties acquired after 1980 and before 1986, for example, are subject to a 15% credit. Here, as with the regular ITC, the base for the credit is "qualified investment." The credit for energy properties is in addition to the regular ITC.[16] If property is acquired that qualifies for the regular credit and the energy credit, the rate is 20 to 25% (plus an additional 1 or 1.5% for the Employee Stock Option Plans).

Example 19: T constructed a plant for the extraction of petroleum from shale, a qualified energy property. Most of the cost was for "equipment," tangible, personal property that qualifies for the regular ITC also. The rate for these properties is 20%. Other costs, e.g., plant building, qualify for the 10% energy credit only.

For energy properties placed in service after 1982, the basis is reduced by 50% of the credit claimed. Also, the basis reduction cannot be avoided by electing a lower rate, an election applicable only to the regular credit.

Unlike the regular ITC, the energy credit can offset 100% of the gross tax liability. Taxpayers apply the regular credit first up to the limit ($25,000 of gross tax plus 85% of amount over $25,000) and then any energy credit is used to offset the remaining liability.[17] The energy credit not allowed currently is carried back three years and forward 15 years.

The energy credit discussed here applies to properties acquired for use in a trade or business and should not be confused with the credits allowed homeowners who spend money for energy conservation measures. The "residential" energy credits are explained later in the chapter.

OTHER BUSINESS-RELATED TAX CREDITS

The law contains several other credits related to business operations not discussed here in detail because they are either temporary or limited in scope.

TARGETED JOBS CREDIT[18] This credit, which expires at the end of 1985, provides tax relief for taxpayers who employ individuals who are members of groups where unemployment is high (ex-convicts, economically disadvantaged Vietnam-era veterans, etc.). The credit is based on

FORM 5884

[16] Sec. 46(a)(2)(c).

[17] Sec. 46(a)(9).

[18] Sec. 51.

the FUTA (Federal Unemployment Tax Act) wages paid and is generally 50% of such wages in the first year of employment and 25% for the second year, but subject to numerous technical limitations designed to prevent abuse.

CREDITS FOR ALTERNATIVE FUELS In addition to the energy credits discussed earlier, the statute also provides two credits to encourage the manufacture and/or use of alternative fuels. Section 29 provides a nonrefundable credit for taxpayers who produce oil, gas, steam, and synthetic fuels from nonconventional sources, e.g., garbage, cow manure, etc. Section 40 provides a credit for the production, sale or use of alcohol or alcohol-blend fuels.

CREDIT FOR RESEARCH ACTIVITIES Taxpayers who spend increased amounts for research and experimentation during the period between June 30, 1981 and January 1, 1986 are entitled to a credit for the *qualified, incremental* expenditures.

FORM 6765 The credit is generally 25% of *excess* qualified expenditures for the year over the average base period expenditures.[19] Qualified expenditures include both in-house and contract research and experimentation but with numerous restrictions. Section 30-F also contains specific rules for computation of the base-period average. While this credit is scheduled to expire after 1985, a bill that would make the credit permanent was introduced in Congress in early 1985. Prospects for passage, given our severe budgetary problems, are not bright.

CREDITS RELATED TO INDIVIDUALS

The credits in the preceding section were enacted by Congress to encourage business investment generally or in specific activities necessary for economic growth. Most other credits are included in the law to provide relief for some perceived social problem. For example, the child-care credit is designed to encourage the proper daytime care of small children in households where both parents work. Similarly, the credit for the elderly provides tax relief for older citizens with limited incomes. Other credits discussed in this section include those for earned income, political contributions, and residential energy conservation.

BACKGROUND

As noted earlier, the extensive use of credits to accomplish the policy objectives of the government is a relatively new development. This trend toward the use of credits is mirrored by the development of the credit for child (dependent) care.

Continued

[19] Sec. 30.

BACKGROUND

This credit addresses the problem of tax equity where both spouses are gainfully employed (but applies equally when there is only one adult breadwinner in the household). If one spouse stays at home to do the housework and tend the children, no tax is levied on the value of such services. If both work, both incomes are taxed and some tax relief is needed if they employ a third person to perform the tasks normally handled by the nonworking spouse.

The child-care credit began as a deduction in 1954, with a limit of $600 on the amount deductible. The deduction was liberalized several times; a substantial increase was made in 1971. Finally, the deduction was converted to a credit in 1976 and the credit provision has been changed several times since, usually to increase its benefits.*

---

*Bittker, *Federal Taxation of Income, Estates, and Gifts*, (Boston: Warren, Gorham and Lamont, 1981) Volume 2, p. 37-2.

CHILD (DEPENDENT)-CARE CREDIT

Though commonly called the "child-care credit," this credit is accurately described in the title of Section 21 as the credit for "expenses for household and ***dependent-care*** services necessary for gainful employment." Only taxpayers who are gainfully employed and who incur expenses for the care of qualified individuals are entitled to the credit. This credit was revised substantially in 1981 and the rules explained here are for years beginning in 1982 and later.

DEPENDENT-CARE EXPENSES Often called "child-care" expenses, dependent-care expenses are amounts spent for housekeeping, cooking, nursing, and baby-sitting, where a qualified dependent is cared for in the taxpayer's home.

GENERAL REQUIREMENTS To qualify for this credit a taxpayer must (*a*) incur "employment-related" expenses, (*b*) for the care of a "qualified individual."[20] An expense is employment-related only if paid to enable the taxpayer to be gainfully employed, and if either spent for household services or for the care of a qualified person in the taxpayer's home. A qualified person is:

- A dependent of the taxpayer under 15 years of age,
- A dependent of the taxpayer who is physically or mentally incapable of self care, or
- The taxpayer's spouse who is physically or mentally incapable of self care.

Generally, expenses qualify for the credit only if incurred within the taxpayer's residence. However, the care can be outside the home if the qualifying individual is a dependent under 15, or is a disabled dependent or spouse, so long as such disabled person spends eight hours each day in the taxpayer's home.

---

[20] Sec. 21(b)(1) and (2).

Example 20: T, divorced, operates her own business. She pays M to keep T's house clean and to cook. M also looks after T's 10-year-old son before and after the son's school day. The amounts paid M for all activities are "employment-related expenses" that qualify for the credit.

Example 21: In Example 20, T also pays G a salary to maintain the gardens surrounding her home. The payments to G are *not* for household or dependent-care services.

Example 22: H and W both work. They leave their 4-year-old daughter in a day-care center during the work day. Amounts paid to the center are "employment-related expenses."

Example 23: W works and supports her husband H, who is mentally disabled. Amounts spent for the care of H either in W's home or outside the home (if H spends eight hours a day in W's home) are "employment-related expenses."

Where the care outside the home is in a dependent care center, as opposed to a private home for example, the center must comply with all applicable laws and regulations of the state or local government. A dependent care center is a facility which provides care for more than six individuals and receives a fee for such care.[21]

RATE AND BASE FOR THE CREDIT The credit allowed is generally 30% of the base as defined below.[22] However, the 30% rate is reduced by 1% for each $2,000 or fraction thereof of adjusted gross income in excess of $10,000. In no event is the rate less than 20%.

Example 24: T, divorced, pays a day-care center for care of his 3-year-old daughter. If T's gross income is $10,000 or less, the rate for the credit is 30%. If T's AGI is $15,000, the applicable rate is 27%. If T's AGI is $35,000, the rate is only 20%.

Because of the relationship between the rate and adjusted gross income, married couples must file a joint return (showing their combined AGI).[23] Where married persons live apart, a joint return is not required for the spouse who pays over half the cost of maintaining the home, provided the other spouse is not a member of the household during the last six months of the year.[24]

The base for the credit is the amount paid for "employment-related expenses," but subject to several limits and qualifications.

---

[21] Sec. 21(b)(2)(c) and (d).

[22] Sec. 21(e)(6).

[23] Sec. 21(a)(2).

[24] Sec. 21(e)(2) and (4).

DOLLAR LIMIT The amount of the employment-related expenses taken into account for any year may not exceed $2,400 if there is one qualifying individual, or $4,800 if there are two or more qualifying individuals.

Example 25: T, divorced, pays a day-care center $2,100 for care of her 4-year-old daughter. T's AGI is less than $10,000. T's child-care credit is $630 ($2,100 times 30%). If T pays the center $3,000 during the year, the base is only $2,400 and the credit is $720 ($2,400 × 30%).

Example 26: H and W have a combined AGI of $60,000. They pay a maid $7,200 during the year to care for their home and for their two children, aged 8 and 12, before and after school. The base is limited to $4,800 and the credit is $960. ($4,800 × 20%).

EARNED INCOME LIMIT In addition to the maximum dollar limit just explained, the base cannot exceed the ***earned income*** of the taxpayer. For a married couple the base is limited to the earned income of the spouse with the lower earned income.[25] This limit assures that the credit is allowed only where taxpayers are gainfully employed.

EARNED INCOME As used here and elsewhere in the law, earned income is the opposite of passive income from property. Earned income arises from labor, salaries, wages, fees, commissions, etc.; passive income arises from capital, interest, dividends, gains, etc.

Example 27: H and W pay a maid $7,200 during the year to care for their home and their 2-year-old child. W is an advertising executive and earns $80,000. H dabbles in various lines of work and earned only $1,500 during the year. The base for the credit is $1,500, H's earned income.

A spouse who is either a full-time student or incapable of self care is *assumed* to have earned income equal to the maximum dollar limits ($2,400 for one dependent, $4,800 for two or more).[26] If the spouse's status as a student or disabled person runs for only part of the year, the earned income is imputed to that spouse pro rata—$200 per month for one dependent, $400 per month for two or more dependents.

Example 28: In Example 27, assume that H is a full-time medical student throughout the year. The base for the credit is $2,400.

OTHER RULES A child of divorced parents is treated as the dependent of the spouse who has custody for the longest period of time during the year. However, the child-care credit can apply to a custodial spouse only if over one-half of the child's support is provided by both parents and only if the child is in the custody of a parent for over six months of the year.[27] Note that under this rule the custodial parent must claim the credit even when the noncustodial parent claims the dependency exemption.

---

[25] Sec. 21(d).

[26] Sec. 21(d)(2).

[27] Sec. 21(e)(5).

No credit is allowed for amounts paid to a dependent of the taxpayer or to a dependent of the taxpayer's spouse, or for payments made to a taxpayer's child who is under 19.[28]

FORM 2441 The child-care credit is reported on Form 2441.

CREDIT FOR THE ELDERLY AND DISABLED

The credit for the elderly provides limited tax relief for our elder citizens as well as for citizens who retire because of a disability. To qualify for the credit the taxpayer must be 65 years old before the end of the taxable year, or must be retired on a disability that is both permanent and total.[29] Because of the phase-out based on adjusted gross income which is explained later, only taxpayers with lower incomes qualify for this credit.

The credit is 15% of a base called the "initial amount," an arbitrary amount based on filing status, less certain excluded income and the AGI phase-out. The initial amounts are:[30]

- $5,000 for a single individual.
- $5,000 on a joint return when only one spouse is eligible.
- $7,500 on a joint return where both spouses are eligible.
- $3,750 for married taxpayers filing separate returns.

Married taxpayers must file jointly unless they maintain separate households throughout the taxable year.[31]

The initial amount for a disabled taxpayer who has not attained the age of 65 is limited to the taxpayer's disability income.[32] Disability income is the disabled taxpayer's retirement pay or amounts received under an employer's health and accident plan that represents compensation or payments in lieu of wages. Special rules apply to the determination of the initial amount for married taxpayers where one is 65 and the other is under 65 but disabled.

Beginning with one of the initial amounts above, reductions are made for:

- Excluded income—While the usual instances are Social Security and railroad retirement payments, any pension or annuity income excluded from taxation reduces the basic amount. However, no reduction is required for the amounts excluded under the annuity formula or for the taxpayer's cost of qualified pension plans.[33] Workmen's compensation benefits that are treated as social security benefits under the Social Security Act also reduce the initial amount.

---

[28] Sec. 21(e)(6).
[29] Sec. 22(b).
[30] Sec. 22(c)(2).
[31] Sec. 22(e)(1).
[32] Sec. 22(c)(2)(b).
[33] Sec. 22(c)(3).

■ Phase-out for adjusted gross income—The basic (initial) amount is also reduced by 50% of the taxpayer's adjusted gross income in excess of:[34]

Single individual—$7,500
Joint return—$10,000
Married filing separately—$5,000.

Example 29: T, a 70-year-old widow, has adjusted gross income of $6,000 and received excluded Social Security payments of $4,200, her only excluded income. T's credit is:

Basic amount for a single person		$5,000
Less: Excluded income	$4,200	
AGI phase-out	-0-	4,200
Base for credit		$ 800
Percentage		.15
Credit allowed		$ 120

Note that T's credit is zero if her Social Security payments equal or exceed $5,000, commonly the case for covered individuals.

Example 30: H and W, both over 65, have AGI of $12,500 on their joint return and receive Social Security payments of $5,500, their only excludable income. Their credit is calculated as follows:

Basic amount—two qualified persons—joint		$7,500
Less: Social Security payments	$5,500	
one-half of AGI of $12,500 over $10,000	1,250	(6,750)
Base for credit		$ 750
Percentage rate		.15
Credit		$ 112

As Examples 29 and 30 illustrate, any increase in Social Security payments, adjusted gross income, or other excluded income would eliminate the credit entirely.

Example 31: T, a bachelor who is 60, retired last year due to a stroke that resulted in his total and permanent disability. During the current year, T received $4,000 from his employer's noncontributory pension fund. T also received $6,000 from social security. T's initial amount is $4,000, the disability income, and not $5,000. However, T's credit is zero because the social security benefits exceed the initial amount.

[34] Sec. 22(d).

All taxpayers who claim the credit for the elderly or disabled must file Schedule R. This credit is nonrefundable and is therefore limited to the gross tax liability.

EARNED-INCOME CREDIT

The earned-income credit is a special tax break for low income families that live at or near the poverty level. The credit is refundable and in some instances works like a negative income tax, where the government pays money to the taxpayer.

To be eligible for the credit, a taxpayer must be:

- Married and entitled to a dependency deduction for a child;
- A surviving spouse with a dependent child; or
- A head-of-household by reason of the fact that a child resides with the taxpayer.

In every case, the child must have the same principal place of abode as the taxpayer claiming the credit.[35] In short, the credit can be claimed only by a family unit consisting of at least a parent and child. Also, the credit is available only to residents of the U.S. whose earned income is from a U.S. source.

Taxpayers entitled to this credit obtain the amount of the credit from a table provided by the IRS. The table for 1984 is reproduced in Appendix D. The table for 1985 and later years will be substantially different from the 1984 table because of an increase in the credit passed by Congress in 1984. For 1985 and later, the table will be based on: a credit of 11% of earned income up to $5,000 giving a maximum credit of $550. This maximum credit is reduced by 12⅔% of taxpayer's adjusted gross income or earned income, whichever is larger, in excess of $6,500. Because of this phase-out, taxpayers whose earned income or adjusted gross income is $11,000 or greater are not entitled to the credit.

Example 32: T, divorced, maintains a home for her 2-year-old son. T has earned income of $7,500. She also claims a deduction for AGI of $500 for employee transportation, making her AGI $7,000. As a head-of-household with a dependent child, she qualifies for the earned income credit. The credit is:

11% of earned income up to $5,000	$550.00
Less: 12⅔% of $500 ($7,000 − $6,500)	(61.00)
Credit allowed	$489.00

If the credit exceeds T's gross tax, she may claim a refund for such excess.

[35] Sec. 32(c)(1).

Example 33: Assume the same facts as in Example 32 except that T also has interest (unearned) income of $2,000. Thus, T's AGI is $9,000 and the credit is:

Maximum allowed on earned income	$550.00
Less: 12⅖% of $2,500 ($9,000 − $6,500)	(305.56)
Credit allowed	$244.44

The credit is thus reduced by earned or unearned income in excess of the $6,500 limit.

Married individuals must file a joint return showing their combined AGI in order to claim the credit.[36] If the taxpayer can predict that the credit will result in a refund, the refund can be obtained in installments from the taxpayer's employer by filing a Form W-5.[37]

FORM W-5

CREDIT FOR POLITICAL CONTRIBUTION

Taxpayers who make contributions to political parties and candidates for political office can claim a limited, nonrefundable credit. Congress included this provision to encourage widespread support of our democratic processes. What constitutes a political contribution is loosely defined and includes such payments as those to form committees for candidates, tickets to political fund-raising affairs, etc.

The amount of the credit is 50% of contributions up to $100 for single individuals and $200 for married persons.[38] The maximum credit is thus $50 ($100 on a joint return).

Example 34: H and W contributed $175 to the campaign of Mayor Y and paid $100 for two tickets to a Democratic dinner for Senator X. Their credit is $100, 50% of contributions up to $200. If they had not bought the dinner tickets, their credit would have been only $87.50, 50% of the $175 contribution to Y's campaign.

RESIDENTIAL ENERGY CREDIT

The statute contains two temporary credits intended to encourage the conservation of energy used in a taxpayer's residence. One is a credit for ***energy-conservation expenditures*** and the other is for renewable energy sources. Both credits are allowed only for expenditures made *before 1986*.

ENERGY-CONSERVATION EXPENDITURES Expenditures for insulation, storm doors, storm windows, and similar items related to the taxpayer's residence are energy-conservation expenditures that qualify for the residential energy credit.

ENERGY CONSERVATION Amounts spent to conserve energy, such as for storm doors and windows and insulation, qualify for a credit of 15%

[36] Sec. 32(d).

[37] Sec. 3509.

[38] Sec. 24(b).

with a ceiling of the expenditures of $2,000 for each residence. A taxpayer who acquires a different residence is entitled to an additional $2,000 limit. The expenditures must be made on a residence that was substantially completed prior to April 20, 1977. The $2,000 limit is cumulative for all years per residence.[39] Credit of $10 or less cannot be claimed.

FORM 5695

Example 35: Last year, T spent $1,200 for storm windows on his residence (built in 1960) and claimed a credit for these expenditures. In the current year, he spent $1,000 for additional insulation on the same residence. The credit allowed this year is 15% of $800, or $120.

A credit not allowed because it exceeds the gross tax may be carried forward and claimed in a later year. However, no carryover is allowed after 1987.[40]

RENEWABLE ENERGY SOURCES Related to the residential energy credit, renewable energy sources are primarily solar heating units (including water heaters) and wind generating units.

RENEWABLE ENERGY SOURCES Expenditures for devices such as solar water heaters, wind generating units, and other ***renewable energy sources*** give rise to a credit of 40% up to a maximum expenditure of $10,000. Thus, the maximum credit for renewable energy sources is $4,000.[41] (The rate of this credit and the maximum limit is less for expenditures made before 1980.) Unlike conservation expenditures, this credit applies to expenditures made relative to a new residence. The $10,000 limit is cumulative for all years. Unused credits are carried forward but must be used before 1988, and only expenditures made before 1986 qualify.

OTHER TAX CREDITS

Some credits are included in the law because some payments made by taxpayers are really prepayments of the federal income tax, even though paid for a different reason. This rationale applies to the credit for off-highway use of petroleum products and to the credit for foreign income taxes.

OFF-HIGHWAY USE OF PETROLEUM PRODUCTS

Petroleum products, such as gasoline and lubricating oils refined for use in automobiles, are subject to a federal excise tax. This tax goes to the federal highway construction fund and is used for highway construction and repair. Taxpayers can claim a credit against the income tax for the amount of the fuel tax paid for certain off-highway use of these products.[42]

Off-highway uses that result in a credit are limited to the following

---

[39] Sec. 23(b)(1).

[40] Sec. 23(b)(5).

[41] Sec. 23(b)(2).

[42] Sec. 34(a).

business uses: operation of a farm, operation of public land transportation (taxicabs), and certain nontaxable ventures. If the cost of the fuel is deductible for tax purposes, the amount of the credit is included in gross income and thus reduces the deduction allowed (since a tax prepayment is not a deductible expenditure). Like the earned income credit, this credit is refundable where credits and prepayments exceed the gross tax liability. The credit is completed on Form 4136 or 4136T (Taxis). **FORM 4136**

FOREIGN TAX CREDIT

Citizens and residents of the U.S. must generally pay the U.S. tax on their worldwide income. Exceptions to this rule include the exclusion for foreign earned income and income excluded from double taxation by treaty. With these exceptions, a citizen or resident is often subject to the U.S. tax and a tax by the host country for foreign source income. The U.S. law therefore provides a credit against the U.S. tax for income taxes paid to foreign countries.[43]

All foreign taxes, including income taxes, are often deductible by taxpayers as trade or business expenses under Section 162 or as taxes under Section 164. Taxpayers therefore can elect to take a credit or to deduct foreign income taxes. The credit, with rare exceptions, results in the greatest reduction in the U.S. tax liability.

The foreign tax credit is limited by several provisions beyond the scope of this text. In no event can the credit claimed for foreign taxes exceed the taxes assessed by the U.S. on the foreign source income. This upward limit is calculated as follows:

$$\text{Limit} = \frac{\text{Foreign-source taxable income}}{\text{Worldwide taxable income}} \times \text{U.S. income tax before credits}$$

Example 36: T, a single individual, had a worldwide taxable income of $120,000 in 1983. The U.S. tax on this income from Schedule X is $49,473. T had taxable income of $50,000 derived from country X and he paid country X an income tax of $20,000. The limit for the foreign tax credit is:

$$\frac{\$50{,}000}{\$120{,}000} \times \$49{,}473 = \$20{,}613.75$$

Therefore T can claim a credit for $20,000 and reduce his U.S. tax to $29,473.

If T had claimed the $20,000 foreign tax as a deduction, his taxable income would have been $100,000 and his U.S. tax $39,473, $10,000 more than from use of the credit.

The foreign tax credit is reported on Form 1116. **FORM 1116**

[43] Sec. 27 and Sec. 901.

P L A N N I N G   W O R K S H O P

Most credits discussed in this chapter offer little opportunity for tax planning. This generalization is especially true for those credits included in the law for social objectives. A wife and mother, for example, does not seek gainful employment because of the child-care credit, though the amounts she pays for child care may be affected by the credit. The business-related credits do, however, afford some opportunities for planning.

OPTIMIZATION OF ITC

The ITC necessarily influences decisions related to acquisitions of new business properties, especially their timing. The entire credit is allowed even when properties are placed in service at the end of a year. Taxpayers can reduce their tax bills in good years by accelerating plans for asset acquisitions. Note, however, that mere acquisition is not enough; the new property must actually be placed in service.

ITC recapture rules may sometimes dictate a postponement of asset retirements. Premature dispositions carry a price tag. When the scrap or resale value of an asset is low, continued use in a back-up capacity may be preferable.

Here, as elsewhere, the tax planning tail should not wag the fiscal dog. The ITC provisions may affect decisions about property acquisitions and dispositions, but usually at the margin. The credit will not rescue a basically unsound business decision.

ELECTING THE REDUCED RATE

For years after 1982 the law provides for a reduction in the basis of ITC property equal to 50% of the credit claimed. As an alternative, a taxpayer can elect to use an 8% rate (4% for 3-year property). Generally, the basis reduction carries the lowest tax price tag.

Assume the acquisition of a qualifed 5-year property costing $100,000 by a taxpayer with a marginal rate of 50%. The "full" credit is $10,000, the reduced credit at 8%, $8,000, a $2,000 difference. If the full credit is claimed, the asset's basis and the resulting depreciation is reduced by $5,000 over the next 5 years. But claiming the deductions will reduce the tax only by $2,500, given the 50% marginal rate for the taxpayer. (If the taxpayer's marginal rate is 40%, the deductions are worth only $2,000, the credit forgone to obtain the deductions.) So the taxpayer's choice is between a $2,000 credit now and $2,500 of tax reductions from deductions over 5 years. With interest rates where they are these days, the $2,000 in hand now is usually the better choice. For taxpayers with lower marginals, espe-

Continued

PLANNING WORKSHOP

cially below 40%, the full credit with basis reduction is preferable in most circumstances.

This conclusion will not hold if the tentative credit for the year exceeds the limit based on the gross tax *and* the credit cannot be offset against the tax in one of the three carryback periods. The taxpayer gains nothing if the credit is added to a carryforward that may or may not reduce future taxes. In this case, the deduction, which yields a greater absolute benefit, is the better choice. The election to use the reduced rate and avoid the basis reduction is available on a property-by-property basis. This permits taxpayers to "fine tune" the credit and avoid the limitations.

REHABILITATION CREDITS

The credit for rehabilitation of old buildings varies from 15 to 25% of the rehabilitation expenditures. In some areas the cost of these older buildings is very low and the investment in the land on which the structure is situated can be a sound one. Thus, except for the land costs, the largest expenditure is often the rehabilitation cost subject to the credit. Aided substantially by this credit, attorneys, accountants, and other professionals with good incomes have acquired impressive and distinctive office space.

KEY POINTS TO REMEMBER

1. The properties that qualify for the regular ITC are primarily depreciable, tangible personal property and depreciable real property (other than buildings) serving as an integral part of a productive process. Separate definitions apply to qualified energy properties and rehabilitation expenditures.
2. The tentative ITC is calculated by applying the appropriate rate to the qualified investment for the year. The rate is generally 10%. Qualified investment includes 100% of the costs of qualified properties except for 3-year properties, where only 60% of the cost is included. The credit allowed each year is the tentative credit for the year, plus carrybacks and carryforwards from other years, but subject to a limit based on the gross tax.
3. The premature disposition of ITC property results in a recapture of the "unearned" credit. The amount recaptured differs for properties placed in service after 1980 compared to those placed in service before that date.
4. The basis of ITC property placed in service after 1982 is reduced by 50% of the credit claimed unless the taxpayer agrees to reduce the basic rate of the credit by 2%.

5. The tax law contains several credits related to business operations other than the ITC. These include the targeted-jobs credit (scheduled to expire in 1985), the credit for incremental research expense (available through 1985), and the credits for alternative fuels.
6. The credit for dependent-care expenses offers relief for certain households where all adult members are gainfully employed. The basic credit is 30% of amounts spent on care up to $2,400 ($4,800 if two or more dependents require care). The rate is scaled down to 20% as the AGI rises from $10,000 to $30,000. Various other limits apply to the credit.
7. The earned-income credit is a refundable credit designed to encourage gainful employment by low-income taxpayers. To qualify, a taxpayer must maintain a residence for a dependent child. The credit is 11% of earned income up to $5,000 but is phased out as the earned income (or AGI) rises from $6,500 to $11,000. This credit works as a "negative" income tax when the credit exceeds the tax liability.
8. The credit for the elderly affords some tax relief for taxpayers 65 or older (and younger taxpayers retired because of a disability). The credit, however, is tied to Social Security benefits and as a result is not available to most taxpayers.
9. Other credits included in the law, along with the objectives of each, are: the residential energy credit designed to encourage energy conservation at home; the credit for political contributions designed to encourage widespread participation in our democratic processes; the foreign tax credit that eliminates a double tax where income is subject to both the U.S. tax and that of a foreign government; and the credit for off-highway uses of fuel designed to refund the highway tax where fuels are used for other purposes.

SELF-STUDY QUESTIONS

1. Eric Ross, who is single and has no dependents, had an adjusted gross income of $80,000 in 1983. During 1983, Eric contributed $500 to the political committee of an elected public official. How much of a tax credit can Eric claim on his 1983 return for the $500 political contribution?

   a) $250

   b) $100

   c) $ 50

   d) $0

   (AICPA adapted)

2. Foster Corporation's tax liability for the year ended December 31, 1981, was $15,000 before claiming an investment tax credit. On July 1, 1981, Foster purchased a new truck for $180,000. The truck is appropriately categorized by Foster as 5-year property under the acceler-

ated cost recovery system. Foster's allowed investment credit for 1981 is

a) $ 9,000

b) $12,000

c) $15,000

d) $18,000

(AICPA adapted)

3. During 1975, the Alex Corporation purchased new equipment for $600,000 that had an estimated 10-year life and qualified for the investment tax credit. The corporation's tax liability for 1975 was $50,000, before claiming an investment tax credit.

   What is the maximum investment tax credit that Alex Corporation can claim for 1975?

   a) $ 5,000

   b) $37,500

   c) $46,250

   d) $50,000

   (AICPA adapted)

4. In December 1979, Margate Corporation paid $650,000 for a used machine for use in its business. The machine had an estimated remaining useful life of ten years, and was put in service on December 15, 1979. Margate's tax liability for the year ended December 31, 1979, was $75,000, before claiming an investment tax credit. What is the maximum investment tax credit that Margate can utilize for 1979?

   a) $0

   b) $10,000

   c) $12,500

   d) $65,000

   (AICPA adapted)

5. On July 1, 1981, Pemberton Corporation bought a new drill press for $20,000, which was placed in service the same day. The drill press qualifies as 5-year accelerated cost recovery system property, for which an investment credit of $2,000 was claimed. If Pemberton disposes of this drill press on May 31, 1983, how much of the investment credit must be recaptured in 1983?

   a) $0

   b) $1,200

   c) $1,600

   d) $2,000

   (AICPA adapted)

6. For the year 1978, Roberta Collins, who is divorced, reported the following items of income:

Interest income	$ 100
Wages	4,000
Earnings from self-employment	3,000

She maintains a household for herself and her 5-year-old son who qualifies as her dependent. What is the maximum earned income credit available to her for 1978?

a) $ 90

b) $137.50

c) $362.50

d) $500

(AICPA adapted)

7. Nancy and Dennis Martin are married and file a joint income tax return. Both were employed during 1979 and earned the following salaries:

Dennis	$32,000
Nancy	14,000

In order for Nancy to work she incurred at-home child care expenses of $6,000 for their 2-year-old daughter and 4-year-old son. What is the amount of the child care credit that they can claim for 1979?

a) $0

b) $ 489

c) $ 960

d) $1,200

(AICPA adapted)

8. Amos Kettle, a single taxpayer, age 66, filed his income tax return for 1976, and reported an adjusted gross income of $6,000. He received a total of $1,200 in social security benefits for the year and has no other excludable pension or annuity amounts. What amount can Kettle claim as a tax credit for the elderly?

a) $555

b) $570

c) $750

d) $900

(AICPA adapted)

9. Melvin Crane is 66 years old, and his wife, Matilda, is 65. They filed a joint income tax return for 1980, reporting an adjusted gross income of $7,800, on which they paid a tax of $60. They received $1,250 from social security benefits in 1980. How much can they claim on Schedule R of Form 1040 in 1980 as a credit for the elderly?

a) $0

b) $ 60

c) $375

d) $937.50

(AICPA adapted)

10. During 1980 William and Jane Conley made the following energy-conserving component additions to their personal residence (a 5-year-old house purchased by them in July 1980):

Aluminum siding (for the north side of the house)	$1,000
Insulation	750
Automatic setback thermostat	150
Used storm windows (purchased from an unrelated party)	300

Assuming that the Conleys have a tax liability of $3,000 without any other credits against their tax for 1980, what amount can they claim as a residential energy credit on their 1980 income tax return?

a) $135

b) $180

c) $300

d) $330

(AICPA adapted)

11. In 1981, Pianca Corporation bought the following new assets, both of which are in the 5-year class under the accelerated cost recovery system:

ASSET	COST
Solar panels	$ 8,000
Shredder for recycling of aluminum cans	12,000

Pianca claimed the regular investment credit in 1981 for the qualifying property. What is the total amount of the above-mentioned assets eligible in 1981 for the business energy credit?

a) $0

b) $ 8,000

c) $12,000

d) $20,000

(AICPA adapted)

12. During 1980 Bell Corporation had worldwide taxable income of $675,000 and a tentative U.S. income tax of $270,000. Bell's taxable income from business operations in Country A was $300,000, and foreign income taxes imposed were $135,000 stated in U.S. dollars.

How much should Bell claim as a credit for foreign income taxes on its U.S. income tax return for 1980?

a) $0

b) $ 75,000

c) $120,000

d) $135,000

(AICPA adapted)

13. One of the requirements for claiming the earned income credit is that the individual's

a) earned income must be $10,000 or more

b) earned income must be $10,000 or less

c) adjusted gross income must be less than $10,000

d) adjusted gross income must be equal to earned income

(AICPA adapted)

14. Orna Corp., a calendar-year taxpayer, had an unused investment credit of $8,000 at December 31, 1982, its first taxable year. For how many years can Orna carry over this unused investment credit?

a) 15

b) 7

c) 5

d) 3

(AICPA adapted)

QUESTIONS

1. Define the term "qualified-investment property". Does it include "personal" property? "Real" property?

2. Which of the following qualify for the "regular" investment tax credit:

   a) An automobile used in a business?

   b) An automobile held for personal use and enjoyment?

   c) An electric transmission line of a public utility?

   d) The office building of a manufacturing concern?

   e) A greenhouse used by a florist to raise flowers?

3. If a property qualifies for the energy credit, can it also qualify for the regular ITC?

4. Can a property that qualifies for the rehabilitation tax credit also qualify for the regular ITC?

5. Can the regular ITC offset 100% of a taxpayer's gross tax liability? If not, how is the limit calculated?

6. Is the basis of an asset affected by the ITC in every case? Explain. Do the same rules apply to the energy credit? The rehabilitation credit?

7. How is the ITC affected by an asset's estimated useful life?
8. What is meant by a "premature disposition" of ITC property? How does the "recaptured" credit affect the current year's ITC?
9. What expenditures qualify for the rehabilitation credit? Are the costs of acquiring or enlarging a property included?
10. Are the energy credits a permanent part of our tax law? If not, when do the various provisions expire?
11. Briefly define the following: Targeted-jobs credit; credit for alternative fuels; research-activities credit.
12. What does the term "qualified individual" mean relative to the dependent-care credit?
13. What employment-related expenses qualify for the dependent-care credit? Does that term include amounts paid to housekeepers? Cooks?
14. The basic rate for the dependent-care credit is 30%, but in some cases is as low as 20%. Explain. How is the rate determined for a particular taxpayer?
15. What is the maximum base for the dependent-care credit if there is one qualified individual? Two qualified individuals? Three?
16. How does the earned-income limit for the dependent-care credit work when one spouse is a full-time student? When spouse is disabled and is therefore a qualified individual?
17. Under what circumstances does a taxpayer qualify for the credit for the elderly?
18. How is the credit for the elderly computed? Why do most taxpayers 65 or older fail to qualify for the credit?
19. Ms. T is an unwed mother. She supports her two-year-old child who lives with Ms. T. Is Ms. T eligible for the earned-income credit?
20. What is the maximum credit allowed for earned income? How is this maximum phased out as a taxpayer's income rises?
21. Mr. T is eligible for an earned-income credit of $375 for the current year. However, because of deductions, Mr. T has a zero gross tax liability. Does he lose the benefit of the credit? Explain.
22. Mr. T contributed $300 during the current year to various political campaigns. How much credit can Mr. T claim if he is single? Married?
23. What is the maximum credit allowed for energy-conservation expenditures relative to a personal residence? For renewable energy sources related to a residence?
24. A citizen of the U.S. earns income in a foreign country and pays an income tax to that country. Is the foreign income also subject to the

U.S. tax? If so, what provisions does our U.S. tax law include to eliminate or mitigate the double tax?

25. If a U.S. citizen pays a foreign income tax that is deductible as a trade or business expense, will he or she be wiser to claim a deduction or the foreign tax credit? Explain.

PROBLEMS

1. Jeb Jones is a self-employed contractor. Jeb is married and files a joint return. During 1985 he purchased the following assets for use in his business:

DESCRIPTION	COST	GUIDELINE LIFE
Patent	$15,000	Remaining legal life is 10 years.
Land	20,000	———
Equipment (new)	12,000	5 years
Office building (used)	40,000	50 years
Office furniture (new)	5,000	10 years
Warehouse (new)	20,000	40 years
Truck (used)	3,000	3 years

   a) Explain the options available to Jeb relative to ITC. What would you recommend, based on the general rule?

   b) Calculate Jeb's tentative ITC assuming he elects the 10% rate.

2. During 1985, John Hancock, an insurance agent, purchased the following assets:

ASSETS	GUIDELINE LIFE (YEARS)	COST
Calculator	10	$ 300
Typewriter	6	500
New residence	35	66,000
New automobile	4	8,000
Dictaphone (used)	3	400

The new residence included a large office attached to the garage. John intends to use this office exclusively for business purposes. One-sixth of the total cost of the new home can be allocated properly to this office. The car will be used 90% of the time for business purposes and 10% of the time for personal uses.

   a) What is John's investment tax credit for 1985? (Assume that his tax liability is larger than this tentative credit, that the energy credit is not applicable, and that he uses the 10% rate.)

   b) Suppose that six years later (1991) John is still using the same dictaphone purchased in 1985. What effect, if any, will this fact have on John's tax liability for 1985? For 1991?

c) Suppose that after using the automobile purchased in 1985 for 2½ years, John decides to trade it in for a new car to avoid costly repairs. What effect, if any, will John's decision to dispose of this car have on this 1989 tax liability? Explain in detail.

d) Suppose that instead of trading the automobile (as suggested above), John sold his wife's older car and gave her the 2-year-old model to use as a family car. He then purchased a new car for business purposes. Would this decision have any tax advantages over the trade-in suggested above? Explain.

3. In 19X3, Expanding Corporation (not a public utility) purchased enough qualified property to give it a tentative regular investment credit of $56,000. The corporation's tax liability before the investment tax credit for 19X3 was $27,000. Its tax liabilities for other years are: 19X0, zero (a loss was incurred in its first year of operations); 19X1, $2,000; 19X2, $12,000; 19X4, $18,000 (it has no investments in qualified property in 19X4).

   a) What is the corporation's net tax liability for 19X3? Assume that 19X3 is a tax year after 1982.

   b) What can Expanding Corporation do with the "excess" investment tax credit in 19X3?

4. Exeter Company made the following asset acquisitions in 1985:

ASSETS	COST	ESTIMATED LIFE (YEARS)
Automobiles	$ 20,000	3
Warehouse	140,000	25
Plant machines	80,000	10
Delivery equipment	42,000	7
Common stock of affiliate	100,000	———

   a) Compute Exeter's tentative investment credit for 1985 using the 10% rate. The energy credit is not available for these assets.

   b) What is the allowable credit for 1985 if Exeter's tax liability before the credit is only $20,000?

   c) Assume that the credit disallowed in 1985 is carried back and absorbed in the three preceding years. What is the effect on the corporation's tax liability for 1989 if the automobiles are sold in the second year of use?

5. During the current year, New Corporation made the following asset acquisitions:

Regular ITC property	$1,500,000
"Energy" property (10% rate)	500,000

   The energy property is also tangible, personal property used in the business (but amount is not included in the $1.5 million for regular ITC property).

a) Compute New's tentative ITC for the year, assuming the 10% rate is used for the regular ITC.

b) New's gross tax liability for the year before the ITC is $225,000. Compute New's net tax liability after the credit and the disposition of the unused ITC, if any.

c) What is New's basis in the properties acquired?

6. In January 1985 Peter Whimsey, an attorney, purchased an old home close to the downtown area. The home was 75 years old and in bad condition when acquired. He refurbished the building throughout, though the exterior walls were left intact. On September 1, 1985 Peter began use of the building as an office for his practice. Amounts spent were:

Acquisition price of home ($75,000 was allocated to the land)	$175,000
Renovation costs	120,000
Furniture and fixtures	50,000

a) If the building is *not* a certified historical structure, compute:
   (1) Peter's tentative ITC, assuming only the above properties are acquired in 1985 and assuming the 10% rate is used.
   (2) Use of the tentative credit if Peter's gross tax before the credit is $30,000.
   (3) Peter's depreciation deduction for 1985, using the maximum recovery rates available. The furniture and fixtures were also placed in service on September 1.

b) Calculate the amounts above if the building is a certified historical structure.

7. For 1985 Tom Wolfe had the following tentative credits related to the operation of business as a proprietor:

Regular ITC	$60,000
Rehabilitation credit	15,000
Targeted jobs credit	15,000

Tom's gross tax liability before considering these credits was $80,000.

a) What is the amount allowed as a credit in 1985 for each tentative credit above?

b) How are disallowed credits, if any, treated for other years?

8. H and W are married and file a joint return showing adjusted gross income of $35,000. During the year H and W spent $6,000 to care for their two dependent children, ages 4 and 6, in a "qualified" child care center. What is the amount of the dependent care credit if H is employed as an accountant but:

a) W is not gainfully employed during the year?

b) W has a part-time job and earns $2,000 during the year?

c) W is a full-time student?

d) W is physically incapable of self care and the $6,000 includes amounts spent for her care?

e) W earns $10,000 as a model?

9. In each of the following independent cases, compute the "earned-income credit" for 1985:

   a) Taxpayer and spouse file a joint return. They have no dependents. Their income consists of salaries of $6,800 and interest of $600. Gross tax liability is $240.

   b) Taxpayer and spouse file a joint return. They maintain a household for their dependent 14-year-old child. Their combined adjusted gross income is $7,400, all from wages. Gross tax liability is zero.

   c) Same facts as part (b), except that their total adjusted gross income of $8,400 is made up of $7,800 wages and $600 of interest. Gross tax liability is $240.

   d) Same facts as part (b), except that their adjusted gross income was $3,600 consisting solely of wages. Gross tax liability is zero.

   e) Same facts as part (b), except that their adjusted gross income was $3,800, consisting solely of taxpayer's net profit from a small motor repair shop. Gross tax liability is zero.

10. In each of the following independent cases, determine the amount, if any, of the taxpayer's credit for child-care expenses. Assume that payment is made to enable taxpayer to be gainfully employed unless otherwise stated.

    a) Taxpayer is a widow employed as a corporate controller. She earns $88,000 during the current year. In order to be gainfully employed, she pays her cousin $150 per month to take care of her 6-year-old child in the cousin's home.

    b) Taxpayer is unmarried, earns $17,000 per year, and supports her two younger brothers, ages 8 and 17. During the year she paid a baby-sitter $250 per month to care for the 8-year-old.

    c) Sue is divorced. She earned $8,200 during the current year, but had to pay a housekeeper $200 per month to care for her two children, ages 4 and 5, while she worked. The housekeeper also cleaned the house and prepared all the meals. It is estimated that the housekeeper spends one-half of her time caring for the children and the other one-half doing housework.

    d) Margaret is unmarried. She has two dependent children, ages 8 and 14. Both children attend school, but she paid the 14-year-old $480 during the year to take care of the younger child after school until 5:30 P.M. each day. Margaret earned $8,000 during the year.

    e) John is a bachelor and supports his aged parents who live with him. John pays a neighbor $300 per month during the year to take care of his parents, both of whom are bedridden, while John works. John's income was $18,000 for the year.

11. Matte Harmon, a widow, aged 67, had adjusted gross income of $8,000 during the current year. Matte also received $1,800 during the year from Social Security.
    a) What is Matte's credit for the elderly?
    b) What is her credit if her Social Security benefits amount to $5,500?

12. Dave, a bachelor, suffered a severe heart attack last year at the age of 60. His employer retired Dave on a disability pension. Dave has no income except for his pension and social security payments. He also uses the zero bracket amount. Calculate the amount of Dave's disability credit for this year if:
    a) The disability pension is $4,500 and Dave receives $3,600 from social security.
    b) The disability pension is $7,000 and Dave receives $3,600 from social security.
    c) The disability pension is $7,000 and Dave receives $6,000 from social security.

13. H and W file a joint return and provide a home for their dependent 10-year-old child. H earns $8,000 during the year (after 1984) as a part-time construction worker. W is not employed. Calculate the earned income credit for H and W if:
    a) They have no other income and no deductions for AGI.
    b) They have no other income but H incurs deductible transportation expenses of $300 related to his employment.
    c) H and W have interest income of $3,000 and $300 of deductions for AGI.

14. In each of the following independent cases, compute the taxpayer's credit for dependent care expenses. Assume the payments are necessary for gainful employment unless otherwise stated.
    a) Macomb and his wife have five small children, ranging in age from 2 to 9. During the current year Macomb earned $7,400; his wife earned $8,200. They paid a baby-sitter $200 per month to care for the children while they both worked. They filed a joint return.
    b) Assume the same facts as in part (a), except that they paid the sitter $410 per month for caring for the children.
    c) Ann, a widow, was employed throughout the year, earning $10,200. She paid a baby-sitter $70 per month throughout the year to care for her two children. The younger is 9, the other became 15 on August 1 of this year.
    d) The taxpayer, a widow, works as an interior decorator and has income of $50,000. During the year she paid $400 per month for

maid service including care of her two dependent children, ages 10 and 12. The amount allocated to child care was $1,500.

e) The taxpayer, a widow with AGI of $12,000, paid her mother $100 per month during the year to care for her 5-year-old dependent child. The mother is not a dependent of the taxpayer.

f) John and Sue are married and file a joint return. John is a full-time student but earned $1,000 from part-time jobs during 19X1. Sue is employed and earned $9,400 during the year. In order for Sue to work and John to attend classes, they paid a baby-sitter $900 ($75 per month) to take care of their 2-year-old child.

g) Ray and Ellen are married and file a joint return. Ray is employed and earned $20,000 during 19X1. Ellen is not gainfully employed, but paid a college student $600 during the year to take care of her small child while Ellen did her shopping, attended meetings, and so on.

15. In each of the following independent cases, determine the amount of the credit for political contributions. In each case, the gift "qualifies," e.g., is made to a candidate or to an appropriate organization.

a) T, a single individual, contributes $75.

b) T, a single individual, contributes $175.

c) H and W, married filing jointly, contribute $175.

d) H and W, married filing jointly, contribute $275.

16. T's personal residence was constructed in 1965. In 1984 he spent $1,500 for storm doors and windows. T had not previously claimed the residential energy credit.

a) What is T's residential energy credit for 1984?

b) Assume that T spends $1,500 in 1985 for insulation of the residence. How much energy credit can he claim in 1985?

c) If, in 1985, T also spends $5,000 for a solar water heater, how much credit can he claim?

17. Pertinent facts about a married couple filing a joint return for 1985 are:

a) Total salaries earned $8,800. This is also the amount of adjusted gross income.

b) Exemptions claimed, three (husband, wife, and 4-year-old child).

c) Income tax withheld from earnings, $300.

d) Gross tax liability before credits, $220.

e) During the year taxpayers paid $600 for qualified child-care expenses.

f) During the year they paid political contributions of $80.

g) Also, during the year they spent $300 to insulate their home constructed in 1965.

Compute the net amount of tax they still owe, or the amount of refund they have coming.

18. T's taxable income for the current year is $80,000 and his gross tax for 1985 as a single individual is $29,473. T had dividend income of $5,000 from a Canadian corporation that withheld $750 of the dividend under Canadian income tax law.
    a) Should T claim the $750 as a deduction (and reduce his taxable income to $79,250) or should he claim a foreign tax credit?
    b) If he claims the credit, what amount is allowed?

TAX PLANNING PROBLEMS

1. John Quincy plans to spend $100,000 for 5-year ACRS property this year. This property also qualifies for the ITC. John's gross tax liability will absorb the ITC in the current year. Should he elect the 10% rate or the 8% rate if:
   a) His marginal tax rate is 50% in all years?
   b) His marginal tax rate is only 25% in all years?
2. Hiram Friedman is an attorney who practices as a sole proprietor. He has decided to build a fancy office for his practice but cannot decide between two alternatives—construction of a new fieldstone and glass building at a cost of $200,000 plus land costs of $50,000, or the purchase and rehabilitation of a 50-year-old residence. The residence would cost $125,000 of which $50,000 would be allocated to land. The rehabilitation would cost $125,000 (all qualifying for the credit).

   Hiram judges the two locations to be equally attractive and considers the other aesthetic considerations to be equal. Hiram's marginal tax rate is 50%. He currently borrows money at 12% and he will use 18-year straight-line depreciation for the structure.

   Based on the tax law, what choice should Hiram make? Support your choice with a complete present-value analysis.

CASE PROBLEM

Clyde Cooper began a new machinery repair business in January, 1985. Early in the year he acquired the following properties:

- January 20—New pick-up truck, $11,000 cost
- Feb. 2—Used machines, $40,000 cost
- Feb. 18—New machines $20,000 cost
- Feb. 20—Metal building to house business, $110,000 cost, of this, $20,000 was allocated to the land

Clyde wants to accelerate to the maximum the rate of capital recovery.

Results from operations of the business for 1985:

Repair income	$120,000
Labor expense	(40,000)
Other operating expense	(22,000)
Interest expense	(8,000)

Clyde is married and files a joint return with his wife, Mary (both under 65 and with good vision). Mary earned $12,000 as a secretary. Her employer withheld income tax of $3,000 from her pay. Clyde and Mary have a 3-year-old son. They paid a qualified day care center $1,800 during 1985. Other items related to their 1985 return are:

Dividend income—U.S. Corporations	$2,000
Medical expenses	(400)
State and local taxes*	(3,200)
Home mortgage interest	(3,000)

*This includes state sales taxes

Clyde did not pay estimated taxes for 1985.

a) Should Clyde elect to expense $5,000 of the cost of properties under Sec. 179? Explain.

b) Without prejudice to your answer to question (a), calculate the next tax liability for Clyde and Mary.

RESEARCH PROBLEMS

1. Anderson Grain Co. buys grain directly from farmers but is not itself engaged in the farming business. This year Anderson built two new concrete grain storage bins. While Anderson does not "produce" the grain in a farming sense, it does store, dry, aerate, bind, and finally ship the grain to Anderson's customers. Do the costs of these storage bins qualify for the investment credit?

2. Mary Lou has a 4-year-old son who stays in a qualified day-care center for six hours each day at a cost of $4,000 for this year. Until last year, Mary Lou was married to Mark, who now pays Mary Lou alimony and child care of $5,000 per month. The son is left in the center because Mary Lou spends her days painting landscapes. She also spends one day each week as a volunteer hostess at the local art museum. During this year, Mary Lou sold three pictures for $200 each. However, she is getting better and thinks that her art will produce substantial income later. Is she entitled to the child care credit?

Chapter Objectives

1. Identify the three types of expenditures deductible under Sec. 212, along with examples of each.
2. Explain the income tax treatment to a lessor of prepaid rents, damage deposits, and leasehold improvements which revert to the lessor.
3. Identify the special loss limitation rules applicable to vacation rental homes.
4. Explain the tax implications to a lessor and a lessee if a transaction is treated as (*a*) a lease and (*b*) a purchase.
5. Explain how the IRS Guidelines require the presence of nontax considerations in qualifying leases.
6. Identify the special deduction provisions available for exploration, development, and intangible drilling costs associated with the exploitation of natural resources.
7. Compare the cost and percentage methods of calculating depletion.
8. Explain the basic purpose of tax shelter investments, and identify the common tax advantages of such investments in real estate, equipment leasing, and oil and gas activities.

15 Investment Properties: Income, Deductions, and Tax-Shelter Opportunities

Chapters 6 and 8 were concerned primarily with business income and business expenses. The present chapter deals with the tax considerations applicable to rents, royalties, and other sources of passive income, and introduces the basic principles of tax-sheltered investments.

The first part of this chapter reviews the events leading up to the enactment of Sec. 212, which authorized deductions for expenses attributable to income-producing activities. This is followed by a discussion of the federal income tax treatment of rent and royalty expenses. The last part of this chapter contains an introduction to tax shelter activities, with practical examples illustrating how such investments are used to shelter other sources of income.

SEC. 212 EXPENSES

As mentioned in Chapter 7, Sec. 212 was enacted in 1942 to authorize deductions for expenses incurred in activities which were profit-oriented but did not meet the statutory definition of a trade or business. This provision was enacted primarily in response to two court cases which denied taxpayers deductions for expenses incurred in connection with income-producing activities. In Deputy v. Dupont,[1] the Supreme Court denied a deduction for expenses a noncontrolling investor incurred in purchasing

---

[1] *Deputy v. Dupont*, 308 U.S. 488 (1940).

a block of securities which were distributed to the corporate officers in order to increase management efficiency. Similarly, in Higgins v. Commissioner,[2] the Supreme Court denied deductions for expenses incident to the managing of a sizable portfolio of securities, even though the taxpayer maintained an office and staff to manage the investments. In both cases, the Court ruled that the activities of an investor did not meet the statutory definition of a trade or business.

Sec. 212 overcomes this definitional problem by authorizing deductions for ". . . any ordinary and necessary expenses paid or incurred during the year—(1) for the production or collection of income; (2) for the management, conservation, or maintenance of property held for the production of income; or (3) in connection with the determination, collection, or refund of any tax." (The third category was actually added in 1954.) As noted in the committee reports, the changes were made

> . . . not by disturbing the Court's definition of "trade or business" but by following the pattern that had been established since 1916 of (enlarging) the category of incomes with reference to which expenses were deductible.[3]

Several points should be noted in evaluating the deductibility of expenses covered by Sec. 212. The first category of expenses for the "production or collection of income" covers a wide range of expenditures, and is the general authority for deducting most rent, royalty, and investment expenses. However, expenditures incurred in certain activities, such as hobbies, personal pursuits, or perfecting title to property are not deductible as ***Sec. 212 expenses***.[4]

SEC. 212 EXPENSES All ordinary and necessary expenses paid or incurred in (*a*) producing income, (*b*) maintaining or preserving income-producing property, or (*c*) determining or litigating a tax liability.

The second category of expenses incurred "in maintaining or conserving income-producing property" also covers a variety of expenditures. For example, expenditures incurred in repairing rental properties are deductible under this provision, as well as the costs of trips by an owner to inspect the property. It is interesting to note that such expenses are deductible even though the property is not currently generating rental income. A personal residence is considered to be converted to rental property when efforts are made to rent the property.

Example 1: A purchases a new residence and lists her old residence as available for rent. Any expenses incurred in maintaining or conserving the residence from this point will be deductible. This will be true even if the old residence is concurrently listed for sale.[5]

The deduction for expenses incurred in the determination, collection, or refund of any tax was added to Sec. 212 in the *Revenue Act of 1954*. This deduction is available for expenses associated with any type of tax.

---

[2] *Higgins v. Commissioner*, 61 S. Ct. 475 (1941).

[3] *House of Representatives Report No. 2333*, 77th Congress, 2nd session, p. 46.

[4] Reg. Sec. 1.212-1(c).

[5] *William C. Horrmann*, 17 T.C. 903 (1951) (Acq.).

Thus expenses incurred in contesting a federal gift tax deficiency are deductible. A deduction is also available for fees paid for tax planning advice, although such expenses must be clearly distinguishable from nondeductible legal costs.

Example 2: Of the $3,100 of legal expenses incurred by B in a divorce action filed against her former spouse, a total of $800 is properly allocable to negotiations for alimony payments which will be taxable to B under Sec. 71. This portion of the legal fees is deductible by B under Sec. 212;[6] the remaining portion is considered to be a nondeductible personal expenditure.

In summary, Sec. 212 authorizes deductibility for expenses related to income-producing activities which do not meet the definitional requirements of a trade or business. However, it is still important to differentiate trade or business and income-producing activities. You may recall that all trade or business expenses are deductions *for* adjusted gross income for individuals. On the other hand, expenses attributable to rents and royalties are the only two income-producing activities listed under Sec. 62 which qualify as deductions *for* adjusted gross income. Expenses associated with any other income-producing activities must be taken as miscellaneous itemized deductions (*from* adjusted gross income).

Example 3: During 19X1 C incurred $180 of miscellaneous expenses in connection with his oil royalty income. The expenses are deductible *for* adjusted gross income.

Example 4: During 19X2 D paid $48 for a safety deposit box rental. The deposit box is used to store D's stock and bond investments. The rental fee is deductible under Sec. 212, since the investments would be an income-producing activity. However, the fee must be taken by D as a miscellaneous itemized deduction.

RENTAL INCOME AND EXPENSES

Although rental expenses and trade or business expenses are both deductions *for* adjusted gross income, it is still important to distinguish the two types of activities. For example, the special one-year deferral of prepaid services income permitted by Revenue Procedure 71-21 (see Chapter 4) is not available for prepaid rents. Similarly, Sec. 1402(a)(1) excludes rental income from the definition of income subject to the tax on net earnings from self-employment (see Chapter 13). However, in both cases the rendering of significant services by the lessor to the occupants may reclassify the income as trade or business income, which would be eli-

[6] Reg. Sec. 1.262-1(b)(7).

gible for the deferral election and would also be considered as earnings from self-employment.

The distinction between passive rental income and active services income is sometimes difficult to determine. Generally, services are considered to be significant if they are primarily for the occupant's convenience and are other than those customarily provided with the rental of rooms only.[7]

Example 5: E operates the Shady Motel and Tourist Lodge. E provides heat, lights, and trash collection for each cabin. These activities do not constitute significant services. However, if E provides maid service for each cabin, then the services are considered to be significant. Such a service is considered to be primarily for the occupant's convenience.

TAX ACCOUNTING FOR RENTAL RECEIPTS

The taxability of rental payments to a lessor is usually governed by the claim-of-right doctrine. Generally, any advance payment received by a lessor and not subject to a restriction as to disposition is taxable when received, regardless of the lessor's method of accounting. Prepayments of future months' rent (including a payment for the last month), as well as bonus payments for executing a lease, are taxable immediately. Lease cancellation payments to a lessor are treated as substitute rental payments and are therefore fully taxable.[8] Additionally, the payment of expenses and taxes of the lessor by the tenant are treated as being constructively received by the lessor as additional rent.[9]

Example 6: F, an accrual-basis, calendar-year taxpayer, receives $21,000 in 19X1 for 19X1 rentals and $3,200 as prepayments for 19X2 rentals. Additionally, a tenant paid the quarterly property taxes of $875 on the rental property as consideration for canceling her lease contract. All three payments are taxable to F in 19X1.

Amounts paid in advance as refundable deposits are not considered to be taxable income to the lessor if such payments are designed to secure a tenant's performance under a lease (e.g., deposits for damages). The possibility of a refund is considered to be a significant restriction on the use of the funds, even though the lessor has temporary use of the money during the interim period. However, any amounts not subsequently refunded because of the tenant's lack of performance are taxable when the restrictions as to usage are removed.[10]

---

[7] Reg. Sec. 1.1402(a)-4(c)(2).

[8] *Hart v. Commissioner*, 61 S. Ct. 757 (1941).

[9] Reg. Sec. 1.61-8(c).

[10] *John Mantell*, 17 T.C. 1143 (1952). In this case the Tax Court emphasized the importance of differentiating security payments from prepayments of rent. For example, a prepayment of the last month's rent under the lease is not a security deposit and is therefore taxable when received.

Example 7: G collects a $400 damage deposit from all tenants at the inception of a lease. At the end of tenant H's lease, G withholds $300 of the deposit for damage done to the apartment and refunds the remaining $100 to H. The $300 is taxable to G at that time. G cannot exclude this amount on the grounds that the $300 is merely reimbursement for a deductible repair expense. If in fact G later spends the $300 on legitimate repairs, a deduction will be allowed at that time.

BACKGROUND

One of the goals of the many tax accounting rule changes instituted by the Tax Reform Act of 1984 was to curb perceived abuses in situations where Congress believed that taxpayers were benefitting from a mismatching of income and deductions. For example, a cash-basis taxpayer recognizes no rental income until the rents are actually received, even though immediate deductions are taken for such expenses as interest, taxes, insurance, and depreciation. This front-loading of deductions could also be accomplished by using a deferred-payment lease, which provides for proportionately higher levels of rent over the life of the lease. This mismatching problem is further magnified when the lessee is on the accrual basis, since the rental expense would be deducted as incurred, rather than deducted as paid.

Congress responded to this problem by enacting Sec. 467, which will essentially place cash-basis lessors and lessees on the accrual basis of accounting if the timing of rent payments is mismatched with the incurrence of the expense. Specifically, Sec. 467 imposes a uniform method of income and expense recognition for lessors and lessees who have entered into a "deferred payment rental agreement," defined in Sec. 467(d)(1) as an agreement for the use of tangible property and services that contain either a step-rate (increasing rent) provision or a provision for the deferral of one or more rent payments more than one year after the year of incurrence. In general, both the lessor and the lessee must include in income and expense, respectively, the present value of the portion of any deferred rental payment relating to the current rental period, as well as *imputed* interest on accrued but unpaid rentals of prior years. The Treasury Department will issue regulations detailing the specific procedures to be used in making such computations.

Occasionally a lessee will make substantial improvements to leased property during the life of the lease. If these improvements revert to the owner at the end of the lease term, a question arises as to the taxability to the lessor of such improvements. Initially the courts took the approach of taxing the lessor on the fair market value of the improvements at the end of the lease. Congress eventually enacted Sec. 109, which specifically excludes the value of such improvements from the income of the lessor. However, the lessor's tax basis in the improvements is zero, so the exclusion is in effect a deferral of gain. The lessor will eventually realize the gain on a subsequent disposition of the property. Additionally, any improvements made in lieu of rent payments are not eligible for the exclusion.

Example 8: T enters into a lease agreement with H Corporation for the years 19X1 through 19X5, with rent payments specified at $6,000 per year. At the beginning of 19X4, T constructs an addition to the property at a total cost of $9,600. Under the terms of the lease, such an improvement reverts to H Corporation at the end of the lease; however, T may reduce remaining rental payments a total of $6,000. The addition has a value of $10,000 at the end of the lease. H Corporation must recognize the $6,000 rent reduction as taxable income, since this represents a rent substitute. The remaining $4,000 value of the improvement is excludable; however, H Corporation can increase the basis of the property by the $6,000 of recognized income only (i.e., H Corporation constructively received the $6,000 rent and reinvested it in the property).[11]

BACKGROUND

The first authoritative decision on the taxability of leasehold improvements reverting to a lessor occurred in 1917, when the Treasury Department ruled that the value of such improvements were taxable income to the lessor at the termination of a lease.* In 1935 the Court of Appeals of the Second Circuit ruled that the value of such improvements was not taxable to the lessor, since the improvement was not detachable from the land.† Because of the conflicting decisions, the Supreme Court agreed to review a case involving this question in 1939. In a landmark decision, the Court ruled that such improvements were taxable to the lessor, based on the following rationale:

> It is not necessary to recognition of taxable gain that he should be able to sever the improvement begetting the gain from his original capital. If that were necessary, no income could arise from the exchange of property . . .‡

This Court case was criticized because after the decision potentially large amounts of income would have to be telescoped into one

Continued

[11] See *Isidore and Gladys Brown*, 22 T.C. 147 (1954).

BACKGROUND

taxable year for the lessors. To avoid such possibilities, lessors could have been tempted to construct such improvements themselves and charge higher rents, or renegotiate rents downward in order to induce lessees not to abandon their leases. These possibilities led Congress in 1942 to enact the present Sec. 109, which excludes the value of the improvements from the lessor's income. Note that the lessor "pays" for this exclusion privilege by not being permitted to assign any tax basis to the improvement. In this respect, the tax treatment is similar to the so-called nontaxable exchange provisions of the Code (see Chapter 12).

---

*T.D. 2442, 1917.

† *Hewitt Realty Co. v. Commissioner*, 75 F(2d) 880 (1935).

‡ *Helvering v. Brunn*, 60 S. Ct. 631 (1939).

RENTAL EXPENSES

Generally the deductibility of rental expenses depends on the same criteria as trade or business expenses (e.g., ordinary, necessary, and reasonable in amount). For example, fees and commissions paid by the lessor for collecting rent and managing the property will ordinarily meet the criteria for deductibility. However, expenditures which are incurred in trying to obtain a lessee (advertising, attorney's fees, and broker's fees) should be capitalized and amortized over the life of the lease.[12] The same treatment would be applicable to expenses incurred in altering the premises for a particular lessee.

When a lessor pays an amount to a lessee in order to cancel the remaining term of a lease, usually the payment must be amortized over what would have been the remaining term of the lease.[13] However, if the payment is made in order to allow the lessor to enter into a new lease on the property, there is some authority for viewing such a payment as a cost of acquiring a new lease.[14] In this case, the payment should be amortized over the new lease term.

Example 9: With eight years remaining on a lease agreement, J (the lessor) pays $6,000 to the lessee in order to cancel the remaining lease term. This payment was made so that J can enter into a more profitable leasing contract of five years. J may amortize the $6,000 cost over the 5-year life of the new leasing agreement.[15]

---

[12] Rev. Rul. 70-408, 1970-2 C.B. 168.

[13] Rev. Rul. 71-283, 1971-2 C.B. 168.

[14] *Montgomery Co.*, 54 T.C. 986 (1970), Acq.

[15] A question arises as to the taxability of the $6,000 payment to the lessee. This payment is either capital-gain or ordinary income, depending on the character of the lease to the lessee.

FORM 1040—SCHEDULE E

Schedule E is used to report rental income and expense, as well as other sources of supplemental income. This form is illustrated in Figure 15-1.

VACATION RENTAL HOMES

The Tax Reform Act of 1976 established specific limitations on the deductions which may be taken by persons renting out their vacation homes. As discussed later in the chapter, rental activities sometimes provide a convenient tax shelter by creating tax savings with deductible losses even though the investment creates a positive cash flow. The restrictions created by the 1976 Act were intended to limit such loss deductions when such a home was also used for personal purposes during the tax year.

VACATION RENTAL HOME A second, or vacation home, also used for rental income. For tax purposes, special loss limitation rules may apply to rental expenses incurred if home is used for personal purposes more than the greater of 14 days or 10% of the total days rented during the taxable year.

Sec. 280A establishes three basic rules applicable to ***vacation rental homes***. The rule applicable to a particular situation depends on the number of days rented and the number of days used by the owner for personal purposes. These rules may be described as follows:

1. *De Minimus Rule*—If the vacation rental home is rented out for fewer than 15 days during the taxable year, both the income and expenses attributable to the rental property are ignored in computing the owner's taxable income. (However, deductions for interest, taxes, and casualty losses are still allowed as itemized deductions.)
2. *Insignificant Personal Usage*—If the home is not used for personal reasons more than the *greater* of 14 days or 10% of the total days rented, then rental expenses attributable to the rental days are deductible, subject to the application of the hobby-loss rules of Sec. 183. For example, the failure to show a profit in at least two out of five consecutive years from the activity may limit the expense deductions in all years to the gross rental income.
3. *Significant Personal Usage*—If the home is used for more than the *greater* of 14 days or 10% of the total days rented, then Sec. 280A limits the rental business deductions to the gross rental income from the property. Thus, the loss limitation rule is applied automatically without reference to the two out of five year test of the hobby-loss rules.

Several points should be noted in applying these rules. First, a rental of the property to a related party (as defined in Sec. 267) will be considered to be personal use of the property (for the days test) unless a fair rental is charged to the relative.[16] Secondly, if a taxpayer's principal residence is converted to rental property, the period that the home was used as the taxpayer's personal residence will not be counted as personal-use days.[17] Finally, in applying the expense-limitation rules (item (3) above), interest, taxes, and casualty losses must be deducted first from gross rental income. The reason for this rule is obvious; a taxpayer could circumvent

[16] Sec. 280A(d)(3).

[17] Sec. 280A(d)(4).

FIGURE 15-1

SCHEDULE E (Form 1040)
Department of the Treasury
Internal Revenue Service (0)

Supplemental Income Schedule

(From rents and royalties, partnerships, estates, and trusts, etc.)
▶ Attach to Form 1040. ▶ See Instructions for Schedule E (Form 1040).

OMB No. 1545-0074
1984
13

Name(s) as shown on Form 1040: Ralph and Wanda Wilson
Your social security number: 633 48 7077

Part I Rent and Royalty Income or Loss

1 Did you or a member of your family use for personal purposes any rental property listed below for more than the greater of 14 days or 10% of the total days rented at fair rental value during the tax year? ☐ Yes ☐ No

2 **Description of Properties** (Show kind and location for each)
Property A Rental Duplex, 1060 Grove Avenue, Dekalb, Illinois 60115
Property B
Property C

Rental and Royalty Income	Line	Properties A	Properties B	Properties C	Totals (Add columns A, B, and C)
3 a Rents received		9,600			3
b Royalties received					
Rental and Royalty Expenses					
4 Advertising	4				
5 Auto and travel	5	50			
6 Cleaning and maintenance	6	110			
7 Commissions	7	–			
8 Insurance	8	425			
9 Interest	9	2,400			
10 Legal and other professional fees	10	150			
11 Repairs	11	600			
12 Supplies	12	–			
13 Taxes (Do **not** include Windfall Profit Tax here. See Part III, line 37.)	13	1,540			
14 Utilities	14	960			
15 Wages and salaries	15				
16 Other (list) ▶					
17 Total expenses other than depreciation and depletion. Add lines 4 through 16	17	6,235			17
18 Depreciation expense (see Instructions), or depletion	18	4,360			18
19 Total. Add lines 17 and 18	19	10,595			
20 Income or (loss) from rental or royalty properties. Subtract line 19 from line 3a (rents) or 3b (royalties)	20	(995)			

21 Add properties with profits on line 20, and write the total profits here	21	
22 Add properties with losses on line 20, and write the total (losses) here	22	(995)
23 Combine amounts on lines 21 and 22, and write the net profit or (loss) here	23	(995)
24 Net farm rental profit or (loss) from Form 4835, line 49	24	
25 Total rental or royalty income or (loss). Combine amounts on lines 23 and 24, and write the total here. If Parts II, III, and IV on page 2 do not apply to you, write the amount from line 25 on Form 1040, line 18. Otherwise, include the amount in line 39 on page 2 of Schedule E	25	(995)

For Paperwork Reduction Act Notice, see Form 1040 Instructions. **Schedule E (Form 1040) 1984**

the loss limitation by deducting these amounts as itemized (personal) deductions and offsetting the rental receipts with such expenses as depreciation, utilities, and repairs.

Example 10: K owns a cabin by the beach which was held out for rent for the entire year of 19X1. K actually rented the cabin for 120 days and used the cabin for 30 days personal vacation. K received $2,850 gross rents for the 120-day period and incurred the following total expenses in 19X1: taxes, $1,200; interest, $1,600; repairs, $500; utilities, $800; and depreciation, $1,500. Since K's personal usage (30 days) exceeded the greater of 14 days or 10% (12 days) of the rental period, K's expense deductions attributable to the rental period will be limited as follows:

Gross Rental Receipts		$2,850
Less Rental Expenses Otherwise Deductible:		
Taxes ($1,200 × 120/150)	960	
Interest ($1,600 × 120/150)	1,280	(2,240)
Net Rental Income After Taxes and Interest		610
Less Remaining Rental Expenses:		
Repairs ($500 × 120/150)	400	
Utilities ($800 × 120/150, limited to $210)	210	(610)
Net Rental Income		0

Note that $430 of the utilities ($640 − 210) and $1,200 of depreciation ($1,500 × 120/150) are not allowed as deductions because of the expense-limitation rule. Since the depreciation was not allowed, the basis of the cabin will not be reduced. Also, the $240 of taxes ($1,200 × 30/150) and $320 of interest ($1600 × 30/150) attributable to the personal use days may be deducted if K itemizes. (In no case will any of the repairs, utilities, or depreciation attributable to the personal use days be deductible.)

Note in the calculations above that 150 days was used as the denominator in the fraction for all of the deductible expenses. However, in a recent Tax Court Case—*Dorrance D. Bolton*, 77 T.C. 104 (1981)—a taxpayer used 365 days as the denominator for the interest and tax deductions, since these expenditures were incurred for the entire taxable year, rather than just the actual days that the vacation home was in use. This calculation benefits the taxpayer, since the smaller interest and tax deductions on the rental portion allow larger deductions for the other rental expenses which otherwise would not be deductible (because of the loss-limitation rules). The remaining interest and tax deductions would then be taken as itemized deductions. The IRS continues to oppose this calculation.

Finally, the vacation rental home rules also apply to the rental of a principal residence. Although the intent of the rules was to limit deductions, the *de minimus* rule may work to a taxpayer's advantage when exorbitant rentals are charged for rental periods of less than 15 days (e.g., a one-week rental during the Olympic Games). In such a case, the rental expenses *and income* are ignored for tax purposes.

LEASE VERSUS PURCHASE

Sec. 162(a)(3) specifically limits the deduction for rental payments to those on ". . . property to which the taxpayer has not taken or is not taking title or in which he has no equity." Unfortunately, it is sometimes very difficult to separate rental activities from transactions which are in substance a purchase of the rental property. Obviously the tax implications of such a classification are important. If the transaction is in substance a purchase, then the rental payments are not deductible by the lessee, who will be entitled to a depreciation deduction (and possibly an investment tax credit) on the property. In the case of the lessor, the rental payments are actually installment payments on a purchase price of the property (along with imputed interest income).

Despite the importance of this classification problem, no general rule can be given for separating leases and sales of property. (This problem has also plagued financial accounting reporting procedures as well.) One of the earliest guides for classifying such transactions was Revenue Ruling 55-40,[18] which stated that the following factors are indicative of a purchase rather than a lease:

1. Portions of the periodic payments are applicable to an equity interest to be acquired by the lessee.
2. The lessee acquires title after payment of a stated amount of rentals required under the contract.
3. The total rental payments for a relatively short period of usage represent an inordinately large portion of the sum necessary to acquire title.
4. Rental payments materially exceed the current fair rental value of the property.
5. The property may be acquired at a price which is relatively nominal when compared to either the value of the property or to total payments made under the lease.
6. Some portion of the rental payments are specifically designated as interest.
7. The lease may be renewed at nominal rentals for the remaining useful life of the property.

The lease versus purchase distinction is especially important in the case of ***sale/lease-back transactions***. Frequently, a company in a loss position can realize benefits indirectly from a newly-purchased asset by selling the asset to a profitable company and in turn leasing back the same asset. The profitable company is now considered to be the owner of the asset and is therefore entitled to the tax benefits of ownership (depreciation deductions and investment tax credit). The loss company can then

SALE/LEASE-BACK TRANSACTION A procedure whereby a taxpayer purchases an asset, sells it to another party, and then leases the asset from that party. Frequently such transactions are arranged to provide the tax benefits of ownership to the lessor and immediate cash benefits to the lessee.

[18] Rev. Rul. 55-540, C.B. 1955-2, 39.

realize some of these tax benefits indirectly by paying rents less than the fair rental value of the property.

Prior to 1981 the tax treatment of such sale/lease-back transactions was determined on a case-by-case basis. In some cases the IRS successfully contended that no sale had occurred and therefore denied the tax benefits of ownership to the purchaser/lessor. In such cases the transaction is viewed merely as a "financing arrangement" between the profitable company and the loss company.

Several revenue procedures were issued to assist in distinguishing sale/lease-back arrangements from financing arrangements. For example, Rev. Proc. 75-21[19] indicated that a true sale/lease-back arrangement would require that the lessor have a 20% minimum investment (based on asset cost) at risk in the property throughout the lease term. Additionally, the lessee should not be guaranteed the right to purchase the property at less than fair market value.

Sec. 168(f)(8) was enacted as part of the *Economic Tax Recovery Act of 1981* to provide a "safe-harbor" election which guarantees sale/lease-back treatment to certain transactions if specific requirements are met. The purpose of this provision was to make it easier for loss companies to "sell" their tax benefits accruing on new asset purchases by entering into sale/lease-back transactions with profitable companies. The intent was to generate an immediate cash flow for such loss companies, rather than deferring the benefits through carryover provisions. If the safe harbor conditions were met, the transaction would be treated as a lease, even though the transaction did not comply with prior IRS guidelines. The safe harbor provisions were quite liberal and encouraged sale/lease-back transactions which essentially involved an exchange of cash for anticipated future tax benefits. This was accomplished by selling the asset on an installment basis to the profitable company with annual payments equal to the rent payments charged by the profitable company.

Example 11: L Company, in a loss position in 1983, purchases new equipment for $100,000. The equipment is then sold to P Company (in a profit position) for $100,000, payable as follows: $15,000 down, and 10 annual payments which include 12% interest on the unpaid balance. P Company then leases the equipment to L Company at an annual rental of $15,044. Thus, the rental payments due P Company exactly offset the installment payments due L Company, and the only cash changing hands is the $15,000 down payment. This $15,000 represents in effect a payment to L Company for the tax benefits of ownership accruing to P Company, the new owner of the equipment. Normally, the agreement would also provide that the asset would pass back to the loss company at the end of the lease for some nominal amount (such as $1).

---

[19] Rev. Proc. 75-21, 1975-1 C.B. 715.

The safe-harbor lease provisions were significantly revised by the *Tax Equity and Fiscal Responsibility Act of 1982*. The changes were made in order to correct perceived abuses in the application of the rules and also to help reduce projected budget deficits. The safe-harbor provisions are repealed for properties placed into service after 1983.[20] For sale/lease-back agreements entered into after 1983, the 1982 Act creates a new lease category called "finance leases." However, as one of the revenue-raising measures of the 1984 Tax Reform Act, Congress postponed the effective date of the finance leasing provisions until 1988.

BACKGROUND

It is somewhat ironic that the success of the safe-harbor leasing provisions led to their own demise. The underlying logic of the provisions was to increase the profitability of struggling businesses by offering them incentives to purchase new machinery and equipment. However, much of the public's attention was focused on the potentially enormous profitability of such transactions to the lessor companies. For example, much media attention was given to the safe-harbor leasing arrangement between IBM and Ford Motor Company. The provisions were sometimes portrayed as welfare to wealthy lessor companies, rather than to struggling lessee companies. A combination of public reaction and a real cost of billions of dollars to the Treasury because of the popularity of such transactions led to the repeal of safe-harbor leasing for tax years after 1983.

The new ***finance-lease*** classification will represent a hybrid of the safe-harbor lease rules and the traditional lease rules (primarily Rev. Proc. 75-21). In order to qualify as a finance lease, a sale/lease-back transaction must meet several requirements designed to restrict the benefits of tax-motivated leases. For example, the lessor must allocate any investment credit over a 5-year period, as opposed to using the entire credit in the year of purchasing the property from the lessee.

FINANCE LEASE A sale/lease-back transaction which is treated as a lease for tax purposes if the requirements of Code Sec. 168(f)(8) are met.

Until the finance lease provisions become effective in 1988, sale-lease-back transactions will be guided by pre-1981 IRS rulings and restrictions. Perhaps the most significant of these restrictions is the requirement that the lessor must have a reasonable expectation of profit from the transaction *independent* of the tax benefits. This imposes an economic reality test which was not part of the 1981 safe-harbor provisions (but which was a requirement of Rev. Proc. 75-21). As a practical matter, agreements meeting these requirements can no longer be structured with only a net exchange of cash at the front end of the agreement (see Example 11). To

[20] Code Sec. 168(f)(8). In addition, the requirements for safe-harbor leases entered into between July 1, 1982 and December 31, 1983 were significantly altered in order to reduce the tax benefits available to lessors under safe-harbor leasing. Most of these restrictions still apply to the new "finance leases" described above.

show a profit *independent* of the tax benefits, it will be necessary for a lessor either to (*a*) charge an annual rental larger than the annual installment note payment to the lessee, (*b*) sell the asset back to the lessee at the end of the lease for more than a nominal amount, or (*c*) use a combination of increased rental payments and increased repurchase prices.

The requirement to show a profit has been interpreted to mean a net positive cash flow (without reflecting time value of money considerations). Interestingly, the cash flow need only be positive; it does not have to constitute a "reasonable return."

Example 12: Loss Company purchases a machine for $100,000 on 3/1/84 and sells the machine to Profit Company on 4/1/84 in a sale/lease-back arrangement. Loss Company receives $15,000 cash and a 10-year installment note for the balance of $85,000, payable in ten equal installments with 12% interest on the unpaid balance. The annual installment payment on the note is computed to be $15,044 (same as Example 11). However, to show a profit on the transaction, Profit Company will have to charge enough rent (or increase the repurchase price) to cover the down payment of $15,000 (an annual rental of $15,044 would only offset the annual cash outflow on the $85,000 note). Thus, Profit Company would need to charge an annual rent of approximately $16,550 (or increase the repurchase price) to create a net cash inflow over the life of the lease. This is verified as follows:

Total annual rents ($16,555 × 10)	$165,550
Total installment payments ($15,044 × 10)	(150,440)
Total down payment	(15,000)
Net cash inflow before tax considerations	110

INVESTMENTS RELATED TO NATURAL RESOURCE DEVELOPMENT

Because of the various tax incentives available for the extractive industries, investments in natural resource development have become very popular in recent years. In discussing the tax provisions relating to these investments, it is important to distinguish the income and expenses of the producer/operator from those of the royalty holder. The producer/operator is the taxpayer who is engaged in the active trade or business of natural resource exploitation, and the royalty holder is generally the person who owns and leases the land to the operator in return for an income (royalty) interest based on production. Furthermore, a third-party investor may provide the necessary capital to an operator in return for a share of the profits. The most common arrangement is for the venture to be organized as a partnership, with investors purchasing partnership shares.

The following discussion is based primarily on the tax consequences of such investments to royalty holders and investors. However, it will be necessary to discuss some of the special deductions available to an active trade or business, since these may be allocated to investors and the operator/producers in the partnership.

ROYALTY RECEIPTS AND PRODUCTION INCOME

Royalties may be defined in general as payments for the use of property. Royalties are sometimes distinguished from rents in that royalties are payments based on a percentage or per-unit basis of production. Additionally, the use of royalty property frequently results in the physical exhaustion of the property (for example, a mine). Royalties may include payments received from books, stories, plays, copyrights, trademarks, formulas, patents, and also payments from the exploitation of such natural resources as gas, oil, coal, copper, and timber.[21]

Royalty payments are usually taxed as ordinary income, in much the same manner as rental income. This is true even though state law may characterize the lease as a sale of minerals.[22] However, legislative exceptions have been developed for payments received for patents and timber, as well as coal and iron ore royalties. These payments may qualify for capital-gains treatment (see the discussion in Chapter 11).

The claim-of-right doctrine applies to advance royalties and bonus payments received upon executing a royalty agreement. Generally such payments are includable in gross income in the year received, regardless of whether the taxpayer is on the cash or accrual basis.[23]

Example 13: Q leased 320 acres of land to an oil company in 19X2 and received a lease bonus of $120,000. Additionally, Q is entitled to a 1/8th royalty interest in the gross value of oil produced each year. This percentage of 19X2 production totaled $48,500. Q must include $168,500 in her 19X2 gross income. All payments are taxable when received.

DEDUCTIONS ATTRIBUTABLE TO NATURAL RESOURCES

ROYALTY EXPENSES IN GENERAL Expenses incurred in the production of royalty income are deductible as nonbusiness expenses under Code Sec. 212. For an individual taxpayer, such items are taken as deductions *for* AGI.[24] Royalty property includes intangible as well as tangible property, so cost recovery deductions are allowable on such items as patents and copyrights (generally over the useful life of the property).

In most instances questions of deductibility of expenses associated with royalty income can be answered by applying the basic requirements of Code Sec. 212. However, special considerations are present in the taxation of royalties derived from the exploitation of natural resources. In some cases the tax law has been used to subsidize investments in the ex-

---

[21] Reg. Sec. 61-8(a).

[22] *Strother v. Burnet*, 287 U.S. 314 (Sup. Ct.).

[23] Reg. Sec. 1.61-8(b).

[24] Sec. 62(a)(5).

DEPLETION A systematic cost recovery deduction for an owner's or operator's economic interest in a natural resource.

tractive industries by permitting special deductions to offset some of the high risk inherent in such ventures. For example, the ***depletion*** deduction (cost recovery for natural resource investments) is somewhat different from ACRS recovery. Some of the more important provisions are summarized in the following sections.

EXPLORATION EXPENDITURES Sec. 617 (a)(1) defines a mining exploration expenditure as ". . . a payment incurred for the purpose of ascertaining the existence, location, extent, or quality of any deposit of ore or other material . . . incurred before the beginning of the development stage of the mine." Ordinarily such expenditures would have to be capitalized as part of the total asset cost. Sec. 617, however, permits mine operators to elect to deduct all ***exploration costs*** in the year incurred. (These costs include depreciation on capital equipment used in the exploration.) However, the deducted costs must eventually be "recaptured" by either (*a*) including the deducted costs for a specific mine in income when the mine reaches a productive stage, and increasing the basis for depletion accordingly, or (*b*) deferring the depletion deduction on a specific mine until the total exploration cost related to that mine is recovered.[25] This election (made annually) in effect allows a mine operator to accelerate deductions which otherwise must be capitalized and taken as part of the depletion deduction over the useful life of the mine.

EXPLORATION COSTS All ordinary and necessary costs incurred in determining the existence, location, extent, or quality of any natural resource deposit.

Example 14: Z, a mine operator, incurs $60,000 of 19X1 exploration expenses in developing a coal mine. The mine becomes productive in 19X2, and Z's total depletable cost (exclusive of the $60,000) is $120,000. Assume that Z deducts the $60,000 exploration costs in 19X1. In 19X2, Z must either (1) include the $60,000 in gross income and increase the total depletable cost to $180,000, or (2) compute depletion deductions on the $180,000 and defer all depletion deductions until the $60,000 would have been recovered (based on the estimated total recovery).

It is important to note that the Sec. 617 election applies only to *mining* exploration costs; expenditures incurred in discovering oil and gas deposits must be capitalized. These capitalized exploration costs become part of the depletable basis of the minerals. However, these expenses may be charged off as losses from worthless properties if no minerals are found and the location is abandoned. These are sometimes referred to as "dry-hole costs."

Example 15: X Company, an oil producer, leases 1,500 acres of land in 19X1 and divides the property into three areas of interest, A, B, C. Area A is eventually abandoned in 19X4 because no evidence of minerals was found. X may deduct in 19X4 any direct costs of exploration associated with area A, as well as a portion of any general costs of exploration associated with the entire tract of 1,500 acres.

---

[25] Sec. 617(b)(1).

DEVELOPMENT EXPENDITURES ***Development costs*** are those expenditures incurred in preparing a natural resource deposit for production. These expenditures are incurred after the discovery of minerals is confirmed. Sec. 616(a) permits a mining operator to deduct such expenditures in the year paid or incurred. (These costs also include depreciation on related equipment.) Alternatively, the taxpayer may elect to deduct such expenses proportionately as the mineral or ore related to such expenditures is sold. These deferred expenses are not considered to be part of the depletable basis, however; they are amortized separately.[26]

DEVELOPMENT COSTS All ordinary and necessary costs incurred in preparing a natural resource deposit for production after discovery.

Example 16: After discovering a mineral deposit in 19X1, B incurs $13,000 of development expenses, which includes $3,000 ACRS recovery on equipment used in the development process. B may elect to deduct the $13,000 currently. Alternatively, B may elect to recover these costs ratably over the period of production. For example, if the total projected recovery is 65,000 tons of ore, B may deduct $.20 for each ton of ore sold. Furthermore, if the interest is sold before full recovery, B may recover the unamortized development costs as part of the adjusted basis of the property.

The Code Sec. 616 election for development expenditures does not apply to oil and gas wells. Instead, a special election is available for certain "intangible drilling and development costs," as described below.

INTANGIBLE DRILLING AND DEVELOPMENT COSTS Sec. 263 permits an oil or gas deposit operator the option of either capitalizing (and depleting) or immediately expensing certain ***intangible drilling costs*** and development costs. These costs include the intangible expenditures of drilling from the surface to the deposit. Among the qualifying costs are labor, taxes, repairs, supplies, power, and equipment rentals (tangible equipment must be depreciated separately). The expensing election must be made on the tax return for the first year in which such costs are incurred. If an operator has elected to capitalize these costs, an additional election is available if the well proves to be unproductive. Such unamortized costs may be deducted as an ordinary loss, if an election is made in the year that the unproductive well is completed.[27]

INTANGIBLE DRILLING COSTS All necessary intangible expenditures incurred in drilling from the surface to the natural resource deposit.

Example 17: Y Company discovered a significant oil deposit on a leased property in 19X4. Expenses incurred in 19X4 during the drilling operation included the following: $26,000 labor, $4,000 power, $18,000 supplies, and $4,000 repairs. In addition, the drilling operation involved the use of $80,000 of machinery purchased in 19X4. If a Sec. 263 election is made, Y Company may deduct $52,000 of expenses as intangible drilling costs (the labor, power, supplies, and repairs). In addition Y Company may take a regular ACRS deduction of $11,400 (15% of $76,000, the recovery basis after reduction for

---

[26] Sec. 616(b).

[27] Reg. Sec. 1.612-4(b).

one-half of the investment tax credit) on the machinery, assuming that it is 5-year ACRS property. Tangible equipment used in the production is never subject to an immediate expensing option.

Intangible drilling and development costs paid or incurred after 1975 are subject to ordinary income recapture upon disposition of the oil or gas property. These recapture rules are discussed in Chapter 11. Additionally, the excess of such deductions over what would have been a 10-year straight-line recovery is a tax preference item for purposes of the maximum tax (see Chapter 13).

DEPLETION Once normal operations commence on a mine or oil and gas operation, all production costs are generally treated as currently deductible expenses. In addition, a cost recovery deduction is allowed for the investment in the natural resource, since the property has a limited usefulness and is being gradually exhausted. The term depletion refers to the capital recovery procedures used for natural resources.

A depletion deduction is allowed to anyone with an economic interest in the oil or minerals in place.[28] In the normal situation, this would include both the operator (lessee) and the landowner (lessor), since each has a capital investment in the venture. In this respect, an economic interest must be distinguished from an economic advantage.

Example 18: A Company enters into a contract with Big Oil Company to refine crude oil from production of a new location. Although A Company enjoys an economic advantage from the production, it has no economic interest (capital investment) in the oil production and is therefore not entitled to the depletion deduction.

The amount subject to the depletion allowance (the economic interest) depends on whether the taxpayer is the lessor or the lessee. Typically, the person who owns the land also owns the mineral deposits. The owner usually leases the land to a producer (operator). The operator's depletable cost will be the total amount paid to the lessor (the lease bonus) and other costs not currently deducted (e.g., exploration, development, and intangible drilling costs). For the owner lessor, the lease bonus would be subject to depletion, as well as the royalty payments received (as explained below).

The depletion calculation differs significantly from the ACRS recovery deductions associated with fixed assets. Each year a taxpayer computes potential depletion deductions under two methods, the cost method and the percentage (statutory) method, and the taxpayer is required to deduct the larger of the two amounts. (An exception is made for timber; only cost depletion can be used for this natural resource.)

The *cost method of depletion* is somewhat similar to the units-of-

---

[28]Sec. 611(b).

production depreciation method described in Chapter 8. An estimated cost per unit of natural resource is calculated each year, and this unit cost is multiplied by the number of units sold during the tax year. The calculation may be expressed by the following formula:

$$\text{Cost Depletion} = \frac{\text{Unrecovered Depletable Cost at End of Year}}{\text{Estimated Remaining Units Recoverable at Beginning of Year}} \times \text{Number of Units Sold in Current Tax Year}$$

The estimated recoverable units is not necessarily a fixed number, and may be revised periodically by geological or engineering studies. It is important to note that the number of units *sold*, and not the number of units produced, is used in the calculation. Finally, it should be noted that cost depletion, like depreciation or ACRS recovery, can never exceed the historical cost of the investment.[29]

Example 19: N, an oil and gas operator, paid $210,000 to acquire all oil rights to Blackacre. This was N's only depletable basis in the property. It is estimated that the deposit contains 700,000 barrels of usable crude oil. During the year 19X3, 180,000 barrels of oil were produced and 150,000 barrels of oil were sold. N's cost depletion deduction for 19X3 would be $45,000, computed as follows:

$$\text{Cost Depletion} = \frac{\$210{,}000}{700{,}000} \times 150{,}000 = \$45{,}000$$

Note that the recoverable depletion basis would not include any tangible equipment used in the operation; these would be depreciated under normal procedures.

The *percentage method of depletion* is determined by multiplying a statutory percentage times the gross income from the property. However, the deduction is limited to 50% of the taxable income from the property.[30] The gross income from the property is defined as the total value of the natural resource when extracted. For a lessor, this is the total value of the mineral or metal less any royalty interest paid to a lessee, since the lessee will deplete this amount. The net income from the property is the gross income less all other operating costs, which includes general overhead and any development or intangible drilling costs expensed during the taxable year.

The statutory percentage is specified in Sec. 613, and varies from 5% to 22%. A representative listing of these percentages is given in Table 15-1. For tax years after 1975, most large oil and gas companies are not permitted to use percentage depletion. This change ended a widely debated controversy.

[29] Sec. 612.

[30] Sec. 613(a).

TABLE 15-1
Examples of Statutory Percentage Depletion

RESOURCE	PERCENTAGE RECOVERY
Gravel, peat, sand, and stone	5%
Clay and shale used to manufacture sewer pipe or brick	7%
Coal, lignite, and perlite	10%
Rock asphalt, vermiculite	14%
Gold, silver, oil shale, geothermal deposits	15%
Sulphur, uranium, and various U.S. metals	22%

Example 20: Z leases land from T, who is given a one-eighth royalty interest. Z extracts a mineral qualifying for the 22% statutory depletion rate. During 19X2, Z realized a total of $400,000 sales proceeds from the mining operation (of which $50,000 was paid to T in royalties) and incurred $220,000 of operating expenses. Z's 19X2 depletion deduction would be $65,000, determined as follows:

Gross Receipts from property	$400,000
Less Royalty Interest Paid to T	(50,000)
Gross Income to Z	$350,000
Statutory Percentage	×.22
Tentative Percentage Depletion	$ 77,000
Limited to 50% of Taxable Income:	
$130,000 ($350,000 minus $220,000) × .50	$ 65,000

The percentage depletion deduction is limited to 50% of the taxable income from the property (if this is still larger than the cost depletion calculation).

Example 21: Refer to Example 20. T, the lessor, would be entitled to a percentage depletion deduction of $11,000 ($50,000 × .22), assuming that T had no related expenses. If T had received a bonus at the inception of the lease, this amount could be recovered by cost or percentage depletion.

Prior to 1984, lease bonuses and advance royalties did not qualify for depletion deductions until actual production had begun. However, in Engle, 104 Sct 597, the Supreme Court ruled that percentage depletion is available on such payments even if there is not production during the year. In Rev. Ruls. 84-64, IRB 1984-23, 58, the IRS permits such deductions for the year in which such payments are included in income.

In comparing cost and percentage depletion procedures, it is important to note that percentage depletion can be deducted as long as the property produces a gross income. Unlike cost depletion calculations, the deduction is not limited to the adjusted basis of the property. Thus, percentage depletion may still be taken after a full basis recovery. This may create a minimum tax problem, since this excess is treated as a tax preference item (see Chapter 13).

BACKGROUND

For tax years prior to 1976, oil and gas qualified for the maximum (statutory) percentage depletion allowance of 22% (27.5% before 1969). This provision, when combined with the liberal deductions available for intangible drilling and development costs, was viewed by some critics as providing an unfair competitive advantage to oil and gas companies. Others defended these tax incentives as compensation for the risks involved in producing a supply of minerals and metals vital to a self-sufficient economy.

The unusually large profits reported by the large oil companies during the oil embargo period of the early 1970s caused Congress to act in 1975. After an initial attempt by the House to eliminate percentage depletion on all oil and gas ventures completely, a modified version of the bill essentially eliminated the percentage allowance for large oil and gas producers. Exempted from the repeal provision were certain independent producers and royalty owners.*

To eliminate the depletion deduction for the large integrated companies but leave an incentive for the small, high-risk producer the term "independent producers" was defined in terms of maximum retail sales and maximum output quotas.† Perhaps more controversial was the exemption of the oil or gas royalty owner from the repeal of percentage depletion. This taxpayer essentially plays a passive role in the venture with no real capital at risk, and yet the percentage deduction is still available to him or her if the venture generates large profits.

*The applicable percentage, however, was scheduled to be reduced gradually to 15% by 1984.

†Independent producers and royalty owners may use 15% percentage depletion for production which does not exceed a daily average allowance of 1,000 barrels per day. For these purposes, 6,000 cubic feet of gas is considered to be the equivalent of one barrel of oil. Retailers may use the percentage method if gross receipts from oil and gas sales do not exceed $5 million during the year. Finally, refiners can use the percentage method if the production from refining does not exceed 50,000 barrels on any day during the taxable year.

WINDFALL PROFITS TAX Due to the deregulation of oil and natural gas prices, the Crude Oil Windfall Profit Tax of 1980[31] created a temporary excise tax on the production and sale of crude oil. The tax is imposed on an oil producer's "windfall profits," a number derived from a rather complex calculation based on the difference between selling price (less

[31]Sec. 4986.

state severance taxes) and a base price as defined in the Code. A producer is defined as the holder of an economic interest, so this tax is imposed on both the operator (lessee) and the royalty owner (lessor). This excise tax is deductible for federal income tax purposes. A detailed examination of the calculation of the tax is beyond the scope of this text.[32]

TAX SHELTER ACTIVITIES: AN INTRODUCTION

The term "tax shelter" has been applied to a variety of investment activities designed to minimize the effects of the income tax on wealth accumulation. Using this definition, a ***tax shelter investment*** could include a contribution to an Individual Retirement Account, since the corresponding deduction defers the incidence of the income tax until the amounts are withdrawn by the taxpayer (presumably during lower-income retirement years). This definition of tax shelter would also include investments in state or municipal bonds, as the interest income on these obligations is exempt from the federal income tax. A similar analogy can be made for investments in corporate stocks with growth potential, since a disposition at a gain receives preferential tax treatment if the stock is held on a long-term basis.

TAX SHELTER INVESTMENTS Tax-motivated investments usually generating immediate tax losses used to offset other sources of income. Frequently the losses are somewhat artificial in that such noncash-flow items as ACRS deductions create the tax loss.

In tax practice, the term "tax shelter" is sometimes given a more limited meaning by including only those investments which generate significant tax losses as a result of the allowable deductions associated with the investment. These losses are available to reduce the tax liability attaching to the other unrelated (and often primary) income of the taxpayer. In other words, the investment "shelters" a portion (or all) of the other sources of income from taxation.

Eventually, the taxpayer will have a final tax reckoning on the liquidation of the investment. However, the losses permit a deferral of these tax effects, and frequently the taxpayer is able to convert the earlier ordinary expense deductions into capital gains income. In fact, "good" tax shelters accomplish two goals: a deferral of taxation and the conversion of ordinary income (caused by deductions) into capital gain.

The remainder of this chapter discusses the tax advantages and disadvantages of three common tax investments: residential real estate, oil and gas ventures, and equipment leasing. In addition, an introduction to methods of evaluating tax shelter investments is included in the discussion of real estate shelters.

Before discussing these tax shelter investments, a few basic concepts concerning tax-motivated investments should be clarified. First, many of the tax advantages inherent in these activities represent a conscious attempt by Congress to attract investment capital to certain activities having a high national priority and/or involving a high degree of risk. Examples include the tax incentives to invest in low-income residential housing and oil or gas ventures. Although some critics feel that direct subsidies to

---

[32] This tax is scheduled to expire no later than September 30, 1993. The Act exempts Alaskan oil from the tax, although this exemption was recently challenged unsuccessfully in the courts.

such areas would be a better way to achieve these goals, the tax law has been used for this purpose.

Secondly, it is true that the deductible tax losses generated by such activities create significant tax savings. For example, a 50% bracket taxpayer investing $8,000 in a venture which creates a $3,000 deductible loss in the first year has a net cost in the venture after the first year of only $6,500 ($8,000 − $1,500 tax savings). However, it is important to realize that creating losses is by no means the only objective of tax shelter investments; the cash-flow effects and a host of other economic effects must be considered. After all, a taxpayer having a large uninsured deductible theft loss would hardly consider such a transaction to be an attractive tax shelter!

Finally, there is seldom a guarantee that a tax shelter investment will be successful. Many factors beyond the taxpayer's control can alter significantly the expected returns from an investment. You may recall that many tax incentives were created because of either low returns or the high degree of risk inherent in the venture. A different though equally important type of risk in tax shelters is the possibility of IRS scrutiny. The potential profitability of some tax investments has led to several loophole-closing provisions, such as the at-risk rules, the hobby-loss rules, and the depreciation-recapture rules.

BACKGROUND

Congress has become increasingly concerned in recent years with the proliferation of tax shelter investment opportunities. Many of these investment offerings are legitimate investment ventures designed to show a profit eventually. Unfortunately, some of these offerings are little more than houses of cards propped up with promises of large tax savings. Such offerings often collapse once they are subject to IRS scrutiny since many lack economic substance. As our society has become more and more affluent, each year a larger and larger number of taxpayers seek shelter in those ventures offering such exaggerated claims as "$3 or $4 of deductions for each $1 invested." The sheer number of these potentially abusive shelter offerings in recent years has severely strained the administrative capabilities of the IRS.

As part of the Tax Reform Act of 1984, Congress enacted several provisions designed to assist the IRS in its attempts to uncover and regulate abusive tax shelters. For example, Sec. 6111 requires any tax shelter organizer to register the shelter* with the IRS on the day that the first offering for sale of such interests occurs. After furnishing various details of the offering to the IRS in the registration statement, the organizers will then be given a registration number which must be furnished to each investor, who in turn must include the number on his or her income tax return. In addition, Sec. 6707 provides penalties for (1) an organizer's failure to register a shelter (the

Continued

BACKGROUND

greater of $500 or 1% of the aggregate assets invested, limited to $10,000), (2) an investor's failure to include the registration number on his or her return ($50 per failure), and (3) an organizer's failure to retain a list of all investors for a period of at least seven years ($50 per omission, up to $50,000 maximum per year).

---

*For purposes of these provisions, Sec. 6111(c)(1) defines a tax shelter as any investment offering which appears to promise a tax savings (deductions and credits) to investment cost ratio of more than 2 to 1 at any time during the first five years of investment.

Frequently, tax shelter investments are organized as partnerships. The partnership form of organization offers several tax and nontax advantages. For example, it is often possible for a partnership to make special allocations of certain income and expense items; these allocations may be designed to confer many of the special tax deductions to the tax shelter investors. Additionally, a partnership can be organized to accept tax shelter investors as *limited* partners, so that their potential maximum loss from the venture is limited to the amount of their investment. Finally, a partner's tax basis (for cost recovery purposes) includes his or her share of the outstanding partnership liabilities. This can increase significantly a partner's maximum loss deduction for tax purposes.

AT-RISK RULES Sec. 465 provisions which deny tax loss deductions based on properties subject to nonrecourse financing (where the debtor is not personally liable).

In 1976 Congress enacted Sec. 465, which can limit the loss deductions of a tax shelter investor in a particular year. These provisions are known as the ***at-risk rules***, in that they are designed to eliminate artificial tax loss deductions caused by the use of nonrecourse debt in financing an activity. A nonrecourse debt is a liability secured only by the underlying property; the debt-holder may not proceed against the debtor as an individual. Congress felt that a taxpayer is not "at risk" economically in such a circumstance and should not be rewarded with a tax deduction based on a recovery of the debt cost.

Example 22: A contributes the following properties to a farming operation: $10,000 cash, equipment with a $20,000 adjusted basis which is subject to a mortgage on which he is personally liable, and equipment with a $32,000 basis which is financed on a nonrecourse basis (no personal liability). A's amount at risk is $30,000; the nonrecourse debt cannot be included in this total. Future loss deductions will be limited to this amount, although the excess losses will be deductible in future years if A's amount at risk increases (through additional contributions to the venture, additional income, or conversions of nonrecourse debt into recourse debt).

It is interesting to note that investments in real estate are exempted from the at-risk rules. This exemption has been somewhat controversial, in that it serves as a tax incentive for real estate investments. Of course, the construction and real estate markets are vital segments of our economy, and in that respect, Congress continues to justify this exemption.

REAL ESTATE TAX SHELTERS

Investments in real estate offer several tax and nontax advantages. Tax advantages accrue from such factors as (*a*) the profitable use of leveraging, (*b*) the use of ACRS recovery, (*c*) the dual benefits of tax losses and positive cash flow, and (*d*) the beneficial tax treatment accorded gains upon disposition. The following comprehensive example will be used to illustrate each of these points, as well as introducing a procedure for evaluating tax shelter investments.

Example 23: Audrey Rosen, single, age 30, inherited $20,000 from her aunt's estate. She is considering a January 1986 investment in a 15-year-old rental duplex. The duplex costs $80,000 ($70,000 is properly allocable to the building), and can be purchased with a down payment of $16,000, with the balance of $64,000 financed with a special 25-year, 10% mortgage. Audrey would spend the remaining $4,000 of her inheritance on furniture and appliances for the duplex.

Audrey has been advised that she could rent the duplex initially for $750 a month ($375 each side), with an 8% increase in rent every two years. Tenants will pay all utilities, and annual out-of-pocket expenses are expected to average $1,500 for property taxes and $300 for repairs. The building and land are expected to appreciate in value at the rate of 5% a year, and the value of the furniture and appliances after five years is considered to be negligible.

Audrey is a manager in a CPA firm with a current annual salary of $40,000 (expected to increase 8% a year). She does not have other sources of income, and normally does not itemize her deductions. She asks you to evaluate the profitability of this investment based on the assumptions given above, including a projection of after-tax cash if she sells the duplex at its expected fair market value at the end of 1991 (6 years from now). She can invest idle funds in the money market at an average 10% rate of return.

Before analyzing this investment alternative, it is important to note that the entire analysis depends on the accuracy of the projected inflows, outflows, and appreciations. Investment analyses sometimes seem to imply a much higher degree of accuracy than warranted by the underlying assumptions. It is very important to emphasize this point when making these calculations. Nevertheless, the potential margin of error may be an acceptable risk when compared with the alternative of making no projections at all.

A good starting point in analyzing this investment is to mention the concept of leveraging and how it applies to real estate. In the example, Audrey will have a $70,000 depreciable investment in the building for an initial cash outlay of only $16,000 (the down payment). This is because a taxpayer's basis in a property is determined by the total cost of the property, regardless of the method of financing. The tax savings from the ACRS deduction on 18-year property alone in the first tax year will cover over one-sixth of this down payment. Furthermore, the interest on the

TABLE 15-2
Comparison of Taxable Income and Cash Flow Calculations for First Year of Realty Investment

	TAXABLE INCOME (LOSS)	CASH INFLOW (OUTFLOW)
Rental receipts	$9,000	$9,000
Property taxes	(1,500)	(1,500)
Repair expenses	(300)	(300)
ACRS–Furniture and appliances	(600)[*]	—
ACRS–Duplex building	(6,300)[†]	—
Mortgage Payments—Interest	(6,372)	(6,372)
Mortgage Payments—Principal	—	(609)
Total before tax effect	(6,072)	219
Income tax savings from loss:		
Tax on $38,960[‡] $9,132		
Tax on $32,888[§] (6,929)	—	2,203
TOTAL	($6,072)	$2,422

*$4,000 Cost × .15 (ACRS Factor, 5-Year Personalty Class, First Year)
†$70,000 Cost × .09 (ACRS Factor, 18-Year Realty Class, First Year)
‡$40,000 Salary less $1,040 Exemption (Taxable Income Without Investment)
§$40,000 Salary less $1,040 Exemption less $6,072 Rental Loss (Taxable Income with Investment)

LEVERAGING The process of acquiring large tax (or nontax) benefits by using minimal initial cash outlays.

mortgaged amount is deductible. This process of using limited cash outlays to acquire much larger benefits is known as ***leveraging***.

Perhaps the most frequently cited advantage of real estate investments is the opportunity to create deductible tax losses and yet receive positive cash flows from the investment. This can be illustrated by referring to the facts of the example. Table 15-2 compares the calculation of net taxable income (loss) and net cash inflows (outflow) of the proposed investment for the first year of the investment, 1986. (The amounts for mortgage interest and principal payments are taken from a monthly amortization schedule for a 25-year, 10% mortgage.)

Table 15-2 indicates that the rental property will produce a $6,072 deductible loss and a $2,422 positive cash flow. Note particularly the income tax effect (based on 1985 tax rates); the $6,072 deductible loss reduces Audrey's federal tax liability by $2,203. This amount is calculated on a marginal basis, by comparing the tax due without the rental investment ($9,132) with the tax due including the rental investment ($6,929).[33]

This same analysis can be prepared for all years of the assumed investment. In order to do this, an assumption needs to be made on the treat-

[33] In many cases the tax effects of an investment are simplified by assuming that a constant marginal tax rate is applicable for the taxpayer. However, note in the above example that the rental loss dropped Audrey's taxable income from the 38% tax bracket to the 34% tax bracket (1985 rates).

ment of each year's cash flow. In Example 23, it is assumed that Audrey invests idle cash in a taxable money market fund which is expected to pay an average 10% interest rate over the period. Thus, each year's net cash inflow from the rental investment is assumed to be invested in this fund.

Table 15-3 displays a procedure for evaluating the cash inflows and outflows associated with an investment activity. (For simplicity, a constant personal exemption deduction of $1,040 is assumed.) The first portion of the table includes a calculation of taxable income and the calculation of the net tax savings (or tax cost) caused by the rental investment. Note that the net tax cost of $13,659 in 1991 is caused by the tax on the gain from liquidating the investment at the end of the year. In all other years the rental loss "shelters" salary income by reducing net taxable income. Although the amount of detail in this table is somewhat overwhelming, the reader is encouraged to examine the results of each year in order to understand the basic mechanics of analyzing a tax shelter opportunity.

The last section of Table 15-3 summarizes the calculation of net cash inflows available to invest in the money market fund. Note that the non-cash flow rental items (ACRS–Furniture and ACRS–Duplex) are added back to the rental loss to convert the rental results to a cash basis. (Adjustments are also made for the nondeductible mortgage principal payments and the net tax savings from the investment.) In order to simplify the analysis, it is assumed that all cash flows occur at the end of the year. Thus, the net cash inflow invested in the money fund at the end of 1986 ($2,422) earns no interest, although $242 ($2,422 × .10) is earned in 1987. The same procedure is used for each year of the investment, with the fund balance increased each year by that year's net cash inflow.

The 1991 results include the effects of liquidating the investment at the end of the year. The original assumption was that the land and building would increase in value at a rate of 5% a year. Under this assumption, the land has a value of $13,401 and the building has a value of $93,807. The entire gain on the land ($3,401) would be taxed as a long-term gain through the operation of Sec. 1231 (discussed in Chapter 11). The gain on the building would also be taxed as a long-term gain except for $7,700 of "excess depreciation" ($32,200 ACRS depreciation taken less $24,500 straight-line recovery on the same property). This "excess depreciation" is taxed as ordinary income under the Sec. 1250 rules applicable to residential realty.

The analysis in Table 15-3 projects that the initial $20,000 investment of 1986 will be worth $52,660 at the end of 1991 (after the property is sold). Of course, these projections are only estimates which depend entirely on the accuracy of the projected revenues, expenses, and appreciations. The real value of this evaluation technique is the opportunity to use the same procedure to evaluate other investment opportunities and compare the results of the different investment alternatives. For example, if Audrey invests the $20,000 in an 8% nontaxable municipal bond at the beginning of 1986 and sells the bonds (at cost) at the end of 1991, the final cash fund balance will be estimated to be $44,555.

The implications of investing in real estate as a tax shelter can be re-

TABLE 15-3
Cash Flow Analysis of Real Estate Investment

	1986	1987	1988	1989	1990	1991
Computation of Rental Income (Loss):						
Rental Receipts	9000	9000	9720	9720	10498	10498
Property Taxes	(1500)	(1500)	(1500)	(1500)	(1500)	(1500)
Repair Expenses	(300)	(300)	(300)	(300)	(300)	(300)
ACRS - Furniture	(600)	(880)	(840)	(840)	(840)	0
ACRS - Duplex Building	(6300)	(6300)	(5600)	(4900)	(4900)	(4200)
Mortgage Payments - Interest	(6372)	(6308)	(6239)	(6161)	(6076)	(5979)
Rental Income (Loss)	(6072)	(6288)	(4759)	(3981)	(3118)	(1481)
Other Taxable Income and Expense Items:						
Salary	40000	43200	46656	50388	54419	58773
Interest on Reinvested Funds[a]	0	242	518	834	1144	1513
Taxable Gain on Sale of Land	0	0	0			1360[b]
Taxable Gain on Sale of Building	0	0	0			27023[b]
Adjusted Gross Income	33928	37154	42415	47241	52445	87188
Personal Exemption	(1040)	(1040)	(1040)	(1040)	(1040)	(1040)
Taxable Income	32888	36114	41375	46201	51405	86148
Tax on (Salary-Exemption) Only	9132	10348	11758	13326	15019	16859
Tax on Taxable Income	(6929)	(8051)	(10050)	(12004)	(14190)	(30518)
Tax Savings (Cost) of Investment	2203	2297	1708	1322	829	(13659)
Calculation of Cash Flows:						
Rental Income (Loss)	(6072)	(6288)	(4759)	(3981)	(3118)	(1481)
ACRS - Furniture	600	880	840	840	840	0
ACRS - Duplex	6300	6300	5600	4900	4900	4200
Mortgage Payments - Principal	(609)	(673)	(742)	(820)	(905)	(1002)
Interest on Reinvested Funds[a]	0	242	518	834	1144	1513
Sales Proceeds - Land and Building	0	0	0	0	0	107208
Payment of Outstanding Mortgage	0	0	0	0	0	(59249)
Tax Savings (Cost) of Investment	2203	2297	1708	1322	829	(13659)
Net Cash Inflow (Outflow) from Investment	2422	2758	3165	3095	3690	37530
Add Beginning Balance of Cash Fund	0	2422	5180	8345	11440	15130
Ending Balance, Cash Fund	2422	5180	8345	11440	15130	52660

[a] Beginning Balance of Cash Fund x .10

[b] Taxable Gain on Sale of Investment	Land	Building	Total
Selling Price (FMV @ 12-31-88)	13401	93807	107208
Adjusted Basis	(10000)	(37800*)	(47800)
Total Gain	3401	56007	59408
Less 60% Long Term Deduction:			
$3,401 x .60	(2041)		(2041)
($56,007 - 7,700**) x .60		(28984)	28984
Taxable Gain	1360	27023	(28383)

*$70,000 Cost - $32,200 Accumulated Depreciation

**$7,700 Represents Excess Depreciation, Taxed as Ordinary Income Under Code Sec. 1250 (Chapter 11.)

viewed by summarizing the advantages and disadvantages. Among the tax advantages of such investments are the following:

- Leveraging can be used to obtain relative large bases in the depreciable assets for relatively small cash outlays. (Recall also that real estate is exempted from the nonrecourse financing limitations of the at-risk rules.)
- The combination of ACRS deductions, property tax deductions, and interest expense deductions usually leads to a net rental loss which can shelter other sources of income from tax.
- Although a rental loss is shown on the tax return, the cash flow from the rental activity is usually positive because of the large ACRS (noncash) deductions.
- In the past, realty has not only held its value but in many cases has actually increased in value over the years. This offers the investor the pleasing prospect of recognizing an additional bonus when the property is liquidated. Much or all of this gain is taxable as capital gain.

There are some potential disadvantages associated with real estate investments. These include the following:

- Investments in real estate may not be feasible because of high interest rates and/or large down payment requirements. Although the interest is deductible, the large monthly payments at current interest rates may eliminate the positive cash-flow possibility.
- Unforeseen problems invariably occur. These may include failure to find tenants, unreimbursed damages, and property tax reassessments.
- The combination of declining ACRS deductions and interest deductions may eventually cause the rental property to show a tax profit, which of course eliminates the shelter feature.
- The expected appreciations in value of the property may not occur. Note in the example of Table 15-3 that much of the ending fund balance associated with the investment was due to the net proceeds realized from the sale of the property.
- If the property is rented to commercial enterprises (as opposed to residential tenants), the ordinary income recapture costs at disposition under Sec. 1250 can be substantial. These provisions were discussed in detail in Chapter 11. Basically, the gain will be taxed as ordinary income to the extent of all depreciation taken on the building (as opposed to being limited to the "excess" depreciation as in the above example).
- The use of accelerated (ACRS) recovery on the building may generate a minimum tax problem, since the excess depreciation is considered to be a tax preference item (see Chapter 13).

OTHER TAX SHELTER INVESTMENTS

Tax shelter investments are available for a variety of activities. A whole industry of packaging tax shelter investments has flourished in recent years, and promoters are constantly looking for those unique opportunities which will attract investor capital. Two of the most popular vehicles for tax shelter investments are equipment leasing companies and oil and gas ventures.

EQUIPMENT LEASING Equipment leasing ventures have been a popular form of tax shelter, especially when organized as a partnership arrangement. In some arrangements, a partner will purchase a limited partnership interest, which basically limits his or her liability to the investment in the activity. All income, losses, and credits are allocated to the partners based on their profit and loss sharing ratios. Limited partnership shares are a popular means of raising equity capital for tax shelter ventures, and an abundance of these programs is offered to the public by various promoters.

The tax benefits of equipment leasing operations relate primarily to the front-end tax benefits generated by ACRS deductions and investment credits. Again, a key ingredient is the ability to generate tax losses and positive cash flows simultaneously.

The potential advantages of these types of tax shelter include the following:

- The investment offers a lot of immediate tax benefits, with a 5-year ACRS write-off and the investment credit. The potential tax savings of these early years may return a significant portion of the taxpayer's original investment.
- This investment also offers a possible opportunity to take advantage of leveraging by financing the equipment purchases with minimal down payments.
- The demand for equipment leasing may be fairly strong, particularly during times of tight money and high interest rates. More and more taxpayers may be forced to lease rather than buy.

Just like other tax-motivated investments, equipment leasing shelters are subject to potential problems. These include the following:

- Unless investments are continually made in new equipment, the venture may begin to show large profits, since most of the tax benefits occur in the first two or three years of equipment usage. Of course, if the profits are large enough a taxpayer may not mind paying the additional taxes; however, the ability to shelter other income from taxation is lost.
- Special restrictions are placed on the availability of the investment tax credit to individuals and other noncorporate lessors. Generally, Sec. 46(e)(3) limits the availability of the credit to those noncorporate taxpayers who (*a*) actually manufacture the leased property or

(*b*) engage in the trade or business of making short-term leases. The latter categorization is met only if (*a*) business deductions on the property exceed 15% of the rental income of the first 12 months of the lease and (*b*) the lease period is less than 50% of the property's recovery period.

- Gain on the sale of the equipment is usually taxed as ordinary income under Sec. 1245. Therefore, a significant tax cost may be associated with the disposition of the asset. In addition, investment credit recapture may be a problem on premature dispositions.
- Accelerated depreciation on leased personalty is a tax-preference item for purposes of the minimum tax.
- Other than certain closely-held corporations, taxpayers investing in equipment leasing ventures are subject to the at-risk rules of Sec. 465. If equipment purchases are financed on a nonrecourse basis, the taxpayer may not include this portion of cost as part of his or her investment basis. As a consequence, the taxpayer's potential loss deductions may be limited.
- Investments in equipment leasing activities may involve significant repair and maintenance costs. Though deductible, these expenditures will adversely affect cash-flow projections.

OIL AND GAS VENTURES The previous discussion of the special tax incentive provisions relating to oil and gas ventures helps explain why investments in these activities are popular tax shelters. Again, a limited partnership is often used as the vehicle for organizing these investments. As an additional "sweetener" to attract new participants, promoters frequently offer special profit and loss sharing ratios to favor those investors seeking tax shelter. For example, the partnership agreement may provide that deductions attributable to intangible drilling and dry holes are allocated to the limited partners. Usually, such special profit and loss ratios will be accepted by the IRS.

The list of tax advantages associated with oil and gas ventures is impressive. Some of the primary advantages are:

- The special expensing elections available for exploration, development, and intangible drilling costs can create significant tax losses which can be used to shelter other types of income.
- The depletion calculation for an investor is a significant noncash deduction, and it may be possible for the investor to recover more than his or her investment because of the allowance of the percentage method. Recall that percentage depletion for oil and gas ventures is still available for small independent producers and royalty holders.
- Although the costs of tangible equipment used in a venture cannot be immediately expensed, ACRS deductions and investment credits are still available for such acquisitions.

- In the event that a well proves successful, the potential windfall gains from production may erase any fears of showing a taxable profit (after all, the income tax rates are never 100%).
- Achieving energy independence is a high national priority, and this factor alone may help insure beneficial income tax treatment for natural resources in the future.

Oil and gas ventures are not without their risks, however. These include both tax and nontax risks such as the following:

- A host of recapture provisions may apply to the disposition of the investment. These include depreciation recapture, recapture of intangible drilling costs, and investment credit recapture. Therefore, the tax costs of liquidating the investment may be large.
- Because of the potentially large tax savings associated with such ventures, Congress has enacted various provisions which "charge" the taxpayer for the privilege of using these special deductions. For example, the use of percentage depletion for the intangible drilling costs will create tax-preference items which may expose the taxpayer to a minimum-tax liability (discussed in Chapter 13).
- Oil and gas activities are subject to the at-risk rules of Code Sec. 465. Therefore, the use of nonrecourse debt in financing the activity may limit a participant's loss deduction, which in turn may eliminate any tax advantages of using leverage.
- Most ventures are very speculative in nature and are usually offered for tax shelter created by losses, rather than potential profitability.
- Though successful wells may generate large profits, these amounts will potentially be subject to a windfall-profit tax.
- Because of the popularity of these types of tax shelter offerings, they continue to receive close scrutiny by the IRS.

PLANNING WORKSHOP

SEC. 212 EXPENSES

Sec. 212 is the authority for deducting a variety of expenditures associated with income-producing activities. Occasionally taxpayers will miss some of these deductible items in preparing their tax returns. For example, an investor would be permitted to deduct the cost of an investment newsletter and a safety deposit box rental (if used to store the securities). The basic requirement is that the expenditure be related to the income-producing activity.

Investments in rental properties are popular these days, and it is

Continued

PLANNING WORKSHOP

important for a taxpayer to be aware of the tax implications of rental agreements. For example, the wording of a lease agreement may be important in distinguishing a deposit from a prepayment of rent. Additionally, a taxpayer should be aware of the tax implications of using a rental home for personal reasons for a portion of the year. The vacation rental home rules will limit deductions when the personal usage exceeds the greater of 14 days or 10% of the days rented. Recall also that rentals to a related party are counted as personal usage in these tests unless a fair rental amount is charged.

LEASE VERSUS PURCHASE

It is important for a taxpayer to understand the tax implications of leasing agreements. The tax consequences of leasing property are vastly different from the consequences of purchasing property. This is true for both the lessor and lessee. Reclassification of a transaction can have disastrous tax consequences for one or both parties.

Unfortunately no definite set of rules can be applied to determine whether a transaction is in substance a lease or a sale. Rulings issued by the IRS prior to 1980 represent attempts to develop specific guidelines for tax-motivated leasing arrangements. If properly followed, these guidelines present unique opportunities to both profitable and unprofitable companies.

For an unprofitable company, a finance lease may represent an opportunity to "cash in" on the tax benefits of purchasing new property by entering into a sale/lease-back transaction with a profitable company. This is especially true when the company does not anticipate profits in the foreseeable future; in this case, loss and credit carryovers associated with property ownership are of little value. On the other hand, the cash down payment received on the sale of the asset may provide some much-needed current capital.

For a profitable company, the finance lease provisions may represent an opportunity to make a profitable investment. In a capital budgeting sense, the down payment in a typical sale/lease-back arrangement may be thought of as the present cost of a stream of tax benefits (ACRS and investment credits) to be received in the future. These proposals can be evaluated easily using common discounted cash-flow techniques.

TAX SHELTER INVESTMENTS

Most tax sheltered investments offer participants immediate opportunities to recover a significant portion of their investment in the first few years of the activity. These promises of "$1 for $1", or "$2 for $1" deductions for each dollar invested are appealing, but do not represent the total story. Significant tax costs may be incurred when

Continued

PLANNING WORKSHOP

the venture "turns the corner" and proves profitable. (These are sometimes referred to as "burned out" tax shelters.) Furthermore, attempts to bail out of the venture before this occurs can entail significant tax recapture costs. One possible solution to this problem would be to reinvest in other loss shelters to offset the profits generated by current shelters. This is sometimes referred to as "pyramiding" tax shelters, which only postpones the final reckoning. One author compared this to ". . . riding a tiger: it poses severe problems in getting off."*

An evaluative technique incorporating time value of money concepts is needed to properly analyze and compare the tax implications of various tax alternatives. The method proposed in this chapter is essentially a future value model, in that projections of cash flow are made for future years and each annual cash flow is reinvested at a specified return. An alternative evaluative technique would be to sketch all cash inflows and outflows and discount these values back to the present using a predetermined acceptable rate of return. This method could also be used to calculate an expected rate of return on a given investment alternative. Regardless of the evaluative technique used, the tax consequences of disposing of the investment should always be considered.

One final point should be made in reference to tax-motivated investments. Many tax-sheltered investment opportunities offered to the public represent legitimate ventures designed to assist an investor in accomplishing a variety of tax and non-tax objectives. However, some of the proposed investments will not stand up to IRS scrutiny. Although the characteristics of the venture may conform somewhat to the form of the law, the economic substance of the venture may be highly questionable. In the final analysis, the IRS will be trying to determine if the investment venture makes economic sense, apart from the question of tax avoidance. The investigation of potential tax-sham ventures has received a high priority in the assignment of IRS personnel in recent years.

---

*Benjamin Benson, "The Strategy of Tax Shelter," *The Journal of Accountancy* CXL (July, 1975), p. 52.

KEY POINTS TO REMEMBER

1. Sec. 212 provides deductions for income-producing activities which do not qualify as a trade or business. These include expenses of producing income, expenses of maintaining or conserving income-producing property, or expenses incurred in determining or litigating a tax liability.
2. Rental income is generally taxed when received. Exceptions are made

for refundable deposits and leasehold improvements which revert to the lessor at the end of the lease.

3. Expense deductions associated with vacation rental homes will be limited to rental receipts if the personal use of the second home exceeds the larger of 14 days or 10% of the days rented.
4. The classification of a transaction as a lease or purchase has significant tax implications for both the lessor and lessee. This is especially true for tax-motivated sale/lease-back transactions.
5. For tax years before 1988, a sale/lease-back transaction will be treated as a lease if certain requirements of IRS guidelines are met. Chief among these requirements is the provision that a lessor must show a profit (no matter how small) independent of the tax benefits accruing from the lease.
6. Royalty income represents payments for the use of property calculated on a percentage or per-unit basis of production. The deductibility of most royalty-related expenses is determined by Sec. 212.
7. Special elections provide for current deductibility of exploration and development costs associated with natural resources. A similar election provides for current deductibility of intangible drilling costs associated with oil and gas ventures.
8. Depletion refers to the cost recovery deductions for economic interests in natural resources. The two methods of calculating depletion are the *cost* method (a unit cost is assigned to each unit sold) and the *percentage* method (a statutory percentage times the gross income from the property).
9. Percentage depletion may allow cost recovery in excess of the adjusted basis of the property. This excess is a tax-preference item for purposes of the minimum tax.
10. Tax shelter investments are usually designed to create losses, during the early years of the investment, which offset other sources of income of the taxpayer. These front-end losses are usually caused by a combination of ACRS deductions, interest deductions, and/or investment credits.
11. Some tax shelter investments offer tax loss deductions and positive cash flows in the early years. Among the most popular investments are real estate, equipment leasing, and oil and gas ventures.

SELF-STUDY QUESTIONS

1. Bill McDonald, a cash-basis taxpayer, is the owner of a house with two identical apartments. He resides in one apartment and rents the other apartment to a tenant under a five-year lease dated March 1, 19X9, and expiring on February 29, 19Y4. The tenant made timely monthly rental payments of $500 for the months of January through November 19Y0. Rents for December 19Y0 and January 19Y1 were paid by the tenant on January 5, 19Y1. The following additional information for 19Y0 was available:

Fuel and utilities	$3,600
Depreciation of building	3,000
Maintenance and repairs (rental apartment)	400
Insurance on building	600

What amount should McDonald report as net rental income for 19Y0?

a) $2,200

b) $2,000

c) $1,700

d) $1,500

(AICPA adapted)

2. Paul Bristol, a cash-basis taxpayer, owns an apartment building. The following information was available for 19X2:

   An analysis of the 19X2 bank deposit slips showed recurring monthly rents received totaling $50,000.

   On March 1, 19X2, the tenant in Apartment 2B paid Bristol $2,000 to cancel the lease expiring on December 31, 19X2.

   The lease of the tenant in Apartment 3A expired on December 31, 19X2, and the tenant left improvements valued at $1,000. The improvements were not in lieu of any rent required to have been paid.

   In computing the rental income for 19X2, Bristol should report gross rents of

   a) $50,000

   b) $51,000

   c) $52,000

   d) $53,000

   (AICPA adapted)

3. On November 1, 19V8, Sam Lerner leased a building to Kenneth Tate for a period of 15 years at a monthly rental of $400 with no option to renew. At that date the building had a remaining useful life of 20 years.

   Prior to taking possession of the premises, Tate made improvements at a cost of $20,000. These improvements had an estimated useful life of 20 years at the commencement of the lease period. The lease expired on October 31, 19X3, at which point the improvements had a fair market value of $3,000. The amount Lerner should include in his 19X3 gross income resulting from the leased building is

   a) $12,000

   b) $ 9,000

   c) $ 7,000

   d) $ 4,000

   (AICPA adapted)

4. Donald Duval owns a two-family home. He rents out the first floor and resides on the second floor. The following expenses attributable

to the building were incurred by Duval for the year ended December 31, 19X0:

	EXPENSES FOR:		
	ENTIRE BUILDING	FIRST FLOOR	SECOND FLOOR
Depreciation	$2,000		
Realty taxes	1,800		
Mortgage interest	1,200		
Utilities	1,000		
Repairs		$300	
Painting			$400

What portion of the expenses can Duval deduct on Schedule E of Form 1040?

a) $1,800

b) $3,300

c) $6,000

d) $6,300

(AICPA adapted)

5. Refer to Question 4. What portion of the expenses can Duval take as itemized deductions on Schedule A of Form 1040?

a) $1,500

b) $1,900

c) $3,400

d) $6,400

(AICPA adapted)

6. Adam Ant owns a vacation rental home in Colorado. He rented this home at a fair rental value for a total of 190 days in 19X3 (30 of these days to his sister Alicia). Adam Ant will not be automatically required to limit his rental deductions to the amount of rental income unless his personal usage of the vacation home exceeds

a) 14 days

b) 16 days

c) 19 days

d) 175 days

7. Phil Collins owns numerous oil leases in the Southwest. During 19X8 he made several trips to inspect oil wells on the leases and to consult about future oil wells to be drilled on these sites. As a result of these overnight trips, he paid the following expenses:

Plane fares	$4,000
Hotels	1,000
Meals	800
Entertaining lessees	500

Of the $6,300 in expenses incurred, he can deduct:

a) $6,300

b) $5,800

c) $5,500

d) $5,000

(AICPA adapted)

8. The Nugget Mining Corporation mines mineral deposits that were acquired in 19X0 for $800,000. For 19X5, the corporation will have gross income of $500,000 and taxable income of $190,000 from its mining operations, before claiming a deduction for depletion. In prior years, percentage depletion totaling $700,000 was claimed and allowed. The percentage depletion rate for the mineral is 22%.

   For 19X5, the corporation can claim percentage depletion of

   a) $ 41,800

   b) $ 95,000

   c) $100,000

   d) $110,000

   (AICPA adapted)

9. In analyzing the consequences of an investment, the effects of any income tax savings and/or tax costs are usually computed on a marginal basis (i.e., by comparing total projected tax liabilities with and without the investment). This procedure is not necessary when

   a) the marginal tax rate is below 50%

   b) the marginal tax rate is expected to increase

   c) the marginal tax rate is between 14% and 50%

   d) the marginal tax rate is expected to be a constant 50%

10. Which of the following is not a tax advantage of real estate?

    a) accelerated depreciation

    b) net losses which can offset other sources of income

    c) positive cash flows

    d) investment tax credits

QUESTIONS

1. What is the one characteristic of a Sec. 162 expense which is not required of a Sec. 212 expense? Explain.

2. What are the three types of deductible expenditures authorized by Sec. 212? Give an example of each.

3. What is the key question to be answered in determining whether rental income is considered to be earnings from self-employment?

4. "For an individual, all Sec. 212 expenditures are deductions *for* adjusted gross income." Do you agree? Explain.

5. Under the terms of a 1-year rental agreement, the lessee must make a $400 deposit for possible apartment damages and also prepay the last month's rent of $450. Will these amounts be taxed differently to the lessor? Explain.

6. "A leasehold improvement which reverts to the owner of the property at the end of the lease is not taxable to the owner; however, the potential gain is merely deferred, rather than eliminated." Explain.

7. Sec. 280A limits the deduction for rental expenses associated with vacation homes when "significant personal usage" has occurred. Describe the Sec. 280A test for significant personal usage, including the effects of renting the property to a related party.

8. Little Company, in a loss position, needs a new machine. Large Company agrees to purchase the needed machine and lease it to Little Company. The lease will be designed to cover the expected useful life of the machine, and Little Company can purchase the machine at the end of the lease for $1. What are the tax implications to Little and Large if the IRS reclassifies the leasing arrangement as a purchase of the asset by Little Company?

9. Under the old IRS guidelines, a nominal lessor in a sale/lease-back transaction must show a profit "independent of the related tax benefits." How is this profit computed? What options are available to the lessor to ensure that this test is met?

10. In some cases the Tax Code has been used to encourage investments in the extractive industries by permitting special elections for certain expenditures. Describe the special options available for (*a*) exploration expenditures, (*b*) development expenditures, and (*c*) intangible drilling and development costs.

11. A depletion deduction is available to anyone with an "economic interest" in the natural resource. Explain what is meant by an economic interest, and give an example.

12. "Percentage depletion represents a significant departure from normal cost recovery procedures." Do you agree? Explain.

13. One common characteristic of most tax shelter investments is the creation of a tax deductible loss and a positive cash flow from the investment in the same year. Explain what factor(s) make this possible for investments in (*a*) real estate, (*b*) equipment leasing, and (*c*) oil and gas ventures.

14. The tax consequences of an investment should always be evaluated on a marginal basis. Explain the correct procedure for making this analysis. Are there situations where this procedure may not be necessary?

15. What is meant by "leveraging" a tax investment? How do the at-risk rules of Sec. 465 affect a taxpayer's ability to use leveraging?

16. What are the tax consequences to a lessor who (*a*) receives a lease cancellation payment? (*b*) makes a lease cancellation payment in order to enter into a more profitable lease with another tenant?

17. What is the rationale for requiring that forfeited damage deposits be included in income at the time of forfeiture?

18. If the owner of a vacation rental home has significant personal usage as defined in Sec. 280A, which expenses are deducted first in determining the net rental income or loss? Explain.

19. Explain how percentage depletion can create a cost recovery in excess of the depletable basis of a natural resource.

20. How will the Tax Reform Act of 1984 assist the IRS in detecting, monitoring, and auditing potentially abusive tax shelters?

21. Real estate investments usually offer excellent leverage opportunities. Explain.

22. What tax advantages are offered by an equipment leasing venture?

PROBLEMS

1. For each of the following expenditures, classify the item as either (*a*) deductible under Sec. 162, (*b*) deductible under Sec. 212, or (*c*) nondeductible (personal expenditure):
   a) $35 paid by an individual to have her income tax return prepared;
   b) $850 depletion deduction of a royalty holder (owner of the property);
   c) $300 paid by an individual to perfect title to a vacant lot;
   d) $50 monthly payment by a self-employed dentist to a bookkeeping service;
   e) $40 advertising fee paid to a newspaper by an individual in connection with renting a former residence (property has never been rented in the past).

2. Individuals Allen, Baker, and Carter all subscribe to the *Wall Street Journal*. Allen deducts her subscription cost *for* adjusted gross income, Baker deducts his subscription cost *from* adjusted gross income, and Carter is not permitted to deduct the fee. Explain how these differences in tax treatment may occur.

3. Graham owns a residential apartment complex consisting of 20 apartments, one of which Graham uses as his personal residence. During 19X3 Graham received the following amounts in connection with the rental:

- $184,000 cash from rents, of which $13,000 represents late payments of 19X2 rents and $15,500 represents prepayments of January 19X4 rents;
- $12,500 prepayments of rent for the last month of new leases entered into in 19X3;
- $8,200 of damage deposits on new rentals (refundable if no damage exists at the end of the lease);
- $1,600 forfeited deposits on leases expiring in 19X3 (Graham expects to spend this amount in the near future on deductible repair expenses);
- $830 value of a painting given to Graham by a tenant in lieu of two months rent;
- $1,040 value of a greenhouse room addition to an apartment left by a tenant at the end of the lease (as a condition for constructing the greenhouse, Graham agreed to reduce the rent $100 for each of the six months remaining on the lease);

How much must Graham report as gross rental income on his 19X3 tax return assuming that he uses the cash basis?

4. Taxpayer Graham in problem (3) incurred the following expenditures in 19X3 in connection with the apartment complex (including his own apartment): $4,800 property taxes, $1,500 utilities, $23,400 mortgage interest, $14,800 ACRS deductions (on total cost of building), $650 advertising, and $3,200 repairs (of which $350 related to his own apartment). Additionally, Graham refunded $3,200 of damage deposits for leases expiring in 19X3. Assuming that Graham itemizes his deductions, determine his total deductions (*a*) *for* adjusted gross income and (*b*) *from* adjusted gross income.

5. Under the terms of a 10-year lease, Telly (the lessee) agrees to construct an addition to the rental building. The building will revert to Holly (the lessor) at the end of the lease. Telly will pay a monthly rent of $800, which is $150 a month below the normal rent payment for similar leases issued by Holly. The building addition cost $26,000 and was worth $24,000 at the end of the lease. Describe the tax consequences of this rental agreement to Holly, the lessor. What will be Holly's adjusted basis in the building addition?

6. With seven years remaining on a lease, Green (the lessor) pays $6,000 to Markowitz (the lessee) in 19X3 in order to cancel the lease immediately. Green subsequently issues a new 4-year lease to O'Brien on October 1, 19X3 at a substantially higher annual rental. How should Green report the $6,000 payment on her 19X3 tax return? Explain.

7. Halder purchased a mountain cabin on March 1, 19X3 to use as both a vacation home and rental property. Halder rented the property a total of 200 days in 19X3 to unrelated parties. After apportioning expenses

between business and personal usage, Halder computes a $1,200 loss on the rental property ($2,600 receipts less $3,800 expenses). How much of this loss is deductible by Halder in 19X3, assuming that his personal use of the cabin was:

a) 12 days?

b) 18 days?

c) 24 days?

d) 16 days, not including 30 days that Halder rented the cabin to his father at a fair rental value (the 30 days aren't included in the 200 days described above)?

8. Randolph purchased a second home in North Carolina on June 12, 19X3. The cabin was used for 30 days for a family vacation in 19X3 and was rented to the Bradley family for 170 days. The home was vacant for the remainder of the year. Randolph received $4,400 of gross rents during the year and incurred the following expenses related to the cabin for the 200 days of usage in 19X3: $2,850 mortgage payments (of which $2,000 represents interest), $1,700 property taxes, $860 utilities, $400 repairs and $40 advertising expense. The appropriate ACRS deduction on the property based on 100% rental usage would be $3,600.

   a) Determine Randolph's taxable income (loss) from the rental property.

   b) Would any of the expenditures be deductible *from* adjusted gross income?

9. Refer to Problem 8. How would your answer change if the personal use of the cabin was only 16 days? Explain.

10. Seller Company sells machinery to Rich Company for $100,000, payable as follows: $20,000 down and an $80,000, 10-year, 12% note for the balance (payable in ten equal $14,159 payments). Rich Company then leases the property to Seller Company under a 10-year lease calling for annual payments of $15,500. At the end of the lease Seller Company can repurchase the property for $1. Will Seller Company be treated as the owner of the property for tax purposes under the IRS guideline provisions? Explain, including any actions that Seller Company might take to ensure lease treatment.

11. Getto Oil Company is a small independent producer. During the current year Getto incurred $800,000 of total costs in drilling five wells ($160,000 per well). Two of the wells proved to be dry holes, and the other three contained deposits sufficient to justify production.

    a) What options does Getto have in reporting the $800,000 costs for tax purposes?

    b) How would Getto report the cost of any tangible equipment used in the drilling operation?

12. Ackley, a small independent oil and gas operator paid $450,000 to ac-

quire all oil rights to North Property. The deposits contain an estimated 500,000 barrels of oil. Ackley's results for 19X4 were as follows:

Sales (100,000 barrels @ $14)	$1,400,000
Royalty payments to property owners	(112,000)
Gross income from property	1,288,000
Direct expenses of operations	(948,000)
Taxable income from property	$ 340,000

a) Compute Ackley's depletion deduction using the cost method.

b) Compute Ackley's depletion deduction using the percentage (15%) method.

c) Which amount would Ackley deduct for tax purposes?

13. Zeiko Company's undepleted cost basis in a coal mine on January 1, 19X3 was $123,000. The computed cost depletion deduction for 19X3 is $111,000, and the computed percentage-depletion deduction is $146,000. What is Zeiko's depletion deduction for 19X3?

14. Henry Strong earned a salary of $54,000 as a CPA in 19X3. He invested $10,000 in a partnership share of an oil and gas venture which provided allocations as follows: $2,500 of cash revenues, $1,500 of cash operating expenses, $2,000 of depletion deductions, and $1,000 of depreciation deductions. What was the net after-tax cash inflow (outflow) from the partnership investment?

15. An investment in real estate generated the following revenues, expenditures, and ACRS deductions:

Rental receipts	$14,400
ACRS—building	10,600
ACRS—furniture	2,300
ACRS—appliances	1,700
Mortgage payments (including $9,200 interest)	11,800
Property taxes	1,700
Utilities expense	1,800
Repair expenses	800
Advertising expenses	200

Assuming that the investor-taxpayer is in the 50% marginal-tax bracket (before and after considering the investment effects) determine (*a*) the taxable income (loss) generated by the investment and (*b*) the after-tax cash inflow (outflow) from the investment.

16. On January 1, 19X6, Abe Lemons received $800 from a new tenant under a 12-month lease. Of this total, $300 represents the January rent, $300 represents the last month's rent, and $200 represents a refundable damage deposit. Under the applicable state law, lessors must pay tenants 4% annual interest on any refunded damage deposits. During 19X6, the tenant made all rent payments on time, and Lemons refunded the tenant $156 at the end of the lease ($50 was

withheld for damages, and $6 interest was paid on the $150 refund). Assuming that Lemons had invested the $200 deposit in a 9% certificate for the year, explain how these items would be reported on his 19X6 return.

17. Refer to Problem 16. Assume that Lemons used $30 of the $50 damage deposit withheld to repair a cabinet in the apartment. The $30 was for replacement handles, and Lemons estimates that the value of his time to repair the cabinet was $25 for two hours work. How would this affect his 19X6 return?

18. Zelmo Beatty, a mine operator, incurred $36,000 of exploration expenses in developing a coal mine in 19X6. The mine becomes productive in 19X7, and Beatty's total depletable cost (exclusive of the $36,000 exploration costs) is $84,000. How will Beatty's 19X7 depletion deduction be affected if he elected to expense the $36,000 exploration costs in his 19X6 return? Explain.

19. Mary Washington received a $50,000 bonus in 19X5 for signing an oil lease with Wildcat Company. The lease permitted Wildcat to exploit any natural resources on the land; however, production did not actually commence until 19X7. What are the tax consequences of the lease bonus to Mary Washington in 19X5?

20. Explain how the following items would affect the taxable income and cash flows of an owner of an apartment complex:
    a) Gross rent collections of $34,500
    b) $32,300 payments on a mortgage on the property (of which $28,400 represents interest)
    c) $8,500 ACRS deductions on the apartment building
    d) $4,200 property taxes on the building
    e) $2,300 ACRS deductions on apartment furniture
    f) $3,250 utility expenses (paid by the lessor per the rental agreement)

TAX PLANNING PROBLEMS

1. Claudia Benson, a 50%-bracket, single taxpayer, lives in Chicago, Illinois, site of the 19X7 International Games. She lives two blocks from the central location of the games, and she has been offered two attractive rental options by a visitor to the games. Under Option 1, she would rent her home to the visitor for $900 a day for a 12-day period. Under Option 2, she would rent her home for $1,000 a day for a 16-day period. She estimates that her allocable deductible expenses for each day of rental would be $30 (interest), $10 (taxes), $8 (utilities), and $80 (depreciation). Which offer should she accept? (Hint: The vacation rental home rules also apply to personal residences)

2. Janet Bissell invested $25,000 in an equipment leasing venture in January 19X3. This amount was used as a down payment on equipment costing $100,000. The $75,000 balance was financed with a 5-year, 12% note, payable in equal installments (beginning on December 15, 19X3) of $20,804. Projected results for the first four years of the investment are as follows:

	19X3	19X4	19X5	19X6
Equipment leasing receipts	$55,000	$60,000	$70,000	$75,000
Operating expenses (cash)	(20,000)	(20,000)	(25,000)	(25,000)
Mortgage payment–Interest	(9,000)	(7,584)	(5,997)	(4,100)
Mortgage payment–Principal	(11,804)	(13,220)	(15,807)	(16,704)
ACRS–Equipment	(14,250)	(20,900)	(19,950)	(19,950)

Janet's marginal income tax rate is 50%, and will be unaffected by the leasing investment. Janet asks you to project the after-tax cash flow generated by this investment as of January 1, 19X7 (after reflecting the cash-flow and the tax effects of selling the property). Any cash inflows each year are invested in a fund paying 12% (taxable) interest. Assume that the equipment will be sold on December 31, 19X6 for an estimated $35,000, and any gain will be fully taxable as ordinary income under Sec. 1245. (NOTE: Janet may take an investment credit of $10,000 in 19X3 directly against her tax liability, but a disposition in December of 19X6 will cause an additional $2,000 tax liability in 19X6 because of investment credit recapture.)

CASE PROBLEM

William Small is a 42-year-old single taxpayer who lives in Davenport, Iowa and reports on the cash basis. Small is employed as an attorney with Littleton, Inc., and in 1985 he received a salary of $68,000, of which $27,000 was withheld in federal income taxes and $1,600 in state income taxes. Most of Small's business-related expenses are reimbursed by his employer; however, the following 1985 expenditures were not reimbursed: $740 travel expenses, $240 entertainment expenses, and $320 professional dues and subscriptions.

Small's other sources of income in 1985 consist of interest, dividends, proceeds from the sale of personal stock holdings, a partnership interest, and a rental property. During 1985 Small received $2,200 interest on certificates of deposit, $1,400 dividends from domestic corporations, and $16,000 from an 8/1/85 sale of Blaine Hotels Corporation stock (originally acquired on 2/2/81 for $21,200). Small is a 20% partner in the RST oil and gas partnership, and during 1985 his allocable share of the partnership loss was $5,800.

Small owns a 5-unit apartment complex in Davenport. Small lives in one of the units and rents the other four units (all apartments are approximately the same size). His cash receipts and disbursements records for the building in 1985 were as follows:

	RECEIPTS	DISBURSEMENTS
Collections of 1985 rents	$28,200	—
Collections of late 1984 rents	4,300	—
Collections of 1986 advance rents	3,600	—
Damage deposits collected on new leases	2,800	—
Interest earned on invested damage deposits	320	—
Deposits withheld for damages at end of leases	640	—
Deposits refunded to tenants in 1985	—	$ 852
Interest paid to tenants on refunded deposits	—	56
Utilities expenses (all 5 apartments)	—	2,708
Painting the interior of all 5 apartments	—	1,250
Advertising expenses (4 rental units)	—	350
Interest expense on building mortgage	—	18,200
Principal payments on building mortgage	—	3,100
Property taxes on building	—	2,900
Repairs to rental units	—	1,220

The building was originally acquired on 1/1/80 for $150,000, and straight-line depreciation was elected (based on a 30-year useful life). Small also acquired $8,400 of furniture on 1/1/80 and elected straight-line depreciation based on a 10-year useful life. Additional furniture was acquired on 12/1/85 for $2,000, and ACRS recovery was elected. (All furniture is used in the four rental apartments.)

Small's other expenditures in 19X5 include $800 state and local sales taxes, $1,200 unreimbursed hospital charges, $800 interest on a personal car loan, and $2,400 of charitable contributions.

Determine William Small's 1985 net tax liability (or refund due).

RESEARCH PROBLEMS

1. In 19X3 Brinson accepted a new job in Houston and placed his old residence in Dallas for sale. After several months on the market, Brinson rented the property, reporting a rental loss on his 19X4 return. In 19X5 Brinson was able to sell the Dallas residence and he immediately

purchased a new personal residence in Houston. Brinson did not report the 19X5 gain on the sale of the Dallas residence because of the special deferral-of-gain rules in Sec. 1034. Can Brinson defer this gain on the sale of the Dallas home and at the same time show a rental loss in his 19X4 return? Explain.

2. In 19X6 Mary Poston offered a furnished apartment for rent for the first time. However, the only tenants that she could locate would lease the apartment only if it was unfurnished. As a consequence, Mary paid $375 to a warehouse to store the furniture during the lease term. Can Mary deduct this expenditure under Sec. 212? Explain.

Chapter Objectives

1. Describe how corporations and other entities are used to reduce the income taxes of individuals.
2. Distinguish corporations from other entities such as partnerships and trusts.
3. Explain the differences between the tax rules for individuals and those for C corporations related to the computation of taxable income and the computation of the income tax.
4. Describe the tax treatment of transactions between C corporations and shareholders, including contributions to capital of the corporation, dividend distributions, redemptions, and liquidations.
5. Explain how mergers and other reorganizations affect the corporate shareholders.
6. Distinguish the tax treatment of partnerships from that of C corporations.
7. Explain how transactions between partnerships and partners are not usually taxable events.
8. Describe how partnership items of income, gains, losses, deductions, and credits flow through to the partners.
9. Distinguish S corporations from C corporations and partnerships.
10. Explain the rules related to the eligibility for the S election and how the S election affects the tax treatment of a corporation, including the flow through of taxable items to the S corporation shareholders.
11. Describe how estates and trusts come into existence and explain how fiduciaries are taxpayers only when their current income is not distributed to beneficiaries.

16 Corporations and Other Entities

The preceding chapters in this text treat the federal income taxation of individuals. In any discussion of taxation, individuals (natural persons) must be the centerpiece because only individuals bear the burden of taxation. Taxes, by definition, are transfers from the private sector to the public sector, and such transfers mean that individual taxpayers eventually have less wherewithal to consume. Nevertheless, several types of *artificial* legal entities play important roles in our tax law and affect the burden of the income tax on individuals. These entities are C corporations, S corporations,[1] partnerships, trusts and estates. The role of these entities in our income tax law is the subject of this chapter.

The tax treatment of these artificial entities varies widely. At one extreme, C corporations are treated as separate entities, apart from their shareholders. As such, C corporations are subject to the income tax. At the other extreme, partnerships are treated as aggregations of the individual interests of the partners. For tax purposes, partnerships are merely conduits and all income, deductions, etc., flow through the entity and impact directly on the tax returns of the partners. S corporations, trusts, and estates fall between these extremes and these entities are sometimes treated as separate from the individual owners or beneficiaries, and sometimes treated merely as conduits for taxable transactions.[2]

---

[1]The rules governing most corporations are found in Subchapter C of the Internal Revenue Code. However, in some circumstances, the shareholders of a corporation can elect the treatment of Subchapter S.

[2]A proprietorship is sometimes treated as an entity in financial accounting. For tax purposes, a proprietorship has no tax standing. Its taxable transactions are always attributed to the individual.

Much of what passes for tax planning today involves the creation of an artificial entity, and its insinuation between a taxpayer and some taxable event, for the reduction of the tax burden of the individuals involved.

Example 1: T, a widow aged 65, has income of $200,000 each year in the form of interest and dividends. She plans to leave the bulk of her wealth to her five teen-aged grandchildren. To avoid high taxes now on income which T does not need, an irrevocable trust is created for each grandchild and income-producing assets transferred to each trust. As a result, five new taxpayers are created and the total tax paid on the $200,000 income is reduced substantially.

In Example 1, the tax plan reduces the taxes by increasing the number of taxpayers and thereby reducing the marginal tax rates applicable to the income. The other artificial entities discussed below play similar roles in tax planning. The remainder of this chapter explains the tax rules applicable to the several entities and how they are used in tax planning.

C CORPORATIONS

C CORPORATION A corporation taxed as a separate entity, as distinguished from an S corporation, so called because it is subject to the rules of Subchapter C of the Internal Revenue Code. A C corporation is often called a "regular" corporation.

C Corporations, also called "regular" corporations, are separate entities for tax purposes. They pay an income tax,[3] deal with their shareholders as with strangers, treat officer-shareholders as normal employees, and their dividend distributions are taxable income to shareholders. Thus, a C corporation is a *tax person*.

Example 2: T has operated his retail clothing business as a proprietorship for several years. Gross income, deductions, and other tax items were reported directly on T's return, primarily on Schedule C. On January 2 of the current year, the assets of the business were transferred to the T Corporation and the business conducted in the corporate name. T owns all of the corporation's stock and serves as chairman of the board and president. T corporation is a new taxpayer. It must file Form 1120 and pay an income tax if it has taxable income. As president, T is an employee of T Corporation and, while T's salary is deductible to T Corporation, it must pay the FICA tax on T's wages and otherwise treat T as an employee. Dividends distributed to T in subsequent years are taxable income to him.

A few "public" corporations, approximately 25,000, are in fact separate from their shareholders. Another two million corporations, however, are closely held, family corporations that owe their existence in large measure to our tax laws. While the same rules apply to public corporations and to closely held corporations, usually only the latter can be manipulated for tax purposes.

---

[3]Sec. 11(b).

FORMING THE CORPORATION

Legal requirements for incorporation under state laws are generally simple. For a nominal fee, an attorney will obtain the necessary charter from the appropriate state agency, draft the necessary bylaws, and conduct the necessary organizational meetings of shareholders and directors. When desirable for a tax plan, the creation of a *de jure* corporation presents no problem. Occasionally, under circumstances where the separate treatment is undesirable, the IRS will argue that a *de facto* corporation exists and that the separate corporate tax is owed.

When two or more people join resources and/or services to earn a joint profit, the resulting entity is usually a partnership. However, when a partnership organized under the limited partnership laws of a state takes on the characteristics of a corporation, the limited partnership may be taxed as an ***association*** or *de facto* corporation. Corporate characteristics (in addition to the joint profit motive) are centralized management, readily transferable ownership shares, limited liability, and unlimited legal life.[4] Regulations provide that a partnership possessing more than two of these characteristics will be treated as an association and subjected to the corporate tax.[5] However, recent attempts of the IRS to treat limited partnerships as associations have failed, based on the rationale that under state law a limited partnership can never possess more than two corporate characteristics.[6] As a result, the classification of partnerships as *de facto* corporations is unlikely.

ASSOCIATION A partnership or trust that possesses the attributes of a corporation is an association. An association is taxed as a corporation.

Trusts used for investment purposes, often in real estate, are sometimes classified as associations when they possess more corporate than noncorporate characteristics. Trusts formed to *hold* investment properties, as opposed to the active *operation* of a business, can never be associations because such trusts lack the basic characteristic of joint proprietary operations. As with partnerships, care exercised in the organization of an investment trust will avoid the association treatment.

TRUST A legal arrangement in which the title to property passes from a grantor into the control of a trustee who administers the property for the beneficiaries in the manner and for the period specified by the trust agreement. A simple trust is one that is required to distribute its income currently. All other trusts are "complex."

CONTRIBUTIONS OF PROPERTY TO CONTROLLED CORPORATIONS

Section 351 permits shareholders to form a corporation, or to transfer property to an existing corporation, without recognition of gain on appreciated property. Normally, our tax law treats a corporation as a separate entity and most transactions between a corporation and its shareholders as taxable exchanges. Section 351 contains a major exception to the general rule. The rationale for this nontaxable exchange is the same as for those discussed in Chapter 12: The taxpayer has a continuing investment in the same property and no wherewithal to pay a tax.

An exchange is nontaxable under Section 351, or partially nontaxable if boot is involved, if the following conditions are met:

---

[4] *Morrissey* v. *Commissioner*, 296 U.S. 344 (1935).

[5] Reg. Sec. 301.7701-2(a)(3).

[6] *Phillip G. Larsen*, 66 T.C. 159 (1976).

TRANSFER OF PROPERTY The shareholders must transfer property to their corporation.[7] Cash is property for this purpose. Property must be distinguished from services and other inchoate rights that do not have the standing of "property" under state law. If a person performs services for a corporation in exchange for the corporation's stock, the person recognizes gross income measured by the fair market value of the securities.[8]

> **Example 3:** A and B transfer real estate to New Corp. in exchange for 90% of New's common stock. C, an attorney, does all legal work relative to the formation of New and receives 10% of the stock. The exchange of property for securities by A and B may be nontaxable: C has gross income (compensation) equal to the fair market value of the stock.

FOR STOCK OR SECURITIES The transferors of the property must receive stock or securities of the tranferee corporation. If some consideration other than stock or securities is received, any realized gains (but not losses) are recognized to the extent of "boot."[9]

The term "securities" means the long-term, registered obligations of the transferee corporation. While the exact dividing line between long-term and short-term is unclear, notes, debentures, etc., due in ten years or longer are clearly securities, while notes due on demand or within one or two years are not securities.

> **Example 4:** T, an individual, owns property with a basis of $50,000 and a FMV of $125,000. He transfers the property to New Corp., a corporation recently formed by T, in exchange for 100% of New Corp.'s common stock and a demand note issued by New Corp. for $20,000. The amount realized by T is $125,000, the fair market value of the stock and the note (really the FMV of New Corp.'s property received from T). T's realized gain is $75,000 ($125,000 less the basis of $50,000). Since the demand note is not a security, T has received boot, and the gain equal to the $20,000 market value of the note is recognized.

TRANSFERORS CONTROL THE CORPORATION To be nontaxable under Section 351, the transferor, or transferors if more than one, must control the transferee corporation immediately following the exchange. Control for this purpose means the ownership of at least 80% of the combined voting power of all stock outstanding, plus ownership of at least 80% of all other classes.[10]

> **Example 5:** A and B, two individuals, transfer property to New Corp. A receives 100% of New's common stock and B receives 100%

[7] Sec. 351(a).
[8] Sec. 61(a)(1).
[9] Sec. 351(b).
[10] Sec. 368(c).

of New's nonvoting preferred stock. Provided the transfers occur at the same time, the exchanges are nontaxable. A and B together, the transferors, meet the control tests.

The test for control must be made immediately after the exchange.

Example 6: Assume in Example 5, that A transfers his property for New's common stock in June, 19X1 and that B transfers his property for New's preferred stock in June, 19X2. The two transactions were not part of a single plan. A's exchange is nontaxable under Section 351 because A has control following the transfer (A owns all New's stock). B's transfer is taxable, however, because B, considered alone in June 19X2, does not meet the control test.

BASIS RULES FOR SECTION 351 EXCHANGES When an exchange is nontaxable or partially nontaxable because of Section 351, the following rules determine the basis for the various properties:

- The basis of the transferor's stock and securities received in the exchange are the same as the basis of the property exchanged, plus any gain recognized less the fair market value of any boot received.[11]
- The basis of the property received by the transferee corporation is the same as the basis in the hands of the transferor, increased by any gain recognized by the transferor.[12]

Example 7: Refer again to the facts in Example 4 where T transferred property with a basis of $50,000 for common stock and a demand note valued at $20,000. Since the note was boot, gain of $20,000 was recognized. T's basis in the stock is:

Basis of property transferred	$50,000
Plus: Gain recognized	20,000
	70,000
Less: Value of boot received	(20,000)
Basis of stock received	$50,000

T's basis for the demand note is $20,000. New Corp. has a basis of $70,000 in the property, T's $50,000 basis plus the $20,000 gain recognized by T.

TRANSFERS OF DEBT TO CORPORATIONS The transfer of debts associated with property to a corporation does not result in the recognition of gain in the usual case under Section 351. The debt transfer is not treated as cash boot as it is in like-kind exchanges.[13]

---

[11] Sec. 358(a)(1).

[12] Sec. 361(b).

[13] Sec. 357(a).

Example 8: T transfers real estate with a basis of $50,000 and a fair market value of $75,000 to a corporation in a transaction that qualifies for nonrecognition under Section 351. The real estate is subject to a mortgage of $40,000. Transfer of the debt to the corporation is not treated as boot and no gain is recognized.

Transfer of debt can result in boot if the liability transferred exceeds the basis of the property or if the liability was incurred shortly before the transfer for a tax avoidance purpose.[14]

While a transferred liability is not boot for purposes of gain recognition, it must be treated as such for purposes of determining the transferor's basis in the stock and securities received.[15] Otherwise, the transferor's basis would be increased by a debt which he or she never pays.

Example 9: In Example 8, assume that T receives all the common stock of the new corporation in exchange for the mortgaged real estate. His basis in the stock is $10,000, the $50,000 basis in the real estate less the $40,000 debt transferred to the corporation.

EXCHANGES OF STOCK FOR PROPERTY Section 351 provides for the nonrecognition of gain or loss to the transferring shareholders. A corresponding rule makes the exchange nontaxable to the corporation that issues the stock. Section 1032 provides that a corporation recognizes neither gain nor loss when it exchanges its own stock for property.

Example 10: New Corp. issues 1,000 shares of its common stock to T for T's property with a basis of $50,000 and a fair market value of $125,000. New Corp. recognizes no gain or loss. It takes T's $50,000 basis in the property, recording a comparable amount in its capital accounts.

Nonrecognition under Section 1032 extends to treasury stock transactions and to other exchanges of the corporation's stock for property.

THE CORPORATE INCOME TAX

C corporations are full-fledged taxpayers and, except as noted below, the rules relating to gross income, exclusions, deductions, and credits throughout this text apply equally to individuals and C corporations. The tax rates applicable to corporations, on the other hand, are quite different from those applicable to individuals.

CORPORATE TAX RATES AND PAYMENTS Traditionally, C corporations have not been subject to the steeply progressive rates applicable to individuals. In addition, the maximum marginal rate applicable to corpo-

[14] Sec. 357 (b) and (c).

[15] Sec. 358 (d).

rations has been lower than that applicable to individuals. The rate schedule applicable to corporations after 1982 is:[16]

IF TAXABLE INCOME IS:		TAX IS:		
OVER	BUT NOT OVER	AMOUNT PLUS	% OF	EXCESS OVER
-0-	$ 25,000	-0-	15	-0-
$ 25,000	50,000	$ 3,750	18	$ 25,000
50,000	75,000	8,250	30	50,000
75,000	100,000	15,750	40	75,000
100,000		25,750	46	100,000

A comparison of the rates above with those applicable to individuals in Appendix A shows that individual rates increase more rapidly, with a maximum rate of 50% compared to the 46% maximum on the corporate schedule. (For a further comparison, see the Corporate Rate Shelter in the Planning Workshop on pp. 16/35–38.)

Example 11: For 1985, X Corporation has taxable income of $60,000. X's gross tax liability is, using the above schedule:

1st $50,000 of taxable income	$ 8,250
30% of excess over $50,000 (.30 × $10,000)	3,000
Gross tax	$11,250

This result is also obtained by applying the marginal rate in each bracket to the income in each bracket:

1st $25,000 at 15%	$ 3,750
Next $25,000 at 18%	4,500
Next $10,000 at 30%	3,000
	$11,250

In the Tax Reform Act of 1984, Congress decided that the low tax rates applicable to the first $100,000 of taxable income made little or no sense for large, profitable corporations. To correct this inequity, the Code imposes (for years after 1983) an additional 5% tax on all corporate taxable income in excess of $1,000,000 but less than $1,405,000.[17]

Example 12: For 1985, Large Corporation had a taxable income of $1,350,000. Large's 1985 gross tax liability is:

Tax on $100,000 (from schedule above)	$ 25,750
Tax at 46% of $1,250,000	575,000
Tax at 5% of $350,000	17,500
	$618,250

[16] Corporate rates changed often in the years between 1975 and 1982. For example, changes in 1981 and 1982 lowered the rates on the first two $25,000 brackets of taxable income 1% each year.

[17] Sec. 11(b).

The maximum additional tax under this provision is $20,250, or 5% of $405,000. The "extra" tax is equal to the value of the "surtax exemption" resulting from the lower rates on income below $100,000, as calculated below:

$25,000 × (46% − 15%) =	$ 7,750
Plus $25,000 × (46% − 18%) =	7,000
Plus $25,000 × (46% − 30%) =	4,000
Plus $25,000 × (46% − 40%) =	1,500
	$20,250

As a result of this provision a corporation with taxable income of $1,405,000 or more is subject to a "flat" tax of 46%.

Where a corporation is a member of a controlled group of corporations, the corporate brackets and rates below $100,000 and 46% must be shared by all members of the group.[18] This rule is included in the law to limit taxpayers' freedom to reduce rates by dividing a business into numerous corporate entities.

Example 13: A and B Corporations are members of a controlled group. Each has taxable income in excess of $100,000. Only $25,000 of the *combined* income of A and B is subject to the 15% rate, another $25,000 of *combined* income is subject to the 18% rate, etc.

The term controlled group includes parent-subsidiary groups where the parent owns 80% of voting stock plus 80% of the total value of all classes of stock.[19] The term also includes brother-sister groups where five or fewer persons own 80% of the stock in two or more corporations and where the "identical" ownership of all corporations is at least 50%.[20]

Example 14: Individuals X and Y own the common stock (only class outstanding) of Corporations A and B in the following pattern:

INDIVIDUAL	COMMON STOCK OF A	COMMON STOCK OF B	IDENTICAL OWNERSHIP
X	30%	70%	30%
Y	70%	30%	30%
	100%	100%	60%

A and B are members of a brother-sister controlled group. X and Y together own 100% of both corporations. In addition, the identical or common ownership is 60%.

[18] Sec. 1561(a).
[19] Sec. 1563(a)(1).
[20] Sec. 1563(a)(2).

BACKGROUND

For most of the years since World War II, our corporate tax rates contained a two-step progression. A relatively low rate, 22% for many years, applied to the first $25,000 of taxable income, and a much higher rate, 48%, applied to all income above $25,000. This 2-step progression was gradually increased to the current five steps during the late 1970s.

Before 1969, a common tax planning strategy was the subdivision of a business into numerous corporations to get the maximum advantage from the low rate applicable to the first $25,000 of taxable income. The IRS's only defense against this strategy was court action based on the claim that the multiple corporations were a sham and that only one business existed. This defense was inadequate. Taxpayers were able to devise apparently sound business reasons for the extra corporations. For example, where the business consisted of a chain of retail stores, it was not unreasonable to insist that each unit had different risks and deserved separate incorporation.

Congress came to the rescue of the IRS with a statutory solution beginning in 1969. That solution gradually evolved into the rules for controlled groups at Sections 1561 through 1564. Because of the 1984 change to the corporate rates, multiple corporations will serve no purpose where each corporation's income is at least $1,405,000. For 1984 and later years, these corporations are subject to a flat tax rate of 46%.

The gross tax is reduced by the tax credits and by prepayments of the estimated tax to determine the amount due with the return. Corporations, like individuals, must pay their taxes in advance quarterly to avoid the penalty for underpayment. The return is made on Form 1120 and is due on the 15th day of the third month following the end of the taxable year,[21] or March 15 for calendar year corporations.

FORM 1120

ALTERNATIVE TAX FOR NET CAPITAL GAINS Individuals who have net capital gains (an excess of net long-term capital gains over net short-term capital losses) for their taxable years are entitled to a deduction equal to 60% of the net capital gains (see Chapter 10). Corporations are not entitled to the net capital gain deduction and 100% of such gains are included in taxable income. However, a corporation's tax on net capital gains cannot exceed 28%.[22] When a corporation has a net capital gain, its tax liability is the lesser of: (*a*) the regular tax (based on the rates above) on the total taxable income; or (*b*) the alternative tax. The ***alternative tax*** is the sum of (*a*) the regular tax on taxable income less net capital gains plus (*b*) 28% of net capital gain.

ALTERNATIVE TAX The maximum rate applicable to the net capital gains of corporations is 28%. The alternative tax that applies when it is less than the regular tax is the sum of the regular tax on ordinary taxable income plus 28% of the net capital gain.

[21] Sec. 6072 (B).

[22] Sec. 1201(a).

Example 15: X Corporation has taxable income for the current year of $135,000, including a $25,000 net capital gain. The regular tax (using rates above) is:

Tax on $100,000	$25,750
Excess of $35,000 at 46%	16,100
Regular tax	$41,850

The alternative tax is as follows:

Regular tax on $110,000 (taxable income less $25,000 net capital gain):	
Tax on $100,000	$25,750
Excess of $10,000 at 46%	4,600
Regular tax	$30,350
Plus 28% of $25,000	7,000
Alternative tax	$37,350

Corporation X will pay the alternative tax of $37,350 because it is less than the regular tax.

Note in Example 15 that $25,000 net capital gain is taxed at a marginal rate of 46% in the regular tax computation—the last $25,000 of taxable income falls in the bracket above $100,000 that is taxed at 46%. In this case, the alternative tax, which limits the rate on net capital gains to 28%, will clearly produce a lower tax. If the marginal rate applicable to the net capital gain in the regular computation is less than 28%, the alternative tax produces no benefits.

Example 16: Y Corporation has taxable income of $45,000 including a $10,000 net capital gain. Y's regular tax is:

Tax on $25,000	$3,750
Excess $20,000 at 18%	3,600
	$7,350

The alternative tax is:

Tax on taxable income less net capital gain:

Tax on $25,000	$3,750
Excess $10,000 at 18%	1,800
	$5,550
Plus 28% of net capital gain	2,800
Alternative tax	$8,350

Here, the alternative tax is higher because the highest marginal rate used in the regular computation is only 18%.

Where the corporation's regular taxable income exceeds $50,000, the rate applicable to the net capital gain will exceed 28%, and the alternative tax will be lower.

COMPUTATION OF CORPORATE TAXABLE INCOME A C corporation is a taxpayer and, as such, must make all elections related to taxable years and accounting methods, as discussed in Chapter 6. Where inventory is a material income-producing factor, the corporation must use the accrual method for purchases, sales, and inventories.

> **Example 17:** T has operated a TV repair shop as a sole proprietorship for several years. For this business, T used the cash method and filed his personal return on the calendar-year basis. On January 2 of the current year, T incorporates the business. The corporation is a new taxpayer and it can elect any tax year and can use any approved accounting method.

As noted earlier, tax rules related to gross income, exclusions, deductions, and credits generally apply to corporations as well as to individuals. There are, however, many important exceptions to this generalization. One has already been noted: corporations are not allowed a deduction for net capital gains (but are entitled to the alternative tax). Other important exceptions are explained in the following sections.

NO PERSONAL OR ITEMIZED DEDUCTIONS. Some deductions allowed individuals are included in the law solely for natural persons and clearly have no application to the corporate setting. Deductions in this category are medical expenses, alimony, and moving expenses. The concept of personal or itemized deductions (and the zero-bracket amount) has no application to corporations, and the division of deductions into the categories *for* and *from* adjusted gross income (AGI) is unnecessary for corporations. Section 212, which allows deductions for the production of income or for the maintenance of income-producing property, applies only to individuals.

These restrictions on deductions do not mean that corporations are at a disadvantage in this regard. The deductions allowed for trades or businesses in Section 162 normally cover all corporate expenses.

> **Example 18:** X Corporation pays the medical expenses of its employees. The amounts paid cannot be deducted as medical expenses under Section 213. However, the amounts paid or incurred are ordinary and necessary expenses in the conduct of the corporate business and are deductible under Section 162.

Just as some deductions apply only to individuals by their nature, some exclusions have the same limited scope. The exclusion for *personal* damages and the exclusions for fringe benefits of employees are examples.

NO DEDUCTIONS FOR NET CAPITAL LOSSES. As previously noted, corporations get no deduction for net capital gains. In addition, corporations are not allowed a deduction for net capital losses. Individuals can deduct net capital losses but are generally limited to $3,000.

Example 19: In 19X3, X Corporation has net long-term capital losses of $15,000 and net short-term capital gains of $7,000. The net capital loss is $8,000. X Corporation cannot deduct the $8,000 in 19X3. If X were an individual, a deduction of $3,000 would be allowed.

The net capital loss of a corporation, while not deductible, can be carried back for three years and carried forward for five years. (Individuals get no capital loss carrybacks and an unlimited carryforward.) Capital losses of corporations are always treated as short-term losses in the years to which they are carried. This means that carrybacks and carryforwards reduce short-term capital gains first and these gains are taxed at regular rates, not the 28% alternative rate.

Example 20: To continue Example 19, X Corporation first carries the 19X3 $8,000 loss to the third preceding year, 19X0. Note that the $8,000 loss is long-term. Despite this fact, the carryback is treated as a short-term loss. Assume that X Corporation had a short-term gain of $20,000 in 19X0 and that its total taxable income before such gain exceeded $100,000. The short-term gain was thus taxed at a 46% marginal rate and the $8,000 carryback will produce a refund of $3,680 ($8,000 × 46%).

Example 21: Assume instead in Example 21 that X Corporation has a $20,000 long-term gain in 19X0 and no short-term gain. Since the regular taxable income exceeds $50,000 the $20,000 net capital gain is taxed at 28%. The carryback produces a refund of $2,240 ($8,000 × 28%).

Except for the differences noted here, all other major rules relating to property dispositions (Chapters 10 and 11) are the same for individuals and corporations. This includes the rules in Section 1231 and the related recapture provisions.

CHARITABLE CONTRIBUTIONS. Corporations, like individuals, are allowed a deduction for charitable contributions. The rules explained in Chapter 9 relating to qualified organizations and to the amount of the contribution when noncash property is contributed apply to corporations also, except that certain corporate contributions of ordinary income property receive more favorable treatment.[23] Corporate contributions, however, are limited to 10% of the corporation's *taxable* income, computed before the contribution deduction, the dividends-received deduction discussed below, and any capital or net operating loss carrybacks.[24] Contributions in excess of the limit are carried forward for a period of five years.[25]

---

[23] Sec. 170(e)(3) and (4).

[24] Sec. 170(b)(2).

[25] Sec. 170(d)(2).

Example 22: During 19X1, X Corporation had gross income of $100,000 and Section 162 deductions of $80,000. X Corporation received no dividends and had no carrybacks to 19X1. The Corporation made a $5,000 contribution in 19X1. Only $2,000 of the contribution is allowed in 19X1 (10% of $100,000 less $80,000). The remaining $3,000 is carried forward for five years.

While contributions are generally deductible only in the year paid, an accrual-basis corporation can accrue contributions provided they are approved by the board of directors before the year's end and are actually paid before the due date of the return.[26]

SPECIAL DEDUCTIONS ALLOWED CORPORATIONS The statute contains several deductions for corporations only. With two exceptions, these deductions have limited application, relating mainly to foreign operations. The exceptions are the deductions for dividends received and amortization of organizational expenditures.

DIVIDENDS-RECEIVED DEDUCTION. Corporations are allowed a deduction equal to 85% of taxable dividends received from domestic corporations subject to the U.S. income tax.[27] When a corporation is a member of a controlled group, the deduction is 100% of taxable dividends received from other members of the group. The dividends-received deduction is included in the law in response to the concern over "double taxation" of corporate earnings.

BACKGROUND

While our tax law treats corporations as separate entities, many people remain unhappy with how dividend payments are taxed under the general concept. These people claim that the taxation of dividends results in a "double" taxation of corporate income.

As a separate entity, a C corporation pays the income tax on its taxable income. Subsequently, when a corporation makes a distribution out of past earnings, the dividend is income to its shareholders and is taxed again. The dividend distribution is not a deduction to the distributing corporation. The limited exclusion for dividends available to individuals (see Chapter 5) is included in the law as a response to the argument of "double" taxation. The 85% dividends-received deduction allowed corporations thus avoids a "triple" tax on corporate income that passes through more than one corporate intermediary before reaching an individual shareholder.

Proposals made to eliminate the perceived inequity of double taxation either allow the paying corporation a deduction for dividends paid or permit the shareholder to claim a credit for taxes previously paid at the corporate level.

---

[26] Sec. 170(a)(2).

[27] Sec. 243(a).

The dividends-received deduction is 85% of the dividends (except for members of a controlled group where the deduction is 100%), but is limited to 85% of the corporate taxable income computed without regard for the dividends-received deduction and net operating loss deductions. However, this limit does not apply when the corporation has a net operating loss in the current year, even when the net operating loss is created by the dividends-received deduction.

Example 23: For 19X1, X Corporation's operations resulted in the following:

Gross income from operations	$150,000
Dividends received	20,000
Operating deductions	110,000

Based on these facts, the dividends-received deduction is $17,000, 85% of $20,000. The limit is $51,000, 85% of taxable income of $60,000 before the dividends-received deduction, and it does not apply in this case.

ORGANIZATIONAL EXPENSES Costs incurred by a corporation to obtain its charter, for accounting fees related to organization, and for fees paid to the state. Organizational expenses are subject to special amortization by the corporation.

AMORTIZATION OF ORGANIZATIONAL EXPENSES. The ***organizational expenses*** of a corporation are capital expenditures and without the special deduction explained here they would be deductible only when the corporation liquidates or ceases to do business. The statute, however, permits the amortization and deduction of these costs over a period of not less than 60 months at the election of the corporation.[28] The amortization period begins the month when the corporation begins business.

Example 24: X Corporation began business in May 19X1. It incurred organizational expenses of $5,000. The deduction allowed for 19X1 is $667 ($5,000 ÷ 60 months × 8 months).

The term organizational expenses includes legal services incidental to acquiring the corporate charter and other organizational functions: accounting services connected with organization, fees paid to the state related to incorporation, and expenses of temporary directors and organizational meetings.[29] The term does not include the costs connected with issuing or selling the corporation's stock.

ADD-ON MINIMUM TAX In addition to the regular (or alternative) tax explained above, corporations are subject to a minimum tax based on their tax preferences. This minimum tax is an add-on tax, unlike the *alternative* minimum tax paid by individuals explained in Chapter 13.

The ***add-on minimum tax*** is computed in the following manner:[30]

ADD-ON MINIMUM TAX A tax, levied at the rate of 15%, on a corporation's total tax preferences, less an exemption. This tax is levied as an addition to the regular tax as penalty on the use of preferences.

[28] Sec. 248(a).

[29] Reg. Sec. 1.248-1(b)(2).

[30] Sec. 56(a).

Total tax preferences	xx
Less exemption: greater of	
(a) $10,000 or (b) the regular tax liability	− x
Base for tax	xx
Rate	× 15%
Add-on preference tax	$ x

For purposes of the exemption above, the regular tax liability is the gross tax less the tax credits, except for the credit related to employee stock ownership in Section 41, and the refundable credits allowed, usually the credit for off-highway uses of gasoline in Section 34.[31]

Example 25: X Corporation has total tax preferences of $50,000 for 19X1. Its regular tax liability for 19X1 is $12,000. The add-on minimum tax is computed as follows:

Total preferences	$50,000
Less: Regular tax liability (which is more than $10,000)	(12,000)
Base	$38,000
Rate	× .15
Add-on minimum tax	$ 5,700

A detailed discussion of the various tax preferences is beyond the scope of this introductory text because most preference items arise from complicated tax provisions. The following preferences are the ones that affect most corporations:[32]

- Excess of accelerated depreciation over straight-line depreciation for Section 1250 properties (real estate). For real estate subject to ACRS, straight-line depreciation is based on a 15-year life.
- Net capital gains—The preference is equal to 39.13% of the net capital gain. This percentage is the rate reduction that results from the use of the 28% alternative rate compared to the 46% maximum rate (46 − 28 = 18, or 39.13% of 46%).
- Excess of statutory depletion allowed for natural resources over the adjusted basis of the property.

A measure passed in 1982 reduces some tax preferences to 71.6% of their usual amounts effective for 1983 and later years. Net capital gains from the disposition of Section 1250 property, for example, are affected by this provision.[33]

FORM 4626

[31] Sec. 56(c).

[32] Sec. 57(a).

[33] Sec. 57(b) and Sec. 291.

DIVIDEND DISTRIBUTIONS

DIVIDEND A transfer of cash or other property from a corporation to its shareholders out of the earnings and profits of the corporation. A dividend is ordinary income to the shareholder.

Corporate distributions of property with respect to its own stock, but not in exchange for its stock, are commonly called ***dividend*** distributions. (Distributions of a corporation in exchange for its stock are explained in the following section.) More precisely, the law provides the following treatment for such distributions:[34]

- First, the distribution is ordinary income (a dividend) to the shareholder to the extent of the corporation's earnings and profits (E&P).
- Second, amounts distributed in excess of the corporation's E&P are a return of the shareholder's basis in his or her stock.
- Third, amounts distributed in excess of basis are treated as received in exchange for the corporate stock and are therefore capital gains.

Example 26: T, an individual, owns 100 shares of the common stock of X Corporation with a basis of $1,200. In the current year, X distributes $3,000 cash to T, not in exchange for T's stock. Of this amount, $1,000 is out of X's E&P. The distribution is taxed to T as follows: ordinary dividend, $1,000; return of basis $1,200; capital gain, $800.

Most distributions from corporations are dividends to the shareholders because earnings and profits usually exceed the distributions.

EARNINGS AND PROFITS (E&P) An account maintained for C corporations primarily. The balance of the account is the sum of past taxable income less net operating losses, federal income taxes, dividend distributions and other adjustments. Earnings and profits determine the extent to which corporate distributions are treated as dividends to shareholders.

MEANING OF EARNINGS AND PROFITS A C corporation that realizes income pays an income tax on its taxable income. Since a C corporation is treated as a separate entity, the tax law treats the corporation's realized income as income to its shareholders only when such income is distributed to them. A corporation's ***earnings and profits*** account is a record of its *realized* income and serves as a basis for the measurement of dividend income to shareholders. Corporate distributions in excess of earnings and profits are returns of the shareholder's capital and are not dividends.

The E&P account of a corporation is roughly equivalent to the retained earnings account used for financial accounting. The E&P account is increased by taxable income and by realized nontaxable income, and is decreased by income taxes paid as well as by nondeductible expenses and the amount of distributions.

Example 27: X Corporation began operations in January, 19X1. For its taxable year ended December 31, 19X1, X had taxable income of $20,000 and $2,000 of tax-exempt interest. It paid income taxes of $3,000 on its 19X1 income. X's E&P account has a balance of $19,000 ($20,000 + $2,000 − $3,000) as a result of 19X1 operations.

[34] Sec. 301(c).

Section 312 provides for numerous other adjustments to taxable income in the determination of E&P. For example, E&P must be increased by the excess of accelerated depreciation over straight-line depreciation.[35]

The law provides that distributions are made out of the earnings and profits of the current year first and that a distribution is a dividend if covered by the current E&P, even if the accumulated E&P for past years shows a deficit.[36]

Example 28: X Corporation was organized in January, 19X1. Its operations for 19X1 and 19X2 resulted in net losses. As a consequence its accumulated E&P showed a deficit of $30,000 on January 1, 19X3. X's 19X3 operations were profitable and its current E&P for 19X3 was $20,000. During 19X3 X distributed $15,000 cash to its shareholders. The distribution is a dividend in its entirety because it is covered by current E&P, despite a deficit from operations for the 3-year period.

NONCASH PROPERTY DISTRIBUTIONS When a corporation distributes cash to its shareholders, the *amount* of the distribution is obvious. The dividend is the amount of cash distributed and no questions concerning basis or gain or loss arise. When noncash property is distributed, its fair market value will usually be more (or less) than its basis to the distributing corporation and this difference creates some problems.

DISTRIBUTING CORPORATION. A corporation that distributes appreciated property to its shareholders must generally recognize gain to the extent the fair market value exceeds the property's basis.[37] (Losses are not recognized but usually, depreciated property will not be used for dividend purposes.) The distributing corporation reduces its E&P account by the basis of the property, but note that the basis is the same as fair market value after the corporation has recognized the gain.

Example 29: X Corporation distributes as a dividend property with a basis of $8,000 and a fair market value of $15,000. X's E&P is reduced by $15,000 as a result of this distribution, the $15,000 being the basis of the property after recognition of the $7,000 gain.

This rule that corporations recognize gain on distributed properties does not apply to liquidating distributions (complete or partial) or to distributions of "qualified" dividends on "qualified" stock. A qualified dividend is a distribution of property used actively in a business; qualified stock is generally stock held for at least ten years.[38]

---

[35] Sec. 312(k).

[36] Sec. 316(a).

[37] Sec. 311 (d).

[38] Sec. 311 (e)(1) and (3).

INDIVIDUAL SHAREHOLDERS. An individual shareholder of a corporation who receives a noncash property distribution out of earnings and profits recognizes a dividend equal to the fair market value of the property.[39] The shareholder's basis is also fair market value.

> **Example 30:** T, a shareholder of X corporation, receives as a dividend from X a parcel of land with a fair market value of $10,000 and a basis to X Corporation of $7,000. The distribution is out of X's earnings and profits. T's dividend income is $10,000 and T's basis in the property is $10,000.

CORPORATE SHAREHOLDERS. A corporate shareholder that receives a non-cash dividend recognizes dividend income equal to the lesser of (1) the fair market value of the property, or (2) the distributing corporation's basis.[40] Note, however, that the distributing corporation's basis will be equal to the fair market value of the property because the distributing corporation must recognize the appreciation as gain.

> **Example 31:** T Corporation owns some stock in X Corporation. X distributes out of its E&P to T property with a basis of $10,000 and a fair market value of $15,000. The property is not "qualified" property. X must recognize a $5,000 gain; the recognition of this gain increases X's basis in the property by $5,000, to $15,000. T Corporation recognizes a dividend of $15,000. (T's basis in the dividend property is also $15,000).

DISTRIBUTIONS OF STOCK AND STOCK RIGHTS Corporations commonly distribute to their shareholders the corporation's own stock or rights to acquire its stock. Such distributions are either nontaxable events or are treated as taxable property distributions, depending on the type of shares distributed.

NONTAXABLE STOCK DIVIDENDS. A pro rata distribution of common stock (or the rights to acquire common stock) to the holders of common stock is a nontaxable dividend. A pro rata distribution of preferred stock (or rights to acquire preferred stock) to common stockholders is also nontaxable. The recipient of the ***stock dividend*** allocates his or her basis in the old shares to total shares now held.[41]

STOCK DIVIDEND A distribution of a corporation's own stock to its shareholders, not in exchange for stock, is a stock dividend.

> **Example 32:** T owns 100 shares of the common stock of X Corporation. Her basis in the shares is $2,800. She receives an additional ten shares of X common as a nontaxable stock dividend. T has no dividend income and each share of X Corporation now has a basis of $25.45 ($2,800 ÷ 110 shares).

---

[39] Sec. 301 (b)(1)(A).

[40] Sec. 301 (b)(1)(B).

[41] Sec. 307(a).

When nontaxable ***stock rights*** are received, the basis of the old shares is allocated between the old shares and the rights based on relative fair market value. However, the basis allocation is elective unless the value of the rights is 15% or more of the value of the underlying shares.

STOCK RIGHTS A stock right is a contract that entitles the holder to acquire the stock of a corporation.

Example 33: T owns 100 shares of X Corporation common stock with a basis of $3,000. T receives 100 rights to acquire additional shares of common stock. When the rights are received, their value is $500 and the value of the underlying shares is $5,000. Since the fair market value of the rights is less than 15% of the stock's value, no allocation of basis is required. If T wishes, he can allocate his basis as follows:

$$\text{Basis of Rights} = \frac{\text{FMV of Rights } \$500}{\text{Total FMV } \$5{,}500} \times \text{Stock basis of } \$3{,}000 = \$273$$

Each right would have a basis of $2.73 ($273 ÷ 100 rights). The remaining basis of $2,727 ($3,000 − $273) is the basis of the 100 shares of stock.

If nontaxable stock rights are sold, the taxpayer's gain is reduced by the basis allocated to the rights sold. If nontaxable rights are exercised, the allocated basis of the rights is added to the cost of the new shares acquired to obtain the basis of the new shares. If the nontaxable rights lapse, any allocated basis is added back to the basis of the shares originally held by the taxpayer.

TAXABLE STOCK DIVIDENDS. Except for pro rata distributions of common on common or preferred on common, distributions of stock dividends and rights are treated as taxable property distributions.

Example 34: T owns 100 shares of Class A Common of X Corporation. He receives ten additional shares of Class A common with a fair market value of $1,500 as a stock dividend. At the same time, the holders of X Corporation's Class B common receive a distribution of X Corporation's preferred stock. Since the common stock dividend is not pro rata to all common shareholders it is a taxable distribution. T has dividend income of $1,500; his basis in the shares is also $1,500.

Generally, taxable stock dividends are those that, singly or over a period of time, substantially change the beneficial interest in corporate profits and capital. Also a taxable stock dividend results in every case where the shareholder has the right to take cash in lieu of stock.[42]

[42] Sec. 305 (b)(1).

DISTRIBUTIONS IN EXCHANGE FOR STOCK

For purposes of tax law, corporate distributions in exchange for a corporation's own stock are classified as either redemptions or liquidations. The distinction between the two types is very important, as explained below. Also, the law at this point is complex. The general rules explained here are subject to numerous qualifications and exceptions.

REDEMPTION A distribution of its assets by a corporation in exchange for its stock, but not in liquidation, is a redemption of stock.

REDEMPTIONS The question here is: can the recognition of dividend income be avoided upon the distribution of property from a corporation if the transaction is structured as a ***redemption*** wherein the shareholder exchanges his or her stock for property? If so, the recognition of ordinary, dividend income can be avoided and the transaction treated as the sale of a capital asset resulting in a capital gain to the shareholder.

As a general rule, redemptions of stock are treated as dividend distributions and not as a sale or exchange of the corporate stock.

> **Example 35:** S and T, two unrelated individuals, each own 1,000 shares of X Corporation's common, the only stock outstanding. Their basis is $50 per share. X is a profitable operation and has earnings and profits of $200,000. S and T enter into a sales agreement with X wherein each agrees to sell X 100 shares of stock for $50,000 cash. This transaction is a redemption but is treated as a dividend, not as an exchange of stock qualifying for capital-gains treatment. The $100,000 distributed is covered by the earnings and profits and each shareholder has dividend income of $50,000. The surrender of stock is ignored and the basis of the shares surrendered is assigned to the remaining shares.

A stock redemption that is disproportionate (as defined by the statute), a redemption that completely eliminates the interest of one shareholder, and certain other redemptions are treated as a sale or exchange.[43]

> **Example 36:** Assume the same facts as in Example 35. Instead of a pro rata redemption, S agrees to sell all of her shares to X for $300,000 cash. S will sever all relations with X Corporation following the sale. Since this redemption eliminates S's interest, it is treated as an exchange. S has a $250,000 capital gain ($300,000 realized less $50,000 basis).

A corporation that uses appreciated property to redeem its stock must generally recognize the gain resulting from the distribution.[44] But here, as elsewhere, important exceptions exist.

LIQUIDATION The transfer of a corporation's assets in exchange for its stock, to wind up the corporate business, is a liquidation. Similar transfers by partnerships to partners are also called liquidations.

LIQUIDATIONS Amounts received by shareholders in complete ***liquidation*** of a corporation are treated as amounts realized upon sales of

[43] Sec. 302 (b).
[44] Sec. 311 (d).

stock, and *not* as dividends.[45] A distribution that is one in a series leading to complete liquidation is treated as a distribution in liquidation.[46]

Example 37: Refer to Example 35. Assume that S and T decide to liquidate X Corporation. As a result, X distributes all its assets to S and T in exchange for their stock. S receives assets valued at $300,000. She has a capital gain of $250,000 ($300,000 realized less $50,000 basis), not a dividend. S's basis in the properties received is $300,000.

Generally, a corporation does not recognize gain or loss when it distributes property in liquidation, except for LIFO inventory, installment obligations, and property subject to depreciation recapture.[47]

PARTNERSHIPS

While a C Corporation is a separate entity for tax purposes, a partnership is treated as nothing more than an aggregation of the proprietary interests of the partners. A partnership does not pay an income tax on its transactions. Instead, conceptually, each transaction of a partnership is divided among the partners and affects their individual tax returns. With some notable exceptions discussed below, transactions between a partnership and its partners are not taxable events and do not create gain or loss to the partners or partnership.

A thin line divides the existence of a partnership from the mere joint ownership of property. A partnership exists only when two or more people join together as proprietors with a joint profit motive.

Example 38: S and T own an undivided one-half interest in real estate as tenants in common. They rent the property to a single tenant but each collects his share of the rent and pays his half of the expenses connected with the property. This arrangement is not a partnership; it lacks the necessary joint proprietary profit motive.

Example 39: Assume that S and T jointly provide various services (janitorial, food, etc.) to the tenant. S and T share profits from these activities. Now, a partnership exists and rules discussed in this part apply.

The existence or absence of a partnership can have a substantial tax effect on the participants. As explained below, for some purposes, e.g., accounting elections and sale of a partnership interest, the tax law treats partnerships as separate entities.

---

[45] Sec. 331 (a).

[46] Sec. 346 (a).

[47] Sec. 336 (a) and (b).

CONTRIBUTIONS TO PARTNERSHIPS

No gain or loss is recognized to the contributing partner nor to the partnership upon the contribution of property to a partnership. The basis of the property to the contributing partner becomes the basis to the partnership and the contributing partner's basis in the partnership is increased by the same amount.[48]

Example 40: S and T, two individuals, form Partnership ST for the purpose of developing and selling home building sites. T contributes $100,000 cash; S contributes land with a basis of $25,000 and a fair market value of $100,000. Each partner receives a 50% interest in partnership profits and capital. S recognizes no gain upon the transfer of his appreciated land. T could not, of course, have gain upon the transfer of cash. Partnership ST has a basis of only $25,000 in the land contributed by S.

The rule is that no gain or loss is recognized upon the contribution of property to a partnership even if the contributing partner or partners do not "control" the partnership.

Example 41: Two years following the formation of Partnership ST in Example 40, U contributes land valued at $75,000 with a basis of $30,000 to ST for a 20% interest in profits and capital. U has no gain and STU's basis in U's land is $30,000.

Nonrecognition of gain or loss encompasses only contributions of property. A person who performs services for a partnership in exchange for an interest in partnership capital must usually recognize ordinary income in the amount of the fair market value of the capital interest received.[49]

Section 707(c) provides that a partner may deal with his or her partnership in a capacity other than as a partner. An alternative to a contribution to capital is thus a taxable sale or exchange. A taxable transfer might be preferable, for example, where an appreciated asset is a capital asset to the partner but will be an ordinary asset to the partnership.

Example 42: Refer to Example 40. Assume that S's land is a capital asset in S's hand. The land will be inventory to the partnership. If S contributes cash of $100,000 for his 50% interest and then sells the land to the partnership, S will recognize a $75,000 capital gain. However, the partnership's basis is now $100,000, the cost of the land, not $25,000, S's old basis. The partnership's ordinary income from resale of the land as inventory is $75,000 less under this alternative and capital gains are not converted to ordinary income.

---

[48] Sec. 721, 722 and 723.

[49] Reg. Sec. 1.721 (b)(1) and Sec. 83(a).

OPERATING THE PARTNERSHIP

While a partnership is merely an aggregation of the partners' proprietary interest for most purposes, a partnership is a separate entity for most elections.

ELECTIONS When a new partnership comes into existence, most elections related to the computation and reporting of partnership items are made at the partnership level, and not by individual partners.[50] This includes the election for the general method of accounting, as well as elections related to specific transactions, e.g., replacement of involuntarily converted property, installment recognition, and inventory methods.

Example 43: S and T form Partnership ST. S is on the cash basis, T on the accrual basis. Partnership ST is a new entity for purposes of most elections and it can elect any general accounting method.

Example 44: ST, a partnership, sells property under a threat of condemnation and realizes a gain. The election to acquire qualified replacement property and thereby defer the gain must be made by the Partnership ST, not by the partners, S and T.

A partnership must also elect a taxable year as though the partnership were a taxpayer. The taxable year adopted must generally be the same as the taxable year used by all principal partners,[51] meaning a partner with a 5% or more interest in capital or profits. This rule usually requires the use of the calendar year by most partnerships because most individuals use that year. When the principal partners have different taxable years, the partnership must elect the calendar year unless the Commissioner gives permission for the use of a proposed fiscal year.[52]

ALLOCATION OF PARTNERSHIP ITEMS Conceptually, all partnership items of income, gains, losses, deductions, credits, etc., flow through the partnership and are reported directly by the partners. As a mechanical process, the partnership information return, Form 1065, requires the computation of the partnership's "ordinary" taxable income or loss, which consists of items of income, gains, losses and deductions that receive no special treatment in the tax law. All partnership items that receive special treatment under the law are allocated separately to the partners.[53] This would include such items as contributions (because of the limits), short-term and long-term capital gains and/or losses, Section 1231 gains and losses, and dividends and interest subject to the exclusion.

Example 45: Partnership ST had the following items in the current year:

---

[50] Sec. 703 (b) contains five exceptions.

[51] Sec. 706 (b).

[52] Reg. Sec. 1.706-1 (b)(1)(ii).

[53] Sec. 702 (a).

Gross income from sales	$100,000
Trade or business expenses	60,000
Depreciation	15,000
Gain on sale of land used in business	6,000
Short-term capital loss	(1,600)

S has a 50% interest in the profits and losses of ST. For the year, S reports $12,500 ordinary taxable income (50% of $100,000 minus $60,000 plus $15,000), $3,000 Section 1231 gain, and $800 short-term capital loss.

FORM 1065—SCHEDULE K-1

A partnership must provide each partner with a Schedule K-1 to Form 1065 which shows the partner's share of the partnership items.

As a general rule, partnership items of income, gain, loss, deductions, and credits are allocated to the partners based upon the partnership agreement.[54] When a partnership agreement does not specify how items are allocated to the partners, the allocation is made based upon each partner's interest in the partnership, taking into account all relevant factors.[55] The law gives partners maximum flexibility in allocating partnership items so long as the allocations have "substantial economic effect."

Example 46: S and T, two individuals, join together in Partnership ST. They agree to share all income and profits equally but that any losses from the operation will be allocated entirely to S, because S is in a higher tax bracket. This allocation, agreed on by the partners, is permissible if it has substantial economic effect.

An allocation has substantial economic effect generally if it may affect the amounts eventually received upon liquidation of the partnership.

BASIS OF PARTNERSHIP INTERESTS

When a person contributes property to a partnership for an interest, a new tax property comes into existence, the partnership interest. A partnership is generally treated as a separate entity for purposes of accounting for the partnership interests of the partners. The basis of a partnership interest becomes important for purposes of measuring gain or loss upon sale of the interest or upon liquidation of the partnership. Also, partnership losses are deductible by a partner only to the extent of his or her basis in the partnership interest.[56]

Example 47: S, an individual, is a partner in ST. S's basis in the ST interest is $25,000. If S sells his interest, the $25,000 basis is used to compute gain or loss on the disposition. Also, this basis operates as a limit on the losses of ST deductible by S on his individual return.

---

[54] Sec. 704 (a).
[55] Sec. 704 (b)(1).
[56] Sec. 704 (d).

A partner's basis in his or her interest is the same as the basis of property contributed to the partnership, increased by his or her share of partnership items of income and gains, and decreased by his or her share of partnership deductions and losses (and the basis of property distributed).[57]

Example 48: S contributes land with a basis of $25,000 and fair market value of $100,000 to the ST partnership. Subsequently, ST operations result in a loss of $8,000, of which $4,000 is S's share. Following the loss, S's basis in his interest is $21,000, the $25,000 basis of the contributed property less the $4,000 loss allocated to him.

The basis of a partnership interest also includes the partner's share of any partnership liabilities.[58] Partnership liabilities "flow through" the partnership and are treated as liabilities of the partners for purposes of the basis computation.[59] For this reason, partnerships are widely used in the real estate business when substantial tax losses are expected from highly leveraged ventures.

Example 49: S and T plan to join together to build and operate an office building. Each will contribute $50,000 cash but $2 million will be borrowed from a savings institution. For the first five years of operations, they expect the project to produce tax losses of $400,000, which will be shared equally by S and T. A partnership is the desirable entity, in this instance, as opposed to a C or an S corporation. Each partner has a basis of $1,050,000 in his interest, $50,000 contributed plus one-half of the $2 million liability, more than enough to absorb the expected losses.

SALE OF A PARTNERSHIP INTEREST

A partnership interest is generally treated as a capital asset, and gain or loss upon the sale or other disposition of such an interest is a capital gain or loss.[60] Note that for this purpose the partnership interest is treated like the capital stock of a corporation, not as an aggregation of the partner's proprietary interest in each partnership asset.

Example 50: S is a partner in ST and has a $25,000 basis in his interest. He sells his interest to R for $40,000. S realizes and recognizes a gain of $15,000. The gain is capital in nature.

A major exception to the above rule applies when the partnership has unrealized receivables or substantially appreciated inventory.[61]

---

[57] Sec. 722 and 705.

[58] Sec. 722.

[59] Treatment of nonrecourse liabilities and liabilities of limited partnerships are more complicated and beyond our scope.

[60] Sec. 741.

[61] Sec. 751(a).

Example 51: S, a lawyer, is a partner in RST law firm. The firm uses the cash method and therefore recognizes income only upon the collection of fees. A major asset of the firm is its "unrealized" fees. If S sells his interest in RST, he cannot escape the ordinary income from his share of uncollected fees. A part of his gain will be ordinary income.

The rationale in Example 51 also applies to appreciated inventory held by the partnership as well as to the ordinary income potential from depreciation recapture.

DISTRIBUTION TO PARTNERS

With two major exceptions noted below, distributions of partnership properties to partners are not taxable events. Neither the distributing partnership nor the partner receiving the distribution recognizes gain or loss.[62] This general rule applies to both current distributions and to distributions that liquidate a partner's interest. When noncash property is distributed, the partnership's basis usually becomes the basis to the partner receiving the distribution.

Example 52: S owns a 50% interest in partnership ST. S's basis in his interest is $30,000. In the current year, ST distributes $12,000 cash to S as "drawings" for S's living expenses. S has no income; his basis in his interest is reduced to $18,000.

Example 53: Assume the same facts as in Example 52 except that, instead of cash, ST distributes other property with a fair market value of $12,000 and a basis of $8,000. No gain or loss is recognized by ST or by S upon the distribution. S's basis in the property is $8,000, the same as ST's, and his basis in his interest is $22,000 ($30,000 less $8,000).

When a distribution of noncash property liquidates a partner's entire interest, the basis of his or her interest in the partnership becomes the basis of the property received.[63]

Example 54: R is a partner in RST and has a $20,000 basis in his interest. In liquidation of his interest, R receives cash of $5,000 and property with a fair market value of $30,000 and a basis to the partnership of $18,000. R recognizes no gain. His basis in the partnership interest is first assigned to the cash of $5,000, leaving $15,000. The basis of the property to R is not $18,000, the partnership's basis, but $15,000, R's remaining basis in his interest.

Two major exceptions apply to the general rule that partnership distributions result in no gain or loss. First, a partner who receives a distri-

---

[62] Sec. 731.

[63] Sec. 732 (b).

bution of cash in excess of his or her basis in the partnership interest must recognize gain in the amount of such excess.[64] Gain, in this instance, is treated as gain from sale of the interest. A loss may result when cash is received in complete liquidation of an interest and the basis in the interest exceeds the cash received.

A second exception applies to distributions of property that result in a change of interest among the partners in unrealized receivables and/or substantially appreciated inventory.[65] These rules prohibit the shifting of ordinary income between the partners.

S CORPORATIONS

The shareholders of an "eligible" corporation can elect the tax treatment of Subchapter S of the Internal Revenue Code. The resulting S corporation is treated like a partnership for many important purposes under the tax law. An S corporation is not a taxpayer, with some minor exceptions noted later, and the S corporation's income, gains, losses, deductions, and credits flow through to its shareholders and are reported directly by them.

BACKGROUND

The Subchapter S rules were first added to the law in 1958 and the basic rules adopted then remained unchanged until 1982 when the "S" rules were substantially revised.

Under the rules in effect from 1958 through 1982, an S corporation's net taxable income and net operating losses flowed through to the shareholders, but it was treated as a "regular" corporation in every other respect. As a result, S corporations usually had earnings and profits and some distributions to shareholders were taxable dividends. Also, under the rules in effect before 1983, shareholders were often denied deductions for corporate losses because of peculiar limits on such deductions.

These complications often resulted in tax traps for taxpayers who were not well advised. The Subchapter S Revision Act of 1982 eliminated many of the problems encountered under the old law. Now, for most important purposes, an S corporation is "a corporation taxed as a partnership," a generalization that did not apply earlier.

There still remain, however, some important differences between S corporations and partnerships relating to contributions to the entity, distributions from the entity, and the deductibility of losses. For simplicity, we will cover only the rules applicable to years after 1982.

---

[64] Sec. 731 (a)(1).

[65] Sec. 751 (b).

ELIGIBILITY AND TERMINATION

Subchapter S status is elective and is available only to corporations that meet the following definition:[66]

1. A corporation that has 35 or fewer shareholders. Generally, a husband and wife are treated as one shareholder.
2. All shareholders are individuals, estates, or qualified trusts. The latter term refers to voting trusts and certain other qualified trusts defined in the statute.
3. No shareholder is a nonresident alien.
4. The corporation has only one class of stock.

Even though S corporations are referred to as "small business corporations," nothing in the definition above limits the amount of assets owned by the corporation or the amount of income.

The S election is made by filing Form 2553, along with a consent to the election filed by each shareholder. If the election is made on or before the 15th day of the third month of the corporation's taxable year, S status is available for that year.

Example 55: X Corporation is formed in January of 19X1 and begins business in February of that year. The corporation plans to use the calendar year. A valid election (with the consent of shareholders) filed on or before March 15, 19X1 assures S status for 19X1.

If an election is filed after the 15th day of the third month it becomes effective for the following taxable year.

Example 56: In Example 55, X Corporation does not get its election filed until March 20, 19X1. X is a C corporation for 19X1 but enjoys S status for 19X2.

Once made, the S election is binding on all subsequent years until the corporation ceases to meet the definition above or until the election is revoked. When a corporation becomes disqualified, as, for example, when some of its stock is transferred to another corporation, the S status continues until the date of disqualification and the corporation is a C corporation only for the remainder of its taxable year.[67]

Example 57: X Corporation, on a calendar year, has been an S corporation for several years. On May 15, 19X1, due to a transfer of stock, X obtains its 36th shareholder and fails to qualify for S status. For the period January 1 through May 14, 19X1, X files as an S corporation; for the remainder of the year, as a C corporation.

An S election can be revoked if shareholders owning more than one-half of the corporation's stock consent to such a revocation. If made be-

---

[66] Sec. 1361 (b).

[67] Sec. 1362 (e).

fore the 15th day of the third month of the corporation's year, the revocation is for that entire year. If made later, the revocation applies to the subsequent year.[68]

Example 58: X Corporation is an S corporation using the calendar year. On March 1, 19X1, it files a revocation of its S election, accompanied by the consents of shareholders owning 60% of its stock. X Corporation is a C corporation for all of 19X1.

A revocation can specify a prospective date for termination of the election. Once the S election is revoked, a new election cannot be made for a period of five years without consent of the Commissioner.

CONTRIBUTIONS OF CAPITAL

While the 1982 revision of Subchapter S provides for the general treatment of S corporations as partnerships, the rules of Subchapter C, as explained early in this chapter, still govern many transactions of S corporations. This is true for transactions in which shareholders contribute capital to a corporation in exchange for stock or securities. Such an exchange is a taxable event unless the nonrecognition rules of Section 351 apply (see pp. 16/3–7).

Example 59: S and T, two individuals, own all the stock of X, an S corporation which has operated for several years. R, another individual, exchanges with X property having a fair market value of $60,000 and a basis to him of $40,000, for newly-issued common stock of X. Following the transfer, R owns only 20% of X's stock. In this instance, Section 351 does not apply because R, the transferor of the property, does not control X after the transfer. R must recognize a gain of $20,000 on this transaction.

Under partnership rules, contributions to capital are not taxable events; for an S corporation, they may be taxable.

EFFECTS OF S ELECTION

The basic effect of the S election is the exemption of the corporation from the income tax.[69] Taxable items of income, gains, losses, deductions and credits flow through the S corporation and are reported directly by the shareholders, based on stock holdings throughout the year.[70] The character of the items also flows through. Thus, Example 45, relating to partnerships, applies equally to S corporations.

Each shareholder's pro rata share of an S corporation's taxable items is determined by assuming that each item accrues uniformly throughout

---

[68] Sec. 1362 (d)(1).

[69] In rare instances, an S corporation may be subject to a tax on capital gains (Sec. 1374) and on unusually high passive income over an extended period (Section 1375).

[70] Sec. 1366(a).

the year. Allocation is then made based on stock ownership for each day of the year.[71]

Example 60: Until December 11, 19X1, a year with 365 days, A owned all of the stock of S Corporation. On that day, A sold 25% of his stock to B. For 19X1, S had a long-term capital gain of $36,500. First, this gain is assigned to each day of the year ($36,500 ÷ 365 days), or $100 per day. B owned a 25% interest for 20 days and his share of the gain is $500 ($25 × 20 days). The remaining $36,000 is allocated to A. Similarly, each item is allocated between A and B.

As with partnerships, taxable items that do not receive special treatment are grouped into "ordinary" taxable income (or loss) for allocation purposes.

S corporations, not each shareholder, make the various elections required to account for taxable income and taxable year. New S corporations can use only a permitted year, which is either December 31 or a fiscal year approved by the Commissioner because it serves a business purpose.[72]

Shareholders of S corporations can deduct the losses of their corporations, but always limited to their basis in their stock.[73] Unlike partnerships, the S corporation's indebtedness does not increase the shareholder's basis in his or her stock. However, the basis of an S corporation's indebtedness to a shareholder increases that shareholder's limit on losses.[74]

Example 61: S corporation was organized in January 19X1. A, an individual, contributed $10,000 for 25% of S's stock. Later, in 19X1, A loaned S $5,000. S operated at a loss in 19X1 and A's share of the loss was $12,000. A can deduct the entire $12,000; his limit is $15,000, the basis of his stock plus the basis of the indebtedness.

When a shareholder's losses exceed the basis of his or her stock, plus the basis of indebtedness, the excess loss is carried forward indefinitely until absorbed by future increases in basis.[75]

Another effect of the S election is the disallowance of fringe benefits for employees of the electing corporation who own more than 2% of the corporate stock at any time during the year.[76]

Example 62: T, an individual, owns 25% of the stock of Blessco, Inc., an S corporation. T is also president of Blessco. During the year, the corporation pays a $1,500 premium on health insurance for

---

[71] Sec. 1377 (a)(1).
[72] Sec. 1378 (b).
[73] Sec. 1366 (d).
[74] Sec. 1366 (d)(1).
[75] Sec. 1366 (d)(2).
[76] Sec. 1372 (a).

T. T is not an employee of Blessco and cannot exclude the premium from his gross income.

In some cases, the loss of fringe benefits for officer-stockholders may cause the S election to be unwise.

BASIS ADJUSTMENTS, SALES OF STOCK, AND DISTRIBUTIONS

A shareholder of an S corporation adjusts his or her basis in the S corporation's stock for the S corporation items that flow through to the shareholder. As explained previously, S corporation losses reduce the basis (but not below zero) of the stock. In a similar way, items of income and gains increase the basis. Thus, while the shareholder currently pays taxes on income or takes a deduction for a loss, subsequent gain or loss on the sale of the stock is reduced or increased accordingly.

Example 63: T, an individual, contributed $10,000 for a 10% interest in S corporation in 19X1. For 19X1 and 19X2, T reported and paid taxes on $8,000 as his share of S's taxable income. On January 2, 19X3, T sold his shares in S Corp. for $25,000. T's gain is $7,000, the sales price less a basis of $18,000, the original $10,000 plus the upward adjustments to basis of $8,000.

Stock in an S corporation, like other stock, is a capital asset and gain or loss upon the disposition of such stock is usually a capital gain or loss.

Cash distributions from an S corporation to its shareholders are not taxable events but only reduce the shareholders' bases in their stock.[77] If cash distributions exceed a shareholder's basis, such excess is usually a capital gain.

Example 64: Assume the same facts as in Example 63, except that T does not sell his stock on January 2, 19X3. Instead, S Corp. distributes $12,000 in cash to T on January 2, 19X3. This distribution is treated as a return of capital to T and reduces his basis in the stock from $18,000 to $6,000.

An S corporation that distributes noncash appreciated property to its shareholders must recognize gain as though such property were sold to the shareholders.[78] Any gain recognized by the S corporation must then be reported by its shareholders.

Example 65: T owns all the stock of S Corp. with a basis of $100,000. In 19X1, S Corporation distributes inventory to T. The inventory has a basis of $10,000 and a fair market value of $25,000. T treats the dis-

[77] Sec. 1368 (b). Some S corporations have accumulated earnings and profits and distributions may be taxable dividends. This is the case, for example, where a corporation was a C corporation prior to the S election.

[78] Sec. 1363 (d).

tribution as a return of capital of $25,000 and reduces his basis by that amount. S Corporation must recognize the $15,000 appreciation as ordinary income. This income flows through to T and is reported by him.

Presumably, no losses are recognized on distributions of depreciated property. The shareholder's basis is reduced by the fair market value of the property and his or her basis in the distributed property becomes the fair market value. For depreciated property, the S corporation should sell the property, recognize the loss (which flows through to the shareholders), and distribute the resulting cash proceeds.

Distributions in liquidation of an S corporation are taxed under Subchapter C rules and not like liquidating distributions of partnerships. The S Corporation's shareholders recognize gain or loss for the difference between the fair market value of the assets received and the basis of their stock. The gain or loss is generally capital in nature. The liquidating S Corporation does not recognize gain or loss on the liquidating distribution, with some exceptions noted earlier (on p. 16/21).

TRUSTS AND ESTATES

FIDUCIARY A general term for a person responsible for property held in trust or during the administration of an estate. For a fee, the fiduciary represents all parties with a legal interest in the property.

ESTATE Upon death, property of the decedent comes under the control of some form of probate court and an executor designated by the decedent's will (or an administrator if no will exists). The taxable entity during this period is the estate, which exists until the property passes finally to the decedent's heirs.

EXECUTOR The person named in a will to administer the property during the estate's life (executrix, if a female). Where there is no will, the court appoints an administrator (administratrix).

Trusts and estates, also called ***fiduciaries***, receive unique treatment under our income tax laws. They are conduits like partnerships and S corporations to the extent that their current taxable income is distributed to their beneficiaries. They are taxable separate entities like C corporations to the extent that their income is retained.

Estates come into existence upon the death of a natural person. The decedent's assets typically come under the control of an ***executor*** or administrator until the estate is settled and title of the property passes to the

BACKGROUND

Our first income tax law passed in 1913 provided that all income from estates and trusts would flow through and be taxed to the beneficiaries. Under this scheme, the executor, trustee, or other fiduciary was viewed as the agent of the beneficiary. Receipt of income by an agent is tantamount to receipt by the principal.

This policy was shortsighted. Tax planners had grantors create trusts for the benefit of *unborn* beneficiaries, leaving no natural person to report the income. The original scheme also ignored the problems that arose when the identity of the eventual recipient of the trust property was not apparent.

To cure these defects, the law was changed in 1918, making the fiduciary responsible for the tax payment in situations where the current income is not distributed to beneficiaries.

beneficiaries named in the will, or to heirs by operation of law. During this period of administration, from death to final settlement, an estate exists for income tax purposes. Note that death also triggers the federal estate tax, as well as the inheritance or estate tax for the state of residence.

Trusts are created when property passes into the control of ***trustees*** who hold and administer the property for the ***beneficiaries*** for the period prescribed in the trust instrument. A trust may be endowed by gift during the life of the grantor (*inter vivos* trusts) or may arise from the settlement of an estate where the decedent leaves property in trust for his or her heirs (testamentary trusts).

TRUSTEE The "legal" person who administers a trust is a trustee. A trustee may be a natural person as well as a bank or other "corporate" trustee.

BENEFICIARY A person who enjoys the financial benefits of a trust is a beneficiary. The word is also loosely used for estates.

TRANSFERS TO AND FROM FIDUCIARIES

Transfers of property to an estate or trust are not taxable events. The ***grantor*** or decedent receives no consideration for the enabling transfers and therefore no gain or loss can result.

GRANTOR The person who transfers property to a trust.

> **Example 66:** G transfers corporate stock with a basis of $100,000 and a fair market value of $250,000 to a trust for the benefit of her grandchild. This transfer does not result in gain to G.

While these transfers are not taxable events for purposes of the income tax, the transfers may be taxable as gifts or subject to the federal estate tax. A brief introduction to these transfer taxes is given in Chapter 1.

Transfers from an estate or trust to its beneficiaries are also not taxable events and do not give rise to gain or loss to the fiduciaries. Moreover, distributions from estates or trusts are not income to the beneficiaries unless, as explained in the following section, the distributions are "out of" current or accumulated income of the fiduciary.

> **Example 67:** A is the beneficiary of a trust created several years ago by A's grandmother, G. The trust property is a block of stock with a basis of $100,000 and a fair market value of $350,000. During the life of the trust, dividends from the stock were distributed to A currently. Under the terms of the trust, the stock is distributed to A on his 30th birthday. This transfer to A is not a taxable event to the fiduciary and the $350,000 value received by A is not income.

Trusts and estates are not separate entities for tax purposes. They serve as conduits for income arising from the property held.

TAXATION OF FIDUCIARY'S INCOME

Some trusts are required by the trust instrument to distribute all income currently. For tax purposes, such a trust is called a "simple" trust. Other trusts give trustees power either to distribute or accumulate income, usually in accordance with some standard in the trust instrument. These trusts are called "complex" trusts. Estates are treated as if they were complex trusts.

Estates and trusts file an annual return on Form 1041, reporting their taxable incomes. The tax rules applicable to individuals generally apply to trusts and estates.[79] The individual rules for gross income, exclusions, capital gains and losses, deductions, credits, etc., are used to calculate the fiduciary's taxable income. However, instead of the $1,000 personal exemption allowed individuals, the exemptions are:[80] complex trusts, $100; simple trusts, $300; estates, $600. Trusts and estates pay an income tax based on the rate schedule at Appendix E, which is the same as the rate schedule applicable to married persons filing separately, but without benefit of the zero-bracket amount.

Example 68: For 1985, Z Trust had interest income from corporate bonds of $6,000 and long-term capital gains of $5,000. Z Trust paid trustee fees of $700 during the year. The trust made no distributions. Z's taxable income is:

Gross income ($6,000 + $5,000)		$11,000
Deductions:		
Net capital gains	$3,000	
Trustee fees under Sec. 212	700	
Exemption (complex trust)	100	(3,800)
Taxable income		$ 7,200

Z's tax liability (using Appendix E) is $1,032.50.

DISTRIBUTION DEDUCTION Trusts and estates are entitled to a special deduction for the amounts distributed to beneficiaries. If the fiduciary distributes all of its current income, this deduction eliminates any tax on the estate or trust.

While individual rules generally apply to the calculation of taxable income, trusts and estates are allowed a ***distribution deduction*** for distributions made to beneficiaries.[81]

Example 69: To continue Example 68, assume instead that Z trust distributes cash of $10,300 to its beneficiary, A. This amount is the $11,000 income less the trustee fees. Z is allowed a deduction for this distribution (technically limited to its distributable net income, a concept beyond our scope here) and Z has no taxable income and pays no tax. The income is reported by A, the beneficiary.

Where a trust or estate distributes only a part of its income, the tax burden falls partly on the fiduciary and partly on the beneficiary. The deduction is allowed for distributions made during the taxable year, and during the first 65 days of the following year, if the fiduciary so elects.[82]

---

[79] Sec. 641 (b).
[80] Sec. 642 (b).
[81] Sec. 651 (a) and 661 (a).
[82] Sec. 663 (b).

The tax character of taxable items is not affected by a distribution to a beneficiary. Income distributed to a beneficiary has the same character to the beneficiary as it had in the hands of the fiduciary.[83]

Example 70: A, the beneficiary of Z Trust in Example 69, reports the distribution received as interest income and long-term capital gain. A is then entitled to the net capital gain deduction and to any exclusions related to the income.

A complex trust or an estate may distribute an amount in excess of its current income. Generally, such *accumulation* distributions by estates are treated as distributions of corpus and are not taxable to the recipients. However, if the tax rates applicable to the fiduciary of a trust on the accumulated income were lower than the rates that would have applied to such income if it had been distributed currently to the beneficiaries, the additional taxes may be levied on the accumulation distribution.[84] This rate adjustment is referred to as the "throw back" rule.

PLANNING WORKSHOP

The artificial entities discussed in this chapter are major tools used in tax planning. As stated earlier, much tax planning involves nothing more than the positioning of these entities between an individual taxpayer and economic activity for the purpose of reducing the tax burden. Some common examples of this planning strategy are illustrated in this workshop.

C CORPORATION AS A RATE SHELTER

Many nontax factors exist for the incorporation of a business. Indeed, the successful operation of large, public businesses in any other legal form would be well-nigh impossible. Many corporations exist, nevertheless, primarily for tax reasons. The maximum corporate tax is 46% compared to 50% for individuals. Corporate rates are substantially lower at other points on the schedule. For example, the corporate rate on taxable income from $25,000 to $50,000 is only 18%; the rates on married individuals filing jointly with comparable incomes rise from 25% to 38% (using the 1985 Rate Schedule).

Continued

[83] Sec. 651 (c) and 661 (c).

[84] Sec. 665 through 668. In computing the hypothetical tax to the beneficiaries, an average marginal-tax rate of three of the past five tax years is used. (The marginal-tax rates of the highest and lowest of the preceding five years are omitted from the average.)

PLANNING WORKSHOP

Sizable savings result, therefore, from the incorporation of many businesses.

Example 71: Two individuals, A and B, each operate a business that is their only source of income. A's business produces an income of $100,000 per year and B's business produces income of $200,000 per year. Assume that both are married and file a joint return (with no dependents) and that neither A nor B has itemized deductions in excess of the zero-bracket amount. The tax year is 1984. If operated as proprietorships, the gross tax liabilities are:

	A	B
Gross income from business after deductions *for* AGI	$100,000	$200,000
Exemptions	2,000	2,000
Taxable income	$ 98,000	$198,000
Gross tax liability from Schedule Y (Joint)	$ 31,500	$ 80,400

Now, assume that the businesses are incorporated and that A draws a salary of $40,000 and B a salary of $40,000. The corporations become separate entities and the salaries paid to A and B would be ordinary and necessary business deductions to the corporation even though A and B own all the stock of their respective corporations and control them absolutely. Of course, the salaries will be taxable income to A and B. After incorporation the total tax liability of each is:

	A	B
Tax on corporation:		
Net income from business	$100,000	$200,000
Less salary of officer-owner	40,000	40,000
Taxable income of corporation	$ 60,000	$160,000
Tax on corporation	$ 11,250	$ 53,350
Tax on individuals:		
Salary from corporation	$ 40,000	$ 40,000
Less exemptions	2,000	2,000
Taxable income	$ 38,000	$ 38,000
Tax on $38,000 from Schedule Y (Joint)	$ 7,198	$ 7,198
Combined tax on corporation and individual	$ 18,448	$ 60,548
Tax before incorporation	31,500	$ 80,400
Tax saved	$ 13,052	$ 19,852

Continued

PLANNING WORKSHOP

For A, the savings above represents approximately 40% of tax liability before incorporation; for B, the savings are approximately 25% of the tax before incorporation. In this example, any increase in B's income results in only a 4% savings from incorporation. At B's level of income, the corporate marginal rate is 46% compared with 50% applicable to individuals.

The tax savings illustrated in Example 65 result only if the after-tax income of the corporations is reinvested in the businesses. If the corporations distribute substantial ordinary dividends, the double tax that results when the tax is paid by the shareholders eliminates the advantage.

Once a business is incorporated, a second or double tax on the corporate income is usually inevitable. Even if current dividends are avoided, the eventual distribution in liquidation of the retained earnings results in a capital gain to the shareholders. Incorporation is feasible, then, only if the taxes saved are reinvested over several years so that the growth in value of the tax savings more than pays for the double tax upon liquidation.

Another reason for the use of corporations in tax planning is the availability of employee fringe benefits for shareholder-officers. Once incorporated, shareholders who work for the corporation are employees and the wage package for these employees can include the usual "perks." The cost of these fringe benefits, e.g., pension, health insurance, etc., are deductible to the corporate employer and their value is excluded from income of the employee.

Prior to 1983, many S corporations were formed to obtain the tax savings from fringe benefits for shareholder-employees. In years after 1982, a person who owns, directly or indirectly, more than 2% of the stock of an S corporation at any time during a year cannot be an employee entitled to fringe benefits.*

PARTNERSHIPS AND REAL ESTATE VENTURES

Our tax law makes the partnership ideally suited for many real estate ventures. In real estate the capital needed for projects such as apartment houses and shopping centers is great enough to require the combined resources of two or more people. The ventures commonly produce large tax losses in their early years because of large depreciation deductions. Also, the projects are usually leveraged and interest payments in the early years are high.

Our partnership rules permit the flow-through to the partners of the resulting losses. And while the losses deductible by a partner are limited to his or her basis in the partnership interest, the debt of the partnership also flows through and increases the partner's basis. As a result, the partners can in effect *deduct* dollars borrowed by the partnership.

Continued

PLANNING WORKSHOP

Example 72: In 19X1, T, an individual, invested $20,000 for a 10% interest in Boway Apartments, a general partnership. The partnership borrowed $1 million. In 19X1, 19X2 and 19X3, T's share of Boway's losses totaled $50,000. Boway made no principal payments on the mortgage indebtedness. T's basis in his interest is $120,000, his $20,000 contribution plus 10% of the partnership indebtedness. T can deduct all of his $50,000 share of the losses of the partnership, as this amount is less than his $120,000 basis.

The at-risk rules in Section 465 sometimes limit the deductibility of partnership losses when a partner is not personally liable for the partnership debts. The at-risk rules, however, do not apply to real estate.[†]

S corporations are less suited for the type of real estate venture that produces large tax losses using borrowed funds. In an S corporation, the shareholders' deductible losses are limited to their basis in the stock and their basis is not increased by the corporation's indebtedness.

MULTIPLE TAXPAYERS USING TRUSTS

Trusts are commonly used by wealthier taxpayers to reduce the total tax burden on their incomes by dividing up the income between several taxpayers. A person in a high tax bracket can transfer income-producing properties to one or more trusts and reduce the total tax paid because the taxable income of each trust is taxed beginning with the lowest rates on the schedule.

Example 73: T, a 65-year-old widow, has taxable income of $150,000 primarily from interest and dividends. She has five grandchildren, all minors, who are the natural heirs to her estate. She transfers stocks and bonds to a trust for each grandchild sufficient to produce income of $10,000 for each. Prior to this transfer, T's marginal rate on the last $50,000 of income was 50%. Once divided between five trusts, the top marginal rate on this income will be 22% or less.

The effect described above is also obtained by making direct gifts of property to beneficiaries, provided the donees do not have substantial income in their own rights. A trust is preferable, however, for minor children and for irresponsible adults.

---

[*] Sec. 1372 (a).

[†] Sec. 465 (c)(3)(D).

KEY POINTS TO REMEMBER

1. The formation of corporations and other entities described in this chapter can result in the reduction of the income taxes of individuals because such entities benefit from reduced tax rates and special tax provisions.
2. *De facto* corporations, or associations, are treated as C corporations even though the taxpayers planned a partnership or trust. Partnerships and trusts are treated as associations if they possess a majority of requisite corporation characteristics.
3. Appreciated property can be transferred to a corporation in exchange for stock without the recognition of gain, provided the transferors control the corporation at the time of the transfer. Also, liabilities assumed by the corporation in such transfers are not treated as boot.
4. C corporations generally compute their taxable income using the rules applicable to individuals, though special rules exist for dividends received, capital gains and losses, and other items. Corporate tax rates are quite different from those for individuals.
5. Distributions from C corporations to its shareholders are generally dividends to the shareholders to the extent of the corporation's earnings and profits. Redemptions are also treated as dividends, with limited exceptions. However, when a corporation distributes its property in liquidation, shareholders realize a capital gain or loss.
6. Partnerships are aggregations of the proprietary interest of the partners, not separate entities.
7. Contributions of property to partnerships and distributions of property from partnerships are not usually taxable events and do not result in gains or losses to the parties involved. Gain or loss is deferred by substituting the property's basis.
8. Partnership items of income, gains, losses, deductions, and credits are allocated to the partners based on the partnership agreement and each partner reports his share of the items. The agreement can specify special allocations of partnership items if the allocation has substantial economic effect.
9. An electing S corporation is not generally a taxpayer and its income, gains, losses, deductions and credits are reported by its shareholders based on the stock ownership throughout the year. Otherwise, S corporations are subject to the usual corporate rules.
10. Only corporations that meet the definition of a "small business corporation" are eligible for S corporation status. To qualify, a corporation must have 35 or fewer shareholders, only one class of stock, and must meet other requirements.
11. Trusts and estates do not pay an income tax if they distribute their incomes currently.

c) $220,000

d) $232,000

(AICPA adapted)

5. In computing a corporation's taxable income, a net capital loss is
   a) deductible in full in the year sustained
   b) deductible to a maximum extent of 50% in the year sustained
   c) not deductible at all in the year sustained
   d) limited to a maximum deduction of $3,000 in the year sustained

   (AICPA adapted)

6. James Bell, CPA, a sole practitioner reporting on the cash basis, incorporated his accounting practice in 1984, transferring the following assets to the newly formed corporation:

Cash	$5,000
Office furniture and equipment:	
Adjusted basis	$35,000
Fair market value	45,000

   No liabilities were transferred, and there were no other stockholders. The corporation's total basis for the transferred assets is
   a) $35,000
   b) $40,000
   c) $45,000
   d) $50,000

   (AICPA adapted)

7. In 1977, its first year of operation, the Champion Corporation, not a dealer in securities, realized taxable income of $64,000 from the operation of its business. In addition to its regular business operations, it realized the following gains and losses from the sale of marketable securities:

Short-term capital gain	$ 5,000
Short-term capital loss	(2,000)
Long-term capital gain	6,000
Long-term capital loss	(16,000)

   What is Champion's total taxable income for 1977?
   a) $57,000
   b) $62,000
   c) $64,000
   d) $75,000

   (AICPA adapted)

8. In 1977, its first year of operation, Commerce Corporation had a gross profit from operations of $360,000 and deductions of $500,000 exclud-

ing any special deductions. Commerce also received dividends of $100,000 from unaffiliated domestic corporations. What is the net operating loss for 1977?

a) $34,000

b) $40,000

c) $55,000

d) $125,000

(AICPA adapted)

9. The Cresap Corporation, an accrual-basis taxpayer, was formed and began operations on May 1, 1972. The following expenses were incurred during its first tax period, May 1–December 1, 1972:

Expenses of temporary directors and of organizational meetings	$500
Fee paid to state for incorporation	100
Accounting services incident to organization	200
Legal services for drafting the corporate charter and bylaws	400
Expenses of printing stock certificates	420

If Cresap Corporation makes an appropriate and timely election, the maximum organization expense that it can properly deduct for 1972 would be

a) $160

b) $216

c) $324

d) $0

(AICPA adapted)

10. For the year ended December 31, 1974, Fendel Corporation had net income per books of $120,000. Included in determining net income were the following items:

Insurance premiums on the life of the president (Company is not the beneficiary)	$3,000
Net capital losses	2,200
Penalty for failure to deposit withholding taxes	500
Contributions to charitable organizations	10,000

If all other items included in book income were appropriately includable in the calculation of taxable income, and reasonableness of compensation was not at issue, what was Fendel's taxable income for 1974? (In 1974, limit was 5%, not 10%.)

a) $107,300

b) $122,700

c) $126,065

d) $128,915

(AICPA adapted)

11. Trulor Corporation, not an S corporation, had a deficit of $80,000 at the end of 1975. Its net income after taxes in 1976 was $40,000 (including a long-term capital gain of $10,000). It made distributions to shareholders of $20,000 in 1976. Trulor should describe the payments as

a) ordinary dividends 50%; return of capital 50%

b) ordinary dividends 50%; long-term capital gain 50%

c) ordinary dividends 75%; long-term capital gain 25%

d) ordinary dividends 100%

(AICPA adapted)

12. Lonky Corporation's condensed income statement for the year ended December 31, 1982, was as follows:

Business income	$500,000
Business costs and expenses	475,000
Operating income	$ 25,00
Charitable contributions	5,000
Income before income taxes	$ 20,000

The maximum amount deductible by Lonky for charitable contributions in its 1982 income tax return is

a) $1,000

b) $1,250

c) $2,000

d) $2,500

(AICPA adapted)

13. On May 1, 1984, John Alda was admitted to partnership in the firm of Bartok & Benson. Alda's contribution to capital consisted of 500 shares of stock in Asch Corp., purchased in 1973 for $20,000, which had a fair market value of $100,000 on May 1, 1984. Alda's interest in the partnership's capital and profits is 25%. On May 1, 1984, the fair market value of the partnership's net assets (after Alda was admitted) was $400,000. What was Alda's gain in 1984 on the exchange of the Asch stock for Alda's partnership interest?

a) $0

b) $80,000 ordinary income

c) $80,000 long-term capital gain

d) $80,000 Section 1231 gain

(AICPA adapted)

14. An S corporation may

a) have both common and preferred stock

b) have a corporation as a shareholder

c) be a member of an affiliated group

d) have as many as 35 shareholders

(AICPA adapted)

15. During 1975, Luction Corporation exchanged 5,000 shares of its $10 par value common stock for a parcel of land with a fair market value of $70,000. The fair market value of Luction's common stock at the time of the exchange was $13 per share. For 1975, Luction should report a taxable gain of

a) $0

b) $5,000

c) $10,000

d) $20,000

(AICPA adapted)

QUESTIONS

1. For tax purposes, C corporations are treated as separate entities. Explain generally what this means when: (a) shareholders transfer assets to a C corporation in exchange for stock in the corporation; (b) C corporations distribute their earnings to shareholders; and (c) C corporations distribute their assets in liquidation.
2. To avoid the corporate income tax, a group of investors decides to conduct a business in the form of a trust. Will this plan be successful in every event? If not, under what conditions will the trust be taxed as a corporation?
3. A, an individual, transfers appreciated property to a corporation in exchange for the corporation's stock. Under what conditions is this transfer a nontaxable exchange?
4. Does a corporation recognize gain or loss when it issues its stock to shareholders in exchange for property?
5. T owns 75% of the stock of X Corporation. X is insolvent and T transfers appreciated property to X to shore up its finances. Does T recognize a gain or loss on this transfer?
6. List the major differences between the rules for the calculation of taxable income of C corporations as compared to individuals.
7. Are the corporate tax rates higher or lower than the rates applicable to individuals? At all levels of income? Is the differential greater, or less, now as compared to the past?
8. What is the purpose of the alternate tax applicable to C corporations? How is this effect obtained for individual taxpayers?

9. X Corporation made a "qualified" charitable contribution of $50,000. Are corporations allowed deductions for these gifts? Is the deduction, if allowed, limited? Explain.

10. What is the purpose of the 85% dividends-received deduction allowed C corporations? Why doesn't the law allow a similar deduction to individual shareholders?

11. What is the basic difference between the minimum tax levied on individuals and the one levied on C corporations?

12. X corporation distributes cash to its shareholders. What determines the tax treatment of this "dividend" to the shareholders?

13. Can C corporation's earnings and profits be determined by adding up its past taxable income? Explain.

14. T owns 60% of the stock of X Corporation. T received as a dividend from X land with a fair market value of $10,000 and a basis of $6,000. What is the amount of T's dividend income (assuming ample E&P)? What if T is a corporation? Does X recognize a gain?

15. T owns 100 shares of Giant, Inc. common stock and receives ten additional common shares with a value of $60 each. T paid $35 per share for 100 shares several years ago. How does this distribution affect Giant? T? What is T's basis in the 10 shares?

16. Assume in Question 15 that T's 100 shares are preferred stock and that the dividend is common stock. How does this change your answers?

17. Under what circumstances does a stock redemption result in capital gain or loss to the shareholder whose stock is redeemed?

18. Why does a shareholder usually realize a capital gain or loss upon the complete liquidation of a corporation, but not from a pro rata redemption of stock not in liquidation?

19. For tax purposes, a partnership is treated as an aggregation of the proprietary interests of the partners. Following this concept, what is the tax effect of: (a) contributions of appreciated property to a partnership by its partners; (b) distributions of assets from a partnership to partners; and (c) realization of income by a partnership?

20. In the current year, RS partnership recognizes ordinary income of $30,000 and a $10,000 long-term capital gain. R, an individual, has a 50% interest in RS's profits and losses. However, RS made no distributions of cash or other property to R during the year. How do the RS operations affect R's personal return under these circumstances?

21. Must all partnership items be allocated to the partners in the same manner? Explain.

22. How do the liabilities of a partnership affect the basis of a partner in his partnership interest? Explain how a partner is able to deduct partnership losses in excess of the basis of the property and/or cash contributed to the partnership?
23. Under what conditions does a partner recognize gain or loss when property is distributed from a partnership?
24. List the characteristics that a corporation must possess before it can make the "S" election. Do these characteristics deal directly with the corporation's size?
25. What major differences exist between the tax treatment of partnerships and S corporations?
26. How do the liabilities of an S corporation affect a shareholder's stock basis?
27. X Corporation, formed in 1983, is an S corporation and it distributes appreciated property to its shareholders. Does X recognize gain on the distribution? Do the shareholders recognize dividend income?
28. Under what conditions is a trust or an estate subject to the federal income tax?
29. Does a grantor recognize gain or loss when property is transferred to a trust? What federal tax often applies to such transfers?
30. What is meant by the term "corporate rate shelter"? Explain how the use of a corporation can save taxes despite the "double" tax levied on corporate income.
31. Explain why partnerships are often used for the development of real estate.

PROBLEMS

1. ABC Corporation received the following items of income in the current year:

Revenue from sales of merchandise	$130,000
Dividends from domestic corporations	10,000
Interest from State of Kansas bonds	5,000

In addition, ABC Corporation incurred the following expenses:

Cost of merchandise sold	$80,000
Other operating expenses	12,000
Contributions	5,000

a) What is ABC's taxable income for the year?

b) What is ABC's gross tax for the year?

c) Calculate ABC's current earnings and profits for this year's operations.

2. A and B, two individuals, form AB, Inc. for the operation of a new business. Both transfer assets as follows to AB in exchange for AB's common stock:

	A	B
Basis of property	$20,000	$55,000
Fair market value	60,000	40,000

A receives 6,000 shares and B receives 4,000 shares. C, a lawyer, received 200 shares valued at $2,000 for his legal work connected with the organization.

a) How much gain or loss do A and B recognize as a result of this exchange and what is their basis in the shares received?

b) How is C affected by the receipt of his shares?

c) How much gain or loss does AB, Inc. recognize from these exchanges? What is AB's basis in the property?

3. James Madison and Henry Clay formed a corporation on July 1 of this year. Madison transferred to the corporation the assets of his existing hardware business, which had a basis of $8,000, while Clay transferred assets that had a basis of $18,000. Each individual received 200 shares of stock in the new corporation, each share having a fair market value of $80 per share. In addition, Madison's wife was issued one share of stock on the investment of $80 in cash. Discuss the tax consequences of this transaction, including the basis of shares received and the basis of the corporation in the property.

4. Kyle, Dan and Bob decided to pool some assets in a new corporate business to be known as KDB Company. Kyle agreed to contribute $4,000 cash plus equipment with a fair market value of $26,000 and a tax basis of $15,000. Dan agreed to contribute land with a fair market value of $30,000 and a tax basis of $40,000. Bob agreed to contribute $20,000 cash and a good deal of work, which all parties agreed was worth $10,000. In exchange, each of the three received 1,000 shares of KDB stock.

a) If all the contributions are made under a single plan so that the transaction qualifies under Sec. 351(a):
   1. How much taxable income or loss will each man recognize in the year because KDB incorporated?
   2. What is the tax basis of the 1,000 shares of KDB each man owns?
   3. What is the tax basis of the equipment and land owned by KDB Company?
   4. Why might Dan strongly prefer to arrange the incorporating transaction in a way that would not qualify it under Sec. 351(a)?
   5. Why might Kyle strongly prefer to keep the transaction as it is currently arranged?

b) If the incorporation plans were revised so that initially Dan were to contribute $30,000 cash and subsequently, in a wholly separate transaction, KDB Company were to purchase the land from Dan at a cost of $30,000, why might both Kyle and Dan be satisfied?

c) Under either plan (a) or (b) above each of the owners has contributed $30,000 in cash or equivalent property and/or services to KDB Company in exchange for 1,000 shares of stock. Nevertheless, in one important sense Kyle has not contributed his fair share. Explain.

5. For the current year, Titus, Inc. has *ordinary* taxable income of $120,000 and the following gains and losses from property:

L-T capital gain	$40,000
S-T capital loss	(12,000)
Net Section 1231 gain	5,000

a) What is Titus's gross tax liability for the year?

b) Assume the L-T gain of $40,000 is instead an L-T loss. What is Titus's gross tax? What use does Titus make of the net capital loss? Explain.

6. Gummo, Inc. has the following items of income and deductions for the year:

Income:	
Gross income from sales of inventory	$200,000
Net capital gain	20,000
Dividends from domestic corporations	40,000
Deductions:	
Operating expenses	90,000
Loss on sale of machinery	6,000
Contributions	20,000

Gummo was formed two years ago and at that time incurred organizational costs of $5,000.

a) Calculate Gummo's taxable income for the year.

b) Calculate Gummo's gross tax for the year.

7. Individuals Able, Baker and Cooke together own 100% of three corporations. Each corporation operates a separate "discount store" located in three different cities. Each store has annual income of $80,000.

a) If each shareholder owns 33-1/3% of each corporation's stock, compute the additional tax liability due for the current year (1985) compared to an arrangement in which Able, Baker, and Cooke each owned one of the corporations. Benefits from all brackets are allocated equally among the companies.

b) Devise a scheme of ownership whereby Able, Baker and Cooke can own the three corporations jointly and avoid treatment as a controlled corporate group.

c) Discuss why the three individuals would hesitate to adopt the pattern of ownership you devised in part (b). For this purpose, assume that the stores have been in existence only for a brief period.

8. Big Burn, Inc. has a taxable income of $1,250,000 for 1985.
   a) Calculate Big Burn's gross tax liability.
   b) Calculate the tax liability if the taxable income is $1,500,000.
   c) Why did Congress increase the corporate tax rates in this manner in 1984?

9. Nasrullah, Inc. had the following preference items in 1985:

Excess of accelerated over straight-line depreciation on real estate	$70,000
Net capital gain	50,000

   Nasrullah's gross tax (before the add-on minimum tax) was $22,000 for 1985.
   a) Calculate Nasrullah's add-on minimum tax.
   b) Is this tax an alternative to the regular tax? Or an addition to the regular tax? Explain.

10. Tom Tulle owns 100 shares of Argus, Inc. Tom's basis in the stock is $10,000. During the current year, Tom receives a cash dividend of $8,000 from Argus. However, only $5,000 of this distribution is out of the earnings and profits of Argus.
    a) How does Tom treat the $8,000 distribution for tax purposes?
    b) How would your answer change if the distribution were $12,000?

11. T, an individual, owns 40% of the shares of Shecky, Inc. During the year, Shecky distributed to T real estate with a value of $60,000 and a basis of $35,000. This distribution is a dividend out of earnings and profits.
    a) Does Shecky recognize gain or loss because of this distribution? If so, how much?
    b) How much dividend income must T recognize? What is T's basis in the real estate?
    c) If T is a corporate shareholder, how do your answers to above change?
    d) Why does the law make a distinction between corporate and noncorporate shareholders in this case?

12. At the beginning of the year, Mite Corporation had a deficit of $100,000 in its earnings and profits account. For the current year, earnings and profits are $40,000 (leaving a deficit over all of $60,000). The directors decide to distribute cash of $50,000 in the current year and thereby avoid a dividend for its shareholders.
    a) Will this plan work?
    b) How is the $50,000 distribution treated by Mite's shareholders?

13. Nancy Deer owns 1,000 shares of Nijinsky, Inc. common stock with a basis of $25,000. During the year, Nancy received a dividend of 100 shares of Nijinsky common with a value of $10,000.

   a) How much income must Nancy recognize because of this distribution?

   b) What is Nancy's basis in the shares received?

   c) Assume that Nancy had the option of receiving 100 shares or $10,000 in cash from Nijinsky, and selected the stock. How does this change affect your answers in (a) and (b) above?

14. Jane Deer owns 1,000 shares of Basin Corporation common stock with a basis of $30,000. During this year, Basin distributes to Jane 1,000 stock rights. For five rights and $35, Jane can acquire an additional share of Basin common. On the day the Basin shares went "ex-rights," the common stock had a value of $50 and each right was valued at $3.

   a) Must Jane allocate her basis to the rights? Explain.

   b) Assume that Jane exercises the 1,000 rights. What is the basis of Jane's new 200 shares if she: (1) allocates basis; (2) does not allocate basis?

   c) Assume that Jane sells the rights for $3.50. How much gain must Jane recognize?

   d) What is the tax effect if Jane lets the rights expire?

15. Baker Corporation's common stock is owned entirely by James and Charles Baker. James owns 4,000 shares with a basis of $60,000; Charles owns 6,000 shares with a basis of $75,000. The corporation has been profitable and holds cash and other appreciated property with a basis of $450,000 and fair market value of $800,000. Earnings and profits are $250,000. James and Charles want to get cash out of the corporation without paying ordinary rates on a dividend. To this end, Baker Corporation redeems 1,000 shares of James's stock and 1,500 shares of Charles's stock for cash of $80 per share.

   a) How does this redemption affect the returns of James and Charles?

   b) Assume instead that Baker Corporation completely liquidates, exchanging its assets for all shares outstanding. How does this transaction affect James and Charles?

16. James Hampton, a client of yours, owns a large city lot that cost him $15,000 several years ago. He has been leasing the lot, which has a fair market value of $250,000, to a used car dealer. James has been approached by Henry Simon about building an office building on the property. Simon proposes to put $250,000 cash into the deal and then obtain a mortgage loan of $12 million to cover the building costs. James and Henry would operate the office building for five or six years and then sell it at a profit. List the advantages and disadvantages if the new venture is (a) a corporation, (b) an S corporation, and (c) a partnership.

17. M and N, two individuals who use the calendar year, formed a partnership in January of the current year. Each partner has a 50% interest in profits, losses, and capital. For his capital interest, M contributed property with a basis of $60,000 and a fair market value of $100,000. During the year, partnership MN had the following items:

Ordinary loss from operations	($30,000)
Short-term capital gain	$10,000

At December 31, MN owed creditors $25,000. In December, each partner withdrew cash of $7,500.

a) Does M recognize gain on his contribution to MN? If so, what is its nature?

b) What taxable year must MN use?

c) How does the MN operation affect M's personal return?

d) How does the $7,500 withdrawal affect M's personal return?

e) Calculate M's basis in his partnership interest at the end of the year.

18. S and T, two individuals, form a partnership for purposes of building a small apartment house. Each contributes cash of $50,000 and the partnership ST then borrows $900,000. The $1 million is used by the partnership to buy land and construct an apartment house. Because of high interest charges and large depreciation, ST shows a loss of $70,000 for its first year of operations and $60,000 for its second year.

a) If S and T share these losses equally, will they be allowed a deduction for the full amounts? Explain.

b) S and T agree that S will receive all losses from this venture. Will this agreement be recognized for tax purposes? Explain.

19. N is a partner in MNO, a partnership engaged in farming. N has a basis of $75,000 in his interest. His share of MNO's net assets are valued at $160,000. N has decided to dispose of his interest.

a) If N sells his interest for $160,000 cash, what is the tax effect on N (assume that MNO has no unrealized receivables or appreciated inventory)?

b) If MNO distributes land to N in liquidation of his interest, what is the tax effect on N? The land has a value of $160,000 and a basis to the partnership of $60,000. Would the partnership recognize gain from this distribution?

20. Jack Warden, who files a joint return, is a successful banker who owns a small country bank. His income and deductions for recent years have been constant and, as a result, his taxable income has been about $103,400 per year for the past several years. In January 19X1, Jack decided to open a seed and fertilizer store in the rural town in which his bank is located. He found an experienced and dependable manager and initiated the new operation in January 19X1. The

new venture was incorporated as the Community Seed and Fertilizer Company, Inc., of which Jack owns 100% of the stock. The operating results of the corporation were as follows:

	GAIN (LOSS)
19X1	($50,000)
19X2	(30,000)
19X3	5,000

a) Calculate the combined tax of the corporation and Warden for 19X1 through 19X3 (assuming that Warden's taxable income was $103,400 per year). Use the current year's tax rates. The corporate losses can be carried forward (but not back, since 19X1 was the first year of operation).

b) Calculate the total tax for Warden for 19X1 through 19X3, assuming that Warden made a proper election under Subchapter S for the years involved. Use the current year's tax rates. Warden's cost of his stock exceeds the losses.

c) Assume that Warden contributed cash of $60,000 for the stock of Community in 19X1 and that other funds needed by the corporation were obtained on a loan from a bank in a neighboring town. How does this affect your answers in (a) and (b) above?

21. In January, 19X1 Lew Archer paid $50,000 for a 10% interest in the common stock of Ross, Inc. For 19X1, Lew reported a loss of $3,000 as his share of the Ross loss. For 19X2, Ross earned a profit of $40,000 and Lew reported his $4,000 share of this profit. What is the tax effect, assuming that Ross, Inc. is a qualified Subchapter S corporation if, on January 1, 19X3:

    a) Lew sells his shares for $65,000 cash?

    b) Ross distributes cash of $10,000 to Lew?

22. Hunt Trust is a complex trust formed to provide for the education of Melissa Hunt's granddaughter. During 19X1, the trust realized dividend income of $6,000 and a long-term capital gain of $4,000. Administrative expenses were $500.

    a) Calculate the income tax of Hunt Trust for 19X1, assuming no distributions.

    b) If the trust beneficiary, Brenda, aged 14, has no income, what advice would you give the trustee?

23. The statements below describe some major tax characteristics of one or more of the entities (other than individuals) discussed in this chapter—corporations, S corporations, trusts, partnerships. For each statement, which is the appropriate entity or entities?

    a) A separate entity for all purposes under the tax law.

    b) An entity that serves only as a conduit for income and deductions.

c) An entity that functions as a taxpayer only to the extent that its income is not distributed.

d) An entity that serves as a rate shelter because it is subject to lower tax rates.

e) An entity that serves as a rate shelter only because it increases the number of taxpayers.

TAX PLANNING PROBLEMS

1. Twenty years ago Bob and Ray jointly invested in an 80-acre tract of vacant land at a cost of $8,000. Today that land is ready to be developed into a first-class residential area. Conservative estimates place the value of the land at $88,000. Bob and Ray are considering the possibility of joining with two builder-developers in a corporate business that would actually develop this land. What good tax reasons might Bob and Ray have to prefer a taxable transfer of their land to the new corporation rather than a nontaxable transfer under Section 351(a)? Explain.

2. Charles Goodnight owns a successful men's clothing store, which he operates as a proprietorship. Charles estimates that the net profits of the business will be $110,000. He wonders if he can gain a tax advantage by incorporation. He has no other source of income, and he would need a salary of $40,000 from the corporation. Calculate the tax savings from incorporation if Charles is single, under 65, with no dependents, and has itemized deductions less than the zero-bracket amount. Use rates in effect for 1985.

3. Herman Irish is married and has two small children who are dependent on him for support. For the current year, Herman expects to receive the following income:

Salary	$80,000
Dividends from taxable domestic corporations	6,000

The dividends will be paid on stock owned jointly by Herman and his wife, Betty. Herman expects the following deductions:

Unreimbursed travel and transportation related to employment	$4,000
Itemized deductions	6,000
Exemption deductions for Herman, Betty, and two children	4,000

Herman's tax consultant has recommended that the stock owned by Herman and Betty be transferred to two trusts, one for each child. The trustees would be instructed to accumulate income and pay out the accumulated income as needed for the college education of the children after they reach their majority. The corpus of the trust, plus any accumulated income, would be paid to each child when he or she reaches the age of 30. The tax consultant also recommends that Herman and Betty retain enough stock to produce dividends of $200.

a) Compute Herman and Betty's tax liability for the current year, assuming they do not create the trusts.

b) Compute the combined liabilities of Herman and Betty and the two trusts, assuming the trusts are established on January 1 of the current year (ignore the federal gift taxes).

c) How much tax is saved by the trust arrangement?

CASE PROBLEM

James Agee is president of the local bank and dabbles in real estate. In January, 1985, James decided to subdivide a tract of land and sell the lots for homesites. Since he holds several other tracts of land as investments, he decided to conduct the subdivision in a corporate shell. To this end, he formed a new corporation, Sunset Acres, and transferred the land (basis $50,000; fair market value, $250,000) and $75,000 in cash to the corporation in exchange for 10,000 shares of Sunset common, the only stock outstanding.

For January through May, Sunset spent $60,000 for streets, sewer, etc. Sales began in June, 1985 with the following results by year end for Sunset:

Sales price of lots (representing 40% of those available)	$300,000
Sales commissions and expenses	35,000
Other operating expenses	22,000

Because of excess available cash, Sunset distributed $20,000 cash to James in October, 1985.

In November, 1985, James sold 2,500 shares of Sunset stock for $140,000. This sale was made to another officer at the bank but was not planned in January, 1985.

James is married and has two dependent children. Information for 1985 relative to his personal financial affairs is:

Salary	$100,000
Interest earned on savings	4,000
Interest paid	(22,000)
State and local taxes (including sales)	(2,700)
Contributions	(4,000)

Make the following computations for 1985:

a) Sunset's gross tax liability

b) Agee's gross tax liability

RESEARCH PROBLEMS

1. RST Partnership was formed in 1979 for purposes of constructing and operating an apartment building. Each of the three partners contributed $100,000 in cash. The partnership then borrowed $3 million from a S & L association. Since this loan was made under a program insured by FHA, the loan was non-recourse. The apartment project was completed at a cost of $3.3 million in early 1980 and operations from 1980 through 1984 produced net losses of $800,000. On Oct. 31, 1984, RST defaulted on the mortgage note and the S & L association took possession of the property under the mortgage arrangement. At that time the complex had a basis of $2.5 million but a fair market value of only $2.2 million. The unpaid balance of the note was $2,990,000. RST had no other assets.

   Since the fair market value of the complex was less than the amount due on the note, RST reported neither gain nor loss from the foreclosure. Is this treatment correct? If not, specify the correct treatment.

2. A, B, and C—three individuals—formed a new corporation, New Co. The properties and services contributed by A, B, and C and the stock of New received by A, B, and C were:

TRANSFERRED TO NEW	FMV	NUMBER OF SHARES RECEIVED
A—Real estate	$100,000	1,000
B—Tangible personal property	100,000	1,000
C—Services	?	580
C—Cash	2,000	20

   Except for the stock issued by New, no other shares are outstanding. The above transfers were made on the same day. Does this transaction qualify under Sec. 351?

TAX RETURN CASE

1 Control number		OMB No. 1545-0008	
2 Employer's name, address, and ZIP code Arco, Inc. 1140 Fifth Avenue Fairfax, VA 22030		3 Employer's identification number 33-60677	4 Employer's State number 33-60677
		5 Statutory employee [X] Deceased [ ] Legal rep [ ]	942 emp [ ] Subtotal [ ] Void [ ]
		6 Allocated tips	7 Advance EIC payment
8 Employee's social security number 583-44-8002	9 Federal income tax withheld $13,280	10 Wages, tips, other compensation $40,200	11 Social security tax withheld $2,646
12 Employee's name, address, and ZIP code Patricia Nelson 1240 Sunnyvale Drive Fairfax, VA 22030		13 Social security wages $37,800	14 Social security tips
		16	
		17 State income tax $2,460 / 18 State wages, tips, etc. $40,200	19 Name of State VA
		20 Local income tax -- / 21 Local wages, tips, etc. --	22 Name of locality --

Form **W-2 Wage and Tax Statement** — **Copy B To be filed with employee's FEDERAL tax return** — This information is being furnished to the Internal Revenue Service — Department of the Treasury Internal Revenue Service

Richard and Patricia Nelson, ages 39 and 38, respectively, are married taxpayers who live at 1240 Sunnyvale Drive, Fairfax, Virginia 22030. Richard's social security number is 582-22-6611, and Patricia's number is 583-44-8002. Richard and Patricia provide all of the support for their twin 4-year-old daughters, Melissa and Phyllis. They also provide 75% of the support of Richard's 67-year-old mother, Alice, whose only sources of income in 1984 were $200 dividends on Ford Motor Co. stock, $830 interest on City of Baltimore bonds, and $1,300 social security benefits.

Richard and Patricia moved to Fairfax during the first week of January, 1984. Prior to this time, they lived and worked in Philadelphia, Pennsylvania. Patricia is a divisional plant manager with Arco, Inc., of Fairfax. Her 1984 Form W-2 is disclosed on this page. Most of Patricia's business-related expenses are paid for directly by Arco; however, the following legitimate expenses were paid for out of her own personal funds and were not reimbursed by the company:

Travel expenses (metrobus) to related companies	$230
Entertainment of prospective buyers	134
Long-distance business phone calls from home	83
Professional society dues	151
Professional journal subscriptions	82
Business usage of personal auto—220 miles	—

Richard owns and operates his own appliance sales and repair business. His cash-basis records for 1984 reveal the following information (inventories are based on the first-in, first-out method, and are considered to be a significant component of income):

	RECEIPTS	DISBURSEMENTS
Cash appliance sales and account collections	$192,480	—
Cash payments for services and on account	144,320	
Cash payments on account for purchases		$126,400
Gross salary payments (four employees)		89,652
Advertising expenses		3,406
Insurance expense (expires 12/31/84)		4,820
Operating expenses for delivery trucks		6,340
Bad debts written off (merchandise sales only)		2,560
Rent for building location		12,000
Payroll taxes (employer's share)		7,643
Self-employment (FICA) tax (for 1983, paid in 1984)		3,822
Supplies expense		2,322
Utilities expense		8,240

The following assets were used by Richard in the business during 1984:

ASSET	DATE ACQUIRED	COST	ACRS CLASS	RECOVERY METHOD	PRIOR YEARS' DEDUCTIONS
Business building*	1/2/81	$96,000	15 yr.	SL	$19,200
Display counters†	1/2/81	6,200	5 yr.	ACRS	3,596
Personal computer	1/17/81	4,600	5 yr.	ACRS	2,668
Delivery vans	2/15/82	24,850	3 yr.	ACRS	15,655
Office furniture	4/2/82	6,250	5 yr.	ACRS	2,312
Business auto	8/1/82	8,320	3 yr.	ACRS	5,242
Office equipment‡	1/9/84	6,320	5 yr.	ACRS	—

*The business building, located in Philadelphia, was sold on 1/4/84 for $82,400. Richard now leases office space in the Fairfax location.

†The counters were also sold on 1/4/84 to a different buyer for $4,100. An investment tax credit of $620 was claimed on the property in 1981.

‡Richard elects to immediately expense as much of this cost as possible, and claim a 10% investment tax credit on the balance.

The accounting records also disclose the following account balances:

	12/31/83	12/31/84
Accounts receivable	$12,300	$12,950
Accounts payable	8,420	8,010
Merchandise inventory	20,620	27,430

CASE

2

9292 ☐ VOID ☐ CORRECTED For Official Use Only

Type or machine print PAYER'S name, street address, city, state, and ZIP code			OMB No. 1545-0112	**Interest Income**
Fox Valley Savings & Loan 1239 Burk Road Fairfax, VA 22030			19 Statement for Recipients of	
PAYER'S Federal identification number 22-65654	RECIPIENT'S identification number 583-44-8002	1 Earnings from savings and loan associations, credit unions, bank deposits, bearer certificates of deposit, etc. $752		**Copy A For Internal Revenue Service Center** For Paperwork Reduction Act Notice and instructions for completing this form, see Instructions for Form 1099 Series, 1098, 5498, and 1096.
Type or machine print RECIPIENT'S name (first, middle, last) Patricia Nelson		2 Amount of forfeiture	3 U.S. Savings Bonds, etc.	
Street address 1240 Sunnyvale Drive		4 Federal income tax withheld		
City, state, and ZIP code Fairfax, VA 22030		5 Foreign tax paid (if eligible for foreign tax credit)	6 Foreign country or U.S. possession	
Account number (optional)				

Form **1099-INT** Department of the Treasury - Internal Revenue Service

Do NOT Cut or Separate Forms on This Page

☐ VOID ☐ CORRECTED

PAYER'S name, street address, city, state, and ZIP code			OMB No. 1545-0110	**Dividends and Distributions**
International Business Machines 1212 Avenue of the Americas New York, NY 10023		1 Gross dividends and other distributions on stock $623	Statement for Recipients of	
		2 Dividends qualifying for exclusion $623		
PAYER'S Federal identification number 54-66453	RECIPIENT'S identification number 582-22-6611	3 Dividends not qualifying for exclusion	4 Federal income tax withheld	**Copy C For Payer**
RECIPIENT'S name (first, middle, last) Richard Nelson		5 Capital gain distributions	6 Nontaxable distributions (if determinable)	For Paperwork Reduction Act Notice and instructions for completing this form, see Instructions for Form 1099 Series, 1098, 5498, and 1096.
Street address 1240 Sunnyvale Drive		7 Foreign tax paid	8 Foreign country or U.S. possession	
City, state, and ZIP code Fairfax, VA 22030		**Liquidation Distributions**		
Account number (optional)		9 Cash	10 Noncash (Fair market value)	

Form **1099-DIV** Department of the Treasury - Internal Revenue Service

The Nelson's other sources of income in 1984 included interest (per Form 1099-INT above), dividends (per Form 1099-DIV above), $3,600 from the sale on 2/14/84 of 90 shares of IBM stock (originally acquired on 12/3/83 for $4,100), a $696 prize (per Form 1099-MISC, on next page) and $9,600 of rent receipts from a rental property located at 1122 Chainbridge Road, Fairfax. The new rental condominium was acquired on 8/8/84 for $60,000 (ACRS recovery), and the Nelsons spent $3,000 for furniture and appliances to furnish the apartment on 8/12/84. Expenses incurred on the property in 1984 include $980 property taxes, $4,210 interest, and $180 repairs.

The Nelsons sold their Philadelphia residence on 1/18/84 for $92,300.

9595 ☐ VOID ☐ CORRECTED For Official Use Only

Type or machine print PAYER'S name, street address, city, state, and ZIP code		1 Rents	OMB No. 1545-0115	**Miscellaneous Income**
Heck Department Stores 1220 B Street Washington, D.C. 22010		2 Royalties	Statement for Recipients of	
PAYER'S Federal identification number 66-43432	RECIPIENT'S identification number 583-44-8002	3 Prizes and awards $696	4 Federal income tax withheld	**Copy A For Internal Revenue Service Center**
Type or machine print RECIPIENT'S name (first, middle, last) Patricia Nelson		5 Fishing boat proceeds	6 Medical and health care payments	For Paperwork Reduction Act Notice and instructions for completing this form, see Instructions for Form 1099 Series, 1098, 5498, and 1096.
Street address 1240 Sunnyvale Drive Fairfax, VA 22030		7 Nonemployee compensation	8 Substitute payments in lieu of dividends or interest	
City, state, and ZIP code		9 Payer made direct sales of $5,000 or more of consumer products to a buyer (recipient) for resale ▶ ☐		
Account number (optional)				

Form **1099-MISC** **Do NOT Cut or Separate Forms on This Page** Department of the Treasury - Internal Revenue Service

The residence was originally acquired on 2/12/80 for $73,400, and selling expenses of $4,600 were incurred on the sale. The Nelsons purchased a new residence in Fairfax on 1/2/84 for $82,850. (NOTE: The Nelsons elect to deduct as much of the selling expenses as possible on the moving expense calculation, with the balance reducing the amount realized on the sale of the old residence.)

On 12/28/84, the Nelsons sold a five-acre plot of land located in Hollywood, Florida. The land was originally acquired on 2/3/77 for $9,440, and was sold for a total consideration of $16,100, payable as follows: $4,100 down payment, and three annual payments of $4,000 plus 12% interest on the unpaid balance, beginning on 12/28/85. The Nelsons incurred $220 of selling expenses on the transfer of the property.

The Nelsons have prepared the following list of 1984 personal expenditures for consideration as possible deductions in the preparation of their 1984 return:

$10,962	unreimbursed damages to their recreational vehicle by fire on 1/15/84 (the vehicle was acquired on 2/12/80 for $12,000, and the Nelsons had inadvertently allowed the insurance coverage to lapse)
1,032	payment to United Van Lines to move personal effects to Fairfax
126	meal and lodging expenses incurred in the move from Philadelphia to Fairfax (additionally, the two family cars were each driven 290 miles in the move)
84	contribution to the Democratic National Party
352	premiums on homeowner's insurance policy

68	interest expense paid on Mastercharge credit card in 1984
22	federal excise taxes paid on phone installations in Fairfax
296	cost of eyeglasses for Richard and Melissa
2,124	unreimbursed hospital expenses for Alice Nelson, Richard's mother
1,346	real estate taxes on personal residence in Fairfax
90	dues to professional business society (Richard)
120	fee for preparation of 1983 federal and state income tax returns
6,320	interest paid on home mortgage
346	interest paid on personal automobile loan at First National Bank
4,960	payments to Childworld Nursery to care for Melissa and Phyllis while Richard and Patricia were at work
1,296	premiums for health insurance coverage for the family
660	payment to insulate the Fairfax residence (which was originally constructed in 1972)
50	fee for car licenses ($25 flat fee per automobile)
2,420	contributions to First Methodist Church of Fairfax
230	unreimbursed physician charges
300	contribution to the Heart Fund
86	vaccinations for the family cats
924	state sales taxes, based on actual receipts (assume that the amount is larger than the amount provided in the optional sales tax tables)
403	state sales tax on new personal automobile (not included in the $924)

Richard furnishes the following record of 1984 federal and state estimated tax payments related to his self-employment income:

DATE	FEDERAL	STATE
4/12/84	$4,600	$1,000
6/10/84	4,600	1,000
9/18/84	4,600	1,000
12/20/84	4,600	1,000

Finally, Richard and Patricia believe that they may benefit from income averaging in 1984, and they furnish the following combined taxable incomes for the three prior tax years:

1981	$22,300
1982	28,500
1983	38,400

REQUIRED: Prepare in good form a 1984 Form 1040 for Richard and Patricia Nelson, with accompanying Schedules A, B, C, D, E, G, SE, and W, and Forms 2106, 2119, 2441, 3468, 3903, 4255, 4562 (business), 4562 (rental property), 4684, 4797, 5695, and 6252. The Nelsons do not elect to contribute to the Presidential Election Campaign Fund. The forms necessary to complete this problem begin on the next page.

Form **1040** Department of the Treasury—Internal Revenue Service
U.S. Individual Income Tax Return **1984** (0)

For the year January 1-December 31, 1984, or other tax year beginning , 1984, ending 19 | OMB No. 1545-0074

Use IRS label. Otherwise, please print or type.

Your first name and initial (if joint return, also give spouse's name and initial) | Last name | **Your social security number**

Present home address (Number and street, including apartment number, or rural route) | **Spouse's social security number**

City, town or post office, State, and ZIP code | Your occupation | Spouse's occupation

Presidential Election Campaign ▶ Do you want $1 to go to this fund? Yes No
If joint return, does your spouse want $1 to go to this fund? Yes No

Note: *Checking "Yes" will not change your tax or reduce your refund.*

For Privacy Act and Paperwork Reduction Act Notice, see Instructions.

Filing Status

Check only one box.

1 Single
2 Married filing joint return (even if only one had income)
3 Married filing separate return. Enter spouse's social security no. above and full name here.
4 Head of household (with qualifying person). (See page 5 of Instructions.) If the qualifying person is your unmarried child but not your dependent, write child's name here.
5 Qualifying widow(er) with dependent child (Year spouse died ▶ 19). (See page 6 of Instructions.)

Exemptions

Always check the box labeled Yourself. Check other boxes if they apply.

6a Yourself | 65 or over | Blind
b Spouse | 65 or over | Blind
Enter number of boxes checked on 6a and b ▶

c First names of your dependent children who lived with you
Enter number of children listed on 6c ▶

d Other dependents:

(1) Name	(2) Relationship	(3) Number of months lived in your home	(4) Did dependent have income of $1,000 or more?	(5) Did you provide more than one-half of dependent's support?

Enter number of other dependents ▶

e Total number of exemptions claimed (also complete line 36). Add numbers entered in boxes above ▶

Income

Please attach Copy B of your Forms W-2, W-2G, and W-2P here.

If you do not have a W-2, see page 4 of Instructions.

Please attach check or money order here.

7 Wages, salaries, tips, etc. | 7
8 Interest income *(also attach Schedule B if over $400)* | 8
9a Dividends *(also attach Schedule B if over $400)* , 9b Exclusion
c Subtract line 9b from line 9a and enter the result | 9c
10 Refunds of State and local income taxes, from the worksheet on page 9 of Instructions *(do not enter an amount unless you itemized deductions for those taxes in an earlier year—see page 9)* | 10
11 Alimony received | 11
12 Business income or (loss) *(attach Schedule C)* | 12
13 Capital gain or (loss) *(attach Schedule D)* | 13
14 40% of capital gain distributions not reported on line 13 (see page 9 of Instructions) | 14
15 Supplemental gains or (losses) *(attach Form 4797)* | 15
16 Fully taxable pensions, IRA distributions, and annuities not reported on line 17 | 16
17a Other pensions and annuities, including rollovers. Total received | 17a
b Taxable amount, if any, from the worksheet on page 10 of Instructions | 17b
18 Rents, royalties, partnerships, estates, trusts, etc. *(attach Schedule E)* | 18
19 Farm income or (loss) *(attach Schedule F)* | 19
20a Unemployment compensation (insurance). Total received | 20a
b Taxable amount, if any, from the worksheet on page 10 of Instructions | 20b
21a Social security benefits. (see page 10 of Instructions) | 21a
b Taxable amount, if any, from the worksheet on page 11 of Instructions | 21b
22 Other income (state nature and source—see page 11 of Instructions) | 22
23 Add lines 7 through 22. This is your **total income** ▶ | 23

Adjustments to Income

(See Instructions on page 11.)

24 Moving expense *(attach Form 3903 or 3903F)* | 24
25 Employee business expenses *(attach Form 2106)* | 25
26a IRA deduction, from the worksheet on page 12 | 26a
b Enter here IRA payments you made in 1985 that are included in line 26a above ▶
27 Payments to a Keogh *(H.R. 10)* retirement plan | 27
28 Penalty on early withdrawal of savings | 28
29 Alimony paid | 29
30 Deduction for a married couple when both work *(attach Schedule W)* | 30
31 Add lines 24 through 30. These are your **total adjustments** ▶ | 31

Adjusted Gross Income

32 Subtract line 31 from line 23. *This is your* **adjusted gross income.** *If this line is less than $10,000, see "Earned Income Credit" (line 59) on page 16 of Instructions. If you want IRS to figure your tax, see page 12 of Instructions.* ▶ | 32

Tax Computation

(See Instructions on page 13.)

33 Amount from line 32 (adjusted gross income) 33

34a If you itemize, attach Schedule A (Form 1040) and enter the amount from Schedule A, line 26 . . . . 34a

Caution: If you have unearned income and can be claimed as a dependent on your parent's return, check here ▶ ☐ and see page 13 of the Instructions. Also see page 13 if:
- You are married filing a separate return and your spouse itemizes deductions, OR
- You file Form 4563, OR
- You are a dual-status alien.

34b If you do not itemize deductions, and you have charitable contributions, complete the worksheet on page 14. Then enter the allowable part of your contributions here 34b

35 Subtract line 34a or 34b, whichever applies, from line 33 35

36 Multiply $1,000 by the total number of exemptions claimed on Form 1040, line 6e 36

37 Taxable Income. Subtract line 36 from line 35 37

38 Tax. Enter tax here and check if from ☐ Tax Table, ☐ Tax Rate Schedule X, Y, or Z, or ☐ Schedule G 38

39 Additional Taxes. (See page 14 of Instructions.) Enter here and check if from ☐ Form 4970, ☐ Form 4972, or ☐ Form 5544 39

40 Add lines 38 and 39. Enter the total . . . . ▶ 40

Credits

(See Instructions on page 14.)

41 Credit for child and dependent care expenses *(attach Form 2441)* 41

42 Credit for the elderly and the permanently and totally disabled *(attach Schedule R)* 42

43 Residential energy credit *(attach Form 5695)* 43

44 Partial credit for political contributions for which you have receipts 44

45 Add lines 41 through 44. These are your total personal credits 45

46 Subtract line 45 from 40. Enter the result (but not less than zero) 46

47 Foreign tax credit *(attach Form 1116)* 47

48 General business credit. Check if from ☐ Form 3800, ☐ Form 3468, ☐ Form 5884, ☐ Form 6478 48

49 Add lines 47 and 48. These are your total business and other credits 49

50 Subtract line 49 from 46. Enter the result (but not less than zero) . . . . ▶ 50

Other Taxes

(Including Advance EIC Payments)

51 Self-employment tax *(attach Schedule SE)* 51

52 Alternative minimum tax *(attach Form 6251)* 52

53 Tax from recapture of investment credit *(attach Form 4255)* 53

54 Social security tax on tip income not reported to employer *(attach Form 4137)* 54

55 Tax on an IRA *(attach Form 5329)* 55

■

56 Add lines 50 through 55. This is your **total tax** . . . . ▶ 56

Payments

Attach Forms W-2, W-2G, and W-2P to front.

57 Federal income tax withheld 57

58 1984 estimated tax payments and amount applied from 1983 return . 58

59 Earned income credit. If line 33 is under $10,000, see page 16 . 59

60 Amount paid with Form 4868 60

61 Excess social security tax and RRTA tax withheld (two or more employers) 61

62 Credit for Federal tax on gasoline and special fuels *(attach Form 4136)* 62

63 Regulated Investment Company credit *(attach Form 2439)* 63

64 Add lines 57 through 63. These are your **total payments** . . . . ▶ 64

Refund or Amount You Owe

65 If line 64 is larger than line 56, enter amount **OVERPAID** . . . . ▶ 65

66 Amount of line 65 to be **REFUNDED TO YOU** . . . . ▶ 66

67 Amount of line 65 to be applied to your 1985 estimated tax . . . ▶ 67

68 If line 56 is larger than line 64, enter **AMOUNT YOU OWE.** Attach check or money order for full amount payable to "Internal Revenue Service." Write your social security number and "1984 Form 1040" on it . . ▶ 68

(Check ▶ ☐ if Form 2210 (2210F) is attached. See page 17 of Instructions.) $

Please Sign Here

Under penalties of perjury, I declare that I have examined this return and accompanying schedules and statements, and to the best of my knowledge and belief, they are true, correct, and complete. Declaration of preparer (other than taxpayer) is based on all information of which preparer has any knowledge.

Your signature | Date | Spouse's signature (if filing jointly, BOTH must sign)

Paid Preparer's Use Only

Preparer's signature | Date | Check if self-employed ☐ | Preparer's social security no.

Firm's name (or yours, if self-employed) and address | E.I. No. | ZIP code

☆ U.S.GPO:1984-0-423-073 ☆ E.I.#430814328

SCHEDULES A&B (Form 1040)

Department of the Treasury
Internal Revenue Service (0)

Schedule A—Itemized Deductions

(Schedule B is on back)

▶ Attach to Form 1040. ▶ See Instructions for Schedules A and B (Form 1040).

OMB No. 1545-0074

1984

07

Name(s) as shown on Form 1040

Your social security number

Section	Line	Description	Box	Amount	Total line	Total
Medical and Dental Expenses	1	Prescription medicines and drugs; and insulin	1			
(Do not include expenses reimbursed or paid by others.)	2 a	Doctors, dentists, nurses, hospitals, insurance premiums you paid for medical and dental care, etc.	2a			
(See Instructions on page 19)	b	Transportation and lodging	2b			
	c	Other (list—include hearing aids, dentures, eyeglasses, etc.) ▶	2c			
	3	Add lines 1 through 2c, and write the total here	3			
	4	Multiply the amount on Form 1040, line 33, by 5% (.05)	4			
	5	Subtract line 4 from line 3. If zero or less, write -0-. **Total** medical and dental ▶			5	
Taxes You Paid	6	State and local income taxes	6			
(See Instructions on page 20)	7	Real estate taxes	7			
	8 a	General sales tax (see sales tax tables in instruction booklet)	8a			
	b	General sales tax on motor vehicles	8b			
	9	Other taxes (list—include personal property taxes) ▶	9			
	10	Add the amounts on lines 6 through 9. Write the total here. **Total** taxes ▶			10	
Interest You Paid	11 a	Home mortgage interest you paid to financial institutions	11a			
(See Instructions on page 20)	b	Home mortgage interest you paid to individuals (show that person's name and address) ▶	11b			
	12	Total credit card and charge account interest you paid	12			
	13	Other interest you paid (list) ▶	13			
	14	Add the amounts on lines 11a through 13. Write the total here. **Total** interest ▶			14	
Contributions You Made	15 a	Cash contributions. (If you gave $3,000 or more to any one organization, report those contributions on line 15b.)	15a			
(See Instructions on page 20)	b	Cash contributions totaling $3,000 or more to any one organization. (Show to whom you gave and how much you gave.) ▶	15b			
	16	Other than cash (attach required statement)	16			
	17	Carryover from prior year	17			
	18	Add the amounts on lines 15a through 17. Write the total here. **Total** contributions ▶			18	
Casualty and Theft Losses	19	Total casualty or theft loss(es). (You must attach Form 4684 or similar statement.) (see page 21 of Instructions) ▶			19	
Miscellaneous Deductions	20	Union and professional dues	20			
(See Instructions on page 21)	21	Tax return preparation fee	21			
	22	Other (list type and amount) ▶	22			
	23	Add the amounts on lines 20 through 22. Write the total here. **Total** miscellaneous ▶			23	
Summary of Itemized Deductions	24	Add the amounts on lines 5, 10, 14, 18, 19, and 23. Write your answer here.			24	
(See Instructions on page 22)	25	If you checked Form 1040 { Filing Status box 2 or 5, write $3,400; Filing Status box 1 or 4, write $2,300; Filing Status box 3, write $1,700 }			25	
	26	Subtract line 25 from line 24. Write your answer here and on Form 1040, line 34a. (If line 25 is more than line 24, see the Instructions for line 26 on page 22.) ▶			26	

For Paperwork Reduction Act Notice, see Form 1040 Instructions.

Schedule B—Interest and Dividend Income

08 OMB No. 1545-0074

Name(s) as shown on Form 1040 (Do not enter name and social security number if shown on other side.)

Your social security number

Part I Interest Income

(See Instructions on pages 8 and 22)

Also complete Part III.

If you received more than $400 in interest income, you must complete Part I and list ALL interest received. If you received interest as a nominee for another, or you received or paid accrued interest on securities transferred between interest payment dates, or you received any interest from an All-Savers Certificate, see page 22.

Interest income		Amount
1 Interest income from seller-financed mortgages. (See Instructions and show name of payer.) ▶	1	
2 Other interest income (list name of payer) ▶	2	
3 Add the amounts on lines 1 and 2. Write the total here and on Form 1040, line 8 ▶	3	

Part II Dividend Income

(See Instructions on pages 8 and 22)

Also complete Part III.

If you received more than $400 in gross dividends (including capital gain distributions) and other distributions on stock, or you are electing to exclude qualified reinvested dividends from a public utility, complete Part II. If you received dividends as a nominee for another, see page 22.

Name of payer				Amount
4			4	
5 Add the amounts on line 4. Write the total here			5	
6 Capital gain distributions. Enter here and on line 15, Schedule D.*	6			
7 Nontaxable distributions. (See Schedule D Instructions for adjustment to basis.)	7			
8 Exclusion of qualified reinvested dividends from a public utility. (See page 23 of Instructions.)	8			
9 Add the amounts on lines 6, 7, and 8. Write the total here			9	
10 Subtract line 9 from line 5. Write the result here and on Form 1040, line 9a ▶			10	

**If you received capital gain distributions for the year and you do not need Schedule D to report any other gains or losses, do not file that schedule. Instead, enter 40% of your capital gain distributions on Form 1040, line 14.*

Part III Foreign Accounts and Foreign Trusts

(See Instructions on page 23)

If you received more than $400 of interest or dividends, OR if you had a foreign account or were a grantor of, or a transferor to, a foreign trust, you must answer both questions in Part III.	Yes	No
11 At any time during the tax year, did you have an interest in or a signature or other authority over a bank account, securities account, or other financial account in a foreign country? (See page 23 of the Instructions for exceptions and filing requirements for Form TD F 90-22.1.)		
If "Yes," write the name of the foreign country ▶		
12 Were you the grantor of, or transferor to, a foreign trust which existed during the current tax year, whether or not you have any beneficial interest in it? If "Yes," you may have to file Forms 3520, 3520-A, or 926.		

For Paperwork Reduction Act Notice, see Form 1040 Instructions.

SCHEDULE C (Form 1040)

Department of the Treasury
Internal Revenue Service

Profit or (Loss) From Business or Profession
(Sole Proprietorship)

Partnerships, Joint Ventures, etc., Must File Form 1065.

▶ **Attach to Form 1040 or Form 1041.** ▶ **See Instructions for Schedule C (Form 1040).**

OMB No. 1545-0074

1984
09

Name of proprietor | **Social security number**

A Main business activity (see Instructions) ▶ Product or Service ▶

B Business name and address ▶ C Employer ID number

D Method(s) used to value closing inventory:
(1) ☐ Cost (2) ☐ Lower of cost or market (3) ☐ Other (attach explanation)

E Accounting method: (1) ☐ Cash (2) ☐ Accrual (3) ☐ Other (specify) ▶

	Yes	No
F Was there any change in determining quantities, costs, or valuations between opening and closing inventory? If "Yes," attach explanation.		
G Did you deduct expenses for an office in your home?		

Part I Income

1 a Gross receipts or sales	1a	
b Less: Returns and allowances	1b	
c Subtract line 1b from line 1a and enter the balance here	1c	
2 Cost of goods sold and/or operations (from Part III, line 8)	2	
3 Subtract line 2 from line 1c and enter the **gross profit** here	3	
4 a Windfall Profit Tax Credit or Refund received in 1984 (see Instructions)	4a	
b Other income	4b	
5 Add lines 3, 4a, and 4b. This is the **gross income** ▶	5	

Part II Deductions

6 Advertising		23 Repairs	
7 Bad debts from sales or services (Cash method taxpayers, see Instructions)		24 Supplies (not included in Part III below)	
8 Bank service charges		25 Taxes (Do not include Windfall Profit Tax here. See line 29.)	
9 Car and truck expenses		26 Travel and entertainment	
10 Commissions		27 Utilities and telephone	
11 Depletion		28 a Wages	
12 Depreciation and Section 179 deduction from Form 4562 (not included in Part III below)		b Jobs credit	
		c Subtract line 28b from 28a	
		29 Windfall Profit Tax withheld in 1984	
13 Dues and publications		30 Other expenses (specify):	
14 Employee benefit programs		a	
15 Freight (not included in Part III below)		b	
16 Insurance		c	
17 Interest on business indebtedness		d	
18 Laundry and cleaning		e	
19 Legal and professional services		f	
20 Office expense		g	
21 Pension and profit-sharing plans		h	
22 Rent on business property		i	

31 Add amounts in columns for lines 6 through 30i. These are the **total deductions** ▶	31	
32 **Net profit or (loss).** Subtract line 31 from line 5 and enter the result. If a profit, enter on Form 1040, line 12, and on Schedule SE, Part I, line 2 (or Form 1041, line 6). If a loss, you **MUST** go on to line 33	32	

33 If you have a loss, you **MUST** answer this question: "Do you have amounts for which you are not at risk in this business (see Instructions)?" ☐ Yes ☐ No
If "Yes," you **MUST** attach **Form 6198.** If "No," enter the loss on Form 1040, line 12, and on Schedule SE, Part I, line 2 (or Form 1041, line 6).

Part III Cost of Goods Sold and/or Operations (See Schedule C Instructions for Part III)

1 Inventory at beginning of year (if different from last year's closing inventory, attach explanation)	1	
2 Purchases less cost of items withdrawn for personal use	2	
3 Cost of labor (do not include salary paid to yourself)	3	
4 Materials and supplies	4	
5 Other costs	5	
6 Add lines 1 through 5	6	
7 Less: Inventory at end of year	7	
8 **Cost of goods sold and/or operations.** Subtract line 7 from line 6. Enter here and in Part I, line 2, above.	8	

SCHEDULE D
(Form 1040)

Department of the Treasury
Internal Revenue Service (0)

Capital Gains and Losses

(Also reconciliation of sales of stocks, bonds, and bartering income from Forms 1099-B)

▶ **Attach to Form 1040.** ▶ **See Instructions for Schedule D (Form 1040).**

OMB No. 1545-0074

1984

12

Name(s) as shown on Form 1040 | **Your social security number**

Part I Short-term Capital Gains and Losses-Assets Held One Year or Less (6 months if acquired after 6/22/84)

a. Description of property (Example, 100 shares 7% preferred of "Z" Co.)	**b.** Date acquired (Mo., day, yr.)	**c.** Date sold (Mo., day, yr.)	**d.** Gross sales price	**e.** Cost or other basis (see instructions)	**f.** LOSS If column (e) is more than (d) subtract (d) from (e)	**g.** GAIN If column (d) is more than (e) subtract (e) from (d)
1						

2 Short-term gain from sale or exchange of a principal residence from Form 2119, lines 7 or 11	2		
3 Short-term gain from installment sales from Form 6252, lines 22 or 30	3		
4 Net short-term gain or (loss) from partnerships, S corporations, and fiduciaries	4		
5 Add lines 1 through 4 in columns f and g	5	( )	
6 Combine columns f and g of line 5 and enter the net gain or (loss)		6	
7 Short-term capital loss carryover from years beginning after 1969		7	( )
8 Net short-term gain or (loss), combine lines 6 and 7		8	

Part II Long-term Capital Gains and Losses-Assets Held More Than One Year (6 months if acquired after 6/22/84)

a	b	c	d	e	f	g
9						

10 Long-term gain from sale or exchange of a principal residence from Form 2119, lines 7, 11, 16, or 18	10		
11 Long-term gain from installment sales from Form 6252, lines 22 or 30	11		
12 Net long-term gain or (loss) from partnerships, S corporations, and fiduciaries	12		
13 Add lines 9 through 12 in columns f and g	13	( )	
14 Combine columns f and g of line 13 and enter the net gain or (loss)		14	
15 Capital gain distributions		15	
16 Enter gain from Form 4797, line 6(a)(1)		16	
17 Combine lines 14 through 16		17	
18 Long-term capital loss carryover from years beginning after 1969		18	( )
19 Net long-term gain or (loss), combine lines 17 and 18		19	

Note: *Complete the back of this form. However, if you have capital loss carryovers from years beginning before 1970, do not complete Parts III or IV. See Form 4798 instead.*

Name(s) as shown on Form 1040 (Do not enter name and social security number if shown on other side) | Your social security number

Part III Summary of Parts I and II

20 Combine lines 8 and 19, and enter the net gain or (loss) here 20

Note: *If line 20 is a loss, skip lines 21 through 23 and complete lines 24 and 25. If line 20 is a gain complete lines 21 through 23 and skip lines 24 and 25.*

21 If line 20 shows a gain, enter the smaller of line 19 or line 20. Enter zero if there is a loss or no entry on line 19. 21

22 Enter 60% of line 21 22

If line 22 is more than zero, you may be liable for the alternative minimum tax. See Form 6251.

23 Subtract line 22 from line 20. Enter here and on Form 1040, line 13 23

24 If line 20 shows a loss, enter one of the following amounts:

a If line 8 is zero or a net gain, enter 50% of line 20;

b If line 19 is zero or a net gain, enter line 20; or

c If line 8 and line 19 are net losses, enter amount on line 8 added to 50% of the amount on line 19 . 24

25 Enter here and as a loss on Form 1040, line 13, the smallest of:

a The amount on line 24;

b $3,000 ($1,500 if married and filing a separate return); or

c Taxable income, as adjusted. 25

Part IV Computation of Post-1969 Capital Loss Carryovers from 1984 to 1985

(Complete this part if the loss on line 24 is more than the loss on line 25)

26 Enter loss shown on line 8; if none, enter zero and skip lines 27 through 30, then go to line 31 26

27 Enter gain shown on line 19. If that line is blank or shows a loss, enter zero 27

28 Reduce any loss on line 26 to the extent of any gain on line 27 28

29 Enter smaller of line 25 or line 28 29

30 Subtract line 29 from line 28. This is your short-term capital loss carryover from 1984 to 1985 . . . 30

31 Subtract line 29 from line 25. (Note: If you skipped lines 27 through 30, enter amount from line 25) 31

32 Enter loss from line 19; if none, enter zero and skip lines 33 through 36 32

33 Enter gain shown on line 8. If that line is blank or shows a loss, enter zero 33

34 Reduce any loss on line 32 to the extent of any gain on line 33 34

35 Multiply amount on line 31 by 2 35

36 Subtract line 35 from line 34. This is your long-term capital loss carryover from 1984 to 1985 36

Part V Complete this Part Only If You Elect Out of the Installment Method and Report a Note or Other Obligation at Less Than Full Face Value

☐ Check here if you elect out of the installment method.

Enter the face amount of the note or other obligation. ▶ ....

Enter the percentage of valuation of the note or other obligation. ▶ ....

Part VI Reconciliation of Forms 1099-B With Tax Return (Complete this part if you received one or more Forms 1099-B or equivalent statement reporting sales of stock, bonds, etc. or bartering income.)

SECTION A.—Reconciliation of Sales of Stocks, Bonds, etc.

37 Total sales of stock, bonds, etc. from Forms 1099-B or equivalent statement received from your brokers 37

38 Proceeds from sale or exchange of capital assets reported on Schedule D, but not included in line 37 38

39 Add lines 37 and 38. 39

40 Part of line 37 not reported on Schedule D this year, attach explanation 40

41 Subtract line 40 from line 39 41

Note: *The amount on line 41 should be the same as the total of all amounts on page 1, lines 1 and 9 of column d.*

SECTION B.—Reconciliation of Bartering Income

Indicate below the amount of bartering income reported on each form or schedule | Amount of bartering from Form 1099-B or equivalent statement

42 Form 1040, line 22. 42

43 Schedule C (Form 1040) 43

44 Schedule D (Form 1040) 44

45 Schedule E (Form 1040) 45

46 Schedule F (Form 1040) 46

47 Other (identify) (if not taxable, indicate reason—attach additional sheets if necessary) ▶ 47

48 Total (add lines 42 through 47) 48

Note: *The amount on line 48 should be the same as the total bartering on all Forms 1099-B or equivalent statements received.*

☆ U.S. GOVERNMENT PRINTING OFFICE: 1984-423-091

SCHEDULE E (Form 1040)
Department of the Treasury
Internal Revenue Service (0)

Supplemental Income Schedule

(From rents and royalties, partnerships, estates, and trusts, etc.)
▶ **Attach to Form 1040.** ▶ **See Instructions for Schedule E (Form 1040).**

OMB No. 1545-0074
1984
13

Name(s) as shown on Form 1040 | **Your social security number**

Part I Rent and Royalty Income or Loss

1 Did you or a member of your family use for personal purposes any rental property listed below for more than the greater of 14 days or 10% of the total days rented at fair rental value during the tax year? . . . ☐ Yes ☐ No

2 Description of Properties (Show kind and location for each)

Property A ....

Property B ....

Property C

Rental and Royalty Income		**Properties** A	B	C	**Totals** (Add columns A, B, and C)	
3 a Rents received					3	
b Royalties received						
Rental and Royalty Expenses						
4 Advertising	4					
5 Auto and travel	5					
6 Cleaning and maintenance	6					
7 Commissions	7					
8 Insurance	8					
9 Interest	9					
10 Legal and other professional fees	10					
11 Repairs	11					
12 Supplies	12					
13 Taxes (Do **not** include Windfall Profit Tax here. See Part III, line 37.)	13					
14 Utilities	14					
15 Wages and salaries	15					
16 Other (list) ▶						
....						
....						
....						
....						
....						
....						
....						
....						
....						
17 Total expenses other than depreciation and depletion. Add lines 4 through 16	17				17	
18 Depreciation expense (see Instructions), or depletion	18				18	
19 Total. Add lines 17 and 18	19					
20 Income or (loss) from rental or royalty properties. Subtract line 19 from line 3a (rents) or 3b (royalties)	20					

21 Add properties with profits on line 20, and write the total profits here	21	
22 Add properties with losses on line 20, and write the total (losses) here	22	( )
23 Combine amounts on lines 21 and 22, and write the net profit or (loss) here	23	
24 Net farm rental profit or (loss) from Form 4835, line 49	24	
25 Total rental or royalty income or (loss). Combine amounts on lines 23 and 24, and write the total here. If Parts II, III, and IV on page 2 do not apply to you, write the amount from line 25 on Form 1040, line 18. Otherwise, include the amount in line 39 on page 2 of Schedule E	25	

For Paperwork Reduction Act Notice, see Form 1040 Instructions.

Name(s) as shown on Form 1040 (Do not enter name and social security number if shown on other side) | Your social security number

Part II Income or Losses from Partnerships, Estates or Trusts, or S Corporations

If you report a loss below, and have amounts invested in that activity for which you are not at risk, you may have to file Form 6198. See instructions.

	(a) Name	(b) Check if foreign partnership	(c) Employer identification number	(d) Net loss (see instructions for at-risk limitations)	(e) Net income
Partnerships					
	26 Add amounts in columns (d) and (e) and write the total(s) here		26	( )	
	27 Combine amounts in columns (d) and (e), line 26, and write the net income or (loss) here			27	
	28 Deduction for section 179 property (from Form 1065, Schedule K-1). (See Instructions for limitations.)			28	( )
	29 Total partnership income or (loss). Combine amounts on lines 27 and 28. Write the total here and include in line 39 below			29	
Estates or Trusts					
	30 Add amounts in columns (d) and (e) and write the total(s) here		30	( )	
	31 Total estate or trust income or (loss). Combine amounts in columns (d) and (e), line 30. Write the total here and include in line 39 below			31	
S Corporations					
	32 Add amounts in columns (d) and (e) and write the total(s) here		32	( )	
	33 Combine amounts in columns (d) and (e), line 32, and write the net income or (loss) here			33	
	34 Deduction for section 179 property (from Form 1120S, Schedule K-1). (See Instructions for limitations.)			34	( )
	35 Total S corporation income or (loss). Combine amounts on lines 33 and 34. Write the total here and include in line 39 below			35	

Part III Windfall Profit Tax Summary

36 Windfall profit tax credit or refund received in 1984 (see Instructions)	36	
37 Windfall profit tax withheld in 1984 (see Instructions)	37	( )
38 Combine amounts on lines 36 and 37. Write the total here and include in line 39 below	38	

Part IV Summary

39 TOTAL income or (loss). Combine lines 25, 29, 31, 35, and 38. Write total here and on Form 1040, line 18 ▶	39	
40 Farmers and fishermen: Write your share of GROSS FARMING AND FISHING INCOME applicable to Parts I and II.	40	

Part V Depreciation Claimed in Part I.—Complete only if property was placed in service before January 1, 1981. For more space, use a separate sheet. If you placed any property in service after December 31, 1980, use Form 4562 for all property; do NOT complete Part V.

	(a) Description of property	(b) Date acquired	(c) Cost or other basis	(d) Depreciation allowed or allowable in prior years	(e) Depreciation method	(f) Life or rate	(g) Depreciation for this year
Property A							
	Totals (Property A)						
Property B							
	Totals (Property B)						
Property C							
	Totals (Property C)						

☆ U.S. GOVERNMENT PRINTING OFFICE: 1984-423-095 23 188 5979

Schedule G (Form 1040)
Department of the Treasury
Internal Revenue Service

Income Averaging

▶ See instructions on back. ▶ Attach to Form 1040.

OMB No. 1545-0074

1984
16

Name(s) as shown on Form 1040 | Your social security number

Step 1 Add your income from 1981—1983

1981	1	Fill in the amount from your 1981 Form 1040 (line 34) or Form 1040A (line 12). If less than zero, enter zero	1	
1982	2	Fill in the amount from your 1982 Form 1040 (line 37), Form 1040A (line 16), or Form 1040EZ (line 7). If less than zero, enter zero	2	
1983	3	Fill in the amount from your 1983 Form 1040 (line 37), Form 1040A (line 19), or Form 1040EZ (line 7). If less than zero, enter zero	3	
Total	4	Fill in all income less deductions earned outside of the U.S. or within U.S. possessions and excluded for 1981 through 1983 (include housing exclusion in 1982 and 1983)	4	
	5	Add lines 1 through 4	5	

Step 2 Figure your averageable income

6	Divide the amount on line 5 by three (3)	6	
7	Multiply the amount on line 6 by 140% (1.4)	7	
8	Fill in your taxable income for 1984 from Form 1040, line 37	8	
9	If you received a premature or excessive distribution subject to a penalty under section 72, see instructions	9	
10	Subtract line 9 from line 8	10	
11	If you live in a community property state and are filing a separate return, see instructions	11	
12	Subtract line 11 from line 10. If less than zero, enter zero	12	
13	Write in the amount from line 7 above	13	
14	Subtract line 13 from line 12. This is your averageable income. If this line is $3,000 or less, do not complete the rest of this form	14	

Step 3 Figure your tax

15	Multiply the amount on line 14 by 25% (.25)			15	
16	Write in the amount from line 7 above			16	
17	Add lines 15 and 16			17	
18	Write in the amount from line 11 above			18	
19	Add lines 17 and 18			19	
20	Tax on amount on line 19 (from Tax Rate Schedule X, Y, or Z)			20	
21	Tax on amount on line 17 (from Tax Rate Schedule X, Y, or Z)	21			
22	Tax on amount on line 16 (from Tax Rate Schedule X, Y, or Z)	22			
23	Subtract line 22 from line 21	23			
24	Multiply the amount on line 23 by 3			24	
	If you have no entry on line 9, skip lines 25 through 27 and go to line 28.				
25	Tax on amount on line 8 (from Tax Rate Schedule X, Y, or Z)	25			
26	Tax on amount on line 10 (from Tax Rate Schedule X, Y, or Z)	26			
27	Subtract line 26 from line 25			27	
28	Add lines 20, 24, and 27. Write the result here and on Form 1040, line 38 if less than the tax figured using the tax rate schedules or table. Also, check the Schedule G box			28	

SCHEDULE SE (Form 1040)

Department of the Treasury
Internal Revenue Service

Computation of Social Security Self-Employment Tax

▶ See Instructions for Schedule SE (Form 1040).

▶ Attach to Form 1040.

OMB No. 1545-0074

1984

18

Name of **self-employed** person (as shown on social security card) | Social security number of **self-employed** person ▶

Part I Regular Computation of Net Earnings from Self-Employment

Note: *If you performed services for certain churches or church-controlled organizations and you are not a minister or a member of a religious order, see the instructions.*

1 Net profit or (loss) from Schedule F (Form 1040), line 56 or line 89, and farm partnerships, Schedule K-1 (Form 1065), line 17a . . .	1		
2 Net profit or (loss) from Schedule C (Form 1040), line 32, Schedule K-1 (Form 1065), line 17a (other than farming), and Form W-2 wages of $100 or more from an electing church or church-controlled organization (See instructions for other income to report.) . . .	2		

Note: ☐ Check here if you are **exempt** from self-employment tax on your earnings as a minister, member of a religious order, or Christian Science practitioner because you filed **Form 4361**. See instructions for kinds of income to report. If you have other earnings of $400 or more that are subject to self-employment tax, include those earnings on this line.

Part II Optional Computation of Net Earnings from Self-Employment (See "Who Can Use Schedule SE")

Generally, this part may be used **only** if you meet any of the following tests:

A Your gross farm profits (Schedule F (Form 1040), line 31 or line 87) were not more than $2,400, or

B Your gross farm profits (Schedule F (Form 1040), line 31 or line 87) were more than $2,400 and your net farm profits (Schedule F (Form 1040), line 56 or line 89) were less than $1,600, or

C Your net nonfarm profits (Schedule C (Form 1040), line 32) were less than $1,600 and also less than two-thirds (⅔) of your gross nonfarm income (Schedule C (Form 1040), line 5).

See instructions for other limitations.

3 Maximum income for optional methods . . .	3	$1,600	00
4 Farm Optional Method—If you meet test A or B above, enter: two-thirds (⅔) of gross profits from Schedule F (Form 1040), line 31 or line 87, and farm partnerships, Schedule K-1 (Form 1065), line 17b, or $1,600, whichever is smaller . . .	4		
5 Subtract line 4 from line 3 . . .	5		
6 Nonfarm Optional Method—If you meet test C, enter: the smaller of two-thirds (⅔) of gross nonfarm income from Schedule C (Form 1040), line 5, and Schedule K-1 (Form 1065), line 17c (other than farming), or $1,600, or, if you elected the farm optional method, the amount on line 5 . . .	6		

Part III Computation of Social Security Self-Employment Tax

7 Enter the amount from Part I, line 1, or, if you elected the farm optional method, Part II, line 4 . . .	7		
8 Enter the amount from Part I, line 2, or, if you elected the nonfarm optional method, Part II, line 6 . . .	8		
9 Add lines 7 and 8. If less than $400, you are not subject to self-employment tax. Do not fill in the rest of the schedule. (**Exception:** If this line is less than $400 and you are an employee of an electing church or church-controlled organization, complete the schedule unless this line is a loss. See instructions.) . . .	9		
10 The largest amount of combined wages and self-employment earnings subject to social security or railroad retirement tax (Tier I) for 1984 is . . .	10	$37,800	00
11 a Total social security wages and tips from Forms W-2 and railroad retirement compensation (Tier I). **Note:** U.S. Government employees whose wages are only subject to the 1.3% hospital insurance benefits tax (Medicare) and employees of certain church or church-controlled organizations, should not include those wages on this line (see instructions) . . . **11a**			
b Unreported tips subject to social security tax from Form 4137, line 9, or to railroad retirement tax (Tier I) . . . **11b**			
c Add lines 11a and 11b . . .	11c		
12 a Subtract line 11c from line 10. . . .	12a		
b Enter your "qualified" U.S. Government wages if you are required to use the worksheet in Part III of the instructions. **12b**			
c Enter your Form W-2 wages from an electing church or church-controlled organization. **12c**			
13 Enter the smaller of line 9 or line 12a . . .	13		
If line 13 is $37,800 or more, fill in $4,271.40 on line 14. Otherwise, multiply line 13 by .113 and enter the result on line 14 . . .		.113	
14 Self-employment tax. Enter this amount on Form 1040, line 51 . . .	14		

For Paperwork Reduction Act Notice, see Form 1040 Instructions.

Schedule W **(Form 1040)**
Department of the Treasury Internal Revenue Service

Deduction for a Married Couple When Both Work

▶ For Paperwork Reduction Act Notice, see Form 1040 Instructions.
▶ Attach to Form 1040.

OMB No. 1545-0074
1984
20

Names as shown on Form 1040 | Your social security number

Step 1 Figure your earned income

		(a) You		(b) Your spouse
1 Wages, salaries, tips, etc., from Form 1040, line 7. (Do not include nondisability pensions or annuities.)	1		1	
2 Net profit or (loss) from self-employment (from Schedules C and F (Form 1040), Schedule K-1 (Form 1065), and any other taxable self-employment or earned income)	2		2	
3 Add lines 1 and 2. This is your total earned income	3		3	

Step 2 Figure your qualified earned income

		(a) You		(b) Your spouse
4 Adjustments from Form 1040, lines 25, 26a, 27, and any repayment of sub-pay included on line 31. (See instructions below.)	4		4	
5 Subtract line 4 from line 3. This is your qualified earned income. (If the amount in column (a) or (b) is zero (-0-) or less, stop here. You may not take this deduction.)	5		5	

Step 3 Figure your deduction

6 Compare the amounts in columns (a) and (b) of line 5. Write the smaller amount here. (Write either amount if 5(a) and 5(b) are exactly the same.) ***Do not write more than $30,000***	6	
7 Percentage used to figure the deduction (10%)	7	x .10
8 Multiply the amount on line 6 by the percentage on line 7. This is the amount of your deduction. Write the answer here and on Form 1040, line 30 ▶	8	

Instructions

Complete this schedule and attach it to your Form 1040 if you take the deduction for a married couple when both work. You may take the deduction if both you and your spouse:

- work and have qualified earned income, and
- file a joint return, and
- do not file **Form 2555** to exclude income or to exclude or deduct certain housing costs, and
- do not file **Form 4563** to exclude income.

There are three steps to follow in figuring the deduction on Schedule W.

Step 1 (lines 1, 2, and 3).—Figure earned income separately for yourself and your spouse.

Step 2 (lines 4 and 5).—Figure qualified earned income separately for yourself and your spouse by subtracting certain adjustments from earned income.

Step 3 (lines 6, 7, and 8).—Figure the deduction based on the **smaller** of:

- the qualified earned income entered in column (a) or (b) of line 5, whichever is less, **OR**
- $30,000.

Earned income.—This is generally income you receive for services you provide. It includes wages, salaries, tips, commissions, certain disability income, sub-pay, etc. (from Form 1040, line 7). It also includes income earned from self-employment (from Schedules C and F of Form 1040 and Schedule K-1 of Form 1065), and net earnings and gains (other than capital gains) from the disposition, transfer, or licensing of property that you created. Earned income does not include interest, dividends, social security or tier 1 railroad retirement benefits, IRA distributions, unemployment compensation, deferred compensation, or nontaxable income. It also does not include any amount your spouse paid you.

Caution: *Do not consider community property laws in figuring your earned income.*

Qualified earned income.—This is the amount on which the deduction is based. Figure it by subtracting certain adjustments from earned income.

These adjustments (and the related lines on Form 1040) are:

- Employee business expenses (from line 25).
- Payments to an IRA (from line 26a).
- Payments to a Keogh plan (from line 27).
- Repayment of supplemental unemployment benefits (sub-pay) included in the total on line 31. See the instructions on repayment of sub-pay on page 12 of the Form 1040 Instructions.

Enter the total of any adjustments that apply to your or your spouse's earned income in the appropriate column of line 4.

Example.—You earned a salary of $20,000 and had $3,000 of employee business expenses (line 25 of Form 1040). Your spouse earned $17,000 and put $1,000 into an IRA (line 26a of Form 1040). Your qualified earned income is $17,000 ($20,000 minus $3,000) and your spouse's is $16,000 ($17,000 minus $1,000). Because your spouse's qualified earned income is less than yours, the deduction is figured on your spouse's income. Therefore, the deduction is $1,600 ($16,000 x .10).

Form **2106**

Department of the Treasury
Internal Revenue Service

Employee Business Expenses

(Please use Form 3903 to figure moving expense deduction.)

▶ **Attach to Form 1040.**

OMB No. 1545-0139

1984

54

Your name	Social security number	Occupation in which expenses were incurred

Part I Employee Business Expenses Deductible in Figuring Adjusted Gross Income on Form 1040, Line 32

1 Reimbursed and unreimbursed fares for airplane, boat, bus, taxicab, train, etc.	1	
2 Reimbursed and unreimbursed meal, lodging, and other expenses while away from your tax home	2	
3 Reimbursed and unreimbursed car expenses from Part II	3	
4 Reimbursed and unreimbursed outside salesperson's expenses other than those shown on lines 1 through 3. **Caution:** *Do not use this line unless you are an outside salesperson (see instructions).*	4	
5 Reimbursed expenses other than those shown on lines 1 through 3 (see instructions)	5	
6 Add lines 1 through 5	6	
7 Employer's payments for these expenses only if not included on Form W-2	7	
8 If line 6 is more than line 7, subtract line 7 from line 6. Enter here and on Form 1040, line 25	8	
9 If line 7 is more than line 6, subtract line 6 from line 7. Enter here and on Form 1040, line 7	9	

Part II Car Expenses (Use either your actual expenses or the mileage rate.)

	Car 1	Car 2	Car 3
A Number of months you used car for business during 1984	months	months	months
B Total mileage for months on line A	miles	miles	miles
C Business part of line B mileage	miles	miles	miles
D Date placed in service	/ /	/ /	/ /

Actual Expenses (Include expenses on lines 1 and 2 only for the months shown on line A, above.)

		Car 1	Car 2	Car 3
1 Gasoline, oil, lubrication, etc.	1			
2 Other	2			
3 Total (add lines 1 and 2)	3			
4 Divide line C by line B, above	4	%	%	%
5 Multiply line 3 by line 4	5			
6 Depreciation (see instructions)	6			
7 Business parking fees and tolls	7			
8 Add lines 5 through 7. Also enter in Part I, line 3.	8			

Mileage Rate

9 Enter the smaller of (a) 15,000 miles or (b) the total mileage (Car 1+ Car 2+ Car 3) from line C, above	9	miles
10 Multiply line 9 by 20½¢ (.205) (11¢ (.11) if applicable, see instructions)	10	
11 Enter the total mileage, if any (Car 1 + Car 2 + Car 3) from line C that is over 15,000 miles	11	miles
12 Multiply line 11 by 11¢ (.11) and enter here	12	
13 Business part of car interest, parking fees, tolls, and State and local taxes (except gasoline tax)	13	
14 Total (add lines 10, 12, and 13). Enter here and in Part I, line 3.	14	

Part III Information About Educational Expenses Shown in Part I or on Schedule A (Form 1040)

1 Did you need this education to meet the minimum educational requirements for your business or profession? ☐ Yes ☐ No

2 Will this study program qualify you for a new business or profession? ☐ Yes ☐ No

Note: *If your answer to question 1 or 2 is "Yes," stop here. You cannot deduct these expenses, even if you do not intend to change your business or profession.*

3 If "No," list the courses you took and their relationship to your business or profession ▶

Changes You Should Note

New rules apply that may limit the amount of your recovery deduction for depreciation and investment credit for certain property used in your trade or business and placed in service after June 18, 1984.

- For calendar year 1984, the recovery deduction for a "passenger automobile" may not exceed $4,000, and the investment credit may not exceed $1,000. In figuring your recovery deduction, for purposes of this limitation, the section 179 expense deduction is treated as a recovery deduction. These amounts are reduced if your business use is less than 100%.
- The section 179 expense deduction and investment credit are not allowed for certain property such as "passenger automobiles" and other transportation property used 50% or less in your trade or business. Additionally, if you use the property 50% or less in a trade or business, you must use the straight-line method of depreciation.
- No deduction for recovery depreciation or investment credit will be allowed for an employee's "passenger automobile" or other transportation property unless such use is for the convenience of the employer and required as a condition of employment.
- New recordkeeping rules for trade or business expenses will apply beginning in 1985. See **Important Tax Law Changes** on page 2 of your 1984 Form 1040 Instructions.

See **Publications 572**, Investment Credit and **534**, Depreciation, for more detail on the kinds of property to which the above limitations apply. Also, see **Forms 3468**, Computation of Investment Credit, and **4562**, Depreciation and Amortization, for additional information.

For Paperwork Reduction Act Notice, see instructions on back.

Form **2119**

Department of the Treasury
Internal Revenue Service

Sale or Exchange of Principal Residence

▶ See instructions on back.

▶ Attach to Form 1040 for year of sale (see instruction B).

OMB No. 1545-0072

1984
21

Do not include expenses that you deduct as moving expenses.

Name(s) as shown on Form 1040 | **Your social security number**

1 (a) Date former residence sold ▶

(b) Enter the face amount of any mortgage, note (for example, second trust), or other financial instrument on which you will receive periodic payments of principal or interest from this sale ▶

2 (a) If you bought or built a new residence, enter date you occupied it; otherwise enter "none"

(b) Are any rooms in either residence rented out or used for business for which a deduction is allowed? ☐ Yes ☐ No
(If "Yes" do not include gain in line 7 from the rented or business part; instead include in income on Form 4797.)

Part I Gain and Adjusted Sales Price

3 Selling price of residence. (Do not include selling price of personal property items.)		**3**	
4 Commissions and other expenses of sale not deducted as moving expenses		**4**	
5 Amount realized (subtract line 4 from line 3)		**5**	
6 Basis of residence sold	**6**		
7 Gain on sale (subtract line 6 from line 5). If zero or less, enter zero and do not complete the rest of form. Enter the gain from this line on Schedule D, line 2 or 10*, unless you bought another principal residence or elect the exclusion in Part III.	**7**		
If you haven't replaced your residence, do you plan to do so within the replacement period? ☐ Yes ☐ No (If "Yes" see instruction B.)			
8 Fixing-up expenses (see instructions for time limits.)		**8**	
9 Adjusted sales price (subtract line 8 from line 5)		**9**	

Part II Gain to be Postponed and Adjusted Basis of New Residence

Do not complete this part if you check "Yes" to 14(d) to elect the Age 55 or over Exclusion in Part III.

10 Cost of new residence	**10**	
11 Gain taxable this year. (subtract line 10 from line 9). If result is zero or less, enter zero. Do not enter more than line 7. Enter the gain from this line on Schedule D, line 2 or 10.*	**11**	
12 Gain to be postponed (subtract line 11 from line 7)	**12**	
13 Adjusted basis of new residence (subtract line 12 from line 10)	**13**	

Part III 55 or over Exclusion, Gain to be Reported, and Adjusted Basis of New Residence

	Yes	No
14 (a) Were you 55 or over on date of sale?		
(b) Was your spouse 55 or over on date of sale? (If you answered "No" to 14(a) and (b), do not complete this part.)		
(c) Did the one who answered "Yes" to 14(a) or (b) own and use the property sold as his or her principal residence for a total of at least 3 years (except for short absences) of the 5-year period before the sale? (If "No," see Part II.)		
(d) If you answered "Yes" to 14(c), do you elect to take the once in a lifetime exclusion of the gain on the sale? (If "Yes," complete the rest of Part III. If "No," see Part II.)		
(e) At time of sale, was the residence owned by: ☐ you, ☐ your spouse, ☐ both of you?		
(f) Social security number of spouse, at time of sale, if different from number on Form 1040 ▶ (Enter "none" if you were not married at time of sale.)		

Do not complete rest of Part III if you did not check "Yes" to line 14(d).

15 Enter the smaller of line 7 or $125,000 ($62,500, if married filing separate return)	**15**	
16 Part of gain included (subtract line 15 from line 7)(If the result is zero, do not complete the rest of form.)	**16**	
17 Cost of new residence. If you did not buy a new principal residence, enter "None." Then enter the gain from line 16 on Schedule D, line 10,* and do not complete the rest of form	**17**	
18 Gain taxable this year. (subtract line 15 plus line 17 from line 9). If result is zero or less, enter zero. Do not enter more than line 16. Enter the gain from this line on Schedule D, line 10.*	**18**	
19 Gain to be postponed (subtract line 18 from line 16)	**19**	
20 Adjusted basis of new residence (subtract line 19 from line 17)	**20**	

***Caution:** If you completed Form 6252 for the residence in 1(a), do not enter your taxable gain from Form 2119 on Schedule D.

For Paperwork Reduction Act Notice, see back of form.

Form **2441**

Department of the Treasury
Internal Revenue Service

Credit for Child and Dependent Care Expenses

▶ Attach to Form 1040.
▶ See Instructions below.

OMB No. 1545-0068

1984
23

Name(s) as shown on Form 1040 | Your social security number

1 Write the number of qualifying persons who were cared for in 1984. (See the instructions below for the definition of qualifying persons.) . . . ▶ **1**

2 If payments listed on line 3 were made to an individual, complete the following: | Yes | No

a If you paid $50 or more in a calendar quarter to an individual, were the services performed in your home? . . . **2a**

b If "Yes," have you filed appropriate wage tax returns on wages for services in your home (see instructions for line 2)? **2b**

c If the answer to **b** is "Yes," write your employer identification number. . . . ▶ **2c**

3 Write the amount of qualified expenses you incurred and actually paid in 1984, but **do not** write more than $2,400 ($4,800 if you paid for the care of two or more qualifying persons) . . . **3**

4 You **must** write your earned income on line 4. See the instructions for line 4 for the definition of earned income.

- If you were **unmarried** at the end of 1984, write your earned income on line 4, **OR**
- If you are **married,** filing a joint return for 1984,
  - a write your earned income $ ____________, and
  - b write your spouse's earned income $ ____________, and
  - c compare amounts on lines 4a and 4b, and write the **smaller** of the two amounts on line 4. . . . **4**

5 Compare amounts on lines 3 and 4, and write the **smaller** of the two amounts on line 5 . . . **5**

6 Write the percentage from the table below that applies to the adjusted gross income on Form 1040, line 33. . . . **6**

If line 33 is: Over— But not over—	Percentage is:	If line 33 is: Over— But not over—	Percentage is:
0–$10,000	30% (.30)	$20,000–22,000	24% (.24)
$10,000–12,000	29% (.29)	22,000–24,000	23% (.23)
12,000–14,000	28% (.28)	24,000–26,000	22% (.22)
14,000–16,000	27% (.27)	26,000–28,000	21% (.21)
16,000–18,000	26% (.26)	28,000	20% (.20)
18,000–20,000	25% (.25)		

7 Multiply the amount on line 5 by the percentage shown on line 6, and write the result. . . . **7**

8 Multiply any child and dependent care expenses for 1983 that you paid in 1984 by the percentage that applies to the adjusted gross income on Form 1040, line 33, for 1983. Write the result. (See line 8 instructions for the required statement.) . . . **8**

9 Add amounts on lines 7 and 8. Write the total here and on Form 1040, line 41. This is the maximum amount of your credit for child and dependent care expenses. . . . **9**

General Instructions

Paperwork Reduction Act Notice.—We ask for this information to carry out the Internal Revenue laws of the United States. We need it to ensure that taxpayers are complying with these laws and to allow us to figure and collect the right amount of tax. You are required to give us this information.

What Is the Child and Dependent Care Expenses Credit?

You may be able to take a tax credit for amounts you paid someone to care for your child or other qualifying person so you could work or look for work in 1984. The credit will lower the amount of your tax. The credit is based on a percentage of the amount you paid during the year. The most you may take as a credit is $720 if you paid for the care of one qualifying person, or $1,440 if you paid for the care of two or more qualifying persons.

Additional information.—For more information about the credit, please get **Publication 503**, Child and Dependent Care Credit, and Employment Taxes for Household Employers.

Who Is a Qualifying Person?

A qualifying person is any one of the following persons:

- Any person under age 15 whom you claim as a dependent (but see the special rule later for **Children of divorced or separated parents**).
- Your disabled spouse who is mentally or physically unable to care for himself or herself.
- Any disabled person who is mentally or physically unable to care for himself or herself and whom you claim as a dependent, or could claim as a dependent except that he or she had income of $1,000 or more.

Children of divorced or separated parents.—If you were divorced, legally separated, or separated under a written agreement, you may be able to claim the credit even if your child is not your dependent. Your child is a qualifying person if **all four** of the following apply:

1. You had custody for the longer period during the year; and

2. The child received over half of his or her support from one or both of the parents; and

3. The child was in the custody of one or both of the parents over half of the year; and

4. The child was under age 15, or was physically or mentally unable to care for himself or herself.

(Continued on back)

Form **3468**

Department of the Treasury
Internal Revenue Service

Computation of Investment Credit

▶ Attach to your tax return.
▶ Schedule B (Business Energy Investment Credit) on back.

OMB No. 1545-0155

1984
24

Name(s) as shown on return | Identifying number

Part I Elections (Check the box(es) below that apply to you (See Instruction D).)

A I elect to increase my qualified investment to 100% for certain commuter highway vehicles under section 46(c)(6) . . . . ☐

B I elect to increase my qualified investment by all qualified progress expenditures made this and all later tax years . . . . ☐
Enter total qualified progress expenditures included in column (4), Part II ▶ ____________

C I claim full credit on certain ships under section 46(g)(3) (See **Instruction B** for details.) . . . . ☐

Part II Qualified Investment (See instructions for new rules on automobiles and certain property with any personal use)

1 Recovery Property		Line	(1) Class of Property	(2) Unadjusted Basis	(3) Applicable Percentage	(4) Qualified Investment (Column 2 x column 3)
Regular Percentage	New Property	(a)	3-year		60	
		(b)	Other		100	
	Used Property	(c)	3-year		60	
		(d)	Other		100	
Section 48(q) Election to Reduce Credit (instead of adjusting basis)	New Property	(e)	3-year		40	
		(f)	Other		80	
	Used Property	(g)	3-year		40	
		(h)	Other		80	

2	Nonrecovery property—Enter total qualified investment (See instructions for line 2)	2	
3	New commuter highway vehicle—Enter total qualified investment (See **Instruction D(1)**)	3	
4	Used commuter highway vehicle—Enter total qualified investment (See **Instruction D(1)**)	4	
5	**Total qualified investment in 10% property**—Add lines 1(a) through 1(h), 2, 3, and 4 (See instructions for special limits)	5	
6	Qualified rehabilitation expenditures—Enter total qualified investment for:		
	a 30-year-old buildings	6a	
	b 40-year-old buildings	6b	
	c Certified historic structures (You must attach NPS certification—see instructions).	6c	

Part III Tentative Regular Investment Credit

7	10% of line 5	7	
8	15% of line 6a	8	
9	20% of line 6b	9	
10	25% of line 6c	10	
11	Credit from cooperatives—Enter regular investment credit from cooperatives	11	
12	Regular investment credit—Add lines 7 through 11	12	
13	Business energy investment credit—From line 11 of Schedule B (see back of this form)	13	
14	Current year investment credit—Add lines 12 and 13	14	

Note: *If you have a 1984 jobs credit (Form 5884), credit for alcohol used as fuel (Form 6478), or employee stock ownership plan (ESOP) credit (Form 8007), in addition to your 1984 investment credit, you must stop here and go to new* ***Form 3800****, General Business Credit, to claim your 1984 investment credit. If you have only the investment credit (which may include business energy investment credit) or an investment credit carryforward from 1983, you may continue with lines 15 through 22 to claim your credit.*

15	Carryforward of unused regular or business energy investment credit from 1983	15	
16	Total—Add lines 14 and 15.	16	

Part IV Tax Liability Limitations

17	**a** Individuals—From Form 1040, enter amount from line 46 . . . . **b** Estates and trusts—From Form 1041, enter tax from line 26a, plus any section 644 tax on trusts . . **c** Corporations—From Form 1120, Schedule J, enter tax from line 3 (or Form 1120-A, Part I, line 1). **d** Other filers —Enter tax before credits from return	17	
18	**a** Individuals—From Form 1040, enter credits from line 47, plus any orphan drug, nonconventional source fuel, and research credits . . . . **b** Estates and trusts—From Form 1041, enter any credits from line 27d . . . . **c** Corporations—From Form 1120, Schedule J, enter credits from lines 4(a) through 4(e) (Form 1120-A filers, enter zero) . . . . **d** Other filers—See instructions for line 18d	18	
19	Income tax liability as adjusted (subtract line 18 from line 17).	19	
20	**a** Enter smaller of line 19 or $25,000. (See instructions for line 20)	20a	
	b If line 19 is more than $25,000—Enter 85% of the excess.	20b	
21	Investment credit limitation—Add lines 20a and 20b	21	
22	Total allowed credit—Enter the smaller of line 16 or line 21. This is your **General Business Credit** for 1984. Enter here and on Form 1040, line 48; Form 1120, Schedule J, line 4(f); Form 1120-A, Part I, line 2 ; or the proper line of other returns	22	

For Paperwork Reduction Act Notice, see separate instructions.

Form **3903**

Department of the Treasury
Internal Revenue Service

Moving Expense Adjustment

▶ **Attach to Form 1040.**

OMB No. 1545-0062

1984

62

Name(s) as shown on Form 1040 | **Your social security number**

a What is the distance from your **old** residence to your **new** work place? ________ miles

b What is the distance from your **old** residence to your **old** work place? ________ miles

c If the distance in **a** above is 35 or more miles farther than the distance in **b** above, complete the rest of this form. If the distance is less than 35 miles, you may not take a deduction for moving expenses. This rule does not apply to members of the armed forces.

1 Transportation expenses in moving household goods and personal effects			1
2 Travel, meal, and lodging expenses in moving from old to new residence			2
3 Pre-move travel, meal, and lodging expenses in looking for a new residence after getting your job	3		
4 Temporary living expenses in new location or area during any 30 days in a row after getting your job	4		
5 Add lines 3 and 4	5		
6 Enter the smaller of line 5 or $1,500 ($750 if married, filing a separate return, and, at the end of the tax year, you lived with your spouse who also started work during the tax year)		6	
7 Expenses of (check one): **a** ☐ selling or exchanging your old residence; or **b** ☐ if renting, settling an unexpired lease on your old residence		7	
8 Expenses of (check one): **a** ☐ buying your new residence; or **b** ☐ if renting, getting a lease on your new residence		8	
9 Add lines 6, 7, and 8		9	
10 Enter the smaller of line 9 or $3,000 ($1,500 if married, filing a separate return, and, at the end of the tax year, you lived with your spouse who also started work during the tax year)			10
Note: *Use any amount on line* ***7a*** *not deducted because of the $3,000 (or $1,500) limit to decrease the gain on the sale of your residence. Use any amount on line* ***8a*** *not deducted because of the limit to increase the basis of your new residence. See* ***No Double Benefit*** *in the instructions.*			
11 Add lines 1, 2, and 10. This is your moving expense deduction. Enter here and on Form 1040, line 24 ▶			11
Note: *If your employer paid for any part of your move (including the value of any services furnished in kind), report that amount on* ***Form 1040, line 7.*** *See* ***Reimbursements*** *in the instructions.*			

General Instructions

Paperwork Reduction Act Notice.—We ask for this information to carry out the Internal Revenue laws of the United States. We need it to ensure that taxpayers are complying with these laws and to allow us to figure and collect the right amount of tax. You are required to give us this information.

Purpose of Form.—Use Form 3903 if you moved to a new principal work place within the United States or its possessions and you qualify to deduct your moving expenses.

Note: *Use* ***Form 3903F,*** *Foreign Moving Expense Adjustment, instead of this form if you are a U.S. citizen or resident alien who moved to a new principal work place outside the United States or its possessions.*

Additional Information.—For more information about moving expenses, please get **Publication 521,** Moving Expenses.

Who May Deduct Moving Expenses.—If you moved your residence because of a change in the location of your job, you may be able to deduct your moving expenses. You may qualify for a deduction whether you are self-employed or an employee. However, you must meet certain tests of distance and time, explained below.

Distance Test.—Your new work place must be at least 35 miles farther from your old residence than your old work place was. For example, if your old work place was 3 miles from your old residence, your new work place must be at least 38 miles from that residence. If you did not have an old work place, your new work place must be at least 35 miles from your old residence. (The distance between two points is the shortest of the more commonly traveled routes between the points.)

Time Test.—If you are an employee, you must work full time for at least 39 weeks during the 12 months right after you move. If you are self-employed, you must work full time for at least 39 weeks during the first 12 months and a total of at least 78 weeks during the 24 months right after you move.

You may deduct your moving expenses for 1984 even if you have not met the time test before your 1984 return is due. You may do this if you expect to meet the 39-week test by the end of 1985 or the 78-week test by the end of 1986. If you have not met the test by then, you will have to do one of the following:

- Amend your 1984 tax return on which you deducted moving expenses. To do this, use **Form 1040X,** Amended U.S. Individual Income Tax Return; or
- Report as income on your tax return for the year you cannot meet the test the amount you deducted on your 1984 return.

If you do not deduct your moving expenses on your 1984 return, and you later meet the time test, you may file an amended return for 1984, taking the deduction. To do this, use Form 1040X.

Exceptions to the Distance and Time Tests.—You do not have to meet the time

Form **4255** (Rev. Nov. 1982) Department of the Treasury Internal Revenue Service

Recapture of Investment Credit

(Including Energy Investment Credit)

► Attach to your income tax return

OMB No. 1545-0166 Expires 11-30-85

65

Name(s) as shown on return	**Identifying number**

Properties	**Kind of property—State whether recovery or nonrecovery (see Form 3468 instructions for definitions). If energy property, show type. Also indicate if rehabilitation expenditure property.**
A	
B	
C	
D	
E	

Original Investment Credit

Computation Steps: (see Specific Instructions)	A	B	C	D	E
1 Original rate of credit					
2 Date property was placed in service					
3 Cost or other basis					
4 Original estimated useful life or class of property					
5 Applicable percentage					
6 Original qualified investment (line 3 times line 5)					
7 Original credit (line 1 times line 6)					
8 Date property ceased to be qualified investment credit property					
9 Number of full years between the date on line 2 and the date on line 8					

Computation of Recapture Tax

	A	B	C	D	E
10 Recapture percentage					
11 Tentative recapture tax—Line 7 times line 10					

12 Add line 11, columns A through E	
13 a Enter tax from disposed qualified progress expenditure property (attach separate computation)	
b Enter tax from any part of property ceasing to be at risk (attach separate computation)	
14 Total—Add lines 12, 13a and 13b	
15 Portion of original credit (line 7) not used to offset tax in any year (Do not enter more than line 14—see instructions)	
16 Total increase in tax—Subtract line 15 from line 14. Enter here and on the proper line of your tax return. Do not use this amount to reduce current year's investment credit figured on Form 3468, Computation of Investment Credit. Any unused credit on line 15 cannot be used in any year as a carryback or carryover	

For Paperwork Reduction Act Notice, see instructions on back.

Form **4562**

Department of the Treasury
Internal Revenue Service (O)

Depreciation and Amortization

▶ See separate instructions.
▶ Attach this form to your return.

OMB No. 1545-0172
1984
67

Name(s) as shown on return | **Identifying number**

Business or activity to which this form relates

Part I **Depreciation** For transportation equipment (e.g. autos), amusement/recreation property, and computer/peripheral equipment placed in service after June 18, 1984, and used 50% or less in a trade or business, the section 179 deduction is not allowed and depreciation must be taken only on line 2(h).

Section A.—Election to expense recovery property (Section 179)

A. Class of property	B. Cost	C. Expense deduction
1 Total (not more than $5,000). (Partnerships or S corporations—see the Schedule K and Schedule K-1 Instructions of Form 1065 or 1120S)		

Section B.—Depreciation of recovery property

A. Class of property	B. Date placed in service	C. Cost or other basis	D. Recovery period	E. Method of figuring depreciation	F. Deduction
2 Accelerated Cost Recovery System (ACRS) (see instructions): *For assets placed in service* **ONLY** *during taxable year beginning in 1984*					
(a) 3-year property					
(b) 5-year property					
(c) 10-year property					
(d) 15-year public utility property					
(e) 15-year real property—low-income housing					
(f) 15-year real property other than low-income housing					
(g) 18-year real property					
(h) Other recovery property				**S/L**	
				S/L	
3 ACRS deduction for assets placed in service prior to 1984 (see instructions)					

Section C.—Depreciation of nonrecovery property

4 Property subject to section 168(e)(2) election (see instructions)	
5 Class Life Asset Depreciation Range (CLADR) System Depreciation (see instructions)	
6 Other depreciation (see instructions)	

Section D.—Summary

7 Total (Add deductions on lines 1 through 6). Enter here and on the Depreciation line of your return (Partnerships and S corporations—DO NOT include any amounts entered on line 1.)	

Part II **Amortization**

A. Description of property	B. Date acquired	C. Cost or other basis	D. Code section	E. Amortization period or percentage	F. Amortization for this year
Total. Enter here and on Other Deductions or Other Expenses line of your return					

See Paperwork Reduction Act Notice on page 1 of the separate instructions.

U.S. GOVERNMENT PRINTING OFFICE 1984-423-237 (31-0598032)

Form **4562**

Department of the Treasury
Internal Revenue Service (O)

Depreciation and Amortization

▶ See separate instructions.

▶ Attach this form to your return.

OMB No. 1545-0172

1984

67

Name(s) as shown on return | **Identifying number**

Business or activity to which this form relates

Part I **Depreciation** For transportation equipment (e.g. autos), amusement/recreation property, and computer/peripheral equipment placed in service after June 18, 1984, and used 50% or less in a trade or business, the section 179 deduction is not allowed and depreciation must be taken only on line 2(h).

Section A.—Election to expense recovery property (Section 179)

A. Class of property	B. Cost	C. Expense deduction
1 Total (not more than $5,000). (Partnerships or S corporations—see the Schedule K and Schedule K-1 Instructions of Form 1065 or 1120S)		

Section B.—Depreciation of recovery property

A. Class of property	B. Date placed in service	C. Cost or other basis	D. Recovery period	E. Method of figuring depreciation	F. Deduction
2 Accelerated Cost Recovery System (ACRS) (see instructions): *For assets placed in service* **ONLY** *during taxable year beginning in 1984*					
(a) 3-year property					
(b) 5-year property					
(c) 10-year property					
(d) 15-year public utility property					
(e) 15-year real property—low-income housing					
(f) 15-year real property other than low-income housing					
(g) 18-year real property					
(h) Other recovery property				**S/L**	
				S/L	
3 ACRS deduction for assets placed in service prior to 1984 (see instructions)					

Section C.—Depreciation of nonrecovery property

4 Property subject to section 168(e)(2) election (see instructions)	
5 Class Life Asset Depreciation Range (CLADR) System Depreciation (see instructions)	
6 Other depreciation (see instructions)	

Section D.—Summary

7 Total (Add deductions on lines 1 through 6). Enter here and on the Depreciation line of your return (Partnerships and S corporations—DO NOT include any amounts entered on line 1.)	

Part II **Amortization**

A. Description of property	B. Date acquired	C. Cost or other basis	D. Code section	E. Amortization period or percentage	F. Amortization for this year
Total. Enter here and on Other Deductions or Other Expenses line of your return					

See Paperwork Reduction Act Notice on page 1 of the separate instructions.

U.S. GOVERNMENT PRINTING OFFICE 1984-423-237 (31-0598032)

Form **4684**

Department of the Treasury
Internal Revenue Service

Casualties and Thefts

▶ **See separate instructions.**

▶ **To be filed with Form 1040, 1041, 1065, 1120, etc.**

Use a separate Form 4684 for each different casualty or theft.

OMB No. 1545-0177

1984

26

Name(s) as shown on tax return | **Identifying Number**

SECTION A.— Personal Use Property

*(Casualties and thefts to property that is **not** used in a trade or business or for income-producing purposes.)*

	Item or article	Item or article	Item or article	Item or article
1 (a) Kind of property and description				
(b) Date of purchase or acquisition				
2 Cost or other basis of each item				
3 Insurance or other reimbursement you received or expect to receive for each item				
Note: *If line 2 is more than line 3, skip line 4*				
4 Gain from casualty or theft. If line 3 is more than line 2, enter difference here and skip lines 5 through 13				
5 Fair market value before casualty or theft				
6 Fair market value after casualty or theft				
7 Subtract line 6 from line 5				
8 Enter smaller of line 2 or line 7				
9 Subtract line 3 from line 8				

10 Casualty or theft loss. Add amounts on line 9	
11 Enter the amount from line 10 or $100, whichever is smaller	
12 Subtract line 11 from line 10	
Caution: *Use only one Form 4684 for lines 13 through 18.*	
13 Add the line 12 amounts from all Forms 4684, Section A	
14 Add the line 4 amounts from all Forms 4684, Section A	
15 If line 14 is more than line 13, enter difference here and on Schedule D, and do not complete the rest of form. Otherwise, enter zero and complete lines 16 through 18 (see instructions). If line 14 is equal to line 13, do not complete the rest of form	
16 If line 13 is more than line 14, enter difference	
17 Enter 10% of adjusted gross income (Form 1040, line 33). Estates and trusts, See instructions	
18 Subtract line 17 from line 16. If zero or less, enter zero. Enter on Schedule A(Form 1040), line 19. Estates and trusts, see instructions	

For Paperwork Reduction Act Notice, see page 1 of separate instructions.

Name(s) as shown on tax return (Do not enter name and identifying number if shown on other side)	Identifying Number

SECTION B.— Business and Income-Producing Property

*(Casualties and thefts to property that **is** used in a trade or business or for income-producing purposes.)*

PART I. Casualty or Theft Gain or Loss (Use a separate Part I for each different casualty or theft.)

	Item or article	Item or article	Item or article	Item or article
1 (a) Kind of property and description				
(b) Date of purchase or acquisition				
2 Cost or other basis of each item				
3 Insurance or other reimbursement you received or expect to receive for each item.				
Note: *If line 2 is more than line 3, skip line 4* **4** Gain from casualty or theft. If line 3 is more than line 2, enter difference here and on line 11 or 16, column C. However, see instructions for line 15. Also, skip lines 5 through 10				
5 Fair market value before casualty or theft				
6 Fair market value after casualty or theft				
7 Subtract line 6 from line 5				
8 Enter smaller of line 2 or line 7				
Note: *If the item was totally destroyed by a casualty, or lost from theft, enter on line 8, in each column, the amount from line 2.*				
9 Subtract line 3 from line 8				

10 Casualty or theft loss. Add amounts on line 9. Enter here and on line 11 or 16.

PART II. Summary of Gains and Losses (From separate Parts I)

(A) Identify casualty or theft	(B) Losses from casualties or thefts: (i) Trade, business, rental or royalty property	(B) (ii) Income-producing property	(C) Gains from casualties or thefts includible in income
Casualty or Theft of Property Held One Year or Less (6 months if acquired after 6/22/84)			
11			
12 Totals. Add amounts on line 11 for each column			
13 Combine line 12, columns (B)(i) and (C). Enter the net gain or (loss) here and on Form 4797, Part II, line 9. (If Form 4797 is not otherwise required, see instructions.)			
14 Enter the amount from line 12, column (B)(ii) here and on line 19 of Schedule A (Form 1040). Partnerships, S Corporations, Estates and Trusts, see instructions			
Casualty or Theft of Property Held More Than One Year (6 months if acquired after 6/22/84)			
15 Casualty or theft gains from Form 4797, Part III, line 28			
16			
17 Total losses. Add amounts on line 16, columns (B)(i) and (B)(ii)			
18 Total gains. Add lines 15 and 16, column (C)			
19 Add amounts on line 17, columns (B)(i) and (B)(ii) *Partnerships, enter the amount from line 20 or line 21 on your Schedule K-1, line 6. S Corporations, enter the amount from line 20 on your Schedule K-1, line 5.*			
20 If the loss on line 19 is more than the gain on line 18: **(a)** Combine line 17, column (B)(i) and line 18. Enter the net gain or (loss) here and on Form 4797, Part II, line 9. (If Form 4797 is not otherwise required, see instructions.)			
(b) Enter the amount from line 17, column (B)(ii) here and on line 19 of Schedule A (Form 1040). Estates and Trusts, see instructions			
21 If the loss on line 19 is equal to or smaller than the gain on line 18, combine these lines and enter here and on Form 4797, Part I, line 2. (If Form 4797 is not otherwise required, see instructions.)			

☆U.S.GPO:1984-0-423-241 E.I.#430814328

Form **4797**

Department of the Treasury
Internal Revenue Service (O)

Supplemental Schedule of Gains and Losses

(Includes Gains and Losses From Sales or Exchanges of Assets Used in a Trade or Business and Involuntary Conversions)

▶ **To be filed with Forms 1040, 1041, 1065, 1120S, 1120, etc.—See Separate Instructions**

OMB No. 1545-0184

1984

27

Name(s) as shown on return | **Identifying number**

Part I Sales or Exchanges of Property Used in a Trade or Business, and Involuntary Conversions From Other Than Casualty and Theft—Property Held More Than 1 Year (6 Months if Acquired After 6/22/84) (Except for Certain Livestock)

Note: *Use Form 4684 to report involuntary conversions from casualty and theft.*

Caution: *If you sold property on which you claimed the investment credit, you may be liable for recapture of that credit. See Form 4255 for additional information.*

Note: *If you report a loss below and have amounts invested in the activity for which you are not at risk, you will have to file Form 6198. (See instructions under "Special Rules.")*

a. Description of property	**b.** Date acquired (mo., day, yr.)	**c.** Date sold (mo., day, yr.)	**d.** Gross sales price	**e.** Depreciation allowed (or allowable) since acquisition	**f.** Cost or other basis, plus improvements and expense of sale	**g.** LOSS (f minus the sum of d and e)	**h.** GAIN (d plus e minus f)
1							

	g. LOSS	h. GAIN
2 Gain, if any, from Form 4684, Section B, line 21		
3 Section 1231 gain from installment sales from Form 6252, line 22 or 30		
4 Gain, if any, on line 28 from other than casualty and theft		
5 Add lines 1 through 4 in column g and column h	( )	

6 Combine columns g and h of line 5. Enter gain or (loss) here, and on the appropriate line as follows:

(a) For all except partnership returns:

(1) If line 6 is a gain, enter the gain as a long-term capital gain on Schedule D. See specific instructions for Part I.

(2) If line 6 is zero or a loss, enter that amount on line 7. (S corporations, enter on Schedule K (Form 1120S), line 6.)

(b) For partnership returns: Enter each partner's share of line 6 above, on Schedule K-1 (Form 1065), line 7.

Part II Ordinary Gains and Losses

a. Description of property	**b.** Date acquired (mo., day, yr.)	**c.** Date sold (mo., day, yr.)	**d.** Gross sales price	**e.** Depreciation allowed (or allowable) since acquisition	**f.** Cost or other basis, plus improvements and expense of sale	**g.** LOSS (f minus the sum of d and e)	**h.** GAIN (d plus e minus f)
7 Loss, if any, from line 6(a)(2)							
8 Gain, if any, on line 27							
9 Net gain or (loss) from Form 4684, Section B, lines 13 and 20(a)							
10 Ordinary gain from installment sales from Form 6252, line 21 or 29 (Applies only to sales before 6/7/84)							
11 Recapture of section 179 deduction (see instructions)							
12 Other ordinary gains and losses (include property held 1 year or less, (6 months or less if acquired after 6/22/84)):							
13 Add lines 7 through 12 in column g and column h						( )	

14 Combine columns g and h of line 13. Enter gain or (loss) here, and on the appropriate line as follows:

(a) For all except individual returns: Enter the gain or (loss) from line 14, on the return being filed. See instructions for Part II for specific line references.

(b) For individual returns:

(1) If the loss on line 7 includes a loss from Form 4684, Section B, Part II, column B(ii), enter that part of the loss here and on line 19 of Schedule A (Form 1040). Identify as from "Form 4797, line 14(b)(1)"

(2) Redetermine the gain or (loss) on line 14, excluding the loss (if any) on line 14(b)(1). Enter here and on Form 1040, line 15

For Paperwork Reduction Act Notice, see page 1 of separate instructions.

Part III Gain From Disposition of Property Under Sections 1245, 1250, 1252, 1254, 1255

Skip section 1252 on line 23 and in the instructions, if you did not dispose of farmland, or if a partnership files this form.

15 Description of sections 1245, 1250, 1252, 1254, and 1255 property:	Date acquired (mo., day, yr.)	Date sold (mo., day, yr.)
(A)		
(B)		
(C)		
(D)		

Relate lines 15(A) through 15(D) to these columns ► ► ► ►	Property (A)	Property (B)	Property (C)	Property (D)
16 Gross sales price				
17 Cost or other basis plus expense of sale				
18 Depreciation (or depletion) allowed (or allowable)				
19 Adjusted basis, subtract line 18 from line 17				
20 Total gain, subtract line 19 from line 16				
21 **If section 1245 property:**				
(a) Depreciation allowed (or allowable) (see instructions)				
(b) Enter smaller of line 20 or 21(a)				
22 **If section 1250 property:** (If straight line depreciation used, enter zero on line 22(g) unless you are a corporation subject to section 291.)				
(a) Additional depreciation after 12/31/75				
(b) Applicable percentage times the smaller of line 20 or line 22(a) (see instructions)				
(c) Subtract line 22(a) from line 20. If line 20 is not more than line 22(a), skip lines 22(d) and 22(e)				
(d) Additional depreciation after 12/31/69 and before 1/1/76				
(e) Applicable percentage times the smaller of line 22(c) or 22(d) (see instructions)				
(f) Section 291 amount (For Corporations only.)				
(g) Add lines 22(b), 22(e), and 22(f)				
23 **If section 1252 property:**				
(a) Soil, water, and land clearing expenses				
(b) Line 23(a) times applicable percentage (see instructions)				
(c) Enter smaller of line 20 or 23(b)				
24 **If section 1254 property:**				
(a) Intangible drilling and development costs deducted after 12/31/75 (see instructions)				
(b) Enter smaller of line 20 or 24(a)				
25 **If section 1255 property:**				
(a) Applicable percentage of payments excluded from income under section 126 (see instructions)				
(b) Enter the smaller of line 20 or 25(a)				

Summary of Part III Gains (Complete Property columns (A) through (D) through line 25(b) before going to line 26)

26 Total gains for all properties (add columns (A) through (D), line 20)	
27 Add columns (A) through (D), lines 21(b), 22(g), 23(c), 24(b), and 25(b). Enter here and on Part II, line 8	
28 Subtract line 27 from line 26. Enter the portion from casualty and theft on Form 4684, Section B, line 15; enter the portion from other than casualty and theft on Form 4797, Part I, line 4.	

Part IV Complete this Part Only if You Elect Out of the Installment Method And Report a Note or Other Obligation at Less Than Full Face Value

☐ Check here if you elect out of the installment method.

Enter the face amount of the note or other obligation ► ____________

Enter the percentage of valuation of the note or other obligation ►

☆ U.S. GOVERNMENT PRINTING OFFICE: 1984-423-247 (31-0598032)

Form **5695** Department of the Treasury Internal Revenue Service

Residential Energy Credit

▶ Attach to Form 1040. ▶ See Instructions on back.

▶ For Paperwork Reduction Act Notice, see Instructions on back.

OMB No. 1545-0214

1984

30

Name(s) as shown on Form 1040 | **Your social security number**

Enter the address of your principal residence on which the credit is claimed if it is different from the address shown on Form 1040.

If you have an energy credit carryover from a previous tax year and no energy savings costs this year, skip to Part III, line 24.

Part I Fill in your energy conservation costs (but do not include repair or maintenance costs).

1 Was your principal residence substantially completed before April 20, 1977? (See instructions) ▶ ☐ Yes ☐ No

Note: *You MUST answer this question. Failure to do so will delay the processing of your return. If you checked the "No" box, you CANNOT claim an energy credit under Part I and you should not fill in lines 2a through 12 of this form.*

2 a	Insulation	2a	
b	Storm (or thermal) windows or doors	2b	
c	Caulking or weatherstripping	2c	
d	A replacement burner for your existing furnace that reduces fuel use	2d	
e	A device for modifying flue openings to make a heating system more efficient	2e	
f	An electrical or mechanical furnace ignition system that replaces a gas pilot light	2f	
g	A thermostat with an automatic setback	2g	
h	A meter that shows the cost of energy used	2h	
3	Total (add lines 2a through 2h)	3	
4	Enter the part of expenditures made from nontaxable government grants and subsidized financing	4	
5	Subtract line 4 from line 3	5	
6	Maximum amount of cost on which credit can be figured	6	$2,000 00
7	Enter the total energy conservation costs for this residence. Add lines 2 of your 1978, 1979, and 1980 Forms 5695 and line 3 of your 1981, 1982, and 1983 Forms 5695	7	
8	Subtract line 7 from line 6. If line 7 exceeds line 6, enter zero here and on line 12	8	
9	Enter the total nontaxable grants and subsidized financing used to purchase qualified energy items for this residence. Add the amount on line 4 of this form and your 1981, 1982, and 1983 Forms 5695	9	
10	Subtract line 9 from line 8. If zero or less, do not complete the rest of Part I	10	
11	Enter the amount on line 5 or line 10, whichever is less	11	
12	Enter 15% of line 11 here and include in amount on line 23 below	12	

Part II Fill in your renewable energy source costs (but do not include repair or maintenance costs).

13	**a** Solar ______ **13b** Geothermal ______ **13c** Wind ______ Total ▶	13d	
14	Enter the part of expenditures made from nontaxable government grants and subsidized financing	14	
15	Subtract line 14 from line 13d	15	
16	Maximum amount of cost on which the credit can be figured	16	$10,000 00
17	Enter the total renewable energy source costs for this residence. Add line 5 of your 1978 Form 5695, line 9 of your 1979 and 1980 Forms 5695, and line 13d of your 1981, 1982, and 1983 Forms 5695	17	
18	Subtract line 17 from line 16. If line 17 exceeds line 16, enter zero here and on line 22	18	
19	Enter the total nontaxable grants and subsidized financing used to purchase qualified energy items for this residence. Add the amount on line 14 of this form and your 1981, 1982, and 1983 Forms 5695	19	
20	Subtract line 19 from line 18. If zero or less, do not complete the rest of Part II	20	
21	Enter the amount on line 15 or line 20, whichever is less	21	
22	Enter 40% of line 21 here and include in amount on line 23 below	22	

Part III Fill in this part to figure the limitation.

23	Add lines 12 and 22. If less than $10, enter zero	23	
24	Enter your energy credit carryover from a previous tax year. **Caution**—Do not make an entry on this line if your 1983 Form 1040, line 49, showed an amount of more than zero.	24	
25	Add lines 23 and 24	25	
26	Enter the amount of tax shown on Form 1040, line 40	26	
27	Add lines 41, 42, and 44 from Form 1040 and enter the total	27	
28	Subtract line 27 from line 26. If zero or less, enter zero	28	
29	Residential energy credit. Enter the amount on line 25 or line 28, whichever is less. Also, enter this amount on Form 1040, line 43. Complete Part IV below if this line is less than line 25	29	

Part IV Fill in this part to figure your carryover to 1985 (complete only if line 29 is less than line 25).

30	Enter amount from Part III, line 25	30	
31	Enter amount from Part III, line 29	31	
32	Credit carryover to 1985 (subtract line 31 from line 30)	32	

Form **6252**

Department of the Treasury
Internal Revenue Service

Computation of Installment Sale Income

▶ See instructions on back. ▶ Attach to your tax return.
Use a separate form for each sale or other disposition of property on the installment method.

OMB No. 1545-0228

1984

79

Name(s) as shown on tax return | **Identifying number**

A Description of property ▶ ____________

B Date acquired (month, day, and year) ▶ ________ C Date sold (month, day, and year) ▶ ________

D Was property sold to a related party after May 14, 1980? (See instruction C) . . . ☐ Yes ☐ No

E If the answer to D is "Yes," was the property a marketable security? . . . ☐ Yes ☐ No

If you checked "Yes" to question E, complete Part III.
If you checked "No" to question E, complete Part III for the year of sale and for 2 years after the year of sale.

Part I Computation of Gross Profit and Contract Price *(Complete this part for year of sale only.)*

1	Selling price including mortgages and other indebtedness (Do not include interest whether stated or unstated)		1	
2	Mortgages and other indebtedness buyer assumes or takes property subject to (Do not include new mortgages from a bank or other source.)	2		
3	Subtract line 2 from line 1	3		
4	Cost or other basis of property sold	4		
5	Depreciation allowed or allowable	5		
6	Adjusted basis (subtract line 5 from line 4)	6		
7	Commissions and other expenses of sale	7		
8	Income recapture from Form 4797, Part III (see instructions)	8		
9	Add lines 6, 7, and 8		9	
10	Subtract line 9 from line 1. If result is zero or less, do not complete rest of form		10	
11	If question A is a principal residence, enter the sum of Form 2119, lines 12,15, and 19		11	
12	Gross profit (subtract line 11 from line 10)		12	
13	Subtract line 9 from line 2. If line 9 is more than line 2, enter zero		13	
14	Contract price (add line 3 and line 13)		14	

Part II Computation of Taxable Part of Installment Sale

(Complete this part for year of sale and any year you receive a payment.)

15	Gross profit ratio (divide line 12 by line 14) (for years after the year of sale, see instructions)		15	
16	For year of sale only—enter amount from line 13 above; otherwise enter zero		16	
17	Payments received during year (Do not include interest whether stated or unstated)		17	
18	Add lines 16 and 17		18	
19	Payments received in prior years (Do not include interest whether stated or unstated)	19		
20	Taxable part of installment sale (multiply line 18 by line 15)		20	
21	Part of line 20 that is ordinary income under recapture rules (applies only to sales before 6/7/84)		21	
22	Subtract line 21 from line 20. Enter on Schedule D or Form 4797		22	

Part III Information and Computation for Related Party Installment Sale

(Do not complete this part if you received the final installment payment this tax year.)

F Name, address, and taxpayer identifying number of related party ____________

G Did the related party, during this tax year, resell or dispose of the property? . . . ☐ Yes ☐ No

H If the answer to question G is "Yes," complete lines 23 through 30 below unless one of the following conditions is met (check only the box that applies).

☐ The first disposition was a sale or exchange of stock to the issuing corporation.

☐ The second disposition was an involuntary conversion where the threat of conversion occurred after the first disposition.

☐ The second disposition occurred after the death of the original seller or purchaser.

☐ It can be established to the satisfaction of the Internal Revenue Service that tax avoidance was not a principal purpose for either of the dispositions. If this box is checked, attach an explanation. (See instruction C.)

23	Selling price of property sold by related party	23	
24	Enter contract price from line 14 for year of first sale	24	
25	Enter the smaller of line 23 or line 24	25	
26	Total payments received by the end of your 1984 tax year. Add lines 18 and 19	26	
27	Subtract line 26 from line 25. If line 26 is more than line 25, enter zero	27	
28	Multiply line 27 by the gross profit ratio on line 15 for year of first sale	28	
29	Part of line 28 that is ordinary income under recapture rules (applies only to sales before 6/7/84)	29	
30	Subtract line 29 from line 28. Enter on Schedule D or Form 4797	30	

For Paperwork Reduction Act Notice, see back of form.

APPENDIX A

1985 Tax Rate Schedules

Caution: Do not use these Tax Rate Schedules to figure your 1984 taxes. Use only to figure your 1985 estimated taxes.

SCHEDULE X—Single Taxpayers

If line 5 is: Over—	but not over—	The tax is:	of the amount over—
$0	$2,390	—0—	
2,390	3,540	------- 11%	$2,390
3,540	4,580	$126.50 + 12%	3,540
4,580	6,760	251.30 + 14%	4,580
6,760	8,850	556.50 + 15%	6,760
8,850	11,240	870.00 + 16%	8,850
11,240	13,430	1,252.40 + 18%	11,240
13,430	15,610	1,646.60 + 20%	13,430
15,610	18,940	2,082.60 + 23%	15,610
18,940	24,460	2,848.50 + 26%	18,940
24,460	29,970	4,283.70 + 30%	24,460
29,970	35,490	5,936.70 + 34%	29,970
35,490	43,190	7,813.50 + 38%	35,490
43,190	57,550	10,739.50 + 42%	43,190
57,550	85,130	16,770.70 + 48%	57,550
85,130	--------	30,009.10 + 50%	85,130

SCHEDULE Z—Heads of Household

If line 5 is: Over—	but not over—	The tax is:	of the amount over—
$0	$2,390	—0—	
2,390	4,580	------- 11%	$2,390
4,580	6,760	$240.90 + 12%	4,580
6,760	9,050	502.50 + 14%	6,760
9,050	12,280	823.10 + 17%	9,050
12,280	15,610	1,372.20 + 18%	12,280
15,610	18,940	1,971.60 + 20%	15,610
18,940	24,460	2,637.60 + 24%	18,940
24,460	29,970	3,962.40 + 28%	24,460
29,970	35,490	5,505.20 + 32%	29,970
35,490	46,520	7,271.60 + 35%	35,490
46,520	63,070	11,132.10 + 42%	46,520
63,070	85,130	18,083.10 + 45%	63,070
85,130	112,720	28,010.10 + 48%	85,130
112,720	------	41,253.30 + 50%	112,720

SCHEDULE Y—Married Taxpayers and Qualifying Widows and Widowers

Married Filing Joint Returns and Qualifying Widows and Widowers

If line 5 is: Over—	but not over—	The tax is:	of the amount over—
$0	$3,540	—0—	
3,540	5,720	------- 11%	$3,540
5,720	7,910	$239.80 + 12%	5,720
7,910	12,390	502.60 + 14%	7,910
12,390	16,650	1,129.80 + 16%	12,390
16,650	21,020	1,811.40 + 18%	16,650
21,020	25,600	2,598.00 + 22%	21,020
25,600	31,120	3,605.60 + 25%	25,600
31,120	36,630	4,985.60 + 28%	31,120
36,630	47,670	6,528.40 + 33%	36,630
47,670	62,450	10,171.60 + 38%	47,670
62,450	89,090	15,788.00 + 42%	62,450
89,090	113,860	26,976.80 + 45%	89,090
113,860	169,020	38,123.30 + 49%	113,860
169,020	--------	65,151.70 + 50%	169,020

Married Filing Separate Returns

If line 5 is: Over—	but not over—	The tax is:	of the amount over—
$0	$1,770	—0—	
1,770	2,860	------- 11%	1,770
2,860	3,955	$119.90 + 12%	2,860
3,955	6,195	251.30 + 14%	3,955
6,195	8,325	564.90 + 16%	6,195
8,325	10,510	905.70 + 18%	8,325
10,510	12,800	1,299.00 + 22%	10,510
12,800	15,560	1,802.80 + 25%	12,800
15,560	18,315	2,492.80 + 28%	15,560
18,315	23,835	3,264.20 + 33%	18,315
23,835	31,225	5,085.80 + 38%	23,835
31,225	44,545	7,894.00 + 42%	31,225
44,545	56,930	13,488.40 + 45%	44,545
56,930	84,510	19,061.65 + 49%	56,930
84,510	------	32,575.85 + 50%	84,510

1984 Tax Rate Schedules

Caution: These rates are for 1984 taxes. Schedules for 1985 taxes are printed on the inside front cover of this book and on the preceding page.

SCHEDULE X—Single Taxpayers

If line 5 is: Over—	but not over—	The tax is:	of the amount over—
$0	$2,300	—0—	
2,300	3,400	------- 11%	$2,300
3,400	4,400	$121 + 12%	3,400
4,400	6,500	241 + 14%	4,400
6,500	8,500	535 + 15%	6,500
8,500	10,800	835 + 16%	8,500
10,800	12,900	1,203 + 18%	10,800
12,900	15,000	1,581 + 20%	12,900
15,000	18,200	2,001 + 23%	15,000
18,200	23,500	2,737 + 26%	18,200
23,500	28,800	4,115 + 30%	23,500
28,800	34,100	5,705 + 34%	28,800
34,100	41,500	7,507 + 38%	34,100
41,500	55,300	10,319 + 42%	41,500
55,300	81,800	16,115 + 48%	55,300
81,800	------	28,835 + 50%	81,800

SCHEDULE Z—Heads of Household

If line 5 is: Over—	but not over—	The tax is:	of the amount over—
$0	$2,300	—0—	
2,300	4,400	------- 11%	$2,300
4,400	6,500	$231 + 12%	4,400
6,500	8,700	483 + 14%	6,500
8,700	11,800	791 + 17%	8,700
11,800	15,000	1,318 + 18%	11,800
15,000	18,200	1,894 + 20%	15,000
18,200	23,500	2,534 + 24%	18,200
23,500	28,800	3,806 + 28%	23,500
28,800	34,100	5,290 + 32%	28,800
34,100	44,700	6,986 + 35%	34,100
44,700	60,600	10,696 + 42%	44,700
60,600	81,800	17,374 + 45%	60,600
81,800	108,300	26,914 + 48%	81,800
108,300	------	39,634 + 50%	108,300

SCHEDULE Y—Married Taxpayers and Qualifying Widows and Widowers

Married Filing Joint Returns and Qualifying Widows and Widowers

If line 5 is: Over—	but not over—	The tax is:	of the amount over—
$0	$3,400	—0—	
3,400	5,500	------ 11%	$3,400
5,500	7,600	$231 + 12%	5,500
7,600	11,900	483 + 14%	7,600
11,900	16,000	1,085 + 16%	11,900
16,000	20,200	1,741 + 18%	16,000
20,200	24,600	2,497 + 22%	20,200
24,600	29,900	3,465 + 25%	24,600
29,900	35,200	4,790 + 28%	29,900
35,200	45,800	6,274 + 33%	35,200
45,800	60,000	9,772 + 38%	45,800
60,000	85,600	15,168 + 42%	60,000
85,600	109,400	25,920 + 45%	85,600
109,400	162,400	36,630 + 49%	109,400
162,400	--------	62,600 + 50%	162,400

Married Filing Separate Returns

If line 5 is: Over—	but not over—	The tax is:	of the amount over—
$0	$1,700	—0—	
1,700	2,750	---------- 11%	$1,700
2,750	3,800	$115.50 + 12%	2,750
3,800	5,950	241.50 + 14%	3,800
5,950	8,000	542.50 + 16%	5,950
8,000	10,100	870.50 + 18%	8,000
10,100	12,300	1,248.50 + 22%	10,100
12,300	14,950	1,732.50 + 25%	12,300
14,950	17,600	2,395.00 + 28%	14,950
17,600	22,900	3,137.00 + 33%	17,600
22,900	30,000	4,886.00 + 38%	22,900
30,000	42,800	7,584.00 + 42%	30,000
42,800	54,700	12,960.00 + 45%	42,800
54,700	81,200	18,315.00 + 49%	54,700
81,200	------	31,300.00 + 50%	81,200

1984 Tax Table

Based on Taxable Income
For persons with taxable incomes of less than $50,000.

Example: Mr. and Mrs. Brown are filing a joint return. Their taxable income on line 37 of Form 1040 is $25,325. First, they find the $25,300–25,350 income line. Next, they find the column for married filing jointly and read down the column. The amount shown where the income line and filing status column meet is $3,646. This is the tax amount they must write on line 38 of their return.

	At least	But less than	Single	Married filing jointly *	Married filing separately	Head of a household
			Your tax is—			
	25,200	25,250	4,633	3,621	5,770	4,289
	25,250	25,300	4,648	3,634	5,789	4,303
→	25,300	25,350	4,663	(3,646)	5,808	4,317
	25,350	25,400	4,678	3,659	5,827	4,331

If line 37 (taxable income) is—		And you are—			
At least	But less than	Single	Married filing jointly *	Married filing separately	Head of a household
		Your tax is—			
$0	$1,700	$0	$0	$0	$0
1,700	1,725	0	0	[a]1	0
1,725	1,750	0	0	4	0
1,750	1,775	0	0	7	0
1,775	1,800	0	0	10	0
1,800	1,825	0	0	12	0
1,825	1,850	0	0	15	0
1,850	1,875	0	0	18	0
1,875	1,900	0	0	21	0
1,900	1,925	0	0	23	0
1,925	1,950	0	0	26	0
1,950	1,975	0	0	29	0
1,975	2,000	0	0	32	0
2,000					
2,000	2,025	0	0	34	0
2,025	2,050	0	0	37	0
2,050	2,075	0	0	40	0
2,075	2,100	0	0	43	0
2,100	2,125	0	0	45	0
2,125	2,150	0	0	48	0
2,150	2,175	0	0	51	0
2,175	2,200	0	0	54	0
2,200	2,225	0	0	56	0
2,225	2,250	0	0	59	0
2,250	2,275	0	0	62	0
2,275	2,300	0	0	65	0
2,300	2,325	[b]1	0	67	[b]1
2,325	2,350	4	0	70	4
2,350	2,375	7	0	73	7
2,375	2,400	10	0	76	10

If line 37 (taxable income) is—		And you are—			
At least	But less than	Single	Married filing jointly *	Married filing separately	Head of a household
		Your tax is—			
2,400	2,425	12	0	78	12
2,425	2,450	15	0	81	15
2,450	2,475	18	0	84	18
2,475	2,500	21	0	87	21
2,500	2,525	23	0	89	23
2,525	2,550	26	0	92	26
2,550	2,575	29	0	95	29
2,575	2,600	32	0	98	32
2,600	2,625	34	0	100	34
2,625	2,650	37	0	103	37
2,650	2,675	40	0	106	40
2,675	2,700	43	0	109	43
2,700	2,725	45	0	111	45
2,725	2,750	48	0	114	48
2,750	2,775	51	0	117	51
2,775	2,800	54	0	120	54
2,800	2,825	56	0	123	56
2,825	2,850	59	0	126	59
2,850	2,875	62	0	129	62
2,875	2,900	65	0	132	65
2,900	2,925	67	0	135	67
2,925	2,950	70	0	138	70
2,950	2,975	73	0	141	73
2,975	3,000	76	0	144	76
3,000					
3,000	3,050	80	0	149	80
3,050	3,100	85	0	155	85
3,100	3,150	91	0	161	91
3,150	3,200	96	0	167	96
3,200	3,250	102	0	173	102
3,250	3,300	107	0	179	107
3,300	3,350	113	0	185	113
3,350	3,400	118	0	191	118

If line 37 (taxable income) is—		And you are—			
At least	But less than	Single	Married filing jointly *	Married filing separately	Head of a household
		Your tax is—			
3,400	3,450	124	[c]3	197	124
3,450	3,500	130	8	203	129
3,500	3,550	136	14	209	135
3,550	3,600	142	19	215	140
3,600	3,650	148	25	221	146
3,650	3,700	154	30	227	151
3,700	3,750	160	36	233	157
3,750	3,800	166	41	239	162
3,800	3,850	172	47	245	168
3,850	3,900	178	52	252	173
3,900	3,950	184	58	259	179
3,950	4,000	190	63	266	184
4,000					
4,000	4,050	196	69	273	190
4,050	4,100	202	74	280	195
4,100	4,150	208	80	287	201
4,150	4,200	214	85	294	206
4,200	4,250	220	91	301	212
4,250	4,300	226	96	308	217
4,300	4,350	232	102	315	223
4,350	4,400	238	107	322	228
4,400	4,450	245	113	329	234
4,450	4,500	252	118	336	240
4,500	4,550	259	124	343	246
4,550	4,600	266	129	350	252
4,600	4,650	273	135	357	258
4,650	4,700	280	140	364	264
4,700	4,750	287	146	371	270
4,750	4,800	294	151	378	276
4,800	4,850	301	157	385	282
4,850	4,900	308	162	392	288
4,900	4,950	315	168	399	294
4,950	5,000	322	173	406	300

*This column must also be used by a qualifying widow(er).

Continued on next page

a If your taxable income is exactly $1,700, your tax is zero.
b If your taxable income is exactly $2,300, your tax is zero.
c If your taxable income is exactly $3,400, your tax is zero.

1984 Tax Table (*Continued*)

If line 37 (taxable income) is— At least	But less than	And you are— Single	Married filing jointly *	Married filing sepa-rately	Head of a house-hold
		Your tax is—			
5,000					
5,000	5,050	329	179	413	306
5,050	5,100	336	184	420	312
5,100	5,150	343	190	427	318
5,150	5,200	350	195	434	324
5,200	5,250	357	201	441	330
5,250	5,300	364	206	448	336
5,300	5,350	371	212	455	342
5,350	5,400	378	217	462	348
5,400	5,450	385	223	469	354
5,450	5,500	392	228	476	360
5,500	5,550	399	234	483	366
5,550	5,600	406	240	490	372
5,600	5,650	413	246	497	378
5,650	5,700	420	252	504	384
5,700	5,750	427	258	511	390
5,750	5,800	434	264	518	396
5,800	5,850	441	270	525	402
5,850	5,900	448	276	532	408
5,900	5,950	455	282	539	414
5,950	6,000	462	288	547	420
6,000					
6,000	6,050	469	294	555	426
6,050	6,100	476	300	563	432
6,100	6,150	483	306	571	438
6,150	6,200	490	312	579	444
6,200	6,250	497	318	587	450
6,250	6,300	504	324	595	456
6,300	6,350	511	330	603	462
6,350	6,400	518	336	611	468
6,400	6,450	525	342	619	474
6,450	6,500	532	348	627	480
6,500	6,550	539	354	635	487
6,550	6,600	546	360	643	494
6,600	6,650	554	366	651	501
6,650	6,700	561	372	659	508
6,700	6,750	569	378	667	515
6,750	6,800	576	384	675	522
6,800	6,850	584	390	683	529
6,850	6,900	591	396	691	536
6,900	6,950	599	402	699	543
6,950	7,000	606	408	707	550
7,000					
7,000	7,050	614	414	715	557
7,050	7,100	621	420	723	564
7,100	7,150	629	426	731	571
7,150	7,200	636	432	739	578
7,200	7,250	644	438	747	585
7,250	7,300	651	444	755	592
7,300	7,350	659	450	763	599
7,350	7,400	666	456	771	606
7,400	7,450	674	462	779	613
7,450	7,500	681	468	787	620
7,500	7,550	689	474	795	627
7,550	7,600	696	480	803	634
7,600	7,650	704	487	811	641
7,650	7,700	711	494	819	648
7,700	7,750	719	501	827	655
7,750	7,800	726	508	835	662
7,800	7,850	734	515	843	669
7,850	7,900	741	522	851	676
7,900	7,950	749	529	859	683
7,950	8,000	756	536	867	690

If line 37 (taxable income) is— At least	But less than	And you are— Single	Married filing jointly *	Married filing sepa-rately	Head of a house-hold
		Your tax is—			
8,000					
8,000	8,050	764	543	875	697
8,050	8,100	771	550	884	704
8,100	8,150	779	557	893	711
8,150	8,200	786	564	902	718
8,200	8,250	794	571	911	725
8,250	8,300	801	578	920	732
8,300	8,350	809	585	929	739
8,350	8,400	816	592	938	746
8,400	8,450	824	599	947	753
8,450	8,500	831	606	956	760
8,500	8,550	839	613	965	767
8,550	8,600	847	620	974	774
8,600	8,650	855	627	983	781
8,650	8,700	863	634	992	788
8,700	8,750	871	641	1,001	795
8,750	8,800	879	648	1,010	804
8,800	8,850	887	655	1,019	812
8,850	8,900	895	662	1,028	821
8,900	8,950	903	669	1,037	829
8,950	9,000	911	676	1,046	838
9,000					
9,000	9,050	919	683	1,055	846
9,050	9,100	927	690	1,064	855
9,100	9,150	935	697	1,073	863
9,150	9,200	943	704	1,082	872
9,200	9,250	951	711	1,091	880
9,250	9,300	959	718	1,100	889
9,300	9,350	967	725	1,109	897
9,350	9,400	975	732	1,118	906
9,400	9,450	983	739	1,127	914
9,450	9,500	991	746	1,136	923
9,500	9,550	999	753	1,145	931
9,550	9,600	1,007	760	1,154	940
9,600	9,650	1,015	767	1,163	948
9,650	9,700	1,023	774	1,172	957
9,700	9,750	1,031	781	1,181	965
9,750	9,800	1,039	788	1,190	974
9,800	9,850	1,047	795	1,199	982
9,850	9,900	1,055	802	1,208	991
9,900	9,950	1,063	809	1,217	999
9,950	10,000	1,071	816	1,226	1,008
10,000					
10,000	10,050	1,079	823	1,235	1,016
10,050	10,100	1,087	830	1,244	1,025
10,100	10,150	1,095	837	1,254	1,033
10,150	10,200	1,103	844	1,265	1,042
10,200	10,250	1,111	851	1,276	1,050
10,250	10,300	1,119	858	1,287	1,059
10,300	10,350	1,127	865	1,298	1,067
10,350	10,400	1,135	872	1,309	1,076
10,400	10,450	1,143	879	1,320	1,084
10,450	10,500	1,151	886	1,331	1,093
10,500	10,550	1,159	893	1,342	1,101
10,550	10,600	1,167	900	1,353	1,110
10,600	10,650	1,175	907	1,364	1,118
10,650	10,700	1,183	914	1,375	1,127
10,700	10,750	1,191	921	1,386	1,135
10,750	10,800	1,199	928	1,397	1,144
10,800	10,850	1,208	935	1,408	1,152
10,850	10,900	1,217	942	1,419	1,161
10,900	10,950	1,226	949	1,430	1,169
10,950	11,000	1,235	956	1,441	1,178

If line 37 (taxable income) is— At least	But less than	And you are— Single	Married filing jointly *	Married filing sepa-rately	Head of a house-hold
		Your tax is—			
11,000					
11,000	11,050	1,244	963	1,452	1,186
11,050	11,100	1,253	970	1,463	1,195
11,100	11,150	1,262	977	1,474	1,203
11,150	11,200	1,271	984	1,485	1,212
11,200	11,250	1,280	991	1,496	1,220
11,250	11,300	1,289	998	1,507	1,229
11,300	11,350	1,298	1,005	1,518	1,237
11,350	11,400	1,307	1,012	1,529	1,246
11,400	11,450	1,316	1,019	1,540	1,254
11,450	11,500	1,325	1,026	1,551	1,263
11,500	11,550	1,334	1,033	1,562	1,271
11,550	11,600	1,343	1,040	1,573	1,280
11,600	11,650	1,352	1,047	1,584	1,288
11,650	11,700	1,361	1,054	1,595	1,297
11,700	11,750	1,370	1,061	1,606	1,305
11,750	11,800	1,379	1,068	1,617	1,314
11,800	11,850	1,388	1,075	1,628	1,323
11,850	11,900	1,397	1,082	1,639	1,332
11,900	11,950	1,406	1,089	1,650	1,341
11,950	12,000	1,415	1,097	1,661	1,350
12,000					
12,000	12,050	1,424	1,105	1,672	1,359
12,050	12,100	1,433	1,113	1,683	1,368
12,100	12,150	1,442	1,121	1,694	1,377
12,150	12,200	1,451	1,129	1,705	1,386
12,200	12,250	1,460	1,137	1,716	1,395
12,250	12,300	1,469	1,145	1,727	1,404
12,300	12,350	1,478	1,153	1,739	1,413
12,350	12,400	1,487	1,161	1,751	1,422
12,400	12,450	1,496	1,169	1,764	1,431
12,450	12,500	1,505	1,177	1,776	1,440
12,500	12,550	1,514	1,185	1,789	1,449
12,550	12,600	1,523	1,193	1,801	1,458
12,600	12,650	1,532	1,201	1,814	1,467
12,650	12,700	1,541	1,209	1,826	1,476
12,700	12,750	1,550	1,217	1,839	1,485
12,750	12,800	1,559	1,225	1,851	1,494
12,800	12,850	1,568	1,233	1,864	1,503
12,850	12,900	1,577	1,241	1,876	1,512
12,900	12,950	1,586	1,249	1,889	1,521
12,950	13,000	1,596	1,257	1,901	1,530
13,000					
13,000	13,050	1,606	1,265	1,914	1,539
13,050	13,100	1,616	1,273	1,926	1,548
13,100	13,150	1,626	1,281	1,939	1,557
13,150	13,200	1,636	1,289	1,951	1,566
13,200	13,250	1,646	1,297	1,964	1,575
13,250	13,300	1,656	1,305	1,976	1,584
13,300	13,350	1,666	1,313	1,989	1,593
13,350	13,400	1,676	1,321	2,001	1,602
13,400	13,450	1,686	1,329	2,014	1,611
13,450	13,500	1,696	1,337	2,026	1,620
13,500	13,550	1,706	1,345	2,039	1,629
13,550	13,600	1,716	1,353	2,051	1,638
13,600	13,650	1,726	1,361	2,064	1,647
13,650	13,700	1,736	1,369	2,076	1,656
13,700	13,750	1,746	1,377	2,089	1,665
13,750	13,800	1,756	1,385	2,101	1,674
13,800	13,850	1,766	1,393	2,114	1,683
13,850	13,900	1,776	1,401	2,126	1,692
13,900	13,950	1,786	1,409	2,139	1,701
13,950	14,000	1,796	1,417	2,151	1,710

*This column must also be used by a qualifying widow(er).

Continued on next page

1984 Tax Table (*Continued*)

If line 37 (taxable income) is—		And you are—			
At least	But less than	Single	Married filing jointly *	Married filing separately	Head of a household
		Your tax is—			
14,000					
14,000	**14,050**	1,806	1,425	2,164	1,719
14,050	**14,100**	1,816	1,433	2,176	1,728
14,100	**14,150**	1,826	1,441	2,189	1,737
14,150	**14,200**	1,836	1,449	2,201	1,746
14,200	**14,250**	1,846	1,457	2,214	1,755
14,250	**14,300**	1,856	1,465	2,226	1,764
14,300	**14,350**	1,866	1,473	2,239	1,773
14,350	**14,400**	1,876	1,481	2,251	1,782
14,400	**14,450**	1,886	1,489	2,264	1,791
14,450	**14,500**	1,896	1,497	2,276	1,800
14,500	**14,550**	1,906	1,505	2,289	1,809
14,550	**14,600**	1,916	1,513	2,301	1,818
14,600	**14,650**	1,926	1,521	2,314	1,827
14,650	**14,700**	1,936	1,529	2,326	1,836
14,700	**14,750**	1,946	1,537	2,339	1,845
14,750	**14,800**	1,956	1,545	2,351	1,854
14,800	**14,850**	1,966	1,553	2,364	1,863
14,850	**14,900**	1,976	1,561	2,376	1,872
14,900	**14,950**	1,986	1,569	2,389	1,881
14,950	**15,000**	1,996	1,577	2,402	1,890
15,000					
15,000	**15,050**	2,007	1,585	2,416	1,899
15,050	**15,100**	2,018	1,593	2,430	1,909
15,100	**15,150**	2,030	1,601	2,444	1,919
15,150	**15,200**	2,041	1,609	2,458	1,929
15,200	**15,250**	2,053	1,617	2,472	1,939
15,250	**15,300**	2,064	1,625	2,486	1,949
15,300	**15,350**	2,076	1,633	2,500	1,959
15,350	**15,400**	2,087	1,641	2,514	1,969
15,400	**15,450**	2,099	1,649	2,528	1,979
15,450	**15,500**	2,110	1,657	2,542	1,989
15,500	**15,550**	2,122	1,665	2,556	1,999
15,550	**15,600**	2,133	1,673	2,570	2,009
15,600	**15,650**	2,145	1,681	2,584	2,019
15,650	**15,700**	2,156	1,689	2,598	2,029
15,700	**15,750**	2,168	1,697	2,612	2,039
15,750	**15,800**	2,179	1,705	2,626	2,049
15,800	**15,850**	2,191	1,713	2,640	2,059
15,850	**15,900**	2,202	1,721	2,654	2,069
15,900	**15,950**	2,214	1,729	2,668	2,079
15,950	**16,000**	2,225	1,737	2,682	2,089
16,000					
16,000	**16,050**	2,237	1,746	2,696	2,099
16,050	**16,100**	2,248	1,755	2,710	2,109
16,100	**16,150**	2,260	1,764	2,724	2,119
16,150	**16,200**	2,271	1,773	2,738	2,129
16,200	**16,250**	2,283	1,782	2,752	2,139
16,250	**16,300**	2,294	1,791	2,766	2,149
16,300	**16,350**	2,306	1,800	2,780	2,159
16,350	**16,400**	2,317	1,809	2,794	2,169
16,400	**16,450**	2,329	1,818	2,808	2,179
16,450	**16,500**	2,340	1,827	2,822	2,189
16,500	**16,550**	2,352	1,836	2,836	2,199
16,550	**16,600**	2,363	1,845	2,850	2,209
16,600	**16,650**	2,375	1,854	2,864	2,219
16,650	**16,700**	2,386	1,863	2,878	2,229
16,700	**16,750**	2,398	1,872	2,892	2,239
16,750	**16,800**	2,409	1,881	2,906	2,249
16,800	**16,850**	2,421	1,890	2,920	2,259
16,850	**16,900**	2,432	1,899	2,934	2,269
16,900	**16,950**	2,444	1,908	2,948	2,279
16,950	**17,000**	2,455	1,917	2,962	2,289

If line 37 (taxable income) is—		And you are—			
At least	But less than	Single	Married filing jointly *	Married filing separately	Head of a household
		Your tax is—			
17,000					
17,000	**17,050**	2,467	1,926	2,976	2,299
17,050	**17,100**	2,478	1,935	2,990	2,309
17,100	**17,150**	2,490	1,944	3,004	2,319
17,150	**17,200**	2,501	1,953	3,018	2,329
17,200	**17,250**	2,513	1,962	3,032	2,339
17,250	**17,300**	2,524	1,971	3,046	2,349
17,300	**17,350**	2,536	1,980	3,060	2,359
17,350	**17,400**	2,547	1,989	3,074	2,369
17,400	**17,450**	2,559	1,998	3,088	2,379
17,450	**17,500**	2,570	2,007	3,102	2,389
17,500	**17,550**	2,582	2,016	3,116	2,399
17,550	**17,600**	2,593	2,025	3,130	2,409
17,600	**17,650**	2,605	2,034	3,145	2,419
17,650	**17,700**	2,616	2,043	3,162	2,429
17,700	**17,750**	2,628	2,052	3,178	2,439
17,750	**17,800**	2,639	2,061	3,195	2,449
17,800	**17,850**	2,651	2,070	3,211	2,459
17,850	**17,900**	2,662	2,079	3,228	2,469
17,900	**17,950**	2,674	2,088	3,244	2,479
17,950	**18,000**	2,685	2,097	3,261	2,489
18,000					
18,000	**18,050**	2,697	2,106	3,277	2,499
18,050	**18,100**	2,708	2,115	3,294	2,509
18,100	**18,150**	2,720	2,124	3,310	2,519
18,150	**18,200**	2,731	2,133	3,327	2,529
18,200	**18,250**	2,744	2,142	3,343	2,540
18,250	**18,300**	2,757	2,151	3,360	2,552
18,300	**18,350**	2,770	2,160	3,376	2,564
18,350	**18,400**	2,783	2,169	3,393	2,576
18,400	**18,450**	2,796	2,178	3,409	2,588
18,450	**18,500**	2,809	2,187	3,426	2,600
18,500	**18,550**	2,822	2,196	3,442	2,612
18,550	**18,600**	2,835	2,205	3,459	2,624
18,600	**18,650**	2,848	2,214	3,475	2,636
18,650	**18,700**	2,861	2,223	3,492	2,648
18,700	**18,750**	2,874	2,232	3,508	2,660
18,750	**18,800**	2,887	2,241	3,525	2,672
18,800	**18,850**	2,900	2,250	3,541	2,684
18,850	**18,900**	2,913	2,259	3,558	2,696
18,900	**18,950**	2,926	2,268	3,574	2,708
18,950	**19,000**	2,939	2,277	3,591	2,720
19,000					
19,000	**19,050**	2,952	2,286	3,607	2,732
19,050	**19,100**	2,965	2,295	3,624	2,744
19,100	**19,150**	2,978	2,304	3,640	2,756
19,150	**19,200**	2,991	2,313	3,657	2,768
19,200	**19,250**	3,004	2,322	3,673	2,780
19,250	**19,300**	3,017	2,331	3,690	2,792
19,300	**19,350**	3,030	2,340	3,706	2,804
19,350	**19,400**	3,043	2,349	3,723	2,816
19,400	**19,450**	3,056	2,358	3,739	2,828
19,450	**19,500**	3,069	2,367	3,756	2,840
19,500	**19,550**	3,082	2,376	3,772	2,852
19,550	**19,600**	3,095	2,385	3,789	2,864
19,600	**19,650**	3,108	2,394	3,805	2,876
19,650	**19,700**	3,121	2,403	3,822	2,888
19,700	**19,750**	3,134	2,412	3,838	2,900
19,750	**19,800**	3,147	2,421	3,855	2,912
19,800	**19,850**	3,160	2,430	3,871	2,924
19,850	**19,900**	3,173	2,439	3,888	2,936
19,900	**19,950**	3,186	2,448	3,904	2,948
19,950	**20,000**	3,199	2,457	3,921	2,960

If line 37 (taxable income) is—		And you are—			
At least	But less than	Single	Married filing jointly *	Married filing separately	Head of a household
		Your tax is—			
20,000					
20,000	**20,050**	3,212	2,466	3,937	2,972
20,050	**20,100**	3,225	2,475	3,954	2,984
20,100	**20,150**	3,238	2,484	3,970	2,996
20,150	**20,200**	3,251	2,493	3,987	3,008
20,200	**20,250**	3,264	2,503	4,003	3,020
20,250	**20,300**	3,277	2,514	4,020	3,032
20,300	**20,350**	3,290	2,525	4,036	3,044
20,350	**20,400**	3,303	2,536	4,053	3,056
20,400	**20,450**	3,316	2,547	4,069	3,068
20,450	**20,500**	3,329	2,558	4,086	3,080
20,500	**20,550**	3,342	2,569	4,102	3,092
20,550	**20,600**	3,355	2,580	4,119	3,104
20,600	**20,650**	3,368	2,591	4,135	3,116
20,650	**20,700**	3,381	2,602	4,152	3,128
20,700	**20,750**	3,394	2,613	4,168	3,140
20,750	**20,800**	3,407	2,624	4,185	3,152
20,800	**20,850**	3,420	2,635	4,201	3,164
20,850	**20,900**	3,433	2,646	4,218	3,176
20,900	**20,950**	3,446	2,657	4,234	3,188
20,950	**21,000**	3,459	2,668	4,251	3,200
21,000					
21,000	**21,050**	3,472	2,679	4,267	3,212
21,050	**21,100**	3,485	2,690	4,284	3,224
21,100	**21,150**	3,498	2,701	4,300	3,236
21,150	**21,200**	3,511	2,712	4,317	3,248
21,200	**21,250**	3,524	2,723	4,333	3,260
21,250	**21,300**	3,537	2,734	4,350	3,272
21,300	**21,350**	3,550	2,745	4,366	3,284
21,350	**21,400**	3,563	2,756	4,383	3,296
21,400	**21,450**	3,576	2,767	4,399	3,308
21,450	**21,500**	3,589	2,778	4,416	3,320
21,500	**21,550**	3,602	2,789	4,432	3,332
21,550	**21,600**	3,615	2,800	4,449	3,344
21,600	**21,650**	3,628	2,811	4,465	3,356
21,650	**21,700**	3,641	2,822	4,482	3,368
21,700	**21,750**	3,654	2,833	4,498	3,380
21,750	**21,800**	3,667	2,844	4,515	3,392
21,800	**21,850**	3,680	2,855	4,531	3,404
21,850	**21,900**	3,693	2,866	4,548	3,416
21,900	**21,950**	3,706	2,877	4,564	3,428
21,950	**22,000**	3,719	2,888	4,581	3,440
22,000					
22,000	**22,050**	3,732	2,899	4,597	3,452
22,050	**22,100**	3,745	2,910	4,614	3,464
22,100	**22,150**	3,758	2,921	4,630	3,476
22,150	**22,200**	3,771	2,932	4,647	3,488
22,200	**22,250**	3,784	2,943	4,663	3,500
22,250	**22,300**	3,797	2,954	4,680	3,512
22,300	**22,350**	3,810	2,965	4,696	3,524
22,350	**22,400**	3,823	2,976	4,713	3,536
22,400	**22,450**	3,836	2,987	4,729	3,548
22,450	**22,500**	3,849	2,998	4,746	3,560
22,500	**22,550**	3,862	3,009	4,762	3,572
22,550	**22,600**	3,875	3,020	4,779	3,584
22,600	**22,650**	3,888	3,031	4,795	3,596
22,650	**22,700**	3,901	3,042	4,812	3,608
22,700	**22,750**	3,914	3,053	4,828	3,620
22,750	**22,800**	3,927	3,064	4,845	3,632
22,800	**22,850**	3,940	3,075	4,861	3,644
22,850	**22,900**	3,953	3,086	4,878	3,656
22,900	**22,950**	3,966	3,097	4,896	3,668
22,950	**23,000**	3,979	3,108	4,915	3,680

*This column must also be used by a qualifying widow(er).

Continued on next page

1984 Tax Table (*Continued*)

If line 37 (taxable income) is— At least	But less than	And you are— Single	Married filing jointly *	Married filing sepa-rately	Head of a house-hold
		Your tax is—			
23,000					
23,000	**23,050**	3,992	3,119	4,934	3,692
23,050	**23,100**	4,005	3,130	4,953	3,704
23,100	**23,150**	4,018	3,141	4,972	3,716
23,150	**23,200**	4,031	3,152	4,991	3,728
23,200	**23,250**	4,044	3,163	5,010	3,740
23,250	**23,300**	4,057	3,174	5,029	3,752
23,300	**23,350**	4,070	3,185	5,048	3,764
23,350	**23,400**	4,083	3,196	5,067	3,776
23,400	**23,450**	4,096	3,207	5,086	3,788
23,450	**23,500**	4,109	3,218	5,105	3,800
23,500	**23,550**	4,123	3,229	5,124	3,813
23,550	**23,600**	4,138	3,240	5,143	3,827
23,600	**23,650**	4,153	3,251	5,162	3,841
23,650	**23,700**	4,168	3,262	5,181	3,855
23,700	**23,750**	4,183	3,273	5,200	3,869
23,750	**23,800**	4,198	3,284	5,219	3,883
23,800	**23,850**	4,213	3,295	5,238	3,897
23,850	**23,900**	4,228	3,306	5,257	3,911
23,900	**23,950**	4,243	3,317	5,276	3,925
23,950	**24,000**	4,258	3,328	5,295	3,939
24,000					
24,000	**24,050**	4,273	3,339	5,314	3,953
24,050	**24,100**	4,288	3,350	5,333	3,967
24,100	**24,150**	4,303	3,361	5,352	3,981
24,150	**24,200**	4,318	3,372	5,371	3,995
24,200	**24,250**	4,333	3,383	5,390	4,009
24,250	**24,300**	4,348	3,394	5,409	4,023
24,300	**24,350**	4,363	3,405	5,428	4,037
24,350	**24,400**	4,378	3,416	5,447	4,051
24,400	**24,450**	4,393	3,427	5,466	4,065
24,450	**24,500**	4,408	3,438	5,485	4,079
24,500	**24,550**	4,423	3,449	5,504	4,093
24,550	**24,600**	4,438	3,460	5,523	4,107
24,600	**24,650**	4,453	3,471	5,542	4,121
24,650	**24,700**	4,468	3,484	5,561	4,135
24,700	**24,750**	4,483	3,496	5,580	4,149
24,750	**24,800**	4,498	3,509	5,599	4,163
24,800	**24,850**	4,513	3,521	5,618	4,177
24,850	**24,900**	4,528	3,534	5,637	4,191
24,900	**24,950**	4,543	3,546	5,656	4,205
24,950	**25,000**	4,558	3,559	5,675	4,219
25,000					
25,000	**25,050**	4,573	3,571	5,694	4,233
25,050	**25,100**	4,588	3,584	5,713	4,247
25,100	**25,150**	4,603	3,596	5,732	4,261
25,150	**25,200**	4,618	3,609	5,751	4,275
25,200	**25,250**	4,633	3,621	5,770	4,289
25,250	**25,300**	4,648	3,634	5,789	4,303
25,300	**25,350**	4,663	3,646	5,808	4,317
25,350	**25,400**	4,678	3,659	5,827	4,331
25,400	**25,450**	4,693	3,671	5,846	4,345
25,450	**25,500**	4,708	3,684	5,865	4,359
25,500	**25,550**	4,723	3,696	5,884	4,373
25,550	**25,600**	4,738	3,709	5,903	4,387
25,600	**25,650**	4,753	3,721	5,922	4,401
25,650	**25,700**	4,768	3,734	5,941	4,415
25,700	**25,750**	4,783	3,746	5,960	4,429
25,750	**25,800**	4,798	3,759	5,979	4,443
25,800	**25,850**	4,813	3,771	5,998	4,457
25,850	**25,900**	4,828	3,784	6,017	4,471
25,900	**25,950**	4,843	3,796	6,036	4,485
25,950	**26,000**	4,858	3,809	6,055	4,499

If line 37 (taxable income) is— At least	But less than	And you are— Single	Married filing jointly *	Married filing sepa-rately	Head of a house-hold
		Your tax is—			
26,000					
26,000	**26,050**	4,873	3,821	6,074	4,513
26,050	**26,100**	4,888	3,834	6,093	4,527
26,100	**26,150**	4,903	3,846	6,112	4,541
26,150	**26,200**	4,918	3,859	6,131	4,555
26,200	**26,250**	4,933	3,871	6,150	4,569
26,250	**26,300**	4,948	3,884	6,169	4,583
26,300	**26,350**	4,963	3,896	6,188	4,597
26,350	**26,400**	4,978	3,909	6,207	4,611
26,400	**26,450**	4,993	3,921	6,226	4,625
26,450	**26,500**	5,008	3,934	6,245	4,639
26,500	**26,550**	5,023	3,946	6,264	4,653
26,550	**26,600**	5,038	3,959	6,283	4,667
26,600	**26,650**	5,053	3,971	6,302	4,681
26,650	**26,700**	5,068	3,984	6,321	4,695
26,700	**26,750**	5,083	3,996	6,340	4,709
26,750	**26,800**	5,098	4,009	6,359	4,723
26,800	**26,850**	5,113	4,021	6,378	4,737
26,850	**26,900**	5,128	4,034	6,397	4,751
26,900	**26,950**	5,143	4,046	6,416	4,765
26,950	**27,000**	5,158	4,059	6,435	4,779
27,000					
27,000	**27,050**	5,173	4,071	6,454	4,793
27,050	**27,100**	5,188	4,084	6,473	4,807
27,100	**27,150**	5,203	4,096	6,492	4,821
27,150	**27,200**	5,218	4,109	6,511	4,835
27,200	**27,250**	5,233	4,121	6,530	4,849
27,250	**27,300**	5,248	4,134	6,549	4,863
27,300	**27,350**	5,263	4,146	6,568	4,877
27,350	**27,400**	5,278	4,159	6,587	4,891
27,400	**27,450**	5,293	4,171	6,606	4,905
27,450	**27,500**	5,308	4,184	6,625	4,919
27,500	**27,550**	5,323	4,196	6,644	4,933
27,550	**27,600**	5,338	4,209	6,663	4,947
27,600	**27,650**	5,353	4,221	6,682	4,961
27,650	**27,700**	5,368	4,234	6,701	4,975
27,700	**27,750**	5,383	4,246	6,720	4,989
27,750	**27,800**	5,398	4,259	6,739	5,003
27,800	**27,850**	5,413	4,271	6,758	5,017
27,850	**27,900**	5,428	4,284	6,777	5,031
27,900	**27,950**	5,443	4,296	6,796	5,045
27,950	**28,000**	5,458	4,309	6,815	5,059
28,000					
28,000	**28,050**	5,473	4,321	6,834	5,073
28,050	**28,100**	5,488	4,334	6,853	5,087
28,100	**28,150**	5,503	4,346	6,872	5,101
28,150	**28,200**	5,518	4,359	6,891	5,115
28,200	**28,250**	5,533	4,371	6,910	5,129
28,250	**28,300**	5,548	4,384	6,929	5,143
28,300	**28,350**	5,563	4,396	6,948	5,157
28,350	**28,400**	5,578	4,409	6,967	5,171
28,400	**28,450**	5,593	4,421	6,986	5,185
28,450	**28,500**	5,608	4,434	7,005	5,199
28,500	**28,550**	5,623	4,446	7,024	5,213
28,550	**28,600**	5,638	4,459	7,043	5,227
28,600	**28,650**	5,653	4,471	7,062	5,241
28,650	**28,700**	5,668	4,484	7,081	5,255
28,700	**28,750**	5,683	4,496	7,100	5,269
28,750	**28,800**	5,698	4,509	7,119	5,283
28,800	**28,850**	5,714	4,521	7,138	5,298
28,850	**28,900**	5,731	4,534	7,157	5,314
28,900	**28,950**	5,748	4,546	7,176	5,330
28,950	**29,000**	5,765	4,559	7,195	5,346

If line 37 (taxable income) is— At least	But less than	And you are— Single	Married filing jointly *	Married filing sepa-rately	Head of a house-hold
		Your tax is—			
29,000					
29,000	**29,050**	5,782	4,571	7,214	5,362
29,050	**29,100**	5,799	4,584	7,233	5,378
29,100	**29,150**	5,816	4,596	7,252	5,394
29,150	**29,200**	5,833	4,609	7,271	5,410
29,200	**29,250**	5,850	4,621	7,290	5,426
29,250	**29,300**	5,867	4,634	7,309	5,442
29,300	**29,350**	5,884	4,646	7,328	5,458
29,350	**29,400**	5,901	4,659	7,347	5,474
29,400	**29,450**	5,918	4,671	7,366	5,490
29,450	**29,500**	5,935	4,684	7,385	5,506
29,500	**29,550**	5,952	4,696	7,404	5,522
29,550	**29,600**	5,969	4,709	7,423	5,538
29,600	**29,650**	5,986	4,721	7,442	5,554
29,650	**29,700**	6,003	4,734	7,461	5,570
29,700	**29,750**	6,020	4,746	7,480	5,586
29,750	**29,800**	6,037	4,759	7,499	5,602
29,800	**29,850**	6,054	4,771	7,518	5,618
29,850	**29,900**	6,071	4,784	7,537	5,634
29,900	**29,950**	6,088	4,797	7,556	5,650
29,950	**30,000**	6,105	4,811	7,575	5,666
30,000					
30,000	**30,050**	6,122	4,825	7,595	5,682
30,050	**30,100**	6,139	4,839	7,616	5,698
30,100	**30,150**	6,156	4,853	7,637	5,714
30,150	**30,200**	6,173	4,867	7,658	5,730
30,200	**30,250**	6,190	4,881	7,679	5,746
30,250	**30,300**	6,207	4,895	7,700	5,762
30,300	**30,350**	6,224	4,909	7,721	5,778
30,350	**30,400**	6,241	4,923	7,742	5,794
30,400	**30,450**	6,258	4,937	7,763	5,810
30,450	**30,500**	6,275	4,951	7,784	5,826
30,500	**30,550**	6,292	4,965	7,805	5,842
30,550	**30,600**	6,309	4,979	7,826	5,858
30,600	**30,650**	6,326	4,993	7,847	5,874
30,650	**30,700**	6,343	5,007	7,868	5,890
30,700	**30,750**	6,360	5,021	7,889	5,906
30,750	**30,800**	6,377	5,035	7,910	5,922
30,800	**30,850**	6,394	5,049	7,931	5,938
30,850	**30,900**	6,411	5,063	7,952	5,954
30,900	**30,950**	6,428	5,077	7,973	5,970
30,950	**31,000**	6,445	5,091	7,994	5,986
31,000					
31,000	**31,050**	6,462	5,105	8,015	6,002
31,050	**31,100**	6,479	5,119	8,036	6,018
31,100	**31,150**	6,496	5,133	8,057	6,034
31,150	**31,200**	6,513	5,147	8,078	6,050
31,200	**31,250**	6,530	5,161	8,099	6,066
31,250	**31,300**	6,547	5,175	8,120	6,082
31,300	**31,350**	6,564	5,189	8,141	6,098
31,350	**31,400**	6,581	5,203	8,162	6,114
31,400	**31,450**	6,598	5,217	8,183	6,130
31,450	**31,500**	6,615	5,231	8,204	6,146
31,500	**31,550**	6,632	5,245	8,225	6,162
31,550	**31,600**	6,649	5,259	8,246	6,178
31,600	**31,650**	6,666	5,273	8,267	6,194
31,650	**31,700**	6,683	5,287	8,288	6,210
31,700	**31,750**	6,700	5,301	8,309	6,226
31,750	**31,800**	6,717	5,315	8,330	6,242
31,800	**31,850**	6,734	5,329	8,351	6,258
31,850	**31,900**	6,751	5,343	8,372	6,274
31,900	**31,950**	6,768	5,357	8,393	6,290
31,950	**32,000**	6,785	5,371	8,414	6,306

*This column must also be used by a qualifying widow(er).

Continued on next page

1984 Tax Table (*Continued*)

If line 37 (taxable income) is—		And you are—			
At least	But less than	Single	Married filing jointly *	Married filing sepa-rately	Head of a house-hold
		Your tax is—			
32,000					
32,000	**32,050**	6,802	5,385	8,435	6,322
32,050	**32,100**	6,819	5,399	8,456	6,338
32,100	**32,150**	6,836	5,413	8,477	6,354
32,150	**32,200**	6,853	5,427	8,498	6,370
32,200	**32,250**	6,870	5,441	8,519	6,386
32,250	**32,300**	6,887	5,455	8,540	6,402
32,300	**32,350**	6,904	5,469	8,561	6,418
32,350	**32,400**	6,921	5,483	8,582	6,434
32,400	**32,450**	6,938	5,497	8,603	6,450
32,450	**32,500**	6,955	5,511	8,624	6,466
32,500	**32,550**	6,972	5,525	8,645	6,482
32,550	**32,600**	6,989	5,539	8,666	6,498
32,600	**32,650**	7,006	5,553	8,687	6,514
32,650	**32,700**	7,023	5,567	8,708	6,530
32,700	**32,750**	7,040	5,581	8,729	6,546
32,750	**32,800**	7,057	5,595	8,750	6,562
32,800	**32,850**	7,074	5,609	8,771	6,578
32,850	**32,900**	7,091	5,623	8,792	6,594
32,900	**32,950**	7,108	5,637	8,813	6,610
32,950	**33,000**	7,125	5,651	8,834	6,626
33,000					
33,000	**33,050**	7,142	5,665	8,855	6,642
33,050	**33,100**	7,159	5,679	8,876	6,658
33,100	**33,150**	7,176	5,693	8,897	6,674
33,150	**33,200**	7,193	5,707	8,918	6,690
33,200	**33,250**	7,210	5,721	8,939	6,706
33,250	**33,300**	7,227	5,735	8,960	6,722
33,300	**33,350**	7,244	5,749	8,981	6,738
33,350	**33,400**	7,261	5,763	9,002	6,754
33,400	**33,450**	7,278	5,777	9,023	6,770
33,450	**33,500**	7,295	5,791	9,044	6,786
33,500	**33,550**	7,312	5,805	9,065	6,802
33,550	**33,600**	7,329	5,819	9,086	6,818
33,600	**33,650**	7,346	5,833	9,107	6,834
33,650	**33,700**	7,363	5,847	9,128	6,850
33,700	**33,750**	7,380	5,861	9,149	6,866
33,750	**33,800**	7,397	5,875	9,170	6,882
33,800	**33,850**	7,414	5,889	9,191	6,898
33,850	**33,900**	7,431	5,903	9,212	6,914
33,900	**33,950**	7,448	5,917	9,233	6,930
33,950	**34,000**	7,465	5,931	9,254	6,946
34,000					
34,000	**34,050**	7,482	5,945	9,275	6,962
34,050	**34,100**	7,499	5,959	9,296	6,978
34,100	**34,150**	7,517	5,973	9,317	6,995
34,150	**34,200**	7,536	5,987	9,338	7,012
34,200	**34,250**	7,555	6,001	9,359	7,030
34,250	**34,300**	7,574	6,015	9,380	7,047
34,300	**34,350**	7,593	6,029	9,401	7,065
34,350	**34,400**	7,612	6,043	9,422	7,082
34,400	**34,450**	7,631	6,057	9,443	7,100
34,450	**34,500**	7,650	6,071	9,464	7,117
34,500	**34,550**	7,669	6,085	9,485	7,135
34,550	**34,600**	7,688	6,099	9,506	7,152
34,600	**34,650**	7,707	6,113	9,527	7,170
34,650	**34,700**	7,726	6,127	9,548	7,187
34,700	**34,750**	7,745	6,141	9,569	7,205
34,750	**34,800**	7,764	6,155	9,590	7,222
34,800	**34,850**	7,783	6,169	9,611	7,240
34,850	**34,900**	7,802	6,183	9,632	7,257
34,900	**34,950**	7,821	6,197	9,653	7,275
34,950	**35,000**	7,840	6,211	9,674	7,292

If line 37 (taxable income) is—		And you are—			
At least	But less than	Single	Married filing jointly *	Married filing sepa-rately	Head of a house-hold
		Your tax is—			
35,000					
35,000	**35,050**	7,859	6,225	9,695	7,310
35,050	**35,100**	7,878	6,239	9,716	7,327
35,100	**35,150**	7,897	6,253	9,737	7,345
35,150	**35,200**	7,916	6,267	9,758	7,362
35,200	**35,250**	7,935	6,282	9,779	7,380
35,250	**35,300**	7,954	6,299	9,800	7,397
35,300	**35,350**	7,973	6,315	9,821	7,415
35,350	**35,400**	7,992	6,332	9,842	7,432
35,400	**35,450**	8,011	6,348	9,863	7,450
35,450	**35,500**	8,030	6,365	9,884	7,467
35,500	**35,550**	8,049	6,381	9,905	7,485
35,550	**35,600**	8,068	6,398	9,926	7,502
35,600	**35,650**	8,087	6,414	9,947	7,520
35,650	**35,700**	8,106	6,431	9,968	7,537
35,700	**35,750**	8,125	6,447	9,989	7,555
35,750	**35,800**	8,144	6,464	10,010	7,572
35,800	**35,850**	8,163	6,480	10,031	7,590
35,850	**35,900**	8,182	6,497	10,052	7,607
35,900	**35,950**	8,201	6,513	10,073	7,625
35,950	**36,000**	8,220	6,530	10,094	7,642
36,000					
36,000	**36,050**	8,239	6,546	10,115	7,660
36,050	**36,100**	8,258	6,563	10,136	7,677
36,100	**36,150**	8,277	6,579	10,157	7,695
36,150	**36,200**	8,296	6,596	10,178	7,712
36,200	**36,250**	8,315	6,612	10,199	7,730
36,250	**36,300**	8,334	6,629	10,220	7,747
36,300	**36,350**	8,353	6,645	10,241	7,765
36,350	**36,400**	8,372	6,662	10,262	7,782
36,400	**36,450**	8,391	6,678	10,283	7,800
36,450	**36,500**	8,410	6,695	10,304	7,817
36,500	**36,550**	8,429	6,711	10,325	7,835
36,550	**36,600**	8,448	6,728	10,346	7,852
36,600	**36,650**	8,467	6,744	10,367	7,870
36,650	**36,700**	8,486	6,761	10,388	7,887
36,700	**36,750**	8,505	6,777	10,409	7,905
36,750	**36,800**	8,524	6,794	10,430	7,922
36,800	**36,850**	8,543	6,810	10,451	7,940
36,850	**36,900**	8,562	6,827	10,472	7,957
36,900	**36,950**	8,581	6,843	10,493	7,975
36,950	**37,000**	8,600	6,860	10,514	7,992
37,000					
37,000	**37,050**	8,619	6,876	10,535	8,010
37,050	**37,100**	8,638	6,893	10,556	8,027
37,100	**37,150**	8,657	6,909	10,577	8,045
37,150	**37,200**	8,676	6,926	10,598	8,062
37,200	**37,250**	8,695	6,942	10,619	8,080
37,250	**37,300**	8,714	6,959	10,640	8,097
37,300	**37,350**	8,733	6,975	10,661	8,115
37,350	**37,400**	8,752	6,992	10,682	8,132
37,400	**37,450**	8,771	7,008	10,703	8,150
37,450	**37,500**	8,790	7,025	10,724	8,167
37,500	**37,550**	8,809	7,041	10,745	8,185
37,550	**37,600**	8,828	7,058	10,766	8,202
37,600	**37,650**	8,847	7,074	10,787	8,220
37,650	**37,700**	8,866	7,091	10,808	8,237
37,700	**37,750**	8,885	7,107	10,829	8,255
37,750	**37,800**	8,904	7,124	10,850	8,272
37,800	**37,850**	8,923	7,140	10,871	8,290
37,850	**37,900**	8,942	7,157	10,892	8,307
37,900	**37,950**	8,961	7,173	10,913	8,325
37,950	**38,000**	8,980	7,190	10,934	8,342

If line 37 (taxable income) is—		And you are—			
At least	But less than	Single	Married filing jointly *	Married filing sepa-rately	Head of a house-hold
		Your tax is—			
38,000					
38,000	**38,050**	8,999	7,206	10,955	8,360
38,050	**38,100**	9,018	7,223	10,976	8,377
38,100	**38,150**	9,037	7,239	10,997	8,395
38,150	**38,200**	9,056	7,256	11,018	8,412
38,200	**38,250**	9,075	7,272	11,039	8,430
38,250	**38,300**	9,094	7,289	11,060	8,447
38,300	**38,350**	9,113	7,305	11,081	8,465
38,350	**38,400**	9,132	7,322	11,102	8,482
38,400	**38,450**	9,151	7,338	11,123	8,500
38,450	**38,500**	9,170	7,355	11,144	8,517
38,500	**38,550**	9,189	7,371	11,165	8,535
38,550	**38,600**	9,208	7,388	11,186	8,552
38,600	**38,650**	9,227	7,404	11,207	8,570
38,650	**38,700**	9,246	7,421	11,228	8,587
38,700	**38,750**	9,265	7,437	11,249	8,605
38,750	**38,800**	9,284	7,454	11,270	8,622
38,800	**38,850**	9,303	7,470	11,291	8,640
38,850	**38,900**	9,322	7,487	11,312	8,657
38,900	**38,950**	9,341	7,503	11,333	8,675
38,950	**39,000**	9,360	7,520	11,354	8,692
39,000					
39,000	**39,050**	9,379	7,536	11,375	8,710
39,050	**39,100**	9,398	7,553	11,396	8,727
39,100	**39,150**	9,417	7,569	11,417	8,745
39,150	**39,200**	9,436	7,586	11,438	8,762
39,200	**39,250**	9,455	7,602	11,459	8,780
39,250	**39,300**	9,474	7,619	11,480	8,797
39,300	**39,350**	9,493	7,635	11,501	8,815
39,350	**39,400**	9,512	7,652	11,522	8,832
39,400	**39,450**	9,531	7,668	11,543	8,850
39,450	**39,500**	9,550	7,685	11,564	8,867
39,500	**39,550**	9,569	7,701	11,585	8,885
39,550	**39,600**	9,588	7,718	11,606	8,902
39,600	**39,650**	9,607	7,734	11,627	8,920
39,650	**39,700**	9,626	7,751	11,648	8,937
39,700	**39,750**	9,645	7,767	11,669	8,955
39,750	**39,800**	9,664	7,784	11,690	8,972
39,800	**39,850**	9,683	7,800	11,711	8,990
39,850	**39,900**	9,702	7,817	11,732	9,007
39,900	**39,950**	9,721	7,833	11,753	9,025
39,950	**40,000**	9,740	7,850	11,774	9,042
40,000					
40,000	**40,050**	9,759	7,866	11,795	9,060
40,050	**40,100**	9,778	7,883	11,816	9,077
40,100	**40,150**	9,797	7,899	11,837	9,095
40,150	**40,200**	9,816	7,916	11,858	9,112
40,200	**40,250**	9,835	7,932	11,879	9,130
40,250	**40,300**	9,854	7,949	11,900	9,147
40,300	**40,350**	9,873	7,965	11,921	9,165
40,350	**40,400**	9,892	7,982	11,942	9,182
40,400	**40,450**	9,911	7,998	11,963	9,200
40,450	**40,500**	9,930	8,015	11,984	9,217
40,500	**40,550**	9,949	8,031	12,005	9,235
40,550	**40,600**	9,968	8,048	12,026	9,252
40,600	**40,650**	9,987	8,064	12,047	9,270
40,650	**40,700**	10,006	8,081	12,068	9,287
40,700	**40,750**	10,025	8,097	12,089	9,305
40,750	**40,800**	10,044	8,114	12,110	9,322
40,800	**40,850**	10,063	8,130	12,131	9,340
40,850	**40,900**	10,082	8,147	12,152	9,357
40,900	**40,950**	10,101	8,163	12,173	9,375
40,950	**41,000**	10,120	8,180	12,194	9,392

*This column must also be used by a qualifying widow(er).

Continued on next page

1984 Tax Table (*Continued*)

If line 37 (taxable income) is— At least	But less than	Single	Married filing jointly *	Married filing separately	Head of a household
		Your tax is—			
41,000					
41,000	**41,050**	10,139	8,196	12,215	9,410
41,050	**41,100**	10,158	8,213	12,236	9,427
41,100	**41,150**	10,177	8,229	12,257	9,445
41,150	**41,200**	10,196	8,246	12,278	9,462
41,200	**41,250**	10,215	8,262	12,299	9,480
41,250	**41,300**	10,234	8,279	12,320	9,497
41,300	**41,350**	10,253	8,295	12,341	9,515
41,350	**41,400**	10,272	8,312	12,362	9,532
41,400	**41,450**	10,291	8,328	12,383	9,550
41,450	**41,500**	10,310	8,345	12,404	9,567
41,500	**41,550**	10,330	8,361	12,425	9,585
41,550	**41,600**	10,351	8,378	12,446	9,602
41,600	**41,650**	10,372	8,394	12,467	9,620
41,650	**41,700**	10,393	8,411	12,488	9,637
41,700	**41,750**	10,414	8,427	12,509	9,655
41,750	**41,800**	10,435	8,444	12,530	9,672
41,800	**41,850**	10,456	8,460	12,551	9,690
41,850	**41,900**	10,477	8,477	12,572	9,707
41,900	**41,950**	10,498	8,493	12,593	9,725
41,950	**42,000**	10,519	8,510	12,614	9,742
42,000					
42,000	**42,050**	10,540	8,526	12,635	9,760
42,050	**42,100**	10,561	8,543	12,656	9,777
42,100	**42,150**	10,582	8,559	12,677	9,795
42,150	**42,200**	10,603	8,576	12,698	9,812
42,200	**42,250**	10,624	8,592	12,719	9,830
42,250	**42,300**	10,645	8,609	12,740	9,847
42,300	**42,350**	10,666	8,625	12,761	9,865
42,350	**42,400**	10,687	8,642	12,782	9,882
42,400	**42,450**	10,708	8,658	12,803	9,900
42,450	**42,500**	10,729	8,675	12,824	9,917
42,500	**42,550**	10,750	8,691	12,845	9,935
42,550	**42,600**	10,771	8,708	12,866	9,952
42,600	**42,650**	10,792	8,724	12,887	9,970
42,650	**42,700**	10,813	8,741	12,908	9,987
42,700	**42,750**	10,834	8,757	12,929	10,005
42,750	**42,800**	10,855	8,774	12,950	10,022
42,800	**42,850**	10,876	8,790	12,971	10,040
42,850	**42,900**	10,897	8,807	12,994	10,057
42,900	**42,950**	10,918	8,823	13,016	10,075
42,950	**43,000**	10,939	8,840	13,039	10,092
43,000					
43,000	**43,050**	10,960	8,856	13,061	10,110
43,050	**43,100**	10,981	8,873	13,084	10,127
43,100	**43,150**	11,002	8,889	13,106	10,145
43,150	**43,200**	11,023	8,906	13,129	10,162
43,200	**43,250**	11,044	8,922	13,151	10,180
43,250	**43,300**	11,065	8,939	13,174	10,197
43,300	**43,350**	11,086	8,955	13,196	10,215
43,350	**43,400**	11,107	8,972	13,219	10,232
43,400	**43,450**	11,128	8,988	13,241	10,250
43,450	**43,500**	11,149	9,005	13,264	10,267
43,500	**43,550**	11,170	9,021	13,286	10,285
43,550	**43,600**	11,191	9,038	13,309	10,302
43,600	**43,650**	11,212	9,054	13,331	10,320
43,650	**43,700**	11,233	9,071	13,354	10,337
43,700	**43,750**	11,254	9,087	13,376	10,355
43,750	**43,800**	11,275	9,104	13,399	10,372
43,800	**43,850**	11,296	9,120	13,421	10,390
43,850	**43,900**	11,317	9,137	13,444	10,407
43,900	**43,950**	11,338	9,153	13,466	10,425
43,950	**44,000**	11,359	9,170	13,489	10,442

If line 37 (taxable income) is— At least	But less than	Single	Married filing jointly *	Married filing separately	Head of a household
		Your tax is—			
44,000					
44,000	**44,050**	11,380	9,186	13,511	10,460
44,050	**44,100**	11,401	9,203	13,534	10,477
44,100	**44,150**	11,422	9,219	13,556	10,495
44,150	**44,200**	11,443	9,236	13,579	10,512
44,200	**44,250**	11,464	9,252	13,601	10,530
44,250	**44,300**	11,485	9,269	13,624	10,547
44,300	**44,350**	11,506	9,285	13,646	10,565
44,350	**44,400**	11,527	9,302	13,669	10,582
44,400	**44,450**	11,548	9,318	13,691	10,600
44,450	**44,500**	11,569	9,335	13,714	10,617
44,500	**44,550**	11,590	9,351	13,736	10,635
44,550	**44,600**	11,611	9,368	13,759	10,652
44,600	**44,650**	11,632	9,384	13,781	10,670
44,650	**44,700**	11,653	9,401	13,804	10,687
44,700	**44,750**	11,674	9,417	13,826	10,707
44,750	**44,800**	11,695	9,434	13,849	10,728
44,800	**44,850**	11,716	9,450	13,871	10,749
44,850	**44,900**	11,737	9,467	13,894	10,770
44,900	**44,950**	11,758	9,483	13,916	10,791
44,950	**45,000**	11,779	9,500	13,939	10,812
45,000					
45,000	**45,050**	11,800	9,516	13,961	10,833
45,050	**45,100**	11,821	9,533	13,984	10,854
45,100	**45,150**	11,842	9,549	14,006	10,875
45,150	**45,200**	11,863	9,566	14,029	10,896
45,200	**45,250**	11,884	9,582	14,051	10,917
45,250	**45,300**	11,905	9,599	14,074	10,938
45,300	**45,350**	11,926	9,615	14,096	10,959
45,350	**45,400**	11,947	9,632	14,119	10,980
45,400	**45,450**	11,968	9,648	14,141	11,001
45,450	**45,500**	11,989	9,665	14,164	11,022
45,500	**45,550**	12,010	9,681	14,186	11,043
45,550	**45,600**	12,031	9,698	14,209	11,064
45,600	**45,650**	12,052	9,714	14,231	11,085
45,650	**45,700**	12,073	9,731	14,254	11,106
45,700	**45,750**	12,094	9,747	14,276	11,127
45,750	**45,800**	12,115	9,764	14,299	11,148
45,800	**45,850**	12,136	9,782	14,321	11,169
45,850	**45,900**	12,157	9,801	14,344	11,190
45,900	**45,950**	12,178	9,820	14,366	11,211
45,950	**46,000**	12,199	9,839	14,389	11,232
46,000					
46,000	**46,050**	12,220	9,858	14,411	11,253
46,050	**46,100**	12,241	9,877	14,434	11,274
46,100	**46,150**	12,262	9,896	14,456	11,295
46,150	**46,200**	12,283	9,915	14,479	11,316
46,200	**46,250**	12,304	9,934	14,501	11,337
46,250	**46,300**	12,325	9,953	14,524	11,358
46,300	**46,350**	12,346	9,972	14,546	11,379
46,350	**46,400**	12,367	9,991	14,569	11,400
46,400	**46,450**	12,388	10,010	14,591	11,421
46,450	**46,500**	12,409	10,029	14,614	11,442
46,500	**46,550**	12,430	10,048	14,636	11,463
46,550	**46,600**	12,451	10,067	14,659	11,484
46,600	**46,650**	12,472	10,086	14,681	11,505
46,650	**46,700**	12,493	10,105	14,704	11,526
46,700	**46,750**	12,514	10,124	14,726	11,547
46,750	**46,800**	12,535	10,143	14,749	11,568
46,800	**46,850**	12,556	10,162	14,771	11,589
46,850	**46,900**	12,577	10,181	14,794	11,610
46,900	**46,950**	12,598	10,200	14,816	11,631
46,950	**47,000**	12,619	10,219	14,839	11,652

If line 37 (taxable income) is— At least	But less than	Single	Married filing jointly *	Married filing separately	Head of a household
		Your tax is—			
47,000					
47,000	**47,050**	12,640	10,238	14,861	11,673
47,050	**47,100**	12,661	10,257	14,884	11,694
47,100	**47,150**	12,682	10,276	14,906	11,715
47,150	**47,200**	12,703	10,295	14,929	11,736
47,200	**47,250**	12,724	10,314	14,951	11,757
47,250	**47,300**	12,745	10,333	14,974	11,778
47,300	**47,350**	12,766	10,352	14,996	11,799
47,350	**47,400**	12,787	10,371	15,019	11,820
47,400	**47,450**	12,808	10,390	15,041	11,841
47,450	**47,500**	12,829	10,409	15,064	11,862
47,500	**47,550**	12,850	10,428	15,086	11,883
47,550	**47,600**	12,871	10,447	15,109	11,904
47,600	**47,650**	12,892	10,466	15,131	11,925
47,650	**47,700**	12,913	10,485	15,154	11,946
47,700	**47,750**	12,934	10,504	15,176	11,967
47,750	**47,800**	12,955	10,523	15,199	11,988
47,800	**47,850**	12,976	10,542	15,221	12,009
47,850	**47,900**	12,997	10,561	15,244	12,030
47,900	**47,950**	13,018	10,580	15,266	12,051
47,950	**48,000**	13,039	10,599	15,289	12,072
48,000					
48,000	**48,050**	13,060	10,618	15,311	12,093
48,050	**48,100**	13,081	10,637	15,334	12,114
48,100	**48,150**	13,102	10,656	15,356	12,135
48,150	**48,200**	13,123	10,675	15,379	12,156
48,200	**48,250**	13,144	10,694	15,401	12,177
48,250	**48,300**	13,165	10,713	15,424	12,198
48,300	**48,350**	13,186	10,732	15,446	12,219
48,350	**48,400**	13,207	10,751	15,469	12,240
48,400	**48,450**	13,228	10,770	15,491	12,261
48,450	**48,500**	13,249	10,789	15,514	12,282
48,500	**48,550**	13,270	10,808	15,536	12,303
48,550	**48,600**	13,291	10,827	15,559	12,324
48,600	**48,650**	13,312	10,846	15,581	12,345
48,650	**48,700**	13,333	10,865	15,604	12,366
48,700	**48,750**	13,354	10,884	15,626	12,387
48,750	**48,800**	13,375	10,903	15,649	12,408
48,800	**48,850**	13,396	10,922	15,671	12,429
48,850	**48,900**	13,417	10,941	15,694	12,450
48,900	**48,950**	13,438	10,960	15,716	12,471
48,950	**49,000**	13,459	10,979	15,739	12,492
49,000					
49,000	**49,050**	13,480	10,998	15,761	12,513
49,050	**49,100**	13,501	11,017	15,784	12,534
49,100	**49,150**	13,522	11,036	15,806	12,555
49,150	**49,200**	13,543	11,055	15,829	12,576
49,200	**49,250**	13,564	11,074	15,851	12,597
49,250	**49,300**	13,585	11,093	15,874	12,618
49,300	**49,350**	13,606	11,112	15,896	12,639
49,350	**49,400**	13,627	11,131	15,919	12,660
49,400	**49,450**	13,648	11,150	15,941	12,681
49,450	**49,500**	13,669	11,169	15,964	12,702
49,500	**49,550**	13,690	11,188	15,986	12,723
49,550	**49,600**	13,711	11,207	16,009	12,744
49,600	**49,650**	13,732	11,226	16,031	12,765
49,650	**49,700**	13,753	11,245	16,054	12,786
49,700	**49,750**	13,774	11,264	16,076	12,807
49,750	**49,800**	13,795	11,283	16,099	12,828
49,800	**49,850**	13,816	11,302	16,121	12,849
49,850	**49,900**	13,837	11,321	16,144	12,870
49,900	**49,950**	13,858	11,340	16,166	12,891
49,950	**50,000**	13,879	11,359	16,189	12,912

*This column must also be used by a qualifying widow(er).

50,000 or over—use tax rate schedules

APPENDIX C

1984 Optional State Sales Tax Tables

(If you kept records that show you paid more sales tax than the table for your State indicates, you may claim the higher amount on Schedule A, line 8a.)

Your itemized deduction for general sales tax paid can be estimated from these tables plus any qualifying sales taxes paid on the items listed on page 20.

To use the tables:

Step 1—Figure your total available income. (See note to the right).

Step 2—Count the number of exemptions for you and your family. Do not count exemptions claimed for being 65 or over or blind as part of your family size.

Step 3 A—If your total available income is not over $40,000, find the income line for your State on the tables and read across to find the amount of sales tax for your family size.

Step 3 B—If your income is over $40,000 but not over $100,000, find the deduction listed on the income line "$38,001-$40,000" for your family size and State. For each $5,000 (or part of $5,000) of income over $40,000, increase the deduction by the amount listed for the line "$40,001-$100,000."

Step 3 C—If your income is over $100,000, your sales tax deduction is limited to the deduction for income of $100,000. To figure your sales tax deduction, use Step 3 B, but don't go over $100,000.

***Note:** Use the total of the amount on Form 1040, line 33, and nontaxable income such as veterans' benefits, workmen's compensation, untaxed portion of long-term capital gains or unemployment compensation, nontaxable part of social security and railroad retirement benefits, dividend's exclusion, deduction for a married couple when both work, and public assistance payments.*

Income	Alabama [1] Family size 1	2	3	4	5	Over 5	Arizona [2] Family size 1&2	3	4	5	Over 5	Arkansas [1] Family size 1	2	3	4	5	Over 5
$1-$8,000	91	113	120	130	141	160	105	120	120	127	133	103	128	134	143	153	173
$8,001-$10,000	107	129	140	151	164	185	124	142	142	150	157	120	146	156	167	178	200
$10,001-$12,000	121	144	159	171	185	207	141	162	163	171	179	136	162	176	189	201	224
$12,001-$14,000	135	158	176	190	204	227	157	181	183	192	200	151	177	195	209	223	246
$14,001-$16,000	148	170	192	207	223	246	173	199	203	211	219	165	191	213	228	243	266
$16,001-$18,000	160	182	208	224	240	265	187	217	222	229	238	179	204	230	246	262	286
$18,001-$20,000	172	193	222	240	257	282	201	233	240	247	256	191	216	246	263	280	305
$20,001-$22,000	183	204	236	255	273	298	215	249	258	264	274	203	228	261	279	297	322
$22,001-$24,000	194	214	250	269	288	314	228	265	275	281	291	215	239	276	295	314	339
$24,001-$26,000	204	224	263	283	303	329	241	280	292	297	307	227	249	290	311	330	356
$26,001-$28,000	214	234	276	297	317	344	253	295	308	313	323	238	259	304	326	345	372
$28,001-$30,000	224	243	289	310	331	358	265	309	324	328	338	249	269	317	340	360	387
$30,001-$32,000	234	252	301	323	344	372	277	323	340	343	353	259	279	330	354	375	402
$32,001-$34,000	244	261	313	336	357	385	289	337	355	358	368	269	288	343	368	389	417
$34,001-$36,000	253	269	324	348	370	398	300	350	370	372	382	279	297	356	381	403	431
$36,001-$38,000	262	277	335	360	383	411	311	363	385	386	396	289	306	368	394	417	445
$38,001-$40,000	271	285	346	372	395	423	322	376	399	400	410	298	315	380	407	431	458
$40,001-$100,000 (See Step 3B)	14	14	17	19	20	21	16	19	20	20	21	15	16	19	20	22	23

Income	California [3] Family size 1&2	3&4	5	Over 5	Colorado [2] Family size 1&2	3&4	5	Over 5	Connecticut Family size 1&2	3,4&5	Over 5	Dist. of Columbia Family size 1	2	3	4	5	Over 5
$1-$8,000	125	147	155	164	47	56	59	63	126	139	146	94	112	125	125	132	140
$8,001-$10,000	147	173	183	193	55	66	70	74	150	167	175	110	129	145	146	155	164
$10,001-$12,000	167	198	208	219	63	76	80	85	172	194	203	125	145	164	166	177	186
$12,001-$14,000	186	220	232	243	70	85	90	95	194	220	229	139	159	182	186	197	206
$14,001-$16,000	204	242	255	266	77	94	99	104	214	244	254	152	173	198	205	216	225
$16,001-$18,000	222	263	276	288	83	102	108	113	234	268	279	165	186	213	223	234	244
$18,001-$20,000	238	282	297	309	89	110	117	122	253	291	302	177	198	228	240	252	261
$20,001-$22,000	254	301	317	330	95	118	125	130	271	313	325	189	210	242	256	268	278
$22,001-$24,000	270	320	336	349	101	126	133	138	289	335	347	200	221	256	272	284	294
$24,001-$26,000	285	338	355	368	107	133	141	146	306	357	369	211	232	269	287	300	310
$26,001-$28,000	299	355	373	386	112	140	149	154	323	378	390	222	242	282	302	315	325
$28,001-$30,000	313	372	391	404	117	147	156	162	340	398	411	232	252	295	317	330	340
$30,001-$32,000	327	389	408	422	122	154	163	169	356	418	432	242	262	307	332	345	354
$32,001-$34,000	341	405	425	439	127	161	170	176	372	438	452	252	272	319	346	359	368
$34,001-$36,000	354	421	441	455	132	168	177	183	388	458	472	262	281	330	360	373	382
$36,001-$38,000	367	436	457	471	137	174	184	190	403	477	491	271	290	341	373	387	396
$38,001-$40,000	380	451	473	487	142	180	191	196	418	496	510	280	299	352	386	400	409
$40,001-$100,000 (See Step 3B)	19	23	24	24	7	9	10	10	21	25	26	14	15	18	19	20	20

Income	Florida Family size 1&2	3	4	5	Over 5	Georgia [1] Family size 1	2	3	4	5	Over 5	Hawaii Family size 1&2	3	4	5	Over 5
$1-$8,000	104	123	123	130	139	82	103	110	116	125	141	158	180	183	190	204
$8,001-$10,000	124	145	146	155	164	95	117	127	135	145	161	181	206	209	219	235
$10,001-$12,000	142	166	168	178	187	107	130	143	152	163	180	201	228	234	245	263
$12,001-$14,000	159	186	189	200	209	118	141	157	167	179	198	220	249	256	269	288
$14,001-$16,000	176	204	210	221	230	129	152	171	182	195	214	238	268	277	292	312
$16,001-$18,000	192	222	229	241	250	139	162	184	196	210	229	254	286	297	313	335
$18,001-$20,000	207	239	248	260	269	149	171	196	209	224	244	270	303	315	333	356
$20,001-$22,000	222	255	267	278	288	158	180	208	222	237	258	285	319	333	352	377
$22,001-$24,000	236	271	285	296	306	167	189	219	234	250	271	299	335	350	371	397
$24,001-$26,000	250	287	302	314	324	176	198	230	246	262	283	313	350	366	389	416
$26,001-$28,000	264	302	319	331	341	184	206	240	258	274	295	326	364	382	406	434
$28,001-$30,000	277	317	336	348	357	192	213	250	269	286	307	339	378	397	423	451
$30,001-$32,000	290	331	353	364	373	200	220	260	280	297	319	351	391	412	439	468
$32,001-$34,000	303	345	369	380	389	208	227	270	290	308	330	363	404	426	454	485
$34,001-$36,000	315	359	385	396	405	215	234	279	300	319	341	375	416	440	469	501
$36,001-$38,000	327	373	400	412	420	222	241	288	310	330	352	386	428	454	484	517
$38,001-$40,000	339	386	415	427	435	229	247	297	320	340	362	397	440	467	499	533
$40,001-$100,000 (See Step 3B)	17	19	21	21	22	11	12	15	16	17	18	20	22	23	25	27

Income	Idaho Family size 1	2	3	4	5	Over 5	Illinois [4] Family size 1&2	3&4	5	Over 5	Indiana Family size 1&2	3&4	5	Over 5
$1-$8,000	97	118	127	137	150	169	121	143	153	162	117	139	148	157
$8,001-$10,000	114	135	148	160	174	195	143	169	180	191	137	163	173	183
$10,001-$12,000	130	151	167	181	196	218	163	193	206	217	156	186	197	207
$12,001-$14,000	144	165	185	200	216	240	182	216	230	242	173	207	219	230
$14,001-$16,000	158	178	202	219	236	260	200	238	253	266	189	227	240	252
$16,001-$18,000	171	191	218	236	254	280	217	259	275	288	205	246	260	272
$18,001-$20,000	184	203	234	253	271	298	233	279	296	309	220	264	279	291
$20,001-$22,000	196	214	249	269	288	315	249	299	316	330	234	282	298	310
$22,001-$24,000	208	225	263	284	304	332	264	318	336	350	248	299	316	328
$24,001-$26,000	219	235	277	299	319	348	279	336	355	369	261	316	333	346
$26,001-$28,000	230	245	290	314	334	364	294	354	373	388	274	332	350	363
$28,001-$30,000	241	255	303	328	349	379	308	372	391	407	287	347	366	379
$30,001-$32,000	251	264	316	342	363	394	322	389	409	425	299	362	382	395
$32,001-$34,000	261	273	328	355	377	408	335	406	426	442	311	377	397	411
$34,001-$36,000	271	282	340	368	390	422	348	422	443	459	323	392	412	426
$36,001-$38,000	281	290	352	381	403	436	361	438	460	476	334	406	427	441
$38,001-$40,000	291	298	363	393	416	449	374	454	476	493	345	420	442	456
$40,001-$100,000 (See Step 3B)	15	15	18	20	21	22	19	23	24	25	17	21	22	23

Income	Iowa Family size 1&2	3,4&5	Over 5	Kansas [1] Family size 1	2	3	4	5	Over 5	Kentucky Family size 1&2	3&4	5	Over 5
$1-$8,000	96	107	115	72	90	95	102	108	122	91	104	109	117
$8,001-$10,000	113	127	136	85	104	112	120	127	142	108	124	130	138
$10,001-$12,000	129	146	155	96	116	127	136	144	160	124	143	150	157
$12,001-$14,000	144	164	173	107	128	141	151	160	177	138	161	168	176
$14,001-$16,000	158	181	191	117	138	155	165	176	193	152	178	186	193
$16,001-$18,000	172	197	207	126	148	168	179	191	208	165	195	203	210
$18,001-$20,000	185	212	223	135	158	180	192	205	222	178	211	219	226
$20,001-$22,000	198	227	239	144	167	192	205	219	236	190	226	235	241
$22,001-$24,000	210	242	254	153	176	203	217	232	249	202	241	250	256
$24,001-$26,000	222	256	268	161	184	214	229	245	262	214	256	265	271
$26,001-$28,000	233	270	282	169	192	225	240	257	274	225	270	280	285
$28,001-$30,000	244	284	296	177	200	235	251	269	286	236	284	294	299
$30,001-$32,000	255	297	309	185	208	245	262	281	298	247	298	308	312
$32,001-$34,000	266	310	322	192	215	255	273	293	309	258	312	322	325
$34,001-$36,000	277	323	335	199	222	265	284	304	320	268	325	336	338
$36,001-$38,000	287	336	348	206	229	275	294	315	330	278	338	349	351
$38,001-$40,000	297	348	360	212	236	284	304	325	340	288	351	362	363
$40,001-$100,000 (See Step 3B)	15	17	18	11	12	14	15	16	17	14	18	18	18

Income	Louisiana [5] Family size 1&2	3&4	5	Over 5	Maine [6] Family size 1&2	3&4	5	Over 5	Maryland Family size 1&2	3	4	5	Over 5	Massachusetts [7] Family size 1&2	Over 2
$1-$8,000	67	75	79	83	90	102	107	112	80	90	90	94	98	58	63
$8,001-$10,000	80	91	94	99	107	122	128	134	95	108	108	113	118	69	76
$10,001-$12,000	92	105	109	114	123	141	147	154	110	125	125	131	136	79	89
$12,001-$14,000	104	118	123	128	138	160	166	173	124	141	143	149	154	89	101
$14,001-$16,000	115	131	137	142	152	177	184	191	137	157	160	166	171	98	113
$16,001-$18,000	125	144	150	155	166	194	201	208	150	172	177	182	188	107	124
$18,001-$20,000	135	156	162	168	179	210	218	225	163	186	193	198	203	116	135
$20,001-$22,000	145	168	174	180	191	226	234	241	175	200	209	213	219	124	146
$22,001-$24,000	155	179	186	192	203	241	250	257	187	214	225	228	234	132	157
$24,001-$26,000	164	190	198	204	215	256	265	273	198	227	240	243	249	140	168
$26,001-$28,000	173	201	209	215	227	271	280	288	209	240	255	257	263	148	178
$28,001-$30,000	182	212	220	226	238	285	295	303	220	253	270	271	278	155	188
$30,001-$32,000	191	223	231	237	249	299	310	318	231	265	285	285	292	162	198
$32,001-$34,000	200	233	242	248	260	313	324	332	242	277	299	299	305	169	208
$34,001-$36,000	209	243	253	259	271	327	338	346	253	289	313	313	319	176	217
$36,001-$38,000	217	253	263	269	282	340	352	360	263	301	327	327	332	183	227
$38,001-$40,000	225	262	273	279	292	353	366	373	273	313	341	341	345	190	236
$40,001-$100,000 (See Step 3B)	11	13	14	14	15	18	18	19	14	16	17	17	17	10	12

[1] Local sales taxes are not included. Add an amount based on the ratio between the local and State sales tax rates, considering the number of months each rate has been in effect.

[2] Local sales taxes are not included. Add the amount paid.

[3] The 1¼ percent local sales tax is included. If a ½ of 1 percent local sales tax for transportation is paid all year (Alameda, Contra Costa, Los Angeles, San Francisco, San Mateo, Santa Clara and Santa Cruz counties), add 8 percent to the table amount.

[4] The Illinois table is based on a combined 6 percent rate (5 State, 1 local). Residents of: Du Page, Kane, Lake, McHenry and Will counties can add 5 percent; Cook county can add 19 percent; Chicago can add an additional 19 percent. For other local sales tax, see footnote 1.

[5] If your local sales tax applies to food for home consumption, check your local newspaper during mid-January for the correct deduction. Otherwise, see footnote 1.

[6] Sales tax paid on purchase of electricity of 750 KWH or more per month can be added to the table amounts.

[7] Sales tax paid on the purchase of any single item of clothing for $175 or more can be added to the table amounts.

[8] Sales tax paid on purchases of natural gas or electricity can be added to the table amounts. For local sales tax, see footnote 1.

[9] Local sales taxes are not included. If paid all year, add 26 percent of the table amount for each 1 percent of local sales tax rate. Otherwise, use a proportionate amount. For N.Y. City, add 107 percent of the table amount.

(Footnotes continued on next page)

1984 Optional State Sales Tax Tables—Continued

Income	Michigan				Minnesota [8]		Mississippi					
	Family size 1&2	3&4	5	Over 5	Family size 1&2	Over 2	Family size 1	2	3	4	5	Over 5
$1-$8,000	88	102	108	113	86	99	167	201	215	227	242	271
$8,001-$10,000	103	121	127	133	101	118	194	231	250	264	282	313
$10,001-$12,000	118	138	145	151	115	136	220	257	282	298	318	350
$12,001-$14,000	131	154	161	168	129	152	244	282	312	330	352	385
$14,001-$16,000	144	169	177	184	142	168	266	304	340	360	383	418
$16,001-$18,000	156	184	192	199	154	183	287	326	367	388	413	449
$18,001-$20,000	168	198	207	214	166	198	308	346	392	415	442	478
$20,001-$22,000	180	211	221	228	177	212	327	365	416	441	470	506
$22,001-$24,000	191	224	234	241	188	226	346	384	440	466	496	533
$24,001-$26,000	202	237	247	254	198	240	364	401	462	490	522	559
$26,001-$28,000	212	249	260	267	208	253	382	418	484	513	547	584
$28,001-$30,000	222	261	272	280	218	266	399	435	506	536	571	608
$30,001-$32,000	232	273	284	292	228	279	416	451	527	558	594	631
$32,001-$34,000	242	284	296	304	238	291	432	467	547	580	617	654
$34,001-$36,000	252	295	308	316	247	303	448	482	566	601	639	676
$36,001-$38,000	261	306	319	327	256	315	463	497	585	622	661	698
$38,001-$40,000	270	317	330	338	265	327	478	511	604	642	682	719
$40,001-$100,000 (See Step 3B)	14	16	17	17	13	16	24	26	30	32	34	36

Income	Missouri [1]						Nebraska [1]				Nevada [1]				New Jersey	
	Family size 1	2	3	4	5	Over 5	Family size 1&2	3&4	5	Over 5	Family size 1&2	3&4	5	Over 5	Family size 1&2	Over 2
$1-$8,000	99	119	126	135	145	163	75	86	91	95	94	106	111	115	76	83
$8,001-$10,000	116	137	147	158	169	188	88	102	107	112	112	128	134	138	91	101
$10,001-$12,000	132	153	167	178	191	211	101	117	123	128	129	148	154	159	105	118
$12,001-$14,000	147	168	185	198	211	233	112	131	137	142	145	167	174	179	118	134
$14,001-$16,000	162	181	202	216	230	253	123	144	151	156	160	186	193	199	131	150
$16,001-$18,000	175	194	219	234	248	271	133	157	164	170	174	204	211	217	144	165
$18,001-$20,000	188	207	234	250	266	289	143	169	177	183	188	221	229	235	156	180
$20,001-$22,000	200	219	249	266	282	306	152	181	189	195	202	238	246	253	167	194
$22,001-$24,000	212	230	264	282	298	323	161	192	201	207	215	254	263	270	178	208
$24,001-$26,000	224	241	278	297	314	339	170	203	212	219	228	270	279	287	189	222
$26,001-$28,000	235	251	291	311	329	354	179	214	223	230	241	286	295	303	200	236
$28,001-$30,000	246	261	304	325	343	369	187	225	234	241	253	301	311	319	211	249
$30,001-$32,000	257	271	317	339	357	383	195	235	245	252	265	316	326	335	221	262
$32,001-$34,000	268	281	330	352	371	397	203	245	256	263	277	331	341	350	231	275
$34,001-$36,000	278	291	342	365	384	411	211	255	266	273	288	346	356	365	241	288
$36,001-$38,000	288	299	354	378	397	424	219	265	276	283	299	360	371	380	251	301
$38,001-$40,000	298	307	366	391	410	437	226	274	286	293	310	374	385	394	261	313
$40,001-$100,000 (See Step 3B)	15	15	18	20	21	22	11	14	14	15	16	19	19	20	13	16

Income	New Mexico [1]						New York [9]				North Carolina [10]					
	Family size 1	2	3	4	5	Over 5	Family size 1&2	3&4	5	Over 5	Family size 1	2	3	4	5	Over 5
$1-$8,000	117	144	150	155	165	184	86	99	103	108	92	114	121	130	139	159
$8,001-$10,000	136	164	174	181	193	213	103	118	123	128	108	131	141	151	162	183
$10,001-$12,000	153	183	197	206	219	240	118	136	141	147	123	146	159	171	182	204
$12,001-$14,000	169	200	217	228	242	265	132	152	159	165	137	159	176	189	202	224
$14,001-$16,000	184	216	237	249	265	288	146	168	176	182	150	172	192	206	220	243
$16,001-$18,000	198	231	255	269	286	310	159	183	192	198	162	184	207	222	237	261
$18,001-$20,000	211	245	273	289	306	331	172	198	208	214	174	195	222	237	253	277
$20,001-$22,000	224	259	290	307	326	351	184	212	223	229	185	206	236	252	268	293
$22,001-$24,000	236	272	306	325	345	371	196	226	238	244	196	216	249	266	283	308
$24,001-$26,000	248	284	321	342	363	389	208	240	252	258	207	226	262	280	298	323
$26,001-$28,000	260	296	336	359	380	407	219	253	266	272	217	236	275	293	312	337
$28,001-$30,000	271	308	351	375	397	425	230	266	280	286	227	245	287	306	325	351
$30,001-$32,000	282	319	365	391	414	442	241	278	293	299	237	254	299	319	338	364
$32,001-$34,000	293	330	379	407	430	459	252	290	306	312	247	263	310	331	351	377
$34,001-$36,000	304	341	393	422	446	475	262	302	319	325	257	271	321	343	364	390
$36,001-$38,000	314	351	406	437	462	491	272	314	332	337	266	279	332	355	376	402
$38,001-$40,000	323	361	419	451	477	506	282	326	345	349	275	287	343	366	388	414
$40,001-$100,000 (See Step 3B)	16	18	21	23	24	25	14	16	17	17	14	14	17	18	19	21

Income	North Dakota			Ohio [1]				Oklahoma [1]						Pennsylvania	
	Family size 1&2	3,4&5	Over 5	Family size 1&2	3&4	5	Over 5	Family size 1	2	3	4	5	Over 5	Family size 1&2	Over 2
$1-$8,000	72	83	90	90	102	107	112	71	85	90	95	102	115	77	86
$8,001-$10,000	85	99	107	107	122	128	134	83	97	105	112	119	133	92	103
$10,001-$12,000	98	115	122	123	141	147	154	95	109	119	127	135	150	106	120
$12,001-$14,000	109	129	137	138	159	166	172	106	120	132	141	150	165	120	136
$14,001-$16,000	120	143	151	153	176	184	191	116	130	144	154	164	180	133	151
$16,001-$18,000	131	156	164	167	193	201	208	125	139	156	167	177	193	145	166
$18,001-$20,000	142	169	177	180	209	217	225	134	148	167	179	189	206	157	180
$20,001-$22,000	152	182	189	193	225	233	241	143	156	178	191	201	219	169	194
$22,001-$24,000	162	194	201	206	240	248	257	152	164	188	202	213	231	180	207
$24,001-$26,000	171	206	213	218	255	263	272	160	172	198	213	224	242	191	220
$26,001-$28,000	180	217	224	230	269	278	287	168	180	208	223	235	253	202	233
$28,001-$30,000	189	228	235	242	283	293	302	176	187	218	233	246	264	213	246
$30,001-$32,000	198	239	246	253	297	307	316	184	194	227	243	256	275	223	259
$32,001-$34,000	207	250	257	264	311	321	330	192	201	236	253	266	285	233	271
$34,001-$36,000	215	261	267	275	324	334	344	199	208	245	263	276	295	243	283
$36,001-$38,000	223	272	277	286	337	347	357	206	214	253	272	286	305	253	295
$38,001-$40,000	231	282	287	297	350	360	370	213	220	261	281	295	314	263	306
$40,001-$100,000 (See Step 3B)	12	14	14	15	18	18	19	11	11	13	14	15	16	13	15

Income	Rhode Island		South Carolina						South Dakota [2]					
	Family size 1&2	Over 2	Family size 1	2	3	4	5	Over 5	Family size 1	2	3	4	5	Over 5
$1-$8,000	88	94	110	131	140	149	161	181	110	133	140	149	162	182
$8,001-$10,000	104	113	128	150	163	173	186	209	129	153	164	174	188	210
$10,001-$12,000	120	131	145	167	184	196	210	233	147	171	185	198	213	235
$12,001-$14,000	134	148	161	183	203	217	231	256	164	188	205	219	235	259
$14,001-$16,000	148	164	176	197	221	236	252	277	181	203	224	239	257	281
$16,001-$18,000	161	180	190	211	239	255	271	297	196	218	242	259	277	302
$18,001-$20,000	174	196	204	224	255	272	289	316	211	232	259	277	296	322
$20,001-$22,000	187	211	217	236	271	289	307	334	225	245	276	295	315	341
$22,001-$24,000	199	225	229	248	286	306	324	351	239	258	292	312	333	360
$24,001-$26,000	210	239	241	259	301	322	340	368	252	271	308	329	351	377
$26,001-$28,000	221	253	253	270	315	337	356	384	265	283	323	346	368	394
$28,001-$30,000	232	267	265	281	329	352	371	400	278	294	338	362	385	411
$30,001-$32,000	243	281	276	291	342	366	386	415	290	305	353	377	401	427
$32,001-$34,000	254	294	287	301	355	381	400	430	302	316	367	392	417	443
$34,001-$36,000	265	307	298	311	368	395	414	444	314	327	381	407	432	458
$36,001-$38,000	276	320	308	320	381	408	428	458	326	337	395	422	447	473
$38,001-$40,000	286	333	318	329	393	421	441	471	337	347	408	436	462	487
$40,001-$100,000 (See Step 3B)	14	17	16	16	20	21	22	24	17	17	20	22	23	24

Income	Tennessee [1]						Texas [1]				Utah [11]					
	Family size 1	2	3	4	5	Over 5	Family size 1&2	3&4	5	Over 5	Family size 1	2	3	4	5	Over 5
$1-$8,000	130	157	167	179	192	217	69	81	87	92	136	164	173	184	197	223
$8,001-$10,000	153	180	194	209	223	251	82	97	104	110	160	188	202	216	230	257
$10,001-$12,000	174	201	220	236	252	281	94	112	119	126	181	210	229	244	260	289
$12,001-$14,000	193	221	244	261	279	308	106	126	134	141	202	230	254	271	288	318
$14,001-$16,000	212	239	267	285	304	334	117	139	148	156	221	249	277	296	314	345
$16,001-$18,000	230	256	288	308	328	359	127	152	162	170	239	267	300	320	340	371
$18,001-$20,000	247	272	308	330	350	382	137	165	175	183	256	284	321	343	364	395
$20,001-$22,000	263	287	328	351	372	404	147	177	188	196	273	300	342	365	387	418
$22,001-$24,000	279	302	347	371	393	426	157	189	200	209	289	315	362	387	409	441
$24,001-$26,000	294	316	365	390	413	446	166	200	212	221	305	330	381	407	431	462
$26,001-$28,000	309	330	383	409	433	466	175	211	224	233	320	344	399	427	452	483
$28,001-$30,000	323	343	401	427	452	485	184	222	235	245	335	358	417	447	472	504
$30,001-$32,000	337	356	418	445	471	504	193	233	246	257	350	371	435	466	492	523
$32,001-$34,000	351	369	434	462	489	522	201	244	257	268	364	384	452	484	511	542
$34,001-$36,000	364	381	450	479	506	540	209	254	268	279	378	397	469	502	530	561
$36,001-$38,000	377	393	466	496	523	557	217	264	279	290	391	409	485	520	548	579
$38,001-$40,000	390	404	481	512	540	574	225	274	289	301	404	421	501	537	566	597
$40,001-$100,000 (See Step 3B)	20	20	24	26	27	29	11	14	14	15	20	21	25	27	28	30

Income	Vermont						Virginia [12]						Washington [13]			
	Family size 1	2	3	4	5	Over 5	Family size 1	2	3	4	5	Over 5	Family size 1&2	3&4	5	Over 5
$1-$8,000	44	50	58	58	60	65	88	111	117	127	137	156	136	154	156	165
$8,001-$10,000	53	60	69	69	73	77	104	127	137	148	159	179	162	185	189	198
$10,001-$12,000	61	68	79	80	84	89	118	141	155	166	179	200	187	214	219	230
$12,001-$14,000	68	76	89	91	95	100	131	154	171	184	197	220	210	242	248	259
$14,001-$16,000	75	84	98	102	106	110	143	167	187	201	215	238	232	268	277	288
$16,001-$18,000	82	92	107	112	116	120	155	178	202	216	231	255	254	293	304	315
$18,001-$20,000	89	99	115	122	126	130	166	189	216	231	247	271	274	318	330	341
$20,001-$22,000	96	106	123	132	136	139	177	199	230	245	262	286	294	342	356	367
$22,001-$24,000	102	113	131	142	145	148	188	209	243	259	276	301	314	365	381	392
$24,001-$26,000	108	120	139	151	154	157	198	219	256	273	290	315	333	388	405	417
$26,001-$28,000	114	126	147	160	163	166	208	228	268	286	304	329	351	410	429	441
$28,001-$30,000	120	132	154	169	172	174	218	237	280	298	317	342	369	432	453	464
$30,001-$32,000	126	138	161	178	181	182	227	246	292	310	330	355	387	453	476	487
$32,001-$34,000	132	144	168	187	190	190	236	254	303	322	342	368	405	474	499	510
$34,001-$36,000	138	150	175	196	198	198	245	262	314	334	354	380	422	495	522	532
$36,001-$38,000	143	156	182	204	206	206	254	270	325	345	366	391	439	515	544	554
$38,001-$40,000	148	162	188	212	214	214	263	277	336	356	378	402	455	535	566	575
$40,001-$100,000 (See Step 3B)	7	8	9	11	11	11	13	14	17	18	19	20	23	27	28	29

Income	West Virginia				Wisconsin [14]				Wyoming [1]					
	Family size 1&2	3&4	5	Over 5	Family size 1&2	3&4	5	Over 5	Family size 1	2	3	4	5	Over 5
$1-$8,000	105	119	123	130	103	115	119	125	81	98	104	109	117	132
$8,001-$10,000	125	142	147	154	123	137	142	149	95	112	121	127	136	152
$10,001-$12,000	143	164	170	177	141	158	164	171	107	125	136	144	153	170
$12,001-$14,000	160	184	192	199	158	178	185	192	119	136	151	159	169	187
$14,001-$16,000	176	204	212	220	175	197	205	212	130	147	164	173	184	202
$16,001-$18,000	192	223	232	240	191	216	224	231	140	157	176	187	198	217
$18,001-$20,000	207	241	251	259	206	233	242	250	150	167	188	200	212	231
$20,001-$22,000	222	258	270	278	220	251	260	268	159	176	200	213	225	244
$22,001-$24,000	236	275	288	296	234	268	278	285	168	185	211	225	237	257
$24,001-$26,000	250	292	306	313	248	284	295	302	177	193	222	236	249	269
$26,001-$28,000	264	308	323	330	262	300	312	318	186	201	232	247	261	281
$28,001-$30,000	277	324	340	347	275	316	328	334	194	209	242	258	273	293
$30,001-$32,000	290	340	357	363	288	331	344	350	202	216	252	269	284	304
$32,001-$34,000	303	355	373	379	301	346	360	366	210	223	261	280	294	315
$34,001-$36,000	315	370	389	395	313	361	375	381	218	230	270	290	304	326
$36,001-$38,000	327	385	405	411	325	376	390	396	226	237	279	300	314	336
$38,001-$40,000	339	399	420	426	337	390	405	410	233	244	288	310	324	346
$40,001-$100,000 (See Step 3B)	17	20	21	21	17	20	20	21	12	12	14	16	16	17

[10] The North Carolina table is based on a combined 4 percent rate (3 State, 1 local). If the ½ of 1 percent sales tax is also paid, see footnote 1.

[11] Local ⅞'s of 1 percent sales tax is included. If the ¼ of 1 percent county sales tax for transportation is paid all year, add 5 percent to the table amount. Otherwise, see footnote 1.

[12] Local 1 percent sales tax is included.

[13] The Washington table is based on a combined 7 percent rate (6.5 State, 0.5 local). Border county taxpayers where the combined rate is 5.9 percent (5.4 State, 0.5 local) should use 84 percent of the table amount. For local sales tax, in addition to the ½ of 1 percent included in the table, see footnote 1.

[14] Sales tax paid on the purchase of natural gas or electricity (May through October) can be added to the table amounts.

1984 Earned Income Credit Table

Caution: This is Not a Tax Table

To find your earned income credit: Read down the column titled "If line 3 or 4 of the worksheet is—" and find the appropriate amount from the Earned Income Credit Worksheet on page 16. Read across to the right and find the amount of the earned income credit. Enter that amount on line 5 or 6 of the worksheet, whichever applies.

If line 3 or 4 of the worksheet is—		Your earned income credit is—	If line 3 or 4 of the worksheet is—		Your earned income credit is—	If line 3 or 4 of the worksheet is—		Your earned income credit is—	If line 3 or 4 of the worksheet is—		Your earned income credit is—	If line 3 or 4 of the worksheet is—		Your earned income credit is—
Over	But not over		Over	But not over		Over	But not over		Over	But not over		Over	But not over	
$0	$50	$3	$1,800	$1,850	$183	$3,600	$3,650	$363	$6,350	$6,400	$453	$8,150	$8,200	$228
50	100	8	1,850	1,900	188	3,650	3,700	368	6,400	6,450	447	8,200	8,250	222
100	150	13	1,900	1,950	193	3,700	3,750	373	6,450	6,500	441	8,250	8,300	216
150	200	18	1,950	2,000	198	3,750	3,800	378	6,500	6,550	434	8,300	8,350	209
200	250	23	2,000	2,050	203	3,800	3,850	383	6,550	6,600	428	8,350	8,400	203
250	300	28	2,050	2,100	208	3,850	3,900	388	6,600	6,650	422	8,400	8,450	197
300	350	33	2,100	2,150	213	3,900	3,950	393	6,650	6,700	416	8,450	8,500	191
350	400	38	2,150	2,200	218	3,950	4,000	398	6,700	6,750	409	8,500	8,550	184
400	450	43	2,200	2,250	223	4,000	4,050	403	6,750	6,800	403	8,550	8,600	178
450	500	48	2,250	2,300	228	4,050	4,100	408	6,800	6,850	397	8,600	8,650	172
500	550	53	2,300	2,350	233	4,100	4,150	413	6,850	6,900	391	8,650	8,700	166
550	600	58	2,350	2,400	238	4,150	4,200	418	6,900	6,950	384	8,700	8,750	159
600	650	63	2,400	2,450	243	4,200	4,250	423	6,950	7,000	378	8,750	8,800	153
650	700	68	2,450	2,500	248	4,250	4,300	428	7,000	7,050	372	8,800	8,850	147
700	750	73	2,500	2,550	253	4,300	4,350	433	7,050	7,100	366	8,850	8,900	141
750	800	78	2,550	2,600	258	4,350	4,400	438	7,100	7,150	359	8,900	8,950	134
800	850	83	2,600	2,650	263	4,400	4,450	443	7,150	7,200	353	8,950	9,000	128
850	900	88	2,650	2,700	268	4,450	4,500	448	7,200	7,250	347	9,000	9,050	122
900	950	93	2,700	2,750	273	4,500	4,550	453	7,250	7,300	341	9,050	9,100	116
950	1,000	98	2,750	2,800	278	4,550	4,600	458	7,300	7,350	334	9,100	9,150	109
1,000	1,050	103	2,800	2,850	283	4,600	4,650	463	7,350	7,400	328	9,150	9,200	103
1,050	1,100	108	2,850	2,900	288	4,650	4,700	468	7,400	7,450	322	9,200	9,250	97
1,100	1,150	113	2,900	2,950	293	4,700	4,750	473	7,450	7,500	316	9,250	9,300	91
1,150	1,200	118	2,950	3,000	298	4,750	4,800	478	7,500	7,550	309	9,300	9,350	84
1,200	1,250	123	3,000	3,050	303	4,800	4,850	483	7,550	7,600	303	9,350	9,400	78
1,250	1,300	128	3,050	3,100	308	4,850	4,900	488	7,600	7,650	297	9,400	9,450	72
1,300	1,350	133	3,100	3,150	313	4,900	4,950	493	7,650	7,700	291	9,450	9,500	66
1,350	1,400	138	3,150	3,200	318	4,950	5,000	498	7,700	7,750	284	9,500	9,550	59
1,400	1,450	143	3,200	3,250	323	5,000	6,000	500	7,750	7,800	278	9,550	9,600	53
1,450	1,500	148	3,250	3,300	328	6,000	6,050	497	7,800	7,850	272	9,600	9,650	47
1,500	1,550	153	3,300	3,350	333	6,050	6,100	491	7,850	7,900	266	9,650	9,700	41
1,550	1,600	158	3,350	3,400	338	6,100	6,150	484	7,900	7,950	259	9,700	9,750	34
1,600	1,650	163	3,400	3,450	343	6,150	6,200	478	7,950	8,000	253	9,750	9,800	28
1,650	1,700	168	3,450	3,500	348	6,200	6,250	472	8,000	8,050	247	9,800	9,850	22
1,700	1,750	173	3,500	3,550	353	6,250	6,300	466	8,050	8,100	241	9,850	9,900	16
1,750	1,800	178	3,550	3,600	358	6,300	6,350	459	8,100	8,150	234	9,900	9,950	9
												9,950	9,999	3

APPENDIX E
Unified Rate Schedules

Unified Rate Schedule
(Estates of decedents dying before '88 and gifts made before '88

(A)	(B)	(C)	(D)
Amount subject to tentative tax		Tax on amount in Column A *	Tax rate on excess over amounts in Column A*
exceeding	but not exceeding		Percent
$ ——	$ 10,000	$ ——	18
10,000	20,000	1,800	20
20,000	40,000	3,800	22
40,000	60,000	8,200	24
60,000	80,000	13,000	26
80,000	100,000	18,200	28
100,000	150,000	23,800	30
150,000	250,000	38,800	32
250,000	500,000	70,800	34
500,000	750,000	155,800	37
750,000	1,000,000	248,300	39
1,000,000	1,250,000	345,800	41
1,250,000	1,500,000	448,300	43
1,500,000	2,000,000	555,800	45
2,000,000	2,500,000	780,800	49
2,500,000	3,000,000	1,025,800	53
3,000,000	——	1,290,800	55

* Before credits

Unified Rate Schedule
(Estates of decedents made in '88 and gifts made in '88

(A)	(B)	(C)	(D)
Amount subject to tentative tax		Tax on amount in Column A *	Tax rate on excess over amounts in Column A*
exceeding	but not exceeding		Percent
$ ——	$ 10,000	$ ——	18
10,000	20,000	1,800	20
20,000	40,000	3,800	22
40,000	60,000	8,200	24
60,000	80,000	13,000	26
80,000	100,000	18,200	28
100,000	150,000	23,800	30
150,000	250,000	38,800	32
250,000	500,000	70,800	34
500,000	750,000	155,800	37
750,000	1,000,000	248,300	39
1,000,000	1,250,000	345,800	41
1,250,000	1,500,000	448,300	43
1,500,000	2,000,000	555,800	45
2,000,000	2,500,000	780,800	49
2,500,000	——	1,025,800	50

* Before credits

Unified credit. The law provides for a unified credit against the estate tax. This credit is phased in on the following schedule:

Decedents dying in	*Unified Credit*
'84	96,300
'85	121,800
'86	155,800
'87 and after	192,800

APPENDIX F
Income Tax Rates for Estates and Trusts

If taxable income is:	**The tax is:**
Not over $1,050	11% of taxable income.
Over $1,050 but not over $2,100	$115.50, plus 12% of the excess over $1,050.
Over 2,100 but not over $4,250	$241.50, plus 14% of the excess over $2,100.
Over $4,250 but not over $6,300	$542.50, plus 16% of the excess over $4,250.
Over $6,300 but not over $8,400	$870.50, plus 18% of the excess over $6,300.
Over $8,400 but not over $10,600	$1,248.50, plus 22% of the excess over $8,400.
Over $10,600 but not over $13,250	$1,732.50, plus 25% of the excess over $10,600.
Over $13,250 but not over $15,900	$2,395, plus 28% of the excess over $13,250.
Over $15,900 but not over $21,200	$3,137, plus 33% of the excess over $15,900.
Over $21,200 but not over $28,300	$4,886, plus 38% of the excess over $21,200.
Over $28,300 but not over $41,100	$7,584, plus 42% of the excess over $28,300.
Over $41,100 but not over $53,000	$12,960, plus 45% of the excess over $41,100.
Over $53,000 but not over $79,500	$18,315, plus 49% of the excess over $53,000.
Over $79,500	$31,300, plus 50% of the excess over $79,500.

Solutions to Self-study Questions

Chapter 1
1-d; 2-c; 3-d; 4-a; 5-c; 6-b; 7-d; 8-b; 9-d; 10-a.

Chapter 2
1-d; 2-b; 3-a; 4-b; 5-d; 6-b; 7-a; 8-d; 9-b; 10-a.

Chapter 3
1-b; 2-d; 3-b; 4-c; 5-d; 6-c; 7-c; 8-b; 9-c; 10-d.

Chapter 4
1-c; 2-d; 3-d; 4-a; 5-d; 6-b; 7-a; 8-e; 9-c; 10-b.

Chapter 5
1-a; 2-b; 3-a; 4-d; 5-d; 6-c; 7-d; 8-c; 9-a; 10-b; 11-a; 12-a; 13-a; 14-a; 15-d.

Chapter 6
1-d; 2-a; 3-c; 4-b; 5-c; 6-d; 7-c; 8-d; 9-b; 10-d.

Chapter 7
1-a; 2-d; 3-a; 4-c; 5-c; 6-d; 7-c; 8-a; 9-a; 10-d; 11-b; 12-a; 13-c.

Chapter 8
1-c; 2-c; 3-d; 4-b; 5-d; 6-d; 7-b; 8-b; 9-d; 10-c.

Chapter 9
1-c; 2-a; 3-b; 4-b; 5-b; 6-d; 7-b; 8-c; 9-d; 10-c; 11-b; 12-b; 13-b.

Chapter 10
1-c; 2-a; 3-c; 4-d; 5-d; 6-b; 7-b; 8-c; 9-b; 10-b; 11-b; 12-b; 13-c.

Chapter 11
1-a; 2-b; 3-a; 4-c; 5-b; 6-b; 7-d; 8-d; 9-a; 10-d.

Chapter 12
1-b; 2-a; 3-a; 4-a; 5-d; 6-b; 7-c; 8-d; 9-d; 10-c.

Chapter 13
1-b; 2-b; 3-b; 4-c; 5-b; 6-b; 7-c; 8-b; 9-d; 10-d.

Chapter 14
1-c; 2-c; 3-c; 4-c; 5-c; 6-c; 7-c; 8-b; 9-b; 10-a; 11-d; 12-c; 13-c; 14-a.

Chapter 15
1-d; 2-c; 3-d; 4-b; 5-a; 6-c; 7-a; 8-b; 9-d; 10-d.

Chapter 16
1-a; 2-b; 3-b; 4-d; 5-c; 6-b; 7-c; 8-d; 9-a; 10-b; 11-d; 12-d; 13-a; 14-d; 15-a.

Subject Index

A

B

C

D

E

F

G

H

I

J

K

L

S

T

U

V

W

Z

Index of Code Sections Cited

A 5
B 6
C 7
D 8
E 9
F 0
G 1
H 2
I 3
J 4